Drafting Corporate & Commercial Agreements

Legal Drafting Guidelines,
Forms & Precedents

Drafting Corporate & Commercial Agreements

Legal Drafting Guidelines, Forms & Precedents

Rodney D Ryder
Advocate

Universal
Law Publishing Co. Pvt. Ltd.

2005 Edition
Reprint 2007

ISBN : 81-7534-444-X

© Publishers

No part of this publication can be reproduced or transmitted in any form or by any means, without prior permission of the Publishers.

Published by
UNIVERSAL LAW PUBLISHING CO. PVT. LTD.
C-FF-1A, Dilkhush Industrial Estate,
(Opp. Hans Cinema, Azadpur) G.T. Karnal Road,
Delhi-110 033
Tel : 011-27438103, 27215334, 42381334
Fax : 011-27458529
E-mail *(For sales inquiries)* : sales@unilawbooks.com
E-mail *(For editorial inquiries)* : edit@unilawbooks.com
Website : www.unilawbooks.com

Recommended citation: *Corporate and Commercial Agreements*, Rodney D. Ryder, (New Delhi: Universal Law Publishing Co. Pvt. Ltd., 2005)

This publication is being sold on the condition and understanding that the information, comments, and views it contains are merely for guidance and reference and must not be taken as having the authority of, or being binding in any way on, the author, editors, publishers, and sellers, who do not owe any responsibility whatsoever for any loss, damage, or distress to any person, whether or not a purchaser of this publication, on account of any action taken or not taken on the basis of this publication. Despite all the care taken, errors or omissions may have crept inadvertently into this publication. The publishers shall be obliged if any such error or omission is brought to their notice for possible correction in a future edition. In the case of binding defect, misprint, missing pages, etc., the publishers' liability is limited to replacement of the defective copy within one month of its purchase by a copy of the same edition or reprint. All disputes are subject to the jurisdiction of competent courts in Delhi.

Computer Typeset at Aesthetic & *Printed* at Glorious Printer, New Delhi.

PREFACE

The text is aimed at assisting lawyers, legal counsel and managers in drafting and structuring commercial agreements. The forms and precedents used in this text are examples of drafting and should be used as a guide.

Counsels are advised to structure their agreements based on the drafts, but it is also important to create drafts afresh using the forms and structure provided in the text.

This prefatory note also contains acknowledgements to persons, institutions, governments and companies who have contributed in making the text richer in meaning and experience. My family and friends, I can never thank enough! I am deeply indebted to them. My eternal gratitude to the three 'forces' in my life, Mummy, Gunjan and Podgie. This text is dedicated to them. A book, especially a reference text, can never be the work of a single individual. I would like to thank all who made this effort possible. My gratitude to my family, my parents who have been the most solid rock on which our life's foundations have been built. My parents-in-law for believing in me and supporting me at each step of the way. Gaurav for his support and encouragement. Gunjan, without whom there would be no purpose and perhaps no light in my life. My brother, for always thinking that the effort was worth it and for believing in me. K.J., for walking with me all these years and never stopping.

To 'College' [St. Stephen's College, Delhi] I owe a great debt. To those who taught me the art of the essay, Dr. David Baker, Dr. Upinder Singh, Dr. S. Menon, Ms. T. Suhrawardy, Ms. S. Sharma-Luthra, Dr. R. Wanchoo and Prof. P.S. Dwivedi. My special thanks to Dr. Anil Wilson, who conceived of and has mentored the School for Legal Studies and always has the time for new ideas.

My dear friends and colleagues at National Law School of India University (NLSIU) and the National Academy of Legal Science And Research (NALSAR). Special thanks to Prof. (Dr.) Ranbir Singh, Prof. A. Jayagovind, Prof. V.C. Vivekanandan, Prof. T. Ramakrishna, Prof. Ghanshyam Singh and Prof. V. Nagraj, all the institutions who have invited me and been a part of the 'process' over the years, The International Bar Association (IBA), The Inter Pacific Bar Association (IPBA), The All India Management Association (AIMA), The Institute of Company Secretaries of India (ICSI) and Institute of Chartered Accountants of India (ICAI). Special thanks due, to educational institutions such as The Amity Law School, New Delhi, National Law University, Jodhpur, Indian Institute of Management, Lucknow, Integrated Academy of Management Technology, Ghaziabad.

My special thanks to my good friends in the Legal Publishing fraternity, academics, lawyers and others. It is impossible to name everyone.

For their encouragement, support and personal enthusiasm, my publishers Universal Law Publishing Co. Pvt. Ltd. For Manish who made the end product a possibility.

I do hope this text is useful to all readers. I need to record my gratitude and appreciation to all who made this possible.

Finally I would say that although I have had a great deal of assistance from various quarters, the mistakes and omissions in this text are entirely my own. Organisations are advised to treat this text as merely a starting point for discussion and study and not as a blue print for establishing their organisation's policy. Organisations should always remember that their brands are individual and unique. A careful and determined policy has to be sculpted using perhaps available literature and other materials.

RODNEY D. RYDER
rodney@preconcept.org

GENERAL CONTENTS

- *Preface* — v
- *Detailed Contents* — ix
- *Table of Cases* — xvii

1. DRAFTS, FORMS, PRECEDENTS—A PRELIMINARY NOTE — 1
2. COMPANY LAW: FORMS AND PRECEDENTS — 40
3. GENERAL COMMERCIAL AGREEMENTS — 100
4. INTELLECTUAL PROPERTY — 368
5. FRANCHISE AGREEMENTS — 514
6. PROJECT FINANCE — 538
7. DEEDS — 659
8. BONDS — 678
9. PLEDGES — 704
10. ARBITRATION — 715
11. LEASE — 727
12. TRUST — 764
13. SOCIETY — 794
14. POWER OF ATTORNEY — 808

- *Subject Index* — 812

DETAILED CONTENTS

- *Preface* v
- *General Contents* vii
- *Table of Cases* xvii

CHAPTER 1
DRAFTS, FORMS, PRECEDENTS— A PRELIMINARY NOTE

DEED DRAFTING AND CONVEYANCING IN INDIA	2
FORMS OF CONVEYANCE	3
Deeds poll	3
Indentures bilateral	3
Simple words	3
PARAGRAPHS, PUNCTUATION AND CAPITALS	4
FIGURES AND WORDS	4
General requirements of deed of transfer	4
DIVISION OF DEED	5
(a) Description of the deed	5
(b) Date	5
(c) Parties to the deed	6
(d) Recitals	13
Caution	14
ORDER OF RECITALS	14
FORM OF RECITALS	15
(e) Testatum	15
(f) Consideration	15
(g) Receipt	15
(h) Operative words	16
(i) Parcels	16
(j) Exceptions and reservations	19
(k) Habendum	19
(l) Covenants and undertakings	19
(m) Testimonium	20
(n) Signatures and attestation	20
Sign	21
FORMS OF ATTESTATION	22
Illiterate persons	22
Delivery	22
ERRORS AND OMISSIONS	23
POSTSCRIPT	23
ENDORSEMENT AND SUPPLEMENTAL DEEDS	23
FORM OF ENDORSEMENT	23
FORM OF SUPPLEMENTAL DEED	24

STAMP DUTY BY WHOM PAYABLE	24
STAMP DUTY ON ENDORSEMENTS AND SUPPLEMENTAL DEEDS	24
REGISTRATION	25
PRECAUTIONS	25
Rules of Construction Deeds	26
NOTES ON THE INDIAN LAW OF CONTRACT	27
Introduction	27
General Concepts	28
Breach	29
Excuses for non-performance	30
Indemnity and Guarantee	30
Bailments and Pledges	30
Bona fide Purchases	31
Interpretation of Contracts and Applicable Law	31
Capacity to Contract	32
Formal Requirements	32
Written Agreements	32
Commencement	34
CONTRACT DRAFTING AND CONTRACT MANAGEMENT	34
Engagement Phase	35
Analytical Phase	35
Drafting Phase	35
Execution Phase	36
Contract Administration Phase	36
TYPES OF CONTRACTS	36
CONTRACTS	36
DATA COLLECTION DURING THE ENGAGEMENT PHASE	36
Check-list	36
STANDARD CLAUSES CHECKLIST	37

CHAPTER 2

COMPANY LAW: FORMS AND PRECEDENTS

TYPES OF COMPANIES	41
Public and Private Companies	41
Formation procedure (private limited company)	41
PRECEDENTS	
• Application Form for availability of names	44
• Memorandum of Association	45
• Articles of Association	59
• Legal Due Diligence	70
• Due Diligence Report	74

CHAPTER 3

GENERAL COMMERCIAL AGREEMENTS

PRECEDENTS	
• Contract of Employment—(For A Junior Level Employee)	101
• Contract of Employment—(For A Senior Level Employee)	104

- Employee Innovation And Proprietary Information Agreement ... 109
- Consultancy Agreement ... 111
- Consulting Services Agreement ... 115
- Termination Clause ... 154
- Consultant's Non-disclosure & Non-compete Agreement ... 159
- Agency Agreement ... 163
- Supply Contract ... 165
- Software Services Supply Agreement ... 171
- ERC Facilities Agreement ... 181
- Facilities Sharing Agreement ... 191
- Financial Collaboration Agreement ... 196
- Marketing Assistance Agreement ... 206
- Office Refurbishment Agreement ... 218
- Research And Development Agreement ... 239
- Agreement for sale made by a vendor in favour of purchaser, the purchaser to execute a mortgage deed for balance of purchase money ... 251
- Agreement extending the time for completion of a purchase and otherwise modifying terms of the contract supplemental to the original contract ... 252
- Agreement for sale of property with usual provisions ... 253
- Exclusive Reseller Agreement ... 254

A GUIDE TO DRAFTING JOINT VENTURE DOCUMENTATION ... **271**
- Joint Venture Agreement ... 275
- Company, Management and Project ... 285
- Shareholders' Agreement ... 295
- Shareholders' Agreements and the Articles of Association ... 316
- Share Transfer Agreement ... 319
- Transfer of Shares (Specimen Clause) ... 331
- Share Acquisition and Reconstruction Agreement ... 337
- Transfer of Undertaking Agreement ... 347
- Subscription Agreement ... 354

CHAPTER 4
INTELLECTUAL PROPERTY

ASSIGNMENT OF COPYRIGHT ... **369**
   Disputes as to Assignment ... 371
      Infringement ... 371
"PASSING OFF" ACTIONS UNDER INDIAN LAW ... **374**
   The history of passing off actions under English Common Law ... 374
   Modern formulation of the law of passing off ... 375
   Remedies ... 376
   Proof of damage ... 376
   Means adopted for passing off ... 377
   Passing off in professional practice ... 377
   "Passing off" in Indian Courts: Remedies available ... 378
   Mareva Injunctions in India ... 379
PRECEDENTS ... **380**
On Trademark and Brand Protection
- Trademark License Agreement ... 380

- Trade Name License Agreement — 386
- Deed of Assignment — 392

On Copyright (Media Entertainment)
- Writer Employment Agreement — 394
- Sound Recording and Distribution License Agreement — 398
- Co-production Agreement — 405
- Deed of Assignment of Copyright — 409
- Dialogue and Vocal Replacement Agreement — 411
- Actor Employment Agreement — 425
- Memorandum of understanding between two Media Companies — 430
- Patent Agreement for Employees — 442
- Patents, Patent Licensing and Protection in India — 443
- Technology Transfer and License Agreement — 446
- Technology and Marketing Collaboration Agreement — 460
- Assignment of Rights in Invention — 483
- Technology Assignment Agreement — 484

On Confidentiality and non-disclosure
- Know-How Assignment Agreement — 487
- Confidentiality Agreement (Between A Company and an individual) — 492
- Confidentiality Agreement - Both party obligations — 496
- Consultancy Agreement — 499
- Confidentiality and Non-discloser Agreement — 503
- Employees non-disclosure and non-compete agreeement — 506
- Non-disclosure and non-compete agreeement — 509

CHAPTER 5
FRANCHISE AGREEMENTS

OUTLINING THE SPHERE OF LAW RELATING TO FRANCHISE — 515
- Direct Franchising — 515
- Franchising through Subsidiary or Branch Office — 516
- Area Development Agreement — 516
- Master Franchising Agreement — 516
- Franchising through Joint Venture — 516

PRECEDENTS
- Franchise Agreement — 517
- Draft Version of Franchise Agreement — 521
- Franchising Agreement — 526

CHAPTER 6
PROJECT FINANCE

THE RISK MATRIX — 539
DUE DIGILENCE — 542
SECURITY — 542
FORCE MAJEURE — 543
WHEN THINGS GO WRONG — 544
- Contract Damages — 544
- Liquidated Damages — 544

CONCLUSION	545
POWER PURCHASE AGREEMENTS - PITFALLS AND REMEDIES	545
Definitions	546
Tariff	546
Counter Guarantee	547
Financing	547
Price Mechanism	548
Pricing Risk	548
Payment Risk	548
Third Party Sale	549
Tax Holidays	549
Judicial Inquiry	549
Force Majeure	549
Conclusion	550
FUEL SUPPLY AGREEMENT - BANKABLE OFFTAKES	**550**
Infrastructure	551
Pricing	551
Payment	551
Force Majeure	551
Dispute Resolution	551
Transportation	552
Scheduling; Metering and Weighing	552
Quality and Rejection	552
Default	552
Remedies for Breach	553
DUE DILIGENCE	553
TYPICAL DUE DILIGENCE DELIBERATIONS IN A PROJECT FINANCING STRUCTURE	554
The Project Sponsor	554
The Site of The Project	554
Political, Economical & Legal Considerations	554
Financial Parameters	554
Construction Commitments	554
Input Agreements	555
Off-take Agreements	555
General Contract Review	555
Environmental Considerations	555
Critique	555
PRECEDENTS	556

CHAPTER 7
DEEDS

PRECEDENTS

• Assignment of Business with Goodwill and Tenancy Rights	660
• Assignment of Simple Contract Debts	663
• General Power of Attorney	664
• Special Power of Attorney in respect of entering into and concluding one Transaction	670

- Special Power of Attorney for Admitting Execution before Sub Registrar of Document already executed — 672
- Release and Indemnities — 673
- Guarantees — 673
- Guarantee, Deposit and Charge as Security for Advances to a Third Person — 674
- Agreement of Reference – To Arbitration — 676

CHAPTER 8
BONDS

FORM	679
USE OF BONDS	679
HEIRS AND REPRESENTATIVES	680
TWO RATES OF INTEREST	680
STAMP DUTY	681
REGISTRATION	681
PRECEDENTS	

- Simple Money Bond for money borrowed — 681
- Simple Money Bond, for Money due with Recitals — 681
- Instalment Bond — 682
- Equated Instalments Bond — 682
- Bond by a Debtor and his Surety for a Loan — 683
- Bond by a Debtor and his Surety for an Existing Liability — 683
- Instalment Bond, with Surety, for an Existing Liability (in the form of a deed) — 683
- Bond with Sureties for a Loan Repayable in Equated Instalment with Hypothecation of Property (in the form of a deed) — 684
- Bond with Sureties for Loan (in the form of a deed) with Provision for lower Rate of Interest in case of Punctual Payments — 685
- Administration Bond by a Person Obtaining Letters of Administration (section 291, Succession Act) — 686
- Security Bond given for the Grant of a Succession Certificate (section 375, Succession Act) — 687
- Administration Bond by Guardian Appointed under the Guardians and Wards Act — 687
- Security Bond by a Debtor (under section 21, Provincial Insolvency Act) — 688
- Security Bond by a Receiver Appointed in a Suit: Order 40, Rule 3(a), C.P.C. — 688
- Cash Security Bond by an Employee of Government (in the Form of Agreement) — 689
- Personal Security Bond by an Employee, with Sureties, Pending the Execution of a Hypothecation Bond — 690
- Security Bond by Sureties on behalf of a Claimant to Money due from Government to his Deceased Ancestor — 691
- Security Bond by Surety of the Manager of an Estate (Hypothecating Property) — 692
- Security given by a Legatee under a Lost Will to a Purchaser of Bequeathed Property (with Hypothecation) — 693
- Security Bond with two Sureties, the Principal Agreeing to Deposit Cash Security by Monthly Deduction from Pay — 694
- Bond by Sureties of a Student Admitted to a College to Secure the Performance of an Agreement — 695
- Bond by Surety for Due Observance by Another of Terms of Partnership Deed — 696
- Bond by a Trainee (if minor, by his Guardian) with Sureties — 697

- Performance Guarantee Bond — 697
- Deed of Indemnity — 699
- Indemnity Bond — 700

CHAPTER 9
PLEDGES

"PLEDGE", "PAWNOR AND "PAWNEE" DEFINED	704
DOCUMENTS AND SECURITIES	704
PRECEDENTS	
• Pledge Deed	705
• Pledge of Term Deposit as Additional Security for NCDs subscribed by *Beta* Bank	713

CHAPTER 10
ARBITRATION

DISPUTE SETTLEMENT: ALTERNATE DISPUTE RESOLUTION	715
DRAFTING AN ARBITRATION AGREEMENT/CLAUSE	715
Arbitration Agreement	716
Judicial Analysis	717
Halsbury's Laws	719
A brief epilogue	719
INTERNATIONAL COMMERCIAL ARBITRATION	719
Advantages of alternative dispute resolution	720
Disadvantages of alternative dispute resolution	720
ENFORCEMENT OF ARBITRAL AWARDS	**721**
Detrimental Reliance	721
ARBITRATION CLAUSE	**722**
DAMAGES IN ARBITRATION	**725**

CHAPTER 11
LEASE

PARTIES	727
CONSIDERATION	727
COVENANTS ENTERED INTO BY THE LESSEE	727
COVENANTS BY THE LESSOR	**728**
PROVISO FOR RE-ENTRY	**728**
AGREEMENT OF LEASE	**728**
PRECEDENTS	
• Agreement of Lease	731

CHAPTER 12
TRUST

THE GOVERNING LEGISLATION	764
The Nature of an Indian Trust	764
Requirements of a Trust	765

Trust deed	766
Complete constitution of a trust	766
Legislation relating to trusts	766
Trustees	767
Trustees' Duties	768
REGULATORY ENVIRONMENT AND LIMITATION ON TRUSTS	**770**
Courts	770
Breach of Trust	772
Limitation on trusts	773
Perpetuities and accumulations	773
Remuneration	773
Exoneration clauses	774
Public policy	774
Who can act as a trustee?	775
REASONS FOR THE CREATION OF TRUSTS AND THEIR USES	**775**
Personal or Private Trusts	775
Pension and employee benefits	776
Collective investment schemes	776
Charities	776
Non-Charitable Purpose Trusts	777
CONCLUSION	**777**
PRECEDENTS	
• Agenda of meeting of Board of Trustees	777
• Appointment of additional members to Board of Trustees	778
• Deed of Family Trust Settlement	779
• Rules and Regulations Governing the Management of "Nature For Children"	784
• Trust Deed	788
• Alteration of A Trust Deed	793

CHAPTER 13
SOCIETY 794

CHAPTER 14
POWER OF ATTORNEY

DEFINITION	**808**
ELEMENTS OF POWER OF ATTORNEY	**808**
PRECEDENTS	**809**
• Irrevocable Power of Attorney	809
• Power of Attorney – 1	810
• Power of Attorney – 2	811
• *Subject Index*	812

TABLE OF CASES

A

A. & B.C. Chewing Gum Ltd. (in re:), (1975) 1 AU ER 1017	318
Abdur Rahim Khan v. Fakir Md. Shah, AIR 1946 Nag 401: ILR 1946 Nag 518	14
Adbulla Ahmad v. Animendra K. Mitter, AIR 1950 SC 15	26
Agarwal Engg. Co. v. Technoimpex, (1977) 4 SCC 367	26
Alopi Parshad & Sons Ltd. v. Union of India, AIR 1960 SC 588	30
Angurbala v. Debabrata, AIR 1951 SC 293	7, 8
Anton Piller AG v. Manufacturing Processes Ltd.	372, 378

B

Badri Prasad v. Abdul Karim, 11 ALJ 260 (262)	22
Bal Krishna Gupta v. Swadeshi Polytex Ltd., AIR 1985 SC 520	704
Beer v. Bowden, 1981 (1) All ER 1070 (Ca)	33
Bengal Waterproof Ltd. v. Bombay Waterproof Mfg. Co., (1977) 1 SCC 99	373, 378
Bhaggabhor Mandal v. Mohini Mohan, AIR 1918 Cal 1027	8
Bhikraj Jaipuria v. Union of India, AIR 1962 SC 113: 1962 (2) SCJ 479: (1962) 2 SCR 880	12
Bholanath v. Balbhadra, AIR 1964 All 527	8
Bhopatrao v. Shri Ram Chandra, 96 IC 1004	7
Bihar Fisherman Society v. Sinai Singh, 1977 (4) SCC 145	12
Bisgood v. Henderson's Transvaal Estates Ltd., 1908 (1) Ch 743	316
Blanchard v. Hill, (1742) 2 Atk 484	374
Blofeld v. Payne, (1833) 4 B & Ad 410	374
Board of Trustees, Ayurvedic and Unani Tibia College v. State of Delhi, AIR 1962 SC 458	8
Boothlinga Agencies v. V.T.C. Periaswami Nadar, AIR 1969 SC 110	30
British Medical Association, (1931) 48 RPC 565 (574)	377

C

Charanjit Lal v. Union of India, AIR 1951 SC 41 para 43	8
Compare, Gujarat Ginning Co. v. M.H.S. & W. & Co., 31 BLR 1310	33
Crawshay v. Thompson, (1842) 4 Man & G 357	375
Currimbhay & Co. v. Creet, AIR 1933 PC 29: 69 IA 297	33
Consorzio del Prosciutto di Parma v. Marks & Spencer plc, [1991] RPC 351	376

D

Daniel v. Mariamma, AIR 1951 Mad 466	8
Delhi Transport Corp. v. D.T.C. Mazdoor Congress, AIR 1991 Supp (1) SSC 600	28
Dhyan Chand v. Savitri Devi, AIR 1998 HP 37	22
Dixon v. Fawcus, (1861) 3 E & E 537	375
Dobson v. Groves, 1844 (6) QB 637, 647	725
Dullichand v. CIT, AIR 1956 SC 354	11
Duncan Gilmour & Co Ltd. (in re:), (1952) 2 All ER 871	317

Dunlop Pneumatic Tyre Co. *v.* Selfridge & Co., 1915 AC 847	33
Dwarkadas & Co. *v.* Dalu Ram, AIR 1951 Cal 10	33

E

E.W. Savoy *v.* World of Golf, (1914) 2 Ch 566 CA.	371
East Coast Shipping Limited *v.* M. J. Scrap Pvt. Ltd., 1997 (1) CHN 444	153
East India Co. *v.* Nuthum, 7 Moo PC 482	33
Ebrahim Peer Mohamed *v.* K. Gopal Bagree, AIR 1937 Cal 180	766
Edelsten *v.* Edelsten, (1863) 1 De GJ & Sm 195	374
Erven Warnink *v.* Townend, (1980) RPC 31 at 93 (HL)	375

G

Gee (in re:), 1948 Ch D 284	774
Girja Dutt *v.* Gangotri, AIR 1955 SC 346	22
Godhra Electricity Co. *v.* State of Gujarat, (1975) 1 SCC 199	18
Gopal Das *v.* Sri Thakurji, AIR 1943 PC	25
Great American Insurance Co. *v.* Mandanlal, 1935 (59) Bom 656	8
Gujarat Bottling Co. Ltd. *v.* Coca Cola Co., (1995) 5 SCC 545.	373, 379
Gujarat S.F.C. *v.* Lotus Hotel, AIR 1983 SC 848: 1983 (3) SCC 379	12
Gurumukh Singh *v.* Amar Singh, (1991) 3 SCC 79	34

H

Hall *v.* Barrows, (1863) 4 De GJ & Sm 150	374
Hayes *v.* Bristol Plant Hire, 1957 (1) All ER 685	317
Howitt *v.* Hall	370
Hutchins (*Ex Parte*), (1879) 4 BD 483 CA	371

I

Inderjeet Singh *v.* Karam Chand Thapar; (1995) 6 SCC 166: AIR 1996 SC 247	26

J

Jamna Das *v.* Ram Autar, (1911) 391 1A 7 PC	33
Jankidas *v.* Mohanlal, AIR 1951 SC 144	29
Jaykant *v.* Durgashankar, AIR 1970 Guj 106	9
Jonathan Cape *v.* Consolidated Press, (1954) 3 All ER 253: (1954) 1 WLR 1313	369
Jyoti Prakash *v.* Mukti Prakash, 22 CWN 297: 33 IC 89	704
Judi's Musical Composition (*in re:*), (1907) 1 Ch 651 CA.	371

K

K. Sriramalu *v.* Ashwatha Narayana, AIR 1968 SC 1028	33
K.N. Vidhyadharan *v.* State of Kerala, AIR 1980 Ker 212	12
K.P. Chowdhry *v.* State of Madhya Pradesh, AIR 1967 SC 203	12
K.P. Subbarama Sastri *v.* K.S. Raghvan, (1987) 2 SCC 424: AIR 1987 SC 1257	679
K.S. Nanji & Co *v.* Jatashankar, AIR 1961 SC 1474	16
Kalyanpur Lime Works Ltd. *v.* State of Bihar, AIR 1954 SC 165	29

Table of Cases

Keele v. Wheeler, (1844) 7 man and Gr. 665	23
Khwaja Mohd. Khan v. Husaini Begum, (1910) 37 1A 152 PC	34
Knight Sugar Co. Ltd v. The Alberata Railway & Irrigation Co., 173 UC 88 (PC)	27
Kondal Rao Naidu v. Dhanakoti Ammal, AIR 1938 Mad 81: 1937 MWN 1027: 176 IC 173	26
Kovuru v. Kumar Krishna, AIR 1945 Mad 10	33

L

L'Estrange v. F. Graucob Ltd., 1934 (2) KB 394, DC	33
Laminar v. Telecom, Dist. Manager, AIR 1998 Kant 67	11
Laxman Waman v. Balmukund Jainarain, AIR 1954 Nag 142	27
Learoyd v. Whitely, (1887) 12 App Cas 727	768
Life Insurance Corporation of India v. Dharam Vir Anand, (1998) 7 SCC 348	27
Loew's Inc. v. Littler, (1958) Ch 650: (1958) 2 All ER 200 CA.	370
London Printing and Publishing Alliance v. Cox, (1891) 3 Ch 291 CA	371
Lucknow Development Authority v. M.K. Gupta, 1993 (3) CPJ 7 SC: 1994 CPR 569	238

M

M.V. Rama Subbiar v. Manicka Narasimhachari, AIR 1979 SC 671	769
M.C. Chacko v. State Bank ot Travancore, (1969) 2 SCC 343	33
M.C. Mohapatra v. R. Mohapatra, AIR 1951 Ori 132	767
M.L. Abdul Jaffar v. Venkatashastri, AIR 1969 SC 1147	22
M.M.T.C. Ltd v. Sterlite Industries (India) Ltd, AIR 1997 SC 605	717
M.P. Sugar Mills v. State of U.P., AIR 1969 SC 621	722
Mackintosh Burn Ltd. v. Shivakali Kumar, AIR 1933 Cal 668	768
Mahabir Prasad v. Peer Bux, AIR 1972 All 466	681
Manik Chandra v. Ram Chandra, AIR 1981 SC 519: (1980) 4 SCC 22	8, 10
Mareva v. International Bulkcarriers, (1975) (2) Lloyd's Rep 509	379
Marquess of Londonderry's Settlement (in re:), 1964 Ch 594	770
May v. Beloona, (1905) 2 Ch. 605	19
Messager v. British Broadcasting, (1929) AC 151 HL	370
Micheletti's Estate (in re:), 24 Cal 1944 2d 904	773
Millington v. Fox, (1838) 3 My & Cr 338	374
Motilal Padampat Sugar Mills v. State of UP., AIR 1979 SC 621: 1979 (2) SCC 409	12
Motley v. Downman, (1837) 3 My & Cr 1	374
Mulchand v. State of MP, 1968 (3) SCR 214: AIR 1968 SC 1218	12
Multichannel (India) Ltd. v. Kavitalaya Productions Ltd., AIR 1999 Mad 59 (DB)	33
Municipal Corporation of Delhi v. Children Book Trust, (1992) 3 SCC 390.	777

N

N. Chordiya Family Beneficial Trust v. Income Tax Office, 1989 30 ITD 373 (Pune)	773
Nagewaraswami v. Viswasundara, AIR 1953 SC 370	680
Nagulapati Lakshamma v. Mupparaju, (1998) 5 SCC 285	22
New Marine Coal Co. v. Union of India, AIR 1964 SC 152	13

Nilamani Poricha v. Appanna Poricha, AIR 1936 Mad 14 — 770
Nippon Yusen Kaisha v. Karageorgis, (1975) (1) WLR 1093 — 379

O

O'Rourke v. Darbishire, 1920 AC 581 — 769
Orwell's W.T. (in re:), [1982] 3 All ER 177 — 774

P

Parker v. South Eastern Railway Co., 1877 (2) CPD 416, CA — 33
Parma v. Marks & Spencer plc, [1991] RPC 351 — 376
Pierce Leslie & Co. Ltd. v. Miss Violet Ouchterlony Wapshare, AIR 1969 SC 843 — 769
Plestin KAB Co-op Society v. Govt. of Palestine, AIR 1948 PC 207 — 18

Q

Quin & Axtens Ltd. v. Salmon, 1909 AC 442 — 317

R

R. v. Bow Street (Magistrates Court, March, 1994) — 237
Raghava Chariar v. Srinivasa, 1917 (40) Mad 308 (FB) — 8
Raghuber Singh v. Jai Indra Bopander Singh, AIR 1919 PC 55: ILR 42 All 158 — 8
Rajratha Naranbhai Mills Co Ltd. v. STO, (1991) 3 SCC 283 — 34
Ram Gopal v. Nandlal, AIR 1951 SC 139 — 26
Ramchandra v. Chinubhai, AIR 1944 Bom 76 — 33
Ramji Dayawala & Sons (P) Ltd v. Invest Import, AIR 1981 SC 2085 — 717
Raneegunge Coal Association Ltd. v. Tata Iron and Steel Co. Ltd., AIR 1940 PC 151 (153) — 27
Rattan Chand Hira Chand v. Askar Nawaz Jung, (1991) 3 SCC 67 — 34
Reckitt & Coleman v. Borden, (1990) RPC 341 (HL) — 376
Rodgers v. Nowill, (1847) 5 CB 109 — 375
Royal Talkies v. ESIC, (1978) 4 SCC 204 — 25

S

S. Rathnammal v. Mattadu, 1998 AIHC 3094 (Mad) — 25
Sant Ram v. Rajinder Lal, AIR 1978 SC 1601: (1979) 2 SCC 274: (1979) 1 SCWR 175 — 25
Sarkar Barnad v. Alak Manjary, AIR 1925 PC 89: 26 BLR 737: 83 IC 170 — 22
Satyabhrata Ghose v. Mugneeram Bangur and Co., AIR 1954 SC 44 — 27
Savitri Devi v. Dwarka Prasad, AIR 1939 All 305 — 371
Shamu Patter v. Abdul Kadir, 35 M 607 — 22
Shanmuga Mudali v. Arungiri Mudali, AIR 1932 Mad 658 — 770
Shanti Devi v. State, AIR 1982 Del 453 — 776
Shanti Vijay and Co. v. Princess Fatima Fouzia, (1979) 4 SCC 602 — 770
Shapoor F Mazda v. Durga Prosad, AIR 1961 SC 1236 — 26
Sheodutt v. Pandit Vishnudutta, AIR 1955 Nag 116 — 718
Shyam Sunder v. Delta International Ltd., AIR 1998 Cal 233 (DB) — 26
Singer Manufacturing Co. v. Loog, (1882) App Cas 15 — 374
Singer Manufacturing Co. v. Wilson, (1876) 2 ChD 434 — 374, 375

Table of Cases

Society of Accountants & Auditors, (1907) 1 Ch 489	377
Sohanlal Pachisia & Co. *v.* Bilasrav Khemani, AIR 1954 Cal 179	27
Southern *v.* How, (1618) Poph 143	374
Sree S M Jew *v.* B K Vyas, AIR 1952 Cal 763	770
Sri Yadagiri Lakshmi Narasimha Swami Temple *v.* Induru Pattabhirami Reddi, AIR 1967 SC 781	769
State of Bihar *v.* Usha Martin Industries Ltd., 1987 (Supp) SCC 710	12
State of Haryana *v.* Lal Chand, 1984 (3) SCC 634 (para 10).	12
State of Himachal Pradesh *v.* Ganesh Wood Products, 1995 (6) SCC 363	722
State of Orissa *v.* Titlaghur Paper Mills, AIR 1985 SC 1293: (1985) Supp. SCC 280	26
State of Punjab *v.* Okara Grain Buyers Syndicate Ltd., AIR 1964 SC 669	27
State of UP *v.* Murari Lal and Bros., AIR 1971 SC 2210: 1971 (2) SCC 449	12
State of West Bengal *v.* B.K. Mondal, AIR 1962 SC 779: 1962 Supp (1) SCR 876	12, 13
Sykes *v.* Sykes, (1824) 3 B&C 541	374

T

Than Singh *v.* Barelal, AIR 1974 MP 24	10
Thomson *v.* Butcher, (1625) 3 Buls 300	23
Thyssen Stahlunion GmbH *v.* Steel Authority of India Ltd., unreported, 7th October 1999; Civ. App. 6036 of 1996 SC	152
Trustees of Govardhandas Family Charitable Trust *v.* Income Tax Commissioner, AIR 1952 Bom 145	777

U

U.P. Rajkiya Nirman Nigam Ltd. *v.* Indure (P) Ltd, AIR 1996 SC 1373	717
Union Carbide Corporation *v.* Union of India, 1991 (4) SCC 584 (para 107)	12
Union of India *v.* A.L. Rallia Ram, AIR 1963 SC 1685	12
Union of India *v.* Amar Singh, AIR 1960 SC 233	29, 31
Union of India *v.* Godfrey Philips, (1985) 4 SCC 369: AIR 1986 SC 806	12, 722
Union of India *v.* N.K. Private Limited, AIR 1972 SC 915: 1973 (1) SCJ 107	12
Union of India *v.* Raman Iron Foundry, (1974) 2 SCC 231	34
United Commercial Bank *v.* Bank of India, AIR 1981 SC 1426	153

V

V. Narasimharaju *v.* V. Gurumurthyraju, AIR 1963 SC 107	29
Venugopal Setty *v.* Suryakanta, (1992) PTC 55 (Karn HC)	371
Vishnudas Trading *v.* Vazir Sultan Tobacco Co. Ltd, (1977) 4 SCC 201	373, 378

W

Watchman *v.* Attorney General of East Africa Protectorate, (1919) AC 533 PC	18

Z

Zafar Ahsam *v.* Zubaida Khatun, 1929 (27) All LJ 1114	8

CHAPTER 1
DRAFTS, FORMS, PRECEDENTS—
A PRELIMINARY NOTE

SYNOPSIS

DEED DRAFTING AND CONVEYANCING IN INDIA
FORMS OF CONVEYANCE
    Deeds poll
    Indentures bilateral
    Simple words
PARAGRAPHS, PUNCTUATION AND CAPITALS
FIGURES AND WORDS
    General requirements of deed of transfer
DIVISION OF DEED
        (a) Description of the deed
        (b) Date
        (c) Parties to the deed
        (d) Recitals
    Caution
ORDER OF RECITALS
FORM OF RECITALS
        (e) Testatum
        (f) Consideration
        (g) Receipt
        (h) Operative words
        (i) Parcels
        (j) Exceptions and reservations
        (k) Habendum
        (l) Covenants and undertakings
        (m) Testimonium
        (n) Signatures and attestation
    Sign
FORMS OF ATTESTATION
    Illiterate persons
    Delivery
ERRORS AND OMISSIONS
POSTSCRIPT
ENDORSEMENT AND SUPPLEMENTAL DEEDS
FORM OF ENDORSEMENT
FORM OF SUPPLEMENTAL DEED
STAMP DUTY BY WHOM PAYABLE
STAMP DUTY ON ENDORSEMENTS AND SUPPLEMENTAL DEEDS
REGISTRATION

PRECAUTIONS
    Rules of Construction Deeds
NOTES ON THE INDIAN LAW OF CONTRACT
    Introduction
    General Concepts
    Breach
    Excuses for non-performance
    Indemnity and Guarantee
    Bailments and Pledges
    Bona fide Purchases
    Interpretation of Contracts and Applicable Law
    Capacity to Contract
    Formal Requirements
    Written Agreements
    Commencement
CONTRACT DRAFTING AND CONTRACT MANAGEMENT
    Engagement Phase
    Analytical Phase
    Drafting Phase
    Execution Phase
    Contract Administration Phase
TYPES OF CONTRACTS
CONTRACTS
DATA COLLECTION DURING THE ENGAGEMENT PHASE
    Check-list
STANDARD CLAUSES CHECKLIST

Deed Drafting and Conveyancing in India

Conveyancing[1] in India has its origins in the presidency towns and adjoining mofussil areas where drafting was done by solicitors trained in the English system of conveyancing. The work since the earliest days has usually been in the hands of scribes (deed writers[2]) who have had no legal education or training but are only conversant with certain set forms of various kinds of deeds in common use in the country, and acquire by experience the knack of adapting them to their requirements. The origin of these vernacular forms is not known but the forms are very old and have been handed down from generation to generation. These lawyers, who have ordinarily had no education in conveyancing, generally get hold of some English forms from a solicitor in Calcutta or Bombay and adapt them to their needs, or take the help of some book containing English precedents of conveyancing[3]. The art of conveyancing in India has developed without the assistance of the formalised structure of legislation, in contrast to the legislative solutions available in England[4], laying down what a conveyance should, and

---

1. Conveyancing has been defined in various texts; it has been described as the "art of creating, transferring and extinguishing interests in property both in dealing with substantive law and providing examples to illustrate its principles" in Goodeves' Real Property (1929) p. 72.
2. The North Indian vernacular being 'vasika nawis'.
3. Mogha's Indian Conveyancer, Eleventh Edition.
4. Namely, the Conveyancing Act, 1881 (sec. 2 interpretation of various terms) and the Law of Property Act, 1925. The latter Act, contains among other things (many of which are covered by our Transfer of Property Act, Trusts Act, Contract Act, Registration Act, etc.) standard forms in the same manner as our Civil Procedure Code contains standard

what it need not contain, and providing a set of authority forms. In the last decade, global legal traditions have benefited from interaction. India has benefited no less in exchanging drafting techniques with the rest of the world.

Forms of Conveyance

The form in which a conveyance is drafted is immaterial but as English forms have, by long usage, obtained a sort of sanctity, the same may be retained with necessary alterations. In England deeds are drafted either as deeds poll or as indentures.

Deeds poll[1]

Deeds poll are those in which there is one party only and are so called because they were at one time polled or cut level at the top. They are chiefly used for the purpose of granting powers of attorney and for exercising power of appointment or setting out an arbitrator's award. They are drawn in first person.

Indentures bilateral[2]

Indentures are those deeds in which there are two or more Parties. Indentures were so called as at one time they were indented or cut with an uneven edge at the top. In old times the practice was to make as many copies or parts, as they were called, of the instrument as there were parties to it, which parts taken together formed the deed, and to engross all of them on the same skin or parchment. Then a word, usually Cyrographum, was written between the two or more copies, and the parchment was cut in a jagged line through this word. The idea was that the difficulty of so cutting another piece of parchment that it would fit exactly into this cutting and writing constituted a safeguard against the fraudulent substitution of a different writing for one of the parts of the original. This practice of indenting deeds has ceased long ago and even in England the practice of calling them indentures has largely fallen into disuse.

Indian usage: In India the Stamp Act, 1899 uses the word "instrument" for every document by which any right or liability is, or purports to be, created, transferred, limited, extended, extinguished or recorded, *vide* sec. 2(14). In the Registration Act, 1908 the word "document" has been used instead. In this book, for the sake of uniformity, the word "deed" has been used generally.

Simple words

In English conveyances several words in old English form are used, *e.g.*, "witnesseth", "doth covenant", etc. We can however as well use their modern equivalents, *e.g.*, "witnesses", "covenants", etc.

---

forms of pleadings, etc. Its sec. 46 empowers the Lord Chancellor to prescribe other forms of agreements as well. Its secs. 61, 62 and 63 also contains rules of interpretation applicable to deeds generally, subject to special provisions to the contrary as may be specified in a deed. Some other provisions, which may be usefully adapted, is one in sec. 15 (The persons expressed to be parties to any conveyance shall, until the contrary be provided, be presumed to be of full age at the date thereof.").

1. *See* notes to sec. 57 Law of Property Act, 1925 in Halsbury's Statutes, Vol. 27, p. 435.
2. *Ibid.*

Paragraphs, Punctuation and Capitals

In England, deeds were formerly all written in one paragraph without punctuation, but the practice of dividing the deed into paragraphs is now growing. As the division of a deed into paragraphs makes it more easily intelligible, this practice is recommended. The commencement of every important part of a deed is marked by putting the first word or phrase in capital letters and this was very necessary when the deed was not divided into paragraphs as a reader who wanted to refer only to a particular part could easily find what he wanted without having to read the whole. With the division of deed into paragraphs the use of capital letters is not absolutely necessary but is continued in practice.

Although a free use of punctuation marks is not desirable, as a mistake in punctuation sometimes alters the sense, yet a full stop or semicolon, as may be proper, at the end of each paragraph would be suitable. The language of the deed should be such that the intention of the parties should be clearly understood without the aid of punctuations.

A deed poll is generally drawn in the first person and an indenture always in the third person.

Deeds poll generally commence with:

"Know all men by these presents",

If, there are no recitals, then with:

"To all whom these presents shall come Greeting."

If there are recitals, the date is written at the end of the deed in the testimonium clause, thus:

"IN WITNESS WHEREOF I, the said................. have hitherto set my hand this................. day of.................".

The form in which deed poll and other deeds (hitherto known as indentures) are drafted will be given later under appropriate headings and the exact requirements of such forms will be dealt with in the preliminary notes. The most common and important transactions for which deeds are required are those of various kinds of transfer of immovable property. The general requirements of all deeds of transfer are dealt with in the next part.

Figures and Words

Date, sums and numbers should, in order to avoid mistake, be preferably stated in words or in words as well as in figures.

General requirements of deed of transfer

In this part it is proposed to deal with the general requirements of all deeds of transfer and to notice the various clauses, of which a deed of transfer is generally composed, and to show in what way each clause should be framed. The particular and special requirements of particular kinds of transfer deeds and any modifications necessary in the case of a particular kind of transfer will be noticed in the "preliminary note" to the precedents relating thereto.

Division of Deed

An ordinary deed of transfer may conveniently be divided into the following parts:

Description of the deed; Date; Parties; Recitals; Testatum; Consideration; Receipt; Operative words; Parcels; Exceptions and Reservations (if any); Habendum; Covenants (if any); Testimonium.

The part of the deed, which precedes the habendum, is termed "the premises"[1]. Each of these parts will now be separately considered.

(a) Description of the deed

Although the necessity of indenting was abolished long ago in England by sec. 5 of the Real Property Act, 1845, which section was later replaced by sec. 56 of the Law of Property Act, 1925, deeds are still sometimes described as indentures, such is the conservatism of English lawyers! Sec. 57 of the Law of Property Act, 1925 provides that a deed may be described as a deed simply according to the nature of the transaction. In some of the latest books on conveyancing this has been followed and the word "indenture" has been discarded.

In India there never was any reason for calling a deed "indenture", but as solicitors generally copied the English style of conveyancing the word has come to be adopted here also. All deeds should now be described by the name of the transaction which they evidence, such as "THIS DEED OF MORTGAGE", "THIS DEED OF SALE", "THIS LEASE", "THIS DEED OF GIFT", etc. When the deed is of a complex character and evidences different transactions known by different legal names, or the conveyancer is not sure what name should properly be given to it, it would be best to describe it simply as 'THIS DEED". This description is usually written in capitals.

(b) Date

After the description of the deed is stated, the date on which it is executed, thus:

> "THIS LEASE made on the .... day of February, one thousand nine hundred and ninety nine".

The date is, strictly speaking not an essential part of the deed and a deed is perfectly valid if it is undated or the date given is an impossible one, *e.g.* the 30th day of February, and if no date is given, oral evidence will always be admissible to prove the date of execution if it becomes necessary to determine it. It is, however, always a matter of great importance to know the date from which a particular deed operates. In India, as there is a short period of four months (sec. 23, Registration Act, 1908) from the date of execution within which a deed

---

1. Black's Law Dictionary (1992 Edn.) defines "premises" (in conveyancing) as "that part of deed which precedes the habendum, in which are set forth the names of the parties with their titles and additions, and in which are recited such deeds, agreements, or matters of fact as are necessary to explain the reasons upon which the present transaction is founded; and it is here, also, the consideration on which it is made is set down and the certainty of the thing granted."

which requires to be registered must be presented for registration, the date of execution is always the first matter for inquiry by the registering officer. Similarly, in the case of a deed of transfer of land in respect of which mutation of names is necessary, the date of execution is ascertained for mutation purposes. The date is further important for the purposes of the application of law of limitation. In view of the extreme importance of the date of execution, and of the great risk in leaving the same to be determined by oral evidence, a deed should always be dated, and this should be regarded as an essential requirement.

The date of a deed is the date on which it is signed by the party or parties executing it. When there is only one party to a deed, as in the case of deed poll, or when all the parties sign it on one and the same date, or when, though there are several parties to a deed, all do not sign and those who sign do so on one date, there is no difficulty. But if several parties to a deed sign it on different dates, the question is which date should be entered as the date of deed. The practice is to regard the last of such dates as the date of the deed. This does not, however, seem to be universally correct as there might be parties who execute a deed only for the sake of the formality and the deed operates even without their signature. For example, in the case of a sale deed the transfer operates on its execution by the vendor and without the purchaser's signature on the deed, or when a person is impleaded as a party to a deed simply in order to give him notice of the transaction to obtain his consent though such consent is not legally necessary to validate the transaction. In all such cases the dates on which such persons sign the deed may be discarded from consideration, because the date of deed is really the date on which the deed operates.

The date should, in order to avoid mistake and risk of forgery, be written in words and not in figures. Figures may be added within parenthesis, if desired thus—

"The ..... day of ....., two thousand ...."

In every case in which a deed is executed by more than one person, the date on which each signs the deed must be shown in the deed, preferably against his signature.

(c) Parties to the deed

(i) *Transferee*: After the date, the names and description of the parties to the deed are mentioned. Who are the necessary and proper parties to a deed depends on the circumstances of each case. In England, the custom is to make both the transferor and the transferee parties to all deeds of transfer. This was necessary in former times as no person could take an interest under an indenture who was not named as a party therein but since the passing of the Real Property Act, 1845 (later replaced by the Law of Property Act, 1925) an estate or interest in any property and the benefit of a condition or covenant respecting the same may be taken, although the transferee is not named as a party (*see* sec. 5 of the 1845 Act now sec. 56 of the 1925 Act). The practice of naming the transferee as a party, however, still continues. In India, except in the case of leases which, under section 107 of the Transfer of Property Act, 1882 require to be executed both by the lessor and the lessee, the transferee is not a necessary party to any deed of transfer, and in the forms used in Indian languages transferees are not normally named as parties and do not execute the deeds. But in all cases where any covenant has to be made by the transferee also, he becomes a necessary party.[1]

(ii) *Third Person*: Sometimes, it is necessary or expedient, in order to validate a transfer or to give a complete title to the transferee, or to avoid possible disputes or doubts in that regard, to obtain the consent or concurrence of a third person. In such cases, such third person may also be joined as a party. For instance, prior to the enactment of the Hindu Succession Act, 1956 [sec. 14(1), a reversioner used to be joined in the case of a transfer by a Hindu widow of absolute title in her husband's property. Again in the case of sale of lessee's right the lessor may be joined if the lessee has no power to transfer his rights without the lessor's permission. (Such permission is generally required under rent control laws; its absence may result in the lessee forfeiting his protection under such laws]. Sometimes other persons also make some covenants in the deed and are joined for this purpose. In all such cases the transferor is placed first, any person whose concurrence is necessary or who enters into any covenant comes next, and the transferee last. If different portions of the estate transferred are owned by different persons as the mortgagor and mortgagee, lessor and lessee, reversioner and life owner and full estate is transferred by all such persons, the person who has the legal estate should be placed first, and those who have the equitable estate next.

(iii) *Description* : Full description of the parties so as to prevent difficulty of identification should follow the name. In India, parentage, occupation and residence including municipal or survey number, street and city and in the case of resident of a rural area the village, sub-division, tehsil and/or development block are generally regarded as sufficient to identify a man, but if there is any other description which is sufficient, the same may be normally adopted. It should not be considered necessary to specify the caste or religion as it is desirable to discourage emphasis on communal or caste distinctions in our republic. But where the transferor is a member of a scheduled caste or scheduled tribe for whose protection the statute places restrictions on his right to transfer it may be necessary to mention such caste or tribe while reciting the fact of permission for the transfer having been obtained from the competent authority.

(iv) *Juridical person* : A party to a transfer need not be a living individual but may be a company, or association or body of individuals (sec. 5 of Transfer of Property Act, 1882), or an idol[2] or a corporation sole or

---

1. In this context, *see* "Covenants and undertakings", post.
2. *Bhopatrao v. Shri Ram Chandra*, 96 IC 1004; see *Angurbala v. Debabrata*, AIR 1951 SC 293 (In all Hindu religious endowment the entire ownership of the dedicated property is transferred to the deity or the institution itself as juristic person, and the shebait or mahant - unlike a trustee under the English Law in whom the property vests for the benefit of *cestui que* trust - is mere manager).

aggregate.[1] or in fact any juridical person capable of holding property and entering into contracts. A court is not a juridical person capable of holding property or entering into contracts, and security bonds which are given to courts must, therefore, be made in favour of a named officer of the court and not in favour of the court.[2] Care should be taken that companies, associations and corporations are described by their correct names. It is better also to refer to the Act under which they are registered or incorporated thus:

"...................... (name), a company within the meaning of the Companies Act, 1956, and having its registered office at ...."

"...................... (name), a society Registered under the Societies Registration Act, 1860;

"...................... (name) a body incorporated under the U.P. State Universities Act, 1973".

(v) *Idol*: As an idol has to act through some natural person[3], the name of the latter should be disclosed, thus:

"The idol of .... (name) installed in the temple at .... (place), acting through its .... (name), son of .... (name) of ....".

(vi) *Persons under disability*: Persons under disability (namely minors, persons of unsound mind and persons disqualified from contracting by any law to which they are subject) cannot enter into a contract and cannot therefore transfer property (*See* sec. 7 of the Transfer of Property Act read with secs. 11 and 12 of the Contract Act and sec. 3 of Majority Act)[4]. They cannot by themselves even take a transfer, if the same involves entering into any covenant, as all contracts made by them are void. But if no promise is made by the person under disability as a consideration of the transfer or where there remains nothing for the minor to do there is nothing to make the contract unenforceable at his instance.[5] However, some statutory obligations attach to a transferee even in the absence of

---

1. *Board of Trustees, Ayurvedic and Unani Tibia College* v. *State of Delhi*, AIR 1962 SC 458 (para 9). A company is a Corporation aggregate (sec. 34, The Companies Act, 1956); it has a legal personality distinct from its shareholders (*Charanjit Lal* v. *Union of India*, AIR 1951 SC 41 para 43). For illustrations of corporation sole *see* the Administrators - General Act, 1963 (sec. 5) and the Charitable Endowments Act, 1890 (sec. 3). Universities, State Electricity Boards, Life Insurance Corporation of India and nationalised banks are instances of corporation aggregate.
2. *Raghuber Singh* v. *Jai Indra Bopander Singh*, AIR 1919 PC 55: ILR 42 All 158 (*See* precedent No. 10 under BOND).
3. *Angurbala* v. *Debabrata*, AIR 1951 SC 293.
4. *See* discussion of case law in *Manik Chandra* v. *Ram Chandra*, AIR 1981 SC 519: (1980) 4 SCC 22.
5. *Raghava Chariar* v. *Srinivasa*, 1917 (40) Mad 308 (FB) (if minor has fulfilled his part of the contract the other party cannot resist its enforcement on the ground of voidness); *Zafar Ahsam* v. *Zubaida Khatun*, 1929 (27) All LJ 1114; *Bhaggabhor Mandal* v. *Mohini Mohan*, AIR 1918 Cal 1027; *Daniel* v. *Mariammu*, AIR 1951 Mad 466; *Bholanath* v. *Balbhadra*, AIR 1964 All 527; *The Great American Insurance Co.* v. *Mandanlal*, 1935 (59) Bom 656 (per Beaumond C.J.).

a specific covenant on their part, *e.g.* in Transfer of Property Act, sec. 55(5) in a case of sale and sec. 109 in a case of lease. Thus a lease in favour of a minor is not enforceable even at his instance if he himself and not his guardian is the executant.[1] Sec. 68, Contract Act lays down an exception to the effect that a person who supplies necessaries to a person under disability is entitled to reimbursement from the latter's property.

(vii) *Minors*: Minors are persons, male or female who are below the age of 18 years. If, however, a guardian has been appointed or declared by court for him before his attaining that age, the minor does not attain majority until, he is 21. A transfer of his immovable property can (except short-term lease for which no permission is required, as hereinafter stated) be made by his natural guardian or guardian appointed by Will or other instrument or appointed or declared by the court under the Guardians and Wards Act only with the permission of the court. Even for transfer of movables or for lease for a short-term it is necessary that the transfer should be for the benefit of the minor or for the realisation, protection or benefit of his estate and that there should be no personal covenant binding the minor. The powers of a testamentary guardian may be further restricted by the terms of the Will (sec. 28, Guardians and Wards Act).

The usual form is...

"*AB*, a minor, acting through *CD* his guardian:

The authority of the guardian should be either recited in the recital, thus:

"The Vendor is a minor and the said *CD* is the certificated guardian of his property appointed by order of the District Judge of .... dated....."

Or it may be shortly stated in the heading itself thus:

"*AB*, a minor, acting through *CD* his guardian appointed by the District Judge, ..., by order dated...."

Or "*AB*, a minor, acting through his father and natural guardian *CD*:"

In case of transfer of a minor's property the circumstances which gave the guardian or *Karta* power to make the transfer should be mentioned in the recitals, *e.g.* in case of natural guardian or manager of a Hindu family, the legal necessity of the transfer (except a lease for a period not exceeding five years) without the sanction of the court (sec. 29, Guardian and Wards Act). The powers of a natural guardian of a Hindu minor are now defined in sec. 8 of the Hindu Minority and Guardianship Act, 1956. In fact, it gives statutory recognition to certain powers enjoyed by natural guardian under the Old Hindu Law. Under that provision the natural guardian shall not mortgage or charge or transfer by sale, gift, exchange or otherwise any part of the immovable property of the minor, or lease any part of such property for a term exceeding five years or for a term exceeding more than one year beyond the date on which the minor will attain majority, except with the previous permission of the court. Such permission should be referred to in the recitals thus:

"The District Judge of .... has by order dated.. in miscellaneous case no.... of ... permitted the said *AB* to make the said sale."

---

1. *Jaykant* v. *Durgashankar*, AIR 1970 Guj 106.

If the guardian in his personal capacity also joins in making a conveyance the two may be described thus:

"*AB* acting for himself and as guardian of *CD*, a minor", or

"*AB* etc. and *CD* etc. a minor acting by his guardian the said *AB*".

A transfer of immovable property by a guardian in contravention of sub-sec. (1) or sub-sec. (2) of sec. 8 of the Hindu Minority and Guardianship Act or sec. 28 or sec. 29 of the Guardians and Wards Act is voidable, at the instance of the minor or any person claiming under him. The other party as well as a minor, however, can enforce a contract for sale of property entered into by a natural guardian if the contract is for the benefit of the minor.[1] The restriction imposed under sec. 8 is against alienation of minor's property by a natural guardian but the latter can purchase any property without court's permission if the purchase is for the minor's benefit.[2]

(viii) *Mentally ill Persons*: A mentally ill person means a person who is in need of treatment by reason of any mental disorder other than mental retardation. A manager appointed by the court can alone transfer such person's property with the permission of the court (sec. 59, Mental Health Act, 1987). The above-mentioned directions about guardian of a minor apply to the manager of the property of a mentally ill person as well.

(ix) *Insolvent*: The property of an insolvent vests in the official assignee in the presidency towns and in the official receiver elsewhere, and the official assignee or the official receiver alone can transfer it (sec. 68, Presidency Towns Insolvency Act, 1909 and sec. 59 of the Provincial Insolvency Act, 1920).

As the property vests in the official receiver (sec. 56) or the official assignee (sec. 51), the transfer should be made by him in his own name, and the fact of the insolvency of the owner and the vesting of the property in the transferor should be mentioned in the recitals.

(x) *Trustees*: If a property vests in trustees, the transfer should be by the trustees themselves in their own name, as

"*AB, CD* and *EF* trustees of the estate of *XY*".

The facts showing the estate came to be vested in the trustees should be mentioned in the recitals.

The powers of trustees in regard to transfer of trust property depend on the terms of the trust deed. *See* precedents of "Miscellaneous Clauses and Conditions of Trust" under TRUSTS, *post*.

(xi) *Hindu Coparcenary*: The manager or *Karta* may execute the deed in his name alone or all members of the Coparcenary may join it. In either case the fact of the property being joint family property should be mentioned in the recitals. See "(d) Recitals", *post*.

---

1. *Manik Chand* v. *Ram Chander*, AIR 1981 SC 519.
2. *Than Singh* v. *Barelal*, AIR 1974 MP 24.

(xii) *Attorney* : An attorney may be made party either in his own name (sec. 2, Power of Attorney Act, 1882), thus:

"*AB* attorney of *CD*".

Or the name of the principal may be shown as a party, thus:

"*CD* acting by his attorney *AB*"

The latter form is preferable.

(xiii) *Firm* : Every partner has, under sec. 19 of the Partnership Act, 1932, an implied authority to bind the firm by acts done to carry on the business of the firm in the usual way. In case of emergency a partner may do any reasonable act (sec. 21). The acts mentioned in sec. 19(2) including transfers of immovable property must be done by all the partners; other acts done and instruments executed by one partner must be done and executed by him in the firm's name or in any other manner expressing or implying an intention to bind the firm (sec. 22). Thus:

"*AB*, etc., a partner of and acting for and on behalf of the firm carrying on business under the name and style of – (firm's name)".

"Firm - acting through *AB*, etc., its managing partner".

It may, however, be added that strictly speaking, a firm unlike a corporation, is not a juridical person,[1] and only its partners are juridical persons. Hence if it is desired to execute a deed of transfer in the firm name it should be ensured that the deed is signed either by all its partners or by a partner holding a power of attorney on behalf of all partners. As regards sec. 19 it is to be noted that it does not confer an implied authority on any partner to buy or sell property for or on behalf of the firm. Commercial agreements may, however, be entered into by the managing partner in the ordinary course of business.

(xiv) *Government*: Contracts made in exercise of the power of the Union and all assurances of property vested in the Union are to be expressed in the name of the President while those relating to a State are to be made in the name of the Governor[2] of that State, as laid down by Article 299(1) of the Constitution. Notifications under Article 299(1) authorizing Secretaries of the various Ministries of the Government of India and the Secretaries to Governments of the various departments in the States as well as some heads of department and various other officers for entering into contracts or executing assurances of property on behalf of the President or the Governor, as the case may be, have been issued from time to time.

---

1. See *Dullichand* v. *CIT*, AIR 1956 SC 354.
2. While the agreement or the deed of lease, sale etc., may at the outset mention the President or the Governors so that it may be expressed in his name it is customary to add within brackets the words "(hereinafter called the Government of India the State Government, the said Government)", as the case may be, so that the office of the President or the Governor may not have to be referred to repeatedly in subsequent clauses. It is sufficient to give it only in the beginning for fulfilling the constitutional requirement. *See* e.g., the agreement quoted in *Laminar* v. *Telecom, Dist. Manager*, AIR 1998 Kant 67 (Para 5).

If the contract or transfer is not made in accordance with Article 299 of the Constitution, it is void.[1] Such a contract is not capable of being ratified, nor does estoppel become applicable, nor can there be implied contract between the Government and another person.[2] A formal contract in accordance with Article 299 is however, necessary only when Government acts in its Executive capacity and not when a particular statutory authority, as distinguished from the Union or the States, enters into contract in exercise of a statutory power, such as a contract whereby a licence is granted for vend of liquor after acceptance of bid at an auction under the relevant State excise law,[3] unless the statutory provision itself contemplates or requires that a formal deed between the contractor and the Government be executed.[4] Moreover, absence of a formal contract with Government or a public corporation will not stand in the way of a citizen pleading promissory estoppel against the Government or such corporation on the basis that on the assurance or promise made by the latter he has acted to his prejudice.[5] Estoppel is however inoperative to defeat a statutory obligation of an unconditional character. Invalidity based on public policy is a good defence to the objection of consent.[6]

It is well settled that Article 299 does not by itself prohibit a contract with Government coming into existence without a formal deed as it can, notwithstanding the use of the word "executed" in that Article, result from correspondence between an authorised officer of Government, acting expressly on behalf of Government, and a private party, *e.g.*, when a tender for purchase of goods in pursuance of an invitation issued by or on behalf of Government is accepted in writing by the authorised officer on behalf of Government.[7]

However, as clause (1) of Article 299 adds that all such contracts and all assurances of property shall be executed on behalf of the President or the Governor by such persons and in such manner as he may direct or authorise, it is open to the Government concerned to direct that contracts of a specified class shall be made only through formal deed. Even in the absence of a valid contract, where a party has done something for or supplied something to the Government under an informal agreement and the Government has taken advantage thereof,

---

1. *Bihar Fisherman Society* v. *Sinai Singh*, 1977 (4) SCC 145; *Bhikraj Jaipuria* v. *Union of India*, AIR 1962 SC 113: 1962 (2) SCJ 479: (1962) 2 SCR 880; *State of W. Bengal* v. *B.K. Mandal*, AIR 1962 SC 779; *State of UP* v. *Murari Lal and Bros.*, AIR 1971 SC 2210: 1971 (2) SCC 449; *Union of India* v. *N.K. Private Limited*, AIR 1972 SC 915: 1973 (1) SCJ 107; *K.P. Chowdhry* v. *State of MP*, AIR 1967 SC 203; *K.N. Vidhyadharan* v. *State of Kerala*, AIR 1980 Ker 212.
2. *Mulchand* v. *State of MP*, 1968 (3) SCR 214: AIR 1968 SC 1218; *State of Haryana* v. *Lal Chand*, 1984 (3) SCC 634 (para 10).
3. *State of Haryana*, supra (para 10).
4. *K.P. Chowdhry*, Supra: *Mulchand*, supra; (distinguished on this ground in *State of Haryana*, supra, para 11).
5. *Motilal Padampat Sugar Mills* v. *State of U.P.*, AIR 1979 SC 621: 1979 (2) SCC 409; *Gujarat S.F.C.* v. *Lotus Hotel*, AIR 1983 SC 848: 1983 (3) SCC 379; *Union of India* v. *Godfrey Philips*, AIR 1986 SC 806; *State of Bihar* v. *Usha Martin Industries Ltd.*, 1987 (Supp) SCC 710.
6. *Union Carbide Corporation* v. *Union of India*, 1991 (4) SCC 584 (para 107).
7. *Union of India* v. *A.L. Rallia Ram*, AIR 1963 SC 1685.

the latter can be required to compensate the other party (the former) under sections 65 and 70 of the Contract Act.[1]

(xv) *Reference Labels of Parties*: In order to avoid the repetition of the full name and description at every place, the parties are generally referred to in the body of the deed by some easy and convenient names, which generally have reference to the character in which they join in the deed, such as "the vendor", "the purchaser", "the lessor", and "the lessee". In England, in order to avoid mistakes in writing words resembling each other for opposite parties, *e.g.*, a combination of "mortgagor" and "mortgagee" or vendor" and "vendee", they prefer to use a combination of "borrower" and "mortgagee" or "vendor" and "purchaser". If no such name is adopted, the parties can be referred to as "the party of the first part" (or "the first party"), "the party of the second part" (or "the second party"), "the said *AB*", "the said *CD*", but it is always preferable to give each party some short name for reference. Whatever short name is adopted the party should be referred to throughout by the same name.

The form, in which the Parties will describe in the beginning of the deed would thus be as follows:

"This SALE DEED is made on the .... day of .... between *AB*, etc. (hereinafter called the "the vendor") of the one part and *CD*, etc. (hereinafter called "the purchaser") of the other part".

If the transferor alone is made a Party, this clause will run as follows:

"This SALE DEED is made on the......... day of......... by *AB* etc. (hereinafter called 'the vendor')"

Of there are more than two Parties instead of the words "of the one part" and "of the other part" the words "of the first part", "of the second part", "of the third part", etc., should be used.

(d) Recitals

Recitals are of two kinds: (1) Narrative recitals, which relate the past history of the property transferred and set out facts and instruments necessary to show the title and the relation of the parties to the subject matter of the deed; and (2) Introductory recitals, which explains the motive for the preparation and execution of the deed.

(i) *Narrative recitals* : If the transferor is an absolute owner of the property transferred, his title and the mode in which he acquired it need not generally be recited, but when he is not an absolute owner, recitals showing the extent of his interest and the title under which he holds it, will be necessary. So also when the transferor transfers under some power given to him by another instrument or by any special law, such instrument or law must be recited, *e.g.*, in the case of a transfer by a guardian of a minor, the fact of his appointment as such guardian by a deed or order of court and in the latter case, the fact of his having obtained the permission of the court to make the transfer, must be recited. Similarly, in a

---

1. *State of West Bengal* v. *B.K. Mondal*, AIR 1962 SC 779: (1962) Supp (1) SCR 876; *New Marine Coal Co.* v. *Union of India*, AIR 1964 SC 152.

transfer of leasehold or mortgagee rights, the lease or mortgage under which the transferor holds should be recited. When the transferor is authorised to transfer only in certain circumstances, it would be advisable to narrate those circumstances in the recital to avoid future disputes, although their omission in the recital cannot estop the transferee from proving them if the transfer is impugned. For instance, in case of a *Karta* of a Hindu Coparcenary he should better recite the legal necessity for which the transfer is being made.

(ii) *Introductory recitals* : Among the introductory recitals, which come after the narrative recitals, the chief one is of the agreement, which the deed is intended to give effect to. If the agreement is in writing, it is not necessary to give particulars of the date and place of such agreement but it may be expressed in brief and general terms. Any other recitals, which may be necessary to connect the narrative recitals with the rest of the deed by showing why and how, the state of things previously existing is about to be altered by the deed should also be entered.

Caution

Recitals should be inserted with great caution because they may control the operative part of the deed if the same is ambiguous, and may operate as estoppel by estopping the parties and their representatives from showing the existence of a different state of things from that stated in the recitals. In any case, they may be good evidence of the facts recited, either as admissions under sec. 21 or as substantive evidence under section 32 or corroborative previous statements under sec. 157 of the Evidence Act, though as admission they are not ordinarily admissible in evidence against persons not parties to the document.[1] If, however, the operative part of the deed is clear and unambiguous nothing contained in the recital will control it. Persons drafting should therefore take the greatest care to avoid unnecessary recitals and to ensure that all recitals are both correct and judicious. The tendency of the modern conveyancers is to do away with recitals, and in simple cases of sale, lease or gift no recitals are generally needed. But recitals are necessary whenever the deed itself does not clearly imply for what purpose any person joining in it is made a party or whenever the covenants into which he enters show that he has only a qualified interest in the property transferred. It is unnecessary to recite conclusions of law or negative events.

Order of Recitals

If it is necessary to have numerous and lengthy recitals, they should be inserted in chronological order. In the case of narrative recitals, the different instruments and acts, which ultimately result in vesting the property in the transferor, should be recited in strict, chronological order. When the property comes to the transferor partly under one and partly under another title, each title should be traced separately and in chronological order.

Facts and events contained in the introductory recitals also should be inserted in the sequence in which they have happened or occurred.

---

1. *Abdur Rahim Khan* v. *Fakir Md. Shah*, AIR 1946 Nag 401: ILR 1946 Nag 518.

Form of Recitals

Recitals generally begin with the word "Whereas", but, when there are several recitals, one can either repeat the word before every one of them, by beginning the second and subsequent ones with the words "And whereas", or divide the recitals into numbered paragraphs with the word "Whereas" at the top thus:

"Whereas—

1

2

3

etc.,"

(e) Testatum

The next division of a deed consists of the operative part. It commences with a witnessing clause termed the 'testatum", which refers to the introductory recitals of the agreement (if any) and also states the consideration (if any) and recites acknowledgement of its receipt. The witnessing clause usually begins with the words "Now this deed witnesses". These words of testatum are of no importance as affecting the operation of the deed and their sole use is to direct attention to the object, which the deed is intended to effect. If the deed is intended to serve several objects, use the words "as follows" after the testatum, thus:

"Now this deed witnesses as follows:

1

2

3

4

etc."

(f) Consideration

As contracts are necessarily for consideration (sec. 10 of the Contract Act), it is advisable to express the consideration. This is necessary in many cases of transfer for ascertaining the stamp duty payable on the deed as sec. 27 of the Indian Stamp Act requires that the consideration should be fully and truly set forth in the deed. The penalty for omission to comply with this requirement is fine, which may extend to Rs. 5,000 (*vide* sec. 64).

(g) Receipt

Acknowledgment of receipt of consideration may be embodied in the deed itself instead of passing a separate receipt. Thus:

"now this deed witnesses that in pursuance of the aforesaid agreement and in consideration of Rs............. paid by the purchaser to the vendor before the execution hereof, the receipt of which the vendor hereby acknowledges."

(h) Operative words

Then follow the real operative words, which vary according to the nature of the estate and of the transaction. What words are necessary in a particular kind of transaction will be dealt with in the preliminary note to the precedents relating to that kind of transaction.

(i) Parcels

This is a technical expression meaning description of the property transferred and it follows the operative words. Care must be taken, on the one hand, to include in the particular or in general words, all the lands, etc., which are intended to pass so that no doubt may arise as to the extent and operation of the deed; and, on the other hand not insert words which will pass more than what is intended. If the description is a short one, it may be given in the body of the deed in full but if it is a long one it is better to give it in details in a schedule at the foot of the deed, describing it shortly in the body of the deed and referring to the Schedule, thus:

> "The house known as Glenco and situated at Nainital and fully described in the Schedule hereto"

The practice of entering the full description in a schedule is a convenient one and should generally be followed as it makes the reading of the deed easier and clearer.

Map: Sometimes it is necessary to have a map or a plan of the property in order to avoid mistake about its identity and to indicate the actual property conveyed with greater definiteness and precision. In such cases such plan or map should be appended to the deed and referred to in the parcels, stating how the property transferred has been shown on it, *e.g.*, by being coloured, or by coloured boundaries or by letters, etc., thus:

> "Which land is for greater clarity (or, by way of further identification), delineated on the plan annexed hereto and thereon shown as coloured red (or, with its boundaries coloured blue), (or, thereon marked with letters ABCDE)".

It is always desirable to make it clear whether the description in the deed controls the plan or vice versa. The words "for greater clarity" or "by way of further identification" are added to indicate that the description controls the plan. If plan is intended to control description, we may say thus:

> "All that portion of the compound of house known as No. ...., which is indicated by letters ABCD on the plan annexed hereto and which contains an area of 1500 sqm. approximately."

A map referred to in a transfer deed is treated as incorporated in the deed, and if it is drawn to scale and demarcates the boundaries clearly it is not permissible to attempt to correct them with reference to revenue records.[1]

Great care should be taken in describing the property, as a slight mistake or omission may cause immense loss to a party and if the property is described both

---

1. *K.S. Nanji & Co* v. *Jatashankar*, AIR 1961 SC 1474.

in the body and the Schedule, a conflict between the two should be carefully avoided.

In English conveyancing, different technical words are used to denote different kinds of property. For example:

(i) Messuage denotes a dwelling house without houses and gardens.
(ii) Tenement property means land and anything, which is subject to tenure but is generally used as equivalent to a messuage.
(iii) Hereditament applies to all interests in land.
(iv) Land includes not only the surface of earth but everything under it or over it such as mines, woods and houses.
(v) Water is used to denote only the right to water and not the land it covers while 'pool' cover both water and the land.

In India, however, there is no need to use such technical words. Instead, words of ordinary use which are commonly understood, such as, land, house, trees, etc., should be used, and so long as the description is sufficient to show with certainty what the subject matter of a conveyance is, it is of no concern what words are employed, but care should always be taken that the whole interest conveyed is clearly and fully described.

General words: After a specific description of the property conveyed, there formerly came what were known as the "general words" giving minute details of the easements and legal incidents intended to be conveyed, but this is unnecessary in India in view of the provision of sec. 8 of the Transfer of Property Act.

Sec. 8 is subject to a different intention expressed or necessarily implied. Hence if it is intended to exclude any easement or legal incident it should be expressly mentioned. Likewise if it is intended to include in the transfer any right the inclusion of which is not implied by these provisions, the same should be specifically mentioned, *e.g.*, if a garden attached to a house is transferred with the house, the same should be specifically mentioned. No fixed rule can be laid down as to how a particular kind of property should be described in the parcels, but care should be taken that the description used is full, sufficient, precise, definite and unambiguous.

As laid down in sec. 3, Transfer of Property Act, standing timber, growing crops or grass are not included in immovable property, hence if they are also to be transferred specific mention should be made in that behalf.

The following are the particulars usually necessary for the description of different kinds of property in India—

Agricultural land: The numbers and areas of the plots, and the names of the village, pargana, tahsil and district should be given. The tenure on which the land is held, with the amount of revenue, if any, fixed on the land should be given. If the land is a part of a plot, the area transferred and its position with reference to a map (to be annexed to the deed) should be clearly stated and, if possible, boundaries may also be given.

Non-agricultural land: The exact situation, area and boundaries of the land should be given. If any number is assigned to it in municipal or village register, the same should also be given.

House: Should be described by its name, if any. The number of the house, if there is one, and the name of the street in which it is situate should also be given as well as its boundaries. If there are any separate out-houses, stables, garages or gardens or open land attached to it, the same should be mentioned unless the description of the house as given in the deed is wide enough to include them. Sometimes the area of the land is also given. If house alone is transferred (and not the land covered by it, *e.g.*, when the land belongs to another person), the fact should be made clear in the deed, by adding the words "but without the land occupied by the said house" after the description of the house. Sometimes the length and breadth of the house or of the whole compound are also entered. It is not necessary to mention specifically the fixtures and fittings of the house, *e.g.*, doors, windows, etc., and other things provided for permanent use therewith, nor any easement annexed to it (sec. 8 of the Transfer of Property Act), but if there are any machineries fixed in the house and they are included, they should be specifically mentioned.

Trees: Pass with the land on which they stand, but if they are separately transferred, they should be described correctly by their position and their species.

Grove: The name, if any, with the correct position of the grove and the number, if any, in village or municipal registers should be given. The area and the boundaries should also be mentioned.

Area: Wherever area is given, care should be taken that it is correct. To be on the safe side, it is advisable that after the area the word "approximately" or the words "more or less" may be added so that there may not be any trouble if the area is found to be incorrect.

The normal rule is that in case of conflict, a description by fixed boundaries should be preferred to a description by area, which would be rejected as false demonstration[1]. Where, however, in a deed the boundaries of the land conveyed and the area marked in the plan disagreed but the parties had always treated the area marked in the plan as the truce area conveyed, this conduct of the parties was held to be relevant for upholding the plan in preference to the boundaries recited.[2] The boundaries stated in the description of the property at the foot of the deed should be read along with the document as a whole including any plan annexed thereto and also, if two conveyances have been simultaneously executed in respect of adjacent properties, the terms of the other conveyance so executed simultaneously.

Description of the property to be conveyed should, as far as practicable, be the same as in former title deeds. If the description in former title deeds is found to be wrong or has been changed owing to change of circumstances, the correct

---

1. *Plestin KAB Co-op Society v. Govt. of Palestine,* AIR 1948 PC 207.
2. *Watchman v. Attorney General of East Africa Protectorate,* (1919) AC 533 PC; referred to with approval in *Godhra Electricity Co. v. State of Gujarat,* (1975) 1 SCC 199 (para 13).

present description should be given and a reference may, if necessary, be made connecting the parcels with the former description, thus:

"The house now known as .... (name) situate at .... (place) which was formerly known as .... ".

For forms of parcels see under general forms post.

(j) Exceptions and reservations

All exceptions and reservations out of the property transferred should follow the parcels.

An exception is something in existence at the date of transfer which, if not expressly excepted, would pass the property as described in the parcels, such as trees.

A reservation is something not in existence at the date of the transfer but is newly created by the grant, *e.g.*, when the vendor reserves a right of way over the property. But since both "excepting and reserving" are used in practice it is immaterial whether what follows is an exception or a reservation.

Strictly speaking, as a reservation operates as a new grant by the transferee to the transferor, deed should be executed by the transferee also, otherwise on reservation of an easement no legal easement is created but only an equitable right.[1]

(k) Habendum

This is the familiar "to have and to hold" (in Latin, *habendum et tenendum*) clause of the English precedents. In India such phrases as "to have and hold" or such an expression as "to the use of the purchaser" are not strictly necessary but there is no harm in continuing the established practice.

See Preliminary Notes to SALE, post on "Habendum, when Several Purchasers".

(l) Covenants and undertakings

If, the Parties to a transfer enter into covenants, such covenants should be entered after the Habendum. While drafting covenants, regard should be had to the statutorily implied covenants, which operate subject to any contract to the contrary. For instance, sec. 55 (sale), secs. 65 and 67 (mortgage), sec. 108 (lease) of the Transfer of Property Act should be kept in mind.

Where several covenants follow each other, they may run on as one sentence, each being introduced with the words "and also" or by the words "First", "secondly" etc. or they may be sent out in paragraph form with the heading:

"The vendor hereby covenants with the purchaser as follows:—"

> It is better to put in the transferor's and the transferee's covenants separately, and any covenants separately, and any covenants mutually entered into by the parties with each other may be inserted separately. If the transferor's and transferee's covenants are separately mentioned in the

---

1. *May* v. *Beloona*, (1905) 2 Ch 605.

deed, care should be taken that no covenant which should really be the covenant of one party is entered in the covenants of the other. For example, if a lessee is given the right to cut trees of a certain kind and not to cut trees of a different kind, the latter covenant is a covenant by the lessee and the former is a covenant by the lessor and both should not be inserted in one covenant by either. When it is found inconvenient or awkward to split up, what really is one covenant into two parts, it is better to insert such a covenant as a mutual covenant by the Parties.

Sometimes the terms and conditions of a transfer cannot be conveniently separated into transferor's covenants and transferee's covenants. In such cases, it would be better to include all the covenants under one head as parties' covenants thus: "The parties aforesaid hereto hereby mutually agree with each other as follows:

(m) Testimonium

The last part of a deed is the testimonium, which sets forth the fact of the parties having signed the deed. This is not an essential part of the deed, but as it marks the close of the deed there is no harm in continuing the established practice. The usual English form of testimonium is as follows:

"In witness whereof the parties hereto have hereunto set their respective hands and seals the day and year first above written".

The use of seal is not common in India except in cases of companies and corporations, and the proper form in simple language would be somewhat as follows:

"In witness where of the parties hereto have signed this deed on the date first above written."

(n) Signatures and attestation

After testimonium should allow the signatures of the executants and those of attesting witnesses. If the executant is not competent to contract or is a juristic person, the deed must be signed by the person competent to contract on his or its behalf. Thus if the deed is executed:

(i) on behalf of a minor or a mentally ill person it must be signed by his natural guardian or where a guardian has been appointed by a competent court, then by such guardian, as guardian of .....;

(ii) by a firm, then by any partner or partners of the firm, authorised (impliedly under sec. 19, Partnership Act, or expressly by power of attorney), on behalf of the firm;

(iii) by a corporation such as a university or a local authority or other statutory corporation, then by a person or the persons authorised in this behalf by or under the statute incorporating such body. Whether it is also to be sealed depends on the provisions of such statute;

(iv) by a company or co-operative society or a society registered under the Societies Registration Act, 1860, then by a person authorised in this behalf by or under the articles of association or rules or regulations or bye laws, as the case may be section 48 of the Companies Act, 1956 requires that the common seal of the company should be affixed in the case of a power of attorney. Such seal is not required for other agreements and conveyances (sec. 54);

(v) by a trustee or *mutwalli*, then by such person describing himself as such;

(vi) by an attorney, then by such person describing himself as such and mentioning the date of the deed of the power of attorney;

(vii) by the Government, then by the person authorised in this behalf under Article 299 of the Constitution of India, by and on behalf of the President or the Governor, as the case may be, specifying the official designation and preferably notification or government order under which the authority is conferred. (The other party may well insist on seeing such notification or authorisation.)]

Sign

The word 'sign' means "to write one's name on, as in acknowledging authorship". Sec. 3 (56) of the General Clauses Act, 1897, extends its meaning, with reference to a person who is unable to write his name, to include "mark". The document must be signed by a person in such a way as to acknowledge that he is the party contracting, and it is not very material in what part of the document the signature appears.

The execution of a deed is necessary under the Transfer of Property Act in cases of mortgage, lease (except a tenancy from month to month or for a term up to one year which may be created orally, accompanied by delivery of possession. Sec. 107 of the Transfer of Property Act), gift[1] of immovable property and transfer of actionable claims, and the omission of the signature of the executant will therefore make the deed invalid. But in case of sale there is no such necessity if the property is movable or if the immovable property is sold for less than one hundred rupees.

A deed of transfer need not be signed by the transferee, even though he is mentioned as a party. All conditions and covenants are binding upon him without his executing the conveyance if he consents to it by entering upon the land granted under the conveyance. But if the deed contains any special covenant by the transferee or any reservation (which legally amounts to a re-grant by the transferee), it is always proper to have it signed by the transferee also.

Attestation is necessary in case of some deeds, *e.g.*, mortgage, gift, bond, will and revocation of will. In other cases, though it is not necessary, it is except in the case of negotiable instruments, always safe to have the signature of the executants attested. Attestation in India, whenever required by law, should be by at least two witnesses, who should have seen the executant sign the deed or should have received from the executant personal acknowledgement of his

---

1. The Transfer of Property Act, is, however, not exhaustive, nor is it universally applicable. Muslim gifts are thus governed by Muslim law, *vide* sec. 129, Transfer of Property Act. A deed is not necessary for a gift by a Muslim, but if deed is executed it requires registration.

signature but it is not necessary that both the witnesses should have been present at the same time. (*See* definition of "attested" in sec. 3 of the Transfer of Property Act and also sec. 63, Indian Succession Act).

A deed is normally signed at the end on the right side of its last page and the attesting witnesses may sign on the left side. If both parties sign, transferor may sign on the right and the transferee on the left and witnesses to each signature may sign below the signature. However, as noted earlier, the place at which the signatures occur has no legal effect. It is also expedient to ensure that preceding pages are also initialled or signed by the Parties.

Forms of Attestation

There is no particular form of attestation but it should appear clearly that a witness intended to sign as an attesting witness. The practice in Indian forms is to write the word "Witness" above the signature. In English forms between the signatures of the executants and witnesses the words "in the presence of" are added. It has been held that the signature of the scribe or of an identifying witness or of a third party approving the transaction or of the registering officer at the bottom of a deed does not by itself, amount to attestation.[1] If the scribe intends to sign as an attesting witness, this should clearly appear from the deed by the addition of the word "Witness", or otherwise. The *animus* to attest is necessary for any such person to be treated as an attesting witness.[2] In the case of a will it is further noteworthy that while the testator may sign or affix his mark himself or direct some other person to sign on his behalf, the attestor is not allowed to so delegate his authority to any other person to sign or make a mark on his behalf.[3]

Illiterate persons

Illiterate persons not able to sign may either put their pen mark or thumb mark. Only the latter is in vogue in modern deeds. As a thumb mark is more satisfactory for identification purposes, the executant or witness should put his thumb mark (as per usage, left thumb mark in the case of males and right thumb mark in the case of females, and if that hand or thumb is defective or injured then of the other thumb), and the scribe or another person should make an endorsement above or under the mark to show whose mark and of which hand's thumb it is. The ancient practice of the executant touching the pen of the scribe and the scribe signing for him is obsolete and unsafe.

Delivery

The last formality to validate a deed in England is 'delivery"[4] but this is not necessary in this country.

---

1. *Sarkar Barnad* v. *Alak Manjary*, AIR 1925 PC 89: 26 BLR 737: 83 IC 170; *Girja Dutt* v. *Gangotri*, AIR 1955 SC 346; *M.L. Abdul Jaffar* v. *Venkatashastri*, AIR 1969 SC 1147.
2. *Badri Prasad* v. *Abdul Karim*, 11 ALJ 260 (262); *Dhyan Chand* v. *Savitri Devi*, AIR 1998 HP 37; *Shamu Patter* v. *Abdul Kadir*, 35 M 607.
3. *Nagulapati Lakshamma* v. *Mupparaju*, (1998) 5 SCC 285 (case law on 'sign').
4. *See* Halsbury 4th Edn. Vol. 12, para 1329.

Errors and Omissions

Any error or omission detected after engrossing a deed on stamped paper but before its completion by signature may be corrected, and the corrections initialled by the parties signing the deed. It is better and safer to have these noted in a memorandum before the testimonium.

Postscript

A new covenant may according to old English practice be added as a postscript after the testimonium and it will have the same effect as one entered before.[1] However, this has now fallen in disuse and the modern practice is either to note the errors before the testimonium or to execute a separate supplementary deed (post).

Endorsement and Supplemental Deeds

When a deed or agreement becomes necessary in pursuance of, or in relation to, a prior deed, this is effected either by endorsement on the prior deed when a short writing would be sufficient, or by a separate deed described as "supplemental" or "intended to be read as annexed to the prior deed" in which case, detailed recitals of the prior deed are unnecessary. For example, if a lessee transfers his rights under the lease to another person such transfer, or if it is intended to alter any covenants in the lease or to surrender the lease, such agreement, may be endorsed on the lease itself (*see* precedents under "Lease"); if a mortgage is redeemed on receipt of mortgage money, the reconveyance may be endorsed on the mortgage deed (see precedents under Mortgage); and appointment of new trustees and revocation of trusts are usually made by endorsements on the deed of trust (see precedents under "Trust"). The same thing can also be done by a separate deed if a short writing is not considered sufficient and the deed, either by reason of large recital or on account of lengthy covenants, promises to be a lengthy and detailed one. The matter is purely one of convenience, but mostly in contracts with the Government, a supplemental deed becomes necessary either because a new term of agreement is sought to be added or because modification of the existing terms has been subsequently agreed upon.

Endorsements, which are of general use and for which no supplemental deed is necessary, relate to part payment or acknowledgement of a debt by a debtor. What is necessary for such an endorsement is that the intention should be expressed by use of specific words. Endorsements are also common for negotiating a negotiable instrument or transfer of a bill of exchange or a policy of insurance or Government Securities. Again no particular form of endorsement is necessary in such cases. What is necessary is that the words should clearly show the transfer of interest in favour of a particular person.

Form of Endorsement

The endorsement may begin either by saying "This deed made on this ...... day of ...... between the within named......... and the within named ...." Or

---
1. *Thomson* v. *Butcher*, (1625) 3 Buls 300; *Keele* v. *Wheeler*, (1844) 7 man and Gr. 665.

directly thus: "The parties to the within written deed hereby agree as follows". The operative part of the deed then follows, usually without any recitals unless any recital is also absolutely necessary in order to make the deed intelligible. The original deed on which the endorsement is made is referred to in the endorsement as the 'within written deed" and the parties, recital, covenant, etc., in the original deed are referred to as "within named lessor" or "within named parties" or "within mentioned covenants" or "within recited ...." Or "within described house" or "the garden described in the schedule to the within written deed", etc. If after one endorsement another is made, the reference in the latter to the former endorsed deed shall be made by the use of the word "above" instead of "within". After the operative part of the endorsement, the usual testimonium clause shall be added, ending with signatures of executants and of attesting witnesses, if necessary.

Form of Supplemental Deed

The form shall be the usual form of deed or agreement in which after the names of parties should be inserted the words "supplemental (or, intended to be read as annexed) to a deed of... dated.... and made between the Parties hereto (or, between.... and ....) hereinafter called the "Principal deed". If the particulars of the principal deed are somewhat lengthy, it is more convenient to refer to the principal deed in the first recital and to say that this deed is supplemental to that deed, thus "whereas this deed is supplemental to a deed of sale made, etc... hereinafter called the "Principal Deed". If the supplemental deed is supplemental to several deeds each should be mentioned specifically. Then should follow such recitals as are considered absolutely necessary in order to make the deed intelligible for facts leading to the execution of the supplemental deed, but recitals about the contents of the principal deed are not necessary. After that, should follow the usual operative part and covenants etc. When referring to matters or persons mentioned in the principal deed, we should say "..... mentioned (or, recited) in the principal deed".

Precedents of endorsement and supplemental deeds are given under the heads of the principal deeds, *e.g.* Lease, Sale, Trust, etc., and all deeds given under the head "rectification and modification" are supplemental deeds.

Stamp Duty by whom Payable

Section 29 of the Stamp Act provides which party, in the absence of an agreement to the contrary, will bear the stamp duty payable on an instrument. This may be kept in view while drafting a deed. Only when the party other than the one mentioned in sec. 29 is to bear the stamp duty need specific provision be made in the deed. Sec. 29 is not exhaustive of all the instruments on which the stamp duty is leviable under the Stamp Act. In cases of instruments not provided for in sec. 29, the stamp duty will be borne by the person who has agreed to pay it.

Stamp Duty on Endorsements and Supplemental Deeds

All endorsements or supplemental deeds should be stamped according to the nature of the transaction which they evidence, *e.g.*, if it is for receipt of money, it should be stamped as a receipt; if it is an agreement, it should be stamped as an agreement. Some documents if endorsed on prior deeds are exempt from stamp duty, *e.g.*, receipt of mortgage money endorsed on mortgage deed, or transfer of a bill of exchange or policy of insurance or securities of Government of India endorsed on those papers.

Registration

Whether a deed is required to be compulsorily registered (sec. 17, Registration Act) will be shown in the Preliminary Note to each deed. Even some documents not compulsorily registrable may be voluntarily got registered (sec. 18) sec. 49 provides that an unregistered document of the nature requiring compulsory registration may be used in evidence for certain collateral purposes, though not as evidence of the transaction itself. Sec. 60(2) provides that the sub-Registrar's endorsement while registering a document is admissible for proving the facts mentioned there. [1]

Precautions

Besides knowing the general requirements of deeds of transfer and the various components, which compose a deed, it is also necessary to know some other essential requirements of drafting specially in light of rules of constructions of documents. In this part it is proposed to point out the precautions, which are to be taken in drafting a document and in the next part to note the various rules of interpretation of documents, which may help a conveyancer to a scientific drafting of deeds.

The object of writing a deed is that the parties should remain bound to their contractual obligations. The deed has therefore to be drawn up in a manner as to give no chance to any party to the deed to resale from the rights and obligations created under the deed. In the words of Sir James Fitzjames Stephen, "in drafting it is not enough to gain a degree of precision which a person reading in bad faith cannot misunderstand"[2]. To achieve this objective the following precautions should be observed.

(1) The deed should contain all the material facts leading to the agreement along with the terms and conditions settled between the parties.

(2) The intention of the parties should be made clear by plain and simple reading of the document as a whole and there should be no ambiguity or inconsistency between paragraphs or clauses of the deed.

(3) The words and expressions should be used in their primary natural and grammatical meanings and the same words and expressions should have same meaning throughout.

(4) The recitals should be kept at the minimum and drafted in consonance with the operative part, otherwise some recital may be interpreted to control the operative part.

1. *Gopal Das* v. *Sri Thakurji*, AIR 1943 PC, followed in *S. Rathnammal* v. *Mattadu*, 1998 AIHC 3094 (Mad).
2. *Sant Ram* v. *Rajinder Lal*, AIR 1978 SC 1601: (1979) 2 SCC 274 (para 8): (1979) 1 SCWR 175; *Royal Talkies* v. *ESIC*, (1978) 4 SCC 204 (para 23).

Rules of Construction Deeds

(a) Relevancy of precedents for interpreting other documents: Unless the language of two documents is identical, an interpretation placed by courts on one document is no authority for the proposition that a document differently drafted, though using partially similar language, should be similarly interpreted.[1] Judicial interpretation of similar documents in the past can[2] and ought[3] to be relied on, but as the effect of the words used must inevitably depend on the context and would be conditioned by the tenor of each document such decisions are not very useful unless the words used are identical.[4]

(b) Description of deed not conclusive: As will be seen under the various Preliminary Notes, such as under LICENCE and under MORTGAGE, post, the description given to a transaction by the parties in the deed is not conclusive. It is the substance and not the form that has to be seen. A document described as licence may be construed as a lease, a deed described as a sale with a condition of repurchase may be construed as a mortgage, a deed described as family settlement may be construed to be a partition, and so on. Numerous cases under the Stamp Act, also show that sometimes parties deliberately misdescribe a deed in order to avoid the need for registration or to evade stamp duty. "The document is weighed by its content, not the title.[5]

(c) Construction of Deed a question of law or a mixed question of law and fact: The interpretation of written document is, as stated in Halsbury's,[6] "generally speaking, a matter of law". But the ascertainment of the meaning of technical or commercial terms used in a written contract, and also, in order to enable the construction of the document, the surrounding circumstances of the particular case, are questions of fact; where there is a latent ambiguity in a written instrument, the question of which meaning was intended is also a question of fact.[7] Sections 91 and 92 of the Evidence Act also point to the same.

(d) Executed and Executory Contracts: Sometimes a contract is completed in two parts. At first an executory contract is executed and later an executed contract. In such cases, too, the same language should be used, so that a different intention may not be made out by difference in language. It should be remembered that a deed is primarily construed from the words and expression used in it and not on the basis of antecedent contract. In case of any difference between the preliminary contract and final contract the terms of the latter must prevail.[8] In some cases the ground for such a view has been stated to be merger

---

1. *Adbulla Ahmad* v. *Animendra K. Mitter*, AIR 1950 SC 15.
2. *Ram Gopal* v. *Nandlal*, AIR 1951 SC 139 (para 23).
3. *State of Orissa* v. *Titlaghur Paper Mills*, AIR 1985 SC 1293: (1985) Supp SCC 280.
4. *Shapoor F Mazda* v. *Durga Prosad*, AIR 1961 SC 1236.
5. *Shyam Sunder* v. *Delta International Ltd.*, AIR 1998 Cal 233 (DB), Folld. *Inderjeet Singh* v. *Karam Chand Thapar*; (1995) 6 SCC 166 (para 13): AIR 1996 SC 247.
6. 4th Edn. Ol. 12 para 1461.
7. The references to judge and jury in Halsbury (*ibid.*) are irrelevant in the Indian context, hence replaced here by questions of law and of fact respectively.
8. *Kondal Rao Naidu* v. *Dhanakoti Ammal*, AIR 1938 Mad 81: 1937 MWN 1027: 176 IC 173; *see* however, *Agarwal Engg. Co.* v. *Technoimpex*, (1977) 4 SCC 367 (para 17).

of the earlier contract into the latter[1], or that the first contract was merely a provisional one.[2] (*see* also the next sub-heading "Reference to earlier deeds", in this context).

(e) Draftsman to be careful in the choice of words and expressions: The language of a deed, in order to convey the intention of the parties, should be simple, so that no other meaning except the primary and natural meaning may be imputed. The sentences should be grammatically correct. The court while construing a document would give to the words used their natural and grammatical meanings.[3] In construing contracts, the courts cannot give the words of the contract an entirely different meaning even to avoid superfluity. The parties intention must be found out form the language in which the parties to the agreement chose to express themselves. This can easily be achieved if in drafting a document the same words and expressions are used to convey the same meaning in different clauses of the deed. Use of different words and language or substituted words, even though the meaning may be same, should be avoided. A draftsman, unlike a literary writer or orator, cannot indulge in the luxury of "elegant variation"[4] As pointed out in *Life Insurance Corporation of India* v. *Dharam Vir Anand*[5], "when the same clause of a contract uses two different expressions, ordinarily those different expressions convey different meanings and both the expressions cannot be held to be conveying one and the same meaning". Because if any inconsistency arises in the literal construction of the words used, the courts in their attempt to reconcile the inconsistency may interpret the clauses in a manner which may not be according to the actual intention of the contracting parties. If the inconsistency cannot be resolved by attributing natural and grammatical meanings, the courts may give the words any other reasonably possible construction that may resolve the inconsistency.[6]

Notes on the Indian Law of Contract

Introduction

The Law of Contract is to be found in the Indian Contract Act of 1872. The Act is in essence a code of English Common Law and like all codes based on an existing authoritative doctrine; it assumes certain knowledge of principles and habits of thought, which are embodied in that doctrine[7]. The English Law has been modified to suit the Indian ethos. Separate statutes govern sale of goods and partnership.

---

1. *Knight Sugar Co. Ltd* v. *Alberata Railway & Irrigation Co.*, 173 UC 88 (PC).
2. *Laxman Waman* v. *Balmukund Jainarain*, AIR 1954 Nag 142; *State of Punjab* v. *Okara Grain Buyers Syndicate Ltd.*, AIR 1964 SC 669.
3. *Sohanlal Pachisia & Co.* v. *Bilasrav Khemani*, AIR 1954 Cal 179 (para 17).
4. Fowler's Modern English Usage (Oxford) does not recommend elegant variation for users of the language. Dictionaries of synonyms such as Roget's Thesarus are available for that purpose.
5. (1998) 7 SCC 348.
6. *Raneegunge Coal Association Ltd.* v. *Tata Iron and Steel Co. Ltd.*, AIR 1940 PC 151 (153).
7. *Satyabhrata Ghose* v. *Mugneeram Bangur and Co.*, AIR 1954 SC 44.

General Concepts

The modifications to the English Law have not been drastic and most of the basic concepts of proposal, acceptance, consideration, free consent, voidable contracts and void agreements, etc., are very similar to those in English Law. The limits concerning revocation of acceptance of a proposal have been broadened so that the promisee might revoke his acceptance before it comes to the knowledge of the promisor. Under English Law, acceptance is complete as soon as communication is dispatched. Under English Law, past consideration is not recognised but as per the Indian Contract Act, it is good consideration. The Indian Contract Act, also recognises some agreements as contracts without consideration, for example, contracts out of natural love and affection or promise to pay a time barred debt. English Law deems consideration to be a vital ingredient of a valid contract and declares all agreements devoid of consideration as null. Contract with a minor is void in India, whereas in England, it is voidable. So too in contracts made by persons under the influence of alcohol, in India all such agreements are void but in England they can be ratified by the drunken party when they are sober.

According to section 10 of the Indian Contract Act, any agreement made by free consent of parties who are competent to contract, for lawful consideration and object and not expressly declared to be void are valid, enforceable contracts. Consent is said to be free when not obtained by coercion, fraud, misrepresentation or undue influence and such a contract is voidable at the option of the party whose consent was so caused. Even though inadequacy of consideration is taken into account by the court in determining whether consent was freely given or not, by itself it does not provide sufficient grounds for avoiding an agreement. It is not the court's duty to bargain an equitable agreement between contracting Parties.

Section 23 of the Act talks about lawful consideration and object. It broadly states that a contract would be enforceable unless its consideration or object is not illegal, not forbidden by law, not opposed to public policy[1], or of such nature that, if enforced, would not defeat the purpose of an already existing legislation. For example, in the case of an agreement extending the time of limitation of a debt, it would appear, *prima facie*, not to be in restraint of legal proceedings and not an attempt to oust the jurisdiction of the court. Nevertheless, it would be declared void under section 23 as tending to defeat the provisions of the Limitation Act.

When the situation arises of the consideration or object of an agreement being partly legal and partly illegal, the Act states that if the lawful and unlawful parts can be severed then the illegal part can be rejected and the legal portion retained. If, however, the two being inseparable, the entire agreement is void. In the case of marriage contracts, whereby a person is bound not to marry or whereby his or her freedom of choice is interfered with, such a contract would be contrary to public policy and therefore void.

---

1. *Delhi Transport Corp.* v. *D.T.C. Mazdoor Congress*, AIR 1991 Supp (1) SSC 600.

When both the parties are mistaken as to the validity of a material fact essential to the contract, the agreement is void. A mistake as to foreign law has the same effect as a mistake of fact but a mistake as to a law in force in India will not vitiate a contract[1] unless it concerns private rights of property or is brought about by a wilful misrepresentation by one of the parties to the contract.

It is provided in section 27 that an agreement by which one is restrained wholly or partly from exercising a lawful profession, trade or commercial transaction of any kind is deemed to be void. The exception to this case lies where in the case of the sale of the goodwill of a business; the seller may contract with the buyer to refrain from carrying on a similar business. As long as the court feels such limitations to be reasonable, the contract will be held valid. Similarly section 28 lays down that all agreements in restraint of legal proceedings are void[2]. What the section prevents is that the rights of the parties should not be withdrawn absolutely from the jurisdiction of the court.

Liability under joint contracts has been made joint and several. In variation of English Law, where two or more parties have made a joint promise, the release of one such person does not discharge the other joint promisors. Wagering agreements are void but not illegal and thus are unenforceable in the eyes of the law.

Sections 68 to 73 deal with certain relations resembling those created by contract. Such relations are termed quasi-contracts. The difference between ordinary contracts and quasi contracts is that in the former, legal obligations are created with the volition of the parties. In the case of the latter, the Act provides, that where a person does something for another without intending it to be a gratuitous act and the other person enjoys the benefit of this Act, the latter is bound to compensate the former[3].

Breach

Sections 73 to 75 deal with the consequences of breach of contract. There are three remedies for such breach:

(i) Payment of damages

(ii) Specific performance

(iii) Injunction

While the Indian Specific Relief Act of 1963, governs the latter two, the first remedy is dealt with by the Indian Contract Act, 1872. The fundamental principle governing the measurement of extent of damages to be awarded is that the loss or damage must have naturally arisen in the usual course of events from the breach or which the Parties knew likely to result from breach[4].

If the contract provides for a sum to be paid by the defaulting party on breach of contract then the court must decide whether the sum stipulated is a penalty in *terrorem* of breach or whether it is an actual fair estimation of loss or

---

1. *Kalyanpur Lime Works Ltd.* v. *State of Bihar*, AIR 1954 SC 165.
2. *V. Narasimharaju* v. *V. Gurumurthyraju*, AIR 1963 SC 107.
3. *Union of India* v. *Amar Singh*, AIR 1960 SC 233.
4. *Jankidas* v. *Mohanlal*, AIR 1951 SC 144.

damage caused by breach. The court does not decide the validity of the penalty clause by its name but delves into the nature of the stipulation and then awards reasonable compensation not more than the amount stipulated for in the contract. The measure of damages is generally the difference between the price contracted for and the market price of the goods on the day of the breach.

Excuses for non-performance

There are certain circumstances under which a Party need not perform his part of the contract. In cases where the act to be performed is unlawful or impossible, such agreements are void. However, if a party knew or could have known with ordinary diligence that the act to be performed was illegal or impossible then that party must compensate the other contracting party for loss caused due to non-performance. It is also, provided that if a Party through his own actions frustrates performance then he is not entitled to claim for damages[1]. Other circumstances would be outbreak of war, strike by employees, etc., in cases where time is the essence of the contract and where performance is delayed the contract is voidable at the option of the other Party. However, commercial impossibility or unfeasibility alone shall not determine a contract[2].

Indemnity and Guarantee

The law being substantially the same as in England it has been laid down that a contract of indemnity is an agreement by which one party promises to save the other party from any loss suffered by him due to the conduct of the promisor or any other person. Indian Law differs from English Law on the point that in the latter even loss suffered due to natural disasters is covered by the indemnity. This is not so in India. A contract of guarantee is an agreement to perform the promise or discharge the liability of a third Party in case of his default. The Party that gives the guarantee in this case is known as the surety. So, in essence, the difference between contracts of indemnity and guarantee is that a contract of indemnity is simply for the reimbursement of loss whereas, a contract of guarantee is for the security of the creditor. In contracts of indemnity there is only one contract between two parties. In contracts of guarantee, there are three contracts, two expressed and one implied between three parties i.e., the creditor, the principal debtor and the surety. Guarantee obtained by concealment of material facts or by misrepresentation renders the guarantee invalid. The other topics dealt with under this heading are surety's liability, continuing guarantee, discharge of surety's liability etc.

Bailments and Pledges

Section 148 defines bailment as the delivery of goods by one person to another for some purpose, upon a contract that they shall, when the person is accomplished, be returned or otherwise disposed of according to the directions of the person delivering them. The Act goes onto state that the bailor would be held liable for damages if he fails to disclose defects in the goods supplied. The bailee is barred from making unauthorised use of the goods supplied and is

---

1. *Boothlinga Agencies v. V.T.C. Periaswami Nadar*, AIR 1969 SC 110.
2. *Alopi Parshad & Sons Ltd. v. Union of India*, AIR 1960 SC 588.

bound to take care of them as an ordinary man of prudence[1]. In the event of mixture of goods by bailee with his own goods there are three scenarios:
  (i) If the mixture is with the consent of the bailor then the bailor and bailee have an interest in proportion to their respective shares in the mixture thus produced.
  (ii) If the bailee, without the consent of the bailor, mixes the goods with his own goods and the goods can be separated and divided, the property in the goods remain in the parties respectively. In this case the bailee is bound to bear the expenses of separation or division, and any damage arising from the mixture.
  (iii) If the bailee, without the consent of the bailor, mixes the goods of the bailor with his own goods, in such a manner that it is impossible to separate the goods bailed, from the other goods and deliver them back, the bailor is entitled to be compensated by the bailee for the loss of the goods.

Section 170 deals with the liens of a bailee who has rendered service involving exercise of labour and skill in respect of goods bailed. Pledge is the bailment of goods as security for the payment of debts or performance of promise. If pledger makes default in the performance of his promise or in payment of the debt then the Act provides that the pledgee may either file suit or sell the goods after giving notice and if the sale proceeds are not sufficient, recover damages from the pledger.

Bona fide Purchases

In English common law, it is an established principle that no person can give better title than he himself possesses. Section 178 of the Indian Contract Act, states that mercantile agents who are in possession of goods or documents of title to goods with the consent of the owners are entitled to pledge the goods so long as:
  (i) they are acting in good faith;
  (ii) they have not, at the time of the pledge, notice that the pawnor has no authority to pledge.

Interpretation of Contracts and Applicable Law

The construction of a written contract involves the ascertainment of the words used by the parties and the determination, subject to any rule of law, of the legal effect of those words. The object sought to be achieved in construing any contract is to ascertain what the mutual intentions of the Parties were as to the legal obligations each assumed by the contractual words in which they sought to express them. There is no intention independent of the meaning of the words they have used. The proper construction of contract is a question of law. However, the ascertainment of the meaning of a particular word is a question of fact. The general presumption is against implying terms into written contracts. The more detracted and apparently complete the contract, the stronger the

---

1. *Union of India* v. *Amar Singh,* AIR 1960 SC 233.

presumption. The contract must be construed as a whole and no clause should be taken in isolation. The court will not by the purpose of construction correct a mistake as to the legal effect of a written contract. However, such a mistake can be corrected by rectification. The materials available to the courts for the purpose of construing a contract are documents to be construed, consideration of deleted words to construe the words that remain, antecedent agreements, drafts and preparatory negotiations along with expressly incorporated terms. As to the applicable law enforced in contracts, the proper law is deemed to be the law of the country according to whose laws the contracting parties wish to be governed. If such intention does not exist the applicable law is objectively determined as the law of the country with which the contract is primarily concerned.

Capacity to Contract

Capacity to buy and sell is regulated by the general law concerning capacity to contract and to transfer and acquire property. Where necessaries are sold and delivered to a minor or to a person who by reason of mental incapacity or drunkenness is incompetent to contract, he must pay a reasonable price for them. 'Necessaries' in this connection mean goods suitable to the condition in life of the minor or other person to whom they are sold and delivered, and such goods must be suitable to his actual requirements at the time of the sale and the delivery.

A local authority may enter into all such contracts as are necessary for the discharge of its functions. A State is not immune from proceedings relating to a commercial transaction, or to an obligation of the State, which, by virtue of a contract, fails, to be performed wholly or partly in India.

Formal Requirements

In general, contracts for the sale of goods may be made in writing, as a deed or otherwise, or by means of oral communication, or partly in express form and partly oral. In respect of certain kinds of goods there is a statutory requirement that the seller shall supply the buyer with prescribed particulars as to the nature, condition and quality of the goods.

Written Agreements

It is advisable and desirable for contracts [in all but the simplest cases] to be reduced to writing, the partie's contractual obligations clearly defined. Written agreements are registrable in accordance with the appropriate law[1]. This is often done in general commercial situations by an order form, invoice or quotation being expressed as subject to the general conditions of the seller. Where a specified article or articles are to be supplied, and in particular, where installation or servicing or both are required, a formal contract is often to be

---

1. If an agreement does not by itself create an interest in immovable property, its registration is not compulsory under sec. 17(2); but if it creates an interest in immovable property worth Rs. 100 or more its registration is compulsory. Other agreements not relating to immovable property are not compulsorily registrable. In UP, however, an agreement to sell immovable property is also compulsorily registrable if the agreement is accompanied by delivery of possession.

preferred[1]. A Letter of Intent may or may not be a concluded contract, depending on the facts and circumstances of the case.[2]

In preparing an agreement it is necessary and important that the intention of the Parties should be set forth explicitly so as to leave no room for doubt or further controversy. Only a concluded contract can be enforced. An agreement is a legally enforceable contract only if it is made by the free consent of the Parties competent to contract, for a lawful consideration and with a lawful object and is not expressly declared by the provisions of the Contract Act, or any other law to be void (sec. 10 Contract Act). The language should be simple and the words used should be definite and precise; the use of loose expression such as "proper", "reasonable", should, as far as possible, be avoided. The essence of a valid agreement is that the parties consciously agree about the subject matter at the same time and in the same sense (*consensus ad idem*).

The provisions of the Contract Act, about the essential conditions and legality of agreements (sections 2 to 30) should be studied and nothing should be introduced or left out which would make the agreement void. Where under an agreement, a party agreed to pay the other party a sum of money "after deduction as would be agreed upon", it was held that the clause offended against section 29 (Agreement void for uncertainty) and no suit could be brought on such agreement. (*Kovuru* v. *Kumar Krishna*, AIR 1945 Mad 10). But, if the material terms of an agreement are clear and specific, omission of certain details which can be worked out by consent of parties or in its absence be settled by court will not invalidate the agreement.[3] However, normally, it is not for the court to make a contract for the parties if the parties have left the terms vague or ambiguous. (*Dwarkadas & Co.* v. *Dalu Ram*, AIR 1951 Cal 10.).

Normally, a third party cannot gain any right under a contract [*Dunlop Pneumatic Tyre Co.* v. *Selfridge & Co.*, 1915 AC 847; *M.C. Chacko* v. *State Bank of Travancore*, (1969) 2 SCC 343; *Jamna Das* v. *Ram Autar*, (1911) 391 1A 7 PC.] unless he is beneficiary under a trust created by a contract to which he is not a party.[1]

Under the English Common Law a genuine pre-estimate of damages by mutual agreement is regarded as a stipulation naming liquidated damages and binding between the parties: a stipulation in a contract in *terrorem* is a penalty and the court refuses to enforce it, awarding to the aggrieved party only reasonable compensation, section 74 of the Contract Act, has sought to cut across the web of rules and presumptions under the common law by enacting a uniform principle applicable to all stipulations naming amounts to be paid in case of

---

1. As a general rule this is not mandatory, though desirable for convenience. At common law the writing may be incorporated into the contract in one of the ways: [1] by signature (the rule in *L'Estrange* v. *F. Graucob Ltd.*, 1934 (2) KB 394, DC; [2] by notice (the rule in *Parker* v. *South Eastern Railway Co.*, 1877 (2) CPD 416, CA).
2. *Multichannel (India) Ltd.* v. *Kavitalaya Productions Ltd.*, AIR 1999 Mad 59 (DB) paras 7, 8, 10; *K. Sriramalu* v. *Ashwatha Narayana*, AIR 1968 SC 1028; *Currimbhay & Co.* v. *Creet*, AIR 1933 PC 29: 69 IA 297.
3. *Ramchandra* v. *Chinubhai*, AIR 1944 Bom 76 (82) (Chagla J); [Compare, *Gujarat Ginning Co.* v *M.H.S. & W. & Co.*, 31 BLR 1310; *East India Co.* v. *Nuthum*, 7 Moo PC 482 at 497; *Beer* v. *Bowden*, 1981 (1) All ER 1070 (Ca)].

breach, and stipulations by way of penalty, and according to this principle, even if there is a stipulation by way of liquidated damages, a party complaining of breach of contract can recover only reasonable compensation for the injury sustained by him, the stipulated amount being merely the outside limit. Thus, like a claim for unliquidated damages, a claim for liquidated damages also does not give rise to a debt until the liability is adjudicated and damages assessed by a decree or order of a court or other adjudicatory authority.[1]

Sections 23 to 30 of the Contract Act pertain to the legality of agreement. The provisions contained therein have to be borne in mind to ascertain what considerations and objects are lawful and what are not. Agreement between the Parties with the object that one of them should wield influence with government to have the Nawab recognised as the heir to the estate in return for being given a share in the amount to be recovered by the Nawab, was nullified, being opposed to public policy. Contract having tendency to injure public welfare is regarded opposite to public policy. The public policy is not static. With the changing time and the needs of the society it varies. The march of law must match with the 'felt needs' of the society: the fact situation.[2] Agreement between two bidders at an auction sale to bid jointly but not intended to peg down the price or to defraud Government to knock out the sale at a lower price was held not to be against public policy and as such not unlawful and void. The Agreement, was only to bid jointly, it may be noted, and not to bid against each other.[3]

Commencement

Agreements generally begin with "An Agreement" or "This Agreement" or "Articles of Agreement" or "Memorandum of Agreement". The latter two expressions are generally used in cases where the covenants are lengthy. After the title follows the date, then the names of the parties with their addresses, as in the case of transfer deed. Then follow recitals, if necessary (For detailed instructions about parties and recitals see Part II of the Introduction.

The covenants are introduced by some such phrase as:

"Whereby the Parties mutually agree with each other as follows" (if there are no recitals, then by......)

Contract Drafting and Contract Management

In an ideal world the drafting of a contract runs parallel to the negotiations on its subject matter. In reality however, the drafting will start somewhat into the negotiations requiring the drafters, or those who review the draft, to educate themselves quickly about the transaction.

There are five stages in the "life" of an international contract and the involvement of the finance and contract departments therewith:

---

1. *Khwaja Mohd. Khan* v. *Husaini Begum*, (1910) 37 1A 152 PC, approved in M.C. Chacko, supra.
2. *Union of India* v. *Raman Iron Foundry*, (1974) 2 SCC 231; (see also *Rajratha Naranbhai Mills Co Ltd.* v. *STO*, (1991) 3 SCC 283.
3. *Rattan Chand Hira Chand* v. *Askar Nawaz Jung*, (1991) 3 SCC 67.
4. *Gurumukh Singh* v. *Amar Singh*, (1991) 3 SCC 79; Halsbury's Laws of England (4th ed. Vol. 9 para 392 at p. 266).

Engagement Phase

At a certain point in the negotiations the question arises if there is the need for an extensive written agreement. Immediately followed by the question (or suggestion), if a "one-pager" or a "gentlemen's agreement" would suffice. The answer to that second question should almost always be a resounding no! As a result the need arises to seek the assistance of the contract or finance departments. Gathering information is the main objective of this phase. The assembled data will be analyzed in the next phase. What one is looking for is information about the purpose of the agreement, the subject matter, the contracting parties, responsibilities, long, or short-term relationships, etc. It is very important to realize, being a newcomer to an existing relationship, that one is not just looking for problems, but for raw data and possible solutions to eventual problems.

Analytical Phase

During the phase immediately following the data collection all the raw information gathered will have to be sorted and hence analyzed and checked for compliance with the requirements of both the contracting parties and the legal system that will govern the contract. Of course the determination of exactly which set of laws and regulations will govern the contract is one of the questions to be answered to begin with. Some further issues to be dealt with in this phase are, for example: the fiscal consequences of the proposed transaction, what financial/legal problems are to be expected in the execution of the contract and what surprises "popped up" during the negotiations recently. By now the format and contents of the eventual contract should become clear.

Often this is also the time when preliminary, pre-contractual, agreements are construed by the parties to the negotiation. In international negotiations the legality (read: enforceability) of such pre-contractual documents is an interesting, yet complicated concept because of the ever increasing role of good faith and reliance in international law.

Drafting Phase

In this phase the issues are of a more practical nature. Which party will, for instance, write the first draft of the contract? It is not uncommon that the buyer comes up with the first draft. This can be a substantial advantage on the side of the buyer. There are advantages and disadvantages to one-sided contract clauses though, mostly they will be interpreted *contra proferentum* by a judge or arbitration panel. The actual wording of contract clauses, should the need arise to draft some, is easily obtained from standard conditions. There are considerable risks involved with using "boilerplate" documents and it is advisable to check each article of such a "boilerplate" contract against the overall purpose of the agreement.

One must not forget to agree, at the start of the negotiations, what language will be the "official" language of the contract. Most legal terms and concepts cannot be translated across jurisdictional borders and confusion will be the result. If one of both the parties prefer to negotiate based on contract drafts in their "home-language", certified translations should be used.

Execution Phase

After the negotiations the parties will be ready to sign the contract. The signatories must have the authority to legally bind their companies and that all parties should perform their obligations at signing.

Contract Administration Phase

Per definition an international contract requires more attention. Checklists, timeliness, etc. are useful tools to make the transaction a success. It is best if the finance department "translates" the document requirements from the letter of credit (if applicable) as to timely instruct all departments and freight forwarders about what documents are needed at collection time.

Types of Contracts

In general there are three types of contracts to be distinguished: A Simple oral contract, without any preceding negotiations, with no terms or conditions specified (grocery purchases etc.) A simple contract with specific terms and conditions. A negotiated custom-made contract with specific clauses and stipulations. In all legal systems there are substantive laws that influence and regulate the contract and its execution.

Contracts

More generalities: international commercial contracts are longer and more complicated than national commercial contracts. This is not such a big surprise if we take into account that these international contracts have to regulate within their "four corners" such issues as; letters of credit, international shipping, international tax-issues, currency crisis, and outside influences such as; wars, political turmoil and export/import regulations. The negotiations and the drafting of high-dollar international contracts are therefore slow, time-consuming processes.

Data Collection during the Engagement Phase

International business requires the exporting company to consider a number of factors unique to the new marketplace. Below is a checklist of political, legal and economic issues to be considered in international trade. The listing is not conclusive, but it gives the most important issues that should be investigated when engaging in international trade.

Background information on the other contract party, legal entity, financial information, product and markets, etc. Responsibilities of all parties during the term of the contract. For instance: who is responsible for marketing, price-setting, quality control, shipping, financing, audits, taxes, liabilities, profit-sharing.

Check-list

Intellectual property rights and what to do to protect your company's IP.
Legal requirements as to the quality of goods or services, specifications, labeling laws, packing and marking. Retention of title.
Government licenses and fees, and anti-trust regulations.
Restrictive governmental policies.

Currency exchange control and currency transfer restrictions.
Tariffs and quota restrictions.
Expropriation risks.
Export/Import licensing.
Trade embargoes.
Anti-dumping legislation.
Taxation.
Overall political climate.
Language problems.
Product liability laws.
Protective laws for commercial agents or distributors.
Labour laws and labour union issues.
Force Majeure laws.

Standard Clauses Checklist

As described above, it is normal practice that the seller receives a draft contract from the buyer. There are a number of issues that need to be dealt with in an agreement for the international sale of goods. Listed below are the minimum requirements for such a contract, which can double as checklist for contract review. Once again, this list is not definitive and various cultural, legal and trade customs around the world determine the validity and interpretation of the clauses as they are used.

Preamble: A carefully worded preamble saves a lot of work for the drafters as it clearly describes the "reason for being" of the contract and that in turn helps with interpretation issues in case of a contractual disputes long after the original drafters left for greener pastures.

Parties: Each contracting party should be clearly named, and its legal status and location described. When dealing with a multinational or a (privatised) government operation not determining the parties to the contract properly can lead to confusion and all kinds of jurisdictional problems.

Definitions: Specifically contracts for the sale of high-tech equipment or contracts that regulate long-term or turn-key projects are well served with a concise list of definitions, if only to forego confusion later on.

Offer and acceptance: It never hurts to determine what the offer was all about and how it was accepted.

Obligations: This clause should, in detail, describe what the parties have agreed upon and include matters such as the transportation costs, packaging, marking, etc.

Conditions: Always include the conditions precedent and subsequent directly effecting the contractual relationship between the parties.

Indemnification and Exoneration: Limitations on the liability of parties is an issue easily "forgotten" in the heat of the negotiations.

Environmental responsibilities: Besides listing possible risks it should be determined which party is responsible in case an environmental issue arises.

Security: It is common sense to strive for a secured transaction when dealing international. Retention of title and the necessary perfection of the security interest can be difficult in an international setting and requires sufficient study during the analytical phase.

Delivery: One finds many contracts in which it is not properly defined what constitutes delivery and acceptance of the goods and services. International contracts do not always have the luxury of such a gap-filler and it is advisable to utilize the 'Incoterms' from the International Chamber of Commerce.

Insurance, Risk of Loss: Parties should carefully determine who carries the responsibility for damage or loss to the goods and is responsible for insuring them. For example: in France the risk of loss transfers to buyer at the moment of contract signing as opposed to "upon delivery" as under the Uniform Commercial Code.

Price and Currency indexes: Long term contracts, or contracts that deal in foreign currency, need to contain articles that make sure that the economics of the underlying deal remain intact.

Force Majeure and hardship clause: In light of the fact that every legal system has its own definition of what constitutes *Force Majeure*, or, for that matter, impossibility, it is advisable to refer a standard definition, such as the one from the ICC, publication No. 421.

Default, Termination and Expiration: Besides actually determining when a contractual relationship ends, it is advisable to determine what constitutes default and what procedures need to be followed in order to terminate the contract as a remedy against the default.

Assignment: Are the parties allowed to transfer their rights and duties under the contract to a third party.

Options: Specifically if one of the objectives of the contract is to build a long-term relationship, or if a change of type of contract is expected, there should be room to facilitate these changes in the contract.

Intellectual Property Rights: If the subject matter of the contract concerns or contains Patents, Trademarks or the use or licensing thereof the IP in question should be mentioned (fully described) in the contract.

Confidentiality and Non-compete: For obvious reasons one should always include these clauses. Enforceability, of course, differs from jurisdiction to jurisdiction.

Penalties and Liquidated Damages: Not every legal system in the world views contractual damages all too positive, (in most common law systems penalties are illegal) and it should be carefully reviewed if such a clause will be enforceable under the governing legal system. It is the writer's preference to include a stipulation in the same article that the delinquent party should pay the costs connected to the collection. In many legal systems that is automatic, but a clearly stated, and agreed to, clause will make it easier to enforce.

Delay, non waiver-clause: A clause that is very useful for those legal systems where partial use of one's rights leads to waiver of the entire set of rights.

Notice Clause: In those cases where the (international) contract partners are located in different countries, or where the communication lines are untrustworthy, it is good practice to determine to whom and where "official" communications should be directed.

Publicity clause: In order to forego any unexpected publicity and the risk of having to deal with unwanted press questions one should reach agreement on what can and cannot be communicated to the outside world.

Language clause: It is essential that the contract stipulates which language prevails. Translating legal concepts from the one language to the other often leads to confusion.

Required activity: In order to forego (bad faith) non-cooperation from the other party, any type of activity essential to the success of the contract should be written down and consequences listed for non-compliance by each of the contracting parties. (most often used in settlement agreements)

Merger and "Four Corner" clauses: The introduction of pre-contractual statements or collateral contracts into the relationship should be excluded on forehand. Even though good faith cannot be removed as such in most legal systems, stipulations that limit free-ranging interpretations of the contract, and the underlying relationship, will limit the risk of a "surprise" ruling in a court case or arbitration.

Choice of law and Venue: One of the more important clauses in an international agreement. The consequences of the choices made here can be enormous in case of disputes. In many international commercial contracts the parties opt for arbitration.

CHAPTER 2
COMPANY LAW: FORMS AND PRECEDENTS

SYNOPSIS

TYPES OF COMPANIES
Public and Private Companies
Formation procedure (private limited company)

PRECEDENTS
- APPLICATION FORM FOR AVAILABILITY OF NAMES
- MEMORANDUM OF ASSOCIATION
- ARTICLES OF ASSOCIATION
- LEGAL DUE DILIGENCE
- DUE DILIGENCE REPORT

It is important for a draftsman to remember that the principal form of commercial enterprise in India, apart from statutory corporations owned by the Government, is a Company incorporated with limited liability[1]. Indian law makes a distinction between corporate body and Company. 'Corporate Body" includes a Company incorporated outside India. "Company" means a company formed and registered under the Indian Companies Act, 1956 or any other previous Companies Act[2].

Companies incorporated in India and branches of foreign corporations are regulated by the Indian Companies Act, 1956[3]. The Act, in general is more restrictive than the English Act, and is more comprehensive. However, several provisions of the Act do not apply to branches of foreign corporations and the Companies Act is in fact far less stringent with regard to such branches.

Companies incorporated under the Companies Act are usually limited liability companies having a share capital. Companies limited by guarantee or unlimited companies, though permissible, are relatively uncommon.

The distinction between the following types of companies is important, because the applications of the provisions of the Act may vary accordingly. The

---

1. It is important to note that banking, insurance and electric utility companies are subject to special legislation.
2. The term "corporate body" includes both Indian and foreign companies, whereas "Company" refers only to an Indian Company.
3. The Act in its unamended form was in many respects similar to the English Companies Acts.

provisions are more stringent in the case of public companies and less so for private companies. A private company that is a subsidiary of a public company is, with a few exceptions, treated as a public company.

Types of Companies

Public and Private Companies

A Company may be incorporated, as either a public or a private company. To qualify as a private company, its articles of association must restrict the right to transfer its shares, limit the number of shareholders to 50 (excluding employees and former employees) and prohibit any invitation to the public to subscribe to shares or debentures. There are certain requirements of the Act from which private companies are exempt, but the requirement to file annual accounts with the Registrar of Companies applies to all companies.

The Companies Act, provides that a private company becomes a deemed public company, if any of the following conditions are met:

- 25 per cent or more of its paid-up share capital is held by one or more corporate bodies.
- It holds 25 per cent. or more of the paid-up share capital of a public company.
- Its average annual turnover is above a prescribed amount (at present Rs. ....(amount)).
- It accepts deposits from the public after an invitation to accept is made by an advertisement or renews its public deposits. Deposits from shareholders, directors and their relatives are not treated as public deposits.

All companies, other than private companies are public companies[1].

Subsidiaries

A Company is a subsidiary of its holding Company, if the following conditions are met:

(1) The composition of the Board of Directors is controlled by the holding Company.

(2) The holding Company controls more than one-half of the total voting power in the subsidiary.

(3) The subsidiary is a subsidiary of any other Company that is itself the subsidiary of the holding Company.

Formation procedure (private limited company)

The law under which a Company is incorporated in India is the Indian Companies Act, 1956, which extends to the whole of India.

---

1. The Central Government exercises considerable control over the affairs of companies. Its sanction or approval is necessary in several important matters of internal administration, particularly in matters concerning managerial personnel [directors and managers]. Such controls are less stringent in the case of private limited companies.

Detailed below are the steps to incorporate a private limited company in India:

1. Select, in order of preference, a few suitable names, not less than four, each of which should indicate as far as possible the main object of the proposed company.
2. Out of the four proposed names, one name will be the main name, and other three are to be mentioned in order of preference.
3. Avoid names, which resemble too closely or are the same, as the names of any other company already registered, and avoid names with the words "Stock Exchange" as part of the names.
4. Apply to the Registrar of Companies to ascertain which of the names selected by you is available.
5. An application in Form No. 1A is to be submitted to the Registrar of Companies in this regard, and a fee of Rs. ....(amount) is payable with each application[1].
6. *See* that one of the promoters is also a subscriber to the memorandum and articles of association of the proposed Company.
7. Pay the fee for the application for availability of name (Form 1A) in cash to the Registrar of Companies.
8. The Registrar of Companies will ordinarily inform you within a period of seven to fourteen days from the submission of your application, whether any of the names applied for is available.
9. If, none of the names is available, you will have to apply again, selecting fresh names, along with required application fee.
10. Get the memorandum and articles of association suitable for a private limited company drafted.
11. Get both the memorandum and articles of association stamped as per the Indian Stamp Act, or the relevant State Act and the notifications thereunder in force in your State.
12. Get both the memorandum and articles of association signed by at least two subscribers, each of whom will also write in his own hand, his father's name, occupation, address and the number of shares subscribed for.
13. There will be at least one witness to these signatures, as mentioned above who will sign and write in his own hand, his father's name, occupation and address.
14. Their agents duly authorised by power of attorney may sign the aforesaid two documents on behalf of the subscribers.
15. Both the documents will then be dated.
16. *See* that the date given on these documents is any date after the date of stamping of them and not before that date.

---

1. The formal application should be done at the same time, as the memorandum and articles of association.

17. Get the following forms duly filled up and signed:
    (i) Declaration of compliance in Form No.1 by an advocate of the Supreme Court or of a High Court, an attorney or a pleader entitled to appear before a High Court or a Secretary or a Chartered Accountant in whole-time practice in India who is engaged in the formation of company, or by a person named in the articles as a director, manager or secretary of the company that all the requirements of the Companies Act, 1956 and the rules thereunder have been complied with in respect of registration and matters precedent and incidental thereto.
    (ii) Notice of the situation of the registered office of the company in Form No.18.
    (iii) Particulars of directors, manager or secretary in Form No. 32 in duplicate.
    (iv) Declaration in favour of one of the subscribers to the Memorandum of Association or any other person authorising him to file the documents and papers for registration and to make necessary corrections, if any. This should be executed on non-judicial stamp paper of the requisite value.

    (Forms stated in sub-items (ii) and (iii), though required to be filed within 30 days of the incorporation of the company, are generally filed together with the memorandum and articles of association.)

18. File the following with the Registrar of Companies within six months from the date of availability of name with necessary registration and filing fees. Minimum registration fee is Rs. ....(amount) and the maximum is Rs. ....(amount) lakhs:—
    (i) The stamped and signed copy of the memorandum and articles of association;
    (ii) The forms mentioned in item 17 above;
    (iii) Any other Agreement, if referred to in memorandum and articles of association, as in that case, it will form a part of the Memorandum and Articles;
    (iv) Any Agreement which the company to be incorporated proposes to enter into with any individual for appointment as its managing or whole-time director or manager;
    (v) Original copy of the Registrar of Companies' letter intimating about the availability of name.

19. Pay the registration and filing fee by way of cash or demand draft or treasury challan for registration of the memorandum of association and for filing of the articles of association and the forms mentioned in item 17, depending on the authorised share capital of the proposed Company.

20. If, paid by way of demand draft, then draw the demand draft in favour of either the concerned Registrar of Companies of the State or Union Territory or Pay and Accounts Officer, Department of Company Affairs, New Delhi, or Mumbai, or Calcutta or Chennai, as the case may be.

21. If, paid by way of treasury challan, then obtain three copies of treasury challan from the specified branches of the appropriate bank, fill up the details, and deposit along with the fee in cash to the said branch of the bank.

22. The description of the head of account of the treasury challan should be as prescribed under Rule 22(1) of the Companies (Central Government's) General Rules and Forms, 1956 and as amended up-to-date.

23. Two copies of the challans will be given to the depositor one of which should be sent to the Registrar of Companies along with the forms and documents mentioned in item 17.

24. The Registrar of Companies will then scrutinise the documents and papers filed for registration and, if necessary, on intimation, the authorised person will make necessary correction to them under his initials.

25. The Registrar of Companies will then register the Company and issue the certificate of incorporation.

26. The date given by the Registrar of Companies on the certificate of incorporation will be the date of incorporation of the Company and on that date, the Company will come into being as a separate legal entity.

27. The private limited company, so registered can commence business and exercise borrowing powers immediately after obtaining the certificate of incorporation from the Registrar of Companies.

PRECEDENTS

APPLICATION FORM FOR AVAILABILITY OF NAMES

The Registrar of Companies.

Sir,

Subject: Availability of names—Information—Furnishing of:

We, the following applicants, are desirous of forming a company to be registered under Companies Act, 1956, in the State of ....

1. Name and full address of the person(s) applying for the availability of the name. (in block capitals)..........................

2. Proposed name of the company..........................

3. State whether public or private.................................

4. In case the proposed name mentioned in item 2 is not available, 3 names to be considered in the order of preference.

5. Main object of the proposed company.

6. Names and addresses of the prospective directors, promoters, etc.

7. Particulars of the names and situation of registered offices of other companies in the group or under the same management.

8. Proposed authorised capital. Rs......................................

9. Please furnish particulars and results of any application moved to this or any other Registrar previously for availability of name.

10. Particulars of remittance of fee (Draft/IPO) Rs. ....

Situation...................

Dated.......................   Signature of the applicant

MEMORANDUM OF ASSOCIATION

Memorandum of Association is charter of a company. It is the fundamental document pertaining to the formation of a company. It contains the basic conditions on the basis of which the company is incorporated. In other words the Memorandum of Association is the constitution of the company, which defines and confines the area of operation of the company. It demarcates the area beyond which the action of the company cannot go. Any transaction outside the objects and powers given in the memorandum is *ultra vires* and cannot be ratified by the company in the general meeting.

Drafting of Memorandum of Association

Draftsmen should know that a Memorandum of Association is the basic document upon which the whole structure of the company is formed. As the Memorandum of Association is the charter of the company, it shall define the area of its activity and extent of power it could exercise. Section 13, of the Companies Act, 1956 deal with contents of Memorandum of Association. The provisions of section 13 could be summarised as below:

  (i) Name clause (Name of the company)—As per section 13(1)(a), the words 'limited' or 'private limited', as the case may be, shall be added as the last words to the name made available by Registrar of Companies (ROC).

  (ii) Registered office clause: (Registered office of the company) As per section 13(1)(b) the State in which the registered office of the company would be situated, is to be mentioned here.

  (iii) Objects clause: (objects for which the company is established) As per section 13(1)(d) the objects clause is required to state (i) the main objects to be pursued by the company on its incorporation and objects incidental or ancillary to the attainment of the main objects;

(ii) other objects of the Company not included in above sub-clause (1).

As per section 13(1)(e) in the case of companies (other than trading corporations), with objects not confined to one State, the States to whose territories the objects extend.

(iv) The memorandum of a company limited by shares or by guarantee shall also state that the liability of its members is limited.

(v) The memorandum of a company limited by guarantee shall also state that each member undertakes to contribute to the assets of the company in the event of its being wound up while he is a member or within one year after he ceases to be a member, for payment of the debts and liabilities of the company, or of such debts and liabilities of the company as may have been contracted before he ceases to be a member as the case may be. It should also state that each member undertakes to contribute for the charges, costs and expenses of winding up and for adjustment of the rights of the contributories among themselves such amount as may be required, not exceeding a specified amount.

(vi) In the case of a company having a share capital—

(a) If the company is a limited company, the memorandum shall also state the amount of share capital with which the company is to be registered and the division thereof into a shares of a fixed amount.

(b) No subscriber of the memorandum shall take less than one share; and

(c) each subscriber of the memorandum shall write opposite to his name the number of shares he takes.

TOTAL VALUE OF WORKS

Less Payments Previously Certified

BALANCE DUE TO CONTRACTOR

2. The Purchaser shall pay the amount due to the Contractor within (30) days after the date hereof.

3. Payment by the Purchaser of the amount due to the Contractor hereunder shall constitute conclusive evidence that the Purchaser has performed all its obligations under the Contract, provided that it is not so conclusive:

(a) to the extent that fraud or dishonesty relates to or affects any matter dealt with in this Certificate, or

(b) if any arbitration or court proceedings under the contract have been commenced by either Party before the expiry of 90 days after the date hereof.

MEMORANDUM OF ASSOCIATION
OF
ALPHA PVT. LTD.

(Registered under the Companies Act, 1956)

I. The name of the Company is "*Alpha* Private Ltd."

II. The Registered Office of the Company is situated in the National Capital Territory of Delhi.

III. The objects for which the Company is established are:

(A) THE MAIN OBJECTS OF THE COMPANY TO BE PURSUED BY IT ON ITS INCORPORATION ARE:

1. To carry on trade, business of or otherwise in any other way venture into the activity of mining, extracting, exploring, producing, washing, managing, mobilising, supplying, expanding, developing, processing, buying, selling, re-selling, importing, exporting, exchanging, distributing, transporting, acting as agents and dealing in all kinds of fuel, including coal including but not limited to lignite and washed coke, naphtha, diesel, other hydro-carbon, natural gas in liquefied or vaporised form etc. (for the sake of brevity, hereinafter referred to as the fuel) for the purpose of supplying, transmitting, marketing, distributing, entering into contract with, franchising, transporting the fuel to any power projects in India or abroad including externally aided projects and non-pithed fast track power projects.

(2) To acquire (whether by purchase, lease, grant, hire or otherwise); establish, develop, exploit, operate and maintain land, airspace, foreshore, claims, walls, mines, washeries, oil refineries, licenses, consents or authorisations, concessions, drilling and mining rights, exploration and production rights, and rights and interests of all descriptions in or relating to the same which may seem to the company capable or possibly capable of affording or facilitating the purchase, generation, supply, distribution, transformation, conversion, transmission, production, manufacture, processing, development, storing, carrying, import and export of, or dealing in the fuel or by-products derived from or connected with any such activity (including limitation scheme) or affording supply of natural or other gas, petroleum or other hydrocarbons, coal and other minerals, heat, steam, solar, hydro, wind, wave, geothermal, biological and all other forms of energy, or chemicals.

3. To construct, operate, maintain and acquire storage, regasification, liquification and other associated facilities for Liquefied Natural Gas.

4. To construct, operate, acquire and maintain pipelines and other modes of transport including automobile tankers, ships for transport, supply and distribution of fuel.

5. To promote, undertake, sponsor and provide research and development services associated with fuel.

(B) THE OBJECTS INCIDENTAL OR ANCILLARY TO ATTAINMENT OF MAIN OBJECTS ARE:

(1) To acquire and hold controlling and other interests in any company or companies and in particular in companies (a) in the business of development of infrastructure for the regasification of the Liquefied Natural Gas (LNG) required for power plants and other users of gas; (b) in the power sector; (c) in the business of exploration, production, sale, purchase, import, export, storage or transportation of the fuel, (d) in the business of construction, maintenance, operation and ownership of a pipeline distribution system to transport natural gas to power plants and other users of gas.

(2) To act as a holding company and to give guarantees and indemnities, to invest or use moneys and property of the Company in such manner as the Board may think fit and without limiting the generality of foregoing, to advance deposit or lend moneys, securities and property to or with such persons, companies or corporations on such security or without security and on such terms and conditions as to the directors may deem expedient and to issue on commission, subscribe for, take, acquire, hold, sell and exchange share stocks, bonds, obligations, debentures, mortgages or securities of any government or other competent authority, company or persons, and to provide financial, managerial and administrative advice, services and assistance for any company in which this Company is interested, and for any other Company, firm or persons.

(3) To plan, locate, design, establish, build, construct, equip, operate, make use, administer, manage and maintain service, improve, inspect, enlarge, alter, protect, develop, extend, repair, replace, refurbish, pull down and remove and carry out work (including without limitation dredging works) in respect of the whole or any part or parts of a fuel receipt, storage, processing treatment and handling facility, a port and harbour facility, jetty, harbour, support vessels, pumping stations, buildings, plants, equipment and any facilities ancillary to the operation or use of the aforesaid or any of them including structures, erections, pipes, pipelines, offices, works, warehouses, plants, platforms, derricks, liquefied natural gas revaporisation equipment, laboratories, research stations, transport facilities, roads, railways, bridges and structures of all kind and to purchase or otherwise, lease, charter, and take or let or hire part of, any operation in respect of the same and to acquire, operate and maintain the licenses, consents, authorisations, wayleaves, easements and other rights capable or possibly capable of facilitating the aforesaid.

(4) To install in any premises or plant and to operate, use, inspect, maintain, service, repair, refurbish and remove meters or other devices for assessing the quantity and/or quality of supplies of the fuel and other substances and forms of energy and further purposes connected with such supplies.

(5) To do anything that an electricity generator, electricity supplier or electricity transmitter, oil refinery, coal washeries, coal mines etc., are empowered, enabled, or required to do under or by virtue of, or under license or exemption granted under any enactment or statutory instruments.

(6) To do any of the business of procurers, suppliers, distributors, extractors, producers, developers, purchasers, refiners, distillers, processors, converters, storers, carriers, importers and exporters of, explorers and prospectors for the dealers in natural gas and other gases, petroleum and other hydrocarbon, minerals, metals, chemicals, and other products, other than the Fuel derived from or connected with any of them for the purposes of the main objects of the Company.

(7) To enter into partnership or into any arrangement for sharing profits, union or interest, co-operation, joint venture, reciprocal concessions or otherwise, or collaborate with any person or company, carrying on or engaged in, any business or transaction either in India or abroad which this Company is authorised to carry on or engage or in any business or transaction, capable of being conducted so as directly or indirectly to benefit the Company.

(8) To make donations to such persons or institutions either of cash or any other assets as may be thought directly or indirectly conducive to any of the Company's objects or otherwise and in particular to remunerate any person or corporation introducing business to the Company and also to subscribe, contribute or otherwise assist, or guarantee for money for charitable, scientific, religious, benevolent, national, public, cultural, educational or other institutions or objects or for any exhibition of any public, general or other objects.

(9) To train, establish training facilities for or pay for training in India or abroad of any of Company's employees or officers or any candidate in the interest of or furtherance of the Company's objects.

(10) To expend money in experimenting, developing, planning and testing and improving or seeking to improve any patents, rights, inventions, discoveries, processes or information of the Company or which the Company may acquire or propose to acquire.

(11) To establish, provide, maintain and conduct or otherwise subsidise, research laboratories and experimental workshops for scientific and technical research and experiments and to undertake and carry on with all scientific and technical research, experiments and tests of all kinds and to promote studies and research both scientific and technical investigations and inventions by providing, subsidising, endowing or assisting laboratories, workshops, libraries, lectures, meetings and conferences and by providing remuneration to scientific and technical professors and teachers and by providing for the award, scholarships, prizes, grants to students or independent students or otherwise and to encourage, promote and award studies, researches, investigations,

experiments, tests and inventions of any kind that may be considered likely to assist any of the businesses which the Company is authorised to carry on.

(12) To set up a productivity enhancement, support centre to bring about improvements in product engineering, quality control and procurement management.

(13) To buy, purchase, take on lease, exchange or otherwise machinery, plant and equipment, trademarks and stock in trade, acquire lands, buildings, flats, and hereditaments of any tenure or description in India or elsewhere whether for residential, business or other purposes and any rights, easements, advantages and privileges relating thereto and either for investment or resale and to turn the same into account as may seem appropriate or expedient, and to construct, alter, improve, decorate, develop, furnish and maintain offices, flats, houses, buildings, and structures, works and conveniences of all kinds on any of the land, or immovable properties, purchased or acquired by the company and to lease, sell, mortgage, exchange, convey, transfer, deal in or to otherwise dispose of the same.

(14) Subject to the directions of the Reserve Bank of India in this behalf, to borrow or raise moneys or loans from any person, firm, body corporate, financial institutions, banks, or association of persons for the purposes of the Company by promissory notes, Bills of Exchange, Hundies, and other negotiable or transferable instruments or by mortgage, charge, hypothecation or pledge, or by debentures or debenture stock, perpetual or otherwise, charged upon all or any of the Company's properties and assets both present and future, movable and immovable, including its uncalled capital, upon such terms as the directors may deem appropriate or expedient or in such other manner, or to take money on deposit or otherwise (merely for the purpose of financing the business of the Company) with or without allowance of interest thereon and to lend money to customers and others having dealings with the Company and to guarantee the performance of contracts by such person and to execute all deeds, writings and assurances for any of the aforesaid purposes.

(15) To open current, overdraft or fixed deposit accounts with any banks, bankers, shroffs or merchants and to pay into and draw moneys from such accounts.

(16) To draw, make, accept, endorse, discount, execute and issue promissory notes, bills of exchange, bills of lading, warrants, debentures, and other negotiable or transferable instruments.

(17) To invest the funds of the Company from time to time in such assets, properties, securities, shares, bullion, specie or investment or otherwise as may from time to time be determined appropriate by the directors and from time to time sell or vary all such investments and to execute

all assignments, transfers, receipts and documents that may be necessary in that behalf.

(18) Upon any issue of shares, debentures, or any other securities of the Company, to employ brokers, commission agents and underwriters, and to provide for the remuneration of such persons for their services by payment in cash or issue of shares, debentures or other securities of the Company, by granting the option to take the same or in any other manner permitted by law.

(19) To act in conjunction with, unite or amalgamate with, create or constitute or assist in creating or constituting any other company or association of a kind similar, wholly or partially to this Company for the purpose of acquiring all or any of the properties, rights and liabilities of the Company and to buy or absorb all or any part of the business or properties of any such company or association and to acquire and secure membership seat or privilege in and of any of the associations, exchange, market, or institution in India or any part of the world.

(20) To enter into any arrangements with any Government or authorities, municipal, local or otherwise or any persons or companies in India or abroad, that is or may be conducive to the object of the Company or any of them and to obtain from any such Government authorities, persons, or companies, any rights, privileges, charters, contracts, licenses and concessions which the Company deem desirable and to carry out, exercise and comply therewith.

(21) To alter, manage, develop, exchange, lease, transfer, mortgage, and give in gift, or otherwise dispose of, improve or deal with the lands, properties, assets and rights and resources and undertakings of the Company or any part thereof for such considerations as the Company may think fit and in particular for shares, debentures, securities, of any other Company having object altogether or in part similar to those of this Company and to distribute amongst the members of the Company in cash or in specie any properties or assets of the Company, provided that no such distribution amounts to reduction of share capital of the Company except in accordance with the provisions of the Companies Act, 1956, in this behalf.

(22) To pay all costs, charges and expenses incurred or sustained in or about the promotion and establishment of the Company or which the Company shall construe to be preliminary, including therein the cost of advertising, commission for underwriting, brokerage, printing and stationery and the expenses attendant upon the formation of agencies and local boards.

(23) To pay all preliminary expenses of any company promoted by the Company or any company in which the Company is or may contemplate be interested and preliminary expenses may include all or any part of the costs and expenses of owners of any businesses or properties acquired by the Company.

(24) To procure the incorporation, registration or other recognition of the Company in India, and to establish and regulate agencies for the purposes of the Company's business and to apply or join in applying to governmental, local, municipal or other authorities or bodies for concessions, orders, rights or privileges, that is, or may be conducive to the Company's objects or any of them and to oppose any proceedings or applications which are or may be calculated directly or indirectly to prejudice the Company's interests.

(25) To provide for welfare of the Directors or the employees or former employees of the Company, and the wives, widows and families of such persons, by building or by contributing to the building of houses, dwelling houses or by grant of money, pensions, allowances, bonus or other payments or by creating and from time to time subscribing to provident and other funds and providing or subscribing towards schools, places of instruction and recreation and hospitals, dispensaries, medical and other attendants and other assistants as the Company shall think fit, and to form, subscribe to or otherwise aid benevolent, religious, scientific, national, public or other institutions or objects or purposes.

(26) To acquire and undertake the whole or any part of the business, property and liabilities of any person carrying on the main business of the Company and to carry on or possession of property suitable for the purpose of the main objects of the Company.

(27) To dispose of or transfer the business, property and undertaking of the Company or any part thereof for any consideration which the Company may deem fit to accept and in particular for shares, debentures, debenture stock, bonds or securities of any other company or companies for the purpose of its or their acquiring all or any of the property, rights or liabilities of this Company or for any other purpose which may seem calculated to benefit this Company.

(28) To create any reserve fund, sinking fund, insurance fund, dividend equalisation fund or any other special fund, whether for depreciation or for repairing, improving, extending or maintaining any of the property of the company or for any other purposes conducive to the interests of the Company.

(29) Subject to the provisions of the Companies Act, 1956 to place, to reserve or to distribute as dividend or bonus shares among the members or otherwise to apply, as the Company may from time to time think fit, any moneys belonging to the Company including those received by way of premium on shares or debentures issued by the Company at a premium and any moneys received in respect of forfeited shares and moneys arising from the reissue by the Company of forfeited shares.

(30) To do all or any of the things hereby authorised either alone or in conjunction with, or in partnership with any person, firm or body corporate or as factors, trustees, or agents of any other companies or persons or by or through any factors, trustees, or agents.

(31) To do all and everything necessary, suitable or proper for the accomplishment of any of the purposes or the attainment of any of the objects or the furtherance of any of the powers herewith set forth, either along or in association with other corporate bodies, firms, or individuals, and to do every other act or acts, thing or things incidental or appurtenant to or growing out of or connected with the aforesaid business or powers or any part or parts thereof.

(32) To appoint or employ, temporarily or permanently, or obtain on deputation any person or persons, remunerate any person, firm or company for rendering services to the Company whether in cash or by allotment of shares or securities (including debentures) of the Company credited as paid in full or in part or otherwise as may be thought expedient.

(33) To accept gifts of property, shares or assets in connection with the attainments of main objects of the Company.

(34) Subject to the provisions of the Companies Act, 1956, to enter into arrangements for rendering and obtaining of technical know-how services and/or technical collaboration with individuals, firms, research laboratory, body corporate whether in or outside India.

(35) To buy wholesale or retail, repair, alter and exchange, let on hire, import all kinds of articles and things which may be required for the purpose of any of the main businesses or which is commonly supplied or dealt with by persons engaged in any such business or which may seem capable of being profitably dealt with in connection with any of the main businesses.

(36) To apply for purchase or otherwise, acquire any patent, patent right, copyright, trade marks, formula, license, know-how, lease, concessions, conferring any exclusive or limited right to use or other information as to any invention which may seem capable of being used for any of the purposes of the Company or the acquisition of which may directly or indirectly benefit the Company, and to use, exercise, develop or grant licenses in respect of the property rights, or information so acquired.

(37) To lend and advance money to the credit of any person or company, to give a guarantee or indemnity for the payment of money or the performance of contracts or obligations by any person, to secure or undertake in any way the repayment of moneys lent or advanced to, or the liabilities incurred by any person subject to the provisions of the Companies Act, 1956 and Regulations made thereunder and directives issued by the Reserve Bank of India.

(38) To adopt such means of making known and advertising the business and products of the Company as may be expedient.

(39) To issue or allot fully or partly paid shares in the Capital of the Company in payment of or part payment of any movable or immovable property purchased or otherwise acquired by the Company or any services rendered to the Company.

(40) To control, manage, finance, subsidise, co-ordinate or otherwise assist any company or companies, including subsidiaries, in which the Company has a direct or indirect financial interest, to provide secretarial, administrative, technical, commercial and other services and facilities of all kinds for any such Company or Companies and to make payments by way of subvention or otherwise and any other arrangements which may seem desirable with respect to any business or operations of or generally with respect to such Company or companies.

(41) To arrange for the marketing in India and abroad and sale of services of the Company and purchase of raw materials, goods and articles, as are necessary for carrying on the business of the Company and, for that purpose, either to establish its own shop, agency, or marketing organization, or to appoint selling or buying agents or distributors of both (whether individuals, firms, bodies corporate) in any place in or outside India and to allot, specify, alter or modify their areas of operation or the terms and conditions of their appointment and to pay remuneration to such selling or buying agents or distributors or both by way of such commission or in such other manner as the Company may deem fit.

(42) To institute and defend any suit, appeal, application for review or revision or any other application of any nature whatsoever, to take out executions, to enter into agreements, to refer to arbitration and to enforce and where need be to contest any award and for all such purposes to engage or retain counsels, attorneys and agents and when necessary to remove them.

(43) To carry out research, investigation, development and experimental work of every description in relation to computer hardware and software and its application and use.

(44) To undertake and execute any trusts the undertaking of which may seem to the Company desirable and either gratuitously or otherwise.

(45) To insure the whole or any part of the property of the Company, either fully or partly, and to protect and indemnify the Company from liability or loss in any respect.

(46) To construct, assemble, erect, maintain, run and establish factories for making pre-fabricated houses or apartments or structures in connection with the main business of the Company.

(47) To indemnify members, officers, directors, secretaries and servants of the Company against proceedings, damages, claims and demands in respect of anything done or ordered to be done by them for and in the interest of the Company or for any loss, damages, or misfortunes which may happen in the execution of the duties of their office or in relation thereto.

(48) To promote any company or companies for the purpose of acquiring all or any of the properties and liabilities of this Company or for any other

such purpose connected with the main business of the Company carried or in pursuance of its aforesaid objects.

(49) To import or prepare for market revise, clean, restore, recondition, treat and otherwise manipulate and deal and turn to account by any process of means, by-products, re-use and waste, and other products capable of being manufactured or produced out of or with the use of all or any raw materials, ingredients, substances or commodities used in the manufacture of all or any of the products which the Company is entitled to manufacture or deal in and to make such use of the same as may be thought fit for the attainment of the main objects of the Company.

(50) To do any of the business as buyers, sellers, traders, importers, exporters, distributors, general merchants, stockists, warehouses, commission agents, advertising agents, agents for promotion of sales, clearing and forwarding agents and the business of sourcing of all kinds of goods and materials, either manufactured, semi-manufactured or raw materials of all materials and descriptions and to offer all services in relation to the above and to carry on agency business of all kinds.

(51) To guarantee the payment of money, unsecured by or payable under or in respect of bonds, debentures, debenture stocks, contracts, mortgages, charges, obligations and other securities of any company or of any authority, Central, State, Municipal, local or otherwise or of any person whatsoever, whether incorporated or not and generally to transact all kinds of guarantee business, to guarantee the issue of or the payment of interest on the shares, debentures, debenture-stock or other securities or obligations of any company or association, and to pay or provide for brokerage, commission and underwriting in respect of any such issue and to transact all kinds of trust and agency business.

(52) To purchase, charter, lease, take or let on hire, operate, use, employ or turn to account, build, equip, service, repair, maintain, supply, and deal in tankers and other ships and vessels and crafts of every description (including without limitation submersible crafts), hovercraft, motor vehicles, aircraft, airships, railway, locomotives, wagons, trucks, and many means of transport and parts and accessories of all kinds for any of the same.

(C) THE OTHER OBJECTS ARE:

(1) To invent, design, develop, construct, manufacture, produce, erect, assemble, test, import, export, alter, install, maintain, repair, renovate, refurbish, recondition, utilise, operate, manage, acquire, sell, hire, hire out, supply, and otherwise deal in plant, equipment and apparatus for the purposes of communications of all kinds (including, without prejudice to the generality of the foregoing, plants, equipment and apparatus which is intended for, or capable of, or designed for use in, with, in connection with, in conjunction with, connected directly or indirectly, to, or ancillary to, all, part or parts of telecommunication, data processing, information storage or retrieval or process control,

systems, services, facilities, apparatus, plant and equipment, as the case may be), and anything capable of being used for or in connection with or ancillary to such plant, equipment and apparatus as aforesaid.

(2) To provide remotely located offices and services and systems (including without prejudice to the generality of the foregoing telephone answering, calling and related services and computer bureau) and remotely located services and systems for the control of machinery utilising telecommunication or data processing facilities, to act as business and office managers, secretaries, messengers, telephone operators, commercial agents, mail order bureau, market researchers and to provide services in connection with the reception, processing and forwarding of signals and information by telephone, telemessage, telegram, telex, letter, wireless telegraphy and (without limitation) any other means of communications and the processing, ordering and payment for and dispatch and delivery of goods, articles and services of all kinds by any means whatsoever.

(3) To acquire, produce, transmit, publish, print and reproduce in any form whatsoever (including, without prejudice to the generality of the foregoing, visual or audible form and forms capable of being used by, in, or in connection with computers) and to buy, sell, supply and otherwise deal in directories, brochures, manuals, journals, periodicals, magazines, newspapers, books, pictures, photographs, stationary and other documents.

(4) To establish, acquire, operate, manage, supply, sell, hire, hire out, maintain and otherwise deal in facilities, plant, apparatus, and equipment (including but not limited to radio and television stations and studios) used or designed for use for the purposes of receiving and broadcasting or otherwise transmitting (by wireless telegraphy, closed circuits, cables or otherwise) and of making, producing, recording replaying or producing programmes and cinematographic films for radio and television and for any other means of communication, sound and visual recordings and other products of all kinds (whether pre-recorded or not) for recording in permanent or semi-permanent form, and replaying or reproducing sounds, images and signals of all kinds.

(5) To carry on all or any of the businesses of, and provide services associated with, engineers, (including without limitation, telecommunications, mechanical, chemical, electrical, civil, heating and ventilation engineers), bankers, financiers, factors, underwriters and dealers in securities, insurers, insurance brokers, share brokers and agents, insurance underwriters, property developers, freight contractors, carriers by land, water and air of freight and passengers, forwarding agents, shipping agents, travel agents, employment agents, estate agents, surveyors, architects, wharfingers, warehousemen, garage proprietors, motor mechanics, storage contractors, electricity supply undertakers, general traders, licensed restaurateurs, food processors, manufacturers and distributors, painters, decorators, producers of oil exhibitions and displays, entertainers, photographers, cartographers,

couriers and retailers, wholesalers and mail order operators for the sale, hire or other supply of any products or services.

(6) To render engineering, technical, management and other types of skilled and other services of all types of industries or organisations in India or abroad including for office, advertising, accounting, computer, secretarial and taxation matters and without limiting the generality of the above to act as consultants.

(7) To undertake, carry out, promote and sponsor rural development including any programmes for promoting the social and economic welfare or, the upliftment of the public in any rural area and to incur any expenditure or any program of rural development and to assist the execution and promotion thereof either directly or indirectly or through an independent agency or in any other manner. The words rural area shall include such areas as may be regarded as rural areas under section 35CC of the Income-tax Act, 1961, or any other law relating to rural development for the time being in force or as may be regarded by the Directors as rural areas and the Directors may at their discretion, in order to implement any of the above mentioned objects or purposes, transfer without consideration or at such fair or concessional valuer as the Directors may think fit and divest the ownership of any property of the Company to or in favour of any Public institutions or Trusts of Funds whose object is rural development or upliftment.

(8) To acquire or set up and run hospitals, clinics, nursing homes, maternity and family planning units or pathological laboratories and optician shops.

(9) To carry on in India or elsewhere the business of importers and exporters of and dealers in all such items that are permissible under the prevailing Import and Export Trade Policy of the Government of India and also to buy and sell, either as principal to principal or as broker, Import Replenishment License as per the policy of the Government of India.

(10) To carry on the business of building construction, civil contractors and undertake construction work on turnkey project based in India and abroad.

(11) Subject to the approval of RBI if necessary under RBI Act, 1934, as amended by RBI (Amendment) Act, 1997, to carry on the business of finance, hire purchase, leasing and investment. The Company shall, however, not carry on any business of Banking as defined under the Banking Regulation Act, 1949.

(12) To carry on all or any of the business of and provide services associated with engineers (including without limitation, electrical, gas, petroleum, environmental, drilling, construction, mechanical, heating, ventilation, civil, chemical, telecommunications, computer and data information engineers), environmental biologists, physicists, chemists, physicians and specialists in medicine, mechanics, technicians, geologists, draftsmen, designers, surveyors, architects, builders, painters and decorators.

(13) To carry on all or any of the businesses of procurers, suppliers, distributors, converters, producers, processors, developers, storers, carriers, importers and exporters of, and dealers in, hydrocarbon fuels, fuel handling equipment and machinery and fuel handling facilities thereto and any products or by products derived from any such business (including without limitation distillate fuel oil and natural gas whether in liquefied or vaporised form) and to carry on all or any of the businesses of construction, maintenance, running and owning a pipeline distribution system and import, export, store, sell, market and transport the natural gas to power plants and other users of gas by way of laying pipelines or through any other transportation means.

(14) To plan, locate, design, establish, build, construct, equip, operate, make use, administer, manage and maintain, service, improve, inspect, enlarge, alter, protect, develop, extend, repair, replace, refurbish, pull down and remove and carry out works in respect of the whole or any part or parts of any electricity generating station (including without limitation combined heat and power stations), generating sets, sub-station, transformer station, pumping station, building, plant, equipment, electric main works and any facilities ancillary to the operation or use of the aforesaid or any of them including structures, erections, pipes, pipelines, machinery, engines, shops and showrooms, offices, factories, works, warehouses, plants, platforms, derricks, transmission towers or pylons, rigs, wind structures, dams and associated structures, testing sites, offshore wave structures, installations, (including without limitation solar power and geothermal installations), depots, distribution stations and sub-stations, wharves, jetties, terminals, transport facilities, canals, roads, railways, branches, or sidings, bridges, reservoirs, water courses, tunnels, airports, and structures of all kinds, whether for the purposes of the Company or for sale or hire to, or in return for any consideration from any person, and to purchase or otherwise acquire, lease, charter and take or let on hire any of the same and to contribute to, or assist in, or carry out any part of, any operation in respect of the same and to acquire, operate and maintain the licenses, consents, authorisations, wayleaves, easements and other rights capable of facilitating the aforesaid.

(15) To do any of the businesses of procurers, suppliers, distributors, designers, developers, manufacturers, installers, fitters, repairers, maintainers, importers and exporters of, and dealers in electrical appliances, electrical plants and machinery, and all kinds of goods, equipment, fittings, machinery, materials and installation connected with the generation, transformation, transmissions, supply and use of electricity for domestic, industrial, commercial or other purposes or with conservation of electricity and other forms of energy for the purpose of main objects of the Company.

IV. The liability of the Members is limited.

V. The Authorised Share Capital of the Company is Rs. .... (Amount in figure) .... (Amount in words) divided into Rs. .... (Amount in figure) .... (Amount in words) Equity Shares of Rs. .... (Amount in figure) .... (Amount in words) each.

We, the several persons whose names, addresses and descriptions are subscribed hereunder, are desirous of being formed into a Company in pursuance of this Memorandum of Association and we respectively agree to take the number of shares in the Capital of the Company set opposite our respective names.

S No.	Name, address, description and occupation of the Subscriber	No. of Equity Shares taken by each Subscriber	Signature of Subscriber	Signature of Witness with address and occupation
1		10 (Ten)		
2.		10 (Ten)		
	TOTAL	20		
	Twenty (only)			

Dated..................
Place....................

ARTICLES OF ASSOCIATION

Introduction

The Articles of Association is an important document which is framed with the object of carrying out the aims and objective of the company as contained in Memorandum. The Articles are regulations for the internal management of a company and are subordinate to the Memorandum. It constitutes a contract between the company and its members and members *inter se*.

Drafting of Articles of Association.—Articles of association of a company may be drafted in any one of the forms given in Tables 'A', 'C', 'D' and 'E' of Schedule 1 of the companies Act as may be applicable or in a form as near thereto as circumstances admit. The companies are, however free to make provisions contained in any of the tables adopted by the Company.

The articles of association usually contains provisions relating to the following matters:

1. Exclusion wholly or in part of Table 'A';
2. Issue of sweat equity shares;
3. Issue of preference shares;

4. Allotment of shares;
5. Dematerialisation;
6. Lien of shares;
7. Call on shares;
8. Transfer of shares;
9. Transmission of shares;
10. Nomination;
11. Forfeiture of shares;
12. Buy-back of its own shares;
13. Conversion of shares into stock;
14. Share warrants;
15. Alteration of capital;
16. General meetings and proceedings, thereat;
17. Voting rights of members, voting and proxies;
18. Minimum and maximum number of directors;
19. Directors, managing/whole-time directors/their appointment, remuneration, qualifications, powers and proceedings of the Board of Directors;
20. Dividends and reserves;
21. Managing and/or Secretary;
22. Accounts and Audit;
23. Borrowing powers;
24. Common sale;
25. Capitalisation of profits;
26. Secrecy;
27. Winding up; and
28. Execution or adoption of preliminary agreements.

COMPANY LIMITED BY SHARES
ARTICLES OF ASSOCIATION
OF
Beta (Plumbing) Private Limited

Table 'A'

1. Regulations contained in Table 'A' in the First Schedule to the Companies Act, 1956 (hereinafter referred to as Table 'A') shall apply to the Company in so far as they are not inconsistent with these Articles.

2. Regulations 36 to 43 and 64 to 66 of Table A shall not apply to the Company.

Definitions

3. The following expressions shall have the meaning assigned to them herein below unless there be something in the subject or context inconsistent therewith:

"*The Act*" means the Companies Act, 1956, as amended from time to time.

"*The Agreement*" shall mean the Shareholder's Agreement between *Alpha* .... and *Beta* .... Private Limited dated.................... , 20..... along with annexures thereto and shall include any modification, alteration, addition or deletion thereto agreed between the parties in writing after the effective date of this Agreement.

DGO B.V *Alpha* .... B.V means a company organised and existing under Dutch law and having its registered office in .... (place/State) and place of business at .... (address).

The "..................... Group" means Mr. .... (name) son of Mr. .... (name), resident of .... (address), representing himself and certain other companies, individuals and entities specified in Schedule 1 to Shareholders Agreement, all of whom are collectively referred to hereinafter as the "*Beta* Private Limited"

"*Board*" means the Board of Directors of the company or the Directors present at a duly convened meeting of the Directors at which quorum is present.

"*Company*" means Beta .... Private Limited.

"*Director(s)*" means the Director(s) for the time being of the company including Additional Director(s) and Alternate Director(s) as the case may be, the Directors assembled at a Board, or acting under a Circular Resolution under the Articles.

"*Office*" means the Registered Office for the time being of the company.

"*The Register*" means the Register of Members to be kept pursuant to the Act.

"*The Chairman*" means the Chairman of the Board of Directors for the time being of the Company.

"*Documents*" including summons, notice, requisition other legal process and registers, whether issued, sent or kept in pursuance of this or any other Act or otherwise.

"*Members*" means the duly registered holders, from time to time of the shares of the Company and includes the subscribers to the Memorandum of the Company.

"*Month*" means the calendar month.

"*The Registrar*" means the Registrar of the Companies,.................................

"*The Register of Members*" means the register of members to be kept pursuant to section 150 of the Act.

"*Shares*" means the shares or stocks into which the capital of the Company is divided and interest corresponding with such shares or stocks except where a distinction between stocks and shares is expressed or implied.

"*Year*" means the calendar year and "Financial Year" shall have the meaning assigned thereto by section 2(17) of the Act.

Private Company

4. The company is a Private Limited Company, within the meaning of section 3(1)(iii) of the Companies Act, 1956 and accordingly:

   (a) The number of members of the Company (exclusive of the persons who are in the employment of the Company and persons or who having been formerly in the employment of the Company, were members of the Company while in that employment and have continued to be members after the employment ceased) is not to exceed fifty. Provided that where two or more persons hold one or more shares in the Company jointly, they shall for the purposes of this clause be treated as a single member;

   (b) Any invitation to the public to subscribe for any shares or debentures of the Company is hereby prohibited; and

   (c) The right of transfer of shares shall be restricted as hereinafter provided.

Authorised Capital

5. The Authorised share capital of the company is Rs. .... (amount in figures and words) divided into .... (quantity of shares in figures and words) Equity shares of Rs. .... (amount in figures and words) each payable in the manner as may be determined by the Directors, from time to time, with power to increase, reduce, sub-divide or to repay the same or to divide the same into several classes and to attach thereto any right and to consolidate or sub-divide or re-organise the shares subject to the provisions of the Act, to vary such rights as may be determined in accordance with the regulations of the Company.

6. In regulation 13 of Table 'A' the words "provided that no call shall exceed one fourth of the nominal value of the share or be payable at less than one month from the date fixed for the payment of the last proceeding call" shall be omitted.

7. The shares may be issued against consideration other than cash.

8. The calls on any partly paid up shares in the Company and any further issue of shares shall be made by the Company in accordance with the provisions of Articles and upon taking into account financial requirements of the Company.

Issue of Capital

9. If and when the Company desires to increase the paid-up share-capital, whether by a further issue of equity shares or preference shares, the additional shares shall be offered in the first instance to the existing holders of the shares by way of rights issue in proportion to the capital paid-up on the shares (whether equity or preference) held by them at the time so as to maintain the ownership structure within the Company except when issued under Article 13 hereof.

10. The new shares shall be issued upon such terms and conditions and with such rights and privileges annexed thereto as the general meeting resolving upon

the creation thereof, shall direct and if no direction shall be given, as the Board shall determine, and in particular such shares may be issued with a preferential or qualified right to dividends, and in the distribution of assets of the Company and with a special or without any voting right.

Additional Contribution

11. The Shareholders shall contribute additional capital to the Company, in proportion to their respective shareholding percentages (each such contribution being referred to as an "Additional Contribution"), as required by the Company to implement its projects envisaged in the Agreement.

12. Each Shareholder shall, unless otherwise specified herein, pay the amount of its pro-rata share of the Additional Contribution, in accordance with the following procedure:

- a. The Board of Directors shall issue a notice ('Payment Notice') to the Shareholders setting forth each Shareholder's pro-rata share, based on its shareholding percentage of such contribution and specifying the date on which payment is required to be made.
- b. The Shareholders shall, on or before the date specified in the Payment Notice, remit immediately available funds as specified in the Payment Notice to the Company's bank account(s) designated in the Payment Notice.
- c. Against the amounts contributed by the Shareholders pursuant to this Article the Board of Directors shall issue to each Shareholder such additional number of Shares, credited as fully paid, as are necessary to reflect such Shareholder's pro-rata share of the relevant contribution.

13. The Board of Directors may issue the further share to the person(s) who may not be the shareholders of the Company with previous approval of the Shareholders accorded by passing a resolution at a general meeting by consensus vote.

Transfer of Shares

14. The Company shall keep a register of transfers, and therein shall be fairly and distinctly entered particulars of every transfer or transmission of any Share.

15. The instrument of transfer shall be in writing and all the provisions of section 108 and other applicable provisions of the Act shall be duly complied with in respect of all transfers of Shares and registration thereof. The Company shall not charge any fee for registration of transfer of Shares.

16. Except where the transfer is made pursuant to Article 21 hereof the person proposing the transfer of any share (hereinafter called 'the Proposing Transferor') shall give notice in writing (hereinafter called a 'Transfer Notice') to the Company that he desires to transfer the shares. A Transfer Notice shall specify the number of shares proposed to be transferred, the sum the Proposing Transferor fixed as the fair value, and shall constitute the Company his agent for the sale of the share to any member or person selected by the Board, willing to purchase the share (hereinafter called "the Proposed buyer") at the price so fixed, or at the fair value to be fixed in accordance with Article 19 hereof. The Transfer

Notice may include several shares and in such case shall operate as if it were a separate notice in respect of each share. The transfer Notice shall not be revocable without the sanction of the Board.

17. On receipt of the Transfer Notice the Company shall within fifteen (15) days inform all the Shareholders (except the Proposing Transferor)

18. If the Company shall within three months after being served with a Transfer Notice, find a Proposed buyer, shall give notice thereof to the Proposing Transferor. On receipt of the notice and upon payment of the fair value as fixed in accordance with Article 16 or 19 hereof the Proposing Transferor shall be bound to transfer the share to Proposed buyer.

19. In case any difference arises between the Proposing Transferor and the Proposed buyer as to the fair value of a share, the fair value shall be calculated as the norms given in Article 22 and Auditors of the Company shall on the application of either party, certify in writing the sum which, in their opinion, is the fair value, as per the norms given in Article 22 hereof and such sum shall be deemed to be the fair value, and in so certifying the Auditors shall be considered to be acting as experts and not as arbitrators, and as such the Arbitration and Conciliation Act shall not apply.

20. If the Proposing Transferor, after having become bound as aforesaid, makes default in transferring the share, the Company may receive the purchase money and the Proposing Transferor shall be deemed to have appointed any on Director or the secretary of the Company as his agent to execute the Transfer Deeds or any other documents as may be necessary to transfer the shares in favour of the Proposed buyer, and upon the execution of such Transfer Deed the Company shall hold the purchase money in trust for the Proposing Transferor. The receipt of the purchase money by the Company shall be a good discharge to the Proposed buyer, and after his name has been entered in the register of members in purported exercise of the aforesaid power, the validity of the proceedings shall not be questioned by any person.

21. If the Company is unable to find, within a period of three months after being served with a Transfer Notice, a Proposed buyer, the company shall give notice to the Proposing Transferor. On receipt of such notice the Proposing Transferor shall at any time within three months of this notice, be at liberty, to sell and transfer the share(s) to any person and at any price not below the price mentioned in the Transfer Notice.

Transfer Price

22. The transfer price shall be calculated as follows:

The Transfer price shall be greater of:

(a) The book value determined according to the method of the evaluation used in the balance sheet of the previous year.

22.1 The price of the proposed sale of Shares to BLS and or its nominee shall be the fair value of such Shares determined on the basis of a valuation report by *Delta* or one of the other firms of Chartered Accountants of similar international repute. If so requested by DGO, such valuation report shall take into account the price offered by the potential buyer. Provided that if the approval of the Reserve Bank of India is required. Such shares shall be valued in accordance with the method/s acceptable to the Reserve Bank of India for the purpose of granting approval for the said transfer. BLS may convey, in writing, its acceptance to the offer to DGO within a reasonable period, which shall be not later than sixty (60) days from the date of receipt of offer from DGO along with the valuation report of the firm of chartered accountants.

23. Refusal to register transfer of shares

1. Subject as aforesaid, the Board may at any time in their absolute and uncontrolled discretion decline to register any proposed transfer of shares. This clause shall apply to a case where the proposed transferee is also a member of the Company.

2. The Board may also decline to register any transfer of shares on which the Company has a lien. The Board may also suspend the registration of transfers during the fourteen days immediately preceding the annual general meeting in each year.

3. The Board may also decline to recognise any instrument of transfer unless the instrument of transfer is accompanied by the certificate of the shares to which it relates and such other evidence as the Board may reasonably require to show the right of the transferor to make the transfer.

Directors

24. Unless otherwise determined by a general meeting, the number of Directors shall not be less than and not more than

25. The First Directors of the Company shall be...

26. A Director shall not be required to hold any qualification shares nor required to retire by rotation. Once appointed they shall continue in office until they are removed by the general meeting or die or resign or become permanently incapacitated. The Directors are entitled to notice of general meetings and to attend and speak thereat.

27. Subject to the provisions of the Companies Act, 1956:

   (a) The remuneration of every Director for his services shall be such sum as the Board may from time to time determine for each meeting of the Board or a meeting of any committee attended by him.

   (b) If any Director, being willing, shall be called upon to perform extra services (which expression shall include work done by the Director as a member of any committee formed by the Directors) or to make any special exertions for any of the purposes of the Company or to give special attention to the business and affairs of the Company, the Board may remunerate such Director either by paying a fixed sum or a percentage of profits or both or any other manner, and may allow to such Director at the cost and expense of the Company such facilities or amenities as the Board may determine from time to time.

28. If the office of the Director is vacated due to death, resignation or otherwise, the resulting vacancy shall be filled in by the Board at a duly convened meeting of the Board.

29. Subject to the provision of section 313 of the Companies Act, the Board may appoint an alternate Director to act for one or more Directors (hereinafter called the 'Original Director') during his/their absence for a period of not less than three months from the state in which the meetings of the Board are usually held and such appointment shall have effect and such appointee, whilst he holds office as an alternate Director, shall be entitled to notice of meetings of the Board and attend and vote on behalf of the Original Director he is representing. If the alternate Director is himself a director, he shall be entitled to exercise in addition to his vote, a vote on behalf of the Original Director to whom he is alternate. An alternate director appointed under this clause shall be a person nominated by the party who nominated the Original Director.

30. The Company may have other Directors, *i.e.* Directors, not representing either or provided this is agreed in writing by both and such Directors shall be in addition to the number of Directors mentioned in Article 24 provided, however, that shall be entitled to nominate for each such new Director one additional Director to ensure its casting vote under Article 46.

31. The Board may appoint and, at their discretion, remove or suspend such/officers by whatever designation called, managers, secretaries, engineers, experts, legal advisers, solicitors, clerks, agents, salesmen, workmen and other servants or professionals for permanent, temporary or special service, as the Board may, from time to time, think fit and determine their duties, fix their remuneration, salaries or emoluments, and delegate to or confer upon them such powers, including the power to sub-delegate, authorities and discretion as the Board may think fit.

32. The Board may authorise or empower any Director or Directors or the Secretary of the Company either by name or by virtue of office or otherwise, or any other person or persons, either singly or jointly, to exercise such powers, functions and authorities subject to such restrictions, limitations and conditions, if any, and either generally or in specific cases, as the Board may think fit.

Managing Director

33. Subject to the necessary approvals, there shall be two Managing Directors of the Company, each nominated by the Board and the day to day management of the Company shall be entrusted by the Board of Directors to the Managing Directors, who shall manage the affairs of the Company under the supervision and control of the Board. The Board shall if deems fit and proper, define duties and responsibilities of the Managing Directors.

34. The Managing Directors shall be appointed for such term and with such powers and at such remuneration whether by way of salary or commission or participation in profits or partly in one way and partly in another, as the Board may think fit.

35. Subject to the control, direction and supervision of the Board, the Managing Directors shall be delegated with maximum operational responsibilities. Provided the decisions on the matters as set out hereunder shall be subject to the approval of the Board of Directors:

(a) annual planning, budget and long term corporate planning (as well as substantial changes of and deviations from the plans approved);

(b) selection of auditors, tax advisors, attorneys and management consultants for the Joint Venture Company;

(c) fundamental issues of business policy and organisation including significant changes of the organisation;

(d) increase or reduction in the authorised share capital of the Joint Venture Company, transfer of shares;

(e) any one time borrowing or guarantee of loans exceeding the limits fixed by the Board of Directors and/or borrowings, which exceed the paid-up share capital and free reserves of the Joint Venture Company;

(f) the annual accounts and distribution of profits;

(g) measures and activities concerning the company's management including any increase or reduction in the number of Directors;

(h) formulation of the product range policy of the Joint Venture Company including the discontinuation or significant changes of an existing line of business or product range;

(i) any amendment or alteration of the Joint Venture Company's Memorandum and Articles of Association;

(j) merger or amalgamation with another company as well as reorganisation or reconstruction and winding-up of the Joint Venture Company;

(k) purchase, sale and encumbrance of real estate and real estate rights;

(l) contracts regarding intellectual property (patents, licenses, etc.);

(m) other matters of particular significance like particularly important, risky, a typical or exceptional business transactions, contract measures or activities.

36. In case the Managing Directors fail to take decisions on any matter by consensus, the matter shall be delegated to the Board of Directors and the Meeting of the Board may be convened for that purpose by any Managing Director by giving at least seven *business days* notice to other directors.

37. The Company shall have Auditors (belonging to an International Chartered Accountant firm such as .... , *Delta*, etc.) to be agreed and appointed at the first meeting of the Board of Directors.

Borrowing Power

38. 1. The Board may from time to time at their discretion raise or borrow money or secure payment of any sum or sums of money for the purposes of the Company.

2. The payment or repayment of such money may be secured in such manner and upon such terms and conditions as the Board of Directors may think fit, and in particular by the issue of bonds, perpetual or redeemable debentures of the Company charged upon all or any part of

the property of the Company, both present and future, include its uncalled capital for the time being, and the debentures and other securities may be made assignable free from any equities between the Company and the person to whom the same may be issued.

3. The working capital requirements shall be financed by a debt/equity ratio of 1.5 : 1. If a debt/equity ratio of 1.5 : 1 is not sufficient to enable the company to borrow the remaining necessary funds without providing further securities or guarantees, then the debt/equity ratio has to be improved to a sufficient level whereby the contribution shall be made by *Bravo* and *Delta* in the ratio of 49 : 51.

Meetings of the Board of Directors

39. The Managing Director or Secretary of the Company may convene meetings of the board. A written notice of every meeting of the board shall be given to every Director at least seven (7) days in advance thereof. In case of a Director residing outside India, notice of meetings of the board shall be given to such Director by cable, telex or fax at least twenty one (21) days in advance of the meeting.

40. Every notice convening a meeting of the Board shall set out the agenda of the business to be transacted thereat in full and sufficient detail.

41. The quorum for a meeting of the Board of Directors shall be one-third of the total strength of the Board or two Directors whichever is higher. Quorum shall not be complete unless one director each nominated by .... (name) and .... (name) is present at the meeting.

42. Resolutions to be passed at the meeting of the Board shall be passed by a majority of votes.

43. No resolution shall be deemed to have been duly passed by the Board by circulation, through facsimile transmission or otherwise, unless the resolution has been circulated in draft together with necessary papers, if any, to all the Directors or their alternates or to all members of the committee as are entitled to vote on the resolution.

Chairman

44. After he has been nominated by the Board as the Director of the Company, shall be the Chairman for all Board and General meetings. In the absence of the Chairman, the Board shall from among their members elect a Chairman of the Board or the General meeting.

45. The Chairman of the Board or General meeting shall not have a casting vote.

46. When there is a tie of votes cast in favour and against any resolution at the Board or General meeting, the Managing Director nominated by the Board shall have a casting vote. If the such Managing Director is not present at any meeting, any other director nominated by the Board and present at the meeting shall have a casting vote.

General Meetings

47. The quorum for general meetings shall be the presence of two shareholders.

Common Seal

48. The Board of directors shall provide for a common seal for the purpose of the Company, and shall have power from time to time to destroy the same and substitute a new seal in lieu thereof and the Board shall provide for the safe custody of the Seal and the Seal shall not be used except by the authority of a resolution of the Board of Directors, previously given. Every deed or instrument to which the Seal of the Company is required to be affixed shall unless the same is executed by a duly constituted attorney for the Company be signed by one Director and the Seal shall be affixed thereto in his presence, subject, however to Rule 6 of the Companies (Issue of Share Certificates) Rules, 1960.

Indemnity

49. Subject to section 201 of the Companies Act, 1956, every officer or agent for the time being of the Company shall be indemnified out of the assets of the Company against any liability incurred by him in defending any proceedings, whether civil or criminal, in which judgment is given in his favour or in which he is acquitted or in connection with any application under section 633 of the Companies Act, 1956 in which relief is granted to him by the Court.

50. Subject to section 201 of the Companies Act, 1956, no Director or other officer of the Company shall be liable for the acts, receipts, neglects or defaults of any other Director or officer of the Company for joining in any receipt or other act for conformity or for any loss or expense happening to the Company through the insufficiency of title to any property acquired by order of the directors for or on behalf of the Company or for the insufficiency or deficiency of any security in or upon which any of the moneys of the Company shall be invested or for any loss or damage arising from the bankruptcy, insolvency, or tortoise act of any person with whom any moneys, securities or effects shall be deposited or for any loss occasioned by any error of judgement or oversight on his part or for any other loss, damage whatever, which shall happen in the execution of the duties of his office or in relation thereto.

....

Name, description occupation and address of subscribers

....

Signature of Subscriber, Signature of Witness with address and occupation

Place....................

Date......................, 20....

LEGAL DUE DILIGENCE

List of Documents

The Legal Due Diligence Report is based on the documents supplied by the Companies.

ALPHA Limited

1. Copy of the Memorandum and Articles of Association
2. Minutes of Board and General Meetings (Original)
3. Copies of Register of—
   (a) Transfer of Shares
   (b) Directors
   (c) Contracts
   (d) Directors' Shareholding
   (e) Charges
4. Copy of list of Shareholders as on .... 20..... (date)
5. Copy of the release of first hypothecation charge for Rs. .... (amount) by .... Bank dated....................
6. Copy of the Sale Deed dated ...., between *Beta* and *Alpha* in respect of property bearing numbers ....
7. Copy of the Sale Deed dated ...., between .... (name) and *Alpha* in respect of property bearing number ....
8. Copy of letter dated ...., of .... (name) regarding allotment of industrial sheds number .... to *Alpha*.
9. Copy of the Notice under .... (name).
10. Copy of the Sale Deed dated .... (name), between *Gama* .... (name) and *Alpha* in respect of industrial sheds number .... Address
11. Copy of Memorandum of Settlement under the Industrial Disputes Act, 1947, between the Workman and the Management of the Company.
12. Copy of the Directors' Report to the Shareholders twenty first Annual Report and Accounts of the Company.
13. Copy of the Auditors' Report for the year ending ....
14. Copy of the Hypothecation of Book Debts Agreement and Hypothecation of Goods Agreement dated ...., with .... (bank).
15. Copy of the Loan Agreement for vehicle financing dated ....
16. Copy of the Loan Agreement for Auto Loan and Guarantee dated ....
17. Copy of the Hire-Purchase Agreement dated ...., with .... (name of company)

18. Copy of the Equipment Lease Agreement dated ...., with ....(name of company)
19. Copy of the Lease Deed dated ...., with ....Pvt. Ltd.
20. Copy of the Trust Deed dated ...., with Insurance Company.................. under the Employee Group Gratuity cum CA Scheme and Copy of the Deed of variation to the Trust Deed dated ....
21. Copies of Writ Petitions, Notifications, Orders passed by the High Court, proposition notices, reply to the said notices in respect of matter relating to litigation.
22. Copy of the Assessment Order of Deputy Commissioner of Income Tax dated ....
23. Copy of Notice of Demand under section 156 of Income Tax dated ....
24. Copy of the Appeal to the Deputy Commissioner of Income Tax dated ....

Beta Private Limited
1. Copy of Memorandum and Articles of Association
2. Copy of Deed of Dissolution dated....................
3. Copy of the Certificate of Incorporation dated ....
4. Copy of the fresh Certificate of Incorporation dated ....
5. Copy of the list of Shareholders as on ....
6. Copy of Form 24AA, Notice of Interested Directors (pursuant to section 299 of the Act).
7. Copy of Memorandum of Settlement under section 2(p) read with section 18(3) of the Industrial Disputes Act, 1947.
8. Register of Charges and Contracts (original).
9. Copy of Minutes of Board and General Meetings.
10. Copy of the Auditors report for the year ending March....................
11. Copy of Application filed by Workman of the Company for Unfair Labour Practices.
12. Copies of show cause-cum-demand notices from the Excise Authority, Company's reply to the said notices and copy of the legal opinion sought by the Company in this matter.
13. Copy of the Appeal filed by the Company before the Asst. Commissioner of Income Tax, Appellate Tribunal, ... against the orders of Assistant Commissioner of Income tax dated ....
14. Copy for the documents pertaining to creation of Equitable Mortgage by deposit of title deeds on .... on Company's immovable property at .... in favour of .... (bank) for credit facilities and modification of the charge dated ....

15. Copy of the Hypothecation of Goods Agreement dated .... with .... (bank) and Supplemental Agreement dated ....
16. Copy of the Agreement for Hypothecation of Assets for credit facilities dated ....
17. Copy of the Agreement for Hypothecation of Movable Assets dated March...................., with .... (bank).
18. Copy of the Agreement for Hypothecation of Book Debts and Agreement of Hypothecation of Goods dated ....
19. Copy of the Composite Loan Agreement for Auto Loan and Guarantee dated ...., with .... (bank).
20. Copy of the Trust Deed dated ...., under the Employees Group Gratuity cum Life Assurance Scheme amended by a Deed of Variation dated ....
21. Copy of the Sale deed between .... Pvt. Ltd. and *Beta*...................., in respect of ....and Survey Nos. ....(Address)
22. Copy of Memorandum of Satisfaction of Charges dated ...., of Rs. .... (amount)
23. Copy of the Auditors' Report for the year ending ....

Beta India (J&K) Private Limited

1. Copy of Certificate of Incorporation.
2. Copy of Memorandum and Articles of Association.
3. Copy of Certificate of SSI Unit.
4. Copy of the Auditors Report for the year ending ....
5. Copy of the Minutes of the Board and General Meetings.
6. Register of Members (original).
7. Copy of the Register of—
   (a) Contracts, Companies and Firms in which the Directors, etc., are interested.
   (b) Mortgages and Charges.
   (c) Directors, Managing Directors, Manager and Secretary.
   (d) Contracts.
8. Copy of letter pertaining to variation in the letter of appointment of .... (name), dated ....
9. Copy of the list of Share Transfers of the last three years.
10. Copy of the Lease Deed dated .... in respect of .... (address) in favour of *Beta* Pvt. Ltd.
11. Copy of the Rectification Deed dated ...., in respect of ....(adderss) in favour of *Beta* Pvt. Ltd.

12. Copy of the Appointment letter of .... as Authorised Sales Representative of the Company, dated ....
13. Copy of the Hypothecation of Book Debts Agreement dated .... with .... (bank) and Promissory Note in favour of .... (bank) for Rs. ....(amount).
14. Copy of the Hypothecation of Goods Agreement dated .... with .... (bank) for Rs. .... (amount) and copy of Promissory Note in favour of .... (bank) for Rs. ....(amount).
15. Copies of the letters pertaining to renewal/enhancement of credit facilities to the Company, by .... (bank)

BETA India Private Limited
1. Copy of the Certificate of Incorporation.
2. Copy of Memorandum and Articles of Association.
3. Copy of the Minutes of the Board and General Meetings.
4. Copy of the Register of—
   (a) Contracts, Companies and Firms in which the Directors etc. are interested.
   (b) Mortgages and Charges.
   (c) Directors, Managing Directors, Manager and Secretary.
   (d) Contracts.
5. Copy of the list of Share Transfers of the last three years.
6. Lease Agreement dated .... with .... in respect of, ...(adderss)
7. Agreement dated .... with .... in respect of premises bearing No. ....
8. Lease Agreement dated .... with .... in respect of Industrial Shed No. ....
9. Agreement dated .... with .... for what purpose.
10. Letter by .... Ltd., pertaining to payment of Rs. ....(amount) towards trade advance on ....
11. Copy of the Letter(s) of Hypothecation dated .... and Documents relating to registration of charge.
12. Copy of the Term Loan Agreement dated .... with .... (bank) for Rs. ....(amount).
13. Copy of the search Report dated ...., stating the particulars of the assets charged.
14. Copy of the letter pertaining to grant of credit facilities to the Company, by .... (bank) dated ...., and ....
15. Litigation papers of ....(name of Company), Sales Tax Matter.

16. Litigation papers of Sales Tax Appeal pending in the High Court of ....

17. Litigation papers of Labour case pending before Labour Court ....

DUE DILIGENCE REPORT

Alpha PACKAGING PRIVATE LIMITED

1. Organisation and Existence

1.1 *Alpha* Private Limited, (hereinafter "the Company") was incorporated on .... in the name of .... Pvt. Ltd., as a private limited company under the Indian Companies Act, 1956 (hereinafter the 'Act').

    1.2.1 The Company became a partner in a partnership firm called Alpha Traders/Alpha Engineering Company in .... (year). The said partnership firm was dissolved on .... (date) and the Company became entitled to the said business and its assets and goodwill together with the ownership rights to the business premises and have been accordingly continuing the said business on their own account from the date of dissolution of the said partnership firm. A copy of the Deed of Dissolution, dated .... is annexed hereto as Annexure 1

    1.2.2 The name of the Company was changed from .... Pvt. Ltd. to Alpha Pvt. Ltd. A copy of the fresh Certificate of Incorporation consequent to change of name of the Company, dated .... is annexed hereto as Annexure 2.

    1.3.1 The Registered Office of the Company is situated in the State of .... at the following address:

    ....

    ....(address)

    1.3.2 According to Clause III (A) of the memorandum of association of the Company, the main objects to be pursued by the Company on its incorporation are:

        1. To carry on the business of manufacturers, buyers, sellers, importers, exporters and dealers in electro-pneumatic valves, air-operated valves, both hand-operated and foot-operated, solenoid valves, low watt consumption valves, intrinsically safe valves for operation by air, hydraulics and liquids, and generally of valves of every kind and description; air cylinders including single and double operated, low friction and with or without cushion and cylinders of every other kind and description; pneumatic and

electric tools such as drills including Auto Feed, Screw Drivers, etc.; balances including Sky Climbers' equipment of every size and weight; electro-pneumatic sequence control systems for machine tools, industrial machinery and any automation device incorporating valves and cylinders or otherwise, manufactured by the Company as well as by others; special purpose machines to be operated by valves and cylinders or otherwise, manufactured by the Company as well as by others; electro-heating induction equipment for welding on high, low and contact frequency rating and electro-pneumatic machinery of every kind, nature or description, machinery of every kind incorporating pneumatic, electro-pneumatic or electro-magnetic devices.

2. To manufacture, buy, sell, import, export and otherwise deal in:
   (a) all accessories and spares required for the use in and manufacture of the aforesaid articles and things, including drill chucks, drill collates, couplings, compressors, air filtration, regulation, lubrication equipment, Pneumatic Hoist, etc.;
   (b) Corrugated cardboard rolls, sheets and boxes, including their printing and waxing; and flat stitching wire, flexible and other packaging items.

1.3.3 The Objects clause III (B) in the Memorandum of Association of the Company includes objects incidental and ancillary to the attainment of the main objects and other objects. A copy of the Memorandum of Association is annexed hereto as Annexure 3.

1.3.4 According to clause IV of the memorandum of association, the liability of the members of the Company is limited.

1.3.5 According to clause VA of the memorandum of association, the authorised share Capital[1] of the Company is Rs. ....(amount) (amount in words) divided into ....(quantity of equity shares) equity shares of Rs. ....(amount) each.

2. Share Capital

2.1 As on ...., the Authorised Share Capital of the Company was Rs. ....(amount) divided into (quantity of equity shares) equity shares of Rs. .... (amount) each.

2.2 As on March...................., the issued subscribed and paid-up Capital of the Company was Rs. .... (amount) divided into (Quantity of equity shares) equity shares of Rs. .... (amount) each, fully paid-up.

---

1. For a company limited by shares, the amount of the share capital with which the Company is to be registered is called the authorised capital, which must be stated in the Memorandum. The Authorised capital sets the limit of capital available for issue and the issued capital can never exceed that limit. [Section 13 (4) of the Companies Act].

2.3 There are no restrictions under the memorandum of association on changes in the capital structure of the Company.

3. Internal Regulations

3.1 The internal regulations of the Company are contained in the Articles of Association (hereinafter 'the Articles'). A copy of the articles of association is annexed hereto as Annexure 4[1].

3.2 The regulations contained in Table 'A'[2] to the Act, shall not apply to the Company except as adopted by the articles.

3.3 The articles authorise the Company to issue shares at a premium or at par or subject to the provisions of section 79 of the Act[3], at a discount and "to give to any person the option to call for or be allotted any shares either at par or at a premium during such time and for such consideration as the Board thinks fit". (Article 11)

3.4 Certain restrictions are placed on the transfer of shares to a person who is not a member of the Company. Therefore, a member desirous of selling his shares shall offer the same to the existing members at the first instance by giving a notice to the Board of Directors (Article 23 to Article 27 contain the procedure for transfer of shares to non-members). However, such restrictions as contained in Articles 20 to 25 and Article 27 shall not apply to transfer of shares to existing

---

1. Under section 9 of the Act, any provision contained in the memorandum, articles, Agreement or Resolution to the extent to which it is repugnant to the provisions of this Act become or be void, as the case may be.
2. As per section 28 of the Companies Act, the Articles of Association of a company limited by shares may adopt all or any of the regulations contained in Table A in Schedule I.
3. Section 79 of the Act:
   (1) A Company shall not issue shares at a discount except as provided in this Section.
   (2) A Company may issue at a discount shares in the company of a class already issued, if the following conditions are fulfilled, namely—
      (i) the issue of the shares at a discount is authorised by a resolution passed by the company in a general meeting, and sanctioned by the Company Law Board;
      (ii) the resolution specifies the maximum rate of the discount at which the shares are to be issued;
      (iii) not less than one year has at the date of the issue elapsed since the date on which the company was entitled to commence business; and
      (iv) the shares to be issued at a discount are issued within two months after the date on which the issue is sanctioned by the Company Law Board or within such extended time as the Company Law Board may allow.
   (3) Where a company passes a resolution authorising the issue of shares at a discount, it may apply to the Company Law Board for an order sanctioning the issue; and on any such application the Company Law Board, if, having regard to all the circumstances of the case, it thinks proper so to do, may make an order sanctioning the issue on such terms and conditions as it thinks fit.
   (4) Every prospectus relating to the issue of the shares shall contain particulars of the discount allowed on the issue of the shares or of the shares or of so much of that discount as had not been written off at the date of the issue of the prospectus.

members or to a person selected by the Board and in certain other cases (Article 28).

3.5 Article 29 provides that "the Directors may, in their absolute and uncontrolled discretion and without being bound to give any reason, refuse to register transfer of any share"[1]. Articles 31 to 34 contain the procedure as to transfer of shares.

3.6 The provisions relating to joint holders of a share are contained in Article 42.

3.7 Article 45 provides, that any General Meeting (annual or extra ordinary) of the Company may be called by giving not less than 7 days notice in writing[2]. However, a General Meeting[3] may be called by giving a shorter notice than 7 days[4].

---

1. Section 111 of the Companies Act, deals with power to refuse registration and appeal against refusal:

    If a Company refuses, whether in pursuance of any power of the Company under its articles or otherwise, to register the transfer of, or the transmission by operation of law of the rights to, any shares or interest of a member in, or debentures of, the Company, it shall within two months from the date on which the instrument of transfer, or the intimation of such transmission, as the case may be, was delivered to a Company, send notice of the refusal to the transferee and the transferor or to the person giving intimation of such transmission, as the case may be, giving reasons for such refusal to the transferor or transferee, or the person who gave intimation of the transmission by operation of law, as the case may be, may appeal to the Company Law Board against any refusal of the Company to register the transfer or transmission, or against any failure on its part within the period referred to in sub-section (1) either to register the transfer or transmission or to send notice of its refusal to register the same.

2. Section 171(1) of the Act

    Length of notice for calling meeting: A general meeting of a company may be called by giving not less than twenty one days notice in writing.

    The said provisions are not applicable to private companies unless otherwise specified in its Articles (Section 170).

3. Section 166 of the Act:

    (1) Every company shall in each year hold in addition to any other meeting, a general meeting as its annual general meeting and shall specify the meeting as such in the notices calling it; and not more than fifteen months shall elapse between the date of one annual general meeting of a Company and that of the next.

4. Section 171(2) of the Act:

    A general meeting may be called after giving shorter notice than that specified in sub section (1), if consent is accorded thereto:

    (i) in the case of an annual general meeting, by all the members entitled to vote thereat; and

    (ii) in the case of any other meeting, by members of the company (a) holding, if the company has a share capital, not less than 95 per cent of such part of the paid up share capital of the company as gives a right to vote at the meeting, or (b) having, if the company has no share capital, not less than 95 per cent of the total voting power exercisable at that meeting.

3.8 Article 46 provides, that "where any special business[1] is to be transacted at a general meeting, no explanatory statement need to be annexed to the notice of the meeting". The Article excludes the applicability of section 173(2)[2].

3.9 To constitute a quorum for a General Meeting, two members are required to be present in person[3].

3.10 The Articles provide as under with respect to voting rights of members[4]:

(a) Upon a show of hands or on poll, every member present in person or the proxy shall be entitled to vote in proportion to his share of the paid-up equity capital viz. he shall have one vote for one equity share.

(b) In the case of equality of votes, the Chairman of the General Meeting shall, have a second or casting vote, both on show of hands and on a poll, in addition to the vote/votes to which he may be entitled as a member. (Article 52)

(c) Article 53 provides that a member can only appoint another member as a proxy to attend and vote instead of himself. Article 53 contains the provisions relating to Proxies[5].

---

1. Under section 173(1)

    In the case of an annual general meeting, all business to be transacted at the meeting shall be deemed special, with the exception of business relating to:

    (i) the consideration of the accounts, balance sheets and the reports of the Board of Directors and auditors,

    (ii) the declaration of the dividend,

    (iii) the appointment of directors in the place of those retiring, and

    (iv) the appointment of and the fixing of the remuneration of the auditors.

2. Section 173(2):

    Where any items of business to be transacted at the meeting are deemed to be special as aforesaid, there shall be annexed to the notice of the meeting a statement setting out all material facts concerning each such item of business, including in particular, the nature of concern or interest,

    A private company, which is not a subsidiary of a public company, may exclude the application to itself of the provisions of section 173(2).

3. This is in accordance with section 174(1) of the Act.

    Section 174(1):

    (1) Unless the articles of the company provide for a larger number, five members personally present in the case of a public company (other than a public company which has become such by virtue of section 43A) and two members personally present in the case of any other Company, shall be the quorum for a meeting of the Company.

4. Section 41 of the Companies Act defines 'Members' as:

    (1) the subscriber of the memorandum of a Company shall be deemed to have agreed to become members of the Company, and on its registration, shall be entered as members in its register of members.

    (2) every other person who agrees in writing to become a member of a Company and whose name is entered in its register of members, shall be a member of the Company.

5. Section 176 of the Act deals with proxies. The said section applies to the Company with such modifications as stated in the clause to Articles 53.

3.11 Unless otherwise determined in a General Meeting, the Company is required to have not less than two and not more than seven Directors (Article 59). No qualification by way of holding shares is required of any Director (Article 63). The Directors are empowered to fill up a casual vacancy or as an addition to the Board. A Director so appointed shall hold office up to the date up to which the Director in whose place he is appointed would have held office if it had not been vacated. Any Director appointed as Additional Director shall hold office only up to the date of the next Annual General Meeting but shall be eligible for re-appointment at such meeting (Article 62).

3.12 The provisions of sections 255[1] and 256[2] of the Act shall apply to appointment and retirement by rotation of Directors (Article 60).

1. Section 255 of the Act:
   Appointment of directors and proportion of those who are to retire by rotation
   (1) Unless the articles provide for the retirement of all the directors at every annual general meeting, not less than two-thirds of the total number of directors of a public company, shall—
      (a) be persons whose period of office is liable to determination by retirement of directors by rotation; and
      (b) save as otherwise expressly provided in this Act, be appointed by the Company in a general meeting.
   (2) The remaining directors in the case of any such Company, and the directors generally in the case of a private company which is not a subsidiary of a public Company, shall, in default of and subject to any regulation in the articles of the Company, also be appointed by the company in general meeting.
2. Section 256 of the Act:
   Ascertainment of directors retiring by rotation and filling of vacancies
   (1) At the first annual general meeting of a public company, or a private company which is a subsidiary of a public company held next after the date of the general meeting at which the first directors are appointed in accordance with section 255 and at every subsequent annual general meeting one-third of such of the directors for the time being as are liable to retire by rotation, or if their number is not three or a multiple of three, then, the number nearest to one-third, shall retire from office.
   (2) The directors to retire by rotation at every annual general meeting shall be those who have been longest in office since their last appointment, but as between persons who became directors on the same day, those who are to retire shall, in default of and subject to any Agreement among themselves, be determined by lot.
   (3) At the annual general meeting at which a director retires as aforesaid, the Company may fill up the vacancy by appointing the retiring director or some other person thereto.
   (4) (a) If the place of the retiring director is not so filled up and the meeting has not expressly resolved not to fill the vacancy, the meeting shall stand adjourned till the same day in the next week, at the same time and place, or if that day is a public holiday, till the next succeeding day which is not a public holiday, at the same time and place.
       (b) If at the adjourned meeting also, the place of the retiring director is not filled up and that meeting also has not expressly resolved not to fill the vacancy, the retiring director shall be deemed to have been re-appointed at the adjourned meeting, unless—
           (i) at that meeting or at the previous meeting a resolution for the reappointment of such director has been put to the meeting and lost;

Contd. on next page

3.13 The meeting of Board of Directors shall be held once in every three months and at least four such meetings shall be held every year[1]. (Article 66(b))

3.14 Article 67 provides as under with respect to quorum for a Board Meeting:

"a. The quorum for a meeting of the Board of Directors shall be one-third of the total strength of the Board of Directors (any fraction contained in that one-third being rounded off as one) or two Directors, whichever is higher.

b. For the purpose of clause (a) 'total strength' means the total strength of the Board of Directors of the Company as determined in pursuance of the Act after deducting therefrom the number of the Directors, if any, whose places may be vacant at the time."

3.15 Powers of Directors are contained in Articles 70 to 75[2]. Clause 21 of Article 70 empowers the Board to delegate its powers, authorities and discretions to any person, firm, company or fluctuating body of persons.

3.16 Article 79 provides as under with respect to the inspection of accounts, books and documents of the Company:

"(1) The Board of Directors shall from time to time determine whether and to what extent and at what times and places and under what conditions or regulations the accounts and books of the Company or any of them shall be open to the inspection of members not being Directors.

(2) No member (not being a Director) shall have any right of inspecting any books of account or documents of the Company except as conferred by law or authorised by the Board or by the Company in general meeting."

Contd. from pervious page

(ii) the retiring director has, by a notice in writing addressed to the company or its Board of Directors, expressed his unwillingness to be so re-appointed;

(iii) he is not qualified or is disqualified for appointment;

(iv) a resolution, whether special or ordinary, is required for his appointment or re-appointment by virtue of any provisions of this Act;

1. Section 285 of the Act:

In the case of every Company, a meeting of its Board of Directors shall be held at least once in every three months and at least four such meetings shall be held in a year.

2. Section 292 of the Act

Certain powers to be exercised only at Meetings:

(1) The Board of Directors of a Company shall exercise the following powers on behalf of the company, and it shall do so only by means of resolutions passed at meetings of the Board:

(a) the power to make calls on shareholders in respect of money unpaid on their shares;

(b) the power to issue debentures;

(c) the power to borrow money otherwise than on debentures;

(d) the power to invest the funds of the Company; and

(e) the power to make loans.

3.17 The provisions relating to Dividends are contained in Regulations 85 to 94 of the Table 'A' in the First Schedule to the Act.

4. Directors

4.1 At present, the Company has four Directors. A List of Directors of the Company is annexed hereto as Annexure 5.

4.2 A copy of the list of shareholders as of ...., is annexed hereto as Annexure 6.

4.3 List of companies in which the Directors are interested is annexed hereto as Annexure 7.

5. Agreements

5.1 Certain charges are required to be registered with the Registrar of Companies within 30 days of making the charge[1].

5.2 The Company has maintained a Register of Charges[2].

5.3 An Equitable Mortgage was created in respect of Company's immovable property, ... on .... for Rs. ....(amount) for credit facilities in favour of .... (bank). The charge was modified subsequently and presently the amount of charge has been enhanced to Rs. ....(amount).

5.4 The Company entered into a Hypothecation of Goods Agreement dated ...., with .... Bank for credit facilities wherein a charge of Rs. ....(amount) was created on existing and future plant and machinery installed/to be installed at the premises of the Company at .... or elsewhere. By a Supplemental Agreement dated ...., the credit limit was enhanced to Rs. ....(amount) as and by way of second modification.

---

1. Section 125 of the Act deals with charges, which includes a mortgage. Section 125(4) applies to the following charges:
    (a) a charge for the purpose of securing any issue of debentures;
    (b) a charge on uncalled share capital of the Company;
    (c) a charge on any immovable property, wherever situate, or any interest therein;
    (d) a charge on any book debts of the Company;
    (e) a charge, not being a pledge, on any movable property of the Company;
    (f) a floating charge on the undertaking or any property of the Company including stock-in-trade;
    (g) a charge on calls made but not paid;
    (h) a charge on a ship or any share in a ship;
    (i) a charge on goodwill, on a patent or a licence under a patent, on a trade mark, or on a copyright or a licence under a copyright.
2. Section 143(1): Every company shall keep at its registered office a register of charges and enter therein all charges specifically effecting property of the company and all floating charges on the undertaking or any property of the company, giving in each case:
    (i) a short description of the property charged;
    (ii) the amount of the charge; and
    (iii) except in the case of securities to bearer, the names of the persons entitled to the charge.

5.5 Under the Agreement for Hypothecation of Movable Assets dated ...., a charge of Rs. ....(amount) was created on one gluer machine installed at Company premises at .... or elsewhere for term loan facility for the purchase of machinery. The aforesaid term loan is repayable by monthly instalments of Rs. ....(amount) per month, commencing from .... until the loan account is fully adjusted.

5.6 Under the Hypothecation of Goods Agreement dated ...., with .... (bank) for banking facilities a charge of Rs. ....(amount) was created on existing and future plant machinery installed/to be installed at the premises of the Company at .... or elsewhere. By way of Hypothecation of Assets Agreement for Cash Credit/Overdraft/Demand Loan Facility dated ...., the credit limit was enhanced to Rs. ....(amount) as and by way of first modification.

5.7 An equitable mortgage of the Company's immovable property at .... was created on ...., for Rs. ....(amount) in favour of the .... (bank). The charge was modified on ...., and the credit limit was enhanced to Rs. ....(amount).

5.8 The Company entered into an Agreement for Hypothecation of Movable Assets to secure a Term Loan of Rs. ....(amount) dated ...., for the purchase of machinery. Under the said Agreement, new plant and machinery, including office equipment, tools, vehicles, fixtures, fittings, accessories and parts at the Company premises at ....or elsewhere were hypothecated as and by way of first charge in favour of the Bank. Further, under the said Agreement, the Company shall deal exclusively with .... (bank) for all types of credit facilities in future and shall not obtain any fund/non-fund based credit facility from any other source without the knowledge and concurrence of the Bank in writing.

5.9 Under the Agreement of Hypothecation of Goods and Agreement of Hypothecation of Book Debts dated .... (both the Agreements constituting a single charge) for Rs. ....(amount) stocks of raw materials, work-in-process, finished goods, stores and spares at ....(address) and present and future book debts of the Company were hypothecated in favour of the Bank. The credit facility was enhanced on subsequent dates and by a Supplemental Agreement dated ...., the said credit facility was enhanced to Rs. ....(amount).

5.10 Under the Composite Agreement for Auto Loan and Guarantee dated ...., for Rs. ....(amount) with .... (bank), the Company has to repay the loan by 36 equated monthly instalments of Rs. ....(amount), the first instalment being due on ....(date). We have been informed by the Company that it has been paying the instalments regularly.

5.11 The Trust Deed dated ...., under the Employees Group Gratuity cum Life Assurance Scheme was amended by a Deed of Variation executed on .... pursuant to the amendments to the Payment of Gratuity Act, death of one of the trustees and change of name of the Company.

6. Labour Agreement

A Settlement was entered into between the Workmen and the Management of the Company under section 2(p) read with section 18(3) of the Industrial Disputes Act, 1947. The Settlement will remain in force for a period of three years from ...., to .... either of the parties may after the expiry of the said period, give a written notice, two months in advance to terminate this Settlement in accordance with section 19(2) of the Industrial Disputes Act, 1947. The terms of Settlement are contained in the Memorandum of Settlement, which is annexed hereto as Annexure 8.

7. Title to Properties

The Company has the following immovable properties:

7.1 Property bearing .... along with the building situated at .... The title of the said property is still in the name of M/s *Alpha Traders/Alpha* Engineering Company (Under the Deed of Dissolution ...., Annexure 1, the Company became entitled to the ownership of the said property). Equitable Mortgage was created on the said property in favour of .... (bank). We have not examined the title deeds of the said property.

7.2 Plot Number .... and Survey Nos. ....

7.3 Plot Number .... and Survey Nos. ....

8. Litigation

8.1 Taxation

8.1.1 The Assistant Commissioner of Sales Tax *vide* Order dated ...., rectified the Assessment Order for the financial year ...., demanding additional taxes as under:

    i. Central Sales Tax   ... Rs. ....(amount)

    ii. .... (State) Sales Tax   ... Rs. ....(amount)

    (including interest)

We were informed by the Company that the additional liability i.e. Sales Tax on sale of corrugated boxes is wrongly allowed against Form -'H' worth Rs. ....(amount) and Form 14-B worth Rs. ....(amount). We were further informed that the Company was given Form -'H' and Form 14-B by its customer ....(name) (which exports goods using the corrugated boxes manufactured by the Company). Further the Company has now received the correct forms namely *viz.* Form-'C' against Form-'H' and Form 'N-14' against Form '14-B', and the liability after rectification is likely to be as under:

    i. Central Sales Tax   ... Rs. ....(amount)

    ii. .... (State) Sales Tax   ... Rs. ....(amount)

The above-mentioned liability will be borne by the Company's customer, ...(name). The Company has further informed us that it would be making the necessary application for rectification shortly.

8.1.2 The Company has filed an appeal before the Assistant Commissioner of Income Tax, Appellate Tribunal, ...(city) against the Order of the Asst. Commissioner of Income Tax; .... (city) dated ...., for the assessment year 1991-91. The Company has appealed against the said Order on the ground that the amount of Rs ....(amount) being the provision for gratuity has not been deducted from taxable income of the assessee.

8.2 Central Excise

8.2.1 The Company has received the following Show Cause-cum-Demand Notices which aggregate to Rs. ....(amount):

Notice Date	Period	Amount/Rs.
30-6-97	1994-95	....
30-6-97	1995-96	....
30-6-97	1996-97	....
30-6-97	Penalty	....
	....	
		....
5-12-97	1-8-97 to 31-12-97	....
7-5-98	1-11-97 to 31-3-98	....
	....	
		....

The Company has made a reply to all the above-mentioned notices to the Commissioner of Central Excise wherein it has submitted that the said notices are void and illegal and require to be recomputed taking into consideration, the submissions made in its reply to the said notices. The Company also requested for a personal hearing. At the hearing on ...., the Company reiterated the submissions made in its reply to the show cause notice.

The Company sought a legal opinion on the matter and the Counsel is of the opinion that the question of liability does not arise unless the said show cause notices are converted into a confirmed demand by way of Order-In-Original after complete hearing of the case. Further, the Company has a *prima facie* case in view of the Central Board of Excise and Custom circular clarifying that the corrugated fitments/partitions are inherent part of the corrugated boxes and are not to be classified as separate items.

8.3 Labour

8.3.1 An Application before the Labour Court has been filed by a workman of the Company for unfair labour practice. The Workman was suspended in the year 1996-97, and later on, his services were terminated in the year 1997-98. In the said application, the Workman has prayed for reinstatement, back wages and subsistence allowance.

9. Miscellaneous

9.1 Most of the pages of the Minute Book of the Board Meetings, Annual and

Extra Ordinary General Meeting are not initialled or signed by the Chairman of the Meeting and the last page of the record of the proceeding though signed, is not dated[1] as required by the Act. Pages .... and .... of the Board Minutes are blank and page number .... of the minutes of annual and extra ordinary general meetings is blank.

9.2.1 As per the Auditor's report for the year ending ...., the Company has taken unsecured loans from the directors of the Company, companies and other parties listed in the register maintained under section 301 of the Act. The details of interest paid on unsecured loans during the Financial Year .... are annexed hereto as Annexure 9. The Company has not taken any other loans from firms listed in the register maintained under section 301 of the Companies Act, 1956. The rate of interest paid and other terms and conditions of such loans are not *prima facie* prejudicial to the interest of the Company. The Company has not taken any loans, secured or unsecured from companies under the same management as defined under section 370(1B) of the Companies Act, 1956.

9.2.2 As per the Auditors report for the year ending ...., the Company during the year ...., has not granted any loans secured or unsecured, to companies, firms or other parties listed in the register maintained under section 301 of the Act and/or to the companies under the same management as defined under section 370 (IB) of the Act.

ANNEXURE 5
LIST OF DIRECTORS OF ALPHA PACKAGING PVT. LTD.

1. .... (NAME)
2. .... (NAME)
3. .... (NAME)
4. .... (NAME)

Drafting of

Prospectus: As per section 2(36) of the Companies Act, 1956 "prospectus" means any document described or issued as prospectus and includes any notice, circular, advertisement or other document inviting deposits from the public or inviting offers from the public for the subscription or purchase of any shares in, or debentures of, a body corporate.

Schedule II of the Companies Act, 1956 gives the matters to be specified in

---

1. Section 193 of the Act:
   (1) Every Company shall cause minutes of all proceedings of every general meeting and of all proceedings of every meeting of its Board of Directors or of every committee of the Board, to be kept by making within thirty days of the conclusion of every such meeting concerned, entries thereof in books kept for that purpose with their pages consecutively numbered.

the prospectus. Which is as following—

SCHEDULE II

(*See* sections 44 (2) (a) and 56)

MATTERS TO BE SPECIFIED IN PROSPECTUS AND REPORTS TO BE SET OUT THEREIN

PART I

I. *General information.—*
   (a) Name and address of registered office of the company.
   (b) (i) Consent of the Central Government for the present issue and declaration of the Central Government about non-responsibility for financial soundness or correctness of statements.
       (ii) Letter of Intent/industrial licence and declaration of the Central Government about non-responsibility for financial soundness or correctness of statements.
   (c) Names of regional stock exchange and other stock exchanges where application made for listing of present issue.
   (d) Provisions of sub-section (1) of section 68A of the Companies Act, relating to punishment for fictitious applications.
   (e) Statement/declaration about refund of the issue if minimum subscription of 90 per cent is not received within 90 days from closure of the issue.
   (f) Declaration about the issue of allotment letters/refunds within a period of 10 weeks and interest in case of any delay in refund at the prescribed rate under section 73 (2)/(2A).
   (g) Date of opening of the issue.
       Date of closing of the issue.
       Date of earliest closing of issue.
   (h) Name and address of auditors/and lead managers.
   (i) Name and address of trustee under debenture trust deed (In case of debenture issue).
   (j) Whether rating from Crisil or any rating agency has been obtained for the proposed debenture/preference share issue.
       If no rating has been obtained, this should be answered as "No".
       If yes, the rating should be indicated.
   (k) Underwriting of the issue.

(Names and addresses of the underwriters and the amount underwritten by them.)

(Declaration by Board of Directors that the underwriters have sufficient resources to discharge their respective obligations.)

II. *Capital Structure of the company.—*
- (a) Authorised, issued, subscribed and paid up capital.
- (b) Size of present issue giving separately reservation for preferential allotment to promoters and others.
- (c) Paid-up capital
    - (i) after the present issue,
    - (ii) after conversion of debentures (if applicable).

III. *Terms of the present issue.—*
- (a) Terms of payments.
- (b) Rights of the instrument holders.
- (c) How to apply—availability of forms, prospectus and mode of payment.
- (d) Any special tax benefits for company and its shareholders.

IV. *Particulars of the issue.—*
- (a) Objects.
- (b) Project Cost.
- (c) Means of Financing (including contribution of promoters).

V. *Company, management and project.—*
- (a) History and main objects and present business of the company.
- (b) Subsidiary(ies) of the company, if any (For financial data, refer to auditor's report in Part II).
- (c) Promoters and their background.
- (d) Names, addresses, and occupation of manager, managing director and other directors including nominee directors, whole-time directors (giving their directorships in other companies).
- (e) Location of project.
- (f) Plant and machinery, technology, process, etc.
- (g) Collaboration, any performance guarantee or assistance in marketing by the collaborators.
- (h) Infrastructure facilities for raw materials and utilities like water, electricity, etc.
- (i) Schedule of implementation of the project and progress made so far, giving details of land acquisition, civil works, installation of plant and machinery, trial production, date of commercial production, etc.
- (j) The products:
    - (i) Nature of the Product/s—consumer/industrial and end users.
    - (ii) Approach to, marketing and proposed marketing set up.
    - (iii) Export possibilities and export obligations, if any (In case of a company providing any 'service' particulars, as applicable, be furnished).
- (k) Future prospects—expected capacity utilisation during the first three

years from the date of commencement of production, and the expected year when the company would be able to earn cash profits and net profits.

Stock market data for shares debentures of the company high/low price in each of the last 3 years and monthly high/low during the last six months (where applicable).

VI. Following particulars in regard to the company and other listed companies under the same management within the meaning of section 370 (1B) which made any capital issue during the last 3 years:—

Name of the company

Year of issue

Type of issue

(Public/right/composite)

Amount of issue

Date of closure of issue

Date of completion of delivery of share/debenture certificates

Date of completion of the project, where object of the issue was financing of a project

Rate of dividend paid.

VII. (a) *Outstanding litigation pertaining to.*—(i) matters likely to affect operation and finances of the company including disputed tax liabilities of any nature; and

(ii) criminal prosecution launched against the company and the directors for alleged offences under the enactments specified in Paragraph 1 of Part I of Schedule XIII to the Companies Act, 1956.

(b) Particulars of default, if any, in meeting statutory dues, institutional dues, and towards instrument holders like debentures, fixed deposits, and arrears on cumulative preference shares, etc. (also give the same particulars about the companies promoted by the same private promoters and listed on stock exchanges).

(c) Any material development after the date of the latest balance-sheet and its impact on performance and prospectus of the company.

VIII. Management perception of risk factors (*e.g.* Sensitivity to foreign exchange rate fluctuations, difficulty in availability of raw materials or in marketing of products, cost/time over run, etc.).

PART II

A. *General Information*

1. Consent of directors, auditors, solicitors/advocates, managers to the issue, registrar of issue, bankers to the company, bankers to the issue and experts.

2. Expert opinion obtained, if any.

3. Change, if any, in directors and auditors during the last three years, and reasons thereof.

4. Authority for the issue and details of resolution passed for the issue.

5. Procedure and time schedule for allotment and issue of certificates.

6. Names and addresses of the company secretary, legal adviser, lead managers, co-managers, auditors, bankers to the company, bankers to the issue, and brokers to the issue.

B. Financial Information
Reports to be set out

1. *A report by the auditors of the company with respect to.*—(a) profits and losses and assets and liabilities, in accordance with sub-clause (2) or (3) of this clause, as the case may require; and

(b) The rates of the dividends, if any, paid by the company in respect of each class of shares in the company for each of the five financial years immediately preceding the issue of the prospectus, giving particulars of each class of shares on which such dividends have been paid and particulars of the cases in which no dividends have been paid in respect of any class of shares for any of those years; and if no accounts have been made up in respect of any part of the period of five years ending on a date three months before the issue of the prospectus, containing a statement of that fact (and accompanied by a statement of the accounts of the company in respect of that part of the said period up to a date not earlier than six months of the date of issue of the prospectus indicating the profit or loss for that period and the assets and liabilities position as at the end of that period together with a certificate from the auditors that such accounts have been examined and found correct by them. The said statement may indicate the nature of provision or adjustments made or are yet to be made).

2. *If the company has no subsidiaries, the report shall.*—(a) So far as regards profits and losses, deal with the profits or losses of the company (distinguishing items of a non-recurring nature) for each of the five financial years immediately preceding the issue of the prospectus; and

(b) So far as regards assets and liabilities, deal with the assets and liabilities of the company at the last date to which the accounts of the company were made up.

3. *If the company has subsidiaries the report shall.*—(a) So far as regards profits and losses, deal separately with the company's profits or losses as provided by sub-clause (2) and in addition deal either—

(i) as a whole with the combined profits or losses of its subsidiaries, so far as they concern members of the company; or

(ii) individually with the profits or losses of each subsidiary, so far as they concern members of the company,

or, instead of dealing separately with the company's profits or losses, deal as a whole with the profits or losses of the company, and, so far as they concern members of the company, with the combined profits or losses of its subsidiaries; and

(b) So far as regards assets and liabilities, deal separately with the company's assets and liabilities as provided by sub-clause (2) and in addition, deal either—

   (i) as a whole with the combined assets and liabilities of its subsidiaries, with or without the company's assets and liabilities, or

   (ii) individually with the assets and liabilities of each subsidiary,

and shall indicate as respects the assets and liabilities of the subsidiaries, the allowance to be made for persons other than members of the company.

4. If the proceeds, or any part of the proceeds, of the issue of the shares or debentures are or is to be applied directly or indirectly—

   (i) in the purchase of any business; or

   (ii) in the purchase of an interest in any business and by reason of that purchase or, anything to be done in consequence thereof, or in connection therewith; the company will become entitled to an interest as respects either the capital or profits and losses or both, in such business exceeding fifty per cent, thereof,

a report made by accountants (who shall be named in the prospectus) upon—

   (a) the profits or losses of the business for each of the five financial years immediately preceding the issue of the prospectus; and

   (b) the assets and liabilities of the business at the last date to which the accounts of the business were made up, being a date not more than one hundred and twenty days before the date of the issue of the prospectus.

5. (1) If.—

   (a) the proceeds, or any part of the proceeds, of the issue of the shares or debentures are or is to be applied directly or indirectly in any manner resulting in the acquisition by the company of shares in any other body corporate; and

   (b) by reason of that acquisition or anything to be done in consequence thereof or in connection therewith, that body corporate will become a subsidiary of the company,

a report made by accountants (who shall be named in the prospectus) upon—

   (i) the profits or losses of the other body corporate for each of the five financial years immediately preceding the issue of the prospectus; and

   (ii) the assets and liabilities of the other body corporate at the last date to which its accounts were made up.

(2) *The said report shall.*—(a) Indicate how the profits or losses of the other body corporate dealt with by the report would, in respect of the shares to be acquired, have concerned members of the company and what allowance would have fallen to be made, in relation to assets and liabilities so dealt with for holders of other shares, if the company had at all material times held the shares to be acquired; and

(b) Where the other body corporate has subsidiaries, deal with the profits or losses and the assets and liabilities of the body corporate and its subsidiaries in the manner provided by sub-clause (2) above in relation to the company and its subsidiaries.

6. Principal terms of loan and assets charged as security.

C. Statutory and other information

1. Minimum subscription.
2. Expenses of the issue giving separately fee payable to—
   (a) Advisors.
   (b) Registrars to the issue.
   (c) Managers to the issue.
   (d) Trustees for the debenture-holders.
3. Underwriting commission and brokerage.
4. Previous issue for cash.
5. Previous public or rights issue, if any (during last five years):—
   (a) Date of allotment: Closing Date:
       Date of Refunds:
       Date of listing on the stock exchange:
   (b) If the issue(s) at premium or discount and the amount thereof.
   (c) The amount paid or payable by way of premium, if any, on each share which had been issued within the two years preceding the date of the prospectus or is to be issued, stating the dates or proposed dates of issue and, where some shares have been or are to be issued at a premium and other shares of the same class at a lower premium, or at par or at a discount, the reasons for the differentiation and how any premiums received have been or are to be disposed of.
6. Commission or brokerage on previous issue.
7. Issue of shares otherwise than for cash.
8. Debentures and redeemable preference shares and other instruments issued by the company outstanding as on the date of prospectus and terms of issue.
9. Option to subscribe.

9A. The details of option to subscribe for securities to be debt in a depository.

10. *Purchase of property.*—(i) As respects any property to which this clause applies—
    (a) The names, addresses, descriptions and occupations of the vendors;
    (b) The amount paid or payable in cash, share or debentures to the vendor and, where there is more than one separate vendor, or the company is a sub-purchaser, the amount so paid or payable to each vendor, specifying separately the amount, if any, paid or payable for goodwill;
    (c) The nature of the title or interest in such property acquired or to be acquired by the company;

(d) Short particulars of every transaction relating to the property completed within the two preceding years, in which any vendor of the property to the company or any person who is, or was at the time of the transaction, a promoter, or a director or proposed director of the company had any interest, direct or indirect, specifying the date of the transaction and the name of such promoter, director or proposed director and stating the amount payable by or to such vendor, promoter, director or proposed director in respect of the transaction.

(ii) The property to which sub-clause (1) applies is a property purchased or acquired by the company or proposed to be purchased or acquired, which is to be paid for wholly or partly out of the proceeds of the issue offered for subscription by the prospectus or the purchase or acquisition of which has not been completed at the date of issue of the prospectus, other than property—

(a) the contract for the purchase or acquisition whereof was entered into in the ordinary course of the company's business, the contract not being made in contemplation of the issue nor the issue in consequence of the contract; or

(b) as respects which the amount of the purchase money is not material.

(iii) For the purpose of this clause, where a vendor is a firm, the members of the firm shall not be treated as separate vendors.

(iv) If the company proposes to acquire a business which has been carried on for less than three years, the length of time during which the business has been carried on.

11. (i) Details of directors, proposed directors, whole-time directors, their remuneration, appointment and remuneration of managing directors, interests of directors, their borrowing powers and qualification shares.

Any amount or benefit paid or given within the two preceding years or intended to be paid or given to any promoter or officer and consideration for payment of giving of the benefit.

(ii) The dates, parties to, and general nature of—

(a) every contract appointing or fixing the remuneration of a managing director or manager whenever entered into, that is to say, whether within or more than, two years before the date of the prospectus;

(b) every other material contract, not being a contract entered into in the ordinary course of the business carried on or intended to be carried on by the company or a contract entered into more than two years before the date of the prospectus.

A reasonable time and place at which any such contract or a copy thereof may be inspected.

(iii) Full particulars of the nature and extent of the interest, if any, of every director or promoter—

(a) in the promotion of the company; or

(b) in any property acquired by the company within two years of the date of the prospectus or proposed to be acquired by it.

Where the interest of such a director or promoter consists in being a member of a firm or company, the nature and extent of the interest of the firm or company, with a statement of all sums paid or agreed to be paid to him or to the firm or company in cash or shares or otherwise by any person either to induce him to become, or to qualify him as, a director, or otherwise for services rendered by him or by the firm or company, in connection with the promotion or formation of the company.

12. Rights of members regarding voting dividend, lien on shares and the process for modification of such rights and forfeiture of shares.

13. Restrictions, if any, on transfer and transmission of shares/debentures and on their consolidation/splitting.

14. Revaluation of assets, if any (during last 5 years).

15. Material contracts and inspection of documents *e.g.*
   A. Material contracts.
   B. Documents.
   C. Time and place at which the contracts together with documents will be available for inspection from the date of prospectus until the date of closing of the subscription list.

PART III

Provisions Applying to Parts I and II of the Schedule

16. Every person shall, for the purpose of this Schedule, be deemed to be a vendor who has entered into any contract, absolute or conditional, for the sale or purchase or for any option of purchase, of any property to be acquired by the company, in any case where—

   (a) the purchase money is not fully paid at the date of the issue of the prospectus;

   (b) the purchase money is to be paid or satisfied, wholly or in part, out of the proceeds of the issue offered for subscription by the prospectus;

   (c) the contract depends for its validity or fulfilment on the result of that issue.

17. Where any property to be acquired by the company is to be taken on lease, this Schedule shall have effect as if the expression "vendor" included the lessor, the expression "purchase money" included the consideration for the lease, and the expression "sub-purchaser" included a sub-lessee.

18. If in the case of a company which has been carrying on business, or of a business which has been carried on for less than five financial years, the accounts of the company or business have only been made up in respect of four such years, three such years, two such years or one such year, Part II of this Schedule shall have effect as if references to four financial years, three financial years, two financial years or one financial year, as the case may be, were substituted for references to five financial years.

19. Where the five financial years immediately preceding the issue of the prospectus which are referred to in Part II of this Schedule or in this Part cover a period of less than five years, references to the said five financial years in either Part shall have effect as if references to a number of financial years the aggregate period covered by which is not less than five years immediately preceding the issue of the prospectus were substituted for references to the five financial years aforesaid.

20. *Any report required by Part II of this Schedule shall either.—*
   (a) indicate by way of note any adjustments as respects the figures of any profits or losses or assets and liabilities dealt with by the report which appear to the persons making the report necessary; or
   (b) make those adjustments and indicate that adjustments have been made.

21. *Any report by accountants required by Part II of this Schedule.—*
   (a) shall be made by accountants qualified under this Act for appointment as auditors of the company; and
   (b) shall not be made by any accountant who is an officer or servant, or a partner or in the employment of an officer or servant, of the company or of the company's subsidiary or holding company or of a subsidiary of the company's holding company.

For the purpose of this clause, the expression "officer" shall include a proposed director but not an auditor.

22. *Inspection of documents.*—Reasonable time and place at which copies of all balance sheets and profit and loss accounts, if any, on which the report of the auditors is based, and material contracts and other documents may be inspected.

Note.—Term 'year' wherever used herein, earlier, means financial year.

Declaration.—That all the relevant provisions of the Companies Act, 1956, and the guidelines issued by the Government or the guidelines issued by the Securities and Exchange Board of India established under section 3 of the Securities and Exchange Board of India Act, 1992, as the case may be, have been complied with and no statement made in prospectus is contrary to the provisions of the Companies Act, 1956 or the Securities and Exchange Board of India Act, 1992 or rules made thereunder or guidelines issued, as the case may be.

Place......................
Date......................　　　　　　　　　　　　　　　Signatures of directors)

Prospectus

Alpha Company Limited offering shares for
subscription to the public.

I. General information

I.a. Prospectus of *Alpha* Company Ltd., offering shares to the public for subscription.

(This prospectus has been duly filed with the Registrar Joint Stock Company).

I.b. The subscription list will open on the.................... day of ....20... and will close on or before the.................... day of...........20... The permission of the Central Government has been obtained to this issue, but it must be distinctly understood that in giving this permission the Government do not take any responsibility for the financial soundness of any schemes or for the correctness of any of the statements made or opinions expressed with regard to them.

I.c. This Company is incorporated under the Indian Companies Act, 1956.

II. Capital structure of the company—

II.a. Capital of the company is Rs. .... divided into .... preference shares of Rs............... each; .... equity shares of Rs............ each; .... founders (or management) shares of Rs. ....each.

II.b. The preference shares carry a fixed cumulative preferential dividend @............ % p.a. on the capital for the time being paid up thereon, and rank, both as regards dividend and capital, in priority to the ordinary shares, but without any further right to participate in the profits or assets.

II.c. The founders's shares carry a right (state the rights, also mention who is to get the shares)

III. Terms of the present issue—

III.a. Of the above shares .... ordinary shares and.............. preference shares equal to Rs. .... are to be issued and credited as fully paid.

issued at par

..............preference shares of Rs......................

..............equity shares of Rs.....................

..............founders shares of Rs.....................

Payable as follows:—

    On application of preference shares Rs....................

    On allotment of preference shares of Rs................. the balance payable as and when called by the Directors.

    On application ordering share of Rs.................

    On allotment equity shares of Rs................. the balance payable when called by the Directors.

    The Founders' shares are payable in full on allotment.

III.b. The right of voting at general meetings is one vote for every three preference shares, and one vote for every ordinary share and six votes for every Founder's share.

IV. Company, management and project—

IV.a. The main object of the company is to establish and carry on the business of manufacture of electric goods and in particular to purchase the business carried on by M/s........................ described as Vendors hereafter at..................... (place).

IV.b. A copy of the memorandum is attached which shall be treated as part of the prospectus and provides full details regarding the objects of the company.

IV.c. The following are the names of the signatories of the memorandum.

(State here the names of the signatories, and shares taken by them should be stated opposite each name)

Directors
(Name, address and description)

Bankers
(Name and addresses)

Auditors
(Names, addresses and description)

Legal Advisers
(Names and addresses)

Secretary and Registered office
(Name, Addresses and description)

IV.d. The qualification offered directors is fixed by articles as holding............ unencumbered shares in their own name and remuneration of the Directors is fixed by the Articles as follows:—

(Here give the remuneration fixed by the Articles).

IV.e. The minimum amount which must be raised out of the proceeds of this issue is Rs. .... to provide for the purchase price of the business and other property; Rs. .... for the preliminary expenses and commission payable to any person in consideration of his agreeing to be a subscriber or for procuring or agreeing to procure subscriptions for shares in the company and Rs. .... for working capital.

IV.f. The shares now for offered subscription have been under written by M/s..................... at a commission @...................% and such commission is payable by the Company. The directors are of the opinion that the resources of the underwriters are sufficient to discharge the underwriting obligations.

IV.g. The business which this company has been formed to acquire was carried on by M/s. BETA, hereinafter called the Vendors, for a total price of Rs................ and the purchase price there of is Rs.............. The deed of the contract is.................. which can be seen at the registered office of the company during business hours. Out of the total consideration for the purchase of the business Rs................ is the price of the goodwill of the business. The remaining assets of the business are valued at Rs...........

Stock at cost	Rs..............
Cash at hand and at	
Bank and bills not discounted	Rs..............
Book debt	Rs..............
Less trade discounts (.....%)	Rs..............
Book debts (Retail) after allowing for bad and doubtful debts	Rs..............

Goodwill	Rs.............
Leasehold Premises	Rs.............
Advances on security	Rs.............
Buildings	Rs.............
Plant, Equipment, fittings and fixtures	Rs.............
Vehicles	Rs.............
Less Trade liabilities	Rs.............

The books of the firm have been recently examined by M/s. .... chartered accountants, who have given the following certificate:—

"M/s *Beta*

We have examined your books and we hereby certify that the net profits of your business for the three years ending (the date)............ 20.... have been.......................... A balance sheet made up to this date which is not more than 90 days from date of this issue of prospectus, is attached herewith/mentioned under

Profits for the year ending January...................

Profits for the year ending January...................

Profits for the year ending January...................

Average for the three years.

Yours faithfully
............................."

IV.h. The total consideration for purchase of the aforesaid property of the vendors is Rs......... payable equally to each of them which consideration shall be satisfied as follows:

Rs............. payable to each vendor in cash and the balance shall be satisfied by allotment of............... fully paid up shares to each one of the vendors.

IV.i. The Vendors are to pay the preliminary expenses of and incidental to the formation and floating of the company down to the time when it becomes entitled to commence business, exclusive of the under-writing commission above mentioned, and the estimated amount thereof is Rs...............

IV.j. The sum of Rs............. is to be paid by the vendors to Mr................., in cash, for his service for promotion of the company and Mr............ who has joined the directorate at the request of the vendors is to receive from them a sum sufficient to enable him to pay for his qualification shares.

The following material contracts have been entered into by the company within three years of the issue of this prospectus.

Agreement dated............... made between the company of the one part and M/s. *Beta* of the other part for sale of the business referred to above.

V. Objectives

This company has been formed to acquire the business of manufacture of electric goods carried on by M/s *Beta* at............ . This business was founded in............... by the predecessors of the present vendors. This business is carried on in well built commodious building situated at............ . The premises are held on lease by the Vendors at a low rate of rent. The remarkable development made by the business during the last............ years has pursued the vendors to convert it into a limited company. The business will be taken over by the Company as a going concern as from the date of............... The working capital of the business together with the sale proceeds of the share now offered to the public will be adequate for the purpose of the company.

It is proposed to continue the business without break or interruption upon the lines which have proved so successful in the past, retaining the services of the present Managers and staff who have so largely contributed to that success.

The vendors have agreed to serve the company as Managing Directors for the period of.............. years and during the time of their service shall own at least............ shares in the capital of the company.

It will appear from the above that there are very good prospects before the business and after making every allowance the company expects to pay a worthy return for the capital invested.

Signature of the Directors.

FORM NO. 1

No. of Company..................

THE COMPANIES ACT, 1956

Declaration of Compliance with the Requirements of the Companies Act, 1956, on application for Registration of a Company

(Pursuant to section 33(2))

Name of Company............................ ....Limited/Private Limited

Presented by..

I............................ of.. do solemnly and sincerely declare that I am (a).. who is engaged in the formation of the company, or a person named in the Articles as a Director/Manager/Secretary of the.. Limited/Private Limited.

And that all the requirements of the Companies Act, 1956, and the rules thereunder in respect of matters precedent to the registration of the said company and incidental thereto have been complied with. And I make this solemn declaration conscientiously believing the same to be true.

Date......................

Place...................   Signature

Witness   Designation

(a) An advocate of the Supreme Court or the High Court or an attorney or a Pleader entitled to appear before the High Court or a Secretary or a Chartered Accountant in whole time practice is India.

Registration No.
of company......................
Nominal Capital Rs................

*State whether director, managing/whole time director, manager or secretary.

CHAPTER 3
GENERAL COMMERCIAL AGREEMENTS

SYNOPSIS

PRECEDENTS
- CONTRACT OF EMPLOYMENT—(for a Junior Level Employee)
- CONTRACT OF EMPLOYMENT—(for a Senior Level Employee)
- EMPLOYEE INNOVATION AND PROPRIETARY INFORMATION AGREEMENT
- CONSULTANCY AGREEMENT
- CONSULTING SERVICES AGREEMENT
- TERMINATION CLAUSE
- CONSULTANT'S NON-DISCLOSURE & NON-COMPETE AGREEMENT
- AGENCY AGREEMENT
- SUPPLY CONTRACT
- SOFTWARE SERVICES SUPPLY AGREEMENT
- ERC FACILITIES AGREEMENT
- FACILITIES SHARING AGREEMENT
- FINANCIAL COLLABORATION AGREEMENT
- MARKETING ASSISTANCE AGREEMENT
- OFFICE REFURBISHMENT AGREEMENT
- RESEARCH AND DEVELOPMENT AGREEMENT
- AGREEMENT FOR SALE MADE BY A VENDOR IN FAVOUR OF PURCHASER, THE PURCHASER TO EXECUTE A MORTGAGE DEED FOR BALANCE OF PURCHASE MONEY
- AGREEMENT EXTENDING THE TIME FOR COMPLETION OF A PURCHASE AND OTHERWISE MODIFYING TERMS OF THE CONTRACT SUPPLEMENTAL TO THE ORIGINAL CONTRACT
- AGREEMENT FOR SALE OF PROPERTY WITH USUAL PROVISIONS

Exclusive Reseller Agreement
A Guide to Drafting Joint Venture Documentation
- JOINT VENTURE AGREEMENT
- COMPANY, MANAGEMENT AND PROJECT

Shareholders' Agreement
Shareholders' Agreements and the Articles of Association
- SHARE TRANSFER AGREEMENT

Transfer Of Shares (Specimen Clause)
- SHARE ACQUISITION AND RECONSTRUCTION AGREEMENT
- TRANSFER OF UNDERTAKING AGREEMENT
- SUBSCRIPTION AGREEMENT

An agrement which is enforceable by law is called a contract. Generally when a contract is reduced to writing the document itself is called an agrement.

Agreements embrace a large variety of subjects and are the foundation of all business transactions. It is not difficult to draft a simple Agreement but there are certain kinds of Agreements which are of complex nature and require some skill in drafting.

Employment contracts.—The employment contracts are generally for the guidance of the employer and employee who are not conversant with law, the terms of an Agreement should be as explicit as possible and should be easily intelligible to a layman. Unlike other Agreements and legal documents which need not contain matters presumed or implied by law, it is better in such Agreements to specify even such matters and all other matters so to make it complete code, embodying the rights and duties of each party.

Employment contracts are drafted in same way as other Agreements. Provisions should generally be made for (a) the time or period of employment; (b) Job title (c) the remuneration including pay, allowances, commission etc. (d) duties of employment; (e) powers of the employees; (f) leave and the terms on which it will be granted; (g) modes and grounds of determining the employment during the term and (h) restrictive covenants.

PRECEDENTS

CONTRACT OF EMPLOYMENT
(for a Junior Level Employee)

We are pleased to offer you, the position of (post offered) with *Alpha* Private Ltd. (the 'Company') on the following terms and conditions:

1. Commencement of employment
Your employment will be effective, as of ....

2. Job title
Your job title will be (post offered), and you will report to .... (name and designation).

3. Salary
Your salary and other benefits will be as set out in Schedule 1, hereto.

4. Place of posting
You will be posted at .... You may however be required to work at any place of business which the Company has, or may later acquire.

5. Hours of work
The normal working days are Monday through .... You will be required to work for such hours as are necessary for the proper discharge of your duties to the Company. The normal working hours are from .... to .... and you are expected to work not less than .... hours each week, and if necessary for additional hours depending on your responsibilities.

6. Leave/Holidays

6.1 You are entitled to a paid leave of ...... calendar days per calendar year in addition to casual leave of ...... days.

6.2 You are entitled to ...... working days of paid sick leave.

6.3 Accumulation of leave earned shall be in accordance with Company policy. However, in case of resignation from your side, the leaves pending can be offset against your notice period which will stand reduced accordingly.

6.4 The Company shall notify a list of declared holidays in the beginning of each year. For the purposes of this clause, the Holiday Year shall be 1st............to 31st....................

7. Nature of duties

You will perform to the best of your ability all the duties as are inherent in your post and such additional duties as the Company may call upon you to perform, from time to time. Your specific duties are set out in Schedule II hereto.

8. Company property

You will always maintain in good condition Company property, which may be entrusted to you for official use during the course of your employment and shall return all such property to the Company prior to relinquishment of your charge, failing which the cost of the same will be recovered from you by the Company.

9. Borrowings/accepting gifts

You will not borrow or accept any money, gift, reward or compensation for your personal gains from or otherwise place yourself under pecuniary obligation to any person/client with whom you may be having official dealings.

10. Termination

10.1 Your appointment can be terminated by the Company, without any reason, by giving you not less than .... months' prior notice in writing or salary in lieu thereof. For the purposes of this clause, salary shall mean basic salary (whatever else the Company wishes to be included).

10.2 You may terminate your employment with the Company, without any cause, by giving no less than .... month's prior notice or salary for unsaved period, if any, left after adjustment of pending leaves, as on date.

10.3 The Company reserves the right to terminate your employment summarily without any notice period or termination payment, if it has reasonable ground to believe you are guilty of misconduct or negligence, or have committed any fundamental breach of contract or caused any loss to the Company.

10.4 On the termination of your employment for whatever reason, you will return to the Company all property; documents and papers, both original and copies thereof, including any samples, literature, contracts, records, lists, drawings, blueprints, letters, **notes**, data and the like; **and** Confidential Information, in your possession or under your control relating to your employment or to clients' business affairs.

11. Confidential information

11.1 During your employment with the Company you will devote your whole time, attention and skill to the best of your ability for its business. You shall not, directly or indirectly, engage or associate yourself with, be connected with, concerned, employed or engaged in any other business or activities or any other post or work part time or pursue any course of study whatsoever, without the prior permission of the Company.

11.2 You must always maintain the highest degree of confidentiality and keep as confidential the records, documents and other Confidential Information relating to the business of the Company which may be known to you or confided in you by any means and you will use such records, documents and information only in a duly authorised manner in the interest of the Company. For the purposes of this clause 'Confidential Information' means information about the Company's business and that of its customers which is not available to the general public and which may be learnt by you in the course of your employment. This includes, but is not limited to, information relating to the organization, its customer lists, employment policies, personnel, and information about the Company's products, processes including ideas, concepts, projections, technology, manuals, drawing, designs, specifications, and all papers, resumes, records and other documents containing such Confidential Information.

11.3 At no time, will you remove any Confidential Information from the office without the permission of (the name of the person to whom such employee is reporting).

11.4 Your duty to safeguard and not disclose Confidential Information will survive the expiration or termination of this Agreement and/or your employment with the Company.

11.5 Breach of the conditions of this clause will render you liable to summary dismissal under clause 10.4 above in addition to any other remedy the Company may have against you in law.

12. Notices

Notices may be given by you to the Company at its registered office address. Notices may be given by the Company to you at the address intimated by you in the official records.

13. Applicability of Company Policy

The Company shall be entitled to make policy declarations from time to time pertaining to matters like leave entitlement, maternity leave, employees' benefits, working hours, transfer policies etc. and may alter the same from time to time at its sole discretion. All such policy decisions of the Company shall be binding on you and shall override this Agreement to that extent.

14. Governing Law/Jurisdiction

Your employment with the Company is subject to Indian laws. All disputes shall be subject to the jurisdiction of .... courts only.

15. Acceptance of our offer

Please confirm your acceptance of this Contract of Employment by signing and returning the duplicate copy for my attention within 14 days of receipt of this letter.

We welcome you, and look forward to receiving your acceptance and to working with you.

Yours sincerely,

(name)....................

(Signature)

(....................)

Date....................   Signature:....................

SCHEDULE I

Salary Structure
Basic salary
House rent allowance or furnished accommodation
Medical allowance
Leave travel allowance
Additional Benefits
Performance incentive
Provident Fund
Stock option
Car
Telephone

You will receive salary, and all other benefits forming part of your remuneration package subject to, and after, deduction of tax at source in accordance with applicable law.

SCHEDULE II
Specific Nature of the Employee's Duties
(To be supplied by the company)

CONTRACT OF EMPLOYMENT
(for a Senior Level Employee) on the Company Letter Head

Based on our discussions and on the basis of the representations made by you in your curriculum vitae, we are pleased to offer you, the position of (designation offered) with *Beta* (the 'company') on the following terms and conditions:

1. Commencement of employment

Your employment will be effective, as of ....

2. Job title

Your job title will be (post offered), and you will report to Mr. (Name and designation).

3. Salary

Your salary, perquisites and benefits will be as set out in Schedule 1, hereto.

4. Place of posting

4.1 Your place of posting will be at (......). You may however be required to work at any place of business which the company has or may later acquire. The company may, after giving you reasonable notice, transfer or assign your service to any place of business of the company that may be presently operating, or which may subsequently be acquired or established, in any part of India or abroad.

4.2 The company may also depute you to work, or assign your services to any associate company, sister company, subsidiary or other company/concern/organisation/firm with whom the company may make such arrangement or Agreement.

4.3 You may be required by the company to make such tours as may be necessary in the interest of the company's business or as you may be directed by the company to make. The company shall reimburse to you all reasonable expenses incurred by you as per company policy.

5. Hours of work

The normal working days are Monday through.....................You will be required to work for such hours as are necessary for the proper discharge of your duties to the company. The normal working hours are from....................to ....and you are expected to work no less than....................hours each week, and if necessary for additional hours depending on your responsibilities.

6. Leave/Holidays

6.1 You are entitled to a paid leave of ...... calendar days per calendar year in addition to casual leave of ...... days.

6.2 You are entitled to ...... working days of paid sick leave.

6.3 Accumulation of leave earned shall be in accordance with company policy. However, in case of resignation from your side, the leaves pending can be offset against your notice period which will stand reduced accordingly.

6.4 The company shall notify a list of declared holidays in the beginning of each year. For the purposes of this clause, the Holiday Year shall be 1st............. to 31st....................

7. Nature of duties

You will perform to the best of your ability all the duties, as are inherent in your post and such additional duties as the company may call upon you to perform, from time to time. Your specific duties are set out in Schedule II, hereto.

8. Company property

You will always maintain in good condition company property, which may be entrusted to you for official use during the course of your employment and shall return all such property to the company prior to relinquishment of your charge, failing which the cost of the same will be recovered from you by the Company.

9. Borrowings/accepting gifts

You will not borrow or accept any money, gift, reward or compensation for your personal gains from or otherwise place yourself under pecuniary obligation to any person/client with whom, you may be having official dealings.

10. Termination

10.1 Your appointment can be terminated by the Company, without any reason, by giving you not less than .... months' prior notice in writing or salary in lieu thereof. For the purposes of this clause salary shall mean basic salary, house rent allowance, monthly reimbursements (whatever else the company wishes to be included).

10.2 If, your employment under this Agreement is terminated by reason of reconstruction or amalgamation of the company and you are offered employment with any concern or undertaking resulting from the reconstruction or amalgamation on terms and conditions substantially the same as the terms of this Agreement, then you shall have no claim against the company in respect of the termination of your employment under this Agreement, which claim in any case shall not exceed the compensation set out in 10.1 above.

10.3 You may terminate your employment with the company, without any cause, by giving not less than .... month's prior notice or salary for unsaved period, if any, left after adjustment of pending leaves, as on date.

10.4 The company reserves the right to terminate your employment summarily without any notice period or termination payment, if it has reasonable ground to believe you are guilty of misconduct or negligence, or have committed any fundamental breach of contract or caused any loss to the company.

10.5 On the termination of your employment for whatever reason, you will return to the company all property; documents and papers, both original and copies thereof, including any samples, literature, contracts, records, lists, drawings, blueprints, letters, notes, data and the like; and Confidential Information, in your possession or under your control relating to your employment or to clients' business affairs.

11. Confidential Information

11.1 During your employment with the company you will devote your whole time, attention and skill to the best of your ability for its business. You shall not, directly or indirectly, engage or associate yourself with, be connected with, concerned, employed or engaged in any other business or activities or any other post or work part time or pursue any course of study whatsoever, without the prior permission of the company.

11.2 On the termination of your employment with the company, howsoever arising, and for a period of six months thereafter, you must not, neither on your behalf nor on behalf of any other person solicit business in competition with the company from any clients of the company with whom, you have had dealings at any time during the course of your employment with the company.

11.3 You must always maintain the highest degree of confidentiality and keep as confidential the records, documents and other Confidential Information relating to the business of the company, which may be known to you or confided in you by any means and you will use such records, documents and information only in a duly authorised manner in the interest of the company. For the purposes of this clause 'Confidential Information' means information about the company's business and that of its customers which is not available to the general public and which may be learnt by you in the course of your employment. This includes, but is not limited to, information relating to the organization, its customer lists, employment policies, personnel, and information about the company's products, processes, including ideas, concepts, projections, technology, manuals, drawing, designs, specifications, and all papers, resumes, records and other documents containing such Confidential Information.

11.4 At no time will you remove any Confidential Information from the office without the permission of (the name of the person to whom such employee is reporting).

11.5 Your duty to safeguard and not disclose Confidential Information will survive the expiration or termination of this Agreement and/or your employment with the company.

11.6 Breach of the conditions of this clause will render you liable to summary dismissal under clause 10.4 above in addition to any other remedy the company may have against you in law.

12. Intellectual Property

12.1 All inventions, discoveries, improvements, copyrightable material, trademarks ideas and concepts, which you may make or conceive, either solely or jointly with others, during the period of your employment, shall be deemed to be the sole property of the company and you hereby waive any right, title or interest, if any in the same in favour of the company. Further, it shall be your duty to promptly reduce to writing and to disclose to the company all such inventions, discoveries, improvements, copyrightable material, trademarks ideas and concepts, which you may make or conceive.

12.2 You agree to, at all times, assist the company in every proper way to patent or register the said ideas, concepts, inventions, discoveries, improvements, copyrightable material and/or trademarks in any and all countries and to vest title thereto in the company, its successors, assigns or nominees.

12.3 Your obligations under this clause will survive the expiration or termination of this Agreement and/or your employment with the company.

13. Obligations

13.1 You expressly agree to defend, indemnify and hold the company harmless from and against any and all claims, demands, damages, injuries, expenses and liability arising from your acts or omissions.

13.2 You agree that you will defend, at your own expense, and will indemnify and hold the company harmless from and against any and all damages, demands, expenses, claims, liability, injuries, suits and proceedings asserted or brought against the company on a claim that any materials, software or other writings or articles developed by you for the company during the course of your performance under this Agreement constitute an infringement of any patent or copyright, provided that you are promptly notified in writing.

13.3 You shall not, at any time purchase any securities of the company, in violation of SEBI (Insider Trading Regulations), 1992.

14. Notices

Notices may be given by you to the company at its registered office address. Notices may be given by the company to you at the address intimated by you in the official records.

15. Applicability of company policy

The company shall be entitled to make policy declarations from time to time pertaining to matters like leave entitlement, maternity leave, employees' benefits, working hours, transfer policies etc., and may alter the same from time to time at its sole discretion. All such policy decisions of the company shall be binding on you and shall override this Agreement to that extent.

16. Governing law/jurisdiction

Your employment with the company is subject to Indian laws. All disputes shall be subject to the jurisdiction of .... courts only.

17. Acceptance of our offer

Please, confirm your acceptance of this contract of employment by signing and returning the duplicate copy for my attention within 14 days of receipt of this letter.

We welcome you and look forward to receiving your acceptance and to working with you.

Yours sincerely,

(name)....................

(Signature)

Place....................

Date....................   Signature:....................

SCHEDULE I

Salary Structure
Basic salary
House rent allowance or furnished accommodation
Medical allowance
Leave travel allowance
Additional Benefits
Performance incentive
Provident Fund
Stock option
Car
Telephone

You will receive salary, and all other benefits forming part of your remuneration package subject to, and after, deduction of tax at source in accordance with applicable law.

SCHEDULE II
Specific Nature of the Employee's Duties
(To be supplied by the Company)

EMPLOYEE INNOVATION AND PROPRIETARY INFORMATION AGREEMENT

(To be completed in triplicate)

Distribution: original copy to Human Resource Manager; second copy to the employee and third copy to Legal Counsel.)

To......................

In consideration of my employment by....................("the Company") and of the salary or wages paid to me, I agree:

(a) to disclose and assign to the Company as its exclusive property, free from any obligations to me, all copyrightable works, inventions and technical or business innovations developed or conceived by me solely or jointly with others during the period of my employment, (1) that are along the lines of the businesses, work or investigations of the Company or its affiliates to which my employment relates or as to which I may receive information due to my employment, or (2) that result from or are suggested by any work which I may do for the Company or (3) that are otherwise made through the use of Company time, facilities or materials;

(b) to execute all necessary papers and otherwise provide proper assistance (at the Company's expense), during and subsequent to my employment, to enable the Company to obtain for itself or its nominees, patents, copyrights, or other legal protection for such copyrightable works, inventions or innovations in any and all countries;

(c) to make and maintain for the Company adequate and current written records of all such copyrightable works, inventions or innovations, in addition to this, to set forth below a complete listing of all inventions, if any, which I made prior to or since my employment by the Company and which I wish to exclude from the scope of this Agreement, subject to acceptance in writing by the Company;

(d) at the Company's request, or upon any termination of my employment to deliver to the Company promptly all items which belong to the Company or which by their nature are for the use of Company employees only, including, without limitation, all written and other materials which are of a secret* or confidential* nature relating to the business of the Company or its affiliates;

(e) not to use, publish or otherwise disclose (except as my Company duties may require), either during or subsequent to my employment, any secret or Confidential Information or data of the Company or any information or data of others which the Company is obligated to maintain in confidence; and

(f) not to disclose or utilize in my work with the Company any secret or Confidential Information of others (including any prior employers), or any inventions or innovations of my own which are not included within the scope of this Agreement.

This Agreement supersedes and replaces any existing Agreement between the Company and me relating generally to the same subject matter. It may not be modified or terminated, in whole or part, except in writing signed by an authorized representative of the Company. Discharge of my undertakings in this Agreement shall be an obligation of my executors, administrators, or other legal representatives or assigns. If any provision contained in this Agreement is held to be invalid or unenforceable, the remaining provisions of this Agreement shall be construed as if such provision did not exist, and the unenforceability or invalidity of such provision shall not be held to render any other provision of this Agreement unenforceable or invalid.

I represent that, except as stated below, I have no Agreements with or obligations to others in conflict with the foregoing.

These terms are used in the ordinary sense and do not refer to official security classifications of any government. The Company generally considers "secret" or "confidential" information or data which is not generally known - regardless of whether such information or data is in oral, written, machine readable or other form. When in doubt, you should assume that information or data is secret or confidential unless or until determined otherwise. Without limitation, examples of information or data which may be of a secret or confidential nature are: drawings, manuals, notebooks, reports, models, inventions, formulas, processes, machines, compositions, computer programs, accounting methods, business plans and information systems. For further information, you should consult your company's assigned legal counsel.

(TYPE OR PRINT IN INK, USING FIRM PRESSURE)

Full Name.. Component..
Permanent Account No./Passport No................................ Location...................

.... (Signed)................................
Witness (The Employee's immediate manager or other appropriate representative of the Company)   (Employee's signature-to include employee's first name in full)

....   (Date)...............................
Position
Countersigned - Authorized Company Representative
(Required only when this Agreement supersedes prior Agreement)

The following are the only Agreements to which I am a party, which may be in conflict with the obligations undertaken above:

....
....

CONSULTANCY AGREEMENT

.................(Name of Foreign Company)

THIS CONSULTANCY AGREEMENT (the "Agreement") is entered into on this ...... day of ...., 20.....

BETWEEN

Alpha........................., a Company organised and existing under the laws of ....(a Foreign country) and having its registered office at .... , through its Chief Executive Officer Mr. .... (hereinafter called *"Alpha"* which expression shall, unless repugnant to the meaning or context hereof, be deemed to include its successors and permitted assigns), of the FIRST PART;

AND

Beta, a company duly incorporated under the Companies Act, 1956 and having its registered office at ...., India, through its authorised signatory Mr. ....(hereinafter referred to as "CONSULTANT" which expression shall, unless repugnant to the meaning or context hereof, be deemed to include its successors and permitted assigns), of the SECOND PART.

(*Alpha* and Consultant are collectively referred to as "Parties" and individually as a "Party").

A. WHEREAS, (A) a registered society set up by the Government of India (B) in furtherance of its plan to enter into the field of Mobile Telephony Services along with Department of Telecommunication, ("DOT"), has floated a global tender ("Tender") inviting vendors for undertaking survey, planning, design, supply of equipment, installation, testing, commissioning and handing over the systems on a turnkey basis;

B. WHEREAS, ...(name) Limited, a company duly incorporated under the Companies Act, 1956, having its registered office at ...., India, ("*Beta*"), is engaged in the manufacture and marketing of the telecommunication equipment including GSM Cellular equipment (BSS) and has a Technical Collaboration Agreement with *Alpha*;

C. WHEREAS, *Beta* has submitted its bid in respect of the Tender at the *behest* of *Alpha* and in doing so has availed the assistance and services of the Consultant which has requisite expertise and knowledge of the telecommunication sector in India;

D. WHEREAS, the Parties understand that the Tender is only a pilot program and that there would be more orders in respect of Mobile Telephony Services in India in future, either by way of repeat orders from or in the form of fresh tenders to be floated by, either A or B , in association with each other or in association with a third party or individually ("Subsequent Tender").

E. WHEREAS, *Alpha* desires that the Consultant provide further assistance to *Beta* in respect of the Tender and Subsequent Tender and whereas the Consultant has agreed to extend its assistance for the same, the Parties have mutually agreed to record their entire understanding by way of this Agreement.

NOW THEREFORE, for good and valuable consideration, the receipt and sufficiency of which is acknowledged by the Parties and on the terms and conditions as hereinafter set forth, the Parties agree as follows:

1. Consultant's Obligations

A. The Consultant agrees to assist and advice *Alpha* on the various aspects of the Tender and Subsequent Tenders, if any. The Consultant shall assist in the preparation and submission of bids in respect of the aforesaid tenders.

B. The Consultant shall carry out surveys and conduct market studies to provide necessary inputs to *Alpha* to make the quotations/bids of *Beta* competitive. The Consultant shall endeavour to obtain any clarifications which would be required from (A)/(B) / other Government Departments in respect of the Tender or any Subsequent Tenders, as the case may be.

C. The Consultant shall also undertake necessary liaison work as may be required from time to time with the officials of the concerned departments. The Consultant shall, at all times, work diligently to promote the interests of *Alpha*.

D. Save and except the representations and warranties stated in this Agreement, the Consultant makes no representations or warranties of any kind or nature with regard to the business, financial viability of the project.

E. The Consultant represents and warrants that it shall comply with all applicable laws, rules and regulations and shall not indulge in any act, which constitutes an offence or a corrupt practice under the Indian laws and/or the ....(country) laws.

2. Alpha's Obligation

A. Upon award of the Tender to *Beta*, *Alpha* undertakes to make payment of five (5) per cent of the "Tender Amount" ("Commission") to the Consultant in the manner given below:

- $1/3^{rd}$ of the Commission on the date of award of the Tender ("Tender Date");
- (——) of the Commission within (......) months of the Tender Date;
- (——) of the Commission within (......) months of the Tender Date; and

B. Upon award of any Subsequent Tender(s) to *Beta*, *Alpha* shall make payment of five (5) per cent of the aggregate value of such Subsequent Tender(s) ("Subsequent Commission") to the Consultant in the manner given below:

- $1/3^{rd}$ of the Subsequent Commission on the date of award of the Subsequent Tender ("Subsequent Tender Date");

- (———) of the Subsequent Commission within (……) months of the Subsequent Tender Date; and
- (———) of the Subsequent Commission within (……) months of the Subsequent Tender Date.

C. It is understood that the payment to be made by *Alpha* in terms of this section in lieu of the services and the assistance rendered by the Consultant shall be inclusive of any out of pocket expenses incurred by the Consultant in carrying out its obligation under this section. All payments to be made under this clause shall be net of taxes and shall be made by *(mode of payment)*.

D. It is clarified that upon the award of the Tender or any Subsequent Tender(s), *Alpha* would be bound to make all payments to the Consultant in the manner and within the time stated above, notwithstanding any allegations, accusations, contentions raised by *Alpha* regarding the role played by the Consultant.

E. *Alpha* agrees not to appoint any other person to act as a Consultant in addition to/substitution of the Consultant without a written consent of the Consultant.

3. Damages

Alpha shall indemnify and keep indemnified the Consultant from and against all claims, proceedings, cost and damages suffered by the Consultant resulting from any breach of this Agreement by *Alpha* including any default of payment in terms of section 2 of the Agreement. Without prejudice to any other remedy that the Consultant may have under law, *Alpha* shall pay (……………) as liquidated damage for any fundamental breach.

4. Secrecy

The Parties shall not at any time during or after the term of this Agreement, divulge, or allow to be divulged, to any person, any Confidential Information (including, but not limited to, any information relating to the accounts, finance, contractual arrangement, products, business or affairs of the Parties) unless the said information comes in public domain without breach by either Party. Notwithstanding anything contained in this section, no Party shall be precluded from disclosing any information to the extent required in the legal proceedings.

5. Termination

This Agreement shall terminate on the occurrence of any of the following events:

- A. *Expiry of Term*: This Agreement shall terminate upon the expiry of …… years[1] from the date of this Agreement.
- B. *Fundamental Breach*: On the occurrence of any of the following events which are fundamental breaches of this Agreement: (a) failure to comply with the terms of any "Default Notice" (as hereinafter defined) within the time stipulated, or (b) *(Other events to be specified)*.

---

1. This could be 10 years.

6. Termination Consequences

Default Notice: In the event of a breach by either Party of any of the provisions of this Agreement other than a Fundamental Breach, the non-breaching Party may serve notice requiring the breach to be remedied within the time stipulated in that notice (a 'Default Notice').

Existing Rights: The expiry or termination of this Agreement shall be without prejudice to any rights, which have already accrued, to either of the parties under this Agreement.

7. Governing Law/Dispute Resolution/Arbitration

Governing Law: This Agreement shall be governed by and construed in accordance with the Indian law.

Arbitration: Any dispute, controversy or claim arising out of or relating to or in connection with this Agreement, or the breach, termination or validity hereof shall be finally settled by an arbitral tribunal (the "Tribunal") in accordance with the Indian Arbitration and Conciliation Act, 1996, as in force at the time such arbitration is commenced (the "Arbitration Act"). Each Party will appoint an arbitrator within thirty (30) days of the receipt by a Party at the other Party's request to initiate arbitration. The two arbitrators so appointed will then jointly appoint a third arbitrator within thirty (30) days of the date of appointment of the second arbitrator, where third Arbitrator will act as Chairman of the Tribunal. Arbitrators not appointed within the time limit set forth in the preceding provision shall be appointed in accordance with the Arbitration Act. The place of the arbitration shall be ....(place), India. The language of the arbitration and award shall be English.

8. Miscellaneous

Compliance: Both Parties agree not to do anything contrary to law or which would be treated as a corrupt practice under Indian or Foreign law.

Waiver: There shall be no waiver of any term, provision or condition of this Agreement unless such waiver is evidenced in writing and signed by the waiving Party. No omission or delay on the part of any Party in exercising any right, power or privilege hereunder shall operate as a waiver thereof, nor shall any single or partial exercise of any such right, power or privilege preclude any other or further exercise thereof or of any other right, power or privilege. The rights and remedies herein provided are cumulative with, and not exclusive of, any rights or remedies provided by law.

Modifications: Modifications of and amendments to this Agreement shall be effective only if made in writing and signed by duly authorised representatives of the Parties.

Notices: Any notice required or permitted to be given hereunder shall be in writing and sent by registered mail, postage prepaid or facsimile transmission and shall be addressed to the Parties at the address mentioned below:

if addressed to *Alpha*,

Facsimile #

if addressed to the Consultant,

Facsimile #

or such other addresses and numbers as any of the Parties may from time to time designate by notice in writing to the other. The notice shall be deemed to be served when first received.

Assignment: Save as otherwise expressly provided under this Agreement, all rights and obligations hereunder are personal to the Parties hereto and may not be assigned at law or in equity without the prior written consent of the other Party.

Entire Agreement: This Agreement sets forth the entire understanding of the Parties with respect to the subject matter hereof and supersedes all prior Agreements between them relating thereto.

IN WITNESS WHEREOF, the Parties hereto have duly executed this Agreement as of the date first above written.

ALPHA —   WITNESSES:

1......................................

2......................................

By:....................

Chief Executive Officer

Consultant

By:....................

CONSULTING SERVICES AGREEMENT

This Consulting Services Agreement (the "Agreement") is made and entered into as of this......day of, ... , 20..... (the "Effective Date") by and between ("*Alpha Pvt. Ltd.*"), and *Beta Pvt. Ltd.* Technologies Limited, an Indian corporation, located at .... (address) India ("*Beta Pvt. Ltd.*").

WHEREAS, *Alpha Pvt. Ltd.* has entered into an Agreement with .... (name of company) to license certain sherwood software (the "Product") to be used by and *Alpha Pvt. Ltd.* to create software ("Software") to be used by *Alpha Pvt. Ltd.* and certain related companies ("*Alpha Pvt. Ltd.* Affiliates") and to implement such Software (collectively, the "Project");

WHEREAS, *Alpha Pvt. Ltd.* desires to engage *Beta Pvt. Ltd.* to provide certain consulting services specified by *Alpha Pvt. Ltd.* in this Agreement and in any Statement of Services attached hereto with respect to the implementation of the Software; and

WHEREAS, *Beta Pvt. Ltd.* is in the business of providing such services and represents to *Alpha Pvt. Ltd.* that it has the personnel and expertise to provide the services required by *Alpha Pvt. Ltd.* in a professional and confidential manner.

NOW, THEREFORE, in consideration of the above and the mutual promises set forth in the Agreement, the Parties agree as follows:

1. Services

1.1 Proposal.—Beta Pvt. Ltd. has issued a proposal dated................... (the "Proposal") to Alpha Pvt. Ltd. with respect to the services required by Alpha Pvt. Ltd.. The representations of Beta Pvt. Ltd. in the Proposal are hereby confirmed by Beta Pvt. Ltd. and were relied upon by Alpha Pvt. Ltd. in entering into this Agreement. The Proposal is incorporated herein by this reference.

1.2 Services.—Beta Pvt. Ltd. agrees to provide to Alpha Pvt. Ltd. those services as requested by Alpha Pvt. Ltd. consisting of the performance of various tasks with respect to the implementation of the Software, including but not limited to development of user interfaces (also known as front-end, GUI, screen development & navigation, etc.), communication links to Alpha Pvt. Ltd. or Alpha Pvt. Ltd. Affiliates (as defined herein), interfaces to existing Alpha Pvt. Ltd. or Alpha Pvt. Ltd. Affiliate (legacy) systems, interfaces between the core policy administration system and miscellaneous peripheral system components (*e.g.*, General Ledger, Document Production, H/R, etc.), interfaces to existing Alpha Pvt. Ltd. or Alpha Pvt. Ltd. Affiliate, and systems and solution modelling (collectively, "Services"). Specific Services and the date by which they shall be satisfactorily completed ("Milestone") shall be as described in consecutively numbered Statements of services agreed to by the parties from time to time. Services shall be provided in the phases ("Phases") set forth in a Statement of Services and may be performed by Beta Pvt. Ltd. at Beta Pvt. Ltd.' premises or at any location of Alpha Pvt. Ltd. or Alpha Pvt. Ltd. Affiliate (as defined herein) (each such location, a "Site"). A Statement of Services shall be in a form substantially similar to Exhibit A attached hereto and made a part hereof and shall become effective when signed by both parties. All Statements of Services shall be incorporated into and form part of this Agreement. To the extent there is a conflict between the terms of this Agreement and a Statement of Services, the terms of this Agreement shall control. All Services provided by Beta Pvt. Ltd. shall be performed by employees of Beta Pvt. Ltd. unless otherwise agreed to in advance in writing by Alpha Pvt. Ltd.. "Alpha Pvt. Ltd. Affiliates" shall mean those entities identified to Beta Pvt. Ltd. by Alpha Pvt. Ltd. as being eligible to receive Services hereunder. In performance of the services, Beta Pvt. Ltd. shall cooperate with Alpha Pvt. Ltd., the Alpha Pvt. Ltd. Affiliates, Sherwood, and any third Party authorized by Alpha Pvt. Ltd. to participate in the Project.

1.3 Deliverables.—Beta Pvt. Ltd. shall use its best efforts and ability in performing the Services and in providing Alpha Pvt. Ltd. with any deliverables as described in each Statement of Services ("Deliverables"). Beta Pvt. Ltd. shall cause all deliverables to conform to and be in accordance with the terms of this Agreement and the description thereof in each Statement of Services.

1.4 Change Control Procedure.—From time to time during the term of a Statement of Services, Alpha Pvt. Ltd. may request, in writing, changes in the deliverables, Milestones or other aspects of Beta Pvt. Ltd. performance. Upon receipt of each such request from Alpha Pvt. Ltd. (a "Change Request"), Beta Pvt. Ltd. will evaluate the impact that the Change Request will have on the resources required by Beta Pvt. Ltd. to implement the change. Beta Pvt. Ltd. will notify Alpha Pvt. Ltd. in writing as to the results of such evaluation (the "Change Proposal") as soon as reasonably feasible following receipt of the Change Request, but in no event later than fifteen (15) days from such Change Request. To the extent the changes set forth in the Change Request can, in the reasonable business judgment of *Beta Pvt. Ltd.*, be performed without an increase in the resources or fees, there will be no additional fees payable by *Alpha Pvt. Ltd.* In the event the Change Proposal cannot, in the reasonable business judgment of *Beta Pvt. Ltd.*, be implemented without additional fees, *Beta Pvt. Ltd.* and *Alpha Pvt. Ltd.* shall mutually agree upon the fee and timetable to implement the Change Proposal as well as any changes to the Implementation Plan. The fees for the Services represented by such Change Proposal shall be as agreed to by the Parties.

1.5 *Knowledge Transfer.*—(Need to flush out more details regarding the transfer obligations from .... (name of the affiliate) to *Beta Pvt. Ltd.*)

2. Fees, Expenses, Taxes and Records

2.1 *Fees.—*

(a) *Beta Pvt. Ltd.* agrees to invoice *Alpha Pvt. Ltd.* monthly, in arrears, for the services and Deliverables provided to *Alpha Pvt. Ltd.* by *Beta Pvt. Ltd.* in .... (name of foreign currency) and in accordance with the Schedule of payments set forth in the Payment Schedule attachment to each Statement of services.

(b) Unless otherwise agreed in writing, all invoices shall include the names of all *Beta Pvt. Ltd.* employees who performed the Services being invoiced, their hourly rates and the number of hours spent by each employee in performing such Services related to that invoice. Any invoice for a Deliverable provided under a Statement of Services shall include a detailed breakdown of the charges for such Deliverable in a form acceptable to *Alpha Pvt. Ltd.* All hours of *Beta Pvt. Ltd.* employees must be approved in advance by *Alpha Pvt. Ltd.*.

(c) *Beta Pvt. Ltd.* understands that timely performance is of the essence and that *Beta Pvt. Ltd.* is being compensated hereunder for such timely performance. Consequently, in the event that the date for any Milestone is not met due to delay caused by *Beta Pvt. Ltd.*, as liquidated damages, *Beta Pvt. Ltd.* shall not earn, and *Alpha Pvt. Ltd.* shall not be required to pay, fifteen per cent (15%) of the payment for that Milestone as set forth in the Statement of services, in addition to any other remedy available to *Alpha Pvt. Ltd.*.

2.2 *Expenses.*—In addition to the fees referenced in section 2.1, *Beta Pvt. Ltd.* shall invoice *Alpha Pvt. Ltd.* monthly in arrears for those expenses incurred as a result of performing the Services, which are specifically set forth as authorized by *Alpha Pvt. Ltd.* in the Payment Schedule attachment to the Statement of Services. *Beta Pvt. Ltd.* shall have sole responsibility for all other expenses incurred as a result of performing the Services.

2.3 *Payment.—*

(a) *Beta Pvt. Ltd.* will submit the invoices for fees or expenses for Services performed and the applicable documentation to the *Alpha Pvt. Ltd.*

Project Manager (as defined in section 6.1). Unless otherwise specified in the Statement of Services, the charges or expenses invoiced in accordance with this section, except for any amounts disputed by *Alpha Pvt. Ltd.* or as otherwise provided in Exhibit F, shall be payable by *Alpha Pvt. Ltd.* within sixty (60) (*Beta Pvt. Ltd. proposes 30 days*) days of receipt of each invoice.

(b) If *Alpha Pvt. Ltd.* in good faith believes there is a Dispute (as defined in section 14.1) concerning the accuracy or applicability of any invoiced amount, it will notify *Beta Pvt. Ltd.* of the nature of such Dispute and will provide detailed support for such Dispute within ten (10) business days after giving notice. In such an event, *Alpha Pvt. Ltd.* may withhold payment of such disputed amount but will continue to pay all undisputed amounts. No failure by *Alpha Pvt. Ltd.* to identify a disputed charge or other invoiced amount prior to payment of an invoice will limit or waive any of its rights or remedies with respect thereto, including its right to withhold such disputed amount from payment on subsequent invoices. The withholding of a disputed amount in accordance with this section will not be considered a basis for monetary or other default or grounds for termination under this Agreement. *Beta Pvt. Ltd.* shall continue to provide the Services during the process of resolving an invoice Dispute.

2.4 *Taxes.*—*Alpha Pvt. Ltd.* agrees to pay any sales or use taxes, if any, imposed by any state or local taxing jurisdiction on or with respect to the performance by *Beta Pvt. Ltd.* of the Services; *provided, however,* that *Alpha Pvt. Ltd.* shall not pay or be responsible for any taxes: (a) imposed on or with respect to *Beta Pvt. Ltd.* net or gross income, capital or franchise; (b) in the nature of employee withholding taxes, FICA, Medicare taxes, unemployment insurance or other taxes relating to *Beta Pvt. Ltd.* personnel performing Services hereunder; (c) imposed on, with respect to, or in connection with *Beta Pvt. Ltd.* purchase of any supplies, materials, equipment, software or services for use in providing the Services; (d) in the nature of permits required to provide the Services; (e) imposed by any state or local taxing authority as withholding taxes, or taxes in the nature of withholding taxes, on or with respect to any amounts paid or accrued with respect to the services; or (f) imposed by any foreign taxing jurisdiction.

2.5 *Records.*—*Beta Pvt. Ltd.* shall maintain complete and accurate accounting records in accordance with generally accepted accounting principles, to substantiate *Beta Pvt. Ltd.* fees and expenses hereunder.

2.6 *Billing reviews.*—

(a) Upon reasonable prior notice to *Beta Pvt. Ltd.*, *Alpha Pvt. Ltd.* and/or its designated representative may inspect and review the billing records and other documentation of *Beta Pvt. Ltd.* underlying any *Beta Pvt. Ltd.* invoice solely for the purpose of evaluating the accuracy of such invoice and the fees and expenses set forth therein (such inspection and review, a "Billing Review"); *provided,* that *Beta Pvt. Ltd.* may react from such records and documentation information that is clearly irrelevant to the purposes of the Billing Review, constitutes *Beta Pvt. Ltd.* Confidential Information or reveals the identity of other customers of *Beta Pvt. Ltd.*. *Beta Pvt. Ltd.* will cooperate with and assist *Alpha Pvt. Ltd.* and/or its designated representative in any Billing Review and will provide access to such records, documentation, personnel and facilities as is reasonably necessary in connection with such Billing Review. *Beta Pvt. Ltd.* will maintain such billing records and other underlying documentation for a period of six (6) *(Beta Pvt. Ltd. proposes one year)* years after the date of each invoice, and no Billing Review with respect to such invoice shall be performed later than such date (unless an error in a later invoice indicates a systemic error which may be present in previous invoices). Any Billing Review shall be conducted during *Beta Pvt. Ltd.*' normal business hours at the *Beta Pvt. Ltd.* premises where it maintains such billing records and other documentation, in such a manner as not to interfere with *Beta Pvt. Ltd.*'s normal business activities, or, in *Alpha Pvt. Ltd.*'s sole discretion, at a reasonably convenient location in the .... (name of foreign company) designated by *Alpha Pvt. Ltd.*. In the latter case, *Beta Pvt. Ltd.* will provide access to such records and documentation at *Beta Pvt. Ltd.*' expense.

(b) If, as a result of any Billing Review, it is determined that *Beta Pvt. Ltd.* has overcharged *Alpha Pvt. Ltd.*, *Alpha Pvt. Ltd.* will notify *Beta Pvt. Ltd.* of the amount of such overcharge, and *Beta Pvt. Ltd.* will promptly pay to *Alpha Pvt. Ltd.* the amount of the overcharge, plus interest at the then-current prime rate, as announced from time to time by .... (bank), plus two percent (2%) *(Beta Pvt. Ltd. proposes to delete "plus two percent (2%)")* (or, if lower, the maximum amount allowed by law), calculated from the date of *Alpha Pvt. Ltd.*'s payment of the overcharged amount until the date of repayment by *Beta Pvt. Ltd.* to *Alpha Pvt. Ltd.* In addition, if the amount of the error is in excess of five percent (5%) of the amount invoiced, *Beta Pvt. Ltd.* will be pay the costs of the Billing Review.

2.7 *Performance.—*

(a) Upon reasonable prior notice to *Beta Pvt. Ltd.*, *Alpha Pvt. Ltd.* and/or its designated representative may conduct a performance audit on *Beta Pvt. Ltd.*'s premises or the site of the Services to ensure *Beta Pvt. Ltd.*'s compliance with the terms of this Agreement and to evaluate *Beta Pvt. Ltd.*'s performance with respect thereto (such inspection and review, a "Performance Audit"). *Beta Pvt. Ltd.* will provide to *Alpha Pvt. Ltd.* and/or its designated representative all support services and facilities reasonably necessary in connection with Performance Audit at no charge to *Alpha Pvt. Ltd.* and/or its designated representative for any reasonable use related to the Performance Audit. Any Performance Audit shall be conducted during *Beta Pvt. Ltd.*'s normal business hours in such a manner as not to interfere with *Beta Pvt. Ltd.*'s normal business activities.

(b) Without limiting *Beta Pvt. Ltd.'s* obligations or *Alpha Pvt. Ltd.'s* rights and remedies provided elsewhere in this Agreement, or otherwise, if, as a result of any Performance Audit or at any other time prior to final acceptance (as defined in section 4.1) of the last Deliverable of a Statement of Services, it is determined by *Alpha Pvt. Ltd.* that *Beta Pvt. Ltd.* has not complied with the terms of this Agreement or has failed to perform in accordance with the requirements thereof (each, a "Performance Failure"), *Alpha Pvt. Ltd.* will notify *Beta Pvt. Ltd.*, in writing, of such Performance Failure, and *Beta Pvt. Ltd.* shall: (i) escalate to the appropriate management levels that a problem has occurred; (ii) attempt to isolate the reason for the Performance Failure; (iii) identify potential areas for performance improvement; (iv) develop an action plan, including specific recommendations for performance improvement; (v) review the action plan with *Alpha Pvt. Ltd.*; (vi) reach Agreement with *Alpha Pvt. Ltd.* on the action plan; and (vii) if approval is reached, begin implementation of the action plan and document results. If such Performance Failure is not remedied in accordance with the foregoing within .... days after receipt of *Alpha Pvt. Ltd.'s* notice of such non-compliance, it shall be deemed a material breach of this Agreement.

3. Delivery

3.1 Delivery of deliverables.—*Beta Pvt. Ltd.* shall provide the Services to *Alpha Pvt. Ltd.* and deliver to *Alpha Pvt. Ltd.* the deliverables in accordance with the specifications ("Specifications") therefore set forth in the Statement of Services or agreed to by the Parties in accordance with the implementation plan (the "Implementation Plan") set forth in, or incorporated in the Statement of Services. *Beta Pvt. Ltd.* shall deliver the object code and source code for all software Deliverables. "Object code" shall mean machine readable language compiled or assembled from the source code. "Source code" shall mean the files containing, without limitation: (i) all the program, code, routines, subroutines, diagnostic routines, algorithms, control software and documentation used in building the software deliverables; (ii) all resource files, "make" files describing the structures and relationships of the software deliverable files; (iii) all related files, including underlying code for programs necessary for the operation and assembly of the software Deliverables; and (iv) code which comprises so-called software engines, device drivers, function drivers and links and hooks; navigation logic and implementation; know-how and technology; software tools and utilities; and database managers, as well as the design of database managers.

3.2 Implementation plan.—The Implementation Plan sets forth the timing of the development, delivery and implementation of the Deliverables and the tasks to be performed by *Beta Pvt. Ltd.*. *Beta Pvt. Ltd.* recognizes the importance to *Alpha Pvt. Ltd.* of the timely development, modification, implementation and acceptance of the Software in accordance with the Implementation Plan, and agrees that time is of the essence in the delivery of the Services.

3.3 Delays.—In the event that any performance or delivery of any Milestone set forth in the implementation plan is not met due to a delay caused by *Beta Pvt.*

Ltd. *Beta Pvt. Ltd.* agrees, at no charge to *Alpha Pvt. Ltd.*, to commit such additional resources and personnel as shall be necessary to ensure that such delay does not result in the slippage of later Milestones pursuant to the Implementation Plan and shall cooperate with *Alpha Pvt. Ltd.* by disclosing the details of such additional resources and personnel commitments.

3.4 *Progress reports and meetings.*—*Beta Pvt. Ltd.* shall submit a detailed written progress report ("Progress Report") to the *Alpha Pvt. Ltd.* Project Manager as mutually agreed upon in the Statements of Services. Such Progress Reports will detail the current status of *Beta Pvt. Ltd.* activities, indication of the progress of the work being performed in comparison to the implementation plan and resources expended since the last report, as well as a cumulative total to date, estimated time and cost to complete, and identification of actual and anticipated problem areas, the impact thereof on *Beta Pvt. Ltd.*' work effort, and action being taken or alternative actions to be taken to remedy such problems. If *Alpha Pvt. Ltd.* so requests, *Beta Pvt. Ltd.* shall hold status meetings with the *Alpha Pvt. Ltd.* project manager in order to review the status of *Beta Pvt. Ltd.'s* activities.

4. Acceptance

4.1 *Services.*—For any Services for which an acceptance criteria (as defined below) are not specified in the Statement of Services, acceptance of such Services shall be based on *Alpha Pvt. Ltd.*'s reasonable satisfaction therewith.

4.2 *Acceptance criteria for deliverables.*—

(a) The deliverables shall be subject to acceptance testing by *Alpha Pvt. Ltd.* to verify that such Deliverables satisfy the acceptance criteria mutually agreed to by *Alpha Pvt. Ltd.* and *Beta Pvt. Ltd.* (the "Acceptance Criteria").

(b) The Acceptance Criteria, which shall be included in the Statement of Services, shall be jointly developed and mutually agreed to by *Alpha Pvt. Ltd.* and *Beta Pvt. Ltd.* and shall demonstrate to *Alpha Pvt. Ltd.*'s reasonable satisfaction that, for software deliverables, (i) all of the functions of the software deliverables set forth in the Statement of Services have been provided and the software deliverable is in conformity with the Specifications therefore; (ii) all performance standards for the software deliverables set forth in the Statement of Services have been met or exceeded; and (iii) volume and capacity testing meets or exceeds *Alpha Pvt. Ltd.*'s requirements and, with respect to all other deliverables, such deliverables are compliant with all applicable requirements set forth in the Statement of services and this Agreement.

4.3 *Acceptance testing for deliverables.*—

(a) Acceptance testing may be done by site, or by Phase or both. Acceptance testing for the deliverables, provided under a Statement of Services shall commence within twenty (20) working days of the date on which *Beta Pvt. Ltd.* notifies *Alpha Pvt. Ltd.*'s Project Manager, in writing, that the Deliverables have been satisfactorily completed, in *Beta*

Pvt. Ltd.' opinion, have been delivered, and are ready for acceptance testing by *Alpha Pvt. Ltd.*. Acceptance testing shall continue for the period of time specified in the Acceptance Criteria or, if no such time period has been agreed upon by the parties, for a period of thirty (30) consecutive days (the "Initial Acceptance Period").

(b) In the event that any Deliverable does not conform to the Acceptance Criteria during the Initial Acceptance Period, *Alpha Pvt. Ltd.* shall give *Beta Pvt. Ltd.* written notice thereof. *Alpha Pvt. Ltd.* shall cooperate with *Beta Pvt. Ltd.* in identifying in what respects the Deliverable has failed to conform to the Acceptance Criteria. *Beta Pvt. Ltd.* shall, at no cost to *Alpha Pvt. Ltd.*, promptly correct any deficiencies, which prevent such Deliverable from conforming to the Acceptance Criteria, and correct such deficiency and the effects of such deficiency in prior Phases and Sites. Upon completion of the corrective action by *Beta Pvt. Ltd.*, and at no additional cost to *Alpha Pvt. Ltd.*, the acceptance test will be repeated until the deliverable has successfully conformed to the Acceptance Criteria.

(c) If the Deliverable does not conform to the Acceptance Criteria within sixty (60) days after the end of the Initial Acceptance Period described above, *Alpha Pvt. Ltd.* may (i) immediately terminate this Agreement pursuant to section 7.2, or (ii) require *Beta Pvt. Ltd.* to continue to attempt to correct the differences, reserving the right to terminate as aforesaid at any time.

(d) When the deliverable has successfully satisfied the Acceptance Criteria, *Alpha Pvt. Ltd.* shall give *Beta Pvt. Ltd.* written notice thereof. At the completion of each phase, the deliverables for such Phase and each Site within such Phase shall operate for a period of at least ninety (90) days in full compliance with the Acceptance Criteria. Acknowledgement by *Alpha Pvt. Ltd.* of successful operation of the Deliverables for such ninety (90) day period shall be deemed "Final Acceptance" of those deliverables.

(e) *Final acceptance testing.*—After the Deliverables for all phases and sites have successfully met the Acceptance Criteria, *Alpha Pvt. Ltd.* shall conduct a final Acceptance Test ("Final Acceptance Test"). The Final Acceptance Test shall demonstrate to *Alpha Pvt. Ltd.*'s reasonable satisfaction that (i) all of the functions of all Deliverables have been provided and all Acceptance Criteria for each phase and site have been met. In the event such Acceptance Criteria has not been met for all Phases and Sites, *Beta Pvt. Ltd.* shall, at no cost to *Alpha Pvt. Ltd.*, promptly correct any deficiencies, which prevent any Deliverable from conforming to the Acceptance Criteria, correct such deficiency and the effect of such deficiency in all Phases and Sites. Upon completion of the corrective action by *Beta Pvt. Ltd.*, at no additional cost to *Alpha Pvt. Ltd.*, the Final Acceptance Test will be repeated until all Deliverables conform to the Acceptance Criteria for all Phases and Sites. (*Beta Pvt.*

Ltd. must check to see if Final Acceptance Testing has been budgeted for the project plan).

5. **Beta Pvt. Ltd. Personnel and Service Location**

5.1 *Beta Pvt. Ltd. Personnel.*—*Beta Pvt. Ltd.* shall appoint appropriately qualified and trained staff to provide the Services (the "project staff") as requested by *Alpha Pvt. Ltd.*. *Beta Pvt. Ltd.* further acknowledges its responsibility for specially training members of the Project Staff. The size of the Project Staff and a description of its responsibilities will be set forth in the Statement of Services. *Beta Pvt. Ltd.* shall not subcontract any Services hereunder, or perform such Services by individuals who are not *bona fide* employees of *Beta Pvt. Ltd.*, without the prior written approval of *Alpha Pvt. Ltd.* in each instance.

5.2 *Beta Pvt. Ltd. Project Manager.*—In addition to the project staff, *Beta Pvt. Ltd.* will appoint a qualified member of its staff to act as project manager (the "*Beta Pvt. Ltd.* Project Manager") who will: (i) have overall managerial responsibility for the Services; (ii) act as primary liaison between *Alpha Pvt. Ltd.* and *Beta Pvt. Ltd.*; and (iii) co-ordinate, oversee and monitor the project staff.

5.3 *Qualifications.*—Prior to hiring or otherwise engaging any person who will perform Services (each, a "candidate"), *Beta Pvt. Ltd.* shall provide *Alpha Pvt. Ltd.* with (a) a summary of the Candidate's qualifications and a resume, (b) a description of the tasks the candidate is to perform, (c) an opportunity to consult with *Beta Pvt. Ltd.* regarding the candidate, and (d) upon *Alpha Pvt. Ltd.*'s request, an opportunity to interview the candidate. Upon review of the candidate's qualifications, *Alpha Pvt. Ltd.* may object to the Candidate on the grounds that the candidate is not sufficiently qualified to perform the contemplated tasks.

5.4 *Continuity.*—*Beta Pvt. Ltd.* acknowledges and agrees that the success of the Project is dependent upon the continuity of employees assigned to the Project Staff because such continuity will contribute to the timely delivery and successful completion of the Services. Therefore, any removal or re-assignment by *Beta Pvt. Ltd.* of those of its employees assigned to perform Services hereunder must be with one (1) month's prior written notice to *Alpha Pvt. Ltd.* and with *Alpha Pvt. Ltd.*'s prior written consent as to the removal or re-assignment and as to any replacement employee. Any replacement employee shall have substantially equivalent or better qualifications than the employee being replaced. In the event *Beta Pvt. Ltd.* replaces any of its employees with *Alpha Pvt. Ltd.*'s consent, *Beta Pvt. Ltd.* will promptly provide said replacement. Unless otherwise agreed to in writing by *Alpha Pvt. Ltd.*, *Beta Pvt. Ltd.* shall not remove or replace personnel provided hereunder.

5.5 *Removal.*—In the event that any *Beta Pvt. Ltd.* employee providing Services is found to be unacceptable to *Alpha Pvt. Ltd.*, *Alpha Pvt. Ltd.* shall notify *Beta Pvt. Ltd.* of such fact and *Beta Pvt. Ltd.* shall immediately remove said employee and, if requested by *Alpha Pvt. Ltd.*, provide a replacement acceptable to *Alpha Pvt. Ltd.*, within five (5) days of said notice. *Alpha Pvt. Ltd.* shall be the sole judge as to performance capability. *Beta Pvt. Ltd.* shall also remove and provide a replacement for any other *Beta Pvt. Ltd.* employee if the work product delivered by such employee is unsatisfactory to *Alpha Pvt. Ltd.*

5.6 *Replacements.*—There will be no charge to *Alpha Pvt. Ltd.* for any replacement provided in accordance with the above sections while the replacement employee acquires the necessary orientation and training (including without limitation training in the latest releases of amarta), which shall not exceed five (5) working days.

5.7 *Service location.*—All Project Staff who are performing Services in India shall initially be located at the *Beta Pvt. Ltd.* facility at ....(Address) India. Project Staff shall not perform Services from any other location in India or elsewhere without prior written notice to *Alpha Pvt. Ltd.*, and subject to *Alpha Pvt. Ltd.*'s prior written consent, which consent shall not be unreasonably withheld. (*Beta Pvt. Ltd.* proposes to delete: "*Beta Pvt. Ltd.* shall be responsible for acquiring, operating and maintaining all hardware, equipment and software necessary for the performance of the Services at this facility as well as adequate security.")

5.8 *Visas.*—*Beta Pvt. Ltd.* will pay for and be solely responsible for obtaining and maintaining such visas as may be required for its employees to enter and remain in the country in which Services are rendered in connection with this Agreement.

6. *Alpha Pvt. Ltd.* Project Manager and Facilities

6.1 *Alpha Pvt. Ltd. Project Manager.*—*Alpha Pvt. Ltd.* shall designate a project manager for the Project ("*Alpha Pvt. Ltd.* Project Manager") who shall act as a liaision between *Alpha Pvt. Ltd.* and *Beta Pvt. Ltd.*.

6.2 *Access and security.*—*Beta Pvt. Ltd.* Personnel shall have such access to *Alpha Pvt. Ltd.*'s and *Alpha Pvt. Ltd.* Affiliate's premises as is reasonably necessary to provide the Services in accordance with the terms of this Agreement, subject to the terms of this section 6.2. While at *Alpha Pvt. Ltd.*'s premises or that of an *Alpha Pvt. Ltd.* Affiliate, *Beta Pvt. Ltd.* agrees to comply (and to cause its personnel to comply) with the *Alpha Pvt. Ltd.* Code of business conduct attached hereto as exhibit B, and all safety and security procedures and other rules and regulations regarding personal and professional conduct (including, without limitation, the wearing of identification badges and observance of dress codes) which are in effect, and otherwise to conduct itself and themselves in a business like manner. *Beta Pvt. Ltd.* agrees to cooperate fully and to provide any assistance necessary to *Alpha Pvt. Ltd.* in investigation of any security breaches which may involve *Beta Pvt. Ltd.* or *Beta Pvt. Ltd.*' employees.

6.3 *Telecommunications connection.*—*Alpha Pvt. Ltd.* and *Beta Pvt. Ltd.* shall establish a telecommunications connection to provide *Beta Pvt. Ltd.* remote access to the non-production version of *Alpha Pvt. Ltd.*'s and its Affiliates' computing systems and/or networks for purpose of downloading and uploading necessary files and software. Each party's responsibilities for establishing and maintaining such connection is defined in Exhibit C. *Beta Pvt. Ltd.* shall provide security to prevent unauthorized access to any and all of *Alpha Pvt. Ltd.*'s and its Affiliates' computing systems and/or networks. *Beta Pvt. Ltd.* represents and warrants that: (a) all *Beta Pvt. Ltd.* interconnectivity to *Alpha Pvt. Ltd.*'s and its Affiliates' computing systems and/or networks and all attempts at same shall be only through *Alpha Pvt. Ltd.*'s and its Affiliates' security gateways/firewalls; (b) it will not access, and will not permit unauthorized persons or entities to access, *Alpha Pvt. Ltd.*'s and its Affiliates' computing systems and/or networks without *Alpha Pvt. Ltd.*'s express written authorization, and any such actual or attempted access shall be consistent with any such authorization; (c) it will use the latest available, most comprehensive virus detection/scanning programs prior to any attempt to access any of *Alpha Pvt. Ltd.*'s or its Affiliates' computing systems and/or networks, and upon detecting a virus, shall immediately cease all attempts to access *Alpha Pvt. Ltd.*'s and its Affiliates' computing systems and/or networks and shall not resume such attempts until any such virus has been eliminated.

6.4 *Unauthorized access.*—In the event *Beta Pvt. Ltd.* discovers or is notified of (a) a breach or potential breach of security involving *Alpha Pvt. Ltd.*'s or its Affiliates' computing systems and/or networks, or (b) actual or potential unauthorized or illegal activities by personnel of *Beta Pvt. Ltd.* to obtain money or information from or through *Alpha Pvt. Ltd.*'s or its Affiliates' computing systems and/or networks, *Beta Pvt. Ltd.* will immediately notify *Alpha Pvt. Ltd.* and will cooperate fully with *Alpha Pvt. Ltd.* and its designees in any investigation or action relating to such breach or potential breach.

7. Term and Termination

7.1 *Term.*—This Agreement shall commence on the date hereof as indicated above and shall continue in full force and effect thereafter unless and until terminated in accordance with the provisions of this Agreement or until satisfactory completion of the services provided for herein based on the acceptance criteria set forth in the applicable statement of services.

7.2 *Termination.*—This Agreement may be terminated at any time as follows:

(a) *Termination for material breach.*—For any material breach or failure of performance by either Party, the non-breaching Party may (reserving all other remedies and rights under this Agreement and at law and in equity), terminate this Agreement in whole or in part, by site, phase or statement of service if within thirty (30) days after the giving of written notice to the breaching party of such failure, the breaching party has not cured such failure, or if such failure is incapable of being cured, termination shall be effective upon receipt of notice.

(b) *Termination for failure to deliver or Meet acceptance criteria.*—In the event (a) of slippage of a Milestone by more than thirty (30) days or (b) the Deliverables (or any portion thereof) fail to conform to the Acceptance Criteria within the time period set forth in section 4, *Alpha Pvt. Ltd.* may (reserving all other remedies and rights under this Agreement and at law and in equity), terminate this Agreement in whole or in part, by site, phase or statement of service.

(c) *Termination for convenience.*—*Alpha Pvt. Ltd.* may terminate this Agreement in whole or in part, by site, phase, statement of services or otherwise at any time upon ten (10) days prior written notice to *Beta Pvt. Ltd.* in the event that *Alpha Pvt. Ltd.* determines to terminate the Project or for any reason in its sole discretion. Upon termination pursuant to this paragraph, *Alpha Pvt. Ltd.* shall be under no further obligation to *Beta Pvt. Ltd.*, except upon *Alpha Pvt. Ltd.*'s receipt of the materials described in section 7.2(g), *Alpha Pvt. Ltd.* shall (a) make payment on any Deliverable for which *Alpha Pvt. Ltd.* has indicated Final Acceptance and (b) make payment for the value of Services acceptably performed by *Beta Pvt. Ltd.* in contemplation of receiving the next scheduled Milestone and for which *Beta Pvt. Ltd.* has not, as of the date of termination, received such payment. *Beta Pvt. Ltd.* shall submit to *Alpha Pvt. Ltd.* a detailed invoice (which shall not be binding upon *Alpha Pvt. Ltd.*) of the value of such terminated Services, which value shall be calculated and documented by *Beta Pvt. Ltd.* to *Alpha Pvt. Ltd.*'s reasonable satisfaction based upon a *pro rata* portion of the Milestone payment for work completed.

(d) *Termination for unprofessional performance.*—*Beta Pvt. Ltd.* fails to perform any work in a skilled, professional-like manner, and expeditious manner.

(e) *Termination for bankruptcy/insolvency.*—In the event that *Beta Pvt. Ltd.* is declared to be bankrupt or insolvent, *Beta Pvt. Ltd.* makes an assignment for the benefit of creditors, *Beta Pvt. Ltd.* shall file a voluntary petition in bankruptcy or insolvency or a receiver shall be appointed for *Beta Pvt. Ltd.* and such appointment or bankruptcy or insolvency proceedings, petition, declaration or assignment is not set aside within ...... days.

(f) *Termination for adverse financial condition.*—There has been a material adverse change in the financial condition of *Beta Pvt. Ltd.*, which affects the ability of *Beta Pvt. Ltd.* to perform the work.

(g) *Effects of termination.*—After receipt of a notice of termination and except as otherwise directed by *Alpha Pvt. Ltd.*, *Beta Pvt. Ltd.* shall:

  (i) stop work on the date and to the extent specified in the notice of termination;

  (ii) transfer title or license to *Alpha Pvt. Ltd.* (to the extent that title or license has not already been transferred) and deliver in the manner, at the times, and to the extent directed thereby the Deliverables, work in process, completed work, supplies, and other material produced as a part of, or acquired in respect to the performance of, the work terminated by the notice of termination.

  (iii) deliver to *Alpha Pvt. Ltd.*, and cause its employees to deliver to *Alpha Pvt. Ltd.*, all materials relating to *Alpha Pvt. Ltd.* or this Agreement, or obtained or developed in the course of performance of this Agreement, or containing or derived from *Alpha Pvt. Ltd.* Confidential Information (as defined herein) (a certificate evidencing compliance with this provision shall, if requested by *Alpha Pvt. Ltd.*, accompany such material);

  (iv) continue performance of such part of the work as shall not have been terminated by the notice of termination.

(v) in addition to the other requirements of this section 7.2(g), deliver to *Alpha Pvt. Ltd.* all Developer Tools and *Beta Pvt. Ltd.* shall grant to *Alpha Pvt. Ltd.* at no cost a perpetual, fully paid, non-exclusive and royalty free license to use, reproduce, distribute, perform and display, disclose and otherwise use and exploit all or any part of the Developer Tools to install, use, support, create, revise, modify or enhance the Deliverables. In addition, (aa) *Alpha Pvt. Ltd.* shall have the right to transfer such license to a designated third party which *Alpha Pvt. Ltd.* selects to perform services with respect to the Software and (bb) *Beta Pvt. Ltd.* shall provide such services as are reasonably necessary to transition the Project to *Alpha Pvt. Ltd.* or such third party. "Developer Tools" shall mean any and all tools used by *Beta Pvt. Ltd.* as part of the process of creating the Deliverables, including without limitation, methodologies, tools, knowledge, data, configuration data, specifications, listings, printouts, documentation, documents, notes, flow charts and programming techniques commonly employed by programmers.

Termination of the Agreement in part shall not affect the rights of *Alpha Pvt. Ltd.* and the obligations of *Beta Pvt. Ltd.* with respect to those portions of the Agreement not terminated.

8. Confidential Information

8.1 Confidential information defined.—During the term of this Agreement, *Alpha Pvt. Ltd.* may disclose to *Beta Pvt. Ltd.* certain confidential, proprietary information and/or trade secrets or *Beta Pvt. Ltd.* may have or be given access to certain confidential, proprietary information and/or trade secrets of *Alpha Pvt. Ltd.*, *Alpha Pvt. Ltd.* Affiliates, ... (name of affiliates) or other third party licensors or contractors of *Alpha Pvt. Ltd.* (collectively, "*Alpha Pvt. Ltd.* Confidential Information"). Unless otherwise excluded in this Agreement, *Alpha Pvt. Ltd.* Confidential Information shall mean any and all such information provided to *Beta Pvt. Ltd.* or to which *Beta Pvt. Ltd.* has or is given access, in whatever form, verbal or otherwise, including, but not limited to, business plans, marketing plans, financial records and analysis, research, technical specifications, marketing-sales-pricing data, designs, Agreements, trade secrets, software or other intellectual property, whether or not identified as "*Alpha Pvt. Ltd.* Confidential Information", in whatever media, electronic or otherwise, and any other materials identified in writing as "*Alpha Pvt. Ltd.* Confidential Information." *Beta Pvt. Ltd.* may disclose to *Alpha Pvt. Ltd.* information relating to *Beta Pvt. Ltd.*' past, present or future research, development or business activities (collectively, "*Beta Pvt. Ltd.* Confidential Information.")

8.2 Non-disclosure.—*Beta Pvt. Ltd.* will not, without the prior written consent of *Alpha Pvt. Ltd.*, remove from *Alpha Pvt. Ltd.*'s or *Alpha Pvt. Ltd.* Affiliate's premises or disclose *Alpha Pvt. Ltd.* Confidential Information to any third party, other than those of *Beta Pvt. Ltd.*' employees, directors and officers with a need to know for performance hereunder, or otherwise jeopardize the confidential nature of the *Alpha Pvt. Ltd.* Confidential Information, and *Beta Pvt. Ltd.* will not use such *Alpha Pvt. Ltd.* Confidential Information other than for the purposes of this Agreement. *Beta Pvt. Ltd.* agrees that all *Alpha Pvt. Ltd.* Confidential Information will be held in strictest confidence by *Beta Pvt. Ltd.* and that such *Alpha Pvt. Ltd.* Confidential Information will not be copied, reproduced or altered either in whole or in part by any method whatsoever, unless agreed upon in writing by *Alpha Pvt. Ltd.*. *Beta Pvt. Ltd.* shall cause its employees, officers and directors to whom the *Alpha Pvt. Ltd.* Confidential Information is disclosed to be informed of and agree to be bound by the restrictions upon disclosure and use of *Alpha Pvt. Ltd.* Confidential Information as contained in this Agreement and to sign an Agreement containing the terms set forth in Exhibit D hereto. *Alpha Pvt. Ltd.* agrees that it will not, during or after the term of this Agreement, permit the duplication or disclosure of any *Beta Pvt. Ltd.* Confidential Information to any person (other than an employee, agent or representative of *Alpha Pvt. Ltd.* or .... (name of aplha affiliate) who needs such information for the performance of the obligations hereunder), unless such duplication, use or disclosure is specifically authorized by *Beta Pvt. Ltd.* in writing.

8.3 *Exceptions.*—The terms "*Alpha Pvt. Ltd.* confidential information" and "*Beta Pvt. Ltd.* confidential information" shall not apply to information that:

(a) has been legally in the recipient Party's possession prior to disclosure by the disclosing party and is not subject to any non-disclosure obligations;

(b) has become part of the public domain through no fault of the recipient Party;

(c) has been developed subsequent to, and independent of, disclosure to the recipient Party; or

(d) has been released in writing by the disclosing party so that the recipient party may make public disclosure, or is otherwise deemed by the disclosing party, in writing, to be no longer confidential.

8.4 *Required disclosure.*—Notwithstanding anything to the contrary in this section, if the recipient party learns that it is or may be required by applicable court order, law or regulation to disclose any confidential information, then recipient party shall: (a) as promptly as possible after learning of a possible disclosure requirement, and in any case prior to making disclosure, notify disclosing party of the disclosure requirement so that disclosing party or the appropriate party may seek a protective order or other appropriate relief, (b) provide such co-operation and assistance as disclosing party may reasonably request in any effort by disclosing party or the appropriate party to obtain such relief, and (c) take reasonable steps to limit the amount of Confidential Information so disclosed and to protect its confidentiality.

8.5 *Injunctive relief.*—*Beta Pvt. Ltd.* acknowledges that breach of this section or disclosure of other information which, at law or in good conscience or equity, ought to remain confidential, will give rise to irreparable injury to *Alpha Pvt. Ltd.* or the owner of such information, inadequately compensation in damages. Accordingly, *Alpha Pvt. Ltd.* or such other party may seek and obtain injunctive relief against the breach or threatened breach of the foregoing undertakings, in addition to any other legal remedies, which may be available. *Beta Pvt. Ltd.* acknowledges and agrees that the covenants contained herein are necessary for the protection of legitimate business interests of *Alpha Pvt. Ltd.* and are reasonable in scope and content.

8.6 No License.—Nothing contained in this Agreement shall be construed to grant to *Beta Pvt. Ltd.* any right or license under any Intellectual Property Right of *Alpha Pvt. Ltd..* "Intellectual Property Rights" shall mean copyright rights (including, without limitation, the exclusive right to use, make recordings of, reproduce, modify, adapt, edit, enhance, maintain, support, market, sell, rent, sell for rental, sublicense, distribute copies of, publicly and privately display and publicly and privately perform, exploit, exhibit, the copyrighted work and to prepare derivative works), copyright registrations and applications, trademark rights (including, without limitation, trade names, trademarks, service marks and trade dress) trademark and service mark registrations and applications, patent rights (including without limitation the exclusive right to make, use and sell), patent registrations and applications, mask-work rights, trade secrets, moral rights, author's rights, right of publicity, contract and licensing rights, rights in packaging, goodwill and other intellectual property rights, as may exist now and/or hereafter come into existence, and all renewals and extensions thereof, regardless of whether any of such rights arise under the laws of any state, country or jurisdiction.

8.7 Return of confidential information.—Upon the earlier of (i) a request of the disclosing party; or (ii) the expiration or termination of this Agreement, the recipient party will return all confidential information, in whatever form or media, retaining no copies of the same in any form whatsoever, or destroy such Confidential Information and certify in writing to the disclosing party such destruction has been effected. Recipient Party's obligations hereunder regarding Confidential Information shall survive the return or destruction of such Confidential Information or termination of this Agreement or completion of the services.

9. Title, Proprietary Rights

9.1 Work for hire.—All work performed hereunder, including but not limited to, the Services, deliverables, business methods or processes, programs, systems, processes, data development, modification and enhancement of systems, computer programs, operating instructions, ideas, designs, concepts and all other documentation developed for or relating to *Alpha Pvt. Ltd.* or the Project and all documents, data and other information of any kind, including information incorporating, based upon, or derived from the foregoing, including reports and notes prepared by *Beta Pvt. Ltd.* and its employees and agents, and all software Deliverables and other Deliverables developed, prepared, produced or created for *Alpha Pvt. Ltd.* by *Beta Pvt. Ltd.* hereunder (whether or not completed) together with all modifications, revisions, changes, copies, partial copies, translations, compilations, partial copies with modifications and derivative works of the foregoing (collectively, the "Work Product") are, shall be and shall remain the property of *Alpha Pvt. Ltd.* and may not be used by *Beta Pvt. Ltd.* or its employees for any other purpose except for the benefit of *Alpha Pvt. Ltd..* Beta

Pvt. Ltd. shall not sell, transfer, publish, disclose, display, rent, lease, loan, license or otherwise make available to others any part of the Work Product, or copies thereof and *Beta Pvt. Ltd.* shall treat the same as Confidential Information. All applicable rights to patents, copyrights, trademarks, trade secrets and all other Intellectual Property Rights in and to the Work Product are, shall vest and shall remain in *Alpha Pvt. Ltd.*, and neither *Beta Pvt. Ltd.* nor its employees shall have any property interest in the Work Product, and same are to be considered works made for hire. (*Beta Pvt. Ltd.* proposes to add: "*Beta Pvt. Ltd.* will provide generic hardware and software required for performance of the Services. However, should special or project specific hardware or software be required, these shall be provided on loan by *Alpha Pvt. Ltd.* and set forth in the attached Schedules. All hardware and software provided on a loan basis will be returned to *Alpha Pvt. Ltd.* after the project is completed in the same condition it was delivered, reasonable wear and tear excepted. *Alpha Pvt. Ltd.* shall be responsible for the shipping, handling, insurance, and annual maintenance costs of all loaned hardware and software.")

9.2 *Assignment of rights.*—To the extent the Work Product or any materials contained therein or prepared therefore or the Intellectual Property Rights therein do not vest in *Alpha Pvt. Ltd.* by reason of the same being a work made for hire, *Beta Pvt. Ltd.* hereby grants, assigns and transfers to *Alpha Pvt. Ltd.* all right, title and interest in and to the Work Product and all Intellectual Property Rights thereto and *Beta Pvt. Ltd.* shall not retain any such rights therein. *Alpha Pvt. Ltd.* shall have all authorship rights therein. All Work Product shall belong exclusively to *Alpha Pvt. Ltd.*, with *Alpha Pvt. Ltd.* having the exclusive right to obtain and to hold in its own name, patents, copyright registrations or trademark registrations or such other protection as may be appropriate to the subject matter, and any extensions and renewals thereof, unencumbered by any claim by *Beta Pvt. Ltd.*, its officers, directors, employees, agents or sub-contractors. *Beta Pvt. Ltd.* agrees, at *Alpha Pvt. Ltd.*'s cost, to give *Alpha Pvt. Ltd.* and any person designated by *Alpha Pvt. Ltd.*, reasonable assistance required to perfect the rights defined in this section including execution and delivery of all documents required by *Alpha Pvt. Ltd.* to document or protect *Alpha Pvt. Ltd.* proprietary rights in the Work Product or assistance in filing applications for patent or copyright registration of such materials in the name of *Alpha Pvt. Ltd.* and in making all other necessary or appropriate filings with governmental entities so as to secure and maintain maximum protection for the Work Product. Unless otherwise requested by *Alpha Pvt. Ltd.*, upon the completion of the Services to be performed hereunder, or upon the earlier termination of this Agreement, *Beta Pvt. Ltd.* shall immediately turn over to *Alpha Pvt. Ltd.* all such materials and the Work Product developed pursuant hereto and no copies thereof shall be retained by *Beta Pvt. Ltd.* or its employees without the prior written consent of *Alpha Pvt. Ltd.*. Without limiting the foregoing, *Beta Pvt. Ltd.* hereby waives any and all claims that *Beta Pvt. Ltd.* may now or hereafter have in any jurisdiction to so-called "moral rights" or rights of "droit moral" with respect to the results and proceeds of the Work Product and *Beta Pvt. Ltd.*' services hereunder.

9.3 *Alpha Pvt. Ltd. furnished materials.*—Any materials furnished by *Alpha Pvt. Ltd.* in connection with this Agreement are provided to *Beta Pvt. Ltd.* solely for the use by *Beta Pvt. Ltd.* in furtherance of this Agreement, and all rights, title and interest thereto shall at all times remain in *Alpha Pvt. Ltd.*. All drawings, models, parts, drafts, reports, documentation, computers, work stations, network-related devices, computer equipment, office equipment, software, data storage media, whether machine readable or otherwise, and/or any other property, made, prepared, or acquired by *Beta Pvt. Ltd.* from *Alpha Pvt. Ltd.* in the rendition of services hereunder, and all copies thereof shall be the property of *Alpha Pvt. Ltd.* and shall be, at such times as may be specified by *Alpha Pvt. Ltd.*, delivered to *Alpha Pvt. Ltd.*. Neither *Beta Pvt. Ltd.* nor its employees or *Beta Pvt. Ltd.* may remove any such property from *Beta Pvt. Ltd.*' or *Alpha Pvt. Ltd.*'s or its Affiliates' premises or use same for any other purpose other than providing the services without *Alpha Pvt. Ltd.*'s prior consent.

9.4 *Pre-existing materials.*—To the extent that any pre-existing materials or information owned by *Beta Pvt. Ltd.* or any third party are contained in the Deliverables or are necessary for the use of the Deliverables, including, but not limited to the developers Tools, *Beta Pvt. Ltd.* warrants that it has or will acquire the right to grant and will grant to *Alpha Pvt. Ltd.* and its Affiliates, before delivery of the Deliverables, an irrevocable, non-exclusive, worldwide, royalty-free license to: (i) use, execute, display, copy, perform, modify and prepare derivative works thereof, and (ii) authorize others to do any, some, or all of the foregoing.

9.5 *Alpha Pvt. Ltd. systems.*—Commencing on the effective date and for the term hereof, *Alpha Pvt. Ltd.* will provide to *Beta Pvt. Ltd.*, at no charge to *Beta Pvt. Ltd.*, the right to use and access the systems currently used by *Alpha Pvt. Ltd.* or its Affiliates, or necessary for *Beta Pvt. Ltd.* to perform the functions to be performed by *Beta Pvt. Ltd.* hereunder, including the Software, and any successor systems, as listed in Exhibit E (the "*Alpha Pvt. Ltd.* systems") for use in performing services hereunder, (and all necessary support for *Beta Pvt. Ltd.*' continued use and access thereof.) *Alpha Pvt. Ltd.* shall be responsible for obtaining any necessary consents or assignments from any third party licensors of the *Alpha Pvt. Ltd.* systems prior to the Effective Date to enable *Beta Pvt. Ltd.* to use the *Alpha Pvt. Ltd. systems* in accordance with this section. *Beta Pvt. Ltd.* shall use the *Alpha Pvt. Ltd. systems* only for the purposes of this Agreement and in accordance with any restrictions on such use, which may be provided by *Alpha Pvt. Ltd.* to *Beta Pvt. Ltd.* from time to time. *Beta Pvt. Ltd.* may not copy the *Alpha Pvt. Ltd. systems* or permit same to be copied. *Beta Pvt. Ltd.* shall not modify, decompile, translate or adapt, by reverse engineering or otherwise, the *Alpha Pvt. Ltd.* systems in any way or use the *Alpha Pvt. Ltd. systems* to create a derivative work or attempt to create the source code from the object code. *Beta Pvt. Ltd.* acknowledges that the *Alpha Pvt. Ltd. systems* are the sole and exclusive property of *Alpha Pvt. Ltd.* or its licensors, including .... (name of Alpha's affiliate) all applicable rights to patents, copyrights, trademarks and trade secrets inherent therein and appurtenant thereto. Title in and to the *Alpha Pvt. Ltd. Systems* and any copies thereof shall be and remain the sole and exclusive property of *Alpha Pvt. Ltd.* or its licensors. *Beta Pvt. Ltd.* shall not sell, transfer, publish, disclose, display, rent, lease, loan, license, or otherwise make available any portion of the

Alpha Pvt. Ltd. Systems to others, and shall not permit any other party access or use of such *Alpha Pvt. Ltd.* Systems, other than the employees of *Beta Pvt. Ltd.* who have a need to access or use such Systems for performance of this Agreement. *Beta Pvt. Ltd.* agrees to secure and protect the *Alpha Pvt. Ltd. Systems* in a manner consistent with the maintenance of *Alpha Pvt. Ltd.*'s or its licensors' rights therein and to take appropriate action by instruction or Agreement with all persons who are permitted access to the *Alpha Pvt. Ltd. Systems* to satisfy its obligations hereunder. *Beta Pvt. Ltd.* acknowledges that the *Alpha Pvt. Ltd.* Systems contains proprietary trade secrets of *Alpha Pvt. Ltd.* or its Affiliates or its licensors and hereby agrees to maintain the confidentiality thereof using at least as great a degree of care as *Beta Pvt. Ltd.* uses to maintain the confidentiality of *Beta Pvt. Ltd.*' own most confidential information. *Beta Pvt. Ltd.* agrees to comply with the terms of any Agreement required by any third party licensor of *Alpha Pvt. Ltd. Systems*, which *Beta Pvt. Ltd.* is required to execute by such third Party.

9.6 *Use of Third Party content or technology.*—*Beta Pvt. Ltd.* shall not use any Third Party Content or Third Party Technology in the Deliverables or the provision of the Services without *Alpha Pvt. Ltd.*'s prior written approval and unless: (a) *Beta Pvt. Ltd.* is expressly permitted to use such third party Technology or Third Party Content pursuant to written Agreements with all third party rights holders; and (b) *Beta Pvt. Ltd.* has acquired for *Beta Pvt. Ltd.* and *Alpha Pvt. Ltd.* and *Alpha Pvt. Ltd.* Affiliates, all rights, permissions, clearances, releases or other authorizations necessary to use such Third Party Technology and/or Third Party content, as contemplated by this Agreement. *Beta Pvt. Ltd.* shall be responsible for all payments in connection with the use of Third Party Technology and Third Party content, *Alpha Pvt. Ltd.* shall have the right to review all *Beta Pvt. Ltd.* Agreements with third parties to ensure their acceptability, and *Beta Pvt. Ltd.* shall deliver such Agreements to *Alpha Pvt. Ltd.* within five (5) days of *Alpha Pvt. Ltd.*'s request therefore. For purposes of this Agreement, "Third Party Content" shall mean all content, if any, for which rights, licenses, permissions, or other clearances need to be obtained from any persons other than the parties hereto for the use of such content in the deliverables as contemplated herein. "Third Party Technology" shall mean all systems, tools and/or software, if any (including, without limitation, compilers, diagnostics and data base products) which (i) are required to be licensed from persons other than the parties hereto if the Deliverables require the use of such Third Party Technology, (ii) with which the Deliverables are designed or is based on, or (iii) are required for or used in the provision of the Services.

10. Warranties

10.1 *Beta Pvt. Ltd. warranties.*—*Beta Pvt. Ltd.* represents and warrants that: (a) *Beta Pvt. Ltd.* shall comply with all applicable laws and regulations, including import/export laws and regulations and the Foreign Corrupt Practices Act, as it may be amended from time to time; (b) in rendering the Services, it and its employees have all necessary rights, authorizations, or licenses to provide the Services hereunder and to provide all related materials and services required under this Agreement; (c) each of its employees assigned to perform services under any Schedule shall have the proper skill, training and background so as to be able to perform in a competent and professional manner and that all work will be so performed in accordance with this Agreement and the applicable statement of services; (d) *Alpha Pvt. Ltd.* shall receive free, good and clear title to all Deliverables delivered under this Agreement; and (e) the Deliverables shall be delivered in a manner consistent with good commercial practice, free from defects in material and workmanship, and shall conform to the Specifications for same as set forth in the Statement of Services and shall, for a period of ninety (90) days from the date of Final Acceptance, meet the functional, performance and reliability requirements of *Alpha Pvt. Ltd.* as set forth in the applicable Statement of Services.

10.2 *Warranty period.*—Until ninety (90) days after Final Acceptance for a Phase (the "Warranty Period"), *Beta Pvt. Ltd.* will, at no charge to *Alpha Pvt. Ltd.*, furnish such materials and services as shall be necessary to correct any defects in the Deliverables, promptly correct any deficiencies which prevent such Deliverables from conforming to the acceptance criteria and correct such deficiency and the effects of such deficiency in prior Phases and Sites. *Beta Pvt. Ltd.* warranty service obligations under this section 10.2 shall not apply to the extent that any claimed non-conformity was directly and solely caused by: (a) the improper use of any hardware or software not provided or recommended by *Beta Pvt. Ltd.*, (b) *Alpha Pvt. Ltd.*'s negligence, fault or improper use of a Deliverable, or (c) modifications to or changes in a Deliverable not made or approved by *Beta Pvt. Ltd.*.

10.3 *Additional software warranties.*—*Beta Pvt. Ltd.* represents and warrants that the software Deliverables shall be millennium compliant and that, as of the time of delivery to *Alpha Pvt. Ltd.*, all code as delivered will be free and clear of and contain no threats known as software viruses, salamis, time bombs, logic bombs, Trojan horses, trap doors, or other malicious computer instructions, intentional devices or techniques that can or were designed to threaten, infect, attach, assault, vandalize, defraud, disrupt, damage, disable, or shut down a computer system or any component of such computer system, including its security or user data. *Beta Pvt. Ltd.* further represents and warrants that each module of all software deliverables and components and functions thereof shall be capable or operating fully and correctly on the combination of the computer hardware, telecommunications equipment, the programming language and/or operating system environment specified in the statement of services. For purposes of this Agreement, millennium compliant means fault-free performance in the processing of date and date related data (including, but not limited to, calculating, comparing, and sequencing). Fault-free performance includes the manipulation of data with dates prior to, through, and beyond ....20.... and successful transition into and performance in and after the year 20.... with the correct system date, without human intervention, including leap year calculations, and provision of correct results when moving forward and backward in time across the year 20......

10.4 *Software deliverable reliability.*—Software Deliverables shall be subject to performance and reliability warranties set forth in the statement of services to ensure that there is no degradation in the performance or reliability of the software Deliverables. Such warranty shall provide a performance and reliability standard against which the software Deliverables are to be measured during the Acceptance Test and Warranty Period, and the remedies available to *Alpha Pvt. Ltd.* upon failure of the software Deliverables to meet said standards. Such remedies may include the provision of services and products necessary to make the software Deliverables meet said standards, extension of the Warranty Period, credit toward future payments, or hold-back of current amounts due, as *Alpha Pvt. Ltd.* shall determine in its sole discretion.

10.5 Permits.—The parties acknowledge that certain software and technical data to be provided under this Agreement and certain transactions under this Agreement may be subject to export controls under the laws and regulations of the .... and other countries. *Beta Pvt. Ltd.* will be responsible, as part of the services, for securing all permits, licenses, regulatory approvals and authorizations, whether domestic or international, and including all applicable import/export control approvals (collectively, "Permits") required for *Beta Pvt. Ltd.* to provide the services to *Alpha Pvt. Ltd.* or its designees and will take all lawful steps necessary to maintain such Permits during the term of this Agreement. *Beta Pvt. Ltd.* will have financial responsibility for, and will pay, all fees and taxes associated with obtaining such permits. *Alpha Pvt. Ltd.* will co-operate with *Beta Pvt. Ltd.* in securing such Permits. If *Beta Pvt. Ltd.* is not able to secure the Permits in its own name, *Alpha Pvt. Ltd.* will undertake to secure such Permits at the reasonable direction of *Beta Pvt. Ltd.* and at *Beta Pvt. Ltd.'* expense. *Beta Pvt. Ltd.* shall be solely responsible for compliance with all laws and regulations relating to data protection and privacy and/or trans-border data flow.

10.6 Year 20.... services warranty.—Notwithstanding anything in this Agreement to the contrary, *Beta Pvt. Ltd.* warrants and represents that (i) its ability to provide continuous services as set forth in each Statement of Services will be unaffected by computer problems related to dates beyond ...., 20....; (ii) the *Beta Pvt. Ltd.'* computer systems related to the services shall be millennium compliant.

10.7 Additional warranties.—In the Statement of Services, the parties may agree upon warranties which will apply to the Deliverables to be provided, under that Statement of Services, in addition to those set forth in sections 10.1 through 10.4 inclusive ("Additional Warranties"). The warranties required by sections 10.1 through 10.4 inclusive shall apply to all Statements of Services, whether or not a Statement of Services sets forth Additional Warranties.

10.8 Remedies for breach of warranties.—In the event that the Deliverables or Services do not meet the above warranties, *Beta Pvt. Ltd.* shall provide, at no charge, the necessary Deliverables and services required to attain the levels or standards set forth in said warranties.

10.9 Notice of problem.—In the event that during the term of this Agreement *Beta Pvt. Ltd.* becomes aware of an event, occurrence, error, defect or malfunction which *Beta Pvt. Ltd.* reasonably and in good faith anticipates would adversely and materially affect *Alpha Pvt. Ltd.* or its Affiliates, then *Beta Pvt. Ltd.* will promptly provide *Alpha Pvt. Ltd.* with written notice of the event, occurrence, error, defect or malfunction and the adverse effect anticipated by *Beta Pvt. Ltd.*, as well as a proposed remedy therefore.

10.10 *Business Disruption.*—In performing its Services hereunder, *Beta Pvt. Ltd.* will use diligent efforts to perform such services in a manner that minimizes the risk of undue disruption to the normal business operations of *Alpha Pvt. Ltd.* and its Affiliates.

10.11 *Duly Authorized.*—*Beta Pvt. Ltd.* makes the following representations:

(a) *Beta Pvt. Ltd.* is a corporation registered and in good standing under the laws of India and is qualified and in good standing as a foreign corporation under the laws of any jurisdiction where the ownership of its assets or the conduct of its business require *Beta Pvt. Ltd.* to be so qualified, or if *Beta Pvt. Ltd.* is not so qualified, the failure to so qualify will not have a material adverse effect on the ability of *Alpha Pvt. Ltd.* to enforce this Agreement;

(b) There is no action, suit or proceeding pending or threatened against or affecting *Beta Pvt. Ltd.* before or by any court, administrative agency or other governmental authority which in any way will impair *Beta Pvt. Ltd.*' ability to perform all of its obligations under, or which otherwise brings into question the enforceability or validity of the transactions contemplated by the Agreement;

(c) *Beta Pvt. Ltd.'s* execution, delivery, and performance of this Agreement has been duly authorized by all appropriate corporate action on the part of *Beta Pvt. Ltd.* and this Agreement constitutes the valid and binding obligation of *Beta Pvt. Ltd.* enforceable against *Beta Pvt. Ltd.* in accordance with the terms thereof and hereof;

(d) Neither the execution and delivery by *Beta Pvt. Ltd.* of this Agreement, nor the consummation by *Beta Pvt. Ltd.* of the transactions contemplated hereby, nor compliance by *Beta Pvt. Ltd.* with the provisions hereof, conflicts with or results in a breach of any of the provisions of the certificate of or articles of incorporation or by-laws of *Beta Pvt. Ltd.* or any amendments thereto, or any applicable law, judgment, order, writ, injunction, decree, rule or regulation of any court, administrative agency or other governmental authority, or of any Agreement or other instrument to which *Beta Pvt. Ltd.* is a Party or by which it is bound, or constitute a default under any provision thereof.

10.12 *Warranty disclaimer.*—The warranties of *Beta Pvt. Ltd.* set forth herein are expressly in lieu of all other warranties, express or implied. *Beta Pvt. Ltd.* makes no other warranty, express or implied, of merchantability or fitness for a particular purpose.

11. Indemnification

11.1 *Losses Defined.*—For purposes of this Agreement, "Losses" means all claims, actions, losses, liabilities, damages and costs (including taxes) and all related costs and expenses (including reasonable attorney's fees and disbursements and costs of investigation, litigation and settlement).

11.2 Indemnification and defence.—

(a) *Beta Pvt. Ltd.* will indemnify, defend and hold *Alpha Pvt. Ltd.*, *Alpha Pvt. Ltd.* Affiliates and its and their respective officers, directors, employees, agents, successors and assigns (each, an "*Alpha Pvt. Ltd.* Indemnitee") harmless from and against any and all Losses arising out of or relating to any claim:

   (i) that the services or any Deliverable provided to *Alpha Pvt. Ltd.* or its Affiliates or designees by *Beta Pvt. Ltd.* infringe upon the Intellectual Proprietary Rights of such Third Party;

   (ii) alleging a violation of laws or regulations or a failure by *Beta Pvt. Ltd.* to obtain required permits, rights or licenses or otherwise, including as set forth in section 10.5;

   (iii) alleging a breach by *Beta Pvt. Ltd.* of any obligation, representation or warranty made by *Beta Pvt. Ltd.* in this Agreement or *Beta Pvt. Ltd.'* or its employees' obligations with respect to Confidential Information, and in particular, breach of *Beta Pvt. Ltd.'* obligations under section 9.5;

   (iv) alleging a breach by *Beta Pvt. Ltd.* or its employees of the *Alpha Pvt. Ltd.* policies or procedures in effect at any *Alpha Pvt. Ltd.* facility;

   (v) arising out of or in connection with the injury of or damage to any person or real or tangible personal property to the extent such injury or damage is proximately caused by the negligence or wilful misconduct of any person for whose conduct *Beta Pvt. Ltd.* is liable; or

   (vi) arising out of or in connection with any claim for payment of compensation, salary or benefits asserted by an employee of *Beta Pvt. Ltd.* or arising out of removal of a *Beta Pvt. Ltd.* employee under section 5.5.

(b) *Alpha Pvt. Ltd.* shall, at its own expense, defend any claim, suit, or action brought against *Beta Pvt. Ltd.* by Third Parties (other than liability solely the fault of *Beta Pvt. Ltd.*) for infringement or misappropriation of a third party's copyright, patent, trade secret or other intellectual property rights by any proprietary property provided by *Alpha Pvt. Ltd.* (and not of any Third Party) to *Beta Pvt. Ltd.* under this Agreement, and shall pay any damages or settlement assessed against *Beta Pvt. Ltd.* under such a claim. *Beta Pvt. Ltd.* shall be obligated to give *Alpha Pvt. Ltd.* prompt written notice of, and the parties shall co-operate in, the defence of any claim, suit or action, including appeals and negotiations. This indemnity shall not extend to any claim of infringement or misappropriation resulting from *Beta Pvt. Ltd.'s* unauthorized modification of such intellectual property. Except as specified above, *Alpha Pvt. Ltd.* shall not be liable for any costs or expenses incurred without its prior written authorization.

(c) *Beta Pvt. Ltd.* shall not settle any claim, which adversely affects *Alpha Pvt. Ltd.'s* rights without *Alpha Pvt. Ltd.'s* prior written consent. Furthermore, in the event *Alpha Pvt. Ltd.* should be enjoined in such suit or proceeding from use of any Deliverable, *Beta Pvt. Ltd.*, at its option, shall promptly either (a) at any time, secure termination of the injunction and procure for *Alpha Pvt. Ltd.* the right to use such Deliverable without any obligations or liability, or (b) after a final judicial determination of such infringement, replace such Deliverable with a suitable non-infringing Deliverable or modify the original Deliverable to become non-infringing without affecting its functionality, all at *Beta Pvt. Ltd.'s* sole expense. The party claiming indemnification shall promptly notify the other of any matters in respect of which the indemnity may apply and of which the notifying party has knowledge and shall give the other full opportunity to control the response thereto and the defence thereof, including without limitation any Agreement relating to the settlement thereof. The indemnified party's failure to promptly give notice shall affect the indemnifying party's obligation to indemnify the indemnified party only to the extent the indemnifying party's rights are materially prejudiced by such failure. The indemnified party may participate, at its own expense, in such defence and in any settlement discussions directly or through counsel of its choice and review all documents prepared in connection therewith.

11.3 *No remedies exclusive.* The remedies of *Alpha Pvt. Ltd.* with respect to any matter under this Agreement shall not be limited to the remedies set forth herein; provided, that *Alpha Pvt. Ltd.* shall not receive a duplicative recovery.

12. Limitation of Liability

In no event will either party be liable for consequential, incidental, indirect, punitive, exemplary or special damages, however caused and based on any theory of liability arising out of or relating to this Agreement, even if a party has been advised of the possibility of such damages. *Beta Pvt. Ltd.'s* aggregate liability hereunder shall not exceed amounts paid hereunder by *Alpha Pvt. Ltd. Alpha Pvt. Ltd.'s* aggregate liability hereunder shall not exceed amounts owed to *Beta Pvt. Ltd.* hereunder. The above limitations shall not apply to (i) *Beta Pvt. Ltd.* Obligations under section 11.2; (ii) claims or causes of action which are due to *Beta Pvt. Ltd.'s* gross negligence or wilful misconduct or that of its officers, directors, employees, agents or representatives; and (iii) breach of *Beta Pvt. Ltd.'s* obligations of confidentiality. The parties acknowledge that the limitations set forth in this section are integral to the amount of consideration paid or to be paid under this Agreement.

13. Insurance, Fidelity Bond and Letter of Credit

13.1 *Insurance.*—*Beta Pvt. Ltd.* agrees, at its own expense, to provide and keep in full force and effect during the term of this Agreement, the following kinds and minimum amounts of insurance.

  (a) *Workers' Compensation.*—Workers' Compensation insurance with coverage and limits complying with the requirements of the jurisdiction in which the Services are performed.

(b) *Employer's Liability*—Employer's liability insurance with limits of not less than .... (amount in foreign currency) per accident.

(c) *General Liability*—Commercial general liability insurance including contractual liability, personal injury and broad form property damage, with limits of .... (amount in foreign currency) per each occurrence and .... (amount in foreign currency) as general aggregate limits. *Alpha Pvt. Ltd.* shall be named as an additional insured to this insurance policy.

(d) *Errors and Omissions Liability.*—Errors and omissions (or Professional Liability) insurance with limits of.................... (amount in foreign currency)

(e) *Fidelity Bond* - Commercial Blanket Fidelity Bond insurance including a customer protection endorsement, with limits of........................ said bond shall cover, without limitation, computer crime. *Alpha Pvt. Ltd.* shall be named as an additional insured and a loss payee as its interests may appear. (*Beta Pvt. Ltd.* proposes to delete this paragraph.)

The aforesaid insurance policies shall be maintained with insurers having a minimum rating of 'A' from .... (name) or other comparable insurance rating service. *Beta Pvt. Ltd.'s* insurance will be primary over any other applicable insurance, and any coverage offered under *Alpha Pvt. Ltd.'s* policies will be excess and non-contributory. Certificates of insurance acceptable to *Alpha Pvt. Ltd.* shall be provided to, *Alpha Pvt. Ltd.* before the commencement of services under this Agreement and, as to any secondary supplier, prior to any sub-contractor providing services through *Beta Pvt. Ltd.* to *Alpha Pvt. Ltd.*. *Alpha Pvt. Ltd.* shall be notified in writing at least thirty (30) days prior written notice to *Alpha Pvt. Ltd.*. *Alpha Pvt. Ltd.* shall be notified in writing at least thirty (30) days prior to any insurance cancellation, interruption or reduction in coverage. All insurance premiums, expenses, costs and charges incurred under this Agreement shall be borne by *Beta Pvt. Ltd.*. Secondary suppliers, including any *Beta Pvt. Ltd.* subsidiary and/or affiliate (to the extent not covered under *Beta Pvt. Ltd.'s* coverages) are required to maintain and carry the types and amounts of insurance noted above and be subject to the same conditions and obligations imposed on *Beta Pvt. Ltd.* as specified herein.

13.2 Letter of credit.—Prior to execution of this Agreement and any subsequent Statements of services, *Beta Pvt. Ltd.* shall post an irrevocable letter of credit naming *Alpha Pvt. Ltd.* as beneficiary in a format and on a domestic foreign bank acceptable to *Alpha Pvt. Ltd.* for the amount of the total price set forth in all Statements of Services. The irrevocable letter of credit shall remain in full force and effect until the conclusion of *Beta Pvt. Ltd.'s* obligations hereunder. In the event that *Beta Pvt. Ltd.* does not perform in accordance with the requirements of this Agreement, then *Alpha Pvt. Ltd.* may invoke the letter of credit. (*Beta Pvt. Ltd.* proposes to delete this paragraph.)

13.3 Performance bond.—*Beta Pvt. Ltd.* shall furnish a performance bond, in form and substance reasonably satisfactory to *Alpha Pvt. Ltd.*, in the amount of .... , to secure *Beta Pvt. Ltd.'s* performance of its obligations under this

Agreement. The performance bond shall be executed by *Beta Pvt. Ltd.* and by a surety or sureties approved by *Alpha Pvt. Ltd.* and shall be in effect from the Effective Date through the date of conclusion of *Beta Pvt. Ltd.'s* obligations hereunder. *(Beta Pvt. Ltd. proposes to delete this paragraph)*

14. Dispute Resolution

14.1 Dispute.—In the event of any dispute, controversy or claim arising out of or relating to this Agreement or any subsequent amendments to this Agreement including, without limitation, the breach, termination, validity or invalidity thereof, or any non-contractual issues relating to this Agreement (each, a "Dispute"), each of the parties will appoint a designated officer to meet for the purpose of endeavouring to resolve such Dispute or to negotiate for an adjustment to such provision. No formal proceedings for the judicial resolution of such dispute, except for the seeking of temporary restraining orders or injunctions, may begin until this dispute resolution procedure has been elevated to the Executive Vice President level, in the case of *Alpha Pvt. Ltd.*, and the .... level, in the case of *Beta Pvt. Ltd.*, and either of such officers of *Beta Pvt. Ltd.* or *Alpha Pvt. Ltd.* in good faith conclude, after a good faith attempt to resolve the dispute, that amicable resolution through continued negotiation of the matter at issue does not appear likely. Such attempt to resolve the dispute may be accomplished by conference between such officers of *Alpha Pvt. Ltd.* and *Beta Pvt. Ltd.*, either face-to-face or by telephone, or by the exchange of correspondence.

14.2 Arbitration.—

(a) All disputes, controversies or claims between the Parties hereto arising out of or relating to this Agreement (including, but not limited to, disputes as to the validity, interpretation, performance, breach, or with respect to damages upon termination of this Agreement) which are not settled pursuant to the issue resolution procedures set forth in section 14.1 hereof, will be settled by final and binding arbitration in accordance with the following:

(b) Except as specified herein or otherwise agreed to in writing, the arbitration will be conducted in the English language in the.................... (name of foreign company) and otherwise in accordance with and subject to the Rules of the International Chamber of Commerce in effect at such time (the "Rules"), by a panel of three arbitrators in accordance with the Rules. The arbitrators should be knowledgeable and have expertise in areas relating to the subject matter of the dispute. Each of the parties shall designate an arbitrator within .... days of receipt of a notice of dispute. The two designated arbitrators shall select a third neutral arbitrator who shall be a lawyer, judge or former judge with substantial experience in disputes arising out of computer technology and shall be a citizen of neither .... (name of the country of the Foreign Collaborator's Company) nor India. At least one member of the panel shall be an attorney experienced in the procedures of arbitration.

(c) The arbitration panel is authorized to render awards of monetary damages and injunctive relief (direction to take or refrain from taking action), or both. The arbitration panel may, at its discretion, order one party to reimburse the other party for all or any part of (i) the expenses of the arbitration paid by the other party, or (ii) the attorneys' fees and other expenses reasonably incurred by the other Party in connection with the arbitration. However, the arbitration panel may impose monetary sanctions for conduct contrary to the express direction of the panel. Prior to the start of any arbitration, each party shall deposit with the ICC one half of the estimated costs and fees of the arbitration proceeding. Unless the arbitral award provides otherwise, all costs associated with the arbitration shall be shared equally by *Alpha Pvt. Ltd.* and *Beta Pvt. Ltd.*. The arbitral award shall be in writing setting forth the legal and factual basis for the award and shall be final and binding upon the parties who agree, in writing, to waive all rights of appeal thereon subject to the International Chamber of Commerce, International Court of Arbitration's approval. Notwithstanding anything to the contrary in this Agreement, the arbitration panel shall be bound by the express terms of this Agreement, and shall not change or modify any term of this Agreement clearly expressed herein.

(d) In the event that the arbitration procedures set forth in this section conflict with the Rules, the arbitration procedures set forth in this section shall prevail if and to the extent allowed by the Rules.

(e) Judgment upon the award rendered in any such arbitration may be entered in any court of competent jurisdiction, or application may be made to such court for a judicial acceptance of the award and an enforcement, as the law of such jurisdiction may require or allow.

(f) It is expressly understood and agreed that the pendency of a dispute hereunder shall at no time and in no respect constitute a basis for any modification, limitation or suspension of *Alpha Pvt. Ltd.*'s and *Beta Pvt. Ltd.*'s obligations to fully perform in accordance with the terms of this Agreement.

14.3 Statute of Limitations. Except as otherwise determined by the arbitrator under section 14.2, any statute of limitations will be tolled upon initiation of the dispute resolution procedures under this Article and will remain tolled until the dispute is resolved in accordance herewith; provided, however, that tolling will cease if the party against which the statute of limitations would be applied fails to observe the procedures set forth in this Article.

15. Miscellaneous

15.1 Modification of Agreement.—Except as otherwise provided herein, this Agreement may be modified only by a writing signed by both Parties to this Agreement.

15.2 Assignment.—This Agreement shall be binding on the parties' respective successors and permitted assigns. *Beta Pvt. Ltd.* may not assign, subcontract or transfer this Agreement in any manner or any interest, payment or rights hereunder without the prior written consent of *Alpha Pvt. Ltd.* and any assignment or transfer not so approved shall be considered *null* and *void*. *Beta Pvt. Ltd.* shall be liable for the acts and omissions of its employees and sub-contractors. Any sub-contractors approved by *Alpha Pvt. Ltd.* shall agree in a writing to be provided to *Alpha Pvt. Ltd.* before such sub-contractor begins services, to be bound by the terms of this Agreement, in particular, Article 8.

15.3 Independent contractors.—*Beta Pvt. Ltd.* is acting, in performance of this Agreement, as an independent contractor. *Beta Pvt. Ltd.* shall provide under this Agreement, the services of only those personnel who are employees of *Beta Pvt. Ltd.* for tax purposes. Personnel supplied by *Beta Pvt. Ltd.* hereunder are not *Alpha Pvt. Ltd.*'s employees or agents and *Beta Pvt. Ltd.* assumes full responsibility for their acts. *Beta Pvt. Ltd.* shall be solely responsible for the payment of compensation of *Beta Pvt. Ltd.*' employees assigned to perform services hereunder and such employees shall be informed that they are not entitled to the provision of any *Alpha Pvt. Ltd.* employee benefits. *Alpha Pvt. Ltd.* shall not be responsible for payment of worker's compensation, disability benefits, and unemployment insurance or for withholding and paying employment taxes for any *Beta Pvt. Ltd.* employee, but such responsibility shall be solely that of *Beta Pvt. Ltd.* In the event that any *Beta Pvt. Ltd.* employee performing services hereunder is found to be not an employee of *Beta Pvt. Ltd.* for any purpose, including federal tax purposes, *Beta Pvt. Ltd.* shall immediately take appropriate corrective action or remove said employee from performing services hereunder and, if requested by *Alpha Pvt. Ltd.*, provide a qualified replacement as set forth in Article 5.

15.4 Governing Law and service of process.—This Agreement shall be governed exclusively by and construed in accordance with the laws of the .... (name of the Foreign Collaborator's Company) and the .... (name of the Foreign Collaborator's Company) excluding its conflict of laws provisions. *Beta Pvt. Ltd.* hereby designates (insert name and address of *Beta Pvt. Ltd.* representative) for service of process in any action or proceeding arising under this Agreement and waives any international treaty provisions with respect to such service of process. Service of process in any action or proceeding arising hereunder shall be by mail only. The parties agree that all disputes, controversies of claims arising out of or related to this Agreement will be settled only by final and binding arbitration in accordance with sub-section 14.2; below; provided, however, that *Alpha Pvt. Ltd.* shall not be precluded by the foregoing from seeking equitable relief where appropriate in any court of competent jurisdiction. Further, *Beta Pvt. Ltd.* hereby agrees and covenants not to challenge or dispute the applicability or enforceability of any order, injunction, judgment or other action taken by such court, or any arbitral award, regardless of the location where such application, enforcement or award is sought. Any issue concerning the extent to which any dispute is subject to arbitration, or concerning the applicability, interpretation, or enforceability of these procedures, including any contention that all or part of these procedures are invalid or unenforceable, shall be governed by the .... (name of the Foreign Collaborator's) Arbitration Act and resolved by the arbitrators.

15.5 Validity.—To the extent any provision of this Agreement shall be held to be void, illegal or unenforceable by any court, or regulatory agency, the same shall have no effect on the validity or enforceability of the remaining provisions shall not be affected thereby and this Agreement shall be carried out as if any such invalid or unenforceable provision was not contained herein.

15.6 Remedies cumulative.—The enumeration of specific remedies shall not be exclusive of any other remedies under this Agreement or available under law or equity.

15.7 Attorneys' Fees.—Notwithstanding section 12, *Beta Pvt. Ltd.* shall be responsible and shall reimburse *Alpha Pvt. Ltd.* for any cost or expense, including attorney's fees, incurred by *Alpha Pvt. Ltd.* in enforcing the terms and conditions of this Agreement.

15.8 Notices.—Any notice provided pursuant to this Agreement, if specified to be in writing, shall be in writing and shall be deemed given (a) if by hand delivery, upon receipt thereof, (b) if mailed, ten (10) days after deposit in the .... (name of the Foreign Collaborator's Company) or Indian mails, postage pre-paid, certified mail return receipt requested, (c) if by next day express delivery service, upon such delivery or (d) if by facsimile upon confirmation of receipt. All notices shall be addressed as follows (or such other address as either party may in the future specify in writing to the other):

Alpha Pvt. Ltd.: International, Inc.
.... (Address)
....
Attn:
copy to: Office of General Counsel
....
.... (Address)
....
Attn: *General Counsel*
If to *Beta Pvt. Ltd.* at: *Beta Pvt. Ltd.* Technologies Limited
.... (Address)
....
Attn:....................
Telephone number:....................
Facsimile number:....................

15.9 Entire Agreement.—This Agreement constitutes the entire Agreement between the parties and supersedes any and all prior to contemporaneous Agreement, understanding, negotiation or warranty or representation between the parties in connection with the subject matter of this Agreement. In the event of a conflict between the terms and conditions of this Agreement and any statement of services attached hereto, then the terms of such statement of services shall prevail.

15.10 Waiver.—The failure of either party to promptly enforce or seek remedy for the breach of any provision of this Agreement shall not constitute a waiver of such provision or any part thereof. No term or provision shall be deemed waived, and no breach hereof shall be deemed consented to, unless such waiver or consent shall be in writing and signed by the Party, which has given such waiver or consent. Any such waiver or consent shall not constitute a waiver of, or consent to, any other term or provision.

15.11 Force Majeure.—Neither party shall be liable to the other for any delay or failure to perform due to causes beyond its reasonable control. Performance times shall be considered extended for a period of time equivalent to the time lost because of any such delay, provided that in the event *Beta Pvt. Ltd.* is delayed in its performance by reason of such cause, no such extension shall be made unless notice thereof is presented by *Beta Pvt. Ltd.* to *Alpha Pvt. Ltd.* in writing within five (5) business days after the start of the occurrence of such delay, no payment shall be made by *Alpha Pvt. Ltd.* for any fees or expenses incurred by *Beta Pvt. Ltd.* by reason of such delay, and *Beta Pvt. Ltd.* shall use best efforts to perform its obligations during such period of delay. If *Beta Pvt. Ltd.'s* non-performance continues for a period of greater than thirty (30) days, *Alpha Pvt. Ltd.* may terminate this Agreement by providing written notice to the *Beta Pvt. Ltd.*

15.12 Publicity.—*Beta Pvt. Ltd.* agrees that it will not, without prior written consent of *Alpha Pvt. Ltd.* in each instance (i) use in advertising, publicity or otherwise the name of *Alpha Pvt. Ltd.*, or any affiliate of *Alpha Pvt. Ltd.* or any director, officer, employee or agent of *Alpha Pvt. Ltd.* nor any trade name, trademark, trade device, service mark, symbol or any abbreviation, contraction, or simulation thereof owned by *Alpha Pvt. Ltd.* or its affiliates, (ii) represent directly or indirectly that any product or service provided by *Beta Pvt. Ltd.* has been approved or endorsed by *Alpha Pvt. Ltd.*, or (iii) refer to the existence of this Agreement in press releases, advertising or materials distributed to prospective customers.

15.13 Most favoured customer.—*Beta Pvt. Ltd.* agrees to treat *Alpha Pvt. Ltd.* as its most favoured customer. *Beta Pvt. Ltd.* represents that all of the provisions of this Agreement and any Statement of Services are comparable to or better than the equivalent provisions being offered by *Beta Pvt. Ltd.* to any of its other customers. If *Beta Pvt. Ltd.* offers more favourable provisions to any customer during the term of its contract period than under this Agreement or any statement of services, such provisions shall be made available to *Alpha Pvt. Ltd.*. (*Beta Pvt. Ltd. proposes to delete this paragraph.*)

15.14 Non-solicitation and Non-employment of employees.—During the term of this Agreement and for a period of six (6) months after its expiration or termination, *Beta Pvt. Ltd.* nor any of its employees, agents, or sub-contractors will, without the prior written consent of *Alpha Pvt. Ltd.*, directly or indirectly (a) solicit employees of the *Alpha Pvt. Ltd.* to seek employment or other contractual arrangements with any employees, agents, or sub-contractors of *Alpha Pvt. Ltd.* or (b) employ or otherwise engage the services of any employee of *Alpha Pvt. Ltd.*

15.15 Headings.—The headings have been inserted for convenience and reference only and shall not be construed to affect the meaning, construction or effect of this Agreement.

15.16 Surviving Articles and sections.—All provisions of sections 2.6, 2.7, 8, 9, 11, 12, 13, 14, 15 and 16 shall survive the termination of this Agreement for any reason or the completion of services.

IN WITNESS WHEREOF, the Parties have executed this Agreement as of the date first herein above set forth.

Theta	Beta Pvt. Ltd. Technologies Ltd.
....	....
Signature	Signature
....	....
Name	Name
....	....
Title	Title
....	....
Date	Date

Exhibit A

Form of Statement of Services

Statement of Services

Dated

1. *Services, product and deliverables*:

2. *Special Instructions*:

3. *Delivery/Completion Date*:

IN WITNESS WHEREOF, the Parties hereto have made and executed this Statement of Services as of the date first herein above set forth.

Theta	Beta Pvt. Ltd.
....	....
Signature	Signature
....	....
Name	Name
....	....
Title	Title
....	....
Date	Date

Exhibit B

Alpha Pvt. Ltd. Code of Business Conduct

Exhibit C

Telecommunication...Connection

Exhibit D
Beta Pvt. Ltd. EMPLOYEE TERMS

1. Non-Disclosure

In connection with services which now or in the future are performed by the undersigned for (..................................) ("*Alpha Pvt. Ltd.*"), or for any subsidiary or affiliate of *Alpha Pvt. Ltd.* or for any agent of *Alpha Pvt. Ltd.*, or for any other third party performing services on behalf of *Alpha Pvt. Ltd.*, the undersigned may receive or have access to information concerning the management and business of *Alpha Pvt. Ltd.*, files maintained by *Alpha Pvt. Ltd.*, the business relationships and affairs of *Alpha Pvt. Ltd.* and its clients, the internal policies and procedures followed by *Alpha Pvt. Ltd.* personnel, the formulation of investment strategies and policies and other information developed or obtained by the undersigned in performance of services for *Alpha Pvt. Ltd.* including design concepts, systems, computer programs and related proprietary materials ("Confidential Information"). The undersigned acknowledges and agrees as follows:

(a) Confidential information shall be deemed to be any and all information of any form developed or obtained by the undersigned in performance of services for *Alpha Pvt. Ltd.* and shall be considered the property of *Alpha Pvt. Ltd.* and will be used exclusively for the purposes intended by *Alpha Pvt. Ltd.*

(b) The undersigned will hold such Confidential Information in strict confidence and will not, nor will it permit any agent, servant or employee to copy, reproduce, sell, assign, license, market transfer or otherwise dispose of, give or disclose Confidential Information to any person, firm or corporation, or use Confidential Information for any purpose other than to provide services to *Alpha Pvt. Ltd.*

(c) Upon the termination of the services to be performed by the undersigned (or earlier if requested by *Alpha Pvt. Ltd.*), the undersigned shall return to *Alpha Pvt. Ltd.* all copies of documents, papers or other material relating to *Alpha Pvt. Ltd.* or obtained or developed in the course of performing services for *Alpha Pvt. Ltd.*, or containing or derived from Confidential Information which are in the undersigned's possession, together with a certificate signed by the undersigned, in form and substance satisfactory to *Alpha Pvt. Ltd.*, to the effect that all such Confidential Information has been returned.

(d) The undersigned hereby irrevocably assigns to *Alpha Pvt. Ltd.*, and *Alpha Pvt. Ltd.* shall have, exclusive ownership rights, including without limitation, all patent, copyright and trade secret rights, with respect to all work performed hereunder, including but not limited to business methods or processes, programs, systems, processes, data, developments, modification and enhancement of systems, computer programs, operating instructions, ideas, designs, concepts and all other documentation developed for or relating to *Alpha Pvt. Ltd.* and all documents, data and other information of any kind, including information incorporating, based upon, or derived from the foregoing, including reports and notes prepared by the undersigned, and all software and other Deliverables developed, prepared, produced or created for *Alpha Pvt. Ltd.* by the undersigned (whether or not completed) together with all modifications, revisions, changes, copies, partial copies, translations, compilations, partial copies with modifications and derivative works of the foregoing (collectively, the "Work Product"). Such Work Product will be the property of *Alpha Pvt. Ltd.* and may not be used by the undersigned for any other purpose than the benefit of *Alpha Pvt. Ltd.* Any and all such work product and material containing such work product shall be delivered forthwith to

Alpha Pvt. Ltd. on request by *Alpha Pvt. Ltd.* and in any event at the termination of the undersigned's work for *Alpha Pvt. Ltd.* and no copies thereof shall be retained by the undersigned unless the prior written consent of *Alpha Pvt. Ltd.* is obtained with respect thereto. A certificate evidencing compliance with this provision shall, if requested by *Alpha Pvt. Ltd.*, accompany such materials. The undersigned will execute and deliver all documents required by *Alpha Pvt. Ltd.* to document or perfect *Alpha Pvt. Ltd.*'s proprietary rights in said Work Product. Such Work Product be a work made for hire and the undersigned shall have no proprietary interest herein.

(e) Confidential information shall not be deemed to include information which (i) is or becomes (other than by disclosure by the undersigned) publicly known; or (ii) is clearly and unmistakably a publicly available document, such as annual reports, proxy statements, prospectuses and the like.

2. Non-promotion

The undersigned agrees that the undersigned will not, without the prior written consent of *Alpha Pvt. Ltd.* in each instance: (a) use in advertising, publicity or otherwise the name of *Alpha Pvt. Ltd.* or any trade name, trademark, trade device, service mark, symbol or any abbreviation, contraction or simulation thereof owned by *Alpha Pvt. Ltd.*; or (b) represent directly or indirectly, that any product or any service provided by the undersigned has been approved or endorsed by *Alpha Pvt. Ltd.*

3. Non-employment

The undersigned affirms that the undersigned is not an employee of *Alpha Pvt. Ltd.* for any purpose and that the undersigned is not entitled to exercise any rights, or seek any benefit, accruing to the regular employees of *Alpha Pvt. Ltd.* by virtue of the services rendered by the undersigned to *Alpha Pvt. Ltd.* or otherwise. The undersigned agrees to provide any assistance necessary to *Alpha Pvt. Ltd.* in investigating any illegal or fraudulent activities, security breaches or similar situations.

4. No infringement

The undersigned affirms that the undersigned has all necessary rights, authorization or licenses to provide the services to *Alpha Pvt. Ltd.* and provide all work product and that the provision of such services and Work Product or of any component thereof, and *Alpha Pvt. Ltd.*'s use of concepts, materials or information provided by the undersigned will not constitute a breach of any Agreement to which the undersigned is a party or constitute an infringement of any patent or copyright or constitute an unauthorized use of proprietary information or trade secrets of a Third Party.

The obligations created by this Agreement shall survive the termination of services of the undersigned. The undersigned acknowledges that any violation, breach or other failure on the undersigned's part to strictly comply with this Agreement could materially, adversely affect *Alpha Pvt. Ltd.* and its business, thus giving rise to suit for monetary damages and/or injunctive relief for such violation, breach or other failure.

....(Name)
....(Signature)
....(Print Name)
....(Date)

Exhibit E

Alpha Pvt. Ltd. Systems

Statement of Services # 1

Dated

1. *Services, Product and Deliverables*:

Front-End & Interface Delivery

- *Beta Pvt. Ltd.* will be responsible for the delivery of the front-end (defined as 177 screens) and the interfaces (16 interfaces).
- A base amount of effort associated with "reports' has been included in effort estimates for this project. Any additional reporting requirements will have to be addressed separately.
- Elements:

    Architecture Definition/Training/Knowledge transfer

    Screens

    Interfaces

    Reports (Basic)

    Integration Testing/system test

    Support/Warranty

Back-End Delivery

- For the purposes of this proposal, *Beta Pvt. Ltd.* has used .... (name of the Authorities) estimates for this project
- This part of the project will be managed by.................... (name of *Beta* Pvt. Ltd. Affiliate) & *Beta Pvt. Ltd.* will leverage this project as part of the "skills transfer"
- This work effort will be completed under sub-contract to.................... (name of *Beta* Pvt. Ltd. Affiliate)
- Elements:

    Documentation/DBA/Modelling

    Design/Coding

    Integration testing/System test

    Support

Deliverables

   Requirement Specification Document

   Architecture Document (Phase 1 only)

   Screen Specification and prototype

   Project plan (Phase 1 only)

   CM plan (Phase 1 only)

   Proof of Concept (Phase 1 only)

   System test plan

   Integration Test plan

   Design Document

   Executable system

Terms - Onsite & Offshore

- *Beta Pvt. Ltd.* blended consulting rate for time and materials component:...................... (amount in foreign currency) hour.
- For Onsite work, an additional .... (amount in foreign currency) per day will be charged for each day onsite (for Philippines, Indonesia, Hong Kong, London and Taiwan).
- *Beta Pvt. Ltd.* will make all necessary work and stay arrangements for the...................... (name of Alpha's Affiliate) *Alpha Pvt. Ltd.* personnel stationed in India as part of the project.

Project Costs

- The Front End Effort assumes on onsite component of between 20% - 35%.
- Front End Cost Estimate: .... (amount in foreign currency)
- Work on the Front End will be on a *Fixed Estimate* basis. This estimate will only change if there is any change to the scope or any of our stated assumptions

Web Browser as a FE choice - Features.—

- Web Clients are thin with very much less code on client
- Browser based interface makes the client platform independent
- Shorter life cycle for development
- Ease of integration with application components developed on any language
- Scalable architectures

2. *Special Instructions.—*

   Phased Approach to Execution

   The duration of each phase is closely aligned to Alpha's Affiliate schedule

   Phase 1 Completion Date: ....

   Phase 2 Completion Date: ....

   Phase 3 Completion Date: ....

   Phase 4 Completion Date: ....

3. *Delivery/Completion Date*:

4. *Identification of Key Employees*:

   IN WITNESS WHEREOF, the Parties hereto have made and executed this Statement of Services as of the date first herein above set forth.

Alpha Pvt. Ltd.	*Beta Pvt. Ltd.*
....	....
Signature	Signature
....	....
Name	Name
....	....
Title	Title
....	....
Date	Date

Exhibit F
Bonus/Penalty Scheme
(THIS EXHIBIT 'F' IS SUBJECT TO FURTHER REVIEW)

- The scheme is designed towards better aligning the goals of *Beta Pvt. Ltd.* and *Alpha Pvt. Ltd.* in delivering the *Alpha Pvt. Ltd.*.................. based solution.
- This scheme will apply only to the estimates proposed for the Front-End Project in our proposal dated ...... All references to 'project' in the following clauses refer to the Front-End Project.
- The scheme is designed to reward *Beta Pvt. Ltd.* for exceeding commitments to *Alpha Pvt. Ltd.* on both the timelines and cost estimates fronts and to compensate *Alpha Pvt. Ltd.* if *Beta Pvt. Ltd.* is not able to meet commitments in either area.
- 'Regular Monthly Amount' in the following clauses refers to the amount to be billed to *Alpha Pvt. Ltd.* every month based on agreed billing rates on a time and materials bases – before the application of any of the bonus/penalty percentages described below.
- 5% of the value of the project will be tied to the project coming within 10% of the projected cost estimates. As such, the invoices raised by *Beta Pvt. Ltd.* on a monthly basis will be for the regular monthly amount less than 5%. The line items of the invoice will clearly specify the actual amounts per person billed, and show a final subtraction of 5% of the total, to arrive at the monthly payable. At the end of the project, *Beta Pvt. Ltd.* will send a 'Final Invoice' to *Alpha Pvt. Ltd.* for the 5% withheld from all the previous invoices, showing clearly as line items the amounts referenced in each past invoice. This will be done only if *Beta Pvt. Ltd.* is within budget by +/- 10%. If *Beta Pvt. Ltd.* is over 10% of budget, the 'Final Invoice' will not be raised.
- Also any additional effort involved with delivering the project to *Alpha Pvt. Ltd.* (once it exceeds 10% of the projected cost estimate) will be invoiced to *Alpha Pvt. Ltd.* using an hourly rate discounted at 5% of the agreed upon billing rate.
- Should *Beta Pvt. Ltd.* deliver the project at less than 90% of the projected cost, the savings will be shared equally by both parties.
- Subject to agreed upon scope control parameters, there will be a cap on the overall project budget of 200% of project estimate (*i.e.* actual budget cannot exceed 2% of estimated budget)
- An additional 15% of the regular monthly amount for the project will be tied towards meeting timelines of milestones as defined in Appendix X. The way this will be applied is as follows:—
  - On every super-milestone date a 'Penalty Amount' will be calculated. The 'Penalty Amount' will be calculated as 15% of the sum of all regular monthly amounts from the month of the last super-milestone to the month preceding the current super-milestone date.
  - If any super-milestone is not completed on time, the relevant 'Penalty Amount' will be subtracted from the invoice for the month containing the super-milestone date.
  - If a super-milestone is completed on time, but one or more associated sub-milestones are not completed on time – no subtraction is made from the invoice of the month of the super-milestone. However, if the phase of any of the missed sub-milestones is not completed on time, the 'Penalty Amount' for the super-milestone is subtracted from the invoice of the month the phase is missed.

PHASE	Super Milestone 1 20.....	Super Milestone 2 20.....	Super Milestone 3 20.....	Super Milestone 4 20.....	Super Milestone 5 20.....
1	System Test Complete ....20....	Integration Test Complete ....20....			
2	Screen Prototypes Complete ....20....	Screen Design Complete ....20....	Installation of release complete ....20....		
3		Screen Prototypes Complete .... 20.....	Screen Design Complete .... 200.....		
3			Screen Build Complete .... 20.....	Installation of release complete .... 20.....	
4			Screen Prototypes Complete .... 20.....	System test complete .... 20.....	Installation of release Complete .... 20.....

1. External Dependencies

Beta Pvt. Ltd. Milestone	External Task	External Task - Start Date	External Task - End Date
Phase 1 System Test Complete	Phase 1 Build Phase 1 System Test Starts	....	....
Phase 2 Screen Prototypes complete	Phase 2 Business Modelling	....	....
Phase 1 Integration test complete	Phase 1 System test Phase 1 Integration test starts	....	....
Phase 2 screen design complete	Phase 2 Business modelling	....	....
Phase 3 Screen Prototypes complete	Phase 3 Business modelling	....	....

Phase 2 Installation of Release complete	Alpha Pvt. Ltd. Phase 2 Acceptance test Beta Pvt. Ltd. Phase 2 Receive release from Delta Beta Pvt. Ltd. Phase 2 Set-up Production system	....	....
Phase 3 Screen Design complete	Phase 3 business modelling	....	....
Phase 3 Screen build complete	Phase 3 build	....	....
Phase 4 screen prototypes complete	Phase 4 business modelling	....	....
Phase 3 installation of release complete	Alpha Pvt. Ltd. Phase 3 Acceptance Test Beta Pvt. Ltd. Phase 3 receive release from Delta Beta Pvt. Ltd. Phase 3 Set-up production system	.... 0 .... 0 0	....
Phase 4 System test complete	Phase 4 Build Phase 4 System test Starts	....	 0
Phase 4 Installation of release complete	Alpha Pvt. Ltd. Phase 4 Acceptance test Beta Pvt. Ltd. Phase 4 Receive release from Delta Beta Pvt. Ltd. Phase 4 set-up production system	....	....

All the dates have been picked up from the baseline project plan.

We give below, our comments on the queries raised by you:—

(1) The enforceability in India of the arbitration award granted under the Agreement:

Under the Arbitration and Conciliation Act, 1996, there is no requirement for obtaining a judgment from a competent court on the award[1]. Subject to the powers of the court to allow recourse against an arbitral award, an award will be final and binding on the parties and persons claiming under them respectively[2]. When the time for making an application for setting aside the arbitral award has expired, and if, on such application having been made it has been refused, the award may be enforced under the Code of Civil Procedure, 1908, in the same manner as if it were a decree of the court[3].

An award given when arbitral proceedings commenced before the Arbitration and Conciliation Act, 1996, came into force[4] will be enforced under the provisions of the Arbitration Act, 1940; however, for arbitral proceedings commenced before the coming

---

1. This is in contrast to the position under the Arbitration Act, 1940.
2. Indian Arbitration and Conciliation Act, 1996, Sec. 35.
3. Indian Arbitration and Conciliation Act, 1996, Sec. 36.
4. The Act came into force on August 22, 1996.

into force of the 1996 Act and pending before the arbitrator, the parties can agree that the new Act be applicable to such proceedings[1]. A foreign award given after the commencement of the 1996 Act can be enforced only under that Act; there is no vested right to have the award enforced under the Foreign Awards (Recognition and Enforcement) Act, 1961[5].

Under the Indian Arbitration Act, an Award is enforceable on its own force without the need for any ratification or approval by the court.

However, an opportunity to challenge the award is afforded to the aggrieved party. Under section 34 (a) of the Arbitration Act, an Award can be challenged only on certain limited grounds, as follows:

(i) incapacity of the Party;

(ii) invalidity of the Arbitration Agreement;

(iii) lack of proper notice to the aggrieved party of the appointment of the arbitrator or of the arbitration proceedings;

(iv) inability of a party to present his case;

(v) The arbitral award dealing with disputes not contemplated by or falling within the terms of submission to arbitration;

(vi) the procedure not being in accordance with the Agreement of the parties.

An Award can also be set aside under sub-section (b) of section 34, if the court finds that the subject matter of the dispute is not capable of settlement by arbitration or that the arbitration award is in conflict with the "public policy" of India. Public policy is not defined. The Explanation to section 34 states that the Award is bad on the grounds of public policy, if it is induced or affected by fraud or corruption or is contrary to section 75 (duty of conciliator to maintain confidentiality) or section 81 (non-admissibility of evidence relating to conciliation proceedings). Mere error of law would not render an award bad on the ground of public policy.

The time limit for filing objection to an award is three months, extendable by 30 days at the discretion of the court. An appeal would lie from the order of the court, setting aside or refusing to set aside the award. Thereafter a second appeal may lie to the Supreme Court, purely at the discretion of the court. This would only be if an important question of law or of public interest is involved. Subject to the aforesaid, an award is executable, as soon as the period for filing objections is over.

(2) Enforcement in India of foreign judgment

The Indian Code of Civil Procedure under section 13 provides for the execution of a foreign judgment. The section states that a foreign judgment shall be conclusive as to any matter thereby directly adjudicated upon between the same parties or between parties under whom they or any of them claim litigating under the same title except—

(a) where it has not been pronounced by a court of competent jurisdiction;

(b) where it has not been given on the merits of the case;

(c) where it appears on the face of the proceedings to be founded on an incorrect view of international law or a refusal to recognise the law of India in cases in which such law is applicable;

(d) where the proceedings in which the judgment was obtained are contrary to the principles of natural justice;

---

1. *Thyssen Stahlunion GmbH* v. *Steel Authority of India Ltd.*, unreported, 7th October 1999; Civ. App. 6036 of 1996, SC. The parties could so agree even before the coming into force of the Arbitration and Conciliation Act, 1996.

(e) where it has been obtained by fraud;

(f) where it sustains a claim founded on a breach of any law in force in India.

With respect to reciprocating territories.—The Indian Code of Civil Procedure ('CPC') under section 44A provides that a decree passed by a Court of a "reciprocating territory" may be executed in India as a decree, as if it were passed by the Indian Courts. The United Kingdom is a reciprocating territory, but the United States of America is not. Where the decree is of a court, which is not a reciprocating territory, the procedure is not so straight forward. In such cases, foreign judgment can only be enforced by a suit upon the judgment. In such cases, the courts would generally not go into the question whether the judgment is correct in facts or in law but the judgment can be impugned on several stated grounds, such as inherent lack of jurisdiction, denial of natural justice, fraud, amongst other grounds.

(3) Sections 13.2 and 13.3:

Typically, in Agreements of this nature, the contracting (Indian) company usually obtains a guarantee from a bank. This is under ordinary circumstances a surer remedy in case of default. A performance bond still runs the additional burden of its enforceability. A Corporate Guarantee (given in draft form below) as sought by the Indian Company (Beta Pvt. Ltd.) will not run the risk of enforceability. Indian courts will ordinarily desist from interfering with the enforcement of bank guarantees, and will not interfere by way of injunction to prevent their due implementation[1]. The Corporate Guarantee will take in its ambit concerns apropos the Letter of Credit (clause 13.2) and the Performance Bond (clause 13.3).

(4) Possibility of obtaining injunctive relief in Indian Courts

(a) Interim relief in arbitral proceedings

Interim relief may be granted at any time before, during or after commencement of the arbitration. In *East Coast Shipping Limited v. M. J. Scrap Pvt. Ltd.*, 1997 (1) CHN 444, a single judge of the Calcutta High Court held that an Indian court cannot grant interim relief under section 9 of the Indian Arbitration Act, where the place of Arbitration is outside India. This view is based on a restrictive interpretation of section 2(2) of the Indian Arbitration Act, 1996, which states that:

> "This Part (*i.e.* Part which includes section 9 relating to the powers of the court to grant interim relief) shall apply where the place of arbitration is in India."

In view of the above section, the court held:

> "Sub-section (2) of section 2 leaves no room for doubt that Part I of the 1996 Act, ... will apply *only* in cases where the place of arbitration is in India... In my view the provisions of sub-sections (3), (4) and (5) of section 2 are controlled by sub-section (2) and widen the scope thereof to include arbitral proceedings being conducted outside India... Sub-section (5) cannot be read in isolation of sub-section (2) as an exception thereto as otherwise the provisions of sub-section (2) will be rendered otiose. Sub-section (5)... does not extend the application of Part-I to arbitral proceedings where the place of arbitration is not in India". (*Emphasis supplied*)

Another reason given in support of this view is that unlike Article 1(2) of the Model Law, which allows for court-imposed interim relief even when the seat of arbitration is in a different country, section 2(2) of the Indian Arbitration Act deviates from the Model Law by restricting the court's powers to grant interim relief in arbitrations where the place of arbitration is in India.

---

1. *United Commercial Bank v. Bank of India,* AIR 1981 SC 1426.

"We cannot also lose sight of the fact that the global scope of Article 1(2) of the UNCITRAL Model Law on International Commercial Arbitration was consciously omitted from the 1996 Act, thereby confirming the scope of Part I thereof only to arbitration proceedings where the place of arbitration is in India. According to Article 1(2) of the Model Law, the provisions of Articles 8, 9, 35 and 36 would apply even if the place of arbitration was not within the territory of the particular State and the remedy thereunder would be international in character. Sub-section (2) of section 2 of the 1996 Act does not provide for such an exception and clearly indicates that the provisions of Part I will apply to arbitration proceedings where the place of arbitration is in India. The deviation from the Model Law reveals the intention of the legislature to limit the scope of Part I of the Act to arbitration proceedings where the place of arbitration is in India".

(b) Injunctions under the Indian Code of Civil Procedure are of two kinds, temporary and perpetual. A party against whom a perpetual injunction is granted is thereby restrained *for ever* from doing the act complained of. A perpetual injunction can only be granted by a *final decree* made at the hearing and upon the merits of a suit. A temporary or interim injunction, on the other hand, may be granted on an interlocutory application at any stage of the suit. The injunction is called temporary, for it endures only until the suit is disposed of or until the further order of the court.

TERMINATION CLAUSE

Distributor's Remediable Events:

1. Each of the following shall be a Distributor's Remediable Event:—

The occurrence of any of the following:—

  (i) The marketing of the products by Distributor outside the Territory in violation of this Agreement.

  (ii) The selling of any product by Distributor with respect to which it has received a notice of recall as per clause 11 of this Agreement.

  (iii) The conviction of Distributor or a Controlling Entity for a felony of a type which, in the reasonable judgement of the Company, may adversely affect sales of the products or the goodwill of the Company or of Gucci.

  (iv) Distributor ceasing, without the prior written consent of the Company, to purchase and sell any of the products.

  (v) Occurrence of a control change without the prior written consent of the Company.

  (vi) Any breach by Distributor of any of its obligations under this Agreement, or any other material breach of this Agreement by Distributor.

  (vii) Failure by Distributor to provide the requested documentation as listed in section 13 within .... days of written notice from the Company that such reports are due;

(viii) Any of Distributor's representations and warranties, after the effective date, being or becoming untrue;

Procedure upon Distributor's Remediable Events:

Upon the occurrence of any Distributor's Remediable Event, the following procedure shall apply:

(a) The Company may give a notice (the "Cure Notice") to Distributor, specifying Distributor's Remediable Event giving rise to such Cure Notice, and the date by which Distributor is required to cure Distributor's Remediable Event, which date shall not be less than 10 days after the date of such notice;

(b) During the period of 10 days (or such longer period set forth in the Termination Notice or as the Parties may agree to in writing) following the giving of such Cure Notice ("Cure Period"), Distributor shall make all efforts to cure such Distributor's Remediable Event, and the Parties shall consult as to what steps shall be taken with a view to mitigating or remedying the consequences of such Event having regard to all circumstances.

Distributor's Non-Remediable Events:

1. Each of the following Events shall be a Distributor's Non-Remediable Event:—

The occurrence of any of the following:

(i) If, on the expiry of the Cure Period referred to in clause ......(b), unless the Parties shall have otherwise agreed in writing, the Event giving rise to the Cure Notice shall not have been occured;

(ii) The passing of a resolution for the bankruptcy, insolvency, winding up, liquidation or other similar proceedings;

(iii) The appointment of a trustee, liquidator, custodian, provisional manager or similar person in a proceeding referred to in clause (i) above, which appointment has not been set aside or stayed within (60) days of such appointment;

(iv) The making by a court having jurisdiction of an order of winding up or otherwise confirming the bankruptcy or insolvency of Distributor which order has not been set aside or stayed within 60 days;

(v) The transfer, assignment, sharing or division by Distributor of any or all of its rights, duties and/or benefits under this Agreement in breach of its terms;

(vi) Distributor engaging in any fraudulent conduct in its dealings with the Company or Gucci, including, but not limited to, offering for sale any imitation of the Products or merchandise infringing any of the Gucci Marks, or purchasing the products from any source other than the Company or Gucci;

(vii) Any of Distributor's representations and warranties, on or before the effective date, being untrue;

(viii) Distributor knowingly or wilfully causing damage to the Gucci Image, the Gucci Marks and/or the goodwill associated therewith;

(ix) Distributor engaging in practices of transhipping;

(x) Failure by Distributor to pay any amount, including, but not limited to, any amount for purchases of products within ten (10) days of written Notice from the Company that such payment is due in accordance with the terms of this Agreement.

Termination upon Distributor Non-Remediable Events:

Upon the occurrence of any Distributor's Non-Remediable Event, the following procedure shall apply:

(a) The Company may give a notice (the "Termination Notice") to Distributor, specifying Distributor's Non-Remediable Event giving rise to such Termination Notice, and the date on which the Company proposes to terminate this Agreement, which date shall not be less than 10 days after the date of such notice;

(b) at any time after the expiry of the period referred to in clause (a) ...... above, unless the parties shall have otherwise agreed in writing, the Company may terminate the Agreement:

Provided, however, that for any Distributor's Remediable Event which continues beyond the Cure Period, the Company or Gucci may, in lieu of terminating this entire Agreement in accordance with clause (b) .... above, terminate the portion of this Agreement granting Distributor the exclusive rights to sell the products listed in Schedule 1 in the Territory for the Term.

Termination Other than upon Distributor's Non-Remediable Events:

1. *Termination in the Event of Force Majeure.*—If any Event of *Force Majeure* prevents, or the Parties agree that such an Event of *Force Majeure* will prevent, Distributor from fulfilling its obligations under this Agreement for a continuous period of more than six (6) months; either Party may terminate this Agreement upon twenty eight (28) days prior written notice to the other Party.

2. *Termination for Convenience:* The Company may terminate this Agreement at any time by giving not less than thirty (30) days notice thereof to Distributor.

Force Majeure

1. An "Event of *Force Majeure*" shall mean any circumstance not within the reasonable control, directly or indirectly, of the Party affected, but only if and to the extent that:

(i) such circumstances, despite the exercise of reasonable diligence, cannot be or be caused to be prevented, avoided or removed by such Party.

(ii) such Event materially adversely affects (in cost and/or time) the ability of the party to perform its obligations under the Agreement, and such Party has taken all reasonable precautions, due care and reasonable alternative measures in order to avoid the effect of such Event on its ability to perform its obligations under the Agreement and to mitigate the consequences thereof, and

(iii) such Event is not the direct or indirect result of the failure of such Party to perform any of its obligations under this Agreement.

Subject to the foregoing, the Events of *Force Majeure* shall include:

(a) wars, invasions, acts of foreign enemies;

(b) revolutions, riots, civil commotion, insurrection, rebellion or sabotage;

(c) explosions, major fires, floods, earthquakes or other exceptional natural calamities and exceptional acts of God;

(d) the adoption, enactment or application to either Party of any legal requirements of any Government instrumentality of India not existing or not applicable to such Party on the date hereof or any change in any such legal requirements or the application or interpretation thereof by a governmental instrumentality of India after the date hereof, but not including any such legal requirements or application or interpretation thereof in existence at such date which by its terms became or will be effective and applicable to either Party after such date.

2. Relief under this clause shall not be given unless the Party intending to claim relief has, by notice to the other Party within 10 days of becoming aware of an Event of *Force Majeure* or if later, within 10 days of an Event of *Force Majeure* having an effect upon the performance of such Party's obligations under this Agreement, inform the other Party that it desires to claim relief under this clause. Such notice shall include such relevant information as is available, including without limitation, a description of the Event and the date of its occurrence, the effect of such Event upon the performance of such Party's obligations, the expected duration of such Event of *Force Majeure* and its effects and the actions it is taking in order to comply with this clause

3. As soon as, practicable after the occurrence of an Event of *Force Majeure*, the Party affected shall:

(a) use its best endeavours to prevent and reduce to a minimum and mitigate the effects of the Event of *Force Majeure*, including where appropriate and without limitation by having recourse to alternate acceptable sources of services, equipment and materials; and

(b) use its best endeavours to perform its obligations to the maximum extent practicable. Relief under this clause .... shall cease to be available to a Party if it fails to use such best endeavours.

4. Subject to clauses 2 and 3, either Party shall be relieved from liability and shall not be construed to be in default in respect of any obligation hereunder to the extent that and for so long as the failure to perform such obligation shall be due to an Event of *Force Majeure*.

5. If an Event of *Force Majeure* has occurred that results in delay of the obligations of the Parties, in excess of three (3) months, the Parties may, at the option of the Company, enter into good faith negotiations regarding adjustments of the terms of this Agreement. If any Event of *Force Majeure* prevents, or the Parties agree that such an Event of *Force Majeure* will prevent, Distributor from fulfilling its obligations under this Agreement for a continuous period of more

than six (6) months; either Party may terminate this Agreement in accordance with the provisions of this Agreement.

Arbitration

All disputes, controversies and/or claims arising out of or in relation to or in connection with this Agreement, or the breach, termination or validity hereof, shall be settled by an arbitral tribunal (the "Tribunal") in accordance with the International Rules of the .... Chamber of Commerce as in force at the time such arbitration is commenced (the "Arbitration Rules"). The seat of the arbitration shall be in .... and the number of arbitrators shall be three. The Parties shall appoint one arbitrator each, who shall then jointly appoint a third arbitrator. The third arbitrator shall act as the Chairman of the Tribunal. The language of the arbitration proceedings, and of the award, shall be English. The decision of the Tribunal shall be final and binding on the Parties.

Miscellaneous

1. *Languages and measures.*—This Agreement is being executed and delivered in the English language and all modifications, amendments, waivers of any provisions of this Agreement, all documents, notices and communications between the Parties under this Agreement shall be in the English language. The metric system of measurement shall be exclusively used in this Agreement.

2. *Severability of provisions.*—The invalidity, illegality or unenforceability in whole or in part of any of the provisions of this Agreement shall not affect or impair the validity, legality or enforceability of the remaining provisions of this Agreement.

3. *Waiver.*—Save where this Agreement otherwise expressly provides, neither Party shall be deemed to have waived any right under this Agreement, unless such Party shall have delivered to the other Party a written waiver signed by an authorised officer of such waiving Party. No failure or delay in exercising any right, power or remedy under this Agreement shall operate as a waiver, default or acquiescence thereof, nor shall any single or partial exercise of any right, power or remedy preclude the exercise of any other or further exercise of the same.

4. *Amendments and modifications.*—This Agreement may only be amended or modified by a written instrument signed by each of the Parties.

5. *Further Acts and assurances.*—Each of the Parties agree to execute and deliver all such further instruments, and to do and perform all such further acts and things, as shall be necessary or convenient to carry out the provisions of this Agreement.

6. *Expenses.*—Each Party shall pay its own costs and expenses (including without limitation the fees and expenses of its agents, representatives, advisors, counsel and accountants) necessary for the negotiation, preparation, execution, delivery, performance of and compliance with this Agreement.

7. *No partnership or agency.*—Nothing contained in this Agreement shall or shall be deemed to create an agency, association, trust, partnership, or joint venture or impose or create an agency relationship, trust or partnership duty, obligation, or liability on or with regard to either Party.

8. *Compliance with laws.*—In the performance of their obligations under this Agreement, the Parties shall, and shall cause their respective affiliates, officers, directors, agents and employees, to comply strictly with all applicable laws.

CONSULTANT'S NON-DISCLOSURE & NON-COMPETE AGREEMENT

This CONSULTANT'S NON-DISCLOSURE & NON-COMPETE AGREEMENT has been entered into this day of .... 20..... by and

BETWEEN

Alphacare Limited., an Indian firm having its registered offices at ....(hereinafter called "Alphacare" which expression unless repugnant to the context shall mean and include its subsidiaries, and its successors and assigns)

AND

...................., a Consultant of *Alphacare* and residing at ...., (hereinafter referred to as "Consultant" which expression unless repugnant to the context shall include all beneficiaries of the said Consultant)

1. Definitions

Consultant.—Consultant shall mean an independent individual not being an employee of *Alphacare*, who is an appointed distributor and meets criteria set out by *Alphacare* to qualify for the leadership Seminar. The term Consultant shall also be inclusive of the terms "Gold Achiever", "Star director", President Star Consultant, Consultants who qualified for the preceding years Seminar and have achieved one level higher than the preceding qualifying standard. *Alphacare* shall be the final quantifier of the aforesaid terms as are exhaustively detailed in ANNEXURE A.

Confidential Information.—Confidential Information means the database in print and/or electronic form, Trade secrets, literature, training methods, Marketing methods and other proprietary information whether affixed or demonstrated and/or divulged/disclosed/forwarded in print and or electronic form to all Consultants, Star Directors and other Consultants who become such under terms created by *Alphacare*, also as used in this Agreement, the term "Confidential Information" means (i) the terms and conditions of this Agreement inclusive of but not limited to any other prior confidentiality Agreement whether explicit or implied, that is subsisting on the date of this Agreement; (ii) *Alphacare's* trade secrets, proprietary Information, business plans, strategies, methods and/or practices; and (iii) any other information relating to *Alphacare* or its business that is not generally known to the public, including but not limited to information about *Alphacare's* personnel, products, formulations, customers, marketing strategies, services or future business plans.

WHEREAS,

a. Consultant during his/her normal course of business has upon achieving targets set by *Alphacare* based upon its points value system and other indicia, been deemed eligible to participate in the Leadership Seminar/Cruise organized by *Alphacare*.

b. Certain grades of Consultants shall also be required to pay *Alphacare* a certain sum of Money

c. Consultant before, during and after the said seminar shall be exposed to the Confidential Information owned by *Alphacare* either in its disembodied form or in the form of a package. *Alphacare* treats this preparation as being in the nature of confidential information.

d. *Alphacare* will invest a substantial amount of monies and other efforts upon the Consultant during and subsequent to this seminar. Both Parties agree that such expense by *Alphacare* upon Consultant shall be deemed to be adequate and fair consideration in lieu of the non-disclosure and non-compete terms agreed to by the Consultant in this Agreement.

e. The unauthorised disclosure by Consultant of the said Confidential Information could expose *Alphacare* to irreparable harm in monetary terms as well as in terms of reputation and goodwill.

f. *Alphacare* thus wishes to safe guard against the wrongful or inadvertent disclosure of its confidential information.

2. Acknowledgement of Confidentiality

a. Consultant hereby acknowledges that all Confidential Information that he/she is made privy to during his/her course of association with *Alphacare* are in the nature of confidential and proprietary information and protected as such.

3. Agreement Not to Disclose

a. Consultant hereby agrees that he/she shall hold in confidence and hereby agrees that he/she shall not use, commercialize or disclose except under terms of association of *Alphacare* and only at the specific behest of *Alphacare*, any Confidential Information to any person or entity, or else under provision governed by this memorandum. *Alphacare* may provide such approval in writing.

b. Even upon termination of his/her association with *Alphacare*, Consultant undertakes not to make use of the Confidential Information in his/her business, or provide the same to third parties in pursuance of their business whether in the role of a Consultant or employee. Consultant undertakes to use at least the same degree of care in safeguarding the Confidential Information as he/she uses or would use in safeguarding his/her own Confidential Information, and shall take all steps necessary to protect the Confidential Information from unauthorized or inadvertent disclosure.

c. Consultant undertakes to surrender all material print based or in electronic form comprising the Confidential Information to Alphacare. Any material owned by *Alphacare*, in the possession of Consultant shall be deemed to be a breach of this Agreement and shall make the Consultant liable to the full extent of the Law.

4. Remedies for Breach of Confidentiality

a. Consultant agrees and acknowledges that any disclosure, advertent or inadvertent, of any Confidential Information prohibited herein or any breach of the provisions herein may result in irreparable injury and damage to *Alphacare* which will not be adequately compensatable in monetary damages, that *Alphacare* will have no adequate remedy at law therefor, and that *Alphacare* may, in addition to all other remedies available to it at law or in equity, obtain such preliminary, temporary or permanent mandatory or restraining injunctions, orders or decrees as may be necessary to protect *Alphacare* against, or on account of, any breach by the Consultant, ex-Consultant of the provisions contained herein, and Consultant agrees to reimburse the reasonable legal fees and other costs incurred by *Alphacare* in enforcing the provisions of this Agreement.

5. Non-compete

a. Consultant inclusive of his/ her direct beneficiaries in business, interest and title in recognition of the disclosure of confidential and proprietary information owned by *Alphacare* hereby agrees not to directly or indirectly compete with the business of *Alphacare* and its successors and assigns during the term of the association of the Consultant with *Alphacare* and for a period of Three Years following the expiration or termination of this contract and notwithstanding the cause or reason for termination.

6. Jurisdiction

a. Any action arising out of or pertaining to this Agreement shall be initiated and maintained in a court of competent jurisdiction at the High Court of ....

7. Term

This Agreement shall subsist during the course for Consultant's association with *Alphacare* as well as for a period of three years thereafter.

8. General Provision

a. This document constitutes the entire Agreement between the parties with respect to the subject matter hereof and supersedes all other communications, whether written or oral.

b. This Agreement is expressly limited to its terms and may be modified or amended only by writing, signed by both parties.

c. Neither this Agreement nor any rights or obligations inherent in *Alphacare's* confidential information, know-how, trade secrets and other property and intellectual property hereunder may be transferred or assigned without *Alphacare's* written consent respectively. Any attempt to the contrary shall be void.

9. Severability

a. The provisions of this Agreement shall be deemed severable, and the unenforceability of any one or more of its provisions shall not affect the enforceability of any of the other provisions. If any provision is declared to be unenforceable, the parties shall substitute an enforceable provision that, to the maximum extent possible in accordance with applicable law, preserves the original intentions and economic positions of the parties. Waiver of any provision hereof in one instance shall not preclude enforcement thereof on future occasions.

The parties hereto consider the restrictions contained to be reasonable as to protect *Alphacare's* interests and rights.

10. *Force Majeure*

a. Neither party will be responsible for any failure to perform its obligations under this Agreement due to causes beyond its control, including but not limited to acts of God, war, riot, embargoes, acts of civil or military authorities, fire, floods or accidents.

11. Notice

a. All notices and communications required or permitted under this Agreement shall be in writing and any communication or delivery shall be deemed to have been duly made if actually delivered, or after three (3) days after mailing, if mailed by registered post addressed.

IN WITNESS WHEREOF, the parties hereto have caused this Agreement to be executed as of the date first written above.

Alphacare Limited

....

Address....................

Dated....................

Consultant

....

Address....................

Dated....................

Witness:

Witness:

Romeo/Agreements/ Charlie - Agreement

III. Agency and Distributions.—In commercial usage the term "Agency" is often applied to relationships which may not be strictly agencies at all. An example which occurs is the use of the term "distributing agency" or some such equivalent term to describe the function of a distributor of manufactured goods which he obtains from a supplier under a sale Agreement (usually an exclusive sales agrement) in such a relationship, the distributor doesn't come as an agent between a principal who sells and a customer who buys, but is himself buyer of the goods for resale to his own customers.

The law of various countries of the world show considerable differences with regard to the legal status of commercial agents and in many cases contain particularly detailed provisions governing the relationship between the principal and such an agent. Therefore it is essential to procure that nothing contained in a commercial agency contract shall be repugnant to emphasise provisions of the law of any country in which such a contract or any part there of has to be carried into effect.

AGENCY AGREEMENT

THIS AGREEMENT is entered into on this ...... day of ...., 20....

BETWEEN

Alpha, a Company duly incorporated under the Companies Act, 1956 and having its registered office at ....(address), India, through its Chief Executive Officer Mr. ....(name) (hereinafter referred to as *"Alpha"* which expression shall, unless repugnant to the meaning or context hereof, be deemed to include its successors and permitted assigns), of the FIRST PART;

AND

Beta, a Company duly incorporated under the Companies Act, 1956 and having its registered office at .... (address), India, through its authorised signatory Mr. ....(hereinafter referred to as *"Beta"* which expression shall, unless repugnant to the meaning or context hereof, be deemed to include its successors and permitted assigns), of the SECOND PART.

WHEREAS

A. ....a registered Society set up by the Government of India, in furtherance of its intention to enter into the field of Mobile Telephony Services along with Department of Telecommunication, ("DOT"), has floated a global tender dated ....("Tender"), inviting bids for undertaking survey, planning, design, supply of equipment, installation, testing, commissioning and handing over the systems on a turnkey basis;

B. *Gamma*, a Company duly incorporated under the Companies Act, 1956, having its registered office at ...., India, (*"Beta"*), is engaged in the manufacture and marketing of the telecommunication equipment including ....Cellular equipment (BSS) and has a Technical Collaboration Agreement with *Theta*;

C. *Theta* has submitted its bid in respect of the Tender in collaboration with.................... (name of entity);

D. ....'s services (as described herein below) shall be required in relation to the Tender and for Subsequent Tenders;

E. The Parties recognise that the Tender is only for a pilot program and that there would be more orders in respect of Mobile Telephony Services in future, either by way of repeat orders or in the form of fresh tenders to be floated by, either ....or ...., in association with each other or in association with a third party or individually ("Subsequent Tender").

NOW THEREFORE, for good and valuable consideration, the receipt and sufficiency of which is acknowledged by the Parties and on the terms and conditions as hereinafter set forth, the Parties agree as follows:

1. Scope of ....'s services

In relation to the Tender/Subsequent Tenders, if any, ... (*Gama* Company) shall carry out the following services:

(i) Assist and advice *Theta* on the various aspects of the Tender and Subsequent Tenders, if any.

(ii) Assist in the preparation and submission of bids in respect of the aforesaid tenders.

(iii) Provide necessary inputs to *Beta* to make the quotations/bids of .... (name of the entity) competitive.

(iv) Obtain any clarifications, as may be required, from C-DOT/DOT/other Government Departments in respect of the Tender or any Subsequent Tenders, as the case may be.

(v) Undertake necessary liaison work, as may be required, from time to time with the officials of the concerned departments.

2. *Alpha*'s obligation

(i) Upon award of the Tender to *Gamma*, it undertakes to make payment to ...., amounting to five (5) percent of the value of the award, as fees in the manner stated below:

(a) 33% of the fees on the date of award of the Tender ("Award Date");

(b) 47% of the fees within (......) months of the Award Date;

(c) 20% of the fees within (......) months of the Award Date;

(ii) The Parties recognise that the Tender is only for a pilot program and that there would be Subsequent Tenders. Accordingly, ...shall be entitled to its fee in relation to Subsequent Tenders. Upon award of any Subsequent Tender(s) to *Theta* ("Subsequent Award"), *Gamma* shall make payment of .... per cent of the value of such Subsequent Award to .... ("Subsequent Fees") in the same manner as in 3(i) above;

(iii) It is clarified and agreed upon that .... shall be entitled to its fees as stated in 3(i) and 3(ii) above, irrespective of any contingencies such as cancellation, suspension, termination of Award or Subsequent Award by ..../.......... due to any reason including *Force Majeure* reason, any allegation of any shortcomings, accusations, contentions, etc., raised by *Alpha* regarding the services performed by ....;

(iv) Any payments outstanding beyond a period of .... days from due date shall carry an interest of .... p.a. without prejudice to any other rights of .... All payments shall be net of present or future taxes, if any. The fees payable to .... is lump sum, all-inclusive and it shall not be entitled to any other compensation towards out of pocket expenses etc.

3. Exclusive Agreement

Alpha agrees not to appoint any other person to act as an agent, etc., in relation to the Tender/Subsequent Tender in addition to/substitution of .... without its prior written consent. Similarly, ...shall not act as an agent for any other party on the subject matter of the Tender without prior written consent of *Theta*.

4. Secrecy

The Parties shall not, at any time, during or after the term of this Agreement, divulge, or allow to be divulged, to any person, any Confidential Information (including, but not limited to, any information relating to the accounts, finance, contractual arrangement, products, business or affairs) of the Parties unless the said information comes into the public domain. Notwithstanding anything contained in this Clause, no Party shall be precluded from disclosing any information to the extent required in compliance with law.

5. Dispute Resolution/Arbitration

Any dispute, controversy or claim arising out of or relating to or in connection with this Agreement, or the breach, termination or validity hereof shall be finally settled by arbitration in accordance with the Indian Arbitration and Conciliation Act, 1996, as in force (the "Arbitration Act") by reference to a sole arbitrator. The venue of the arbitration shall be ....(place).

6. Miscellaneous

Compliance: Both Parties agree not to do anything contrary to law or which would be treated as a corrupt practice under Indian or foreign law.

SUPPLY CONTRACT

BETWEEN

ALPHA a company construed under the laws of (foreign country) foreign................................ represented by its legal representative, hereafter called the manufacturer, ON THE FIRST PART,

AND

BETA a company construed under the laws of India, represented by its legal representative, hereafter called the company, ON THE SECOND PART,

WHEREAS

(1) The manufacturer has developed and finalized an emergency contraception product, hereafter referred to as the product or the products that allows for an emergency contraception treatment.

    (a) The product is made of one tablet of ....

    (b) The treatment is made of two tablets of the product.

(2) The company wishes to market the product in India.

(3) The manufacturer wishes to supply the product to the company.

THEREFORE

Section I: Supply

A. The manufacturer agrees to supply the product to the company for marketing within the territory as referred to in section VIB and hereafter referred to as the territory.

1. The manufacturer will at its discretion decide the places of manufacture of the products and of the persons and/or companies in charge of such manufacture.
2. The company may not refuse delivery in consideration of such discretionary decision by the manufacturer.

B. The company will:
1. market the product exclusively within the territory;
2. not acquire and/or market in the territory directly or through any other company, any other emergency contraceptive treatment.

C. The manufacturer:
1. is free to supply the product for marketing in the territory:
   (a) with another trademark than the trademark referred to in section VIB hereafter and hereafter referred to as the trademark;
   (b) to *Omega*, a company construed under the laws of India, whose registered office ...., who is registered at the Registrar of Companies of ....and ...., number ....;
   (c) to any Sub-contractor of *Omega*;
   (d) to any non-governmental organizations or international agencies for marketing through their network;
2. may not supply the product to any other party than those specified in paragraph C hereabove, unless the company fails to keep in line with the minimum purchase quantities specified in section III-8 hereafter;

in case of such failure, the manufacturer will be free to supply the product to any party, without prejudice of section V-C-2 and section VIII hereafter.

Section II: Obligations of the Manufacturer

A. The manufacturer agrees to:
1. deliver the product to the company under the terms and conditions of section IV hereafter;
2. subscribe and keep throughout the duration of the present contract, a liability insurance especially in regard to the storage, the production, the exploitation and the distribution of the product without prejudice to the obligations of the company;
3. provide the company with all the necessary scientific assistance, especially for the registration and the promotion of the product and in case of any litigation upon the territory implying the product, its fabrication and/or its distribution.

B. The manufacturer guarantees that upon delivery, the product will conform with the specifications required by the authorities of the territory for authorizing its sale, if it has been informed by the company of these requirements in conformity with section III hereafter.

C. If and when the manufacturer has other projects in regard of the territory and needs a local partner thereof, it will inform the company and enter *bona fide* discussions with it;

such information and discussion will not bind the manufacturer to unveil any of its proprietary information.

Section III: Obligations of the Company

The company agrees to:

1. obtain the necessary authorisation for the sale of the product within the territory ;
2. inform the manufacturer of the product's specifications required by the authorities of the territory and of any modification of these specifications, as soon as possible and not later than thirty days from the decision of these authorities;
3. carry on under its own liability, the entire promotion, publicity, sale, distribution and invoicing of the products within the territory, and the collecting of the debts;
4. commercialize the product :
   (a) under the trade name chosen in compliance with section VIB hereafter;
   (b) in the private sector such as chemist shops, pharmacies, doctors office and any retail store;
   (c) in the public sector;
5. not commercialize the product in the networks of non-governmental organizations funded by international organization, except if previously agreed in writing by the manufacturer
6. not use any trademark of the manufacturer for whatever purpose;
7. pay each invoice of the manufacturer, within the terms and conditions of section IV hereafter;
8. order each calendar year from the launch of the product, a minimum quantity of the product, i.e.:
   (a) ....(amount) treatments the first calendar year, reduced *prorata temporis* in case of launch in the course of a calendar year;
   (b) for each following calendar year, the amount ordered the previous year plus a .... per cent. increase;

for determining the second calendar year minimum quantity orders, the first calendar year orders will be increased *prorata temporis,* in case of launch in the course of a calendar year;

9. address to the manufacturer:
   (a) a monthly statement of the sales made within the territory, in value and in quantity;
   (b) a provisional statement of its quarterly needs for the next year, ... days before the end of the running year;
   (c) a monthly statement of its needs for the following six months;
10. maintain within the premises chosen by the company and located in the territory, the stock immediately necessary to face the needs of the market for a minimum period of .... days;

11. inform the manufacturer as soon as possible and within a maximum delay of .... days starting from the knowledge of each Event:
    * of any damage of any nature and of any secondary effect, occurred within the territory, because of the product;
    * of any procedure of any nature, engaged within the territory, in regard of the product;
12. respect the legal obligations of the territory regarding the declaration of adverse reactions or secondary effects and address to the manufacturer a copy of any declaration of adverse reactions or secondary effects not later than two days after it has been done;
13. in case of litigation:
    * inform the manufacturer of any proceeding, of its evolution and of the arguments and demands exposed by the parties;
    * require the scientific advice of the manufacturer upon the arguments and grievances exposed regarding the product;
14. keep the secret upon the knowledge and not use except for the execution of the present contract, the information and the know-how relating to the product and more generally relating to the activity of the manufacturer, to the terms of the present contract and/or to the manufacturer, for all the duration of the present contract and for a minimum period of ten years after the end of the present contract and as long as the knowledge, the information and the know-how will not be in the public domain;
15. subscribe and keep for all the duration of the present contract, a liability insurance especially in regard to the exploitation and the distribution of the product;
16. pay at cost all travel expenses of the manufacturer, when required by the company.

Section IV: Property Transfer and Delivery

A. The property transfer of the products, will take place after their proper payment by the company to the manufacturer.

B. Delivery:

1. The delivery of the products will take place ex-factory according to Incoterms 2000 at the manufacturer's premises, by its clearance by the company, sixty days after the receipt by the manufacturer of the company's order.
   (a) The product will be delivered in blisters of two products hereafter referred to as the blister product, bearing the print of its expiry date and of its batch number.
   (b) Any other delivery requirement may be agreed by the parties.
2. After the delivery of the product, and even though the payment and the property transfer have not occurred, the product will be:
   (a) at the company's risk of any damage that could occur;

(b) under the company's responsibility regarding any issue, including local packaging and labeling legal requirements.

Section V: Orders, Price, Payments
A. Orders:
1. The products will be exclusively sold by minimum batches of .... of two tablets each.
2. No orders inferior to one batch will be accepted.

B. Prices:
1. The manufacturer's sale price to the company of the blister product works according to ...., exclusive of tax and ready for shipment at the manufacturer's premises, is .... of an ....(foreign amount) for one packed product.
   (a) A seven cents of an .... (foreign amount) rebate will be granted to the company for each packed product ordered in excess of .... packed products over the company's annual minimum orders.
   (b) Such rebate will be increased by seven cents of an .... (foreign amount) for each order in excess of each next .... packed products.
   (c) Such extra rebates will be limited so that the packed products price will never come below .... of an ....(foreign amount).
2. Any special requirement of the company, not covered by the present contract, will be charged at cost, on top of the price of the product.
3. The price may be modified by the manufacturer in regard to its costs with a three months notice, in mutual Agreement with the company.

C. Payment:
1. Any invoice of the manufacturer will be issued upon receipt of the company's order and will be paid by the company, by a bank draft accepted by a foreign bank, due for payment within thirty days from its issue and received by the manufacturer at least two days before delivery.
2. The payment of the minimum annual order referred to in section III-8 will remain due eventhough such minimum order is not reached and eventhough section I-C-2 or section VIII and IX-C are implemented as a consequence of such failure, in which case the remaining due payment will be invoiced by the manufacture at the end of the relevant year and paid by the company, by a bank draft accepted by a foreign Bank, issued and sent to the manufacturer on receipt of the relevant invoice and due for payment within thirty days from its issue.
3. Any failure by the company to pay any invoice of the manufacturer will allow the manufacturer to suspend any delivery until the complete payment of all due debts.

Section VI: Territory - Trade Mark

A. The territory is the territory of India; the territory may be extended to .... and .... in accordance with any further decision of the parties.

B. The company will choose and own the trademark under the condition that it is not similar to any trademark of the manufacturer.

Section VII: Duration - Act of God

A. The contract is agreed from the day of its signature until the end of the fifth calendar year following the year of its signature.

B. Unless this contract is terminated by either party by a registered letter with return receipt, addressed to the other party, six months before the expiration of the ongoing period, the contract will be automatically renewed for another period of three years and at the end of this new period, will continue for fixed periods of three years, unless terminated in the terms hereabove mentioned, ... (period) before the expiration of the ongoing period.

C. Any act of God, *i.e.* any event irresistible and unpredictable, will bring a suspension of this contract, for all the duration of such act of God.

Section VIII: Termination

A. The present contract may be terminated at any time:

1. by either party, if the other party:
   (a) is declared insolvent, enters into receivership or liquidation whether amicable or judicial, makes a composition with its creditors or is in any similar situation;
   (b) remains in breach of any of its obligations in regard to the present contract, after a period of .... days following a notice to comply with the present contract, sent by registered letter with return receipt, by the non-defaulting party;
2. by either party if any suspension of this contract because of an act of God, lasts over six months;
3. by the manufacturer:
   (a) if the company fails within twelve months from the signature of the present contract to obtain the necessary authorization for the sale of the product within the territory;
   (b) if no Agreement is reached regarding a price modification issue leaving the manufacturer in a non-profit making situation.

B. Such termination will take place, as soon as notified by the terminating party to the other party, by registered letter with return receipt.

C. Any tolerance observed by a party in regard to any infringement by the other party to any term of the contract, will not imply a renunciation to the benefit of this stipulation and will not prevent the enforcement of section VIII paragraphs A and B hereabove in regard to that infringement.

Section IX: Consequences of the end of Contract

A. After the end of the contract and within thirty days from the formal request by the manufacturer, the company will transfer to the manufacturer or any person, firm or corporation designated by the manufacturer, all the products that it may have and all documentation or items regarding the product or belonging to the manufacturer.

B. At the end of the contract, no indemnity of any kind will be due by either party to the other party.

C. Nevertheless, if the contract is terminated in accordance with section VIII, for any breach by the company, the price of the minimum annual orders referred to in section III-8, for the period running from the date of early termination until the end of the ongoing contractual period, will become immediately due.

1. The manufacturer will issue an invoice of the due amount.
2. The company will pay such invoice by a bank draft accepted by a foreign bank, due for payment thirty days after its issue and issued at receipt of the manufacturer's invoice.

Section X: Address

1. For the delivery of the products, the manufacturer's premises are any place in the territory or in ...., where the product will be achieved, and which will be notified to the company by the manufacturer at the first order of the company.

2. For any other purpose, including any order or letter, the manufacturer's address is marked at the beginning of the present contract.

3. For any purpose, the company's address is marked at the beginning of the present contract.

4. any modification by one party of its address, will need to be notified to the other party, by registered letter with return receipt.

Section XI: Applicable Law

The present contract is subjected to Indian law.

Section XII: Judicial Competence

Any litigation regarding the present contract and all eventual addenda will be submitted at first to the Commercial Tribunal of ....

ALPHA   *BETA*

SOFTWARE SERVICES SUPPLY AGREEMENT

THIS AGREEMENT (hereinafter referred to as the "Agreement") dated the day of ...., 20......

BETWEEN

Alpha, a ....company with its principal place of business at.................... *Alpha* on behalf of itself, its affiliates and subsidiaries hereinafter called "*Alpha*" which expression unless repugnant to the context includes its successors in business and interest on one part

AND

Beta, a joint venture of ITI Limited ("ITI"), *Alpha* and The Industrialization Fund for Developing Countries ("IFU"), a company incorporated under the Indian Companies Act 1956, having its Registered Office at ...., and works at ...., hereinafter called "*Beta*" which expression unless repugnant to the context includes its successors in business and interest on the other part

WITNESSETH:

WHEREAS *Alpha* and *Beta* in 1995 successfully have entered into a Technology and License Agreement regarding SDH equipment and now the Parties have a desire to extend the business relationship so *Beta* will act as a sub supplier to *Alpha* in accordance with this Agreement;

WHEREAS *Beta* has acquired from *Alpha* the assets from its Indian software center "*Alpha*," in ....("TCI") and *Beta* intends to offer software services using the methodology already deployed by *Alpha*.

WHEREAS, *Alpha* is engaged in the business of manufacture and sale of telecom products and is desirous of engaging the services of *Beta* for development of software required by it;

NOW, THEREFORE in consideration of the premises and the mutual rights and obligations herein set forth, the Parties hereto agree as follows:

Definitions

"*Confidential Information*" means information shared with *Beta* and designated by *Alpha* as Confidential Information about *Alpha*'s business and/or that of its customers and/or other third parties which is not available to the general public and which may be learned, and/or generated, made, conceived, or contributed to by *Beta* towards performance of this Agreement. This includes, without limitation, information relating to *Alpha*'s organization, its Software (as hereinafter defined), intellectual property, business and customer information, trade secrets, customer lists, employment policies, personnel, and information about *Alpha*'s products, processes, including ideas, concepts, projections, know-how, technology, manuals, drawings, designs, specifications, all data, documents, applications, statements, programs, plans, papers, resumes, records and other documents containing and/or relating to such confidential information, and any and all information of value to *Alpha*, or which gives *Alpha* an edge over competition, which *Alpha* is legally obliged to treat as confidential, and which *Alpha* treats and designates as confidential.

"*Software*", means software in any and all various stages of development and/or final form, and includes, without limitation, the literal elements of a program (source code, object code or otherwise), its audio-visual components (menus, screens, structure and organisation), any human or machine readable form of the program, and any writing or medium in which the program or the information therein is stored, written or described, including, without limitation, diagrams, flow charts, designs, drawings, specifications, models, data, bug reports and customer information.

"Know-how" means technical information, possessed by *Alpha* and includes hardware and software manuals, test procedure manual, relevant proprietary / confidential data, related drawings, documentation, engineering skills, data sheets, literature, patentable or not which is presently owned and / or used by *Alpha* and which *Beta* receives from *Alpha* in connection with this Agreement.

"Software Services" shall mean and include any services towards software development, software support, software project management services, software error corrections, development of new applications, maintenance or upgrade or rework on any existing software products/applications, customer support etc. or any other services provided through software engineers (SW Personnel) of *Beta*.

"Work Product" shall mean the results of SW Personnel's activities during the course of its performance under this Agreement, including all ideas, concepts, developments, know-how techniques, processes, methods, discoveries, innovations and inventions, including without limitation all information developed regarding technical, (such as design, manufacturing, and procurement specifications, procedures, manufacturing processes) and physical embodiments of all such information (such as drawings, specification sheets, computer storage media, documentation, reports, manuals, correspondence, and samples).

"SW Personnel" shall mean *Beta* employees who are technically skilled in making Software development and have been trained on Software development on *Alpha* products, allocated to provide Software Services to *Alpha* as per this Agreement.

"Man-year" means 365 salary paid calendar days of one SW Person or 12 salary paid calendar months of one SW Person.

1. Engagement

1.1 *Alpha* hereby engages *Beta* to provide to *Alpha* the Software Services as defined in this Agreement.

1.2 *Beta* will make available trained SW Personnel to *Alpha* so as to meet *Alpha* requirement for required number of Man-years of Software Services. These SW personnel shall render Software Services as per *Alpha* instructions and shall deliver services as per the transmission mode agreed between the parties.

1.3 *Alpha* will within a period of .... years from the effective date of this Agreement avail from *Beta* .... Man-years of Software Services,.

Alpha will avail itself of total .... Man-years of Software Services over three years as follows:

year 1 .... Man-years

year 2 .... Man-years

year 3 .... Man-years

The numbers for year 2002 are to be understood as indicative and may be changed based upon how many .... employees will actually join *Beta*. *Alpha* expects to have available SW Personnel of about ...... employees per year. In future years the number of SW Personnel may be adjusted upwards or downwards after mutual Agreement. *Alpha* does not expect *Beta* to reduce the number of SW Personnel by more than ..... employees relative to the said ..... SW Personnel employees per year.

If *Alpha* requests *Beta* to increase the number of SW Personnel beyond the number above, *Alpha* will allow *Beta* a four months ramp-up period exclusive of training period.

The parties will however at best effort basis accommodate requirements for changes in the allocated SW Personnel at shortest possible notice.

1.4 The price for one Man-year corresponds to .... (amount) The total price for Software Services according to this Agreement amounts to ....(amount)

1.5 Charges and other terms for any Software Services ordered by *Alpha* beyond the .... Man-years mentioned in Section 1.3 will be mutually agreed between *Alpha* and *Beta*.

2. Term of the Agreement

This Agreement shall be effective on .... (date) regardless of the date of execution hereof, and shall continue .... years from the Effective Date at which time it shall automatically expire.

3. Charges and Payment

3.1. *Beta* shall raise invoices at the end of each month for the number of salary paid days of SW Personnel during that month. All invoices shall be raised in .... (amount).

3.2. *Beta* will certify number of days for which salary has been paid to SW Personnel every month (person and days specified). On quarterly basis *Beta* will provide details of salary paid days and leaves availed for each SW Personnel.

3.3. All invoices shall be subject to verification prior to payment. Invoices submitted by *Beta* will:

(i) Identify any authorized expenses incurred hereunder; and

(ii) Make reference to this Agreement, or otherwise identify the invoice in such manner as *Alpha* may reasonably require.

3.4. The agreed upon payment terms for services performed by *Beta* shall be .... days upon date of invoice. *Beta* shall submit invoices in duplicate to *Alpha* as follows:

ALPHA

......................(address)

4. Reimbursable Expense

4.1. *Alpha* shall reimburse *Beta* the expenses for travel (air coach fares on economy class), boarding & lodging and public ground transport to and from *Alpha* offices for all SW Personnel, incurred as a result of the work performed by *Beta* at *Alpha* at *Alpha*'s request. *Alpha* will also reimburse daily allowances for such SW Personnel working on-site as per local regulations, currently @ .... per day. *Alpha* shall also reimburse *Beta* the expenses for travel (air coach fares on economy class) up to one round trip *Alpha-Beta-Alpha* per quarter for SW

Personnel staying at *Alpha* on *Alpha's* request for more than 3 months, *Beta* shall invoice *Alpha* for these expenses and *Alpha* shall pay *Beta* as per the terms outlined in Section 3. *Alpha* will make no direct payments to SW Personnel.

4.2. *Alpha* has the right to find accommodation for SW Personnel appropriate to their respective position when they come to work at *Alpha*.

5. Supplies, Equipment and Management

5.3. Save as provided through the assets *Beta* acquires from *Alpha*, *Alpha* shall supply *Beta*, on no charge, returnable basis; SW or HW tools or other items of capital nature (except required for maintaining basic infrastructure related to building/ leasehold improvement and IT as specified at 5.4 below) which may be required by *Beta*, in order to perform its services according to this Agreement.

However, if *Alpha* faces any legal complication in providing these SW tools to *Beta*, *Alpha* shall re-imburse to *Beta* all costs on actual basis required for acquiring the said tools etc. *Alpha* shall provide *Beta* the project management, technical leadership and priority setting, and source code management ("SCM") deemed necessary by *Alpha* in order to let *Beta* to perform its services according to this Agreement. *Beta* is not allowed to use anything listed in this section or any other supplies or equipment for any other purpose than according to this Agreement.

5.4. *Alpha* warrants that the personnel who have been transferred from *Alpha* to *Beta* have been fully trained in *Alpha's* products, and thus shall be considered SW Personnel.

5.5. In case new personnel are required to be allocated for providing Software Services, both *Beta* and *Alpha* will jointly select such personnel. *Beta* warrants that the personnel providing services to *Alpha* are provided the necessary tools and proper training. Training needs of these personnel shall be mutually agreed between *Alpha* and *Beta* and will not exceed two months in total duration. If this training requires that *Beta* employees travel to *Alpha*, *Beta* will pay for travel and boarding/lodging expenses whereas *Alpha* will provide training free of charge. If *Beta* requests and training takes place in India, *Beta* will pay travel and boarding/lodging expenses for the *Alpha* trainers. *Beta* employees will not be considered SW Personnel until they have either (i) completed two months of required training either at *Beta* or at *Alpha* or (ii) been certified by *Alpha* to be fully trained, whichever is earlier.

5.6. *Alpha* shall have the right to communicate directly with SW Personnel to ensure that each employee understands his tasks and deadlines. If SW Personnel in *Alpha's* opinion requires additional training then any expense including payment for SW Personnel's time as per 1.4 incurred in connection with such training will be borne by *Alpha* as per Section 4 above.

5.7. *Beta* will provide the IT infrastructure including but not limited to internet access with the necessary standard MS office applications required for employees to work efficiently with the team in *Alpha*.

5.8. Any SW or HW tools or other items of capital nature provided by *Alpha* to *Beta* according to this Agreement shall promptly be returned by *Beta* to *Alpha* upon request.

6. Software License

To the extent *Alpha* provides *Beta* with computer programs contained on a magnetic tape, disc, semiconductor device, or other memory device or system memory ("Software") under this Agreement, *Beta* is hereby granted a revocable, nonexclusive, nontransferable, indivisible personal license to use the Software only to perform its services under this Agreement. Software shall be treated as the exclusive property of *Alpha* and *Beta* shall: (1) treat such Software as information provided to *Beta* by *Alpha* pursuant to section12.1; (2) utilize such Software or any portions or aspects thereof (including any methods or concepts utilized therein) solely for performance of services under this Agreement; (3) forthwith return to *Alpha* all memory media, documentation and/or other material that has been modified, updated, or replaced; (4) not modify, disassemble, or decompile such Software, or reverse engineer any portion of the Software, or permit others to do so, without *Alpha's* written consent; (5) return such Software, and any copies, in whole or in part, to *Alpha* upon *Beta's* request; and (6) not reproduce or copy such Software in whole or in part except for backup and archival purposes or as otherwise permitted in writing by *Alpha* or as required to perform the development performed for *Alpha's*. *Alpha* provides such Software "AS IS". The obligations of this section shall survive the expiration or termination of this Agreement.

7. Development Process

7.1. The parties' intent is to continue to use the methodologies already deployed with *Alpha* and *Alpha* in the future development work including but not limited to review of test and design documents, design architecture and project reporting.

7.2. The parties will work closely together to ensure that tools and methodologies are harmonized with the aim of ensuring that Software developed by *Alpha* using own resources or SW Personnel and Software developed by *Beta* remain compatible. This means that the software tools already in place will continue to be used and upgraded as *Alpha* upgrade their tools.

8. Communications and Administration

For and on behalf of *Alpha*, liaison and general administration of the Agreement for *Alpha* shall be through the person designated below. All reports, loaned supplies and equipment shall be sent directly to this individual or his designate:

ALPHA

....................(address)

Att.: ....

For and on behalf of *Beta*, liaison and general administration of the Agreement for *Beta* shall be through the person designated below:

Beta

.................(address)

Attn. ....

9. Rights in Work Product

9.1. The Work Product which SW Personnel, conceive or reduce to practice whether alone or with others, during the course of its performance under this Agreement, shall be the exclusive property of *Alpha*.

9.2. The Work Product shall be deemed *Alpha* proprietary information and shall not be disclosed to anyone outside of *Alpha*, or used by *Beta* or others without the prior, written consent of *Alpha*. *Beta* shall restrict its disclosure of the Work Product for their performance under this Agreement.

9.3. *Beta* hereby assigns to *Alpha* all its rights, title and interest in or to any inventions, any ideas, patentable or not, conceived or made by SW Personnel working on the Subject Matter of this Agreement alone or with others, during substantially the period of time in which *Beta* is engaged by *Alpha*, and that are Work Product, or related in any way to the Subject Matter of this Agreement, or to the actual or prospective business of *Alpha* or its subsidiaries. The "Subject Matter of this Agreement" includes the engagement set forth in Section 1, the Work Product, and any information received by *Beta* from *Alpha* under and during the term of the Agreement.

9.4. During the term of this Agreement and within ..... months thereafter when called upon to do so by *Alpha*, *Beta* shall execute patent applications, assignments to *Alpha*, and other papers and agrees to render such other assistance which *Alpha* believes necessary to secure for *Alpha* the full protection and ownership of all rights in and to the Work Product of the Software Services performed by *Beta*. The filing of patent applications on inventions made by *Beta* shall be decided by *Alpha* and shall be for such countries as *Alpha* shall elect. *Alpha* shall bear the expenses in connection with the preparation, filing, and prosecution of applications for patents and for all matters provided in this subsection requiring the time and/or assistance of *Beta* in securing protection and ownership of *Alpha* for such inventions.

9.5. All Subject Matter of this Agreement capable of copyright protection within the Work Product, prepared by *Beta* under *Alpha*'s supervision ("Written Data"), including without limitation, any drawing, schematic, disclosure, article, paper, treatise, computer program, or report, shall be considered a "work made for hire" of *Alpha* under the copyright laws of ...., and as such shall be the exclusive property of *Alpha*. If any Subject Matter of this Agreement capable of copyright protection within Written Data should not qualify as a "work made for hire", *Beta* hereby assigns all rights, title and interest in and to such Subject Matter of this Agreement capable of copyright protection within the Written Data, including the copyright, and all extensions and renewals thereof, to *Alpha*. Upon *Alpha*'s request, *Beta* shall execute any document and render such other assistance as reasonably necessary to establish, preserve and enforce the full right, title, and interest worldwide in the Written Data, including formal conveyance of copyright. Written Data shall not be published or submitted for publication by *Beta* without the prior, written approval of *Alpha*. No license is hereby granted to *Beta* regarding said Written Data.

10. Insurance

The parties will be responsible for all insurance related to their respective scope of work as per this Agreement.

11. Warranties and Indemnity

11.1. *Beta* warrants that it pays and/or withholds all employment related taxes for SW Personnel.

11.2. All other warranties than those expressly stated in this agreement by the parties is hereby disclaimed by the parties.

12. Confidential Information

The obligations of this section shall survive the expiration or termination of this Agreement.

12.1. *Beta* shall maintain confidential and secret all written, recorded, photographic, machine-readable, or other physical form which may be disclosed or provided to *Beta*, by *Alpha* or at *Alpha's* direction and *Beta* shall not disclose this information to any other person (including *Alpha* employees in any other division, group, or entity), firm, or corporation. *Beta* shall also maintain confidential the "Know-how" and future plans of *Alpha* relating to the fields of endeavor in which *Beta* performs investigations, evaluations, and services for *Alpha* as well as the nature of work projects to which *Beta* is exposed and the identity of persons working on those projects.

12.2. As between *Alpha* and *Beta*, all information referred to in section 12.1 shall remain the property of Tellabs, and such information and all copies thereof shall be promptly returned to *Alpha* upon *Alpha's* request for such return. Except as expressly stated in this Agreement, nothing contained in this Agreement shall be construed as granting to or conferring upon *Beta* any rights, by license or otherwise, express or implied, in such information, other than the right to use such information for performing services under this Agreement. Any copies of such information made by *Beta* shall reproduce proprietary marking and legends included therein, but the provisions of this Agreement supersede any provisions of such legends inconsistent herewith.

12.3. The existence of this Agreement and the terms and conditions hereof shall not be disclosed by *Beta* to others, except with the prior, written consent of *Alpha* or as may be required by law or as necessary to establish its rights hereunder. *Beta* shall not use the name of *Alpha* in any, public announcement or advertisement, in relation to this Agreement without the prior, written consent of *Alpha* except for generic reference to products and services being offered by *Beta* to its customers

12.4. If, in connection with its performance, *Beta* discloses to *Alpha* any ideas, developments, or inventions conceived or actually reduced to practice by *Beta* prior to this Agreement, no relationship, confidential or otherwise, express or implied, is established with *Alpha* by the disclosure thereof. With respect to any such disclosure, no obligation of any kind is assumed by, nor may be implied against, *Alpha*, its subsidiary, or associated companies unless a formal, separate, written contract regarding the subject of disclosure is consummated by the Parties, and then the obligation shall be only as expressed in the separate contract. *Alpha* and *Beta* shall agree and sign a Non-Disclosure Agreement ("NDA") to cover any such disclosures anticipated by *Beta* to *Alpha*.

13. Consulting Agreement

Beta warrants that it is not a party to any other existing Agreement which would prevent *Beta* from entering into this Agreement or which would adversely affect this Agreement.

14. Independent Party

It is understood and agreed that *Beta* shall be acting as an independent party and not as an agent or employee of *Alpha*. Accordingly, *Beta* assumes all risks and hazards encountered in its performance of this Agreement and, further, *Beta* shall be solely responsible for all injuries, including death, to all persons and all loss or damage to property which are attributed to *Beta's* performance under this Agreement or that of any agent, employee, or subcontractor engaged by *Beta*.

All SW Personnel allocated to provide Software Services to *Alpha* under the provisions of this Agreement are solely the employees of *Beta* and nothing in this Agreement shall be construed or interpreted as creating an employer-employee relationship between *Alpha* and the said employees of *Beta*. Accordingly *Beta* shall be solely responsible for all employee related issues such as but not limited to compensation and other employee related payments and social security contributions.

15. Termination

15.1. This Section shall not be deemed to waive, prejudice, or diminish any rights which the parties may have at law or in equity for an unlawful termination or other breach of this Agreement by the other.

15.2. This Agreement may be terminated in the following circumstances :

In the event of any material breach of, or material default under, this Agreement by *Alpha* or *Beta*, the non-defaulting party shall give the other party written notice of such breach or default. The other party shall have a period of thirty (30) days from the date of receipt of such written notice within which the breach or default may be rectified. In the event of failure to cure such breach or default, this Agreement may be terminated immediately by written notice of the non-breaching or non-defaulting party's election to terminate to the other party.

15.3. Either party may terminate this Agreement immediately, upon written notice of termination to the other party, if the other party goes into bankruptcy or voluntary dissolution, is declared insolvent, fails to pay its debts as they become due, makes an assignment for the benefit of creditors, becomes subject to any proceeding under any bankruptcy or insolvency law or suffers the appointment of a receiver or trustee over all or substantially all of its assets or properties; and

15.4. *Beta* shall submit to *Alpha*, within thirty (30) calendar days of such termination, a written report of all fees owed by *Alpha* for services performed prior to the termination date. *Alpha* shall pay the service fees owed to *Beta* within thirty (30) calendar days of submission of said report by *Beta*.

16. Performance Criteria

16.1. *Beta* agrees that, upon request, *Beta* will remove from *Alpna* assigned Software Services work hereunder any SW Personnel who, in Tellabs's sole opinion, may be guilty of improper conduct or is not qualified to perform the work assigned.

16.2. Any failure by either Party to carry out any of its obligations shall not be deemed to be a breach of this Agreement if such failure is caused by a *force majeure* event. For the purposes of this Agreement *force majeure* shall include, *inter alia*, strikes, lockouts, boycotts, embargoes, governmental restrictions, wars, war-like actions, civil commotion, riots, uprising, revolutions, epidemics, fires, floods, storms, earthquakes, other natural occurrence or any other event beyond the control of such Party.

The performance of the Parties' obligations shall be suspended for as long as the *force majeure* event continues to exist. It is understood that such Party shall take all reasonable steps to limit the effect of *force majeure* by resorting to alternative measures. If such *force majeure* continues in existence for more than .... months, either Party, at its option, shall have the right to terminate this Agreement. Such termination shall be without prejudice to the rights of either Party, which may have accrued up to the date of termination.

Notice in writing of *force majeure* shall be made within .... days of its occurrence. If such notice is made later it shall have effect only concerning the proceeding .... days. A Party in default may not invoke *force majeure*, occurring subsequent to such default as an excuse therefore.

17. Binding Agreement

This Agreement shall be binding upon and inure to the benefit of the heirs, legal representatives, successors and assigns of *Alpha* and shall be binding upon and inure to the benefit of *Beta*'s heirs, legal representatives, successors, and assigns.

18. Applicable Law

18.1. The terms and conditions of this Agreement and performance hereunder shall be construed in accordance with the laws of India.

18.2. In the event of breach of this Agreement both Parties shall make reasonable efforts to reach an amicable settlement thereof. If the Parties cannot reach an amicable settlement all disputes arising in connection with this Agreement shall be settled without recourse to any court of law under the laws of Arbitration and Conciliation Act, 1996 of India by three arbitrators appointed in accordance with the said rules. Arbitration shall be held in India. The language of the proceedings shall be English.

19. Assignment

19.1. This Agreement shall not be assignable by *Beta* without the written consent of *Alpha*, and any purported assignment, including full or partial assignment or delegation to any agent, subcontractor, not permitted hereunder shall be void.

19.2. *Alpha* shall have the right at any time without the prior written consent of *Beta* to assign this Agreement to any other member of the *Alpha* group of companies.

20. Modification

This Agreement and any attachment hereto shall be modified only by an instrument in writing and signed by duly authorized representatives of the Parties. Representatives of the Parties who sign this Agreement and any modification thereto personally warrant and represent that they have been duly authorized by their respective party to sign such Agreement and/or modification on behalf of such party.

21. Entirety of Agreement

This document constitutes the entire Agreement between the Parties with respect to the Subject Matter of this Agreement hereof, and supersedes all previous communications, representations, understandings, and Agreements, either oral or written, between the Parties or any official or representative thereof.

IN WITNESS WHEREOF:

Both parties hereto cause this Agreement to be executed in duplicate, each copy of which shall be considered an original, by their representative, duly authorized as of the day, month and year first above written.

ALPHA A/S
By:................................
Name:............................
Title:.............................
Date:.............................

BETA Limited
By:................................
Name:............................
Title:.............................
Date:.............................

ERC FACILITIES AGREEMENT

This Agreement is made at .... on this ...., day of ...., 20....

BETWEEN

ALPHA Springs Ltd. a public limited company incorporated in India under the Companies Act, 1956, and having its registered office at .... (address), India (hereinafter referred to as "*Alpha*", which expression shall include, unless repugnant to the meaning or context thereof, its successors and permitted assigns) of the ONE PART;

AND

.................., a company incorporated under the Companies Act, 1956 and having its registered office at .... (address), (hereinafter referred to as the "Company", which expression shall include, unless repugnant to the meaning or context thereof, its successors and permitted assigns) of the OTHER PART.

(*Alpha* and the Company are hereinafter individually referred to as "Party" and collectively as "Parties").

WHEREAS:

A. The company is a joint venture between *Alpha* and (name of The Gamma Company affiliate), a company registered under the laws of the ...., and having its registered office at.................. (hereinafter referred to as "*Gamma*", which expression shall include, unless repugnant to the meaning or context thereof, its successors and permitted assigns) proposed to be managed in accordance with a Shareholders' Agreement entered into between *Alpha*, *Gamma* and the Company being executed simultaneously herewith (the "Shareholders' Agreement"), and is engaged in the activity of manufacturing and selling multi-leaf springs, parabolic springs and spring assemblies for automotive suspension systems and commercial vehicle suspension systems.

B. The company acquired the.......................... (address) Unit (the "Unit") of *Alpha* situated at plot No. .... (address) pursuant to the Transfer of Undertaking Agreement dated...............entered into between the Company and *Alpha*;

C. *Alpha* has, within its factory complex at .... (address), infrastructure and facilities in respect of the engineering, research, testing and sample development of leaf and parabolic springs ;

D. *Alpha* was sharing its said facilities at .... (address) with the Unit prior to the acquisition of the same by Company;

E. For the effective operations of the Unit, the Company is desirous that *Alpha* continues to share the said facilities with the Company, and *Alpha* is agreeable to making the same available to the Company on a continuous basis;

E. Based on the representations and assurances given by *Alpha*, the Company has agreed to utilize the facilities referred to above and described in detail hereinafter subject to the terms and conditions contained herein.

NOW THEREFORE in consideration of the mutual covenants and obligations herein, it is hereby agreed to between the Parties as under:

1. Definitions

"*Agreement*" shall mean this ERC Facilities Agreement and the Annexures hereto, including any and all modifications and alterations thereto made in writing after the date of execution, hereof;

"ERC Facilities"	shall mean the engineering and research facilities more particularly described at Annexure A, hereto[1];
"Effective Date"	shall mean the Effective Date of the Shareholders' Agreement;
"Products"	shall mean multi-leaf springs, parabolic springs and spring assemblies for automotive suspension systems and commercial vehicle suspension systems, and any other products for automotive and commercial vehicles as may be mutually agreed by the Parties from time to time.

2. Provision of ERC Facilities

2.1 *Alpha* shall share and make available to the Company, on a day-to-day basis, ERC Facilities, in accordance with the terms and conditions hereof, to enable the Company to effectively and efficiently operate the Unit.

2.2 The proposed organisation of the ERC Facilities shall be in accordance with Annexure B hereto.

3. Obligations and Responsibilities of *Alpha*[2]

3.1 It is hereby agreed between the Parties hereto, that the Company has entered into this Agreement based on *Alpha*'s assurances that it has appropriate and sufficient infrastructure, equipment and skilled manpower to provide ERC Facilities to the satisfaction of the Company. Accordingly, it is agreed that *Alpha* shall be responsible for:

   (a) ensuring that the ERC Facilities shall be provided to the Company in a prudent, competent, efficient and timely manner;

   (b) paying salaries, benefits, statutory dues and the like to all its employees that are engaged by *Alpha* to provide the ERC Facilities to the Company. *Alpha* shall ensure on its own and in due compliance with all laws and regulations relating to its employees, their employment with *Alpha* and otherwise. *Alpha* shall hold the Company harmless and keep it indemnified in respect of any claims or demands made against it in respect of such salaries and benefits etc.;

   (c) causing its employees to make best efforts to ensure that the ERC Facilities are provided to the Company in accordance with this Agreement;

---

1. From the definition of the term 'ERC Facilities' it appears that certain services would be provided by ALPHA to the Company pursuant to the Agreement. Is it so intended, or is it intended that the Company have the right to use the engineering research infrastructure of ALPHA? The definition would have to be modified accordingly.

2. Obligations and Responsibilities of ALPHA (Clause 3)

   Whether it is services or infrastructure that ALPHA is supposed, to provide or make available to the company, the Agreement does not lay down any standards therefore. The only indication is contained in clause 2.1, which provides that the Facilities to be provided by ALPHA should "enable the company to effectively and efficiently operate the Unit".

(d) co-operating at all times with the Company in making available the ERC Facilities as per the specifications if any, provided by the Company to *Alpha*;

(e) performing its obligations, duties and functions within the scope of this Agreement in such manner so as to ensure that the designs of the products conform to the specifications of the Products, provided by, and are fit for the use of such Products indicated by, the customers of the Company. However, *Alpha* shall not be responsible for the quality of the Products, which are manufactured by the Company;

(f) the day-to-day operations and functioning of all its utilities/ departments that are within the scope of the engineering and research centre of *Alpha*;

(g) making employees available as per the requirements of the Company for the purposes of this Agreement and for the ERC Facilities, to be provided hereunder;

(h) obtaining approvals, licenses or consents, if any, required to execute this Agreement and perform all its obligations under this Agreement;

(i) providing the employees of the Company access to the ERC Facilities for inspection and use thereof;

(j) ensuring that the equipment and facilities of *Alpha* are updated from time to time and as reasonably requested by the Company.

4. Charges for ERC Facilities and Consideration[1]

4.1.1 In consideration for the ERC Facilities provided hereunder and for the expenses to be incurred by *Alpha* therefore, the Company shall make to *Alpha*:

(a) a lump sum payment of Rs............. ...., which shall be the capital requirement needed to allow for the testing by the ERC Facilities of Products for heavy duty commercial vehicles, payable on execution of this Agreement; and

(b) monthly charges of Rs. .... on the basis of the relative percentage of revenues of the entities availing services similar to the ERC Facilities.

4.1.2 The charges relating to the travel expenses, hotel accommodation, lodgings, meals and other miscellaneous expenses for any Company personnel receiving training at the ERC Facilities shall be on actuals and shall be borne by the Company.

---

1. Charges for ERC Facilities and Consideration (Clause 4)

    Clause 4.1 - The Agreement should also (a) identify what exactly the payments will be for; (b) specify the cost centres for providing/making available the facilities; and (c) require ALPHA to produce the details of the expenses incurred in providing/making available the facilities.

    Clause 4.2 - The clients should consider adding the parameters on which the review of the monthly consideration would take place. One factor that would substantially reduce the consideration could be the company setting up its own facilities.

4.2 Charges under sub-clause (b) of clause 4.1.1 will be reviewed and fixed mutually by the Parties on each anniversary of the Agreement.

4.3 *Alpha* shall raise monthly invoices for the ERC Facilities rendered by it. The invoices shall be raised by *Alpha* within the first week of the month succeeding the month for which the invoice is raised. Such invoices would be payable by the Company net of applicable taxes within fifteen (15) business days of the receipt of the invoices.

4.4 *Alpha* shall provide such details of the charges invoiced by it as may be reasonably requested by the Company from time to time.

5. Representation and Warranties of *Alpha*

5.1 *Alpha* represents and warrants to the Company that:

(a) it has full legal right, power and authority to enter into, execute and deliver this Agreement and to undertake and perform the obligations set forth, herein;

(b) this Agreement has been duly and validly executed and delivered by *Alpha* and constitutes its legal, valid and binding obligation, enforceable against it, in accordance with the terms hereof;

(c) ERC Facilities will be made available to the company as per the requirements specified by the company to *Alpha*, in accordance with the terms hereof;

(d) the use of the ERC Facilities by *Alpha* and/or third parties shall not in any manner whatsoever affect the availability of the ERC Facilities to the company;

(e) neither the execution nor delivery of this Agreement by *Alpha*, nor the fulfilment nor compliance by *Alpha* with the terms and provisions hereof: (i) will conflict with, or result in a breach of, terms, conditions or provisions of, or constitute a default under, or result in any violation of its Memorandum and Articles of Association, or any Agreement or arrangement to which *Alpha* is a party or any laws, regulations or orders to which *Alpha* is or has been subject to, or (ii) require any consent, approval or other action by any court or administrative or governmental body

(f) *Alpha*, in performing its obligations under this Agreement, shall comply with all applicable laws, rules, regulations and Government orders.

6. Term and Termination

6.1 Term

This Agreement shall take effect and become binding upon the Parties on the Effective Date of the Shareholders' Agreement and shall remain in full force until the earlier of the termination of the Shareholders' Agreement or notice by the company to *Alpha* pursuant to clause 6.2.3, that it is terminating this Agreement.

6.2 Termination

6.2.1 Notwithstanding anything contained in this Agreement, and without prejudice to its other rights in law or equity and without any liability and judicial intervention, this Agreement may be terminated by the Party not in default (the "Non-Defaulting Party") by giving a thirty (30) days' written notice to the Party in default (the "Defaulting Party"), if any of the following events (hereinafter referred to as an "Event of Default") occurs:

(a) Either Party commits a breach of this Agreement and such breach, if capable of remedy, is not remedied by the Defaulting Party within the aforesaid thirty (30) days' notice period;

(b) Any change in control of either Party. For the purpose of this sub-clause, the Party in respect of which a change in control occurs will be deemed to be the Defaulting Party; or

(c) If either Party goes into liquidation (other than a voluntary liquidation for the purposes of reconstruction and where all the rights and obligations are validly assigned), administration or receivership or ceases to carry on its business or is otherwise insolvent or unable to pay its debts on time.

6.2.2 This Agreement may be terminated by the mutual written consent of the Parties.

6.2.3 The Company, without cause, may terminate this Agreement by serving a notice of ( ) months. The Company shall not be obliged to give reasons for such termination. Upon the expiry of the aforesaid notice period, this Agreement shall stand terminated.

6.2.4 Notwithstanding clause 6.1, this Agreement may be terminated by the Company (or shall stand terminated) upon the Company setting up or acquiring its own facilities for research and engineering.

6.3 Cessation of rights and obligations

Subject to clause 6.4 herein below, upon termination of this Agreement for whatever reason, all the rights and obligations of the Parties, hereunder shall cease.

7. Confidentiality

7.1 *Alpha* agrees that all information, including all documents, applications, papers, statements, programs, plans and other trade secrets, confidential knowledge or information (hereinafter collectively referred to as "*Information*"), provided to *Alpha* by the Company in connection with this Agreement is, shall be and shall remain the sole property of the Company and shall be of a strictly private and confidential nature and shall be treated as confidential by *Alpha*.

7.2 During the term of this Agreement and thereafter, *Alpha* shall not in any way make use of any such information for any purpose, whatsoever which is not necessary for the discharge of its obligations under this Agreement, or to the disadvantage of the Company, nor shall it divulge any such information to any one other than the Company or persons designated by the Company unless or until such information has been publicly released by the Company or becomes generally known to the public from other sources.

7.3 All information shall be returned forthwith by *Alpha* to the Company on the expiry or termination of this Agreement; provided that *Alpha* shall, upon demand by the Company at any time during the term of this Agreement, return to the Company any and all information.

7.4 The provisions of this clause shall survive the termination or expiry of this Agreement.

8. Indemnification

8.1 *Alpha* shall indemnify, the company and hold it harmless against any claims or demands made against the company or its employees or shareholders by any of *Alpha*'s employees, workers, Consultants, sub-contractors or the like, or the sub-contractors' employees, workers, Consultants or the like.

8.2 *Alpha* shall indemnify and hold harmless the company from and against all losses, costs, actions, damages, liabilities, fines, penalties of any kind or nature whatsoever resulting from or relating to the negligence, default, act or omission on the part of *Alpha*, its employees, workers, Consultants, sub-contractors, or the like, or the employees, workers or Consultants of such sub-contractors in the performance of or failure to perform, *Alpha*'s obligations hereunder.

8.3 The Company shall indemnify and hold harmless *Alpha* from and against all losses, costs, actions, damages, liabilities, fines or penalties of any kind or nature whatsoever with respect to any harm caused to *Alpha* and disruption caused to *Alpha*'s operations at the factory complex resulting from or relating to the negligence or default on the part of the Company.

9. Governing Law and Arbitration

9.1 This Agreement shall be construed in accordance with the law of India.

9.2 Any dispute, difference, controversy or claim ("Dispute") arising between the Parties out of or in relation to or in connection with this Agreement, or the breach, termination, effect, validity, interpretation or application of this Agreement or as to their rights, duties or liabilities hereunder, shall be settled by the Parties by mutual negotiations and Agreement. If, for any reason, such dispute cannot be resolved amicably by the Parties, the same shall be referred to and settled by way of arbitration proceedings by three arbitrators, one to be nominated by each Party and the third to be appointed by the two appointed arbitrators. The arbitration proceedings shall be held in accordance with the Arbitration and Conciliation Act, 1996, or any subsequent enactment or amendment thereto (the "Arbitration Act"). Each of the Parties shall appoint an arbitrator within .... days of the receipt by a Party of the other Party's request to initiate arbitration. The two arbitrators so appointed shall then jointly appoint a third arbitrator within .... days of the date of appointment of the second arbitrator, such third arbitrator shall act, as the Chairman of the tribunal. Arbitrators not appointed within the time limit set forth in the preceding sentence shall be appointed in accordance with the Arbitration Act. The decision of the arbitrators shall be final and binding upon the Parties. The venue of arbitration proceedings shall be .... The language of the arbitration and the award shall be English.

10. Entire Agreement

This Agreement and the Schedules and Annexures, hereto represent the entire Agreement as to the subject, matter hereof, and supersede any and all prior understandings between the Parties on the subject-matter, hereof.

11. *Force Majeure*

Notwithstanding anything to the contrary in this Agreement, neither Party shall be liable by reason of failure or delay in the performance of its duties and obligations under this Agreement if such failure or delay is caused by acts of God, war, riot, fire, civil commotion, strikes, lock outs, embargoes, any orders of governmental, quasi-governmental, or local authorities or any other similar cause beyond its control and without its fault or negligence.

12. Notice

All notices required or permitted hereunder shall be in writing and in the English language and shall be sent by internationally recognised courier or by facsimile transmission (with confirming facsimile receipt) addressed to the address of each Party set forth below, or to such other address as such other Party shall have communicated to the other Party in writing. Notice shall be deemed to have been served when received (and in case of a facsimile transmission, provided that a confirming copy is sent to the other Party, in accordance with the non-facsimile notice delivery requirements).

If to *ALPHA*:

....
....

If to **the Company**:

....
....

13. Waiver

Save where this Agreement expressly provides, neither Party shall be deemed to have waived any right, power, privilege or remedy under this Agreement unless such Party shall have delivered to the other Party a written waiver signed by an authorised officer of such waiving Party. No failure or delay on the part of either Party in exercising any right, power, privilege or remedy hereunder shall operate as a waiver, default or acquiescence thereof, nor shall any waiver on the part of either Party of any right, power, privilege or remedy hereunder operate as a waiver of any other right, power, privilege or remedy, nor shall any single or partial exercise of any right, power, privilege or remedy hereunder preclude any other or further exercise thereof or the exercise of any other right, power, privilege or remedy hereunder.

14. Remedies

No remedy conferred by any of the provisions of this Agreement is intended to be exclusive of any other remedy, which is otherwise available at law, in equity, by statute or otherwise, or any other remedy given hereunder or now or hereafter existing at law, in equity, by statute, or otherwise, except as stated to the contrary in this Agreement. The election of any one or more of such remedies by any of the Parties hereto shall not constitute a waiver by such Party of the right to pursue any other available remedy.

15. Severance

If any provision of this Agreement or part, thereof is rendered void, illegal or unenforceable in any respect under any law, the same shall be replaced by, and any omission shall be remedied, by way of a corresponding provision which comes as close as legally and commercially possible to the express or implied intention of the Parties, and the validity, legality and enforceability of the remaining provisions shall not in any way be affected or impaired thereby.

16. Survival of Rights, Duties and Obligations

Termination of this Agreement for any cause whatsoever shall not release a Party from any liability which, at the time of termination, has already accrued to the other Party or which may thereafter accrue in respect of any act or omission prior to such termination.

17. No Partnership or Agency

Nothing contained herein shall or shall be deemed to create any partnership, agency, association, trust, or joint venture between *Alpha* and the company, or their representatives and employees and nothing herein shall be deemed to confer on any Party any authority to incur any obligation or liability on behalf of the other Party.

18. Employees

All employees, workers, Consultants and the like engaged by *Alpha* in connection with the discharge of its duties and obligations under this Agreement shall be in the sole employment of *Alpha* and *Alpha* shall be solely responsible for their salaries, wages, statutory payments and the like. Under no circumstances shall the company be liable for any payment or claim or compensation (including but not limited to compensation on account of injury/death/termination) of any nature to such employees, workers and Consultants at any point of time during the currency of this Agreement or after its termination.

19. Sub-contracts

Alpha shall itself perform its services, obligations and duties under this Agreement. However, with the company's prior written approval, *Alpha* may sub-contract any part of the facilities. The company's approval to such sub-contract shall not create any relationship between the company and such sub-contractor nor shall it discharge *Alpha* from its responsibilities for performance of its services, obligations and duties under this Agreement. *Alpha* shall be absolutely responsible and liable for all acts and omissions of such sub-contractor and shall always keep and hold the company harmless and indemnified in this regard.

20. Assignment

Neither of the Parties hereto shall be entitled to assign this Agreement, or any of their rights, powers, obligations and/or duties hereunder without the prior written consent of the other Party.

21. Amendments

No amendments and/or modifications to this Agreement shall be valid unless executed in writing and signed by both Parties.

22. Further Acts and Assurances

Each Party shall co-operate with the other and execute and deliver to the other such instruments and documents and take such other actions as may be reasonably requested by the other Party from time to time in order to carry out, give effect to or confirm its rights, and for the intended purpose of this Agreement.

23. Survival

The provisions of the following clauses of this Agreement shall survive the termination or expiry hereof: clauses.

24. Interpretation

24.1 Headings are inserted for ease of reference only and have no legal effect.

24.2 References to clauses are references to clauses of this Agreement.

24.3 The schedules, annexures and appendices referred to in this Agreement and attached hereto form a part of this Agreement.

IN WITNESS WHEREOF, the Parties hereto have signed this Agreement on the day and year first above written.

For and on behalf of:	For and on behalf of:
The Company	*ALPHA*
Signature :	Signature:................................
Name :	Name:.....................................
Designation :	Designation:............................

ANNEXURE "A"

1. Multi leaf/ parabolic spring designing for all domestic and overseas customers; Cooperation with *Gamma* including despatch of personnel to *Gamma* for spring designing for all customers procured by *Gamma*; such co-operation to be provided in accordance with the provisions of the Agreement attached, hereto.

2. Technical support to the Company in new product development.

3. Setting up design testing facilities and carrying out testing of Products designed for the Company's customers;

4. Monitoring product development plan.

5. Failure and warranty analysis; and

6. Training of the Company's personnel.

ANNEXURE B

Suggested Additions

The Agreement should, subject to the intention of the parties, also provide that the Company shall have the right to (a) send its employees or representatives to use the Engineering Research Center of *Alpha*; (b) require up-gradation of the equipment, etc.; (c) inspect the facilities; and (d) priority in use of the facilities over third parties using the center.

FACILITIES SHARING AGREEMENT

This Agreement is made at .... on this .... day of ...., 20.....

BETWEEN

ALPHA PVT. LTD., being a company registered under the Companies Act, 1956 and having its registered office at .... (address) (hereinafter referred to as *"Alpha"*) of the FIRST PARTY;

AND

BETA PVT. LTD., a company incorporated under the Companies Act, 1956 and having its registered office at .... (address) (hereinafter referred to as *"Beta "*) of the SECOND PARTY

WHEREAS *Alpha* has acquired the undertaking of *Gamma Ltd.*, a company incorporated in India and having its registered office in .... (address) (hereinafter referred to as "JPSL") situated at plot no. ....(address) and *vide* lease deed dated ...., 20.... entered into between *Alpha* and *Beta* , *Beta* has taken on lease, subject to the terms and conditions mentioned therein, a portion of the aforesaid premises measuring .... located within the aforesaid factory complex for the purposes of operating its air suspension business for an initial period of five years (hereinafter referred to as "the Plant"); and

WHEREAS for the effective running of the Plant, *Beta* requires certain facilities, amenities and utilities (as defined herein) on a continuous basis; and

WHEREAS *Alpha* has, within its factory complex at .... District, the necessary infrastructure in respect of the facilities, amenities and utilities required by *Beta* and is in position to share the same with *Beta*, and

WHEREAS *Beta* is desirous of sharing such facilities, amenities and utilities from *Alpha*. *Alpha* is agreeable to make the same available to *Beta*; and

WHEREAS based on the representations and assurances given by *Alpha*. *Beta* has agreed to utilize the facilities, amenities and utilities referred to above and described in detail hereinafter subject to the terms and conditions contained herein; and

WHEREAS *Alpha* and *Beta* desire to set forth and define the terms and conditions pursuant to which *Alpha* shall share and make available the necessary facilities to *Beta*.

NOW, THEREFORE in consideration of the mutual covenants and obligations herein, it is hereby agreed to between the parties as under:

1. Scope of Facilities

From the effective date of this Agreement, *Alpha* shall share and make available to *Beta* , on a day-to-day basis, certain facilities, amenities and utilities, more particularly described in the *Schedule hereto* and forming part of this Agreement, to enable *Beta* to effectively and efficiently operate its air suspension business at .... (address) (hereinafter referred to as *"the Facilities"*).

The employees/officers of *Alpha* that will be responsible for the facilities to be made available and shared by *Alpha* with *Beta* are specified in the Schedule. In case of a change in any such employee/officer, *Alpha* shall give reasonable notice to *Beta* in writing and furnish the name of the replacement employee or officer along with his qualification, experience and profile.

2. Obligations and Responsibilities of *Alpha*

It is hereby agreed between the parties hereto that *Beta* has entered into this Agreement based on *Alpha's* assurances that the facilities hereunder shall be adequate and sufficient for the efficient running of the air suspension business by *Beta* . Accordingly, it is agreed that *Alpha* shall be responsible for the following:

(a) making available the facilities (as described in the Schedule hereto), during the term of this Agreement to *Beta* from the effective date hereof;

(b) ensuring that the facilities shall be provided to *Beta* in a prudent, competent, efficient and timely manner;

(c) paying salaries, benefits, statutory dues and the like to all its employees that are engaged by *Alpha* to provide the Facilities to *Beta* . *Alpha* shall ensure on its own and in due compliance of all laws and regulations relating to its employees, their employment with *Alpha* and otherwise. *Alpha* shall hold *Beta* harmless and keep it indemnified in respect of any claims or demands made against it in respect of the aforesaid;

(d) causing its employees to make best efforts to ensure efficient operations of *Beta*;

(e) co-operating at all times with *Beta* in making available the facilities as per the specifications if any:

Provided by *Beta* to *Alpha* and at the cost referred to in Article 3 hereunder;

(f) day-to-day operation and functioning of all its utilities departments that are within the scope of the facilities;

(g) making employees available as per the requirements of the *Beta* for the purposes of this Agreement and facilities to be provided hereunder.

(h) obtaining approvals, licenses or consents, if any required to execute this Agreement and perform all its obligations under this Agreement.

3. Costs for Facilities and Consideration

3.1 In consideration for the facilities provided hereunder and for the expenses to be incurred by *Alpha* therefor, *Beta* shall pay *Alpha* monthly compensation as per the rates fixed under the Schedule attached hereto.

3.2 The rates shall be mutually reviewed after such intervals as specified in the said Schedule. The rates shall be reviewed on the basis of the costs during the year preceding the review. *Alpha* shall provide the cost data for the review of rates and *Beta* shall be entitled to inspect *Alpha*'s accounts for verifying the cost data furnished by *Alpha*. The rates shall be revised with mutual consent in accordance with the formula enumerated in the Schedule.

3.3 *Alpha* shall raise monthly invoices for the facilities rendered by it. The invoices shall be raised by *Alpha* within the first week of the month succeeding the month for which the invoice is raised. Such invoices would be payable by *Beta* within fifteen business days of the receipt of the invoices.

4. Representation and Warranties

Alpha represents and warrants to *Beta* that:—

(a) it has full legal right, power and authority to enter into, execute and deliver this Agreement and to undertake and perform the obligations set forth herein;

(b) this Agreement has been duly and validly executed and delivered by *Alpha* and constitutes its legal, valid and binding obligation, enforceable against it in accordance with the terms hereof;

(c) facilities will be made available to *Beta* as per the requirements specified by *Beta* to *Alpha* in accordance with the terms hereof and Schedule I hereto;

(d) the use of the facilities by *Alpha* and/or third parties shall not in any manner whatsoever affect the availability of the facilities to *Beta* as per Schedule;

(e) the execution and delivery of this Agreement by *Alpha* and performance of the obligations hereunder by *Alpha* shall not violate, conflict with or result in the breach of any of the terms, conditions or provisions of the Memorandum and Articles of Association of *Alpha* or any Agreement or arrangement to which *Alpha* is a party or any laws, regulations or orders to which *Alpha* is or has been subject to.

5. Term and Termination

5.1 This Agreement shall take effect and come into force on .... (hereinafter referred to as the "*Effective Date*") and shall continue till the time *Beta* continues to operate its air suspension business at *Alpha*'s factory complex, unless terminated earlier in terms hereof.

5.2 Notwithstanding anything contained in this Agreement, either party shall be entitled to terminate this Agreement forthwith upon the happening of any or all the following events:—

(a) Upon any party committing a breach of any of the terms and conditions of this Agreement and failing to rectify such breach within a period of thirty days of the notice of such breach;

(b) Upon termination of the Sub-lease Deed dated ...., 20.... entered into between the parties.

(c) *Beta* shall be entitled to terminate this Agreement due to a *force majeure* as provided under Article 9 hereof preventing *Alpha* from providing the facilities or part thereof for a period of 30 days.

5.3 Termination of this Agreement shall not affect the rights and liabilities of the parties accrued during the subsistence of the Agreement.

5.4 Upon termination of the Agreement, *Beta* may request *Alpha* and *Alpha* may at its option continue to perform facilities or any portion thereof for up to 360 days following termination to enable *Beta* to make alternate arrangements on mutually agreeable terms and conditions.

6. Indemnification

6.1 *Alpha* shall indemnify *Beta* and hold it harmless against any claims or demands made by *Alpha*'s employees or sub-contractors or their employees against *Beta* or its employees or its shareholders, on the ground that such persons are rendering services to *Beta*.

6.2 *Alpha* shall indemnify and hold harmless *Beta* from and against all losses, costs, actions, damages, liabilities, fines, penalties of any kind or nature whatsoever resulting from or relating to the negligence or default on the part of *Alpha* in performing or failing to perform its obligations hereunder.

6.3 *Beta* shall indemnify and hold harmless *Alpha* from and against all losses, costs, actions, damages, liabilities, fines or penalties of any kind or nature whatsoever with respect to any harm caused to *Alpha*'s employees and disruption caused to *Alpha*'s operations at the factory complex resulting from or relating to the negligence or default on the part of *Beta*.

7. Governing Law and Arbitration

7.1 All disputes arising in connection with this Agreement shall, to the extent possible, be settled amicably by prompt good faith negotiations between the representatives of the Parties. In default of such amicable settlement within thirty days (or such period as agreed between the parties) of the commencement of discussions, the dispute shall be finally settled under the Rules of International Chamber of Commerce ("*ICC*") by three arbitrators, appointed in accordance with the said Rules, whose decision the parties shall recognize and respect as final and binding upon the parties without any right of appeal or review on any grounds whether in law or equity before any judicial or government body. The venue of arbitration proceedings shall be .... (place). The governing law for the arbitration shall be the law of India.

7.2 This Agreement shall be construed in accordance with the applicable laws of India. Any or all disputes arising out of this Agreement shall be subject to the exclusive jurisdiction of the courts in .... (place).

8. Entire Agreement

This Agreement and the Schedule hereto represent the entire Agreement as to the subject-matter hereof and supersedes any prior understandings between the parties on the subject-matter hereof, save and except that nothing herein contained shall affect the Transfer of Business Agreement.

9. Force Majeure

Notwithstanding anything to the contrary herein contained, nothing herein shall apply if either party is prevented from discharging its obligation hereunder due to any cause arising from or related to any act of God, war, riot, fire, civil commotion, strikes lock out or any orders of governmental, quasi-governmental, or local authority or any similar cause.

10. Notice

A notice to be given or other communications to be provided hereunder shall be in writing addressed to the parties at their respective addresses set out herein above, unless *Alpha* or *Beta* shall have given notice of a different address.

11. Waiver

No delay on the part of either party hereto in exercising any right, power or privilege hereunder shall operate as a waiver thereof, nor shall any waiver on the part of the either party of any right, power or privilege hereunder operate as a waiver of any other right, power, or privilege hereunder, nor shall any single or partial exercise of any right, power or privilege hereunder preclude any other or further exercise thereof or the exercise of any other right, power or privilege hereunder.

12. Miscellaneous

12.1 This Agreement shall not be assigned by *Alpha* without the prior written consent of *Beta* .

12.2 The appendices referred to in this Agreement form a part and parcel of this Agreement.

12.3 All rights and obligations that have arisen up to the date of termination shall survive after the termination date until they are completely performed by either party.

12.4 Article headings are inserted for convenience of reference only and shall not be deemed to affect the interpretation of this Agreement or of any clause.

12.5 Both the Parties shall co-operate with the other and execute and deliver to the other such instruments and documents and take such other actions as may be reasonably requested from time to time in order to carry out, give effect to and confirm their rights and the intended purpose of this Agreement.

IN WITNESS WHEREOF the parties hereto have signed this Agreement on the day and year first above written.

For and on behalf of	For and on behalf of
BETA	*ALPHA*
Signature:	Signature: ....
Name:	Name: ....
Designation:	Designation: ....
Date:	Date : ....
Place:	Place: ....

FINANCIAL COLLABORATION AGREEMENT

This agreement is made this...day of .... 20.....

BETWEEN

ALPHA, a Company incorporated (hereinafter called "*Alpha*", which expression shall unless repugnant to the context or meaning thereof, include its permitted assigns and successors), of the ONE PARTY.

AND

Mr. .... residents of .... (hereinafter collectively called "*BETA*", which expression shall, unless repugnant to the context and meaning thereof include their assigns permitted and successors), of the OTHER PART,

WHEREAS *Beta*, *Alpha* and .... Affiliate of *Alpha*), with place of registry in .... (address), and having an office at .... (address), (hereinafter referred to as .... Affiliate of *Alpha*) which expression shall unless repugnant to the context thereof include its assigns and successors), have under a Memorandum of Understanding dated ...., 20.... agreed to set up a joint venture private limited company in India (hereinafter called "the company") for manufacture and marketing of garment and finishing equipment and provision of associated and incidental services;

AND, WHEREAS .... (Affiliate of *Alpha*), is engaged in the manufacture of garment and finishing equipment and is in possession of extensive know-how and technical information concerning the manufacture of such products;

AND, WHEREAS, *Beta* have requested .... (name of *Alpha*'s Affiliate), to furnish know-how and technical assistance to the Company.

AND, WHEREAS, ... (name of *Alpha*'s Affiliate), is willing to provide the Company such know-how and assistance for the manufacture of the aforesaid products;

NOW, it is hereby mutually agreed and declared as follows:

Article 1: Definitions

1.1 "*Effective Date*" shall mean the date on which this Government shall commence in accordance with Article 2, hereunder;

1.2 "*Shares*" shall mean equity shares of the Company to be subscribed for by the Parties hereto;

1.3 "*Know-how*" shall mean the technical information as defined in the technical collaboration agreement between .... (name of *Alpha*'s Affiliate) and the Company;

1.4 "*Affiliated Company*" shall mean any body corporate which is a wholly owned subsidiary of any party hereto or the holding Company wholly owning such part or a wholly owned subsidiary of such holding Company;

1.5 "*Date of Incorporation*" shall mean the date on which the certificate of incorporation of the Company is granted to it by the Registrar of Companies at .... (name of the place).

Article 2. Commencement and Term

2.1 This Agreement shall commence on the date on which approval is obtained from the Government of India and/or the Reserve bank of India to the investment in foreign currency by *Alpha* in the shares of the Company to the extent and in the manner provided herein;

2.2 This agreement shall remain in force unless terminated earlier in accordance with the provisions herein.

Article 3: Promotion of the Company

As soon as, possible after the effective date, the parties hereto agree to cause the Company to be incorporated and registered under the Companies Act, 1956 with the principal object of manufacturing and marketing of certain garment and finishing equipment, more particularly described in Annexure. I.

Article 4: Structure of the Company

4.1 The Company shall initially be formed as a private limited company. The registered office of the Company shall be located in ....(name of the place). The initial subscribed and paid up capital of the Company shall be Rs. .... (Rupees .....) and its authorised capital shall be Rs..... (Rupees....);

4.2 Subject to the provisions hereinafter appearing *Alpha* and *Beta* shall subscribe and participate in the capital of the Company at all times in the following proportions:

Beta: 50%

Alpha 50%

All further issues of capital by the company shall be subscribed and paid for by the parties hereto in the aforesaid proportions. The parties agree to maintain the above proportions at all times, except as hereinafter provided or unless otherwise agreed to in writing by the Parties.

4.3 The name of the company shall be........................ (name of the joint venture company) or such other name as is acceptable to the Registrar of Companies which shall be mutually agreed. However, in the event that the participation of *Alpha* in the equity capital of the Company falls below the percentage set out in Article 4.2 above, the Parties hereto agree to take such steps as are necessary to discontinue the use of the word "*Alpha*" in the name of the Company and to accordingly change the name of the company. The memorandum and articles of association of the Company shall be in form and substance as, mutually agreed upon and approved by *Alpha* and *Beta*.

4.4 All measures and expenses required for incorporating the Company shall be undertaken by *Beta*. These expenses shall be chargeable to the Company's account after the company is formed.

Article 5: Board of Directors of the Company

To the extent legally permissible, the articles of association of the Company shall at all times contain provisions regulating the following matters and independently of the Articles of Association, the parties hereto solemnly declare and undertake that they shall at all times ensure that:

5.1 The number of Directors of the Company shall (initially)... be two (and during the life of the company be six), it being agreed that the number of Directors shall always be an even number and that the Directors will be appointed by *BETA* and *ALPHA* in equal number and the parties hereto shall vote and procure accordingly.

5.2 The Board shall appoint as alternate Director for any Director during his absence for a period of not less than three months from India such person as is nominated or approved in writing by the party hereto represented by the original Director in whose place he is appointed.

5.3 Unless otherwise agreed to by the Directors designated and appointed by the parties hereto or their alternates, written notice of every meeting of the Board shall be received by every Director atleast 28 days in advance thereof. In the case of a Director residing outside India notification of such meeting shall be sent to him by fax atleast 28 days in advance of such meeting.

5.4 Every notice convening meeting of Board of Directors shall set out the agenda of the business to be transacted thereat in full and sufficient details and any item not included in the agenda transacted a meeting in which a nominee of the parties hereto may not be present shall not be deemed to have been carried unless the nominee of the parties hereto confirms his affirmative vote whether before or afer such meeting.

5.5 No Director shall be removed except with the approval of the party he represents.

5.6 A quorum at a Board Meeting shall be constituted only when the number of *Beta* directors (directors nominated by *Beta* or their alternates) present equals the number of *Alpha* directors (directors nominated by *Alpha* or other alternates) present, except where for a particular meeting the said requirement for quorum for their respective nominee's presence is waived in writing by any of the Directors nominated by the parties hereto respectively. If a quorum shall not be present within fifteen minutes from the time appointed for holding a meeting of the Board, the meeting shall be adjourned to the same day in the next month at the same time and place or to such other date, time and place as may be decided by the Directors present of which notice in writing be given again to all Directors.

5.7 The parties hereto agree that in case a Director dies, resigns or is otherwise removed prior to the completion of his term, then *Beta* and *Alpha* will vote on their shares and take such other action as may be necessary to appoint or cause to be appointed, as replacement for such deceased, resigned or removed Director, a Director nominated by the party who nominated by the Director whose death, resignation or removal created the vacancy, as soon. as possible after such vacancy occurs.

5.8 Subject to the restrictions contained in the Companies Act, 1956, the Board of Directors of the Company may delegate any of their powers to a committee of the Board consisting of two or more members of its body, as it thinks fit.

5.9 No resolution shall be deemed to have been duly passed by the Board or by a Committee thereof by circulation unless the resolution has been circulated in draft together with necessary papers, if any to all the directors or their alternates or to all the members of the Committee as are entitled to vote on the resolution.

5.10 The parties hereto agree at all during the effective period of this Agreement to cause their representatives on the Board of Directors of the Company to exercise their votes in consonance with and in compliance of the terms of this Agreement.

5.11 One of the directors nominated by *Beta* shall at all times be the Managing Director of the company, *Alpha*, however, shall have the right to appoint a Joint Managing Director who will be one of the Directors nominated by *Alpha*.

5.12 The day-to-day management of the affairs of the Company shall be entrusted by the Board of Directors to the Managing Director who shall manage the affairs of the Company under the supervision and control of the Board.

5.13 The Managing Director/s shall be accountable to the Board for the exercise of powers vested in him. During the month of November every calendar year, the Managing Director shall present a Business Plan for the following financial year to the Board. The Board shall pass the Business Plan with such modifications as it deems fit within 45 days. In the event that the Board fails to pass the Business Plan within the said period, the Business Plan then in force shall be deemed to have been passed for the following financial year, with an upward revision of 15% in the budgeted figures.

5.14 There shall be two (2) chairmen of the Company one each nominated by *Alpha* and by *Beta*. The Chairman nominated by *Beta* will be normally present in India and will act as Chairman of the Company except when the chairman nominated by *Alpha* visits India and attends a Board Meeting, he will be given the honour of chairing the Meeting.

5.15 The chairmen shall not have a casting vote.

Article 6: Technical Collaboration Agreement

6.1 *Alpha* agrees to provide to the company through its affiliate, *(name of Alpha's Affiliate)* the know-how and technical services which would enable the Company to manufacture certain garment finishing equipment.

6.2 The terms and conditions for the provision of the know-how and technical services will be clearly set out in a separate technical collaboration agreement between the......................*(name of Alpha's Affiliate)* and the company.

Article 7: Roles of Contracting Parties

7.1 *Beta* and *Alpha* shall give their respective assistance to the company according to their respective roles as stipulated in this Agreement that will aid the company to become a successful venture.

7.2 *Beta'* assistance to the company shall include, *inter alia*, the following aspects:

(a) business contacts in India,

(b) procurement of Indian raw materials and equipment,

(c) ensuring credit facilities in India,

(d) personnel recruitment,

(e) administrative, fiscal and legal services, and

(f) sales, distribution, marketing and servicing infrastructure at the most favourable terms.

7.3 *Alpha*'s assistance to the company shall include, *inter alia*, the following aspects:

(a) transfer of know-how,

(b) international marketing,

(c) procurement of foreign raw materials and equipment, and

(d) training the company's employees in.................. (name of the place).

7.4 Both the parties shall from time to time assign to the Company their qualified employees in such numbers and on such terms and conditions as mutually agreed upon for providing suitable services as may be necessary.

Article 8: Memorandum and Articles of Association

The Memorandum and Articles of Association of the Company shall be in such form as the parties hereto shall mutually agree.

Article 9: Subscription of Shares and Further Issue of Capital

9.1 The parties shall pay for their respective shares in the Company in cash at par and/or in kind. The calls on the shares shall be made as the Board of the Company may decide taking into account the financial requirements of the Company.

9.2 If and when the Company desires to increase the paid up share capital, the additional shares shall be offered in the first instance to the existing holders of the equity shares of the Company by way of rights issues in proportion to the capital paid-up on the shares held by them at that time.

Article 10: Trade marks

It is mutually agreed that if the Company uses any of the trade marks of *Alpha*, the Company and *Alpha* will enter into a separate agreement governing the rights and obligations of the parties with respect thereto.

Article 11: Mutual understanding on certain matters

11.1 The Company shall not without the prior written consent of *Beta* and *Alpha* pass any special resolution at any General Meeting, in particular not, to—

(a) increase or re-organize its capital,

(b) alter its memorandum and articles of association, commence any new line of business,

(c) change the name of the company,

(d) grant loans or provide credit or guarantees to another party except in the ordinary course of business, and

(e) wind-up the Company voluntarily.

11.2 The following matters which may be decided by the Board of Directors of the Company shall require the affirmative vote of at least one of the *Alpha* Directors or his/their alternate(s):

(a) approval of the annual expenditure budget of the Company;

(b) capital expenditure in relation to a single transaction in excess of an amount equal to 10% of the paid-up capital of the Company;

(c) issue of shares or debentures of the Company;

(d) aggregate borrowings in excess of an amount equal to the paid-up capital and free reserves of the Company;

(e) disposal of any fixed assets of the Company in excess of an amount equal to 2.5% of the paid-up capital of the Company;

(f) sub-licensing of the know-how to a third Party;

(g) appointment and remuneration and terms of service of Directors and senior executives of the Company, including Director (Technical), General Manager and Managing Director;

(h) appointment or removal of the Company's auditors;

(i) export of the Company's products or services;

(j) appointment of selling agents or distributors for the Company's products;

(k) appropriation/utilisation of profits of the Company;

(l) acquisition of any company by the Company and/or establishment of office of the Company in India or abroad;

(m) selling, leasing or otherwise disposing of the whole or any part of the undertaking of the Company;

(n) borrowing money from parties hereto;

(o) changing of composition of shareholding of the Company;

(p) addition/deletion in the products of the Company;

(q) filling casual vacancy in the Board of Directors;

(r) sales policy-domestic and exports;

(s) appointment of foreigners and their remuneration;

(t) purchasing or selling immovable property;

(u) giving guarantees;

(v) entering into contracts with relatives of directors or with companies in which directors are interested;

(w) entering into co-operation agreements with other Companies;

11.3 A general meeting of the Company shall be called only after giving not less than twenty eight days' notice in writing by fax and registered Air-mail.

11.4 The parties hereto shall exercise their voting powers to appoint such firm of Chartered Accountants as the statutory auditors of the Company as may be proposed by *Alpha*.

Article 12: Sale of Shares

12.1 No shares of the Company shall be transferred to any legal entity other than an affiliated company without the consent of the other shareholders and without the affiliated company agreeing to be bound by the terms and conditions of this Agreement as if he were a party hereto.

12.2 Notwithstanding provisions of clause 12.1 hereof, in the event of either party transferring the shares held by them in the Company to any person other than a party to this Agreement in accordance with the Articles of Association of the Company the transferee of such Shares shall enter into an Agreement with the parties hereto (except the Vendor of the Shares who has sold all his shares) agreeing to be bound by the terms and conditions of this Agreement as if he were a party hereto.

12.3 In the event that *Alpha* is constrained to divest its shareholding in the Company due to reasons beyond its control, including but not limited to, the change of political regime in................ (name of place), *Alpha* may transfer its shareholding to any of its affiliates it deems fit and *Beta* shall not object to such transfer, provided that all requisite approvals for such transfer are obtained and the transferee signs and abides by this Agreement.

12.4 In the event of material breach hereof by *Beta*, mismanagement by *Beta* and/or commission of financial irregularities by *Beta*, *Alpha* shall have the right to terminate the Agreement, transfer its shares in accordance with the Articles of Association, terminate the Technical Collaboration Agreement and/or terminate the Trade Mark License Agreement.

Article 13: Non-Competition

Beta shall not during the term hereof, or for a period of three years after the termination hereof, directly or indirectly, compete in any part of India either with *Alpha* or the Company in any manner whatsoever by directly or indirectly forming or being interested in any business or undertaking which is engaged in or concerned with, or enter into any contract with respect to products and services which are similar to or compete with those of the company, without prior written approval of *Alpha*.

Article 14: Agreement of the New Company

The parties hereto will have the Company upon its incorporation ratify, consent to and agree to be bound by this Agreement.

Article 15: Reporting and Inspection of Books and Records

15.1 The Company shall send monthly reports to *Alpha* regarding the affairs of the Company within the first fifteen (15) days of the following month and shall maintain close contact by means of telephone or other mode of communication in the event that *Alpha* is not able to participate in the day-to-day affairs of the Company covering such matters as may be requisited by *Alpha* including the following:

(a) Net sales.
(b) Values and changes in finished, semi-finished goods material stocks.
(c) Purchases of materials, supplies and services.
(d) Manufacturing capacities.
(e) Wages of production staff and salaries and wages of other staff.
(f) Expenses incurred.
(g) Sundry Debtors, Sundry Creditors and other debtors and creditors.
(h) Amounts of loan utilised and investments made.
(i) Amounts of depreciation chargeable.
(j) Projected cash flow for coming month.
(k) Compliance with all laws applicable to the Company and the parties by virtue of activities of the Company.
(l) Disbursement on behalf of the Company in accordance with the annual financial and Business Plan.
(m) Filing with appropriate authorities any tax and other reports of the Company required by law.

15.2 The Company shall give to each of the Parties hereto, and its representative, so long as such party shall then be a shareholder of the Company, full access during normal business hours to all of the premises, physical properties, books, records and agreements of the Company, including the right to make copies of or abstracts from any of such books, records and Agreements.

Article 16. Termination

16.1 In the event of either party committing a breach of any of the provisions of this Agreement, the other party shall, without prejudice to other rights and remedies available, have the right to terminate this Agreement, by giving the defaulting party a 30 days prior notice in writing, specifying *inter alia* the nature of the claimed default and the intention of termination unless such default is cured by the defaulting party within 30 days following receipt of the said notice.

16.2 In addition to the above, *Alpha* shall have the option of terminating this Agreement, if changes in Government policy or Government actions require *Alpha* to reduce its present shareholding in the Company, prevent *Alpha* from receiving dividends of the Company or from repatriation of capital or profits, or *Alpha* is effectively excluded from participation in the management or control of the Company, as provided in this Agreement.

16.3 Should *Alpha* exercise its option to sell its shares on terminating the Agreement, *Beta* shall purchase the shares at the fair market value as determined by the Company's auditors on the "Net assets" basis which will include a fair amount for "Goodwill".

Article 17: Exports

17.1 The Company shall not export any of its products without the consent of *Alpha*.

17.2 The parties agree that they will endeavour to export the Company's products and services as and when the international markets present a profitable opportunity, and in the opinion of *Alpha* the products and services are of *Alpha*'s international standards in terms of price, quality and delivery. In this event the Company shall appoint *Alpha* or one or several of its affiliated companies as its exclusive distributor/sole selling agent for the export of the Company's products and services, on terms and conditions to be mutually agreed to between the *Alpha* and the Company, provided that *Alpha* shall have the right to decline such appointment.

17.3 Products of the Company that are for sale outside India shall be marked only with the trade marks of *Alpha* and strictly in accordance with the instructions of *Alpha*. Such products shall not bear the name "*Beta*", either by itself or in conjunction with other names or marks.

17.4 Upon incorporation of the Company, the parties hereto shall exercise their voting powers to pass necessary resolutions to give effect to the terms of this Article.

Article 18: Confidentiality

Each of the parties (and its affiliated companies, directors and employees) and the Company shall keep secret all the know-how, trade secrets and other confidential information received by the Company from......................(name of *Alpha's* Affiliate) and shall not use any of such confidential information except as previously authorized in writing by *Alpha* and subject to such terms and conditions as are imposed by *Alpha*. This obligation shall survive termination of this Agreement, but shall cease to apply to any information after it has come into the public domain.

Article 19: *Force majeure*

If, the performance of the obligations under this Agreement is prevented by reason of any contingencies, which could not have been reasonably avoided and are beyond the control of the parties, the party so affected shall not be liable to the other for damages to the extent of such prevention. Such contingencies include strikes of workers, fire, flood, explosion, riots sabotage, acts of God and war or enemy action.

Article 20: Notices

Any notice required or permitted to be given hereunder shall be in writing and sent by registered air mail, postage pre-paid, and shall be addressed to the parties at the following addresses or such other addresses as either of the parties may from time to time designate by notice in writing to the other. The notice shall be deemed to be served when received.

Alpha:

Beta:

Article 21: Arbitration

21.1 In the event, that any dispute or differences arises out of this Agreement or in relation thereto, including any dispute relating to its validity or effect, each of *Alpha* and *Beta* shall immediately appoint one high ranking executive of any of their companies as their representative for the purpose of this clause. The two representatives shall meet and try to resolve the dispute or disputes amicably.

21.2 In the event that the disputes or differences are not resolved for a period of two weeks from the date of arising of the dispute or difference, the parties will try to resolve the dispute through mediation for a further period of two weeks by appointing a mediator, who shall be a mutually acceptable and respectable person. If no such person(s) is/are appointed or are able to decide to parties satisfaction within the aforesaid period, then clause 22.3 of this Agreement will apply.

21.3 In the event that the dispute or difference is not resolved under Article 22.1 or 22.2 such dispute or difference shall be settled finally in accordance with the Rules of the........................ (name of the national arbitration body). The arbitration proceedings shall be initiated by the party asking for arbitration submitting its request for arbitration to the Secretariat of the Court. The other party shall nominate its arbitrator in its answer to the request for arbitration, which shall be supplied to the party asking for arbitration and the Court within a period of thirty days of the receipt of the request for arbitration. The two arbitrators thus appointed shall within a further period of thirty days elect the Chairman of the Arbitration Tribunal. In the event that the other party should fail to appoint its arbitrator within the thirty days or in the event the two arbitrators appointed for the parties do not agree on the appointment of the Chairman within thirty days of their appointment the court shall make the appointment of the Chairman or the appointment of one the arbitrators not timely made or as the case may be, and any such appointment shall be final and binding upon the parties. The venue of the arbitration shall be in................... (name of the place). The parties shall contribute in equal proportion towards the expenses of the arbitration proceedings. However the Arbitration Tribunal shall decide the proportion in which the parties are to bear the expenses ultimately.

21.4 For the purpose of obtaining any interim relief from the Courts, arbitration proceedings shall be deemed to have commenced from the date of arising of the dispute or difference/notice as per clause 22.1

Article 22: Severability

The invalidity of any portion of this Agreement shall not affect the remaining portions of this Agreement or any part thereof, and this Agreement shall be construed, as if such invalid portion or portions had not been inserted therein.

Article 23: Government Approvals

23.1 *Beta* and *Alpha* shall use their best efforts to obtain from the appropriate agencies of the Indian and .... Governments all the consents and approvals required for the execution and performance of this agreement by the Company.

23.2 In the event that such consents and approvals are not obtained within one hundred and eighty (180) days from the date of this Agreement, and unless extension of the said period is agreed upon in writing by *Beta* and *Alpha*, either party shall have the right to declare this Agreement *null* and *void*.

IN WITNESS WHEREOF, the parties hereto have set and subscribed their respective hands and seals the day and year first hereinabove written.

For and on behalf of	For and on behalf of
Alpha	*Beta*
Signature:	Signature: ....
Name:	Name: ....
Designation:	Designation: ....
Date:	Date: ....
Place:	Place: ....

MARKETING ASSISTANCE AGREEMENT

This Agreement is made at .... (place) on this.................... day of 20....

BETWEEN

Alpha, a Company registered under the Companies Act, 1956 and having its office at .... (place) through its authorised signatory (hereinafter referred to as the "Company", which expression shall include, unless repugnant to the meaning or context thereof, its successors and permitted assigns) of the ONE PART;

AND

Delta (Name of The Omega Company's Affiliate), a company registered under the laws of ....(country), and having its registered office at .... through its authorized signatory (hereinafter referred to as "*Delta*", which expression shall include, unless repugnant to the meaning or context thereof, its successors group companies, and permitted assigns) of the OTHER PART.

(The Company and *Delta* are collectively referred to as "Parties" and individually a "Party").

WHEREAS

A. The Company is a joint venture between Alpha Ltd. (a public limited company incorporated in India and having its registered office at .... (address), hereinafter referred to as "*Alpha*", which expression shall include, unless repugnant to the meaning or context thereof, its successors and permitted assigns), and *Delta*, managed in accordance with a Shareholders' Agreement among *Alpha*, *Delta* and the Company being executed simultaneously herewith (the "Shareholders' Agreement"), and is engaged in the activity of manufacturing and selling multi-leaf springs, parabolic springs, and spring assemblies for automotive suspension systems and commercial vehicle suspension systems.

B. *Delta* is engaged in the business of manufacturing and selling suspension systems and components, such as, multi-leaf springs, parabolic springs, air suspension springs and systems and spring assemblies for commercial vehicles, and has substantial marketing experience and an established worldwide marketing network.

C. For the purpose of promoting and establishing its business in the Territory (as defined hereinafter), the Company is desirous of availing marketing assistance from *Delta* and *Delta* is agreeable to rendering the same to the Company.

NOW THEREFORE, in consideration of the mutual promises contained herein and intending to, be legally bound, the Parties have agreed as follows:

1. Definitions

In this Agreement the following expressions shall have, where the context so admits, the meanings assigned thereto:—

1.1 *"Agreement"* shall mean this Marketing Assistance Agreement;

1.2 *"Assistance"* shall mean the marketing and sales promotion and customer development services as more elaborately described in Annexure A hereto;

1.3 *"Effective Date"* shall mean the Effective Date of the Shareholders' Agreement;

1.4 *"Products"* shall mean leaf springs, parabolic springs, and spring assemblies for automotive suspension systems and commercial vehicle suspension systems and any other products for commercial vehicles that may be mutually agreed by the Parties from time to time;

1.5 *"Territory"* shall mean the territory allotted to *Delta* under the market matrix provided in Annexure B hereto;

1.6 *"Net Price"* shall mean the invoice price of the Products sold by the Company excluding any applicable Indian taxes and duties, transportation costs and special packing costs in respect of the Products.

2. Scope of Work

Delta hereby agrees to provide to the Company, and the Company hereby agrees to avail, the Assistance in the Territory in respect of the Products in the manner and on the terms and conditions hereinafter contained in a clause.

3. Assignment and Sub-contracting

3.1 Neither of the Parties hereto shall be entitled to assign this Agreement or any of their rights, powers, benefits, obligations and/or duties hereunder without the prior written consent of the other Party.

3.2 *Delta* shall by itself, or, at its discretion, through a sub-contractor appointed by it, render the Assistance and discharge its obligations and duties under this Agreement; provided that such sub-contractors shall be absolutely accountable to *Delta*.

3.3 *Delta* shall be absolutely responsible and liable for all acts and omissions of any such sub-contractors and shall always keep and hold the Company harmless and indemnified in this regard provided that the Company shall not be entitled to directly deal or contract with such sub-contractors without the express, written consent of *Delta*. In case of such direct dealing by the Company with the sub-contractors, the Company shall be absolutely responsible for all the acts and omissions of the sub-contractors, and for all the costs and expenses involved. The Company shall keep and hold *Delta* harmless and indemnified in case of any direct dealing by the Company with the sub-contractors.

3.4 The Company may, at its sole option and at its sole cost and responsibility, acquire by purchase, lease or otherwise any warehouse or depot or branch office other than the warehouses or depots or branches forming part of the existing marketing network of *Delta*. The obligations of *Delta* under this Agreement shall not extend to such warehouses, depots or branch offices unless otherwise agreed to between the Parties.

4. Orders

4.1 All orders from customers shall be addressed and forwarded to the appropriate office of the Company and shall be subject to acceptance by the Company. Immediately upon acceptance of an order, the Company shall intimate HIC and forward a copy of the accepted order to *Delta*. Subject to clause 4.4, the Company shall have the absolute discretion to decline or accept any order. No remuneration shall be due to *Delta* on orders not accepted by the Company.

4.2 On acceptance of any order by the Company from customers, all dealings between the *Alpha* and the customers shall be on a principal to principal basis.

4.3 Upon the acceptance of an order by the Company, the Company shall be responsible to the customer for the execution of, and supplies against, the order in accordance with its terms and conditions. *Delta* shall not, to any extent, be liable or responsible therefore.

4.4 Notwithstanding anything contained in this Agreement, the Company shall not be entitled to refuse an order from a customer referred to the Company by *Delta* as a result of the assistance other than on the following grounds:

(i) if the manufacture or sale of the product for which the order is placed has been discontinued by the Company;

(ii) if sale pursuant to such an order would violate applicable laws;

---

1. *Remuneration (Clause 5)*

    Sub-clause (i) of clause 5.1.1 - Details of any existing marketing arrangements with *Delta* with respect to the .... Unit should be inserted in the Agreement.

    Please note that there should be a mention of this lumpsum consideration in the minutes of the meeting between the two joint venture partners. Has the lump sum consideration been negotiated? What would be the terms of this payment? These should be inserted in the Agreement.

5. Remuneration

5.1.1 In consideration of the Assistance provided by *Delta* under this Agreement, and upon acceptance by the Company of the orders resulting therefrom, *Delta* shall be entitled to a fee equivalent to 2½ (two and a half) percent of the Net Price of the Products under an order accepted by the Company[1].

5.1.2 *Delta* shall raise its invoice for the fees under clause 5.1.1 within.................... days of an order being accepted by the Company. The fee shall be paid by the Company within 30 days of the date of such invoice in respect of the fee. Backup documentation, such as.................... shall be provided with each invoice.

5.1.3 In addition to the payments under clause 5.1.1, *Delta* shall be entitled to be reimbursed by the Company in respect of any costs and expenses incurred by *Delta* with the prior written approval of the Company. Such reimbursable costs and expenses shall be included in the invoice raised by *Delta* under clause 5.1.2 and shall be paid by the Company along with the fee[1].

5.1.4 All payments under this Agreement to *Delta* shall be made in U.S. Dollars after deduction of applicable taxes at the address of *Delta* as set forth in this Agreement.

5.1.5 The payments as provided for in this Agreement shall at all times be subject to being permitted and valid under applicable policies, laws, orders, and regulations.

5.1.6 It is expressly clarified that no remuneration shall be payable by the Company to *Delta* on a direct sale by the Company to *Delta*.

6. Terms and Shipments

6.1 *Delta* shall endeavour to ensure that orders procured by it as a result of the assistance include the following terms:

(i) All shipments of the products to the customers shall be made in accordance with the Company's standard terms and conditions as amended and provided to *Delta* from time to time.

7. Obligations of Delta

7.1 *Delta* undertakes to (a) purchase from the Company, and/or (b) procure orders for the Company in respect of, the Products, in the aggregate value of (x) .... (amount) during the period of 12 months commencing from the effective date, and (y) .... (amount) during the immediately following period of 12 months.

---

1. The basis for calculation of the additional payment due to the Company for "sales by the *Alpha* to customers existing on the date of the transfer of the undertaking" is not clear. Would the calculation be based on the balance of the trade debtors account? Which date would be used as a cut-off date of the transfer of undertaking agreement or the closing pursuant thereto?

   Moreover, in view of the lump sum consideration under sub-clause (i) of clause 5.1, no additional consideration should be payable for the sales 'existing on the date of the transfer'.

7.2 The orders procured by *Delta* for the Company will be subject to a mutual agreement between the Parties with respect to all significant factors in the production process.

7.3 The value of orders procured by *Delta* for the Company which comply with clause 6.1, but which are not accepted by the Company for reasons other than those stated under sub-clauses (i) and (ii) of clause 4.4, shall reduce the obligation of *Delta* to procure orders for, or purchase from, the Company under clause 7.1.

7.4 *Delta* further undertakes to:
  (i) co-operate to the fullest extent with the Company in implementing its sales programmes and directions;
  (ii) maintain a sales organisation capable of fulfilling its obligations under this Agreement;
  (iii) assist the Company in securing customers' agreement to the Company's standard terms and conditions of sale;
  (iv) notify the Company if *Delta* is aware that any customer is purchasing the Company's products for resale or for unlawful use;
  (v) furnish to the Company such detailed market analysis and reports as the Company may reasonably request or as may be reasonably and materially necessary to keep the Company informed of such matters.

7.5 *Delta* shall designate a person responsible as in charge of all Assistance to the Company and for day to day co-ordination between the Company and *Delta*.

7.6 Forecasts of Purchases; Reports to be furnished:
  (i) *Delta* shall furnish the Company, on a monthly basis, with a statement of orders for the Products procured by *Delta* during the preceding calendar month.
  (ii) HIC shall also furnish to *Alpha* mid-year and year-end such other reports or information as *Alpha* may reasonably request concerning the position of sale of the products in the Territory and information on the customers.
  (iii) HIC shall also furnish to *Alpha* reports and analysis on competitors activities at mutually agreed frequencies.

8. (Intentionally left Blank).

9. Non Competition

(i) The Parties recognize that the scope of work as provided in clause 2 hereinabove shall be in accordance with the market matrix provided in Annexure B hereto.

(ii) *Delta* shall not solicit customers for the products outside the territory without the prior written consent of the Company.

(iii) The Company shall not directly or through any third party solicit business in respect of the products from any customers in the territory.

10. Confidentiality

10.1 Each of the Parties recognizes, accepts and agrees that all information obtained or disclosed, including but not limited to all data, documents, applications, papers, statements, slips, programmes, plans and/or any business/customer information, marketing strategies/plans and any and all other trade secrets, confidential knowledge or information of either Party relating to its business, practices and procedures (hereinafter collectively referred to as "*Information*") which may be provided or communicated by such Party to the other Party in connection with this Agreement and/or in the course of performance under this Agreement, is, shall be and shall remain the sole property of the Party providing such Information and shall be of a strictly private and confidential nature and shall be treated as confidential by the other Party.

10.2 During the term of this Agreement and thereafter, neither Party shall make use of any such Information for any purpose whatsoever which is not necessary for the discharge of its obligations under this Agreement, or to the disadvantage of the Party providing such Information, nor shall the Party receiving such Information divulge it to any one other than the Party providing the Information or persons designated by such Party.

10.3 All Information shall be returned forthwith by the Party receiving such Information to the Party providing the Information on the expiry or termination of this Agreement:

Provided that the Party receiving such Information shall, upon demand by the Party providing it at any time during the term of this Agreement, return to the Party providing it, any and all Information.

10.4 The obligations of each of the Parties contained in this clause shall continue for the term of this Agreement and five (5) years after the termination of this Agreement but shall not apply to any Information which: (a) is or hereafter comes into the public domain otherwise than through a breach by any Party of its obligations under this Agreement; (b) is, at the time of disclosure, already known to the Party receiving the Information as evidenced by such Party's written documentation; (c) is independently developed by employees of the Party receiving the Information who have not had access to or received any such Information under this Agreement; or (d) is required to be disclosed for the purpose of providing Assistance hereunder subject to the other Party's prior consent to the same:

Provided, however, that nothing contained in this clause shall prevent any Party from disclosing such Information to the extent required in or in connection with legal proceedings arising out of this Agreement or any matter relating to or in connection therewith.

10.5 Neither Party shall issue any public statement concerning these arrangements or disclose the contents hereof or matters related thereto to the public or any third party except with the express prior written approval of the other Party or except as required under applicable law.

10.6 The provisions of this clause shall survive the termination or expiry of this Agreement.

11. Exclusivity

11.1 It is expressly agreed between the Parties that the arrangement with *Delta* under this Agreement is on an exclusive basis. The Company shall not enter in to any arrangement and/or Agreement with respect to the Assistance contemplated herein in the Territory with any other person(s)/entity(ies) any time during the currency of this Agreement without prior written consent of *Delta*.

11.2 *Delta* confirms and agrees not to undertake any assignment or enter into any arrangement to provide services similar to the Assistance hereunder with respect to products similar to the Products to any person(s)/entity(ies) in India, directly or indirectly engaged in activities competing to or similar to that of the Company during the term of this Agreement.

12. Principal to Principal Relationship

12.1 This Agreement is being entered into on a principal to principal basis and it shall not create any employer-employee relationship; nor shall this Agreement be deemed to create any partnership, joint venture, agency, association or trust between the Company and *Delta* or their representatives and employees. All employees, workers, consultants and the like engaged by *Delta* to render Assistance to the Company hereunder shall be in the sole employment of *Delta* and *Delta* shall be solely responsible for their salaries, wages, statutory payments and the like. The Company shall not be liable for any payment or claim or compensation (including but not limited to compensation on account of injury/death/termination) of any nature to such employees, workers and consultants at any point of time during the currency of this Agreement or after its termination.

12.2 *Delta* shall not have the authority to direct the actions of any employee of the Company or to bind the Company to any agreement with any third party without the prior consent of the Company.

12.3 *Delta* shall have no right to enter into any contracts or commitments in the name of or on behalf of the Company, or to bind the Company in any respect whatsoever. In addition, *Delta* shall not obligate or purport to obligate the Company by issuing or making any warranties or guarantees with respect to the Products to any third party.

13. Invalid Provisions

If any provision of this Agreement or any part thereof is held by a court of competent jurisdiction to be invalid or is rendered void, illegal or un-enforceable in any respect under any law, the same shall be replaced and any omission shall be remedied by a corresponding provision which comes as close as legally and commercially possible to the express or implied intention of the Parties and the validity, legality and enforceability of the remaining provision shall not in any way be affected or impaired thereby.

14. Term and Termination

14.1 This Agreement shall take effect and become binding upon the Parties on the Effective Date and shall remain in full force and effect until the termination of the Shareholders' Agreement.

14.2 Notwithstanding anything contained in this Agreement, and without prejudice to its other rights in law or equity and without any liability and judicial intervention, this Agreement may be terminated by the Party not in default (the "Non-Defaulting Party") by giving a thirty (30) days' written notice to the Party in default (the "Defaulting Party") if any of the following events (hereinafter referred to as an "Event of Default") occurs:

(a) Either Party commits a breach of this Agreement and such breach, if capable of remedy, is not remedied by the Defaulting Party within the aforesaid thirty (30) days' notice period;

(b) Any change in control of either Party. For the purpose of this sub-clause, the Party in respect of which a change in control occurs will be deemed to be the Defaulting Party; or

(c) If either Party goes into liquidation (other than a voluntary liquidation for the purposes of reconstruction and where all the rights and obligations are validly assigned), administration or receivership or ceases to carry on its business or is otherwise insolvent or unable to pay its debts on time.

14.3 This Agreement may be terminated by the mutual written consent of the Parties.

14.4 Upon termination of this Agreement for whatever reason, all the rights and obligations of the Parties hereunder shall cease.

15. Indemnification

Delta shall indemnify and hold harmless the Company, its directors, officers, employees, customers, subsidiaries, affiliates, sub-contractors and assignees, or any of them, from and against:

(i) Any losses, damages, liabilities, expenses (including reasonable attorney's fees) costs, claims, suits, demands, actions, causes of action, proceedings, judgements, assessments, deficiencies and charges resulting from third Party claims occasioned by, arising out of or resulting from any material misrepresentation of any of the terms of this Agreement by *Delta* to the customers; and

(ii) All costs resulting from, caused by, relating to or arising out of performance by *Delta* of its obligations hereunder, and negligent acts or omissions or wilful misconduct by *Delta* in connection with the conduct of *Delta*'s performance of its obligations hereunder, including any assertions regarding unfair competition or violations of laws, rules or regulations by the customers.

(iii) Any claims or demands made against the Company or its employees or shareholders by any sub-contractors, employees, workers, consultants and the like engaged by *Delta* in connection with the Assistance hereunder.

16. Mutual Representations

16.1 Each Party hereto represents and warrants to the other that:

(i) it has full legal power and authority to carry on its business and to enter into this Agreement and perform all of its obligations hereunder; and

(ii) neither the execution nor delivery of this Agreement, nor the fulfilment nor compliance with the terms and provisions hereof; (a) will conflict with, or result in a breach of, terms, conditions or provisions of, or constitute a default under, or result in any violation of its charter or by-law, if any, or any agreement, restrictions, instrument, order, judgement, decree, statute, law, rule or regulation to which it is subject, or (b) require any consent, approval or other action by any court or administrative or Governmental body.

16.2 Each of the Parties agrees, in performing its obligations under this Agreement, to comply with all applicable laws, rules, regulations and Government orders.

16.3 Each of the Parties agrees that no action (or failure to take action) by it or any of its employees, agents or representatives shall cause the other Party to violate or incur any penalty or loss of taxable benefits under any applicable laws, rules or regulations under the .... Export Administration Act, the Foreign Corrupt Practices Act, and the anti-boycott provisions of the Internal Revenue Code in effect as of the date of this Agreement and as amended from time to time. Each Party represents and warrants that neither it, nor any of its owners, officers, directors, employees, agents or representatives is (or will be at any time during the term of this Agreement) an official agent or employee of, or in any manner connected with, any Government or any entity, agency, instrumentality of sub-division of such Government, or any corporation or other entity owned or controlled thereby. Further, no part of any payment made by either Party to the other under this Agreement shall be illegally paid to or accrue for the benefit of, directly or indirectly, any Government or any entity, agency, instrumentality or sub-division of such Government, or any corporation or other entity owned or controlled thereby. Further, neither Party shall pay or permit the payment of directly or indirectly, any part of any payments made by the other under this Agreement to any such person.

16.4 Each Party acknowledges that certain laws, customary business ethics and corporate policies of the other, prohibit offers, promises or payments, directly or indirectly, to customers or other parties for the purpose of kick-backs, commercial bribes or other legally impermissible, unjust or unfair benefits or trade practices. Each Party agrees that no part of its fees paid hereunder shall be offered, promised or paid, directly or indirectly, in any such manner for the benefit or any other person, including any owner, officer, director, employee, agent or representative (including family members thereof) of a customer.

17. Governing Laws and Arbitration

17.1 Any dispute, difference, controversy or claim ("Dispute") arising between the Parties out of or in relation to or in connection with this Agreement, of the breach, termination, effect, validity, interpretation or application of this Agreement or as to their rights, duties or liabilities thereunder, or as to any act, matter or thing arising out of, consequent to or in connection with this Agreement, shall be settled by the Parties by mutual negotiations and agreement. If, for any reason, such Dispute cannot be resolved amicably by the Parties, the same shall then be referred to and settled by way of arbitration proceedings in accordance with the Arbitration and Conciliation Act, 1996 or any subsequent enactment or amendment thereto (the "Arbitration Act"). Each of the Parties shall appoint an arbitrator within ..... days of the receipt by a Party of the other Party's request to initiate arbitration. The two arbitrators so appointed shall then jointly appoint a third arbitrator within ..... days of the date of appointment of the second arbitrator, such third arbitrator shall act as the Chairman of the tribunal. Arbitrators not appointed within the time limit set forth in the preceding sentence shall be appointed in accordance with the Arbitration Act. The decision of the Arbitrators shall be final and binding upon the Parties. The venue of arbitration proceedings shall be .... (place). The language of the arbitration and the award shall be English.

17.2 This Agreement shall be construed in accordance with the law of India.

18. *Force Majeure*

Notwithstanding anything to the contrary in this Agreement, neither Party shall be liable by reason of failure or delay in the performance of its duties and obligations under this Agreement if such failure or delay is caused by acts of God, strikes, lockouts, war, riots, embargoes, civil commotion, any orders of governmental, quasi-governmental or local authorities, or any other similar cause beyond its control and without its fault or negligence.

19. Notice

All notices required or permitted hereunder shall be in writing and in the English language and shall be sent by internationally recognised courier or by facsimile transmission (with confirming facsimile receipt) addressed to the address of each Party set forth below, or to such other address as such other Party shall have communicated to the other Party in writing. Notice shall be deemed to have been served when received (and in case of a facsimile transmission, provided that a confirming copy is sent to the other Party, in accordance with the non-facsimile notice delivery requirements).

If to *Delta*:

....
....

If to the Company:

....
....

20. No Waiver

Save where this Agreement expressly provides, neither Party shall be deemed to have waived any right, power, privilege or remedy under this Agreement unless such Party shall have delivered to the other Party a written waiver signed by an authorised officer of such waiving Party. No failure or delay on the part of either Party in exercising any right, power, privilege or remedy hereunder shall operate as a waiver, default or acquiescence thereof, nor shall any waiver on the part of either Party of any right, power, privilege or remedy hereunder operate as a waiver of any other right, power, privilege or remedy, nor shall any single or partial exercise of any right, power, privilege or remedy hereunder preclude any other or further exercise thereof or the exercise of any other right, power, privilege or remedy hereunder.

21. Miscellaneous

21.1 This Agreement and the Schedules, Annexures and Appendices hereto represent the entire Agreement between the Parties as to the subject matter hereof and supersede all prior understandings between the Parties on the subject-matter hereof.

21.2 No amendments and/or modifications to this Agreement shall be valid unless executed in writing and signed by both Parties.

21.3 The Schedules, Annexures and Appendices attached to this Agreement form a part of this Agreement.

21.4 Termination of this Agreement for any cause whatsoever shall not release a Party from any liability which, at the time of termination, has already accrued to the other Party or which may thereafter accrue in respect of any act or omission prior to such termination.

21.5 Article headings are inserted for convenience of reference only and shall not be deemed to affect the interpretation of this Agreement or of any clause.

21.6 Each Party shall co-operate with the other and execute and deliver to the other such instruments and documents and take such other actions as may be reasonably requested from time to time in order to carry out, give effect to and confirm their rights and the intended purpose of this Agreement.

21.7 No remedy conferred by any of the provisions of this Agreement is intended to be exclusive of any other remedy which is otherwise available at law, in equity, by statute or otherwise, or any other remedy given hereunder or now or hereafter existing at law, in equity, by statute, or otherwise, except as stated to the contrary in this Agreement. The election of any one or more of such remedies by any of the Parties hereto shall not constitute a waiver by such Party of the right to pursue any other available remedy.

21.8 The provisions of the following clauses of this Agreement shall survive the termination or expiry hereof:

IN WITNESS WHEREOF, the parties hereto have signed this Agreement on the day and year first above written.

Signed and delivered by

For and on behalf of *Delta*   For and on behalf of the Company

By: .... By: ....
Title: .... Title: ....

ANNEXURE A

(I) The Assistance

Delta shall provide the Assistance to the Company in the Territory in the field of marketing and sales promotion and customer development in respect of the Products including but not limited to the following:—

1. Complete liaison on behalf of the Company with the customers for the Company's customer development including regular contacts with their divisions or departments such as Engineering, Product Development, Purchasing, Supplier/Vendor Development and with all plants of the customers receiving components from the Company.
2. Assisting the Company in price fixation, quotation, submission and all sample and PPAP submissions to customers, and assistance in scheduling, customs clearing, warehousing and shipping information:

    Provided, however, that the Company shall pay *Delta* a reasonable fee for storing Products at any of its facilities.
3. Customer relations and service including negotiations for claim settlements. Also acting as the liaison between the overseas warehouse and the customers to ensure customer satisfaction with delivery schedules and inventory levels.
4. Arranging on time deliveries of Products to the customers.
5. Keeping sales and other relevant records.
6. Arranging timely submission and transmission of information to the Company including but not limited to the customer's production Schedules, customer off-take reports, warehouse inventory levels, payment advises, rejection reports, customer's new model development reports, marketing surveys or any other intimation from the customers or the warehouse or any other source directly relevant to the sale of Products by the Company.
7. Monitor safe receipts and clearances of Products exported by the Company.
8. Arranging for any sorting of components on the instruction of the Company or the customer and on the Company's request arranging for the rework, if any, the cost of which will be borne by the Company.
9. Education of the Company's sales staff.

ANNEXURE-B

MARKET MATRIX

Description	North America	Europe	India	Rest of World
Class 5-8 (Medium & Heavy OEMs)				
Class 1-4 Light duty OEM				

Class 5-8

After market

Class 1-4

After market

Any other

* *Alpha* and *Delta* jointly in these territories (marked *) on mutually agreeable terms.

OFFICE REFURBISHMENT AGREEMENT

THIS OFFICE REFURBISHMENT AGREEMENT is executed at .... (name of place) .... (name of state) on this .... day of .... 20....

BETWEEN

Alpha, a Company registered under the provisions of the Indian Companies Act, 1956, having its registered office c/o .... (address) .... name of state) (hereinafter referred to as the 'EMPLOYER', which expression shall, unless repugnant to the context or meaning thereof, mean and include its successors in title, legal representatives, permitted assigns, associates, affiliates, subsidiaries, group companies) of the ONE PART.

AND

Beta, a... having its principal place of business at ....(Address)..................(name of place) (hereinafter referred to as the 'VENDOR', which expression shall, unless repugnant to the context or meaning thereof, mean and include its successors in title, legal representatives, permitted assigns) of the OTHER PART.

The Employer and the Vendor shall hereinafter individually be referred to as the "Party" and collectively as the "Parties".

WHEREAS the Employer has entered into a Lease Agreement dated .... 20.... (hereinafter the "Lease Agreement") with .... (name), resident of .... (address), ... (name of state), for the lease of the premises situated at .... (address) .... (name of State) consisting of a building comprising of the basement admeasuring .... sq. ft. the ground floor admeasuring .... sq. ft. the first floor admeasuring .... sq.ft, and the second floor admeasuring .... sq. ft. having a total built up area of .... sq .ft. and other areas such as access area, rear lawns and terrace (hereinafter the "Demised Premises");

WHEREAS the Employer has the right, under the Lease Agreement, at its own cost and expense, to furnish and decorate the Demised Premises for the purposes of its business operations;

WHEREAS the Employer has expressed its desire to carry out certain refurbishment and decoration works at the Demised Premises;

WHEREAS the Vendor has prepared and presented to the Employer Drawings (as defined hereinbelow), a Bill of Quantities (as defined hereinbelow) with respect to the Works (as defined hereinbelow), which have been accepted by the Employer;

WHEREAS the Employer has prepared and presented to the Vendor a Schedule of Works (as defined hereinbelow), which has been accepted by the Vendor;

WHEREAS on the basis of the Drawings, the Bill of Quantities and the Schedule of Works, and in accordance with the terms of this Agreement, the Employer now wishes the Vendor to carry out the Works and the Vendor wishes to carry out the Works in connection with the Demised Premises;

NOW, THEREFORE THIS AGREEMENT WITNESSETH AND IT IS HEREBY AGREED BY AND BETWEEN THE PARTIES HERETO AS HEREUNDER:

I. Definitions and Interpretation

1. Definitions

1.1 Unless otherwise required by the context, the following capitalized terms, when used in this Agreement, shall have the meanings set forth below (with the terms defined in the singular having the corresponding meaning when used in the plural and *vice versa*):

"Agreement" shall mean this Office Refurbishment Agreement.

"Bill of Quantities" shall mean the bill prepared by the Vendor and presented to the Employer relating to the Items and Materials proposed to be utilised, subject to the Employer's approval in accordance with Article .... hereof, for and in carrying out the Works in connection with the Demised Premises, their quantities, qualities, specifications, the costs and prices thereof, etc., attached hereto as *Annexure 'A'*.

"Completion Date" shall have the meaning set forth in clause 12.1.2 hereinbelow.

"Demised Premises" shall have the meaning set forth in the Recitals hereinabove.

"Drawings" shall mean the set of drawings, floor plans, illustrations, diagrams and representations prepared by the Vendor and presented to the Employer representing the proposed Works to be carried out in connection with the Demised Premises, attached hereto as *Annexure 'B'*.

"Effective Date" shall mean the date of execution of this Agreement by both the Parties.

"Items and Materials" shall mean any and all raw and other materials, including, but not limited to, wood, ply, particle boards, block boards, paints,

laminates, varnishes, polishes, nuts, bolts, brick, mortar, cement, blinds, wiring, furniture, fixtures, fittings, units, items, electronic goods, items and components, furnishings, furbishing etc., proposed to be utilised for and in carrying out the Works in connection with the Demised Premises.

"Lease Agreement" shall have the meaning set forth in the Recitals hereinabove.

"New Price" shall have the meaning set forth in clause 9.1.4 herein below.

"Organisational" shall mean, with respect to either Party, its documents, memorandum of association, articles of association, charter, bye-laws and any and all other documents of similar venture, as in effect at the relevant time.

"Price" shall have the meaning set forth in clause 9.1.1 hereinbelow.

"Schedule of Works" shall mean the proposed schedule of the Works to be carried out in connection with the Demised Premises prepared by the Employer and presented to the Vendor, attached hereto as *Annexure 'C'*.

"Site" shall mean the Demised Premises.

"Stage(s)" shall have the meaning set forth in clause 3.1 hereinbelow.

"Term" shall have the meaning set forth in clause 12.1.1 hereinbelow.

"Works" shall mean the refurbishment and redecoration works to be carried out in connection with the Demised Premises, in accordance with the Drawings, the Bill of Quantities and the Schedule of Works.

1.2 Other References

Unless otherwise provided or unless the context clearly requires otherwise, all references to "Articles" and "Clauses" are to Articles and Clauses of this Agreement, and all references to "Annexures", "Exhibits" or "Schedules" are to Annexures, Exhibits and Schedules to this Agreement, each of which is an integral part of this Agreement for all purposes; references to either gender include the other; all uses of "include" or "including" mean without limitation.

II. Scope of Works

2.1 The Vendor agrees, on the terms and conditions stated hereinbelow, to carry out the Works in accordance with the Drawings, the Bill of Quantities and the Schedule of Works in such a manner as to conform to the specifications approved or provided by the Employer therefor, and to ensure that the refurbished and redecorated Demised Premises are fit for the intended use and purpose thereof, as indicated by the Employer and of a standard and quality fit for the purposes of and use by a software technology centre of international standards and standing.

2.2 The Vendor agrees to carry out and execute, as the Works, all works, acts, etc., which may be required for and/or be incidental to ensuring that the refurbished and re-decorated Demised Premises conform to the specifications approved or provided by the Employer therefor, with the exception only of those works, acts, etc., listed in *Annexure 'D'* attached hereto.

2.3 The Vendor agrees that, in carrying out the Works, they shall confine their operations to the space designated by the Employer at the Demised Premises therefor.

2.4 The Parties agree that any further or additional works and/or deviation in the Works shall be carried out by the Vendor only upon the express written request and authorisation by the Employer therefor, and as may be mutually agreed to between the Parties in writing from time to time. The cost and expense of such further and additional Works and/or deviation in the Works shall be adjusted into the Price.

III. Schedule of the Works

3.1 Payments for the Works carried out shall be made upon completion of the following stages, more particularly described in the Schedule of Works attached hereto as *Annexure 'C'*: (i) commencement; (ii) 40%, (iii) 70%; (iv) 90%; and (v) completion ("Stage(s)")

3.2 The Vendor shall notify the Employer in writing of the completion of each Stage of the Works.

3.3 Subject to Articles VIII and IX, the payment of the price of the Works shall be paid for each Stage of the Works upon completion of that Stage of the Works.

IV. Employer Approvals for Line outs, Mock-UPS, Samples, etc.

4.1 The Vendor agrees that, before the commencement of the Works, or any part of the Works, as the case may be, at the Site, they shall draw a line out on the Site or part of the Site, as the case may be, representing the Works or part of the Works proposed to be carried out on the Site or part of the Site with paper tape fixed on to the floor of the Site or part of the Site, and shall have the same approved by the Employer. The Vendor agrees that they shall not commence the Works or any part of the Works, as the case may be, without the Employer's prior written approval for such line out(s).

4.2 The Vendor agrees that, before the commencement of the Works, or any part of the Works, as the case may be, they shall prepare and present to the Employer for their approval, life-size mock-ups and samples of the Works or any part of the Works, and of any and all Items and Materials proposed to be utilised for and in connection with carrying out the Works. In the event such life-size mock-ups and samples are impractical or unfeasible, the Vendor may, with the prior written permission of the Employer, prepare and present to the Employer for their approval, smaller mock-ups and samples. The Vendor agrees that they shall not commence the Works or any part of the Works, as the case may be, without the Employer's prior written approval for such mock-ups and samples.

4.3 The Vendor agrees that, before the commencement of the Works, or any part of the Works, as the case may be, they shall present to the Employer for their approval, all the specifications with regards to any and all Items and Materials proposed to be utilised for and in carrying out the Works, including, but not limited to, quality, quantity, colour, shade, size, dimensions, polish, painting, laminates and the like thereof or with respect thereto. The Vendor agrees that they shall not commence the Works or any part of the Works, as the case may be, without the Employer's prior written approval for the above specifications.

4.4 In the event the Employer does not grant their approval for any or all of the above line out, mock-ups and samples, and specifications for and in connection with the Works, any part of the Works, and Items and Materials to be utilised therefor or therein, the same shall be substituted by the Vendor by line outs, mock-ups and samples and Items and Materials of the same, or similar, quality, quantity and specifications, subject, once again, to the Employer's approval therefor in accordance with this Article.

4.5 In the event the Vendor wishes to substitute the Works, any part of the Works, and/or any Items and Materials already approved by the Employer, the Vendor agrees to present such substituted Works, any part of the Works, and/or Items and Materials to the Employer for their approval in accordance with the provisions of this Article. The Vendor agrees that they shall not substitute the Works or any part of the Works, and/or Items and Materials or utilise such substituted Works or any part of the Works and/or Items and Materials for any purpose whatsoever, without the Employer's prior written approval therefor.

4.6 In the event the Vendor commences the Works or any part thereof, as the case may be, without the Employer's prior written approval for the abovementioned line outs, mock-ups and samples, and specifications, any and all costs and expenses resulting from such Works or any parts thereof, as the case may be, including the costs and expenses of dismantling and/or redoing any such Works, any costs and expenses resulting from damage to or displacement of Items and Materials as a result thereof, shall be borne by the Vendor.

4.7 In the event the Employer, after having granted their approval for any or all of the abovementioned line outs, mock-ups and samples and/or specifications, seeks any changes, alterations or variations therein, the costs and expenses incurred on the Works, or any part of the Works, already having been commenced, until the time such change, alteration or variation is requested shall be borne by the Employer. The amount of such costs and expenses shall be mutually agreed to between the Parties in writing.

V. Obligations of the Vendor

5.1 The Vendor undertakes to ensure that the Works are carried out in a prudent, competent, efficient and timely manner in accordance herewith, with the Drawings, the Bill of Quantities and the Schedule of Works in such a manner as to conform to the specifications provided by the Employer therefor, and to ensure that the re-furbished and re-decorated Demised Premises are fit for the intended use and purpose thereof, as indicated by the Employer.

5.2 The Vendor undertakes that it shall perform its obligations, duties and functions within the scope of this Agreement in such a manner so as to ensure that the Works, and the re-furbished and re-decorated Demised Premises shall conform to the specifications provided by the Employer therefor, and shall be fit for the intended use and purpose thereof, as indicated by the Employer.

5.3 The Vendor undertakes, subject to clause ...., to carry out and complete the Works within the Term of this Agreement.

5.4 The Vendor undertakes that they shall carry out the Works and utilise Items and Materials and equipment therefor and in connection therewith subject to Article IV hereinabove. The Vendor further undertakes that they shall carry out only those Works and parts of the Works that have been approved by the Employer and shall utilise only those Items and Materials for and in connection with the Works which have been approved by the Employer.

5.5 The Vendor undertakes to ensure that the Works are carried out in a manner that causes the minimum of inconvenience to the Employer and that will comply with any and all security requirements, whether or not of the Employer.

5.6 The Vendor undertakes that they shall be responsible for the buying and procurement of all the Items and Materials, and all the equipment required for and proposed to be utilised for and in the Works, with the exception only of those Items and Materials, and equipment, that the Employer, from time to time, in its sole discretion, chooses to procure directly provided that the Employer shall before doing so, inform the Vendor by means of a written notice of its intention to do so.

5.7 Subject to Clause 9.1.2, the Vendor undertakes that, upon the Employer handing over to the Vendor any and all Items and Materials and equipment purchased directly by the Employer to be utilised for and in connection with the Works, the Vendor shall be responsible for co-ordinating the use of, and for utilising, such Items and Materials and equipment for and in connection with the Works and shall do all necessary deeds and actions to ensure that they are so utilised.

5.8 The Vendor undertakes that, unless otherwise expressly specified in writing, all Items and Materials utilised in and for the Works, and any and all substitutes therefor, shall be new and of the best quality, and the Vendor shall, as and when required by the Employer to do so, furnish satisfactory evidence as to the kind or quality of any or all of the raw and other materials used in and for the Works.

5.9 The Vendor undertakes that any and all substitutes for any Items and Materials shall be of the same quality, quantity, specifications etc., as the substituted Items and Materials.

5.10 The Vendor undertakes that the workmanship employed in carrying out the Works shall, without exception, be of a high quality and shall be substantial and neat and shall be executed in the best manner known to each trade used in and for the Works and shall be to the complete satisfaction of the Employer.

5.11 The Vendor undertakes to supervise the Works in an efficient and competent manner using his best skills and attention.

5.12 The Vendor undertakes to employ a competent, skilful and efficient superintendent, together with necessary assistants, to supervise the Works and to ensure that the Works are being carried out in a timely, efficient, competent and prudent manner in accordance herewith. Such superintendents and assistants shall be employed subject to the approval of the Employer. Such superintendent shall be empowered by the Vendor to act in their name.

5.13 The Vendor undertakes to employ and maintain, at all times, sufficient numbers of trained and skilled workmen, sub-contractors, agents, representatives, supervisors, superintendents and the like to carry out the Works and to ensure the rapid and orderly progress of the Works. The Vendor further undertakes that he shall not, at any time, employ and maintain, for the purpose of carrying out any part of the Work, any workmen, sub-contractors, agents, representatives, supervisors, superintendents and the like unfit or unskilled in the part of the Works assigned to such workmen, sub-contractors, agents, representatives, supervisors, superintendents and the like. The Vendor further undertakes that he shall not employ, and if such a workman, sub-contractor, agent, representative, supervisor, superintendent and the like has been employed, not maintain or continue to employ, any workman, sub-contractor, agent, representative, supervisor, superintendent and the like deemed unsatisfactory by the Employer.

5.14 The Vendor undertakes, at all times, to enforce and ensure strict discipline and good order amongst their employees and workmen, sub-contractors, agents, representatives, supervisors, superintendents and the like.

5.15 The Vendor undertakes that, in the event it becomes necessary for their employees and workmen to stay overnight at the Site in order to ensure that the Works progress rapidly and are completed within the Term of this Agreement, they shall provide the Employer reasonable prior notice thereof and shall seek the Employer's prior permission therefor.

5.16 The Vendor undertakes to liaise and coordinate with any and all sub-contractors, suppliers of Items and Materials, equipment suppliers and the like, who may be engaged either by the Vendor or directly by the Employer to provide and/or supply services, Items and Materials and equipment to be utilised for and/or in connection with the Works.

5.17 The Vendor undertakes that they shall confine their operations for the carrying out of the Works to the space designated by the Employer at the Demised Premises therefor.

5.18 The Vendor shall be responsible for paying salaries, benefits, statutory dues and the like to the employees, workmen, sub-contractors, agents, representatives, supervisors, superintendents and the like of the Vendor who are engaged in carrying out the Works. Under no circumstances shall the Employer be liable for any payment, claim, demand or compensation (including but not limited to compensation on account of injury/death/termination) of any nature to such employees, workmen, sub-contractors, agents, representatives, supervisors and the like of the Vendor at any point of time during the currency of this Agreement or after its termination; and the Vendor shall indemnify the Employer therefore.

5.19 The Vendor undertakes to ensure to employees and representatives of the Employer access to the areas of the Site where the Works are being carried out for the inspection and use thereof.

5.20 The Vendor undertakes that they shall progressively, with the commencement and completion of the Works and any parts of the Works, remove from the Site all waste, *malba,* rubbish, debris etc. resulting from the carrying on of the Works.

VI. Obligations of the Employer

6.1 The Employer undertakes that they shall provide at the Site, adequate electricity and water required by the Vendor for the carrying out of the Works without charge to the Vendor. Such water and electricity shall be provided at certain supply pint mutually determined and decided and determined by the Parties.

6.2 The Employer undertakes to make available to the Vendor for the duration of the Works, one telephone line and connection for the use of the Vendor in connection with the Works. The cost, expense and bills incurred for such telephone line and connection during the duration of the Works shall be borne by the Vendor.

6.3 The Employer undertakes, upon reasonable request by the Vendor, to grant permission for and make reasonable and suitable overnight arrangements for such employees and workmen of the Vendor who shall be required to stay overnight at the Site in connection with the Works.

6.4 The Employer undertakes to procure all necessary permissions, if any, which may be required for carrying on the Works at the Site twenty-four (24) hours a day.

6.5 The Employer undertakes that it shall, pursuant to mutual agreement in writing by the Parties, from time to time, buy and procure certain Items and Materials, and equipment required for and proposed to be utilised for and in connection with the Works. Such Items and Materials and equipment shall be handed over by the Employer to the Vendor for utilisation for and in connection with the Works.

VII. Mutual Representations and Warranties

Each Party hereto represents and warrants to the other as follows:

7.1 That it is duly organised and validly existing, and has full legal power and authority to own, lease and operate its assets and properties and to carry on its business;

7.2 That it has full corporate power and authority to execute and deliver this Agreement and to perform all of its obligations hereunder. The execution, delivery and performance of this Agreement by either Party has been authorised by all necessary corporate action, and does not and will not (i) require any consents, except for such consents and approvals as have already been obtained, (ii) violate any applicable law, (iii) violate its Organisational Documents, or (iv) contravene any provision of, or constitute a default under, any other agreement or instrument to which it is a party or by which it or its assets or properties may be bound;

7.3 That this Agreement is a legal, valid and binding obligation of each of the Parties, enforceable against either Party in accordance with its terms, except as the enforceability thereof may be limited by applicable bankruptcy, insolvency, liquidation, moratorium and other laws of general application relating to or affecting the rights of creditors or by general principles of equity;

7.4 *Compliance with laws.*—Each of the Parties represents and warrants to the other that the following are, as of the date hereof, true and correct in all material respects: (i) it has conducted and shall conduct its affairs and activities in respect of its business in accordance with applicable law, (ii) it has ensured and shall ensure that all invoices, financial settlements, reports and billings in respect of the Party thereto reflect properly the facts about all activities and transactions that are the subject thereof, and (iii) it has notified and shall notify the other promptly upon the discovery of any non-compliance with the foregoing.

7.5 The right to indemnification or other remedy based on the representations and warranties of the Parties contained in this Agreement will not be affected by any investigation conducted, except to the extent that a Party was provided specific information (through due diligence investigation or otherwise) or reasonably could have inferred from such information disclosed to it, the inaccuracy of any such representation or warranty.

VIII. Progress Reports and Reviews, Inspections

8.1 The Parties shall each appoint suitable representatives to be members of a committee, which shall liaise on matters relating to the Works.

8.2 The Employer's representatives shall, at all times during the Term of this Agreement and for the duration of the Works, have the right to carry out inspections of the Works and any parts of the Works without the prior permission of the Vendor and without any prior notice having to be given to the Vendor thereof.

8.3 After the Effective Date during the Term of this Agreement, and for the duration of the Works, a minimum of one representative each of the Parties shall meet formally once every calendar week to discuss and review the progress made on the Works that week and until that time. All such progress reviews shall take place at the Site or at any other location as may be mutually agreed to between the Parties.

8.4 The Vendor shall, once every calendar week from the Effective Date, provide to the Employer weekly progress reports on the Works in such format as may be agreed to between the Parties.

8.5 Upon the Vendor notifying the Employee in writing of the completion of each Stage of the Works, a minimum of one representative each of each of the Parties shall inspect the Works and shall mutually agree as to whether that Stage of the Works has been completed to the complete and total satisfaction of the Employer. In the event it is determined in writing that such Stage of the Works has been completed to the complete and total satisfaction of the Employer, the Vendor shall raise their invoice for that Stage of the Works in accordance with clause .... In the event it is determined that such Stage of the Work has not been completed to the complete and total satisfaction of the Employer, the Vendor shall not raise their invoice for that Stage of the Works until such time as it is mutually determined by the Parties upon inspection thereof by representatives of the Parties that such Stage of the Works has been completed to the complete and total satisfaction of the Employer.

IX. Price, Advance, Invoices and Payment

9.1 Price

9.1.1 Subject to Clause 9.1.2, the price for the Works shall be ...., calculated before the commencement of the Works for the entire Works on the basis of Items and Materials proposed to be utilised for and in connection with the Works, subject to the Employer's approval thereof, labour charges for the Works etc. ("Price").

9.1.2 If the Employer procures directly, any Items and Materials, cost of which has been taken into consideration for the purpose of Clause 9.1.1 to reckon the Price, then the Price shall be reduced by an amount equal to the price of such Items and Materials, as quoted by the Vendor in the Bill of Quantities provided that the Vendor shall be still be entitled to a fee of ten percent (10%) of the cost of such Items and Materials to the Employer if the Employer seeks, in writing, any consultancy and/or coordination from the Vendor in respect thereof.

9.1.3 The Employer may, from time to time, issue instructions in writing as to the expenditure by the Vendor of any provisional sums, which instructions and provisional sums shall be valued on a fair and reasonable basis mutually by the Parties in writing. An inclusive price shall be agreed to between the Employer and the Vendor in writing upon such valuation of the instructions and provisional sums prior to the Vendor carrying out such instructions. This inclusive price shall be added onto the Price.

9.1.4 The Employer may, from time to time, issue written instructions to the Vendor for the procurement and utilisation in the Works of items and materials in addition to those Items and Materials already approved by the Employer for utilisation in the Works and used for the calculation of the Price in accordance with clause 9.1.1. The value/price of such additional items and materials shall be as per the market value/price for such items and materials at the time of procurement thereof. The actual cost and expense of such additional items and materials shall be added onto the Price.

9.1.5 In the event there is a change or variation in the Price as a result of clauses 9.1.2, 9.1.3 and 9.1.4 the Parties shall mutually agree in writing on a new Price ("New Price").

9.2 Advance

9.2.1 The Employer shall pay to the Vendor, within four (4) days after the Effective Date, an amount of Rs. ...., being fifteen per cent (15%) of the Price, as an advance payment for the Works.

9.3 Invoices

9.3.1 Subject to clause 8.7, the Vendor shall raise their invoice for each Stage of the Works upon completion of that Stage of the Works.

9.3.2 The Vendor shall raise invoices for the following amounts at the completion of each Stage of the Works:

(i) 40% - for Rs. ...., being forty per cent (40%) of the Price, or for 40% of the New Price, as the case may be, *minus* the amount paid as advance under clause 9.2.1

(ii) 70% - for Rs. ...., being seventy per cent (70%) of the Price, or for 70% of the New price, as the case may be, *minus* 40% of the Price or the New Price, as the case may be,

(iii) 90% - for Rs. ...., being ninety per cent (90%) of the Price, or for 90% of the New Price, as the case may be, *minus* 70% of the Price or the New Price, as the case may be.

(iv) On completion – for Rs. ...., being one hundred per cent (100%) of the Price, or for 100% of the New Price, as the case may be, *minus* 90% of the Price or the New Price, as the case may be.

9.3.3 Each invoice raised by the Vendor in accordance with the provisions of this Article shall contain a brief description and details of the Works carried out by the Vendor up to the Stage for which such invoice is being raised, along with the quantities, specifications, etc., of the Items and Materials utilised in the Works up to that Stage.

9.4 Payment

9.4.1 The Employer shall make payments of the invoices raised in accordance with clauses 9.3.2 (i), (ii) and (iii) within five (5) working days of the receipt thereof, and of the invoice raised in accordance with clause 9.3.2 (iv) within fourteen (14) working days of the receipt thereof.

9.4.2 The Employer shall, at the time of making payments of the amounts raised in the invoices against accomplishment of 40%, 70% and 90% Stage of the Works, retain 15% of the invoiced amount.

9.4.3 The total amounts withheld by the Employer in accordance with clause 9.4.2 shall be paid by the Employer to the Vendor along with the balance Price or New Price, as the case may be, within fourteen (14) days of the receipt by the Employer of the final invoice raised by the Vendor in accordance with clause 9.3.2 (iv) hereinabove.

9.4.4 Payment shall be made by way of crossed cheque payable at .... (name of the place) ....

X. Indemnity

10.1 The Vendor shall indemnify the Employer and hold it harmless against any claims or demands made against the Employer or its employees, directors, representatives, agents or shareholders by any of the Vendor's employees, workmen, sub-contractors, agents, representatives, supervisors, superintendents and the like, or the sub-contractors' employees, workers, consultants or the like.

10.2 The Vendor shall indemnify and hold harmless the Employer from and against all losses, costs, actions, damages, liabilities, fines, penalties of any kind or nature whatsoever resulting from or relating to the negligence, default, act or omission on the part of the Vendor, its employees, workmen, sub-contractors, agents, representatives, supervisors, superintendents and the like, or the sub-contractors' employees, workers, consultants or the like in the performance of or failure to perform, the Vendor's obligations hereunder.

XI. Warranty

11.1 The Vendor shall, along with the Vendor's final invoice raised in accordance with clause 9.3.2(iv) hereinabove, present to the Employer a written warrantee and guarantee warranting all the Items and Materials, and all the workmanship utilised for and in connection with the Works against any and all defects of any sort whatsoever, normal wear and tear, and defects arising out of factors outside the scope of the Vendor's obligations under this Agreement excepted, for a minimum period of one (1) year from the date of such final invoice.

11.2 The Vendor, in the abovementioned warranty and guarantee, shall undertake, at no further cost and expense to the Employer, to repair and/or replace, to the complete and total satisfaction of the Employer, the defective Works, or any part of the defective Works, as the case may, and any and all defective Items and Materials which become defective for any reason whatsoever at any time during the period of the said warranty and guarantee. The Vendor shall further undertake to repair and/or replace any and all of the Works, any part of the Works, and any and all Items and Materials which may have been damaged as a result of such defects and/or which may have been displaced in carrying out such repairs and/or replacements in, to or of the Works, any part of the Works, and Items and Materials.

11.3 Notwithstanding clause 11.1 hereinabove, in the event any or all of the Items and Materials, and equipment utilised for and in connection with the Works is covered by a warranty and/or guarantee by the original supplier or manufacturer of such Items and Materials and/or equipment, such warranty and/or guarantee shall apply to the Items and Materials and/or equipment in addition to the Vendor's warranty and guarantee under clauses 9.1 and 9.2.

XII. Term and Termination

12.1 Term

12.1.1 The term of this Agreement shall be three months and fifteen days (................... months) from the Effective Date of this Agreement ("Term").

12.1.2 The date for the completion of the Works shall be ...., being the date three months and fifteen days (.................... months) form the Effective Date ("Completion Date").

12.2 Termination

Notwithstanding clause 12.1 hereinabove, the Employer shall have the right to terminate this Agreement any time during the Term of this Agreement by giving the Vendor one (1) week's prior written notice thereof in the event of any breach by the Vendor of any of their duties and obligations under this Agreement.

XIII. Penalties

13.1 Subject to clause....................., in the event the Works are not completed by the Vendor within the Term and no later than the Completion Date, the Vendor shall pay to the Employer, by way of penalty for the delay, ... of the Price or the New Price, as the case may be, per week of the delay, subject to a total maximum limit of .... per cent (....................) of the Price or New Price, as the case may be.

13.2 In the event any period of delay is less than one (1) week, the amount of the penalty payable by the Vendor to the Employer for such period shall be calculated on a *pro rata* basis.

13.3 In the event the Works are not completed within four (4) weeks of the Completion Date, the Vendor shall not be entitled to raise their final invoice under clause 9.3.2 (iv), and the Employer shall be entitled to withhold payment of the final amounts of the Price or New Price, as the case may be, including the amounts withheld by the Employer the Price or New Price pursuant to Article IX.

XIV. Governing Law and Dispute Resolution

14.1 Governing law

This Agreement shall be governed by and construed in accordance with the laws of India.

14.2 Dispute resolution

14.2.1 Any difference, dispute, controversy or claim ("Dispute") which may arise between the Parties out of or in relation to or in connection with this Agreement, or the breach, termination, effect, validity, interpretation or application of this Agreement or as to their rights, duties or liabilities hereunder, other than a dispute for which provision is specifically made in this Agreement, shall be settled by the Parties, in the first instance, by mutual negotiations and agreement between Mr. .... (name of the employee) of the Employer and Mr. .... of the Vendor, and such other representatives of the Parties as the Parties may wish.

14.2.2 If, for any reason, such Dispute cannot be resolved amicably by the Parties, the same shall be settled by way of arbitration proceedings in accordance with the Arbitration and Conciliation Act, 1996, or any subsequent enactment or amendment thereto (the "Arbitration Act"). The Dispute shall be referred to the

sole arbitration of Mr. .... (name of the Advocate), of M/s. ....
(name of the firm). The decision of the arbitrator shall be final and binding upon the Parties. The venue of the arbitration shall be .... (place), India. The language of the arbitration and the award shall be English. The Employer has disclosed to the Vendor that Mr. .... (name of the Advocate) is a partner in M/s .... (name of the firm), which has its offices at .... (address). The Employer has further disclosed to the Vendor that M/s .... (name of the firm) have advised the Employer in connection with this Agreement and that Mr. .... (name of the Advocate) has not himself been personally associated with the aforesaid advice. After the aforesaid disclosure, the Vendor agrees that they do not and shall not have any objection to the appointment of Mr. .... (name of the Advocate) as the sole arbitrator.

XV. Force Majeure

15.1 Notwithstanding anything to the contrary in this Agreement, neither Party shall be liable by reason of failure or delay in the performance of its duties and obligations under this Agreement if such failure or delay is caused by acts of God, war, riot, fire, civil commotion, strikes, lock outs, embargoes, curfews, any orders of governmental, quasi-governmental, or local authorities or any other similar cause beyond its control and without its fault or negligence.

15.2 In the event the timely and efficient progress of the Works is interrupted or suspended because of any of the aforementioned events of *force majeure*, the Term of the Agreement shall be extended to include the number of days for which the progress of the works was so interrupted or suspended, and the Completion Date shall be pushed back accordingly. Any such extension of the Term and new Completion Date shall be mutually agreed to between the Parties in writing.

XVI. Assignment

16.1 The Vendor shall not be entitled to assign this Agreement or any of their rights, powers, obligations and/or duties hereunder without the express prior written consent of the Employer.

XVII. Miscellaneous

17.1 Notices

All notices required or permitted hereunder shall be in writing and in the English language and shall be sent by internationally recognised courier or by facsimile transmission (with confirming facsimile receipt) addressed to the address of each Party set forth below, or to such other address as such other Party shall have communicated to the other Party in writing. Notice shall be deemed to have been served when received (and in the case of a facsimile transmission, provided that a confirming copy is sent to the other Party, in accordance with the non-facsimile notice delivery requirements).

If to: The Employer

....

....

If to: The Vendor

....

....

17.2 Remedies

No remedy conferred by any of the provisions of this Agreement is intended to be exclusive of any other remedy which is otherwise available at law, in equity, by statute or otherwise, and each and every other remedy given hereunder or now or hereafter existing at law, in equity, by statute or otherwise except as stated to the contrary in this Agreement. The election of any one or more of such remedies by any of the Parties hereto shall not constitute a waiver by such Party of the right to pursue any other available remedy except as aforesaid.

17.3 Severance

If any provision of this Agreement or part thereof is rendered void, illegal or unenforceable in any respect under any law, the validity, legality and enforceability of the remaining provisions shall not in any way be affected or impaired thereby.

17.4 Survival of Rights, Duties and Obligations

Termination of this Agreement for any cause shall not release a Party from any liability which at the time of termination has already accrued to another Party or which thereafter may accrue in respect of any act or omission prior to such termination.

17.5 Entire Agreement

This Agreement, and the Schedules, Annexures and Exhibits hereto constitute the entire agreement between the Parties as to the subject matter hereof and supercede any and all prior understandings between the Parties on the subject-matter hereof.

17.6 Further Acts and Assurance

Each Party shall co-operate with the other and execute and deliver to the other such instruments and documents and take such other actions as may be reasonably requested by the other from time to time in order to carry out, give effect to or confirm its rights, and for the intended purpose of this Agreement.

17.7 Amendments and Modifications

No amendments and/or modifications of any of the provisions of this Agreement shall be effective unless made in writing specifically referring to this Agreement and duly signed by the Parties hereto.

17.8 Waiver

Save where this Agreement expressly provides, neither Party shall be deemed to have waived any right, power, privilege or remedy under this Agreement unless such Party shall have delivered to the other Party a written waiver signed by an authorised officer of such waiving Party. No failure or delay on the part of either Party in exercising any right, power, privilege or remedy hereunder shall operate as a waiver, default or acquiescence thereof, nor shall any waiver on the part of either Party of any right, power, privilege or remedy hereunder operate as a waiver of any other right, power, privilege or remedy, nor shall any single or partial exercise of any right, power, privilege or remedy hereunder preclude any other or further exercise thereof or the exercise of any other right, power, privilege or remedy hereunder.

IN WITNESS whereof this Agreement has been entered into the day and year first above written.

Signed by, for and on behalf of

....

THE EMPLOYER

....

THE VENDOR

PRODUCT LIABILITY AND CONSUMER PROTECTION

PRODUCT LIABILITY: AN ANALYSIS

Two major lessons for successful global trade management emerge from the last fifty years of world trading system. *First*, globalization is essential to avoid backsliding into protectionism and mercantilism. *Second*, international discipline in product manufacturing is essential to meet the consumers' demands for safe and high quality products in international markets.

The intermingling of world economies has heralded an era of somewhat homogenous product standards throughout the globe. In recent years, the number of technical regulations and standards adopted by countries has grown significantly. Liability for defective and unsafe products is a strong manifestation of the growing concern to protect consumers.

International Regulations and Standards

In 1996, the United States imposed restrictions on import of fuel oil from Venezuela, because of its failure to meet the domestic fuel standards of the United States. These restrictions resulted in a dispute relating to the implementation of the .... domestic legislation known as the Clean Air Act, of 1990 ("CAA") and, more specifically, to the regulations enacted by the United States Environmental Protection Agency ("EPA") pursuant to the provisions of the CAA. These regulations were enacted to control toxic and other pollution caused by the combustion of gasoline manufactured in or imported into the United States.

In May, 1997, Canada requested consultations with the European Community, when France prohibited import and sale of asbestos and products containing asbestos from Canada. It was argued by Canada, that these measures had severely damaged its trade interests. Similarly, the United States prohibited import of wearing apparels from India on the ground, that they were flammable. These are only some of the many such examples of the growing restrictions imposed by the domestic markets when the exporting countries fail to align their manufacturing standards with those of the domestic markets.

In March 2000, Norway joined the three Baltic countries of Lithuania, Latvia and Estonia in banning most Danish meat imports after neighboring Denmark reported a case of Mad Cow disease. Norway and other nations also want the import of these products banned because the contaminated meat has been linked to a deadly human brain ailment, Creutzfeldt-Jakob disease.

About, eight European countries, in 1999, sought some sort of a prohibition on the sale of PVC toys. This ban, perhaps, has prompted the world's largest toy maker to announce a major new initiative aimed at making its plastic toys out of environmentally friendly, organically based materials derived from edible oils and plant starches. Mattel Inc., the maker of Barbie, Power Wheels and Fisher-Price toys, hopes to start making products from renewable materials as early as 2001. This initiative has been announced to replace polyvinyl chloride and a controversial group of chemical additives called phthalates that are used in soft plastic toys. Some phthalate compounds have been linked to cancer, kidney and liver damage in animals. Their threat to humans is being studied. It is not surprising that Mattel's announcement came just as the European Union met to formally approve an emergency ban on phthalates in polyvinyl chloride (PVC) toys, such as baby rattles and teething toys, designed to be chewed by children, under 3 years of age.

In December, 1999, Greenpeace, the international environmental group, founded by late Jacques Cousteau, had identified over 60 ships containing hazardous substances which had arrived from the OECD (Organization for Economic Co-operation and Development) and other countries, and were dismantled at India's west coast. This was in alleged violation of the norms of the Basel Convention, 1994, which had banned export of hazardous wastes from the OECD to the non-OECD countries. Consequently, export *via* such ships was not only a violation of the convention but also of the norms of the European Union and of the 1997 order of the Indian Supreme Court under which import of hazardous wastes was specifically banned. Such vessels were exported to India, and other ship-breaking yards of Asia *viz.* Bangladesh, China, Philippines and Pakistan, ostensibly for scrapping, but covertly for carrying toxic materials dangerous to health and environment.

All these issues raise the question of lack of uniform product standards and product liability laws globally. Domestic laws are the reflection of the economic, social and general well-being of the country. In an international economy, this creates problems when domestic standards are applied to goods imported from abroad. For a less technically and economically developed country, this, then, directly amounts to adoption of superior manufacturing standards in compliance with the manufacturing standards of the importing country. However, this does not answer the question in cases where a country with superior manufacturing standards of exports goods to countries with less developed or poorly enforced product standards. It leaves a lot of room for manoeuvering of standards by the country with superior standards and consequently dumping of inferior goods in the country with lower standards.

Impact on International Trade

Although, it is difficult to give a precise estimate of the impact on international trade of the need to comply with different foreign technical regulations and standards, it certainly involves significant costs for producers and exporters. In general, these costs arise from the translation of foreign regulations, hiring of technical experts to explain foreign regulations, and adjustment of production facilities to comply with the requirements. In addition, there is the need to prove that the exported products meet the foreign regulations.

If, a firm must adjust its production facilities to comply with diverse technical requirements of multiple markets, production costs per unit are likely to increase. This imposes handicap particularly on small and medium enterprises. Exporters are normally at a disadvantage *vis-à-vis* domestic firms, in terms of adjustment costs, if confronted with new regulations. Manufacturers may also have difficulties in securing approval of their products from foreign markets because of disagreement of testing experts on optimal testing procedures, bureaucratic inertia, or even manipulation of the testing process by the protectionist groups. Perhaps one of the main difficulties faced by exporters who sell in multiple markets is costly multiple testing or certification of products. These costs would be drastically reduced if a product could be tested once and the testing results be accepted in all the markets. Of course, the additional markets made available for the marketing of the products, however, suitably compensate the costs incurred in complying with the technical regulations.

Agreement on Technical Barriers to Trade ("TBT") and Agreement on Sanitary and Phytosanitary Measures ("SPS"), creatures of the World Trade Organization, too have acted as catalysts to promote consumer and environment-friendly societies across the globe. The question, however, is whether these regulations merely serve to strengthen the existing manufacturing standards of countries with high product guidelines or if they are really helping to evolve higher product consciousness and criteria in countries with less developed economies and standards.

WTO and the Technical Barriers to Trade

In the Tokyo Round of multilateral trade negotiations (1974-79), an Agreement on Technical Barriers to Trade was negotiated ("TBT" Agreement or "Standards Code") with a view to harmonize product standards worldwide. The TBT Agreement was followed by an Agreement on the Application of Sanitary and Phytosanitary Measures ("SPS Agreement") entered into with the establishment of the World Trade Organisation on January 1, 1995. The two Agreements have some common elements, including basic obligations for non-discrimination. However, the scope of these two Agreements is different. The SPS Agreement covers all measures whose purpose is to protect human or animal health from food borne risks, and animals, and plants from pests and diseases. The TBT Agreement, on the other hand, covers all technical regulations, voluntary standards and various procedures for industrial and agricultural products.

SPS measures, by their very nature, may result in restrictions on trade. Similarly, a large number of TBT standards are aimed at protecting human safety and health. Increasingly, national regulations require motor vehicles to be equipped with seat belts to minimize injury in the event of road accidents, and electric sockets to be manufactured in a way to protect users, especially children from electric shocks. Another very good example of regulation whose objective is to protect the human health is labelling of cigarettes to indicate that they are harmful to health. Regulations that protect animal and plant life and health are also very common. These are intended to ensure that animal or plant species endangered by water, air or soil pollution do not become extinct.

There is, however, a very thin line between TBT and SPS regulations established by the importing countries and the same being used as protectionist measures. A GATT working group set up to evaluate the impact of non-tariff barriers in international trade has concluded that technical barriers are the largest category of non-tariff barriers faced by exporters. GATT/WTO, therefore, provide for a Government to challenge another country's food safety and plant and animal health laws, and technical regulations.

A number of trade disputes alleging violations on the SPS Agreement have been brought to the Dispute Settlement Body since 1995. These include, a complaint by the United States against Korean shelf-life requirements and a separate US complaint against Korean inspection procedures (1995); complaints by Canada and the United States against Australia's restrictions related to fish diseases (1995), and complaints by the United States and Canada against the European Community's ban on imports of hormone-treated meats (1996). The disputes, under TBT Agreement, include Canada's complaint against European Community involving an order by the French Government prescribing the official trade description of scallops (1996), complaint by Venezuela and Brazil against U.S. Gasoline Regulation (1996), and complaint filed by U.S. against European Commission's import measures on meat and meat products (1996).

Product Liability Law Suits

The greatest incentive, perhaps, for the shift in attitude towards product safety and standards, has been promoted by the product liability lawsuits. Ford Motor Company no longer produces a car that explodes and bursts into a ball of flames when struck from behind. Life threatening birth control and other medical devices are being removed from the market and infants' toys are safer. Unfortunately, these lawsuits are more common place and well received only in the well-developed economies.

The world does not have a homogeneous legal system and therefore there cannot be any generalization of the product liability laws in various jurisdictions. However, the developments in the product liability laws in a jurisdiction indicate a refinement and sophistication in the market and laws of the concerned jurisdiction.

U.S. product liability laws are different from most other countries and provide for punitive damages in civil proceedings. Product liability claims in U.S. can be based on negligence, strict liability, or breach of warranty of fitness depending on the jurisdiction where the claim is based. There is no federal product liability law in the U.S. Many States have enacted comprehensive product liability statutes. These statutory provisions can be very diverse, so the United States Department of Commerce has promulgated a Model Uniform Products Liability Act, (MUPLA) for voluntary use by the States.

In U.S., an Oregon jury awarded the petitioner $ 500,000 in punitive damages, over five times the amount of the compensatory damages award. The petitioner in this case had sustained injuries while driving a three wheeled all terrain vehicle manufactured and sold by Honda Motor Co. In addition to the punitive damages awarded frequently by the U.S. juries, product liability lawsuits in the U.S. witnessed another revolution in the 80's in the form of mass personal injury litigation. Hundreds and thousands of people sued scores of corporations for losses due to injuries or diseases that they attributed to defective pharmaceutical products or toxic substances. In the 90's, too, there has been massive litigation involving tobacco products, breast implants and asbestos. The grounds for fixing liability and the quantum of damages awarded in the U.S. have made it an often misunderstood and dreaded jurisdiction for product liability lawsuits.

In U.K., the Consumer Protection Act, 1987, is the implementation of the European Directive of 1985 for harmonization of laws in the European Union in respect of product liability. In *R. v. Bow Street* (Magistrates Court, March, 1994), the magistrate held that a piece of bone found in the jar of baby food, *prima facie* proved that the defendant did not exercise due diligence in its conduct. A significant trial in class action relating to infection with Hepatitis from blood transfusion in "the Hepatitis Litigation" is due to start in October, 2000. In U.K., too, punitive damages can be awarded, but the courts are generally reluctant to make such awards.

A significant development in the product liability lawsuits in U.K. has been the concept of contingency fee. This type of funding had been regarded an anathema for long. However, only four years back the same was permitted in personal injury and other actions.

In Japan, the Diet in 1995, enacted a new law that has changed the face of product liability issues. While the Japanese distributors and consumers have always been extremely quality conscious, this new law will increase the importance of product manuals, and the use of warning labels. The new law has also generated an interest in quality assurance programs of the manufacturers. Special agencies in Japan offer certain safety approvals for many products sold in Japan *viz.* "SG" ("safety goods") mark for consumer products from the Product Safety Association, and the "ST" ("safety toy") mark from the Japan Toy Association.

Though, the application of this law is still relatively untested, the first ever product liability suit in Japan registered an inclination towards U.S. style practice. A restaurant owner sought $ 9,100 in compensation for a minor injury suffered in the left thumb, while opening a paper container for black tea. The percentage of product liability claims in Japan, however, remains highest in the field of pharmaceuticals.

The product liability law in Germany, based on the European Directive of 1985, has been a fairly well settled law since the enactment of the Product Liability Act, in 1990. Punitive damages are not allowed and the awards in product liability litigation are limited in amount and include medical expenses and loss in income, if any. In July, 1997, a new statute was enacted by the .... Parliament, which deals with the safety standards to be applied to consumer products. The Product Safety Act acknowledges the right of the State Authorities to impose upon the manufacturer the duty to warn or to recall the products. The consumer would perhaps now even be able to claim damages against a manufacturer for violation of the order of the State Authority.

The South African law has no statutory provision relating to product liability. Nevertheless, the South African Courts have recognized that there is a need to protect the consumer and have held that the production of a defective article that causes physical or pure economic damage to any person constitutes a wrongful act. However, until the time that the legislature formulates all the aspects of a product liability law, the principles of contract and tort would provide the required protection.

Kenya, too, does not have a statutory provision relating to product liability. The Kenya Sale of Goods Act, which is virtually identical to the U.K. Sale of Goods Act, affords the only protection available to the consumers.

The societies, which allow recourse to product liability lawsuits, are undoubtedly more considerate towards the needs of consumers. The fact, however, remains that manufacturing safe products is still the best way to avoid any liability, irrespective of the laws prevailing in a jurisdiction.

Product Liability and Product Standards in India

Considering the revolution of the world markets in the form of phenomenal increase and steady exchange of goods across the borders, Indian markets and laws too have endeavoured to maintain their pace in the race. Unfortunately, though, there is no general statutory provision relating to "product liability" in India. Basically, the principles of laws of contract provide protection to the consumers. Laws of torts are still in their rudimentary stages as far as India is concerned. However, an important development in the field of law of torts has been the Consumer Protection Act of 1986. This Act provides relief to those who have suffered loss either for some defects in the goods purchased or hired for consideration or for any deficiency in services they have or have not received. The importance of the Act lies in promoting the welfare of the society by enabling the consumers to participate directly in the market economy, *Lucknow Development Authority v. M.K. Gupta*, 1993 (3) CPJ 7 SC: 1994 CPR 569.

The law of tort in India is yet to extend its principles to the field of product liability in a major way. However, the law of tort does give redress for damages suffered due to defective or unsafe products on the basis of negligence.

Today, in India, there is a conspicuous lack of precedents imposing tort liability for defective products. Tobacco litigation has not made its way into India as yet, non-flammability of wearing apparel has not been made a condition precedent to the marketing of such clothes, gas stoves have not been made consumer safe nor does manufacturing of toxic toys evoke strict sanctions. Yet, fierce competition and free market economy are slowly propelling India towards a consumer conscious society.

Emerging Scenario

The consumers are now armed with two effective weapons to fight against dangerous and unsafe products. At a macro level, they can ban imports of unwanted products and services by taking recourse to various multilateral Agreements like TBT and SPS. At the micro level, more and more countries are allowing the consumers to go to courts to challenge, through product liability lawsuits, the safety and desirability of products and services they buy.

However, these lawsuits are still not, as favorable, simple or commonplace in countries with less developed economies. The status, though, is rapidly changing in the wake of growing consumerism and dissolving boundaries. Active participation of the countries in international organizations, phenomenal inroads made inside the country by international trade and the ensuing liabilities are, slowly but surely, moving the whole world towards a more consumer friendly global village.

RESEARCH AND DEVELOPMENT AGREEMENT

This RESEARCH AND DEVELOPMENT AGREEMENT (the "Agreement") dated, as of ...., and executed in .... is made by and among:

.... (name of the *Gamma* Company affiliate), a company organized and existing under the laws of .... and having its registered office at .... (hereinafter referred to, as "*Beta*" which expression shall, unless repugnant to the context meaning thereof, mean and include its successors and permitted assigns) of the FIRST PART.

AND

.... (name of the JVC), a company registered under the Indian Companies Act, 1956 and having its registered office at ...., ... (place), India (hereinafter referred to as the "Company" which expression shall, unless repugnant to the context or meaning thereof, mean and include its successors and permitted assigns) of the SECOND PART.

(*Beta* and the Company shall hereinafter individually be referred to as "Party" and collectively as "Parties").

WHEREAS, the Company is a joint venture between *Beta* and *Alpha* Springs Limited (a public limited company organized and existing under the laws of India and having its registered office at .... (address), India, hereinafter referred to as "*Alpha*" which expression shall, unless repugnant to the context or meaning thereof, mean and include its successors and permitted assigns).

WHEREAS, the Company is proposed to be managed in accordance with a Shareholders' Agreement dated .... entered into between *Beta*, *Alpha* and the Company (the "Shareholders' Agreement"), and is engaged in the activity of manufacturing and selling multi-leaf springs, parabolic springs and spring assemblies for automotive suspension systems and commercial vehicle suspension systems, and the research and development of multi-leaf springs, parabolic springs, air springs, spring assemblies and suspension systems;

WHEREAS, the Company acquired the .... (place) Unit (the "Unit") of *Alpha* situated at.., ... pursuant to the Transfer of Undertaking Agreement dated.. entered into between the Company and *Alpha*;

WHEREAS *Beta* and *Alpha* have agreed to establish and organize a second joint venture company (the "Second JVC") to research, develop, manufacture and sell air springs assemblies and suspension systems;

WHEREAS *Beta* has scientific expertise and know-how relating to air springs, air spring assemblies and suspension systems, and has a long term interest in the R&D Work;

WHEREAS *Alpha* has expressed a willingness to fund the R&D Work, and the Company has agreed to carry out the R&D Work at the Unit;

WHEREAS, it is anticipated that by the end of the R&D Work, one or more Air Spring Prototypes will have been developed;

WHEREAS, the Parties have agreed that any and all tangible and intangible rights, present and future, in and pertaining to the R&D Work and the Air Spring Prototypes that may result from the R&D Work shall be the exclusive property of *Beta*, and the Company has agreed to transfer and assign the same to *Beta*;

NOW, THEREFORE, in consideration of the mutual covenants and in reliance on the representations and warranties contained herein, and for good and valuable consideration, the receipt and sufficiency of which are hereby acknowledged, the Parties hereto, intending to be legally bound, hereby agree as follows:

Article I. Definitions

1.1 Definitions

Unless otherwise required by the context, the following capitalized terms, when used in this Agreement, shall have the meanings set forth below (with the terms defined in the singular having the corresponding meaning when used in the plural and *vice versa*):

"*Agreement*" means this Research and Development Agreement.

"Air Spring Prototype(s)" means a prototype(s) of air springs, air spring assemblies and suspension systems for automotives and commercial vehicles and any and all air suspension automotive products for automotives commercial vehicles, including improvements and/or advancements thereon or thereof, that may be developed as a result of the R&D Work

"Confidential Information" has the meaning set forth in section 7.2.1.

"Consents" means all non-governmental approvals, consents or waivers of shareholders, board of directors, other third Parties etc., and all governmental approvals required to be obtained in connection with the execution, delivery and performance of this Agreement.

"Dispute" has the meaning set forth in section 9.2.

"Dollars" or *"US$"* means the lawful currency of the United States of America.

"Effective Date" means the date of execution of this Agreement.

"Organisational Documents" means, with respect to either party, its memorandum of association, articles of association, charter, bye-laws and any and all other documents of similar venture, as in effect at the relevant time.

"Prototype Rights" has the meaning set forth in section 7.1.1.

"R&D Work" means the research and development work to be carried out by the Company in accordance with the programme of research and development attached hereto as *Annexure 'A'* entitled (....................).

"Research Committee" has the meaning set forth in section 3.1.

"Rupees" or *"Rs."* means the lawful currency of the Republic of India.

"Term" has the meaning set forth in section 8.1.1.

"Unit" has the meaning set forth in the recitals hereinabove.

1.2 Other References

Unless otherwise provided or unless the context clearly requires otherwise, all references to "Articles" and "Sections" are to Articles and sections of this Agreement, and all references to "Annexures", "Exhibits" or "Schedules" are to Annexures, Exhibits and Schedules to this Agreement, each of which is an integral part of Agreement for all purposes; references to either gender include the other; all uses of "include" or "including" mean without limitation.

Article 2. Scope of R&D Work

2.1 The Company agrees, on the terms and conditions stated hereinbelow, to carry out the R&D Work with a view to developing spring assemblies (....................).

2.2 The R&D Work shall be carried out by the Company in accordance, with the programme of research and development entitled (....................) attached hereto, as Annexure 'A'.

2.3 During the Term of this Agreement, the Company shall not enter into any agreement with a third party relating to the R&D Work or undertake any work for a third Party which would come within the scope of the R&D Work.

Article 3. Progress Reviews and Reports

3.1 The Parties shall each appoint suitably qualified representatives to be members of a committee, which shall liaise on matters relating to the R&D Work (the "Research Committee").

3.2 During the Term of this Agreement, the Research Committee shall meet formally at intervals of 6 (six) calendar months, or at such other intervals as may be mutually agreed to between the Parties in writing, to discuss the progress of the R&D Work and the results obtained therefrom.

3.3 Unless otherwise agreed to between the Parties in writing, the first meeting of the Research Committee shall be held on a date 6 (six) months from the Effective Date. All meetings of the Research Committee shall be held at the Unit, or at any other location, which may be mutually agreed to between the Parties in writing.

3.4 Notwithstanding sections 3.2 and 3.3 above, *Beta* may at any time during the Term of this Agreement, upon giving the Company 2 (two) calendar weeks' prior written notice thereof, schedule a meeting of the Research Committee.

3.5 Beginning 6 (six) months from the Effective Date, the Company shall, every 6 (six) calendar months during the Term of this Agreement, submit to GIC a written report on the progress of the R&D Work and the development of any air spring prototype(s).

3.6 Notwithstanding section 3.5 above, *Beta* may at any time during the Term of this Agreement, upon giving the Company 1 (one) calendar month's prior written notice thereof, require the Company to submit to it a written report on the progress of the R&D Work and the development of any air spring prototype(s).

Article 4. Funding for R&D Work and Consideration

4.1 *Beta* undertakes to fund the R&D Work based on the actual costs and expenses incurred by the Company in carrying out the R&D Work.

4.2 The Company shall raise monthly invoices for the R&D Work carried out by it in that month, which shall state the actual amount of the costs and expenses incurred by it in that month, in carrying out the R&D Work. Each invoice shall also contain a brief description and details of the R&D Work carried out by the Company in the month for which such invoice is being raised. The invoices shall be raised by the Company within the first week of the month succeeding the month for which the invoice is raised.

4.3 Invoices shall be payable by *Beta* net of the applicable taxes within 15 (fifteen) business days of the receipt thereof. Payment shall be made in .... (foreign amount) and shall be made by way of (....................).

Article 5. Obligations of the Company

5.1 The obligations and responsibilities of the Company are as follows:

5.1.1 The Company shall ensure that the R&D Work is carried out in a prudent, competent, efficient and timely manner;

5.1.2 The Company shall be responsible for paying salaries, benefits, statutory dues and the like to the employees of the Company who are engaged in carrying out the R&D Work. Under no circumstances shall *Beta* be liable for any payment, claim, demand or compensation (including but not limited to compensation on account of injury/death/termination) of any nature to such employees at any point of time during the currency of this Agreement or after its termination; and the Company shall indemnify *Beta* therefore;

5.1.3 The Company shall, at its cost and expense, obtain approvals, licenses and consents, if any, which may be required for the execution and performance of this Agreement;

5.1.4 The Company shall, provide employees and representatives of *Beta* access to the Unit for the inspection and use thereof;

5.1.5 The Company shall ensure that the R&D Work is carried out in accordance, with this Agreement.

Article 6. Mutual Representations

6.1 Each Party hereto represents and warrants to the other as follows:

6.1.1 That it is duly organised and validly existing, and has full legal power and authority to own, lease and operate its assets and properties and carry on its business;

6.1.2 That it has full corporate power and authority to execute and deliver this Agreement and to perform all of its obligations hereunder. The execution, delivery and performance of this Agreement by either Party have been authorised by all necessary corporate action, and do not and will not (i) require any Consents, except for such consents and approvals as have already been obtained, (ii) violate any applicable law, (iii) violate its Organisational Documents, or (iv) contravene any provision of, or constitute a default under, any other agreement or instrument to which, it is a party or by which it or its assets or properties may be bound;

6.1.3 That this Agreement is a legal, valid and binding obligation of each of the Parties, enforceable against either Party in accordance with its terms, except as the enforceability thereof may be limited by applicable bankruptcy, insolvency, liquidation, moratorium and other laws of general application relating to or affecting the rights of creditors or by general principles of equity;

6.2 *Compliance with laws.* Each of *Beta* and the Company represents and warrants to the other that the following are, as of the date hereof, true and correct in all material respects: (i) it has conducted and shall conduct its affairs and activities in respect of its business in accordance with applicable law, (ii) it has complied and shall comply with any law, rule or regulation under the laws of India and of the .... (country) which is or may be applicable to it in the conduct of its business relating to the business of the Company, (iii) mindful of the principles of the United States Foreign Corrupt Practices Act, 1977, it has not made and shall not make or authorise any payment, and has not given and shall not give anything of value directly or indirectly to an official of India or of any other government for the purpose of influencing an act or decision in his official capacity or inducing him to use his influence with that government with respect to the business of the Company, (iv) likewise, it has not made and shall not make, and has not authorised and shall not authorise any payment to any government agency, political party or political candidate for the purpose of influencing any official act or decision, or inducing such entity or person or entity to use any influence with that government with respect to the person or entity, (v) it has not taken and shall not take any action with respect to the business of the Company that would subject any Party hereto to liability or penalty under any and all of the foregoing laws, rules and regulations of India or of the ....(country), (vi) it has ensured and shall ensure that all invoices, financial settlements, reports and billings in respect of the Party thereto reflect properly the facts about all activities and transactions that are the subject thereof, and (vii) it has notified and shall notify the other promptly upon the discovery of any non-compliance with the foregoing.

6.3 The right to indemnification or other remedy based on the representations and warranties of the Parties contained in this Agreement will not be affected by any investigation conducted, except to the extent that a Party was provided specific information (through due diligence investigation or otherwise) or reasonably could have inferred from such information disclosed to it, the inaccuracy of any such representation or warranty.

Article 7. Prototypes Rights and Confidentiality

7.1 Prototype Rights

7.1.1 The Parties agree that any and all tangible and intangible rights, title and interest, present and future, in and pertaining to the R&D Work and the air spring prototypes that may result from the R&D Work, including, but not limited to, all tangible and intangible rights in or to any and all inventions, discoveries, improvements, advancements on, copyrightable material, patentable material, ideas and concepts which may be conceived or developed by the Company in connection with the R&D Work and the air spring prototypes during the carrying out of the R&D Work ("Prototype Rights") shall be the exclusive property of *Beta*. *Beta* may license, assign, transfer, commercially exploit or otherwise deal with any and all Prototype Rights at its discretion as and when it deems fit.

7.1.2 The Company hereby waives any right, title and interest, if any, in and to any Prototype Rights, present and future, in favour of *Beta*, and hereby expressly transfers and assigns the same to *Beta*.

7.1.3 Notwithstanding section 3.5 above, the Company hereby undertakes to promptly, and no later than 2 (two) calendar weeks thereafter, reduce into writing and to disclose to *Beta* all the results of the R&D Work including, but not limited to, any and all inventions, discoveries, improvements, advancements on, copyrightable material, patentable material, ideas and concepts which may be conceived or developed by the Company in connection with the R&D Work and air spring prototypes during the carrying out of the R&D Work.

7.1.4 The Company agrees, at *Beta's* request, to render all reasonable assistance to *Beta* to enable it to patent or register any Prototype Rights in any countries, and to vest title thereto in *Beta* and/or its nominees.

7.2 Confidentiality

7.2.1 Each of the Parties recognizes, accepts and agrees that all information obtained or disclosed including, but not limited to, all data, documents, applications, papers, statements, programmes, plans and/or any business/customer information, marketing strategies/plans and any and all other trade secrets, confidential knowledge or information of either Party relating to its business, practices and procedures (hereinafter collectively referred to as "Confidential Information") provided or communicated by such Party to the other in connection with this Agreement and/or in the course of performance under this Agreement is, shall be and shall remain the sole property of the Party providing such Confidential Information and shall be of a strictly private and confidential nature, and shall be treated as confidential by the Party receiving such confidential information.

7.2.2 During the term of this Agreement and thereafter, neither Party shall make use of any such Confidential Information for any purpose whatsoever which is not necessary for the discharge of its obligations under this Agreement, or to the disadvantage of the Party providing such Confidential Information, nor shall the Party receiving such Confidential Information divulge it to any one other than the Party providing the Confidential Information or persons designated by such Party.

7.2.3 All Confidential Information shall be returned by the Party receiving such Confidential Information to the Party providing the Confidential Information on the expiry or termination of this Agreement; provided that the Party receiving such Confidential Information shall, upon demand by the Party providing it at any time during the term of this Agreement, return to the Party providing it, any and all Confidential Information.

7.2.4 The obligations of each of the Parties contained in this Clause shall continue for the Term of this Agreement and 5 (five) years after the termination of this Agreement but shall not apply to any Confidential Information which (i) is or hereafter comes into the public domain otherwise than through a breach by any Party of its obligations under this Agreement, (ii) is, at the time of disclosure, already known to the Party receiving the Confidential Information as evidenced by such Party's written documentation; or (iii) is independently developed by employees of the Party receiving the Confidential Information who have not had access to or received any such Confidential Information under this Agreement:

Provided, however, that nothing contained in this section shall prevent any Party from disclosing such Confidential Information to the extent required in or in connection with legal proceedings arising out of this Agreement or any matter relating to, or in connection with the Company.

7.2.5 Neither Party shall issue any public statement concerning these arrangements or disclose the contents hereof, nor matters related thereto to the public or any third Party except with the express written approval of the other Party or except as required under applicable law.

7.3 Survival

The provisions of this Article shall survive the expiration or prior termination of this Agreement.

Article 8. Term and Termination

8.1 Term

8.1.1 This Agreement shall take effect and become binding upon the Parties on the effective date hereof, and shall remain in full force for a maximum period of 2 (two) years from the Effective Date ("Term").

8.1.2 The Company shall make every reasonable effort to complete the R&D Work within the Term; if some cause beyond the reasonable control or foresight of the Company shall interrupt the progress of the R&D Work, *Beta* may, at its discretion, allow the Company a reasonable additional period of time to complete the R&D Work upon such terms and conditions as may be mutually agreed to between the Parties in writing.

8.2 Termination

8.2.1 Notwithstanding anything contained in this Agreement, and without prejudice to its other rights in law or equity and without any liability and judicial intervention, this Agreement may be terminated by the Party not in default (the "Non-Defaulting Party") by giving a thirty (30) day written notice to the Party in default (the "Defaulting Party") if any of the following events (hereinafter referred to as an "Event of Default") occurs:

  (i) Either Party commits a breach of this Agreement and such breach, if capable of remedy, is not remedied by the Defaulting Party within the aforesaid thirty (30) day notice period;

  (ii) Any change in control of either Party.—For the purpose of this sub-clause, the Party in respect of which a change in control occurs will be deemed to be the Defaulting Party; or

  (iii) If either Party goes into liquidation (other than a voluntary liquidation for the purposes of reconstruction and where all the rights and obligations are validly assigned), administration or receivership or ceases to carry on its business or is otherwise insolvent or unable to pay its debts on time.

8.2.2 This Agreement may be terminated by the mutual written consent of the Parties.

8.2.3 This Agreement may be terminated by *Beta*, without cause, by serving a notice of (..............................) months. *Beta* shall not be obliged to give reasons for such termination. Upon the expiry of the aforesaid notice period, this Agreement shall stand terminated.

8.2.4 Notwithstanding, section 8.1, this Agreement may be terminated by *Beta* by serving a notice of (....................) months upon *Beta* and *Alpha* establishing and organizing the Second JVC. Upon the expiry of the aforesaid notice period, this Agreement shall stand terminated.

Article 9. Governing Law and Dispute Resolution

9.1 Governing law

This Agreement shall be governed by and construed in accordance with the laws of India.

9.2 Dispute resolution

Any difference, dispute, controversy or claim ("Dispute") which may arise between the Parties out of or in relation to or in connection with this Agreement, or the breach, termination, effect, validity, interpretation or application of this Agreement or as to their rights, duties or liabilities hereunder, other than a dispute for which provisions specifically made in this Agreement, shall be settled by the Parties by mutual negotiations and agreement. If, for any reason, such Dispute cannot be resolved amicably by the Parties, the same shall be settled by way of arbitration proceedings by three arbitrators, one to be nominated by each Party and the third to be appointed by the two appointed arbitrators. The arbitration proceedings shall be held in accordance with the Arbitration and Conciliation Act, 1996, or any subsequent enactment or amendment thereto (the "Arbitration Act"). Each of the Parties shall appoint an arbitrator within thirty (30) days of the receipt by a Party of the other Party's request to initiate arbitration. The two arbitrators so appointed shall then jointly appoint a third arbitrator within thirty (30) days of the date of appointment of the second arbitrator, which third arbitrator shall act as the Chairman of the tribunal. Arbitrators not appointed within the time limit set forth in the preceding sentence shall be appointed in accordance with the Arbitration Act. The decision of the arbitrators shall be final and binding upon the Parties. The venue of the arbitration shall be ...., ... The language of the arbitration and the award shall be English.

9.3 Survival

The provisions of this Article shall survive the expiry or prior termination of this Agreement.

Article 10. Indemnification

10.1 Each Party hereto shall indemnify the other Party and its directors, officers, employees, agents and representatives from all costs, losses, claims, damages and liabilities including reasonable attorney's fees, incurred by it, resulting from or arising out of (i) the gross negligence or wilful misconduct of the indemnifying Party or its representatives or (ii) any breach by the indemnifying Party of any obligation, covenant, representation or warranty contained in this Agreement.

10.2 In no event shall a Party hereto or its agents be liable whether in contract, tort, negligence, strict liability or otherwise for any special, indirect, incidental, or consequential loss or damage whatsoever arising under or incurred in connection with this Agreement, or for lost profits, even if advised of the possibility of the same.

Article 11. Miscellaneous

11.1 Expenses

Each of the Parties hereto shall bear its own expenses, including fees and expenses of any attorneys, accountants, consultants, investment bankers, brokers, finders or other persons or entities engaged by it, and incurred in connection with this Agreement and the transactions contemplated hereby.

11.2 Notices

All notices required or permitted, hereunder shall be in writing and in the English language and shall be sent by internationally recognised courier or by facsimile transmission (with confirming facsimile receipt) addressed to the address of each Party set forth below, or to such other address as such other Party shall have communicated to the other Party in writing. Notice shall be deemed to have been served when received (and in the case of a facsimile transmission, provided that a confirming copy is sent to the other Party, in accordance with the non-facsimile notice delivery requirements).

  If to: Beta

      ....

      ....

  If to: The Company

      ....

      ....

11.3 Force Majeure

Notwithstanding anything to the contrary in this Agreement, neither Party shall be liable by reason of failure or delay in the performance of its duties and obligations under this Agreement if such failure or delay is caused by acts of God, war, riot, fire, civil commotion, strikes, lock outs, embargoes, any orders of governmental, quasi-governmental, or local authorities or any other similar cause beyond its control and without its fault or negligence.

11.4 Remedies

No remedy conferred by any of the provisions of this Agreement is intended to be exclusive of any other remedy which is otherwise available at law, in equity, by statute or otherwise, and each and every other remedy given hereunder or now or hereafter existing at law, in equity, by statute or otherwise except as stated to the contrary in this Agreement. The election of any one or more of such remedies by any of the Parties hereto shall not constitute a waiver by such Party of the right to pursue any other available remedy except as aforesaid.

11.5 Severance

If any provision of this Agreement or part thereof is rendered void, illegal or unenforceable in any respect under any law, the validity, legality and enforceability of the remaining provisions shall not in any way be affected or impaired thereby.

11.6 Survival of Rights, Duties and Obligations

Termination of this Agreement for any cause shall not release a Party from any liability which at the time of termination has already accrued to another Party or which thereafter may accrue in respect of any act or omission prior to such termination.

11.7 Entire Agreement

This Agreement, and the Schedules, Annexures and Appendices hereto constitute the entire agreement between the Parties as to the subject-matter hereof and supersede any and all prior understandings between the Parties on the subject-matter hereof.

11.8 Assignment

Neither of the Parties hereto shall be entitled to assign this Agreement or any of their rights, powers, obligations and/or duties hereunder without the prior written consent of the other Party.

11.9 Further Acts and Assurance

Each Party shall co-operate with the others and execute and deliver to the others such instruments and documents and take such other actions as may be reasonably requested by the others from time to time in order to carry out, give effect to or confirm their rights, and for the intended purpose of the Agreement.

11.10 Counter parts

In the event this Agreement is executed in several counter parts, each of the Parties may execute one or more counter parts and the counter parts so executed shall constitute one Agreement and be binding on the Parties, as if they had all executed the same document. This Agreement shall be deemed to have been entered into at such time, as all the Parties hereto have signed a counter part of it.

11.11 Amendments and Modifications

No amendments and/or modifications of any of the provisions of this Agreement shall be effective unless made in writing specifically referring to this Agreement and duly signed by the Parties hereto.

11.12 Waiver

Save where this Agreement expressly provides, neither Party shall be deemed to have waived any right, power, privilege or remedy under this Agreement unless such Party shall have delivered to the other Party a written waiver signed by an authorised officer of such waiving Party. No failure or delay on the part of either Party in exercising any right, power, privilege or remedy hereunder shall operate as a waiver, default or acquiescence thereof, nor shall any waiver on the part of either Party of any right, power, privilege or remedy hereunder operate as a waiver of any other right, power, privilege or remedy, nor shall any single or partial exercise of any right, power, privilege or remedy hereunder preclude any other or further exercise thereof or the exercise of any other right, power, privilege or remedy hereunder.

IN WITNESS, where of the Agreement has been entered into the day and year first above written.

Signed by,

for and on behalf of

....

Beta

....

The Company

ANNEXURE 'A'
(Programme of research and development)

VI SALE OF GOODS (NOTES AND OBSERVATIONS)

The Sale of Goods is regulated by the Indian Sale of Goods Act, 1930, (Act 3 of 1930). The sections now enacted by the Indian Sale of Goods Act, 1930, originally formed part of the Indian Contract Act, 1872. A contract of sale may be oral or in writing.

The Act makes a distinction between conditions and warranties, a condition being a stipulation essential to the main purpose of the contract, the breach of which gives the right to repudiate the contract, whereas a warranty is a stipulation collateral to the main purpose of the contract, the breach of which gives rise to a claim for damages, but not the right to reject the goods or repudiate the contract. The Act lays down specific rules as to when the property in the goods passes from the seller to the buyer. It also deals with the right of the unpaid seller against the goods and gives him a lien to retain possession until payment, if the goods are in his possession, and if the goods are not in his possession there is also the right of the unpaid seller to stop the goods in transit. In cases of breach, the party in default may be sued for the price of the goods or for damages and in case of failure to deliver specific or ascertained goods the court may decree specific performance of the contract if the contract is such as should be specifically enforced.

Warranties. In a contract for sale of goods, there is no implied warranty or condition as to quality or fitness for any particular purpose unless: (1) Buyer has, relying on the seller's skill and/or judgement, made known to him particular purpose for which goods are required and seller ordinarily deals in such goods; or (2) sale is by description from seller who deals in goods of that description; or (3) such implied warranty is annexed by usage of trade.

AGREEMENT FOR SALE MADE BY A VENDOR IN FAVOUR OF PURCHASER, THE PURCHASER TO EXECUTE A MORTGAGE DEED FOR BALANCE OF PURCHASE MONEY

An agreement of sale made this.................day of...................between *Alpha* (hereinafter called the vendor) of the one part, and *Beta* of etc. (hereinafter called the purchaser) of the other part:

It is agreed as follows:

1. The vendor will sell and the purchaser will buy the house, known as.................... bearing Municipal No .... with all the rights belonging or reputed to belong to it and more fully described in the schedule attached hereto.

2. The price shall be Rs. .... of which the sum of Rs. .... as a deposit is paid to the vendor and the further sum of Rs. .... shall be paid on .... the date fixed for the completion of the purchase and the balance Rs. .... shall be secured by a mortgage of the property as hereinafter provided.

3. The Vendor's title is well-known and shall be accepted by the purchaser and he shall not be entitled to the delivery of any abstract or to make any investigation, objection or requisition in respect thereof but shall be satisfied with the assurance of the property executed by the vendor.

4. The Vendor reserves to himself the right to way as incident to the ownership of his neighbouring property known as .... for all purposes over the property hereby agreed to be sold between the points marked X and Y in the plan attached herewith.

5. The purchase shall be completed on the day .... when the purchaser shall pay the sum of Rs. .... and execute a mortgage-deed for secure payment of Rs. .... the balance of purchase money and then shall be entitled to the delivery of a proper sale-deed executed by the Vendor.

6. Immediately after the execution of the said sale-deed the purchaser shall execute in favour of the vendor a mortgage of the property hereby agreed to be sold for securing the payment to the vendor of Rs. .... being the balance of the purchase-money with interest at the rate of .... p.a. with the proviso that so long as interest is paid regularly, the principal mortgage money shall not be payable for a period of .... years. The mortgage shall also contain a covenant for the personal liability of the purchaser and as well as the liability of mortgaged property.

7. All expenses for preparation of the assurance and all charges on account of stamp and registration shall be borne by the purchaser.

8. Any error, mis-statement or omission in the description of the property shall not annul the sale, nor shall any compensation be allowed in respect thereof.

9. The rents and profits of the property shall be received or shall belong to the vendor, and all outgoings, taxes and rates shall be discharged by him up to the time hereinbefore fixed for completion of the sale, and as from, that date all outgoings shall be discharged by, and the rents and profits shall belong to, the

purchaser. The purchaser shall not be entitled to possession or rents and profits of the property until the actual completion of the purchase.

10. If the purchaser shall fail to comply with the terms and conditions hereinbefore mentioned, his deposit shall be forfeited and the vendor, shall be at liberty to re-sell the property, either by public auction or private treaty and recover the deficiency and expenses from the purchaser's person and property and any excess in price on re-sale shall belong to the vendor.

The schedule above referred to—

The plan above referred to—

In witness whereof the parties hereto have set their respective signatures on this.................... day of.................... in the presence of witnesses.

AGREEMENT EXTENDING THE TIME FOR COMPLETION OF A PURCHASE AND OTHERWISE MODIFYING TERMS OF THE CONTRACT SUPPLEMENTAL TO THE ORIGINAL CONTRACT

This agreement made this.................... day of.................... between *Alpha* of the etc., (hereinafter called the vendor which expression shall, wherever the context, so permits, include his successor and assigns) of the one part, and *Beta*, of etc. (hereinafter called the 'purchaser'. which expression wherever the context so permits, shall include his heirs, executors, administrators and assigns) of the other part, supplemental to an agreement dated.................... and made between the same parties for the sale by the vendor to the purchaser of the properties mentioned therein for the sum of Rs. .... (hereinafter called the original agreement):

1. Whereas by the original agreement between the parties hereto it was agreed, *inter alia*, as under—

   (a) The vendor agreed to sell and the purchaser agreed to purchase 9 properties specified in the Schedule "A" attached thereto for a lump sum of Rs. ....

   (b) The purchaser paid Rs. .... as an earnest money and agreed to pay Rs. .... in the month of.................... and the balance of the purchase money was agreed to be paid within two years from the date of the execution of the said agreement with interest at the rate of .... p.a. for the first year and at the rate of .... p. a. for the second year.

   (c) The vendor agreed to execute the sale-deed in favour of the purchaser or his nominee when called upon within two years from, the date of the execution of the said agreement, provided that before demanding the execution of the sale-deed the purchaser shall pay the balance of the purchase money with interest in the manner aforesaid.

   (d) The vendor shall give possession to the purchaser of the properties.

   (e) In case the purchaser fails to pay the balance of the purchase money with interest at the aforesaid rate within two years from the date of the execution of the said agreement, the vendor shall be entitled to sell the properties by private sale or public auction and recover the amount with interest.

2. And whereas the purchaser has paid the vendor as per details given below:—

    (a) Rs. .... as earnest money paid at the time of the execution of the said agreement.

    (b) Rs. .... paid, as agreed, in the month of....................

    (c) Rs. .... as price of the house No. .... which has been sold by the vendor to Mr. .... as nominee of the purchaser and at his instance, and the balance of amount of purchase money due from the purchaser is Rs. ....

3. Whereas the period of two years fixed for the completion, of the sale expires on.................... and the purchaser being unable to complete the sale by that time has approached the vendor to extend the period for such completion and has applied to the vendor to give him further time of two years and the vendor has agreed to the proposed extension subject to the conditions and terms as mentioned hereafter.

Now this agreement witnesseth and it is agreed between the parties as under:—

1. The vendor grants to the purchaser further extension of two years for completion of sale as from.................... up to....................

2. The purchaser before the expiry of extended period shall pay up the balance of the purchase-money amounting to Rs. .... with interest at the rate of .... p.a. and have the sale-deed executed and registered, the interest to be paid half yearly.

3. In case the purchaser fails to pay the balance of purchase-money with interest on the aforesaid money, the vendor shall be entitled to recover the possession of the properties unsold and shall be entitled to sell the properties and appropriate the sale proceeds towards the balance of the purchase money with interest as aforesaid still due and recover the deficiency from the purchaser.

4. The original agreement dated.................... as hereby varied shall remain in full force and subject to the provisions of this agreement shall be carried into effect.

In witness whereof the parties hereto have herewith affixed their signatures in the presence of witnesses.

AGREEMENT FOR SALE OF PROPERTY WITH USUAL PROVISIONS

An agreement made the day of.................... between *Alpha* of etc., (hereinafter called the vendor) of the part and *Beta* of etc., hereinafter called the purchaser) of the other part:

It is further agreed that the draft of deed of sale shall be submitted by the vendor to the purchaser a fortnight prior to the date of the intended execution, and, after approval thereof by the purchaser, the vendor undertakes to obtain the concurrence of the lessee to the deed of sale which shall be executed and presented for registration within two months of the date of this agreement.

It is further agreed that the purchaser shall pay interest at Rs. .... per cent, per annum to the vendor on any sum out of the aforesaid price which shall remain unpaid to the vendor as from the date of the registration of the deed of sale pursuant to this agreement.

The vendor undertakes to pay all rates, taxes or other assessments levied or leviable on the said premises up to the date of registration of the sale-deed, whereafter the purchaser shall be responsible to pay the said public charges.

In witness whereof, the parties aforementioned have executed this deed of sale in token of acceptance thereof

    1. Witness....................   Vendor....................

    2. Witness....................   Purchaser....................

    3. Witness....................   Lessee....................

EXCLUSIVE RESELLER AGREEMENT

Alpha   *Beta*

Address....................   Address....................

Reseller Agreement Effective Date....................

WHEREAS, Manufacturer appoints Reseller as its exclusive Representative and Reseller in Reseller's Territory to sell, license, market and distribute Manufacturer's Products, and WHEREAS, Reseller accepts the appointment and agrees to sell and distribute Manufacturer's Products within its Territory, NOW, THEREFORE, in consideration of the mutual covenants and premises hereinabove and hereinafter set forth, the Parties hereby agree as follows:

Section 1. Definitions

The following terms shall have the meanings indicated:

(1) *"Agreement"* (also referred to herein as the "Contract Documents", "Contract", "Agreement"): this Reseller Agreement, exhibits, Addendums, Schedules and Amendments attached hereto.

(2) *"Manufacturer"* means a party and its subsidiaries engaged in manufacturing products.

(3) *"Reseller"* means a party duly authorized to sell products or services to the public or to an end user.

(4) *"Equipment"* means hardware, materials, and accessories.

(5) *"Software"* means executable Software object code or binary code and firmware be embedded in Equipment.

(6) *"Work"* means any ongoing or one-time Services furnished by Manufacturer or Reseller.

(7) *"Documentation"* means any specifications, manuals, drawings or other technical data in electronic format or other media provided for Equipment, Software or Work.

(8) *"Products"* means all current and future Software, Equipment, Documentation and Work provided by Manufacturer.

(9) *"Territory"* means any location within the political borders of the ....

(10) *"System"* means the combination of Products from various Manufacturers.

(11) *"End User"* or *"Customer"* means a person or entity to whom Reseller distributes a copy of the Software, Equipment and Documentation for private use, who has agreed to be bound by all the terms of the Software License Agreement, or any other Agreement applicable to the distribution of Manufacturer's Products by Reseller.

(12) *"Distributor"* means a party that purchases Products from Manufacturer, adds other hardware or software, and resells the systems with its own branding and after-sale support and warranty for specific applications.

(13) *"Sub-Distributor"* means third parties which, pursuant to a sub-distribution agreement entered into with Reseller ("Sub-Distribution Agreement"), shall purchase Products from Reseller for distribution solely to End Users.

(14) *"Competition"* means rivalry between two or more parties seeking or striving for the same Customer or market.

(15) *"Compete"* means to seek or strive for the same Customer or market.

(16) *"Acceptance"* (also referred to as "Sign-Off") means the point in time when consistent with industry standards the Work has been completed and the Products have been delivered without exceptions.

(17) *"List Price"* means, with respect to a Product, Manufacturer's standard and published list price for the Product in the Territory.

(18) *"Customer Price"* means the price for products a Customer agrees to pay.

(19) *"Reseller Discount"* means the applicable percentage discount from the Customer Price of Manufacturer's products.

(20) *"Software License Agreement"* means a license agreement governing the use of the Software.

(21) *"Update"* means any change to the Products or Documentation provided by Manufacturer to Reseller following prior delivery of the particular Product or Documentation.

(22) *"Customization"* means changes to the Software required for a specific Customer.

(23) *"OEM"* means Original Equipment Manufacturer. A Party who sells its Products to another party for distribution of Products with the branding and support of such other party.

Section 2. Exclusivity

(1) Subject to Reseller's compliance with terms and conditions set forth in this Agreement, Manufacturer agrees not to appoint any other indirect sales organization for distribution of its products within Reseller's Territory, and agrees that any sale to any end-user within Reseller's territory will be effected by Reseller, except for (i) OEM agreement: In the event Manufacturer enters into an OEM agreement through a direct sales effort by Manufacturer, Reseller would not be entitled to any compensation. Manufacturer shall not appoint OEM Resellers that would compete with Reseller's business. OEM Agreements brokered by Reseller shall be eligible for standard discounts/commissions to Reseller; (ii) Direct sales: Reseller agrees that Manufacturer shall conduct direct sales. Direct sales within Reseller's territory shall not be considered as a sale made by Reseller. Manufacturer agrees not to make direct sales which would compete with Reseller; however, to the extent Reseller is involved for the purposes of local support requirements for the above exceptions, Reseller would be eligible for commissions or discounts, agreed to in writing on a case to case basis.

(2) Subject to Manufacturer's compliance with terms and conditions setforth in this Agreement, Reseller agrees not to market products that compete with Manufacturer's Products within Reseller's Territory. This non-compete provision shall apply to Manufacturer's Products in existence before the Effective Date of this Agreement, or as otherwise agreed to in writing.

(3) Reseller shall use commercially reasonable efforts to ensure that it does not make sales outside the Territory. Without limiting the foregoing, Reseller shall require End User to affirm in writing or over the Internet by click-wrap, under penalty of perjury, that they are resident within the Territory. If, now or in the future, Reseller can through reasonable commercial efforts and at minimal costs determine the location of a prospective customer, then Reseller shall from that time utilize such measures and/or technology and shall not sell the Software to anyone with a location so indicated to be outside the Territory.

(4) The parties acknowledge and agree that legal damages shall not be an adequate remedy for any breach or attempted breach of the provisions of this Section 2 and agree that equitable relief, including injunctive relief, shall be required in appropriate circumstances. The parties hereby waive any 'requirement for the securing or posting of any bond in connection with the obtaining of any such injunctive relief.

Section 3. License and Distribution

(1) Subject to Reseller's compliance with terms and conditions set forth in this Agreement, Manufacturer grants Reseller, and Reseller accepts, during the term of this Agreement, a transferable, exclusive license and right (i) to store one or more copies of its Software, Products and Documentation in Reseller's facility for the purpose of distribution to Customers or for demonstration to Customers;

(ii) to distribute the Products and Documentation to Customers in the Territory; and (iii) to demonstrate, market and promote the Software to Customers.

(2) Reseller's Purchase Orders shall contain the following information: (1) name and address of Customer; (2) detailed description of the Products to be purchased; and (3) confirmation of Purchase Price to be paid to Manufacturer by Reseller for each Product.

(3) Reseller shall submit a Software License Agreement covering the applicable Products duly executed by the End User.

(4) Any Sub-Distribution Agreement(s) entered into by Reseller must have terms and conditions which shall be substantially similar to, and in no event less restrictive than, those set forth in this Agreement. Upon request of Manufacturer, Reseller shall provide Manufacturer with copies of Sub-Distribution Agreements.

(5) Reseller shall not make representations or warranties other than those contained in Manufacturer's Documentation.

Section 4. Sales, Marketing, and Minimum Sales Quota

(1) The Parties agree to use commercially reasonable efforts to promote the sale of Manufacturer's Products in the Territory according to the plan outlined in Exhibit C "Marketing Plan".

(2) Reseller agrees to provide Manufacturer with quarterly sales forecasts outlining the quantities of Products anticipated to be purchased and sold by Reseller during the next subsequent quarter.

(3) The Parties agree to jointly review all promotional and advertising materials for the Products prior to use.

(4) Reseller shall not make any contracts or commitments on behalf of Manufacturer not make any warranties or other representations regarding the Products other than those authorized by Manufacturer in writing.

(5) Reseller agrees to a minimum sales quota beginning from the signature date herein:

- a. Quarters One and Two, 1 each so-called 'Beta Site' account with an aggregate revenue to Manufacturer of .... (amount in foreign currency)
- b. Quarters Three and Four, 4 each so-called 'Early Adopter' reference accounts with an aggregate revenue to Manufacturer.................... (amount in foreign currency)
- c. Year 2 .... (amount in foreign currency).

(6) The Parties agree to negotiate in good faith sales quotas for each subsequent year 3 months prior to the renewal date of the Agreement.

(7) Manufacturer acknowledges that its own performance is of the essence to allow Reseller to achieve its quota. Manufacturer's performance includes, but is not limited to, delivering products and services free of defects or deviations from specifications described in the then current brochures and promotional materials or specific agreements with Customers, and timely delivery of accepted Reseller

purchase orders. Manufacturer therefore acknowledges that its failure to perform shall give Reseller the right to reasonably reduce its sales quota without being considered to be in violation of this Section 4 of this Agreement.

(8) Reseller acknowledges that missing sales quotas by more than 10% due to reasons within its reasonable control shall grant Manufacturer the right to appoint other Resellers at its discretion in Reseller's territory.

(9) Reseller covenants that it shall use commercially reasonable efforts to fulfill its contractual and legal obligations to Customers. Reseller further covenants that it will (i) provide Customers with quality sales and technical support for Manufacturer's Products sold by Reseller; (ii) promptly, courteously and appropriately respond to Customers; and (iii) generally approach Customers in a professional manner to add to the good reputation of Reseller and Manufacturer. To the extent that Reseller is unable to fulfill these obligations to Customers, Reseller agrees that Manufacturer shall elect to fulfill those obligations, or any portion thereof, and Reseller shall reimburse Manufacturer reasonable costs and expenses so incurred by Manufacturer.

(10) Taxes, Tariffs, Fees.—Manufacturer's Suggested Prices and Per Copy Fees are FOB Resellers place of Business in .... (place) and do not include any other national, State or local sales, use, value added or other taxes, customs duties, or similar tariffs and fees which shall be required to be paid or collected upon the delivery of the Products or upon collection of the prices for the Products or the Per Copy Fees to Customer. Should any additional tax or levy be made, Reseller agrees to pay such tax or levy and indemnify Manufacturer against any claim for such amount. Reseller represents and warrants to Manufacturer that all Software acquired hereunder is for redistribution in the ordinary course of Reseller's business, and Reseller agrees to provide Manufacturer with appropriate resale certificate numbers and other documentation satisfactory to the applicable taxing authorities to substantiate any claim of exemption from any such taxes or fees.

Section 5. Schedule and Receipt

(1) Manufacturer shall deliver the Products at Reseller or Customer facility, as instructed by Reseller.

(2) The Parties acknowledge that delivery time is of the essence.

(3) Upon receipt regardless of its location specified in 5.1 above, Reseller shall inspect the Products and shall within 30 (thirty) days of receipt give written notice to Manufacturer of any claim of damage or missing items. Should Reseller fail to give such notice, or fail to obtain an extension of such thirty (30) day period from Manufacturer receipt shall be deemed to be accepted by Reseller. Manufacturer will reasonably accommodate Reseller's request to replace its master copy of software, which becomes corrupted or damaged. Reseller shall contractually require its End Users to report any claim of damage or shortages for Software shipped to them within thirty (30) days of the End Users receipt of such package (or the time required by applicable law, if longer). This paragraph addresses exclusively the act of physical receipt of Products and does not

constitute Acceptance or Sign-off of Product's or Manufacturer's performance, as described in Section 6 below.

(4) If a Party's performance of any of its obligations under this Agreement is delayed or impaired by reason of any act of God, war, civil disturbance, strike, adverse weather conditions, delays in transportation, inability to obtain or delays in obtaining any permits or any law, rule or order of any governmental agency or official or for any other cause not reasonably within the party's control and not due to any fault or negligent act or omission on such party's part, then that party shall be entitled to an extension of time for a period equivalent to the lost time; provided, however, that the affected Party must give the other Party notice within ten (10) business days (unless circumstances require immediate notification) of the commencement of such claimed delay or impairment. Neither party shall be liable for any damages, whether direct or indirect, special, exemplary or consequential as a result of non-performance or late performance arising out of these circumstances.

(5) In addition to the above specified circumstances, the time for delivery of the Products shall be extended if and to the extent (i) Reseller fails to make payments when due; and/or (ii) Reseller fails to approve Manufacturer's submittals requiring approvals within reasonable times, or (iii) Reseller fails to satisfy any of its other obligations.

(6) Except as otherwise provided herein, Manufacturer shall ship by whatever means it deems appropriate for Delivery of the Products within agreed delivery times, and shall have the right to designate and control agents and brokers (including freight forwarders and transportation agents).

Section 6. Acceptance

(1) Manufacturer accepts that Reseller shall give its Customer a Notice of Completion when the Product is fit for its intended use, upon which Customer shall inspect the Product, Work, and/or Customization and shall either: (i) accept the Product, Work and/or Customization in writing, or (ii) in good faith reject the same or portions of either by specifically stating the reasons therefore in writing. If Customer rejects the Products or Work or any portion of either, then Manufacturer shall diligently work to correct the noted deficiencies and shall give Reseller notice of work completion, and Reseller shall submit Notice of Completion to Customer. Customer shall inspect and either accept or in good faith reject the Products or Work in the manner set forth in this Section within five (5) days from such notice; if the Customer again so rejects same, then Manufacturer shall diligently work to correct noted deficiencies until Customer finally accepts same. Such process shall be repeated until noted exceptions shall be corrected. When Customer accepts the Products without exceptions to the mutually agreed-to specifications, the Products shall be "delivered". Modifications are commonly accepted on a separate schedule.

(2) The Parties acknowledge that this acceptance manner shall not affect either Party's right to seek appropriate relief against the other at law due to the Customer's failure to reasonably and in good faith accept the Products or Manufacturer's failure to correct noted deficiencies.

(3) Reseller acknowledges that neither the failure nor malfunction nor late delivery nor system malfunction caused by other Equipment, Software, Systems or Work and not provided by Manufacturer shall be grounds for rejection of the Products.

Section 7. Customization

(1) The Parties shall collaborate in scheduling Product Customization and Delivery.

(2) Manufacturer shall diligently work to deliver the Customization of Products in accordance with the terms and conditions of this Agreement and an agreed to Scope of Work.

(3) Manufacturer shall supervise and direct the Work and be responsible for its means, methods, techniques, sequences and procedures and for the coordination. Except as otherwise noted, Manufacturer shall purchase or provide all labour, materials, Equipment, tools, machinery, and other services necessary for the prosecution and completion of the Customization Work.

Section 8. Payments, Taxes

(1) Manufacturer invoices shall reference a respective Customer or Reseller's Project Number.

(2) Invoices shall be payable in 30 days.

(3) Reseller shall not make any subtraction or deduction from any payment unless Reseller received an official credit memorandum authorizing such subtraction or deduction.

(4) If Reseller fails to make any payment to Manufacturer when due, Manufacturer shall upon ten (10) working days prior written notice to Reseller, suspend execution of the Work until such payment is received in full and the period of suspension shall be added to the time at which Manufacturer is required to complete performance of the Work.

(5) Manufacturer shall establish the prices payable by Reseller for the Products (the "Prices"), which shall be based on a discount from Customer Price, unless otherwise agreed to be the Parties in writing.

(6) List Prices shall be set forth in Exhibit A. Manufacturer shall increase or decrease any of the prices upon mutual written agreement.

(7) Manufacturer's prices shall be FOB Reseller's or Customer's place of business, freight pre-paid, unless otherwise agreed to in writing.

(8) Manufacturer shall use its best efforts to timely deliver accepted Orders of Reseller.

Section 9. Title Transfer, Risk of Loss

(1) Title to each item of Equipment, Software or materials shall pass to Reseller upon Reseller's Acceptance and payment for same.

(2) Risk of loss of each item of Equipment shall pass to Reseller upon Delivery.

(3) The Parties certify that they maintain adequate insurance coverage for the regular course of their business, including liability insurance and legally required insurance, such as workman's compensation.

Section 10. Restrictions

(1) Reseller shall not modify, supplement, enhance or bundle the Software, except where permitted by the use of Visual Basic for Applications (VBA) licensed in the Software, and shall distribute the Software solely in the form in which it was provided to Reseller by Manufacturer or customized by Manufacturer. Reseller shall not have the right to sublicense the Software or Documentation, and Reseller shall ensure that all Customers execute the then-current Software License Agreement with Manufacturer before they shall be permitted to use or access the Software.

(2) Reseller agrees not to: (i) disassemble, de-compile or otherwise reverse engineer the Software or otherwise attempt to learn the source code, structure, or algorithms underlying the Software; (ii) take any action contrary to Manufacturer's Software License Agreement except as expressly allowed under this Agreement.

(3) Manufacturer shall not appoint any other Resellers for sale or distribution of the Products within the Territory without prior written consent by Reseller, which it shall give at its sole discretion, except for provisions made specifically in this Agreement.

(4) Manufacturer shall not change the Territory without prior written consent by Reseller, which it shall give at its sole discretion.

Section 11. Intellectual Property, Infringement and Indemnification

(1) Manufacturer warrants and certifies that each product or service provided by Manufacturer or bearing Manufacturer's name or logo shall be free of any known and rightful claim of patent, trademark or copyright infringement.

(2) Ownership.—As between Manufacturer and Reseller, Manufacturer owns and retains all rights, title, and interest in and to all Software and Documentation; all trademarks, service marks or trade names associated with the Software or Documentation (the "Trademarks"); all copyrights, patents, trade secret rights, and other intellectual property rights therein (collectively, together with the Software, Documentation, and Trademarks, the "Property"). Except as expressly granted herein, Manufacturer does not grant to Reseller any right or license, either express or implied, in the Software, Documentation or Property. Reseller shall not reverse engineer, disassemble, de-compile, or otherwise attempt to derive source code from the Software.

(3) Product Indemnity.—Manufacturer will indemnify, defend and hold Reseller and its subsidiaries (each, an "Indemnified Party"), harmless from and against any and all claims, losses, costs, liabilities and expenses (including reasonable attorneys' fees), arising as a result of or in connection with any claim that the Software or Documentation provided by Manufacturer infringes any intellectual property right of a third party provided: (i) the Indemnified Party promptly gives written notice of any claim to Manufacturer; (ii) the Indemnified

Party provides any assistance which Manufacturer shall reasonably request for the defense of the claim (with reasonable out of pocket expenses paid by Manufacturer); and (iii) Manufacturer has the right to control of the defense or settlement of the claim, provided, however, that the Indemnified Party shall have the right to participate in, but not control, any litigation for which indemnification is sought with counsel of its own choosing, at its own expense. Additionally, if an injunction or order issues restricting the use or distribution of any of the Software or Documentation, or if Manufacturer determines that the Software or Documentation are likely to become the subject of a claim of infringement or violation of any proprietary right of any third party, Manufacturer shall in its discretion and, at its option (a) procure the right to continue using, reproducing, and distributing the Software and Documentation; (b) replace or modify the Software and Documentation so that they become non-infringing, provided such modification or replacement does not materially alter or affect the specifications for or the use or operation of the Software; require return of the Software to Manufacturer and refund any licensing fees relating to the future use of the Software.

(4) Protection of Proprietary Rights.—Reseller shall reasonably co-operate without charge (provided that Manufacturer will reimburse out of pocket expenses as agreed in advance in writing), in Manufacturer's efforts to protect Manufacturer's rights in the Property. Reseller shall promptly notify Manufacturer of any infringements of Manufacturer's Property Rights that come to Reseller's attention. Manufacturer shall have the exclusive right to institute infringement or other appropriate legal action against alleged infringers of its Property Rights. Manufacturer shall incur all expenses in connection therewith and shall retain all monetary recoveries received there from.

(5) Reseller shall not obtain or claim any ownership interest in the Software or Documentation, or any portion thereof, or any Intellectual Property therein, unless otherwise agreed to in writing.

(6) Trademarks; Property.—During the term of this Agreement, Reseller shall have the right to use and reproduce the Trademarks in connection with Reseller's marketing, advertising, promotion and distribution of the Software. Reseller's use of the Trademarks shall not create any right, title or interest therein. Reseller shall use the Trademarks only in a manner, which complies in all material respects with Manufacturer's reasonable policies in effect from time to time, a copy of which shall be delivered to Reseller, and all such use shall be for Manufacturer's benefit and Reseller shall reproduce, on every copy of the Software and Documentation made by or for it, all patent, copyright, trademark, service mark or other markings or legends contained therein or thereon. Reseller shall not remove, obscure or alter Manufacturer's copyright notice or the Trademarks from the Software or Documentation. If Reseller, in the course of distributing the Software, acquires any goodwill or reputation in any of the Trademarks, all such goodwill or reputation shall automatically be transferred to and shall vest in Manufacturer when and as, on an ongoing basis, such acquisition of goodwill or reputation occurs, as well as at the expiration or termination of this Agreement, without any separate payment or other

consideration of any kind to Reseller, and Reseller agrees to take all such actions necessary to effect such vesting. Reseller shall not contest the validity of any of the Property or Manufacturer's exclusive ownership of them. Reseller shall not adopt, use, or register, whether as a corporate name, trademark, service mark or other indication of origin, any of the Trademarks, or any word or mark confusingly similar to the Trademarks in any jurisdiction.

(7) The Parties shall not register any of each other's trademarks, logos, domain names or brands, or confusingly similar trademarks, logos, domain names or brands, anywhere in the world.

(8) Manufacturer shall, at its own expense, defend, indemnify and hold harmless Reseller and its directors, officers, employees and agents from and against any suit or claim brought against them, or award of damages and costs (including reasonable attorneys' fees and costs) by any court, including a court of last resort, resulting from any claim of infringement by Manufacturer's Products of any patent, trademark or copyright of the .... In case of a similar infringement by Reseller, any related claims and liabilities would be to Resellers account.

Section 12. System Warranties and Disclaimers

(1) Reseller shall include the first year of Manufacturer mandatory First Year Software Maintenance Agreement in any sale to a Customer. Subsequent yearly Maintenance Agreements shall be optional.

(2) Manufacturer warrants for a period of three hundred sixty (360) days from the date of Acceptance, that the Work shall conform in all material respects to the highest applicable workmanship standards, and that all Products shall be free from defects.

(3) Manufacturer shall assign to Reseller the warranty and warranty terms for the Products for transfer to the Customer.

(4) Manufacturer shall have no liability or obligation to Reseller or Customer with respect to any portion of the System materially damaged or altered by abuse, improper use, negligence, accident, modification, End-User errors and omissions in operating or maintenance procedures, attempted repair by non-qualified personnel, operation of the Products outside of the normal environmental and electrical specifications, provided that such damage or alteration was not caused by Manufacturer.

(5) Manufacturer warrants the merchantability and/or fitness of the Products for their intended purpose.

(6) Reseller shall take necessary action to ensure that (i) the Software or Documentation stored on Reseller's servers or computer systems is appropriately secured so that the Software or Documentation can only be viewed, copied, or utilized by licensed End Users; and (ii) that the object code of the Software can only be accessed by employees authorized by Manufacturer and cannot be copied or downloaded by any of Reseller's licensees or by any other third party. In addition, Reseller shall make its offices and equipment available in person, upon reasonable notice, and to the extent feasible remotely, to Manufacturer to

inspect and test Reseller's physical and technical setup to ensure that Reseller is complying with its obligations under this Section.

Section 13. Maintenance and Support

(1) Manufacturer shall provide Reseller and Customer with the support defined in Exhibit B, to include the distribution of Product Updates.

(2) Reseller shall provide Sub-Distributors and End Users with Reseller Support as set forth in Exhibit B.

(3) Manufacturer shall provide Reseller with the sales, marketing and product training set forth in Exhibit B. Reseller shall be solely responsible for the training of Sub-Distributors and/or End Users.

(4) Reseller shall and shall cause each of its Sub-distributors to maintain accurate books and records of: (1) all licenses granted for the Products; (2) the name, address and contact person for each End User and Sub-distributor; (3) all support and maintenance provided to End Users ("Product Records"). Reseller shall provide resulting records to Manufacturer periodically.

(5) Reseller shall deliver to Manufacturer the name, address and contact person for each End User or Sub-distributor within thirty (30) days of sale. Reseller and Sub-distributors shall deliver a summary of all maintenance provided to End Users on a quarterly basis. Upon reasonable notice to Reseller, and no more frequently than four (4) times per year, Reseller shall make Product Records available to Manufacturer at Reseller's place of business during normal business hours.

Section 14. Permits, Compliance, Government Provisions

(1) The Parties shall at their own cost and expense: (i) obtain all consents, licenses, permits, approvals, authorizations and inspections from any government authorities, agencies or officials required for the performance of obligations under this Agreement; (ii) comply with all laws, ordinances, rules, regulations, codes, standards, orders, and notices required for the performance of obligations under this Agreement.

(2) Unless otherwise provided under this Agreement, no term or condition required in any Government contract or subcontract shall be deemed a part hereof.

(3) The Parties shall comply with all laws and regulations applicable to their respective marketing and distribution of the Software hereunder. Without limiting the generality of the foregoing, the Parties shall, at their own expense, make, obtain, and maintain in force at all times during the term of this Agreement, all filings, registrations, licenses, permits and authorizations required for the performance of their respective obligations under this Agreement. The Parties shall provide each other with English language copies of evidence of compliance with applicable laws upon reasonable request.

Section 15. Confidentiality

(1) The Parties shall reveal to the other certain confidential, proprietary and/or trade secret information concerning its business, operations, products, features

and/or services in whatever form provided, which is "Confidential Information" and shall remain the property of such Party.

(2) Each Party shall make use of that information or data disclosed to it by the other Party, only for the purpose of effectuating this Agreement.

(3) Confidential Information shall at all times be kept within each Party's organization and shall not be disclosed in any way by the party, its employees, agents, attorneys, accountants, or advisors. Each party shall inform its agents, employees, attorneys, accountants and advisors of the confidential nature of all information disclosed by the other party to it and shall require that such persons or entities be bound by the provisions of the Agreement with respect to the disclosure of that information.

(4) The Parties agree that the restrictions set out herein shall not apply to Confidential Information of a party, which is or becomes, through no fault of the other Party information available in the public domain.

(5) The Parties shall not use or refer to this Agreement or any element thereof or any representation thereof in any promotional materials, including advertisements or other public promotional materials without prior written consent of the other party.

Section 16. General Indemnity

(1) Each Party shall defend, indemnify and hold the other (including its holdings, officers, directors, employees, and agents) harmless from and against any and all claims or suits for losses, damages, liabilities, costs, and expenses (including reasonable attorneys' fees and costs) which, arise from or shall be incident to any death, bodily injury, or tangible property damage proximately caused by such party's negligence, willful misconduct, or strict liability in tort with respect to the subject matter of this Agreement, provided the indemnifying Party has sole control over the defense and settlement of any such claims or suits.

(2) Except as otherwise provided for elsewhere in this Agreement, Manufacturer's or its licensors' liability to Reseller or any third party arising out of this Agreement shall not exceed the total amount actually received by Manufacturer hereunder during the previous six (6) months. In no event shall any party or Manufacturer's licensors be liable to another party or any third party for loss of data, costs of procurements of substitute goods or services or any indirect, incidental, special, or consequential damages under any cause of action, even if such party has been advised of the possibility of such damages.

(3) Reseller shall indemnify and hold Manufacturer harmless from and against any and all damages, liabilities, costs and expenses (including reasonable attorney's fees) which Manufacturer incurs as a result of any claim based on any breach of any representation or warranty, covenant or agreement by Reseller under this Agreement or any breach of this Agreement by Reseller; provided: (i) that Manufacturer promptly gives written notice of any claim to Reseller; (ii) at Reseller's expense, Manufacturer provides reasonable assistance which Reseller shall reasonably request for the defense of the claim; and (iii) Reseller has the right to control the defense or settlement of the claim, provided, however, that

Manufacturer shall have the right to participate in, but not control, any litigation for which indemnification is sought with counsel of its own choosing, at its own expense.

Section 17. Term and Termination

(1) The initial Term of this Agreement shall be for three years of the effective date and shall thereafter automatically renew in successive 12 month terms ("Renewal Term"). Either Party shall cancel this Agreement effective on the last day of the Initial Term, or any Renewal Term, by serving written notice of such termination on the other Party at least forty-five (45) days prior to the effective date thereof.

(2) Manufacturer shall terminate the Agreement for convenience prior to its Term in the event Manufacturer ownership and/or corporate governance changes. In such event, Manufacturer agrees to: Either (i) compensate Reseller for the premature termination through an "Agreement Dissolution Fee" as shall be negotiated at the time of the termination; or (ii) enter into an OEM Agreement with Reseller, whose terms and conditions are agreed to at the time of such termination request, and which the parties agree to negotiate in good faith. This OEM Agreement shall include provisions for support, favourable pricing and compensation for capital investments made by Reseller.

(3) In the event a termination for convenience is requested for, by Manufacturer within the first 6 months from the effective date of this Agreement, the aforementioned provisions of Section 17 Paragraph 2 shall not apply, except for the compensation to Reseller for any unsold inventories and equipment procured by Reseller exclusively to support Manufacturers products.

(4) Except as otherwise provided for herein, either Party shall terminate this Agreement upon giving Notice to the other in the event that such other party shall breach or be in default of any of the covenants, obligations, warranties, representations, terms or conditions of this Agreement and such other party fails to cure such breach or default within .... days after Notice thereof from the party not in default. Such Notice shall provide in reasonable detail the basis upon which the breach is claimed. In the event of such non-performance, especially with respect to revenue targets, Manufacturer, after providing all such notices and grace periods to Reseller as shall be required, shall be entitled to appoint other Resellers in the Territory or to terminate this Agreement to enter into the exclusive appointment of another reseller.

(5) The Parties agree to continue their co-operation in order to effect an orderly termination of their relationship and termination of this Agreement shall be adjourned for a period not to exceed three (3) months, during which time Reseller shall continue to market and distribute its inventory of the Products. During such three (3) month period, Reseller shall have no right to order or receive any additional copies of the Products. Within four (4) days of termination, Reseller shall return all copies of promotional materials, marketing literature, written information and reports pertaining to the Products that have been supplied by Manufacturer. Manufacturer agrees to indemnify and hold Reseller harmless in the event a termination causes Reseller loss of profits or investments made or for like causes.

(6) Upon the expiration or termination of this Agreement, Reseller shall, within thirty (30) days, pay to Manufacturer all amounts when due hereunder, return to Manufacturer all products and demonstration copies received from Manufacturer, erase any and all of the foregoing from all computer memories and storage devices within Reseller's possession or control and, if requested, provide Manufacturer with a signed written statement that Reseller has complied with the foregoing obligations. All rights and licenses granted by Manufacturer hereunder shall terminate, provided such termination shall not result in the termination of end user licenses for copies of the Software which already have been purchased by end users in accordance with the provisions of this Agreement.

(7) Notwithstanding other provisions herein, Manufacturer shall not be liable to Reseller because of such termination for compensation, reimbursement or damages on account of the loss of prospective profits or anticipated sales or on account of expenditures, inventory, investments, leases or commitments in connection with the business or goodwill of Reseller.

Section 18. Representations

(1) Reseller represents and warrants to Manufacturer as follows: (i) Reseller is a limited liability company duly organized, validly existing and in good standing under the laws of the .... (place) (Reseller). (ii) Reseller's signing and delivery of this Agreement, and its performance of its obligations hereunder have been duly authorized by all necessary corporate action; and do not conflict with any terms or conditions of its Articles of Organization or By-laws; and do not violate any law, regulation, order, judgment or decree by which it shall be bound; and shall not violate or result in a breach, acceleration or default under any agreement or understanding to which it is a party or by which it shall be bound which shall materially affect its ability to perform its obligations hereunder.

(2) Manufacturer represents and warrants to Reseller as follows: (i) Manufacturer is a corporation duly organized, validly existing and in good standing under the laws of the State of .... (place) (ii) Manufacturer's signing and delivery of this Agreement, and its performance of its obligations hereunder have been duly authorized by all necessary corporate action; and do not conflict with any terms or conditions of its Articles of Organization or By-laws; and do not violate any law, regulation, order, judgment or decree by which it shall be bound; and shall not violate or result in a breach, acceleration or default under any agreement or understanding to which it is a party or by which it shall be bound which shall materially affect its ability to perform its obligations hereunder.

Section 19. Dispute Resolution

(1) Management Escalation. The parties agree that in the event any dispute arising out of or related to this Agreement is not resolved in the ordinary course of business, the parties shall in good faith attempt to resolve the dispute through negotiation by their representatives who shall be at a higher level of management

than those involved in the day to day administration of the Contract and who have authority to settle the dispute. Accordingly, each party agrees that it shall not commence legal action against the other in connection with such dispute without first attempting to resolve the dispute in accordance with the following procedure: (a) Written notice of the dispute (Notice of Dispute) shall be issued to the other (for purposes of this Section the party issuing the Notice of Dispute shall be referred to as the "Claimant" and the other party shall be referred to as the "Respondent"). Such notice shall state the nature of the dispute, the Claimant's position, and its reasons supporting its position. Within thirty (30) days of Respondent's receipt of the Notice of Dispute, representatives of each party who have authority to settle the dispute shall, meet at a mutually agreeable time and place to attempt to negotiate a resolution to the dispute. If these representatives fail to resolve the dispute within forty-five (45) days of the Recipient's receipt of the Notice of Dispute, then either party shall commence legal action as permitted by law. (b) All negotiations pursuant to this Section shall be confidential and treated as settlement discussions for purposes of the Federal Rules of Evidence and applicable State rules of evidence.

(2) Arbitration.—Any controversy or claim arising out of or relating to this Agreement, or the breach thereof, not resolved by Management Escalation shall be settled by binding arbitration in California, under the Commercial Arbitration Rules of the .... and judgment upon the award rendered by the arbitrator(s) shall be entered in any court having jurisdiction over the subject matter of the controversy.

Section 20. Notices

All notices and other communications required or permitted to be given under this Agreement ("Notice") shall be in writing and shall be delivered personally, or mailed by registered or certified mail, return receipt requested, postage prepaid, or by telex, telecopy or other form of rapid transmission, confirmed by mailing as described above, addressed as follows:

If to Reseller	If to Manufacturer
Alpha	*Beta*
....	....
.... (address)	.... (address)

Any Notice so addressed and delivered personally or by rapid transmission shall be deemed given upon receipt. Any Notice so addressed and mailed shall be deemed given as of the date it is deposited in the mails. Either party shall change its address by giving the other written Notice thereof in the manner provided in this Section.

Section 21. General Provisions

(1) The headings of the sections and sub-sections of this Agreement shall be for general information and reference only and they in no way define, limit or describe the scope of the provisions of such sections and shall not be 'considered in the interpretation or enforcement of this Agreement.

(2) Either party's waiver or failure to enforce any of the terms and conditions of this Agreement in any instance shall not be deemed or construed to be a waiver of such term or condition for that instance or of any subsequent breach thereof.

(3) Nothing contained in this Agreement is intended to create, or does create, a joint venture or partnership or any other relationship between the parties other than the relationship of independent contractor between Reseller and Manufacturer nor to make Manufacturer or Reseller the agent of the other. Manufacturer and Reseller each agree not to hold itself out as an employee, partner, agent or representative of the other. Nothing contained herein shall be deemed to limit Manufacturer from entering into any agreement with any other party.

(4) The Parties shall act in good faith and refrain from activities that attempt to overtly induce each other's staff to leave each other's respective employ, or to interfere with the Party's relationship with its employees. Further, the Parties agree that during the term of this Agreement or for 6 months after its completion, Purchaser shall not in any way, directly or indirectly (i) induce or attempt to induce any of its employees to quit employment; (ii) otherwise interfere with or disrupt the Party's relationship with its employees; or (iii) solicit, entice, or hire away any employees of the other Party.

(5) Whenever possible each provision of this Agreement shall be interpreted in such manner as to be effective and valid under applicable law, but if any provision of the Agreement shall be prohibited by or invalid under applicable law, such provision shall be ineffective only to the extent of such prohibition without invalidating the remainder of such provision or the remaining provisions of this Agreement.

(6) All the representations and warranties made by either party in this Agreement and all the obligations of the parties intended by their terms to survive the signing and delivery of this Agreement and its expiration or termination shall so survive.

(7) If there is any litigation between the parties regarding this Agreement, the prevailing party (*i.e.*, the party entitled to recover the costs of suit at such time as all appeals have been exhausted or the time for taking such appeals has expired) shall be entitled to recover reasonable attorneys' fees and court costs in addition to such other relief as the court shall award. This Agreement shall be construed and enforced in accordance with the local law of the District of .... (place) without reference to or application of its rules governing conflicts of law. The Parties hereby consent and submit to the jurisdiction of the federal and State courts located in .... (place) and agree that any action or suit arising out of or related to this Agreement shall be brought only in the federal or State courts located in .... (place) that have proper jurisdiction over the subject matter of the action or suit.

(8) The parties consent that any process, or notice of motion or other application to any State or federal court located or a judge thereof where the action is brought, or any notice in connection with any proceedings, shall be

served inside or outside the State where the action is brought by registered or certified mail, return receipt request directed to Reseller at the address set forth below, or of which Reseller advises Manufacturer in writing, and service so made shall be deemed complete five (5) days after the same shall be posted, or in such manner as shall be permissible under the rules of said Courts.

(9) Unless separately agreed to in writing, no provision required in a Government contract or subcontract shall be a part of this Agreement or imposed upon or binding upon Manufacturer.

(10) This Agreement shall be modified only by a written instrument signed by both parties, making specific reference to this Agreement and to the charges to be made.

(11) This Agreement shall be deemed to have been made and executed in the .... (State) and any dispute arising hereunder shall be resolved in accordance with the local laws of the .... (place), without reference to or application of its rules governing conflicts of law.

(12) If any provision of this Agreement is determined by a court of competent jurisdiction to be invalid or enforceable, such determination shall not affect the validity or enforceability of any other part or provision of this Agreement.

(13) The failure of either Party to insist upon or enforce strict performance by the other Party or any provision of this Agreement or to exercise any right under this Agreement shall not be construed as a waiver or relinquishment to any extent of such Party's right to assert or rely upon any such provision or right in that or any other instance; rather, the same shall be and remain in full force and effect.

(14) The Parties agree to inform each other immediately of any changes in its organization or method of doing business, which might affect the performance of the Party's duties hereunder.

(15) This Agreement shall be binding upon and inure to the benefit of the Parties and their respective administrators, executors, legal representatives, successors and permitted assigns, which will include without limitation any successor to all or substantially all of the Parties' assets or any acquirer of a majority of the voting power of the Parties' capital stock.

(16) This Agreement incorporates the parties' entire understanding and there shall be no warranties, representations, or understandings of any kind, nature, or description whatsoever made by either party to the other, except such as shall be expressly noted.

In witness whereof, the parties by their duly authorized representatives have executed this Agreement as of the date first indicated above.

"Reseller"	"Manufacturer"
NAME	NAME
TITLE	TITLE

Exhibit A: Price List and Standard Terms of Sale
Exhibit B: Support
Exhibit C: Joint Marketing.

A GUIDE TO DRAFTING JOINT VENTURE DOCUMENTATION[1]
NOTES: JOINT VENTURE (CHECKLIST)

Meeting with Mr. ...., A.G.M. (Corporate Affairs) at the Corporate Office of THETA

Date of Meeting: ....
Time   11:25 hrs to 17:05 hrs.
Present   ....(quorum)

A. Background

- The Business was started in, 1955 by Mr. *Alpha* as a partnership firm
- In ....(year), the firm was converted into Company (*Theta*);
- In ....(year), ... made its first public issue;
- In ....(year), ... entered into a Technical Collaboration with .... to manufacture leaf springs;
- In ....(year), ... entered into a Technical Collaboration with .... for the manufacture of Parabolic Springs;
- *Delta* made its first public issue of shares in ....(year);
- In ....(year), ... made a public issue of shares on rights basis to finance its .... Unit;
- In ....(year), *Delta* also made rights issue for expansion of its .... Unit;
- In ....(year), ... and *Delta* both made a preferential issue to .... whereby .... acquired .....% of the equity share capital of each of the two companies.
- Mr. *Alpha* is about 68 years. Has two sons, ... (name) (40) and .... (name) (36) who are in the family business. The senior .... (name) also has two daughters of which ....(name), the elder daughter was a director in *Delta* until last year.
- The .... Group manufactures various kinds of springs, which form part of Suspension of four wheelers. There are four kinds of springs; Leaf; Parabolic; Coil and Air (in order of technical advancement).
- In ...., ... transferred its Stabiliser Parts Gwalior Unit to a company, *Alpha* in which the shareholding pattern is as follows.

    | .... | 58% |
    | .... | 15% |
    | .... | 24% |
    | .... | 03% |

- *Alpha* also manufactures Coil spring at its .... Unit.

---

1. The names and references to commercial entities used herein are fictitious and have been utilised purely for the purposes of illustrating a corporate checklist.

- .... has a Marketing Agreement with *Alfa*.
- As of date, *Delta* has two Units – in .... (place) and in .... (place). The .... Unit is older and manufactures mainly for vehicle manufacturers using relatively old technology. The .... Unit has various QS and ISO certifications and manufactures for more modern four wheeler manufacturers including Ford and Daewoo. The .... Unit also caters to the demand in .... India and to the replacement market. The .... Unit was set up in, ... (year) while .... Unit was set up in .... (year).

B. Incorporation of New Undertaking of New Company

- The new Company, ... Suspension Systems Private Limited with its registered office in the State of .... had already been incorporated to implement the proposed transaction with the .... Company. .... (name) and .... (name) are the subscribers to the memorandum of the new company. It is proposed that the .... Unit will be transferred to the new Company on a going concern basis in consideration for shares in the new company.
- The transaction would involve the following steps:
  i. Sale of .... Unit on a going concerned basis to the new company by *Delta* – this would be a slump sale for income tax purposes;
  ii. .... will invest in to the new company by subscribing to its share at a premium – the overall figures have been decided but the details are yet to be worked out;
  iii. (a) The new company will pay all debt with the funds received as subscription money from .... so as to reduce its debt obligation to .... (foreign amount) – all the debts specific to the .... Unit and the IFCI Corporate Loan are being transferred to the new Company.
  (b) The new company will pay certain consideration to .... and/or *Delta* for giving up their market share in favour of the new company.

C. Sales and Procurement Contract

Delta typically does not enter into any long term supply contract with its customers. *Delta* is the OEM (Original Equipment Manufacturer) for various vehicle manufacturers and supplies to them on the basis of the demand forecast received by it from the manufacturers. The purchase orders are placed with *Delta* and on a monthly basis, the supplies are made.

It was later informed that *Delta* itself have long term contracts with certain customers such as .... (company name) Limited. A copy of the Agreement has been requested. It appears that there are no contracts, which require supplies to be made from both .... Unit and the .... Unit. Accordingly, the supply contracts relating to the .... Unit are easily identifiable and will be transferred as a part of the business being transferred to the new Company. The reason for separate contracts is that geographical consideration.

There is no long term contract for purchase of raw material entered into by *Delta*. However there are certain contracts, which are negotiated at the 'group level' or even at the 'company level', although the arrangement for purchase of raw material is made on a 'unit to unit' basis. Even in this case, there are no contracts benefit of which will be lost by the .... Unit because of the transfer of undertaking to the new company.

The main raw materials are:
1. Steel (80% of the cost of product)
2. Fuels
3. Parts
4. Steel Shots
5. Quenching Oil
6. Components

Even for disposal of scrap, agreements are entered into on a 'unit to unit' basis.

D. Statutory Records of *Delta*

The following records were made available for review:
1. Minute books of General Meetings (date..................... onwards)
2. Minute Books of Board Meetings (date..................... onwards)
3. Minute Books of Share Transfer Committee Meetings;
4. Register of Directors
5. Charge Register
6. Register of Investment
7. Register of Directors' Shareholding
8. Register of contracts.

E. Review of the Minute Books of Board Meetings

It is noticed that the Company had changed its auditors in the recent past. For more details see below.

A Board resolution has been passed on .... (date) authorising the Company to invest upto 100% in the equity share capital of a company, ... (company name) Limited. We were informed that the Company did not invest upto 100%.

On .... (date), another board resolution was passed to purchase the goodwill of ....(company name).

A board resolution was passed on .... (date) for the change of the name of the Company from .... (company name) Limited to .... (company name) Limited. In response to our queries, we were informed that even though the Registrar of Companies had made available the new name for the Company, the name was not changed. Also, see resolution of .... (date).

On .... (date), a resolution was passed to merge *Delta* with a company called .... (company name) Limited. Earlier on .... (date), the board had resolved to provide Technical services to ....

During the Board meetings held on .... (date) (Excise matter search) .... (date) (Ropar Excise Raid – Criminal complaint), ... (date) (Chief Judicial Magistrate), and in another meeting (.................... High Court Writ – Sales tax matter), the board authorised the officials of the Company to represent the company before certain authorities in connection with the litigation, investigation etc. The details of these proceedings have been requested.

It was observed, that board meetings were being called at very short intervals, sometimes after a gap of a couple of days only. This raises a doubt about the compliance with the formalities related to the calling of board meetings such as, giving of proper notice and also to the general organisation of the affairs of the company. As indicated above there were several board resolutions, which were passed, and also the same matters were taken up and resolved at the General meetings. However, no follow-up action was taken. It appears that the Board resolutions were passed even though there was no need to pass the same or the intention to implement the same.

At the Board meeting held on .... (date), the financial year of the company for the purpose of Companies Act was changed from .... (date). In response to our query, it was explained that this was done for the sake of better presentation of the financial results of the company so that the commencement of commercial production at the .... Unit can also be reflected in the accounts. Please also see separate note on change of auditors below.

The last board meeting of *Delta* was held on ...., 20...... Wherein the transfer of undertaking and other related matters were discussed. A copy of the minutes of the said meeting has been requested.

It is also noticed, that for availing some loans personal guarantees of the promoters have also been given.

The Company has an FDR Scheme in operation. The Company is no longer accepting the deposits either fresh or by renewal. However, it still has certain outstanding on account of the Fixed Deposit Scheme.

F. Change of Auditors

For quite some time the auditors of *Delta* has been .... Associates. However, for the .... months ended on .... (date), the accounts have been audited by .... (name) and Associates. The resignation of the earlier auditors was accepted some time towards the end of .... (date). Thereupon, an extra ordinary General Meeting was called for the appointment of .... (name) and Associates. It is to be noted that by the time, the earlier auditors resigned, the audit of the period upto earlier financial year (i.e., March 31) must have been completed and the auditors must have been in a position to issue their financial report. Despite this, the new auditors were appointed.

It was further informed that the earlier auditor resigned since the fee being paid to them was not acceptable and that it was not cost effective for them to continue to audit the accounts of the Company in a place as far as .... The explanation needs to be considered in view of the facts to change in auditors took place much after the end of the financial year and that the appointment of the auditors takes place at the Annual General Meeting called for to consider the previous years financial statement.

G. Documents Requested

During the course of the meeting we requested that the following documents be made available to us:

1. Technical Collaboration Agreement between *Delta* and ....;
2. Further document prepared at the time of *Delta's* issue (1988);
3. Further Document for *Delta's* rights issue (1994);
4. Shareholders Agreement for preferential issue between .... and ....;
5. Shareholders Agreement for Preferential Issue between *Delta* and ....;
6. Memorandum of Understanding .... (year);
7. Long term contract between .... (company name) and *Delta*;
8. Write-up on Purchase policy and procedure;
9. Notice of General Meeting;
10. Details of contractors;
11. Schedules of loans, pending charges and outstanding;
12. List of Group companies
13. Documentation related to .... (place) Sales Tax Exemption
14. Copy of the board meeting minutes dated ....;
15. Details relating to litigation as noted above.
16. Memorandum of Articles of Association of the new Company;
17. Photocopies of correspondence to follow-up of the appointment of auditors of the new Company;
18. Fuel quota and license.

JOINT VENTURE AGREEMENT

This Joint Venture Agreement (the "Agreement") is entered on the (...................) day of ...., 20.....

BETWEEN

Alpha a company incorporated in India under the Companies Act, 1956 and having its Registered Office at .... (address) India (hereinafter referred to as the "OIL")

AND

Beta, a partnership firm of (Mr. ...., Mr. .... and Mr. ....) formed and registered under the laws of .... (country) (with the liability of the partners limited to their contribution) having its principal office at (.................) (hereinafter referred to as the "ABC").

Each of the OIL and the ABC are also referred to herein as a "Party" and collectively as "Parties".

Whereas the OIL is carrying on the business of manufacturing, developing and marketing of various products in the area of information technology, computer hardware, computer software and other related activities in India; and

Whereas the partners of ABC have substantial experience in the area of computer software development, marketing and providing after sales support; and

Whereas the Parties are interested in carrying on business jointly in the .... (foreign) in area of computer software development, system designing, data collection and reporting, (.................) (herein after the "Business"); and

Whereas the Parties have decided to carry on Business jointly by establishing private, limited liability limited under the laws of the State of (.................) .... (foreign) (the "................. Company"); and

Whereas the Parties have entered in to a Memorandum of Understanding dated (.................) to provide for the basic terms and conditions for entering into the Agreement.

NOW THEREFORE, in light of mutual terms and conditions promises contained herein and other good and valuable consideration, the receipt and sufficiency of which is hereby acknowledged the Parties and the .... agree as follows:

1. Definitions

The following words and expressions shall, unless the context otherwise require, have the following meaning:

"Act" The (Companies Act of State of .... (foreign) where the company is proposed to be incorporated), as amended from time to time, or any statutory re-enactment thereof, and wherever the context requires, any statutory rules framed thereunder;

"Agreement" This Shareholders Agreement entered into between OIL and the ABC;

"Articles" the Articles of association of the JVCO venture company to be incorporated pursuant to the Agreement;

"Board" the Board of Directors of the JVCO;

"Director" a Director of the JVCO;

"JVCO" Joint Venture Company to be incorporated pursuant to the Agreement in the name of .... (company name) or in such other name permitted by the authorities;

"*Shares*" the Equity Shares of ten .... (foreign amount) each in the share capital of the JVCO;

"*Shareholders*" OIL and the ABC collectively, or where Shares in the JVCO are held by OIL's affiliates or nominee, that affiliate or nominee holding Shares in the JVCO.

2. Transfer of Business from the ABC to JVCO

2.1 The whole of the business (including all assets, liabilities, rights, title and interest in any intellectual property and goodwill) as was being carried out by the partners of ABC and owned and run by the ABC shall be transferred by the ABC to JVCO in consideration of the 49% Shares in the capital of the JVCO.

2.2 Atleast 10 days before the date fixed for allotment of Shares to the parties the ABC shall prepare a detailed statement of its accounts and finances as of (, 20...) showing clearly the assets and liabilities which are intended to be transferred/assumed by the JVCO. The JVCO shall be liable only for the declared liabilities and such other liabilities arising out of the declared liabilities and none other.

3. Capitalisation and Shareholding of JVCO

3.1 Immediately after the execution of the Agreement ABC shall take steps for the incorporation of the JVCO with the authorised capital of .... (foreign amount in figures and words) divided in to (No. of Shares) equity shares (common stock) of .... (foreign amount in figures and words) each.

3.2 The entire share capital of the JVCO shall be held by the Parties in the following proportion:

OIL	49%
ABC	49%
Non-Resident Indians	2%

(At the option of OIL)

3.3 Of the proposed twenty million Shares, ... (No. of Shares) Shares aggregating to a total face value of .... (foreign amount) (representing 49% stake in the JVCO) reduced by any Share(s) already held shall be issued by the JVCO to the ABC in consideration of the ABC's transferring (having transferred) its entire business to the JVCO.

3.4 Of the proposed twenty million Shares .... (No. of Shares) Shares aggregating to a total face value of .... (foreign amount) (representing an interest of 49%) shall be issued to OIL against the cash subscription paid by OIL to the JVCO.

3.5 The balance of the proposed twenty million Shares, *i.e.* .... (No. of Shares) Shares aggregating to a face value of .... (foreign amount) shall be allotted by the JVCO to such persons who are non-resident Indians and selected by OIL.

3.6 If and when the JVCO desires to increase the paid-up share-capital, by way of further issue of Shares, the additional Shares shall be offered in the first instance to the existing holders of the Shares by way of rights issue in proportion to the Shares held by them at that time so as to maintain the ownership structure within the JVCO.

4. Board of Directors

4.1 The management of the JVCO shall be vested in the Board of Directors consisting of five Directors other than nominee Director(s) of financial institutions and banks, if any. Of the seven Directors, three Directors shall be appointed by OIL and three by the ABC and one Director shall be nominated by the non-resident Indian Shareholders. In the event that financial institutions and/or, banks advancing loans to the JVCO impose conditions as to the composition of the Board, OIL and the ABC shall enter into discussions to arrive at a mutually acceptable solution to comply with the requirements of the said lenders. The Directors shall not be required to hold any shares as a condition or qualification for holding office of directors of the JVCO.

4.2 The Parties shall ensure that the JVCO shall enter into a separate agreement with the Directors nominated by ABC for their appointment as the Whole time Directors of the JVCO. The terms and conditions of their appointment shall be substantially as set out in Schedule –I hereto.

4.3 The chairman of the Board of Directors (the "Chairman") and for the meetings of the Shareholders' of the JVCO shall be a person nominated by OIL.

4.4 The operational powers and responsibilities of the Board shall, subject to the provisions of the Act, be as determined in a general meeting in accordance with the Articles.

5. Management

5.1 *Chairman:* At the first meeting of the Board of Directors, held after the allotment of shares to the Parties as envisaged in section 3 of the Agreement, a Director nominated by OIL shall be appointed the Chairman of the JVCO and such Chairman shall preside over all meetings of the Board and of the Shareholders at which he is present.

5.2 Notwithstanding anything contained in the Act the Chairman shall not have a casting or second vote.

5.3 *Voting:* Subject to the provisions hereof, all decisions of the Board shall be by a majority vote of all the Directors (excluding the Directors nominated by the lenders).

5.4 Any of the following actions:

   (a) Change in the dividend policy
   (b) Alteration of the Memorandum and Articles of Association of the JVCO
   (c) Change in the capital structure of the JVCO.
   (d) Change in the name of the JVCO, its registered office or its constitution.
   (e) Appointment of any exclusive marketing associate.
   (f) Any scheme of arrangement or compromise or restructuring of the JVCO.

(g) Incurring or agreeing to incur capital expenditure exceeding 10 per cent of the net worth of the JVCO.

(h) Any change or action or proposal affecting rights or obligations of the Parties.

(i) Investment in other companies by way of equity, loan or otherwise.

(j) Borrowing other than normal credit in routine course of business.

(k) Appointment of chief executive/whole time Directors.

(l) Changing the constitutions of the Board of Directors other than nominee directors appointed by the financial institutions pursuant to loan agreement, if any.

(m) Appointment of a relative or contract with a relative as defined under the Act.

(n) Any contract of outsourcing where the cumulative value in a year exceeds 10% of the turnover of the previous year.

(o) Change in the remuneration structure of a Director.

(p) Any agreement containing clauses giving right to a person to subscribe to share capital whether it is express or contingent or any other condition which may affect any or all of the above issues mentioned in this article.

(q) Change in the business plan approved by the Board.

Shall require prior approval by:—

(a) OIL and the ABC, in the case of those matters customarily requiring shareholder approval or,

(b) In the case of all other matters, whether being passed at a Board meeting or by circulation, a majority of the Directors comprising at all times at least one Director each appointed by OIL and the ABC,

5.5 The Parties shall at all times during the effective period of this Agreement cause their representatives on the Board to exercise their votes in consonance with and in compliance with the terms of this Agreement.

6. Meetings of the Board

6.1 Meeting of the Board shall be held at least once in a quarter. The minimum number of meeting required to be held under the Act shall always be complied with. The meeting of the Board shall normally be held in ( ) unless otherwise agreed upon by the Parties.

6.2 At least fourteen (14) days' prior written notice of all meetings of the Board shall be given to each of the Directors. There shall be attached to each notice of the meeting of the Board an agenda of the matters to be discussed and decided at the Board meeting. The Board shall not be entitled to take any decision on the matters not provided in the agenda. However, in case of urgency any meeting of the Board can be held at a shorter notice with the approval of all the Directors.

6.3 Quorum for the meeting of the Board shall not be complete unless one representative of each Party is present at the meeting. However, if at a duly convened meeting of the Board, a representative of either of the Parties are not present (the "Absenting Party"), the meeting shall be reconvened by the JVCO. If at the reconvened meeting also a representative of the Absenting Party is not present the quorum shall be deemed to be complete and the Board shall be entitled to take decision on the items mentioned in the agenda. However, the Absenting Party shall have the right to express its consent or dissent on the matters through telephone or Internet.

7. Operations of JVCO

7.1 Unless the Parties agree otherwise, the day to day management of the JVCO will be conducted/carried out by the whole time Directors who shall, however, be accountable to the Board of Directors. However, an adequate "Management Information System" by way of Internet, periodical reports in writing, shall be developed and implemented within a period of one month of signing of the allotment of Shares so as to enable OIL to know about the functioning of the JVCO. In particular, such Management Information System shall provide information relating to matters contained in the Schedule-II to the Agreement.

7.2 In addition to the Management Information System the JVCO shall prepare its Balance Sheet, Profit and Loss Accounts and such other financial statement as may be directed by the Board on a quarterly basis and submit the same within a period of 15 days from the close of each quarter for the approval of the Board.

7.3 Unless otherwise agreed by the Parties, the JVCO shall distribute at least two thirds of its profit after tax by way of dividend.

8. Meetings of the Shareholders

8.1 General meetings of the JVCO shall be called from time to time to direct and control the business of the JVCO and the Board shall decide the time, place and agenda for convening such meetings subject to the Articles and the applicable requirements of the Act.

8.2 Notwithstanding anything contained herein, at all times, atleast twenty one (21) days' prior written notice of any meeting of the Shareholders of the JVCO shall be given to all the Shareholders and Director.

8.3 No business shall be transacted at any meeting of Shareholders or any adjournment thereof, unless a quorum as provided under clause 8.4 hereof is present at the time when the meeting proceeds to business and throughout the meeting.

8.4 A quorum for a general meeting shall not be deemed to have been constituted unless one representative of OIL and one representative of the ABC is present. However, if at a duly convened meeting of the Shareholders, a representative of either of the Parties are not present, meeting shall be reconvened by the JVCO. If at the reconvened meeting also a representative of the Absenting Party is not present the quorum shall be deemed to be complete and the Shareholders shall be entitled to take decision on the items mentioned in the agenda. However, the Absenting Party shall have the right to express its consent or dissent on the matters through telephone or Internet.

9. Books of Accounts, other records and Audit

9.1 The JVCO shall ensure that its books and records are maintained with a view to accurately reflect its financial positions and are kept in accordance with the requirements of the Act and to support the Management Information System as provided in the Agreement.

9.2 A reputed and mutually acceptable firm of Accountants shall be appointed as the Auditors of the JVCO to carry out the statutory audit of the JVCO. However, the Parties shall be free to appoint at their cost any firm of Chartered Accountant or any other qualified person to carry out the independent audit or inspection of the financial position of the JVCO or a management audit of the functioning of the JVCO.

9.3 Not later than (45) days after the end of each fiscal year, audited balance sheets of the JVCO as of the end of that fiscal year, together with the related audited statements of the income, retained earnings and cash flow for that fiscal year, setting forth in comparative form the information for the preceding fiscal year shall be presented before the Board for its consideration and approval.

10. Articles of Association

10.1 Within one month of the allotment of Shares as envisaged in section 3 of the Agreement, the Articles shall be amended to remove any and all provisions which are not in accordance with the provisions of this Agreement and to provide for management of the JVCO in accordance with the provisions of this Agreement.

10.2 The Parties shall take all action to ensure that at all times the Articles reflect the provisions of this Agreement. The Parties agree to do all such things and take all such actions to ensure that the provisions of this Agreement are put into effect. In case of any conflict between the provisions of the Agreement and the Articles, the provisions of this Agreement shall prevail between the Parties.

11. Non-Competition/Confidentiality

11.1 Each of the Parties agree that from the date hereof and for so long as it holds shares in the JVCO it will not engage or be interested whether as principal, agent, consultant, employee or even otherwise in any trade occupation or business worldwide competing directly or indirectly with the JVCO without prior consent in writing of the other Party:

Provided, however, that OIL shall not require any consent of the ABC for accepting the directorship and/or holding/acquiring any stake in any other company carrying on similar business unless the OIL proposes to acquire substantial stake in that company.

11.2 Each of the Parties shall keep confidential all information (written or oral) concerning the business and affairs of the JVCO or any subsidiary of the JVCO or of the other Party that it shall have obtained or received as a result of the discussion leading upto entering into or implementation of the Agreement or its association with the JVCO or any subsidiary of the JVCO save that which is:

(a) trivial or obvious;

(b) obtained lawfully and other than as a result of a breach of this Article from Third Parties; or

(c) in the public domain prior to the signing of the Agreement.

12. Effective Date, Term and Termination

12.1 In the event of either Party committing a breach of any of the provisions of this Agreement, the other Party shall, without prejudice to other rights and remedies available, have the right to terminate this Agreement, by giving the defaulting party a thirty (30) days' prior notice in writing, specifying, *inter alia*, the nature of the alleged default and the intention of termination, unless such default is cured by the defaulting Party within the next thirty (30) days following receipt of the said notice. However the notice of default shall not be valid and effective unless given within a period of ninety (90) days of the event of default or within one month of the default coming to knowledge of the non-defaulting party whichever is later.

12.2 The Agreement shall terminate automatically if at any time as a result of a transfer of shares made in accordance with the Agreement (and the Articles), either the OIL or its nominee or the ABC or their nominee hold no Share in the paid up capital of the JVCO, but without prejudice to any rights which either OIL or the ABC may have against the other party arising prior to such termination.

13. Miscellaneous

13.1 The JVCO shall at all times maintain an independent identity, as distinct from that of the ABC or OIL. OIL shall however, be free to project the JVCO as one of the group companies. However, OIL's; liability in the affairs of JVCO shall be limited to the extent of its equity participation.

13.2 Parties undertake that they will not dispose of their share holding in the first three years of the Agreement except that OIL may transfer its shares to any Company which is within the promoter's group as defined under the guidelines issued by Securities & Exchange Board of India. Provided that such transferee company agrees to be bound by this Agreement. Thereafter if either of them wishes to dispose of its shareholding to a third party, it can do so only upon satisfaction of the following conditions:—

(a) an offer must first be made to the other Party by delivery of ninety day's prior notice in writing, to purchase the shares proposed to be transferred on the same terms and conditions as would be offered to any third Party;

(b) within such ninety days period, the other Party shall have either failed to purchase or declined in writing to purchase the Shares proposed to be sold or a part thereof on the terms and conditions offered to the other Party;

(c) on the expiry of the ninety days period from the original offer, the transferor shall be free to offer the shares to any third party on terms and conditions including prices which are in no way more favourable than that offered to the other Party;

(d) any transaction with the third party shall be concluded within the period of sixty days after the expiry of ninety days period referred to in clause 13.2 (i) above.

(e) It shall be a precondition of any negotiations with any third party that the third party shall be bound by the terms of this Agreement to the same extent as the transferor.

13.3 If at any time during the term of this Agreement, the Parties mutually decide to introduce any Third Party or offer certain percentage of Shares to the public, each of the Parties shall dispose of Shares in proportion to their shareholding in the JVCO.

13.4 Both the Parties shall cause the JVCO to take all actions to implement the provisions of this Agreement both in letter and spirit, to the extent permissible under law.

13.5 Both the ABC have joint and several liability for the actions of each other and guarantee each other's obligations. Whenever any act is to be done by the ABC or any right is vested in the ABC, the same can be exercised or performed by any one of the ABC and OIL. ABC or OIL shall not be liable or responsible for any contention that the said act did not have the authorisation or the sanction of the other Promoter.

14. Representations and Warranties

14.1 *Representation of OIL.*—OIL represents and warrants that the execution, delivery and performance of the Agreement is not impaired by any other valid agreement.

14.2 *Representation and Warranties of the ABC*

The ABC individually and collectively represents and warrants that:—

(a) the execution, delivery and performance of this Agreement by them will not conflict with, result in the breach, termination or acceleration of, or constitute a default under, any agreement, commitment or other instrument to which either it or one of its partners is a Party or bound;

(b) since the incorporation of the JVCO, they have operated its business in the ordinary course and that they have not caused the JVCO to do anything that is calculated to result in any adverse change in the business, financial condition or operations of JVCO.

(c) JVCO has no liability, contingent or crystallised as on the date of the Agreement except as declared under the provisions of clause 2.2;

(d) except for the creditors in the normal course of business (as mentioned in Schedule III to the Agreement) Firm has no liability, contingent or crystallised as on the date of the Agreement;

(e) the promoters warranty that they have joint and several liability for the actions of each other and guarantee due performance of each other's obligations.

15. Dispute Resolution/Arbitration

Any dispute, controversy or claim arising out of or relating to or in connection with this Agreement, or the breach, termination or validity hereof shall be finally settled by arbitration in accordance with the Rules of arbitration of the Indian Council of Arbitration and the award made in pursuance thereof shall be binding on the Parties. The seat of arbitration will be at .... (place).

16. General

16.1 *Waiver:* There shall be no waiver of any term, provision or condition of this Agreement unless such waiver evidenced in writing and signed by the waiving party. No omission or delay on the part of any Party in exercising any right, power or privilege hereunder shall operate as a waiver thereof, nor shall any single or partial exercise of any such right, power or privilege preclude any other or further exercise thereof or of any other right, power or privilege.

The rights and remedies herein provided are cumulative with, and not exclusive of, any rights or remedies provided by law.

16.2 Modifications of and amendments to this Agreement shall be effective only if made in writing and signed by the parties and in their absence, the duly authorised representatives of the Parties.

16.3 *Notice.* Any notice required or permitted to be given hereunder shall be in writing and sent by registered airmail, postage prepaid or facsimile transmission or by Regd. *Post AD* and shall be addressed to the addresses mentioned below:

If addressed to the ABC,
Mr. ....
....

If addressed to OIL,
Mr. ....
....

If addressed to JVCO,
At the registered office of JVCO

or such other addresses and numbers as any of the Parties may from time to time designate by notice in writing to the other. The notice shall be deemed to be served when first received.

16.4 *Severability.*—The invalidity of any portion of this Agreement shall not affect the remaining portion of this Agreement or any part thereof and this Agreement shall be construed as if such invalid portion or portions had not been inserted therein. The Parties will replace an invalid provision or fill a gap with valid provision, which most closely approximates the intent and economic effect of the invalid provision.

16.5 *Assignment.*—Save as otherwise expressly provided under this Agreement, all rights and obligations hereunder are personal to the Parties hereto and may, not be assigned at law or in the equity without the prior written consent of the other Party.

16.6 *Entire Agreement.*—This Agreement (together with the documents referred to herein) constitutes the entire agreement between the parties in connection with the subject matter of this Agreement. All previous documents, undertakings or agreements, whether verbal, written or otherwise between the Parties concerning the subject matter hereof including the memorandum of understanding (dt. ....) are hereby superseded by this Agreement and shall not affect or modify any of the terms or obligations set forth in this Agreement.

IN WITNESS whereof the Parties hereto have duly executed this Agreement the day and year first above written.

OIL   ABC

Witnesses

1. ....

2. ....

SCHEDULE I

Terms and Conditions of the Appointment of Whole Time Director

Salary
Perquisites
Term of Appointment
Responsibilities
Termination of Appointment

SCHEDULE II

Management Information System

SCHEDULE III

Sundry Creditors and other Liabilities of the Firm

COMPANY, MANAGEMENT AND PROJECT

1. History and Present Business of the Company

Alpha, promoted by .... (name), ... (company name) and .... (address), was incorporated under the name of .... (company name) Limited. The name of the Company was changed to .... (company name) Limited with effect from .... (date). *Alpha* obtained certificate of commencement of business on .... (date). The Company entered into a technical assistance Agreement on .... (date) with *Beta*. The Company commenced operation in .... (month/year), for the manufacture of .... however, does not have any shareholding in *Alpha* at present. The abovementioned agreement with *Beta* has been revived with certain revisions on .... (date) for a further period of .... (years).

Presently the Company is supplying springs to the Original Equipment (OE), Replacement and the Overseas Markets, *Alpha* is the sole supplier of .... Company's other OE customers include *Omega* and *Delta*.

2. Promoters and their Background

Alpha, as stated earlier, was promoted by .... However, the promoters bought back .... entire equity stake in *Alpha* as per the agreement. Therefore, at present .... does not hold any shares in the company. .... (name) is a matriculate and also the Chairman-cum-Managing Director of *Theta*. .... (name) has had vast experience in his career spanning 36 years in the automobile, engineering/auto component and railway springs industry, especially in the area of leaf springs.

Theta was founded by .... (name) as a partnership firm in 1955 under the name of *Theta*. It was taken over on .... (date) by *Theta* Limited [incorporated on .... (date)], and was converted into a Public Limited company on .... (date). *Theta* is a manufacturer of Spring and Spring Leaves and specialises in the manufacture of laminated springs for automobiles. *Theta* is an original equipment supplier to leading automobile manufacturers in the Country such as .... (company name) vehicle Factory .... (place) and Premier Automobiles. It is also recognised, as an approved supplier to various State Transport Undertakings throughout the country and is also on the approved list of DGS&D for meeting bulk replacement demand of defence vehicles. *Theta* entered into a technical collaboration agreement in 1985 with .... (company name and place) for leaf springs and consequent to expiry of this agreement in .... (year) revived the same in .... (year) for another period of .... years and also entered into another agreement with *Beta* in .... (year) for supply of know-how for the manufacture of stabiliser bars.

Theta at its existing plant at .... (place) has an aggregate installed capacity of .... *Theta* is in the process of implementation of an expansion project at .... (place) for the manufacture of auto coil springs, stabilizer bars and Parabolic/tapered leaf springs. The commercial production of Phase I (i.e., Tapered Leaf Springs) has already started with effect from .... (date) and the unit has commenced commercial production for Phase II in .... (year). The financial highlights of *Theta* are given below.

(Rupees in Lacs)

PERIOD ENDED

3. Technical Arrangements

Alpha has entered into a Technical Assistance Agreement with *Beta* .... (place) on .... (date) (Approved by the Government of India *vide* their letter No. ..../Comp. SCS dated....................) as amended by the addendum dated .... for the manufacture of Parabolic Springs. The Agreement expired in .... (year). Subsequently to revive the said

Agreement with certain revision in line with the technical requirement of the expansion scheme, the Company has entered into a Technical Assistance Agreement with *Beta* .... (place) on .... (date) for the design and manufacture of Parabolic Leaf Springs. The extension of foreign collaboration for .... years has been approved by the Government of India *vide* their letter No. .... dated ....

ALPHA PRIVATE LIMITED

1. Organization and Existence

1.1 *Alpha* Pvt. Ltd. (hereinafter 'the Company') was incorporated on September 15, 1980 as a private limited Company under the Companies Act, 1956. A copy of the Certificate of Incorporation is annexed hereto as Annexure 1.

1.2.1 The Registered Office of the Company is situated in the State of ...., at the following address:

....

.... (address)

1.2.2 According to clause III(A) of the memorandum of association of the Company, the main objects to be pursued by the Company on its incorporation are:

"1. To carry on the business of manufacturers of and dealers in containers, boxes, packings, packages, wrappings, wrappers and receptacles of all kinds made from paper and boards, including cardboard and plywoods, plastic, plastic materials, polythene, metal, alloy, glass, veneers and other material of all kinds whether synthetic or not, for trade and industries of every description.

2. To carry on the business of manufacturers of and dealers in paper, pulp and boards of all kinds and articles made from papers, pulp and boards of every description, and materials used in the manufacture or treatment of paper and board, including card boards."

1.2.3 The objects clause III (B) in the memorandum of association of the Company includes several objects incidental or ancillary to the attainment of the above main objects and other objects. A copy of the memorandum of association of the Company is annexed hereto as Annexure 2.

1.2.4 According to clause IV of the memorandum of association, the liability of the members of the Company is limited

1.2.5 According to clause V of the memorandum of association, the Authorised Share Capital[1] of the Company is Rs. .... (amount) divided into .... (No.) equity shares of Rs. .... (amount) each.

---

1. For a Company limited by shares, the amount of the share capital with which the Company is to be registered is called the authorised capital, which must be stated in the memorandum of association. The authorised capital sets the limit of capital available for issue and the issue capital can never exceed that limit [Section 13(4) of the Companies Act].

2. Share Capital

2.1 As on .... (date) the Authorised Share Capital of the Company was .... equity shares of Rs. .... each.

2.2 As on March 31, 1997 the Issued, Subscribed and Paid Up Share Capital of the Company was .... (no.) equity shares of Rs. .... (amount) each.

3. Internal Regulations

3.1 The internal regulations of the Company are contained in its Articles of Association (the 'Articles'). A copy of the Articles is annexed hereto as Annexure 3.[1]

3.2 Article 2 of the Company states that the provisions contained in 'Table A'[2] so far as applicable to private companies, shall be the Regulations of the Company.

3.3 The provisions relating to Company's lien on shares are contained in Article 6 and the said Article excludes the application of Regulation 9 of 'Table A' in this regard.

3.4.1 The Articles of the Company restrict the right of members to transfer their shares. A member[3] cannot transfer any shares to a person who is not a member, so long as any member is willing to purchase the same at a fair value. Please see Article 7(a) to (g).

3.4.2 The Articles provide that the Board of Directors "may in its absolute and uncontrolled discretion refuse to register any proposed transfer of shares and shall not be bound to give any reasons for such refusal"[4]. (Article 7(h))

---

1. Under section 9 of the Companies Act the provisions of the Company's Memorandum, Articles, Agreement or Resolution are void to the extent they are inconsistent with the provisions of the Companies Act.
2. As per section 28 of the Act, the Articles of Association of a Company limited by shares may adopt all or any of the regulations contained in 'Table A' in Schedule I.
3. Section 41 of the Companies Act defines 'Members' as:
   (1) The subscribers of the memorandum of a company shall be deemed to have agreed to become members of the company and on its registration, shall be entered as members in its register of members.
   (2) Every other person who agrees in writing to become a member of a company and whose name is entered in its register of members, shall be a member of the company.
4. Section 111 of the Companies Act deals with power to refuse registration and appeal against refusal.
   (1) if a company refuses, whether in pursuance of any power of the Company under its articles or otherwise, to register the transfer of, or the transmission by operation of law of the rights to, any shares or interest of a member in, or debentures of, the company, it shall within two months from the date on which the instrument of transfer, or the intimation of such transmission, as the case may be, was delivered to a company, send notice of the refusal to the transferee and the transferor or to the person giving intimation of such transmission, as the case may be, giving

Contd. on next page

3.5 The Company is required to hold its Annual General Meeting ("AGM")[1] once in every calendar year and such meeting shall be held within six months of the date upto which the balance sheet and profit and loss account to be laid before the meeting are made up. Further, not more than 15 months shall elapse between the date of one AGM and that of the next[2]. (Article 8)

3.6 The Articles provide as under with respect to the voting rights of the members:

"Subject to the provisions of the Act and Regulation 56 of Table 'A', every member present in person shall have one vote on show of hands and on poll every member present in person or by proxy shall have one vote for every ordinary share held by him in respect of which he is entitled to vote (Article 9). A member entitled to attend and vote at a general meeting shall be entitled to appoint another person as his proxy to attend and vote instead of himself and such proxy need not be a member of the Company (Article 10).

3.7 The Articles provide that the number of directors shall not be less than two and unless otherwise determined by the Company in a General Meeting, not more than twelve (Article 11(a)). No qualification share is required by any Director (Article 19).

Contd. from pervious page

reasons for such refusal to the transferor or transferee, or the person who gave intimation of the transmission by operation of law, as the case may be, may appeal to the Company Law Board against any refusal of the company to register the transfer or transmission, or against any failure on its part within the period referred to in sub-section (1) either to register the transfer or transmission or to send notice of its refusal to register the same.

(14) *In this section "company" means a private company and includes a private company which had become a public company by virtue of section 43A of this Act.*

1. Under section 173(1) of the Act, in the case of an annual general meeting, all business to be transacted at the meeting shall be deemed special with the exception business relating to:
   (i) the consideration of the accounts, balance sheets and the reports of the Board of Directors and auditors,
   (ii) the declaration of the dividend,
   (iii) the appointment of Directors in the place of those retiring, and
   (iv) the appointment of and the fixing of remuneration of the auditors.
2. Section 166(1) of the Act:
   (1) Every Company shall in each year hold in addition to any other meetings a general meeting as its annual general meeting and shall specify the meeting as such in the notices calling it; and not more than fifteen months shall elapse between the date of one annual general meeting of a Company and that of the next.

3.8 To constitute a quorum[1] for a General Meeting two members are required to be present in person (Article 49[2] of Table 'A').

3.9 The Directors of the Company shall retire by rotation, according to the provisions of section 256 of the Act (Article 12)[3].

---

1. Section 174 of the Act:
   (1) unless the articles of the Company provide for a larger number, five members personally present in the case of public company (other than a public company which has become such by virtue of section 43 A), and two members personally present in the case of any other Company, shall be the quorum for a meeting of the company.
2. Article 49 of Table 'A' of the Act:
   (1) No business shall be transacted at any general meeting unless a quorum of members is present at the time when the general meeting proceeds to business.
   (2) Save as herein otherwise provided, five members present in person, (in the case of a public Company) - two members present in person, (in the case of a private Company) shall be the quorum.
3. Section 256 of Companies Act
   Ascertainment of directors retiring by rotation and filling of vacancies—
   (1) At the first annual general meeting of a public company, or a private company which is a subsidiary of a public company held next after the date of the general meeting at which the first directors are appointed in accordance with section 255 and at every subsequent annual general meeting one-third of such of the directors for the time being as are liable to retire by rotation, or if their number is not three or a multiple of three, then, the number nearest to one-third, shall retire from office.
   (2) The directors to retire by rotation at every annual general meeting shall be those who have been longest in office since their last appointment, but as between persons who became directors on the same day, those who are to retire shall, in default of and subject to any agreement among themselves, be determined by lot.
   (3) At the annual general meeting at which a director retires as aforesaid, the Company may fill up the vacancy by appointing the retiring director or some other person thereto.
   (4) (a) If the place of the retiring director is not so filled up and the meeting has not expressly resolved not to fill the vacancy, the meeting shall stand adjourned till the same day in the next week, at the same time and place, or if that day is a public holiday, till the next succeeding day which is not a public holiday, at the same time and place.
   (b) If at the adjourned meeting also, the place of the retiring director is not filled up and that meeting also has not expressly resolved not to fill the vacancy, the retiring director shall be deemed to have been re-appointed at the adjourned meeting, unless—
      (i) at that meeting or at the previous meeting a resolution for the re-appointment of such director has been put to the meeting and lost;
      (ii) the retiring director has, by a notice in writing addressed to the company or its Board of Directors, expressed his unwillingness to be so re-appointed;
      (iii) he is not qualified or is disqualified for appointment;
      (iv) a resolution, whether special or ordinary, is required for his appointment or re-appointment in virtue of any provisions of this Act; or
      (v) the proviso to sub-section (2) of section 263 [The words "or sub-section (3) of section 280" in sub-section (4)(b)(v) and sub-section (5) were omitted by section 30 of the Companies (Amendment) Act (XXXI of 1965) (w.e.f. 15-10-1965)] is applicable to the case.

3.10 The Board of Directors are empowered to fill up any casual vacancy and a person so appointed shall hold office upto the date upto which the Director in whose place he is appointed, would have held office if he had not vacated before the expiry of his term of office (Article 13). The Directors have power to appoint any person to be a Director either to fill a casual vacancy or as an addition to existing Directors but the total number of Directors shall not exceed the number fixed by or in accordance with the Articles (Article 14). Any Director so appointed shall hold office upto the next AGM and shall be eligible for re-election and shall not be taken into account in determining the Directors who are to retire by rotation at such meeting. A Managing Director shall not during his tenure as Managing Director retire by rotation nor shall he be counted for determining the number of Directors to retire (Article 20).

3.11 The Board of Directors may appoint Alternate Directors (Article 15).

3.12 The Articles of the Company provide that whenever the Company enters into any contract with any Government/Bank/Financial Institution or any other person, the Directors shall have power to enter into an agreement with such Government/Bank/Financial Institution or any other person whereby such Government/Bank/Financial Institution or any other person shall have the right to appoint or nominate, by giving a notice in writing to the Company, one or more Directors on the Board. The regulations relating to removal, retirement, powers and privileges of Directors so appointed/nominated are contained in Article 16.

3.13 The Board has the power to delegate any of its powers to committees consisting of such member or members of its body as it thinks fit. Any committee so formed shall, in the exercise of the powers so delegated, conform to any regulations that may be imposed on it by the Board. (Regulation 77 of Table 'A'). We were informed by the Company that the Board has not constituted any such committee.

3.14 The provisions relating to Dividends are contained in Regulation 85 to 87 of Table 'A' of the Act.

4. Directors

4.1 At present the Company has three Directors. The names of Directors as mentioned in the Register of 'Directors, Managing Director, Manager and Secretary of the Company' is annexed hereto as Annexure 4.

4.2 A copy of the shareholding pattern of the Company as, provided to us by the Company is annexed hereto as Annexure 5.

4.3 A copy of the list of companies in which the directors are interested is annexed hereto as Annexure 6.

5. Agreements

5.1 Certain charges are required to be registered with the Registrar of Companies within 30 days of making the charge[1].

---

1. Section 125 of the Act deals with charges which includes a mortgage. Section 125 (4) applies to the following charges:

Contd. on next page

5.2 The Company has maintained a Register of Charges[1].

5.3.1 The Company entered into a Hypothecation of Book Debts Agreement dated, ... (date) with Bank, Finance Bank, ... (place) for credit facilities of Rs. .... (amount) wherein a charge was created over the Company's present and future book debts, outstanding money receivable, claims, bills, contracts, securities investments rights and assets. The Company has also executed a Promissory Note in favour of Bank for Rs. .... (amount).

5.3.2 The Company entered into a Hypothecation of Book Debts Agreement dated, ..., 20..... with .... (Bank), New Delhi for credit facilities of Rs. .... wherein a charge was created over the Company's present and future products, goods and movable property of any kind belonging to/lying in the Company's .... (address). The Company has also executed a Promissory Note for Rs. .... (amount) in favour of Bank.

5.3.3 The Company entered into a Hypothecation of Book Debts Agreement dated, ... (date) with Bank, Finance Bank, ... (place) for credit facilities of Rs. .... wherein a charge was created over the Company's present and future products, goods and movable property of any kind belonging to/lying in the Company's .... (address). The Company has also executed a Promissory Note for Rs. .... (amount) in favour of Bank.

5.3.4 The Company entered into a Hypothecation of Book Debts Agreement dated, ... (date) with Bank, ... (place) for credit facilities of Rs. .... (amount) wherein a charge of Rs. .... (amount) was created on all the present and future movable assets including stock of raw material, goods in process and semi-finished goods, all present and future book debts outstanding in Company's godown at .... (address).

Contd. from pervious page

(a) a charge for the purpose of securing any issue of debentures;
(b) a charge on uncalled share capital of the Company;
(c) a charge on any immovable property, wherever situate, or any interest therein;
(d) a charge on any book debts of the Company;
(e) a charge, not being a pledge, on any movable property of the Company;
(f) a floating charge on the undertaking or any property of the Company including stock-in-trade;
(g) a charge on calls made but not paid;
(h) a charge on a ship or any share in a ship;
(i) a charge on goodwill, on a patent or a license under a patent, on a trade mark, or on a copyright or a license under a copyright.

1. Section 143(1): Every Company shall keep at its registered office a register of charges and enter therein all charges specifically effecting property of the company and all floating charges on the undertaking or any property of the company, giving in each case:
    (i) a short description of the property charged;
    (ii) the amount of the charge; and
    (iii) except in the case of securities to bearer, the names of the persons entitled to the charge.

5.3.5 As per the Register of Mortgage and Contracts, a charge of Rs. .... (amount) was created on all present and future movable assets including stocks of raw material, goods in process, semi-finished goods and all present and future book debts by way of first charge by letter of hypothecation dated .... (date). An Equitable Mortgage of the plant and machinery of the Company was also created as second charge.

As informed by the Company, the aforesaid charge was subsequently modified on various dates:

(a) to Rs. ....(amount) and Rs. ....(amount) on May 24, 1983

(b) to Rs. ....(amount) on .... (date)

(c) to Rs. ....(amount) on .... (date)

(d) to Rs. ....(amount) on .... (date)

(e) to Rs. ....(amount) on .... (date)

(f) to Rs. ....(amount) on .... (date)

We were informed by the Company that the aforesaid charge of Rs. .... (amount) is the only charge subsisting as on date and all other charges have been satisfied. A copy of the particulars of the aforesaid charge as entered into the Register of Mortgage and Charges is annexed hereto as Annexure 7. The copies of the letters dated .... (date) issued by the .... (Bank) enhancing the credit facilities in favour of the Bank is annexed hereto as Annexure 8.

(Please note that we have not examined the various letters of hypothecation, other documents relating to modification of charges and documents relating to creation of Equitable Mortgage over the Company's plant and machinery as mentioned in the Register of Mortgage and Charges.)

5.4. The Register of Mortgage and Charges shows that a charge of Rs. .... (amount) created vide Hypothecation of Goods Agreement dated .... (date) for Term Loan Agreement and Guarantee was satisfied on .... (date). *(Please note that we have neither examined the said Agreement nor the certificate of Satisfaction of charge).*

5.5 The Register of Charges shows that a charge of Rs. ....(amount) created vide Mortgage Deed dated .... (date) for Term Loan Agreement and Guarantee was satisfied on .... (date) *(Please note that we have neither examined the said Agreement nor the certificate of Satisfaction of Charge).*

5.6 The Company has taken on Lease property bearing Nos. .... (address) for a period of .... years commencing from .... (date). The Lease Deed was initially in the name of *Alpha* and was subsequently transferred to .... *vide* Deed of Rectification dated .... (date).

6. Litigation

We have been informed by the Company that there is no litigation pending on behalf of or against the Company.

7. Title to Property

7.1 The Company does not have title to any immovable property.

8. Miscellaneous

8.1 *Alpha* is registered as a Small Scale Industry (SSI) unit.

8.2 In the Board Meeting, dated .... (date), a resolution was passed for transfer of one equity share held by .... (name) and of one equity share held by .... (name) to .... (name). However, the necessary entries in this regard have not been made in the Register of Members maintained by the Company.

8.3 The pages of the Minutes Book of the Board and general meetings kept by the Company are not initialed or signed by the Chairman of the meeting and the last page of the record of each meeting although signed, is not dated as required by the Act. The pages of the Minutes of the Board and General Meetings are not consecutively numbered as required by the Act[1].

8.4 The appointment of .... (name) and Associates as the Company's sales representative was renewed w.e.f .... vide letter dated .... (name) and Associates are entitled to a commission of .... % on the net value of orders procured from its existing clients and also on new business developed by it.

8.5 The appointment of .... (company name) as the Company's sales representative was renewed w.e.f. .... vide letter dated .... (name) is entitled to a commission of .... % on the net value of sales effected to parties such as (i) .... Ltd. (ii) .... (iii) Exporters of all types (iv) outstation customers (v) Defence force supplies etc.

---

1. Section 193 of the Act:
    1. Every Company shall cause minutes of all proceedings of every general meeting and of all proceedings of every meeting of its Board of Directors or of every committee of the Board, to be kept by making within thirty days of the conclusion of every such meeting concerned, entries thereof in books kept for that purpose with their pages consecutively numbered.
    1A. Each page of every such book shall be initialed or signed and the last page of the record of proceedings of each such meeting in such books shall be dated and signed:

    (a) in the case of minutes of proceedings of a meeting of the Board or of a committee thereof, by the chairman of the said meeting or the chairman of the next succeeding meeting;

    (b) in the case of minutes of proceedings of a general meeting, by the chairman of the same meeting within the aforesaid period of thirty days or in the event of the death or inability of that chairman within that period, by a director duly authorised by the Board for the purpose.

SHAREHOLDERS AGREEMENT

THIS AGREEMENT is entered into on the .... day of ...., 20.....

BETWEEN

(1) *ALPHA*, a Company organised and existing under .... law and having its registered office in .... and place of business at .... The .... (address), hereinafter called "...................." (which expression shall, unless repugnant to the meaning or context thereof, be deemed to include its successors, assigns and affiliates), represented by its duly authorised representative, of the FIRST PART;

AND

(2) *BETA*, son of Mr. .... , resident of .... , hereinafter called "....................", representing himself and certain other companies, individuals and entities specified in Schedule I to this Agreement, all of whom (including ....) are collectively referred to hereinafter as the "*Beta* Group" (which expression shall, unless repugnant to the meaning or context thereof, be deemed to include its successors and assigns), of the SECOND PART;

AND

(3) *GAMA* .... Private Ltd., a Company registered under the Indian Companies Act, having its registered office at ...., hereinafter called the "Company" (which expression shall, unless repugnant to the meaning or context thereof, be deemed to include its successors and assigns), of the THIRD PART.

WHEREAS

A. Various agreements, including the following have been entered into:

(a) English Consent Letter Agreement dated .... among ...., ("....................") and ("....................") relating to the acquisition by .... of approximately ....% of equity share capital of ("....................");

(b) An agreement between .... and .... relating to the re-acquisition of up to ....% of equity share capital of .... by .... from .... by .... (date), which agreement has not been seen by, and does not bind, ...;

(c) Share Acquisition and Reconstruction Agreement among ...., ... and the *Beta* Group executed contemporaneously with this Agreement relating to (i) the reconstruction of .... whereby all assets, property obligations, liabilities, licences and personnel of the Brass Valves Division of .... would be transferred to the Company; (ii) the issue of shares in the Company resulting in .... holding ....% and the *Beta* Group holding ....% of the total paid up capital of the Company in consideration for the said transfer of the Brass Valves Division to the Company; and (iii) the grant of a loan by .... to the Company, part of which would be convertible into equity shares in the Company at the option of ....

B. The equity share capital of .... is on the date of signing hereof owned as to ....% by ...., ...% by .... and as to ....% by the *Beta* Group; and ....% (.................... equity shares of Rs. .... each) by .... (name).

C. .... and the *Beta* Group have agreed to enter into this Agreement for the purpose of setting out and agreeing the basis upon which the Company will be operated and managed.

D. The purpose of the Company is to manufacture all kinds of copper and brass based plumbing products, including valves, for sale in India and abroad (the 'Business').

NOW THEREFORE, in consideration of the mutual promises, covenants hereinafter set forth, the parties agree as follows:

1. Definitions

The following words and expressions shall, unless the context otherwise require, have the following meanings:

"Act" the Indian Companies Act, 1956, as amended from time to time, or any statutory re-enactment thereof, and wherever the context requires, any statutory rules framed thereunder, in the current version;

"Agreement" this Shareholders Agreement entered into among ...., the *Beta* Group and the Company;

"Articles" the Memorandum and Articles of association of the Company attached as Annexure A hereto;

"Board" the Board of Directors of the Company or the Directors present at a duly convened meeting of the Directors at which a quorum is present;

"Business" the Business of the Company as defined in Recital D;

"Director" a Director of the Company holding office pursuant to appointment or nomination by .... on behalf of the *Beta* Group or by ....;

"Rs. or Rupees" the Lawful currency of India;

"Overall Business Plan" the Overall Business Plan of the Company, including a financial and strategic plan for the following three years (....................) years and budgets and cash flow forecasts, prepared jointly by the Parties;

"Shares" the Equity Shares of Rs. .... each in the capital of the Company;

"Shareholders" the *Beta* Group and .... collectively, or where Shares in the Company are held by affiliates, their respective affiliates holding Shares in the Company; and

"Beta Group Entity" .... or any individual, Company or other entity included in Schedule I.

2. Nomination by the *Beta* Group and ....

2.1 For the purposes of this Agreement, the *Beta* Group and its affiliates shall at all times act collectively, identically and in complete unison.

2.2 The acts, representations and decisions of .... shall be irrevocably binding on the *Beta* Group. .... shall neither be removed nor replaced by the *Beta* Group without the consent in writing of .... Each of the *Beta* Group Entities shall take such action as is necessary to ensure that .... has at all times full authority to represent such *Beta* Group Entity. In the event that .... is replaced by another *Beta* Group Entity, the provisions of this section 2.2 shall apply *mutatis mutandis* with respect to such *Beta* Group Entity. In the event that the *Beta* Group Entities are not able to nominate and appoint one of them to represent them as above within .... days of the inability of .... to represent the *Beta* Group, this Agreement shall terminate and .... may either sell its Shares or buy the *Beta* Group's Shares. However, ... shall not be obliged to exercise either of the foregoing options. .... may exercise its option to sell its Shares only after giving a written offer to sell its Shares to the *Beta* Group. If within .... days of the offer being made to the *Beta* Group, the *Beta* Group has not accepted the same and paid the price, ... may sell its Shares to any third party. In the event that .... exercises its option to buy the *Beta* Group's shares in the Company, the *Beta* Group shall be obliged to offer to .... all its shares in the Company.[1]

2.3 .... shall, by a resolution of its Board of Directors or other governing body or by such other action as is necessary under law applicable to it, authorise such person as it thinks fit to act as its representative at any meeting of the Company. The person authorised as aforesaid (the '.................... Representative') shall be entitled to exercise the same rights and powers (including the right to vote by proxy) on behalf of .... that ....could exercise as if it were an individual member. The acts, representations and decisions of the .... Representative shall be irrevocably binding on ....

3. Representations and Warranties of .... and the *Beta* Group

.... and each of the other *Beta* Group Entities hereby represent and warrant as follows.

3.1 *Authorization*.—The execution, delivery and performance of this Agreement by each of the *Beta* Group Entities has been duly authorized by all necessary individual/collective/corporate actions of the *Beta* Group Entities and this Agreement constitutes the valid and binding obligations of each of the *Beta* Group Entities, enforceable against each of them in accordance with its terms, except to the extent enforceability may be limited by bankruptcy, insolvency, reorganization, moratorium or other similar laws affecting the enforcement of their rights in general and subject to general principles of equity.

---

1. As pointed out by ....(name), this section does not specify how the price for the sale of shares would be arrived at, particularly in the event that .... opts to buy the *Beta* Group's shares in the Company. Please consider providing for the application of the same mechanism as in section 18.2.

3.2 *Consents of third parties.*—The execution and performance of this Agreement by the *Beta* Group will not:

(a) violate or conflict with the memorandum of association and articles of association or other constitutional document of a *Beta* Group Entity;

(b) conflict with, result in the breach, termination or acceleration of, or constitute a default under, any agreement, governmental approval, commitment or other instrument to which a *Beta* Group Entity is a party or bound;

(c) constitute a violation of any law regulation order writ, judgment; or

(d) result in the creation of any material lien upon the properties or assets of the Company.

3.3 *Absence of Certain Changes.*—Since the incorporation of the Company, the Company has/will have operated its business in the ordinary course and the *Beta* Group has not caused the Company to do anything that is calculated to result in any adverse change in the business, financial condition or operations of the Company.[1]

3.4 *Consents, Authorizations, etc.*—No consent, authorization, approval, permit or order of or filing with any governmental authority or agency, or regulatory authority is required for the *Beta* Group to execute, deliver and perform this Agreement.

3.5 *Authorisation of.*—Each of the *Beta* Group Entities other than ...., has taken all such action as is necessary and desirable to nominate and appoint .... to represent its interests as a Shareholder of the Company. A copy of the Power of Attorney executed by each of the *Beta* Group Entities in this regard is attached hereto and marked collectively as Schedule II[2]. No further action is required on the part of any of such *Beta* Group Entities to authorise .... to represent its interests as aforesaid or to make the acts and omissions of .... with respect to such interest binding and enforceable against each of such *Beta* Group Entities.

On and as of the date of issue of Shares to .... and the *Beta* Group as envisaged under the ...., and on and as of the date of .... owning ....% of the issued and paid-up equity capital of the Company, ... and each of the other *Beta* Group entities shall be deemed to repeat the aforementioned representations and warranties.

4. Representations and Warranties of ....

.... hereby represents and warrants as follows. In the event of an affiliate of .... becoming a Shareholder, the following representation and warranties shall be deemed to be given by such .... affiliate *mutatis mutandis*.

---

1. Since the proposal is to incorporate the Company before execution of this Agreement, this representation has been retained in its original version.
2. Board resolutions of the corporate *Beta* Group Entities authorising execution of Power of Attorney should also please be furnished.

4.1 *Authorization.*—The execution, delivery and performance of this Agreement by .... has been duly authorized by all necessary individual/collective/corporate actions of .... and this Agreement constitutes the valid and binding obligations of ...., enforceable against it in accordance with its terms, except to the extent enforceability may be limited by bankruptcy, insolvency, reorganization, moratorium or other similar laws affecting the enforcement of their rights in general and subject to general principles of equity.

4.2 *Consents, Authorizations, etc.*—[No consent, authorization, approval, permit or order of or filing with any governmental authority or agency, or regulatory authority is required for .... to execute, deliver and perform this Agreement.][1]

4.3 *Consents of Third Parties.*—The execution and performance of this Agreement by .... will not:

(a) violate or conflict with the memorandum of association and articles of association or other constitutional document of ....;

(b) conflict with, result in the breach, termination or acceleration of, or constitute a default under, any agreement, governmental approval, commitment or other instrument to which .... is a party or bound;

(c) constitute a violation of any law, regulation, order, writ, judgment; or

(d) result in the creation of any material lien upon the properties or assets of the Company.

5. Structure of the Company and Capital Contribution

5.1 Initially and until the loan proposed to be advanced by .... to the Company pursuant to the .... is converted into Shares, the *Beta* Group and .... shall hold, and participate in, the issued equity capital of the Company in the following proportions:

The *Beta* Group ....%

....%

5.2 Subject to the provisions of the ARA, the *Beta* Group and .... shall hold, and participate in, the issued equity capital of the Company in the following proportions after the aforementioned loan (or part thereof, at the option of ....) is converted into Shares:

The *Beta* Group ....%

....%

The Parties agree to maintain their equity shareholding in the Company as above, at all times, except as herein provided or unless otherwise agreed to in writing by the Parties.

5.3 If and when the Company desires to increase the paid-up share-capital, whether by a further issue of equity shares or preference shares, the additional

---

1. This is subject to review by UK and Dutch lawyers of our Clients.

shares shall be offered in the first instance to the existing holders of the shares by way of rights issue in proportion to the capital paid-up on the shares (whether equity or preference) held by them at that time so as to maintain the ownership structure within the Company.

5.4 The calls on any partly paid up shares in the Company and any further issue of shares shall be made by the Company in accordance with the provisions of Articles and upon taking into account financial requirements of the Company.

5.5 If an issue of further shares is proposed and a Shareholder does not wish or is unable for any reason to subscribe in cash for its proportionate entitlement of such shares, the Shareholders shall seek to agree on mutually suitable alternative form of funding. However, if an issue of shares is proposed by the Company after the date which is .... years from the date hereof and a Shareholder does not wish, or is unable for any reason, to subscribe in cash for its proportionate entitlement of such shares, then the issue of shares shall nevertheless take place and the other Shareholders shall be entitled to subscribe for any shares offered for subscription by the Company to the Shareholder which are not subscribed for by that Shareholder, thereby altering the shareholding pattern of the Company.

6. Meetings of the Shareholders

6.1 *General Meetings of Shareholders.*—General meetings of the Company shall be called to direct and control the business of the Company and the Board shall decide the time, place and agenda for convening such meetings subject to the Articles and the applicable requirements of the Act.

6.2 *Notice.*—At all times, prior written notice of any general meeting of the Company in accordance with the requirements of the Act shall be given to all the Shareholders and each of the Directors .... days in advance.

6.3 *Quorum.*—No business shall be transacted at any general meeting of the Company or any adjournment thereof, unless a quorum of Shareholders is present at the time when the meeting proceeds to business and throughout the meeting. A quorum for a general meeting shall not be deemed to have been constituted unless one representative of .... and one representative of the *Beta* Group are present.

6.4 *Voting.*—Unless otherwise provided under the Act, decisions at a general meeting of the Company shall be by majority of the votes of the members present in person or by proxy.

6.5 *Minutes.*—.................... and .... shall cause the Company to ensure that the minutes of the proceedings of the general meetings are recorded and signed in accordance with the requirements of the Act.

7. Decisions requiring consent of Shareholders

7.1 The Shareholders shall own and operate the Company in good faith in accordance with the provisions of this Agreement.

7.2 Unless the Parties agree otherwise, the Company shall not:
   (a) enter into any agreement, transaction or arrangement, whether verbal or written with either a *Beta* Group Entity or .... or with any

person, firm or entity connected directly or indirectly with either of them;

(b) sell, transfer, lease, license, assign or otherwise dispose of the whole or any material part of its business, undertaking, property and/or assets, except in so far as the same is done in the normal and ordinary course of business, as envisaged in the Business Plan; or

(c) create or issue any debenture, mortgage, charge or other security or increase the amount of any borrowings capable of being secured, except in so far as the same is done in the normal and ordinary course of business as envisaged in the Business Plan, in an amount exceeding £ .... [amount in figures and words] or its equivalent.

8. Board

8.1 *Board.*—The Board shall consist of .... members other than nominees, if any, of financial institutions, banks or any other party that lends to the Company (including any Party hereto). In the event that financial institutions, banks, etc. advancing loans to the Company impose conditions as to the composition of the Board, ... and .... shall enter into discussions to arrive at a mutually acceptable solution to comply with the requirements of the said lenders. The Directors shall not be required to hold any shares as a condition or qualification for holding office.

8.2 *Nominees.*—Unless otherwise agreed to by the Parties, the *Beta* Group and .... shall take all steps including but not limited to exercising their voting rights to ensure the representation of .... and the *Beta* Group on the Board in accordance with the terms hereof.

8.3 *Beta Group Nominees.*—For so long as the *Beta* Group Entities are between them registered as the holders of at least 60 per cent of the issued equity share capital of the Company, the *Beta* Group shall have the right exercisable by notice in writing signed by a duly authorised officer to require the appointment of 3 Directors of the Company from time to time and by like notice to require the removal of any such Director and appointment of another person to act in place of such Director. For so long as the *Beta* Group Entities are between them registered as the holders of at least 49 per cent of the issued equity share capital of the Company, the *Beta* Group shall have the right exercisable by notice in writing signed by a duly authorised officer to require the appointment of 2 Directors of the Company from time to time and by like notice to require the removal of any such Director and appointment of another person to act in place of such Director.

8.4 .... *Nominees.*—For so long as .... and/or any member of the *Alpha* Group are between them registered as the holders of at least .... per cent of the issued equity share capital of the Company, ... shall have the right exercisable by notice in writing signed by a duly authorised officer to require the appointment of two Directors of the Company from time to time and by like notice to require the removal of any such Director and the appointment of another person to act in place of such Director. For so long as .... and/or any member of the *Alpha* Group are between them registered as the holders of at least .... per cent of the issued equity share capital of the Company, ... shall have the right exercisable by notice in writing signed by a duly authorised officer to require the appointment of three Directors of the Company from time to time and by like notice to require the removal of any such Director and the appointment of another person to act in place of such Director.

8.5 *Removal of Nominee*.—If at any time .... gives written notice to the Company of its wish to remove a Director previously designated by ...., the *Beta* Group shall vote all Shares owned by them in favour of removing such .... Director and take all other actions incidental to that vote requested of them by .... to cause the .... Director to be removed. Notwithstanding, anything to the contrary contained herein, no resolution for the removal of any director nominated/appointed by .... shall be taken or passed unless the affirmative vote of .... has been obtained. Likewise, if .... gives a written notice to the Company of his wish to remove a Director previously designated by the *Beta* Group, ... shall vote all the Shares owned by them in favour of removing such a designated Director and take all other actions, incidental thereto, to cause the said Director to be removed. Notwithstanding anything to the contrary, no resolution for the removal of any such Director appointed/nominated by the *Beta* Group shall be taken or passed unless the affirmative vote of .... has been obtained.

8.6 *Notice*.—Notice of any appointment or removal required under this article 8 shall be given to the Company at its registered office.

8.7 *Consultation*.—Without prejudice to their rights hereunder, it is agreed that any Party proposing to require the appointment or removal of a Director under this article will consult with the other Party before giving notice under this article.

8.8 *Casual Vacancy*.—If for any reason, including removal, any Director nominated/appointed by .... ceases to hold office, ... may designate an individual to fill the vacancy so created for the unexpired term, and the *Beta* Group shall, and shall cause their representative Directors to, vote and take all other reasonable actions to cause the individual so designated to be elected to fill the vacancy. The Board shall use its best efforts to ensure that the individual designated by .... in accordance herewith is appointed. Likewise, if for any reason, including removal, any Director nominated/appointed by the *Beta* Group ceases to hold office, the *Beta* Group may designate an individual to fill the vacancy so created for the unexpired term and .... shall, and shall cause their representative Directors to, vote and take all reasonable actions to cause the individual so designated to be elected to fill the vacancy.

8.9 *Appointment of Alternates*.—The Board shall appoint as an alternate director (an "Alternate") for any Director (an "Original Director") during the absence of an Original Director for a period of not less than three (3) months from India, such person as is nominated or approved in writing by, and upon the request of, the Party represented by the Original Director in whose place the

Alternate is to be appointed. An Alternate shall vacate office if and when the Original Director returns to India.

8.10 *Powers.*—The operational powers and responsibilities of the Board shall, subject to the provisions of the Act, be as determined in a general meeting in accordance with the Articles.

9. Management

9.1 *Chairman.*—The Chairman of the Company shall be one of the Directors appointed/nominated by the *Beta* Group. The Chairman of the Company shall preside over all meetings of the Board and of the Shareholders at which he is present.

9.2 *Managing Director.*—The Managing Director of the Company shall be one of the Directors appointed/nominated by .... shall have the right to remove and replace the Managing Director at any time. The Managing Director shall report to the Board.

9.3 *Voting.*—Subject to the provisions hereof, all decisions of the Board shall be by a majority vote of the Directors nominated/appointed by the Shareholders (including in their capacity as lenders to the Company), whether or not present at a meeting. The Parties shall at all times during the effective period of this Agreement cause their representatives on the Board to exercise their votes in consonance with and in compliance with the terms of this Agreement. Each Director present shall have one vote. The Chairman shall not have a casting or second vote.

9.4 *Compliance with law.*—The Company shall carry on its management and administration and other affairs in compliance with the provisions of the Act and other applicable law, including but not limited to the following:

  (a) .... and .... shall cause the representative Directors to disclose their interest in the transactions with the Company, and

  (b) The Company shall comply with the provisions of the Payment of Gratuity Act, 1972.

10. Meetings of the Board

10.1 *Meetings of the Board.*—Meetings of the Board shall be held quarterly. The minimum number of meetings required to be held under the Act shall always be complied with.

10.2 *Notice.*—At all times, prior written notice of any meeting of Directors shall be provided as follows:

  (a) in the case of regularly scheduled Board meetings, at least 14 days' prior written notice to each of the directors of the Company and

  (b) in the case of any other meetings, such prior notice to each of the Directors as is reasonable under the circumstances.

10.3 *Contents of Notice.*—Every notice convening meeting of the Board shall set out the agenda of the business to be transacted there at in full and sufficient detail. At such meeting, Directors may act only with respect to matters set forth in said notice.

10.4 Notwithstanding the provisions of Articles 10.2 and 10.3, meetings of the Board may be held without conforming to such provisions when written consent thereto has been obtained prior to or after the meeting, from all the Directors.

10.5 *Venue of Meetings.*—The venue of all meetings of the Board shall be in .... (name of the place) or such other place as the Parties may agree and the travel expenses for attending the Board meetings shall be borne by the respective Parties.

10.6 *Quorum.*—The quorum for meetings of the Board shall be two Directors comprising at least one Director nominated/appointed by .... and one Director nominated/appointed by the *Beta* Group present at the commencement and throughout the meeting. In the event that at a Board meeting to consider the yearly Plan and Budget the quorum as stipulated herein is not complete, due to the absence of a Director as aforesaid, the Board meeting shall be adjourned to be reconvened after .... days. At the reconvened meeting, the presence of a Director nominated/appointed by the Party, none of whose nominee Directors was present at the originally convened meeting, shall not be necessary for completion of the quorum.

10.7 *Decisions by Circulation.*—No resolutions shall be deemed to have been duly passed by the Board by circulation unless the resolution has been circulated in draft, together with necessary papers if any, to all the Directors or their Alternates as are entitled to vote on the resolution.

10.8 *Minutes.*—The *Beta* Group and .... shall cause their representative Directors to ensure that the minutes of the proceedings of the Board and the resolutions passed by circulation are recorded and signed in accordance with the requirements of the Act.

11. Business Plan and Monthly Reporting

11.1 *Yearly Business Plan.*—Each year not later than date...................(month), a Business Plan for the following calendar year shall be drawn up by the Company, submitted to the Board for approval and approved by the Board. The Board shall discuss and decide upon the Business Plan and subsequent updates during the year.

11.2 *Monthly Reporting.*—The Company shall prepare and submit to the Directors a monthly report regarding the affairs of the Company within the first 10 days of the following month. The monthly report shall include a simple trading summary of the Company prepared in the approved form annexed hereto as *Annexure* B.

12. Right of Pre-emption and Transfer of Shares

12.1 *Permitted Transfers.*—Notwithstanding anything contained in this Agreement, a *Beta* Group Entity may transfer Shares to another *Beta* Group Entity, provided that .... has no objection to such transfer. Notwithstanding anything contained in this Agreement, ... may transfer its Shares, and assign its rights hereunder, to a person or entity in control of, controlled by, or under common control with ...., provided that .... has no objection to such transfer.

12.2 *Transfer to Third Parties.*—If at any time .... or ....'s transferee (as mentioned in Article 12.1) wishes to sell any of its Shares to any other party/parties, other than in accordance with Article 12.1, ... shall, by notice to ...., disclose the identity of such potential buyer and offer to .... all such Shares sought to be sold. .... may nominate a *Beta* Group Entity for the purchase of Shares offered by .... The price for the proposed sale of Shares to .... and or its nominee shall be the fair value of such Shares determined on the basis of a valuation report by *Omega* or one of the other firms of chartered accountants of similar international repute. If so requested by ...., such valuation report shall take into account the price offered by the potential buyer. Provided that if the approval of the Reserve Bank of India is required, such Shares shall be valued in accordance with the method(s) acceptable to the Reserve Bank of India for the purposes of granting approval for the said transfer. .... may convey, in writing, its acceptance to the offer of .... within a reasonable period, which shall not be later than .... days from the date of receipt of offer from .... along with the valuation report of the firm of chartered accountants. The fee of the firm of chartered accountants so engaged shall be borne by ....

12.3 In the event that for any reason whatsoever .... does not accept the offer of .... in terms of this article, ... may sell the Shares offered to the notified potential buyer. If .... wishes to sell the offered Shares to a person other than the notified potential buyer, the procedure in article 12.2 hereof shall be followed again.

12.4 If at any time, a *Beta* Group Entity wishes to sell any of its Shares other than in accordance with section 12.1 hereof, then .... shall, by a notice to ...., disclose the identity of such potential buyer and offer all such Shares sought to be sold to .... may nominate a person or entity in control of controlled by, or under common control with .... for the purchase of Shares offered by the *Beta* Group Entity. The price for the proposed sale of Shares to .... and or its nominee shall be the fair value of such Shares determined on the basis of the valuation report by *Omega* or one of the other firms of chartered accountants of similar international repute. If so requested by ...., such valuation report shall take into account the price offered by the potential buyer. Provided that if the approval of the Reserve Bank of India is required, such Shares shall be valued in accordance with the method/s acceptable to the Reserve Bank of India for the purposes of granting approval for the said transfer. .... or any nominees thereof may convey, in writing, its acceptance of the offer to ....,................ within a reasonable period, which shall not be later than .... days from the date of receipt of offer from .... along with the valuation report of the firm of chartered accountants. The fee of the firm of chartered accountants so engaged shall be borne by ....

12.5 In the event that for any reason whatsoever .... does not accept the offer of the *Beta* Group Entity in terms of this article, such *Beta* Group Entity may transfer the Shares offered to the notified potential buyer. If the *Beta* Group

Entity wishes to sell the offered Shares to a person other than the notified potential buyer, the procedure in Article 12.4 hereof shall be followed again.

13. Corporate Governance

13.1 The *Beta* Group and .... shall cause the Company to take all actions to implement the provisions of this Agreement both in words and spirit, to the extent permissible under law.

13.2 Any of the following actions:—

   (a) re-organization of the capital of the Company,
   (b) alteration of the Memorandum and Articles of Association of the Company,
   (c) commencement of any new line of business (other than the Business),
   (d) changing the name of the Company,
   (e) granting loans or providing securities and giving guarantees to other parties except as may be required in ordinary course of business,
   (f) winding-up of the Company voluntarily,
   (g) incurring or agreeing to incur capital expenditure exceeding Rs. .... (amount) otherwise than in accordance with the yearly Business Plan and budget,
   (h) disposing of assets of the Company, where the sale consideration exceeds Rs. .... (amount) otherwise than in accordance with the yearly Business Plan, or
   (i) passing the yearly Business Plan

   shall require prior approval by

   (A) .... and ...., in the case of those matters customarily requiring Shareholder approvals in international joint ventures or,
   (B) in the case of all other matters, whether being passed at a Board meeting or by circulation, a majority of the Directors comprising at all times at least one Director each nominated/appointed by .... and the *Beta* Group.

13.3 .... or .... shall not unreasonably withhold approval with respect to the actions listed in Article 13.2 above.

14. Books, Records and Affairs of the Company

14.1 *Books and Records.*—The Company shall ensure that its books and records are maintained with a view to accurately reflect the financial position of the Company and are kept in accordance with the requirements of the Act, as well as, generally accepted accounting principles ("GAAP") consistently applied, provided, however, that yearly financial statements shall also be prepared in accordance with such guidelines as may be submitted to the Company by .... and ....

14.2 *Statements.*—The Company shall furnish to .... and ....
  (a) not later than 45 days after the end of each of the first 3 fiscal quarters of each fiscal year, unaudited balance-sheets of the Company as of the end of that fiscal quarter, together with the related unaudited statements of income, retained earnings and cash flows for that fiscal quarter and the year to date, prepared in accordance with GAAP and setting forth in comparative form the information for the corresponding periods of the previous fiscal year,
  (b) not later than .... days after the end of each fiscal year, audited unconsolidated balance sheets of the Company as of the end of that fiscal year, together with the related audited unconsolidated statements of income, retained earnings and cash flow for that fiscal year, prepared in accordance with GAAP and setting forth in comparative form the information for the preceding fiscal year, and the yearly budget together with the related audited report of the Company's independent auditors.

14.3 *Auditing.*—The Company shall cause its books and records to be audited at the end of each fiscal year during the term of this Agreement by an independent firm of chartered accountants appointed by the Shareholders at a general meeting. However, ... at their own cost shall have the right at all times to appoint *Omega* or a firm of chartered accountants of comparable international repute to inspect the books of accounts and other records of the Company; and .... at its own cost shall have the right at all times to appoint a firm of chartered accountants of its choice to inspect the books of accounts and other records of the Company.

14.4 *Statutory Records.*—The Company shall at all times maintain its registers and records in compliance with the provisions of the Act, including (but not limited to) the register of members, register of assets, the register of charges and the register of contracts.

15. Articles of Association

15.1 Subject to compliance with Indian law, to the extent that any of the provisions of this Agreement conflict with any of the provisions of the Articles, the provisions of this Agreement shall prevail.

15.2 The Shareholders shall take all action to ensure that at all times the Articles reflect the provisions of this Agreement. To the extent that any of the provisions contained herein are additional to the provisions contained in the Articles, the Shareholders agree to do all such things and take all such actions to procure that the provisions of this Agreement are put into effect.

16. Earnings and Distributions

Subject to the requirements of the Act, the *Beta* Group and .... shall cause the reserves and incomes of the Company to be applied in the following manner, with the objective of maximising returns by way of dividends:

(i) first, to pay operation, maintenance and financial expenses, including fuel, the funding of major maintenance reserves, taxes, duties and other governmental or statutory charges relating to the Company,

(ii) next, to pay debt obligations,

(iii) apportionment towards the reserves of the Company under the annual plan and budget and/or as deemed appropriate to meet the specific business needs of the Company,

(iv) the remainder shall be appropriated with the aforesaid objective of maximising dividends and in a manner as may be approved by the Board of Directors from time to time.

17. Certain Rights of Shareholders

17.1 .... and ...., subject to the provisions of the Act, may cause the Company to convene general meetings of the Shareholders and discuss the affairs, finances, accounts and policies of the Company.

17.2 Except as expressly provided in this Agreement, a *Beta* Group Entity and .... shall not, through reorganization, consolidation, merger, dissolution or sale of assets, or by any other voluntary Act, (i) avoid or seek to avoid the observance or performance of any of the covenants or agreements to be performed under this Agreement, (ii) adversely affect the interest of each other in the Company and its business.

17.3 .... and .... shall have the right to depute its duly authorised senior executives from time to time, to visit the Company and inspect the properties, records and accounts of the Company, and discuss the affairs of the Company with the Company's senior management at such reasonable times as .... or .... may wish and the Company's senior management shall be available in a manner that does not interfere with or disrupt the business in any material respect.

18. Deadlock

18.1 In the event of any differences relating to any of the matters listed under Articles 7.2 and 13.2 hereof between or among the Directors or Shareholders of the Company which cannot be resolved or settled by the Directors or Shareholders in accordance with the provisions hereof, the Party to this Agreement who raised the issue or proposal at the Board or at the general meeting (the 'Declaring Party') may declare a "Deadlock", for that particular issue by a written notice to the other Party to this Agreement stating "Deadlock" and describing the issue and nature of the "Deadlock" and proposing the resolution thereof. After declaration of the Deadlock, the Parties shall negotiate and try to settle the matter within 90 days from the date of the written notice of "Deadlock".

18.2 If the negotiation fails to resolve the matter, the Declaring Party may, within 10 days of the expiry of the 90 day period for negotiation under Article 18.1 hereof send a written offer to the other Party, stating a price per Share at which it is willing to buy all the Shares of the other Party (the 'Offer Price'). The other Party may either sell all its Shares to the Declaring Party at the Offer Price or buy all the Shares of the Declaring Party at the Offer Price. In the event that the other Party neither sells all its Shares nor buys the Shares of the Declaring Party within .... days of the offer being made by the Declaring Party, either Party may refer the matter to arbitration in accordance with section 23.2. If the Declaring Party does not make an offer under this article 18.2 within the .... days period for negotiation under Article 18.1 hereof, then the other Party may refer the matter to arbitration in accordance with section 23.2.

19. Intellectual Property Rights

19.1 Except where it is necessary to do so for compliance with the statutory regulations, the Shareholders shall not at any time during the term of this Agreement or thereafter in any way or manner whatsoever make known divulge or communicate technical, industrial or market information relating to the establishment or operation and management of the Company or any of the Parties or relating to the manufacture of the products of the Company, furnished by or exchanged by the Company to any other person or company and shall take and maintain such information under strict security precautions to prevent any disclosure. The Company shall use the said information for the purpose of achieving the objectives contemplated hereunder.

19.2 It is mutually agreed that if the Company uses any of the trade marks, trade names or corporate names of .... or its affiliates or a *Beta* Group Entity[1], the Company and ...., its affiliate or the *Gama* Group entity (as the case may be) will enter into a separate agreement governing the rights and obligations with respect thereto, failing which the Company will have no rights.

20. Non-competition/Confidentiality

20.1 Each of the Shareholders agree that from the date hereof and for so long as it holds Shares it will not engage or be interested whether as principal, agent, consultant, employee or otherwise in any trade occupation or business in India competing directly or indirectly with the Business without prior consent in writing of the other Shareholders or as otherwise provided in this Agreement.

20.2 Each of the Shareholders agree that it, or any of its affiliates, shall not for a period of two[2] years following its ceasing to be a Shareholder in the Company on its behalf or on behalf of any third party with whom it may be associated (whether as partner, director, employee, consultant or Shareholder or otherwise) engage or be interested whether as principal, agent, consultant, employee or otherwise in any trade occupation or business in India competing directly or indirectly with the Business without prior consent in writing of the other Shareholders.

20.3 Each of the Shareholders agree that it will not for a period of one year following its ceasing to be a Shareholder in the Company on its behalf or on behalf of any third party with whom it may be associated (whether as partner,

---

1. *Gama* Group is not a defined term. It would be more accurate to refer to a particular legal entity.
2. *Gama* Group insist that this be one year.

director, employee, consultant or shareholder or otherwise) solicit or employ any person who was an employee of the Company or a subsidiary of the Company at any time during the twelve months prior to the date of so ceasing.

20.4 Each of the Shareholders shall keep confidential all information (written or oral) concerning the business and affairs of the Company or any subsidiary of the Company or the other Shareholders that it shall have obtained or received as a result of the discussions leading upto or the entering into or implementation of this Agreement or its association with the Company or any subsidiary of the Company save that which is:

    (a) trivial or obvious;

    (b) obtained lawfully and other than as a result of a breach of this article from Third Parties; or

    (c) in the public domain other than as a result of a breach of this Article.

20.5 Each of the Shareholders undertakes to take all such steps as shall from time to time be necessary to ensure compliance with the provisions of Article 20.3 hereof by its employees, agents and sub-contractors.

20.6 A Shareholder on ceasing to be a Shareholder of the Company will hand over to the Company within a period of seven (7) days all correspondence, budgets, schedules, documents, papers and records belonging to or relating to the Business of the Company, provided that a Shareholder may keep copies of documents that are required for compliance with a statutory requirement and shall thereafter keep confidential all information, including (without limitation) copies of documents and materials, relating to the Company or its Business.

20.7 While the restrictions in sections 20.1, 20.2 and 20.3 hereof are considered by the Shareholders to be reasonable in all the circumstances, if any one or more of such restrictions shall either be taken by itself or themselves together be adjudged to go beyond what is reasonable in all the circumstances for the protection of the Company's legitimate interest but would be adjudged reasonable if any particular restriction or restrictions were deleted or any part or parts of the wording thereof were deleted, restricted or limited in any particular manner, then the said restrictions shall apply with such deletions, restrictions or limitations as the case may be.

20.8 .... and .... shall be entitled to have reasonable access to the accounting and other books and records of the Company, subject to keeping the information contained therein confidential at all times.

21. Costs

Each Party shall bear the fees and disbursements of its own professional advisers in connection with the negotiation and preparation of this Agreement and all agreements supplemental hereto.

22. Effective Date, Term and Termination

22.1 This Agreement shall become effective and binding on the Parties on the date that the Shares in the Company are issued to the *Beta* Group and .... in accordance with the scheme of reconstruction of NSSL sanctioned by court. It.

is acknowledged by the Parties that the representations and warranties contained in this Agreement are true on the date of signing hereof and shall remain so until the effective date.

22.2 This Agreement shall continue in full force and effect and shall bind the Parties until terminated in accordance with the provisions of this article.

22.3 .... and .... shall be entitled to terminate this Agreement immediately by notice in writing to the other Party (but not after .... days of the event in question first coming to the attention of the Party entitled to give the notice) if any of the events set out below shall occur:

(a) in the event of either any *Beta* Group Entity or .... committing a breach of any of the provisions of this Agreement, the other Party shall, without prejudice to other rights and remedies available, have the right to terminate this Agreement, by giving the defaulting party a thirty (30) days' prior notice in writing, specifying *inter alia* the nature of the claimed default and the intention of termination unless such default is cured by the defaulting Party within the next thirty (30) days following receipt of the said notice;

(b) in the event that any of the representations and warranties given by .... or any of the *Beta* Group Entities is found to be not true or correct, the other Party may terminate this Agreement and shall be entitled to such remedies as are available to it in law, including, but not limited to, the right to recover damages; or

(c) if the other Party (being a company) shall go into liquidation whether compulsory or voluntary (except for the purposes of a *bona fide* reconstruction or amalgamation with the consent of the First Party such consent not to be unreasonably withheld) or if the other Party shall have an administrator appointed or if an administrative receiver or manager shall be appointed over any part of the assets or undertaking of the other Party.

22.4 This Agreement shall terminate if at any time as a result of a transfer of Shares made in accordance with this Agreement (and the Articles) either .... or the *Beta* Group holds no Shares, but without prejudice to any rights which either .... or the *Beta* Group may have against the other Party arising prior to such termination.

22.5 This Agreement shall terminate immediately if a resolution is passed to wind up the Company or if a liquidator is otherwise appointed (but without prejudice to any rights either .... or the *Beta* Group may have against the other arising prior to such termination).

22.6 .... shall have the option of terminating this Agreement, if changes in Government policy or Government actions require .... to reduce its shareholding in the Company, prevent .... from receiving dividends from the Company or from repatriation of capital or profits, or effectively exclude .... from participation in the management or control of the Company as provided in this Agreement.

22.7 .... shall have the option of terminating this Agreement, if changes in Government policy or Government actions require the *Beta* Group to reduce their shareholding in the Company, prevent the *Beta* Group from receiving dividends from the Company, or effectively exclude the *Beta* Group from participation in the management or control of the Company as provided in this Agreement.

23. Governing Law/Dispute Resolution/Arbitration

23.1 This Agreement shall be governed by and construed in accordance with the Indian law.

23.2 Any dispute, controversy or claim arising out of or relating to or in connection with this Agreement, or the breach, termination or validity hereof shall be finally settled by an arbitral tribunal (the "Tribunal") in accordance with the Indian Arbitration and Conciliation Act, 1996 as in force at the time such arbitration is commenced (the "Arbitration Act"). Each Party will appoint an arbitrator within thirty (30) days of the receipt by a Party of the other Party's request to initiate arbitration. The two arbitrators so appointed will then jointly appoint a third arbitrator within thirty (30) days of the date of appointment of the second arbitrator, which third will act as Chairman of the Tribunal. Arbitrators not appointed within the time limit set forth in the preceding sentence shall be appointed in accordance with the Arbitration Act. The site of the arbitration shall be ....(place), India. The language of the arbitration and award shall be English.

24. Miscellaneous

24.1 *Waiver.*—There shall be no waiver of any term, provision or condition of this Agreement unless such waiver is evidenced in writing and signed by the waiving party. No omission or delay on the part of any Party in exercising any right, power or privilege hereunder shall operate as a waiver thereof, nor shall any single or partial exercise of any such right, power or privilege preclude any other or further exercise thereof or of any other right, power or privilege. The rights and remedies herein provided are cumulative with, and not exclusive of, any rights or remedies provided by law.

24.2 *Modifications.*—Modifications of and amendments to this Agreement shall be effective only if made in writing and signed by duly authorized representatives of the Parties.

24.3 *Notices.*—Any notice required or permitted to be given hereunder shall be in writing and sent by registered air mail, postage prepaid or facsimile transmission and shall be addressed to the Parties at the address mentioned below:

    if addressed to ....,
        The Financial Manager
        Alpha Group Overseas
        ....
        ....

....
.... (address)

with a copy to:
The Company Secretary
Delta Engineering Holdings Limited
....
....
.... (address)

if addressed to ....,
Beta
....
....
.... (address)

if addressed to the Company,
....
....
....

or such other addresses and numbers as any of the Parties may from time to time designate by notice writing to the other. The notice shall be deemed to be served when first received.

24.4 *Severability*.—The invalidity of any portion of this Agreement shall not affect the remaining portions of this Agreement or any part thereof and this Agreement shall be construed as if such invalid portion or portions had not been inserted therein. The Parties will replace an invalid provision or fill a gap with valid provisions which most closely approximate the intent and economic effect of the invalid provision or, in case of a gap, the Parties' presumable intentions.

24.5 *Assignment*.—Save as otherwise expressly provided under this Agreement, all rights and obligations hereunder are personal to the Parties hereto and may not be assigned at law or in equity without the prior written consent of the other Party.

24.6 *Force Majeure*.—Neither Party shall be liable for delay in performance of its responsibilities hereunder, where any such failure or delay is beyond its control and which may be caused by an act of God, embargo, trade restrictions, blockades, war or consequences of war, fire, flood, natural calamity, riot, civil commotion, epidemic, plague, accident or any other similar extraordinary cause which is beyond the reasonable control of the Parties seeking to rely on this clause. Should the event of *force majeure* subsist for a duration longer than thirty (30) days, the Party seeking to rely on such event of *force majeure* shall give the other party a notice specifying the commencement of such event and the Parties shall mutually agree upon the further course of action. If no mutually agreed resolution is reached within sixty (60) days of commencement of *force majeure* event, the matter will be referred to arbitration as per the provisions of this Agreement.

24.7 *Announcements, etc.*—Each of the Parties agrees, on behalf of itself and its officers, directors, employees, agents and shareholders, not to make any public disclosures or communications with the press regarding the Company outside India and regarding ....'s investment in the Company within India without ....'s prior approval. The Company, each Party and any affiliates thereof shall not use the name of the Company, or of any affiliates thereof in the conduct of its any other businesses. Subject to the first sentence of this section 24.7, the Parties acknowledge that the second sentence of this section 24.7 is not intended to preclude a Party from mentioning, as an introduction, that the Party has an interest in the Company or has a joint venture with the other Party. Neither the making of its Agreement nor its terms shall be disclosed by any Party without the prior consent of the other Parties unless disclosure is required by law or the rules of any recognised stock exchange and disclosure shall then be made only to the person or persons and in the manner required by law or the rules or regulations of the Stock Exchange in question (as the case may be) or as otherwise agreed between the Parties. Notice of such disclosure being made shall be given to the Company within a reasonable time.

25. Entire Agreement

This Agreement (together with the documents referred to herein) constitutes the entire Agreement between the Parties in connection with the subject matter of this Agreement.

IN WITNESS whereof the parties hereto have duly executed this Agreement the day and year first above written.

SIGNED by Mr. ....

Duly Authorised

For and on behalf of ....

SIGNED By *BETA*

Acting on his own behalf and duly authorised

for and on behalf of THE *BETA* GROUP

SIGNED By Mr. ....

Title

For and on behalf of THE COMPANY

ANNEXURE A

Company					Period Ended:			
	MONTH		YEAR TO DATE		BUDGET FOR YEAR	FORECAST		
	Actual	Budget	Actual	Budget		1 month ahead	2 months ahead	3 months ahead
TURNOVER								
-Home								
-Export								
(Direct Material)								
Per Original Budget								
Metal Price Adjustment								
(Direct Labour)								
(Variable Costs)								
- Distribution								
- Other								
CONTRIBUTION								
Fixed expenses:								
(Works)								
- Stock movement								
- Other								
(Administration)								
(Distribution)								
TRADING PROFIT								
Interest								
PROFIT AFTER INTEREST								
CAPITAL EXPENDITURE								
CASH FLOW								
Bank								
Group Loans								
External Borrowings								
TOTAL								

*Forecast to be completed as follows:

January	February	March	April	May & June
February	March	April	May	June
March	April	May	June	—
April	May	June	July	—
May	June	July	August	—
June	July	August	September	Oct. Nov., Dec.
July	August	September	October	Nov. & Dec.
August	September	October	November	December
September	October	November	December	—
October	November	December	January	—
November	December	January	February	—
December	January	February	March	April, May & June

SHAREHOLDERS' AGREEMENTS AND THE ARTICLES OF ASSOCIATION

The balance enabled by law between the respective rights of shareholders may not be the appropriate one for every situation. It is not uncommon, therefore, to find that the members of a company wish to engineer adjustments to that balance. This may be done by special provisions contained in the articles of association or by a separate agreement between the shareholders ('shareholders' agreement') or by a combination of the two agreements of this nature may be made between some or all of the shareholders and frequently join in the Company itself as a Party.

Shareholders' agreements are predominantly made between the members of private companies; not least because public companies commonly have large memberships, thus making the use of such Agreement impractical. For this reason, my analysis principally extends to shareholders agreements as they relate to private companies. Shareholders of private companies are usually faced with restrictions on the transferability of their shares and with the absence of a market in those shares, especially if they are not in a controlling position. Not surprisingly, a person acquiring shares in a private company without obtaining control will be inclined to seek special protections and rights to safeguard his position. Shareholders' agreements are necessarily supplemented to the articles of association and their analysis must first begin with an understanding of the nature and effect of the articles.

Nature and effect of the articles, purpose of the articles of association

The articles of association are the creation of company law and are the primary means by which a company governs its internal management and administrative affairs. They regulate a wide range of matters and cover almost every application of company law to individual companies. They are however, subject to the company's memorandum of association and to the requirements of the Act and the principles of company law propounded by the courts.

The effect and enforceability of the articles

Basic principle.—The basic principle is that the articles impose binding obligations on the members in their dealings with the company (but only as shareholders and not in some other capacity), on the company in its dealing with the members (but only in their capacity as members) and on the members in their dealings with each other (but again only in their capacity as members).

The Company and its members: analysing the relationship

It is clear that each member is obliged to the company to comply with the articles but only in his capacity as a member[1]. The purpose of the memorandum and articles is to define the position of the shareholder as shareholder, not to bind him in his capacity as an individual.

---

1. *Bisgood* v. *Henderson's Transvaal Estates Ltd.*, 1908 (1) Ch 743.

It is also clear that a Company is obliged to its members to comply with the articles of association to the extent that they affect the rights and obligations of the member in their capacity as such. Putting it another way, no article giving an individual a right otherwise than in his capacity as a member may be enforced by that person against the Company, even if he is in fact a member.

No right merely purporting to be given by an article to a person, whether a member or not, in a capacity other than that of a member, as for instance, as solicitor, promoter, director, can be enforced against the Company.

However, this is not the whole picture because it is clear that in some circumstances the courts are willing to allow a member to enforce a right conferred by the articles in a capacity other than as a member. This was the case in *Quin & Axtens Ltd.* v. *Salmon*, 1909 AC 442 and also in *Hayes* v. *Bristol Plant Hire*, 1957 (1) All ER 685 whether or not these and other similar cases form a clearly defined exception to the general principle or are first inconsistent in difficult to determine. It does appear, however, that where a person, who is a 'direct-shareholder' of a company (which is a quasi-partnership) and with a bundle of rights both as member and director, is seeking to enforce a provision contained in the articles, the courts seem less inclined to attempt to disentangle those rights to see which are enforceable and which are not a practical solution.

The note is first a summary of the subject and no doubt the academic debate will continue until these issues come up for further judicial consideration. However, so as to put the matter beyond doubt, there appears to be no reason why the members of the Company cannot agree in a collateral contract that the articles will be enforceable by them in a manner beyond that which the courts are prepared to enforce the statutory contract. A shareholder's agreement which is binding on all the members may provide, for example, that: Each of the parties hereto [namely, the shareholders and the Company] undertake with each of the others fully and promptly to observe and comply with the provisions of the Articles to the intent and effect that each and every provision thereof shall be enforceable by the parties hereto *inter se* and in whatever capacity.

Interpretation of the articles

The articles constitute a statutory contract and unlike ordinary contracts, are not capable of annulment on the grounds of misrepresentation or involve influence and cannot be rectified on the grounds of mistake and, while it may be possible to infer a term in the articles purely by way of constitutional implication, it is not possible to go further and imply or term from extrinsic circumstances. [Practitioners] should be especially careful when drafting articles of association to ensure that the necessary rights and obligations are enshrined expressly and unambiguously. The articles should be read with the memorandum of association but in cases of conflict the memorandum will prevail[1].

Contract between the shareholders, a shareholders' agreement in a contract between the persons, who are parties to it and is enforceable in accordance with normal contractual principles. Ideally, all the shareholders of the Company

---

1. *Duncan Gilmour & Co Ltd. (in re:)*, (1952) 2 All ER 871.

should be joined as parties, as it is not recommended to have a minority hanging outside the Agreement. Where this is not possible for some reason (e.g. where share are to be issued to employees under a share option scheme free of the restrictions on transfer contained in the Agreement), then the shareholder seeking special protections should at least reach Agreement with those shareholders who are in control.

An illustrative case study [English Common Law]

A shareholders' agreement will not normally be exclusive of any remedies which might otherwise be available by law[1], the repudiation by certain shareholders of another shareholder's right to appoint a director under a shareholders' agreement, and thereby participate in management, rendered it just and equitable that the company be wound up under the precursor to section 122(1)(g) of the U.K. Insolvency Act, 1986 although it would be prudent to state this. Where, however, a shareholder has expressly agreed to limit his rights in some way then the courts will not usually interfere unless, of course, the other parties to the agreement are in breach.

The mutual rights and obligations conferred and entered into pursuant to a shareholders' agreement will usually amount to sufficient consideration. However, where a party is not a shareholder (such as a guarantor) or receives benefits but does not incur obligations (or *vice versa*) it may be advisable to execute the agreement as a deed.

It is increasingly common to find that the company itself is joined as a party to the agreement for one or more of the following reasons:

1. To commit the company to obligations in the agreement which might otherwise have been included in the articles of association (*e.g.* restriction on borrowings and directors' remuneration) but which the shareholders prefer to be in the shareholders' agreement. This may be particularly desirable where not all of the shareholders have joined in the agreement; the other parties to the agreement will then be able to rely on the contractual undertakings given by the Company.
2. To place the company under an obligation to recognise and enforce or beneficial owners' rights over shares or to give effect to voting agreements between the shareholders.
3. To bind the directors (indirectly) to give effect to the arrangements when exercising the powers conferred on them. This will be particularly important in the case of a director who is not also a shareholder.
4. To require the company to undertake to exercise appropriate control over its subsidiaries.

---

1. A. & B.C. Chewing Gum Ltd. (in re:), (1975) 1 AU ER 1017.

SHARE TRANSFER AGREEMENT

THIS AGREEMENT is made on the ....day of ....

BETWEEN

ALPHA Healthcare Private Limited, a Company registered under the Indian Companies Act having its registered office at .... (address) (hereinafter referred to as "*ALPHA*" which expression shall unless repugnant to the context or meaning thereof include its successors and permitted assigns) of the FIRST PART,

AND

GAMMA Healthcare Limited, a company registered under the Indian Companies Act having its registered office at "*Alpha* Tower", ... (address) (hereinafter referred to as "*BETA*" which expression shall unless repugnant to the context or meaning thereof include its successors and permitted assigns) of the SECOND PART, and

Mr. ....(name), son of Mr. .... (name), resident of ...., for and on his own behalf and for and on behalf of Mr. .... (name), son of Mr. .... (name), resident of .... (hereinafter referred to as the "Mr. .... [*Gama*]" which expression shall unless repugnant to the context or meaning thereof include its successors and permitted assigns) of the THIRD PART.

Beta and Mr. .... (name) are hereinafter collectively referred to as the 'Sellers'.

Whereas *Gamma*, Mr. .... (name) and Mr. .... (name) hold .... fully paid-up equity shares of Rs. .... (amount) each in .... Healthcare Limited, a company registered under the Indian Companies Act having its registered office at "Alpha Tower", ... [address] (hereinafter referred to as "................ "), constituting 100% of the issued and paid-up share capital of .... (the '................ Shares').

And whereas .... carries on the business of manufacture and sale of certain bulk drugs and formulations;

And whereas the Sellers wish to transfer the .... Shares to ALPHA.

Now therefore, in light of the mutual promises contained herein and other good and valuable consideration, the receipt and sufficiency of which is hereby acknowledged, the Parties agree as follows:

1. Definitions

1.1 '*Assets*' means all rights, properties and assets, whether movable or immovable, tangible or intangible, including Land, owned by .... as set out in *Schedule I* hereto.

1.2 '*Completion Accounts*' means the financial statements, including the balance-sheet and the profit and loss account of .... as of the date of Completion of Transfer.

1.3 '*Completion of Transfer*' means the transfer of the .... Shares from the Sellers to *Alpha* whereupon *Alpha* shall be registered as the holder of the .... Shares in the register of members of ....

1.4 *'FIPB'* means the Foreign Investment Promotion Board.

1.5 *'Land'* means the piece of land known as .... (name of the plot), within the village limits of ....(name), Taluka and Registration Sub-district .... (name), District and Registration District .... (name), admeasuring .... square meters or thereabouts and more particularly described in the Lease Deed and together with all rights, easements, and appurtenances thereto.

1.6 *'Lease Deed'* means the lease deed dated .... (date) between .... and ....

1.7 *'Lien'* means any mortgage, pledge, charge, hypothecation, collateral assignment, deposit arrangement, encumbrance, statutory or other lien, or any other security interest or preferential arrangement of any kind or nature whatsoever, including, without limitation, any conditional sale or other title retention Agreement having substantially the same effect as any of the foregoing.

1.8 *'MIDC'* means the Maharashtra Industrial Development Corporation under the Maharashtra Industrial Development Act, 1961.

1.9 *'SIA'* means the Secretariat for Industrial Assistance.

2. Representations of the Sellers

The Sellers hereby warrant and represent as follows. The representations and warranties in this Article 2 shall remain in full force and effect notwithstanding the Completion of Transfer of .... Shares and so far as such warranties and representations of the Sellers relate in whole or part to present and past matters of fact as on the Completion of Transfer of the .... Shares they shall also be deemed to constitute fundamental representations upon the faith of which this Agreement has been entered into by Alpha. Each of the representations and warranties shall be deemed to be repeated at the time the payments are made to the Sellers under Article 4 hereof.

2.1 With respect to .... and the Sellers

2.1.1 *Status.*—.................... and Gamma are companies duly incorporated and validly existing and have the corporate power to own their assets and carry on their business as is being conducted and to perform their obligations under this Agreement, and .... is the holder of all necessary permissions/licences, required in connection with its Assets and its business and the Sellers know of no reason or of any facts or circumstances which (with or without the giving of notice or lapse of time) would be likely to give rise to any reason why any of them should be suspended, cancelled, revoked or not renewed and there is no order, decree or judgement of any court or any governmental body outstanding which may have a material adverse effect on the business of ....

2.1.2 *Power and Authority.*—The Sellers have the power to execute, deliver and perform their obligations under this Agreement and all necessary corporate, shareholder and other action has been taken to authorise the execution, delivery and performance of this Agreement and the transactions contemplated by this Agreement.

2.1.3 *Legal Validity.*—This Agreement constitutes valid and legally binding obligations of the Sellers, enforceable in accordance with its respective terms.

2.1.4 *Non-Conflict.*—The execution, delivery and performance of this Agreement will not (a) contravene any existing applicable law to which .... and the Sellers are subject, (b) conflict with, or result in any breach of any of the terms of, or constitute a default under, any agreement or other instrument to which .... or any of the Sellers is a party or is subject or by which it or any of the Assets is bound, (c) contravene or conflict with any provision of ....'s or Gamma's constitutional documents or (d) contravene, violate, or conflict with any licenses, approvals, or consents obtained by .... or the Sellers.

2.1.5 *Capital.*—The authorised share capital of .... is Rs. .... (amount in words and figures). As of the date hereof, each shareholder of .... and its legal or beneficial ownership of the .... Shares are as indicated in *Schedule-II* and no other persons, have subscribed or will subscribe, or have entered or will enter into any agreement to subscribe, to any shares, or securities convertible into shares, in ....

2.1.6 *Business until Completion of Transfer.*—During the period between the signing of this Agreement and the Completion of Transfer, nothing will be done in the conduct of the management of the affairs of ...., which would be likely to prejudice the interests of Alpha as a prospective purchaser of the .... Shares.

2.1.7 *Litigation.*—No litigation, arbitration or administrative proceeding is taking place, pending or threatened against .... whether in relation to its assets, liabilities, taxation or otherwise which could have a material adverse effect on the performance of this Agreement, the interest of .... in its assets, the liabilities of .... or the decision of Alpha to enter into and perform this Agreement.

2.2 With respect to the Assets

2.2.1 *Title.*—.................. has good title to all its Assets free and clear of Liens. No person other than .... has any right, title or interest in any of the Assets. The Completion of Transfer shall not affect in any manner the title; ownership and rights of .... to the Assets and .... shall continue to have such ownership, right and title to the Assets following such transfer. Alpha shall have the right to rescind this Agreement by notice to the Sellers if as a consequence of transfer of the .... Shares, the ownership; rights and title to the Assets are affected for reasons not attributable to Alpha. Any costs, expenses, charges or taxes of any nature whatsoever related to perfection of maintenance of ....'s right, title and interest in the Assets, including without limitation any differential premium or other sums payable to MIDC (other than the transfer charges payable at the time of the merger) arising from the transfer of the .... Shares shall be borne and paid by *Gamma*.

2.2.2 *Payment of Rent, Taxes and Service Charges.*—.................. has paid the rent due (to .... under the Lease Deed on the day and in the manner provided for under the Lease Deed); all taxes, rate, assessment outgoings of every description (payable under the Lease Deed in respect of the Land); and recurring fees (to .... in the nature of service charges as may have been due from time to time and/or prescribed by the Government of Maharashtra under the .... Industrial Development Act, 1961 or the Rules framed thereunder in respect of the amenities and common facilities provided by ....). Any rent, taxes service charges or other payments in respect of the Land for the period prior to the Completion of Transfer, which may become due after the Completion of Transfer shall be paid by *Gamma*.

2.2.3 *No excavation.*—.................. has not made any excavation upon any part of the Land nor removed any stone, sand, gravel, clay or earth therefrom except for the purpose of forming foundation of building or for the purpose of executing any work pursuant to the terms of the Lease Deed and in accordance with the terms of the Lease Deed.

2.2.4 *Sanitation.*—.................. has observed and conformed to all rules, regulations and byelaws of the local authorities concerned or any other statutory regulations in any way relating to public health and sanitation in order to keep the Land and surroundings clean and in good condition to the satisfaction of the Executive Engineer and has not, without previous consent in writing of the Executive Engineer, permitted any labourers or workmen to reside upon the Land. Any consents or conditions subject to which such consent has been given have been complied with strictly by ....

2.2.5 *Insurance.*—There are valid and existing policies of insurance against all liabilities and risks and losses against which it is normal and prudent to insure in respect of the Assets owned by and in the business carried on by ....

2.2.6 *No Assignment.*—.................. has not assigned, underlet or parted with the possession of the Assets, or any part thereof or any interest therein and has not entered into an agreement to do any of the foregoing.

2.2.7 *Land - Conditions of the Lease Deed and Law.*—.................. has complied with all the conditions, has performed all its obligations, and is not in breach of or in default, under the Lease Deed or any law, rule, regulation or bye-law applicable to the Land. None of the covenants under the Lease Deed have been breached by .... None of the representations and warranties given by .... under the Lease Deed or in connection therewith are false, whether in part or whole. There are no circumstances, which with the passage of time or the giving of notice will constitute a default or breach under the Lease Deed.

2.2.8 *No Encumbrance.*—There are no encumbrances, mortgages, liens, charges or other security interest subsisting on, or in relation to, the Assets and .... has not entered into any agreement or understanding with a Third Party relating to any of the Assets.

2.3 With respect to the .... Shares

2.3.1 *Validity.*—The .... Shares (a) are duly and validly authorised, issued, allotted and are fully paid; (b) have attached to them the rights and benefits specified in the organisational documents of ....; (c) are not, and will not be, subject to any pre-emptive or other similar rights under the organisational documents of ...., law or any agreement or instrument, or approval to which .... or any shareholder of .... is subject; (d) are, and will be, free from any Lien or other third party claim or interest.

2.3.2 *Percentage.*—The percentage of the issued and outstanding share capital of .... that the .... Shares will constitute as of the Completion of Transfer contemplated under this Agreement is exactly 100%.

2.3.3 *No Option.*—(a) There is no option, right, warrant or other agreement or commitment obligating .... to issue or sell any of its securities and there are no securities convertible into or exchangeable for any equity securities of ...., and (b) no person has any right, option or other agreement or commitment with .... or any of the shareholders of .... to participate in the ownership, investment, management or operation of ....

2.3.4 *Title.*—The Sellers have good and marketable title to the .... Shares.

2.4 *With respect to the liabilities of* ....

2.4.1 *Liabilities and Instruments.*—*Schedule-III* identifies each liability, obligation, undertaking, circumstance, fact, assessment, judgement or order of a court or other *quasi-judicial* or governmental authority, contract, agreement, instrument, consent, approval, permission, authorisation, licence, commitment or other obligation, and all amendments, modifications, extensions and supplements to any of the foregoing (including, without limitation, any contracts or agreements with any workers' union and employee of ....) to which .... is a Party or by which it or its assets or property may be bound, accurate and complete copies of which, including any amendments or supplements thereto, have been provided to Alpha, which may in any way affect the decision of Alpha to purchase the .... Shares. Accurate and complete copies of the current organisational documents of .... have been furnished to *Alpha*. There are no liabilities, contingent or otherwise, other than those identified on *Schedule III*, which can influence the decision of *Alpha* to purchase the .... Shares. .... has not issued any guarantees or indemnities in favour of any person.

2.4.2 *No Default.*—.................. is not in default or in breach, or has alleged any default under or breach of, any of the contracts, agreements, instruments, consents, approvals, permissions, authorisations, licences, commitments or other obligations, or the amendments, modifications, extensions and supplements to any of the foregoing identified in *Schedule III*. Neither .... nor any other Party to any of the said agreements has given, or threatened to give, notice of termination, nor is there any event or circumstance that would, with the passage of time or the giving of notice, constitute a default or breach of any of the instruments identified in *Schedule III*.

2.5 *Information*

The information and reports furnished by the Sellers or .... to *Alpha* in connection with the matters contemplated by this Agreement or with the negotiation of the Agreement are true and accurate in all material respects and not misleading, do not omit material facts and all reasonable enquiries have been made to verify the facts and statements contained therein and there are no other facts the omission of which would make any fact or statement therein misleading.

2.6 With respect to Accounts

2.6.1 *Books and Records.*—The accounting and other books, ledgers, financial and other records of .... are in its possession and have at all times been properly and fully written up in accordance with all applicable laws.

2.6.2 *Accounts.*—The accounts have been prepared and kept in accordance with generally accepted accounting principles and standards consistently applied, and the Companies Act and show a true complete and fair view of the state of affairs, financial position and assets and liabilities of .... as of the date of such accounts.

2.7 Registers and Records

The register of members and all other statutory books and minute books of .... have been properly kept, are up-to-date and contain true, full and accurate records of all matters required to be dealt with therein.

2.8 With respect to environmental matters

2.8.1 *User.*—.................. has used the Land only for the purpose permitted under the Lease Deed and not for the purpose of a factory for any obnoxious industry specified in the annexure to the Lease Deed and has not used the Land or any part thereof for any other purposes nor for the purpose of any factory which may be obnoxious, essence by reason of emission of odour, liquid effluvia, dust, smoke, gas, noise, vibrations or fire hazard.

2.8.2 *Conduct of business.*—The continuing conduct of the business of .... or use of the Assets, and in particular the Land, by .... will not give rise to any claim, proceeding or any action under any applicable law, including environmental laws. The existence and use of the Assets employed in the conduct of the business of .... has been in accordance with the environmental authorisations and laws.

2.8.3 The Land, including without limitation the soil, sub-soil, surface and ground water, is not polluted to a degree violating applicable laws or involving the risk of violating applicable laws.

2.9 Taxes

All taxes, duties and social security charges for which .... may have become liable to be assessed in respect of any period ending on or prior to the date of the completion accounts have either been paid in full or adequate provision therefore has been made in the completion accounts. With respect to all such taxes, duties and charges assessed or accrued prior to the date of the completion of accounts, no further payments; interest or penalties are or will become due. .... will not be liable to repay any investment premiums or subsidies granted to it prior to the date of the completion of accounts.

3. Transfer of .... Shares

3.1 *Agreement to Transfer.*—Subject to, and in accordance with, any conditions imposed under any approval, consent or permission in connection with this Agreement, the Sellers hereby agree to sell, convey, transfer and assign all its rights, title and interest in, or with respect to, the .... Shares whether

·nder an agreement or otherwise, to *Alpha* and a nominee of *Alpha*.[1] ALPHA (relying on the representations and indemnities by the Sellers in this Agreement) shall purchase the .... Shares free from all claims and encumbrances as of the Completion of Transfer. Alpha shall not be obliged to complete the purchase of any of the .... Shares unless the transfer of all the .... Shares is completed simultaneously.

3.2 *Completion of transfer.*—The transfer of the .... Shares from the Sellers to ALPHA shall be completed within fifteen days of the latest of (a) Gamma obtaining all requisite approvals in connection with the transfer of the .... Shares to *Alpha*, in particular the approval of the FIPB or the SIA; (b) the amendment of the memorandum and articles of Association of .... as desired by *Alpha*; and (c) the change of the name of .... to "..." or such other name as is approved by the concerned Registrar of Companies that is acceptable to *Alpha*. At Completion of Transfer, all formalities required under law will be completed and share certificates representing the .... Shares duly endorsed in favour of *Alpha* shall be delivered to *Alpha*. The Parties may agree in writing to extend the said period of fifteen days.

3.3 *Approval of Building Plans.*—Immediately upon the signing of this Agreement, the Sellers shall cause .... to file with ...., applications, along with drawings, plans, etc. relating to the proposed construction on the Land and/or modifications of the buildings thereon, prepared and made available to .... by *Alpha*, for obtaining the approval of .... in respect of the building plans. Upon obtaining the said approval of ...., *Alpha* may cause .... to commence demolition and/or construction on the Land and/or modification of the buildings thereon and shall have the right, without any condition or limitation, to enter upon and bring such equipment, materials and men that it may in its sole discretion consider appropriate in connection with such proposed construction.

3.4 *Following Completion of Transfer.*—Upon Completion of Transfer:

3.4.1 The existing directors of .... shall resign with a written acknowledgement from each that he has no claim whatsoever against ....; the existing auditors of .... shall resign confirming that they have no outstanding claims of any kind;

3.4.2 *Alpha* shall procure that a board meeting shall be held at which such persons as *Alpha* shall nominate be appointed as directors of ....; and auditors shall be appointed as agreed upon by *Alpha*; and

3.4.3 The registered offices of .... shall be shifted to ....

---

1. There must be two shareholders of a deemed public company. Accordingly, the second shareholder can be a nominee of Alpha. The nominee can be any individual or company. If such nominee is a non-resident Indian (individual or company), approval of the Reserve Bank of India would have to be obtained. You could consider making the Escrow Agent the nominee. Upon the Merger being implemented, the nominee would cease to hold the shares in Psi.

4. Consideration

4.1 *Consideration.*—In consideration for the transfer of .... Shares from the Sellers to *Alpha*, *Alpha* shall pay the sum of Rs. .... as follows:

4.1.1 The sum of Rs. .... to *Beta* on the Completion of Transfer under section 3.2 hereof or upon obtaining approval of building plans under section 3.3 hereof, whichever is later;

4.1.2 The sum of Rs. .... to *Beta* upon the production of evidence satisfactory to *Alpha* that the registered office of .... has been shifted to the State of ....; and

4.1.3 The balance sum of Rs. ....[1] to *Beta* upon the production of evidence satisfactory to *Alpha* that the Merger is complete in all respects.

4.2 Upon the payment of the consideration by *Alpha* in accordance with the terms of this Article 4, *Beta* shall be responsible for payment of any sums that may be due to any of the Sellers other than *Beta* or any adjustment of accounts among the Sellers *inter se*, in connection with the transfer of the .... Shares. *Alpha* shall not be liable for the payment of any sums or in any other manner other than in accordance with Article 4.1.

5. Merger

5.1 The Parties shall take all steps to consummate the transfer contemplated hereunder in a manner that is expeditious, tax-efficient and cost-effective for the Parties.

5.2 Upon the Completion of Transfer, the Sellers, in particular *Beta*, shall (a) prepare a scheme for the merger of *Alpha* and .... (the '*Merger*') in the most cost-effective manner; and (b) take all steps to implement the Merger, including obtaining High Court sanction therefor.

5.3 If for any valid reason, the Merger cannot be implemented as envisaged in section 5.2, *Beta* shall obtain necessary approvals and take all other necessary steps, including without limitation payment of all costs, charges, expenses, fees and taxes, for the transfer of Land from .... to Alpha and for the re-transfer of the .... Shares from *Alpha* to the Sellers.[2]

6. Approvals

6.1 *Obligation of the Sellers.*—The Sellers shall take all steps, necessary or desirable, for consummation of the transactions contemplated hereunder or to establish and perfect *Alpha's* right, title and interest in, and to, the .... Shares, including (without limitation) the approval of the .... or the ...., any filing or recording of any document or obtaining the consent, approval or sanction of any Court for the Merger or otherwise, quasi-judicial authority, Government or Government instrumentality, including without limitation ...., or any other person, such as, the lenders of ....

---

1. We suggest a substantial amount be withheld, in order that *Beta* is motivated to expedite the Merger.
2. We suggest that this be contained in a side-letter since this would indicate that the transfer of the Psi Shares is *de facto* a transaction to transfer the Land.

6.2 *Transferee to Support.*—*Alpha* shall extend all such support that .... or the Sellers may reasonably request in connection with section 6.1 hereof, including, if necessary, making joint applications with .... and/or *Beta*.

7. Completion Accounts

7.1 The Sellers shall cause .... to prepare the Completion Accounts as of the date of Completion of Transfer according to the requirements of all relevant statutes and accounting principles generally applied in India and in accordance with accounting principles consistently applied for the annual accounts in the last three business years as far as they are not in conflict with legally determined and generally applied accounting principles in India.

7.2 The completion accounts shall be audited by the auditors of .... The audited completion accounts shall be forwarded to *Alpha* for examination and approval within .... days of completion of transfer. *Alpha* shall have the opportunity to inspect the books and records of .... in connection with the examination of the completion accounts.

8. Expenses, Taxes and Levies

8.1 *Expenses, Taxes and Levies.*—All expenses, taxes, levies, duties, fees or other payments or charges payable under a statute or otherwise, required to be paid for the consummation or legality of the transfer of the .... Shares and the Merger as envisaged under this Agreement ('Transfer Costs') including (without limitation) stamp duty payable on court orders relating to the Merger, share transfer deeds or deed of assignment, any fee payable in connection with the registration of documents, any fee payable to professional advisers or consultants, court fee, any differential premium or transfer charges payable to .... pursuant to .... Transfer Guidelines for Industrial Plots and any charges payable to local authorities, shall, upto a maximum limit of Rs. .... (amount in words and figures), be borne and paid by *Alpha*. Any transfer costs incurred in excess of the said limit shall be borne and paid by *Beta*. Any income tax payable by a Party as a result of the completion of the transfer as envisaged under this Agreement shall be borne and paid by such Party and shall not be included in transfer costs. *Beta* shall keep separate records of Transfer Costs incurred, along with supporting vouchers and external evidence.

8.2 In the event that in the opinion of the professional advisers or engineers representing, or working on behalf of, *Alpha*, the geological, environmental or other similar factors relevant to the land or the modification of the buildings thereon, would result in substantial addition to costs related to construction on the land or modifications of buildings thereon or assumption of inordinate risk, the Parties shall meet to arrive at a mutually acceptable solution, including relating to sharing of additional costs and expenses and, notwithstanding the discussions among the Parties, *Alpha* shall have the right to terminate this Agreement and receive any amount paid pursuant to Article 4.1 hereof.

9. Indemnity

9.1 The Sellers agree to assume liability for, and do hereby indemnify, protect, save and keep harmless *Alpha* and its successors, assigns, agents, directors, servants and shareholders, in particular ...., from and against any and all claims, damages, losses, liabilities, obligations, demands, suits, penalties, judgements or causes of action and all legal proceedings, whether civil or criminal, penalties, fines and other sanctions, and any costs and expenses in connection therewith including, without limitation, legal fees and expenses of whatever kind and nature (whether or not also indemnified against by any other person under any other document), which may result from or grow or arise in any manner out of:

9.1.1 The ownership, title, acceptance, non-acceptance, rejection, delivery, mortgage, possession, return, disposition or use (in each and every case) of the .... Shares;

9.1.2 Any fact or circumstance relating to, or any activity of .... during, the period prior to the completion of the transfer of the .... Shares as envisaged under Section 4.2 hereof;

9.1.3 Any act or omission in the use of the Assets, particularly the land, prior to the completion of the transfer of the .... Shares as envisaged under section 4.2 hereof;

9.1.4 Any claim or dispute as to survival or extinguishment of any Lien in the .... Shares, as the case may be, created, or relating to a date, prior to the completion of the transfer as envisaged under section 4.2 hereof; or

9.1.5 Any warranty or representation of the Sellers made under this Agreement being false.

9.2 *Environmental matters.*—Without limitation to the provisions of section 9.1, in the event of any breach of any representations and warranties with respect to environmental matters given under this Agreement, the Sellers hereby agree to indemnify and hold *Alpha* harmless from and against and to reimburse Alpha for any or all losses, liabilities, damages claims and expenses [including without limitation fines, penalties, clean-up costs, activities, legal obligations, technical consultant's fees incidental and consequential damages ("Environmental Losses")] which may be sustained or suffered by *Alpha* arising out of, based upon or by reason of any environmental warranties being untrue or incorrect or by virtue of any environmental losses incurred by *Alpha* arising out of the use of the Assets, Land or operation of the business of .... prior to completion of Transfer whether or not such liability was known to the Sellers or could have been reasonably known by the Sellers notwithstanding that all reasonable enquiries have been made by the Sellers prior to the completion of transfer.

9.3 *Continuing Indemnity.*—The indemnity given by the Sellers to *Alpha* pursuant to this Article 9 shall not be affected by, and shall survive, the performance, termination or rescission of this Agreement.

10. Exclusivity

During the term of this Agreement none of the Parties or any of their affiliates shall, directly or indirectly, solicit, allow or entertain any discussions with respect to the subject-matter of this Agreement or provide any information with respect thereto.

11. Dispute Resolution

11.1 *Parties.*—For the purposes of this Article 11, the Sellers and .... shall be considered one Party.

11.2 *Initiation of proceedings.*—In the event of any controversy or claim relating to, arising out of or in any way connected to this Agreement, the Parties shall seek to settle their differences amicably between themselves, including entering into non-binding mediation. Any unresolved dispute shall be finally resolved by final and binding arbitration in accordance with this Article. Whenever a Party shall decide to institute arbitration proceedings, it shall give written notice to that effect to the other Party. The Party giving such notice shall refrain from instituting the arbitration proceedings for a period of thirty (30) days following such notice to allow the Parties to attempt to resolve the dispute between them. If the Parties are still unable to resolve the dispute, the Party giving the notice may institute the arbitration proceeding under the rules of Conciliation and Arbitration of the International Chamber of Commerce as then in effect (the "ICC Rules"). This Agreement shall be governed by the laws of India to the exclusion of choice of law principles.

11.3 *Venue, Language and Number of Arbitrators.*—Arbitration shall be held in .... (place), India, in the English language. The arbitration shall be conducted before three arbitrators with each Party to select 1 (one) arbitrator and with the third arbitrator to be appointed in accordance with the ICC Rules.

11.4 *Finality of Award.*—Any award shall be by majority vote and shall be final and binding on the Parties. Nothing contained in this section shall prevent either Party from seeking temporary restraining orders, injunctions or other temporary relief in any court of competent jurisdiction.

12. Termination

12.1 *Termination.*—This Agreement may be terminated by *Alpha* if any of the Sellers breaches any of the provisions hereof or if any of the representations and warranties made hereunder by the Sellers are found to be false, or if the Merger is not complete before .... or such subsequent date as may be fixed by *Alpha*. This Agreement may be terminated by Gamma if *Alpha* breaches any of the provisions hereof.

12.2 *Notice.*—The Party terminating this Agreement shall give a written termination notice of 30 (thirty) days to the other Parties. In the event that after the receipt of the notice the Party in default fails to remedy the breach to the satisfaction of the terminating Party, this Agreement shall terminate upon the expiry of the said period.

12.3 *Transferee's remedy.*—*Alpha*, at its sole option, may choose to seek specific performance of this Agreement.

13. Miscellaneous

13.1 *Errors in Description of Assets.*—Any error, misstatement or omission in the description of the .... Shares or the Assets shall not annul this Agreement or the transfer of the .... Shares, nor shall any compensation be allowed in respect thereof.

13.2 *Force Majeure.*—Neither Party shall be considered in default or be liable to the other Party for any delay in performance or non-performance caused by circumstances beyond the reasonable control of such Party, including but not limited to acts of God, explosion, fire, flood, war, whether declared or not, accident, labour strike or sabotage.

13.3 *Successors and Assigns.*—This Agreement shall be binding upon and inure to the benefit of the Parties hereto and their successors and permitted assigns.

13.4 *Severability.*—All stipulations contained in this Agreement shall be so construed as not to infringe the provisions of any applicable law, but if any such stipulation does infringe any such provision of any applicable law, such stipulation shall be deemed to be void and severable. The Parties undertake to replace invalid stipulations or fill any gap with valid stipulations, which most closely approximate the intent and economic effect of the invalid stipulations or, in the case of a gap, the Parties' presumable intentions. In the event that the terms and conditions of this Agreement are materially altered as a result of the preceding sentence, the Parties will renegotiate the terms and conditions of this Agreement in order to resolve any inequities.

13.5 *Waiver.*—The waiver by a Party of a breach or a default of any provision of this Agreement by the other Party shall not be construed as a waiver of any succeeding breach of the same or any other provision, nor shall any delay or omission on the part of a Party to exercise or avail itself of any right, power or privilege that it has or may have hereunder operate as a waiver of any right, power or privilege by such Party.

13.6 *Modifications and Amendments.*—Modifications and amendments to this Agreement shall be effective only if made in writing. This also applies to a waiver of the written form. Evidence of the contents of this Agreement may only be produced in a form of written documents duly executed by authorised representatives of the Parties hereto.

13.7 *Notices.*—Unless expressly otherwise provided under this Agreement, any notice, report or request required or permitted to be given under or in connection with this Agreement or the subject matter hereof shall be given in the English language by prepaid registered letter, telex, or telefax to the recipient at its address as set forth hereinafter or to such new address as may have therefore been furnished in writing by the recipient to the sending Party. Any such aforementioned notice or request shall be deemed to be effective upon receipt by the Party to which it is addressed.

Any notice to any of the Sellers shall be addressed to:

"*Alpha* Tower", ... (address)

Fax No. ....

Any notice to *Alpha* shall be addressed to:

.... (address)

Fax No. ....

with a copy to .... at:

Any change of these addresses or telefax numbers shall be promptly communicated in writing to the other Party.

13.8 *Headings*: The headings contained in this Agreement are for convenience or reference only and shall not be considered in construing this Agreement.

13.9 *Counterparts*.—This Agreement may be executed in any number of counterparts, each of which shall be deemed an original but all of such together shall constitute one and the same instrument.

13.10 *Governing Law*.—This Agreement shall be governed by the laws of India.

IN WITNESS WHEREOF, the Parties have caused this Agreement to be executed in their names by their properly and duly authorised officers or representatives as of the date first above written.

....

Alpha Healthcare Private Limited

....

Beta Healthcare Limited

....

Mr. .... (name)

....

Psi Healthcare Limited (as Confirming Party)

TRANSFER OF SHARES (SPECIMEN CLAUSE)

1.1 A transfer of shares shall only be admissible in the cases approved by the Board and no share transfer other than the ones permitted by the Board shall be registered by the Company.

1.2 Except where the transfer is made pursuant to Article 21 hereof the person proposing the transfer of any share (hereinafter called 'the Proposing Transferor') shall give notice in writing (hereinafter called a 'Transfer Notice') to the Company that he desires to transfer the shares. A Transfer Notice shall specify the number of shares proposed to be transferred, the sum the Proposing Transferor fixes as the fair value, and shall constitute the Company his agent for the sale of the share to any member or person selected by the Board, willing to purchase the shares (hereinafter called "the Proposed Buyer") at the price so fixed, or at the fair value to be fixed in accordance with Article 19 hereof. The Transfer Notice may include several shares and in such case shall operate as if it were a separate notice in respect of each share. The Transfer Notice shall not be revocable without the sanction of the Board.

1.3 On receipt of the Transfer Notice the Company shall within fifteen (15) days inform all the Shareholders (except the Proposing Transferor)

2. If the Company within three months after being served with a Transfer Notice finds a Proposed Buyer, it shall give notice thereof to the Proposing Transferor ('Notice'). On receipt of the Notice and upon payment of the fair value as fixed in accordance with *Article 16 or 19* hereof the Proposing Transferor shall be bound to transfer the share to Proposed Buyer.

3. In case any difference arises between the Proposing Transferor and the Proposed Buyer as to the fair value of a share, the fair value shall be calculated as per the norms given in Article 22 and Auditors of the Company shall on the application of either party, certify in writing the sum which, in their opinion, is the fair value, as per the norms given in Article 22 hereof and such sum shall be deemed to be the fair value, and in so certifying the Auditors shall be considered to be acting as experts and not as arbitrators, and accordingly the Indian Arbitration and Conciliation Act, shall not apply.

4. If the Proposing Transferor, after having become bound as aforesaid, makes default in transferring the share, the Company may receive the purchase money and the Proposing Transferor shall be deemed to have appointed any one Director or the secretary of the Company as his agent to execute the Transfer Deeds or any other documents as may be necessary to transfer the shares in favour of the Proposed buyer, and upon the execution of such Transfer Deed the Company shall hold the purchase money in trust for the Proposing Transferor. The receipt of the purchase money by the Company shall be a good discharge to the Proposed buyer, and after his name has been entered in the register of members in purported exercise of the aforesaid power, the validity of the proceedings shall not be questioned by any person.

5. If the Company is unable to find, within a period of *three months* after being served with a Transfer Notice, a Proposed buyer, the Company shall give notice to the Proposing Transferor. On receipt of such notice the Proposing Transferor shall at any time within *three months of this notice*, be at liberty, to sell and transfer the share(s) to any person and at any price not below the price mentioned in the Transfer Notice.

6. Transfer Price

The Transfer price shall be calculated as follows:

The Transfer price shall be greater of :

(a) The book value determined according to the method of the evaluation used in the balance-sheet of the previous year, or

(b) The before tax net present value of future profits as determined from the latest approved seven (7) years plan by the Board of Directors subject to an evaluation and verification by an international chartered accountant firm such as ...., *Beta*, etc. to be discounted at a rate of ....%.

The transfer price shall at least cover the paid in capital plus the rate of return equal to the discount rate used in the above formula.

7. Refusal to Register Transfer of Shares

7.1 Subject as aforesaid, the Board may at any time in their absolute and uncontrolled discretion decline to register any proposed transfer of shares. This clause shall apply to a case where the proposed transferee is also a member of the Company.

7.2 The Board may also decline to register any transfer of shares on which the Company has a lien. The Board may also suspend the registration of transfers during the fourteen days immediately preceding the annual general meeting in each year.

7.3 The Board may also decline to recognise any instrument of transfer unless the instrument of transfer is accompanied by the certificate of the shares to which it relates and such other evidence as the Board may reasonably require to show the right of the transferor to make the transfer.

XYZ LTD
TAKE OVER OF THE COMPANY [CHECKLIST]

Sl. No.   Particulars   Purpose/Implications   Assumption

1. Review of the following documents
   — Annual Accounts of the target company for the last five years along with Director's and Auditor's Report.

Commercial

Last available audited balance sheet of the company for .... (financial year) depicts true and fair view about the financial position of the company.

— Articles of Association of the target company.

To understand the restriction, if any on transfer of shares or on a particular block of shares supported by ..../collaboration/ shareholder' agreement, right of first refusal in favour of any shareholder.

There is no restriction on transfer of shares. There is no ..../ collaboration/shareholders' agreement and there is no first right of refusal in favour of any shareholder.

— Any resolution passed by the target company, which is effective and may have impact on the voting percentage or any other rights of the shareholders.

Management of the company might have passed any enabling resolution under section 81(1A) of the Companies Act that can be used as tool to counter the bid by making further allotments.

Under section 81(1A) the board of directors can be authorised by the shareholders to issue further shares otherwise than on rights basis.

The possibility of such a resolution exist for the following reasons:

(a) Statement of the management in the Director's Report at page five that "the management is keeping a close watch on the situation and will take appropriate steps to raise equity resources as and when the capital market improves".

(b) Balance sheet shows unsecured loans of about Rs. .... (amount), a substantial portion of which may be from the promoters, their relatives and associates and the management may consider converting in to equity.

— Offer document/resolution for allotment of preference shares.

To understand the terms on which the existing preference shares of Rs. .... (amount) have been issued, in order to ensure that no possibility exists for conversion of the preference shares in to equity shares.

Preference shares are not convertible in equity shares and the company has not defaulted in the payment of dividend on preference shares so that there is no possibility of giving them the voting rights.

— Offer documents/resolution for allotment of redeemable debentures.

To understand the terms on which the existing debentures of Rs. .... (amount) have been issued, in order to ensure that no possibility exists for conversion of the debenture into equity shares.

Debentures are not convertible into equity shares.

2. Analysis of the following

— Share holding pattern of the company.

To correctly assess the quantum of floating stock available in the market in order to finalise the strategy for the transaction.

Share holding pattern of the company is as under:

Promoters	..........%
Financial Institution	..........%
NRI/Mutual funds etc.	..........%
Public	..........%

It is further assumed that public shareholding is widely scattered.

— Stock market behaviour.

To assess the correlation between the size of the trade and price reaction and judge whether shares are available in blocks.

— Perception of the financial institution about the management of the company.

To assess the chances of the financial institutions supporting the existing management of the company. If the acquirer fails to buy the institutional holding and institutions decide to support the existing management, the whole exercise may turn to be counterproductive. The existing promoters have reasonably good rapport and we may have to apply all sort of tactics to buy institutional holding.

— Performance of other companies in the same group.

To understand market perception about the group and the capacity of the group to arrange finance to counter the bid.

— Reasons of such a low price of the share of the company. 52 weeks high low is just Rs. ....

To assess the pace of upward movement in the share price once the acquisition starts and to judge the future market of the share.

3. Find out the following information about the company

— Ownership pattern of the major assets of the company.

To assess the control of the promoter over the assets of the company and the future value of the company.

— Registrar and share transfer agent of the company.

To see whether some favour can be arranged from the Registrar and to anticipate the extent to which the Registrar can compromise with norms. .... (name of Registrar) is the Registrar and share transfer agent, having reasonably good reputation for its professional approach.

— Is there any ..../collaboration/shareholders' agreement between the shareholders of the company?

If yes, to understand the kind of restriction if any imposed on transfer of shares or the right to first refusal.

— Persons on the Board of the company and their background.

To assess the need to changes in the Board of Directors and at which stage changes would become necessary.

Majority of the members on the board of the company are family members of the promoter. Mr. .... (name) is also one of the directors of the company. Mr. .... (name) was closely associated to Mr. .... (name) in .... securities fraud.

— Auditors of the company.

To judge the authenticity of the accounts and to what extent one can rely on the audited and published balance sheet of the company.

— Promoters financial strength, his market reputation and capacity to arrange funds from organised and unorganised financial market, the details of the shares pledged by the promoters if any.

4. Understand the following

— What kind of legal restriction may be there on the transfer of the shares?

To see the hurdles the acquirer would have to cross to achieve the desired result.

— Whether the company is dominant industrial undertaking or is likely to become such after such acquisition.

Monopolies and Restrictive Trade Practices Act under section ... defines "dominant undertaking" and the Companies Act imposes restriction under sections 108A, 108B on acquisition and transfer of shares of the companies, which are dominant undertaking or would become dominant undertaking after such acquisition.

— Role of the government authorities, if any, in transfer of shares, approval of remittances etc.

Is there any government authority involved or may get involved in the transaction as for instance GOI, FIPB, RBI, SEBI, MOF, Stock Exchanges etc.

STRATEGIC OPTION TO BUY UPTO 10% SHARES OF THE TARGET COMPANY

| Sl. No. | Particulars | Deterrents | Benefits |

1. Option-I

Buy 10% shares from the financial institution out of their total holding of 16% and make a public offer.

   (a) Once the institution comes to know that the intention of the buyer is to acquire the company it would be hard to convince the institution to sell their shares otherwise than public offer.

   (b) After looking at the market reaction institution would demand higher price for their shares.

   (c) If Institution refuses to sell their holding, alternative strategy can be adopted without much trouble.

   (d) It is necessary to ensure that institution shall not vote in favour of the existing management in the event of a share holder's meeting, because in that case the combined holding of the promoter and institution would be more than 50%.

— Institution be persuaded to dispose of their share holding in the stock market or through negotiated deals.

— This would not lead to too much improvement in the price of the shares on the stock exchange.

— The chances of keeping the matter in low profile and confidential are greater.

— Once we have acquired 10% shares from the institution the possibilities of negotiating with the existing management for their smooth exit can be explored.

— Time available with the existing management to defend the bid would be limited.

2. Option-II

Buy 10% shares form the public and make a public offer.

   (a) This would reduce the capacity of the existing management to consolidate their holding because the share price would have gone up by this time.

   (b) This will create an impact in the market, which may be favourable or counter productive.

This option offers less opportunity as compared to risk involved and can be adopted only when the acquirer is confident beyond doubt that:

   (a) The institution can be convinced of the better managerial capability in the relevant field as compared to the existing management.

   (b) The existing management would be able to buy the shareholding of the institution at a price, which we would offer.

SHARE ACQUISITION AND RECONSTRUCTION AGREEMENT

THIS AGREEMENT, is entered into on the .... day of .... 20.....

BETWEEN

A. *Alpha*, a Company organised and existing under .... (country) law and having its registered office in .... and place of business at .... (address), The ....(place), hereinafter called *"Delta"* (which expression shall, unless repugnant to the meaning or context thereof, be deemed to include its successors and assigns), of the FIRST PART;

AND

B. *Beta*, resident of ...., hereinafter called "....................", representing himself and certain other companies, individuals and entities specified in Schedule I to this Agreement, all of whom are collectively referred to hereinafter as the *"Theta* Group" (which expression shall, unless repugnant to the meaning or context thereof, be deemed to include its successors and assigns), of the SECOND PART;

AND

C. *Gama*, a public limited Company registered under the Indian Companies Act, 1956 having its registered office at .... (address), India (hereinafter referred to as '....................', of the THIRD PART.

WHEREAS

(i) The equity share capital of .... is owned as to ....% by .... and ...., ...% by .... and .... [ ]% by the *Theta* Group and as to [ ]% by .... (name);

(ii) By an Agreement between *Delta* and ...., *Delta* has agreed to acquire approximately ....% of the equity share capital of .... and an application to the Reserve Bank of India has been made for the approval of the said transfer;

(iii) By a letter of understanding dated .... (date) among *Delta*, ... and ...., the parties thereto have expressed their preliminary intention to restructure .... by transferring its Brass Valves Division to a separate new Company in consideration of shares in the new company being issued proportionately to the shareholders of ....

(iv) The parties have agreed to enter into this Agreement for the purpose of setting out in detail their understanding.

Now, therefore, in consideration of the mutual promises, covenants hereinafter set forth, the Parties agree as follows:

1. Definitions

The following words and expression shall, unless the context otherwise require, have the following meanings:

"Act" The Indian Companies Act, 1956, as amended from time to time, or any statutory re-enactment thereof, and wherever the context requires, any statutory rules framed thereunder, in the current version.

"Agreement" This Share Acquisition and Reconstruction Agreement entered into among *Delta*, the *Theta* Group and ....

"BVD" The Brass Valves Division of ....

"Company" includes any body corporate.

"Rs. or Rupees" the lawful currency of India.

"Scheme" shall have meaning given to it under Article 7 hereof.

"Shareholders" The *Theta* Group and *Delta* collectively, or where Shares in the Company are held by affiliates, their respective affiliates holding Shares in the Company

"Theta Group Entity" Any individual, company or other entity included in Schedule I.

2. Nomination by the *Theta* Group

2.1 For the purposes of this Agreement, the *Theta* Group Entities and its affiliates shall at all times act collectively, identically and in complete unison.

2.2 The *Theta* Group Entities hereby nominate and appoint, *Omega*, to represent their interests. The acts, representations and decisions of *Omega* shall be irrevocably binding on the *Theta* Group. *Omega* shall neither be removed nor replaced by the *Theta* Group without the consent in writing of *Delta*. In the event that the *Theta* Group Entities are not able to nominate and appoint a representative as above within forty five (45) days of the inability of *Omega* to represent the *Theta* Group, this Agreement shall stand terminated.

3. Representations and Warranties of *Omega*

Omega hereby represents and warrants as follows:—

3.1 *Authorisation*.—The execution, delivery and performance of this Agreement by each of the *Theta* Group Entities has been duly authorised by all necessary individual/collective/corporate actions of the *Theta* Group and this Agreement constitutes the valid and binding obligations of the *Theta* Group, enforceable against each of them in accordance with its terms, except to the extent enforceability may be limited by bankruptcy, insolvency, reorganisation, moratorium or other similar laws affecting the enforcement of rights in general and subject to general principles of equity.

3.2 *Consents of third parties*.—The execution and performance of this Agreement by the *Theta* Group will not:

(a) violate or conflict with the memorandum of association and articles of association or other constitutional document of the *Theta* Group entities;

(b) conflict with, result in the breach, termination or acceleration of, or constitute a default under, any agreement, governmental approval, commitment or other instrument to which any *Theta* Group Entity is a party or bound;

(c) constitute a violation of any law regulation order writ, judgment; or

(d) result in the creation of any material lien upon the properties or assets of the Company or ....

3.3 *Absence of Certain Changes.*—Since the last audited balance sheet date, ... has operated its business in the ordinary course and the *Theta* Group has not caused .... to do anything that is calculated to result in any adverse change in the business, financial condition or operations of the ....

3.4 *Consents, Authorisations, etc.*—No consent, authorisation, approval, permit or order of or filing with any governmental authority or agency, or regulatory authority is required for any of the *Theta* Group Entities to execute, deliver and perform this Agreement.

4. Representations and Warranties of *Delta*

Delta hereby represents and warrants as follows:—

4.1 *Authorisation.*—The execution, delivery and performance of this Agreement by *Delta* has been duly authorised by all necessary individual/collective/corporate actions of *Delta* and this Agreement constitutes the valid and binding obligations of *Delta*, enforceable against it in accordance with its terms, except to the extent enforceability may be limited by bankruptcy, insolvency, reorganisation, moratorium or other similar laws affecting the enforcement of rights in general and subject to general principles of equity.

4.2 *Consents, Authorisation, etc.*—[No consent, authorisation, approval, permit or order of or filing with any governmental authority or agency, or regulatory authority is required for *Delta* to execute, deliver and perform this Agreement]

5. Representations and Warranties of ....

Omega and .... represents and warrants that the following are, as of the date hereof and will be as of the date of the sanction of the scheme by the High Court, true and correct in all material respects:

5.1 .... is an entity duly organised, validly existing and in good standing, under the laws of its jurisdiction; is duly qualified to do business in each relevant jurisdiction and has all requisite corporate power and authority to own, lease and operate its properties and assets and to carry out its business as it is now being conducted and as contemplated hereby;

5.2 The execution, delivery and performance of this Agreement by .... (i) have been authorised by all necessary corporate action, and (ii) do not and will not (A) require any consent or approval of any person, or any clearance or other governmental approval (B) violate any law, or (D) contravene any provision of, or constitute a default under, any other agreement or instrument to which it is a party or by which it or its property or assets may be bound;

5.3 This Agreement is a legal and binding obligation, enforceable against .... in accordance with its terms;

5.4 There is no litigation pending or, to the best of his knowledge, threatened to which .... is a party or which could otherwise adversely affect ...., or any other Party to this Agreement or the transactions contemplated hereby; and

5.5 No third party has or claims, or may have or claim as a result of the transactions contemplated hereby, any interest in .... or the Company through it.

5.6 .... has no obligation pending for importing its products, earning a particular amount of foreign exchange or to deal in a particular manner with its products including the products and business of .... except as mentioned in Annexure.

6. Incorporation of ....

6.1 Immediately upon the signing of this Agreement, a private company with limited liability and having its registered office in the State of .... ('....................') shall be incorporated by the Parties under the name of "...................." or such other name as may be made available by the registrar of companies.

6.2 One representative of the *Theta* Group and one representative of *Delta* shall act as the subscribers to the memorandum and articles of association and the expenses related to incorporation of .... and capitalisation of it shall be borne equally by the *Theta* Group and *Delta*. Any expenses incurred in obtaining advice in relation to the incorporation of .... by the *Theta* Group or *Delta* shall be borne by the *Theta* Group and *Delta* respectively.

6.3 The *Theta* Group and *Delta* shall enter into a separate Shareholders' Agreement to provide for corporate governance and related matters of ....

6.4 Consequent upon the implementation of the Scheme the total paid-up share capital (whether preference or equity) of .... shall be held as follows:

The *Theta* Group	60%
Delta	40%

6.5 Eventually, upon the exercise of the options provided for in this Agreement, the equity share capital of .... shall be held as follows:

The *Theta* Group	49%
Delta	51%

6.6 The Parties shall take all steps necessary to have .... ratify and adopt this Agreement.

6.7. *Omega* shall ensure that .... takes all necessary steps to implement the scheme.

7. Transfer of S&S Shares

7.1 Within two (2) days of .... receiving the approval of the Reserve Bank of India and the completed share transfer deeds relating to the transfer of the S&S Shares from S&S and S&SIA to *Alpha* along with the original share certificates in respect of the S&S Shares:

   (a) *Delta* shall be registered in the records of .... as the shareholder of the S&S Shares;

(b) Share certificates in respect of the S&S Shares duly endorsed in favour of *Delta* shall be delivered to a representative of *Delta* by ....,

(c) .... and the *Theta* Group shall cause .... to, appoint two nominees of *Delta* as directors of ...., who shall remain in office and if necessary, be re-appointed from time to time, until the S&S Shares are transferred by *Delta* to S&S.

7.2 No decision relating to the restructuring of .... or which in any manner impacts directly or indirectly the assets, liabilities or affairs of .... and in particular the .... shall be taken without participation and consent of *Delta*. If such decision requires a Board resolution, the same shall not be passed without the affirmative vote of at least one of the *Delta* Directors or, if such decision requires a resolution of the shareholders, without the affirmative vote of *Delta*.

7.3 During the period that *Delta* holds the S&S Shares no quorum for a Board meeting or general meeting of .... shall be deemed properly constituted unless an *Delta* Director or *Delta* representative, as the case may be, is present.

7.4 Upon the implementation of the Scheme and subject to the necessary approvals being obtained, the S&S Shares shall, at the option of *Delta*, be transferred to S&S for a consideration and terms agreed between *Delta* and S&S.

8. Scheme of Restructuring of ....

8.1 Within .... days of the signing of this Agreement, ... shall prepare a scheme for restructuring of .... (the "Scheme") *inter alia* providing for the following:

(a) transfer of all assets, including plant and machinery, tools and accessories of .... constituting the .... to ....;

(b) transfer to .... of all liabilities of .... relating to ....;

(c) issue of equity shares in .... to the *Theta* Group so that the *Theta* Group holds ....% of the total paid-up capital of ....;

(d) issue of equity shares in .... or, at the option of *Delta*, issue of equity shares and preference shares in .... so that *Delta* holds ....% of the total paid-up capital of ....; and

(e) transfer to .... of all licenses, permits, quotas, approvals, sanctions, authorisations, intellectual property or any other tangible, intangible, direct or indirect rights or benefits available to .... under an agreement or otherwise relating, or in any manner connected to ....

(f) Transfer of employees, skilled workers from .... to .... shall compensate .... for all accrued superannuation benefit of such employees/workers.

8.2 A copy of the Scheme shall be provided to *Delta*, the *Theta* Group and ....

9. Implementation of the Scheme

9.1 .... shall, and *Omega* shall cause .... to take the following steps to implement the Scheme in an expeditious and cost-effective manner:

    (a) for approval of the scheme call meetings of the Board of directors of each of .... and ....;

    (b) convene a shareholders' meeting of each of .... and .... for the approval of the scheme in accordance with the Act;

    (c) submit a joint petition for the sanction of the scheme to the High Court in accordance with the Act;

    (d) convene a shareholders' and creditors' meeting of .... in accordance with the Act and the directions of the High Court;

    (e) file a report of the proceedings of the meetings of the shareholders and creditors of .... and .... with the High Court;

    (f) file copies of the order of the High Court sanctioning the scheme and copies of the Scheme in accordance with the Act with Registrar of Companies, tax authorities, Secretariat of Industrial Assistance, Director General of Foreign Trade and other authorities as may be necessary.

9.2 Within .... days of *Delta* nominees being appointed as directors of .... , a Board meeting of .... shall be held to consider the Scheme of reconstruction as near in form and substance to meet the provisions of this Agreement. At the same Board meeting, an extraordinary general meeting of .... and a meeting of the creditors of .... would be called to obtain the approval of the scheme. The extraordinary general meeting of .... would be called at a minimum notice, not exceeding .... days.

9.3 *Omega* shall, and shall cause all the *Theta* Group Entities, ... and .... to, extend such co-operation as is necessary to expeditiously obtain the approval of SIA, RBI, DGFT and the sanction of the High Court for the scheme.

9.4 Simultaneously with the signing of this Agreement .... shall and shall cause *Theta* to enter into an agreement with .... for sale of plot No. .... measuring.....................

9.5 .... shall grant a lease to .... for the use of the premises where from the .... is presently operating. The period of lease shall not expire/terminate unless .... has acquired new site from *Theta* .... and is in a position to shift the entire activities of .... to the new site.

10. Grant of Loan to the Company *Delta*

10.1 Upon the issue of shares in the Company to the shareholders of .... as envisaged in the scheme sanctioned by the High Court, ... would obtain approval of the RBI for taking an interest-free, convertible (in to equity shares) loan in the sum of .... (foreign amount) from *Delta*, against the security of ....

10.2 *Delta* would remit the said amount of loan to Newco in accordance with the RBI approval. The amount of loan shall be used exclusively for the purpose of acquiring land bearing number .... from *Theta* Fasteners Limited for the purposes of ....

10.3 *Omega* shall cause all steps to be taken and formalities to be completed in connection with obtaining the approval of the RBI for taking loan; for receipt of the principal amount of the loan in India; and for arranging the necessary security for the loan amount.

11. Role of Parties

11.1 *Omega* shall be responsible for all steps to be taken to comply with Indian law, in particular:

(a) have the scheme prepared;

(b) call meetings as may be required for the approval and implementation of the Scheme;

(c) have the scheme sanctioned from the court;

(d) complete formalities before the Registrar of Companies;

(e) take all other steps as may be necessary to implement the Scheme in an expeditious and cost effective manner;

(f) obtain approvals from the RBI, SIA and DGFT in respect of the transactions contemplated hereunder, and

(g) extend full cooperation and support to *Delta* or as may be necessary for the purposes of this Agreement.

11.2 *Delta* shall:

(a) be responsible for all steps to be taken to comply with laws other than Indian law;

(b) shall promptly remit to India funds as approved by the RBI as loan pursuant to article 10 hereof; and

(c) extend full cooperation and support to the other Parties or as may be necessary for the purposes of this Agreement.

12. Term and Termination

12.1 This Agreement shall continue in full force and effect and shall bind the Parties until terminated in accordance with the provisions of this article.

12.2 *Omega* and *Delta* shall be entitled to terminate this Agreement immediately by notice in writing to the other Party (but not after ninety (90) days of the event in question first coming to the attention of the Party entitled to give the notice) if any of the events set out below shall occur:

(a) in the event of either *Omega* or *Delta* committing a breach of any of the provisions of this Agreement, the other Party shall, without prejudice to other rights and remedies available, have the right to terminate this Agreement, by giving the defaulting party a .... day's prior notice in writing, specifying *inter alia* the nature of the claimed default and the intention of termination unless such default is cured by the defaulting Party within the next .... days following receipt of the said notice,

(b) in the event that any of the representations and warranties given by *Delta* or *Omega* are found to be not true or correct, the other Party may terminate this Agreement and shall be entitled to such remedies as are available to it in law, including, but not limited to, the right to recover damages, or

(c) if the other Party (being a company) shall go into liquidation whether compulsory or voluntary (except for the purposes of a *bona fide* reconstruction or amalgamation with the consent of the first Party such consent not to be unreasonably withheld) or if the other Party shall have an administrator appointed or if an administrative receiver or manager shall be appointed over any part of the assets or undertaking of the other Party, or

(d) if there shall be any change in the control of the other Party.

12.3 This Agreement shall terminate immediately if a resolution is passed to wind up .... or .... or if a liquidator is otherwise appointed (but without prejudice to any rights either *Delta* or the *Theta* Group may have against the other arising prior to such termination).

12.4 *Delta* shall have the option of terminating this Agreement, if changes in Government policy or Government actions require *Delta* to reduce its shareholding in ...., prevent *Delta* from receiving dividends from .... or from repatriation of capital or profits, or effectively exclude *Delta* from participation in the management or control of .... or .... as provided in this Agreement.

13. Dispute Resolution

13.1 This Agreement shall be governed by and construed in accordance with the Indian law.

13.2 Any dispute, controversy or claim arising out of or relating to or in connection with this Agreement, or the breach, termination or validity hereof shall be finally settled by an arbitral tribunal (the "Tribunal") in accordance with the Indian Arbitration and Conciliation Act, 1996 as in force at the time such arbitration is commenced (the "Arbitration Act"). Each of *Delta* and *Omega* will appoint an arbitrator within thirty (30) days of the receipt by a Party of the other Party's request to initiate arbitration. The two arbitrators so appointed will then jointly appoint a third arbitrator within thirty (30) days of the date of appointment of the second arbitrator, which third will act as Chairman of the Tribunal. Arbitrators not appointed within the time limit set forth in the preceding sentence shall be appointed in accordance with the Arbitration Act. The site of the arbitration shall be ....(place), India. The language of the arbitration and award shall be English.

14. Miscellaneous

14.1 *Entire Agreement*.—This Agreement constitutes the entire Agreement among the Parties (or any Affiliates) and supersedes all prior agreements and undertakings, written or oral, among them with respect to the subject matter hereof.

14.2 *Amendment and Waiver*.—No amendment or waiver hereto shall be effective or binding on any of the Parties unless in writing and signed by each of the Parties. Any waiver by any of the Parties of any right hereunder or any breach hereof by the other Party shall not constitute a waiver of any other right or any other breach by such other party, whether of a similar or dissimilar nature thereto.

14.3 *Assignment*.—No Party shall assign any of its rights or obligations under this Agreement, other than in accordance with the terms of this Agreement, without the written consent of the other Parties hereto:

Provided, however, that *Delta* may assign all or any part of its rights and obligations hereunder to one or more wholly-owned affiliates of *Delta* without the consent of the other Parties. *Delta* shall not, however, be permitted to assign its obligations hereunder (but shall still be permitted to assign its rights) during the pendency of arbitration of any dispute hereunder. Any prohibited assignment shall be void.

14.4 *Successors and Assigns*.—This Agreement shall be binding upon and inure to the benefit of the Parties, their permitted assigns and successors-in-interest.

14.5 *Indemnity*.—Each Party shall indemnify the other Party and their directors, officers, employees, agents and representatives from all costs, losses, claims, damages and liabilities, including reasonable attorneys' fees, incurred by it, arising out of (1) the gross negligence or wilful misconduct of the indemnifying Shareholder or its representatives or Affiliates, or (2) any breach by the indemnifying Shareholder or any of its Affiliates of any representation, warranty, covenant, agreement or other material obligation contained in this Agreement. The right to indemnification or other remedy based on such obligations, representations or warranties will not be affected by any investigation conducted, any knowledge acquired or waiver granted with respect to the accuracy or inaccuracy of any representation or warranty or compliance with any obligation.

14.6 *No Third Party Beneficiary*.—This Agreement is not intended to and shall not grant or create any rights, interests or benefits under this Agreement or in the Company or any of the Investment Shares in favour of any creditor or third party not a Party to this Agreement, including the Lenders, and none of the provisions of this Agreement shall be enforceable by such creditors or third parties.

14.7 *Notices*.—Any notice to be given hereunder shall be in writing and in English and may be delivered by hand (including without limitation by international express courier against written receipt) or sent by telex or prepaid first class registered letter or (where subsequently confirmed by letter) by facsimile copy to the persons and addresses specified below (or such other person or address as the relevant Party may previously have notified in writing for the purpose). A notice shall be deemed to have been duly served upon receipt. The names and addresses for the service of notices are as follows:

(a) To *Omega*
Attention
Fax No.

(b) To *Delta*
Attention
Fax No.
With a copy to:

(c) To ....
Attention:
Fax No.

14.8 *Invalidity; Illegality.*—The invalidity, illegality or unenforceability of any provision of this Agreement shall not affect the validity or enforceability of its other provisions.

IN WITNESS WHEREOF, the Parties hereto have entered into this Agreement as of the day and year first above written.

Except for the litigations there is no action, suit or proceeding before or by any governmental authority or any arbitration proceeding before any body now pending or, to the best knowledge of ...., threatened, which challenges the Transaction Documents, the transactions contemplated therein, any Project Agreement, the ...., ... interest or proposed interest in the ...., or any government approval issued or obtained in connection with ....

There has not been entered against .... (or otherwise affecting the ....) any decree, order or direction by any governmental authority directing that .... be wound up or liquidated, adjudging "sick" or appointing a receiver, liquidator, assignee, trustee. No other event has occurred which would have an effect analogous to any of those events listed above and .... has not taken any action for the purpose of effecting any of the foregoing.

All of the S&S Shares (a) have been duly and validly authorised, issued, allotted, and fully paid and non-assessable; (b) documents of ....; (c) are not subject to any pre-emptive or other similar rights under the organisational documents of ...., applicable law or any agreement or instrument to which ...., any shareholder or any other person is a party and (d) except for the pre-emptive right of *Omega* as provided under article .... of .... of ....

Except as provided in the transaction documents, (i) there is no option, right, warrant, or other agreement or commitment obligating .... to issue or sell any of its securities and there are no securities convertible into or exchangeable for any equity securities of .... and (ii) no person has any right, option or other agreement or commitment with .... to participate in the ownership, investment, funding, construction, operation, or supply of goods or services to the .... or ....

.................., has good title to all its properties and assets including all properties and assets necessary and appropriate to conduct its business as currently conducted, free and clear of all Liens; no person other than .... has any right, title or interest in any assets or property necessary to the transactions contemplated in the transaction documents, any project agreement or otherwise in connection with ....

No document, certificate or other writing furnished to *Delta* by or on behalf of .... with respect to or in connection with ...., when taken as a whole with all the other written materials and information provided, contains any untrue statement of a material fact or omits to state a material fact necessary to make such information not misleading in any material respect. All documents, information, agreements, correspondence and other materials relating to the .... and .... have been made available to *Delta* and their advisors by or on behalf of ....

Schedule .... to the Agreement contains a complete and accurate list of the employees of ...., together with each such employee's name, salary and title. There are no contracts, agreement or other understandings between any officer, employee, or group of employees and .... or for which .... is or may be responsible which have not been otherwise disclosed in the Schedule and there are no pension plans or other similar benefits extended by .... to any of its employees.

The authorised share capital of .... consists of .... shares, par value Rs. .... (amount) per share of which ....(No. of shares) have been issued, subscribed, allotted and paid for, and are outstanding. As of the date hereof, each shareholder of ...., his, her or its legal and beneficial ownership of the shares issued and outstanding and the price paid by each shareholder of his, her or its shares.

TRANSFER OF UNDERTAKING AGREEMENT

This Agreement is made at .... on this ... day of .... 20....

BETWEEN

Alpha, a public limited company incorporated in India under the Companies Act, 1956, having its registered office at..................... (address) (hereinafter referred to as "*Alpha*" which expression shall unless repugnant in the meaning or context, mean and include its successors, associates and assigns);

AND

Beta, a company incorporated in .... (STATE) and having its registered office at .... (address) (hereinafter referred to as "*Beta*", which expression shall unless repugnant to the meaning or context, mean and include its successors, associates and assigns).

(*Alpha* and *Beta* are hereinafter collectively referred to as "the Parties" and severally as "Party")

Whereas *Alpha* is a group company of .... (".................. ") and is engaged in the business of, *inter alia,* manufacturing leaf and parabolic springs and spring assemblies for automobiles;

And whereas *Beta* is the wholly owned subsidiary of *Alpha*;

And whereas with a view to streamline and develop its business operations, *Alpha* is desirous of transferring its undertaking (as hereinafter defined) to *Beta* as a going concern and *Beta* is desirous of acquiring the undertaking subject to the terms and conditions set forth herein.

Now therefore, in consideration of the mutual promises hereinafter set forth, the Parties hereto agree as follows:

1. Definitions

In this Agreement (including the Recitals), unless the context requires otherwise, the following words and expressions shall have the meanings set out opposite them respectively:

"*Agreement*" means this transfer of undertaking Agreement including any Schedules attached hereto and any amendments and modifications thereof;

"*Assets*" means all movable and immovable assets of *Alpha* to be transferred to *Beta* on the closing date and as more appropriately set out at Schedule A hereof;

"*Closing Date*" means the date on which all Transfer Approvals, to the extent necessary, for the transfer of the undertaking to *Beta* have been received in a form satisfactory to both Parties. The closing date is intended to be ...., or any other date mutually agreed between the Parties;

"*Employees*" means all employees of *Alpha* as of the closing date whose employment is to be transferred to *Beta*;

"*Liabilities*" means the liabilities of *Alpha* to be assumed by *Beta* on the closing date as set out at Schedule B;

"*Undertaking*" means Alpha's existing undertaking situated at .... (address) including its Assets and Liabilities;

"*Purchase Price*" means the lump sum price of Rs. .... payable by *Beta* to *Alpha* in accordance with the terms of clause 3 hereof;

"*Transfer Approvals*" means and includes all approvals, authorisations, permissions, consents and licenses, whether from the governmental authorities, lenders, financial institutions and the like including approvals from *Alpha* shareholders and any other approvals necessary to the transfer of the Undertaking to *Beta*;

The headings to the Articles are inserted for ease of reference and shall not be construed so as to affect the meanings of the Agreement.

2. Transfer of Undertaking

2.1 Subject to the terms and conditions hereof, *Alpha* shall transfer, convey, assign, sell and deliver to *Beta*, and *Beta* shall acquire and assume the undertaking, with such liens as may be existing or specified in respect of the liabilities taken over it.

2.2 To complete the aforesaid transfer, *Alpha* hereby also agrees to initiate and complete all the steps required for such transfer without payment of any additional consideration.

2.3 In pursuance hereof, *Alpha* represents that *Alpha* will, at or as of the Closing Date, transfer the title by delivery of possession to *Beta* of all the movable assets which can pass by delivery and, in respect of assets which require transfer/assignment by instrument or documents, *Alpha* shall execute such instrument or document and the Parties shall cause them to be registered with the appropriate authorities. *Beta* shall deliver to *Alpha* in form and substance satisfactory to *Alpha* an acknowledgement that the delivery of the above has been taken by *Beta* on the Closing Date.

2.4 On or before the Closing Date, *Beta* shall make an offer to the *Alpha* Employees for employment.

3. Purchase Price

3.1 On or not later than .... days of the Closing Date, in consideration for the transfer of the undertaking, *Beta* shall (a) assume the Liabilities and (b) pay the Purchase Price payable to *Alpha* by cheque, bank draft or any other means including by way of issue of shares in *Beta* and/or by take-over/discharge of debts of *Alpha*.

3.2 It is agreed between the Parties that transfer expenses, being stamp duty, registration charges, or any taxes shall, if applicable, be payable by *Beta*.

4. Events of Closing Date

On the Closing Date, *Alpha* shall deliver to *Beta*, in form and substance satisfactory to *Beta*, the following:

(i) good and sufficient instruments of transfer and conveyance as shall be effective to vest in *Beta* good and marketable title to the *Alpha* Assets with such existing or specified liens in respect of the liabilities taken over;

(ii) such good and sufficient instruments as may be required in order to transfer and assign to *Beta*, the Contracts and Permits that are assignable;

(iii) the originals or copies of the records owned by *Alpha* and used in connection with the operations of the undertaking including but not limited to, all employees and other records, accounts, contracts, agreements, arrangements used in connection with the Undertaking and such other customer records and sales data as are maintained by *Alpha*;

5. Representations and warranties of *Alpha*

Alpha hereby represents and warrants to *Beta* as follows:—

(a) Organisation

Alpha is a corporation duly organised, validly existing and in good standing under the laws of India and has all corporate power and authority necessary to

(i) conduct its business as that business is currently conducted, and (ii) execute, deliver and perform this Agreement and consummate the transactions contemplated hereby. *Alpha* has taken all actions necessary for execution, delivery and performance of this Agreement by *Alpha* under applicable law and this Agreement constitutes valid and binding obligations of *Alpha*, enforceable against *Alpha* in accordance with the terms hereof.

(b) Compliance with Laws

Alpha has complied with and is currently in substantial compliance with all laws, ordinances, regulations orders and administrative guidance applicable to *Alpha* Assets.

(c) No Breach

The execution and delivery of this Agreement and consummation of the transactions contemplated hereby will not conflict with or result in the breach or violation of any of the terms or conditions of, or constitute (or with notice or lapse of time or both would constitute) a default under, (i) the Memorandum of Association or Articles of Association of *Alpha*, (ii) any instrument, contract or other agreement to which *Alpha* is a party or by or to which it or any of its assets or properties is bound or subject, or (iii) any statute, law, regulation, order, judgement or decree of any court of governmental or regulatory body.

(d) Actions and Proceedings

Alpha is not a party to, and to Alpha's best knowledge after reasonable inquiry is not threatened with, any litigation or judicial, administrative or arbitration proceedings which if decided adversely to *Alpha* could have an adverse effect upon the transactions contemplated herein. To Alpha's best knowledge after reasonable inquiry, no investigation by any governmental or administrative body or agency is pending which could have a material adverse effect on the Alpha's Assets.

6. Representations and Warranties of *Beta*

Beta hereby represents and warrants to *Alpha* as follows:—

(a) Organisation

Beta is a company duly organised, validly existing and in good standing under the laws of India and has all corporate power and authority necessary to execute, deliver and perform this Agreement and consummate the transactions contemplated hereby. *Beta* will take all actions necessary for the execution, delivery and performance of this Agreement under the applicable law and such Agreement would constitute valid and binding obligations of *Beta*, enforceable against it in accordance with its terms.

(b) Compliance with Laws

Beta has complied with and is currently in substantial compliance with all laws, ordinances, regulations, orders and administrative guidance applicable to it.

(c) No Breach

The execution and delivery of this Agreement and consummation of the transactions contemplated hereby will not conflict with or result in the breach or violation of any of the terms or conditions of, or constitute (or with notice or lapse of time or both would constitute) a default under, (i) the Memorandum of Association or Articles of Association of *Beta*, (ii) any instrument, contract or other agreement to which *Beta* is a party or by or to which it or any of its assets or properties is bound or subject, or (iii) any statute, law, regulation, order, judgement or decree of any court of governmental or regulatory body.

(d) Alpha Employees

Beta will offer employment to all the *Alpha* Employees on the same or better terms as are applicable to them on the Closing Date and upon terms of continuity of service.

7. Conditions precedent to obligations of *Beta*

All obligations of *Beta* under this Agreement are subject to the satisfaction, prior to or on the closing date, of each of the following conditions, any one or more of which may be waived by *Beta*:

(a) *Alpha's* representations and warranties contained in or made pursuant to this Agreement shall be true and correct as of the date of execution, and shall be true and correct as of the closing date as though such representations and warranties were made again on and as of such time;

(b) All Transfer Approvals shall have been obtained and shall be in full force and effect;

(c) No injunction or restraining order shall be in effect which forbids or enjoins the consummation of the transactions contemplated by this Agreement or the transfer of the *Alpha* Transferred Business to *Beta*, and no governmental regulations shall have been enacted which prohibit, restrict or delay the consummation of the transactions contemplated by this Agreement or the transfer of the *Alpha* Transferred Business to *Beta*; and

(d) No action or proceeding by any governmental authority or other person or entity shall have been instituted or threatened which (a) might have a material adverse effect on the transaction contemplated herein or (b) could enjoin, restrain or prohibit, or could result in substantial damages in respect of, any provision of this Agreement or the consummation of the transactions contemplated hereby.

8. Conditions precedent to obligations of *Alpha*

All obligations of *Alpha* under this Agreement are subject to the satisfaction, prior to or on the Closing Date of each of the following conditions, any one or more of which may be waived by *Alpha*.

(a) *Beta* shall have performed or complied with all covenants, agreements and conditions required by this Agreement to have been performed or complied with by it prior to or on the closing date;

(b) All Transfer Approvals shall have been obtained and shall be in full force and effect; and

(c) No injunction or restraining order shall be in effect which forbids or enjoins the consummation of the transactions contemplated by this Agreement or the transfer of the *Alpha* Transferred Business to *Beta*, and no governmental regulations shall have been enacted which prohibit, restrict or delay the consummation of the transactions contemplated by this Agreement or the transfer of the *Alpha* Transferred Business to *Beta*.

9. Indemnification

(a) *Alpha* shall indemnify, save and hold harmless *Beta*, and the successors and assigns, officers, directors, employees and representatives of *Beta* from and against any and all costs, losses, claims, liabilities, damages, lawsuits, judgements and expenses (including, without limitation, legal fees and court or other fees and costs) (collectively, hereinafter the "Costs") in connection with or arising out of or resulting from or incident to any breach of, or inaccuracy with respect to, any covenant or representation or warranty by *Alpha* herein contained;

(b) *Beta* shall indemnify, save and hold harmless *Alpha*, and the successors and assigns, officers, directors, employees and representatives of *Alpha* from and against any and all Costs in connection with or arising out of or resulting from any breach of any covenant by *Beta* herein contained.

10. Expenses

Except as specifically provided below, each Party agrees to be responsible for the payment of all expenses incurred by or on its behalf in connection with the preparation, authorisation, execution and performance of this Agreement, including without limitation all fees of counsel, accountants and consultants. Any taxes or similar levies due and payable in accordance with applicable law or regulations in respect of transfer(s) of *Alpha* Transferred Business shall be paid by *Beta*.

11. Confidentiality

All information supplied by any Party to the others in connection with this Agreement as well as the contents of this Agreement are confidential between the Parties, who will cause their employees, consultants and agents to maintain such confidentiality. Each Party also agrees that it shall not, without the other Party's prior written consent, disclose or allow to be disclosed any such confidential information to anyone, except to its relevant officers and employees and then only to such extent as may be necessary for the performance of its obligations under this Agreement. The Parties shall take all necessary precautions to keep the confidential information secret and confidential and to restrict its use in the manner provided herein.

12. General

12.1 Notices

All notices required or permitted hereunder shall be in writing and in the English language and shall be sent by internationally recognised courier or by facsimile transmission addressed to the address of each Party set forth below, or to such other address as such other Party shall have communicated to the other Party. Notice shall be deemed to have been served when received (and in the case of facsimile transmission, provided that a confirming copy is sent to the other Party in accordance with the non-facsimile notice delivery requirements).

If to *Alpha*: ....

Attention:

If to *Beta*: ....

Attention:

12.2 Assignment

Neither of the Parties hereto may assign its rights and obligations in whole or in part hereunder without the prior written consent of the other Party.

12.3 Variation

Any variation of this Agreement shall be mutually agreed in writing and executed by or on behalf of each of *Alpha* and *Beta*.

12.4 No Waiver

No waiver by any Party of any default with respect to any provision, condition or requirement hereof shall be deemed to be a waiver of any other provision, condition or requirement hereof. No delay or omission of any Party to exercise any right hereunder on one occasion in any manner shall impair the exercise of any such right on any other occasion.

12.5 Severabiltiy

If any provision of this Agreement shall be determined to be illegal or unenforceable, such provision, to the extent it shall be illegal or unenforceable, shall be deemed severed from this Agreement, and shall be substituted by a reasonable provision to be mutually agreed upon.

13. Governing Law

This Agreement shall be governed and construed in accordance with the laws of India.

14. Arbitration and Dispute Resolution

14.1 If any dispute between the Parties as to the effect, interpretation or application of this Agreement, or as to their rights, duties or liabilities thereunder, or as to any act, matter or thing arises out of, consequent to, or in connection with this Agreement (hereinafter referred to as "the Difference") the Parties shall endeavour to resolve the same amicably through negotiations.

14.2 In the event that the Difference is not resolved by means of negotiations within a period of .... days, or such different period as is agreed between the Parties, such Difference shall then be referred to and settled by arbitration by three arbitrators, one to be appointed by each Party and the third to be appointed by the two arbitrators. The arbitration proceedings shall be in accordance with the provisions of the Arbitration and Conciliation Act, 1996 or any subsequent enactment or amendment thereto. The decision of the arbitrator shall be final and binding upon the Parties.

14.3 Unless otherwise agreed to by the Parties, the venue of Arbitration proceedings shall only be ....(place), and the language of the arbitration shall be English.

15. Entire Agreement

This Agreement along with the Schedules hereto represents the entire agreement as to the subject-matter hereof, and supersedes any prior understandings between the Parties on the subject matter hereof.

16. *Force Majeure*

Neither Party shall be liable by reason of failure or delay in the performance of its obligations under this Agreement if such failure or delay is caused by acts of God, strikes, lockouts, war or any other cause beyond its control and without its fault or negligence.

IN WITNESS, WHEREOF the Parties hereto have caused this Agreement to be executed in two (2) copies by their duly authorised representatives as of the date and year first above written.

For and on behalf of
Beta
....
....

For and on behalf of
Alpha

SCHEDULE A
ASSETS

SCHEDULE B
LIABILITIES

SCHEDULE C
CONTRACTS

SUBSCRIPTION AGREEMENT

THIS AGREEMENT made this.................... day of.................... 20....., BETWEEN *Alpha* LIMITED, (hereinafter referred to as "*Alpha*"), a corporation organised under the laws of, having its Registered Office at....................(address), ...: , *Beta* FILTERATION PRIVATE LIMITED (hereinafter referred to as "*Beta*"), a Company incorporated under the Companies Act, 1956, having its Registered Office at .... (address), India, *Beta* (INDIA) LIMITED, a Company incorporated under the Companies Act, 1956 having its Registered Office at .... (address), India (hereinafter referred to as "*Omega*"), ... (name) AND FAMILY (HUF) through its *Karta*

MR. .... (name) S/o DR. .... (name) R/o .... (address), (hereinafter referred to "*Theta*"), ... [name] & SONS (HUF) through its *Karta* MR. .... (name), S/o MR. .... (name) R/o .... (address), (hereinafter referred to as "*Gamma*"), and MRS. .... (name) W/O MR. .... (name), R/o .... (name), (hereinafter referred to as ".................").

WITNESSETH

WHEREAS, *Beta* is a private limited company registered under the Companies Act, 1956, and has an Authorized Share Capital of .... (amount in figures and words) divided into .... (no. of shares) equity shares of Ten Rupees .... (amount per share) each. The issued, subscribed, and paid-up share capital of *Beta* is .... (no. of shares) Shares of .... (amount in figures and words) each fully paid-up equity shares; and WHEREAS, *Beta* has been formed for the main purpose of:

(i) acquiring and taking over as a running concern the existing business of the Filters Division of *Beta* (INDIA) LTD. and;

(ii) establishing and carrying on the business as manufacturer, assemblers, designers, traders, commission and buying agents, distributors, contractors, importers and exporters of all types of Air, Oil and Fuel Filters for Industrial Automotive, Railway & Air conditioning/ ventilation applications, etc.

WHEREAS, *Alpha*, through its holding/associate companies has been engaged for many years, and is a leader in the business of designing, developing, manufacturing and selling a wide range of industrial filters and other dehydration and filtration accessories on a world wide basis. These products are being marketed in various industries and manufactured and sold from plants and operations throughout the world.

WHEREAS, *Alpha* desires to subscribe for .... (no. of shares in figures and words) equity shares of .... (amount in figures and words) each in *Beta* at a premium of .... (amount in figures and words) per share upon and subject to the terms and conditions hereinafter contained.

NOW THIS AGREEMENT WITNESSETH AND IT IS HEREBY AGREED BY AND BETWEEN THE PARTIES HERETO as follows:—

1. Definitions

In this Agreement, save where the context otherwise requires, the following expressions shall have the following meanings:

1.1 "*Shares*" shall mean the (no. of shares in figures and words) equity shares of the nominal value of .... (amount in figures and words) each in *Beta* for which *Alpha* shall subscribe.

1.2 "*Shareholders' Agreement*" shall mean the Shareholders' Agreement of even date between *Alpha* and *Omega*/VE/*Theta*/*Gamma*/.................. (as defined in the Shareholders' Agreement).

1.3 *"Closing"* shall mean the date on which the subscription and allotment of shares shall take place. The closing date shall be within thirty (30) days from the date on which the necessary permission has been obtained from the Reserve Bank of India, or the date on which all of the conditions of this Agreement shall have been satisfied, whichever is later.

1.4 *"VE Partners"* shall have the meaning set forth in the Shareholders' Agreement.

2. Conditions Precedent

2.1 This Agreement shall be conditional upon *Beta* obtaining all necessary governmental approvals and consents in form and substance acceptable to *Alpha* for the transactions and agreements set out herein. This Agreement shall be *null and void* if the necessary approval is not obtained within .... days.

2.2 This Agreement and all related agreements referred to herein shall be null and void and of no effect in the event that the Shareholders' Agreement is terminated in accordance with its provisions.

2.3 The parties hereto agree to use their best endeavours to ensure that all the above conditions of this Agreement are fulfilled and to diligently and energetically pursue the fulfilment thereof in lawful and proper manner.

3. Completion and Corproate Formalities

3.1 *Completion.*—The subscription to and the allotment of shares (the "Completion") provided for in this Agreement will take place at the offices of .... at 10.00 a.m. on the date that is not more than thirty (30) business days following receipt of the last Indian government consent or approval required for the Completion.

3.2 *Completion Obligations of the Parties.*—At the Completion (except with respect to (a)(6) and (a)(7) below):

(a) *Alpha* will deliver to *Beta*

   (1) A duly complete application to subscribe to the Shares of the *Beta*.
   (2) Cashier's check in the amount of Rs. .... (amount) payable to the order of *Beta* or by wire transfer to an account specified by *Beta*.
   (3) The Shareholders' Agreement executed by *Alpha*.
   (4) Trademark License Agreement.
   (5) Trade Name Agreement.
   (6) At the time of issuance of all of the shares subscribed by *Alpha*, cashiers check in the rupee equivalent of .... (foreign amount) payable to the order of *Theta* or by wire transfer to an account specified by *Theta* for payment under the Non-Competition and Confidentiality Agreement.
   (7) Cashiers check in the rupee equivalent of .... (foreing amount) payable to the order of *Gamma* or by wire transfer to an account specified by *Gamma* for payment under the Non-Competition and Confidentiality Agreement.

(b) *Beta* will deliver to *Alpha*:
  (1) Revised Articles of Association of *Beta*.
  (2) Upon receipt of any required approval by the Reserve Bank of India (which may occur post-completion), certificates representing the Shares in the name of *Alpha* issued in accordance with *Beta*'s Articles of Association, along with a copy of the Register of Members of *Beta* showing *Alpha* as the owner of the Shares.
  (3) The Shareholders' Agreement executed by *Omega*/VE/*Theta*/*Gamma*/PSI.
  (4) Trademark License Agreement duly executed by *Beta*.
  (5) Trade Name Agreement duly executed by *Beta*.
  (6) Trademark License Agreement duly executed by *Omega* and *Beta*.
  (7) Non-Competition and Confidentiality Agreement between each of *Theta* & *Gamma*, *Beta* and *Alpha* duly executed by *Theta* & *Gamma*.
  (8) Agreement to Transfer Undertaking (ATU) duly executed by *Omega* and *Beta*.
  (9) A certificate executed by the Managing Director of each of *Beta* and *Omega* representing and warranting to *Alpha* that the sale of the Purchased Business from *Omega* to *Beta* pursuant to the Agreement to Transfer Undertaking Agreement has been completed and that each of *Beta*'s and *Omega*'s representations and warranties in this Agreement were accurate in all respects as of the date of this Agreement and are accurate in all respects as of the Completion Date as if made on the Completion Date and the Agreement is in full force and effect in the form of the executed copy delivered to *Alpha*.
  (10) Non-Competition and Confidentiality Agreement between *Omega*, *Beta* and *Alpha* duly executed by *Omega*.
  (11) Agreement to Sell regarding Immovable Property executed by *Beta* Enterprises as and *Omega*.
(c) *Gamma* and *Theta* shall deliver to *Alpha* and *Beta* a Limited Guarantee and Indemnity Agreement.
(d) *Beta* shall take all actions necessary to cause the shareholdings of *Beta* after completion to be as follows: *Alpha*: .... (no. of shares) shares; VE Partners, ... (no. of shares) shares, including redemptions and cancellations. Unless agreed to by *Alpha*, no cost or expense of any redemptions or cancellations shall be incurred by *Beta* in taking such actions.

3.3 *Corporate Formalities.*—On or before the date of completion the Directors of *Beta* shall convene and duly hold a meeting of the Board of Directors and Shareholders of *Beta* at which:
  (a) The Shares shall be allotted and issued to *Alpha*; and
  (b) The current Board of Directors of *Beta* shall resign. Four individuals selected by *Alpha* shall be elected as Directors of *Beta* and further one of the said Directors nominated by *Alpha* shall be appointed as Chairman of the Board of *Beta* and one individual selected by *Omega* shall be elected as Director of *Beta*.

4. Representations and Warranties

Each of *Omega* and *Beta* represents, warrant to *Alpha*, and agrees with *Alpha* as follows:

4.1 (a) *Organization and Standing.*—Beta is a company duly organized and validly existing under the laws of India. Beta has corporate power and authority to carry on its business as it is now being conducted and to own and operate its assets, properties, and business. Copies of the Memorandum of Association and the original and revised Articles of Association of *Beta*, attached hereto as Schedule "A" are true and complete.

(b) *Capital of BETA.*—The Authorized Share Capital of *Beta* is .... (amount in figures and words) divided into .... (no. of shares) Equity Shares of .... (amount in figures and words) each before the closing. As of the date hereof .... (no. of shares) Shares of .... (amount) is the outstanding share capital of *Beta*, all of which is owned as follows: *Theta*: 20 Shares; KS: 20 shares; and *Omega*: 10 Shares. After giving effect to the issuance of the Shares to *Alpha*, the outstanding share capital of *Beta* shall be as follows: *Alpha*: ....[no. of shares] shares; VE Partners: .... (no. of shares) shares.

(c) *No Other Stock.*—Other than as stated above, no other shares of *Beta* of any kind have been issued. There are no options, warrants or rights to purchase or otherwise acquire shares of *Beta* or other securities convertible into shares of *Beta*, nor are there any outstanding securities or instruments convertible into shares of *Beta*, except for the Deferred Consideration Note (as defined in the Agreement to Transfer Undertaking), which is payable in .... (no. of shares) shares of *Beta*).

(d) *Officers and Directors.*—All Officers and Directors of *Beta* on the date of this Agreement are identified in Schedule "B" attached hereto.

(e) *No Subsidiaries.*—Save as mentioned in Schedule "C" *Beta* does not have any subsidiaries or affiliates, nor does it own any securities of or have any proprietary interest in, any other corporation, partnership, association, business organization, or joint venture; nor does *Beta* control the management or policies of any other corporation, partnership, association, business organization, or joint venture by means of a management contract or otherwise.

4.2 *Financial Statement:* Copies of the following *Omega* Filter Division and *Beta* financial statements are attached hereto as Schedule "D".

(1) *Omega* Filter Division's Balance Sheets as of March 31, 1996, March 31, 1997 and June 30, 1997;

(2) *Omega* Filter Division's Profit and Loss Accounts for the years ended .... (date) and .... (year) and the three months ended .... (date).

(3) *Beta's* Balance Sheet as on Closing Date. Each of the aforesaid financial statements and the related notes thereto presents fairly, as of its date, the financial conditions of *Omega's* Filter Division and *Beta*, respectively, and/or the results of operations of its business for the

fiscal years which they purport to cover, in conformity with generally accepted accounting principles applied on a basis consistent with that of prior periods, where applicable. Whenever reference herein is made to the "Balance Sheet" of *Beta*, it shall, unless otherwise specified, mean *Beta*'s balance sheet as on closing date, and whenever reference is made to the "Balance Sheet Date," it shall unless otherwise specified, mean closing date.

4.3 *Agreement Does Not Violate Other Agreements.*—The execution and delivery of this Agreement and the consummation of the transactions contemplated hereby will not;

(a) Conflict with, result in any breach of any terms or conditions of, or constitute a default under, the Articles of Association of *Beta* or any commitment, mortgage, lease, note, bond, indenture, contract, license, franchise, permit, or other instrument, agreement or obligation to which *Beta* is now a party or by which any of its properties or assets may be bound or affected, or

(b) Result in any violation of any order, writ, injunction or decree of any court, administrative agency or governmental body.

4.4 *Title To And Condition of Assets.*—Schedule "E" hereto is a brief description of all immovable property, buildings, improvements, machinery, equipment, furniture and fixtures valued on the respective records of *Beta* owned or leased by *Beta* or in which it has any other interest. All of the machinery, equipment, furniture, or fixtures owned by *Beta* not held for sale in the ordinary course of business are located on said property. .... has good and marketable title to all immovable property, which it purports to own.

4.5 *Patents and Trademarks.*—Except as set forth in Schedule "F", "*Beta* does not own or use any patents, registered trademarks, or copyrights nor are there any pending applications, therefor. Except as set forth in Schedule "F", the operation of *Beta*, the manufacture, use and sale by it of its products, and the use of its products by its customers for the purposes for which sold, and the publication by *Beta* of its advertising, technical or other literature does not involve infringement or claimed infringement of any Indian or, to *Beta*'s knowledge, other patent, trademark or copyright. No Director, Officer or employee of *Beta* owns, directly or indirectly, in whole or in part, any patents, trademarks or copyrights or applications therefor which *Beta* is presently using or the use of which are necessary for the business of *Beta* as now conducted.

4.6 *Contracts and Commitments.*—Schedule F-1 to this Agreement includes, unless otherwise indicated, the following contracts and commitments:

(i) A list of all agreements between *Beta* and its employees, Officers and Directors;

(ii) All sales agency, distributorship agreements or franchises;

(iii) All collective bargaining agreements, trade union agreements, employment agreements (except those terminable without penalty on thirty (30) days' notice) or agreements providing for the services of an independent contractor;

(iv) All employee benefit plans, agreements or commitments, whether or not legally binding including but not limited to, any profit sharing, pension, stock option, retirement bonus, group life and health insurance plan together with current statements and any related investment agreements, insurance arrangements or funding plans and the certification of governmental authorities obtained or any agreement, plan or benefit, as well as the related applications to the governmental authorities;

(v) All leases or other contracts, agreements, or commitments relating to or affecting immovable property or any interest therein;

(vi) All loan or credit agreements, indentures, mortgages, pledges, conditional sales or other title retention agreements, and all equipment obligations, lease and lease purchase agreements, except leases of office equipment;

(vii) All contracts, agreements, commitments, licenses or sublicenses relating to patents, trademarks, trade name, copyrights, inventions, processes, know-how formulas or trade secrets; and

(viii) All other material contracts or agreements involving a sum not less than .... (amount in figures and words), leases, licenses, plans, arrangements or commitments to which *Beta* is a party or by which it or any of its assets or properties are in any way bound or affected.

Except as specified in the Schedules hereto, all of the above contracts and commitments are valid, binding and in full force and effect and there is no existing default by any party thereunder.

4.7 *Bank Accounts and Power of Attorney*

Schedule "G" hereto is a true and complete list of:

(i) The name of each bank in which *Beta* has an account or safe deposit box and the names of all persons authorized to draw thereon or to have access thereto; and

(ii) The names of all persons, firms, or corporations if any, holding general or special powers of attorney form *Beta*.

4.8 *Litigation.*—Except as described in Schedule "H", there are no suits, actions, claims, inquiries, or known investigations by any governmental body, nor any legal, administrative or arbitration proceedings pending or threatened against or materially adversely affecting *Beta*, or to which *Beta* is or might become a party involving or creating liabilities in the excess of .... (amount in figures and words), and *Beta* does not know of any basis or grounds for any such suit, action, claim, inquiry, investigation or proceeding. There is no outstanding order, writ, injunction or decree of any court, governmental agency or arbitration tribunal against or materially adversely affecting *Beta* or the properties, assets or business of *Beta*.

4.9 *Insurance.*—Schedule "I" hereto contains copies of all insurance policies (and a schedule specifying the insurer, the amount of the coverage, the type of insurance, and the policy number) maintained by *Beta* on its properties, assets, business and personnel. *Beta* is not in any material default with respect to any provision contained in such insurance policies nor has it failed to give any notice or present any material claim thereunder in timely fashion.

4.10 *Licenses and Permits.*—*Beta* has all material governmental licenses and permits (Central, State, Foreign, and local) necessary to conduct its businesses, and such licenses and permits are in full force and effect. No violations are or have been alleged in respect of such licenses or permits, and no proceedings are pending or threatened for the revocation or limitation of any of such licenses or permits which will result in any material loss or damage to *Beta*. *Beta* has complied with all laws, rules, regulations, and orders applicable to its business, including, without limitation, compliance with Monopolies and Restrictive Trade Practices Act insofar as they relate to the purchase, distribution, and sale of its products.

4.11 *Accounts Receivable.*—All notes and accounts receivable by *Beta* have arisen in the ordinary course of business, represent actual transactions and will be collectible in ordinary course of business in the aggregate recorded amounts thereof.

4.12 *Inventory.*—The inventory of *Beta* consists of items of a quality and quantity usable and saleable in the normal course of its businesses.

4.13 *Agreement Authorized.*—*Beta* has full power and authority to execute, deliver, and perform this Agreement, and this Agreement is binding upon and enforceable against *Beta* in accordance with its terms.

4.14 *Compensation.*—Schedule "J" hereto is a true and complete list of the names and current annual salaries of each Director and each of the Officers of *Beta* and of each salaried employee, and the bonus or other forms of compensation (other than salary) paid or payable to or for the benefit of each such person for the last fiscal year of *Beta*.

4.15 *Finder's Fee.*—No broker or finder has acted for *Beta* in connection with this Agreement or the transaction contemplated by this Agreement, and no broker or finder is entitled to any brokerage or finder's fee, or other commission in respect thereof based in any way on agreements, arrangements, or understandings made by or on behalf of *Beta*.

4.16 *Returns.*—All the returns, particulars, resolutions, and other documents required to be filed with or delivered on behalf of *Beta* to the Registrar of Companies pursuant to the provisions of the Act have been correctly and properly prepared and filed or delivered.

4.17 *Contracts or Commitments.*—*Beta* has not made any contract or commitment for capital expenditure in excess of .... (amount in figures and words).

4.18 *Mortgages or charges.*—There are no mortgages, charges, liens, or other encumbrances in respect of the whole or any part of the assets of *Beta* except as, and to the extent, disclosed in the said Balance Sheet.

4.19 *No dividends or other distributions.*—No dividend, bonus or other distribution has been declared, paid or made on any share in the capital of *Beta*. *Beta* agrees and undertakes that no dividend will be paid or made until all the shares have been allotted and issued to *Alpha*.

4.20 *No litigation.*—Save for normal debt collection, *Beta* is not engaged in any litigation or arbitration involving claims or sums in dispute, and *Beta* is not aware of any facts likely to give rise to any such litigation or arbitration. In addition, *Beta* has no reasons to believe that it has any claim against *Omega* in regard to that certain Agreement to Transfer Undertaking dated .... between *Beta* and *Omega*.

4.21 *Representations Complete.*—No representation or warranty made by *Beta* in this section 4 omits any material fact necessary to make the statements herein misleading.

5. Conditions precedent to Alpha's Obligations

All obligations of *Alpha* under this Agreement are subject to the fulfilment, prior to or at the Closing, of each of the following conditions—

(a) The accuracy of all representations and warranties with respect to *Beta* and *Omega*.

(b) *Beta* and *Omega* shall have performed and complied with all covenants, agreements, and conditions required by this Agreement to be performed or complied with prior to or at the Closing.

(c) Approval shall have been obtained from the Foreign Investment Promotion Board and other governmental authorities for the acquisition of the shares of the Company by *Alpha*.

6. Survival of Warranties

All representations and warranties, including financial statements, schedule or attachments, given or made by either party shall:

(a) Survive for three (3) years after the Closing and remain effective regardless of any investigation at any time made by or on behalf of either party or of any information either party may have in respect thereto.

(b) Be true and accurate as of the date hereof any shall be deemed to be made again as of the Closing and shall be true and accurate in all material respects.

7. Termination

Either party hereto shall have the right to terminate this Agreement forthwith at any time by giving notice in writing to the other party upon the happening of all or any of the following events.

(a) The other party making any arrangements or composition with creditors or upon a winding up Order being passed against it or upon the other part going into liquidation, voluntary or otherwise, except for the purposes of amalgamation or reconstruction, or if a receiver is appointed of the property or any portion of the property of the other party, or upon *Beta*, or the equity interest of *Beta*, being nationalized.

(b) Upon any breach or default by the other party of any of the terms and conditions or stipulations herein contained and its failure for a period of not less than thirty (30) days to remedy the same after receipt by it of written notice from the aggrieved party in requiring it to do so.

8. Effect of Termination

The termination or determination of this Agreement shall be without prejudice to the rights of the parties in respect of any antecedent breach, non-performance, or non-observance of any of the obligations herein contained.

9. Indemnity

9.1 *Omega* understands and agrees that all of the business, properties and assets of *Beta* have been acquired from *Omega* under the Agreement to Transfer Undertaking and that all representations and warranties in section 4 relate to the business, properties and assets so acquired. As such, *Omega* hereby represents, and warrants to *Alpha* and undertakes to *Alpha* that, save for any to the extent of disclosures fully and fairly made in the Disclosure Letter as set out in Schedule K, each of the statements set out in section 4 are materially correct and not misleading.

9.2 No claim shall be capable of being made against *Beta* or *Omega* under the warranties, unless written notice thereof (specifying the breach or other event to such claim shall relate and the estimated amount claimed in respect thereof) shall have been given to *Beta* or *Omega* as soon as practicably possible after a claim has arisen and in any event not later than three (3) years after the closing.

9.3 The liability of *Beta* or *Omega* under the warranties shall not exceed the amount equal to the aggregate cash consideration received by *Omega* from *Alpha* or *Beta* in connection with the completion of the transactions contemplated by this Agreement and the Agreement to Transfer Undertaking.

9.4 Further, *Omega* (hereinafter in this Section *Omega* is referred to individually as a "Guarantor") hereby agrees to indemnify and hold *Alpha* harmless against any liability, loss, damage, claim, cost, obligation or expense (including any penalty and any reasonable legal fees and costs) (a "Loss") arising out of or due to:

(a) Breach of any representation or warranty by *Beta* or *Omega* contained herein or in any document delivered hereunder or in the Agreement to Transfer Undertaking.

(b) All liabilities of *Beta* or *Omega* relating to the Assets, whether accrued, absolute, contingent, known or unknown, liquidated or unliquidated, existing at or arising out of a state of facts existing at or prior to the Closing, and any expenses relating thereto, including any environment or tax liabilities, to the extent that such liabilities and expenses are not reflected or reserved against in the Balance Sheet.

9.5 The Guarantor shall only be responsible under this Section with respect to any loss suffered by *Alpha* if such loss, together with the aggregate of all other losses theretofore incurred by *Alpha* shall exceed Rs. .... (amount).

9.6 *Alpha* shall promptly give written notice to Guarantor of any matter, which *Alpha* has determined, has or could give rise to a right of indemnification hereunder, stating an estimate of the amount of the Loss, if known.

9.7 All representations, warranties and indemnification obligations in this Agreement shall survive the Closing and any investigation made by or on behalf of any party. The indemnification obligation of *Omega* shall terminate .... years after the closing. If a claim for indemnification is made prior to termination, such termination shall not affect in any way or impair the rights of *Alpha* to indemnification as to such matter.

9.8 The amount of any Loss arising from the breach of any representation or warranty containing a materiality qualification shall be the entire amount of such Loss and not just the portion that exceeds the relevant materiality.

9.9 In no event shall the aggregate liability of *Omega* under this indemnification provision exceed an amount equal to the aggregate cash consideration received by *Omega* from .... and *Beta* in connection with completion of the transaction contemplated by this Agreement and the Agreement to Transfer Undertaking.

9.10 Each of .... (name) and .... (name), being owners of outstanding shares of *Omega*, hereby agree to indemnify and hold *Beta* and *Alpha* harmless against any loss arising out of or due to the failure of *Omega* to perform fully its indemnification obligation set forth in section 9.1 or the failure of *Omega* to perform any other Agreement contained herein to the extent set forth in the Limited Guaranty and Indemnity Agreement of .... (name) and .... (name) dated .... for the benefit of *Beta* and *Alpha*.

10. General Terms

10.1 *Expenses.*—Except as otherwise agreed to in writing, the parties shall each bear their own expenses with respect to the proposed venture. The reasonable expenses of formation of the Company and other expenses incidental thereto shall be chargeable to the Company's account.

10.2 *Compliance with Laws.*—This Agreement is subject to all laws and regulations of India, in effect, now or hereafter.

10.3 *Relationship of the Parties.*—It is understood that each of *Alpha*, *Beta* and *Omega* are independent entities engaged in the conduct of their own business. Nothing contained herein shall be deemed to create any agency relationship between the parties hereto. It is understood and agreed that *Beta* is not, by this Agreement or anything contained herein, constituted the partner of *Alpha* or *Omega* for any purpose whatsoever, nor shall *Beta* be deemed to have any right or authority to assume any responsibility, express of implied, for, on behalf of, or in the name of *Alpha* or *Omega*, or to bid *Alpha* or *Omega* in any way whatsoever.

10.4 *Waiver.*—The failure of any party to enforce at any time any provision of this Agreement shall not constitute a waiver thereof or the right of the other party to claim damages or to terminate this Agreement for any subsequent default.

10.5 *Exclusion of Assignment.*—This Agreement shall inure to the benefit of and be binding upon the parties hereto, their successors and assigns. It shall not be assignable by either party without the prior written consent of the other party.

10.6 *Notices.*—All notices and other communications with respect to this Agreement shall be given to *Alpha*, *Beta* and *Omega* in English by fax or transmitted by international courier service with proof of delivery at the address set forth below, or such other address as shall hereafter be designated for this purpose:

Alpha
Alpha .... LIMITED
.... (address),
....
....

With a copy to:
....
....
....

Attention: President
Fax:.....................
Beta
Beta Filtration Private Limited
.... (address)
Fax:.....................
With a copy to *Beta* (INDIA) LIMITED
....
.... (address)
Fax:.....................

Notice shall be deemed to have been received and shall be effective fourteen (14) days from the date of mailing.

10.7 *Headings.*—The headings of the Sections of this Agreement have been inserted only to facilitate reference and shall not be taken as being of any significance whatsoever in the construction and interpretation of this Agreement.

10.8 *Entire Agreement.*—This Agreement sets forth the entire agreement and understanding between the parties as to the subject hereof and supersedes all negotiations, commitments and writings prior to the date hereof pertaining to the subject matter of this Agreement.

10.9 *Severability.*—If any provision of this Agreement shall be judged invalid for any reason whatsoever, such invalidity shall not affect the validity or operation of any other provision and such invalid provision shall be deemed to have been deleted from this Agreement.

10.10 *Modifications.*—This Agreement shall not be altered, modified or supplemented except with the prior written approval of the parties hereto:

10.11 *Governing Law.*—This Agreement shall be construed and interpreted in accordance with the laws of the Union of India.

10.12 *Arbitration*

A. All disputes between the parties hereto, arising out of or in connection with the execution, interpretation and performance of this Agreement (including the validity, scope and enforceability of this section 10.12) shall, to the fullest extent permitted by law, be solely and finally settled by a Board of arbitrators consisting to three arbitrators, as set forth below (the term "Arbitrators" shall refer to the board of arbitrators). THE ARBITRATION PROCEEDINGS SHALL BE HELD AT .... (foreign state), AND EXCEPT AS OTHERWISE MAY BE PROVIDED IN THIS section 10.12 SHALL BE CONDUCTED IN

ACCORDANCE WITH THE RULES OF CONCILIATION AND ARBITRATION (THE ICC RULES) OF THE INTERNATIONAL CHAMBER OF COMMERCE, ... (foreign state) ("THE ICC"). The arbitration proceedings shall be conducted in the English language and any award shall be made in .... (foreign currency), unless the dispute is between parties all of which are located in India, in which event any award shall be made in Rupees.

B. If a party hereto determines to submit a dispute to arbitration pursuant to this section 10.12 such party shall furnish the ICC and the other party, with a dated, written notice (the "Arbitration Notice") indicating (I) such party's intent to commence arbitration proceedings pursuant to this section 10.12 (ii) the name and address of such party and a designated officer or agent thereof, (iii) the nature, with reasonable detail, of the dispute, (iv) the remedy such party will seek, and (v) any other information required under the ICC Rules.

C. Within ten (10) days of the date of the Arbitration Notice (the "Selection Date"), the ICC shall select, (and provide written notice of such selection to the parties hereto) the Arbitrators from a list of members of the ICC's Panel of Commercial Arbitrators. Within one hundred twenty (120) days of the Selection Date, the Arbitrators shall conclude all hearings and proceedings relating to the matter under arbitration (the "Final Proceeding Date"). All decisions of the Arbitrators shall be rendered by majority vote in writing stating reasons therefor in reasonable details within ninety (90) days after the Final Proceeding Date.

D. All fees and expenses of the Arbitrators shall be borne equally by the parties hereto. All notices provided pursuant to this section 10.12 shall be given pursuant to the requirements of section 10.12 hereof.

E. To the extent permissible under applicable law, the parties hereto agree that the award of the Arbitrators shall be final and shall not be subject to judicial review except to challenge an award that exceeds the power of such Arbitrators as provided herein. Judgement on the arbitration award may be entered and enforced in any court having jurisdiction over the parties or their assets. For this purpose, all parties hereto submit to jurisdiction before any State or federal court located in .... (Foreign State). It is the intent of the parties that the arbitration provisions hereof be enforced to the fullest extent permitted by applicable law. Further, any arbitration pursuant to this Agreement shall be an International Commercial Arbitration and the award shall be regarded as a "Foreign Award" under the Arbitration and Conciliation Act, 1996.

F. Notwithstanding any other provision of this section 10, 12, a party hereto may seek and receive injunctive relief (whether a temporary restraining order or preliminary injunction or otherwise) or specific performance pending a decision of the Arbitrators and this section 10,12 shall not apply to any such action or procedure (including any court proceeding or self-help).

G. The Arbitrators can render an award only for monetary damages and such monetary damages shall not extend the direct damages for loss or injury caused by a breach of this Agreement. The Arbitrators shall have no authority to award punitive damages, consequential damages or damages for indirect losses or injuries. The Arbitrators shall have no power to provide equitable remedies for any breach of this Agreement; provided that the Arbitrators may direct specific performance of any provision of this Agreement.

10.13 *Consent to Jurisdiction*.—Each of the parties hereto, hereby submits to the non-exclusive jurisdiction and venue of the State and federal courts of .... (Foreign State) for the purpose of enforcing the provisions of section 10.12 or for enforcement of any arbitration award rendered pursuant to section 10.12 hereof.

IN WITNESS WHEREOF, the parties hereto have executed these presents the day, month and year first hereinabove written.

Alpha .... LIMITED.
By:.....................
Title:.....................
By:.....................
Title:.....................
WITNESS:

....
Beta FILTERATION PRIVATE LIMITED
By:.....................
Title:.....................
The Common Seal of *Beta* Filtration Private Limited
has been affixed hereto pursuant to a
resolution of the Board of
Directors passed on the.....................
day of....................., ..., in the
presence of..................... and
.... two of the
Directors of the said Company.
Beta (INDIA) LIMITED
By:.....................
Title:.....................
Name:
Title:
The Common Seal of *Beta* (India)
Limited has been affixed hereto
pursuant to a resolution of the
Board of Directors passed on the
21st day of July, 1997, in
the presence of Mr..................... [name] and
Mrs. .... [name], two of the Directors
of the said Company.
WITNESS:
By:...
Title...
WITNESS:

CHAPTER 4
INTELLECTUAL PROPERTY

SYNOPSIS

ASSIGNMENT OF COPYRIGHT
    Disputes as to Assignment
    Infringement
"PASSING OFF" ACTIONS UNDER INDIAN LAW
    The history of passing off actions under English Common Law
    Modern formulation of the law of passing off
    Remedies
    Proof of damage
    Means adopted for passing off
    Passing off in professional practice
    "Passing off" in Indian Courts: Remedies available
    Mareva Injunctions in India

PRECEDENTS
on Trademark and Brand Protection
- Trademark License Agreement
- Trade Name License Agreement
- Deed Of Assignment

on Copyright (Media Entertainment)
- Writer Employment Agreement
- Sound Recording and Distribution License Agreement
- Co-production Agreement
- Deed of Assignment of Copyright
- Dialogue and Vocal Replacement Agreement
- Actor Employment Agreement
- Memorandum of Understanding between two Media Companies
- Patent Agreement for Employees
- Patents, Patent Licensing and Protection in India
- Technology Transfer and License Agreement
- Technology and Marketing Collaboration Agreement
- Technology Assignment Agreement

on Confidentiality and non-disclosure
- Know-How Assignment Agreement
- Confidentiality Agreement (Between A Company and an individual)
- Confidentiality Agreement - Both party obligations
- Consultancy Agreement
- Confidentiality and Non-discloser Agreement.
- Employees non-disclosure and non-compete agreeement
- Non-disclosure and non-compete agreeement

Assignment of Copyright

Assignment is the legal term for transfer of ownership. It covers all the ways in which ownership of property is transferred from one person to another. Intellectual property, an abstract concept, cannot be physically handed over, so a document is always needed to transfer ownership. An author of a copyright does not exploit the work by himself. He assigns his right to others to exploit it for a consideration. Copyright is a kind of personal movable property. It can therefore be transferred by assignment. The owner of a copyright in an existing work may assign to any person the copyright in the work[1]. Since copyright consists of bundle of rights, the owner may assign the whole of these rights or only some of them. An assignment may be general, *i.e.*, without limitation or subject to limitation. It may be for the whole term of the copyright or any part thereof. Thus, the rights proposed to be assigned are to be clearly indicated in the instrument of assignment. These rights may be:

(i) for assignment of whole copyright;

(ii) for a partial assignment of a copyright;

(iii) for a general assignment;

(iv) for an assignment subject to limitation;

(v) for the whole term of the copyright; or

(vi) for a part of the term of the copyright.

Assignment is in essence a transfer of ownership even if it is partial[2]. Copyright is transmissible by assignment, by testamentary disposition or by operation of law as personal and moveable property. An assignment to pass the legal title to the right assigned must be in writing signed by or on behalf of the assignor. Assignment of copyright is only valid if it is in writing and signed by the assignor or his duly authorised agent. Assignment is usually made on payment of a lump sum whereas licenses are based on royalty payment per copy sold.

In the case of partial assignment[3], the assignees of a copyright in respect of the rights not assigned are treated as owners of the respective rights. An author of a work who has assigned some of the rights can be restrained from exercising these rights by the assignee. A partial assignee can independently sue for infringement of his rights without joining the assignor for he is the exclusive owner of the rights acquired by assignment[4].

---

1. Assignment is the transfer of ownership, so that after the transfer the original owner is now himself excluded from using the property unless the new owner gives him a licence. Hillary Pearson & Clifford Miller, *Commercial Exploitation of Intellectual Property*, First Indian Reprint, Universal Book Publishers.
2. P.A. Narayanan, Intellectual Property Law, Second Edition, p. 254.
3. Partial assignment may take various forms: (1) it may be limited to one or more, but not all, of the acts which the owner of copyright has exclusive right to do, (2) it may be limited to one or more, but not all, of the countries where the owner has the exclusive right, and (3) it may be limited to part of the period for which the copyright subsists. P. A. Narayanan, *Law of Copyright and Industrial Designs*, Second Edition, (10.02), page 104.
4. *Ref. Jonathan Cape* v. *Consolidated Press*, (1954) 3 All ER 253: (1954) 1 WLR 1313.

It has been held that the grant of an exclusive right of performing a play is an assignment of the performing right in the play even though the grant was limited to an area, the consideration was payment of royalty, and in the agreement, the parties were referred to as licensor and licensee[1].

Section 20 expressly provides that if the manuscript of a literary, dramatic or musical work, or an artistic work has been bequeathed to a beneficiary without specifically bequeathing copyright the bequest will carry with it the copyright also unless a contrary intention appears from the Will. When the owner of the copyright becomes bankrupt, the copyright will vest in the official receiver and will pass to the trustee of the bankrupt's estate as assets for distribution among creditors. Section 18 provides that copyright can be assigned even in respect of future works of the author before their coming into existence but in this case, the assignment will take effect only when the work comes into existence. As authors of literary, dramatic, musical or artistic work have a distinctive style of giving form to their ideas, they may be able to produce similar works based on the same ideas on which the assigned work is based but without copying from it. Despite the similarity, it will be difficult to establish infringement in such cases.

Where there is a partial assignment of the copyright to the defendant and that he had become the owner of the particular right mentioned in his agreement and was entitled to take steps to prevent any infringement of that right by the plaintiffs. In cases of partial assignment, the true construction of the agreement is seen. An assignment does not operate to prevent the assignor reproducing his work as new from the original subject though he can be restrained from reproducing the work except to the extent permitted. In other words if the new book is a work which the assignor has produced after further studies and deliberation and represents the results of such fresh work and represents a mature art and a greater wealth, if details of the imaginary is of a superior type there can be no question of infringement of the rights of the assignee.

In *Howitt* v. *Hall*, it appeared that the defendants having brought the copyright for four years in a book, of which the plaintiff was the author, were still continuing several years after the end of the term to sell copies, which they had printed during the four years. The court in refusing an injunction to restrain such sales held that the purchase of the copyright carried the right of printing and that while this right reverted to the author at the end of four years, the publisher was entitled to sell after the expiration of the term, all copies which had been printed in good faith during the term.

It has been held that, it is the Courts duty to give effect to the actual bargain of the parties according to the intimation and when the transaction is in writing the intention of the parties has to be gathered from the actual words used in the instrument unless they are such as not to convey their intention correctly.

---

1. *Messager* v. *British Broadcasting*, (1929) AC 151 (152); *HL Loew's Inc.* v. *Littler*, (1958) Ch 650: (1958) 2 All ER 200 CA.

Disputes as to Assignment

Where there is any dispute as to assignment between the parties, any of the parties may approach the Copyright Board. The Board may after holding enquiry pass such orders, as it may deem fit.

A note on the instrument of assignment

Under Indian Copyright Law, an oral assignment of copyright is invalid[1]. There is no particular form prescribed for assignment and it may be effected even by a letter[2]. To identify the subject matter of the assignment oral evidence may be admitted[3]. An assignment being a conveyance or sale must be stamped in accordance with the relevant provisions of the Indian Stamp Act, 1889.

Copyright does not come within the scope of 'actionable claim' as defined in section 3 of the Transfer of Property Act. Since copyright is a beneficial right in movable property, the owner of the right has actual or constructive possession of the same[4]. There is no prescribed form for assignment. The deed of assignment should contain the following:

- identity of the work;
- the rights assigned and the duration and territorial extent of such assignment;
- the amount of royalty payable, if any, to the author or his legal heirs during the currency of the assignment and the assignment will be subject to revision, extension or termination on terms mutually agreed upon by the Parties.

Infringement

The owner of the copyright has the exclusive right to do certain acts in respect of the work. If any person does any of these acts without authority, he will be committing an infringement of the copyright in the work. Infringement means interference with or the violation of the right of copyright of another. It takes place when a person does anything, which only the owner of the copyright has right to do, or permits for profits any place to be used for the performance constitutes an infringement. The nature of the rights depend upon the nature of the work. Depending upon the kind of Copyright work infringement involves one or more of the following acts:

  (i) reproduction of the work in a material form
  (ii) publication of the work
  (iii) Performance of the work in public
  (iv) making of adaptations and translation of the work and doing any of the above acts in relation to a substantial part of the work.

---

1. *Venugopal Setty* v. *Suryakanta*, (1992) PTC 55 (Karn HC).
2. *London Printing and Publishing Alliance* v. *Cox*, (1891) 3 Ch 291 CA; *Ex Parte Hutchins*, (1879) 4 BD 483 CA; *Judi's Musical Composition (in re:)*, (1907) 1 Ch 651 CA.
3. *E.W. Savoy* v. *World of Golf*, (1914) 2 Ch 566 CA.
4. *Savitri Devi* v. *Dwarka Prasad*, AIR 1939 All 305 (308).

Copyright in a work shall be deemed to be infringed when any person without license granted by the owner of the copyright or in contravention of the conditions of a license so granted permits for profit any place to be used for the communication of the work to the public where such communication constitutes an infringement of the copyright in the work unless he is not aware and had no reasonable ground for believing that such communication to the public would be an infringement of the copyright.

There is no copyright in ideas however original or brilliant in information. What copyright protects is not the raw material from which the work is created but the skill and labour employed by the author in the creation of the work.

The question whether a work is performed or a sound recording film or television broadcasting seen or heard in public is solely one of the facts but certain considerations and tests have been applied among them the question whether there has been any admission with or without payment of any portion of the work to the injury of the author. The Copyright (Amendment) Act, 1994 made many amendments in the existing provisions as relating to what does not constitute infringement.

In the event of infringement of a copyright civil, criminal and administrative remedies are available to the owner. Civil remedies include an injunction, damages, and/or account of profits. In addition, damages can be claimed for conversion that may be very substantial. Criminal remedies include imprisonment, fines, and seizure of infringing copies of the work, which will be delivered to the copyright owner. In appropriate cases courts grant *ex parte* interim injunctions upon motion and in camera require the infringer to enable the plaintiff to enter upon the premises and inspect documents and articles thereon and obtain copies of the infringing materials. However, certain conditions require to be satisfied before obtaining an Anton Piller Order such as a strong *prima facie* case and the seriousness of actual and potential damages.

An illustration of effective orders at the interim stage would be what has come to be known as the Anton Piller Order. In the case of *Anton Piller AG v. Manufacturing Processes Ltd.*, the Court of Appeal in England held that in the most exceptional circumstances, where plaintiffs had a very strong *prima facie* case, actual or potential damage to them was very serious and there was clear evidence that defendants possessed vital material which they might destroy or dispose of so as to defeat the ends of justice before any application *inter partes* could be made, the Court has inherent jurisdiction to order the defendants to permit the plaintiff's representatives to enter the defendants' premises to inspect and remove such material; and that in the very exceptional circumstances the Court is justified in making the order sought on the plaintiff's *ex parte* application. Thus, the Anton Piller Order aims at protecting the plaintiff against the activities of an unscrupulous defendant who may defeat or diminish the plaintiff's chances of success by destroying or removing offending evidence. It is similar to an *ex parte* interlocutory order to inspect the premises of the defendant and take inventory of the offending articles etc., passed in an ordinary suit in India.

In a suit for infringement[1] of trademark, the reliefs, which are usually asked for and granted, are of injunction, and at the option of the plaintiff, either damages or an account of profit. The distinctive feature of an injunction is that it restrains the defendant from doing certain acts. Notwithstanding this, some additional forms of action are available at all times under the Indian law.

In the case of trademarks under the Act, the plaintiff can also file a suit against the defendant for passing off[2] his goods as those of the plaintiff. This claim does not depend on the trademark being registered. The plaintiff brings an action for passing off[3], if the mark, sign or device, which is used by the defendant, is deceptively similar[4] to that of the plaintiff. The principle of a passing off action is that no man is entitled to represent his goods as being the goods of another man. In some jurisdictions, an allied principle of "unfair competition[5]" is applied. Passing off actions are common throughout the developed and developing countries, the reason being that a new entrant or even an existing competitor in trade is often tempted to copy a successful product of another competitor, either by using a similar mark or a label or wrapper of the more successful product.

In an extreme case, there may be a direct false representation that the goods are manufactured by the plaintiff. Normally however, the device is used to adopt a mark, which is colourable intimation of the mark of the plaintiff. On occasion, the essential part of the competitor's name is adopted as part of the defendant's

---

1. Infringement of a trademark gives the proprietor of the registered trademark a statutory remedy due to the exclusivity granted under section 21 of the Act. The proprietor/registered owner of the mark has three courses of action against violation of trademarks rights, that of (a) an injunction under statute (b) a passing off action and (c) criminal action.

2. Passing off is not defined in the Act. It is referred to in sections 27 (2), 105 (c) and 106. Section 27(2) states that the rights of action against any person for passing off goods as the goods of another person or the remedies in respect thereof are unaffected by the provisions of the Act. Section 105 (c) refers to the jurisdiction of courts to try suits for passing off arising out of the use of a trademark. The Act is silent with regard to cases of passing off where no goods or no trademark is involved. Such cases of passing off are also governed by common law.

3. An action for passing off is a common law remedy being an action in substance of deceit under the law of Torts. Wherever and whenever fresh deceitful act is committed the person deceived would naturally have a fresh cause of action in his favour. Thus, every time when a person passes off his goods as those of another he commits the act of such deceit. S.B. Majumdar J., in *Bengal Waterproof Ltd. v. Bombay Waterproof Mfg. Co.*, (1977) 1 SCC 99.

4. Section 12 of the Trademarks Act prohibits registration of deceptively similar trademarks in respect of goods and description of goods, which is identical or deceptively similar to the trademark already registered. For prohibiting registration under section 12(1), in respect of goods or description of goods being same or similar and similar to the trademark already registered. G.N. Ray, J in *Vishnudas Trading v. Vazir Sultan Tobacco Co. Ltd*, (1977) 4 SCC 201.

5. The principle of "unfair trade" involving the restrictions in the right of trade mark in the case of franchise agreements was clarified by the Hon'ble Supreme Court in *Gujarat Bottling Co. Ltd. v. Coca Cola Co.*, (1995) 5 SCC 545.

name. Similarly, as in the case of an infringement, in the case of passing off also, the plaintiff will have to prove damages or ask for an account of profits.

Passing off actions under Indian Law
The history of passing off actions under English Common Law

The action for passing off seems to have been recognised at English Common Law as long ago as during the reign of Elizabeth I[1]. It seems that the action for passing off at common law originally grew out of the action for deceit and like the action for deceit required a false representation made fraudulently, but differed from it, in that the persons deceived were the plaintiff's customers rather than the plaintiff himself[2]. The action at common law was extended to cases where the defendant's customers were not themselves deceived but the defendant sold fraudulently marked goods to retail dealers with express purpose of the goods being resold to the ultimate purchasers as the plaintiff's goods[3]. Although at first equity followed the common law in requiring fraudulent intent on the part of the defendant[4], it was later accepted that an injunction could be granted in equity in the absence of intention to deceive if the defendant's actions would in fact result in deception[5]. It was soon accepted both at law[6] and in equity[7] that it was unnecessary that the goods passed off had to be inferior to the plaintiff's[8].

Equity's willingness to protect the exclusive right to use a trade name or mark even in the absence of fraud was recognised as being based on a right of property, by contrast with the purely personal right to relief at law based on fraud[9]. Equity came to recognise and develop an exclusive property in a trade mark applied to goods acquired by first public use of the mark, which was distinct from the action for passing off founded on misrepresentation; these so-called 'unregistered trade marks' have been superseded by the statutory registration of trade marks and can no longer be enforced, but this does not affect rights of action for passing off[10]. The common law courts maintained the requirement that fraudulent intent had to be proved in an action for passing off until the fusion of the courts of common law and equity[1], and subsequent judicial

---

1. An unreported case was mentioned in the judgement of Doderidge J in *Southern* v. *How*, (1618) Poph 143 at 144, where a defendant fraudulently counterfeited the mark of a clothier from Gloucester; but another report says that the plaintiff was the deceived customer rather than the owner of the mark (Cro Jac 468 at 471), and another that Doderidge J did not make clear which of them was the plaintiff (2 Roll Rep 26 at 28).
2. *Singer Manufacturing Co.* v. *Wilson*, (1876) 2 ChD 434 at 453, CA per Mellish LJ.
3. *Sykes* v. *Sykes*, (1824) 3 B & C 541.
4. *Blanchard* v. *Hill*, (1742) 2 Atk 484 at 485 per Lord Hardwicke LC. Also *Motley* v. *Downman*, (1837) 3 My & Cr 1 at 10 (argument) and at 14 per Lord Cottenham LC.
5. *Millington* v. *Fox*, (1838) 3 My & Cr 338.
6. *Blofeld* v. *Payne*, (1833) 4 B & Ad 410.
7. *Edelsten* v. *Edelsten*, (1863) 1 De GJ & Sm 195.
8. *Singer Manufacturing Co.* v. *Loog*, (1882) App Cas 15 at 30, HL per Lord Blackburn.
9. *Hall* v. *Barrows*, (1863) 4 De GJ & Sm 150 at 158 per Lord Westbury LC.
10. Trade Marks Act, 1994 (English), sec. 2(2).

observations have maintained that passing off in the absence of fraudulent intent is actionable in equity only.

Modern formulation of the law of passing off

Lord Diplock has stated the essential characteristics, which must be present in order to create a valid cause of action for passing off, in *Erven Warnink* v. *Townend (Advocate)*[2], as follows:—

1. misrepresentation, that the plaintiff's goods or services have acquired a goodwill or reputation in the market and are known by some distinguishing feature;
2. made by a person in the course of trade, that there is a misrepresentation by the defendant (whether or not intentional) leading or is likely to lead the public to believe that the goods or services offered by the defendants are goods or services of the plaintiff; and
3. to prospective customers of his or ultimate customers of goods or services supplied by him,
4. which is calculated to injure the business or goodwill of another trader (in the sense that it is a reasonably foreseeable consequence), and
5. which causes actual damage to a business or goodwill of the trader by whom the action is brought brings the action or (in a *quia timet* action) will probably do so. That the plaintiff has suffered or is likely to suffer damage as a result of the erroneous belief engendered by the defendant's misrepresentation.

Lord Fraser of Tullybelton in the same case (at p. 105) expressed the requirements in a different form as follows: The plaintiff must show:—

1. that his business consists, or includes selling in England a class of goods to which the particular trade name applies,
2. that the class of goods is clearly defined and that in the minds of the public, or a section of the public in England, the trade name distinguishes that class from other similar goods,
3. that because of the reputation of the goods, there is goodwill attached to the name,
4. that he, the plaintiff, as a member of the class of those who sell the goods, is the owner of the goodwill in England which is of substantial value, and
5. that he has suffered, or is really likely to suffer a substantial damage to his property in the goodwill by reason of the defendants selling goods which are falsely described by the trade name to which the goodwill is attached.

---

1. *Crawshay* v. *Thompson*, (1842) 4 Man & G 357; *Rodgers* v. *Nowill*, (1847) 5 CB 109. Also *Dixon* v. *Fawcus*, (1861) 3 E & E 537. For a summary of the development of passing off at law and equity refer to *Singer Manufacturing Co.* v. *Wilson*, (1876) 2 Ch D 434 (453), CA per Mellish LJ.
2. (1980) RPC 31 (93) (HL).

In *Reckitt & Coleman* v. *Borden*[1], Lord Oliver of Aylmerton re-formulated the classical formulation of passing off as follows:—

> "the law of passing off can be summarised in one short general proposition – no man may pass off his goods as those of another. More specifically it may be expressed in terms of elements which the plaintiff in such an action has to prove in order to succeed. These are three in number. First, he must establish a goodwill or reputation attached to the goods or services which he supplies in the mind of the purchasing public by association with the identifying get-up (whether it consists simply of a brand name or a trade description of the individual features of labelling or packaging under which his particular goods or services are offered to the public such that the get-up is recognised by the public as distinctive specifically of the plaintiffs' goods or services. Secondly, he must demonstrate a misrepresentation by the defendant to the public (whether or not intentional) leading or likely to lead the public to believe that goods or services offered by him are the goods or services of the plaintiff. Thirdly, he must demonstrate that he suffers or, in a *quia timet* action that he is likely to suffer damage by reason of the erroneous belief engendered by the defendants' misrepresentation that the source of the defendants' goods or service is the same as the source of those offered by the plaintiff.

These principles are sometimes referred to as the classical trinity[2]: goodwill, confusion and damage.

Remedies

The remedies in a passing off action include an injunction, damages or an account of profit and delivery-up of the offending article for erasure or destruction.

Proof of damage

Damage or likelihood of damage to the goodwill of the plaintiff is an essential ingredient for passing off. Although proof of actual damage is not necessary the plaintiff must show that there is a reasonable probability of his being injured by the defendant's action even if the conduct of the defendant might be calculated to deceive the public. If the defendant had been using the mark or name for a long time and no damage was shown to have occurred there could be no reason for supposing that it is likely to occur in the future. But once it is established that the defendants' action will lead to passing off, it will be presumed that damage to the plaintiffs' business will follow a natural consequence.

The object of passing off action is to protect the goodwill of business of the plaintiff. A private individual, therefore, cannot institute a suit for passing off even if the defendant practices deception upon the public unless it is proved that

---

1. (1990) RPC 341 (406) (HL).
2. The "classical trinity" was described in *Consorzio del Prosciutto di Parma* v. *Marks & Spencer plc*, [1991] RPC 351 (368, 369), CA per Nourse LJ ('Parma ham').

the defendants' action is likely to cause damage to that individual. The court will, however, take into consideration the interest of the public, i.e. whether they are going to be deceived or confused.

The adoption of a family name, or the name of a house or an address similar to that of the plaintiff without malicious intention or damage or injury to his trade or business is not an actionable wrong, although it may cause inconvenience or annoyance to the plaintiff.

Means adopted for passing off

The method adopted for passing off include:—

(1) direct false representation,
(2) adoption of a trade mark which is the same or a colourable imitation of the trade mark of a rival trader,
(3) adoption of an essential part of a rival traders' name,
(4) copying the get-up or colour scheme of the label used by a trader,
(5) imitating the design or shape of the goods,
(6) adopting the word or name by which the rival trader's goods or business is known in the market, and many other ingenious methods.

Direct misrepresentation is rare. If a customer orders goods of a particular make under a particular name and received something else, is a case of passing off, although, if he had examined the goods, he would not have been deceived.

The defendant cannot rely on the fact that his statement is literally and accurately true, if, notwithstanding the truth, it carries with it a false representation. The circumstances under which and the reason for which, the trade description was adopted is material.

Passing off in professional practice

It has been held that membership of the society confers a status on its member. It is, therefore, a matter of pecuniary interest to the society that it should have as many members as possible and has a pecuniary interest in preventing persons who are not its members, and therefore, who are not entitled to that status[1].

The British Medical Association had no business in approving proprietary medicines and it was contrary to the principles of the Association to do so. It did not establish the proposition that if a tradesman puts forward a remedy as having been prescribed by, or sold for the benefit, or with the approval, of a medical man, the latter would have no remedy. What is necessary in such a case to prove is, either positive injury, or inaction, a reasonable probability of injury[2]?

---

1. *Society of Accountants & Auditors*, (1907) 1 Ch 489.
2. *British Medical Association*, (1931) 48 RPC 565 (574).

"Passing off" in Indian Courts: Remedies available
Interim Order: Anton Piller

An illustration of effective orders at the interim stage would be what has come to be known as the Anton Piller Order. In the case of *Anton Piller AG v. Manufacturing Processes Ltd.,* the Court of Appeal in England, held that in the most exceptional circumstances, where plaintiffs had a very strong *prima facie* case, actual or potential damage to them was very serious and there was clear evidence that defendants possessed vital material, which they might destroy or dispose off so as to defeat the ends of justice before any application *inter partes* could be made, the court has inherent jurisdiction to order the defendants to permit the plaintiff's representatives to enter the defendants' premises to inspect and remove such material; and that in the very exceptional circumstances the court is justified in making the order sought on the plaintiff's *ex parte* application. Thus, the Anton Piller Order aims at protecting the plaintiff against the activities of an unscrupulous defendant who may defeat or diminish the plaintiffs chances of success by destroying or removing offending evidence.

In a suit for infringement[1] of trade mark, the reliefs which are usually asked for and granted are of injunction, and at the option of the plaintiff, either damages or an account of profit. The distinctive feature of an injunction is that it restrains the defendant from doing certain acts. Notwithstanding this, some additional forms of action are available at all times under the Indian law.

In the case of trademarks under the Act, the plaintiff can also file a suit against the defendant for passing off[2] his goods as those of the plaintiff. This claim does not depend on the trademark being registered. The plaintiff brings an action for passing off[3], if the mark, sign or device, which is used by the defendant, is deceptively similar[4] to that of the plaintiff. The principle of a

---

1. Infringement of a trade mark gives the proprietor of the registered trade mark a statutory remedy due to the exclusivity granted under section 21 of the Act. The proprietor/registered owner of the mark has three courses of action against violation of trade marks rights, that of (a) an injunction under statute (b) a passing off action and (c) criminal action.

2. Passing off is not defined in the Act. It is referred to in ss. 27 (2), 105 (c) and 106. Section 27(2) states that the rights of action against any person for passing off goods as the goods of another person or the remedies in respect thereof are unaffected by the provisions of the Act. Section 105 (c) refers to the jurisdiction of courts to try suits for passing off arising out of the use of a trade mark. The Act is silent with regard to cases of passing off where no goods or no trade mark is involved. Such cases of passing off are also governed by common law.

3. An action for passing off is a common law remedy being an action in substance of deceit under the law of Torts. Wherever and whenever fresh deceitful act is committed the person deceived would naturally have a fresh cause of action in his favour. Thus every time when a person passes off his goods as those of another he commits the act of such deceit. S.B. Majumdar J., in *Bengal Waterproof Ltd. v. Bombay Waterproof Mfg. Co.,* (1977) 1 SCC 99.

4. Section 12 of the Trade Marks Act prohibits registration of deceptively similar trade marks in respect of goods and description of goods, which is identical or deceptively similar to the trade mark already registered. For prohibiting registration under Section 12(1), goods in respect of goods or description of goods being same or similar and similar to the trade mark already registered. G.N. Ray, J. in *Vishnudas Trading v. Vazir Sultan Tobacco Co. Ltd.,* (1977) 4 SCC 201.

passing off action is that no man is entitled to represent his goods as being the goods of another man. In some jurisdictions, an allied principle of "unfair competition[1]" is applied. Passing off actions are common throughout the developed and developing countries, the reason being that a new entrant or even an existing competitor in trade is often tempted to copy a successful product of another competitor, either by using a similar mark or a label or wrapper of the more successful product.

In an extreme case, there may be a direct false representation that the goods are manufactured by the plaintiff. Normally however, the device is used to adopt a mark, which is colourable intimation of the mark of the plaintiff. On occasion, the essential part of the competitor's name is adopted as part of the defendant's name. Similarly, as in the case of an infringement, the case of passing off also, the plaintiff will have to prove damages or ask for an account of profits.

Mareva Injunctions in India

Lord Denning making a historical and comparative survey of seizure of assets before judgement said the following words:

> "...It is said that this new procedure was never know to the law of England. But that is not correct. In former times, it was much used in the city of London by a procedure called foreign attachments. It was originally used so as to compel the Defendant to appear and give bail to attend: but it was extended to all cases when he was not within the jurisdiction. Under it, if the Defendant was not to be found within the jurisdiction of the court, the Plaintiff was unable incidentally, as soon as the plaint was issued to attach any effects of the Defendants, where money or goods, to be found within the jurisdiction of the court.

The two cases of *Nippon Yusen Kaisha* v. *Karageorgis*[2] and *Mareva* v. *International Bulkcarriers*[3] are a part of the evolutionary process. The court was there presented with sets of facts, which called for the intervention of the court, by injunction. The study of those facts will reveal that it was both just and convenient with the court to restrain the debtor from removing his funds from London. Unless an interlocutory injunction was granted, *ex-parte*, the debtor could, and probably would by a single telex or telegraphic message, deprive a rightful person to which he was plainly entitled. So just and so convenient, indeed, is the procedure that has been constantly invoked since in the commercial court with the approval of all the judges and users of that court.

Mareva Injunction has been followed on principle in India where interlocutory injunctions have been granted *ex parte* where a *prima-facie* case has been proved with growing cross-border commercial transactions being carried on in India. It is likely that the Mareva Injunction will prove a useful deal in preventing the misuse of Intellectual property.

---

1. The principle of "unfair trade" involving the restrictions in the right of trade mark in the case of franchise agreements was clarified by the Hon'ble Supreme Court in *Gujarat Bottling Co. Ltd.* v. *Coca Cola Co.*, (1995) 5 SCC 545.
2. (1975) (1) WLR 1093.
3. (1975) (2) Lloyd's Rep 509.

PRECEDENTS

ON TRADE MARK AND BRAND PROTECTION

TRADEMARK LICENSE AGREEMENT

This AGREEMENT entered into this .... day of............... 20.....
BETWEEN *Alpha* BATTERY COMPANY INCORPORATED a Company registered under the laws of the State of .... and having its Registered Office at..............., (hereinafter called ABC) AND *Alpha* INDUSTRIES INDIA LIMITED a company registered under the Indian Companies Act of...............
AND HAVING ITS REGISTERED Office at............... (hereinafter called 'AIIL').

WHEREAS,

1. AIIL is the proprietor of Trademark Registration No. .... for the trademark "*Alpha*" in Class 9, in respect of Batteries, in India, by way of assignment from Union Carbide Corporation dated...............

2. ABC is the proprietor of Trademark Registration No. .... for the trademark "*Alpha*" in Class 9, in respect of Batteries, in .... (name of State).

3. Batteries under the trademark "*Alpha*" are sold by way of a Joint Venture between ABC and AIIL, in India.

4. AIIL is desirous of entering into a Joint Venture (JV) with *Beta*, a Company registered under the laws of .... (name of State), and such JV would thereafter distribute Batteries branded with the trademark "*Alpha*" in the Territory of .... (name of State).

5. ABC is desirous of granting unto AIIL a license whereby AIIL would become the registered user of the Registration No. .... for the Trademark "*Alpha*" in class 9 in respect of Carbon Zinc Batteries (herein after referred to as the 'Product') in the territory of .... (name of State) (herein after referred to as the territory).

6. The terms of such license would allow AIIL to authorise to the 'Joint Venture' the use of the Trademark on the product by virtue of and for the duration of AIIL being party to the said Joint Venture.

1. Grant of license

Subject to the terms and conditions of this agreement ABC hereby grants to AIIL an exclusive license, which will extend to and authorize the use of Trademark by the joint venture in the territory provided that,

(i) AIIL and the Joint Venture maintain ABC's Standards of Quality Control

(ii) The Joint Venture shall be responsible for the payment of royalties to ABC on its net sales as if such net sales were made by AIIL directly, pursuant to the terms and conditions of this license agreement.

2. Exclusivity

(i) AIIL will be the sole Licensee of the Trademark in the territory, in respect of the product.

(ii) ABC agrees that it will not itself market the product branded with the Trademark in the territory, but will confine its use of the Trademark to the setting of the Standard of Quality, the design of the Trademark insignia and press statements of Ownership.

3. Term

This agreement shall come into operation as of the.................... day of .... and shall continue for a period of Five Years and thereafter until either party terminates by.................... months notice to expire at any given time.

4. License fee/Royalty

(i) AIIL agrees to pay to ABC, royalties at the rate of ....% of net sales of product branded with the Trademark sold by AIIL or its joint venture.

(ii) All payments to ABC shall be in .... (foreign amount) and the rates of exchange for such payments shall be the mid-point between the buying and selling rates for ....(foreign amount) as quoted by the.................... Bank at the close of business on the day immediately preceding the day of payment.

5. Ownership of the Trademark

(i) ABC warrants to AIIL that it is the owner of the Trademark and by virtue of this ownership it has the authority to grant to AIIL a license to use the Trademark in respect of the product, in the territory.

(ii) AIIL acknowledges and agrees that all rights, in and to the said trade mark, including all of the goodwill of the business associated therewith, are and shall hereafter continue to be the exclusive property of ABC, and that all use of the said trade mark by AIIL shall enure only to the benefit of ABC.

(iii) AIIL acknowledges and agrees that it does not have and shall not hereafter claim, acquire or assert any ownership rights in, or permanent right to the use of, or challenge the validity or registration of the said trade mark either during the term of this Agreement or after the expiration or termination thereof.

(iv) AIIL acknowledges and agrees that its right to use or authorise to the Joint Venture to use the said trade mark in relation to the Product is dependent at all times upon ABC's authorization and continued consent thereto.

(v) AIIL shall provide in all of the instruments creating and governing the existence and operation of itself and its Joint Venture in the territory, that in the event that this License Agreement with ABC shall expire or be terminated, without being replaced by a new trademark agreement with ABC, then AIIL and its Joint venture, shall, without expense to ABC, promptly do all acts and things which are necessary to change its trade mark to a mark which does not use the said trade mark or any mark which is confusingly similar therewith, or which is a translation or transliteration into any language of the said trade mark or of any mark which is confusingly similar therewith.

6. Use of mark, protection of mark

(a) Proper use

(i) ABC shall approve the form of representation of the Trademark and provide the same to AIIL. All the representations of the Trademark, which AIIL intends to use, shall be the exact copies or representations of those provided by ABC in regard to design colour and other details. AIIL shall submit to ABC the proposed representation of the Trademark to be used on the Product in .... (name of State), before applying the same.

(ii) AIIL shall use and cause the Joint Venture to use the Trademark in a manner that is consistent with the brand image and principles established by ABC. The mechanics to ensure consistency will be included in the guidelines relating to Marketing of the product branded with the Trademark as contained in ANNEXURE....................

(iii) The overall management of the brand image shall vest with ABC. AIIL will ensure that all advertising, marketing and promotional material using the trademark, prepared by AIIL and /or the Joint Venture, shall comply with the guidelines relating to the marketing of the product branded with the Trademark.

(iv) Except as provided by this agreement, AIIL shall not use the said trademark linked with, or in close association with any other trademark or trade name.

(b) Legends; disclaimer

(i) AIIL shall include on all products a trademark legend indicating that the Trademark is owned by ABC, is used under license from ABC, and a disclaimer that AIIL and not ABC has produced the products sold in the territory.

(ii) AIIL agrees to immediately effect any further amendments to the disclaimer if and as required by ABC.

(c) Limitation on use of Trademark

AIIL agrees not to make use of the trademark in connection with products other than the product specified in ANNEXURE....................

(d) Quality standards

(i) AIIL agrees to maintain and enforce, under periodic directions from ABC, with the Joint Venture and any or all sub-contracting parties, a consistent level of quality of products under the Trademark, in conformity with ABC's Standards of Quality Control as laid out in ANNEXURE...................., and substantially equivalent if not higher than the standard found in ABC's products and as well as that which is consistent with general industry standards.

(ii) AIIL understands that ABC may at any point of time during the term of the agreement upgrade the Standards of Quality to be exercised in respect of products branded with the Trademark, and agrees to incorporate the same and immediately act on such incorporation with respect to its own and the Joint Ventures or its sub-contractors' operations, insofar as they are limited to the manufacture, warehousing or storage of products to be branded with the trademark.

(iii) AIIL understands and agrees that failure to immediately act on any future upgradation of ABC's Standard of Quality will be construed by ABC to be a breach of the agreement, and ABC may in its discretion terminate the same in accordance with the relevant provisions of clause 9.

(iv) *Marketing Standards.*—AIIL undertakes to maintain the standards concerning the marketing of the Trademark on the product consistent with the standards laid down by ABC in its Marketing guidelines, ANNEXED AS........................

(e) Monitoring by ABC

(i) AIIL acknowledges that ABC has the right to monitor the use of the trademark in conjunction with the product by AIIL and its Joint Venture.

(ii) Representatives of ABC shall have a right but not an obligation, at all reasonable times, to inspect all aspects relating to the manufacturing, warehousing and distrbution of the product branded with the Trademark, as a part of appropriate quality control.

(iii) This right shall also extend to the Premises of the Joint Venture, its sub-contractors and all other affiliates of the Joint Venture involved in the Manufacture of the Products to be Branded with the Trademark

(f) AIIL's obligations

(i) AIIL agrees to make provisions consistent with the appropriate quality controls set out herewith, with the Joint Venture and any sub-contractors with whom AIIL or Joint Venture may contract and/or employ to manufacture the product, which is branded with the Trademark.

(ii) Should ABC ever notify AIIL that any aspect of the product under the Trademark fails to comply with the standards and specifications set out in ANNEXURE...................., AIIL shall promptly proceed to correct and cause the Joint Venture to correct such defects in accordance with ABC's instructions with respect thereto.

(iii) AIIL shall also refrain from using the Trademark on any defective product, unless such defect shall have been cured to the satisfaction of ABC. Such satisfaction shall be sought and received in writing in order to be effective.

(iv) Failure of AIIL to act in accordance with the aforesaid would constitute a breach of the agreement.

(g) Infringement

(i) ABC will pay all expenses in connection with the application and maintenance of the Trademark.

(ii) AIIL will notify ABC of any alleged infringement of the Trademark in the Territory. ABC on notification of such infringement may take such action within its own discretion, as it deems appropriate to protect the Trademark.

7. Indemnification by AIIL

(i) AIIL agrees to indemnify ABC and to hold it harmless from any and all liability, loss, damages, claims or causes of action including reasonable legal fees and expenses that may be incurred by ABC, arising out of claims by ABC against the joint venture.

(ii) AIIL shall be solely responsible for any claim by any third party arising from the quality of the product branded with the Trademark and distributed by its Joint Venture (notwithstanding ABC's right of Inspection and testing).

(iii) AIIL shall not use or consent to the use of the Trademark except in relation to the product as specified in ANNEXURE..........................

(iv) Failure on the part of AIIL to comply with clause 7(b) (iii) shall be construed a breach of the agreement.

8. ....
9.
10.
11.
12.
13.
14.

Reports, Records, Audits and Inspections

(a) Reports

AIIL undertakes to deliver to ABC, within .... days following the last day of each calendar quarter during the term of the agreement, a written report, in the format illustrated in ANNEXURE.................... showing in reasonable detail, sales of products branded with the trademark by AIIL and its Joint Venture, in such quarter, including, without limitation, the net receipts attributable thereto and any credits given by AIIL or its Joint Venture on previous sales.

(b) Records

AIIL shall maintain, during the term of the agreement, true and complete books and records relating to all sales of product branded with the Trademark either by itself or its Joint Venture.

(c) Audits and Inspections

During the Term of the agreement and for a period of one year thereafter, ABC shall have the right, at its own expense to have AIIL's and the Joint Venture's books and records examined by an independent auditor, in order to verify the Net receipts and sales of products branded with the Trademark.

15. Force Majeure

Neither party will be responsible for any failure to perform its obligations under this agreement due to causes beyond its control, including but not limited to acts of God, war, riot, embargoes, acts of civil or military authorities, fire, floods or accidents.

16. Waiver

No term or provision of this agreement shall be deemed waived, and no breach excused, unless such waiver or consent shall be in writing and signed by the party claimed to have waived or consented.

17. Independent contracts

The parties acknowledge and agree that they are dealing with each other hereunder as independent contractors. Nothing contained in the agreement shall be interpreted as constituting either party as the Joint Venture or partner of the other party or as conferring upon either party the power of authority to bind the other party in any transaction with third parties.

18. Notices

All notices and communications required or permitted under this agreement shall be in writing and any communication or delivery shall be deemed to have been duly made if actually delivered, or after three (3) days after mailing, if mailed by registered post addressed as follows:

If to the *Alpha* Battery Corporation

....

....

If to *Alpha* Industries India Limited

....

....

19. Approvals

(i) AIIL agrees that it will obtain any government approval required in .... (name of State) to enable this agreement to become effective or to enable any Payment thereunder to be made or any obligation thereunder to be observed or performed.

(ii) AIIL agrees that this agreement shall not come into force until that approval has been obtained.

20. Arbitration

All disputes arising in connection with the present agreement shall be finally settled by Arbitration by one or more arbitrators appointed in accordance with the said rules.

21. Termination

(a) This agreement shall terminate upon the following:—
- (i) Termination by either party in accordance with the provisions of section 15 (b) below; or
- (ii) A party's failure to comply with any material provision of this agreement in which case termination shall be subject to the provisions of section 15 (c) below.

(c) This license agreement may be terminated by either party by giving written notice of the intended termination to the other party in accordance with section 3 of this agreement.

(d) On failure or inability of either party to observe or perform a material contractual obligation under this agreement, the non-defaulting party may give written notice to the non-performing party specifying the material failure. The non-performing party shall have a period of .... days from the date of such notification to cure the default or remedy the inability to perform. If said party is unable to do so, the other party may terminate this agreement upon the expiration of .... days.

22. Effect of termination

(i) The termination of this agreement shall not release AIIL or the Joint Venture from their obligation to pay to ABC all royalties which shall have accrued prior to such termination and also shall not release AIIL from any obligations which it may have incurred as a result of such agreement.

(ii) AIIL and its Joint Venture, shall, in particular but without prejudice to the generality of the foregoing, cease in respect of the Trademark, to use the Trademark on its letterheads, packaging, vehicles or elsewhere.

(iii) AIIL and its Joint venture shall be permitted for a period of....................... months to take and fulfil orders of the inventory existing as of date of expiry. AIIL and its Joint Venture shall be liable to the licensor for the payments of royalties and all other payments for all inventories sold during this post-termination phase.

TRADE NAME LICENSE AGREEMENT

BETWEEN

ALPHA HEALTHCARE LIMITED

.... (address)

India

(hereinafter referred to as "*ALPHA*")

AND

BETA HEALTHCARE LTD.

.... (address)

India

(hereinafter referred to as "*BETA*")

Recitals

1. *Beta* Research, a corporation duly organised and existing under the laws of the Federal Republic of .... (State name) having its principal office at .... (address), ... (State name) (hereinafter referred to as "*Beta*

Research") and *Alpha*, a corporation duly organised and existing under the laws of India, have decided to establish a Joint Venture Company in India for the manufacturing and/or marketing of certain pharmaceutical and diagnostic products.

2. This Joint Venture Company has been established under the name "*Beta* Healthcare Limited". The trade names "*Beta*" and "*Theta*" are owned by and registered in India for *Beta* Research and *Alpha*, respectively. *Beta* Research and *Alpha* have agreed upon the general principles of their co-operation with respect to the establishment and business activities of *Beta* in a Joint Venture Agreement dated .... (hereinafter referred to as the "Joint Venture Agreement").

3. In the internal relationship between *Beta* Research and *Beta*, the general principles of the co-operation between *Beta* Research and *Beta* have been laid down in a Distribution and Manufacturing License Agreement (hereinafter referred to as the "License Agreement") as well as a Supply Agreement (hereinafter referred to as the "Supply Agreement").

4. The Parties to this Agreement now wish to establish a legal basis for the right of the Joint Venture Company *Beta* to use the part of the company name "....................". Further, the Parties wish to further concretise their rights and duties with respect to the Company name "*Beta*" of the Joint Venture Company.

5. For the above reasons, *Alpha* and *Beta* agree as follows; capitalised terms not defined under this Agreement refer to the definitions as given in the Joint Venture and License Agreements.

Article 1: Trade Name License

1.1 *Trade Name License.*—Subject to all terms and conditions of this Agreement, ... to *Beta*, and *Beta* accepts, the non-exclusive, non-transferable and non-sub-licensable right and license during the term of this Agreement (i) to use and continue to use the trade name "...................." in its corporate name; and (ii) to carry on and to continue to carry on business under such corporate name including the trade name "....................".

1.2 *Limitations.*—The right and license granted by *Alpha* to *Beta* as set forth in Art. 1.1 hereof is restricted to India and shall not extend beyond such territory except with the prior written approval of *Alpha*, in particular as set forth under the Joint Venture Agreement and the License Agreement. Further, the license hereunder does not include any rights other than those expressly granted in this Agreement.

Beta shall not market, distribute, sell nor cause any Third Party (including, without limitation, its distributors) to market, sell or distribute Products marked with, or otherwise use or caused to be used, the trade name which includes the words "*Beta*" or "...................." that are not within the scope of such territory as agreed under this Article.

Article 2: Intellectual Property Rights in the Trade Name "...................."

Beta acknowledges and agrees that by carrying on business and/or using the corporate and/or trade or business name including the word "....................", it has not acquired and does not and will not acquire at any time hereafter any right or title of any nature whatsoever in the word "...................." either as a name or as a part of the name or otherwise and agrees that it will not at any time take advantage of any legal possibility to acquire rights of its own in and to the word "...................." and renounces any such rights.

Article 3: Use of the Trade Name "...................."

Beta undertakes not to take any measure that might jeopardise the exclusive right of *Alpha* in and to the word "...................." whether as a trademark or as a part of its trade name, and for this purpose it will have regard to any directions given by *Alpha*, and abstain from any actions which may dilute or otherwise adversely affect such right.

Article 4: Intellectual Property Rights in the Trade Name "*Beta*"

4.1 *General Principle.*—Subject to the grant of a related license by *Beta* Research to the trade name "*Beta*", *Alpha* authorises *Beta* to apply for and obtain trademark protection for the trade name "*Beta*" in India as well as the countries covered by the co-operation under the Joint Venture Agreement and License Agreement.

4.2 *Limitations.*—*Beta* undertakes to use the trade name "...................." only in connection with the trade name "*Beta*". *Beta* further undertakes to use the trade name and trademark "*Beta*" strictly for purposes of the implementation of the Joint Venture Agreement, the License Agreement and the Supply Agreement, and not to use such trademark for any other purposes.

Beta shall not use the trade name "...................." in any company or trade name or in combination with any other trademark, service mark, words, symbol, letter or design or on any product other than the Products manufactured by *Beta*, except with the prior written approval of *Alpha*. *Beta* shall use the word "...................." only in the form and manner as authorised under this Agreement and approved in advance by *Alpha*.

Beta acknowledges that this Agreement is conditional upon its not using the trade name "...................." in a manner that is inconsistent with or outside the scope of the terms and conditions of this Agreement and any use in a manner that is inconsistent with or outside the scope of this Agreement shall constitute a material breach of this Agreement.

4.3 *Cancellation.* Subject to the conditions as further described in Art. 7.4 hereof, *Beta* shall cancel the trademark "*Beta*".

Article 5: Defence of Trade Name "*Beta*", Indemnification

5.1 *Notification of Infringements.*—*Beta* agrees to notify *Alpha* promptly in writing of any conflicting use of or application for registration of either the trade name "*Beta*" or the trademark "*Beta*" or of any trademark confusingly similar thereto, or of any known or alleged infringements as well as of unfair competition involving the trade name "*Alpha*" or the trademark "*Beta*" which shall come to its intention.

5.2 *Defence of Trademark Beta.*—*Beta* shall be responsible for the defence of the trademark "*Beta*" and shall defend any proceeding, claim, lawsuit whatsoever, and pay all liability, loss, cost or expense of any nature (including, without limitation, attorney's fees) which may arise or be asserted by Third Parties in connection with the use of the trademark "*Beta*" under this Agreement. *Alpha* undertakes to co-operate with *Beta* and to render *Beta* its best reasonable assistance in the defence of the trademark "*Beta*" free of charge. Any damages and costs recovered shall be for *Beta*'s sole benefit.

5.3 *Rights of Alpha.*—In the event that *Beta* fails to defend the trademark "*Beta*" within sixty (60) days of *Alpha*'s request to do so, *Alpha* shall be entitled to do so at its own expense in coordination with *Beta* Research, and in co-operation and with the best reasonable assistance of *Beta*, such assistance of *Beta* to be rendered free of charge. In this case, any damages and costs recovered shall be for the benefit of *Beta* Research and *Alpha*, as agreed upon by and between *Beta* Research and *Alpha*.

Article 6: Term and Termination

6.1 *Regular Term.*—This Agreement shall come into effect on (insert effective date) and shall continue in full force and effect for the lifetime of the Joint Venture Agreement (the "Regular Term"), commencing from said date and continuing for the Regular Term unless terminated early in accordance with the following provisions, and subject to Article 5.2 with respect to the exercise by *Beta* Research of its Spin-off-Option.

6.2 *Exercise by Beta Research of its Spin-off-Option under the Joint Venture Agreement.*—As further described under Article 9.2 hereof and in line with the provisions of Article 8, in particular Article 8.2 of the Joint Venture Agreement, the following provisions shall apply in case of the exercise by *Beta* Research of its Spin-off-Option under Article 8.1 of the Joint Venture Agreement: The provisions of this Agreement shall, in case of such exercise by *Beta* Research of its Spin-off-Option, continue to apply in the relationship between *Beta* Research or its permitted successors or assigns as shareholder of M&M JVC or R&D JVC on the one side and M&M JVC and/or R&D JVC on the other side; in such case, this Agreement shall apply independently to both M&M JVC and/or R&D JVC, and the Regular Term of this Agreement as defined under Article 6.1 shall run independently for M&M JVC and/or R&D JVC, unless terminated early for M&M JVC and/or R&D JVC in accordance with the following provisions.

6.3 *Termination in Case of Bankruptcy.*—The period of this Agreement shall determine forthwith and without notice if *Beta* passes a resolution to go into liquidation or if a winding-up order is made against *Beta* or if *Beta* suffers appointment of a receiver of the whole or any part of its assets or makes any arrangement or composition with its creditors whatsoever.

6.4 *Termination for Breach.*—*Alpha* shall be entitled to terminate the period of this Agreement without notice period in the event of any breach of the provisions of this Agreement by *Beta* if such breach is not cured within sixty (60) days after written notice from *Alpha* requesting *Beta* to comply with this Agreement.

6.5 *Termination for Exclusion from Participation in Beta.*—*Alpha* shall be entitled to terminate this Agreement without notice period in the event that the shareholding of *Alpha* in *Beta* is for any reason whatsoever reduced below 50 % of the total issued shares.

6.6 *Termination for Exclusion from Participation in Management or Control of BETA.*—*Alpha* shall be entitled to terminate this Agreement without notice period if *Alpha* is effectively excluded from participation in the management or control of *Beta* as provided under Art. 10 and Art. 11 of the Joint Venture Agreement, in particular in case of any restrictions affecting the members of the board of directors to be appointed by *Alpha* and the right of *Alpha* to appoint the Managing Director of the Company.

6.7 *Notice of Termination.*—Notice of termination shall be given in writing by telefax, telegram or registered airmail letter.

6.8 *Survival of Obligations.*—The termination of the period of this Agreement shall be without prejudice to the continuation in force thereafter of the provisions of Art. 7 hereof.

Article 7: Rights and Duties of the Parties upon Termination

7.1 *General Principle.*—The rights and duties of the Parties upon termination as hereinafter described shall, in case of a termination prior to the exercise by *Beta* Research of its Spin-off-Option under Art. 8 of the Joint Venture Agreement, apply with respect to *Beta*; following the exercise by *Beta* Research of such Spin-off-Option, the termination of this Agreement shall affect either M&M JVC or R&D JVC or, in case the reasons of termination persist to both Companies, both M&M JVC and R&D JVC.

7.2 *General Duties of BETA following Termination with Respect to the Trademark "BETA".*—*Beta* or M&M JVC and/or R&D JVC, as the case may be, undertake and agree that upon the termination of this Agreement it (they) shall, subject to Art. 7.5 of this Agreement and Art. 18.6.1 of the License Agreement,

7.2.1 As and when requested by *Alpha* to transfer to *Alpha* such rights if any as may accrue to *Beta* or M&M JVC and/or R&D JVC, respectively, in connection with this Agreement notwithstanding Art. 2 or any other provision of this Agreement;

7.2.2 Not take any measure that might jeopardise the exclusive rights of *Alpha* in and to the business name "...................." whether as a trademark or as a part of its trade name;

7.2.3 Forthwith cease to trade under any trade name which includes the word "....................";

7.2.4 Forthwith cease to trade under any corporate name which includes the word "....................";

7.2.5 Forthwith change any trade or business name of *Beta* including the word "...................." or any other words reasonably capable of confusion therewith;

7.2.6 Forthwith make the necessary arrangements for a shareholders' meeting to pass a Special Resolution to change its corporate name to a name not including the word "...................." and to obtain the requisite approval of the Government of India to such change of name;

7.2.7 Forthwith discontinue any other use of the word "..................." as a trade or business name or as a part of a trade or business name.

7.3 *Termination of Right to use the Trademark and Business Name "...................".*—After the termination of the period of this Agreement, *Beta* or M&M JVC and/or R&D JVC, respectively, shall not use as trade or business name or as part thereof the word "..................." or any other word bearing any resemblance or similarity therewith.

7.4 *Cancellation of Trademark "Beta".*—Immediately following the termination of this Agreement prior to the exercise by *Beta* Research of its Spin-off-Option under Article 8 of the Joint Venture Agreement, *Beta* shall have the trademark "*Beta*" cancelled in all countries where such trademark has been registered. Likewise, immediately following the termination of this Agreement after the exercise by *Beta* Research of its Spin-off-Option under Art. 8 of the License Agreement, M&M JVC and/or R&D JVC, as the case may be, shall likewise have such trademark cancelled, to the extent that the terminated party (M&M JVC or R&D JVC respectively) owns such trademark. To the extent that M&M JVC or R&D JVC, as the case may be, have acquired rights to such trademark in form of a trademark license, such trademark license shall automatically terminate with effect from the termination of this Agreement.

7.5 *Sell-Out Rights.*—In accordance with Article 18.6.1 of the License Agreement, *Beta* or M&M JVC, as the case may be, shall be entitled to sell-out stocks of goods held by or on behalf of *Beta* or M&M JVC respectively, at the date of the termination of this Agreement or sealed packages or containers which are marked with the corporate, business or trade name which includes the words "..................." or "*Beta*" notwithstanding that the said stocks or the said sealed packages or containers are so marked, to the extent that *Beta* Research grants *Beta* related sell-out rights under Article 18.6.1 of the License Agreement.

Article 8: Governing Law and Arbitration

With respect to governing law and arbitration, Article 19 of the License Agreement shall apply, which is hereby integrated into this Agreement by reference.

Article 9: General Provisions

9.1 *Assignment.*—This Agreement may not be assigned by either Party hereto to a Third Party without the other Party's prior written consent. *Alpha* shall be entitled to assign this Agreement to an Affiliate of *Alpha* with *Beta*'s prior written consent, such consent not to be unreasonably withheld.

9.2 *Successors and Assigns.*—This Agreement shall be binding upon and inure to the benefit of the Parties hereto and their successors and permitted assigns. The Parties are in agreement that, should *Beta* Research exercise its Spin-off-Option under Article 8.1 of the Joint Venture Agreement, M&M JVC and/or R&D JVC as further described under Article 8.1 of the Joint Venture Agreement shall be successor or, as the case may be, permitted assign of *Beta* with respect to the rights and duties of *Beta* under this Agreement in accordance with the principles as further laid down in Article 8.1 of the Joint Venture Agreement.

9.3 *Severability.*—All stipulations contained in this Agreement shall be so construed as not to infringe the provisions of any applicable law, but if any such stipulation does infringe any such provision of any applicable law, such stipulation shall be deemed to be void and severable. The Parties undertake to replace invalid stipulations or fill any gap with valid stipulations.

DEED OF ASSIGNMENT

THIS DEED OF ASSIGNMENT dated.................... day of .... 20....., BETWEEN *Alpha* (hereinafter referred to as the "Assignor"), a corporation incorporated under the laws of.................... (name of country), with offices at.................... (name of the place) AND *Beta* (hereinafter referred to as the "Assignee"), a company organised and existing under the laws of.................... (Name of the Country), with offices at.................... (name of the place).

WHEREAS, the Assignor is the proprietor of all rights, title and interest in and to the trade mark, including the goodwill accruing thereto, details of which is set out in the First Schedule hereto (hereinafter referred to as the "Trade Mark").

WHEREAS, a global deed of assignment with respect to the trademark was executed between the Assignor and Assignee on the.................... (Give Data) (hereinafter referred to as 'The Date').

WHEREAS, keeping in view the requirements of .... Trademarks Regulations, the Assignor and Assignee have agreed to execute an assignment deed for the assignment of the trademark in.................... (Name of the Country), which shall be an affirmation of the global assignment deed and shall extend to the territory of ....

WHEREAS, the Assignor and Assignee hereby agree that the present deed of assignment in respect of the Trademark shall be deemed to have taken effect from the date of global assignment of Trademark.

WHEREAS, the Assignor and Assignee hereby agree that in event of conflict between the global assignment deed and the assignment deed executed in .... (name of the country where excuted), the assignment deed executed in .... (name of the country where excuted) shall prevail to the extent of the territory of.................... (name of the country).

WHEREAS, in this Deed of Assignment any reference to the "Trade Mark" and any reference to any goodwill or business is limited to the same, in so far as they relate to the goods set out in the Second Schedule hereto (hereinafter referred to as goods).

WHEREAS, the expression "the Assignor" and "the Assignee", shall include their successors-in-interest and assigns as applicable.

NOW THIS DEED WITNESSETH THAT, in consideration of .... (foreign amount) the receipt of which is duly acknowledged:

the Assignor hereby assigns, to the Assignee with effect from the Date, all rights, title and interest in and to the Trade Mark, *together with* the goodwill of the business in which the Trade Mark has been used and the goodwill appurtenant to, associated with and symbolised by the Trade Mark and all the rights which the Assignor may have acquired through the use and/or the reputation and/or the application for the registration and/or registration of the Trade Mark by or on behalf of the Assignor and/or predecessors of the Assignor and all rights of use and other benefits and advantages in any manner accruing to the Assignor and/or its predecessors, including without limitation, rights derived by reason of the use, reputation and ownership of the Trade Mark which have or are deemed to have vested in or which have or which are deemed to have enured to the benefit of the Assignor.

IN WITNESS WHEREOF the parties hereto have executed this deed on this day of...................., 20.....

Alpha (Assignor)

NAME:....................
DESIGNATION:....................

WITNESS 1:
NAME:
WITNESS 2:
NAME:

Beta Company Limited, (Assignee)

NAME:....................
DESIGNATION:....................

WITNESS 1:
NAME:
WITNESS 2:
NAME

In the presence of

....

Notary Public

THE FIRST SCHEDULE

MARK	APPLICATION NO.	CLASS
....	....	....

THE SECOND SCHEDULE

"Cigarettes, tobacco, tobacco products, smokers' requisites, lighters and matches" falling in international class 34.

PRECEDENTS ON COPYRIGHT (MEDIA ENTERTAINMENT)

WRITER EMPLOYMENT AGREEMENT

Agreement effective .... (date), between *Alpha* Movies Private Limited, a Company incorporated under the Companies Act, 1956, and having its registered office at .... (address) ("Production Company"),

AND

.... (name), S/o...................., R/o.. ("Writer").

1. Employment

Production Company employs Writer to perform and Writer agrees to perform writing services for Production Company's proposed motion picture currently entitled "...................." ("The Picture"), based on the historical events that took place in India in .... (year). Writer shall write dialogues for the Picture in Hindi ("....................").

(a) *Use of Work.*—Production Company has sole, absolute and unfettered discretion to use or not use the Work and/or make any changes in, deletions from or additions to the Work.

(b) *Underlying Property.*—If the Work is based on an original idea or material ("Property") created by Writer, Writer hereby grants Production Company the same rights in the Property as Production Company is acquiring hereunder in the Work. The compensation payable to Writer pursuant to Paragraph 5 includes payment for said rights in the Property and for the writing services of Writer hereunder.

2. Delivery

Writer agrees to complete and deliver each Form of Work and the Work including any changes and revisions required by Production Company as follows:

Hindi Dialogues due by.................... (date).

3. Performance Standards

All of Writer's services shall be rendered promptly in a diligent, conscientious, artistic and efficient manner and Writer shall devote Writer's entire time and attention and best talents and abilities to the services to be rendered, either alone or in collaboration with others. Writer's services shall be rendered in such manner as Production Company may reasonably direct pursuant to the instructions, suggestions and ideas of, and under the control of, and at the times and places reasonably required by, Production Company's duly authorized representatives. Writer, as and when reasonably requested by Production Company, shall consult with Production Company's duly authorized representatives and shall be available for conferences with such representatives for such purposes at such times and places during Writer's employment as may be required by such representatives.

4. Compensation

Conditioned upon Writer's full performance of all of Writer's obligations hereunder, Production Company will pay Writer as full compensation for all services rendered and rights granted as set out hereinbelow. This payment is made for Work created during the course of Writer's employment for the sole purpose of writing dialogues for the Picture and shall constitute a complete buyout of all the rights that Writer may be entitled to exercise. Writer shall not be eligible for any further payments for rendering his services hereunder.

Fixed compensation: Rs. ...., which shall be paid as follows:

i. Rs. ....upon execution of this Agreement.

ii. Rs. ....upon delivery of the last Form of Work due to the Production Company.

5. Warranties, Representations, Indemnities

(a) *Writer Warranties and Representations.*—Writer warrants and represents that each Form of Work and the Work shall be wholly original with Writer, except as to matters within the public domain and except as to material inserted by Writer pursuant to specific instructions of Production Company, and shall not infringe upon or violate the copyright, trademark rights, rights of privacy or publicity of, or constitute a libel or slander against, or violate any common law or any other rights of, any person, firm or corporation.

(b) *Writer's Indemnities.*—Writer shall indemnify Production Company and Production Company's licensees and assigns and its or their officers, agents and employees, from all liabilities, actions, suits or other claims arising out of any breach by Writer of Writer's warranties and representations and out of the use by Production Company of the Work and from reasonable attorneys' fees and costs in defending against the same. The foregoing shall apply only to material created or furnished by Writer, and shall not extend to changes or additions made therein by Production Company, or to claims for defamation or invasion of the privacy of any person unless Writer knowingly uses the name or personality of such person or should have known, in the exercise of reasonable prudence, that such person would or might claim that such person's personality was used in the Work.

(c) *Production Company's Indemnities.*—Production Company shall indemnify Writer to the same extent that Writer indemnifies Production Company hereunder, as to any material supplied by Production Company to Writer for incorporation into the Work.

(d) *Notice and Pendency of Claims.*—The party receiving notice of any claim or action subject to indemnity hereunder shall promptly notify the other party.

6. Ownership

As Writer's employer, Production Company shall solely and exclusively own throughout the world in perpetuity all rights of every kind and nature in the Work, including the right to use the Work in sequels, remakes, etc. and to disseminate it through any media now known or hereinafter devised, and all of the results and proceeds thereof in whatever stage of completion as may exist from time to time, together with the rights generally known as the "moral rights of authors" and more specifically termed "special right of authors" as incorporated under section 57 of the Copyright Act, 1957. Writer acknowledges that the Work is being written by Writer for use as a Motion Picture and that each Form of Work is being written by Writer in the course of Writer's employment by Production Company, and, therefore, Production Company shall be the author and first owner of copyright in the Work.

7. Notices/Payment

(a) *To Writer.*—All notices from Production Company to Writer may be given in writing by mailing the notice to Writer, postage prepaid, or at Production Company's option, Production Company may deliver such notice to Writer personally, either orally or in writing. The date of mailing or of personal delivery shall be deemed to be the date of service. Payments and written notice to Writer shall be sent to Writer at....................(address)

(b) *To Production Company.*—All notices from Writer to Production Company shall be given in writing by mail, message, or cable, addressed as indicated below. The date of receipt of mail, message, cable, telex shall be deemed to be the date of service. Notice to the Production Company shall be sent to .... (address).

(c) *Change of Address.*—The address of Writer and of Production Company set forth herein may be changed to such other address as Writer or Production Company may hereafter specify by written notice given to the other Party.

8. Assignment

This Agreement is non-assignable by Writer. This Agreement shall insure to the benefit of Production Company's successors, assignees, licensees and grantees and associated, affiliated and subsidiary companies. Production Company and any subsequent assignee may freely assign this Agreement, in whole or in part, to any party provided that such party assumes and agrees in writing to keep and perform all of the executory obligations of Production Company hereunder.

9. Name and Likeness

Production Company shall have the right to use and permit others (including any exhibitor or sponsor of the Program or Series) to use Writer's name and likeness for the purpose of advertising and publicizing the Work, any Programme based on the Work, and any of exhibitor's or sponsor's products and services, but not as an endorsement or testimonial.

10. Pay or Play

The rights in this Paragraph shall be in addition to and shall not in any way diminish or detract from Production Company's rights as otherwise set forth. Production Company shall not be obligated to use Writer's services, nor use the results and product of Writers services, nor produce, release, distribute, exhibit, advertise, exploit or otherwise make use of the Programme. Production Company may at any time, without legal justification or excuse, elect not to use Writer's services or to have any further obligations to Writer under this Agreement. If Production Company elects not to use Writer's services pursuant to this Paragraph, Writer shall be paid one-half of the Compensation set forth in Paragraph..................... if Writer performs those services.

11. Credit

The writing credits shall read: "Hindi dialogues by .... (name)" (or another name chosen by Writer), if a substantial amount of Writer's work is incorporated in the Picture and Writer shall receive sole/shared credit.

12. Conditions Affecting or Related to Compensation

(a) *Method of Payment.*—All compensation which shall become due to Writer shall be paid by Production Company by cheque and sent to Writer at the address provided in the Notices and Payments provision of this Agreement.

(b) *Governmental Limitation.*—No withholding, deduction, reduction or limitation of compensation by Production Company which is required or authorized by law ("Governmental Limitation") shall be a breach by Production Company or relieve Writer from Writer's obligations. Payment of compensation as permitted pursuant to the Governmental Limitation shall continue while such Governmental Limitation is in effect and shall be deemed to constitute full performance by Production Company of its obligations respecting the payment of compensation. Notwithstanding the foregoing, if at such time as the Governmental Limitation is no longer in effect there is compensation remaining unpaid to Writer, Production Company shall cooperate with Writer in connection with the processing of any applications related to the payment of such unpaid compensation and Production Company shall pay such compensation to Writer at such times as Production Company is legally permitted to do so.

(c) *Garnishment/Attachment.*—If Production Company shall be required, because of the service of any garnishment, attachment, writ of execution, or lien, or by the terms of any contract or assignment executed by Writer, to withhold, or to pay to any other Party all or any portion of the compensation due to the Writer, the withholding or payment of such compensation or any portion thereof in accordance with the requirements of any such attachment, garnishment, writ of execution, lien, contract or assignment shall not be construed as a breach by Production Company.

(d) *Overpayment/Offset.*—If Production Company makes any overpayment to Writer for any reason or if Writer is indebted to Production Company for any reason, Writer shall pay Production Company such overpayment or indebtedness on demand, or at the election of Production Company, Production Company may deduct and retain for its own account an amount equal to all or any part of such overpayment or indebtedness from any sums that may be due or become due or payable by Production Company to Writer or for the account of Writer and such deduction or retention shall not be construed as a breach by Production Company.

13. Arbitration

This Agreement shall be interpreted in accordance with the laws of India, applicable to agreements executed and to be wholly performed therein. Any controversy or claim arising out of or in relation to this Agreement or the validity, construction or performance of this Agreement, or the breach thereof, shall be resolved by arbitration in accordance with the Arbitration and Conciliation Act (as amended from time to time). The parties agree hereto that they will abide by and perform any award rendered in any arbitration conducted pursuant hereto, that any court having jurisdiction thereof may issue a judgment based upon such award and that the prevailing party in such arbitration and/or confirmation proceeding shall be entitled to recover its reasonable attorneys' fees and expenses. The arbitration will be held in .... (place) and any award shall be final, binding and non-appealable.

IN WITNESS WHEREOF, the parties hereto have signed this Agreement as of the day and year first above written.

"Production Company"   "Writer"

.... (name), ... (name)

Director

on behalf of *Alpha* Movies Private Limited

SOUND RECORDING AND DISTRIBUTION LICENSE AGREEMENT

AGREEMENT MADE AS OF ....20.....

BETWEEN

1. *Alpha* (hereinafter called "Licensor")

AND

2. *Beta* (hereinafter called "Licensee").

IN CONSIDERATION of the mutual promises herein contained, it is agreed:

1. Definitions

"Conversion costs" the costs of converting the Licensed Performance from the Master Recording to use in Records, including, without limitation, re-recording costs, mixing and transfer costs, editing, mastering, equalizing and reference dubs costs, etc.

"Exclusive right" a right granted under this Agreement which the grantor will not itself exercise and will not authorize other persons to exercise

"Master Recording(s)" any original recording, whether on magnetic tape or wire, a lacquer or wax disc, or any other substance or material, whether now known or unknown, which is used in the manufacture of Records

"Person" and *"party"* Include any individual, corporation, partnership, association or other organized group of persons or legal successors or representatives of the foregoing

"Record" a device, at any speed, on any material, now or hereafter known, including, without limitation, disc, wire, tape and film, utilized for the reproduction of sound only

"Suggested retail list price" shall be deemed to be that price which Licensee sells its records to large variety chain stores, record stores, and other like retail stores through normal retail channels in the Territory.

2. Grant

A. Licensor hereby grants to Licensee for the Term and in the Territory the sole and Exclusive right with respect to the Master Recording entitled .... performed by the Artiste (hereinafter called the "Licensed Performance"), to reproduce, manufacture, distribute, sell, communicate to the public, promote and advertise the Licensed Performance.

B. Without limiting the generality of the foregoing, the rights hereby granted by Licensor to Licensee include the following:—

   (a) the Exclusive right to reproduce, manufacture, sell, lease, license, advertise, or otherwise use the Licensed Performance by any and all means and media now known or hereafter devised.

   (b) the Exclusive right to release, advertise, and sell Records embodying the Licensed Performance, and to permit others to do so.

   (c) the Exclusive right to use and allow others to use the name, likeness and biography of the Artiste whose performance is embodied in the Licensed Performance in connection with the advertising, publicity, distribution and sale of Records manufactured therefrom.

   (d) the Exclusive right to perform publicly, or to communicate to the public the Licensed Performance by any and all means and media now known or hereafter devised.

   (e) the Exclusive right to synchronize the Licensed Performance or a portion thereof, in timed-relation with an audiovisual work, including, but not limited to a music video ("A/V work"), and in any and all trailers, radio, television and, other promotions and advertisements of the A/V work, as the same may be exploited in any and all means and media now known or hereafter devised. Where Licensee is responsible for the creation and/or commissioning of such A/V work, the copyright in that A/V work shall vest in Licensee.

   (f) the Exclusive right to combine the Licensed Performance or part thereof together with other Master Recordings of third parties ("third party masters") and to reproduce, publicly perform and distribute such combination of the Licensed Performance along with third party masters by any and all means and media now known or hereafter devised.

   (g) the right to refrain from performing any of the acts or exercising any of the rights granted in this clause 2.

   (h) the right to permit subsidiaries, affiliates, and sub-licensees of Licensee to perform any of the acts or exercise any of the rights granted in this clause 2.

3. Territory

The rights granted herein are exercisable by Licensee in the "Territory" of India, its territories and possessions.

4. Duplication of Licensed Performances

Licensor shall deliver or cause to be delivered to Licensee within 10 days after receipt of a request by Licensee (without charge) any and all materials required by Licensee to enable Licensee or any contractor or sub-contractor of Licensee, to duplicate the Licensed Performance which may be specified by Licensee.

5. Payment

Licensee agrees to pay to Licensor, subject to the regulatory and other government approvals, the following royalties in respect of the sale of Records containing the Licensed Performance:

(a) A royalty at the rate of ten percent (10%) of the suggested retail list price from time to time in respect of net sales of Records embodying the Licensed Performance through normal retail channels in the Territory. As used herein, the term "through normal retail channels in the Territory" shall refer to sales of records by the Licensee through its customary distributors for resale at full price through record and other retail stores;

(b) The royalty payable to Licensor with respect to sales under clause 5(a) above shall be reduced, computed and determined subject to packaging deductions, free goods and discount reductions. Promotional records, free/bonus records as well as excerpts from the recordings used by Licensee for, *inter alia*, publicity and advertising purposes shall be exempted from any royalty payment.

(c) Notwithstanding anything to the contrary contained herein, the royalty payable to Licensor with respect to sales of any Record not consisting exclusively of the Licensed Performance shall be prorated on the basis of the number of royalty-bearing third party masters contained thereon. Royalties on the Master Recording embodying the Licensed Performance, together with the performances of one or more other royalty bearing artists shall be prorated on the basis of the number of artists (including Artiste) whose performances are embodied on such Master Recordings.

(d) Notwithstanding any of the foregoing, no record royalties shall be payable to Licensor unless and until all "conversion costs" relating to the inclusion of the Licensed Performance on any Record, including any Record not consisting exclusively of the Licensed Performance, shall be recouped by the Licensee, from royalties payable to Licensor hereunder. Following such recoupment, Licensor's royalties shall be paid on a prospective basis (*i.e.*, on all Records sold thereafter).

6. Other Obligations

Licensee is responsible for all promotional costs of the Licensed Performance. Licensee has the sole discretion to take decisions with regard to the method, manner and costs of carrying out such promotions.

7. Term

The term of this agreement shall be for a period of twenty-five (25) years commencing upon the date hereof (the "Term").

The Licensee may at its option terminate this Agreement by notice in writing of thirty (30) days to the Licensor.

The Licensor may terminate this Agreement by notice in writing of Ninety (90) days to the Licensee.

For a period one year following the expiration of this agreement for any reason whatsoever Licensee:

(a) shall have the right to sell all Records in its possession which were manufactured by Licensee containing the Licensed Performance; and

(b) all Master Recordings and any other material used in the manufacture of the Records involved herein in the hands of Licensee shall be destroyed by Licensee, and upon written request therefor, a statement regarding said destruction shall be furnished by Licensee.

8. Accounting

Payments by Licensee to Licensor of royalties due pursuant to clause 5 hereof shall be made semi-annually, within sixty (60) days following June, 10th and December, 31st, and each such payment shall be accompanied by a statement setting forth in reasonable detail the computation of the amount thereof. Licensee may establish a reasonable reserve for returns of records shipped. Such reserves shall become payable on the payment date immediately following the second accounting period following the period in which they were established. All royalty statements and all other accounts rendered by Licensee to Licensor shall be binding upon Licensor and not subject to any objection by Licensor for any reason unless specific objection in writing, stating the basis thereof is given to Licensee within seven (7) business days from the date rendered. Licensor shall have the right to appoint a certified public accountant or attorney to examine the books and records of Licensee as the same pertain to this Agreement, provided that such examination shall take place during normal business hours, at Licensee's regular place of business, on reasonable written notice, not more than once in each calendar year or as to any statement and at Licensors' sole cost and expense.

9. Representations and warranties of Licensor

Licensor represents, warrants and agrees that:

(a) Licensor has all necessary authorization, corporate and otherwise, to enter into this agreement and to fully perform the terms hereof, and during the term hereof it shall not be under any liability, restriction or prohibition, either pursuant to agreement or pursuant to any statute, law, order, rule or regulation of any governmental authority, in respect to its right to enter into this agreement and to full perform its terms;

(b) The Licensed Performances were recorded and otherwise prepared in all respects in accordance with the rules and regulations of all unions and similar associations having jurisdiction.

(c) All necessary permissions for the recording, the reproduction and the licensing to Licensee hereunder of all Licensed Performances have been obtained by Licensor. Exercise by Licensee of the rights granted hereunder shall not infringe the rights (whether pursuant to agreement, statute, law order, rule or regulation, or otherwise) of any third party or in any other way contravene any applicable statute, law, order, rule or regulation.

(d) Licensor has all rights necessary to manufacture, advertise, sell or distribute records containing the Licensed Performance for the Term in Territory and hereby grants said rights to Licensee and Licensee shall be under no liability, prohibition, restriction or obligation whatsoever with respect to the manufacture, advertisement, distribution or sale of Records containing the Licensed Performance.

(e) Each person or company who has rendered any service or provided any materials in connection with, or has otherwise contributed in any way, to the making of Licensor's master recordings of the Licensed Performances or the rights granted herein, had the right to grant such rights or render such services or furnish such materials; Licensor warrants and represents that such persons were not bound on the date such performances were recorded or any other date by any agreement with any other person which would in any way prevent or restrict their performance for purposes of making phonograph records of such performances in accordance with the provisions of this Agreement. Licensor will promptly upon request therefor, duly cause to be executed and delivered to Licensee such documents or instruments which in judgment may be deemed necessary or expedient to carry out or effectuate the purpose or intent of this agreement.

(f) Licensor has informed..................... and worldwide distributors for Licensor, that it is entering into this agreement; and both companies have approved of and acknowledged Licensor's right, without any restriction whatsoever, to enter into this agreement; and Licensee shall not be obligated to make any payments of any kind or character whatsoever to..................... or to any person, firm, or entity other than Licensor.

10. Representations and warranties of Licensee

Licensee represents, warrants and agrees that:

(a) Licensee has all necessary authorization, corporate and otherwise to enter into this agreement and to fully perform the terms hereof, and it is not, and during the term hereof it shall not be, under liability, restriction or prohibition, either pursuant to agreement or pursuant to any statute, law, order, rule or regulation of any governmental authority, in respect of its right to enter into this agreement and fail to perform its terms.

(b) Licensee shall not sell or otherwise distribute any of the Licensed Performance, except pursuant to the terms of this agreement.

11. Indemnification

Licensor shall indemnify, save and hold the Licensee harmless from loss or damage arising out of or connected with any claim by a third party which is inconsistent with any of the recitals, agreements, representations or warranties herein. Licensor shall reimburse the Licensee on demand for any payment made by the Licensee at any time after the date hereof in respect of any liability or claim to which this indemnity relates and which has resulted in an adverse final judgment against the Licensee, or a settlement approved by both parties, in which it is determined that the ultimate liability is that of the Licensor. Prompt notice shall be given to the Licensor of any claim to which this indemnity relates and the Licensor shall have the right, at its own expense to control the defense thereof; provided that:

(a) the Licensee shall have the right to cooperate in such defense at its own expense; and

(b) if the Licensor shall not exercise its right to control the defense, then the Licensee shall, in addition to any other indemnity hereunder, be reimbursed for its reasonable expenses (including attorney's fees), if any, incurred in the defense if it shall be determined that the ultimate liability is that of the Licensor.

12. *Force Majeure*

If it shall be impossible or illegal for Licensor substantially to perform hereunder or for Licensee substantially to manufacture, advertise and/or distribute records hereunder, in either case for a temporary period of not more than six months, due to strike, flood or other catastrophe or due to any governmental law, order or regulation, then such impossibility shall not constitute a default hereunder and each of the provisions hereof shall continue with full force and effect; except that, the terms of this agreement (and any renewal term) shall be extended for a term equal to the duration of such temporary impossibility. At the conclusion of such six (6) month period, either party may terminate this agreement upon thirty (30) days written notice to the other.

13. Assignment

Either party, at its election, may assign any or all of its rights under this agreement to any corporation, company, joint venture or other business, if as a condition to any such assignment, the assignee shall be bound by all the terms and conditions of this agreement; and provided further that, such assignment shall not release or alter any undertaking or obligation hereunder of the assignor to the extent not performed by the assignee. Licensor shall not sell, assign license or otherwise transfer any of its rights with resect to the Licensed Performance, unless the assignee thereof or group of assignees thereof, whether or not affiliated or otherwise related, agree in writing to be bound by all of the terms of this agreement. Subject to the foregoing, this agreement shall be binding upon and inure to the benefit of all successors and assigns of the parties hereto.

14. Dispute Resolution

(a) Subject to clause 14(b) any dispute arising in connection with this Agreement shall be finally settled under the Arbitration and Conciliation Act, 1996 by one arbitrator appointed in accordance therewith and the arbitration shall take place in .... (place).

(b) This clause 14 shall not prevent either party from obtaining injunctive, or other similar relief from the court, if so required and pursuant to clause 15.

15. Governing Law and Jurisdiction

Governing Law

(a) The formation, existence, construction, performance, validity and all aspects whatsoever of this Agreement or of any term of this Agreement will be governed by the law of India.

Jurisdiction

(b) Subject to clause 15(c), the courts of India will have non-exclusive jurisdiction to settle any disputes that may arise out of or in connection with this Agreement. The parties irrevocably agree to submit to that jurisdiction.

(c) The agreement contained in clause 15(b) is included for the benefit of Licensee. Accordingly Licensee retains the right to bring proceedings in any other court of competent jurisdiction. Licensor irrevocably waives any objection to, and agrees to submit to, the jurisdiction of such other courts.

(d) The Licensor irrevocably agrees that a judgement or order of any court referred to in this clause is conclusive and binding upon it and may be enforced against it in the courts of any other jurisdiction.

16. Notices

Any notice, demand or communication in connection with this Agreement will be in writing and may be delivered by hand, first class or air-mail pre-paid post or facsimile [(but not by e-mail)], addressed to the recipient at its registered office or its address or facsimile number as the case may be stated herein. The addresses and facsimile numbers for the parties are as follows:

....   *Beta* MUSIC
....   Address
....

....

FAX:.....................   FAX: 91-11-.....................

17. Miscellaneous

(a) No waiver of any provisions of this Agreement or default under this Agreement shall affect any of the parties' rights thereafter to enforce such provisions or to exercise any right to remedy in the event of any default whether or not similar.

(b) The captions and paragraph headings herein are for convenience only, do not constitute a part of this agreement and are not used in the construction hereof.

18. Entire Agreement

This agreement sets forth the entire agreement between the parties hereto with respect to the subject matter hereof and merges all prior discussions and negotiations between them. No modifications, amendment, waiver, termination or discharge of this agreement or of any provision hereof shall be binding unless confirmed by a written instrument signed by the party against which it is sought to be enforced.

IN WITNESS WHEREOF, the parties have executed this agreement the day and year first above written.

Signed by.....................

duly authorised to sign

for and on behalf of

....

CO-PRODUCTION AGREEMENT

THIS AGREEMENT is made on ...., 20.....

BETWEEN

Alpha Entertainment Private Limited (registered under the Companies Act, 1956), whose registered office is located at .... (address) (*"Alpha"*).

AND

Beta Pictures Private Limited (registered under the Companies Act, 1956), whose registered office is located at..................... (*"Beta"*).

BACKGROUND

A. *Beta* and *Alpha* have agreed to co-produce a Feature Film tentatively entitled XYZ (the "Film").

B. *Beta* has developed the project for the Film including the Script, Schedule and Budget and has also decided upon the principal cast. The schedule for the

Film is estimated to be for approximately............(No of days) days between....................., 20..... and..................., 20..... The principal cast includes....................

1. Financing

1.1 *Beta* represents that the Budget of the Film shall, under no circumstances exceed Rs. .... (amount to be mentioned). This amount shall include the personal fee of Mr. ABC ("the fee"). The fee shall be paid for Mr. ABC's services as the Director, Screenwriter, Hindi Dialogue writer, Music Director and for composing the Background Score in the Film. The fee shall not exceed Rs. .... for all Mr. ABC's services except for composing the Background Score. Mr. ABC shall be paid a sum of not more than Rs. .... for his services of composing the Background Score of the Film.

1.2 *Alpha* shall provide an amount of Rs. .... (amount to be mentioned in currency) to *Beta* towards financing the Film from presales/credit/personal resources.

1.3 *Beta* has applied for a loan from IDBI for the balance.................... (amount to be mentioned). In case IDBI does not approve *Beta*'s loan application, *Beta* shall use its best efforts to obtain financing for the Film for the balance Rs. .... ("Amount"). It is agreed that failure to obtain the balance sum of Rs. .... by *Beta* shall be construed as a breach of this Agreement.

1.4 *Alpha* shall exercise sole and exclusive control over the disbursement of monies for all production, marketing and distribution expenses. *Alpha* will maintain two bank accounts for the project: (a) The payments account from which all moneys (apart from *Beta* amount) will be routed to *Beta* for the production; and (b) The Receipts account into which all receipts including sponsorships, promotional revenues and presales shall be deposited.

1.5 At.................... (what is the trigger) payments from the Receipts account shall be made in the following order:

    (a) First, all monies required to ready the Film for release shall be paid out of the account (Through *Beta*);

    (b) Second, all creditors (what kind do you anticipate?) will be paid (Through *Beta*);

    (c) Next, all funds borrowed from IDBI or any other party shall be returned along with interest due thereon (Through *Beta*);

    (d) Next, actual monies paid by *Alpha* (without any finance charge) shall be refunded;

    (e) Next, any fees payable to *Beta* (budgeted but not yet paid) will be disbursed (It is not clear as to what this fee is for. Please elaborate);

    (f) Next, an amount equal to fees paid to *Beta* will be paid to *Alpha* (in lieu of their fee and finance costs etc.)

    (g) All other receipts (isn't this the balance?) will be divided 50:50 between *Alpha* and *Beta* within.................... (no. of days) days of disbursement from/credit into the account.

2. Services provided

2.1 Do you want to make your participation in the project contingent upon the obligation upon .... (name) that only he shall direct/give music/BG Score/write Dialogues, etc.

2.2 *Beta* shall arrange for the facilities, equipment and personnel needed for the production of the Film, within the limits of the budget as set out above.

2.3 *Alpha* shall provide consultative, administrative and managerial support for production of the Film.

2.4 *Alpha* shall also be responsible for marketing, presales and distribution of the Film. However, *Beta* shall be consulted prior to confirmation of all sales and distribution deals. *Beta* shall also be a signatory to all sales deals. It is, however, agreed by the parties that failure to consult *Beta* shall not be construed as a breach of this Agreement by *Alpha*.

2.5 *Alpha* shall assist *Beta* in obtaining a Completion Bond for the Film. *Alpha* shall also work with *Beta* to devise and put in place reporting systems and controls for the Film in order to ensure compliance of the Completion Bond. However, *Alpha*'s obligation to assist *Beta* in obtaining a Completion Bond for the Film is contingent upon *Beta* arranging for the balance amount of Rs. ...., either from IDBI or any other source.

2.6 Nothing in this Agreement shall obligate *Alpha* to produce the Film.

3. Compensation

Please indicate whether there is any further compensation contemplated by the parties in addition to the terms of clause 1 above.

4. Credit

The Film shall carry the either of the following single card credit:

(a) Produced by .... (name) and ABC & a .... Production;
OR
(b) A .... Production & Produced by .... and ....

5. Copyright

Alpha and *Beta* shall jointly own the copyright in the Film. It is also made clear that the physical property in the negative of the Film shall also be held jointly by *Alpha* and *Beta*.

6. Assignment

6.1 *Beta* shall not assign its rights and obligations under this Agreement to any third party.

6.2 *Alpha* may assign its rights and obligations pursuant to this Agreement without the prior written consent of *Beta*.

7. Agency

The parties are entering into this Agreement as independent contractors, and neither party shall have the right to bind the other without the express written consent of the party to be bound.

8. Indemnities & Warranties

8.1 *Beta* warrants and represents that he is free to enter into this Agreement.

8.2 *Beta* also warrants that to the best of his knowledge and belief all the rights and releases necessary for production of the Film have been or will be secured.

8.3 *Beta* further warrants that the production of the Film shall not violate or infringe the rights of any person, company or corporation.

8.4 Both parties agree to hold each other harmless and indemnify each other for any breach of the warranties in this clause, including claims, damages and reasonable attorney's fees.

9. Breach

9.1 In the event *Beta* breaches its obligations under this Agreement, *Alpha* shall have the right to terminate this Agreement after *Alpha* gives written notice to *Beta* of *Beta's* breach, and *Beta* fails to cure the breach within thirty (30) days of his receipt of said notice.

9.2 In order to decide the consequences of breach in terms of the remedy available, we need to talk.

10. Arbitration & Dispute Resolution

10.1 This Agreement shall be interpreted in accordance with the laws of India.

10.2 Any controversy or claim arising out of or in relation to this Agreement or the validity, construction or performance of this Agreement, or the breach thereof, shall be resolved by arbitration in accordance with the Arbitration and Conciliation Act, 1996, as may be amended from time to time.

10.3 Nothing in clause 10.2 shall be construed as taking away the jurisdiction of court in .... (place) to settle any disputes that may arise out of or in connection with this Agreement. The parties irrevocably agree to submit to that jurisdiction.

10.4 The parties agree that the prevailing party in such arbitration and/or litigation proceeding shall be entitled to recover its reasonable attorney fees and expenses.

10.5 The arbitration will be held in .... (place) and any award shall be final, binding and non-appealable.

11. Entire Understanding

This Agreement contains the entire understanding of the parties with respect to the subject matter hereof. The Agreement may not be changed or amended except in writing signed by the parties. This Agreement shall inure to the benefit of, and shall be binding upon, the successors, heirs, executors and administrators of the parties.

AGREED TO AND ACCEPTED:

....
PQR   ABC
Managing Director   Director
Alpha Entertainment Pvt. Ltd.   *Beta* Pictures Pvt. Ltd.
Date: Date:
Witnesses: Witnesses:
1.   1.
2.   2.

DEED OF ASSIGNMENT OF COPYRIGHT

This DEED OF ASSIGNEMENT OF COPYRIGHT is made on this day of .... 20.....

BETWEEN

Alpha Advertising

(hereinafter referred to as "the party of the first part/Assignor")

AND

Beta Limited, a Company incorporated under the Indian Companies Act, having its registered office..................... (address) (hereinafter referred to as "the party of the second part/Assignee")

WHEREAS the Party to the Second part was earlier known as *Theta* Heritage Limited. As a result of the order of the Hon'ble High Court of .... (place) dated..................... with regard to the deamalgamation of the company named as *Gamma* Industries Limited, the scheme of de-meger approved by such order assigned all Intellectual Property rights in the trademark "ABCo" to the company known as *Theta* Heritage Limited later known as *Beta* (I) Limited. The said change of name was duly recorded on the certificate of incorporation of the assignee.

WHEREAS in pursuance thereof, the party to the second part did cause in the year....................., under a contract for services, in exchange for valuable consideration, the receipt of which is acknowledged by the assignor, the creation of the art work for the trademark "ABCo", (hereinafter referred to as "the work")

WHEREAS the said work comprises an original literary work entitled to be protected under the Provisions of the Indian Copyright Act, 1957 as also under common law principles.

WHEREAS as the assignment of all rights to the said work were not due to an inadvertence, transferred to the assignee, in order to finalize and regularize the ownership of the said work and in pursuance to the understandings between the parties in respect thereof, it has been decided to execute this deed of assignment. The said agreement shall be deemed to have effect from.................... (Insert the day//month//year when work was handed over to ....).

THIS DEED NOW WITNESSES AS FOLLOWS:

1. That in consideration of the mutual understanding between the parties and a consideration of Rupees (to be sourced form the receipt for payment for the original work)........................., paid by the Assignee to the Assignors, of which the Assignors acknowledge full and final receipt, the Assignors agree to assign onto the Assignee all rights, interests and titles in the said work.

2. The assignment shall be absolute and valid until the entire tenure of copyright as comprised in the work.

3. The assignment shall be valid for India and also for the rest of the world.

4. No royalty shall be payable by the Assignee to the Assignor during the currency of the Assignment.

5. It is further agreed between the parties that not withstanding the provisions of sections 19 (4) of the Copyright Act, 1957, the Assignment shall not lapse or the right transferred therein revert to the assignor, even if the Assignee does not exercise the rights under assignment within a period of one year from the date of this assignment.

6. The Assignee shall be entitled to file an application before the Registrar of Copyrights to seek registration of copyright comprised in the work in its own name, and the Assignors shall render all possible assistance to the Assignee in seeking such recordals.

7. This assignment shall be binding on all legal heirs, successors and assigns of the Assignors or the Assignee.

8. The terms of this assignment agreement shall be deemed to take effect from......................... (insert the day/month/year in which the work was handed over to ....).

That whereas the parties named above have laid their hands on this deed of assignment on the date, month and year mentioned above.

ASSIGNORS:

Alpha....................

through....................

(Name of authorised signatory)

ASSIGNEE: *Beta* (I) Limited

Through....................

(Mr. XYZ) Managing Director

Witnesses:

1.

2.

DIALOGUE AND VOCAL REPLACEMENT AGREEMENT

("Agreement")

Dated as of:

1. Parties

Alpha

Address....................

Beta

Address....................

2. Subject

This Agreement made by and between the Parties sets forth the rights and obligations for the rendering of *Beta* services in connection with the dialogue and/or vocal replacement for the .... (name of regional language) version of the motion picture entitled "Xfilm" ("Film").

3. Conditions Precedent

All of *Alpha'* obligations in this Agreement are expressly conditional upon *Beta* completing and delivering to *Alpha* signed copies of this Agreement and the assignment of rights and other documents attached hereto as Exhibits 3, 4, 5, 6 and 7 (as applicable) in a form satisfactory to *Alpha*.

4. Dreamworks' Delivery Requirements

Alpha shall deliver to *Beta* the English language version of the Film and such other materials necessary for *Beta* to perform its Services (the "Dubbing Materials") as set forth in Exhibit 1 attached hereto and incorporated herein by reference. Within five (5) business days of *Beta's* receipt of the Dubbing Materials, *Beta* shall notify *Alpha* in writing of any technical, creative or other problems detected during *Beta's* evaluation of the Dubbing Materials and *Alpha* will use its best efforts to rectify any such problems that can reasonably be solved. *Beta* will not make any copies of the Dubbing Materials without *Alpha's* written authorization. In no event shall *Beta* gain any right (other than the right to use the Dubbing Materials in accordance with the terms and conditions herein provided), title or interest in and to the Dubbing Materials as a result of its performance of the Services under this Agreement. All rights, title and interest in the Dubbing Materials shall remain vested in *Alpha* and are all hereby expressly reserved.

5. Approval

Alpha shall have the absolute right of approval over all creative and production elements in connection with *Beta's* Services including, but not limited to, prior written approval of translators, translations, talent (dialogue and vocal), voice characterization (performance, tone and accent) directors, sound engineers, credits, studio or room choice, recording, editing and mixing. *Beta* agrees to seek *Alpha's* prior written approval as early as possible, and at each stage of creative development and production.

6. Services

Beta shall, on a non-exclusive basis, produce and deliver to *Alpha*, its successors, assigns or designee a .... (Dialect) dubbed sound track of the Film in full synchronization and such other materials and services, if any, as more fully set forth in Exhibit 2 attached hereto and incorporated herein by reference ("Services"). *Beta* hereby agrees to furnish at its own cost all utilities, services, personnel and equipment necessary to provide the Services and fulfill its production, delivery and other obligations under this Agreement, subject to *Alpha*' approval rights as set forth herein. *Beta* further agrees to furnish its Services in a timely and efficient manner and in accordance with the highest standards in the ....(country) film industry. The time for the performance of *Beta*'s obligations hereunder shall be of the essence.

7. Delivery costs

(a) *Alpha* will be responsible for shipping and freight costs associated with the delivery of the Dubbing Materials to *Beta* at *Beta*'s address stated herein, and the return of the Dubbing Materials (and all other materials associated with the Film, including, but not limited to, the dubbed tracks and translated script) and the Final Materials (as defined below) to a location or address specified by *Alpha*. All such costs incurred by *Beta* shall be reimbursed by *Alpha* upon presentation of a valid receipt for same.

(b) *Beta* shall be responsible for the payment of all costs incurred in customs clearance and compliance with all applicable laws, in connection with the delivery of the Dubbing Materials and the return of the Dubbing Materials and the Final Materials, including any costs paid to agents for their services and other incidental costs associated with customs clearance. All such costs incurred by *Beta* shall be reimbursed by *Alpha* upon presentation of a valid receipt for same.

8. Delivery Schedule

Beta shall deliver to *Alpha* or its designees the final dubbed tracks, the premix, final mix (if applicable), the inventory copy, the final "as recorded" translated script and lyrics, and other required elements ("Final Materials") pursuant to schedules determined by *Alpha* and set forth on Exhibit 2. Materials shall be accompanied by copies of all agreements with Personnel covering their engagement by *Beta* on the Film. Unless *Alpha* instructs otherwise Dubbing Materials and work materials created by *Beta* or at the request of *Alpha* under this Agreement shall be returned to *Alpha* with the Final Materials.

9. Personnel

Beta shall select and engage all necessary personnel (including but not limited to, dialogue artists, vocal artists, writers, translators, lyricists, adapters, dialogue directors, and vocal directors) and crew to provide the Services hereunder ("Personnel"). *Beta* shall be responsible for managing all Personnel including scheduling the talent and payment of all fees in connection therewith. *Beta* shall select such Personnel to render their respective services and supply their goods and/or works so that production and delivery of all Final Materials occur in accordance with the terms of this Agreement. *Beta* shall pay all compensation, taxes, fees, social security, social charges and other sums required to be paid as a result of *Beta*'s engagement of any Personnel. *Beta*'s engagement of any Personnel shall be subject to *Alpha*' right of prior approval and in accordance with all applicable laws and collective bargaining agreements.

10. Rights

(a) *Beta* shall require all talent and Personnel including, but not limited to, dialogue artists, vocal artists, writers, translators, lyricists, adapters, dialogue directors and vocal directors to assign all of their present and future rights (including all economic and other exploitation rights) in all media forms and technologies now known or hereafter developed, in perpetuity and throughout the universe, as allowable under law, to *Beta* for the benefit of *Alpha* utilizing the assignment of rights forms attached hereto as Exhibits 3, 4, and 5 and incorporated herein by reference. *Beta* shall then assign said acquired rights to *Alpha* and execute the assignment of rights form attached hereto as Exhibit 6 and incorporated herein by reference, and forward the original duly executed assignment of rights documents to *Alpha* or its assignee within five (5) days of recording completion. *Beta* shall be responsible for securing all rights referenced herein from all applicable Personnel providing services hereunder, and will provide *Alpha* with executed documentation of assignment of rights for such Personnel and for *Beta*. *Beta* shall itself waive and shall ensure that all its Personnel waive the right to relinquish copyright under section 21 of the Copyright Act of 1957 as well as their moral rights, that is the right of paternity and the right of integrity under section 57 of the Copyright Act of 1957. In the event the services rendered by any Personnel may constitute a breach of his/her/its agreement with a record label, the *Beta* shall procure from each such record label and forward to *Alpha* a duly signed acknowledgment in the form attached hereto as Exhibit 7 and incorporated herein by reference.

(b) In the event that any of the talent hired by *Beta* hereunder are minors, *Beta* agrees to cause an authorized representative of said minor to review and sign the assignment of rights document in connection with such minor's performance.

(c) *Beta* shall sign any documents and do all such further acts needed to give effect to the assignments of rights to *Alpha* as set forth hereinabove and will continue to assist *Alpha* in this regard following the termination of *Beta*'s engagement by *Alpha*.

(d) If *Beta* has an existing agreement with any Personnel, *Beta* agrees to nevertheless enter into written agreements with all Personnel utilizing the assignment of rights documents attached hereto as Exhibits 3-5. In the event any provisions of the Exhibit conflict with the provisions of the existing agreement, the provisions of the Exhibit shall take precedence.

11. Payment and Assignment

(a) In consideration of *Alpha*' payment to *Beta* of $......................... ("Agreed Amount") for the Services to be rendered by *Beta* and fulfillment by *Beta* of all its obligations as contained herein, *Beta* acknowledges that *Alpha* shall be the sole and exclusive owner of, and hereby irrevocably and unconditionally transfers, sells and assigns to *Alpha* as and when the same come into existence, or as soon as otherwise possible under applicable laws, any and all present and future rights, title and interest throughout the universe in and to the Final Materials (and any other Film related materials) for the exploitation or non-exploitation of same, together with all present and future copyrights, including without limitation, derivative and compilation rights, and other intellectual property rights, economic rights, neighboring rights, and other rights of exploitation of whatever kind existing in the Final Materials (and other Film related materials) for the full period or periods thereof (including any renewals or extensions), in all media forms and technologies now known or hereafter developed. Notwithstanding anything contained in section 19(4) of the Copyright Act of 1957, even if *Alpha* does not exercise the copyright assigned to it within one year of the date of the assignment or otherwise, the same shall not lapse.

OR WHEN NO SUM CAN BE SPECIFIED

(a) In consideration of *Alpha's* payment to *Beta* of an agreed upon amount as set forth in the purchase order (or separate writing) ("Agreed Amount") for the services to be rendered by *Beta* and fulfillment by *Beta* of all its obligations as contained herein, *Beta* acknowledges that *Alpha* shall be the sole and exclusive owner of, and hereby irrevocably and unconditionally transfers, sells and assigns to *Alpha* as and when the same comes into existence, or as soon as otherwise possible under applicable laws, any and all present and future rights, title and interest throughout the universe in and to the Final Materials (and any other Film related materials) for the exploitation or non-exploitation of same, together with all present and future copyrights, including without limitation, derivative and compilation rights, and other intellectual property rights, economic rights, neighboring rights, and other rights of exploitation of whatever kind existing in the Final Materials (and other Film related materials) for the full period or periods thereof (including any renewals or extensions), in all media forms and technologies now known or hereafter developed. Notwithstanding anything contained in section 19(4) of the Copyright Act of 1957, even if *Alpha* does not exercise the copyright assigned to it within one year of the date of the assignment or otherwise, the same shall not lapse.

(b) *Buyout.*—*Beta* agrees that *Alpha'* rights of exploitation hereunder shall constitute a so-called total buy-out of the rights of the *Beta* and Personnel so that: (i) no additional compensation will be payable to *Beta* or Personnel or any party representing or claiming through or under any of them as a result of the exercise of rights of exploitation granted to *Alpha* hereunder; and (ii) no consents will be required from the *Beta* or any Personnel or any other parties before such rights are exercised.

12. Payment Schedule

(a) Subject to sub-paragraph (b) below, *Alpha* will pay *Beta* in accordance with the following payment schedule:

(i) .... percent of the Agreed Amount within .... days after *Beta's* commencement of Services and *Alpha's* receipt and approval of *Beta's* invoice therefore (whichever is the later);

(ii) Thirty-three percent (33%) of the Agreed Amount within thirty (30) days after *Beta*'s completion of the ....(regional language) tracks and upon *Alpha*'s receipt of the recorded dialogue and/or vocal (if applicable) premix, approval thereof and approval and receipt of *Beta*'s invoice therefore (whichever is the later); and

(iii) Thirty-four percent (34%) of the Agreed Amount within thirty (30) days after *Beta*'s completion and *Alpha*'s receipt and approval of all Final Materials including, but not limited to, the final mix (if applicable), all applicable agreements and final approved credits and *Alpha*'s receipt and approval of the *Beta*'s final invoice therefore (whichever is the later). The final invoice will not be paid until and unless *Alpha* has received all the necessary rights documentation including all assignment of rights forms for *Beta* and Personnel.

(b) Without prejudice to *Alpha*'s other rights and remedies against *Beta*, if *Beta* fails to deliver the Final Materials to *Alpha* on schedule or if this Agreement is terminated due to a breach of this Agreement by *Beta*, *Alpha* shall have no obligation to make any further payment to *Beta*.

13. INVOICE INSTRUCTIONS: *Beta* shall send all invoices in connection with the services to:

....

....

(Address where invoice is to be sent)

14. Warranty and Indemnity

(a) *Beta* represents and warrants that it is free to enter into this Agreement and that it is not subject to any obligation or disability which will or might prevent or interfere with its full performance of all the terms and conditions of this Agreement.

(b) *Beta* further represents and warrants that it shall not create or authorize creation of any lien, charge or other encumbrance of any kind over the Dubbing Materials, Final Materials or Film related materials or any of *Alpha*'s rights with respect to any of the same.

(c) *Beta* further represents and warrants that it is duly authorized to enter into this Agreement and has not and will not enter into any agreement which is or may reasonably become inconsistent with the terms of this Agreement.

(d) *Beta* agrees and undertakes to hold harmless and indemnify *Alpha*, its affiliates, successors and assigns from and against any loss, liability, damage, cause of action, cost or expense, including reasonable attorneys' fees, of any kind and character, resulting from or relating to *Beta*'s gross negligence or breach of any representations, warranty or agreement made by *Beta* in this Agreement or any claim brought by Personnel against *Alpha* in connection with *Beta*'s performance of the Services or *Beta*'s delivery of the Final Materials to *Alpha*.

(e) *Beta* further agrees and undertakes to hold harmless and indemnify *Alpha*, its affiliates, successors and assigns from and against any loss, liability, damage, cause of action, cost or expense, including reasonable attorneys' fees, of any kind and character, resulting from any action brought against *Alpha* by a third party in case performance of services under this Agreement by Personnel results in breach of an undertaking owed to the third party by such Personnel.

15. Confidentiality

(a) Other than as may be required by any applicable law, government order or regulation, or by order or decree of any court of competent jurisdiction, *Beta*, its employees, agents or Personnel, shall not in any way divulge or announce, or in any manner disclose to any third party, any secret or confidential information, knowledge, data or matters revealed to *Beta* by *Alpha*, or any of its related companies, or obtained by *Beta* as a result of *Beta*'s engagement hereunder. *Beta* agrees that all information obtained from *Alpha* including, without limitation, ideas, materials (which include but are not limited to, artwork, photographs, scripts, and slides), any information relating to manufacturing techniques, processes, formulas, developments, experimental works, works in progress, business secrets, trade secrets, scripts, plots, characters, records, data, computer programs, software, drawings, schematics, know-how, notes, models, reports, samples or any other matter relating to the artistic creations, film or business of *Alpha*, whether tangible or intangible, together with any material prepared by *Beta* which contains or otherwise relates to such information ("Information") shall be deemed strictly confidential and secret, and shall not, at any time, without the prior written consent of *Alpha*, be disclosed to any unauthorized person, firm or entity, or copied, photographed or reproduced in any manner whatsoever, in whole or in part. *Beta* further agrees not to use the Information for its own benefit or for the benefit of any other person, firm or entity in any manner whatsoever, except as specifically provided for under this Agreement. *Beta* shall enter into written confidentiality agreements with its employees, agents and Personnel, providing that such persons shall not divulge, disclose or announce in any manner the Information, except to the extent as is required in the performance of this Agreement. This clause shall survive the termination or expiration of this Agreement.

(b) *Beta* shall cause its directors, officers, employees, agents or advisers to abide by the confidentiality provisions of this clause 15.

16. Miscellaneous

(a) *Beta* is acting as an independent contractor for all purposes hereunder and shall not subcontract or delegate any of its obligations nor assign any of its rights under this Agreement to a third party. *Alpha* may assign any of its rights hereunder.

(b) Nothing herein contained shall be deemed to create an agency or employment relationship between *Alpha* and *Beta* or between *Alpha* and Personnel. *Beta* agrees to be responsible for any tax (or tax-related) obligations (including, without limitation, the obligation to report taxable income and pay taxes thereon, national insurance, VAT, and all other assessments, taxes contributions or sums payable with respect to or as a result of or in connection with the services performed by *Beta* hereunder) to which *Beta* may be subject.

(c) *Alpha* shall determine the extent, manner, style, form, size and placement of credit (if any) accorded to *Beta* and Personnel in connection with the Services described herein. *Alpha* does not undertake or guarantee that any of the Final Materials will be used or exploited.

(d) *Beta* shall not use the name "*Alpha*" or any of its related companies or any characters or designs of *Alpha* without prior written approval from *Alpha* Business and Legal Affairs Department except to the extent required to produce and deliver the Final Materials under this Agreement.

(e) This Agreement shall be governed by and interpreted in accordance with the laws of India. In case of any discrepancy between the English and.................... (dialect) versions of the Agreement, if any, the English language version shall take precedence. If any provisions hereunder are found to be in conflict with the laws of India, said provisions shall be severed from this Agreement. In such a case, the affected provisions shall be curtailed only to the extent necessary to bring them within the legal requirements, and all other provisions hereunder shall remain in full force and effect. The parties hereto submit and consent to the jurisdiction of the High Court of .... (place) and venue in ....(place), India in any action brought to enforce (or otherwise related to) this agreement.

(f) Both parties shall at all reasonable times be available for meaningful consultation concerning *Beta*'s activities hereunder. *Alpha* reserves the right to have a representative present at all stages of the production and such representative shall be entitled to attend all meetings, all casting, recording, editing and mixing sessions and to review any work in connection with the production of the Final Materials. *Beta* agrees to give *Alpha* reasonable notice of all such events.

(g) In the event of any breach of this Agreement by *Alpha*, *Beta*'s remedy shall be limited to an action at law for damages, if any, and in no event shall *Beta* be entitled to seek injunctive relief or to terminate this Agreement or to seek to enjoin *Alpha's* exploitation of the results and/or proceeds of *Beta*'s Services hereunder.

(h) No payment of any compensation or performance of any obligation by *Alpha* hereunder shall constitute a waiver by *Alpha* of any breach by *Beta* or a waiver of any rights or remedies which *Alpha* may have as a result of such breach.

(i) All notices hereunder shall be given in writing to the parties at the address first specified hereinabove.

17. Entire Agreement

This Agreement together with the Exhibits expresses the entire agreement between *Alpha* and *Beta* and shall replace and supersede all prior arrangements, representations, and agreements (if any), either oral or written, as to the subject matter hereof. This Agreement may not be modified, unless in writing and executed by the parties' authorized representatives.

IN WITNESS WHEREOF, the parties hereto have executed this Agreement by their duly authorized representatives as of the day and year first above written

Beta:
By:...................
Print Name:...............
Its:...................

Alpha
By:...................
Print Name:...................
Its:...................

EXHIBIT 1
DUBBING MATERIALS

EXHIBIT 2
SERVICES AND TECHNICAL REQUIREMENTS

EXHIBIT 3
DIALOGUE AND VOCAL DIRECTOR ASSIGNMENT OF RIGHTS

FILM TITLE: ....Xfilm........................("Film")

DIRECTOR'S NAME: ....

SERVICE(S) PERFORMED: Dialogue Direction Only:...........................

Vocal Direction Only:.................................

Dialogue and Vocal Direction:..................

I, the undersigned Director ("Director"), am duly authorized to enter into this Assignment of Rights and have not and will not enter into any agreement or take any action inconsistent with the terms hereof. I do hereby exclusively and irrevocably assign, transfer and sell to *Beta* ("Beta"), for the benefit of *Alpha*, its successors, assigns and licensees ("Alpha"), throughout the universe and in perpetuity (or to the maximum time according to the relevant law), any and all rights of every kind and character, including all present and future rights, which have or will come into existence from my services for the ....(regional languages) dubbed version of the above mentioned Film. Without limiting the foregoing, this Assignment of Rights includes all of the following and below-detailed intellectual property, economic, exploitation and related rights in and to the performance including but not limited to:

1. All economic and other exploitation rights (their renewals and extensions) including, but not limited to, the right not to exploit, the right of reproduction, the right of distribution and communication to the public by means of sale, lease, loan or in any other manner for public or private use; and 2. All intellectual property rights including, but not limited to, copyrights, neighbouring rights and related rights and their renewals and extensions; and 3. All rights to the use of the dubbed tracks in whole or in part with or independent of visual aspects in all media, technologies and forms, tangible or intangible, now known or later developed or hereafter devised/utilized whether such media, technologies and/or forms are in current use or exist only in research or prototype stages or may be developed in the future such rights to include but not be limited to theatrical, non-theatrical (*e.g.* airlines, ships, hospitals, hotels, etc.), all forms of home video (*e.g.*, video cassettes (1/2"VHS, ¾", 8 mm, Digital Video Cassette, etc.) DVD (digital video disk), laser disk, video on demand, Video CD, mini-CD, sing-alongs, etc.), all forms

of television, no matter what mode of delivery or type (*e.g.* satellite, cable, fiberoptics, video on demand services, pay per view, broadcast HD TV, free TV, pay TV, *via* computer services, *via* internet, *via* digital platform, etc. or any combination thereof, etc.), personal television products, personal video recorders, smart TV services, home servers, digital video recorders, etc. (*e.g.*, TiVo™, ReplayTV™, etc.), all forms of audio exploitation, soundtrack record rights (*e.g.*, phonograms, audio cassettes, compact disks, mini-discs, web-casts, MP3s, read-alongs, sing-alongs, radio transmissions, compilations, etc.), public presentations of any kind (including, but not limited to, live performances/shows, stage shows, theme parks, retail stores, auditoriums, etc.), all forms of consumer products and merchandising (including publishing), all forms of computer products and uses (*e.g.*, CD-ROM, CD-I, DVD-ROM, Internet and all associated on-line services, all interactive formats, solid state devices, etc.), all commercial and non-commercial uses, and all promotional, marketing or advertising uses; and 4. All other intellectual property, economic, exploitation and related rights dealing with the exploitation or use of the dubbed tracks, except any rights expressly considered by applicable law to be non-transferable, non-assignable or not for sale.

As full and final consideration for the dubbing of this Film and the full and irrevocable assignment, transfer and sale to *Beta* as set forth herein, the undersigned understands that *Beta* will pay the undersigned a one-time, lump sum payment for the service(s) performed and that such payment shall include a complete buy-out of rights (such payment to be considered as good and valuable consideration, the receipt and sufficiency of which are hereby acknowledged). The undersigned does hereby irrevocably and unconditionally consent to the assignment by *Beta* of all rights acquired by *Beta* from the Director under this agreement to *Alpha*.

The undersigned expressly waives any and all rights: (i) to credit for the work performed; (ii) to terminate this assignment and/or to prevent or delay the advertising, presentation, distribution or exploitation of the Film; and, (iii) to any action, claim or demand regarding the rights and/or this assignment including without limitation, any such action, claim or demand concerning my moral rights (droit moral) in and/or to the performance in connection with the above titled Film or for any use of the dubbed work in whole or in part.

The Director hereby expresses his/her consent for making changes, deletions and abbreviations to his/her work for the purposes of the exploitation of the dubbed version of the Film as well as for use of his/her work for promotional, advertising and consumer product purposes.

Any amendments to this agreement shall be made in writing and signed by both parties.

Director Signature   Date

Address

Identification Number

Beta Signature   Date

EXHIBIT 4

DIALOGUE AND VOCAL ARTIST ASSIGNMENT OF RIGHTS

FILM TITLE: ....Xfilm....................("Film")

ROLE(S)/CHARACTER NAME(S):   ....

ARTIST'S NAME: ....

SERVICE(S) PERFORMED: Dialogue Artist Only:....................

                          Vocal Artist Only:....................

                          Dialogue and Vocal Artist:....................

I, the undersigned Artist ("Artist"), am duly authorized to enter into this Assignment of Rights and have not and will not enter into any agreement or take any action inconsistent with the terms hereof. I do hereby exclusively and irrevocably assign, transfer and sell to Beta ("Beta"), for the benefit of Alpha, its successors, assigns and licensees ("Alpha"), throughout the universe and in perpetuity (or to the maximum time according to the relevant law), any and all rights of every kind and character, including all present and future rights, which have or will come into existence from my services for the .... *(name of language in which)* dubbed version of the above mentioned Film. Without limiting the foregoing, this Assignment of Rights includes all of the following and below-detailed intellectual property, economic, exploitation and related rights in and to the performance including but not limited to:

1. All economic and other exploitation rights (their renewals and extensions) including, but not limited to, the right not to exploit, the right of reproduction, the right of distribution and communication to the public by means of sale, lease, loan or in any other manner for public or private use; and 2. All intellectual property rights including, but not limited to, copyrights, neighbouring rights and related rights and their renewals and extensions; 3. All rights to the use of the dubbed tracks in whole or in part with or independent of visual aspects in all media, technologies and forms, tangible or intangible, now known or later developed or hereafter devised/utilized whether such media, technologies and/or forms are in current use or exist only in research or prototype stages or may be developed in the future such rights to include but not be limited to theatrical, non-theatrical (*e.g.* airlines, ships, hospitals, hotels, etc.), all forms of home video (*e.g.*, video cassettes (1/2"VHS, ¾", 8 mm, Digital Video Cassette, etc.) DVD (digital video disk), laser disk, video on demand, Video CD, mini-CD, sing-alongs, etc.), all forms of television, no matter what mode of delivery or type (*e.g.* satellite, cable, fiberoptics, video on demand services, pay per view, broadcast HD TV, free TV, pay TV, *via* computer services, *via* internet, *via* digital platform, etc. or any combination thereof, etc.), personal television products, personal video recorders, smart TV services, home servers, digital video recorders, etc. (*e.g.*, TiVo™, ReplayTV™, etc.), all forms of audio exploitation, soundtrack record rights (*e.g.*, phonograms, audio cassettes, compact disks, mini-discs, web-casts, MP3s, read-alongs, sing-alongs, radio transmissions, compilations, etc.), public presentations of any kind (including, but not limited to, live performances/shows, stage shows, theme parks, retail stores, auditoriums, etc.), all forms of consumer products and merchandising (including publishing), all forms of computer products and uses (*e.g.*, CD-ROM, CD-I, DVD-ROM, Internet and all associated on-line services, all interactive formats, solid state devices, etc.), all commercial and non-commercial uses, and all promotional, marketing or advertising uses; and 4. All rights in the roles or characters portrayed by Artist hereunder, including name, likeness and distinctive characterizations thereof, and the right to merchandise and exploit such roles or characters and the right to use Artist's name and likeness in connection therewith, and 5. All other intellectual property, economic, exploitation and related rights dealing with the exploitation or use of the dubbed tracks, except any rights expressly considered by applicable law to be non-transferable, non-assignable or not for sale.

If *Alpha* so requests, Artist shall render promotional services in connection with publicity concerning the release of the Film in any and all media at such times and places as *Alpha* shall designate, subject to Artist's prior *bona fide* professional commitments, provided that Artist shall make reasonable good faith efforts to be available.

As full and final consideration for the dubbing of this Film and the full and irrevocable assignment, transfer and sale to *Beta* as set forth herein, the undersigned understands that *Beta* will pay the undersigned a one-time, lump sum payment for the service(s) performed and that such payment shall include a complete buy-out of rights (such payment to be considered as good and valuable consideration, the receipt and sufficiency of which are hereby acknowledged). The undersigned does hereby irrevocably and unconditionally consent to the assignment by *Beta* of all rights acquired by *Beta* from the Artist under this agreement to *Alpha*.

The undersigned expressly waives any and all rights: (i) to credit for the work performed; (ii) to terminate this assignment and/or to prevent or delay the advertising, presentation, distribution or exploitation of the Film; and, (iii) to any action, claim or demand regarding the rights and/or this assignment including without limitation, any such action, claim or demand concerning my moral rights (droit moral) in and/or to the performance in connection with the above titled Film or for any use of the dubbed work in whole or in part.

The Artist hereby expresses his/her consent for making changes, deletions and abbreviations to his/her work for the purposes of the exploitation of the dubbed version of the Film as well as for use of his/her work for promotional, advertising and consumer product purposes.

Any amendments to this agreement shall be made in writing and signed by both parties.

Artist Signature   Date.....................

Address

Tax Identification Number

Beta Signature   Date.....................

I hereby represent and warrant that I am not a minor....................

(please initial)

If the above is a minor, then this contract must be signed by the above's parents or those having parental responsibility in the space below.

Countersigned by:.................... Date.................... Date....................

Parent Names:.................... [printed]

EXHIBIT 5
WRITER/ADAPTER/LYRICIST/TRANSLATOR ASSIGNMENT OF RIGHTS

FILM TITLE: ....Xfilm....................("Film")

WRITER'S/ADAPTER'S/
LYRICIST'S/TRANSLATOR'S   Name:....................

SERVICE(S) PERFORMED: Writer:.................... Adapter:....................Lyricist:....................
Translator:....................

I, the undersigned writer/adapter/lyricist/translator, am duly authorized to enter into this Assignment of Rights and have not and will not enter into any agreement or take any action inconsistent with the terms hereof. I do hereby exclusively and irrevocably assign, transfer and sell to *Beta* ("*Beta*"), for the benefit of *Alpha*, its successors, assigns and licensees ("*Alpha*"), throughout the universe and in perpetuity (or to the maximum time according to the relevant law), any and all rights of every kind and character, including all present and future rights, which have or will come into existence from my services for the .... (name of language in which) dubbed version of the above mentioned Film. Without limiting the foregoing, this Assignment of Rights includes all of the following and below-detailed intellectual property, economic, exploitation and related rights in and to the performance including but not limited to:

1. All economic and other exploitation rights (their renewals and extensions) including, but not limited to, the right not to exploit, the right of reproduction, the right of distribution and communication to the public by means of sale, lease, loan or in any other manner for public or private use; and 2. All intellectual property rights including, but not limited to, copyrights, neighbouring rights and related rights and their renewals and extensions; 3. All rights to the use of the dubbed tracks in whole or in part with or independent of visual aspects in all media, technologies and forms, tangible or intangible, now known or later developed or hereafter devised/utilized whether such media, technologies and/or forms are in current use or exist only in research or prototype stages or may be developed in the future such rights to include but not be limited to theatrical, non-theatrical (*e.g.* airlines, ships, hospitals, hotels, etc.), all forms of home video (*e.g.*, video cassettes (1/2"VHS, ¾", 8 mm, Digital Video Cassette, etc.) DVD (digital video disk), laser disk, video on demand, Video CD, mini-CD, sing-alongs, etc.), all forms of television, no matter what mode of delivery or type (*e.g.* satellite, cable, fiberoptics, video on demand services, pay per view, broadcast HD TV, free TV, pay TV, *via* computer services, *via* internet, *via* digital platform, etc. or any combination thereof, *etc.*), personal television products, personal video recorders, smart TV services, home servers, digital video recorders, etc. (*e.g.*, TiVo™, ReplayTV™, *etc.*), all forms of audio exploitation, soundtrack record rights (*e.g.*, phonograms, audio cassettes, compact disks, mini-discs, web-casts, MP3s, read-alongs, sing-alongs, radio transmissions, compilations, etc.), public presentations of any kind (including, but not limited to, live performances/shows, stage shows, theme parks, retail stores, auditoriums, etc.), all forms of consumer products and merchandising (including publishing), all forms of computer products and uses (*e.g.*, CD-ROM, CD-I, DVD-ROM, Internet and all associated on-line services, all interactive formats, solid state devices, etc.), all commercial and non-commercial uses, and all promotional, marketing or advertising uses; and 4. All other intellectual property, economic, exploitation and related rights dealing with the exploitation or use of the dubbed tracks, except any rights expressly considered by applicable law to be non-transferable, non-assignable or not for sale.

As full and final consideration for the dubbing of this Film and the full and irrevocable assignment, transfer and sale to *Beta* as set forth herein, the undersigned understands that *Beta* will pay the undersigned a one-time, lump sum payment for the service(s) performed and that such payment shall include a complete buy-out of rights (such payment to be considered as good and valuable consideration, the receipt and sufficiency of which are hereby acknowledged). The undersigned does irrevocably and unconditionally consent to the assignment by *Beta* of all rights acquired by *Beta* from the undersigned under this agreement to *Alpha*.

The undersigned expressly waives any and all rights: (i) to credit for the work performed; (ii) to terminate this assignment and/or to prevent or delay the advertising, presentation, distribution or exploitation of the Film; and, (iii) to any action, claim or demand regarding the rights and/or this assignment including without limitation, any such action, claim or demand concerning my moral rights (droit moral) in and/or to the performance in connection with the above titled Film or for any use of the dubbed work in whole or in part.

The undersigned hereby expresses his/her consent for making changes, deletions and abbreviations to his/her work for the purposes of the exploitation of the dubbed version of the Film as well as for use of his/her work for promotional, advertising and consumer product purposes.

Any amendments to this agreement shall be made in writing and signed by both parties.

Writer/Adapter/Lyricist/Translator Signature	Date....................

Beta Signature	Date....................

EXHIBIT 6
STUDIO ASSIGNMENT OF RIGHTS

STUDIO NAME:	....................*Beta*....................
FILM TITLE:	....................xfilm....................("Film")

I, the undersigned representative of *Beta* ("*Beta*"), am duly authorized to enter into this Assignment of Rights on behalf of the *Beta* and the *Beta* has not and will not enter into any agreement or take any action inconsistent with the terms hereof. *Beta* hereby exclusively and irrevocably assigns, transfers and sells to *Alpha*, its successors, assigns and licensees ("*Alpha*"), throughout the universe and in perpetuity (or to the maximum time according to the relevant law), any and all rights of every kind and character, including all present and future rights, with the sole exception of moral rights, which have or will come into existence for the .... *(name of language in which)* dubbed version of the above mentioned Film. Without limiting the foregoing, this Assignment of Rights includes all of the following and below-detailed intellectual property, economic, exploitation and related rights in and to the .... (name of language in which) dubbed version of the above mentioned Film including but not limited to:

1. All economic and other exploitation rights (their renewals and extensions) including, but not limited to, the right not to exploit, the right of reproduction, the right of distribution and communication to the public by means of sale, lease, loan or in any other manner for public or private use; and 2. All intellectual property rights including, but not limited to, copyrights, neighbouring rights and related rights and their renewals and extensions; 3. All rights to the use of the dubbed tracks in whole or in part with or independent of visual aspects in all media, technologies and forms, tangible or intangible, now known or later developed or hereafter devised/utilized whether such media, technologies and/or forms are in current use or exist only in research or prototype stages or may be developed in the future such rights to include but not be limited to theatrical, non-theatrical (*e.g.* airlines, ships, hospitals, hotels, etc.), all forms of home video (*e.g.*, video cassettes (1/2"VHS, ¾", 8 mm, Digital Video Cassette, etc.), DVD (digital video disk), laser disk, video on demand, Video CD, mini-CD, sing-alongs, etc.), all forms of television, no matter what mode of delivery or type (*e.g.* satellite, cable, fiberoptics, video on demand services, pay per view, broadcast HD TV, free TV, pay TV, *via* computer services, *via* internet, *via* digital platform, etc. or any combination thereof, etc.), personal television products, personal video recorders, smart TV services, home servers, digital video recorders, etc. (*e.g.*, TiVo™, ReplayTV™, etc.), all forms of audio exploitation, soundtrack record rights (*e.g.*, phonograms, audio cassettes, compact disks, mini-discs, web-casts, MP3s, read-alongs, sing-alongs, radio transmissions, compilations, etc.), public presentations of any kind (including, but not limited to, live performances/shows, stage shows, theme parks, retail stores, auditoriums, etc.), all forms of consumer products and merchandising (including publishing), all forms of computer products and uses (*e.g.*, CD-ROM, CD-I, DVD-ROM, Internet and all associated on-line services, all interactive formats, solid state devices, etc.), all commercial and non-commercial uses, and all promotional, marketing or advertising uses; and 4. All other intellectual property,

economic, exploitation and related rights dealing with the exploitation or use of the dubbed tracks, except any rights expressly considered by applicable law to be non-transferable, non-assignable or not for sale.

Beta hereby assigns to *Alpha* all rights, title and interest in and to the above-referenced Film acquired by *Beta* in connection with the Dialogue and Vocal Replacement Agreement and Exhibits thereto.

As full and final consideration for the dubbing of this Film and the full and irrevocable assignment, transfer and sale to *Alpha* as set forth herein, the *Beta* understands that *Alpha* will pay *Beta* an agreed upon lump sum amount for the service(s) performed and that such payment shall include a complete buy-out of rights (such payment to be considered as good and valuable consideration, the receipt and sufficiency of which are hereby acknowledged).

The *Beta* expressly waives any and all rights: (i) to credit for the work performed; (ii) to terminate this assignment and/or to prevent or delay the advertising, presentation, distribution or exploitation of the Film; and, (iii) to any action, claim or demand regarding the rights and/or this assignment including without limitation, any such action, claim or demand concerning moral rights (*droit moral*) in and/or to the services performed in connection with the above titled Film or for any use of the dubbed work in whole or in part.

The *Beta* hereby expresses its consent for making changes, deletions and abbreviations to its work for the purposes of the exploitation of the dubbed version of the Film as well as for use of its work for promotional, advertising and consumer product purposes.

Any amendments to this agreement shall be made in writing and signed by both parties.

Beta:
By:....................
Print Name:....................
Its:....................
Date:....................

Alpha
By:....................
Print Name:....................
Its:....................
Date:....................

EXHIBIT 7

ARTIST'S LABEL ACKNOWLEDGEMENT

ARTIST'S NAME ....("Artist")
ARTIST'S CHARACTER: ....
ARTIST'S LABEL: ....("Label")
FILM TITLE: ....Xfilm....................("Film")

Label hereby acknowledges that it possesses certain exclusive rights with respect to Artist's vocal performance and Artist would like to render vocal performance services to BETA for the benefit of ALPHA ("*Alpha*") in connection with the voice and/or vocal replacement services for the Tamil/Hindi/Malayalam dub version of the Film.

Label agrees and acknowledges that it hereby expressly authorizes Artist to furnish such performance and that rendering such services by Artist will not constitute a breach of Artist's exclusive agreement with Label. Label has read the Artist's Assignment of Rights Form, dated...................., signed by Artist and Label agrees to the terms and conditions contained therein.

Further, Label agrees and acknowledges that *Alpha* and its successors or assigns shall have the right to exploit the performance furnished by Artist in any and all media, and by any and all manners and means of exploiting, marketing, and advertising of the Film or of any other product. Label acknowledges that *Alpha* and its successors and assigns shall have the right to use the Artist's performance also for the purpose of manufacturing, distributing, and selling sound recordings (*e.g.*, soundtrack albums, singles, etc.), without any compensation or credit owing to Label, on any account, for the use of Artist's performance.

LABEL..................... Date.....................
By:.....................
Its:.....................
Alpha..................... Date.....................
By:.....................
Its:.....................

ACTOR EMPLOYMENT AGREEMENT

THIS AGREEMENT is made and entered into as of the..................... (date)
BETWEEN
Alpha (hereinafter "Producer"),
AND
(hereinafter "Actor").

A. Producer intends to produce a theatrical motion picture (hereinafter the "Picture") based upon that certain screenplay tentatively entitled..................... (title of film) (hereinafter the "Screenplay") which Picture is intended for initial theatrical exhibition. The term "Picture" as herein used, shall include, but shall not be limited to, a motion picture produced, recorded, exhibited or transmitted by any means now or hereafter known.

B. Producer wishes to utilize the services of Actor in connection with the Picture upon the terms and conditions herein contained.

ACCORDINGLY, IT IS AGREED AS FOLLOWS:

1. Photoplay, Role, and Consideration: Producer hereby engages Actor to render services as such in the role of ...., in the Screenplay. As full compensation for the services of Actor to be rendered pursuant hereto, and for Actor's undertakings herein specified, the Producer shall, provided the Actor faithfully performs his duties and obligations hereunder, pay the Actor a sum of Rs. .... for his services in the Picture. Actor accepts such engagement upon the terms herein specified and undertakes to perform all the duties and obligations assumed and entered into by him hereunder. This sum shall be payable in the following manner and upon occurrence of the following events:

(a) 20% (initial advance) – Signing this Agreement
(b) ....
(c) ....
(d) ....

2. **Services:** Producer shall cause Actor to render all services customarily rendered by actors in feature-length motion pictures at such times and places designated by Producer and in full compliance with Producer's instructions in all matters. Without limiting the foregoing, Actor's services shall be in accordance with the following:

(a) *Start Date.*—Principal Photography of the Picture shall commence on or about..................... but no later than..................... The Start Date shall be automatically extended without notice for a period equal to the duration of any default, disability and/or *force majeure* (as such terms are defined below and regardless of whether Actor's services are suspended therefor), or due to any location requirements, director and/or cast unavailability, weather conditions, and/or other similar contingencies.

(b) *Exclusivity.*—Actor's services hereunder shall be non-exclusive first priority during the Pre-Production, exclusive during Production Periods, and non-exclusive, but on a first-priority basis, during the Post-Production Period.

(c) *Retakes and Other Services.*—During and after the Term, Actor shall render such services as Producer may desire in producing retakes, added scenes, transparencies, close-ups, sound track (including dubbing and looping), process shots, trick shots and trailers for changes in and foreign versions of the Picture. Compensation set out in paragraph 1 above includes consideration for such services.

(d) *Nights, Weekends, Holidays, Work Time.*—No increased or additional compensation shall accrue or be payable to Actor for services rendered by Actor at night or on weekends or holidays, or after the expiration of any number of hours of service in any period.

3. **Term:** The term of engagement of Actor's services hereunder shall begin on or about the Start Date and continue until....................., or until the completion of the photography and recordation of said role. (Does the industry use any other terminology in place of the given language to define the contours of the term of this contract).

4. **Rights:** Actor grants, and Producer shall have, the perpetual and universal right to photograph and re-photograph Actor (still and moving) and to record and re-record, double and dub Actor's voice and performances, by any present or future methods or means and to use and authorize others to use Actor's name, voice and likeness for and in connection with the Picture, the soundtrack (including a soundtrack album), trailers, and documentary and/or "making of" pictures, and all advertising (including Actor's name and likeness on sleeves, jackets and other packaging for soundtrack albums, video cassettes, videodiscs, written publications and the like), merchandising, commercial tie-ups, publicity, and other means of exploitation of any and all rights pertaining to the Picture and any element thereof. Producer shall own all results and proceeds of Actor's services hereunder, including the copyrights thereof, and as such owner shall have the right (among all other rights of ownership): (i) to include such results and proceeds in the Picture and in advertising and publicity relating to the

Picture, (ii) to reproduce such results and proceeds by any present or future means, (iii) to combine such results and proceeds with photographs and recordings made by others for use in the Picture, (iv) to exhibit and perform such results and proceeds in theatres, on the radio and television, and in, or by any other present or future media, for profit and otherwise, and for commercial or non-commercial purposes and purposes of trade, and (v) to license and assign its rights to any other person or producer. Without in any way limiting the foregoing, the results and proceeds of Actor's services hereunder include any and all material, words, writings, ideas, "gags", dialogue, melody and lyrics composed, submitted or interpolated by Actor in connection with the preparation or production of the Picture (hereinafter referred to as "material"). All said material and the copyright therein, for which valuable consideration is paid in terms of paragraph 1 above, shall automatically become the property of Producer, which shall be deemed the author thereof in terms of the Copyright Act, 1957 ("the Act"). Actor hereby expressly waives and relinquishes any moral rights or "droit morale," or "author's special rights" under section 57 of the Act, in and to any material created by or contributed to the Picture by Actor including all of Actor's performance.

5. Actor's Address and Telephone: All notices which the Producer is required or may desire to give to the Actor may be given either by mailing the same addressed to the Actor at the address listed at the end of this agreement, or such notice may be given to the Actor personally, either orally or in writing.

6. Promotional Film: Producer shall have the exclusive right to make one or more promotional films of thirty (30) minutes or less and to utilize the results and proceeds of Actor's services therein. Actor agrees to render such services for said promotional films during the term of his employment hereunder as Producer may request and Actor further agrees to use by Producer of film clips and behind-the-scenes shots in which Actor appears in such promotional films.

7. Name and Likeness: Producer shall have the exclusive right to use and to license the use of Actor's name, sobriquet, pseudonym, photograph, likeness, voice and/or caricature and shall have the right to simulate Actor's voice, signature and appearance by any means in and in connection with the film and the advertising, publicizing, exhibition, and/or other exploitation thereof in any manner and by any means and in connection with commercial advertising and publicity tie-ups.

8. Merchandising: Producer is also granted the further exclusive right and license, but only in connection with the role portrayed by Actor in the film, to use and to license the use of Actor's name, sobriquet, pseudonym, photograph, likeness, caricature and/or signature (collectively referred to herein as "name and likeness") in and in connection with any merchandising and/or publishing undertakings. In consideration therefor, Producer shall pay Actor a *pro-rata* share (payable among all Actors whose name, etc. is used on a piece of merchandise) of $2\ 1/2\%$ (Two and one-half %) of the gross monies actually derived by Producer after deducting therefrom a distribution fee of fifty percent (50%) thereof as well as a sum equal to all Producer's actual out-of-pocket expenses in connection therewith, for the use of such name or likeness on merchandising and publishing items which utilize Actor's name and likeness, other than in a listing of cast credits.

9. Producer is also granted the further and exclusive right to use and to license the use of and to advertise and publicize the use of Actor's voice from the soundtrack of the film on commercial phonograph records and albums and the exclusive right to use Actor's name and likeness on jackets and labels of such commercial phonograph records and albums.

10. **Screen and Advertising Credits:** Actor shall be accorded credit in accordance with the credit details supplied by Actor, only if Actor has performed substantially all services called for hereunder and appears recognizably in the Picture. The obligation to accord credit to Actor in advertisements shall apply only to paid advertisements issued by Producer, or under its direct control, relating primarily to the picture. This obligation shall in no event extend to so-called "trailors" or other advertising on the screen or by radio or television; or other advertising not relating primarily to the Picture; or to advertising of such nature that Actor has not granted consent to use the Actor's name in connection therewith. All matters relating to Actor's credit, such as size, style of type, placement, colour, etc., shall be at Producer's sole discretion. No casual or inadvertent failure to comply with the provisions of this paragraph and/or the credit details supplied by Actor shall constitute a breach of the Agreement. The rights and remedies of Actor in the event of any breach of this Agreement shall be limited to Actor's right, if any, to recover damages in an action at law and in no event shall Actor be entitled by reason of any such breach to terminate this Agreement or to seek to enjoin or restrain the exhibition, distribution, advertising, exploitation or marketing of the Picture.

11. **Travel:** Solely in the event that Producer requires Actor to render services under this agreement outside of the Mumbai metropolitan area, then Producer agrees to furnish Actor with one (1) business-class round-trip airfare (if available and if used) and ground transportation to and from the airport as well as reasonable hotel accommodations.

12. *Force Majeure*: As used herein the term "force majeure" means epidemic, act of God, strike, lockout, labour condition, unavailability of materials, transportation, power or other commodity, delay of common carrier, civil disturbance, riot, war or armed conflict (whether or not there has been an official declaration of war), the enactment of any law, the issuance of any executive or judicial order or decree, breach of contract by, or disability of, the Producer, Director, other principal cast member, breach of contract by a financier or completion guarantor, or other similar occurrence beyond the control of Producer, which causes an interruption of or materially hampers or materially interferes with the production of the Picture.

13. **Inclusive Payments:** All payments to Actor hereunder shall be deemed to be equitable and inclusive remuneration for all services rendered by Actor in connection with the Picture and to be paid by way of a complete buy-out of all rights granted to Producer hereunder and no further sums shall be payable to Actor by Producer by reason of the exploitation of the Picture and all results and

proceeds of Actor's services hereunder, in any and all media throughout the universe.

14. Withholding: Producer may deduct and withhold from any monies otherwise payable under this Agreement such amounts as Producer may reasonably believe it is legally required to deduct and withhold.

15. Assignment: Producer shall have the right to assign this Agreement and any of the rights granted herein, in whole or in part, to any person, firm, corporation or entity, and nothing contained herein shall imply anything to the contrary. Upon the assignee's assumption of the obligations of Producer with respect to the rights so assigned, Producer shall be relieved of all such obligations. Producer shall also have the right to lend the services of Actor to any person, firm or corporation which is a subsidiary, parent or affiliate of Producer or the successor to Producer by a merger or by a transfer of substantially all of Producer's assets hereunder. In the event of any such lending, Actor agrees to render his services to the best of his ability to the person, firm, or corporation to whom his services are loaned hereunder. Actor may not assign Actor's rights or obligations hereunder.

16. Arbitration: Any controversy or claim arising out of or relating to this agreement or any breach thereof shall be settled by arbitration in accordance with the Arbitration and Conciliation Act, 1996 and the seat of Arbitration shall be at .... (place). The prevailing party shall be entitled to reimbursement for costs and reasonable attorney's fees. In the event of any breach by the Producer of this Agreement, the Actor shall be limited to the Actor's remedy at law for damages, if any, and shall not have the right to terminate or rescind this Agreement or to enjoin or restrain in any way the production, distribution, advertising or exploitation of the Picture.

IN WITNESS WHEREOF, the parties have executed this agreement on the day and year first above written.

AGREED TO AND ACCEPTED:

....

(signature)

....

(print name)

(Actor)

Actor address:

Actor Phone number:

AGREED TO AND ACCEPTED:

...................,

(For Producer)

By:....................

MEMORANDUM OF UNDERSTANDING BETWEEN TWO MEDIA COMPANIES

This MEMORANDUM OF UNDERSTANDING ("MOU") is made and entered into on ...., 20.....

BETWEEN

Alpha, a company limited by guarantee incorporated under section 25 of the (Indian) Companies Act, 1956, having its office at .... (address), (hereinafter referred to as "*Alpha*" which expression shall, unless excluded by or repugnant to the context or meaning thereof, be deemed to include its successors or permitted assigns, through its authorized representative), on the First Part;

AND

Beta, a Non-Governmental Organisation and a Society registered under the Societies Registration Act, 1860, having its registered office at .... (address), (hereinafter referred to as "*Beta*", which expression shall, unless excluded by or repugnant to the context or meaning thereof, be deemed to include its successors or permitted assigns, through its authorized representative), on the Second Part.

The parties to this MOU are individually referred to as the "Party" and collectively referred to as "Parties".

WHEREAS

1. *Alpha* is a collaborative effort between the .... (name of the ministry of a country) and .... (name of the institution) *Alpha* has objects that include working together with industry, non-governmental organizations, government, international organizations, academicia and most importantly ordinary people to bring the latest technological innovations to the common man.

2. *Beta* is a leading regional centre committed to the promotion of Geographic Information Systems (GIS) and its usage in various development activities, which assists the Asian community in developing their capabilities and policies to maximise the benefits of GIS through advocacy, training, information and the provision of expert advice and assistance.

3. The Parties have agreed to undertake a project that pursues the creation of a 'Digital Village' and the development, deployment, transfer and pursuit of standards of 'rurally relevant technology' to the grassroots that can enable the societies a faster and more efficient decision-making process in local governance. The "Digital Village" project will stitch together elements of technology from the other three projects, namely " Bits-for-All", "World Computer" and "Tomorrows Tools" for sustainable deployment of integrated set of technologies relevant for the rural masses. The technology and system integration elements of "Digital Village" will be outlined by *Alpha* on an on-going basis. This project aims to revolutionize rural society by transforming the traditional livelihood with not only digital services and usage but also having an intervention into the development process. ("the Project").

4. Pursuant to the review of the proposal submitted by *Beta* ("Project Proposal"), comprising of the Technical and Management Work Plan ("TMW Plan") annexed hereto in Annexure I, Volume I, the Cost Work Plan ("CW Plan"),

annexed hereto in Annexure I, Volume II and the budget proposal ("Budget Proposal"), annexed hereto as Annexure II, *Alpha* has selected *Beta* for a grant of a maximum of Rs. .... in support of the Project (hereinafter referred to as the "Grant"), which monies shall be disbursed to *Beta* in terms of the provisions of this MOU.

5. The Parties hereto are desirous of recording in writing hereof the terms and conditions for undertaking the Project and the manner in which the Grant shall be utilised.

NOW THEREFORE, in consideration of the promises made in this MOU, *Alpha* and *Beta* agree as follows:

1. Project and Project Administration

1.1 In consideration of *Alpha* providing funds to *Beta* through the Grant, in terms of clause 2 of this MOU, *Beta* shall undertake the Project in accordance with the procedures, processes and other details provided in the Project Proposal.

1.2 The Project shall undertake research and development work by *Beta*, and the Parties shall cooperate to undertake the Project efficiently and expeditiously. *Beta* shall undertake and complete the various goals of the Project within the timelines projected in the Project Proposal, subject to a maximum period of .... months from the Effective Date (as defined in clause 14.1) unless terminated earlier in accordance with clause 12. Upon the expiry of the Term, *Beta* shall submit the Project to *Alpha* for its approval.

1.3 The Parties agree that *Beta* shall be primarily liable to meet the targets and milestones set for the Project according to the Project Proposal. In the event that *Beta* is unable to undertake the Project according to the Project Proposal, it shall be the absolute responsibility of *Beta* to inform *Alpha* of the same as soon as possible, and *Alpha* shall have the right at its option to either (a) propose changes to the Project Proposal under clause 1.9, or (b) terminate this MOU under Clause 12.

1.4 *Beta* shall require its researchers and other personnel involved in the Project to dedicate substantial portion of their time and effort to the Project and shall require that they shall not be involved in any work/ research other than the Project, which would adversely affect the quality of work and performance of such researchers and other personnel in the Project. *Beta* further agrees that it shall bear responsibility for the work performance and research quality of all individual researchers and personnel associated with the Project. (Mention A and B by name)

1.5 The persons involved in the Project shall be those specified in the Personnel Profile of the TMW Plan. The Project Manager Administrative, Project Manager Technical and Accountant , specified as per the said Personnel Profile of the TMW Plan shall constitute the Project Management Committee ("Project Management Committee") and such persons shall bear all responsibilities relating to the Project,. including but not limited to any decision making relating to the undertaking of the Project, application of funds out of the Grant from *Alpha*, incurring expenses in relation to the Project, recruitment of further personnel and researchers for undertaking the Project, providing *Alpha* with all documentation and details as and when required and doing any other acts in relation to the undertaking of the Project. *Beta* acknowledges that the responsibility of the Project Management Committee is administrative in nature and *Beta* shall bear all liability arising out of the actions and omissions of the Project Management Committee, related to the Grant and/or the Project.

1.6 The Project Management Committee shall engage a core staff to carry out the research and development activities and also to maintain the facilities and infrastructure required. The appointment of the said core staff shall be on the basis of the Personnel Profile contained in the TMW Plan. *Alpha* shall be entitled to depute or second any personnel to be involved in the Project and *Beta* agrees that it shall involve such personnel deputed or seconded by *Alpha* for the Project. The Project Management Committee in concurrence with *Alpha* shall determine the terms and conditions of association of the researchers and other personnel involved in the Project. *Beta* shall be responsible to comply with all applicable laws, including any statutes, government notifications, guidelines or executive orders that would apply to the employment of any personnel in relation to the Project.

1.7 The Project Management Committee shall review the progress of the Project. The Project Management Committee shall also submit monthly reviews of the work undertaken by *Beta* in relation to the Project and the proposed estimations of the work to be undertaken in the next month, to *Alpha*. It shall also submit monthly reports to *Alpha* comparing actual progress of the Project with the timelines projected in the TMW Plan.

1.8 *Alpha* shall have the unrestricted and absolute right to monitor and review the developments in the Project at any time during the duration of the Term. *Beta* shall furnish to *Alpha*, all information and details regarding the Project, at any time during the Term, as and when required by *Alpha*.

1.9 *Alpha* shall be entitled to propose any appropriate and reasonable changes to the Project Proposal, in conformity with the objects of the Project as prescribed in the Project Proposal, for undertaking the Project in consultation with *Beta*, which proposed changes shall be intimated in writing to *Beta*. In the event that *Beta* does not accept such changes to the Project Proposal within 15 (fifteen) days of intimation of such proposed changes to the Project Proposal, *Alpha* is entitled to terminate this MOU by giving thirty (30) days prior notice to *Beta* under clause 12.

1.10 In the event that any of the member(s) of the Project Management Committee or any software team leader(s) involved/associated with the Project or as specified in the Project Proposal, leave(s) or disassociate(s) himself/herself/themselves from the Project during the Term, it shall be the absolute responsibility of *Beta* to inform *Alpha* of the same within three days of such formal leave or disassociation. Upon such intimation by *Beta* to *Alpha*, *Alpha* may either (a) approve of any alternative arrangement, or (b) shall be entitled to terminate this MOU under clause 12.

1.11 Notwithstanding anything contained in this MOU, the Parties agree that in the event of any change in the strategy or manner of undertaking the Project or the personnel involved in the Project, in deviation from the Project Proposal, which may materially adversely affect the realization of objectives of the Project as specified in the Project Proposal, *Alpha* shall have the right to terminate this MOU under clause 12. The Parties agree that they may make any changes to the strategy or manner of undertaking the Project or the personnel involved in the Project, in deviation from the Project Proposal by mutual consent.

1.12 The Project shall include field work at places as mutually agreed between the Parties in writing, and research and experiments to be conducted at premises at places as mutually agreed between the Parties in writing. Such field work shall be in conformity with the goals specified in the TMW Plan and the steps laid down therein to achieve the said goals.

1.13 *Beta* shall on a periodic basis as mutually agreed to between Parties in writing, cause the source codes and other programmes, materials or products developed in relation to the Project to *Alpha*, to be backed up and delivered to a destination in a manner to be specified by *Alpha*.

1.14 *Beta* agrees that it shall provide office space admeasuring approximately .... (square feet) at.................... (address), for the purposes of the Project during the Term, free of cost to *Alpha*. *Beta* grants *Alpha*, its employees, affiliates and other authorized representatives, unrestricted access to use the said premises for the purposes of the Project to be called *Alpha* Lab or something to that effect.

2. Grant, Disbursement of Funds and Maintenance of Accounts

2.1 *Alpha* shall provide funds for undertaking the Project through a maximum grant of Rs. .... (amount in currency) (the "Grant") in the manner as provided in this clause 2. The Parties agree that the above-mentioned sum is inclusive of all applicable taxes, and such taxes shall be deducted prior to the granting of the said amounts to *Beta*.

2.2 *Alpha* shall advance funds out of the Grant to *Beta* as monthly advances based on the Budget Proposal annexed herein. Provided that payment for any assets ("Assets") which are to be procured in accordance with the Budget Proposal shall be made by *Alpha* at the beginning of the Project or as and when assets are to be acquired and such payments shall not be included in the monthly advances payable by *Alpha* to *Beta*.

2.3 The estimate of expenses provided by *Beta* in advance shall be in accordance with the general estimate of the cost and expenses to be incurred in undertaking the Project as specified in the Project Proposal.

2.4 Notwithstanding anything contained in this clause 2, the Parties agree that the funds advanced by *Alpha* to *Beta* under clause 2.2 shall be used to reimburse the actual expenses that would be incurred by *Beta* in the month for the Project, and *Beta* shall provide to *Alpha* copies of all bills and/or other documents evidencing the incurring of such expenses, within seven (7) days from the receipt of any demand from *Alpha* for such bills and/or other documents evidencing the incurring of such expenses. *Beta* agrees that in the event that any amounts out of the funds advanced to *Beta* remains unexpended, such unexpended amounts shall be carried forward to the proposed expenses to be incurred by *Beta* during the next month of the Project. The Parties further agree that if any of the funds advanced by *Alpha* to *Beta* under this Clause 2 based on a reasonable estimate of the expenses for the Project, as indicated in the Budget Proposal, remains unexpended at the end of the Term, *Beta* shall reimburse such unexpended amounts within 15 (fifteen) days from the expiry of the Term.

2.5 *Beta* shall use the funds from the Grant solely for the purposes of the Project, and in the manner as indicated in the Budget Proposal. *Beta* shall use the funds from the Grant provided by *Alpha* for each month upto the maximum limits as specified in the Budget Proposal for each of the heads of expenses. *Beta* further agrees that it shall maintain a separate bank account, details of which shall be notified to *Alpha* within seven (7) days of execution of this MOU and all monies in respect of this Project shall be held in such separate bank account.

2.6 Upon disbursement of funds for each month by *Alpha*, the Project Management Committee shall acknowledge receipt of the funds in writing. In the event that this receipt is not forwarded to *Alpha* within three (3) days from the date of the clearance of the cheque in respect of the funds disbursed by *Alpha* to *Beta* under this clause 2, *Alpha* may cancel or suspend any further payments till such time that the Project Management Committee acknowledges receipt of the funds in writing.

2.7 *Alpha* may require *Beta* to account for any misapplied funds or non-utilized monies from the Grant or non-performance or wastage of the funds advanced, and *Beta* shall account for the same notwithstanding any right of general supervision or monitoring that *Alpha* may have retained to itself in accordance with the provisions of this MOU. *Alpha* shall bear no liability for any mismanagement of funds for the Project by *Beta* for any reason whatsoever.

2.8 *Beta* shall maintain full and separate ledger accounts and records of the expenses relating to the Project. At the end of every quarter of the Term and no later than fourteen (14) days from the date of expiry of the quarter, *Beta* shall submit to *Alpha*:

   2.8.1 a complete certified statement of account of the use of the funds from the Grant during the previous quarter, as certified by the auditors of *Beta*;

   2.8.2 a copy of its externally audited financial reports along with the observations and comments of its external auditor appointed for this purpose; and

   2.8.3 a statement of the reasonable estimate of the costs and expenses to be incurred by the Project during the next quarter, with details of the nature and heads of expenses.

2.9 Notwithstanding anything contained in clause 2.8, *Alpha* shall have the right to seek a special audit of the accounts of *Beta* relating to the Project at any time during the Term and for a period of three (3) years from the expiry of the Term by giving a notice to *Beta* of 14 (fourteen) days for such special audit, and to suggest any method of accounting for the purposes of clause 2.8, which shall be followed by *Beta*.

2.10 *Alpha* may at any time at its option after consultation with *Beta*, by a notice of at least fourteen (14) days, vary the total amount of the Grant or vary the maximum limits under each of the heads of expense as specified in the Project Proposal and also alter or modify the nature and heads of expenses in relation to the Project.

2.11 The Parties agree that any Assets, as specified in the Budget Proposal, shall be procured by *Beta* in consultation with *Alpha*, unless otherwise agreed between the Parties, and such Assets shall be placed at the premises where the relevant works related to the Project are undertaken, in consultation with *Beta*. Such Assets shall remain the sole property of *Alpha*. *Alpha* may also at its option permit *Beta* to procure any of the Assets or any additional assets as may be required for undertaking the Project and as may be agreed mutually between the Parties in writing ("Additional Assets"). Funds for such asset purchase shall be advanced by *Alpha* to *Beta* as per clause 2.2. *Beta* agrees that it shall procure such Assets and Additional Assets for the Project in the name of *Alpha*, and such Assets and Additional Assets shall remain the sole property of *Alpha*. All assets used for the Project, whether Assets that are directly procured by *Alpha* or Assets or Additional Assets that are procured by *Beta* at the instance of *Alpha* under this clause 2.11, shall be licensed by *Alpha* to *Beta* for the Term for the limited use of undertaking the Project under this MOU.

2.12 The Parties agree that all assets procured for the purposes of the Project under clause 2.11 shall be returned to *Alpha* on demand, at the end of the Term or earlier.

2.13 The Parties agree that all assets, including all assets and equipments, procured or developed solely or mainly out of the Grant or as a result of any activity under this MOU shall not be used for any purpose other than for the purposes of the Project, and the assets shall not be disposed off or encumbered by *Beta*. *Beta* further agrees that it shall maintain a fixed asset register for all the assets that are procured and are utilized for the purposes of the Project.

3. Representations and Warranties of BETA

Beta represents and warrants as follows:

(a) *Beta* is valid and legally existing society under the Societies Registration Act, 1860 of India.

(b) *Beta* shall not at any time after the date hereof, do any act that may materially/adversely affect the Project.

(c) The Project Proposal is original and *Beta* shall undertake the administration of the research for the Project. *Beta* further represents that it shall take all reasonable endeavours to retain the Project as the first and original work and to the best of their knowledge and belief, the Project has not been previously undertaken, published, discussed or developed by itself or any third party.

4. Intellectual Property Rights

4.1 "Intellectual Property"('IP") shall mean any information, inventions, computer software, semi-conductor topographies (mask works), designs (registered and unregistered) and any works in which copyright and other like rights are recognized by the prevalent laws, including any research reports and other works, (excepting any such work when it is expressed in the form of an artistic or scholarly work), the subject matter of which is invented, discovered, created, acquired or otherwise generated in the course of undertaking the Project under this MOU.

4.2 The Parties agree that all IP, whether individually developed by *Beta* or jointly developed by *Beta* and *Alpha* or acquired by *Beta* or jointly by *Beta* and *Alpha* while undertaking the Project, shall constitute the absolute property of *Alpha*. All such IP shall be fully and promptly disclosed in writing and in confidence by *Beta* to *Alpha*, within seven (7) days from the date of acquiring/development of such IP. *Alpha* shall have the exclusive right to take any action necessary to obtain intellectual property protection of such IP, including the selection of appropriate attorney to file and prosecute such protection. The Parties shall hold the newly disclosed IP in confidence for a period of ninety days from the date of disclosure in order to secure patent, copyright or other intellectual property protections, applications or registrations.

4.3 The Parties agree that in the event that the ownership rights of the IP are deemed to vest with *Beta* under any applicable laws, *Beta* shall be obliged to take all steps to ensure that the ownership rights to the IP are transferred to and vested in *Alpha*, free of all costs, within a period of thirty (30) days from the date of acquiring/development of such IP.

4.4 *Alpha* agrees to grant to *Beta* a royalty free non-exclusive licence of the IP for research usage rights for a period of two (2) years from the date of disclosure of any IP under clause 4.2 where such IP has been developed in the course of the Project. *Beta* shall not grant any sub-license or assign any rights to any third party under such limited licence granted by *Alpha* under this clause 4.4.

4.5 The Parties agree that the IP shall be made available to the sponsors' of *Alpha* through non-exclusive royalty free licenses. The sponsors of *Alpha* will be given the first right to commercially exploit any IP resulting out of the Project, for a period of two (2) years from the date of disclosure of such IP under clause 4.2.

4.6 In the event that *Beta* brings any prior art, owned by *Beta* or any of its researchers/personnel for the Project, *Beta* agrees that it shall provide royalty free licenses of such intellectual property to the sponsors of *Alpha* for the purposes of this Project, or to the extent that such prior art is related to the Project or becomes a part of the Intellectual Property.

5. Publication

5.1 Any publications arising out of works carried out as a part of the Project under this MOU ("Publication(s)"), if any, shall be jointly authored by the relevant research parties of both *Alpha* and *Beta*, in accordance with their contributions to the content of the Publication. Either Party, at their sole discretion, may choose not to contribute authorship to such Publications. In the event that any external third parties have contributed to such Publications, *Alpha* and *Beta* shall mutually agree to their co-authorship. The timing of such Publications shall be decided mutually by the Parties keeping in mind the spirit of the educational and research commitments of *Beta* and the interests of *Alpha*.

5.2 Any written Publication shall contain the following statement: "This Publication is an output from a research project, which is a collaborative effort of *Alpha* and *Beta*, and funded by .... (name of the ministry of a country). The research was carried out in collaboration between Centre for .... in support of the .... programme"

5.3 *Beta* agrees that it shall make any Publication only with the prior written consent of *Alpha*. *Beta* shall give *Alpha* a copy of the subject matter of the Publication, thirty (30) days prior to the Publication, so that *Alpha* may review such proposed Publication to enable *Alpha* to determine whether and what protection should be obtained for the IP involved in the Publication.

5.4 *Alpha* or *Beta*, whichever makes the Publications, within ten (10) days of the date of Publication, shall supply the other Party with as many copies of the written Publication as the other Party may reasonably request and in any event a minimum of two copies.

6. Warranty

6.1 The Parties agree that they shall take reasonable steps to ensure that the IP involved in the technology and know-how developed during or as a result of the Project, does not infringe the intellectual property rights of any third parties.

6.2 Notwithstanding anything contained in clause 6.1, *Beta* warrants that the use or exploitation of the IP will not infringe the rights of any third party or of *Alpha* and, subject to clause 4 above, no license of any rights is granted by *Alpha* to *Beta* in any IP.

7. Confidentiality

7.1 "Confidential Information" shall mean any business, marketing, technical, scientific or other information disclosed which, at the time of disclosure, is designated as confidential (or like designation), is disclosed in circumstances of confidence, or would be understood by the Parties, exercising reasonable business judgment, to be confidential, any work done under this MOU and/or the terms of this MOU. However, "Confidential Information" shall not include any information which:

(a) was previously known by the receiving Party, as evidenced by its business records; or

(b) is lawfully in the public domain, other than through a breach of this MOU; or

(c) was disclosed to the receiving Party by a third party without any restrictions on its use or disclosure, provided the third party is not itself in breach of any obligations of confidence with respect to such information; or

(d) is independently developed by the receiving Party, as evidenced by its business records; or

(e) is authorized by a third party with the right to do so; or

(f) is compelled by law, provided the disclosing Party provides the other Party with prompt notice of any efforts to compel disclosure and reasonably co-operates with other Party's lawful attempts to prevent disclosure or to obtain a protective order.

7.2 Subject to provisions of clause 4, the Parties shall maintain any and all Confidential Information in confidence, and disclose the same only to employees, students, professors, participants and researchers for the purposes of undertaking the Project during the Term. The Parties shall use the same degree of care as each of them uses to protect its own Confidential Information of a similar nature, but no less than reasonable care, to prevent the unauthorized use, dissemination or publication of Confidential Information. Provided that nothing in this clause 7 shall apply to the normal activities of *Alpha* which involve the disclosure of such Confidential Information, except during the ninety day period following the declaration of new IP when patent, copyright, or other protection is being considered or sought.

8. Non-Competition of *Beta*

8.1 *Beta* agrees that it shall not itself or jointly with another party, undertake or set up another organization that undertakes any other activity, project or business that is identical or similar to the Project to be undertaken under this MOU and has the same principal stated objective and scope as the principal stated objective and scope as that of the Project, during the Term, except with the prior written consent of *Alpha*.

8.2 *Beta* further covenants that it shall not discuss with any other organization or person, the details of the Project nor take any grant/ monetary help/ scholarship/ funding or any other form of financing from any other source other than *Alpha* under this MOU, for activities within the scope of the Project, except with the prior written consent of *Alpha*.

9. Indemnification

9.1 Notwithstanding anything contained in this MOU, *Beta* shall defend, indemnify and hold *Alpha*, its sponsors, affiliates, and its employees or agents harmless from and against any and all liability, loss, expense (including reasonable attorneys' fees), or claims for injury or damages arising out of the performance of this MOU but only in proportion to and to the extent such liability, loss, expense, attorneys' fees or claims for injury or damages are caused by or result from the negligence or intentional acts or omissions of *Beta*, its officers, agents, employees, researchers or personnel involved in undertaking the Project under this MOU.

9.2 *Alpha* shall defend, indemnify and hold *Beta* harmless from and against all liability, loss, expense (including reasonable attorneys' fees), or claims for injury or damages arising out of the performance of this MOU but only in proportion to and to the extent such liability, loss, expense, attorneys' fees or claims for injury or damages are caused by or result from the negligence or intentional acts or omissions of *Alpha* under this MOU.

10. Notices

Any Notice hereunder shall be in writing and sent to the following address:

Beta: ....
             ....
             .... (address)

Alpha: ....
             ....
             .... (address)

11. Force Majeure

If the performance of this MOU by *Beta* as per the Project Proposal is delayed, hindered or prevented or is otherwise frustrated by reason of *force majeure*, which shall mean war, civil commotion or disturbances, fire, flood, action by then it shall promptly notify *Alpha* in writing specifying the nature of the *force majeure* and of the anticipated delay in the performance of this MOU, and as of the date of that notification, *Alpha* may suspend the performance of this MOU until the cause of the delay ends. If the period of suspension exceeds 6 months, then, at any time after the six (6) months period of suspension, *Alpha* may terminate this MOU by and upon giving notice to *Beta*.

12. Termination

12.1 Either Party may terminate this MOU by giving the other Party, thirty (30) days prior written notice of termination, in the event of breach of obligations by the other Party under this MOU.

12.2 *Alpha* may terminate this MOU at any time for any reasons whatsoever, by giving sixty (60) days prior written notice of such termination and the reasons for such termination to *Beta*.

12.3 Upon any termination of this MOU under this clause 12, *Beta* shall:

- 12.3.1 ensure that it does not incur any further commitments with respect to the Project;
- 12.3.2 shall reimburse *Alpha* for all unexpended amounts out of the monthly quarterly advance payments made by *Alpha* under clause 2.2, if any amounts have not been expended by *Beta* for the Project

till the date of termination of the MOU by *Alpha* within 15 (fifteen) days from the date of termination; and

12.3.3 deliver possession of all Assets used in the Project and all information and other work products of the Project, including the IP, to *Alpha* within fifteen (15) days from the date of termination.

12.4 In the event of termination of this MOU by *Alpha*, other than under clause 12.1, *Alpha* agrees to pay *Beta* for all costs up to the date of termination, including all uncancellable commitments of *Beta* in accordance with the Project Proposal, if any, which have not been paid for by *Alpha* in the previous monthly advances made by *Alpha* to *Beta* under clause 2.2.

12.5 All clauses intended to survive termination or expiration of this MOU, including but not limited to, the clauses titled "Intellectual Property Rights", "Confidential Information", and "Indemnification" shall survive the termination or expiry of this MOU.

13. Arbitration

Assignablity clause to be included

13.1 In case of any question, dispute or differences between the Parties arising out of or in connection with this MOU or breach, termination or validity thereof ("Dispute"), such Dispute shall be referred to the General Manager, ... (place) of *Alpha* and the Executive Director of *Beta* in the first instance for an amicable solution. In the event that such Dispute does not get resolved within a period of thirty (30) days thereafter, it shall be escalated to the Managing Director of *Alpha* and the Chairman of *Beta* for due resolution.

13.2 If the Dispute cannot be settled amicably, under clause 13.1, either Party, as soon as practicable, but not earlier than 45 days after a request for such amicable settlement to the Managing Director of *Alpha* and the Chairman of *Beta* has been made, give to the other Party a notice in writing of the existence of such Dispute, and the same shall be finally settled by arbitration conducted in .... (place) in accordance with the provisions of the Arbitration and Conciliation Act, 1996 and the rules made thereunder for the time being in force shall apply to the said arbitration proceedings.

13.3 Each of *Beta* and *Alpha* shall appoint one arbitrator each, and such two arbitrators so appointed, *Alpha* shall jointly select a third arbitrator. The award of the arbitrators shall be binding on both the Parties.

14. Effective Date and Duration of MOU

14.1 This MOU shall be effective from .... (date) ("Effective Date"), and shall continue to be effective for a period of .... months from the Effective Date, or upon the termination of this MOU under clause 12, whichever is earlier ("Term"). The Parties may extend the Term at the end of this period by prior mutual consent in writing.

14.2 The Parties agree that all assets/equipments used in the Project and all information and other work products of the Project, including the IP shall, at the end of the Term, be the sole, exclusive and absolute property of *Alpha*.

14.3 In the event that any of the funds advanced by *Alpha* to *Beta* under clause 2 based on a reasonable estimate of the expenses for the Project, as indicated in the Budget Proposal, remains unexpended at the end of the Term, *Beta* shall reimburse such unexpended amounts within .... days from the expiry of the Term.

14A. Publicity

14A.1 *Beta* shall not make any public statements pertaining to this MOU or the work done hereunder to any third parties, orally or in writing, including placing of the same on websites, without obtaining the prior written approval of *Alpha*. *Beta* shall acknowledge and give due credit to *Alpha* in such public statements.

14A.2 *Alpha* shall make all reasonable efforts to acknowledge the participation of *Beta* in the case of any public statements pertaining to this MOU, this Project, or the work done hereunder, in writing, including placing of the same on websites.

14A.3 *Beta* shall provide *Alpha* prior information and notice of all external seminars, conferences and the like that are directly or indirectly related to the Project or the work done under this MOU.

14A.4 All communications to *Alpha* under this section shall be made to the Manager, Corporate Communications Department, *Alpha*.

15. Miscellaneous

15.1 This MOU and any rights or obligations hereunder shall not be assigned or transferred by either party without the prior written consent of the other party; any attempted assignment without the other party's prior written consent shall be void.

15.2 The provisions of this MOU are severable, and, if any provision, or any portion thereof, is deemed by a court or arbitrator of competent jurisdiction to be invalid, illegal, or unenforceable for any reason, the remaining provisions, or remaining portions thereof, shall remain valid and enforceable to the fullest extent permitted by law. The captions used in this MOU are for convenience only and shall not be deemed to have any relevance to the meaning of any of the provisions.

15.3 The provisions and any breach of this MOU shall not be waived, except expressly in writing signed by the waiving party. A waiver on one occasion or of one provision or breach shall not constitute a waiver on another occasion or of another provision or breach. Time is of the essence of this MOU.

15.4 This MOU shall not be amended or cancelled, unless such amendment or cancellation shall be expressly agreed in writing executed by a duly authorized officer of each Party.

15.5 This MOU including all the annexures supersedes any previous negotiations or agreements between the Parties, whether oral or in writing, in relation to the matters dealt with herein and represents the entire understanding between the Parties in relation thereto.

15.6 *Beta* as a research collaborator is an independent contractor and not an agent, joint venture, or partner of *Alpha*.

15.7 This MOU shall be governed by the laws of India, and the courts at .... shall have the exclusive jurisdiction with respect to any matters arising in relation to this MOU.

IN WITNESS whereof the Parties have executed this MOU by their duly authorized representatives, as of the date hereof.

Alpha   Witnessed by:

     By:....................   (1)

     Name:....................   (2)

     Title:....................

     Date:....................

Beta   Witnessed by:

     By:....................   (1)

     Name:....................   (2)

     Title:....................

     Date:....................

PATENT AGREEMENT FOR EMPLOYEES

In consideration of my employment with .... or one of its divisions, subsidiaries, or affiliates (collectively, "..................") and for other good and valuable consideration, the receipt and sufficiency of which are acknowledged, I agree promptly to reduce to writing and to disclose and assign and I do hereby assign to ...., its successors, assigns and nominees, all inventions, discoveries, improvements, copyrightable material, trademarks and ideas and concepts concerning the same, which I may make or conceive, either solely or jointly with others, during the period of my employment, capable of use in connection with the business of ...., or in any way connected with the present business of ...., or any normal extension thereof, or made with the use of the time, material or facilities of ....

I agree without charge to ...., but at its expense, to execute, acknowledge and deliver all such papers, including applications for patent, applications for copyright and trademark registrations and employment thereof, as .... may request and at all times to assist .... in every proper way to patent or register said ideas, concepts, inventions, discoveries, improvements, copyrightable material and/or trademarks in any and all countries and to vest title thereto in ...., its successors, assigns or nominees.

I agree that I will not, during the term of my employment or subsequent thereto, except as required in the conduct of the business of ...., or as authorised in writing on behalf of ...., use, publish, or disclose, or assist or authorise anyone to use, publish or disclose, any secret or confidential information or knowledge concerning any matter relating to the business of ...., which I may in any way learn or acquire by reason of my employment.

I agree that I will, upon leaving my employment at ...., deliver to .... and not otherwise dispose or make use of all original and copies of all................... related information and property, including all equipment, samples, literature, contracts, records, lists, drawing, blue prints, letters, notes, data and the like.

I understand that this Employee's Patent Agreement supersedes any................... Patent Agreement which I may have previously signed and does not apply to any of my inventions for which no equipment, supplies, facility, or trade secret information of .... was used and which was developed entirely on my own time, unless (a) the version relates (i) to the business of .... or (ii) to *Alpha* Infotech's actual or demonstrably anticipated research or development, or (b) the invention results from any work performed by me for ....

I agree that during the term of my employment, I will not engage in, or be employed by, any business competitive to the business of................... I understand that my obligations under this Agreement will survive the expiration or termination of this Agreement and/or my employment by...................

I acknowledge that I have signed and received a copy of this Agreement this .... day of..................., 20.....

EMPLOYEE

SIGNATURE:...................

PATENTS, PATENT LICENSING AND PROTECTION IN INDIA

For the Information Technology industry, patent law is still as relevant as ever. A patent owner is granted certain exclusive rights to a particular invention, including the right to make, use, and sell the invention and obvious extensions of it. One purpose of the patent grant is to enable the inventor to better profit from his efforts in the absence of competition from copycats. In the fast-paced world of computer technology, being the first to develop and patent an invention, which meets an unsatisfied demand in the market, can provide significant leverage over competitors.

The patent owner may also agree to let others make use of the patented invention. Typically, this is done by means of a license agreement, which specifies what the licensee may do with the invention in exchange for a royalty paid to the licensor. Patents and other licences are common in the computer industry, and have in fact shaped major facets of the personal computer market. Consider, for example, the effects of IBM's decision to license the operating system for its PC computer from a small Company named Microsoft.

Patents

What is a Patent?

A Patent is a form of intellectual property rights in, among other things, a new and useful device, design or process. In India, whose laws are fairly typical in key respects, a patent is:—

   (1) right granted by the Government;
   (2) to exclude others;
   (3) from engaging in activities such as making, using, importing, offering to sell or selling an invention.

Consider each one of these characteristics in turn. *First*, the justification for patent law is that granting a limited monopoly right to inventors balances the interest of inventors, who seek compensation for their efforts, competitors, who desire to make use of previous inventions in their own inventions, and the public, which benefits from the availability of new and useful inventions.

Second, a patent right is an exclusionary right; that is, it is a right to exclude others from using the patented invention for the duration of the patent term. It is not an affirmative right to produce the patented invention or to use it for any particular purpose. Production, use, or sale of a patented invention may conflict with the existing laws or other patents, and such activities are not legitimised by the mere existence of a patent.

The *third*, and most significant, aspect of the patent right is what it entitles the patent holder to exclude others from doing, which includes making, using or selling, the patented invention. When someone engages in such activities, they are said to have infringed the patent. A patent may be 'literally' infringed by a device or process that falls within the literal scope of one or more of the patents claims.

When a patent holder believes that his patent has been infringed, a possible recourse is to commence a civil action in a district court. In his defence, the defendant can claim that his invention does not infringe the patent, or that the patent itself is invalid. A successful patent infringement suit typically results in a permanent injunction prohibiting the defendant from engaging in any further acts of infringement. In addition, a successful plaintiff can obtain monetary damages to compensate for the harm caused by infringement.

How is a patent obtained?

Patents in India are obtained by filing a patent application with the Controller of Patents, pursuant to the Patent Act, 1970.

In order to obtain a patent on an invention, the invention must be:

   (1) patentable subject matter;
   (2) novel;
   (3) non-obvious; and
   (4) useful.

Consider each one of these in turn. First, the invention must be of a kind recognised as patentable by the applicable law. Patentable subject-matter includes any 'process, machine, article of manufacture, or composition of matter'. This is a very broad definition and can include computer hardware and software.

Not every idea can be patented. In particular, mere ideas or abstract principles cannot be patented. Similarly, discoveries of the laws of nature and physical phenomena cannot be patented. New, useful, and non-obvious inventions based on such ideas and phenomena, however, can be patented.

In addition to being patentable subject-matter, an invention must be novel in order to be patentable. An invention is 'novel' if, at the time it was invented, it was not 'known or used by others in this country, or patented or described in a printed publication in this or a foreign country'. The knowledge and inventions, which existed at the time the invention was created, is referred to as 'prior art'. Another way, therefore, to describe the novelty requirement is to say that an invention is not novel if it is 'anticipated' by the prior art.

In addition to being novel, an invention must also be 'non-obvious'. This means that to be patentable an invention must be more than a trivial modification of previously existing inventions. This is usually expressed by saying that an invention is obvious if it differs from the prior art in such a way that, the invention as a whole would have been obvious to a person skilled in the relevant art at the time the invention was created.

The last requirement for patentability is usefulness. In order for a patent to be 'useful', it must function as described in the patent application and it must fulfil some purpose. This is a lenient test, which will generally only be failed when the invention is impossible to put into practice.

The process of drafting and filing a patent application and taking all necessary steps to obtain a patent is known as 'patent prosecution'. Although it is possible for an individual to prosecute a patent without an attorney, most inventors retain an experienced patent attorney to obtain a patent. The goal of patent prosecution is to obtain as broad protection for the invention and subsequent improvements on the invention as possible. It is therefore desirable to draft patent claims, which describe the patent in terms, which are as broad as possible. If the claims are too broad, however, the patent office will most likely reject the application on the grounds that the invention does not meet one or more of the statutory requirements (*e.g.* novelty, non-obviousness). Drafting claims, which are as broad as possible without invalidating the patent application, is therefore the ultimate goal of a patent prosecution.

Although each country has its own patent laws, those seeking international patent protection should also be aware of the Paris Convention and the Patent Co-operation Treaty. Approximately 110 countries adhere to the Paris Convention, under which a patent applicant who files in one member nation receives the benefit of that date of filing in all member nations. A patent applicant may also file an application under the Patent Co-operation Treaty, adhered to by approximately 88 nations, effectively allowing the applicant to wait up to twenty (20) months before filing in any other member nation. This can help the applicant avoid some of the cost of filing in multiple countries if the inventor later decides that the patent is not worth prosecuting in one or more countries. An inventor can also file a single application with the European Patent Office E.P.O., which can lead to patent coverage in all European countries that belong to the European Patent Convention. Whether to file with the E.P.O. or with individual European countries will be decided based largely on the number of countries in which patent protection is sought, since obtaining a patent through the E.P.O. is significantly more expensive than obtaining protection from any one nation.

TECHNOLOGY TRANSFER AND LICENSE AGREEMENT

This TECHNOLOGY TRANSFER AND LICENSE AGREEMENT has been entered into this day of .... 20.....

BETWEEN

Alpha, Company having its registered offices in.................... (address) (hereinafter referred to as *"the party of the first part/Licensors*

AND

Beta an Indian firm having its registered offices at ...., (hereinafter referred to as *"the party of the second part/Licensee*

1. Definitions

Intellectual Property: Includes existing and future Intellectual Property in the nature of unregistered or registered rights to any and all patents, copyrights, trademarks and other propriety information not limited to that forming part of the subject-matter transfer, and inclusive of all intellectual property that is the subject of ownership by the Licensor and/or its subsidiaries, venture partners and predecessors in interest business and title.

Copyrights.—Means works of authorship fixed in a tangible medium of expression (including corresponding rights under international agreements and conventions, inclusive of the non-registration and/or registrations, renewal and extensions of any of the foregoing) whether or not containing a copyright notice, which work (s) was/were created before the expiration or prior termination of this agreement.

Trademarks.—The trademarks as provided for in ANNEXURE A in this agreement inclusive of any other trademarks the use of which shall be granted by the Licensor to the Licensee.

Technology.—Means confidential information, trade secrets, technical data such as engineering, manufacturing and assembly information fixed in any medium, drawings performances, specifications, procurements specifications, quality control specifications, inspection and test protocols inclusive of marketing cost, and financial data that the licensor has ownership of and is available and being used by the licensor and the general and specific information not limited to processes, machines, manufactures, composition of matter, know- how, methods, techniques, systems, designs, artwork, drawings, plans, software *(whether in object, source or executable code)* documentation, data *(irrespective of whether human or machine-readable)* pertaining to the design, manufacture and sale of products envisaged by the technology or improved technology.

Improved technology.—Means technology being the subject-matter of transfer in this agreement inclusive of the improvements and customizations to the machinery *(effected by the licensee only with the prior written permission of the licensor)* developed by the licensee pursuant to this agreement including products incorporating such technology and improvements, together with any and all technology and improvements created or first fixed in a tangible medium made, used under this agreement inclusive of any other tasks for which the licensee has been retained for by the Licensor.

Machinery.—Means only the items of present design presently manufactured and sold by the Licensor and any improvement and/or customization thereon made in the future as described in ANNEXURE 'C' setting out the relevant details.

Territory.—The Territory referred to in this Agreement shall include the Country of the Republic of India

WHEREAS,

(a) the Licensor is now engaged and has been engaged for many years, in the development, manufacture and sale of single end washers and slat chain Pastuerisers, whose models are specified in ANNEXURE 'C' (hereinafter referred to as "the Machinery"), and it has developed, and it is the sole owner of the technology pertaining to the manufacturing, packaging, marketing and use of such Machinery, and it is also the owner of certain valuable trademarks and patent rights relating to such Machinery;

(b) The Licensee desires to acquire a license in order to develop, manufacture, distribute, use and sell the Machinery in the licensed territory and in pursuance thereof desires also to utilize the technology and industrial properties of the Licensor in connection therewith.

(c) The Licensor desires to transfer the said technology as well as license its intellectual property to the licensee upon certain terms contained herein.

(d) The Licensee represents that it has all of the required approvals, licenses and other rights, as well the requisite existing level of training, knowledge, expertise and relationship within the Territory, to permit it to enter into this Agreement.

(e) The Licensor is willing to grant such authority and licenses to the Licensee at the terms and conditions hereinafter set forth.

Now therefore, in consideration of the mutual convenants herein contained, the Parties agree as follows:

2. Preliminary undertaking

a. The Licensee undertakes to send at Licensor's premises its personnel or consultants whose performance and trustworthiness must be vouched for by the licensee, for a period of training whose duration shall be decided by the Licensor itself, as well as the number and the level of skill of such a personnel.

b. In any case each training shall be referred to a specific type of Machinery and shall have to be performed before the manufacture of the relevant Machinery within the Territory.

c. Should the Licensor decide to manufacture the initial Machinery at its own premises, then, during the period of the manufacture and assembly of such a Machinery, the Licensor shall provide to the Licensee the technical training needed in order to achieve the know-how suitable to the transfer of technology.

d. A derogation of what stated above shall be possible only if previously agreed in writing between the parties.

e. After the period of the manufacture and assembly of the initial Machinery, the Licensor shall progressively transmit to the Licensee its technology and relevant technical assistance in order to allow the Licensee to manufacture and assemble the Machinery.

f. The Licensee shall adequate its production to the Licensor's standards of production, while the Licensor shall have in any moment the possibility to control and evaluate the Licensee's production as well as its pricing competitiveness.

g. Should the Licensee not be able, for whatever reason to achieve the Licensor's standards of production, or should not be competitive in terms of but not limited to price and delivery, compared with same kind of machines of similar quality and reputation manufactured in the territory, or even should not be able to expand its production capacity to keep pace with increasing demand of the .... market itself, then it shall have six months in order to close such a lack of competitiveness, after having received an advance written notice from the Licensor. Should this period of time have been passed unsuccessfully, then the Licensor shall have the right to terminate this agreement forthwith.

h. Notwithstanding that stated in the present Agreement, the Licensor reserves the right to manufacture the Machinery directly within the Territory.

i. In this case, the Licensor shall not be entitled to any indemnity or similar compensation. This provision does not limit parties right to claim damages for breach of contract.

3. Grant of License and Sales to Market

a. The Licensor grants to the Licensee, for the duration of this Agreement:

(i) a non-transferable exclusive right to manufacture and sell in the Territory, under license, the Machinery as specified in *ANNEXURE 'C'*.

(ii) The Licensor shall not enter into any other similar cooperation. Unless the Licensee agrees it is evident that the Licensee itself cannot expand its production capacity to keep pace with the increasing demand, or fails to be competitive in terms of but not limited to price and delivery, compared with same kind of machines of similar quality and reputation manufactured in the territory, provided that stated in clause 2.g here above.

b. The Licensor reserves the right to sell, either directly or through third companies, the Machinery manufactured under license to all customers outside the territory.

c. If needed the Licensor, either directly or through third companies, shall purchase from the Licensee at terms and conditions which shall be defined at the beginning of ....(month) and .... (month) of each year and shall be indicated in ANNEXURE 'D'.

d. The prices for the machinery forming the subject matter of this agreement shall be agreed each time upon the parties, depending on the relevant layout and specifications. The said prices shall be set forth in ANNEXURE 'E'.

e. The price quoted and invoiced by the Licensee to a customer shall conform to the sale price list, as set forth in ANNEXURE 'F' above, at the beginning of April and October of each year. However, the Licensee may grant to the customer a reasonable discount on the selling price in accordance with normal commercial practice. The Licensee will send to the Licensor a copy of each sale contract and relevant offer/s within .... days from its signature, as well as it will send every three months a periodical report on the offers sent to the customer.

f. All future sales of the Machinery and relevant spare parts will ultimately be subject to the terms and conditions of this Agreement.

g. In the enjoinment of its rights hereunder, the Licensee agrees to make faithful vigorous and diligent efforts to increase its sales and enhance the goodwill of the Machinery in the territory, as well as to perform all convenants herein a manner that will promote the mutual intentions and goals of the parties.

4. Technical Specifications of the Machinery

a. The Technical Specifications and the design of the Machinery are as specified in ANNEXURE 'G'.

b. The Licensee upon written authorization of the Licensor shall use components of local manufacture with the exception of the critical/strategic parts of the Machinery as shall be listed by the licensor, in writing from time to time, which will be purchased from the Licensor only.

c. However, items classified as critical/strategic parts of the Machinery may be manufactured or procured locally by the Licensee only if such local construction will provide to be equivalent to the design and performance standards as indicated in writing by the Licensor.

d. Any eventual extension of the present Agreement, in order to include other machines or strategic critical parts in the future, must be agreed upon in writing by the parties and therefore integrated in this paragraph by way of addendum.

5. Obligations of the Licensor

a. The Licensor will transmit to the Licensee the technology regarding the Industrial property relating to the manufacture of single-end washers and slat-chain pasteurizers.

b. The project of the above mentioned Machinery, with the exception of any critical/strategic parts as provided for, will be made suitable to the Licensee's Country by the Licensee itself, if required, under the supervision of the Licensor at the Licensor's premises.

6. Customization of machinery and ownership thereof

a. The Licensee is entitled to use drawings given to him by the Licensor under clause 5.a herein for the purpose to develop construction drawings suitable to Customer's requirements. The licensee also hereby agrees that all such customizations undertaken by the licensee will be the subject of an immediate non-exclusive license to the licensor.

b. However, any and all construction drawings that may be developed under this clause, shall firstly be checked and evaluated by the Licensor and the construction of any model of Machinery based on such drawings may begin only upon written authorization of the Licensor.

c. The Licensor undertakes to upgrade as and when required by the market designs and know-how relevant to the Machinery and to transfer such upgrading to the Licensee in the form of a non-exclusive license, free of charge.

d. For the purpose of the Licensor to be able to service the Machinery, the Licensor itself will have to receive from the Licensee the below listed technical information for any part of Machinery.

  (i) a list of all commercial parts and components of the Machinery with the indication of the corresponding code number as well as name and address of the local supplier of commercial parts.

  (ii) a complete set of drawings etc., of the Machinery

  (iii) a complete set of instructions and spare parts books in English Language

e. The technical information exchanged between the Licensor and the Licensee under the Agreement shall be in the English language.

f. Before starting the manufacture of any part of Machinery, customized basing on Licensor's drawings and technical documents, the Licensee shall provide the Licensor with a complete set of drawings and technical information regarding changes made for the Machinery to be manufactured. Such documentation will have to be sent from the Licensee to the Licensor's premises and the Licensor will have to authorize the manufacture of such part of Machinery or advise the required technical modifications, if any within.................... (No. days) from the receipt of the technical documentation.

7. Purchase of components from Licensor

a. Components that the Licensee shall purchase from the Licensor, shall always be invoiced at their purchase costs with a handling charge of maximum.................... % but will be.................... % on small consignments of less than.................... (amount).

b. Moreover, the Licensor will assist the Licensee to achieve the best possible terms of importation of components, either from Licensor's official suppliers or from alternative suppliers. If required, the Licensor will procure the components at its own account and upon its own contract rate. Then, it will send them to the Licensee with a handling charge of maximum.................... % but will be.................... % on small consignments of less than.................... (amount).

c. No handling charges shall be payable by the Licensee in case of direct purchase from Licensor's official suppliers or alternative suppliers.

8. Transmittal of technology

In order to transmit to the Licensee all the technology and know how to produce the Machinery, the Licensor will follow this program:

(i) the Licensee shall choose adequate personnel, who will travel to Licensor's premises to receive training, according to the program to be agreed upon by the parties;

(ii) during the manufacturing at Licensee's premises and previous to the mutual consent of the parties, the Licensor will send the number of people that will be disposed for every case by both parties;

(iii) Quality control and performance tests on all the Machinery manufactured by the Licensee will be done under the supervision and discretion of the Licensor. At least one control/test to be performed during the assembly operation and one during the final performance test before the delivery of the Machinery. This procedure will apply until the Licensee will prove to have reached the quality and performance standards of the Licensor.

(iv) Manuals/information regarding suitable standards and methods for inspection of the Machinery and its materials, components and assemblies.

9. Obligations of the Licensee

a. The manufacturer of the Machinery shall obey and comply with all laws and regulations in force in the Territory.

b. The Licensee binds itself to not manufacture any machinery not forming part of this agreement that may be developed based on Licensor's proprietary technology.

c. The Licensee binds itself for all the duration of the present agreement, to not register equal or similar patents, modifications to Licensor's patent in use. All improvement modifications of the patent belonging to the Licensor shall be of its exclusive ownership.

d. The Licensee binds itself to not employ for all duration of the present agreement and a reasonable and sustainable period upon termination or expiry thereof, personnel who was previously under Licensor (either employees or consultants), unless agreed upon by the Licensor itself.

e. The manufacture of the Machinery shall be carried out by the Licensee at.................... premises in.................... The Licensee shall have to communicate each and every possible change of the said location.

f. The Licensee binds itself to transmit every time the specification of the Machinery, which the licensee is going to manufacture.

g. The Licensee will elaborate a detailed order of the material and components, which the Licensor shall have to supply.

h. Any and all modifications made by the Licensee to the original technology must be previously authorized in writing by the Licensor.

i. Such an authorization made by the Licensor shall not in any case relieve the Licensee from its responsibilities and obligations.

j. The Licensee will give to the Licensor all support during the supervision of the manufacture to be carried out. Such a supervision shall be done according to the following points:

(i) Quality control of parts and components not supplied by the Licensor.

(ii) Quality control of all systems of productions.

(iii) Quality and operating control of the Machinery.

k. The Licensee shall manufacture all present and future Machinery in accordance with formulas, processes and procedures and other specifications issued or approved by the Licensor. The quality of all the Machinery and/or ingredients and raw materials in all the Machinery shall be specified and approved by the Licensor.

l. Licensee's requirements of raw materials to be used in the performance of this agreement shall be materials which meet specifications established by the Licensor in order that the Machinery manufactured hereunder meets the quality standards required by this agreement.

m. The Licensee agrees to bear the costs of all materials, labels, containers and other commodities used during the manufacture and sale of the Machinery and shall furnish all buildings, equipment and personnel including sales force, facilities for handling and merchandising the Machinery, for accounting and other office personnel for the proper conduct of the business.

n. If required, at the purpose to simplify the local construction of the Machinery and/or to reduce the costs of it, the Licensor will be entitled to use drawings and parts of the equipment presently produced by the Licensee.

10. Reports, Inspection and Records

a. The Licensor shall have the right to examine, on reasonable notice, at any time during regular business hours, through its employees or agents:

(i) all of Licensee's records that relate to this agreement, including statistics, formulas fixed in any form, advertising materials and similar matters.

(ii) all of Licensee's raw and partially prepared materials, manufacturing facilities, procedures and the Machinery in any stage of manufacture to make certain that the Licensee is meeting all specifications furnished or approved by the Licensor and is attaining the quality specified or approved by the Licensor.

b. The Licensor shall have the right to examine, at any time during regular business hours, through its employees or agents, all financial and other records and book of account of the Licensee in so far as it relates to calculation of royalties' payable for the Machinery. The Licensee agrees that it will make changes and improvements in its reports, as well as in manufacturing, advertising labeling and sale of the Machinery, as may be requested from time to time by the Licensor.

c. Then Licensor has also the right to appoint an independent certified auditor to examine the books of account and other financial records of Licensee in so far as it relates to calculation of royalties payable for the Machinery at any time, as the Licensor so wishes.

d. The Licensee agrees to prepare a regular written semiannual report, and any other reports relevant to this Agreement, as the Licensor may request and in such form as the Licensor may, from time to time, prescribe.

e. The Licensee shall furnish the Licensor with an annual written report within .... days, after the closure of the Licensee's fiscal year. Such annual report shall contain any and all information relating to sales and advertising of the Machinery as the Licensor may request.

f. Inspections by the Licensor of the Machinery and manufacturing facilities of the Licensee shall not relieve the Licensee of its product and warranty obligations.

11. Payments and costs

a. In consideration of the technology, know-how, patent, copyright and trademark rights obtained by the Licensee and the other convenant of the Licensor under this agreement, the Licensor shall receive a down payment equal to:

    (i) .... (foreign amount) for technology and know-how relevant to the Machinery. The drawings are to be delivered by the Licensor to the Licensee at...................., India. Payment shall be upon such a delivery.

    (ii) .... (foreign amount) for technical services and other convenants of the Licensor. Payment shall be made upon rendering of such technical services.

    (iii) Furthermore, the Licensee shall pay to the Licensor within 30 days of each six months ending, in September and March of each calendar year, a royalty calculated on Licensee's net ex-works sales price less returns and statutory taxes. Such a royalty shall be worked out in .... (foreign amount) at the official banker's selling rate in India prevailing on the day when the payment is made.

b. The royalty shall be worked out on the following basis:

    (i) With reference to sales of single end washers the Licensee shall pay a royalty of:

        (a) ....% on ex-works sales of single end washers from the Licensee to the end users less costs of parts imported from the Licensor for manufacture the Machinery, if any.

        (b) ....% on ex-works sales of slat chain pasteurisers.

        (c) ....% on ex-works sales of above said machinery incorporating strategic /crucial parts sourced from the Licensor *(less the ex-factory price of the said strategic /crucial parts so applied to the machinery)*

c. The royalty shall also be worked out on the following basis:
   (i) If the licensee is unable to expand its production capacity to keep pace with the increasing demand, or fails to be competitive in terms of but not limited to price and delivery, compared with same kind of machines of similar quality and reputation manufactured in the territory:
   (ii) No royalty shall be due to Licensor on sales of Machinery, but the Licensor shall purchase as per terms and conditions contained in this agreement and relevant ANNEXURE 'D'.

d. The accrual of the right to royalties for the Licensor shall be at the time of the shipment of the Machinery from the Licensee's premises.

e. Structure and relevancy of the costs liaised to this Agreement are defined in ANNEXURE 'E'.

f. By virtue of the "Double Taxation Avoidance Treaty", subsisting between Italy and India, in making the lump-sum royalty or any other payments relevant to the Agreement, the Licensee shall pay a withholding tax, whose amount shall be deducted from the above mentioned paying in.

g. In such a case the Licensee shall furnish to the Licensor, the relevant certificate stating the payment of the withholding tax in order to allow the Licensor to recover the amount in its country.

12. Non-Competition

a. Throughout the duration of the present Agreement, the parties undertake not to enter similar agreements with other companies for the manufacture and/or sale of the Machinery (and relevant spare parts) anyhow intended for the .... market, except to the extent provided in clauses 2.g and 2.h above.

b. In the event of termination of this Agreement for any reason, the Licensee will not manufacture similar Machinery using Licensor's patents or proprietary technology for a period of .... years from the date of termination.

c. However, the Licensee shall have the right to fulfil any contractual obligations in force at the time of the termination, provided it has been proven by the Licensee to the Licensor.

d. For this reason, at the time of termination of the present Agreement, the Licensee shall have to give to Licensor the list of all pending agreements with any customers.

13. Quality Guarantee

a. The Licensor shall not be responsible towards any third party in any case and for any accident or damage due to the Machinery produced by the Licensee, unless the accident or damage is due to defective parts supplied by the Licensor.

b. In case of defective supply of the initial or strategic/crucial parts by the Licensor, the Licensor shall be responsible to replace such defective parts, free of charge and deliver them at Licensee's premises, provided the Licensor is informed, in writing, of the defects not later than .... months from the date of shipment of such defective parts and these are imputable to defective material, workmanship or design.

c. The Licensor also reserves the right to ascertain any alleged defectiveness of the parts. Should this defectiveness be caused by reason of the Licensee, then the Licensor shall charge the costs to the Licensee itself.

14. Trade Mark

a. The Machinery produced by the Licensee, besides the identifying code of the machine settled by the Licensor, shall be affixed with the trade mark (s)...................., according to the correspondent logotype, under previous written approval by the Licensor.

b. Such trade mark (s) shall belong to the Licensor and shall be duly registered in India on behalf of the same and the Licensee shall have the right to use such trade marks free of charge, provided it is for the Machinery only.

c. Each Machinery shall have a plate with the following inscription:

"*Made in India by BETA, under license of Alpha*",

and a manufacturing progressive number.

d. The Licensee shall promptly notify the Licensor in writing of and submit specimen of, any infringement and/or passing off or violation of other Intellectual Property right that forms subject-matter of this agreement known to the Licensee of the Marks and/or Letter Patent of the Licensor granted in the territory. The Licensee shall likewise notify the Licensor of any information or notice that the Machinery infringes any third party Intellectual property rights. The Licensee shall not, without Licensor's prior specific written consent, file either.

  (i) applications for Letter Patent covering the Machinery or processes relating in any way to the manufacture thereof; or

  (ii) Applications for registration of the trademark (s) or copyright subsisting in any aspect of the technology transmitted to the licensee.

e. The Licensee shall not negotiate with third parties respecting patents covering the Machinery or respecting the Marks or copyright subsisting therein. Further, the Licensee shall not persecute or defend claims relating to label simulation in which the Machinery may be involved.

15. Duration and Termination

a. This agreement shall examine in full effect and force for an initial period of five years.

b. Then it shall continue its effectiveness for an indefinite period of time unless terminated by either party on one year's advance written notice to the other party, excepted on the case set forth in clause 1.3 hereinabove. Notwithstanding this however, if either party is in major default or gross negligence upon any obligation under this agreement, the aggrieved party shall be entitled to give the defaulting party written notice to remedy the breach.

c. If the defaulting party fails to comply with the notice within .... days of receipt of thereof, the aggrieved party shall be entitled to terminate this Agreement forthwith, or to claim specific performance, in either event without prejudice to the aggrieved party's right, including right to claim damages.

d. Upon termination of this agreement for any reason or purpose, all money credits of either party due to the other, shall promptly be paid and accounted for. The Licensee shall also upon termination, promptly deliver to the Licensor all information inclusive of the definition of technology contained in this agreement, formulas cards, processing instructions, correspondence and other data relating to the manufacture processing and packaging of the Machinery and it shall not thereafter use or disclose Licensor's patents or proprietary technology under this agreement. Furthermore, the Licensee shall also, as far as it is able, deliver to the Licensor all correspondence, memoranda or copies thereof, for the .... months preceding termination between the License and its customers relating to the sale of the Machinery, including price list, other documents relating to or containing information about the Licensor's business and/or sale of the Machinery in the territory and all advertising matter relating thereto, in the possession of the Licensee.

e. Upon termination of this agreement, in any manner or for any reason, the Licensee shall not thereafter, either in the territory or elsewhere, adopt, use, register or otherwise claim or have rights in the Marks, package designs or labels for the Machinery, or commercial names of the Licensor or its affiliates or in any closely similar Marks, designs, labels or names.

f. Nor the Licensee shall thereafter either:

   (i) practice any Letter Patents relating to the Machinery which are still then active in the territory; or

   (ii) Utilize any registered or patented design for the Machinery with the exception of any customization effected during pendency of this agreement or containers thereof.

   (iii) Claim right over any trademark forming part of the agreement.

16. Bankruptcy or Receivership or loss of control

The Licensee hereby agrees that, if it makes any assignment of assets or business for the benefit of creditors, or if a trustee or receiver is appointed to administer or conduct the Licensee's business or affairs, or if it is adjudged in any legal action to be either a voluntary or involuntary bankrupt, or their active management of the Licensee as a result of nationalization or for any reason whatsoever, the obligations of the Licensor and the right and privileges of the Licensee under this agreement, shall be deemed to have ceased and terminated immediately prior to such assignment, appointment of trustee or receiver, bankruptcy or loss of or give up of control of active management without the Licensor giving any notice or taking any legal action.

17. Relationship of the Partners

a. Notwithstanding any other provision of the agreement, the Licensee shall not bind or obligate the Licensor in transactions with other and shall be liable to the Licensor for any damage to the Licensor itself arising out of any acts of the Licensee; nor shall anything herein be construed as authorizing the Licensee to conduct its business in the name of, or for the account of the Licensor; nor shall the relationship of Principal and Agent or partners or co-adventurers be deemed to exist.

b. Same provision shall be applicable also to the Licensor.

18. Construction, Enforcement and Assignability

The parties hereto agree that this agreement contains the entire understanding between them. The parties further agree that this agreement may not be assigned by either party. The section titles used in this agreement are for reference purposes only and are not intended to add or to limit or in any other way change the meaning of the language of the agreement.

19. Governing Law and Arbitration

a. This Agreement except for the arbitration rules as provided in this clause shall be governed by and constructed in accordance with laws of India.

b. All disputes arising in connection with the present Agreement shall be finally settled under the Rules of Conciliation and Arbitration of the International Chamber of Commerce in ....(name of country), by three arbitrators appointed in accordance with the said Rules.

c. The place of arbitration will be .... (name of country).

d. The language of arbitration will be the English language.

20. Notice of Parties

a. The parties hereto agree that all notices which may be given by one party to the other under the terms of this agreement, shall be in writing and shall be addressed,

in case of the Licensor to the following address:

....................and

in case of the Licensee, to the following address:

....

b. Provided, however, that any notice deposited in the mails as a registered letter, return receipt requested by either party shall be considered to have been effective when so deposited, and provided further that either of the parties may change the address herein given by express written notice to the other party.

21. Waiver

The failure of the Parties at any time to enforce any of the provisions of this agreement or to exercise any right herein provided, shall not be considered a waiver of such or any other provision or in any way effect the validity of this agreement.

22. Severability

a. It is hereby expressly agreed by both parties that no portion of this agreement is intended to be in violation of any laws of the countries of the contracting parties or of any other country which may, at any time, have jurisdiction over either party hereto, or the agreement itself.

b. Should any portion of this agreement be contrary to, or in violation of any such law, said portion shall be void and of no effect. The reminder of this agreement shall be valid and remain in force notwithstanding the invalidity of such offending portion.

23. Covenant of Secrecy

The Licensee shall exercise and shall require its employees or consultants to exercise the due diligence not to make known, divulge or communicate at any time before or after the termination of this agreement, unless it is necessary for the execution of the Agreement, to any person *(except as necessary to its selected trustworthy employees)* the technology and Confidential Information and/or know-how disclosed and/or recommended to it by the Licensor hereunder, not to do nor suffer to be done or omitted any act or thing in relation to the subject-matter of this agreement whereby said Confidential Information and know-how may become known to any unauthorized person, provided, however, that such information shall not be considered confidential, and this paragraph shall not apply, if such information can be demonstrated to have been in the public domain prior to its disclosure or recommendation by the Licensor, or to have become part of the public domain by any means, except an unauthorized act or omission on the party of the Licensee or any of its employees.

24. *Force majeure*

Neither party shall be in default under this Agreement by reason of its failure or delay in the performance of its obligations, if such failure or delay is caused by actions of God, Government laws and regulations, strikes, lockouts, war or any other cause beyond its reasonable control.

25. Miscellaneous

a. The present Agreement is subject to approval of Government of India.

b. All technical data shall be delivered by the Licensor to the postal address previously indicated in writing by the Licensee.

c. This instrument may not be waived, released, discharged, abandoned, changed or modified in any manner, orally or otherwise except by an instrument in writing signed by duly authorized officers or representatives of the parties hereto.

Date....................

....
Alpha

....
Beta

ANNEXURE A
TRADEMARK SCHEDULE

ANNEXURE B
TECHNICAL SPECIFICATIONS AND DESIGN OF THE MACHINERY
(TO BE FULFILLED ON DUE TIME)

ANNEXURE C
MACHINE MODELS
(TO BE FULFILLED ON DUE TIME)

ANNEXURE D
PURCHASING TERMS AND CONDITIONS
(TO BE FULFILLED ON DUE TIME)

ANNEXURE E
PRICE STATEMENT
(TO BE FULFILLED ON DUE TIME)

ANNEXURE F
SALES PRICE LIST
(TO BE FULFILLED ON DUE TIME)

ANNEXURE G
TECHNICAL SPECIFICATIONS
(TO BE FULFILLED ON DUE TIME)

ADDENDUM III – COSTS' STRUCTURE AND RELEVANCY

	Licensee	Licensor
Licensee personnel in .... (name of country) for training	To pay travel and living expenses of its own personnel	To provide free of charge to its own personnel
Licensor personnel in India (*) for training Licensor personnel in India (*) for QC	Costs, living expenses and time based on agreed fares	
Issue of drawings from Licensor to Licensee		At Licensor charge, covered by royalties and down payment

"Nationalized" Indian drawing from Licensee to Licensor	At Licensee charge
Additional visits in India required by the Licensor	At Licensor charge
Additional visit required by the Licensee (**)	At Licensee charge
Audits required by the Licensor	At Licensor charge

(*) For training and QC of the first machine, it needs 3 visits of 2 weeks per visit.

For the other machines, it needs 2 visits of one week per visit, as far as QC is concerned, with reference to clause 5.7 (iii).

(**) The Licensor, for training personnel and for any other agreed intervention, shall apply the following tariff:

.... (foreign amount) a day, for all personnel

.... (foreign amount) a day, for chief design engineers

Such a tariff shall be revised and agreed upon by the parties at the beginning of each calendar year.

TECHNOLOGY AND MARKETING COLLABORATION AGREEMENT

THIS AGREEMENT is made on................ 20.....

BETWEEN

Alpha (registered number.................) whose registered office is at .... (Registered office to be mentioned).

AND

Beta (registered under the Indian Companies Act, 1956 whose registered office is at...

Background

(A) *Alpha* is possessed of Know-How relating to the Products and has certain skills and the ability to provide consultancy services and technical assistance in the design, marketing, manufacture and sale of the Products.

(B) The Licensee wishes to design windows, doors and partition systems that incorporate the Profiles and to make, extrude, fabricate, sell and install the Products in the Territory.

(C) *Alpha* is willing to provide consultancy services and technical assistance to the Licensee and to license the Licensee to use the Know-How to design windows, doors and partition systems that incorporate the Profiles and to make, extrude, fabricate, sell and install the Products in the Territory on the terms of this Agreement.

1. Definitions

1.1 In this Agreement and the Background the following expressions have the following meanings unless inconsistent with the context:

"*Approved Trade Mark*" the trade marks set out in Part 1 of Schedule 2.

"*Assistance Plan*" the plan set out in Schedule 7 (JB to provide).

"*Associated Company*" any company which is, in relation to another company, its holding company or its subsidiary or a subsidiary of its holding company.

"*Background Information*" all technical know-how and information known to the Parties at the Commencement Date of a confidential nature and not in the public domain, together with all intellectual property rights owned by or licensed to the Parties at the Commencement Date.

"*Business Day*" any day other than Saturday or Sunday or a bank or public holiday.

"*Commencement Date*" the date of this Agreement.

"*Confidential Information*" all information in relation to a party which is commercially sensitive or of a secret nature (in the case of *Alpha* including Know-How), or information which is marked confidential, or which is orally stated to be confidential, relating to any and all aspects of the business and financing of either party. Such information may be expressed in any form including orally, as an idea, as price lists, plans, customer lists or details, computer software, or information concerning either party's relationships with actual or potential clients or customers and the needs and requirements of such persons.

"*Control*" direct or indirect ownership of more than 50% of the share capital or similar right of ownership.

"*Costs*" the costs incurred by *Alpha* specified in Schedule 5.

"*Dry Blend*" a dry powder mixture of Vinyl resin, pigments and various additives which is used as a raw material in the manufacture Profiles.

"*Exclusive*" a right granted under this Agreement which the grantor will not itself exercise and will not authorise other persons to exercise.

"*Government Approval*" written approval from the Ministry of Industry, Government of India, Department of Industrial Policy and Promotion, New Delhi or such other authority or government department from whom approval is required for foreign technology agreements and/or the purposes of this Agreement.

"*Horizontal Sliding*" a multi-element assembly incorporating an outer.

Window System" frame and a number of Sashes depending on the specification which can either be fixed in position or can slide horizontally.

"*Alpha's Bank*" .... (name of the bank with address).

"Improvements" any improvement, modification or adaptation to the Know-How which (whether or not patentable) might reasonably be of commercial interest in the marketing, design, manufacture, quality, presentation or supply of any of the Products and which may be made or acquired by either party during the term of this Agreement.

"Know-How" all knowledge, experience, data, marketing expertise, technical or commercial information, inventions and all other intellectual property rights which might reasonably be of commercial interest to either party in the design, manufacture or supply of the Products. This includes (without limitation) descriptions of manufacturing processes, formulae, and drawings relating to the design, development, manufacture, assembly, repair, testing and use of the Products brief particulars of which are set out in Schedule 1.

"Local Requirements" all relevant statutes, statutory rules or orders or other instruments having the force of law in the country of manufacture or sale (or other disposal) by *Alpha* or the Licensee of the Products (including any such requirements as applicable to health and safety standards, design, manufacture or packaging).

"Man Day" 8 working hours in any day during which a member of *Alpha*'s staff is made available to the Licensee.

"Minimum Sales Value" the minimum aggregate Net Sales Value calculated in ....(foreign currency). Conversion into foreign currency shall be on the basis set out in clause 9.7.1.1 at the rate ruling on the last day of the relevant year.

"Net Sales Value" the invoiced sales price of the Products (after deduction of normal trade discounts actually granted; any rebates; discounts or credits actually given by the Licensee for returned or defective goods; any costs of packing, insurance, carriage, freight, export/import duties and value added tax or any other applicable sales tax or government levies) or such other price which is deemed to be the Net Sales Value pursuant to clause 9.3.

"Non-exclusive" a right granted under this Agreement which the grantor may itself exercise and may authorise and assist any third party to exercise.

"Outer Frame" an assembly which is generally rectangular or square, is manufactured from Outer Frame Profile and incorporates other secondary Profiles, locking devices and accessories.

"Outer Frame Profile" a Profile specifically designed to form the perimeter of the outermost frame assembly of a sliding Sash window that will also accept sliding Sashes.

"Parties" the parties to this Agreement.

"Person" [BM to insert].

"Phase" a phase of the project as set out in the Project Plan.

"Products" Profiles, any Windows, including the Horizontal Sliding Window System, doors and partition systems that incorporate Profiles and any associated accessories and any other product using the Know-How.

"Profile(s)" longitudinal elements, extruded from Dry Blend to a set form, which are subsequently used in the manufacture of windows, doors and partitions.

"Project Plan" the plan set out in Schedule 4 *JB to provide.*

"Quarter" the period of .... months commencing on the date of this Agreement and each consecutive period of .... months thereafter, or any shorter period commencing on a day immediately following the end of a Quarter and ending on the termination of this Agreement, and "Quarterly" shall be construed accordingly.

"Records" all files, records, documents, notebooks, books of accounts, statistics, surveys, blueprints, designs, drawings and specifications, relating to the business of the Licensee including any such information recorded or stored in writing or upon magnetic tape or disc or otherwise recorded or stored for reproduction, whether by mechanical or electronic means and whether or not such reproduction will result in a permanent record being made and all other data necessary for the determination of royalties payable under clause 9.2.

"Sash" a rectangular or square assembly incorporating rollers, locking mechanisms and accessories and panes of glass.

"Sash Profile" a Profile specifically designed to form the perimeter of a sliding Sash which retains the pane(s) of glass with the Sash. Depending on the specification required the Sash Profile may or may not be strengthened with additional metal reinforcing located within an internal hollow chamber.

"Services" the consultancy services and technical assistance to be provided by *Alpha* under this Agreement as more particularly described in the Assistance Plan at Schedule 7.

"Sole" a right granted under this Agreement which the grantor may itself exercise but will not authorise other persons to exercise.

"Specification" as described at Schedule 6 and as shall be more particularly described by *Alpha* from time to time to reflect the on-going design process within the Services.

"Supply" give, sell, lend, let out on hire, lease or otherwise dispose of.

"Territory" India, Nepal, Bangladesh and Bhutan.

"Trade Marks" the trade marks set out in Part 2 of Schedule 2.

"Vinyl" polyvinyl chloride.

"Windows" Vinyl windows incorporating Profiles.

"Year" a period of 365 days from the Commencement Date (or where that period includes a ....).

1.2 Any reference in this Agreement to a clause or Schedule is a reference to a clause or Schedule of this Agreement and references in any Schedule to paragraphs relate to the paragraphs in that Schedule.

1.3 Any reference to a "party" shall mean *Alpha* or the Licensee or both of them as the context requires and "parties" shall be construed accordingly.

1.4 The headings in this Agreement are for convenience only and shall not affect its construction or interpretation.

2. Grant of Rights

2.1 *Alpha* grants to the Licensee with effect from the Commencement Date the Exclusive right and licence subject to clause 9.6 under the Know-How for the duration of this Agreement, to:

2.1.1 Design windows, doors and partition systems that incorporate Profiles; and

2.1.2 Extrude Profiles and make, fabricate and install Products in the Territory; and

2.1.3 Use and Supply Products in the Territory.

2.2 For the duration of this Agreement *Alpha* shall have no right subject to clause 9.6 to:

2.2.1 Make, use, or Supply Products other than to the Licensee or make any other use of the Know-How in any country within the Territory; or

2.2.2 Grant to any other person a licence to do so within the Territory.

2.3 The Licensee shall have no right to manufacture, use or Supply any of the Products, or make any use of the Know-How, for any purpose except for the purpose and under the terms of this Agreement and without first obtaining all Governmental Approvals required for the purposes of this Agreement.

2.4 The Licensee shall not grant or purport to grant to any person any sub-licence or sub-contract of its rights or obligations under this Agreement, save in relation to the fabrication or installation of Products provided that:

2.4.1 The sub-licence is in writing and contains the like obligations and undertakings by the sub-licensee as are contained in this Agreement including in particular (but not limited to) clause 8 (confidentiality), and the Licensee ensures that all sub-licensees duly observe and perform the same; and

2.4.2 The Licensee shall remain responsible for all acts and omissions of such sub-licensees and sub-contractors as though they were made by the Licensee and shall indemnify and keep indemnified the Licensor against all or any losses, costs, claims, damages and expenses incurred by the Licensor or for which the Licensor may become liable as a result of the default or negligence of any sub-licensee or sub-contractor.

3. Know-how

3.1 Subject to the receipt by *Alpha* of evidence of all written Government Approvals in relation to this Agreement, *Alpha* will at appropriate stages in accordance with the Project Plan supply to the Licensee the relevant parts of the Know-How in its possession (which *Alpha* is lawfully permitted to disclose) and which in the opinion of *Alpha* is necessary for the manufacture and use of the Windows in accordance with this Agreement.

3.2 Such Know-How supplied by *Alpha* shall be subject to the provisions of clause 8 (confidentiality) and shall be used by the Licensee only for the purposes of and subject to the terms of this Agreement.

4. Services

4.1 On such dates or at such stages of Phase One as more particularly described in the Project Plan, the Project Director and or other qualified staff or sub-contractors of *Alpha* will provide the services, covering:

4.1.1 Assisting in the transfer of Know-How relating to Windows to the Licensee;

4.1.2 Assisting and training the Licensee with the development of a marketing strategy and marketing techniques for the Products in the Territory as follows:

4.1.2.1 *Alpha* shall use its own knowledge and experience to assist the Licensee to formulate a five year marketing strategy to address issues such as market analysis, segmentation, opportunities, threats and growth potential; routes to market, market creation and barriers to entry; competition evaluation, Product specification and pricing, advertising strategy; location of mixing/blending extrusion and window fabrication facilities; and secondary and or complimentary product ranges;

4.1.2.2 The assistance and/or training outlined at clause 4.1.2.1 shall initially be given to the Licensee at *Alpha*'s site at (....................) and thereafter shall be given by *Alpha* at the Licensee's site in India at such times and for such duration as detailed in the Assistance Plan;

4.1.2.3 For the avoidance of doubt the Licensee shall be responsible for meeting its and *Alpha*'s travel, accommodation and subsistence costs and expenses incurred in connection with the marketing strategy development and training.

4.1.3 Provision of design services whereby *Alpha* shall:

4.1.3.1 Undertake the initial design of Vinyl Profiles, reinforcing profiles, system specific injection moulded components, and locking mechanisms and ancillary products required for the Horizontal Sliding Window System;

4.1.3.2 Conduct a design review by post and telephone with the Licensee of the designs produced pursuant to clause 4.1.3.1;

4.1.3.3. Following the design review, undertake required modification to the initial designs;

4.1.3.4 Visit the Licensee at it's premises to undertake an on-site design review;

4.1.3.5 Implement the results of the design review to finalise the designs which shall be sent by post to the Licensee to be signed-off as agreed by the Licensee. In the event that the designs are not signed-off as agreed by the Licensee, *Alpha* reserves the right to terminate this Agreement;

4.1.3.6 following sign-off of the designs and undertake testing of the designs;

4.1.3.7 Supply to the Licensee stocks of Profiles required in the manufacture of the Horizontal Sliding Window System manufactured by *Alpha* at its own premises to be purchased by the Licensee, such purchase to be subject to *Alpha's* standard terms and conditions of sale and prevailing price rates;

4.1.3.8 Provide at *Alpha's* premises the first set of necessary tooling which the Licensee is obliged to purchase from *Alpha* at a price to be agreed between the Parties but which shall be competitive with the prices of tooling of similar quality, specification, material and output quoted in writing by other tooling manufacturer(s), and such purchase shall be subject to *Alpha's* standard terms and conditions of sale which shall be to the exclusion of any terms and conditions of purchase submitted at any time by the Licensee whether printed or sent with any order form or otherwise which shall be transported by the Licensee to its own premises at its own risk and expense. The Licensee shall be responsible for collection and/or transportation of the tooling to its own premises which shall be at its own risk and expense;

4.1.4 Developing a Dry Blend for white profiles for use within the Territory and supplying the Licensee with details of components, relative quantities used, sources and proposals as to the blending and mixing process and methodology for such Dry Blend;

4.1.5 Making available to the Licensee technical manuals to assist the Licensee to design and manufacture and install Windows to the *Alpha* specification;

4.16. Advising the Licensee and providing specifications as more particularly described at Schedule 3 in connection with infrastructure to enable the Licensee to build and equip:

4.1.6.1 A blending/mixing plant in which to manufacture Dry Blend in the Territory;

4.1.6.2 An extrusion factory in which to manufacture Vinyl Profiles;

4.1.6.3 A Window fabrication factory.

4.1.7 Liaising with architects as necessary in India in connection with clause 4.1.6 *(JB to confirm)*;

4.1.8 Assisting with the fitting out of the extrusion factory and the Window fabrication factory;

4.1.9 Providing training in India to the Licensee's employees who shall be involved in quality systems, blending, extrusion, fabrication and installation of the Products;

4.1.10 Providing training at *Alpha's* site at .... (place) for an appropriate number of the Licensee's personnel involved in the blending, extrusion and fabrication of the Products and quality systems and engineering support.

4.2 On such dates and stages of Phase Two as more particularly described in the Project Plan, the Project Director and or other qualified staff or subcontractors of *Alpha* will:

4.2.1 At such times as *Alpha* shall in its own discretion deem appropriate advise the Licensee as to new or improved technologies relating to any new products that use the Know-How;

4.2.2 If any additional Vinyl Profiles are required by the Licensee, and at the Licensee's reasonable written request to do so, endeavour to design such Vinyl Profiles for the Licensee, and the Licensee shall be charged accordingly by *Alpha* for its provision of those designs by *Alpha* at its applicable standard rate.

4.3 The assistance outlined at clauses 4.1 and 4.2 shall be provided in accordance with the Assistance Plan and will continue for no longer than is reasonably necessary having regard to all the circumstances and in any event will not continue for longer than [number] Man Days in total.

4.4 If the Licensee requires additional assistance to that in the Assistance Plan *Alpha* will use its reasonable endeavours to provide it (for which the Licensee shall be charged at *Alpha*'s applicable standard rate) but accepts no further obligation in this respect.

4.5 The Licensee acknowledges to *Alpha* that *Alpha*'s staff or sub-contractors will attend upon the Licensee merely in an advisory capacity. In particular the Licensee shall be responsible for ensuring that Profiles, Windows and Products are suitable for its purposes. Neither *Alpha* nor such of its staff or sub-contractors shall be liable in any manner whatsoever for any loss (including but not limited to consequential loss, pecuniary loss and loss of profits), damage or injury resulting from any actual or alleged advice or assistance of such staff or sub-contractors and the Licensee shall indemnify and keep indemnified (whether such advice or assistance was negligent or otherwise) *Alpha* against all or any costs claims and expenses or other liability arising in connection with it.

4.6 *Alpha* will be under no liability (whether in negligence or otherwise) under this Agreement for any personal injury, death, loss or damage of any kind whatsoever, whether direct or indirect (including but not limited to, loss of profits, loss of business, depletion of goodwill or otherwise).

4.7 *Alpha* excludes, to the fullest extent permissible in law, all conditions, warranties and stipulations, express (other than those set out in this Agreement) or implied, statutory, customary or otherwise, which, but for such exclusion, would or might subsist in favour of the Licensee.

4.8 *Alpha* shall not be obliged to fulfil its duties and obligations under this Agreement if at any time *Alpha* is prevented from fulfilling its duties by any acts or omissions of the Licensee or the Licensee's personnel including in particular a failure to provide anything to *Alpha* or do anything which the Licensee is obliged to do under this Agreement to enable *Alpha* to be able to perform the Services.

5. Intellectual Property Rights

5.1 For the avoidance of doubt, all Background Information and know-how used shall remain the property of the Party introducing the same.

5.2 Subject to clauses 5.3 and 5.4 all and any intellectual property rights and know-how including, without limitation, copyright, database rights, confidential information, patents, inventions, design rights (whether registered or unregistered) and trade marks developed, created, discovered, invented, designed, written or prepared by in the provision of the Services or otherwise under this Agreement that relate to the Products, shall belong to and vest in the Licensee. *Alpha* agrees at the expense of the Licensee to execute and to procure that its Personnel execute all such documents and do all such things as may be necessary to secure the vesting in the Licensee of all such intellectual property rights and know-how.

5.3 All copyright in the technical manuals supplied to the Licensee by *Alpha* pursuant to clause 4.1.5 shall remain vested in *Alpha* and *Alpha* reserves the Exclusive right to use the .... formulations provided by it to the Licensee pursuant to clause 4.1.4.

5.4 The Licensee shall have the right to use the designs of the Vinyl Profiles which form the .... System and any other components designed by *Alpha* for the .... System pursuant to clause 4.1.3 in the Territory.

6. Trade Marks

6.1 *Alpha* grants to the Licensee an Exclusive licence to use the Approved Trade Mark in the Territory in relation to the Products solely for the purposes of this Agreement.

6.2 *Alpha* agrees that all Products manufactured by the Licensee must be marketed under and by reference to the Approved Trade Mark.

6.3 The Licensee shall not adopt or use any trade mark, symbol or device which incorporates or is confusingly similar to, or is a simulation or colourable imitation of any of the Trade Marks or the Approved Trade Mark or unfairly competes with any of the Trade Marks or the Approved Trade Mark. The Licensee shall not during the period of this Agreement, apply anywhere in the world to register any trade marks identical to or so nearly resembling any of the Trade Marks or the Approved Trade Mark as to be likely to deceive or cause confusion.

6.4 The Licensee shall use the Approved Trade Mark only in connection with Products which conform with the relevant specification and samples approved by *Alpha* and the other requirements of this Agreement.

6.5 The Licensee warrants that all Products shall comply with:

6.5.1 All applicable Local Requirements; and

6.5.2 The Specifications.

6.6 The Licensee shall inform *Alpha* as soon as practicable if it becomes aware that any Products cease to conform with the requirements of this Agreement and shall destroy or correct to meet *Alpha*'s requirements all Products which do not conform with the relevant Specification. The Licensee shall observe all directions given by *Alpha* from time to time as to colour and size and the manner and disposition of the Approved Trade Mark on Products and packaging for the Products as set out in the Specification.

6.7 Unless *Alpha* otherwise agrees in writing, all packaging, advertising and publicity material relating to the Products shall bear the trade mark notices or symbols specified in Part 3 of Schedule 2.

6.8 The Licensee shall not use the Approved Trade Mark in any way which would tend to allow it to become generic, lose their distinct likeness or become liable to mislead the public, nor use the Approved Trade Mark in any way which is materially detrimental to or inconsistent with the good name, goodwill, reputation and image of *Alpha*.

6.9 *Alpha* may by itself or by its authorised agent apply to the appropriate authorities to record or register this Agreement in the registers of the trade marks of the countries in the Territory in order to record the Licensee as the registered user of the Approved Trade Marks and the Licensee shall assist *Alpha* as is necessary for that purpose.

6.10 Upon termination of this Agreement either party shall be entitled to notify the appropriate authorities in the Territory and require cancellation of any entry in any register relating to the Licensee being recorded as a registered user of the Approved Trade Marks.

7. Improvements

7.1 Each party shall disclose to the other in confidence and in such detail as the other may reasonably require all Improvements that it may develop or acquire except insofar as is prohibited by law or by obligation to any other person.

7.2 *Alpha* shall have a Sole, irrevocable, worldwide, royalty-free licence (without limit of time and with the right to assign and to grant sub-licences thereunder) to use all improvements the Licensee is due to disclose to *Alpha* under clause 7.1 of this Agreement, and to use and exploit all intellectual property rights in respect thereof owned by the Licensee or any assignee or successor in title of the Licensee.

7.3 Subject to agreement in writing between the Parties as to relevant terms, *Alpha* shall license the Licensee to use all Improvements that *Alpha* is due to disclose to the Licensee under clause 7.1 for the purpose of the licence granted to the Licensee under clause 2.1.

7.4 Save as otherwise provided in this Agreement, Improvements arising from work carried out by *Alpha* alone shall subject to clause 5.4 remain the exclusive property of *Alpha* and Improvements arising from work carried out by the Licensee alone shall remain the exclusive property of the Licensee.

7.5 Subject to clause 7.7, Improvements arising from work carried out jointly shall belong to the parties equally unless they shall otherwise agree. Each party shall have the irrevocable right to use such joint Improvements independently of the other and to the extent necessary for such use each shall grant to the other a non-exclusive, irrevocable, worldwide, royalty-free licence (without limit of time and with the right to assign and to grant sub-licences) in respect of such jointly held intellectual property rights. Each party undertakes that on request it will confirm to any prospective licensee of the other the right of that other to grant such a licence pursuant to this clause 7.5.

7.6 Without prejudice to the confidentiality obligations in clause 8, where one of the parties develops or acquires an Improvement to which clause 7.1 applies, it shall not publish the same or do anything that might prejudice the validity of any patent that might subsequently be granted on it until the other party has had at least .... Business Days from disclosure in writing of all information relating to it to consider whether patent or other protection should be applied for. The first party will on request notify the other whether it intends to seek any relevant protection.

7.7 Either party may at any time elect not to pursue further an application for patent protection of any Improvement either jointly or on its own behalf, or to maintain any such patent protection as it may have obtained, and the party so electing shall notify the other party and shall, if so requested, assign all rights it may have therein, including, but not limited to, the right to apply for, prosecute and obtain patent and similar protection throughout the world for the Improvement in question and the right to claim priority from the application for patent protection [including under the Paris Convention when making application in countries or territories outside the U.K.], for nominal consideration to that other party, provided that the party electing not to pursue the application or the resulting patent shall be entitled to a full non-exclusive, irrevocable, worldwide, royalty-free licence (without limit of time and with the right to assign and to grant sub-licences thereunder) under all relevant rights.

7.8 Subject to the foregoing, each party shall be free to apply for patent protection for any invention not made in whole or in part by an employee of the other, provided however that the specification in support thereof does not disclose any Know-How and/or other Confidential Information.

7.9 Subject to the provisions of clause 7.7, *Alpha* and the Licensee shall share equally the costs of filing and prosecuting any future joint patent applications.

8. Confidentiality

8.1 Each party agrees during the term of this Agreement and after expiry or termination of this Agreement howsoever arising to keep secret and confidential all Confidential Information obtained from the other. Each party further agrees to use such Confidential Information exclusively for the purposes of this Agreement, and only to disclose the same as follows:

8.1.1 (In the case of *Alpha*) to its licensees who in such event shall enter into a confidentiality undertaking direct with the party whose Confidential Information is being disclosed in terms satisfactory to that party;

8.1.2 (In the case of the Licensee) on a need to know basis to its directors or employees concerned in the manufacture, use or sale of the Products ("Representatives") provided that before any such disclosure takes place the Licensee procures that each of the Representatives concerned shall execute a confidentiality undertaking with *Alpha* and the Licensee. The Licensee warrants that any and all Representatives will comply with the terms of this Agreement; and

8.1.3 In the case of both parties in relation to communications with and from regulatory authorities in the Territory relating to the Products.

8.2 The provisions of clause 8.1 shall not apply to Confidential Information or other information which *Alpha* or the Licensee (as the case may be):

8.2.1 Can prove to have been in its possession (other than under any obligation of confidence) at the date of receipt; or

8.2.2 Which becomes public knowledge otherwise than through a breach of any obligation of confidentiality owed to the party communicating such information to the other; or

8.3 If either party is required to disclose pursuant to an obligation under statute or to a statutory or governmental body it may disclose for that purpose only provided that prior to such required disclosure by the Licensee, the Licensee shall be required to notify *Alpha* of such requirement in writing. Confidential Information disclosed for the purposes of this clause 8.3 must be subsequently and/or otherwise maintained secret and confidential.

8.4 The provisions of this clause 8 shall remain in force following termination of this Agreement.

9. Payments and Royalties

9.1 In consideration of *Alpha* performing its obligations under this Agreement the Licensee shall pay to *Alpha* the fees specified in Schedule 5 as follows:

9.1.1 The Licensee will pay the fee attributable to Phase One of this Agreement in three equal instalments within the period of Phase One, subject to The Government of India Regulations/Directions. The first payment is due seven (7) days after the signing of this Agreement, with the subsequent payments being due as follows [*to be agreed*];

9.1.2 In Phase Two and all subsequent years until this Agreement is terminated or expires the Licensee will pay the annual fee in three equal instalments within that year subject to The Government of India Regulations/ Directions. The first payment for each year is due within 7 days of the commencement of the first month of that year. In the second and all subsequent years the Licensee will pay the royalty within three months of the end of each Licensee financial year.

NB. Phasing and number of payments will be clarified by JB once the length of Phase One and Phase Two has been confirmed.

9.2 In consideration of the rights granted under clauses 2.1 and 3, the Licensee shall during Phase Two of this Agreement pay to *Alpha* a royalty of 4% of the Net Sales Value of all Products supplied and/or installed by the Licensee.

9.3 If the Products are:

9.3.1 Rented, leased, let out or hired or otherwise disposed of to a customer by the Licensee; or

9.3.2 Used by the Licensee for its own commercial purposes; or

9.3.3 Sold to an Associated Company of the Licensee;

the Net Sales Value of each such Product shall be deemed to be equivalent to the Net Sales Value which would have been applicable under this Agreement had such Product been transferred to an independent arm's length customer.

9.4 Payments due under clause 9.2 shall be made within 30 days of the end of each Quarter in respect of all Products Supplied to the Licensee's customer or (if earlier) Supplied to site in readiness for installation in that Quarter.

9.5 If the Licensee does not in any Year specified in column 1 of this clause 9.5 achieve the Minimum Sales Value corresponding to that Year specified in column 2 of this clause, *Alpha* may give notice in writing to the Licensee terminating this Agreement.

(1)	(2)	(3)
Year	£	£
1		
2		
3		
4		
5		]

9.6 If the Licensee does not in any Year set out in column 1 of clause 9.5 achieve the Net Sales Value to maintain exclusivity corresponding to that Year specified in column 3 of clause 9.5 then *Alpha* may license any other person to, or itself, manufacture, use and Supply the Products in the Territory and in such event:

9.6.1 *Alpha* shall notify the Licensee in writing of such licensing; and

9.6.2 Clause 2.1 shall be deemed amended and clause 2.2 deleted accordingly.

9.7 All sums due under this Agreement:

9.7.1 Shall be made in foreign currency to the credit of *Alpha*'s Bank or such other account as may be designated in writing by *Alpha*. Conversion into .... (foreign amount) shall be calculated:

9.7.1.1 In the case of each royalty payment at the middle spot rate ruling in .... (country) on the last Business Day of the Quarter concerned, unless payment is made after the due date, in which case conversions shall be at the rate ruling at the date payment was made if this is more favourable to *Alpha*; and

9.7.1.2 In the case of all other payments at the rate of exchange ruling on the day payment is made or due, whichever is earlier:

Provided always that, where any payment is made after the date required in this Agreement, conversion shall be at the rate ruling at the date of payment if this is more favourable to *Alpha*;

9.7.2 Are exclusive of any value added tax which shall be payable in addition by the Licensee on the rendering by *Alpha* of any appropriate value added tax invoice. The Licensee shall pay any costs, interest and penalties due by reason of late payment of any such value added tax; and

9.7.3 Shall be made in full without deduction of taxes, charges and other duties (including any withholding or other income taxes) that may be imposed, except where the Licensee is required by law to make such deduction or withholding, in which event the Licensee shall:

9.7.3.1 Ensure that the deduction or withholding does not exceed the minimum amount legally required;

9.7.3.2 Pay to *Alpha* such additional amount as shall result in the net amount received by *Alpha* being equal to the amount which would have been received by *Alpha* had no such deduction or withholding been made;

9.7.3.3 Pay to the applicable taxation or other authorities within the period for payment permitted by law the full amount of the deduction or withholding (including, but without prejudice to the generality of the foregoing, the full amount of any deduction or withholding from any additional amount paid pursuant to this clause 9.7.3.3);

9.7.3.4 Furnish to *Alpha*, within the period for payment permitted by law, either an official receipt of the applicable taxation or other authorities for all amounts deducted or withheld as aforesaid or, if such receipts are not issued by the taxation or other authorities concerned on payment to them of amounts so deducted or withheld, a certificate of deduction or equivalent evidence of the relevant deduction or withholding; and

9.7.3.5 Co-operate in all respects necessary to permit *Alpha* to take advantage of such double taxation agreements as may be available.

9.7.4 Are exclusive of the Costs which will be chargeable to the Licensee at cost plus a 10% handling charge. All *Alpha*'s invoices to the Licensee in respect of Costs shall be accompanied by a copy of the original supplier's invoice for such Cost, and shall be payable by the Licensee within .... days of the *Alpha* invoice date.

9.8 If any stamp taxes, registration taxes, turnover taxes, or other taxes, duties or governmental charges are levied on this Agreement by reason of its execution or performance, other than those identified in clause 9.7.3, it shall be the responsibility of the Licensee to pay all such taxes when due. Such taxes shall be in addition to other amounts payable by the Licensee and shall not be set off against any of the amounts due to *Alpha* under this Agreement.

9.9 The Licensee agrees to release and indemnify *Alpha* from and against all liability of whatever nature arising out of the Licensee's failure duly and timely to pay and discharge any of the above-mentioned taxes.

9.9 *Alpha* shall be entitled to charge the Licensee interest on all overdue undisputed payments under this Agreement at an annual rate of 4 per cent. above *Alpha*'s Bank base rate from time to time prevailing. Such interest shall accrue daily and be calculated on a daily basis on all overdue accounts from the date when the payment first became due until the date that payment is made in full.

10. Records

10.1 The Licensee agrees to keep true and accurate Records. The Records shall upon reasonable notice by *Alpha* be open at all reasonable times during business hours for inspection or the taking of copies of Records by *Alpha* or its duly authorised agent or an independent accountant selected by *Alpha* for the purpose of verifying the accuracy of the Licensee's reports. *Alpha* shall be solely responsible for the costs of the accountant unless the accountant certifies that any reports are inaccurate or that the royalty paid to *Alpha* for any relevant period under clause 9 was 5% or more below the royalty to which *Alpha* was entitled during that period in which event the Licensee shall reimburse *Alpha* for all the accountant's costs.

10.2 The Licensee shall submit to *Alpha* within .... days of the end of each Quarter a statement indicating the quantity of Products made, used and or Supplied and the Net Sales Value of Products during that period.

10.3 *Alpha* agrees to maintain confidential all financial information received with respect to the Licensee's operations pursuant to clauses 10.1 and 10.2 except as is reasonably required to recover royalties.

11. Licensee's Obligations

11.1 During the continuance of this Agreement the Licensee shall:

11.1.1 Without prejudice to any obligation on the Licensee pursuant to clause 9.6 use its best endeavours to promote the distribution and Supply of Windows in the Territory providing such advertising and publicity (in a form to be approved by *Alpha*) as may reasonably be expected to bring Windows to the attention of as many customers as possible and in order to maximise demand for Windows in the Territory. The Licensee further agrees to make available all necessary distribution and manufacturing facilities to meet demands for Windows throughout the Territory;

11.1.2 Ensure that all Products Supplied by the Licensee meet the relevant Specification, and to satisfy in performance, quality, construction and use the reasonable requirements of *Alpha*. The Licensee shall upon reasonable notice from *Alpha* give *Alpha* free access at any reasonable time to its premises for the purpose of enabling *Alpha* to assure itself that the Licensee is observing its obligations under this Agreement;

11.1.3 Supply Products to any suitable customers independently of any other products of the Licensee if so required;

11.1.4 Ensure that all literature prepared by the Licensee and relating to Products bears an acknowledgement (approved by *Alpha*) to the effect that they are subject to a licence from *Alpha* and attach to the outer packaging of all Products a label stating that such Products are made under licence from *Alpha*;

11.1.5 [Include in the terms and conditions of sale or other supply of the Products a guarantee to the effect that the Licensee will, during at least the period of .... months from the date of such sale or supply, replace at its own expense and free of charge any Products [Supplied] and/or installed by it that are defective by reason of faulty manufacture or through inadequate workmanship or materials;]

11.1.6 Provide adequate servicing facilities for any Products manufactured and/or fabricated and/or Supplied and/or installed by the Licensee;

11.1.7 Not act as agent of *Alpha*, and specifically not give any indication that it is acting otherwise than as principal, and in advertising or Supplying or installing Products not make any representations or give any warranty on behalf of *Alpha*;

11.1.8 Collaborate as necessary with *Alpha* to enable it to provide the Services and for fulfilment of the Project Plan, such collaboration to include without limitation the following:

11.1.8.1 Subject to clause 8 (confidentiality), the Licensee will provide *Alpha* with such information and data as it may require concerning the Licensee's operations and answers to queries, decisions and approvals which may be necessary for *Alpha* to undertake the Project;

11.1.8.2 The Licensee will provide free of charge to *Alpha* such access to any of its sites, the Licensee's employees and any of the Company's facilities that *Alpha* may require access to, for the purposes of this Agreement;

11.1.8.3 The Licensee shall comply with and fulfil all requirements and obligations upon it in this Agreement and shall not interfere with the provision of the Services by *Alpha*.

12. Infringement or Misuse

12.1 If the Licensee becomes aware of any infringement of the Approved Trade Marks or Trade Marks or misuse of the Know-How it shall promptly notify *Alpha* and provide all details within its knowledge. The Licensee shall also provide *Alpha* with all assistance requested by *Alpha* for the purposes of any infringement action or action for misuse *Alpha* may bring.

12.2 *Alpha* shall be under no obligation to take any action regarding any infringements, whether through the institution of legal proceedings or otherwise, but should *Alpha* in its absolute discretion decide to take any such action, it shall do so at its own cost and the Licensee shall have no claim to any sums recovered by *Alpha*.

13. Term and Termination

13.1 This Agreement comes into effect on the Commencement Date and unless terminated earlier under the provisions of this clause shall remain in full force and effect until the expiry of five years from the Commencement Date.

13.2 *Alpha* may terminate this Agreement by notice in writing if the Licensee is in breach of this Agreement and shall have failed (where the breach is capable of remedy) to remedy the breach within .... days of the receipt of a request in writing from *Alpha* to remedy the breach, such request setting out the breach and indicating that failure to remedy the breach may result in termination of this Agreement.

13.3 In addition to the powers of termination contained elsewhere in this Agreement *Alpha* may by written notice served on the Licensee terminate this Agreement immediately if the Licensee:

13.3.1 Becomes insolvent or goes into liquidation, either compulsory or voluntary (save for the purpose of reconstruction or amalgamation), or if an administrator, administrative receiver or receiver is appointed in respect of the whole or any part of its assets, or if the Licensee makes an assignment for the benefit of, or in composition with, its creditors generally;

13.3.2 Has any distraint, execution or other process levied or enforced on any of its property;

13.3.3 Ceases, or appears in the reasonable opinion of *Alpha* likely or is threatening to cease to trade;

13.3.4 The equivalent of any of the above occurs to that party in the Territory under the jurisdiction to which that party is subject;

13.3.5 Challenges in any way any of the proprietary rights of *Alpha* in the Know-How, the Trade Marks and the Approved Trade Marks.

13.4 The Licensee shall notify *Alpha* of any change in Control of the Licensee (such disclosure being kept confidential by *Alpha* until it becomes a matter of public knowledge) whereupon *Alpha* may terminate this Agreement by serving not less than six months' notice on the Licensee.

14. Consequences of Termination

14.1 All rights and obligations of the parties shall cease to have effect immediately upon termination of this Agreement except that termination shall not affect:

14.1.1 The accrued rights and obligations of the parties at the date of termination; and

14.1.2 The continued existence and validity of the rights and obligations of the parties under those clauses which are expressed to survive termination and any provisions of this Agreement necessary for the interpretation or enforcement of this Agreement.

14.2 Upon termination of this Agreement howsoever occasioned:

14.2.1 The Licensee's rights to use the Know-How under this Agreement shall forthwith cease;

14.2.3 The Licensee shall return promptly to *Alpha*:

14.2.3.1 All technical and promotional material in its possession relating to the Products and all copies of such material, and deliver up to *Alpha* (or to whomsoever *Alpha* shall direct) free of charge all licences and authorities, if any, held by the Licensee in relation to the Products and all or any other industrial property relating specifically to the Products and/or otherwise to this Agreement, whether or not the same shall have been issued in the name of the Licensee by virtue of its functions to be performed under this Agreement. The Licensee undertakes to give all such assistance as may be necessary for the transfer to *Alpha* (or to whomsoever *Alpha* shall direct) of all such licences and authorities and properly to execute any documents which may become necessary to effect any such transfers;

14.2.3.2 Any and all Confidential Information (including any copies of the Confidential Information made by or in the possession of the Licensee;

14.2.3.3 [*Alpha* shall at its discretion either grant the Licensee sufficient time to sell existing stocks of the Products, including stocks on order and in transit at that time which period shall not exceed .... months, and/or purchase from the Licensee all residual stocks in store which are in good and suitable condition, the price for the sale of such stocks being the lower of the cost to the Licensee of such stocks or their market value;]

OR

14.2.4 [The Licensee shall continue to have the right for a period of [NUMBER] months from the date of termination to complete deliveries on contracts in force at that date and to dispose of Products already manufactured subject to payment to the Licensee of royalties thereon in accordance with clause 9]

14.2.5 If either party shall have a claim against the other there shall (in the absence of express written agreement between the parties) be no right of set-off against any money due from the other party. (JB to consider these alternatives)

14.3 The following clauses shall survive the expiry or termination of this Agreement howsoever arising: clause 4.7, clause 4.8, clause 8 (confidentiality) and this clause 14.

15. Product Liability

15.1 The Licensee shall at all times indemnify and keep indemnified *Alpha* against all costs, claims, damages or expenses incurred by *Alpha* or for which *Alpha* may become liable with respect to any product liability claim relating to Products Supplied or put into use by the Licensee pursuant to this Agreement. The Licensee shall maintain adequate product liability insurance [coverage of £(amount), increasing in accordance with the ....(name of the country) Retail Price Index] *(we need to check with the Indian lawyers the equivalent of this)* and shall ensure that *Alpha*'s interest is noted on the policy. The Licensee shall supply *Alpha* with a copy of such insurance policy on request and shall not terminate such policy without prior written notice to *Alpha*.

15.2 The Licensee shall be exclusively responsible for all Products manufactured and/or fabricated and/or installed and/or Supplied by or on behalf of the Licensee and accordingly the Licensee shall indemnify *Alpha* in respect of all costs, claims and expenses or other liabilities incurred as a result of any claims by third parties in tort or otherwise against *Alpha* arising in any way out of the use of any of the Know-How or Products by the Licensee.

16. Restrictions

16.1 The Licensee shall not during the continuance of this Agreement and for a period of .... years following termination of this Agreement either by itself or in conjunction with any other person, firm or company directly or indirectly manufacture and/or Supply any goods which are similar to or competitive with the Products.

17. *Force Majeure*

Neither party will be liable to the other for any failure or delay or for the consequences of any failure or delay in performance of this Agreement if it is due to any event beyond the reasonable control or contemplation of a party to this Agreement including, without limitation, acts of God, war, acts of terrorism, industrial disputes, protests, fire, flood, storm, tempest, explosion and national emergencies and the party so delayed will be entitled to a reasonable extension of time for performing such obligations.

18. Assignment

18.1 *Alpha* may at any time assign the benefit (including any present, future or contingent interest or right to any sums or damages payable by the Licensee under or in connection with this Agreement) or delegate the burden of this Agreement or otherwise sub-contract, mortgage, charge or otherwise transfer or hold on trust any or all of its rights and obligations under this Agreement.

18.2 The Licensee may not assign the benefit (including any present, future or contingent interest or right to any sums or damages payable by either party under or in connection with this Agreement) or delegate the burden of this Agreement or hold this Agreement on trust for any other person.

19. Relationship of the parties

Nothing contained in this Agreement, and no action taken by the parties pursuant to this Agreement, will be deemed to constitute a relationship between the parties of partnership, joint venture, principal and agent or employer and employee. Neither party has, nor may it represent that it has, any authority to act or make any commitments on the other party's behalf.

20. Severability

If any clause or part of this Agreement is found by any court, tribunal, administrative body or authority of competent jurisdiction to be illegal, invalid or unenforceable then that provision will, to the extent required, be severed from this Agreement and will be ineffective without, as far as is possible, modifying any other clause or part of this Agreement and this will not affect any other provisions of this Agreement which will remain in full force and effect unless the substantive purpose of this Agreement is then frustrated, in which case either party may terminate this Agreement on written notice to the other.

21. Entire Agreement/Reliance on Representations

This Agreement and other documents referred to in the Schedules contain all the terms which the parties have agreed in relation to the subject matter of this Agreement and those documents, and supersedes any prior written or oral agreements, representations (excluding any fraudulent misrepresentation) or understandings between the parties in relation to such subject-matter.

22. Variations

No variation of this Agreement shall be valid unless it is in writing and signed by or on behalf of each of the parties by a director or other duly authorised officer of each of the parties.

23. Waiver

No failure or delay by any party to exercise any right, power or remedy will operate as a waiver of it nor will any partial exercise preclude any further exercise of the same, or of some other right, power or remedy.

24. Dispute Resolution

24.1 Subject to clause 24.2 any dispute arising in connection with this Agreement shall be finally settled under the Rules of Conciliation and Arbitration of the International Chamber of Commerce by one arbitrator appointed in accordance with such rules. The Arbitrators shall be appointed by agreement between the Parties hereto or failing agreement by the President for the time being of the International Chamber of Commerce and the arbitration shall take place in ....(name of country) in English.

24.1 This clause 24 shall not prevent either party from obtaining injunctive, or other similar relief from the court, if so required and pursuant to clause 25.

25. Governing Law and Jurisdiction

Governing Law

25.1 The formation, existence, construction, performance, validity and all aspects whatsoever of this Agreement or of any term of this Agreement will be governed by the law of India.

Jurisdiction

25.2 Subject to clause 25.3, the courts of India will have non-exclusive jurisdiction to settle any disputes that may arise out of or in connection with this Agreement. The parties irrevocably agree to submit to that jurisdiction.

25.3 The agreement contained in clause 25.2 is included for the benefit of *Alpha*. Accordingly *Alpha* retains the right to bring proceedings in any other court of competent jurisdiction. The Licensee irrevocably waives any objection to, and agrees to submit to, the jurisdiction of such other courts.

25.4 The Licensee irrevocably agrees that a judgement or order of any court referred to in this clause is conclusive and binding upon it and may be enforced against it in the courts of any other jurisdiction.

26. Notices

26.1 Any notice, demand or communication in connection with this Agreement will be in writing and may be delivered by hand, first class or airmail pre-paid post or facsimile [(but not by e-mail)], addressed to the recipient at its registered office or its address or facsimile number as the case may be stated in clause 26.4 and will be marked for the attention of [*name of position*] (or such other address or facsimile number or person which the recipient has notified in writing to the sender in accordance with this clause 26, to be received by the sender not less than seven Business Days before the notice is despatched).

26.2 The notice, demand or communication will be deemed to have been duly served:

26.2.1 If delivered by hand, at the time of delivery;

26.2.2 If delivered overseas by airmail, 7 Business Days after the date of being posted;

26.2.3 If delivered by facsimile, at the time of transmission:

Provided that, where in the case of delivery by hand or transmission by facsimile, such delivery or transmission occurs either after 4.00 pm local time on a Business Day, or on a day other than a Business Day, service will be deemed to occur at 9.00 am local time on the next following Business Day.

26.3 Service by facsimile is a valid means of service only where service of the original notice, demand or communication is not required.

26.4 The addresses and facsimile numbers for the parties are as follows:

Alpha	[THE LICENSEE]
....	[Address]
....	
.... (address)	[FAX NO.]

27. Costs and Expenses

Except where otherwise expressly provided in this Agreement, each party will pay its own costs and expenses in relation to the preparation, execution, completion and implementation of this Agreement, provided that if *Alpha* lawfully exercises any right to terminate or rescind this Agreement, then, in addition to any other right or remedy which it may have against the Licensee, the Licensee will pay to *Alpha* on demand an amount equal to all such costs and expenses incurred by *Alpha* as aforesaid and incurred in connection with the termination or rescission of this Agreement.

28. Language

This Agreement is made only in the English language. If there is any conflict in the meaning between the English language version of this Agreement and any version or translation of this Agreement in any other language the English version shall prevail.

29. Counterparts

This Agreement may be executed in any number of counterparts, each of which so executed will be an original, but together will constitute one and the same instrument.

SCHEDULE 1

KNOW-HOW

SCHEDULE 2

TRADE MARKS

PART 1

Approved Trade Mark

Territory	Mark	Number	Class
Bangladesh	Spectus		
India	Spectus		
Nepal	Spectus		
Bhutan	Spectus		

PART 2
Trade Marks
Alpha

Heywood Williams

PART 3
Trade Mark Notices

"Spectus is a trade mark of *Alpha*"

"All trade marks acknowledged"

SCHEDULE 3
INFRASTRUCTURE

Alpha will prepare for .... such specifications, information and advice required to enable .... to build and equip a blending plant capable of manufacturing [ ] tonnes of Dry Blend per day at an extrusion factory capable of ultimately manufacturing [ ] tonnes of Vinyl Profiles per annum and a window fabrication factory capable of producing approximately [ ] windows per day. This information will encompass:

Factory Design:
- Floor space required
- Machine layout and configuration
- Electricity supply specification
- Water supply and treatment specification
- Mechanical Handling

Blending/Mixing Plant:
- Raw material handling and storage
- Mixing/blending equipment
- Control systems
- Blended material handling and storage
- Sources of equipment required

Extruders and Downstream Equipment:
- Specification and number of extruders
- Sources of equipment required
- Evaluation of second hand extruders
- Vinyl Profile test equipment

Profile Storage/Warehousing:
- Warehouse layout
- Racking systems
- Mechanical handling

Window Manufacturing:
- Floor space required
- Manufacturing equipment requirements
- Equipment layout and configuration

Electricity supply and requirements and specification
Air supply and specification
Mechanical handling requirements
Labour/headcount requirements
Fabrication test equipment

SCHEDULE 4
PROJECT PLAN

SCHEDULE 5
FEES AND COSTS

Fees

The fees payable will be:

Phase One: [ ] (amount) *(to be advised)*

Phase Two: .... (amount) per annum *(to be confirmed)*

Costs:

The following costs which may be incurred by *Alpha* shall be payable by the Licensee in addition to fees:

Pre-Agreement costs - all travel, accommodation and subsistence costs and expenses incurred by *Alpha*, for the purpose of this Agreement incurred prior to the signing of this Agreement.

Marketing costs - the costs of acquisition of market data from any third party or the costs of provision of any marketing material.

Development/R&D costs - the costs of any materials used by *Alpha* in the preparation of trial and experimental batches of Dry Blend for the Territory.

The costs of any Dry Blend used by *Alpha* in commissioning of any extruders on behalf of the Licensee

Equipment costs - any cost incurred by *Alpha* in purchasing or commissioning or repairing any plant or equipment on behalf of the Licensee.

Testing costs - the costs of any testing of Windows and/or Profiles and/or Products carried out by third parties.

Travel, accommodation and subsistence costs and expenses - incurred by *Alpha* personnel or *Alpha* appointed third party or parties in travelling to, or travelling within, India for the purposes of this Agreement.

Local living expenses incurred in India by *Alpha* personnel or *Alpha* appointed third party or parties for the purposes of this Agreement.

SCHEDULE 6
SPECIFICATION

SCHEDULE 7
ASSISTANCE PLAN

SIGNED by)
duly authorised to sign)
for and on behalf of)
Alpha)

SIGNED by   )
duly authorised to sign   )
for and on behalf of   )
Beta   )

ASSIGNMENT OF RIGHTS IN INVENTION

WHEREAS, I/We
..................(hereinafter referred to as "INVENTORS") have made an invention for

AND, WHEREAS,
.... (hereinafter referred to as "APPLICANT"), are desirous of acquiring the entire right, title & interest in and to said invention in all foreign countries.

NOW, THEREFORE, TO ALL WHOM IT MAY CONCERN, BE IT KNOWN, I/We the "INVENTORS" for valuable consideration of .... (amount), the receipt, adequacy and sufficiency of which is hereby acknowledged, have sold, assigned, transferred and conveyed and by these presents do hereby sell, assign transfer and convey to APPLICANT, the entire right, title and interest in and to said invention for obtaining Letters Patent throughout the world, TO HAVE and TO HOLD the same to the full end of the term for which said Letters Patent may be granted.

AND, I/We, the INVENTORS do hereby covenant and agree to do all lawful acts and things, and make, execute and deliver any and all other instruments in writing, and any and all further applications, papers, affidavits, assignments, and other documents,, which, in the opinion of counsel for said APPLICANT, may be required or necessary more effectively to secure to and vest in said APPLICANT the entire right, title and interest throughout the world in and to said invention, applications, Letters Patent, rights, titles, benefits, privileges and advantages hereby sold, assigned, transferred and conveyed or intended so to be.

Dated this day of
INVENTOR   APPLICANT

....

Witness 1
Signature
Address
Witness 2
Signature
Address

STATE OF
COUNTRY OF

Before me, the undersigned authority, on this day personally appeared................ known to me to be the persons whose names are subscribed to the foregoing instrument and acknowledged to me that they executed the same for the purposes and consideration therein expressed.

Given under my hand and seal of office this....................day of........ ....20....
(Notary Public)

TECHNOLOGY ASSIGNMENT AGREEMENT

This Agreement is entered as of...................,...............
BETWEEN
..................., (the "Company"),
AND
..................., an individual ("Developer"). [The assignment and stock issuance hereunder is intended to qualify for tax-free treatment under Internal Revenue Code Section 351.]

[COMMENT: See the explanation of IRC Section 351 in Section C of Chapter 1; if section 351 criteria are not met, the transaction will likely be taxable even though Developer receives only liquid stock as consideration.]

1. Assignment

Developer hereby assigns to the Company exclusively throughout the world all right, title and interest (choate or inchoate) in (i) the subject matter referred to in Exhibit A ("Technology"), (ii) all precursors, portions and work in progress with respect thereto and all inventions, works of authorship, mask works, technology, information, know-how, materials and tools relating thereto or to the development, support or maintenance thereof and (iii) all copyrights, patent rights, trade secret rights, trademark rights, mask works rights [, *sui generis* database rights] and all other [intellectual and industrial property] rights [of any sort] and all business, contract rights [,causes of action], and goodwill in, incorporated or embodied in, used to develop, or related to any of the foregoing (collectively "Intellectual Property").

[COMMENT: This assignment is intentionally very broad and is designed to provide the Company sufficient protection even if Exhibit A is vague or limited.]

2. Consideration

The Company agrees to issue to Developer.................... shares of common stock of the Company on the date of this Agreement pursuant to the provisions of a Stock Purchase Agreement of even date herewith between the Company and Developer. Such shares shall be the only consideration required of the Company with respect to the subject-matter of this Agreement.

3. Further Assurances; Moral Rights; Competition; Marketing

3.1 Developer agrees to assist the Company in every legal way to evidence, record and perfect the Section 1 assignment and to apply for and obtain recordation of and from time to time enforce, maintain, and defend the assigned rights. If the Company is unable for any reason whatsoever to secure the Developer's signature to any document it is entitled to under this section 3.1, Developer hereby irrevocably designates and appoints the Company and its duly authorized officers and agents, as his agents and attorneys-in-fact with full power of substitution to act for and on his behalf and instead of Developer, to execute and file any such document or documents and to do all other lawfully permitted acts to further the purposes of the foregoing with the same legal force and effect as if executed by Developer.

3.2 To the extent allowed by law, section 1 includes all rights of paternity, integrity, disclosure and withdrawal and any other rights that may be known as or referred to as "moral rights," "artist's rights," "droit moral" or the like (collectively "Moral Rights"). To the extent Developer retains any such Moral Rights under applicable law, Developer hereby ratifies and consents to, and provides all necessary ratifications and consents to, any action that may be taken with respect to such Moral Rights by or authorized by Company; Developer agrees not to assert any Moral Rights with respect thereto. Developer will confirm any such ratifications, consents and agreements from time to time as requested by Company.

[COMMENT: "Moral rights" are rights of individuals akin to copyrights that generally are not assignable. Moral rights, although very limited in the United States, are prevalent elsewhere in the world. Nevertheless, an author in the United States often will be entitled to assert moral rights when a work created in the United States is exploited elsewhere.]

4. Confidential Information

Developer will not use or disclose anything assigned to the Company hereunder or any other technical or business information or plans of the Company, except to the extent Developer (i) can document that it is generally available (through no fault of Developer) for use and disclosure by the public without any charge, license or restriction, or (ii) is permitted to use or disclose such information or plans pursuant to the Proprietary Information and Inventions Agreement by and between Developer and the Company of even date herewith. Developer recognizes and agrees that there is no adequate remedy at law for a breach of this section 4, that such a breach would irreparably harm the Company and that the Company is entitled to equitable relief (including, without limitations, injunctions) with respect to any such breach or potential breach in addition to any other remedies.

5. Warranty

Developer represents and warrants to the Company that the Developer: (i) was the sole owner (other than the Company) of all rights, title and interest in the Intellectual Property and the Technology, (ii) has not assigned, transferred, licensed, pledged or otherwise encumbered any Intellectual Property or the Technology or agreed to do so, (iii) has full power and authority to enter into this Agreement and to make the assignment as provided in Section 1, (iv) is not aware of any violation, infringement or misappropriation of any third party's rights (or any claim thereof) by the Intellectual Property or the Technology, [(v) was not acting within the scope of employment by any third party when conceiving, creating or otherwise performing any activity with respect to anything purportedly assigned in Section 1,] and (vi) is not aware of any questions or challenges with respect to the patentability or validity of any claims of any existing patents or patent applications relating to the Intellectual Property.

6. Miscellaneous

This Agreement is not assignable or transferable by Developer without the prior written consent of the Company; any attempt to do so shall be void. Any notice, report, approval or consent required or permitted hereunder shall be in writing and will be deemed to have been duly given if delivered personally or mailed by first-class, registered or certified ....(country) mail, postage prepaid to the respective addresses of the parties as set below (or such other address as a party may designate by .... days notice). No failure to exercise, and no delay in exercising, on the part of either party, any privilege, any power or any rights hereunder will operate as a waiver thereof, nor will any single or partial exercise of any right or power hereunder preclude further exercise of any other right hereunder. If any provision of this Agreement shall be adjudged by any court of competent jurisdiction to be unenforceable or invalid, that provision shall be limited or eliminated to the minimum extent necessary so that this Agreement shall otherwise remain in full force and effect and enforceable. This Agreement shall be deemed to have been made in, and shall be construed pursuant to the laws of the State of .... and the .... (name of country) without regard to conflicts of laws provisions thereof. The prevailing party in any action to enforce this Agreement shall be entitled to recover costs and expenses including, without limitation, attorneys' fees. The terms of this Agreement are confidential to the Company and no press release or other written or oral disclosure of any nature regarding the compensation terms of this Agreement shall be made by Developer without the Company's prior written approval; however, approval for such disclosure shall be deemed given to the extent such disclosure is required to comply with governmental rules. Any waivers or amendments shall be effective only if made in writing and signed by a representative of the respective parties authorized to bind the parties. Both parties agree that this Agreement is the complete and exclusive statement of the mutual understanding of the parties and supersedes and cancels all previous written and oral agreements and communications relating to the subject-matter of this Agreement.

IN WITNESS WHEREOF, the parties have executed this Agreement on the day and year first indicated above.

By:..
Name:..
Title:..
Address:..
....
:..

EXHIBIT A
TECHNOLOGY ASSIGNMENT AGREEMENT

Services (if the services are for a fixed term, state it here: ....; If no fixed term is stated the term will continue until the services are completed or the agreement is terminated under section 4, whichever occurs first) fees (applicable only where checked and completed) ....hourly fee of .... (Exclusive of travel time; payable monthly in arrears......................... After invoice detailing hours, with a gap of .... In the aggregate...................flat fee of .... Payable days after timely completion of the following milestones prior to termination:

.... Expense reimbursement (if applicable at all, is limited to required, reasonable telephone expenses and long distance coach class (or equivalent)

Travel (transportation, lodging and meals) authorized in writing by company in Advance; payable.................... Days after itemized invoice and delivery of receipts)

PRECEDENTS ON CONFIDENTIALITY AND NON-DISCLOSURE

KNOW HOW ASSIGNMENT AGREEMENT

This KNOW HOW ASSIGNMENT AGREEMENT has been entered into this day of ....(name of month)

BETWEEN

Alpha, an existing company under the Companies Act, 1956 and having its registered office at.......... (hereinafter called *"Alpha"* which expression unless repugnant to the context shall mean and include its subsidiaries, and its successors and assigns)

AND

Beta, an Indian firm having its registered offices at (hereinafter called *"Beta"* which expression unless repugnant to the context shall mean and include its subsidiaries, and its successors and assigns)

1. Definitions

Intellectual Property: Includes all existing Intellectual Property in the nature of unregistered or registered rights to any and all copyrights, trademarks and other confidential/propriety information not limited to that forming part of the subject matter transfer, and inclusive of all intellectual property that is the subject of ownership by *Alpha* and its subsidiaries, venture partners and predecessors in Interest, business and Title and *Beta* and/or its subsidiaries, venture partners and predecessors in interest business and title.

Product: means the .... preparation either as manufactured and packaged by .... by virtue of its agreement with *Beta* or as served in *Beta*'s select restaurants.

Copyrights: means works of authorship whether artistic, literary or otherwise fixed in a tangible medium of expression (including corresponding rights under international agreements and conventions, inclusive of the non-registration and/or registrations, renewal and extensions of any of the foregoing) whether or not containing a copyright notice, which work (s) was/were created before the expiration or prior termination of this agreement.

Trademarks: The trademark .... and other variants thereof, inclusive of any domain names in respect of the said trademarks.

Know how: means confidential/propriety information, trade secrets, recipe, formulation, and preparation information fixed in any medium or otherwise, quality control specifications, inspection and testing protocols, all data *(irrespective of whether human or machine-readable)* inclusive of marketing, cost, financial, survey data that *Beta* has ownership off and will be used by *Alpha* and the general and specific information not limited to processes, compositions, methods, techniques, documentation, pertaining to the recipe/formulation, packaging and sale of products envisaged by the recipe and or formulation as provided in but not limited to ANNEXURE A.

Improved Know How: shall be included in the term know how being the subject matter of assignment in this agreement inclusive of the improvements and customizations to the recipe and or formulation *(effected by Beta and its subsidiaries, venture partners, and other manufacturing parties inclusive of but not limited to ...., or any other authorized entity)* developed by *Beta* and or any other authorized entity prior to this agreement.

Confidential Information: means the know how as defined above. In addition to the following: (i) the terms and conditions of this Agreement; (ii) *Beta's* trade secrets, business plans, strategies, methods and/or practices; and (iii) any other information relating to *Beta* or its business that is not generally known to the public, including but not limited to information about *Beta's* personnel, products, customers, marketing strategies, services or future business plans.

Territory: The Territory referred to in this Agreement shall include the whole of the world.

WHEREAS,

a. *Alpha* Hotels Ltd., (*Beta*), a subsidiary of *Alpha*, operates a well-known chain of hotels in India under the name and style of .... and has under the overall supervision of *Alpha*, developed a specialized cuisine which is served in its ....(name of restaurant) restaurants. One such culinary delight that has gained immense popularity is the ...., a .... (name of preparation) preparation from the cuisine of the North West Frontier region (herein after referred to as the product); Access to the recipe/formulation information of the product is controlled by *Alpha* and *Beta*. The recipe/formulation of the product is in the nature of confidential information and hence protectible as such. *Beta* is also the owner of certain valuable trademarks and copyrights relating to such product.

b. With a view to successfully leverage internal competencies in order to establish a packaged foods business, *Alpha* and *Beta* have decided to make available the .... cuisine across the country and abroad.

c. In this regard *Beta* warrants that it has a subsisting agreement dated ...., with The .... Fruit & Vegetable Products (India) Private Limited, a company incorporated under the Companies Act, 1956 and having its registered office at....to manufacture and package the said product for sale at *Beta*'s select Hotel outlets

d. With such intent to consolidate and rationalize marketing and logistical requirements in order to effect widespread marketing of the product, *Alpha* is now entering into this Know How Assignment agreement with *Beta* to acquire the said proprietary rights from *Beta* in respect of the .... recipe, and method of preparation.

e. *Alpha* represents that it has all of the required approvals, licenses and other rights, as well as the requisite existing level of training, knowledge, expertise by virtue of its subsidiary *Beta* and relationship within the Territory, to permit it to enter into this Agreement.

Now therefore, in consideration of the mutual convenants herein contained, the Parties agree as follows:

2. Preliminary Undertakings

a. *Beta* hereby undertakes to assign to *Alpha*, all ownership rights in the Confidential Information pertaining to the recipe/formulation with regard to the product inclusive of all improvements/modifications effected to the said Confidential Information and inclusive of but not limited to those effected to the product and its constituent elements as well as its packaging during the course of its agreement for manufacture with .... dated ....

b. *Beta* shall cease to cause the manufacture of the said product, ...under the aegis of its said agreement with .... and shall cause .... to hand over rights to all improvements/modification effected to the said recipe/Confidential Information as well as its product packaging during the term of its agreement to manufacture with .... *Alpha* shall also enter into a manufacturing agreement with .... which shall supersede all prior discussions and agreements specifically but not limited to the agreement for manufacture dated .... between *Beta* and .... with respect to the subject-matter hereof.

c. *Alpha* shall continue to cause the said .... to be served at any of its Hotel outlets. In this regard *Alpha* hereby gives *Beta* a non-exclusive license to *Beta* to manufacture and serve the said product at its select Hotel outlets.

3. Transfer of Recipe

Beta hereby assigns to *Alpha* all ownership rights in and to the know-how comprising of the recipe/Confidential Information whether affixed on any medium or otherwise *(inclusive of electronic media)* upon which the said Confidential Information may be stored inclusive of but not limited to the Intellectual Property along with any publicity material generated towards the promotion and sale of the said product. The said documentation shall also include any and all methods/processes relating to the improvement/modification of the said recipe as well as any publicity material, in any media, relating to the promotion of the product afore-mentioned.

4. Confidentiality and Non-compete

Beta covenants that the said recipe/Confidential Information is confidential in nature and has been strictly treated as such. In furtherance of the said transfer *Beta* hereby undertakes to bind all its employees, principal officers, contractors, sub-contractors, consultants etc., that have had, in the normal course of business, access to the said Confidential Information, to terms relating to preserving the confidentiality/non-disclosure of the said recipe/Confidential Information, in conformation with the standard confidentiality/non-compete agreement marked as ANNEXURE B. *Beta* inclusive of its board of directors and their direct beneficiaries, employees, ex-employees, consultants, and any descendants in business, interest and title in recognition of the transfer of confidential and proprietary information to *Alpha* hereby agrees not to directly or indirectly compete with the business of *Alpha* and its successors and assigns in business in relation to the subject matter of this agreement except as provided in clause 2 (c) or as authorized by *Alpha* by virtue of any subsequent written authorization.

5. Consideration for Transfer

The consideration for the transfer of the Confidential Information and all apertuant Intellectual Property rights thereto shall amount to Rs. ...., the receipt of which is hereby acknowledged by *Beta*.

6. Warranty

a. *Beta* represents and warrants to *Alpha* that *Beta* is the sole owner of all rights, title and interest in the Intellectual Property and the know how thereto.

b. *Beta* further represents that it has not assigned, transferred, licensed, pledged or otherwise encumbered the know-how forming the subject matter of this agreement as well as appertuant Intellectual Property or agreed to do so.

c. *Beta* also represents that it has full power and authority and is thus competent to enter into this Agreement and to make the assignment as provided in clause 3 of this agreement.

d. *Beta* is also not aware of any violation, infringement or misappropriation of any third party's rights (or any claim thereof) by the Intellectual Property or the know-how forming the subject-matter of this agreement.

7. Construction, Enforcement and Assignability

The parties hereto agree that this agreement contains the entire understanding between them. The parties further agree that this agreement may not be assigned by either party. The section titles used in this agreement are for reference purposes only and are not intended to add or to limit or in any other way change the meaning of the language of the agreement.

8. Governing Jurisdiction

Any dispute/difference arising from this Agreement shall be subject to the exclusive jurisdiction of the courts in .... (place).

9. Notice of Parties

a. The parties hereto agree that all notices which may be given by one party to the other under the terms of this agreement, shall be in writing and shall be addressed,

in case of *Beta* to the following address:

....and

in case of *Alpha*, to the following address:

....

b. Provided, however, that any notice deposited in the post as a registered letter, acknowledgement due shall be considered to have been effective when so deposited, and provided further that either of the parties may change the address herein given by express written notice to the other party.

10. Waiver

The failure of the Parties at any time to enforce any if the provisions of this agreement or to exercise any right herein provided, shall not be considered a waiver of such or any other provision or in any way effect the validity of this agreement.

11. Severability

a. It is hereby expressly agreed by both parties that no portion of this agreement is intended to be in violation of any law of India or of any other country which may, at any time, have jurisdiction over either party hereto, or the agreement itself.

b. Should any portion of this agreement be contrary to, or in violation of any such law, said portion shall be void and of no effect. The reminder of this agreement shall be valid and remain in force notwithstanding the invalidity of such offending portion.

12. Covenant of secrecy

Beta as well as *Alpha* shall exercise and shall require its employees or consultants to exercise the requisite amount of due diligence not to make known, divulge or communicate at any time before or after the termination of this agreement, unless it is necessary for the execution of the Agreement, to any person *(except as necessary to its selected trustworthy employees)* the know-how and Confidential Information and/or know-how disclosed and/or recommended to it by *Beta* hereunder, not to do nor suffer to be done or omitted any act or thing in relation to the subject matter of this agreement whereby said Confidential Information and know-how may become known to any unauthorized person, provided, however, that such information shall not be considered confidential, and this paragraph shall not apply, if such information can be demonstrated to have been in the public domain prior to its disclosure or recommendation by

Beta, or to have become part of the public domain by any means, except an unauthorized act or omission on the party of *Alpha* or any of its employees.

13. Force Majeure

Neither party shall be in default under this Agreement by reason of its failure or delay in the performance of its obligations, if such failure or delay is caused by actions of God, Government laws and regulations, strikes, lock-outs, war or any other cause beyond its reasonable control.

14. Miscellaneous

a. The present Agreement is subject to approval of Government of India and all its regulatory bodies whether statutory or otherwise.

b. All know-how and appertuant Intellectual property shall be delivered by *Beta* to the postal address previously indicated in writing by *Alpha*.

c. This instrument may not be waived, released, discharged, abandoned, changed or modified in any manner, orally or otherwise except by an instrument in writing signed by duly authorized officers or representatives of the parties hereto.

Date.........................

....

Beta   *Alpha*

CONFIDENTIALITY AGREEMENT (BETWEEN A COMPANY AND AN INDIVIDUAL)

THIS AGREEMENT is made on [*]

BETWEEN

[ ] a company registered in England whose registered office is at [*] (the "Company").

AND

[ ] of [*] (the "Covenantor").

WHEREAS the engagement of the Covenantor by the Company involves the Company placing the Covenantor in a position of special trust in relation to the business of the Company and through the Covenantor gaining knowledge of the Company's valuable secret and confidential know-how, intellectual property, trade secrets, marketing policies, plans, clients, contractual arrangements and trade connections (the "Confidential Information").

IT IS HEREBY AGREED that in consideration of the engagement of the Covenantor by the Company and the continuing disclosure to the Covenantor of Confidential Information:—

1. Definitions

In this Agreement, the following words have the meanings respectively shown opposite, unless the context requires otherwise:

"associated company" means any holding company and/or subsidiary as these terms are defined in section 736 Companies Act 1985;

"engagement" means the engagement of the Covenantor by the Company from time to time whether as employee, consultant or otherwise; and

"engagement contract" means the contract of engagement in force from time to time pursuant to which the Covenantor is engaged by the Company (whether such engagement is as an employee, consultant or otherwise).

2. Obligation not to Disclose

2.1 Subject to clause 2.2 below, the Covenantor shall treat as confidential all Confidential Information which is or may become the property of the Company or any associated company or in respect of which the Company or any associated company may owe an obligation of confidence; and the Covenantor shall not (except insofar as expressly authorised by the Company so to do) during the period of engagement or at any time thereafter disclose or communicate to any person any of the Confidential Information or permit or suffer any act matter or thing by which the Confidential Information may be disclosed or communicated to or ascertained by others; nor will the Covenantor (without the prior written consent of the Company) make use of any part of the Confidential Information for his own purposes.

2.2 The Covenantor shall be entitled to disclose freely to third parties any matter or thing to the extent that it is:

2.2.1 In the public domain at the time of its disclosure to the Covenantor or published after disclosure to him, or becomes part of the public domain otherwise than through the fault of the Covenantor or by the breach of this clause 2 by him; or

2.2.2 In possession of the Covenantor at the time of disclosure to him; or

2.2.3 Lawfully obtained by or on behalf of the Covenantor from a third party source other than in connection with or as a result of his engagement; or

2.2.4 Lawfully now in the possession or at any time after the date of this Agreement acquired by or otherwise obtained by the Covenantor as a result of development work other than development work directly or indirectly related to any business or activity of the Company.

2.3 The Covenantor represents that he does not have in his possession any Confidential Information or documents belonging to others, and will not use, disclose to the Company, or induce the Company to use, any such information or document in relation to his work for the Company. The Covenantor represents that his engagement by the Company will not cause him to violate any obligation to, or confidence of, any other person.

3. Records

The Covenantor shall not during the continuance of the Covenantor's engagement by the Company make (otherwise than for the benefit of the Company) any records or copies of any software or other product marketed or owned by the Company, or any matter concerning any business, operation, dealing, arrangement or activity relating to the affairs of the Company or its associated companies ("Records"); nor shall the Covenantor use or permit to be used any Records otherwise than for the benefit of the Company. All Records made by the Covenantor or in his possession shall be the sole and the absolute property of the Company and shall be delivered to a duly authorised representative of the Company upon the termination of the Covenantor's engagement or at any time on demand of the Company.

4. Inventions

The Covenantor agrees that (subject where applicable to the rights of the Covenantor under the Patents Act, 1977) any invention, design, discovery, secret process or improvement ("Invention") made or developed by the Covenantor at any time during the Covenantor's engagement by the Company (whether before or after the date of this Agreement) and in any way connected with or applicable to any business or operation of the Company or any of its associated companies or capable of being used or adapted for use by the Company belongs solely and absolutely to the Company. The Covenantor shall on receipt of a written request by the Company assign forthwith to the Company by written instrument (or if assignment is impossible, license to the Company) all his right title benefit and interest in and to such Invention. It is agreed between the parties that the inventions made by the Covenantor prior to his engagement by the Company listed on the Exhibit attached to this Agreement are excluded from this scope of this Agreement. The Covenantor represents and warrants that such list is complete.

5. Original Works, etc.

If at any time during the continuance of the Covenantor's engagement by the Company the Covenantor creates or causes to be created any original work (including without limitation any artistic or literary work) and/or any design which in the reasonable opinion of the Company is applicable to the business from time to time carried on by the Company or any associated company, in which there subsists any copyright or any other intellectual property or other right whatsoever, notice and details of such original work shall forthwith be communicated to the Company by the Covenantor and all the Covenantor's rights in that work shall belong to or be assigned to the Company absolutely.

6. Further Assurances

At the request and expense of the Company the Covenantor shall give and supply all information, data and drawings as may be required to enable the Company to use and exploit any and all Inventions pursuant to clause 4 and any and all original works pursuant to clause 5 to the best advantage and the Covenantor shall promptly execute and do all such documents and things as may be necessary or desirable for obtaining patent, copyright or other protection for the same in such part or parts of the world as may be specified by the Company and for vesting the same in the Company or as it may direct.

7. Further obligations of the Covenantor

The Covenantor shall not at any time (whether before or after termination of the Covenantor's engagement):

7.1 whether by way of trade or otherwise and whether or not on his own account, copy or reproduce any products marketed or to be marketed by the Company (or its associated companies) during the period of this engagement or any part of such product, in any manner or do any act which would be an infringement of any rights (including without limitation copyright) of the Company therein;

7.2 challenge or call in question any letters patent or other intellectual property rights of or licensed to the Company or any of its associated companies;

7.3 encourage or assist any other person to do any of such things referred to in this clause 7.

8. Consequences of Termination

8.1 If the Company should terminate the engagement by reason of any material breach by the Covenantor of this Agreement or his engagement contract or if the Covenantor shall terminate his engagement the Covenantor shall not for a period of [twelve] months from the date of such termination be employed, engaged or interested (directly or indirectly) in any part of any business or undertaking being carried on in the .... which would or might compete with any business or prospective business whether actually carried on or in the course of development by the Company at the date of termination of the Covenantor's engagement.

[**Note**: Restrictive clauses are difficult to enforce. The level of protection available will depend on the particular circumstances. See also Attachment 13]

8.2 Further the Covenantor shall not without the Company's prior written consent during such period be employed, engaged or interested (directly or indirectly) in any part of any business or undertaking carried on outside the .... by any licensee, agent, principal or representative of the Company or by any subsidiary holding or associated company of any such licensee agent principal or representative.

9. Miscellaneous

9.1 *Waivers, Remedies Cumulative.*—The rights of the Company under this Agreement are cumulative, may be exercised as often as the Company considers appropriate and are in addition to its rights under the general law. Any failure to exercise or any delay in exercising any of its rights under this Agreement shall not operate as a waiver or variation of that or any other such right; and no act or course of conduct or negotiation on the part of the Company or on its behalf shall in any way preclude it from exercising any such right or constitute a suspension or variation of any such rights.

9.2 *Moral Rights.*—By this Agreement the Covenantor waives unconditionally and irrevocably any and all moral rights which the Covenantor has or may have pursuant to the Covenantor's engagement and howsoever arising.

9.3 *Further Assurances.*—The Covenantor agrees to do or execute any further assurances and documents that may be required by law or that the Company may consider necessary to establish, maintain and protect its rights and generally to carry out the true intent of this Agreement.

9.4 *Amendments.*—No amendment or modification to this Agreement will be effective or binding unless it refers to this Agreement and is in writing signed by both parties.

9.5 *Invalidity of any Provision.*—If at any time any one or more of the provisions of this Agreement becomes invalid; illegal or unenforceable in any respect under any law, the validity, legality and enforceability of the remaining provisions shall not in any way be affected or impaired thereby.

9.6 *Notices.*—Any notice or consent to be given under this Agreement shall be in writing and shall be delivered personally or sent by post or telex to the other party at the address given above or such other address as it notifies in writing from time to time.

9.7 *Assignments.*—The Company may assign its rights under this Agreement to any associated company.

9.8 *Governing Law.*—This Agreement shall be governed by and construed in all respects in accordance with English Law and the parties to this Agreement agree to submit to the jurisdiction of the English Courts.

IN WITNESS whereof the parties hereto have caused this Agreement to be executed the day and year first above written.

Signed by)
for and on behalf)
of the Company in)
the presence of:-)
Signed by the)
Covenantor in)
the presence of:—)

CONFIDENTIALITY AGREEMENT – BOTH PARTY OBLIGATIONS

Parties:

(1)

(2)

RECITALS

For the purpose of trying to negotiate a [business relationship] [merger] [joint venture] between the Parties ("the Negotiations") each of the Parties has agreed to provide to the other and to the professional advisers of that other party Confidential Information (as defined below) relating to each other and their respective subsidiaries.

In consideration of each of the Parties disclosing to the other Confidential Information each Party has agreed to undertake to the other in the terms set out below.

1. Undertakings

Each Party hereby undertakes with the other Party (but so that in this paragraph "Confidential Information" shall mean only Confidential Information which is provided by or on behalf of that other Party):

1.1 to maintain the Confidential Information in strict confidence and, save as provided herein, not to divulge any of the Confidential Information to any third party and in addition not to communicate, indicate or suggest to any third party the existence of the Negotiations;

1.2 not to make use of the Confidential Information other than for the purpose of the Negotiations;

to restrict access to the Confidential Information only to its own responsible employees or professional advisers who need to have such access for the purposes of the Negotiations and to impose upon such persons obligations of confidentiality equivalent to those contained herein (and to be responsible for any breach of the terms of this agreement by its own employees or advisers);

that the disclosure of the Confidential Information shall not be deemed to confer any proprietary rights upon the Party to whom the Confidential Information is disclosed;

to take or to permit to be taken only such copies of any document or other material (in whatsoever medium) embodying any of the Confidential Information as are reasonably necessary for the purposes mentioned herein and forthwith on request at any time to return (and procure the return by any third party to whom disclosure of any of the Confidential Information by it has been made) to the other Party or as it may direct all or any of the documents or other material containing or embodying the Confidential Information together with all copies thereof and extracts therefrom;

to confirm to the other Party in writing at any time on request that it has complied with the provisions hereof;

if one Party receives any communication requesting disclosure of any of the Confidential Information or indicating an intention to obtain or the fact that there has been obtained any order which would oblige that Party in law to disclose any of the Confidential Information, that Party will (immediately and by the fastest means possible, confirmed in writing) communicate to the other Party the fact that the communication has been received and all details of the same with a view to the Parties co-operating in taking all reasonable and proper steps to ensure so far as is possible that the Confidential Information and the negotiations are maintained in the strictest confidence; and that during the period of two years from the date of this agreement each Party shall not, and shall procure that members of the group of companies of which it is a part shall not, directly or indirectly:

solicit or endeavour to entice away any employees of the other Party who at the date of this agreement holds or otherwise has access to the Confidential Information;

in competition with the business of the other Party as carried on at the date of this letter, canvass or solicit the custom of or business from any person, firm or company who has within two years prior to the date of this letter been a customer or business contact of the other Party (and has not within such period been a customer or business contact of the competing Party).

Each party agrees that it considers that the restrictions contained in this paragraph are no greater than is reasonable and necessary for the protection of the other Party's interests.

2. Acknowledgement and confirmation

Each Party hereby further acknowledges and confirms to the other as follows:

neither Party nor any of its subsidiaries, nor any of its or their respective advisers nor any of its shareholders, agents, officers or employees accept responsibility or liability for or make any representation, statement or expression of opinion or warranty, express or implied, with respect to the accuracy or completeness of the Confidential Information or any oral communication in connection therewith unless and save to the extent that such representation, statement or expression of opinion or warranty is expressly incorporated into any legally binding contract executed between the Parties;

the provisions of this agreement shall continue in effect notwithstanding any decision by the Parties not to proceed with the proposed transaction or any return or destruction of the Confidential Information; and

that damages alone would not be an adequate remedy for any breach of the provisions of this agreement and, accordingly, without prejudice to any and all other rights or remedies that either Party may have against the other each shall be entitled without proof of special damage to the remedies of injunction, specific performance and other equitable relief for any threatened or actual breach of the provisions of this agreement.

3. Exemption

The above undertakings shall not apply to Confidential Information which:—

is or becomes publicly available, other than as a result of a breach of this agreement, or becomes lawfully available to the Party to whom it is disclosed for the purposes of the Negotiations from a third party free from any confidentiality restriction; or

either Party is required to disclose;

(a) by law;

(b) by any rule or regulation of any stock exchange;

(c) by any Court procedure; or

(d) by any rule or regulation of any governmental or quasi-governmental authority,

provided that, so far as is practicable to do so the disclosing Party shall consult with the other Party prior to such disclosure with a view to agreeing its timing and content.

4. Definition of Confidential Information

"Confidential Information" means any and all information in whatever form whether disclosed orally or in writing or whether eye readable, machine readable or in any other form including, without limitation, the form, materials and design of any relevant equipment or any part thereof, the methods of operation and the various applications thereof, processes, formulae, plans, strategies, data, know-how, designs, photographs, drawings, specifications, technical literature and any other material made available by one Party to the other Party or gained by the visit by one Party to any establishment of the other Party whether before or after this Agreement is entered into, for the purpose of considering, advising in relation to or furthering the negotiations (and any information derived from such information).

5. Governing Law and Jurisdiction

The provisions hereof shall be governed and construed by English law, and each Party agrees to submit to the exclusive jurisdiction of the English Courts.

Executed by ....

Director

Executed by ....

Director

CONSULTANCY AGREEMENT

THIS AGREEMENT is made on [*]
BETWEEN
[*] (Company no. [*]) whose registered office is at [*] ("the Company").
AND
[*] of [*] ("the Consultant").
RECITALS

(A) The Company [intends to] carr[y/ies] on the business ("the Business") of [*].

(B) The Company has agreed to appoint the Consultant and the Consultant has agreed to serve the Company as Consultant upon the terms and conditions of this Agreement.

IT IS AGREED as follows:—

1. Appointment

The Company appoints the Consultant as a Consultant to the Company and the Consultant accepts the appointment on the terms and conditions in this Agreement.

2. Term

[**Note**: Consultancies may be for fixed terms, unlimited duration or specific projects - this must be considered in drafting this clause].

The appointment (subject to the provisions of Clause [ ]) shall be for a term of [six months] from [*] and shall then continue until terminated by either party serving [three] month's written notice on the other, to expire on, or at any time after, the expiration of the initial period of [six] months.

3. Duties

The duties of the Consultant under this Agreement shall be to:—

3.1 [Render general advice to the Company in connection with the Business and in particular advise on [all financial matters, review management accounts and forecasts, aspects of sales marketing and general management] of the Business at such times and at such place or places as shall be reasonably requested of him by the Board of Directors of the Company ("the Board").]

[**Note:** Defining the scope of the services is vital. Unless the services to be supplied are properly defined, then disputes can arise. Also, there is a risk that the .... Revenue may claim that the relationship is, in reality, that of employment]

3.2 Attend at any meetings of the Board or meetings with customers, suppliers and advisers to the Company at which his presence is reasonably required and whether or not those meetings are during normal business hours.

4. Director

During the subsistence of this Agreement the Consultant shall be a Director of the Company but on termination he will immediately resign as a Director. By this Agreement the Consultant irrevocably appoints the Managing Director of the Company as his attorney for the purposes of signing such a resignation.

[**Note:** If this power of attorney is included the agreement should be executed as a deed. Also, appointing a consultant as a director may lead the Revenue to query whether he is in fact an employee]

5. Fees

The Consultant shall be entitled, by way of remuneration for his services as Consultant, to an [annual] or [monthly] fee of [*] payable [monthly] [quarterly] in arrears on the last day of each [month] [quarter].

[**Note:** Need provision dealing with VAT and a PAYE indemnity]

[**Note:** Some consultancies provide for an initial sum to be paid for know-how followed by a retainer and commission]

6. Loyalty

During the period of this Agreement the Consultant will use skill and care and will faithfully serve the Company. He will use his utmost endeavours to promote its interests and shall co-operate to the fullest extent with the Directors and employees of the Company. The determination as to the interests of the

Company for the purposes of this clause is a matter in the discretion of the Board alone and the Consultant shall at all times act in accordance with policy from time to time laid down by the Board or as instructed by the Board and, in case of doubt, the Consultant shall consult with the Board before taking any action.

7. Confidentiality

[Alternative 1:

7.1 Except as required in the performance of his duties and in accordance with written instructions from the Board of Directors [or a Director of the Company], the Consultant shall not, either himself or acting by or through his servants or agents:-

7.1.1 At any time disclose the private affairs or secrets of the Company which he may learn during his appointment [or as a Director of the Company or any subsidiaries]; or

7.1.2 At any time, directly or indirectly, communicate to any third party or other unauthorised person, firm or company any confidential matters concerning the Company or the Business; or

7.1.3 Directly or indirectly communicate upon any matter concerning the Company or the Business with any of the Company's employees, customers, suppliers, bankers, competitors or other persons or companies with whom the Company does business, except as instructed in the course of his duties as Consultant; or

7.1.4 At any time during this Agreement, or for [ ] months following its termination, solicit or endeavour to entice away from the Company any person, firm, company or public body who was or were customers of the Company [or its subsidiaries] at any time during this consultancy in connection with a business competitive with the Business.

7.1.5 During this Agreement and for a period of [12] months following its termination, solicit, or endeavour to entice away from the Company any person who was an employee of the Company at any time during this Agreement; or

7.1.6 [At any time during this Agreement, or for [ ] months following its termination, carry on, or be engaged, concerned or interested in the carrying on, within the ...., of any business the same or similar to the Business on his own account or jointly with or as agent for any other person, firm or company either directly or indirectly whether as director, employee, shareholder consultant or otherwise PROVIDED ALWAYS that nothing contained in this Agreement shall preclude the Consultant from holding shares or loan capital (not exceeding .... per cent of the shares or loan capital of the class concerned for the time being issued) in any company carrying on any such business and whose shares or loan capital of the class or classes so held are listed on The Stock Exchange or the Unlisted Securities Market; or]

[**Note:** Other restrictive covenants may be appropriate. What is appropriate will depend on the particular circumstances]

7.1.7 At any time use the benefit of any secret process or secret method of production or organisation or the Company; or

7.1.8 At any time take away any documents or data or [ ] of the Company other than as necessary in the course of his duties; or

7.1.9 At any time generally take any action injurious to the interests of the Company or the Business.

7.2 It is agreed between the parties that the provisions of this clause 7 are reasonable for the protection of the Company and the Company was not willing to enter into this Agreement without the benefit of such provisions.

(**Note**: This Clause 7 must be specifically and carefully tailored to the particular business).

(Alternative 2:

The Company and the Consultant shall forthwith enter into the Confidentiality Agreement in the form attached.)

8. Termination

If the Consultant shall be guilty of any breach or non-observance of any of the stipulations contained in this Agreement, or if he becomes bankrupt or makes any composition with his creditors, this Agreement may be determined forthwith. In such event no fee shall be payable to the Consultant in respect of any period subsequent to the determination and such determination shall be without prejudice to any right of action by the Company to claim damages or other relief against the Consultant in respect of any default, breach or non-observance.

(**Note**: It is usual to provide for circumstances in which the agreement can be terminated. These will depend on the nature of the business).

9. Other Interests

Before accepting any full time or part time position, including a consultancy (whether for reward or otherwise), which might conflict with the provisions of this Agreement (and in particular the provisions of clause 7) (or any of them) the Consultant undertakes that he will notify the Company, in writing, of the proposed terms, giving the identity of the other party and sufficient detail of the nature of his duties and the terms of his appointment or engagement.

10. Expenses

The Company shall reimburse the Consultant for such expenses as may be reasonably and properly incurred by him in the proper performance of his duties as Consultant to the Company on production by the Consultant of satisfactory vouchers or evidence.

11. Return of papers

On the termination of this Agreement (for whatever reason) the Consultant shall immediately deliver up to the Company any documents, papers or other written information which either belongs to the Company or relates to the Business and which came into the possession of the Consultant in the performance of his duties under this Agreement.

12. Notices

Any notice under this Agreement shall be given in writing by either party to the other and may be delivered or sent by first class prepaid post addressed, in the case of the Company, to its registered office and, in the case of the Consultant, to his address last known to the Company. Any such notice shall, in the case of delivery, be deemed to have been served at the time of delivery and, in the case of posting on the expiration of twenty four hours after it has been posted by first class mail.

AS WITNESS the hands of the parties to this Agreement or their duly authorised representatives the day and year first before written.

SIGNED by [*]	)
for and on behalf of	)
[*] Limited	)
in the presence of	)
[*]	)
SIGNED by [*]	)
in the presence of	)
[*]	)

CONFIDENTIALITY AND NON-DISCLOSURE AGREEMENT

This confidentiality and non-disclosure agreement is made on the................... day of...................., 20..... BETWEEN...................., a company incorporated under the Companies Act, 1956 and having its principal office at .... (address) (hereinafter referred to as "the Owner") AND.................... (hereinafter referred to as the "the Recipient") on the following terms and conditions:

WHEREAS, in the course of the business relationship between the owner and the recipient, the recipient acknowledges that it may have access to or have disclosed to it certain information of a confidential nature by the owner; and

WHEREAS, the owner is desirous of setting forth the obligations of the recipient with respect to such Confidential Information.

NOW THEREFORE, in consideration of the mutual promises contained herein, the adequacy and sufficiency of which consideration is hereby acknowledged and agreed, the parties hereby agree as follows:—

1. Definitions

Confidential Information means all the information of the owner which is disclosed to the recipient pursuant to the business arrangement whether oral or written and shall include but is not limited to trade secrets, know-how, inventions, techniques, processes, plans, algorithms, software programs, source code, semi-conductor designs, schematic designs, business methods, customer lists, contacts, financial information, sales and marketing plans and business information of the owner.

Materials means including without limitation, documents, drawings, models, apparatus, sketches, designs and lists furnished to the recipient by the owner and any tangible embodiments of the owner's Confidential Information created by the recipient.

2. Covenant not to Disclose

The recipient will use the owner's Confidential Information solely to fulfil its obligations as part of the business relationship with the owner. The recipient shall not disclose any Confidential Information to any person except to its employees, directors, advisors or consultants on a need to know basis, who have prior to the disclosure of or access to any such Confidential Information agreed in writing to receive it under terms at least as restrictive as those specified in this Agreement. In this regard, the agreement entered into between the recipient and any such person shall be forwarded to the owner promptly thereafter. The recipient shall use at least the same degree of care in safeguarding the Confidential Information as it uses or would use in safeguarding its own Confidential Information, and shall take all steps necessary to protect the Confidential Information from any unauthorized or inadvertent use. In particular, the recipient will immediately give notice in writing to the owner of any unauthorized use or disclosure of the Confidential Information and agrees to assist the owner in remedying such unauthorized use or disclosure of the Confidential Information. This confidentiality obligation shall not apply only to the extent that the recipient can demonstrate that:

(a) the Confidential Information of the owner is at the time of disclosure, part of the public domain, except by breach of the provisions of this Agreement; or

(b) the Confidential Information of the owner is required to be disclosed by a government agency to further the objectives of this Agreement or by a proper court of competent jurisdiction; provided however that the recipient will use its best efforts to minimize the disclosure of such information and will consult with and assist the owner in obtaining a protective order prior to such disclosure.

3. Return of the Materials

All Materials shall remain the property of the owner and the recipient shall return to the owner or destroy the Materials and all copies thereof, as instructed by the owner upon the completion of its obligations as part of the business relationship or termination of this Agreement or upon the written request of the owner at any time whether during the course of contemplated communications or after the completion or abandonment.

4. Ownership of Confidential Information

The owner shall be deemed the owner of all Confidential Information disclosed by it or its agents to the recipient hereunder, including without limitation all patents, copyright, trademark, service mark, trade secret and other proprietary rights and interests therein, and recipient acknowledges and agrees that nothing contained in this Agreement shall be construed as granting any rights to the recipient, by license or otherwise in or to any Confidential Information.

5. Remedies for breach of confidentiality

1. The recipient agrees and acknowledges that any disclosure of any Confidential Information prohibited herein or any breach of the provisions herein may result in an irreparable injury and damage to the owner which will not be adequately compensable in terms of monetary damages. The owner will have no adequate remedy at law thereof, and that the owner may, in addition to all other remedies available to it at law or in equity, obtain such preliminary, temporary or permanent mandatory or restraining injunctions, orders or decrees as may be necessary to protect the owner against, or on account of, any breach by the recipient of the provisions contained herein, and the recipient agrees to reimburse the reasonable legal fees and other costs incurred by owner in enforcing the provisions of this Agreement.

2. The recipient agrees and acknowledges that any disclosure, misappropriation, conversion or dishonest use of the said Confidential Information shall, in addition to the remedies mentioned above, make the recipient criminally liable for Breach of Trust under section 405 of the Indian Penal Code.

6. Term

This Agreement shall be effective on the first date written above and shall continue in full force and effect at all times thereafter. This Agreement shall however apply to Confidential Information disclosed by the owner to the recipient prior to, as well as after the effective date hereof. The recipient acknowledges and agrees that the termination of any agreement and relationship with the owner shall not in any way affect the obligations of the recipient set forth herein.

7. Governing Law & Jurisdiction

This Agreement shall be governed by and construed with solely in accordance with the laws of India in every particular, including formation and interpretation. Any proceedings arising out of or in connection with this Agreement shall be brought only before the Court of competent jurisdiction in .... (place).

8. Entire Agreement

This Agreement sets forth the entire agreement and understanding between the parties as to the subject-matter of this Agreement and supersedes all prior or simultaneous representations, discussions, and negotiations whether oral or written. This Agreement may be amended or supplemented only by a writing that is signed by duly authorized representatives of both parties.

9. Waiver

No term or provision hereof will be considered waived and no breach excused by the owner, unless such waiver or consent is in writing signed by or on behalf of the owner. No consent or waiver of a breach by the owner will constitute consent to the waiver of or excuse of any different or subsequent breach by the recipient.

10. Severability

If any provision of this Agreement is found invalid or unenforceable, that part will be amended to achieve as nearly as possible the same effect as the original provision and the remainder of this Agreement will remain in full force.

11. Notices

Any notice provided for or permitted under this Agreement will be treated as having been given when (a) delivered personally, (b) sent by confirmed telecopy, (c) sent by commercial overnight courier with written verification of receipt, or (d) mailed postage prepaid by certified or registered mail, return receipt requested, to the party to be notified, at the address set forth below or at such other place of which the other party has been notified in accordance with the provisions of this clause. Such notice will be treated as having been received upon actual receipt or five days after posting.

IN WITNESS WHEREOF, the parties hereto have executed this Agreement as of the day and the year first above written.

EMPLOYEES NON-DISCLOSURE & NON-COMPETE AGREEMENT

This EMPLOYEES NON-DISCLOSURE & NON-COMPETE AGREEMENT has been entered into this day of.................. 20....

BETWEEN

Alpha Hotels Ltd., an Indian firm having its registered offices at (hereinafter called "*Alpha* HL" which expression unless repugnant to the context shall mean and include its subsidiaries, and its successors and assigns)

AND

........................., an Employee of *Alpha* HL and residing at........................., (hereinafter referred to as "*Employee*" which expression unless repugnant to the context shall include all beneficiaries of the said employee)

1. Definitions

Product: shall mean the final preparation known to *Alpha* HL as .... inclusive of all modifications/improvements etc. *Alpha* HL shall be the final authority to decide the identity of the said product.

Confidential Information: means the recipe/method of preparation/ formulation of the product known as ...., inclusive of any and all improvements/modifications by way of additives, garnishments, preservatives etc., that may have been effected to the recipe/ formulation either by *Alpha* HL or .... pursuant to .... agreement with *Alpha* HL. Also as used in this agreement, the term "Confidential Information" means (i) the terms and conditions of this Agreement inclusive of but not limited to any other prior confidentiality agreement whether explicit or implied, that is subsisting on the date of this agreement; (ii) *Alpha* HL's trade secrets, business plans, strategies, methods and/or practices; and (iii) any other information relating to *Alpha* HL or its business that is not generally known to the public, including but not limited to information about *Alpha* HL's personnel, products, customers, marketing strategies, services or future business plans.

Employee: means any individual who was or is an employee of *Alpha* HL whose status is permanent or contractual in nature on the date of commencement of the manufacture by *Alpha* HL its venture partners or its subsidiaries or beneficiaries or by .... of the product referred to as ....

WHEREAS,

a. Employee during his/her normal course of business has access to the Confidential Information/preparation known as .... in either its disembodied form or in the form of the final preparation. *Alpha* HL treats this preparation as being in the nature of Confidential Information.

b. The unauthorised disclosure by employees or ex-employees of the said Confidential Information could expose *Alpha* to irreparable harm in monetary terms as well as in terms of reputation and goodwill.

c. *Alpha* HL thus wishes to safe guard against the wrongful or inadvertent disclosure of its recipe/ formulation/preparation.

2. Acknowledgement of Confidentiality

.... hereby acknowledges that the recipe and formulation for the product are in the nature of confidential and proprietary information.

3. Agreement not to Disclose

a. Employee hereby agrees that he/she shall hold in confidence and hereby agrees that he/ she shall not use, commercialize or disclose except under terms of employment of *Alpha* HL, any Confidential Information to any person or entity, or else under provision governed by this memorandum except as *Alpha* Co. may approve in writing.

b. Even upon assignment of the Recipe and or formulation to *Alpha* Co., employee undertakes to use at least the same degree of care in safeguarding the Confidential Information as he/she uses or would use in safeguarding his/her own Confidential Information, and shall take all steps necessary to protect the Confidential information from unauthorized or inadvertent disclosure.

4. Remedies for Breach of Confidentiality

Employee agrees and acknowledges that any disclosure of any Confidential Information prohibited herein or any breach of the provisions herein may result in irreparable injury and damage to *Alpha* Co. which will not be adequately compensable in monetary damages, that *Alpha* Co. will have no adequate remedy at law therefor, and that *Alpha* Co. may, in addition to all other remedies available to it at law or in equity, obtain such preliminary, temporary or permanent mandatory or restraining injunctions, orders or decrees as may be necessary to protect *Alpha* Co. against, or on account of, any breach by the employee/ex-employee of the provisions contained herein, and employee agrees to reimburse the reasonable legal fees and other costs incurred by *Alpha* Co. in enforcing the provisions of the proposed transaction.

5. Non-compete

Employee inclusive of his/ her direct beneficiaries in business, interest and title in recognition of the transfer of Confidential and Proprietary Information to *Alpha* Co. hereby agrees not to directly or indirectly compete with the business of *Alpha* Co. and its successors and assigns during the term of the agreement and for a period of five years following the expiration or termination of this contract and notwithstanding the cause or reason for termination.

6. Jurisdiction

Any action arising out of or pertaining to this agreement shall be initiated and maintained in a court of competent jurisdiction at the High Court of .... at ....(place).

7. General Provision

a. This document constitutes the entire agreement between the parties with respect to the subject matter hereof and supersedes all other communications, whether written or oral.

b. This Agreement is expressly limited to its terms and may be modified or amended only by writing signed by both parties.

c. Neither this Agreement nor any rights or obligations inherent in *Alpha* HL Confidential Information, know-how, trade secrets and other property and intellectual property hereunder may be transferred or assigned without *Alpha* HL's written consent respectively. Any attempt to the contrary shall be void.

8. Severability

The provisions of this agreement shall be deemed severable, and the unenforceability of any one or more of its provisions shall not affect the enforceability of any of the other provisions. If any provision is declared to be unenforceable, the parties shall substitute an enforceable provision that, to the maximum extent possible in accordance with applicable law, preserves the original intentions and economic positions of the parties. Waiver of any provision hereof in one instance shall not preclude enforcement thereof on future occasions.

The parties hereto consider the restrictions contained to be reasonable as to protect *Alpha*'s Co. interests and rights.

9. *Force Majeure*

Neither party will be responsible for any failure to perform its obligations under this agreement due to causes beyond its control, including but not limited to acts of God, war, riot, embargoes, acts of civil or military authorities, fire, floods or accidents.

10. Notice

All notices and communications required or permitted under this agreement shall be in writing and any communication or delivery shall be deemed to have been duly made if actually delivered, or after .... days after mailing, if mailed by registered post addressed

IN WITNESS WHEREOF, the parties hereto have caused this Agreement to be executed as of the date first written above their duly authorised representatives.

Alpha Hotels
....
Address:........................
Dated........................
Employee
Address........................
Dated........................
Witness:
Witness:

NON-DISCLOSURE & NON-COMPETE AGREEMENT

This NON-DISCLOSURE & NON-COMPETE AGREEMENT has been entered into this day of....................20..... .

BETWEEN

Alpha, an Indian firm having its registered offices at (hereinafter called "COMPANY" which expression unless repugnant to the context shall mean and include its subsidiaries, and its successors and assigns)

AND

Name of Individual or Entity, residing at........................, *(hereinafter referred to as "Party" which expression unless repugnant to the context shall include all beneficiaries of the said Party)*

1. Definitions

Intellectual Property: Includes existing and future Intellectual Property in the nature of unregistered or registered rights to any and all patents, copyrights, trademarks and other confidential and/or proprietary information limited to that forming part of the subject-matter of the agreement, and inclusive of all intellectual property that is the subject of ownership by Company and/or its subsidiaries, venture partners and predecessors in interest, business and/or title, arising out of the performance of this agreement and/or other business arrangements, inclusive of but not limited to any oral arrangement which Company may have entered into with the Party or other party.

Confidential Information: means, trade secrets, know-how, patents, utility models, formulations, processes/methods of preparation, test data, conducted in-house or by/through collaborative/venture efforts, inclusive of any and all improvements/ modifications, alterations substantial or otherwise etc., that may have been effected to the said Confidential Information by Company. Also as used in this agreement, the term "Confidential Information" means (i) the terms and conditions of this Agreement inclusive of but not limited to any other prior confidentiality agreement whether explicit or implied by terms and relationship of Party with the company and his stated or present functions, that is subsisting on the date of this agreement; (ii) Company's, business plans, strategies, methods and/or practices; (iii) any information relating to Company or its business that is not generally known to the public, including but not limited to information about Company's personnel, products, customers, marketing strategies, services or future business plans, and (iv) Process Information defined as data/test data/ reports/studies in-house or contracted/ details/ quantified steps/ process details whether affixed on paper or transferred by way of oral and/or practical instruction with reference to any product which company may own or be associated with such as manufacturing information, procurement specifications, quality control specifications, inspection and test protocols inclusive of other data that Company has ownership of/retains and is available and being used by Company with reference to its business/ products/ R&D efforts and general and specific information not limited to processes, machines, manufactures, composition of matter, know-how, methods, techniques, systems, software (whether in object, source or executable code) documentation, data (irrespective of whether human or machine-readable) pertaining to the company's products, manufacture and sale of products envisaged by company's know-how or any other improved know-how.

Party: In relation to this agreement, means any individual under a contract of services or contract for services, who was or is an employee of Company, whose status is permanent or contractual in nature on the date of commencement of this agreement or the company's venture partners or its subsidiaries or beneficiaries or by any other entity or person either retained by company or associated with the company.

Compete: In relation to this agreement means the indulging in of any activity, by Party, commercial in nature or otherwise, that may result in a diversion/drop in sales, market share, direct or indirect, with the business of the Company.

WHEREAS,

a. Party during his/her normal course of business has access to the Confidential Information in either its disembodied form or in the form of the final preparation/process/method etc., that company treats as being in the nature of Confidential Information.

b. The unauthorised disclosure by Party, of the said Confidential Information could expose the Company to irreparable harm in monetary terms as well as in terms of reputation and goodwill.

c. Company thus wishes to safe guard against the wrongful or inadvertent disclosure of its Confidential Information.

2. Acknowledgement of Confidentiality

Party hereby acknowledges that the Confidential Information disclosed to or accessed by the Party is in the nature of Confidential and Proprietary Information.

3. Agreement not to Disclose or Assign/License

a. Party hereby agrees that he/she shall hold in confidence and hereby agrees that he/ she shall not assign, license, sell, use, commercialize or disclose except under terms of employment or association with the Company, any Confidential Information, Intellectual Property of the company, to any person or entity, or else under provision governed by this memorandum except as Company may approve in writing.

b. Party undertakes to use at least the same degree of care in safeguarding the Confidential Information/ Intellectual Property as he/she uses or would use in safeguarding his/her own Confidential Information, and shall take all steps necessary to protect the Confidential Information from unauthorized or inadvertent disclosure.

4. Remedies for Breach of Confidentiality

a. Party agrees and acknowledges that any disclosure of any Confidential Information prohibited herein or any breach of the provisions herein may result in irreparable injury and damage to Company which will not be adequately compensable in monetary damages, that Company will have no adequate remedy at law therefor, and that Company may, in addition to all other remedies available to it at law or in equity, obtain such preliminary, temporary or permanent mandatory or restraining injunctions, orders or decrees as may be necessary to protect Company against, or on account of, any breach by the Party, employee/ex-employee of the provisions contained herein.

b. Party agrees to reimburse the reasonable legal fees and other costs incurred by Company in enforcing the provisions of the proposed transaction.

5. Non-compete

a. Party inclusive of his/ her direct beneficiaries in business, interest and title in recognition of the vesting of exclusive rights to the Confidential and Proprietary Information of the Company hereby agrees not to directly or indirectly compete with the business of the Company and its successors and assigns during the term of the agreement.

b. Subsequent to the termination or expiration of terms of employment/ association with the Company, the party undertakes and agrees not to compete with the Company for a period of five years.

c. Following the expiration or termination of this contract and notwithstanding the cause or reason for termination, the Party undertakes and agrees not to compete with the business of the company using the company's Confidential Information in its embodied or disembodied form.

6. Jurisdiction

Any action arising out of or pertaining to this agreement shall be initiated and maintained in a court of competent jurisdiction at the High Court of .... at .... (place).

7. General Provision

a. This document constitutes the entire agreement between the parties with respect to the subject matter hereof and supersedes all other communications, whether written or oral.

b. This Agreement is expressly limited to its terms and may be modified or amended only by writing signed by both parties.

c. Neither this Agreement nor any rights or obligations inherent in Company's Confidential Information, know-how, trade secrets and other property and/or Intellectual Property hereunder may be transferred or assigned without Company's written consent respectively. Any attempt to the contrary shall be void.

8. Term

a. This agreement shall extend for the full and total period of the employment/association of the Party with the company and its successors in business, interest and title. The said agreement in relation shall, after the period of employment/ association comes to an end, extend for a period of five years from the date of end of such relationship.

b. In relation to the preservation of Confidential Information and Intellectual Property owned by the company, this agreement shall extend in perpetuity.

9. Severability

The provisions of this agreement shall be deemed severable, and the unenforceability of any one or more of its provisions shall not affect the enforceability of any of the other provisions. If any provision is declared to be unenforceable, the parties shall substitute an enforceable provision that, to the maximum extent possible in accordance with applicable law, preserves the original intentions and economic positions of the parties. Waiver of any provision hereof in one instance shall not preclude enforcement thereof on future occasions.

The parties hereto consider the restrictions contained to be reasonable as to protect Company's interests and rights.

10. *Force Majeure*

Neither party will be responsible for any failure to perform its obligations under this agreement due to causes beyond its control, including but not limited to acts of God, war, riot, embargoes, acts of civil or military authorities, fire, floods or accidents.

11. Notice

All notices and communications required or permitted under this agreement shall be in writing and any communication or delivery shall be deemed to have been duly made if actually delivered, or after .... days after mailing, if mailed by registered post addressed.

IN WITNESS WHEREOF, the parties hereto have caused this Agreement to be executed as of the date first written above their duly authorised representatives.

Company

....

Address:.........................

Dated.........................

Party

Address:.........................

Dated.........................

Witness:

Witness:

CHAPTER 5
FRANCHISE AGREEMENTS

SYNOPSIS
OUTLINING THE SPHERE OF LAW RELATING TO FRANCHISE
Direct Franchising
Franchising through Subsidiary or Branch Office
Area Development Agreement
Master Franchising Agreement
PRECEDENTS
- Franchise Agreement
- Draft Version of Franchise Agreement
- Franchising Agreement

This introductory note highlights briefly the Indian regulatory regime for franchising in India. The law relating to franchising in India, is still in formation. There is no specific statutory enactment dealing with franchise.

Franchise, as defined in Black's Law Dictionary is a special privilege to do certain things conferred by Government on individual and corporation, and which does not belong to citizens generally of common right. In commercial world, it is a privilege granted or sold such as to use a name or to sell products or services. The right given by a manufacturer or supplier to a retailer to use his products and name on terms and conditions mutually agreed upon. In its simplest form, a franchise is a license from owner of a trademark or trade name permitting another to sell a product or service under that name or mark. In its broadest form in consonance with present day business structure, the concept of franchise has evolved into an elaborate Agreement under which the franchisee undertakes to conduct a business, or sell a product or service in accordance with methods and procedures prescribed by the franchiser. The franchiser usually undertakes to assist the franchisee through advertising, promotion and advisory services.

Apropos the status of franchising in India, franchising has been operating in its elementary and basic form.

The basic elements of franchise are as under:
1. An entrepreneur (the franchiser) develops a workable system of doing business and grants another entrepreneur (the franchisee) the right to use this system.

2. Both the parties are legally and financially independent enterprises. The franchisee invests his own money and takes the risk of losing the money, it has invested if the project/business venture were unsuccessful.
3. The granting of the right to use the franchise system involves the right and privilege of the franchisee to use the franchiser's Intellectual and Industrial Property, knowledge, business and technical methods, procedural system and other Intellectual Property rights.
4. The franchisee in consideration undertakes to allow the methods elaborated by the franchiser and to pay an entrance fee and/or other royalties, the latter of which are normally calculated as a percentage of the turnover.
5. The franchiser retains rights of control over the performance of the franchisee.
6. The franchiser may also undertake providing the franchisee with training and continuing assistance, as may seem appropriate.

Franchise is therefore a package with which *inter alia* includes:
1. Intellectual property rights.
2. Non-patented know-how
3. Training and continued assistance on the part of the franchiser.
4. Franchiser control rights *vis-à-vis* the franchisee and
5. Obligations of the franchisee to follow the instructions of the franchiser, and to comply with the financial terms of the Agreement.

Outlining the sphere of law relating to Franchise

Unlike USA, Canada, France, Australia where franchising is regulated by some specific legislation or code of conduct, India has no separate legislation or code of conduct to regulate franchising. The reason being the complexity of the relationship and the vast areas of law which such relationship involve. The laws regulating franchising includes – law relating to contract, agency, distribution, leasing, assignment, securities, financial investments, intellectual and industrial property competition, companies, immovable and movable properties, labour, foreign investment, insurance, banking, import-export, technology transfer and other legislations which may become applicable in a particular case. The applicability of law depends precisely upon the modes of franchising which may be domestic or transborder. The franchising has been broadly classified under the following four headings.

Direct Franchising

In this type of franchising, the franchiser grants franchise to the franchisee in the foreign country without any intermediary in between. The agreement generally provides for—
   (a) Technology transfer
   (b) Royalty payment

(c) Tax Treatment

(d) Rights of the transfer – Franchisee

(e) Obligations of the franchiser – Franchisee

(f) Assignment or licence for the use of intellectual and industrial property rights

(g) Governing laws

(h) Dispute Resolution

(i) Termination of Agreement

Such, a contract is regulated by all the commercial, economic and fiscal laws. If, the Agreement stipulate for any foreign law as governing law and for jurisdiction of a foreign court in the matter of dispute resolution, then also certain laws relating to import-export, foreign investment, taxation, intellectual and industrial property rights regulate such agreement and the parties must comply with the requirements of these laws.

Franchising through Subsidiary or Branch Office

In case of franchising through subsidiary or branch office the franchiser opens a branch office or forms a subsidiary which is a separate legal entity and enters into franchising agreements through its branch or subsidiary. These franchise agreements attract several provisions of the Foreign Exchange Regulation Act, 1973, (FERA) and Labour laws.

Area Development Agreement

This is the oldest form of franchising widely used in domestic franchise. The franchiser gives a right to the franchisee to open a multiple number of outlets to a predetermined schedule and within a given area. This provides for as many Agreements as the number of units or a single agreement with a schedule of areas. While entering into such Agreement and apart from other legislation the provisions of Monopolies and Restrictive Trade Practises Act, must be kept in view.

Master Franchising Agreement

In this form of agreement the franchiser grants a person in another country, the master franchiser, the exclusive right to open franchise outlet itself and/or to grant franchise to sub-franchisees, within a certain territory. There will be two sets of agreements. One between master Franchiser and the Franchiser and other between the master franchiser and sub-franchisees. There is no privity of contract between the franchiser and sub-franchisee hence in this type of Agreement the provisions for termination, damages etc. must be provided in more specific term.

Franchising through Joint Venture

A joint venture between the franchiser and some native persons are formed, which enters into a master franchise Agreement with the franchiser. In this case, the laws regulating companies become more important.

PRECEDENTS

FRANCHISE AGREEMENT

A specimen copy of the franchise agreement between *ALPHA* LTD., and a partnership firm is given here.

ALPHA LIMITED

This AGREEMENT entered into on the .... day of ...., 20.....;

BETWEEN

ALPHA LIMITED,

A Company incorporate under the Companies Act, 1956, having its Registered Office at ...., represented herein by its .... Shri .... (hereinafter referred to as the '*Alpha* ', which expression shall, whenever the context so requires or admits mean and include its successors and assigns) of the ONE PART;

AND

BETA

A Partnership Firm,

having its place of Business

at....................

represented herein by its Partner—

Shri....................

(hereinafter referred to as the 'AGENT', which expression shall, unless the context so requires or admits mean and include its Partners for the time being, their heirs, legal representatives, executors and permitted assigns) of the OTHER PART;

WITNESSES AS FOLLOWS:

I. WHEREAS *Alpha* is engaged *inter alia* in the business of marketing children products, such as, toys, garments, furniture, utilities and such other goods and are the owners of the trade name and trade mark 'XYZ' and '*Alpha*';

II. WHEREAS the *Alpha* is desirous of promoting children products under its trade name and trade mark by setting up chain or retail outlets all over the country on its own and also by appointing stockist, retailers and franchises for the purpose of setting up of retail outlets;

III. WHEREAS the Agent has offered to set up one such Retail Outlet in the City of .... and has represented to *Alpha* that it is in a position to invest necessary capital and is also possessed of a suitable premises to set up and carry on the Retail Outlet and *Alpha* has accepted the said offer;

IV. NOW THIS AGREEMENT WITNESSES THAT in consideration of the foregoing, the company hereby appoint M/s. .... as its Agent in the City of .... upon the following terms and conditions:

1. The retail outlet for marketing children's products such as toys, garments, utilities, furniture and such other goods under the name and style of 'XYZ' shall be set up and run in the Premises made available by the Agent, which premises is more fully described in the Schedule Premises'. The premises will be made available free of cost or charged to *Alpha* by the Agent during the subsistence of this Agreement.

2. The Agent will meet and bear the entire cost of furnishing and decorating the interior and exterior of the Schedule-Premises in accordance with the specifications and requirements of *Alpha*, particularly touching upon the following aspects – elevation, décor and interior design, selection of furniture, fittings, counters and stands, lighting system, illumination, mannequins, window display, air conditioning, fire fighting equipment, furnishings, flooring, etc. the cost of which is estimated to be of the order of Rs........... He shall also provide necessary warehousing facilities and office space for the *Alpha* representatives.

3. The name of the Shop shall be promptly and clearly displayed as 'XYZ' AND '*Alpha*';

4. *Alpha* will make available from time to time to the Agent, children products like Toys, garments, utilities and furniture and other goods to be manufactured, sold or dealt in by *Alpha* (hereinafter collectively) referred to as 'Stockist') and the Agent will take the stocks on consignment and sell the same in retail at prices fixed from time to time by the *Alpha*. The stocks shall at all times be the property of the *Alpha* and the Agent shall only be entrusted the Stocks for the purpose of enabling their retails sale.

5. The Agent at his cost will employ necessary personnel to man and manage the Retail Outlet to the entire satisfaction of *Alpha*.

V. THE AGENT COVENANTS WITH THE COMPANY AS FOLLOWS:

1. It shall duly and promptly pay the owner of the Schedule Premises rents and other charges and keep the lease subsisting and valid and ensure that the Schedule Premises is always available for running of the Retail Outlet.

2. That it shall not directly or indirectly or in Partnership or Association, with friends or relatives, or companies engaged itself in business, which is same or similar to the one being, carried on by *Alpha*.

3. That is, shall not sell, display or otherwise deal in any goods which are in any way similar to the goods sold or dealt in by *Alpha*.

4. That it shall not use the company's trade name and/or trademark in any manner other than that which is permitted by *Alpha*.

5. That all sales effected by the Agent shall be strictly for cash only.

6. That it shall furnish to *Alpha* at such intervals as they may require certified stocks statement of the stock of all goods held by the Agent giving full and correct particulars thereof.

7. That it shall remit each day the entire sale proceeds of the preceding day to the credit of the designated account of *Alpha*, which may be indicated from time to time and shall forthwith send intimation of such remittances to *Alpha*.
8. That it shall not draw, accept or endorse any Bill on behalf of the *Alpha* or in any way pledge the credit of *Alpha* except with the previous written authorization of *Alpha*.
9. That it shall be at all times responsible to *Alpha* for any damage occasioned to the Stock either on account of the improper or negligent conduct on the part of the Agent, its servants or agents or for any reason whatsoever and shall make good such loss to the *Alpha* as and when demanded without demur.
10. That it shall furnish an irrevocable Bank Guarantee for a sum of Rs.......... in favor of *Alpha* covering the value of the Stocks held by it on consignment and that the said Bank Guarantee shall be enhanced from time to time as may be required by *Alpha* to bring it in conformity with the value of the Stocks held by the Agent.
11. That it shall keep proper accounts of all Stocks received, sold, damaged and furnish to *Alpha* each week full particulars of the Stocks and shall permit *Alpha*, its agents and servants to inspect all Books of Account, Records and vouchers maintained in the Retail Outlet by it at all reasonable times.
12. That it shall be responsible for any loss or damage sustained to the stock while in the custody of the Agent.

DURATION.—The duration of this Agreement shall be for a period of .... years commencing from .... on the expiry of this period or earlier, the Agreement may be extended for such further period and on such terms as the parties may mutually agree in writing.

This Agreement is however terminable as follows:

(a) by either party giving the other .... days notice in writing;

(b) by *Alpha* unilaterally without assigning any reasons (i) if the agent is found guilty of misconduct, or (ii) commits a breach of any of the provisions of the Agreement, or (iii) is dissolved, or (iv) any suit or other proceedings are instituted for its dissolution or winding up, or (v) commits any act of bankruptcy, (vi) suffers any execution or distress.

CONSIDERATION.—In consideration of the foregoing, the Agent shall be entitled to a commission at the rate of ....% of the net sale price realized by it in the Retail Outlet by sale of the Stocks. The expression net sale price shall mean the selling price of the Stocks excluding Sales Tax, local taxes and other levies imposed upon the sale or purchase of the Stocks and/or on the total turnover, packing and forwarding charges and gift wrapping charges.

The commission shall be payable by *Alpha* on or before the .... Day of the succeeding month for which it is due upon receipt of the monthly statement of sales and realization of the sale proceeds.

ASSIGNMENT.—This Agreement or the benefit therefrom shall not be assignable or transferable by the Agent in favor of anyone without prior written consent of the company.

SECURITY DEPOSIT.—In order to ensure *Alpha* the due performance of its obligations under this Agreement, the Agent has this day deposited a sum of Rs .... by Pay Order bearing No. .... dated .... drawn on .... Bank .... Branch, ... (place), in favor of *Alpha* as Security Deposit. The said amount will be refundable upon the termination of this Agreement, free of interest, in the event of there being no outstanding claim against the Agent by *Alpha*. *Alpha* will however be entitled to appropriate and adjust any amounts which may be due to it from the Agent from out of the Security Deposit.

JURISDICTION.—This Agreement is executed at .... city and it is hereby agreed that Court situated in .... city alone will have exclusive jurisdiction over any matter arising under this Agreement to the exclusion of Courts situated in any part of the country.

SCHEDULE

Premises bearing No. .... situated at .... admeasuring and bounded as follows:

MEASUREMENTS

East to West:

North to South:

BOUNDARIES

ON THE EAST	:		By
WEST	:		By
NORTH	:		By
SOUTH	:		By

IN WITNESS WHEREOF the parties above named have executed these presents in the presence of the Witnesses attesting hereunder on the dates and place mentioned herein below:

Place....................

Dated....................

For **ALPHA INDIA LTD.,**

WITNESSES

1. (   )

For *Alpha*

2. (   )

Agent

DRAFT VERSION OF FRANCHISE AGREEMENT

Alpha Shoe Company

This AGREEMENT entered into on the .... day of ...., ...20.....)

BETWEEN

.... *Alpha* Shoe Company;

AND

Beta DISTRIBUTORS

of.................... (hereinafter referred to, for the sake of brevity, as the 'Agent') of the OTHER PART:

WHEREBY IT IS AGREED as follows:

1. THIS AGREEMENT will have effect as from the .... day of ...., 20..... until further notice (subject to determination as hereinafter provided).

2. The Company will supply to the Agent, boots, shoes and other articles and goods usually manufactured, sold or dealt in by the Company (hereinafter collectively referred to as 'Stock') and the Agent will take Stock on consignment and sell the same only in retail at prices fixed from time to time by the company. The Agent will only sell such stock at the address of the Agency as aforesaid and nowhere else.

3. The Company at its discretion will supply to the Agent such furniture and other display material as in the opinion of the Company will help proper display of its stock. The furniture and other material shall remain the absolute property of the company.

4. The agent shall not sell, display or otherwise deal in any goods in any way similar to those manufactured, sold or dealt in by the Company except such as shall be supplied to him by the company.

5. The Agent shall not use the company's trade name and/or trademark in stationery or otherwise, except in the form approved by the Company in writing. The agent shall only use such signboard depicting the word '*Alpha*' as may be supplied by the Company or approved in writing.

6. All instructions issued by the Company from time to time either directly or through their representatives during their inspection visit in connection with the agency under this Agreement shall be strictly followed.

7. (i) During the continuance of this Agreement, the Agent shall, for the sale of Stock, be entitled to commission at the rate of 14% on the net sale price received by him in respect thereof.

(ii) All sale of Stock effected by the Agent shall be strictly for cash only.

8. The Agent shall be solely responsible for and shall discharge all recurring charges and expenses whatsoever incurred or to be incurred in carrying on the said Agency including (but without prejudice to the generality of the foregoing):

   (a) All taxes and other outgoings payable in respect of the premises from time to time occupies by the said Agency.

(b) All wages, salaries, office expenses including telephones, postages, wrapping, bank charges for remitting sale proceeds and charges for lighting and cleaning the said premises;

(c) All charges for local advertising by way of poster, handbills or brochures and for advertising such accessories as may from time to time be supplied to the said Agency by the company;

(d) All charges to be incurred for the carriage of stock from wharf, railway station, bus terminus to the premises of the said Agency;

(e) All charges and expenses to be incurred in connection with the decoration and trimming of the windows of the said premises and the preparation and maintenance of a proper inventory of the Stock, fixtures and fittings therein;

(f) All rent of the premises occupied by the said Agency.

9. (i) On the closing day of *every fortnight the Agent shall deliver* to and on forms to be supplied by the company, full and correct account of all Stock consigned to him, of all sales thereof, and of the balance of stock in hand and of all receipts, payments, transactions and dealings in connection therewith and on the same day or on such day as may otherwise be directed by the company shall remit to the company the full sale price of all stock sold less 14% thereof. The said 14% shall be retained by the Agent on account of the commission payable to him under clause 7(ii) hereof.

(ii) The Agent shall remit the sale proceeds to the company through the collection account of the State Bank of India in places where there are branches of the State Bank of India. In other places it shall be sent in the form of a crossed Demand Draft in favor of the company through one of the Scheduled Banks as may be approved by the company or crossed Indian Postal Order or crossed draft of the Reserve Bank of India, and in no other manner. The Agent's liability in this respect will be discharged by actual receipt of the money by the company.

10. The Agent shall not draw, accept or endorse any bill on behalf of the Company or in any way pledge the credit of the company except in so far as he may have been expressly authorized by the company in writing either generally or in any particular case.

11. (i) All stock, sale proceeds, furniture, signboards and other materials shall remain as exclusive properties of the company and the Agent shall have no right and shall not be entitled to deduct out of the sale products any amount except his commission and shall also not be entitled to retain the sale proceeds in his hands for any reason whatsoever. In case of retention of the sale proceeds or deduction of any amount therefrom except the commission as aforesaid, the Agent will be treated as having committed criminal misappropriation and/or breach of trust and will be liable as such.

(ii) During the continuance of this Agreement the Agent shall be responsible to the company for all damages, whatsoever occasioned to Stock which shall in the opinion of the company be due to improper or negligent conduct on the part of the Agent or any of his servants or agents (or for any loss or losses sustained by reason of delay in the disposal thereof) and the decision of the company as to whether any such damage or loss be final and binding upon the Agent and any sum or sums due to respect thereof shall be immediately debited by the company against the Agent in the Security Account.

(iii) The Agent will remain responsible to properly reserve and look after the stock, furniture and other materials as well as any advertisement accessories furnished by the company.

Stocks, which become 'dead stock' while with the Agent, due to unpopularity of designs or improper fittings will be cleared at the instructions and cost of the company. In case of articles retained by the Agent in spite of manufacturing defects and not returned within two weeks of delivery, such stock will be cleared by the Agent and no claim will be acceptable by the company later on.

12. The Agent shall forthwith furnish to the company a cash deposit of Rs. .... (Amount) to be credited in the name of the Agent (hereinafter referred to as the 'Security Account') and be held by the Company as security for the due performance and observance by the Agent of the Agreements, conditions, stipulations binding upon him hereunder; the Security Account shall be credited by the company with interest at the rate of 10% per annum and the amount thereof and the said interest thereon shall be and remain the property of the Agent but shall be retained by the company until the expiration of a period of two months after the termination of this Agreement (Whether by efflux of time or otherwise) and shall at the expiration of such period be paid to the Agent less any deductions in respect of any moneys owing by the Agent to the company on any account or accounts whatsoever. The security amount deposited by the Agent will be utilized by the company for its purpose at its discretion. The amount of the security may at the discretion of the company be increased from time to time and the Agent shall be bound to deposit such increased amount as security on the same terms as herein.

1. The Agent shall at all times keep or cause to be kept proper accounts and shall every week or fortnight (as may be required from time to time) deliver to the company full and correct accounts on the forms supplied by the company of all stocks, receipts, number of pairs sold and other details specified in the forms, payments, transactions and dealings of all in relation to the business to this Agreement. Such weekly or fortnightly Statements of account will be binding on the Agent unless he points out any error or omission therein within a month from the date of submission thereof to the company and the Agent shall not either himself or by servants remove any of the said books of accounts, cash memos, vouchers, etc. from the place of business of the Agent without the authority in writing of the company. The said books of account shall at all times be open to inspection of any of the officers of the company authorized in this behalf.

2. Any sum or sums of money whatsoever at any time owing by the Agent to the company whether as a liquidated sum or by way of damages of otherwise howsoever may be paid and discharged by the company

without reference to the Agent from the Security Account provided that if at any time the company, repay to the company the amount or amounts so paid or discharged as aforesaid.

3. Retail Manager, Senior District Manager, District Managers and other authorized officers of the company will from time to time inspect, check and make inventories of the stock and sale proceeds, and the Agent and his assistant shall be bound to give all facilities to them in carrying out such inspection and checking and making inventories. If upon inspection, checking and making inventories as aforesaid, a shortage is found in the stock, the Agent will be treated as having committed criminal breach of trust in respect thereof and he will also be liable for the full selling price of the said stock without any deduction whatsoever.

4. In the event of any fire, burglary, theft, loss or damage in any way affecting the stock or any part thereof, the Agent shall forthwith:
   (a) inform the company thereof by telegram within three hours after the discovery of the same;
   (b) investigate the occurrence and establish or cause to be established the amount of loss or damage sustained;
   (c) furnish the company with full particulars of such occurrence including the exact amount of the loss or damage sustained and a full description of the Stock, so burnt, stolen, lost or damaged;
   (d) ensure that the premises occupied by the said Agency remain in the condition in which they were at the time when the fire was extinguished, the burglary or theft committed or the loss of damage sustained until the arrival of a representative of the company;
   (e) report the occurrence to the proper local authority or authorities and preserve all such proofs as may be available until a complete investigation of the occurrence shall have been made by such authorities.

5. The Agent shall have no authority to, and shall not, enter into any agreement on behalf of the company.

   The Agents shall not be entitled to accept any process of law in the name of, or on behalf of the Company, or represent the company without the written permission in that behalf in any matter legal or otherwise. The Agent shall however remain responsible to inform the company in proper time for ascertaining and keeping the company informed from time to time regarding any local action, rules or laws in force in connection with the trade in the locality or transport, or any taxes, or duty, and also for performing or observing them correctly and properly according to the intents and purposes of the rules and law so far as they related to the business under this Agreement.

6. The Agent shall be responsible for and shall discharge the whole loss or damage sustained in any manner or for reason whatsoever in connection

with Stock consigned by the company to the Agent and the Stock shall be at the sole risk of the Agent from the time it leaves the godown or factory of the Company on consignment of the Agent.

7. Such stock as the Agent shall from time to time require for the determination (whether by efflux of time or otherwise). The Company shall be entitled to take possession of all Stock, furniture or other property consigned or supplied by the company to the Agent and to make an inventory thereof and any sum found due to such inventory from the Agent to the company shall be paid and discharged by the Agent immediately and in default may be retained by the Company from the Security Account.

8. On the day preceding that upon which this agreement shall be determination (whether by efflux of time or otherwise). The Company shall be entitled to take possession of all Stock, furniture or other property consigned or supplied by the company to the Agent and to make an inventory thereof and any sum found be paid and discharged by the agent immediately and in default may be retained by the Company from the Security Account.

9. This Agreement may be terminated:
   (a) by either party at any time giving to the other thirty days' notice in writing;
   (b) summarily by the company without assigning any reason if the Agent;
      (i) be guilty of gross misconduct, or
      (ii) commits a breach of any of the provisions hereof, or
      (iii) sells any goods from the said Agency or credit or at higher or lower prices than those from time to time prescribed by the company, or
      (iv) refuses to comply with any lawful order given to him by the Company or its authorized officers, or
      (v) allows any execution or distress to be levied upon any premises belonging to or occupied by the Agent, or
      (vi) commits any act of bankruptcy or has any receiving or adjudication order made against him, or in the case of the company going to liquidation.

10. Any notice requiring to be given hereunder shall be in writing and shall be deemed to be sufficiently served in the case of notice to the Company, if delivered at or sent by Registered Post addressed to Company's Registered Office at......................

    And in case of the agent if delivered at or sent by registered Post addressed to him at his usual or last known place or residence in India and every notice so sent by registered post shall be deemed to have been received on the day and at the time when in the ordinary course of post it would be delivered.

11. If the Agent shall consist of a firm, all the terms and conditions of this Agreement in so far as they are to be observed or performed by the Agent

shall be deemed to have been made by all the partners thereof jointly and severally with the Company and any act of neglect or default of any partner thereof shall for all purposes of this Agreement be deemed to be the act of neglect or default of every partner thereof.

12. In case of termination of this Agreement, the balance of the Security of the agent will be refundable to him only after two months of such termination, and the Company will be at liberty to adjust and recover all moneys payable by the Agent to the Company.

13. The Agent shall render all accounts and pay all dues to the Company and meet all the claims and demands of the Company at the Company Sales Office at....................

14. This Agreement is deemed to be entered at.................... (name of the place) within the jurisdiction of the courts at.................... (name of the place).

IN WITNESS WHEREOF the parties above named have executed these presents in the presence of the Witnesses attesting hereunder on the dates and place mentioned herein below:

Place....................
Dated....................

WITNESSES
1. (....................)
   For *Alpha*
2. (....................)
   Agent

FRANCHISING AGREEMENT

This AGREEMENT is made on.................... day of...................., 20.....
BETWEEN
Alpha Technologies Pvt. Ltd. whose office is at....................;
Beta Overseas Pvt. Ltd. whose office is at.................... (hereinafter collectively referred to as *"the Franchisor"*)
AND
Theta.................... (hereinafter called *"the Franchisee"* which expression shall unless repugnant to the context or meaning thereof, include its heirs, legal representatives, executors, administrators, successors and permitted assigns).

Recitals

A. *Alpha* has developed a business operating under the style BIOTIQUE in the course of which the Franchisor *inter alia*:

   (a) manufactures, distributes and sells by wholesale and retail the Products;
   (b) operates a network of high quality comprehensive and distinctively designed retail outlets to sell the Products;
   (c) has the technical expertise and know-how to operate Ayurvedic Spas to provide "specialized treatments" based on the Methods;

B. *Alpha* Technologies Pvt. Ltd. has expended time, effort and money to develop and acquire knowledge and expertise with regard to the business of manufacturing and marketing Ayurvedic skin, body, hair care and lifestyle products and treatments and constantly endeavours to improve its exclusive range of Products and Services;

C. *Beta* Overseas Pvt. Ltd. is one of the group-company of *Alpha* Technologies Pvt. Ltd. and owns the Trademarks in Germany.

D. That substantial reputation and goodwill has accrued upon the Franchisor's business under the Trademarks and has resulted in substantial demand for its Products and Services;

E. The Franchisee owns and runs the hotel Die *Theta* in ……………… and is desirous of opening an Ayurvedic Spa in its hotel premises;

F. The Franchisee being desirous of obtaining the benefits of the Franchisor's knowledge, expertise and goodwill and the demand for the Products and Services, has requested the Franchisor to grant to the Franchisee the right to establish and operate an Ayurvedic Spa to provide Services and a retail outlet to sell the Products at the Location (hereinafter referred to as *"the Project"*);

1. Definitions

Commencement Date shall be:

Confidential Information shall mean all information or data disclosed (whether in writing, orally or by any other means) by the Franchisor to the Franchisee, and shall include but not be limited to (A) any information ascertainable by the inspection or analysis of the products, (B) any information relating to the Franchisor's business operations, processes, plans, intentions, product information, know-how, trade secrets, market opportunities, customers and business affairs.

Intellectual Property Rights shall include all rights in existing and future Intellectual Property in the nature of registered and unregistered rights to any and all tradenames, trademarks, patents, copyrights, Confidential Information, designs, know-how, business methods, ideas, strategies, database rights and all other Intellectual and Industrial Property rights of any sort (throughout the world), as well as moral rights and similar rights of any type under the laws of any governmental authority, domestic or foreign".

Location shall mean the premises of the Hotel *Theta* at……………… (Name of the Place).

Method shall mean the methods, techniques and processes developed by the Franchisor;

Trademarks shall mean the names, trademarks and service marks owned by the Franchisor and include *inter alia*;

Products shall mean the Ayurvedic skin, body, hair care and lifestyle goods of the Franchisor bearing any of the Trademarks;

Services shall include the range of "specialized treatments" based on the Method.

Term shall mean the period of twenty years from the Commencement Date;

Turnover shall mean gross revenue of the Ayurvedic Spa

2. Grant of Franchise

In consideration of the onetime professional consultancy fees and the other payments, which shall be paid by the Franchisee at the time and in the manner set out in this Agreement and in further consideration of the observance and performance of the undertakings on the part of the Franchisee, the Franchisor grants to the Franchisee the right to establish and operate the Ayurvedic Spa and the Retail Outlet at the Location for the Term.

3. Franchisee's Obligations

The Franchisee covenants and agrees with the Franchisor promptly to perform and observe the following covenants and conditions:

3.1 Commencement

To commence the Project by the Commencement Date.

3.2 Project not to be carried on other than from the Location

Not to carry on the Project or any part thereof other than from the Location without the prior written consent of the Franchisor.

3.5 Promote Business

3.5.1 Actively to promote the Project and to exercise best endeavours in the conduct of the Project to promote the mutual business interests of the Franchisor and the Franchisee and shall cause to be provided at the Location such of the Products as are stipulated by the Franchisor from time to time.

3.5.2 As part of its endeavours to promote the Project, to organize a Media Conference at the time of launch and to organize such other promotional activities including but not limited to media promotions, brochure drops and on-location merchandising display as are mutually decided by the Parties from time to time.

3.6 Products

3.6.1 Only to sell at the Location, the Products, which are specified by the Franchisor and which may be purchased from the Franchisor alone.

3.6.2 In no case will the Franchisee stock or sell any goods other than the Products and goods which the Franchisor otherwise deems to be unsuitable for sale at the Location.

3.6.3 The Franchisee shall pay for all Products acquired by him from the Franchisor according to the terms of payment as notified in writing from time to time by the Franchisor to the Franchisee.

3.6.4 Notwithstanding that risk in any Products supplied by the Franchisor to the Franchisee, shall pass to the Franchisee upon delivery, full legal and equitable title and interest in all and any Products supplied to the Franchisee shall remain in the Franchisor and shall not pass to the Franchisee until the Franchisor shall have received payment in full of all amounts due and owing from the Franchisee to the Franchisor for the time being (including any interest accruing and owing to the Franchisor) and from time to time in respect of all such Products supplied by the Franchisor to the Franchisee at any time.

3.6.5 The Franchisee shall pay the cost of delivery for the Products acquired from the Franchisor.

3.7 Not to tamper with products

To sell the Products in the same condition as that in which it receives them and not to alter or remove or tamper with them or any markings or name plates or indications of the source of origin on them or any packaging supplied by the Franchisor except putting such notices as are required by the packaging laws of .... (Country) and will inform the Franchisor of any such laws and the alterations made for the compliance thereto.

3.8 Not to sell the Products other than to the end users

Not during the term of this Agreement or any renewal or extension thereof without the written approval of the Franchisor, sell the Products other than to end-users.

3.9 Maximum prices

Not to charge customers prices in excess of the prices specified by the Franchisor in writing from time to time.

3.10 Maintain stocks

3.10.1 To commence the Project with a level and type of stock-in-trade of the Products as are in writing specified by the Franchisor and to maintain at all times during the Term, stocks of the Products at a level and of a type approved by the Franchisor from time to time.

3.10.2 To ensure that all stock is maintained in accordance with the Franchisor's instructions and recommendations and to the standards prescribed by the Franchisor in writing from time to time.

3.11 Books of account

3.11.1 To keep such books of account and records and operate such finance and accounting and stock control systems for the Project made up in accordance with proper and accepted accounting practices and accurately maintain them up to date at all times.

3.11.2 To provide the Franchisor with true copies of quarterly audited profit and loss accounts and balance sheets for the Project made up in accordance with proper and accepted accounting practices, which shall be provided no later than 30 days after the end of each quarter.

3.12 Payments & schedule

3.12.1 To pay to the Franchisor (or as the Franchisor directs) as per the relevant dates (time being of the essence):

    (i) One time professional fee of.................... (Amount in any currency) towards providing the professional consultancy for the Project, which shall be payable five months prior to the Commencement Date;

(ii) 4% of the turnover of the Ayurvedic Spa payable on a quarterly basis;

(iii) The salaries of the staff recruited, trained and employed by the Franchisor in relation to the Project and any costs incurred on travel, accommodation or any incidental expenses incurred on recruitment and training of the manpower or in opening and operating the Project with prior sanction of the Franchisee, which the Franchisor shall bill on the actual.

3.12.2 All payments shall be made by the Franchisee by way of a bankers cheque/demand draft made payable at .... (place) in favour of the Franchisor.

3.13 No unauthorised representation

Not to make any representations, statements or warranties about the Project other than those which are expressly permitted by this Agreement or which the Franchisor may first authorise in writing.

3.14 Right of inspection

3.14.1 To permit officers, servants and agents of the Franchisor during normal hours of business to inspect and observe the Project, and all parts of the Location; the stocks of the Products held by the Franchisee and the manner in which the goods are displayed and sold by the Franchisee.

3.14.2 To permit the Franchisor and its servants and agents to inspect and copy, books of account, records, finance and accounting systems at the Location.

3.15 Not to prejudice industrial or intellectual property

Not to be a party to the doing or neglecting to do any act whereby any industrial or intellectual property including trade secrets and business reputation owned by the Franchisor and any company related to it and which the Franchisee is authorised to use (including the goodwill of the business in respect of which this Franchise is granted and used in connection with the Project) may be prejudicially affected either during the Term or afterwards.

3.16 Maintain secrecy

3.16.1 To maintain strict secrecy about the Methods of the Franchisor including any manuals issued by the Franchisor, any technical know-how, trade secrets, product information, market opportunities, advertising and publicity materials belonging to the Franchisor, both during the currency of this Agreement and after it is terminated.

3.16.2 To take all steps necessary to ensure that the Franchisee's nominees, employees, agents and sub-contractors also observe such requirements of secrecy as stipulated in the previous clause and shall cause such nominees, employees, agents or sub-contractors to enter into a secrecy Agreement in a form approved by the Franchisor.

3.16.3 The Franchisee and his nominee, employees, agents or sub-contractors shall not during the currency of this Agreement and after its termination disclose any Confidential Information received by any of them from the Franchisor in the course of the Project unless such disclosure is required by law and will inform the Franchisor of any such disclosure that they are compelled to make.

3.16.4 The Franchisee and his nominees, employees, agents or sub-contractors shall not after the termination of this Agreement and thereafter use such Confidential Information without the prior written consent of the Franchisor.

3.16.5 In order to protect the trade secrets and other Confidential Information as also in lieu of the know-how received by Franchisee from the Franchisor so as to be able to fulfill its obligations as part of the Project, Franchisee agrees that during the Term and even after termination for a period of three years thereof, Franchisee shall not be concerned or interested either directly or indirectly in any business which is involved in the supply of goods which are similar to the Products sold at the Location or in providing services similar to the Services provided as part of the Project.

3.16.6 As part of its obligations to maintain secrecy the Franchisee will not at any time within three years after the termination of this Agreement:

(i) solicit the customers or former customers of the Project with the intent of taking their custom;
(ii) employ or offer to employ any person who immediately before such employment or offer of employment was employed by the Franchisor and not directly or indirectly to induce such person to leave his or her employment.

3.17 Independent Proprietor

3.17.1 To conduct the Project as an independent proprietor under his own name or a name owned by the Franchisee, and not as a partner, representative, agent or employee of the Franchisor and it is also agreed and declared that nothing in this Agreement shall be deemed or construed to constitute a partnership between the Franchisor and the Franchisee.

3.17.2 To evidence the fact that the Franchisee is conducting the Project as an independent proprietor and ensure that customers are aware that any deposits paid by them against sales of any products or services have been received by the Franchisee in his own right and not as agent of the Franchisor.

3.18 Comply with laws

3.18.1 The Franchisee will ensure that it obtains at its own expense all necessary authorizations for the Project including but without limiting the generality, the operation of the Ayurvedic Spa and the sale of the Products at the Location.

3.18.2 To comply at his own expense with any enactments, regulations, bye-laws, notices, directions, orders, requirements or demands of any Government, semi-government or other authority affecting the Project, the Products or the Location.

3.19 Plant, equipment and fittings

Obtain and use for the Project such plant and equipment (including without limitation of the generality of the foregoing, telephone and facsimile equipment) and fixtures and fittings as are prescribed from time to time by the Franchisor and also:

   (i) observe the Franchisor's directions as to the layout and use of such plant and equipment and fixtures and fittings; and

   (ii) maintain such plant and equipment and fixtures and fittings in good repair and good working order.

3.20 Assignment

Not to assign, charge or otherwise deal with the Project in any way without the prior written consent of the Franchisor.

4. The Franchisor's Obligations

The Franchisor covenants and agrees with the Franchisee as follows:

4.1 To permit the Franchisee to carry on the Project

4.1.1 To permit the Franchisee to carry on the business of setting up, operating and promoting the Ayurvedic Spa under the style .... and use the Trademarks or such other names or styles as may be specified in writing by the Franchisor in relation thereto.

4.1.2 To permit the Franchisee to operate the business of providing Products and Services under the style .... and use the Trademarks or such other names or styles as may be specified or approved in writing by the Franchisor from time to time

4.1.3 To permit the Franchisee to use the Intellectual Property Rights in relation to the Project.

4.2 Management advice

4.2.1 To provide the Franchisee, as the Franchisor considers appropriate from time to time, with management, sales and administrative advice in the conduct of the Project and such other advice as the Franchisor considers appropriate to promote the mutual business interests of the Franchisor and the Franchisee.

4.2.2 To furnish the requisite technical expertise and assistance as the Franchisor deems necessary to the Franchisee for the completion, management and promotion of the Project.

4.3 Directions on layout of Location

4.3.1 To provide the Franchisee with directions as to:

   (i) the layout and colour scheme arrangements for the Project at the Location;

   (ii) the plant and equipment and the fixtures and fittings to be used in the Project, as well as for the installation of the same.

4.4 Supply products & services

4.4.1 To exercise its best endeavours to fulfil orders for the Products made by the Franchisee, provided always that the Franchisor shall be under no obligation to fulfil any order for the Products made by the Franchisee, if the Franchisee is at the time in default of his liability to pay his dues.

4.4.2 To provide to the Franchisee the technical know-how and expertise for the entire range of "specialized treatments" as developed and formulated by the Franchisor and to update the Franchisee as regards any improvements thereupon.

4.5 Employ staff & training

4.5.1 To recruit and employ such sufficiently competent staff as the Franchisor deems necessary for the efficient conduct and management of the Project.

4.5.2 To provide initial training to such of the employees as recruited by the Franchisor at the level which in the opinion of the Franchisor is adequate to instruct, in order to efficiently conduct specialized treatments and sell the Products at the Location.

4.5.3 To provide supplementary training as and when the Franchisor deems necessary during the Term as well as further training in new techniques or concepts developed by the Franchisor.

5. Ownership of Intellectual Property Rights

5.1 The Franchisee acknowledges and recognises the exclusive right of the Franchisor to the Intellectual Property rights including without limitation Trademarks as well as the insignia, logo-grams, designs and other Intellectual Property Rights associated with the Franchisor.

5.2 The Franchisee will observe the following requirements in the use of the Trademarks:

(i) Use them in a proper trademark sense in the manner as prescribed by the Franchisor from time to time;

(ii) In the case of such of the Trademarks as are registered indicate that such marks are registered by use of the symbol '®' and that the Franchisee is a licensee of such marks;

(iii) Not encumber, sub-license, assign, transfer or otherwise deal with his rights to the Trademarks;

(iv) Under no circumstances on any occasion will the Franchisee register any business, trade or corporate name or style associated with the Franchisor.

5.3 The Franchisee shall forthwith notify the Franchisor of any infringements of such Intellectual Property Rights of which the Franchisor becomes aware provided however that the prosecution of any claim with respect to any Intellectual Property Rights shall be the sole responsibility and undertaken at the absolute discretion of the Franchisor.

6. Indemnity by the Franchisee

The Franchisee covenants and agrees with the Franchisor that the Franchisee shall assume sole and entire responsibility for and indemnify and save harmless the Franchisor from any and all claims, liabilities, losses, expenses, responsibility and damages by reason of any claim, proceedings action, liability or injury arising out of the Franchisee's conduct of the Project or as a result of the

Franchisee's relations with his customers and other third parties or because of any breach of this Agreement by the Franchisee.

7. Further Term

Provided that there shall not be any prior or existing breaches or non-observances of any of the covenants, conditions, Agreements, and provisos on the part of the Franchisee contained in this Agreement, the Franchisor will upon the written request of the Franchisee given not less than 3 months prior to the expiration of the term of the franchise hereby granted, grant a further term of the franchise for.................... years and the Franchisee will accept such further term upon the Franchisor's then prevailing terms and conditions.

8. Termination

This Agreement shall terminate:

(A) On the expiry of the Term;

(B) On the occurrence of any of the following events which are fundamental breaches of this Agreement terminating it forthwith:

   (i) in the event of a breach by the Franchisee of any provisions of this Agreement and subsequent failure to remedy the breach within thirty days of having been notified by the Franchisor;

   (ii) failure to make the payments on any of the relevant payment dates as specified in the Agreement (time being of the essence);

   (iii) any assignment or disposal of the Project or the Location by the Franchisee;

   (iv) any challenge by the Franchisee to the validity of any part of the Intellectual Property Rights;

   provided that the Franchisor may waive any breach of this Agreement by the Franchisee.

(C) If the Franchisee goes into either compulsory or voluntary liquidation (except for the purpose of reconstruction or amalgamation) or if a receiver is appointed in respect of the whole or any part of its assets or if the Franchisee makes assignment for the benefit of or composition with its creditors generally or threatens to do any of these things or any judgment is made against the Franchisee or any similar occurrence in any jurisdiction affects the Franchisee.

(D) If the Franchisee engages in any conduct prejudicial to the Project or the marketing of the Products or Services generally.

(E) If any material change occurs in the management or control of the Franchisee particularly any change of directors or shareholders.

9. Effects of Termination

9.1 Upon termination of this Agreement for whatever reason the Franchisee shall:

   (i) Immediately cease to operate and conduct the Ayurvedic Spa, provide Services and sell Products, however it shall not be relieved of the obligation to pay any monies due to the Franchisor pursuant to this Agreement;

(ii) Cease to exploit any Intellectual Property Rights owned by the Franchisor or any company related to it and licensed to the Franchisee in respect of the Project;

(iii) Forthwith cease to use any of the Trademarks and to desist from using any trademark confusingly or deceptively similar to the Trademarks or the style BIOTIQUE;

(iv) Deliver to the Franchisor any documentation including without limitation manuals, catalogues, instructions, notes, publicity promotional and advertising material, samples, letterheads, business cards relating to the Project;

(v) The Franchisee will furnish to the Franchisor an inventory of the unsold stock held by it and transfer to the manufacturer or any person, firm or corporation designated by the manufacturer:

(vi) The Franchisee shall if required by the Franchisor sell and deliver to the Franchisor:

(a) the fixtures and fittings and plant and equipment owned and used by the franchisee in the Project as may be selected by the Franchisor;

(b) the Franchisee's unsold stock of the Products which are in good saleable condition as may be selected by the Franchisor.

(vii) The purchase price for such fixtures and fittings and plant and equipment selected by the Franchisor shall be as agreed upon by the Franchisee and the Franchisor and failing Agreement as fixed by a reputed valuer of such items appointed by the Franchisor and shall be paid by the Franchisor to the Franchisee within .... days of the date of termination of the Agreement or within .... days of the date of valuation by a valuer, whichever is later, and the fee of the said valuer shall be paid by the Franchisee.

(viii) The sale to the Franchisor of the Franchisee's unsold stock of the Products selected by the Franchisor shall be at the same price as given by the Franchisor to the Franchisee

(ix) Any freight charges incurred by the Franchisor in the acquisition by it of the Franchisee's fixtures and fittings and plant and equipment and unsold stock of the products as aforesaid shall be paid by the Franchisee.

(x) The Franchisee shall permit and authorise the Franchisor to have reasonable access to the premises at which the fixtures and fittings, plant and equipment and unsold stocks are then located so as to enable the Franchisor to inspect and to take possession of any such items if purchased.

10. Damages

In case of termination of this Agreement by the FRANCHISEE prior to the expiry of the term for any reason whatsoever or in the event of termination by the FRANCHISOR for breach of contract or default by the FRANCHISEE, the FRANCHISEE shall pay a sum of .... only as liquidated damages to compensate the FRANCHISOR for the various losses and damages suffered including the loss of reputation and business opportunity. This is without prejudice to any other remedy available to the FRANCHISOR. The FRANCHISEE agrees to abide by this exit clause in accordance with his acknowledgment that the FRANCHISOR has incurred huge investment and expenditure on behalf of the Centre.

Most specifically the FRANCHISEE acknowledges that:
  (i) the FRANCHISOR has expended considerable time, investment and efforts in:
    (a) locating an appropriate FRANCHISEE at an appropriate location;
    (b) entering into discussions and negotiating with the FRANCHISEE;
    (c) training the FRANCHISEE's personnel;
    (d) helping the FRANCHISEE build up considerable goodwill in its Centre so as to increase business.
  (ii) the premature termination of this Franchise Agreement would result in huge losses to the FRANCHISOR which would then have to:
    (a) locate another appropriate FRANCHISEE;
    (b) invest in the FRANCHISEE Center by training personnel etc.;
    (c) build-up goodwill in the new Centre so that the business of the new FRANCHISEE matches up to that of the earlier FRANCHISEE.

11. Entire Agreement

This Agreement sets forth the entire Agreement and understanding between the parties as to the subject-matter of this Agreement and merges all prior discussions between them and neither of the parties shall be bound by any conditions, definitions, warranties or representations with respect to the subject-matter of this Agreement other than as expressly provided in this Agreement as duly set forth or subsequent to the date in writing and signed by a proper and duly authorized representative of the party to be bound thereby.

12. *Force Majeure*

The Franchisor shall not be liable to the Franchisee for any loss by the Franchisee caused by the failure of the Franchisor to observe the terms and conditions of this Agreement and on his part to be observed and performed where such failure is occasioned by any cause beyond the Franchisor's reasonable control including the failure of the Franchisor to supply or delay in supplying any goods to be supplied by the Franchisor to the Franchisee whether on account of *inter alia* war, insurrection, fire, flood, earthquake, strikes, lock-outs, the unavailability of raw materials or similar cause.

13. WAIVER

Any waiver by the Franchisor of a breach of this Agreement or any other subsequent Agreement to which it may be a party in consequence of this Agreement shall not be deemed to be a waiver of any subsequent breach.

14. Severability

If any provision of this Agreement is invalid or unenforceable, the balance of this Agreement shall remain in effect, and if any provision is inapplicable to any person or circumstances, it shall nevertheless remain applicable to all other persons and circumstances.

15. Proper Law & Jurisdiction

15.1 This Agreement shall be governed by Indian law in every particular including formation and interpretation and shall be deemed to have been made in India.

15.2 Any proceedings arising out of or in connection with this Agreement shall be brought only before the court of competent jurisdictions in ....

16. Notices

16.1 Any notice, request or other communication required to be given under this Agreement shall be served personally or mailed to the other party by registered post, addressed to the parties at their respective addresses set out at the beginning, or at any other address that each party shall provide to the other in writing.

16.2 Any notice served personally shall be considered given at the time of service. Any notice given by registered post shall be deemed to have been received within five days after the date of posting as shown on the post office receipt.

IN WITNESS WHEREOF, the parties hereto have executed this Agreement as of the day and the year first above written.

SIGNED AND DELIVERED BY:
(Name and designation)
On behalf of *Alpha* Technologies Pvt. Ltd.
SIGNED AND DELIVERED BY:
(Name and designation)
On behalf of *Beta* Overseas Pvt. Ltd.
SIGNED AND DELIVERED BY:
(Name and designation)
On behalf of Theta

3.3 Employ staff & training

3.3.1 To employ sufficiently competent employees as recruited and trained by the Franchisor to effectively manage and conduct the Project.

3.3.2 To participate, and cause such of his employees as the Franchisor shall recruit for the Project to participate, in such initial training as the Franchisor may consider necessary to instruct the Franchisee and his employees to efficiently conduct specialized treatments and sell the Products, such training being for such duration as the Franchisor shall prescribe.

CHAPTER 6
PROJECT FINANCE

SYNOPSIS

THE RISK MATRIX
DUE DIGILENCE
SECURITY
FORCE MAJEURE
WHEN THINGS GO WRONG
    Contract Damages
    Liquidated Damages
CONCLUSION
POWER PURCHASE AGREEMENTS - PITFALLS AND REMEDIES
    Definitions
    Tariff
    Counter Guarantee
    Financing
    Price Mechanism
    Pricing Risk
    Payment Risk
    Third Party Sale
    Tax Holidays
    Judicial Inquiry
    Force Majeure
    Conclusion
FUEL SUPPLY AGREEMENT - BANKABLE OFFTAKES
    Infrastructure
    Pricing
    Payment
    Force Majeure
    Dispute Resolution
    Transportation
    Scheduling; Metering And Weighing
    Quality And Rejection
    Default
    Remedies For Breach
DUE DILIGENCE
TYPICAL DUE DILIGENCE DELIBERATIONS IN A PROJECT FINANCING STRUCTURE
    The Project Sponsor
    The Site Of The Project
    Political, Economical & Legal Considerations
    Financial Parameters
    Construction Commitments
    Input Agreements
    Off-take Agreements

General Contract Review
Environmental Considerations
Critique
PRECEDENTS
- Agreement for the Sale and Purchase and Delivery of Coal

Typically, international trade involves a seller in one country providing goods or services to a buyer in another. Projects carry this process one stage further. The international supplier goes to the customer's country and carries out work and/or installations there. Arranging payment and providing credit for such deals brings into play a host of different techniques. Today's financing techniques have shifted the emphasis away from the resources of the country and have transferred the risks towards the customers' production capabilities. This is boosting a trend towards more sophisticated and structured financing packages that divide the risks of non-payment between the financing bank and the supplier in new ways.

The key challenge facing project finance lawyers is to offer solutions, which properly balance the "wants" of the western participants with the "haves" of the hosts' jurisdiction.

Chicken or the egg - which comes first? A project's commercial structure or its financing structure. Actually, the financing structure defining the commercial structure will determine the speed of project implementation, the technology and other components. Typically, project financing will require off-take contracts, proven technologies and a lengthy financial closing process involving a myriad of parties. However, in effect the financial structure determines the commercial structure while the commercial structure is developed in contemplation of the financing structure.

Project finance structure is based on project risk identification and allocation thereof among the parties involved. Because of the importance of risk allocation in the project finance structure, a convenient organised format for identifying the risk and understanding the allocation and mitigation techniques used is helpful. A risk matrix is the tool typically used by project finance participants.

The Risk Matrix

A project developer does not make investment without risk. Risk identification is only a starting point. The unallocated, residual risk is the developer's economic risk for the economic return expected from the project operation. To the extent that return is inadequate in comparison to the expected return on investment, the project should be abandoned.

Sample construction and operation period risk matrix of an electric generation facility is given below:

TYPE OF RISKS INVOLVED	DESCRIPTION OF RISK	PROPOSED SOLUTION	RISK ASSUMED BY
Country Risk	Expropriation Nationalization Interference, Cross border transfer of	Counter guarantee by the government to pay debt and return on equity	Government

TYPE OF RISKS INVOLVED	DESCRIPTION OF RISK	PROPOSED SOLUTION	RISK ASSUMED BY
	payments in respect of principal or interest		
Currency Risk	Potential currency fluctuation and unfavourable exchange rate during construction	Enforceability of any liability denominated in a foreign currency and stand-by finance facility until tariff adjustment is made	Off-take purchaser
Political Risk	Change of law, war, revolution, civil strike, politically motivated violent acts including terrorism and sabotage	Political risk insurance coverage	Insurance company (good argument for opening up the insurance sector)
Technology Risk	Technology proposed for use in implementing the project	Performance guarantee by the contractor	Contractor
Legal Risk	Enforcement of contractual obligations, security, insolvency and regulation of activities related to the project	Engage competent local lawyers familiar with project finance and local laws	Lender, Sponsor
Market Risk	Existence of a market for the product, commodity or service produced by the project and prices that provide anticipated cash flow	Effective due diligence conducted both by lender and sponsor in order to determine the bankability of the project	Project sponsor and lender
Completion Risk	Cost overrun within contractor's control	Fixed price contract	Contractor
	Cost overrun not within contractor's control like subsurface site condition	Stand-by finance facility	Project sponsor
	Cost overrun not within contractor's control like change of law	Stand-by finance facility drawn until tariff adjustment is made	Project sponsor or off-take purchaser
	Completion delay within contractor's control	Fixed completion date in construction contract; daily liquidated damages to cover debt service, fixed operating costs and fuel supply contract, late delivery payments	Contractor

TYPE OF RISKS INVOLVED	DESCRIPTION OF RISK	PROPOSED SOLUTION	RISK ASSUMED BY
	Completion delay that is not within contractor's control insured event	Insurance proceeds	Insurance
	Failure of contractor to satisfy performance guarantees at completion due to contractor fault	Performance guarantee in construction contract; liquidated damages for reduced performance payable by contractor	Contractor
	Increased interest during construction period	Stand-by finance facility drawn until tariff adjustment is made	Purchaser off-take
	Unfavourable exchange rates during construction period	Stand-by finance facility drawn until tariff adjustment is made	Off-take purchaser
Operating Risk	Operating cost overrun government fault	Tariff adjustment	Off-take purchaser
	Operating cost overrun operator failure to satisfy operating guarantees	Performance guarantees in operating agreement; liquidated damages for reduced performance payable by operator	Operator
	Unavailability/ unconvertibility of foreign exchange	Government pays debt and guaranteed equity return to developer	Central or State Governments
	Equipment destruction	Insurance proceeds	Insurance company
	Operator default	Penalties and termination payments	Operator
	Off-take purchaser default	Developer's option to terminate; if terminated, government pays debt and guaranteed equity return to developer	Central government

The lender wants a risk-free project. The lender also wants each of the project finance contracts to be assignable to the lender as collateral for the project finance loan. Additionally, the lender must ensure that if there is a foreclosure, the contracts are assignable to and assumable by the lender and/or by a subsequent project owner. A typical financing structure acceptable to the lender will

emphasise the following issues:
- All costs before construction completion are without recourse to the lender for additional funds.
- The contractor satisfies performance guarantees, as evidenced by performance tests.
- Recourse to other creditworthy project participants for delay and completion costs if the project is abandoned and/or minimum performance levels not achieved.
- Predictable revenue streams that can be applied to service debt, in the currency of the debt (or easily convertible at an adequate exchange rate).
- The revenue streams are long-term, from a creditworthy source and in an amount that covers operating costs and debt service.
- The incentives under the operating agreement ensure that the project will be operated at levels necessary to maximize revenue while minimizing costs, and comply with environmental laws and maintain long-term facility.

The sooner the project financing is closed and construction begins on the project, the sooner the project sponsor starts receiving the financial benefits of its investment.

Since the project sponsor has to negotiate with the host government and the lenders on different issues, it is inevitable that key project documents would well have reached a final shape even before the lenders are involved. Due diligence is the inevitable process which precedes formal appraisal of the status of the project.

Due Digilence

Typically, in a due diligence the lender's advisors check over all work that has been prepared by the sponsor's advisors and confirm whether the figures, assumptions and facts as stated by the sponsors hold up and make the particular project viable and creditworthy to be financed. It is generally very useful, at an early stage, to have a complete list of all the project documentation involved so that appropriate due diligence can take place with respect to each one of these documents. Often the scarcity and inconsistent quality of underlying documents, in particular contracts of supply, permits, etc., as well as the lack of local registries or other public records for search inquiries make the due diligence process extremely onerous. Also, the necessity to conduct due diligence on site in difficult locations and in different languages will often impose practical difficulties to perform appropriate due diligence.

Security

The lender in a project financing structure will look at:
- Cash flow of the project and its ability to meet the project's operating expenses, debt service and other liabilities; and
- The securities likely to be created on project assets.

A type of security in one project may not be the most appropriate in another. What is appropriate will depend largely on the structure of the transaction. Some projects may have local elements, which may require certain licensing, or consents to be obtained. In those types of projects, it is important to be well informed about the particular requirements of each jurisdiction involved. The choice of law to govern the transaction may not circumvent the need for compliance with such local law requirements. As a matter of practicality, it is also important to be aware of the differing levels of bureaucratic efficiency in different locations and to be prepared to adapt the way for the transaction to be handled to allow for such differences.

It is generally understood that security is taken to ensure that the lenders are able to secure repayment as soon as the transaction breaks down. Although, the underlying interest will always be to get access to funds for repayment, some types of security will not be geared towards this as an immediate aim. Rather, security may be taken for various reasons, including prevention of third parties from dealing with the assets, and to enable the lenders to step into the shoes of the project company and operate the business. Such security is not taken for its inherent value, as there is no inherent value to the lenders in a very rapid transport system or a naphtha power plant unless the lenders also have access to the revenue stream that such assets generate.

In India, securities like mortgages on immovable property, hypothecation of moveable property, pledge of shares, assignment of contracts, assignment of insurance and assignment of receivables are generally created in favour of the lender. Apart from this, escrow account arrangements are also increasingly becoming popular. One of the grey areas existing today is the steep stamp duty payable at different rates in different States of India. Stamp duty is levied in accordance with the stamp law of the State where the relevant document is executed. Sometimes the rates are high and do have a substantial impact. For example, stamp duty on a mortgage can be up to 10% of the amount secured and on an assignment of project contracts can be up to 7% of the value of the assignment. Some of the sponsors are able to get a waiver by persuading the State Governments.

Ad-valorem registration duty payable in case of registration of documents in relation to mortgage of an immovable property may also cause problems.

FORCE MAJEURE

The *force majeure* provision in a project contract must also be carefully considered. Inconsistent *force majeure* provisions among the project contracts can result in great risk to the project. For example, if the construction contract provides an extension of time for the contractor to complete the facility upon the occurrence of a *force majeure*, the same relief must be available under the off-take sales agreement. If not, and the off-take sales agreement requires that sales begin on a specified date with no extension permitted for a *force majeure*, the project sponsor would be unable to comply with the sales agreement because the project would not be completed in time. The result could be a terminated sales contract.

Inconsistent *force majeure* provisions can be cured with a so-called "resurrection" clause, in which the contractor agrees with the sponsor/developer that where *force majeure* inconsistencies exist between contracts, the contractor will not receive relief greater than the relief available to the developer under other relevant contracts. In the earlier example the contractor could not have been excused from performance to the extent such excuse would have resulted in a project delay of such length that the off-take sales agreement would be terminated. However, a less extensive delay would be permissible.

Different legal systems can create havoc on well-planned, matched *force majeure* provisions. Despite careful planning, complete elimination of the risk of inconsistencies in *force majeure* provisions may not be possible. Rather than rely on contract provisions, project sponsors may need to seek alternate solutions, such as standby credit, dedication of reserve funds and employment of additional labour to address inconsistent provisions.

When things go wrong

In the end, project financing is dependent on contracts. As such, they are governed by the Indian Contract Act, 1872. Contracts must be carefully reviewed to determine whether the contract terms negotiated by the parties are enforceable. For example, a commitment of one party to prepay the project debt if it breaches a contract may not be enforceable as *liquidated damages*. If the parties desire that a particular contract be performed by a particular party, the laws of *specific performance* must be examined to determine whether that can be enforced.

This legal obstacle course exists in every project financing. More often than not, litigation brought to force a party to perform a contract is a disaster for a project financing structure. Why, then, bother discussing remedies and enforcement at all? It is for two reasons: disincentives must be given in the contract to guard against a breach, and potential remedies often provide negotiating strength if a problem does develop.

Contract Damages

Unless the amount of damages is specifically provided for in the contract, the general rule is that a non-defaulting party is compensated for the loss the defaulting party should have reasonably contemplated (not including any contingent liability) its breach would create. This concept is completely unworkable in the project finance context where a breach under an important project contract could result in an avalanche of damages. There is insufficient time to await the decision of a court or arbitral panel on such questions as foreseeability of the damage and whether the non-defaulting party has a duty to mitigate damages.

Liquidated Damages

Invariably liquidated damages are preferred in almost all project finance contracts. Liquidated damage provisions, sometimes considered sacred to project financiers, are not however, respected by the courts. Damages for breach by either party may be liquidated in the agreement but only at an amount which is reasonable in the light of the anticipated or actual harm caused by the breach, the difficulties of proof of loss, and the inconvenience or non-feasibility of otherwise obtaining an adequate remedy. A term fixing unreasonably large liquidated damages is void as a penalty.

Conclusion

The net effect is that project financing is only one of a number of techniques available to address the financing requirements of large infrastructure projects. Capital markets, tax exempted public finance, securitization and other types of structured finance, all have a role in the analysis of how to achieve an optimal result.

Parties seeking and advising on finances for projects must, therefore, be able to offer expertise in a wide variety of financing resources, and must be capable of applying those resources in circumstances ranging from new project development to acquisitions of existing projects and/or pooling of projects in various combinations.

For all these reasons, for those who are active in the industry, it is a time of great growth and expansion, of applying a wide range of techniques to a wide range of situations.

Power Purchase Agreements - Pitfalls and Remedies

In any power project, a Power Purchase Agreement (PPA), is the linchpin of energy project financing. It is a "Sacrosanct" document that a developer takes to the bank to demonstrate a secure revenue stream. A power purchaser ensures that the power supplier's long term obligations are sustainable and that its own requirements are reflected in the PPA.

To begin with, the PPA should not place constraints on the utility about the way in which plant is dispatched. In many systems, particularly those where there is a shortfall in generation capacity, the availability of plant will, quite reasonably, be of particular concern to the utility. The PPA should therefore, place particular emphasis on this issue and provide for penalties to be exacted in the event of unplanned outages.

One useful approach can be to set a two part tariff based on separate capacity and energy payments. Under that arrangement, the capacity payment is set to cover the project fixed costs including investment, with an element of profit coupled with penalties for failing to meet availability expectations. The energy component can be a pass through arrangement which reflects the actual incremental cost of generation.

The ability of the plant to respond properly after major system incidents and to maintain stability of the interconnective stations is a further important issue for incorporation in the PPA. For instance, utilities may wish to consider means of monitoring this ability. Agreed methods for testing plant on an occasional basis so that the power purchaser is able to satisfy itself that the plant is capable of providing its stated capacity, are also appropriate.

The main risks which a utility or power purchaser may reasonably be expected to accept include matters such as difficulties arising from a site selected by the utility or its agents, changes in the local fiscal conditions and in environmental requirements, certain failures to take power when available under PPA provisions, and changes in the financial environment such as interest rates and forex rates.

The utility may be able to obtain recourse from the government with regard to fiscal changes, and can also provide for cost pass through under some circumstances in the event of changes in environmental requirements. Equally the PPA can include some protective provisions in case of financial disturbances.

Another risk faced by the Independent Power Producers (IPPs) in India, is the absence of a standard PPA. A standard PPA eliminates the need for protracted negotiation between various parties and the right of every government to review the agreements entered into by its predecessors. To mitigate this risk, the Government of India (GOI) is planning to come up with an all-encompassing standard PPA by the end of this year.

A classic non-recourse financing mechanism like PPA has, in general, the following salient features which govern the direction of the project:

Definitions

The definition clause in a PPA should be as unqualified, unambiguous and precise as possible. Qualifications should be preferable in the substantive portions of the PPA, where the SEB has to see that these are equitable, symmetrical, and do not pass on the risk, which ought to be taken by the private company, to the Board and *vice-versa*. This will provide the PPA with a balanced approach towards the interest of both SEBs & IPPs.

Tariff

Tariff is the core of PPA. The Government of India's (GOI's) two-part tariff notification provides only the principles for determining the tariff. The capacity payment should be linked to target availability with substantial penalties for under-availability. Investors and lenders appraise a project primarily on the basis of Internal Rate of Return (IRR) which the project's future cash flow generates for the investor. This is different from the 16% Return on Equity (ROE) allowed as one of the elements in the fixed charges at 68.5% viz. Power Load Factor (PLF). The ROE does not take into account the gestation period and the different levels of risks associated with different fuels *viz.* coal, gas, etc. The return that the promoter starts getting after the commercial operation of the plant has to compensate for the period of construction as well as when the equity could not receive any return. Therefore, longer the construction period, lower will be the IRR corresponding to the 16% ROE. Based on these factors, a 16% ROE could translate into an IRR in the range of 11% – 15%. Hence, higher the cost of project, higher will be the tariff.

The Union Power Ministry has amended the power notification to cap the power tariffs by controlling the incomes of power companies.

The earlier notification was broad based and had allowed all taxes to be recovered from the power tariff. As a result, a promoter was paying no taxes on power generation and also stood to make large profits by improving generation standards. The tax on this additional income was being passed on to the power tariff that would be borne by the consumers ultimately. The government has now clearly defined the income stream available to the power company. It allows power companies, while calculating the ROE, to recover tax from the power tariff for calculating the 16% ROE and on account of the extra rupee liability because of foreign exchange variation. The notification adds that tax on other income streams cannot be recovered from the tariff and will have to be borne by the company. The notification clarifies that any other additional recovery of tax will be adjusted every year on the basis of a certificate from statutory authority.

The National Task Force took a decision on energy tariff that SEB have recently signed PPAs with IPPs will not be bound to open their PPAs for realigning them with available tariff norms. Availability of tariff will typically involve penal provisions against energy overdrawls/underdrawls by bulk constituents and shortfall/surplus generation by a station. Demand will be based on allotted share while supply of energy will depend upon available capacity declared by a station on a prior basis.

Counter Guarantee

The government has clarified that the notification is applicable to projects whose promoter have not signed or finalized PPA with the concerned SEBs. Some of the major projects affected by the new notification include the Reliance promoted 500MW Jayakondam Projects, the 4,000MW CEPA project in Orissa, and the 2,000MW Ennore Project in Tamil Nadu. However, projects like 1,000MW Videocon Project in Tamil Nadu and Dabhol Phase-II, which are close to financial closure, will not be affected by the notification. Counter Guarantee is now being reframed to provide security for the foreign party in a PPA. This will take care of the foreign exchange mechanism of the project. To add to it, there has been an existing incentive policy of 16% ROE in case of foreign exchange fluctuation. Therefore, foreign investors are totally guaranteed for their investment in power sector.

Financing

There should be a bankable PPA with all protection of payment mechanism. Typically, PPA have a two to four years construction period and a total pay-back period varying between ten to twenty years. This calls for finance on terms that would commensurate with the typical long gestation and revenue-earning capacity of power plant. Further, most projects generate only local currency revenue which are susceptible to regulatory and political influences as well as risk associated with wide fluctuation in foreign currencies and corresponding increase in tariff rates. If the foreign currency fluctuations are not allowed as "pass through" in tariff rates, the variability of the project will get affected. A typical solution to the exchange risk fluctuations is to index amounts payable by the power purchaser to the project sponsor under the PPA. The index is designed to reflect the shifting exchange rate between the hard and soft local currencies.

Price Mechanism

PPA with "guaranteed" returns provides little incentive to the power developer to be efficient and minimize cost. The burden is ultimately borne by the consumer. This needs to be replaced by a delivered price mechanism, which in many cases should be based on competitive bidding. For instance, under China's new power policy, developers bid for the contract on basis of the price at which they could produce and deliver electricity, leaving it to them to determine what returns they could get from their offer. If private participation in India is based on the cost-plus approach, it will have to be studied very carefully and the cost calculation must be transparent to be convincing.

Pricing Risk

The "guaranteed off take" and "deemed generation" clauses in PPA are in conflict with merit order dispatch policy being formulated by Ministry of Power. Such a change of law will have a two-fold impact. Firstly, it will make IRR on projects more unpredictable (with revenue streams tied to dispatch) and will create a substantial operational challenge for Load Dispatch Centres. Secondly, it will place the industry in a state of continuous competition, as opposed to the relatively secure returns that could be expected after a hard fought and hopefully bankable PPA. It is only a matter of time before consumer pressure forces merit order dispatch policy.

As SEBs are slowly restructured into separate generation, transmission and distribution entities, a dramatic change will automatically impact the industry. This will again be driven by the ultimate consumer. Private distributors will seek the lowest cost generation and so will transmission agencies. SEBs or central utility generation units will be competing with IPPs and certainly not "backing down" in favor of IPPs. This means competition and renegotiations. No developer can hope to be immune to the inevitable pressures of competition. The solution is to be prepared to renegotiate and to have enough cushion to retain project viability.

Further, as wheeling is permitted to industrial sites to ensure IPP viability, the IPPs that have signed PPAs with SEBs may be put to greater risk. Additionally, SEBs are looking to issue bonds to raise much needed funds. These are likely to take first charge on SEB's revenue and thus impact the sustainability of PPAs further. All these factors increase the medium and long term risk exposure of a PPA.

Typically, pricing risks are dealt with by covering fixed and variable costs including escalations and making strong provisions for pass-through factors *viz.* fuel, taxes etc.

Payment Risk

PPA also contains procedural provisions for the billing and payment of amounts due under the agreement. At the foundation of a PPA is the assumption that there is power requirement and adequate funds to pay for the power. These provisions must be tailored to the other project contracts so that the revenue is received before the time needed to pay debt service, fuel cost and operating expenses. In India, SEBs are reeling under the legacy of political interference, tariff control, entrenched inefficiencies and corruption. It is these constraints of the SEBs that determine the key payment risks in a PPA.

The payment risks in a PPA are dealt with through back-to-back arrangements involving escrow mechanism, LC and letter of guarantee.

Third Party Sale

Whether the project company has the ability to sell power to the purchasers is a subject of negotiation, and varies from project to project. Though, the Indian Electricity Act, 1910 provides for a third party sale subject to the approval of the competent government, the government as a matter of policy does not encourage third party sale. The SEB as a power purchaser has the first right of refusal. These rights are based on the support given by the SEB to the project company, including credit support necessary to finance the project, project development contributions and infrastructure costs, which would be considered before a project company is allowed to make third party sales. Now, when the GOI is opening up electricity sector for private participation, a third party sale would be very lucrative for the private promoters. A pro-rata reduction in capacity charges and other "purchaser provided costs" can be used as the mechanism to allow the project company to make third party sale, while returning to the power purchaser a portion of the benefits it contributed to the project's initial success.

Tax Holidays

Section 80 (1) (A) of the Income Tax Act envisages a five-year tax holiday for the infrastructure sector. However, except for the power and telecom sector, all other sectors have the option to decide as to when they want to enjoy their tax holidays. This is arbitrary, as in the first five years there are hardly any taxable profits on which the promoter would want a tax relaxation. Moreover, India only offers developers a five-year tax holiday whereas this scheme should extend to both developers and lenders, as they are equally losing out on the profit for the money invested and the money advanced.

Judicial Inquiry

The Indian Electricity Act provides for a public notice before setting up any power plant. This procedure should be made more result oriented and obligatory, giving time for all objections to be heard and finally a verdict should be given which should be final and binding, rather than giving a scope for judicial inquiry which would stall the project in between.

Force Majeure

The method of allocating the risk of *force majeure* varies from one contract to the other. This is particularly true in the PPA context. In power projects of developing countries, project sponsors often attempt to place the risk for all *force majeure* events on the power purchaser. In a PPA this clause should be clearly defined and should not be too wide. As the name suggests it should cover only exceptional circumstances and not normal business risks which are in the control of the parties. The manner of intimating to the other party about a *force majeure* situation and the remedy should be spelt out in detail in a PPA instead of simply listing them.

SEB has to take particular care to limit its capacity payments to a specified period in cases of the company's claim of inability to perform on account of *force majeure*. The SEB should also try to incorporate some safeguard for itself in case of inability to take power on account of *force majeure* affecting it. A power purchaser can also protect itself against the risk of uncontrollable events by effective insurance program. This type of insurance will be required under the financing document of the project, and also typically included in the PPA to protect the power purchaser against the risk that the facility will be inoperable and therefore unable to supply it with power. Typically, insurance programs include payment of asset replacement and payment of debt service and fixed costs for a reasonable period of time.

Conclusion

To sum up PPA is a heart and soul of a private power project. It defines the rights and obligations of the project developer and SEB during the development, construction and operation phases of a power plant. Therefore, the PPA along with all other necessary agreements, should be prepared in the early stage of the solicitation process. These interconnected documents should be drafted with clarity keeping in view the technical parameters, commercial and contractual terms and managerial and legal aspect of the power sector.

Fuel Supply Agreement - Bankable Offtakes

India represents a system where policy, demand, supply, structure, fuel, transport, transmission and tariff are all in a state of flux. The performance of the project is dependent on many things: the operator, technical reliability, the grid, the fuel, the fuel transporter and act of God.

Since the Fuel Supply Agreement (FSA) contract has a minimum take or pay requirement therefore prior approval of State Electricity Board (SEB) is normally required. It is important for SEB to appreciate and understand the implication of the subsidiary contracts to which it is directly not a party. SEB should work out an arrangement with the promoter so that it is able to safeguard its interests.

A model FSA has been formulated by the Government of India (GOI) but the buyer and the seller can make changes in the same as per their requirement. However, to reduce undue delays taking place in setting up of power projects, necessary steps must be taken by the GOI to spell out clear guidelines on which the developer and the State Government should or may negotiate.

FSAs have three main concerns in a project financing:
- supply reliability
- transportation reliability and
- cost

The original draft of the FSA, first released in September 1997, was found to be "unbankable" by the financial institutions. Though the new FSA is closer to bankability and perhaps to the expectations of the Independent Power Producers (IPPs), there still remain certain concerns:

Infrastructure

In the new FSA, stress is not laid upon the adequacy of infrastructure for handling and supplying of fuel. This has been pointed out by many oil companies. IPPs and the Indian Government are not willing to give importance to adequacy of infrastructure. They are only concerned about the "quality & quantity guarantee" of the supply of fuel to the project site. Ambiguity with reference to other important infrastructural aspects may lead to lopsided development of the project.

Pricing

Predictability of price over the life of the project is critical to the feasibility and success of a project financing structure. The FSA should contain a clear articulation of price, allocate responsibility for taxes, duties, government charges and basis if any, for price adjustments. There should be a price adjustment for an average expected quality with plus and minus adjustments for variations and penalty for rejection below certain minimum value. While it is a pass through in most FSAs, the fuel supplier should make sure that he is using the optimum pricing/quality/supply solution for the project.

Payment

The FSA should specify in clear and unambigous terms when payments are due, *i.e.* whether on receipt of the seller's invoice or after testing is successfully completed. Also the mode of payment should be specified. Payment can be through Letter of Credit. SEB's payment obligation is being guaranteed by the State Government. Therefore, they seek Central Government guarantee or escrow account to be opened by the SEBs so that the obligations to the lenders are met. The concern is that the lender needs a bankable document based on the creditability of not just the IPP, but also the SEB, who is the ultimate buyer or the grid contractor as per the Electricity Supply Act, 1910. Normative parameters should be taken as ceiling and the SEB should not feel legally debarred from negotiating better terms.

Force Majeure

International/national projects are often structured with and negotiated among many diverse parties. However, most of the time the underlying project contracts contain un-co-ordinated *force majeure* provisions. In such a case, such an anomaly should be removed by inclusion of the "resurrection clause" wherein the contractor and the developer agree that the quantum of relief would be same if they are affected by *force majeure*.

Dispute Resolution

Multiple project documents, multiple parties and potentially inconsistent treatment of the same or similar contract provisions can lead to unacceptable results. Choice of law, forum, panel should be clearly stated. It will be a good idea to lay down a very detailed procedure for dispute resolution through good faith discussions or with the help of experts with the objective of trying to resolve most of the disputes. The FSA should be commercially and financially viable. In order to attract long term financing, it must reflect an acceptable level of certainty of result following an unforeseen event such that certainty prevails in resolving the project's problems and provides adequate comfort with responsibility, rectification and reparation.

Transportation

Model fuel supply and transportation agreements with clear responsibilities fixed on fuel supplier, railways and other similar agencies should be formulated. The railways have, till date, functioned in a certain manner whereby they did not take responsibility for any liquidated damages on account of delays etc. beyond a point. FSA should take care of clauses arising because of transportation difficulties. Transportation risks could be covered by insurance which seems to be more economical but not considered so far by the IPP's.

Scheduling; Metering and Weighing

It is important that the FSA ordering, delivery and scheduling provisions conform to the purchasing schedules of the PPA.

Quality and Rejection

Input quality is an important element of risk in a project financing structure. For example, low fuel quality could increase operating costs or prevent a facility from meeting permit requirements. Also, if the fuel does not meet or exceed the specifications under which the facility was designed, it may not operate at the performance levels needed for a successful project. Consequently, the agreement must set forth a detailed specification of the fuel quality and characteristic requirements.

Besides, a clear statement of the fuel quality and characteristics, a procedure is needed for testing the fuel delivered to the facility. This may be accomplished through an independent laboratory or by operating personnel at the delivery site. A determination should be made as to which party should bear the cost of testing. Finally, a dispute resolution procedure is helpful in resolving disputes relating to compliance with these specifications.

Default

(a) *Termination by Supplier.*—From the perspective of the supplier, the input agreement is typically subject to termination for the following events: non-payment of amounts owed by the project sponsor to the supplier; bankruptcy, acceleration or liquidation of the project sponsor; abandonment of the project (unless due to the fault of the supplier"); termination or material amendment of certain agreed-upon project contracts (other than for good cause or default by the other party); sale of project assets; failure to achieve milestones, including commercial operations, by a definite date; contract repudiation or other action that implies the project sponsor does not intend to perform the contract; and other breaches of material provisions of the agreement.

(b) *Termination by Project Sponsor.*—From the perspective of the project sponsor, the input agreement is typically subject to termination for the following events; non-payment of amounts owed by the supplier to the project company;

bankruptcy, acceleration or liquidation of the supplier; contract repudiation or other action that implies the supplier does not intend to perform the contract; the project sponsor is unable to complete construction or operate the project due to a *force majeure* or supplier fault; and other breaches of material provisions of the agreement. If the supplier is a government entity whose obligations are guaranteed by the host government, the agreement will be terminable if the government, as guarantor, defaults under the guarantee.

(c) *Termination by Project Lenders.*—In some financings, the project lenders agree with the supplier that if it proposes to terminate the contract an alternate party be substituted for the project sponsor. This substitution is subject to reasonable approval rights of the supplier based on operating experience, financial resources, and sometimes, national security.

Remedies for Breach

(a) *Termination Payments.*—If the FSA is terminated for convenience, or due to a default, the party terminating for convenience or in default should pay a high termination payment. If the supplier terminates the agreement for convenience or the contract is terminated due to a supplier default, the project sponsor will need to consider how project debt will be paid, and how it will recover some investment return for the lost opportunity associated with contract operation.

(b) *Specific Performance.*—If the supplier provides one of the only sources of input supply or transportation for a project, with other alternatives too costly to form serious choices, or where the price is crucial to project success, the only remedy that may be acceptable to the project sponsor is that of specific performance. Specific performance would require the party in default to perform the contract as agreed. Local counsel should be consulted to learn whether this is an available remedy.

(c) *Alternative Inputs.*—Another remedy is to require that the supplier supply and transport the needed input to the project from other sources if it is unable to perform the contract from the original source.

In India, the prospective private investors are also wary of fuel related risks. The stakeholders namely the transporters, the utilities, the fuel supplier and the government should evolve an integrated and co-ordinated approach towards fuel supply. Thus, it is important to make sure that the FSA is for a considerable length of time and that it ensures supply either from the Indian sector or from the foreign sectors. Additionally attention must be paid to ensure proper protection for compensation of non-supply of fuel and the opportunity for future negotiations of the rate of tariff.

Due Diligence

For lenders to appraise the viability of a project, financing structure, documentation has to hold the test of the due diligence process. This is to confirm the validity of the assumptions of the project sponsor.

The independent engineer and other consultants are generally retained by the project lender with costs paid by the project sponsor. They are "independent" in the sense that they are disinterested parties, capable of rendering objective opinions.

Typical due Diligence Deliberations in a Project Financing Structure

The Project Sponsor

While conducting due diligence, lenders (through their advisors, consultants, and/or engineers) have to look into the financial status of the project sponsor. They also need to analyse the ownership interest of the sponsor in the project. Additionally the past experience of the sponsor apart from the managerial control structure, capital contribution and the limited recourse liability of each sponsor needs to be validated upon.

The Site of the Project

The terrain and location of the project, terrain of access roads, fuel storage areas, implications of the mountains, jungles, rivers, lakes and other topographical characteristics and other important elements must be studied carefully with an eye on the viability of the project.

Political, Economical & Legal Considerations

Privatization programmes, tax regulations, foreign exchange regulations, guarantees and profit repatriation laws of the host country are to be examined. Lenders must also deliberate upon the specific regulations applicable to the particular project and the need for host country approvals, permits, licenses, concessions, filings and other government actions which may be required in relation to the project.

Financial Parameters

The project construction budget as well as the financial projections should include cost of site development, construction, equipment installation and interest during construction. Additionally, foreign exchange commitments, fuel price fluctuations, inflation and raw material escalation should also be taken into account.

Construction Commitments

Construction cost overruns, change the funding obligations of the project sponsors. Also, the funding commitments of each of the project sponsors during the project development and the construction period should be reflected in the project documentation. This is also true for conditions to these funding commitments.

If the project is in need of additional money due to cost overruns, there should be additional credit facility available. The conditions for use of such funds with or without additional equity contributions, need to be mentioned or explained in detail.

Lenders should also list the potential cost overruns not addressed in firm price contracts, contingency funding obligations or other support mechanisms.

It is preferable to enter into firm price, fixed completion date construction contracts with performance guarantees. The ability, experience and scope of work of the contractor with respect to a particular project are also valuable selection criteria. The liquidated damages to be paid for delays and contractor's failure to perform at guaranteed levels should be compensatory and not retributory in nature.

Input Agreements

The input price should be reasonably based on supply sources. If the input supply is owned or regulated by the government, the conditions under which the prices could change should be mentioned. The delivery schedule, price and damages should be realistic. Also liquidated damages should be stipulated in case of non-delivery or late delivery, as a measure of compensation only, for any increased input costs.

Off-take Agreements

The capacity component of the price should be sufficient to pay for debt service and other costs while the operation component for the variable costs. If the off-take purchaser is owned and controlled by the host government, the conditions under which prices may change or the contract may be liable to be cancelled should be mentioned. The contract term should be sufficient enough to provide revenue predictability of the project for debt service and operating costs payments.

General Contract Review

The dispute resolution process should result in prompt resolution of disputes. The contract should be enforceable and permit collateral assignment to the project lender and subsequent assignment to a purchaser of the project in a foreclosure proceeding.

Environmental Considerations

The technology and the methodology used should be in keeping with the local and the World Bank environmental standards.

Critique

In order to have a relatively, smooth functioning project, it is felt that governments should be involved in some indirect capacity, for example, as the grantor of a concession to run the works, or as a guarantor in case of foreign exchange fluctuations.

Generally, cross border operations involve the host country government as an active participant, specially in India where the markets are being gradually opened up. Projects have to negotiate actively and on a regular basis with either the Central or the State Government or with both. In such cases, regulatory approvals gain primary importance.

The Project sponsors should realize that project documentation has to be sold as a viable package to the lenders. In this respect, if the project documentation has reached final negotiation stage then it becomes more difficult to re-negotiate substantial clauses on behalf of the lenders, should defects be noticed at a later stage.

With the proliferation of securitization, concepts of how to group cash flows from projects are constantly changing and opening up new sources of capital. Where project finance has focused on financing for a single facility, the pooling available with securitization techniques allows what is in effect a capital market subordinated debt to replace what historically would have been equity capital.

In short, due diligence provides the reviewing techniques to check on the different financing techniques used in the project finance structure. To achieve success, parties and their advisors must understand and use the broad range of financing techniques available and mix and match the same to achieve optimal results.

PRECEDENTS

(1) *ALPHA* COAL (PVT.) LIMITED

AND

(2) *BETA* (BVI) LIMITED

AGREEMENT

for the

SALE AND PURCHASE AND DELIVERY OF COAL

THIS AGREEMENT is made on

BETWEEN

Alpha COAL (Pvt) LIMITED ("Supplier") (registered in .... with number ? whose registered office is at ....)

AND

Beta (BVI) LIMITED ("Purchaser"), a company incorporated in the .... with its registered office at ....

WHEREAS:

(A) The Purchaser through its fully owned subsidiary .... is developing the Facility in .... (Address) in the State of ...., India;

(B) The Purchaser requires quantities of coking coal of a certain quality in order to test, commission and operate the .... Plant;

(C) The Supplier has access to quantities of coal of a suitable quality from the Designated Mines; and

(D) The Supplier has agreed to transport by vessel, deliver and sell to the Purchaser and the Purchaser has agreed to purchase from the Supplier, quantities of coking coal and thermal coal, in accordance with the terms and subject to the obligations contained in this Agreement.

IT IS AGREED as follows:

Article 1: Definitions and Interpretation

Definitions.—In this Agreement the following words and/or phrases shall have the following meanings, unless the context requires otherwise:

"Annual Delivery Schedule": is defined in clause 6.3(a) and in the form attached to Schedule 1, Part II;

"Basic Quantity": the sum of the Firm Quantity and the Optional Quantity (if any);

"Binding Certificate of Analysis": the final and binding Certificate of Analysis as specified in clause 10.3;

"Certificate of Analysis": a certificate issued by the Independent Analyst, the Supplier's Analyst or the Umpire Analyst, issued pursuant to clause 10, in each case substantially in the form of Schedule 3, setting out the tested quality and specification of a Shipment supplied under this Agreement;

"Coal": blended coking coal from the Designated Mines, as per specifications enclosed.

"Coke Plant": the Purchaser's .... production plant and associated facilities to be developed, constructed, equipped, installed, tested, commissioned, operated and maintained by the Purchaser at .... (address), ..., India;

"Conditions Precedent": the conditions precedent listed in clause 3.2;

"Contract Period": the period commencing on the Effective Date and, subject to any extensions pursuant to clause 2 and clause 13.11, expiring 15 years thereafter;

"Contract Year": a period of twelve (12) consecutive months commencing, in the case of the first such year, on the Effective Date and in the case of any subsequent year, on the day immediately following the last day of the preceding Contract Year;

"Delivery Schedule": is defined in clause 6.3(b)(ii) and in the form attached to Schedule I, Part III;

"Designated Mines" : the .... and .... mines in ....;

"Direct Agreement": an agreement containing assurances [from the Supplier and the Purchaser] to the Lenders, including, without limitation, consent to the assignment by way of security of this Agreement to the Lenders and the right of the Lenders or their nominee to step-in and perform the obligations of the Purchaser under this Agreement;

"Discharge": has the meaning given in clause 8.14 (and the words "discharged", "undischarged" and "discharge" shall be construed accordingly);

"Discharge Port": the port currently being constructed by ? at .... [Address] in the State of ...., India or if notified by the Purchaser to the Supplier, the port at .... in the State of ...., or such other port notified in writing by the Purchaser to the Supplier;

"...................": the lawful currency from time to time of the .... (place);

"*Effective Date*": the date on which the Provisional Taking over Certificate is issued in respect of the .... Plant;

"*Excess Quantity*": is defined in clause 5.3;

"*ETA*": the estimated time of arrival as stated in clause 8.11;

"*Event of Default*": is defined in clause 14;

"*Expert*": is defined in clause 20.6;

"*Facility*": the Coke Plant and the Power Plant together;

"*Financial Close*": the date when all conditions precedent to the availability of funds to be borrowed by the Purchaser to finance the Facility have been satisfied;

"*Firm Quantity*": is defined in clause 5.2(a);

"*Force Majeure*": is defined in clause 13;

"*Independent Analyst*": any internationally reputable coal inspection authority (other than the Supplier's Analyst or the Umpire Analyst) appointed jointly by the Supplier and the Purchaser for testing the quality and specification of each Shipment at the Discharge Port pursuant to clause 10.1;

"*Initial Delivery Date*": the date on which the Supplier is obliged to commence delivery of the Start-Up Tonnage pursuant to the Start-Up Schedule under clause 6.2;

"*Jetty Operational Requirements*": the requirements for use of the Purchaser's berth at the Discharge Port, as stipulated by the Purchaser, the port authority and/or any other relevant authority at the Discharge Port;

"*JSM Price*": the annual Japanese coking coal market price in ....(amount) per tonne for Australian coking coal under long term contract as certified by an independent Auditor.

"*Laytime*": the time available for the Purchaser to discharge coal from a vessel, in accordance with clause 8;

"*Lenders*": those banks and financial institutions from time to time providing loans to the Purchaser in connection with the development and operation of the Facility;

"*Lenders' Agent*": .... and .... Limited carrying on a banking business from its branch at .... (address)

"*Loading Port*": .... ;

"*Net CV*": [ ];

"*Nomination*": is defined in clause 6.5;

"*Notice of Readiness*": a notice tendered by the master of a vessel or its agent to the Purchaser to the effect that the vessel is in all respects ready to unload a Shipment in or substantially in the form attached at Schedule 1 Part IV;

"*Optional Quantity*": is defined in clause 5.2(b);

"Power Plant": the Purchaser's 100MW cogeneration power plant to be developed, constructed, equipped, installed, tested, commissioned, operated and maintained by the Purchaser at .... (address), ..., India;

"Price": is defined in clause 11;

"Provisional Taking over Certificate": as defined in the engineering, procurement and construction contract for the .... Plant;

"Public Holiday": such days listed in Schedule 4;

"Purchaser's Sample": a sample of Coal of not less than (500 grammes) which is forwarded to the Purchaser for testing and analysis;

"Purchaser's Warranties": the representations and warranties set out in clause 17.1;

"Representative Sample": a sample of Coal of not less than [500 grammes] from a Shipment for testing and analysis by the Umpire Analyst;

"Rejection Limits": the quality parameters entitled "Rejection Limits" set out in Schedule 2;

"Shipment": a cargo of Coal delivered or to be delivered over the applicable vessel's rail to the Purchaser at the Discharge Port;

"Specification": the specification for the Coal set out in Schedule 2;

[*"Standard Tonne"*: the quantity of Coal measured in Tonnes having a heat content (determined on the basis of Net CV) of [ ] kJ;]

"Start-Up Tonnage": the quantity of Coal stipulated in clause 5.1;

"Start-Up Period": the period commencing on the Initial Delivery Date and ending on the day preceding the Effective Date;

"Start-Up Schedule": as referred to in clause 6.2(b) and substantially in the form attached to Schedule 1, Part 1;

"Supplier's Analyst": any internationally reputable coal inspection authority (other than the Independent Analyst or the Umpire Analyst) designated by the Supplier and approved by the Purchaser (such approval not to be unreasonably withheld) to test the quality and specification of the Supplier's Sample;

"Supplier's Sample": a sample of Coal of not less than [500 grams] which is forwarded to the Supplier for testing and analysis;

"Supplier's Warranties": the representations and warranties set out in clause 17.2;

"Surveyor": an internationally reputable marine surveyors firm appointed by the Purchaser and approved by the Supplier (such approval not to be unreasonably withheld) for the weighing of Coal at the Discharge Port;

"Tonne": metric tonne (1000 kilograms);

"Umpire Analyst": any internationally reputable coal inspection authority (other than the Independent Analyst and the Supplier's Analyst) appointed jointly by the Supplier and the Purchaser for the testing of the Representative Sample;

"weather working day": any working day in the State of ...., India, excluding a day on which the Discharge Port's operations have been suspended due to bad weather conditions pursuant to written notice given by the authorities which operate the Discharge Port.

1.2 *Interpretation:* In this Agreement, unless the context otherwise requires:

(a) references to persons shall 'include individuals, bodies corporate, unincorporated associations and partnerships;

(b) the masculine gender shall include the feminine and neuter and the singular shall include the plural and *vice versa*;

(c) headings are inserted for convenience only and shall not affect the construction or interpretation of this Agreement;

(d) references to clauses and Schedules are references to clauses of and Schedules to this Agreement, as amended from time to time;

(e) references to Supplier and Purchaser shall include any successor in title or permitted assign thereof in accordance with this Agreement;

(f) references to any law or act of parliament or any regulation made pursuant to any act of Parliament or to any other directive shall mean such law, act, regulation or directive as from time to time amended, re-enacted or consolidated and including any provision enacted in substitution therefor;

(g) references to a day shall mean a day of the week, including a Saturday or Sunday and to a working day shall mean any day (other than a Saturday or Sunday or a Public Holiday).

Article 2: Commencement and Duration

Initial Term.—This Agreement shall come into force on the date of execution of this Agreement and unless terminated earlier in accordance with its terms or at the Purchaser's written request, extended for a further period up to 15 years, shall terminate automatically on expiry of the Contract Period.

Article 3: Conditions Precedent

3.1 *Exceptions to Conditions Precedent.*—The provisions of this clause 3 shall not apply to clause 1 (Definitions and Interpretation), this clause 3, clause 4.2(c) (Designated Mines), clause 16 (Announcements and Confidentiality), clause 19 (Notices), clause 20 (Governing Law and Dispute Resolution) and clause 21 (Direct Agreement).

3.2 *The Conditions Precedent.*—The obligations of the parties hereunder shall be conditional on the occurrence of the date on which the last of the conditions precedent to be satisfied is satisfied. The conditions precedent are as follows:

(a) written certification by the Lenders' Agent of Financial Close; and

(b) written certification [addressed to the Purchaser] by [an independent consultant approved by the Purchaser] that the recoverable reserves of Coal from the Dedicated Mines are sufficient to enable the Supplier to fulfil its obligations under this Agreement.

3.3 *Supplier to co-operate.*—The Supplier shall co-operate with the Purchaser and the Lenders' Agent to enable the Purchaser to satisfy the Lenders' reasonable conditions precedent to Financial Close to the extent that such conditions precedent relate, either directly or indirectly, to the Supplier and/or this Agreement.

3.4 *Drop dead date.*—If any of the Conditions Precedent have not been fulfilled on or before (....................) or such other date as may be agreed in writing between the parties, this Agreement shall lapse and be of no further force and effect and the parties shall have no further rights against each other and the parties shall be released from all further obligations under this Agreement but without prejudice to any rights or obligations which may already have accrued prior to such date.

3.5 *Financial Close.*—Until Financial Close occurs the Purchaser shall, from time to time, keep the Supplier informed of the likely date of Financial Close.

Article 4: Sale and Purchase

4.1 *Sale and purchase.*—The Supplier shall transport by vessel, deliver and sell to the Purchaser, and the Purchaser shall purchase, take delivery of, and pay for Coal in quantities and of the quality determined under and otherwise in accordance with and subject to the terms of this Agreement.

4.2 *Designated Mines.*—The Supplier hereby undertakes to the Purchaser that it shall:

(1) only obtain Coal for sale under this Agreement to the Purchaser from the Designated Mines;

(2) for the duration of the Contract Period, maintain sufficient quantities of Coal to enable it to supply the Purchaser with the quantities of Coal committed under this Agreement and that it has no other agreements or arrangements, and will not enter into any other agreements or arrangements which will prejudice its ability to supply such quantities of Coal to the Purchaser under this Agreement;

(3) on or before (....................) procure a written report from [an independent coal consultant approved by the Purchaser] as to the extent of the uncommitted recoverable reserves of Coal from the Dedicated Mines; and

(4) at least 30 days before the fifth (5th) and tenth (10th) anniversary of the Effective Date, provide a written report by [an independent coal consultant approved by the Purchaser] stating that the recoverable reserves of Coal from the Dedicated Mines are sufficient to enable the Supplier to continue to fulfil its obligations under this Agreement for the remainder of the Contract Period.

4.3 *Legal title.*—The Supplier undertakes to the Purchaser (on an ongoing basis) that the Supplier will have full legal and beneficial title to all Coal delivered and, on delivery, the Coal delivered will be free from any liens, charges, encumbrances, equities and adverse claims whatsoever and the Supplier hereby indemnifies the Purchaser from and against any losses, damages and expenses (including legal fees) suffered as a result of any breach of this undertaking.

Article 5: Quantities

5.1 *Start-up Tonnage.*—During the Start-Up Period, the Supplier shall sell to the Purchaser and the Purchaser shall buy from the Supplier (....................) Tonnes of Coal (the "Start-Up Tonnage").

5.2 *Contract Quantity.*—During the Contract Period the following shall apply:

(1) Supplier shall sell to the Purchaser and the Purchaser shall buy from the Supplier (....................) Tonnes of Coal each Contract Year (the "Firm Quantity") during the Contract Period.

(2) In addition to the Firm Quantity, the Supplier shall, if requested, sell to the Purchaser (....................) Tonnes of Coal each Contract Year (the "Optional Quantity") during the Contract Period.

5.3 *Excess Quantity.*—In addition to the Basic Quantity, the Supplier shall, if requested, use reasonable endeavours to sell an amount of Coal not exceeding (....................) Tonnes of Coal each Contract Year (the "Excess Quantity") during the Contract Period.

5.4 *Notices.*—If the Purchaser wishes to exercise its entitlement, for a Contract Year, either under clause 5.2(b) and/or clause 5.3 it shall give notice to that effect to the Supplier not later than .... months before the start of that Contract Year.

5.5 *Adjustments.*—The Firm Quantity which the Purchaser is obliged to purchase in each Contract Year shall be reduced by:

(1) any quantity of Coal (in .... Tonnes) of which the Purchaser was prevented from taking delivery due to an event of *Force Majeure* or any default or breach of the Supplier during that Contract Year; and

(2) any quantity of Coal (in .... Tonnes) which the Supplier failed to make available for delivery to the Purchaser due to an event of *Force Majeure* during that Contract Year.

Article 6: Scheduling

6.1 *Transportation and Delivery.*—The Supplier shall transport and deliver Coal to the purchaser in accordance with the provisions of this clause.

6.2 *Start-up Schedule.*—The process for determining the Schedules for delivery of Coal during the Start-Up period shall be as follows:

(1) Not less than .... months before the Start-Up date the Purchaser shall submit to the Supplier a statement with details of the Start-Up Date, the quantity of Coal it requires during the Start-Up Period and the dates on which such deliveries are required to be delivered at the Discharge Port.

(2) Within .... month of the date of such statement the Supplier shall provide to the Purchaser a proposed Start-Up Schedule showing the shipment schedule for the Start-Up Tonnage.

(3) Within .... days of the date of such schedule the Purchaser shall notify the Supplier of any requested changes to the proposed Start-Up Schedule (if any).

(4) The Supplier shall use reasonable endeavours to accommodate the changes requested by the Purchaser and within .... days after receipt of such requested changes, the Supplier shall notify the Purchaser the extent to which it is able to accept the request for change and shall give reasons to the Purchaser for any changes not accepted.

(5) Within .... days thereafter the Supplier shall submit a final Start-Up Schedule which shall be firm and, in accordance with and subject to the terms of this Agreement, binding on the parties and if the Supplier fails to submit such a schedule the schedule provided in accordance with clause 6.2 as amended by the Purchaser's notification pursuant to clause 6.2 shall apply.

6.3 *Contract Period Schedule.*—The process for determining the schedules for delivery of Coal during each Contract Year shall be as follows:

(1) *Yearly and quarterly quantities.*—The process for each Contract Year shall be as follows:

   (1) Not less than .... months before the start of each Contract Year, the Purchaser shall provide the Supplier with its expected requirements for Firm Quantities, Optional Quantities and Excess Quantities of Coal for that Contract Year and the dates on which such deliveries are required to be delivered at the Discharge Port, broken down into quarters (commencing at the beginning of the first Contract Year).

   (2) Within .... days of receipt of such notice from the Purchaser, the Supplier shall provide the Purchaser with a provisional Annual Delivery Schedule, showing the Shipment schedule for such quantities, broken down into quarters.

   (3) Within .... days of the date of such Annual Delivery Schedule, the Purchaser shall notify the Supplier of any requested changes to the proposed Annual Delivery Schedule (if any).

   (4) The Supplier shall give due consideration, and use reasonable endeavours, to accommodate the reasonable changes requested by the Purchaser and within .... days after receipt of such requested changes, the Supplier shall notify the Purchaser the extent to which it is able to accept the request for change and shall give reasons to the Purchaser for any changes not accepted.

(2) *Monthly Quantities.*—The process for each month during a Contract Year shall be as follows:

   (1) Not less than .... before the start of each month during a Contract Year, the Purchaser shall provide the Supplier with its expected requirements for Coal for that month and the dates on which such deliveries are required to be delivered at the Discharge Port for the following month.

   (2) Within .... days of receipt of such notice from the Purchaser, the Supplier shall provide the Purchaser with a

provisional Delivery Schedule, showing the Shipment schedule for such quantities for the following month.

(3) Within .... days of the date of such Delivery Schedule, the Purchaser shall notify the Supplier of any requested changes to the proposed Delivery Schedule (if any).

(4) The Supplier shall use reasonable endeavours, to accommodate the reasonable changes requested by the Purchaser and within .... days after receipt of such requested changes, the Supplier shall notify the Purchaser the extent to which it is able to accept the request for change and shall give reasons to the Purchaser for any changes not accepted.

(5) Within .... days thereafter the Supplier shall submit a final Delivery Schedule which shall be firm and, in accordance with and subject to the terms of this Agreement, binding on the parties and if the Supplier fails to submit such a schedule the schedule provided in accordance with clause 6.3(b)(ii) as amended by the Purchaser's notification pursuant to clause 6.3(b)(iii) shall apply.

6.4 *Variations.*—If the Purchaser anticipates that it will be prevented or restricted from receiving any vessel at the Discharge Port or from accepting or otherwise receiving shipments, the purchaser shall promptly give the Supplier a written request to vary any of the schedules referred to in this clause 6, and the supplier shall use its reasonable endeavours to revise the relevant delivery schedule to address the concerns of the purchaser.

6.5 *Nomination Notice.*—Not later than .... days after the finalisation of the Start-Up Schedule and each Delivery Schedule in accordance with this clause, the Supplier shall provide to the Purchaser a Nomination in which the following shall, without limitation, be specified:

(1) The name, the year built and flag of the vessel;

(2) the ETA at the Discharge Port; and

(3) the quantity of Coal to be discharged.

The Seller shall also forward this information to the relevant port authorities at the Discharge Port.

6.6 *Permissible variation.*—The actual quantity of Coal to be loaded onto the vessel at the Loading Port may vary from the amounts notified by the Supplier to the Purchaser in the Nomination by plus or minus .... percent.

6.7 *Departure.*—As soon as possible after the vessel has sailed from the Loading Port, the Supplier shall (or shall cause the master of the vessel to) notify the Purchaser by radio (or any other means of telecommunications as the Purchaser may approve) of:

(1) the name of the vessel;

(2) the ETA at the Discharge Port at no later than .... days, ... hours, ... hours and .... hours prior to such ETA;

(3) the quantity of Coal on board the vessel.

6.8 *Shipping documents.*—The supplier shall, as soon as possible after payment by the Purchaser for a Shipment, submit to the Purchaser the following documents:

(a) original bill of lading in triplicate;

(b) certificate of weight in triplicate;

(c) certificate of analysis of quality in triplicate; and

(d) certificate of origin in triplicate.

Article 7: Property and Risk

Passing of Property and Risk.—Risk for the loss of Coal and title to the Coal shall transfer to the Purchaser from the Supplier as and when the Coal passes over the vessel's rail at the Discharge Port.

Article 8: Transportation and Delivery

8.1 *Vessels.*—The coal shall be transported at the Supplier's expense in bulk on board a Panamax ungeared vessel with a capacity of between (...................... dwt) and [... dwt] which is designed for continuous cargo discharge, suitable to enter berth, discharge and leave the Discharge Port [with self trimming facilities suitable for grab discharge and mechanical trimming].

8.2 *Age of Vessels.*—The supplier shall ensure that any vessel used to transport and deliver the Coal shall not be older than (....................) years from the date of its manufacture.

8.3 *Approvals.*—The supplier shall ensure that vessels used pursuant to this Agreement shall comply with all laws and governmental approvals applicable to the loading, transportation, delivery and discharge of the Coal. Any additional costs arising from complying with or the failure to comply with these requirements shall be for the sole and exclusive account of the Supplier.

8.4 *Night Discharge.*—The supplier shall ensure any vessel used is equipped with lights and other equipment necessary to permit discharge at night at no cost to the purchaser.

8.5 *Berths.*—For the delivery of the coal the purchaser shall provide, or procure, free of charge, a berth or berths at the Discharge Port which vessels used by the Supplier in accordance with this clause 8 can safely reach and leave and where they can lie and unload safely afloat.

8.6 *Jetty Operational Requirements.*—The Supplier will at all times ensure that vessels berthed at the Discharge Port will comply in all respects with the Jetty Operational Requirements.

8.7 *Shifting berth.*—The Purchaser shall be responsible for any expense of shifting berth after initial berthing unless such shift is for reasons related to the Supplier or the Supplier's vessel.

8.8 *Delivery.*—For the supplies of coal covered by this Agreement, the Supplier shall load each Shipment at the Loading Port.

8.9 *Export Licences and Authorisations.*—The supplier shall obtain at its own risk and cost any export licence or other official authorisation and carry out all customs formalities necessary for the export of Coal.

8.10 *Costs of Shipment.*—The supplier shall pay all costs relating to each Shipment until its discharge at the Discharge Port.

8.11 *Arrival.*—On arrival of a vessel within (....................) km of the Discharge Port the Supplier shall advise the Purchaser of the ETA at the Discharge Port, or ETA at the anchorage offshore if the Discharge Port is occupied with other vessels.

8.12 *Notice of Readiness.*—Notice of Readiness may be given free pratique, between 0800 and 1600 hours during any day, Sundays and holidays included, after arrival of the vessel at the Discharge Port. If given orally, written Notice of Readiness shall be given promptly after the vessel has berthed at the Discharge Port.

8.13 *Unavailability of Purchaser's Berth.*—If the purchaser's berth at the Discharge Port is not available on the vessel's arrival at or off the Discharge Port the vessel shall be entitled to give Notice of Readiness on arrival at the customary offshore anchorage or waiting place at any time as if the vessel were in berth and in all respects ready for discharging.

8.14 *Discharge.*—The purchaser shall carry out unloading of each Shipment at the Discharge Port and discharge shall have taken place when the vessel is at a berth nominated by the Purchaser and the Shipment has been unloaded from the vessel.

8.15 *Rate of discharge.*—The Purchaser shall be responsible for the unloading of each vessel at the Discharge Port at [rate of unloading/Tonnes] per weather working day. The rate of discharge may be increased by the Purchaser.

8.16 *Import licences.*—The purchaser shall obtain at its own risk and cost any import licence or other official authorisation and carry out all customs formalities necessary for the importation of the Coal into India at the Discharge Port.

8.17 *Laytime.*—Subject to clause 8.19 below, Laytime shall commence twelve (12) hours after written Notice of Readiness has been received by the Purchaser in accordance with clause 8.12 whether or not the vessel is in berth provided that if a vessel tenders Notice of Readiness under clause 8.13 and, after berthing at the Discharge Port the vessel is found not to be ready to discharge, all Laytime used shall be cancelled and Laytime shall commence from the time the vessel is in fact ready to discharge.

8.18 *Shifting Anchorage.*—Time spent shifting from anchorage to the Purchaser's berth at the Discharge Port shall not count as Laytime.

8.19 *Laytime to Commence on Weather Working Day.*—Laytime shall only commence on a weather working day and if, pursuant to clause 8.17 Laytime is due to commence on a day other than a weather working day, it shall be deemed to have commenced at 0800 hours on the next day that is a weather working day.

8.20 *Ceasing of Laytime.*—Laytime shall cease;

8.21 *Interruptions of Laytime.*—The following, without limitation, shall be interruptions of Laytime and shall not be taken into account in calculating the total time taken to discharge the vessel:

(1) All periods when coal cannot be discharged as a result of defects in the vessel, the cargo is inaccessible or discharge is stopped to move ship's equipment out of the way;

(2) All periods when the master of the ship orders that discharge should cease, including, without limitation, on account of bad weather conditions;

(3) All periods when the Purchaser determines that weather conditions make it unsafe to operate the Discharge Port's unloading equipment;

(4) All periods when discharge of coal cannot be started because customs or health officials are not present at the Discharge Port [for the reason that it is a Public Holiday];

(5) All periods when discharge of coal cannot be started or continued due to unavailability of shipping documents required to be provided by the Supplier to the Purchaser; and

(6) All periods of *Force Majeure* pursuant to clause 13;

(7) [other]

8.22 *Demurrage.*—In the event that Laytime has expired and the coal delivered to the purchaser by the supplier remains undischarged either in part or in whole, the purchaser shall be liable to pay the supplier demurrage at the rate of (....................) day or *pro rata*. This rate will be reviewed annually [at the time of the annual price negotiations (in clause 11)].

8.23 *Force Majeure and Demurrage.*—If the Purchaser is incurring demurrage in accordance with clause 8.22 when an event of *Force Majeure* occurs the Purchaser shall only be liable to pay (....................)% of the daily demurrage rate (pursuant to clause 8.22) for the period of *Force Majeure*.

8.24 *Remedies for Demurrage to be exhaustive.*—The remedies available to the Supplier, pursuant to clauses 8.22 and 8.23 for delays incurred in discharging a vessel shall be exhaustive and the purchaser shall not be liable to pay to or indemnify the supplier against any further costs, damages or expenses.

8.25 *Despatch.*—In the event that the Purchaser discharges the Coal at a rate in excess of the discharge rate (in accordance with clause 8.15) the Supplier shall be liable to pay despatch to the Purchaser at the daily demurrage rate (pursuant to clause 8.22) per day or *pro rata*. This rate will be reviewed annually [at the time of the annual price negotiations [in clause 11]].

8.26 *Invoicing of Demurrage and Despatch.*—Demurrage and despatch payments shall be reflected in the invoice(s) submitted in accordance with clause 11.

8.27 *Deadfreight.*—The purchaser shall not be liable to pay to the Supplier any deadfreight incurred by the supplier, whether or not relating to shipments pursuant to this agreement.

Article 9: Quality

9.1 *Specification.*—The coal to be transported, delivered at the Discharge Port and sold by the supplier to the purchaser under this Agreement shall conform to the Specification, shall be trimmed and shall be as free as is practicably possible of foreign matter (including, without limitation, wood, iron, non-ferrous materials, or other foreign materials from whatever source).

9.2 *Inspection at Loading Port.*—The supplier shall, before loading any Shipment at the Loading Port, arrange for such Shipment to be quality tested by [an internationally reputable coal inspection authority] and shall promptly notify the Purchaser of the results of such inspection.

9.3 *Rejection at Loading Port.*—If, on receiving notification under clause 9.2 above, the purchaser determines that such Shipment intended to be loaded by the supplier at the Loading Port does not conform to the Specification the purchaser may, but shall not be obliged to, reject and not purchase that Shipment.

9.4 *Rejection following Binding Certificate of Analysis.*—If the supplier delivers or tenders for delivery any shipment that does not conform to the Specification (as evidenced by the Binding Certificate of Analysis pursuant to clause 10.3) the purchaser may, but shall not be obliged to, reject and not purchase the coal that falls outside the rejection limits.

9.5 *Rejection of Coal from Mines other than Designated Mines.*—Should the Supplier sell to the Purchaser, pursuant to this Agreement, coal which is found to be sourced otherwise than from the Designated Mines, then the Purchaser may without prejudice to any other right or remedy which the Purchaser may have, reject and not purchase that coal.

9.6 *Reversion of Risk and Title.*—In the event that the purchaser rejects any Shipment, risk and title to such Shipment will, if it has passed to the Purchaser, revert to the Supplier.

9.7 *Notification of Rejection.*—In the event that the purchaser rejects any coal (pursuant to either clauses 9.3, 9.4 or 9.5) it shall give notice of such intent to the Supplier (such notice, if given orally, to be confirmed in writing thereafter) and the Supplier shall, at the Purchaser's option:

(a) deliver a substitute shipment within .... days of the notice of rejection; and

(b) immediately, at its own expense, receive the shipment and shall be liable for and shall immediately repay to the purchaser all sums of money expended by the Purchaser in respect of the rejected coal and indemnify the purchaser against all costs, losses and damages sustained by the purchaser arising out of or in connection with the Shipment rejected by the purchaser under clause 9.3, 9.4 or 9.5.

In addition, in no circumstances will the purchaser be liable to pay the Supplier for any such coal rejected.

Article 10: Measurement/Testing

10.1 *Quality Testing.*—In relation to each Shipment and as soon as possible after the arrival of each Shipment at the Discharge Port, the Supplier shall procure, at the Supplier's expense, that the Independent Analyst shall:

(1) prior to discharge, take .... samples of coal from each Shipment using mechanical sampling equipment made available at the Discharge Port by the Purchaser, at the Purchaser's expense, which has been independently certified as accurate and bias tested in accordance with the methods laid down by the [International Standards Organisation];

(2) retain one of the three samples referred to in clause 10.1(a) above in a sealed container as a Representative Sample for a period of not less than .... months from the date of discharge of each Shipment;

(3) prepare a supplier's sample from the second of the three samples referred to in 10.1(a) above and, at the supplier's expense, forward the supplier's sample to the supplier by (air freight);

(4) prepare a purchaser's sample from the third of the three samples referred to in clause 10.1(a) above and conduct such tests and analysis on the Purchaser's Sample as are in accordance with the methods laid down by the [International Standards Organisation]; and

(5) complete and forward to the supplier and the purchaser a Certificate of Analysis relating to the Purchaser's Sample.

10.2 *The Supplier's Analyst.*—The supplier may appoint, with the approval of the purchaser (such approval not to be unreasonably withheld), a Supplier's Analyst, who the Supplier may require to:

(1) conduct tests on the supplier's sample in accordance with the methods laid down by the [International Standards Organisation]; and

(2) complete and forward to the Purchaser a Certificate of Analysis in relation to the Supplier's Sample.

10.3 *Binding Certificate of Analysis.*—If, as regard the specification, the Certificate of Analysis prepared by the Independent Analyst and the Certificate of Analysis issued by the supplier's analyst are consistent, then the Certificate of Analysis prepared by the Independent Analyst shall constitute the Binding Certificate of Analysis for such Shipment.

10.4 *Consultation in the Event of Inconsistency.*—If, as regards the Specification, the Certificate of Analysis prepared by the Independent Analyst and the Certificate of Analysis issued by the Supplier's Analyst are not consistent, then the Purchaser and the Supplier shall promptly consult to determine the reasons for such inconsistency and seek to agree which Certificate of Analysis should prevail.

10.5 *Determination by Umpire Analyst.*—If the Supplier and the Purchaser are unable to agree which Certificate of Analysis should prevail either party may by notice to the other require the Umpire Analyst (appointed jointly by the agreement of the Supplier and the Purchaser) to analyse and test the

Representative Sample in accordance with the procedures laid down by the (International Standards Organisation) and, as soon as reasonably practicable thereafter, issue a Certificate of Analysis in relation to the Representative Sample, provided always that neither party shall have the right to require such further analysis by the Umpire Analyst after a period of (......................) days from the date of arrival of the Shipment at the Discharge Port.

10.6 *Determination by Umpire Analyst Final.*—The Umpire Analyst's Certificate of Analysis shall constitute a Binding Certificate of Analysis.

10.7 *Analysis by Lenders' Representative.*—Without prejudice to any of the above provisions, the Purchaser shall have the right to nominate a representative of the Lenders at any time to attend and observe the testing and analysing procedure and [conduct its own tests] at any time, and at the Purchaser's expense, at the Discharge Port.

10.8 *Weight.*—The purchaser shall procure, at the Purchaser's expense, in relation to each shipment that:

(1) the surveyor shall determine by a draft survey at the Discharge Port the weight of each Shipment. (The weight shall be determined at the Discharge Port by means of a survey of the vessel's draft before and after discharge); and

(2) the surveyor shall issue a draft survey Certificate of Weight for each Shipment upon the completion of discharge of the vessel.

10.9 *Certificate of Weight to be Final.*—Subject to clause 10.10 below, the weight shown in the Certificate of Weight for such shipment as provided in clause 10.8(b) above shall be final and binding and relate only to the Coal supplied by the Supplier to the Purchaser.

10.10 *Weighing by Lenders' Representative.*—Without prejudice to any of the above provisions, the purchaser shall have the right to nominate a representative of the lender to attend, observe and test at any time (at the Purchaser's expense) the determination of the weight of each shipment at the Discharge Port.

Article 11: Price

11.1 *Price Components.*—The unit price at which the Supplier shall sell and the Purchaser shall buy each Tonne of Coal under this Agreement shall be equal to the sum of the following:

(1) the Coal price per Tonne calculated in accordance with Schedule [?]; and

(2) the delivery rate, which shall be [...................... (foreign amount) per MT], together referred to as the "Price".

[Note: the Schedule will provide for:

(i) a base price to be adjusted by reference to quality factors;

(ii) yearly indexing of the coal price in accordance with the JSM Price (or such other index, which reflects the .... (name of the country) coal export price);

(iii) yearly indexing of the delivery price in accordance with the (....................... bunker) index.

11.2 *Supplier's Costs.*—Except as specifically set out in this Agreement, all direct and indirect costs for the supply, delivery and transport of Coal to the Discharge Port (including all transportation, weighing, sampling, insurance, handling and mining costs and all taxes) which are incurred by the Supplier in performing its duties hereunder shall be borne exclusively by the Supplier.

11.3 *Substitute index.*—If the .... Price ceases to be published or otherwise ceases to reflect the price of .... coal paid by a majority of .... utilities, the parties shall mutually agree on a substitute index.

Article 12: Invoicing and Payment

12.1 *Delivery of Invoices.*—Within (.....................) days after the date of each shipment, the supplier shall deliver to the Purchaser an invoice calculated according to the Supplier's reasonable and *bona fide* calculations of the Price, setting out the date of the shipment, the quantity of coal delivered to the Purchaser (in tonnes) and the base price based upon the Binding Certificate of Analysis and the Certificate of Weight in accordance with clause 10.

12.2 *Payment of Undisputed Portion.*—Within .... days after receipt of the invoice the purchaser shall pay to the Supplier an amount equal to the undisputed portion of the invoice amount (in accordance with clause 12.3 below) applicable to a Shipment.

12.3 *Invoice Disputes.*—The purchaser shall be entitled to dispute, in good faith and within [....] days of receipt of an invoice, all or any part of an invoice and if the parties fail to agree on such matter the dispute shall be referred to an expert in accordance with clause 20, the decision of whom shall be final and binding on the parties. Any amount determined by the expert to be payable by one party to the other shall immediately be paid, together with interest at a rate of [....%] from the date when payment should originally have been made to the date of payment.

12.4 *Method of Payment.*—All payments to the supplier shall be made by wire transfer in dollars to an account designated in writing from time to time by the supplier.

12.5 *No set-off, etc.*—All payments to be made by either party shall be made without set-off, counterclaim, withholding or deduction for or on account of taxes, except as expressly provided in this Agreement or required by applicable law.

Article 13: *Force Majeure*

13.1 Neither party shall be liable to the other party for any failure or delay in making, receiving and accepting shipments or otherwise performing the terms and provisions or conditions of this Agreement if such performance is hindered or prevented, directly or indirectly by the circumstances listed in clause 13.2, but only if and to the extent that:

(1) such circumstance, despite the exercise of reasonable diligence, cannot be or be caused to be prevented, avoided or removed by such party;

(2) such event materially adversely affects (in cost and/or time) the ability of the party to perform its obligations under this Agreement, and such party has taken all reasonable precautions, due care and reasonable alternative measures in order to avoid the effect of such event on its ability to perform its obligations under this Agreement and to mitigate the consequences thereof; and

(3) such event is not the direct or indirect result of the failure of such party to perform any of its obligations under this Agreement.

13.2 Subject to clauses 13.1 and 13.3, the events of *Force Majeure* shall include:

(1) acts of God;

(2) typhoons, floods or other unusually severe weather conditions;

(3) acts of war (whether declared or undeclared, invasion or civil unrest);

(4) solely with respect to the Purchaser, the Purchaser's inability (despite complying with all legal requirements) to obtain, renew or maintain [any legal and/or governmental approval];

(5) epidemics or quarantine restrictions, earthquakes, explosions, fire and accidents; or

(6) expropriation or compulsory acquisition of any assets of the affected party (including any acquisition resulting from law).

13.3 The following shall not be *Force Majeure* events:

(1) any strike or labour disturbance (except in connection with any lockouts) affecting the Designated Mines the Loading Port or the Discharge Port; or

(2) any delay in or failure to perform of any subcontractor or agent of the supplier except if such delay or failure to perform results from circumstances which would constitute a *Force Majeure* event if such persons were party to this Agreement; or

(3) insufficient supplies of Coal from the Designated Mines;

13.4 *Elimination of Purchaser's requirement for coal.*—The parties expressly agree that performance as aforesaid by the Purchaser shall be deemed to be prevented to the extent that the Purchaser's requirements for Coal are directly or indirectly eliminated or substantially reduced (whether temporarily or permanently) by any of the events listed above.

13.5 *Notification.*—Relief under this clause 13 shall not be given unless the party intending to claim relief has, by notice to the other party within 10 days of becoming aware of an event of *Force Majeure* or if later, within 10 Days of an event of *Force Majeure* having an effect upon the performance of such party's obligations under this Agreement, informed the other party that it desires to claim relief under this clause 13.

13.6 *Contents of notice.*—Such notice referred to in clause 13.5 above shall include such relevant information as is available, including without limitation a description of the event and the date of its occurrence, the effect of such event upon the performance of such party's obligations, the expected duration of such event of *Force Majeure* and its effects and the actions it is taking in order to comply with this clause 13.

13.7 *Outstanding Obligations.*—In the event that due to circumstances covered by the provisions of this clause 13, the full quantities of Coal referred to in clause 5 have not been delivered by the end of the relevant Contract Year, then the Supplier and the Purchaser shall examine together which steps, if any, shall be taken to fulfil any outstanding Shipments, and the terms and conditions to apply thereto, on the principle that such Shipments shall be made up as soon as reasonably practicable at the Purchaser's option.

13.8 *Mitigation.*—As soon as practicable after the occurrence of an event of *Force Majeure*, the party affected shall:

(1) use its best endeavours to prevent and reduce to a minimum and mitigate the effects of the event of *Force Majeure*, including where appropriate and without limitation by having recourse to alternate acceptable sources of services, equipment and materials;

(2) resolve the said *Force Majeure* as rapidly as is reasonable and practicable; and

(3) use its best endeavours to perform its obligations to the maximum extent practicable.

Relief under this clause 13 shall cease to be available to a party if it fails to use such best endeavours.

13.9 *Payment.*—Under no circumstances shall the parties be excused under this clause 13 from their obligations to make payments under the terms of this Agreement.

13.10 *Termination.*—Should performance of any obligation hereunder be delayed or prevented due to an event of *Force Majeure* for a period of more than (....................) then the party, which has not claimed *Force Majeure* relief may terminate this Agreement without penalty.

13.11 *Extension.*—The Contract Period may, at the Purchaser's option, be extended by any period of time during which obligations are suspended due to an event of *Force Majeure*.

Article 14: Termination

14.1 *Events of Default.*—The occurrence of the following shall constitute an Event of Default under this Agreement:

(1) any breach by the supplier of any of its material obligations under this Agreement or any contract made pursuant hereto, including, without limitation:

(1) failure by the supplier to deliver coal in a quantity at least equal to ....% of the aggregate quantity requested by the Purchaser in any two consecutive Shipments or any three Shipments in any Contract Year; or

(2) failure by the supplier to deliver coal conforming to the Specification for any two consecutive Shipments or for more than 33% of the Shipments in any Contract Year; or

(3) failure by the supplier to perform in all respects any other material provision of this Agreement; or

(4) breach in any material respect of the Supplier's Warranties by the Supplier;

(2) any breach by the purchaser of any of its material obligations under this Agreement or any contract made pursuant hereto, including, without limitation, breach in any material respect of the Purchaser's Warranties by the Purchaser;

(3) either party becoming insolvent under any applicable law or making a composition or arrangement with its creditors or putting a proposal to its creditors for a voluntary arrangement for a composition of its debts or a scheme of arrangement or on the presentation of a petition that either party be put into liquidation or administration or on the passing by either party of a resolution putting the other party into voluntary liquidation (other than for the purposes of amalgamation or reconstruction) or on the appointment of an administrator, a provisional liquidator, a receiver, manager or an administrative receiver or on the occurrence of an event which would result in the crystallisation of any floating charge over the business undertaking, property or assets or any part thereof of either party, or on the dissolution of either party; or

(4) either party ceasing or threatening to cease to carry on business; or

(5) any distress, execution or other process being issued, levied or enforced upon the business, undertaking, property or assets or any part thereof of either party; or

(6) a petition being presented or a meeting being convened for the purpose of considering a resolution for the making of an administration order, the winding-up, bankruptcy, or dissolution of either party; or

(7) any act or omission of a party or of its officers, employees or agents which shall in the opinion of the other party in any way prejudice the interests of the first party or bring the name of the first party into disrepute; or

(8) any event analogous to any of the foregoing occurring in any jurisdiction.

14.2 *Notice.*—On the occurrence and during the continuance of an Event of Default the non-defaulting party shall, if it wishes to terminate this Agreement, give .... days' written notice to the defaulting party specifying the Event of Default and if the Event of Default is capable of remedy such notice shall require it to be remedied within .... days of the date of the notice. If the Event of Default is not capable of remedy or, where the Event of Default is capable of remedy but is not remedied within the cure period, the non-defaulting may terminate on giving not less than .... working days' notice.

14.3 *Notice to Lenders.*—Termination of this Agreement by the Supplier shall not be effective unless the Supplier, at the same time, provides a copy of the notice in clause 14.2 to the Lenders' Agent and the Lenders' Agent have been given the opportunity to cure the Event of Default giving rise to the Supplier's termination right in accordance with the requirements of the Direct Agreement.

14.4 *Supplier's Liability for Costs.*—In the event of any termination resulting from the default by the Supplier, the Supplier shall be liable to the Purchaser for any costs incurred by the Purchaser in connection with the purchase of coal for a price in excess of the amount the Purchaser would have incurred under this Agreement as if no such termination had occurred.

14.5 *Termination or Expiry.*—The termination or earlier expiry of this Agreement for whatever cause shall not affect any provision of this Agreement which is expressed to survive or operate in the event of termination or expiry of this Agreement and shall not prejudice or affect the rights of either party against the other in respect of any breach of this Agreement or in respect of any moneys payable by one party to the other in relation to any period prior to termination or expiry.

Article 15: Indemnity

The supplier hereby undertakes to the Purchaser except in so far as the supplier's performance is prevented by any event of *Force Majeure* within clause 13 above that at all times the supplier will duly perform, observe and keep the terms and conditions on the part of the supplier to be performed observed and kept pursuant to this Agreement and that the Supplier will indemnify and keep indemnified the purchaser in respect of any losses costs and expenses sustained by the purchaser through the default of the Supplier with respect to any of its obligations.

Article 16: Announcements and Confidentiality

16.1 *No Announcement Without Approval.*—Unless specifically otherwise agreed in writing or required by law or by The Stock Exchange [or any other financial exchange or governmental body or agency] no public announcement shall be made in respect of the subject matter of this Agreement until after [Financial Close] and in no event shall any announcement permitted hereunder be made by either party without the prior written approval of the other party to its form and content.

16.2 *Undertaking of Confidentiality.*—The parties hereby undertake to each other that they shall not and shall procure that each affiliate, director, officer and employee of them shall not at any time hereafter (whether before or after Financial Close) save with the prior consent in writing of the other party divulge or communicate to any person other than to directors, officers, employees or professional advisers of it [or of any affiliate thereof] whose province it is to know the same, any secret or confidential information concerning the business, financial or contractual arrangements or other dealings or affairs of the other party (or any affiliate thereof) or of any customer or client thereof save to the extent to which such information shall (other than through any unauthorised disclosure by the other party or any affiliate, director, officer or employee thereof) come within the public domain.

Article 17: Representations and Warranties

17.1 *The Purchaser's Warranties.*—The purchaser represents and warrants to the supplier as follows:

(1) the purchaser is a corporation duly organised, validly existing and in good standing under the laws of the ...., and is qualified to do business and is in good standing in each other jurisdiction where the failure so to qualify would have a material adverse effect upon the business or financial condition of the purchaser or the project, and the purchaser has all requisite power and authority to conduct its business, to own its properties and to execute, deliver and perform its obligations under this Agreement;

(2) the execution, delivery and performance by the purchaser of this Agreement have been duly authorised by all necessary corporate action, and do not and will not:

(1) require any consent or approval of the Purchaser's board of directors, shareholders or any third party, other than those that have been obtained (evidence of which shall be delivered, if it has not already been delivered to the Supplier); or

(2) result in a breach of, or constitute a default under, any provisions of the Purchaser's constitutional or incorporation documents, any indenture, contract or agreement to which it is a party or by which it or its assets may be bound, or violate any law, rule, regulation, order, writ, judgement, injunction, decree, determination or award presently in effect and applicable to it;

(3) no legal approval, other than those that have been obtained, is necessary for the due execution and delivery by the Purchaser of this Agreement;

(4) this Agreement constitutes a legal, valid and binding obligation of the purchaser and is enforceable against the purchaser in accordance with its terms; and

(5) except as disclosed in writing by the purchaser to the supplier, as of the date hereof, there is no pending or, to the best of the Purchaser's knowledge, threatened action or proceeding, affecting the Purchaser before any legal authority or arbitrator that could reasonably be expected to materially and adversely affect the financial condition or operations of the Purchaser or the ability of the Purchaser to perform its obligations hereunder, or that purports to affect the legality, validity or enforceability of this Agreement.

17.2 *The Supplier's Warranties.*—The supplier represents and warrants to the Purchaser as follows:

(1) the Supplier is a limited liability company duly organised, validly existing and in good standing under the laws of the State of ....and .... and is qualified to do business and is in

good standing in each other jurisdiction where the failure so to qualify would have a material adverse effect upon the business or financial condition of the Supplier, and the Supplier has all requisite power and authority to conduct its business, to own its properties and to execute, deliver and perform its obligations under this Agreement;

(2) the execution, delivery and performance by the supplier of this Agreement have been duly authorised by all necessary corporate action, and do not and will not:

(1) require any consent or approval of the supplier's board of directors, shareholders or any third party, other than those that have been obtained (evidence of which shall be delivered, if it has not already been, delivered to the Purchaser); or

(2) result in a breach of, or constitute a default under, any provisions of the Supplier's constitutional or incorporation documents, any indenture, contract or agreement to which it is a party or by which it or its assets may be bound or violate any law, rule, regulations, order, writ, judgment, injunction, decree, determination or award presently in effect and applicable to it;

(3) no legal approvals are necessary for the Supplier to export coal from .... and the Supplier is not required to obtain any legal approvals in order to perform any of its obligations hereunder;

(4) this Agreement constitutes a legal, valid and binding obligation of the Supplier and is enforceable against the Supplier in accordance with its terms; and

(5) of the date hereof, there is no pending or, to the best of the Supplier's knowledge, threatened action or proceeding affecting the Supplier before any legal authority or arbitrator that could reasonably be expected to materially and adversely affect the financial condition or operations of the Supplier or the ability of the Supplier to perform its obligations hereunder, or that purports to affect the legality, validity or enforceability of this Agreement.

Article 18: Waivers, Remedies Cumulative, Amendments, etc.

18.1 *No Waiver:* No failure or delay by either party in exercising any right, power or privilege under this Agreement shall operate as a waiver thereof nor shall any single or partial exercise by either party of any right, power or privilege preclude any further exercise thereof or the exercise of any other right, power or privilege.

18.2 *Cumulative Rights:* The rights and remedies herein provided are cumulative and not exclusive of any rights and remedies provided by law.

18.3 *Written agreement to amendment and waiver:* No provision of this Agreement may be amended, modified, waived, discharged or terminated, otherwise than by the express written agreement of the parties hereto nor may any breach of any provision of this Agreement be waived or discharged except with the express written consent of the party not in breach.

Article 19: Notices

19.1 *Notices to be in Writing.*—Any notice or other communication given or made under this Agreement shall be in writing and, without prejudice to the validity of any other method of service, may be delivered personally or by courier or sent by telex or facsimile transmission as follows:

(a) if to ?, to:

....

....

.... (address)

(b) if to ?, to:

....

....

.... (address)

Alternatively, to such other address, or telex or facsimile transmission number as the relevant addressee may hereafter by notice hereunder substitute.

19.2 *Due Service.*—Any such notice or other communication shall be deemed to have been duly served, given or made (i) in the case of delivery, when left at the relevant address; or (ii) in the case of telex when the sender receives the answer back of the addressee at the end of the telex message; or (iii) in the case of a facsimile transmission, upon receipt by the addressee of the complete text in legible form.

Article 20: Governing Law and Dispute Resolution

20.1 *General.*—This Agreement shall be governed by and construed in all respects in accordance with the laws of .... and ....

20.2 *Amicable Settlement.*—The parties shall attempt in good faith to resolve all disputes arising in connection with the interpretation or application of the provisions of this Agreement or in connection with the determination of any matters, which are subject to objective determination pursuant to this Agreement by mutual agreement in accordance with the provisions of this clause 20.

20.3 *Resolution by Company Representatives.*—If a dispute arises under this Agreement, the parties shall, in the first instance, each appoint a company representative who has no involvement in the dispute and shall submit the dispute to the respective representatives for resolution.

20.4 *Resolution of Representatives to be binding.*—Any joint and unanimous decision (which shall be in writing) of the parties' representatives shall be binding upon the parties.

20.5 *Arbitration or Expert Determination.*—If such company representatives fail to resolve the dispute within .... days of the date on which the matter was first submitted to the second company representative for resolution, then either party may submit the dispute to expert determination (where appropriate) in accordance with clause 20.6 or institute arbitration proceedings in accordance with the provisions of clause 20.13. For the avoidance of doubt, each party hereby consents to such arbitration or expert determination.

20.6 *Expert Determination.*—If a dispute is required to be referred to an expert or if the dispute is of a technical nature relating to the Specification or any similar or related matter and the dispute cannot be resolved by the company representatives pursuant to clause 20.3 the dispute may be referred, with the agreement of both parties, for determination to an expert (the "Expert") who shall be deemed to act as expert and not as arbitrator.

20.7 *Selection of Expert.*—The expert shall be selected by mutual agreement or failing agreement, within .... days after a request by one party to the other, shall be chosen at the request of either party by ....

20.8 *Resolution of Expert to be Binding.*—The expert shall be instructed to deliver its determination to the parties within .... days after his appointment and a determination shall be made by all or a majority of them. Decisions of the Expert shall be final and binding and not subject to appeal.

20.9 *Powers of the Expert.*—The expert shall have the same powers to require any party to produce any documents or information to him and the other parties as an arbitrator and each party shall in any event supply to him such information which it has and is material to the matter to be resolved and which it could be required to produce on discovery.

20.10 *The Expert's Fees.*—The fees of the Expert shall be borne equally by the parties, unless otherwise directed by the Expert.

20.11 *Refusal of Determination by Expert.*—If either party does not agree to the dispute being referred for determination in accordance with clause 20.6 then the dispute shall be determined by an arbitrator in accordance with clause 20.12.

20.12 *Arbitration.*—Subject to clauses 20.3 and 20.6 above, any dispute or difference of any kind whatsoever arising between the parties hereto out of or in connection with this Agreement (including, without limitation, any question regarding its existence, validity or termination) shall be referred to and finally resolved by arbitration in .... before a single arbitrator.

20.13 *Appointment by Agreement.*—The parties shall jointly appoint the arbitrator not later than .... days after service of a request in writing by either party to do so.

20.14 *Appointment in default of Agreement.*—If the parties are unable to agree within 28 days as to the appointment of such arbitrator then such arbitrator (hereinafter referred to as "the tribunal") shall be appointed on the application of either party.

20.15 *Location and Language of Arbitration.*—The proceedings shall take place in .... , shall be conducted in the English language (and shall be concluded within .... months of the tribunal being appointed).

20.16 *Expeditious Resolution.*—In the event of a reference to arbitration pursuant to this clause 20, the parties agree to:

    (a) prosecute any such reference expeditiously; and

    (b) do all things or take all steps reasonably necessary in order to enable the tribunal to deliver any award (interim, final or otherwise) as soon as reasonably practicable (and in any event, within .... days of concluding any hearing).

20.17 *No Appeal to Courts on Questions of Law.*—Neither of the parties may apply to any court to determine any question of law arising in the course of the arbitral proceedings. All such questions shall be finally determined by the tribunal on application by either party.

20.18 *Parties' waiver.*—Neither of the parties may appeal to any court on a question of law arising out of an award made in the arbitral proceedings and the parties hereby irrevocably waive any such rights as they might otherwise have had.

20.19 *No Extension of Time Limits by Courts.*—The court shall not have the power set out in Section 79 of the 1996 Arbitration Act to extend time limits relating to arbitral proceedings.

20.20 *Award to be in Writing.*—The award shall be in writing signed by the arbitrator but shall not contain reasons for the award and shall be finalised within [...] days of the hearing.

20.21 *Award to be Binding.*—The award shall be final and binding both on the parties and on any persons claiming through or under them and judgment upon the award rendered may be entered in any court having jurisdiction or application may be made to such court for judicial acceptance of the award and an order of enforcement as the case may be.

20.22 *Continued Compliance.*—Unless this Agreement has already been terminated, each of the parties shall in every case continue to comply with its obligations under this Agreement regardless of the nature of the dispute and notwithstanding the referral of the dispute for resolution pursuant to this clause 20 (but without prejudice to the rights and obligations of the parties in relation to the termination of the Agreement).

Article 21: Direct Agreement

The supplier shall use reasonable endeavours to enter into a Direct Agreement with the Lenders' Agent on or before ....

Article 22: No Assignment

The provisions of this Agreement shall be binding on and ensure to the benefit of the successors and assigns of each party hereto provided that neither Party may (and may not agree to) assign, transfer, charge or otherwise dispose of or subcontract any of its rights or obligations hereunder without the prior written consent of the other party (such consent not to be unreasonably withheld), except that the Purchaser may assign or transfer all or any of its rights and obligations under this Agreement as security for the performance of its obligations to the Lenders without the Supplier's consent (although the Purchaser shall advise the Supplier of such assignment or transfer) and the Supplier agrees to comply will all reasonable requests of the Purchaser and execute all documents reasonably required for such assignment.

Article 23: No Partnership

Nothing herein shall or shall be deemed to create any partnership or joint venture between the parties hereto.

Article 24: Entire Agreement

Each party hereby confirms that this Agreement sets out the entire agreement and understanding between the parties in relation to the transactions hereby contemplated, that it supersedes all previous agreements, arrangements and understandings between them or any of them with regard to such transactions and that it is not entering into this Agreement or any of the arrangements contemplated hereby in reliance upon any representation or warranty not expressly set out herein.

SIGNED by the parties

SIGNED by)
duly authorised for and)
on behalf of)
Alpha COAL (Pte) LIMITED)
SIGNED by)
duly authorised for and)
on behalf of)
Beta (BVI) LIMITED)

SCHEDULE 1
DELIVERY SCHEDULES

Part I: Start-Up Schedule
Part II: Annual Delivery Schedule
Part III: Delivery Schedule
Part IV: Notice of Readiness

SCHEDULE 2
SPECIFICATION

STANDARD ANALYSIS
Specification
Rejection Limits

Total moisture ([air dried]/[as received]))
Net CV
Volatile matter ("VM")
Carbon ([air dried]/[as received]))

Ash ([air dried]/[as received]   )
Sulphur ([air dried]/[as received]   )
Phosphorus (air dried/as received   )
Oxygen ([air dried]/[as received]   )
Hydrogen ([air dried]/[as received]   )
Nitrogen ([air dried]/[as received]   )
Chlorine ([air dried]/[as received]   )
Vitronite ([air dried]/[as received]   )
Size
[not exceeding [mm]
Fines
Grindability (Hardgrove Index)
Ash fusion index

SCHEDULE 3
CERTIFICATE OF ANALYSIS

SCHEDULE 4
PUBLIC HOLIDAYS

EPC CONTRACT
NON-RECOVERY COKE OVEN
PLANT PROJECT

ARTICLES OF AGREEMENT made this .... day of...................., 20.....

BETWEEN

.... (name) a company established under the laws of .... whose principal place of business is at .... (address), ... , ("the Purchaser" which expression shall include the Purchaser's legal successors in title and permitted assigns)

AND

.... (name) GmbH a company established under the laws of .... whose registered office is at .... (address), ("the Contractor", which expression shall include the Contractor's legal successors in title).

The purchaser and the contractor are each referred to herein as "Party" or collectively the "Parties".

RECITALS:

(1) The purchaser wishes to obtain the design, engineering, procurement, manufacture, supply, delivery to site, erection, construction, installation, completion, testing and commissioning, stabilisation of operation, and achievement of Performance Guarantees in relation to a non-recovery type .... oven plant at .... (site location), India with a gross output of .... tonnes per annum of .... on a dry basis and a guaranteed average waste gas generation @ .... NM3/hr/Waste Heat Recovery Boiler @ average temperature of 1100°C, as per Annex 3 D.1 together with

associated facilities, including coal preparation and handling plant and .... screening within battery limits, and training of the purchaser's personnel.

(2) The contractor has submitted a proposal for the design, engineering, procurement, manufacture, supply, delivery to site, erection, construction, installation, completion, testing and commissioning of such plant and the remedying of defects therein all as comprised in the documents attached hereto at Annexure 3 (the Technical Specification) in a fixed sum agreed between the parties (the "Contract Price") and the Purchaser and the contractor have agreed to enter into a contract in respect thereof on the terms of this Agreement

(3) Save as otherwise expressly provided in the contract, the Contractor has familiarised itself with the Site conditions to satisfy itself as to the nature of the site and all relevant conditions affecting the works.

NOW, IT IS HEREBY AGREED as follows:

1. Capitalized terms in these Articles of Agreement shall have the same meanings as are respectively assigned to them in the conditions.

2. Articles 1, 2, 3,4, 6, 7, 8 and 9 (the "Effective Articles") shall come into effect on the date hereof. The remainder of the contract shall come into force on and with effect from, the effective date (as defined below). Prior to the effective date, neither party shall have any responsibility or obligation to the other under the contract (including these Articles of Agreement) except, as provided in the Effective Articles.

3. Prior to the effective date:
   (a) the purchaser shall comply with the obligations on its part to be performed prior to the effective date which are set out in Annexure 2 (the purchaser's obligations), by the times set out therein;
   (b) after the purchaser has complied with its obligations under paragraph 2 of Annexure 2, the contractor shall procure the carrying out of a soil survey of the Site to ascertain the nature of the soil conditions and, in particular, whether Annexure 3G (piling works design) requires modification;
   (c) the contractor shall as soon as reasonably practicable and two weeks prior to effective date notify the Purchaser of the results of the soil survey and the changes (if any) which the contractor proposes to the contract price, time for completion and/or technical specification arising from any of the matters disclosed in that survey;
   (d) the contractor shall as soon as reasonably practicable and within two months of the date of this Agreement develop Annexure 5 (Spare Parts), which is included in the contract in outline at the date hereof, and the contractor shall submit its proposals in relation thereto to the purchaser, together with any consequential adjustments to the contract Price proposed by the contractor;
   (e) the contractor shall as soon as reasonably practicable and within one month of handing over of Site to the contractor as per Annex 3F of the

conditions having consulted with the engineer submit to the purchaser its proposals in relation to the Project Manual, which shall deal with matters such as:

(i) the requirements in relation to the monthly progress reports to be provided by the contractor;

(ii) details of the notifications/ information which either party is required to give to the other party, (e.g. in relation to the time and quantities of coal required by the contractor and interfaces between the various parts of the Project);

(iii) Identify and notify the engineer of the drawings/information/ other requirements of the contractor which relate to any other part of the Project (including the power plant and the Infrastructure) which the contractor requires for the Works.

(f) after submission by the contractor of its proposals in relation to the items referred to in paragraphs (c) (d) and (e) of this Article, the Parties shall consult in good faith to reach agreement on the various issues.

4. The effective date shall, subject to Article 7, be the date upon which all of the following conditions have been satisfied:

(1) the execution of this Agreement;

(2) financial closure has occurred and has been confirmed by the lenders to the contractor;

(3) the purchaser has complied with all of the obligations on its part set out in Annexure 2 (the purchaser's obligations) which are required to be performed prior to the Effective Date;

(4) the contractor has submitted to the Purchaser the Performance Bond and guarantee;

(5) the contractor has submitted to the purchaser the advance payment guarantee and the Purchaser has paid the advance payment to the contractor;

(6) the Purchaser and the contractor have respectively procured the permits which are identified in Annexure 8 (Permits) as being required to be obtained by either of them prior to the Effective Date and any other opermits required by either of them from any governmental instrumentality to the extent such other Permits are required for the commencement of the works;

(7) the contractor has entered into an agreement with the purchaser and the agent and trustee of the lenders in the form set out in Annexure 16. (Form of Direct Agreement);

(8) the contractor and the purchaser have reached agreement in relation to any changes to the contract price, Time for completion, technical specification Annexure 5 (spare parts) , all as referred to in Articles 3(c) and (d); have agreed on the terms of the project manual, and have executed (in the manner required under clause 52.4 of the conditions) an amendment to the contract recording such agreement and;

(9) the purchaser has provided the letter of credit to the contractor in accordance with the contract;

5. Subject only to the fulfilment of the conditions specified in Article 4, the Purchaser shall provide the contractor with a written notice to confirm the occurrence of the effective date, together with such reasonable evidence as the contractor may require that such date has occurred.

6. The purchaser acknowledges that the contract price specified in recital (3) above is based upon the effective date occurring prior to ....(date) (the "tender expiry date") (and is subject to any changes to the contract Price referred to in Articles 3(c) and (d)). If, for whatever reason, the effective date does not occur by the tender expiry date, then, unless otherwise agreed in writing by the Parties, the Parties shall consult in good faith to agree upon appropriate changes to the contract price and/or the Time for completion to take into account the consequences of such delay, and the parties shall execute (in the manner required under clause 52.4 of the conditions) an amendment to the contract recording their agreement in respect of a revised contract price and/or time for completion which shall apply provided that the effective date occurs prior to such later tender expiry date as the Parties agree (the "Extended Tender Expiry Date").

7. If, by the tender expiry date or, (if applicable), the extended tender expiry date:

   (a) the effective date has not occurred; and

   (b) an amendment to the contract referred to in Article 6 has not been entered into so as to extend the tender expiry date or, if applicable, the extended tender expiry date, then, unless otherwise agreed in writing by the parties by the tender expiry date or, as the case may be, the extended tender expiry date, the effective date shall not occur unless and until such an amendment to the contract is subsequently entered into by the parties.

8. If the effective date does not occur solely as a result of:

   (a) any failure on the part of the purchaser to comply with its obligations under Article 3 (a) or Annexure 2; and/or

   (b) Financial Closure not having occurred provided that it is not consequent to a direct action or omission. Then the Purchaser shall reimburse the contractor for the costs incurred by the contractor in relation to the carrying out of the soil survey, within .... days after receipt by the purchaser of documentation from the contractor evidencing (in such detail as the purchaser may reasonably require) the amount of such costs incurred by the contractor.

9. If the effective date does not occur as a result of a failure by the Parties to reach agreement as referred to in Article 3(c), (d) and (e) and, if applicable, Article 6, then (regardless of the reason why the parties failed to reach such agreement), neither Party shall have any right of recourse whatsoever against the other party as a result of the Effective Date not occurring. For the avoidance of doubt, this Article 9 is without prejudice to the contractor's rights under Article 8.

10. The following Annexes, which have been initialled by the parties and bound herewith, shall be deemed to form and be read and construed as part of this Agreement:

Annexure 1 The conditions and the Appendix attached thereto
Annexure 2 Purchaser's obligations
Annexure 3 Technical specification and drawings comprising:
    3A Specification - non recovery .... ovens
    3B Coal and Coke .... handling
    3C Void
    3D1 Testing regimes
    3D2 Liquidated damages
    3E Training
    3F Programme
    3G Piling
    3H Project management
    3I Requirement of O&M personnel
Annexure 4 Excluded works/battery limits
Annexure 5 Spare parts
Annexure 6 Price breakdown and payment schedule
Annexure 7 Insurances
Annexure 8 Permits
Annexure 9 Form of performance bond
Annexure 10 Form of advance payment guarantee
Annexure 11 Form of retention bond
Annexure 12 Form of taking over certificate
Annexure 13 Parent company guarantee ("guarantee")
Annexure 14 Form of defects liability certificate
Annexure 15 Form of final payment certificate
Annexure 16 Form of direct agreement
Annexure 17 Form of latent defects bond
Annexure 18 Cancellation schedule
Annexure 19 Drawings submission and approval procedure
Annexure 20 Contract information
Annexure 21 Dispute resolution procedure
Annexures 22 – 25 Form of payment release bonds.

11. In consideration of the purchaser agreeing to pay the contractor the contract price or such other sum as may become payable by the Purchaser under the contract, the contractor undertakes, subject to and in accordance with the

terms of the contract, to design, engineer, procure, manufacture, supply, deliver to Site, erect, construct, install, test, commission and complete the works, including passing the Performance test within the time for completion, remedying defects therein and doing all other acts and things mentioned in or reasonably to be inferred from the contract in conformity in all respects with the provisions of the contract.

12. The purchaser shall pay to the contractor in consideration of the performance of the obligations referred to in Article 11 and in accordance with clause 39 of the conditions, the contract Price or such other sum as may become payable by the Purchaser under the contract at the time and in the manner prescribed by the contract.

13. Upon the effective date the purchaser shall pay to the contractor the advance payment stated in the Appendix attached to the conditions under the letter of credit.

IN WITNESS whereof, these Articles of Agreement have been signed on behalf of the parties the day and year first above written.

Signed for and on behalf

of purchaser by

in the presence of

or the Common Seal was

affixed etc.

Signed for and on behalf

of contractor by

in the presence of

or the Common Seal was

affixed etc.

ANNEXURE 1
THE CONDITIONS

These are the conditions referred to in the Articles of Agreement, dated
between the Purchaser and the Contractor

Signed by	Signed by
for and on behalf of	for and on behalf of
[Purchaser]	[Contractor]

Article 1: Definitions and Interpretation

1.1 In construing the contract the following words and expressions shall have the following meanings hereby assigned to them unless the context otherwise requires:

"Advance Payment Guarantee".—A bank guarantee from an internationally recognised first class bank acceptable to the Purchaser, in the sum stated in the Appendix to the conditions and in the form set out in Annexure 10 (Form of advance payment guarantee);

"Appendix".—The Appendix to the conditions;

"................... Plant".—................... Plant has the meaning assigned to it in recital (1) to the Articles of Agreement and is more particularly described in the technical specification;

"Cancellation Schedule".—The cancellation Schedule initialled by the Parties and forming part of the contract, as attached as Annexure 18 (Cancellation Schedule) to the Articles of Agreement;

"Change in Legal Requirements" means any of:

(a) the enactment in India of any new legal requirements;

(b) the amendment or repeal in India of an existing legal requirement;

(c) the change in interpretation in India of any Legal Requirement either by consent of the parties or by a competent authority in each of the above cases, after the date of the agreement; or

(d) the imposition in India of a requirement for a permit not required as at the date of the Agreement;

"Change Proposal".—A written proposal by the purchaser to the contractor or by the contractor to the Purchaser made under clause 27 for the addition, deletion or modification of any part of the contract, the works, the .... plant, the programme, the payment Schedule, or the method, sequence or time of performing or completing the works or part thereof.

"Civil Works".—All civil works including excavation works, filling of soil, soil exploration works, PCC/RCC super structures, PCC and RCC Sub-structures and foundations including piling works, water proof treatment for civil structures as per technical specification.

"Conditions".—These conditions attached as Annexure 1 (The conditions and Appendix) to the Articles of Agreement;

"Contract".—The agreement between the purchaser and the contractor for the execution of the works comprising the Articles of Agreement and the annexes thereto referred to at Article 10 thereof;

"Contract Price".—The fixed sum referred to at recital (2) of the Articles of Agreement.;

"Contract Value".—Such part of the contract price, adjusted to give effect to such additions or deductions as are provided for in the contract, as is properly apportionable as determined by the Engineer to the Plant or work in question. In determining contract value the state, condition and topographical location of the plant, the amount of work done and all other relevant circumstances shall be taken into account;

"Contractor".—The party named as such in the Articles of Agreement;

"Contractor Non-Remediable Event".—Contractor Non-Remediable Event has the meaning assigned to it in clause 46.1.2;

"Contractor Remediable Event".—Contractor Remediable Event has the meaning assigned to it in clause 46.1.1;

"Contractor's Equipment".—All appliances or things of whatsoever nature used for the purposes of carrying out the works but this expression does not include Plant;

"Cost".—All expenses and direct costs incurred in carrying out the works, performing the obligation, or otherwise in respect of the matter in question, including overhead and financing charges properly allocable thereto;

"Date for Payment".—In respect of any payment which falls to be made under the contract by either Party to the other, the latest date stated in the contract for such payment, or where no such date is stated, ... days from a written demand by the party entitled to such payment to the other;

"Day".—Calendar day;

"Defects Liability Certificate".—The certificate issued by the engineer pursuant to clause 36.4 in the form set out in Annex 14 (Form of Defects Liability Certificate) to the Articles of Agreement;

"Defects Liability Period".—Defects Liability Period has the meaning assigned to it in clause 36.1;

"Design Documentation".—Dawings, diagrams, details, documents, specifications, samples, models or information (including calculations, logic or sequence overview diagrams and functional design specifications for computer software) prepared by the Contractor for the works;

"Dispute".—Any dispute or difference of whatever nature between the Parties arising under, out of or in connection with the Contract (including any question of interpretation of the Contract) or the works and whether arising during the performance of the works or after completion or abandonment of the same and whether occurring prior to or following termination of the contract;

"Dispute Resolution Procedure".—The procedure referred to in clause 50 and set out in Annexure 21 (Dispute Resolution Procedure) to the Articles of Agreement;

"Effective Date".—Effective Date has the meaning given at Article 4 of the Articles of Agreement;

"Engineer".—.................... (address) or such other person who is experienced in the .... oven production industry as the purchaser may, with the contractor's prior approval (not to be unreasonably withheld) appoint from time to time in writing to act as engineer for the purposes referred to in clause 2 of the conditions;

"Final Payment Certificate".—The certificate to be issued by the Engineer pursuant to clause 39.7 in the form set out in Annex 15 (Form of Final Certificate of Payment) to the Articles of Agreement;

"Financial Closure".—The date the lenders' facility agent notifies the Purchaser that financial close has occurred under the Financing Agreements;

"Financing Agreements".—Collectively, the loan and security agreements entered into in connection with the financing of the project, as the same may be amended from time to time in accordance with the terms and conditions thereof;

"Force Majeure".—Force Majeure has the meaning assigned to it in clause 49.1;

"Good Engineering Practice".—Good Engineering Practice means, at a particular time, those practices, methods and acts as are in accordance with standards of prudence applicable to the .... production industry;

"Governmental Instrumentality".—Any country, and any ministry, department, political sub-division, instrumentality, agency, court, corporation or commission under the direct or indirect control of such country;

"Guarantee".—The guarantee to be procured by the contractor in the form set out in Annexure 13.

"Guarantor".—The party providing the guarantee;

"Imported Equipment".—Tthe meaning given in clause 24.1;

"Indigenous Equipment".—The meaning given in clause 24.1;

"Infrastructure".—Infrastructure includes all civil works, construction, buildings required to be provided at the site other than the works constructions and buildings covered within the scope of the work of this contract, or the EPC power plant contract and includes, all land, construction water, construction power, roads, drainage, sewage line, lighting, civil works, building, dwelling units, stores etc., outside the battery limits of the power plant and the .... plant.

"Interface".—Interface includes the interface information and activities between the contractor and the purchaser and the other contractors during the engineering phase, construction phase and the commissioning phase. The interface is to be co-ordinated by the engineer. The interface activities between the engineer and the contractor shall be subject to the project Manual.

"LC Bank".—The bank approved by the contractor providing each Letter of Credit;

"Legal Requirements".—All laws, legislation, statutes, rules, notifications, directives, orders, by-laws, policies, injunctions, administrative guidance, agreements, treaties and regulations of any governmental instrumentality having jurisdiction over either of the parties, the carrying out of the works or the matter in question, including the requirements of all permits;

"Lenders".—Any of the lenders party to any of the Financing Agreements;

"Lenders' Agent".—Any bank or financial institution appointed as agent for the lenders under the Financing Agreements;

"Lenders' Engineer".—Such company or person as appointed from time to time by the lenders in accordance with the Financing Agreements;

"Letter of Credit".—Each letter of credit to be provided by the Purchaser under the contract from an internationally recognised first class bank acceptable

to the contractor in the form of letter of credit set out in Annexure 6 to the Articles of Agreement or as otherwise acceptable to the contractor, as the same may be extended from time to time;

"*Limit of Total Liquidated Damages*".—As defined in the Appendix to these Conditions;

"*Milestone*".—An event described as such in the Payment Schedule;

"*Milestone Payment*".—The payment to be made in respect of a milestone on the achievement of that milestone;

"*Month*".—A month according to the gregorian calendar;

"*Normal Delivery Date*".—The time for delivery of the relevant plant specified in the Programme, or if no time is specified, at the time appropriate for it to be delivered having regard to the time for completion;

"*O&M Manuals*".—The operation and maintenance manuals submitted by the contractor and approved by the engineer pursuant to clause 15;

"*Payment Schedule*".—The Payment Schedule initialled by the parties and forming part of the contract, as attached as Annexure 6 (Price Breakdown and Payment Schedule) to the Articles of Agreement;

"*Party*" and, collectively "*Parties*".—The purchaser and/or the contractor, as the case may be;

"*Performance Bond*".—A bank guarantee duly executed by an internationally recognised first class bank acceptable to the Purchaser in the sum stated in the Appendix to the conditions in the form set out in Annexure 9 (Form of Performance Bond).

"*Performance Guarantees*".—The meaning attributable thereto in the technical specification;

"*Performance Test*".—The tests so described in the technical specification;

"*Permit*".—Any approval, permit, licence, clearance, consent, authorisation, decree, privilege, filing or other requirement of or required by any Governmental Instrumentality with respect to the project, including those required for all staff and labour of the contractor and its sub-contractors in the carrying out of the works;

"*Plant*".—Machinery, apparatus, materials and all things (including spare parts) to be provided under the contract for incorporation in the works;

"*Power Plant*".—The 100MW cogeneration power plant and ancillary facilities procured pursuant to the Power Plant EPC contract;

"*Power Plant EPC Contract*".—The contracts respectively for the design, engineering, procurement, manufacture, supply, delivery to site, erection, construction, installation, completion, testing and commissioning of the Power Plant, or any of them as the context requires;

"*Power Plant EPC Contractor*".—The contractors engaged in connection with the Power Plant EPC contract, or any of them as the context requires;

"*Power Purchase Agreement*".—The contract entitled "Power Purchase Agreement" made between .... and the purchaser;

"Preliminary Variation".—The submission made by the contractor to the Purchaser in accordance with clause 27.3;

"Programme".—The construction programme so described in the technical specification, as the same may be revised in accordance with clause 14 and/or clause 33;

"Project".—The design, engineering, procurement, financing, manufacture, supply, delivery to Site, erection, construction, installation, completion, testing and commissioning of each of the .... plant and the Power Plant and all related buildings, civil works and infrastructure;

"Project Manual".—The project manual agreed by the Parties pursuant to Article 3 of the Articles of Agreement;

"Purchaser".—The party named as such in the Articles of Agreement;

"Purchaser Remediable Event".—The meaning assigned to it in clause 46.1.3;

"Purchaser Non-Remediable Event".—The meaning assigned to in clause 46.1.4;

"Purchaser's Contractors".—The contractors (excluding the contractor), engaged by the Purchaser to carry out works at the site for the project;

"Purchaser's Risk".—The meaning assigned to it in clause 45;

"Remedial Notice".—The meaning assigned to it in clause 46.1.5;

"Remedial Programme".—The meaning assigned to it in clause 46.1.5;

"Retention Bond".—A bank guarantee from an internationally recognised first class bank acceptable to the purchaser in the sum of ....% of the contract price and in the form set out in Annexure 11 (Form of Retention Bond);

"Senior Debt".—The indebtedness for borrowed money incurred by the Purchaser under the Financing Agreements;

"Site".—The land and other places to be designated by the purchaser, on, under, in or through which the works are to be constructed or which may be used by the contractor in the performance of the contract, as described in Annexure 20 (contract information);

"Spare Parts".—The spare parts listed in Annex 5 to the Articles of Agreement, amended as referred to in Article 4 (8) of the Articles of Agreement, including wear parts;

"Surety".—The party providing the Advance Payment Bond or the Performance Bond (as the case may be);

"Taking Over".—The date when the criteria in clause 29 have been met as stated in the Taking Over Certificate;

"Taking Over Certificate".—The certificate to be issued by the engineer pursuant to clause 29.2, in the form set out in Annexure 12 (Form of Taking Over Certificate) to the Articles of Agreement;

"Technical Specification".—The specifications, drawings and other documents initialled by the Parties and forming part of the Contract and attached as

Annexures 3A to 3I inclusive (the Technical Specification) to the Articles of Agreement;

"*Time for Completion*".—The period stated in the Appendix, or as extended under clause 33;

"*TNEB*".—The Tamil Nadu Electricity Board;

"*Variation*".—The written confirmation, under clause 27.4, clause 27.5 or clause 27.6, of the terms on which a change proposal is to be implemented;

"*Week*".—Any continuous period of 7 days;

"*Works*".—All work and things to be supplied, carried out or done by the contractor under the contract;

1.2 Words importing persons or parties shall include firms, corporations and any organisation having legal capacity and words importing a particular gender include all genders.

1.3 Words importing the singular only also include the plural and *vice versa*, where the context requires.

1.4 Wherever in the contract provision is made for the giving of notice or consent by any person, unless otherwise specified such notice or consent shall be in writing and the word "notify" shall be construed accordingly.

1.5 The headings in the contract shall not be deemed part thereof or be taken into consideration in the interpretation or construction thereof or of the contract.

1.6 References in these conditions to clauses, sub-clauses and paragraphs are references to those contained in these conditions. Except where otherwise stated references in a clause to sub-clause are to a sub-clause of that clause in which the reference appears.

1.7 Where a word or expression is defined in the contract, cognate words and expressions shall be construed accordingly.

1.8 Reference in the contract to the contract, any other agreement or any instrument is to the same as amended, novated, assigned, modified, supplemented or replaced from time to time.

1.9 References in the contract to statutory provisions shall, unless otherwise stated in the contract, be construed as references to those provisions as amended or re-enacted or as their application is modified by other statutory provisions from to time.

1.10 References in the contract to "including" are to be construed without limitation.

Article 2: The Engineer

2.1 The purchaser shall appoint and keep appointed a person to act as the engineer to carry out the duties and functions specified in the contract. The engineer shall exercise the authorities specified in or necessarily to be inferred from the contract, at all times acting reasonably and without unreasonable delay. The appointment of the Engineer by the purchaser shall not in any way relieve the contractor of any of its obligations under the contract. No inspection, examination, testing, approval, consent or similar act by the engineer (including a failure to disapprove any matter) by the Engineer shall relieve the contractor of any liability or any of its obligations under the contract.

2.2 The Engineer shall appoint and keep appointed a representative who is experienced in the .... oven production industry, whose identity shall be notified to the contractor, and who shall carry out such of the duties and functions of the engineer as may be delegated to him and notified to the contractor by the engineer from time to time. In carrying out his duties and functions, the representative shall be bound by all of the obligations of the Engineer hereunder, including under clause 2.7. Any exercise by the representative of the powers delegated to him (or failure to exercise such powers) shall be deemed to be exercised (or not exercised, as the case may be) by the engineer.

2.3 The contractor shall cooperate with the engineer (including in relation to the exercise by the engineer of his powers in relation to co-ordination between the Contractor and the Purchaser's contractors) and the Lenders' Engineer and provide such access, information and assistance as may be reasonably necessary to enable the engineer to perform his duties and shall, subject to clause 2.7, comply with all decisions, instructions and orders made or issued by the engineer.

2.4 Except as expressly provided in the contract, the engineer shall have no authority to relieve the contractor of any of its obligations under the contract; to order any work involving delay or any extra payment by the Purchaser; or to make or authorise any change in the works.

2.5 The purchaser may from time to time in writing delegate to the Engineer any of the powers and authorities vested in the purchaser (or revoke the same) and shall furnish to the contractor a copy of all such written delegations or revocations of powers and authorities. No delegation or revocation shall be effective until the contractor has received notice thereof. Any written instruction or approval given by the Engineer to the contractor within the terms of such delegation, but not otherwise, shall bind the contractor and Purchaser as though it had been given by the Purchaser.

2.6 The contractor may require the Engineer to confirm in writing any decision, instruction or order of the Engineer (or his representative), which is not in writing. The contractor shall, if it requires such confirmation, make such request without undue delay and the Engineer shall confirm in writing his decision, instruction or order without undue delay and in any event within 2 days of receipt of such request. Unless and until the Engineer provides such written confirmation, the decision, instruction or order shall be of no effect.

2.7 Wherever by the conditions the Engineer is required to:

(a) give his decision, opinion or consent; or

(b) express his satisfaction or approval; or

(c) determine any additional cost payable to the contractor or the purchaser or any other addition to or deduction from the contract price; or

(d) determine an extension of time; or

(e) otherwise take any action, which may affect the rights and/or obligations of either of the parties,

he shall do so without unreasonable delay, acting impartially between the Parties, in accordance with the contract, in good faith and having regard to all the relevant circumstances and shall, if reasonably so requested by the contractor or the Purchaser, provide his reasons for such decision, opinion, consent or determination.

2.8 The engineer shall coordinate all the areas of interface (covering the interface information and activities) between the contractor and the power plant EPC contractor and other contractors/parties in such a way that the activities of the relevant contractors are not hindered. The engineer shall require all relevant contractors to attend the co-ordination meetings which may be convened by the Engineer whenever the situation demands and such coordination meeting can be initiated by the engineer. The coordination meeting shall be held at the site as and when the situation demands or fortnightly during the construction/commissioning phases of work. The agenda for such meetings shall be prepared by the Engineer. The Minutes of the Meeting shall be prepared by the engineer and the same shall be duly signed by the parties/contractors who have attended the meeting.

The engineer shall reasonably act in accordance with the contract and the issues as per the contract shall be normally solved by consensus by the contractors. In case of no consensus among the contractors, the engineer's decision shall be final and binding on all the parties/contractors. Any issues that are not reflected in the contract, a decision will be made by the engineer in case the contractors have no consensus. While deciding, the engineer shall consider whether the decision amounts to a change proposal, in which case the provisions of clause 27 shall apply. The Engineer shall be obliged to give reasons to his decision and the contractor shall comply with it.

Article 3: Assignment and sub-contracting

3.1 The contractor shall not assign the benefit of the contract in whole or in part or any of its obligations under the contract. A charge in favour of the contractor's bankers for any moneys due under the contract shall not be considered an assignment.

3.2 The contractor shall not sub-contract the whole of the Works. Except as otherwise expressly provided in the contract, the contractor shall not sub-contract any part of the works without the prior consent in writing of the purchaser (not to be unreasonably withheld or delayed). The contractor shall not require such consent to enter into contracts for:

(i) any items of plant the manufacturer or supplier named in the Technical Specification as an approved supplier; or

(ii) any part of the works to a sub-contractor listed as an approved sub-contractor in the Technical Specification,

but shall notify the Purchaser that it has entered into such contracts.

3.3 Suppliers of any items of plant or sub-contractors of any part of the works who are not identified in the Technical Specification as approved suppliers or approved sub-contractors shall be subject to the approval of the Purchaser (not to be unreasonably withheld or delayed). No such sub-contracting shall relieve the contractor from any liability under the Contract.

3.4 The contractor shall be responsible for all works performed by any sub-contractor and for the acts, defaults and omissions of any sub-contractor, its agents or workmen as fully as if they were the acts, defaults or omissions of the contractor.

3.5 The purchaser may at any time assign its rights, interests and benefits under the contract to the lenders (or to an agent or trustee acting on behalf of the lenders) as security for the financing of the project. An assignment of the Purchaser's rights, interests and benefits under the contract to any other person requires the prior written consent of the contractor (not to be unreasonably withheld). Such assignment shall not relieve the contractor or the purchaser from any of its respective obligations or liabilities under the contract.

Article 4: Contract Documents

4.1 If there is any inconsistency between, the documents forming the Contract, their priority shall be as follows:

(a) the Articles of Agreement;

(b) the conditions and Appendix thereto;

(c) any other document forming part of the contract.

4.2 Subject to clause 4.1, the documents forming the contract are to be taken as mutually explanatory of one another. If the contractor discovers any ambiguity, inconsistency, discrepancy or conflict in or between the documents forming the contract it shall immediately notify the Engineer, who shall issue written instructions resolving the ambiguity, inconsistency, discrepancy or conflict to the contractor and the contractor shall, at its own cost, comply with such instructions.

Article 5: Basis of Tender and Contract Price

5.1 The contractor shall be deemed to have:

(a) thoroughly inspected and surveyed the Site and its surroundings;

(b) satisfied itself fully as to the nature, location and condition of the Site (including the geological, climatic, underground, ecological and hydrological conditions) and circumstances affecting the Site (including without limitation any safety regulations applicable thereto);

(c) satisfied itself as to the available methods of transporting plant, labour, and contractor's equipment to the site;

(d) satisfied itself as to the character, quality, quantity and availability of labour, materials, equipment, facilities, utilities needed for the works and other matters necessary for or affecting the performance of the contract;

(e) generally obtained for itself all necessary information as to any other factors, which would affect its decision to enter into this contract or the terms on which it would do so;

and no such matter shall give rise to any addition to the contract price or extension of time or other claim against the Purchaser, unless otherwise expressly provided for in the contract.

5.2 Without prejudice to its obligations under clause 13, the contractor shall be responsible for any misunderstanding or incorrect information howsoever obtained, including any information provided by the Purchaser or the Engineer except as otherwise expressly provided in the contract. Without prejudice to the generality of clause 5.1, no addition to the contract price or extension of time shall be made on account of any unforeseen conditions whatever, including geological and other underground conditions, hydrological, climatic, environmental or other physical conditions, except, as otherwise provided in the contract.

5.3 The contractor has relied upon the information provided to it by or on behalf of the purchaser set out in Annexure 20 (contract information), which includes certain information pertaining to the matters specified in clause 5.1. The purchaser shall be responsible for the accuracy of this information. If any of the contract information is incorrect or misleading and, as a result, the Contractor, acting reasonably, incurs additional costs and/or delay, which it was not possible for the contractor to avoid or mitigate by the taking of all reasonable steps, the contractor shall, without prejudice to the generality of clause 41, give notice and full particulars thereof to the engineer with a copy to the purchaser and shall submit such further details as the Engineer may reasonably request. After receipt of such notice and details, the Engineer shall, following consultation with the purchaser and the contractor, determine:

(a) any extension of time to which the contractor is entitled under clause 33; and

(b) the amount of any such additional cost, which shall be added to the contract price, subject to and in accordance with clause 39,

and shall notify the Contractor and the purchaser accordingly.

This clause 5.3 shall also apply to any information provided to the contractor by the purchaser or the engineer after the date of this contract regarding interface with the Infrastructure, the power plant and other works not covered within the scope of work of the contractor, provided however, the Parties agree that the said information is material in nature and marked as such.

Article 6: Underground Works

The contractor shall, save as expressly provided in the contract, execute at its own cost all the underground works required for the performance of the works including any relocation, diversion, re-instatement and making good any damage to existing services or structures and, save as aforesaid, all such works as may be necessary or desirable shall be included in the contract price and the programme.

Article 7: Fossils and Antiquities

7.1 All articles, materials or substances of value and structures and other remains or things of geological or archaeological interest discovered on the Site shall, as between the Purchaser and the contractor, be deemed to be the absolute property of the purchaser. The contractor shall take suitable precautions to prevent its workmen or any other persons from removing or damaging any such article or material, substance or thing and shall, immediately upon discovery thereof and before removal, inform the Engineer of such discovery and carry out the engineer's instructions for dealing with the same.

7.2 If, in complying with the instructions of the engineer, the contractor incurs additional costs and/or delay which it was not possible for the contractor to avoid or mitigate by the taking of all reasonable steps, the contractor shall, without prejudice to the generality of clause 41, give notice and full particulars thereof to the Engineer with a copy to the purchaser and shall submit such further details as the engineer may reasonably request. After receipt of such notice and details, the engineer shall, following consultation with the purchaser and the contractor, determine:

(a) any extension of time to which the contractor is entitled under clause 33; and

(b) the amount of any such additional cost, which shall be added to the contract price, subject to and in accordance with clause 39,

and shall notify the contractor and the purchaser accordingly.

Article 8: Monitoring Rights and Report

8.1 The lenders' engineer shall have the right to:

(a) monitor the manufacturing and off-site testing of the plant and its erection, construction, installation, testing and commissioning at the site; and

(b) review and, at its own cost, make copies of all documents required to be obtained and retained by the contractor pursuant to clause 13.7 (other than proprietary information of the contractor or others).

The contractor shall permit the lenders' engineer to conduct such monitoring and review at the site upon giving the contractor reasonable prior notice, during normal business hours twice each month and at such additional times as the Contractor may approve upon the written request of the lenders' Engineer, which approval shall not be unreasonably withheld. In the case of monitoring the manufacturing and off-site testing of the plant, the lenders' engineer shall have the right to conduct such monitoring with the prior approval of the contractor (which shall not be unreasonably withheld) at the times agreed with the contractor, in the presence of a representative of the Contractor at any and all locations inside or outside India at which such equipment and supplies are designed, manufactured, assembled or tested. The contractor shall ensure that its sub-contractors and suppliers provide for the foregoing rights of the lenders' engineer.

8.2 The exercise of any of the rights of the lenders' engineer pursuant to clause 8.1 or otherwise shall not extend to proprietary pricing and cost information of the contractor. The lenders' engineer shall have no authority whatsoever to give any instructions to the contractor.

8.3 The contractor shall supply to the purchaser an activity report at the times and covering the periods and matters stated in the project manual. The contractor shall also provide to the purchaser, the engineer and the lenders' engineer promptly upon becoming aware thereof a report describing the occurrence of any act or condition materially affecting the works or its ability to perform its obligations under the contract.

8.4 The contractor shall within 5 days of the end of each month issue to the purchaser, lenders' engineer and engineer monthly progress reports containing full details of the progress of the works, including milestones, up to the end of such month and identifying any areas of delay or difficulty in such form and detail, as provided in the project manual.

8.5 During the course of the construction of the works the contractor shall take a sufficient number of progress photographs to show the progress and development of the works. The contractor shall issue to the Engineer with its monthly progress report 3 prints of each progress photograph taken during the previous month. Each such progress photograph shall contain the time of day, date, the name of the contractor and the title of the photograph, together with marks identifying the location and direction in which such photograph was taken.

Article 9: Details – Confidential

9.1 The parties shall treat the details of the contract and any information made available by the purchaser, the contractor, the engineer or the lender's Engineer in relation thereto and all information concerning the design, construction and performance of the works as confidential and shall not publish or disclose the same or any particulars thereof to any third parties (save insofar as may be necessary for the purposes of the contract) or make use of the same for purposes not connected with the contract, without the previous consent in writing of the other Party. The Parties shall only divulge confidential information to those of their employees as are directly involved or engaged for the purposes of the contract and who need to know the same and will ensure that such employees are aware of and comply with these obligations as to confidentiality. The contractor shall ensure that its sub-contractors and suppliers are bound by the requirements of this clause. The provisions of this clause 9 shall survive termination of the contract.

9.2 Nothing in this clause 9 shall prevent the communication of any information by either of the Parties to their bankers and professional advisers or others to whom such Party is under a legally enforceable obligation to disclose the same.

Article 10: Notices

10.1 Any notice to be given under the contract and all certificates, instructions and orders to be given by the engineer or the purchaser under the contract (in this clause, referred to as a "notice") shall be served by sending the same to the address set out in the Appendix or such other address, as provided in clause 10.5.

10.2 All notices to be given under the contract shall be sent by registered post, courier or facsimile transmission.

10.3 Any notice sent by facsimile transmission shall be deemed to have been served at the time of receipt of a complete and legible copy of the notice. A notice sent by post or courier shall be deemed to have been served when delivered.

10.4 All written communications between the Parties shall be in the English language.

10.5 Either party may change its address for the service of notices by giving at least 5 days' prior notice to the other Party in accordance with the requirements of this clause.

Article 11: Purchaser's General Obligations

11.1 Upon the effective date the purchaser shall, subject to and in accordance with Annexure 2 (purchaser's obligations), give the contractor access (but not exclusive access) to and possession of each part of the site (but not exclusive possession, save in respect of those areas of the Site where it is provided in Annexure 2 (purchaser's obligations) that the Contractor shall have exclusive possession. The purchaser shall be under no obligation to assist the contractor to gain access to any land outside the site and such matters shall, save as otherwise provided in the contract, be entirely the responsibility of the contractor and at the contractor's risk.

11.2 Not used.

11.3 The contractor shall take such steps as may be reasonably necessary or as the engineer may reasonably direct to co-ordinate the works with other work to be undertaken by or on behalf of the Purchaser in relation to the project so as to minimise any disruption to such other work . The Purchaser shall procure that equivalent obligations as are undertaken by the Contractor under the contract in relation to co-ordination and minimisation of disruption are undertaken by all the Purchaser's Contractors.

11.4 The purchaser shall procure that within the time stated in project manual annexure 19 (Design Approval Procedure, the engineer provides the Contractor with such information and/or documents as the 'contractor requires from the 'purchaser's contractors in accordance with the provisions of the project manual – Annexure 19 (Design Approval Procedure).

11.5 The purchaser shall provide its personnel for the operation and maintenance of the Plant with effect from the date of testing coal handling/first charge of coal and shall comply with the requirements on the purchaser's part set out in Annexure 2/ the contract, including the supply of feed coal in accordance with the specification set out in the technical specification and all consumables required for the operation and maintenance of the Plant. The contractor is responsible of instructions to and control of the Purchaser's Personnel. The above shall be without prejudice to any obligations of the contractor to carry out the Performance Test in accordance with the terms of this contract.

11.6 If:

(i) the Purchaser shall fail to comply with any of its obligations set out in Annexure 2 (purchaser's obligations); or

(ii) as a result of any delay, impediment or prevention caused by any of the purchaser's contractors (including any of their sub-contractors of any tier),

the contractor, acting reasonably, incurs any delay or additional costs as a result which it was not possible to avoid or mitigate by the taking of all reasonable steps, the contractor shall, without prejudice to the generality of clause 41, give notice and full particulars thereof to the Engineer and shall submit such further details as the engineer may reasonably request. After receipt of such notice and details, the Engineer shall, following consultation with the Purchaser and the contractor, determine:

(a) any extension of time to which the contractor is entitled under clause 33; and

(b) the amount of any such additional cost incurred by the contractor which amount shall be added to the contract price, subject to and in accordance with clause 39,

and shall notify the contractor and the Purchaser accordingly.

The purchaser and its respective advisor (RAG-ISG) will select personnel with key functions/qualifications for operating the Plant. The contractor will assist RAG-ISG, in defining necessary qualification of the respective personnel within 3 months after effective date.

Article 12: Legal Requirements, Permits and Licences

12.1(a) The purchaser shall at its own cost comply with, give the notices and obtain all permits required from any governmental instrumentality in India in relation to the construction of the project and all other permits stated to be acquired and/or maintained by the Purchaser in Annexure 8 (permits) and shall pay all fees required to be paid in connection with such permits or legal requirements.

(b) The Contractor shall, where so provided in Annexure 8 (permits), or where otherwise reasonably necessary, take, at the written request of the Purchaser, such reasonable steps (as are notified to the contractor) to assist the Purchaser in obtaining the permits referred to in clause 12.1(a) which relate to the .... plant.

12.2(a) The contractor shall at its own cost comply with, give the notices and obtain all Permits required from any governmental instrumentality outside of India in relation to the construction of the .... plant and all other permits (if any) stated to be acquired and/or maintained by the contractor in

Annexure 8 (permits) and shall pay all fees required to be paid in connection with such permits or legal requirements.

(b) The purchaser shall, where so provided in Annex 8 (permits), or where otherwise reasonably necessary, take, at the written request of the contractor, such reasonable steps (as are notified to the Purchaser) to assist the contractor in obtaining the permits referred to in clause 12.2(a).

12.3 If, by reason of any change-in-legal requirements, the contractor, acting reasonably, incurs:

(i) any delay and/or additional costs which it was not possible to avoid or mitigate by the taking of all reasonable steps; or

(ii) benefits from any reduced costs, the contractor shall, without prejudice to the generality of clause 41, give notice and full particulars thereof to the engineer and shall submit such further details as the Engineer may reasonably request. After receipt of such notice and details, the Engineer shall, following consultation with the Purchaser and the contractor, determine:

(a) any extension of time to which the Contractor is entitled under clause 33; and

(b) the amount of any such additional or reduced cost which shall be added to, or deducted from the contract price (as the case may be), subject to and in accordance with clause 39;

and shall notify the contractor and the Purchaser accordingly.

Article 13: Contractor's Obligations

13.1 If the contractor fails to comply with any of its interface obligations under the contract, and such failure places the Purchaser in breach of the Power Plant EPC contract, the contractor shall indemnify the Purchaser against any liability, which the purchaser may incur to the power plant EPC Contractor as, stated in Appendix.

13.2 The contractor shall subject to and in accordance with the contract and with due skill, care and diligence, design, engineer, procure, manufacture, supply, deliver to site, install, erect, construct, complete, test and commission the .... plant and the works, and shall carry out the performance test within the Time for completion and shall remedy any defect in the works which it is responsible for making good under clause 36 within the defects liability period. The contractor shall provide all labour (save as provided otherwise in the contract), including the supervision thereof, Plant, Contractor's equipment and all other things, whether of a temporary or permanent nature, required for such purposes.

13.3 In lieu of any warranties and conditions implied by law relating to fitness for purpose or quality (which are hereby excluded), and subject to the terms of the contract (including clause 44) the contractor undertakes to the Purchaser that:

(a) the .... plant and the works as completed shall be reasonably fit for the purposes specified in the technical specification;

(b) the .... plant as completed shall be free from defects and deficiencies;

(c) the .... plant as completed shall be in accordance with the requirements stated in the technical specification and where none are so stated, to the reasonable satisfaction of the engineer;

(d) when properly operated in accordance with the O&M manuals, the .... plant as completed shall comply with and operate in accordance with the legal requirements and good engineering practice, in both cases, as at the date stated in the Appendix.

(e) except where otherwise provided in the technical specification, the .... plant shall have been and shall be designed, engineered, specified and tested to the relevant standards referred to in the technical Specification, current as at the date stated in the Appendix or (if not stated), as approved in writing by the Engineer;

(f) the contractor shall within the time for completion successfully complete the performance test.

(g) the contractor has the necessary resources, experience, qualifications and capabilities at its disposal to fulfil all its obligations under the contract;

(h) the contractor shall carry out and be responsible for the design of the Plant and the works, such design to be prepared by qualified designers or other professionals who comply with any relevant criteria set out in the Technical Specification and the Contractor holds out itself, its designers and its relevant subcontractors as having the experience and capability necessary for such design.

(i) at the time for completion the works shall have been constructed in accordance with the design documentation submitted to and approved (or deemed to have approved) by the Engineer in accordance with the contract, and that there will have been, and will be no material departure from, such design documentation except in accordance with clause 27;

(j) that the processes, methods of production and technology incorporated in the .... plant are as stated in the technical specification and, if not so stated, of acceptable standards in India, in both cases, as at the date stated in the Appendix including standards of efficiency, economy, reliability, health and safety;

(k) no infringement of any patent, trade mark, registered design, copyright, design right or any other registrable proprietary or intellectual property right of any kind whether in India or elsewhere will result from the performance of the contract or the operation or ownership of the .... plant by the purchaser;

(l) the .... plant and the works have been and/or shall be designed, engineered and constructed in accordance with good engineering Practice, all applicable legal requirements (including all applicable environmental requirements) and in a manner so as to ensure their operability and maintainability will be in accordance with the standards and practices specified in the technical specification and, if not so specified, in accordance with other applicable acceptable international standards and practices for .... production, in each case, as at the date stated in the Appendix;

(m) the .... plant and the works shall achieve the performance guarantees during the performance test;

(n) the .... plant and the works comprise or will comprise only materials, equipment, plant, machinery and other goods which are new and of appropriate quality and that all workmanship, manufacture and fabrication shall be of standards specified in the technical specification and, if not so specified, in accordance with other applicable internationally acceptable standards for .... production, in each case, as at the date stated in the Appendix;

(o) the contractor shall be responsible for the development and implementation of any additional test procedures called for in the Technical Specification and shall submit the same to the Engineer for approval;

(p) the contractor shall, upon the request of the engineer, provide to the lenders' engineer all such drawings, information required for due diligence relating to the works and such access to the site as the lenders' engineer may reasonably require in the exercise of its rights under the contract, provided that the lenders' engineer, in exercising any right of access to the site, shall have due regard to the works being carried out so as not to interfere with the progress of the works;

(q) the contractor shall comply with all applicable health and safety laws, regulations and guidelines in respect of all the contractor's labour and that of its sub-contractors and suppliers;

(r) the contractor shall not import, sell, give, barter or otherwise dispose of any alcoholic liquor or drugs;

(s) the contractor shall not give, barter or otherwise dispose of to any person or persons any arms or ammunition of any kind;

(t) the contractor shall, in all dealings with the contractor's labour or representatives have due regard to all recognised local festivals, days of rest and religious or other customs;

(u) no person below the age of 18 years shall be employed on or in connection with the works and no female labour shall be employed after darkness;

(v) in the event of any outbreak of illness of an epidemic nature, the contractor shall comply with any applicable regulations, orders and requirements as may be made by any relevant national or state authority or the local medical or sanitary authorities for the purpose of dealing with and overcoming the same;

(w) the contractor shall at all times take all reasonable precautions to prevent any unlawful, riotous or disorderly conduct by or amongst the contractor's labour and for the preservation of peace and protection of persons and property in the neighbourhood of the works against the same;

(x) all employees shall wear identification badges while present at Site;

(y) in the event of any member of the contractor's labour suffering any accident, injury or incapacitating illness while in India and whether there be a claim for compensation or not, the contractor shall without delay notify the relevant authority in such form as that authority may require and shall forward forthwith two copies of such notification to the Engineer; and

(z) the contractor shall be responsible for observance by its sub-contractors, suppliers, agents, representatives or employees of the foregoing provisions.

13.4 The contractor shall provide comprehensive training to designated personnel of the Purchaser in the use, operation, and maintenance of the .... plant, and involve such personnel fully in the commissioning and testing of the .... plant, such training to be as more particularly described in the technical specification for the purpose of providing such training and so as to enable the designated personnel of the Purchaser to familiarise themselves with the works and the .... plant, the contractor shall allow access as necessary for such personnel to the site and shall procure access for such personnel to places off the Site where Plant is being manufactured and tested. The cost of providing such training to the Purchaser's said personnel is included in the contract price (the Purchaser being responsible for all costs in providing such personnel, including their boarding, lodging and transportation).

13.5 The contractor shall, subject to the terms of the contract (including clause 44), so design and construct the .... plant and the works as to comply with all applicable permits, which it is the responsibility of either Party to obtain and maintain under clause 12.

13.6 The purchaser, shall at its own cost, provide fuels, consumables, electricity, telecommunications, water and other utilities required in or about the construction of the .... plant and the works, as provided in Annexure 2 (purchaser's obligations).

13.7 The contractor shall obtain and retain at the Site and supply to the Purchaser as and when the purchaser may reasonably require (the number of copies shall be as per project manual):

(a) for all items of equipment incorporated into the .... plant and identified in the technical specification, copies of the specifications and operation manuals for such equipment;

(b) copies of test results for the Performance Test and any other tests performed on the .... plant and all items of equipment incorporated into the .... plant;

(c) as-built drawings for the .... plant, including all ancillary civil and building works;

(d) copies of all design documentation;

(e) copies of the contract;

(f) copies of any permits which pursuant to Annexure 8 (Permits) it is the responsibility of the contractor to obtain and/or maintain; and

(g) the activity reports, the monthly progress reports and the progress photographs referred to in clause 8.3.

13.8 The contractor shall institute a quality assurance system to demonstrate compliance with the requirements of the contract. Such system shall be in accordance with any relevant details stated in the technical specification. Details of all procedures and compliance documents shall be submitted to the Engineer for his information before each design and execution stage is commenced. The Engineer, acting reasonably, shall be entitled to audit any aspect of the system and require corrective action to be taken.

13.9 The contractor shall afford reasonable access (save to the areas, referred to in clause 11.1, where the contractor will have exclusive possession) for the purchaser's contractors who may be employed in the execution on or near the site of any work not included in this contract or in the performance of any contract which the Purchaser may enter into in connection with the project.

Article 14: Programme

14.1 The contractor shall execute the works in accordance with the order, procedure and dates set out in the programme (as from time to time modified pursuant to the contract) and the Contractor shall not without the Engineer's consent (which shall not be unreasonably withheld), make any alteration thereto. The Contractor shall be entitled to accelerate the works where such acceleration will not have an adverse effect on the carrying out of any other works by the Power Plant EPC Contractor subject to Engineers consent and subject to the Purchaser having sufficient time to comply with its obligations hereunder.

14.2 If (in circumstances which have not arisen as a result of a delay or other default on the part of the contractor) the engineer requires the contractor to alter the order, procedure and/or dates set out in the Programme in order to co-ordinate the works with any other contractors as referred to in clause 11.2 or 14.6 and, in so doing, the contractor, acting reasonably, incurs additional costs and/or delay in so doing which it was not possible to avoid or mitigate by the taking of all reasonable steps, then the contractor shall, without prejudice to the generality of clause 41, give notice and full particulars thereof to the Engineer and shall submit such further details as the Engineer may reasonably request. After receipt of such notice and details, the Engineer shall, following consultation with the Purchaser and the Contractor, determine:

(a) any extension of time to which the Contractor is entitled under clause 33; and

(b) the amount of any such additional cost, which shall be added to, the contract price, subject to and in accordance with clause 39;

and shall notify the Contractor and the Purchaser accordingly.

14.3 Within 1 month before the effective date, the contractor shall submit to the Engineer for approval a project programme showing the sequences and methods in which it proposes to carry out the works including design, engineering, procurement, manufacture, supply, delivery to the Site, installation, erection, construction, completion, testing, commissioning and co-ordination and interfacing with the Purchaser's contractors. The submission to the Engineer of such detailed project programme shall not relieve the contractor of its obligations under the contract. The detailed project programme having been approved by the Engineer shall supplement the programme and the Programme shall be amended to incorporate such approved detailed project programme.

14.4 Save as provided in the contract, the contractor shall not alter the sequences and methods shown in the project programme referred to in clause 14.3 without the written consent of the engineer and shall otherwise adhere to such sequences and methods.

14.5 The Engineer may notify the contractor if in his reasonable opinion the rate of progress of the works or of any part of the works is insufficient to meet the requirements of the programme and/or the project programme referred to in clause 14.3 and such rate of progress is not due to a circumstance or occurrence for which the Contractor is entitled to an extension of time under clause 33.1.

Upon receipt of such notice, the contractor shall take such steps as may be necessary and as the Engineer may approve to achieve the requirements of the programme and/or the project programme referred to in clause 14.3. The Contractor shall as and when instructed by the Engineer make such modifications to the programme and/or the project programme referred to in clause 14.3 as may be necessary to reflect actual and anticipated progress and shall submit such proposed modifications to the Engineer for approval. The Contractor shall not be entitled to any additional payment for taking such steps.

The provisions of this clause 14.5 shall be without prejudice to clause 34.

14.6 The contractor shall, subject to and in accordance with the reasonable instructions of the Engineer, liase with and cooperate fully with the power plant EPC contractor and Purchaser's other contractors, in connection with the programme for commissioning and testing the .... plant and the power plant and the Contractor shall take whatever steps may be necessary and/or as the Engineer may reasonably instruct in connection therewith.

Article 15: Design Documentation

15.1 Where there is any ambiguity, discrepancy or conflict within the Technical Specification the contractor shall (without prejudice to clause 4.2) inform the Engineer in writing of its proposed amendment to resolve such ambiguity, discrepancy or conflict and the Engineer shall either resolve such ambiguity, discrepancy or conflict or otherwise may accept the contractor's proposed amendment and shall inform the contractor accordingly and the Contractor shall comply with the decision or acceptance by the Engineer without cost to the Purchaser nor delay to the progress of the works.

15.2(a) The contractor shall submit to the engineer:

   (i) within the times stated in Annexure 19 (Design Approval Procedure) such Design Documentation as may be called for therein for the approval of the Engineer including such Design Documentation as may be called for therein for the information of the Power Plant EPC contractor;

   (ii) during the progress of the works within such reasonable times as the Engineer may specify such further design documentation as may be specified in the contract or as the Engineer may reasonably require.

(b) The engineer, acting reasonably, shall signify his approval or disapproval of all such design documentation. The Engineer shall be entitled to disapprove the design documentation only if it fails to comply with the requirements of the contract. If he fails to signify his approval or disapproval within the time given in Annexure 19 (Design Approval Procedure) or, if not so stated, within 14 days from receipt, such design information shall be deemed to have been approved.

If the Engineer requires any changes to be made to the design documentation other than as required to comply with the contract then he shall be deemed to have issued a change proposal under clause 27.1 in relation to such changes.

(c) All design documentation shall be signed or otherwise identified by the Engineer as and when approved pursuant to clause 15.2(b).

(d) Any design documentation, which the Engineer may disapprove within the time referred to in clause 15.2(b), shall be modified by the contractor to comply with such comments and requirements and re-submitted by the contractor without delay. The provisions of clause 15.2(b) shall apply in relation to the resubmission of such modified Design Documentation, save that the time limit there referred to shall be 14 days from receipt.

(e) If pursuant to clause 15.2(a), Design Documentation in respect of a part of the works requires the approval of the Engineer, construction of such part of the works shall not commence until the Engineer has approved (or is deemed to have approved) the design documentation in respect of such part. Subject to clause 27, construction of such part shall be in accordance with the design documentation, which has been so approved.

(f) If the Engineer instructs that further design documentation is necessary prior to carrying out any part of the works, the contractor shall upon receiving such instruction prepare such design documentation and submit the same to the Engineer for approval pursuant to clause 15.2(a). The provisions of clause 15.2(b) shall apply in relation to the resubmission of such further design documentation, save that the time limit there referred to shall be as soon as reasonably practicable and, in any event, within 14 days from receipt.

15.3 The Contractor shall submit to the Engineer for information:

(a) within the times stated in Annexure 19 (Design Approval Procedure) such Design Documentation as may be called for therein for information;

(b) within the times stated in the Project Manual/Annexure 19 (Design Approval Procedure) such comments as may be reasonably required and appropriate regarding drawings and information provided by the purchaser's contractor (as referred to in the Project Manual/Annexure 19 (Design Approval Procedure) and made available to the contractor by the Engineer as part of his functions in relation to co-ordination between the contractor and purchaser's contractors;

(c) such further design documentation as the Engineer may reasonably consider necessary from time to time to explain or amplify any part of the Technical Specification or the co-ordination of the works with the works of the Purchaser's Contractors.

15.4 The Engineer shall have the right at all reasonable times to inspect all drawings and other information relating to any part of the works as per Annexure 19.

15.5 In accordance with the project manual, prior to the commencement of performance test the contractor shall supply for the engineer's approval draft operating and maintenance manuals. The O&M Manuals shall be in such detail as will enable the Purchaser to operate and maintain the .... plant and repair and replace all major parts of the .... plant. The provisions of clause 15.2 (b), (c) and (d) shall apply, *mutatis mutandis*.

The contractor shall supply copies of such final draft manuals (or if available on computer disc, hard copies and computer disc) as so revised within such reasonable period before taking over, as stipulated in the project manual.

15.6 After completion of the performance test and taking over, the contractor shall as soon as reasonably practicable submit to the Engineer for approval any revisions which may be required to the final draft O&M Manuals in the light of the performance test. The provisions of clause 15.2 (b), (c) and (d) shall apply, *mutatis mutandis*.

15.7 The contractor shall supply as per the project manual copies of each as built drawing supplied pursuant to clause 13.7 within two months after taking Over. The built drawings and O&M Manuals will be submitted as per the Project Manual on paper print and if required one set of transparency or 35 mm negative. After supplying the revised O&M Manual and as built drawings the contractor will receive a milestone payment of 0.5% of the contract price (against Bank Guarantee).

15.8 All copyright and design rights, which may subsist in Design Documentation, shall (as between the Parties) remain vested in the contractor. The contractor hereby grants to the Purchaser a royalty free non-exclusive, irrevocable licence to copy and use the Design Documentation and to reproduce the designs contained in them as may be reasonably necessary for the purpose of completing, maintaining, operating and repairing the .... plant (but not otherwise without the prior written consent of the contractor). The Purchaser shall be entitled to assign the benefit of the licence to use the design documentation, subject to the contractor's prior consent and the contractor shall not unreasonably withhold such consent. The contractor shall not be liable for any use by the Purchaser (or any assignee) of the design documentation for any purpose other than for the purpose for which they were prepared by the contractor or for any purpose other than completing, maintaining, operating and repairing the .... plant. The provisions of this clause 15.8 shall survive this contract.

15.9 Any drawings and information supplied by the purchaser or the Engineer to the contractor (including drawings and information provided by the Power Plant EPC contractor as referred to in the project manual/Annexure 19 (Design Approval Procedure) for the purposes of the contract shall remain the property of the Purchaser. They shall not without the consent of the Purchaser be used, copied or communicated to a third Party by the contractor unless:—

(a) such distribution is necessary for the purposes of the contract; and

(b) the contractor has caused the recipients of such drawings and information to agree to the confidentiality provisions of the contract.

Article 16: Errors in Design Documentation

16.1 Notwithstanding approval by the Engineer of design documentation under clause 15.2 or submission to the Engineer of design documentation under clause 15.3 the contractor shall, subject as provided in this clause 16.1, be and remain responsible for any failure thereof to comply with or achieve the requirements of the Purchaser's requirements as set out in the preamble to the Technical Specification and for any error, omission or discrepancy therein. No comment of the Engineer or the Purchaser (whether under clause 15.2 or otherwise) in connection with design documentation shall relieve the contractor from any of its obligations under the contract unless and to the extent that:

(i) the contractor has notified the Engineer that it disagrees with any comments made by the Engineer on the design documentation pursuant to clause 15.2;

(ii) such notice sets out the reasons for its disagreement and the adverse consequences which the contractor considers may result from amending the design documentation in accordance with such comments; and

(iii) such adverse consequences in fact arise.

16.2 If the contractor is responsible for any error, omission or discrepancy referred to in clause 16.1, it shall, at its own expense, promptly remedy the same and carry out all work made necessary thereby.

Article 17: Contractor's Representatives

17.1 The contractor shall at all times employ a competent representative to superintend the carrying out of the works on the site. The representative shall be present on the site during working hours, and any instruction, which the Purchaser or the Engineer may give to such representative, shall be deemed to have been given to the contractor. The representative (together with such other representatives of the contractor as the purchaser may reasonably require) shall attend all meetings with the purchaser and the Engineer at times and frequency reasonably required by the Engineer. The contractor shall not replace any such representative without the prior written consent of the Engineer. Any such representative shall be fluent in written and spoken English.

17.2 The Engineer shall be entitled by notice to the contractor to object to any representative or person employed by the contractor in the execution of or otherwise about the works who shall, in the reasonable opinion of the Engineer, misconduct himself or be incompetent or negligent or otherwise undesirable, and the contractor shall forthwith remove such person from the works and replace him within a reasonable time, at its own cost, with a suitably qualified person.

Article18: Site Services and Clearance

18.1 The purchaser shall, subject to and in accordance with the provisions of Annexure 2 (purchaser's obligations), be responsible for clearance and preparation of the site and the provision of security, and temporary roadways and footways therein (save as mentioned in clause 18.2).

18.2 The contractor shall be responsible for proper fencing (where appropriate) and security for the areas (referred to in clause 11.1) which it has exclusive possession of; lighting and watching of the works until taking over; and the provision of all necessary temporary roadways and temporary footways within the above mentioned areas.

18.3 From time to time during the progress of the works the contractor shall clear away and remove from the site all surplus materials and rubbish and, as soon as reasonably practicable following taking over, all contractor's equipment except any contractor's equipment required on Site until completion of the Performance Test. The contractor shall at all times keep the Site and the works clean and in a safe and workmanlike condition to the Engineer's reasonable satisfaction.

Article19: Staff and Labour

19.1 The contractor shall subject to the provisions of the contract, make its own arrangements for the engagement of all its staff and labour, local or otherwise and for their payment, housing, feeding and transport.

19.2 The contractor shall not recruit, or attempt to recruit, any staff or labour from amongst persons in the service of the purchaser or the Engineer.

19.3 Without prejudice to the generality of clause 52.9:

(a) the contractor shall comply with all relevant labour laws applying to its employees;

(b) the contractor shall require all its employees and those of its sub-contractors to obey all applicable laws and regulations concerning safety at work; and

(c) the purchaser shall require all its employees and shall procure that all other contractors operating on the site (other than the contractor and its sub-contractors) obey all applicable laws and regulations concerning safety at work.

19.4 Work shall be carried out on the site during normal working hours and shall not be carried out during the night or on locally recognised days of rest or at other times prohibited by or pursuant to any law or regulation or any licence or Permit granted pursuant thereto without the consent of the Engineer (which shall not be unreasonably withheld) unless such work is unavoidable or necessary for the protection of life or property or for the safety of the works, in which case the contractor shall immediately advise the Engineer.

The contractor shall be responsible for obtaining any necessary Permit or other approval or licence for extended working hours.

19.5 The contractor shall provide and maintain all necessary accommodation and welfare facilities for its and its sub-contractors' staff and labour. The contractor shall be entitled to establish a camp for its employees by the fabrication yard at the Site (or at such other location within the Site as may be agreed between the Parties) and shall not permit any of its employees to maintain any temporary or permanent living quarters within the structures forming part of the .... plant.

19.6 Precautions shall be taken by the contractor to ensure the health, safety and welfare of its staff and labour and those of its sub-contractors, including the provision of first aid facilities, the provision of a sufficient number of personnel who are trained in administering first aid and ensuring that suitable arrangements are made for all necessary welfare and (save to the extent to be provided by the Purchaser under Annexure 2 (purchaser's obligations), hygiene requirements. The contractor shall maintain records and make reports concerning health, safety and welfare of persons, and damage to property, as the Engineer may reasonably require.

19.7 The contractor shall provide all necessary superintendence during the works. Such superintendence shall be provided by persons having adequate knowledge of the operations to be carried out for the satisfactory and safe execution of the works.

19.8 The contractor shall employ (or cause to be employed) only persons who are appropriately qualified, skilled and experienced in their respective trades or occupations.

19.9 The contractor shall, on or before the tenth day of every month, send to the Engineer a return detailing the number of supervisory staff and labour from time to time employed by the contractor and its sub-contractors on the site during the previous month together with an estimate of the number of supervisory staff and labour that will be employed during the current month. The returns shall be provided in such form and with such frequency as the Engineer may reasonably require.

Article 20: Safety

The contractor shall be responsible for the adequacy, security, stability and safety of its operations on the Site.

Article 21: Extraordinary Traffic

21.1 The contractor shall use every reasonable means to prevent damage to the highways and bridges on the routes to the Site by any of the Contractor's vehicles or those of its sub-contractors.

21.2 Save as provided in Annexure 2 (purchaser's obligations), the contractor shall at its own cost take all necessary steps to protect or strengthen any highway or bridge on, along or over which the Contractor intends to transport any plant or contractor's equipment so as to prevent damage thereto.

21.3 The contractor shall indemnify the purchaser against any claim in respect of damage to any highway or bridge arising out of the execution of the works and in respect of any proceedings, costs and expenses incurred by the purchaser in relation thereto save to the extent that such proceedings, costs and expenses arose due to a failure by the Purchaser to comply with its obligations under Annexure 2 (Purchaser's Obligations).

21.4 The foregoing provisions of this clause 21 shall be construed as though the word "highway" included a lock, dock, sea-wall or other marine structure.

Article 22: Setting Out

22.1 The contractor shall be responsible for the true and accurate setting out of the works. If during the execution of the works any error appears in the positions, levels, dimensions or alignment of the works, the Contractor shall rectify such error at its own cost.

22.2 The contractor shall protect and preserve benchmarks, sight rails, pegs and other things used in setting out the works.

Article 23: Inspection and Testing

23.1 The purchaser and/or the Engineer and/or (as provided in clause 8) the lenders' Engineer shall be entitled at all reasonable times to inspect, examine and test at the site or at the place of manufacture (whether the premises of the contractor or any supplier or sub-contractor) the materials, workmanship and performance of any part of the works to be supplied under the contract. Such inspection, examination or testing shall not relieve the contractor from any of its obligations under the contract.

23.2 The contractor shall give due notice to the Engineer and the lenders' Engineer before covering up or putting out of view any part of the works identified in the inspection and procedures plan referred to in clause 23.3 as falling within the scope of this provision. The Engineer and/or the lenders' Engineer shall each without unreasonable delay either together carry out an inspection, examination or test or notify the contractor that it is considered unnecessary for either/both of them to do so. If the contractor fails to give such notice, or fails to give such access for such inspection, examination or test, it shall, when required by the Engineer, uncover such work and thereafter reinstate and make good at its own cost.

23.3 Within 1 month after the effective date, the contractor shall submit to the Engineer and the lenders' Engineer a preliminary draft inspection and procedures plan including witness points for approval and clause 15.2(b) shall apply, *mutatis mutandis*. The contractor shall thereafter develop a more detailed inspection, procedures plan for approval, and clause 15.2(b) shall apply, *mutatis mutandis*. The more detailed inspection and procedures plan shall then supersede the preliminary plan.

23.4 The contractor shall give the Engineer and the lenders' Engineer (with a copy to the purchaser) such notice as is provided in the inspection and procedures plan in relation to the part of the works identified therein (and, if not so provided, the notice period shall be 14 days) prior to the date on which such part of the works will be ready for testing or inspection in accordance therewith, and the proposed location of such testing or inspection. The Engineer shall give the contractor at least 24 hours' notice of its (and the Lenders' Engineer's) intention to attend such test or inspection (save in cases where the period of notice specified in the inspection and test plan is less than 24 hours). If the Engineer or the lenders' Engineer fails to attend at the place and date agreed, the contractor may proceed with the test or inspection, which shall be deemed to have been made in the Engineer's and the lenders' Engineer's presence. The contractor shall forthwith forward to the Engineer and the lenders' Engineer duly certified copies of the results of such tests or inspections.

23.5 Where the contract provides for tests or inspection on the premises of the contractor or of any supplier or sub-contractor, the contractor shall provide free of charge such assistance, labour, materials, electricity, fuel, stores, apparatus and instruments as may be necessary and/or as may reasonably be requested to carry out such test or inspection.

23.6 If after inspecting, examining or testing any part of the works the Engineer, acting reasonably, shall decide that such part of the works is defective or not in accordance with the contract, he may reject such part by a notice stating the grounds for such rejection. As soon as reasonably practicable following receipt of any such notice the Contractor shall make good or otherwise repair or replace the rejected part of the works and at its own cost resubmit the same for test or inspection in accordance with this clause 23. Any additional direct cost reasonably incurred by the Purchaser, the Engineer or the lenders' Engineer in attending such re-testing or inspection shall be borne by the contractor and deducted from the contract price or paid to the purchaser on demand.

23.7 No inspection, examination or testing by the Purchaser, the Engineer or the lenders' Engineer of the works or any part of the works, or the rejection and re-testing of the same pursuant to clause 23.5 shall relieve the contractor of any of its obligations under the contract.

Article 24: Delivery

24.1 The contractor shall notify the Engineer of its intention to deliver any major item of Plant or major item of contractor's Equipment to the Site. In the case of any such plant or contractor's equipment which is to be imported into India (the "imported equipment") such notification shall include details of the shipment date, port of embarkation, expected date of arrival at the designated port of arrival and all such other shipping information as the Purchaser may reasonably require. In the case of any such Plant or contractor's Equipment, which is indigenously supplied (the "Indigenous Equipment"), such notification shall include details of the date of dispatch, the expected date of arrival at site and such other information relating to the consignment as the Purchaser may reasonably require. All Plant and contractor's Equipment arriving at the Site shall be promptly unloaded, transported and stored by the contractor. The contractor shall be responsible for examining all shipments and deliveries, and shall notify the Engineer immediately of any damage, discrepancy or shortage. The contractor shall be responsible for any loss or damage during transit, unloading, storage and erection at the site. Road permits as applicable shall be provided by the purchaser.

24.2 In relation to each item of imported equipment, the contractor shall supply to the Engineer within 15 days of the date of shipment of such item, 8 copies of each of the following documents:

  (a) bill of lading (or, where payment is due under clause 25.3, a warehouse storage receipt);
  (b) invoice;
  (c) packing list;
  (d) test certificate, wherever applicable;
  (e) certificate of country of origin;

24.3 In relation to each item of indigenous equipment, the contractor shall supply to the Engineer within 3 days of the date of despatch of such item, copies of each of the following documents:

  (a) invoice;
  (b) lorry way bill (or, where payment is due under clause 25.3, a warehouse storage receipt);
  (c) packing list;
  (d) test certificate, wherever applicable

Article 25: Suspension of Works

25.1 The Engineer may at any time instruct the contractor to suspend progress of the works or any part thereof. If, at the time of issuing the instruction, it is not reasonably practicable for the contractor to suspend any part of the works, then the instruction of the Engineer shall not take effect, in respect of such part of the works, until such time as it is reasonably practicable for the contractor to do so. During suspension, the contractor shall protect, store, secure and (to the extent required by the Purchaser) insure the works so affected against any deterioration, loss or damage.

25.2 If the contractor, acting reasonably, incurs any delay or incurs any additional costs in carrying out the Engineer's instructions or complying with any other obligations under this clause 25 which it was not possible for the contractor to avoid or mitigate by the taking of all reasonable steps, the contractor shall, without prejudice to the generality of clause 41, give notice and full particulars thereof to the Engineer with a copy to the Purchaser and shall submit such further details as the Engineer may reasonably request. After receipt of such notice and details, the Engineer shall, following consultation with the purchaser and the contractor, determine:

(a) any extension of time to which the contractor is entitled under clause 33; and

(b) the amount of any such additional cost, which shall be added to the contract price, subject to and in accordance with clause 39,

and shall notify the Contractor and the purchaser accordingly, provided that the contractor shall not be entitled to any such extension of time or reimbursement of additional cost if the suspension is due to any breach of contract, negligence or default of the Contractor.

25.3 The contractor shall be entitled to payment for any Plant on which at the normal delivery date, work or delivery to Site has been suspended for more than 28 days in total following instructions under clause 25.1. The contract value of such Plant as at the date of suspension may be included by the contractor in an application for an interim payment certificate under clause 39, provided that the contractor shall have marked such plant as the Purchaser's property in accordance with clause 37.3 and notified insurers as if it were on Site and provided further that the suspension is not due to any breach of contract, negligence or other default of the contractor.

25.4 At any time following an instruction under clause 25.1 the Engineer may give notice to the contractor to resume the works the subject of such instruction. Upon receipt of such notice, the contractor shall examine the parts of the works affected by the suspension. The contractor shall make good any deterioration, defect or loss that may have occurred during suspension.

If the contractor acting reasonably incurs any additional cost in making such examination, making good and resuming work which it was not possible to avoid or mitigate by the taking of all reasonable steps, the same shall be determined by the Engineer and added to the contract price, according to the procedure in clause 25.2, unless such suspension was necessitated by any breach of contract, negligence or other default of the contractor or for the proper execution or safety of the works, in which case all additional costs shall be borne by the contractor. The contractor shall not be entitled to be paid any cost incurred in making such examination or in making good any deterioration, defect or loss if the suspension continued for less than 28 days or if any deterioration, defect or loss was caused by defective materials or workmanship or by the contractor's failure to comply with any instructions of the Engineer under clause 25.

25.5 If suspension under this clause 25 has continued for more than .... days and the suspension is not due to any breach of contract, negligence or default of the contractor, the contractor may by notice to the Engineer require the Engineer to instruct the contractor to proceed with all of the suspended works within .... days. If the Engineer does not issue such an instruction within the said period then (where the suspension affects part of the works) the Engineer shall be deemed to require the contractor to issue a preliminary variation and (where the suspension affects the whole of the Works), the contractor shall be entitled to issue a termination notice on the grounds of purchaser remediable event under clause 46.1.3(b) (save that the period of notice specified in that clause shall be .... days and not .... days).

Article 26: Defects Before Taking Over

Without prejudice to any of the contractor's obligations under the contract, if, in relation to any part of the works which has not achieved taking over, the Engineer, acting reasonably, at any time:

(a) decides that any work done or Plant supplied or used by the contractor or any of its sub-contractors is defective or not in accordance with the contract, or does not fulfil the requirements of the contract (all such matters being in this clause called "defects"); and

(b) as soon as reasonably practicable notifies the contractor of such decision, specifying particulars,

the Purchaser shall so far as may be necessary place the plant at the contractor's disposal and the contractor shall with all speed and at its own expense, make good the defects so specified. If the contractor fails so to do the purchaser may, provided it does so without undue delay, take such steps as may in all the circumstances be necessary to make good such defects and any additional direct cost to the Purchaser of such steps shall be borne by the contractor and deducted from the contract price or paid on demand. All plant provided, by the purchaser to replace defective Plant shall comply with the contract. Nothing contained in this clause shall affect the right of the Purchaser to liquidated damages under clauses 28 and 34 nor any other right or remedy which may be available under the contract.

Article 27: Variations

27.1 The Engineer may, subject as provided in this clause, at any time issue to the contractor a change proposal. Any such proposal by the Engineer shall be in writing and shall include such details as may reasonably be necessary for the contractor to prepare a preliminary variation. For the avoidance of doubt, the Engineer shall not be entitled to require any change proposal omitting any part of the works, which are subsequently carried out by another contractor employed by the Purchaser.

27.2 The contractor may at any time issue to the Purchaser a change proposal if in the contractor's opinion such proposal if implemented will reduce the cost of constructing, maintaining or operating the works or the .... plant or will otherwise be for the benefit of the Purchaser. Any such change proposal by the contractor shall include such information and data (including drawings, specifications, patterns, samples or calculations) as may be reasonably necessary to enable the Purchaser and the Engineer to assess the proposal. The Engineer may at his sole discretion and without any obligation or liability to the contractor either reject such change proposal or instruct the contractor to prepare a preliminary variation with respect to all or part of such change proposal.

27.3 Forthwith upon receipt from the Engineer of a change proposal issued in accordance with clause 27.1 or an instruction under clause 27.2 the contractor

shall prepare a Preliminary Variation and submit it to the Engineer. The preliminary variation shall include:
  (a) a description of any proposed design and/or work to be performed and a programme for its execution;
  (b) any proposed modification to the Programme and/or the Payment Schedule;
  (c) any proposed addition to or deduction from the contract price, Time for completion or performance test period or other amendment to the contract;
  (d) such other information as may reasonably be requested by the Engineer in connection with such proposal or instruction;
  (e) the grounds of any objection the contractor may have to the implementation of the matters instructed or proposed.

27.4 Upon receipt from the contractor of a preliminary variation the Engineer shall review and assess the contents thereof and may request (and the contractor shall forthwith submit) such further information as the Engineer may reasonably require. The Engineer shall as soon thereafter as reasonably practicable respond to the Contractor with the Engineer's approval or rejection of or comments on the Preliminary variation. In the event that the Engineer indicates that it wishes to proceed the Parties may thereupon meet in good faith in order to agree the terms of an appropriate variation and, in the case of a preliminary variation referred to in clause 27.5, the Parties shall meet in good faith in order to agree the terms of an appropriate variation. If so agreed, the contractor shall immediately implement such variation, which shall indicate the full, final, and unconditional agreement of each Party with the terms and matters prescribed therein and the contract shall be deemed amended accordingly. Provided, however, that the contractor shall be so obliged if it receives an extended or a new letter of credit in the amount of the proposed variation where so entitled in terms of this clause 27.

27.5 If within 14 days after receipt by the Engineer of a preliminary variation pursuant to clause 27.3 the parties have reached agreement as to all the terms and/or contents of an appropriate variation other than:
  (a) any addition to or deduction from the contract price which may in all the circumstances be reasonable; or
  (b) any adjustment to the Payment Schedule or to the programme which may in all the circumstances be reasonable and necessary; or
  (c) any extension to the time for completion or performance test period to which the contractor may be entitled under clause 33,

the Engineer may nevertheless issue a variation signed only by the Purchaser and subject to determination of such outstanding matters by agreement or by reference to the disputes resolution procedure and the contractor shall immediately implement such variation pending determination of such outstanding matters.

27.6 If within .... days after receipt by the Engineer of a preliminary variation referred to in clause 25.5, the Parties have not reached agreement as to any of the matters specified therein the Engineer shall nevertheless issue a variation signed only by the purchaser subject to determination of all such outstanding matters as provided in clause 27.5.

27.7 For the avoidance of doubt, any cost, risk or matter deemed to have been allowed for by the contractor in the contract price, including any cost incurred by the contractor in providing design, engineering, procurement, construction, testing and commissioning services and all plant (and components thereof) and contractor's equipment, and any other additional items not specifically described in the contract shall not constitute a variation, nor be taken into account in evaluating any addition to or deduction from the contract price or extension to the Time for completion in relation to a variation, if:

(a) it may reasonably may be inferred in accordance with standards employed by leading international contractors in the .... plant construction industry that the provision of such items was intended as part of the scope of works; and

(b) the provision of such items is necessary in order for the Contractor to satisfy its obligations under the contract.

Article 28: Performance Test

28.1 The Performance Test shall be carried out, as soon as is reasonably practicable as per Annexure 3.D.1 (Testing Regime and Guarantees) and within the time for completion and subject to:

(a) the contractor having delivered to the Purchaser's project site store all spare parts required pursuant to Annexure 5 (Spare Parts); and

(b) the Purchaser having complied with all of the obligations on its part set out in Annexure 2 (Purchaser's obligations) required to enable the contractor to carry out the performance test.

The contractor shall give to the Engineer not less than .... days' notice of the date on which the Performance Test starts. Unless otherwise agreed, such Performance Test shall start on the day notified by the contractor. The results of the Performance Test shall be compiled and evaluated by the Engineer and the contractor. The contractor is entitled to carry out up to two repeat Performance Test.

If the works (or any part thereof) fail to pass the performance test the contractor shall take whatever steps may be necessary to enable the works (or such part) to pass the Performance Test and the Performance Test shall be repeated, within such reasonable time as the contractor requires. However within the contractually stipulated periods. Where it is reasonably necessary for the contractor to prepare design documentation in order to take such steps, it shall submit the same to the Engineer pursuant to clause 15.2.

28.2 If on carrying out the performance test (or any of the repeat tests) the Contractor is unable to demonstrate that the performance guarantees (or any of them) are satisfied, the contractor shall pay to the Purchaser, as liquidated damages for its failure to achieve the applicable performance guarantees, the respective amounts stated in the Annexure 3.D.2. The contractor has the option to pay such liquidated damages or to repeat a performance test (up to two repeat performance test).

Amounts accruing under this clause shall be due and payable not later than .... days after receipt by the contractor of an invoice from the Purchaser following the performance test setting forth the purchaser's claim under this clause.

Payment of liquidated damages in accordance with this clause shall be in full satisfaction of the liability of the contractor to the purchaser in relation to any failure by the contractor to achieve the performance guarantees.

28.3 The contractor shall promptly pay all amounts due under this clause to the purchaser or as the purchaser shall direct. If any amount remains unpaid .... days after a written demand therefor the purchaser shall be entitled to charge interest on the amount unpaid calculated daily at the rate of 2% per annum over the base lending rate. Payment of liquidated damages by the contractor shall be made in respective contractual currencies. The purchaser, at its sole discretion, shall be entitled to set off amounts due under this clause against any amount otherwise due to the contractor under or in connection with the contract.

28.4 The contractor's aggregate liability for liquidated damages under this clause shall not exceed the amount named in the Appendix as the Limit of Damages for performance guarantees.

28.5 If on the performance test or the two repeat performance tests carried out pursuant to this clause, the contractor is unable to demonstrate that the works satisfy the minimum performance criteria, as stipulated in Annexure 3.D.2. the purchaser may instead of deducting liquidated damages pursuant to this clause terminate the contract in which event the purchaser shall have the same remedies as are provided under clause 46, such failure being deemed to be a contractor non-remediable event.

Article 29: Taking Over

29.1 The works shall be deemed to have been taken over by the purchaser after the following criteria have been met:

(a) the works have been completed in accordance with the contract (except in minor respects that do not affect its use for the purposes for which it is intended);

(b) the works have passed (or are deemed, under the terms of the contract, to have passed) the performance test; or if on such performance test the contractor is unable to demonstrate that the .... plant satisfies the performance guarantees (or any of them), upon receipt by the purchaser of the liquidated damages referred to in clause 28.

29.2 The contractor may apply by notice to the Engineer for a taking over certificate when in the contractor's opinion the works have satisfied the criteria in clause 29.1(a). The Engineer shall within .... days after receipt of the contractor's application either:

(a) issue the taking over certificate stating the date on which the works satisfied the criteria in clause 29.1(a) and (b) (except in the case of 29.1(a) in minor respects, recorded on such taking over certificate, that do not affect its use for the purposes for which it is intended); or

(b) reject the application giving his reasons and specifying the work required to be done to enable the taking over certificate to be issued: the contractor shall then complete such work before issuing a further notice under this sub-clause.

29.3 Upon the date referred to in the taking over certificate, the purchaser shall be deemed to have taken over the works and shall take possession of the works and the risk of loss or damage to the works shall pass to the Purchaser (other than any parts thereof excluded by the terms of the Taking Over Certificate).

29.4 The contractor shall rectify or complete to the reasonable satisfaction of the Engineer within the time stated in the Taking Over Certificate any outstanding items of work or Plant noted as requiring rectification or as incomplete. If the contractor fails to do so, the purchaser may arrange for the outstanding work to be done by others and the reasonable costs thereof shall be deducted from the contract price or paid to the Purchaser by the contractor forthwith on demand.

29.5 The ...., ... fines and waste heat gases produced by the .... plant and all revenues derived therefrom (including revenues derived from the power plant) at any time during the term of the contract shall be solely for the benefit of the Purchaser.

Article 30: Use Before Taking Over

31.1 If, by reason of any default on the part of the contractor, a taking over certificate has not been issued in respect of the works within one week after the works have passed the performance test the Purchaser shall without prejudice to the purchaser's other rights hereunder, be entitled but not obliged to use any part of the works, provided the same is reasonably capable of being used. The contractor shall be afforded the earliest possible opportunity of taking such steps as may be necessary to permit the issue of the taking over certificate. The Purchaser shall be responsible for all risk of loss or damage to the works and any Plant; the provisions of clauses 43.1, 43.2 and 43.3 shall not apply to part of the works while being so used by the Purchaser, and clause 36 shall apply thereto as if a taking over certificate had been issued from the date the part was taken into use. Subject as provided in this clause 30, the Purchaser's exercise of its rights under this clause 30 shall not relieve the contractor of its obligations under the contract.

Article 31: Interference with Tests

31.1 If solely by reason of any unjustified act or omission of the purchaser, the engineer, any other contractor employed by the purchaser or any other person for which the Purchaser is responsible, or any breach by the Purchaser of any of its obligations set out in Annexure 2 (purchaser's obligations), the contractor shall be delayed in carrying out and completing the Performance Test or any part thereof, the contractor shall be entitled to an extension of time subject to and in accordance with clause 33 and the contractor shall be entitled to be paid any additional costs reasonably and properly incurred as a consequence thereof, subject to clause 41.

31.2 If the contractor shall be so delayed in carrying out and/or completing the Performance Test and such delay shall continue for a period of .... days or more, the Contractor may by written notice to the Engineer require him to give notice to proceed within .... days. If notice to proceed is not given within that time the Contractor may by further written notice to the Engineer require that this clause shall have effect, in which case, unless in the meantime the works are in the opinion of the Engineer not substantially in accordance with the contract, the Purchaser shall be deemed to have taken over the Works.

31.3 In any case where the works are deemed to have been taken over pursuant to clause 31.2 the contractor shall carry out, or as the case may be complete, the Performance Test during the defects liability period as and when instructed by the Engineer. Such allowances shall be made from the results required to be attained in the Performance Test as may be reasonable having regard to any use of the works by the Purchaser prior to such Performance Test and to any deterioration therein which may have occurred as a result.

31.4 If the performance test are carried out during the defects liability period pursuant to clause 31.3 and in consequence the contractor, acting reasonably, incurs any additional cost, the contractor shall, without prejudice to the generality of clause 41, give notice and full particulars thereof to the Engineer with a copy to the Purchaser and shall submit such further details as the Engineer may reasonably request. After receipt of such notice and details, the Engineer shall, following consultation with the Purchaser and the contractor determine the amount of any such additional cost reasonably and unavoidably incurred, which shall be added to the contract price subject to and in accordance with clause 39. The Engineer shall notify the contractor and the purchaser accordingly.

Article 32: Time for Completion

The contractor shall so execute the works that the works shall be complete and pass the performance Test within the time for completion.

Article 33: Extension of Time

33.1 The contractor may apply to the Engineer at any time for an extension of the time for completion if it is or will be delayed by any of the following:

(a) any matter in respect of which the contractor is expressly entitled to an extension of the Time for Completion by any provision of the contract (save to the extent that an extension of the time for completion is agreed or determined in respect thereof pursuant to such provision); or

(b) *Force Majeure* or the occurrence of a Purchaser's Risk; or

(c) a variation (save to the extent that an extension of the time for completion is agreed or determined in respect thereof pursuant to clause 27); or

(d) any delay, impediment or prevention caused either by a breach by the Purchaser of any of its obligations under the contract or caused by any act or omission of the Engineer which is not in accordance with the contract; or

(e) any delay, impediment or prevention caused by any other contractor of the Purchaser (including the Power Plant EPC contractor and any of their respective sub-contractors of any tier):

Provided that in all such cases the contractor shall have taken such steps as may be reasonable in the circumstances to avoid or prevent the delay the contractor incurs. The contractor shall give notice and full particulars to the Engineer of any reasonable costs incurred by it in avoiding or preventing the delay and, after receipt of such notice and particulars, the Engineer shall, following consultation with the Purchaser and the contractor, determine the amount of any additional cost, which shall be added to the contract price.

33.2 The contractor shall, within 28 days of the occurrence of the event giving rise to the delay or, if later, within 28 days after such occurrence should have become apparent to an experienced contractor, give notice to the Engineer of the contractor's intention to apply for an extension of time. The contractor shall keep such contemporary records as may be necessary to substantiate any such application and such other records as may reasonably be requested by the Engineer, and shall not be entitled to receive any extension of time to the extent that it is unable to substantiate its claim as a result of any failure to keep such records.

33.3 The contractor shall, as soon thereafter as reasonably practicable submit full supporting details of its application and such further details as the Engineer may reasonably instruct and the Engineer shall, as soon as reasonably practicable after receipt of all such information and details consult with the contractor and the Purchaser, and shall thereafter promptly (and in any event, within .... days after receipt of all such information and details) determine such extension of the time for completion and such adjustments to the programme as may be reasonable in all the circumstances.

33.4 The contractor shall not be entitled to an extension of time in respect of any such event or circumstance unless it shall have complied strictly with the requirement to give notice under clause 33.1, and in default of strict compliance the contractor shall be deemed to have waived all such rights to which it might otherwise have become entitled.

33.5 In all cases where the contractor has given notice under clause 33.1 the contractor shall thereafter comply with all reasonable instructions which the Engineer may give in order to overcome or minimise any actual or anticipated delay, and shall not be entitled to an extension of time to the extent that any delay is incurred due to its failure to do so. In circumstances where the contractor is entitled to an extension of time pursuant to clause 33.1 and the contractor, acting reasonably, incurs additional costs in complying with the Engineer's instructions to take measures to avoid or reduce such delay, the contractor shall, without prejudice to the generality of clause 41, give notice and full particulars thereof to the Engineer and shall submit such further details as the Engineer may reasonably request. After receipt of such notice and details, the Engineer shall, following consultation with the Purchaser and the contractor, determine the amount of any additional Cost, which shall be added to the contract price, subject to and in accordance with clause 39.

Article 34: Delay

34.1 Subject to clause 34.2, if the contractor fails to complete the works in accordance with the contract within the time for completion (for the purposes of this clause 34.1 completion of the works shall mean meeting the criteria in clause 29.1(a) and (b)), the contractor shall pay to the Purchaser (by deduction from the contract Price or otherwise as the Purchaser shall direct) the relevant sum named in the Appendix as liquidated damages for delay for every completed Week which shall elapse between the expiry of the time for completion stated in the Appendix or extended time for completion and the date recorded in the taking over certificate under clause 29.2(a).

34.2 Payment of such liquidated damages in accordance with the contract shall not relieve the contractor of its obligation to complete the works but shall be in full satisfaction of the liability of the contractor to the Purchaser in relation to any delay by the contractor. By way of abundant caution, it is clarified that the remedies for under clauses 13.1, 34.4 and 46.1.2(c) shall not be affected by the provisions of this clause.

34.3 The contractor's aggregate liability for liquidated damages for delay under clause 34.1 shall not exceed the amount named in the Appendix as the limit of damages for delay.

34.4 If the Purchaser has become entitled pursuant to clauses 34 to damages up to the limit provided in clause 34.3 and the works remain uncompleted, the purchaser may by notice to the contractor require it to complete the works and the contractor shall so complete. Such notice shall fix a final time for completion, which shall be reasonable having regard to such delay as has already, occurred and to the extent of the work required for completion. If for any reason other than an event of *Force Majeure* or one for which the purchaser is responsible the contractor fails to complete within such time, the purchaser may by further notice to the contractor terminate the contract and otherwise proceed in accordance with clause 46.

34.5 The contractor shall promptly pay all amounts due under this clause to the Purchaser or as the Purchaser shall direct. If any amount remains unpaid 30 days after a written demand therefor the purchaser shall be entitled to charge interest on the amount unpaid calculated daily at the rate of 2% per annum over the Base Lending Rate. Payment of liquidated damages by the contractor shall be made in respective contractual currencies. The purchaser, at its sole discretion, shall be entitled to set off amounts due under this clause against any amount otherwise due to the contractor under or in connection with the contract.

Article 35: Taxes & Duties

(Note: Refer to .... dated ....)

Article 36: Defects Liability

36.1 In these conditions the expression "Defects Liability Period" in respect of the works means the period commencing on taking over and ending on the from such taking over, together with any extension thereof pursuant to this clauses 36 but subject to the proviso set out in clause 36.5 and 36.6.

36.2 The contractor shall be responsible for rectifying or making good by correction, repair or replacement with all possible speed at its expense any error or defect in or damage to any part of the works or any other failure of the works to comply with the contract which may appear or occur during the relevant defects liability period and which arises either:

(a) from any defective materials, workmanship or design (excluding, for the avoidance of doubt, normal wear and tear); or

(b) from any act or omission of the contractor its agents, suppliers or sub-contractors.

For the avoidance of doubt, the contractor shall in no circumstances be liable for replacing any worn out parts during the defects liability period.

36.3 If any defect shall appear or damage occur which the contractor is responsible for making good under clause 36.2, the purchaser or the Engineer shall promptly on becoming aware thereof notify the contractor stating the nature of the defect or damage, and shall afford to the contractor such access to and facilities at the .... plant as are required by the contractor to enable it to remedy the same. Making good shall include, where appropriate, modification, repair or replacement, and provision of modified design documentation and O&M Manuals.

36.4 When the defects liability period has expired and the contractor has completed to the reasonable satisfaction of the Engineer all such making good (if any) as the contractor is responsible for under clause 36.2, the Engineer shall promptly issue the defects liability certificate. The Engineer shall promptly give notice to the Contractor of any making good, which has not been carried out to his reasonable satisfaction, and if he does not issue the defects liability certificate promptly upon the expiry of the defects liability period, he shall notify the contractor of the reasons why he has not done so.

36.5 The provisions of this clause 36 shall apply to any portion of the works so made good under clause 36 until the date falling .... months after the date of completion of such making good and the defects liability period shall be extended accordingly, provided that in no case will the defects liability period expire later than .... months after taking over.

36.6 The defects liability period in respect of any portion of the works not falling within the scope of clause 36.5, but which could not be used as a result of any defect or damage referred to in that clause, shall be extended by a period equal to the period during which such portion of the works could not be used by reason of such defect or damage, provided that in no case will the defects liability period expire later than .... months after taking over.

36.7 If the purchaser has complied with its obligations under clause 36.3 but any such error, defect or damage for which the Contractor is responsible for making good under clause 36.2 is not remedied within a reasonable time, the Purchaser may proceed to do or complete the work at the Contractor's risk and expense provided that the Purchaser gives prior notice to the contractor of its intention so to do. The Purchaser shall promptly give notice to the contractor of the amount of costs reasonably and directly incurred by the Purchaser in carrying out such work, together with documentation in reasonable detail in support thereof, and such documented costs shall be deducted from the contract Price or paid by the contractor to the Purchaser on demand.

36.8 The Contractor may, with the consent of the Engineer, remove from the Site any part of the works which is defective or damaged, if the nature of the defect or damage is such that repairs cannot be expeditiously carried out on the Site.

36.9 If, the repairs or replacements are of such a character as may affect the operation of the works or any part thereof in a significant manner, the Purchaser may within 3 months of completion of such repair or replacement give to the contractor notice requiring that such further tests as may be appropriate in all of the circumstances be carried out in order to verify that the repaired or replaced plant is in accordance with the contract, in which case such further tests shall be carried out.

36.10 The contractor shall, if required by the Purchaser in writing during the defects liability period, search for the cause of any defect or damage. Unless such defect or damage is one which the contractor is responsible for making good under clause 36.2, the cost of the work carried out by the Contractor in searching shall be borne by the Purchaser and added to the contract price.

36.11 Notwithstanding any other provision to the contrary, upon the issuance of the defects liability certificate the contractor shall have no further liability, whether under the contract or otherwise, including by reason of breach of contract or statutory duty or otherwise, in respect of any defects in or damage or loss of whatsoever kind attributable to, any defects or damage or any work done or service or advice rendered in connection therewith, save only as provided in clause 36.12.

36.12 Notwithstanding the issue of the defects liability certificate, the contractor shall remain liable in respect of latent design defects resulting in major damages to the civil works until .... years after the issue of such defects liability certificate, on which date the Contractor shall cease to have any further liability whatsoever save in respect of any latent design defects resulting in major damages to the civil works in respect of which proceedings were commenced prior to such date.

36.13 The contractor shall obtain warranties and guarantees with respect to the materials, workmanship and equipment comprising the .... plant, which shall be standard for the international .... production industry in all material respects. All such warranties and guarantees shall provide that they shall apply notwithstanding any Purchaser's, Engineer's and/or Lenders'

Engineer's inspection, tests and approvals. The contractor shall ensure that the benefit of all such warranties shall be assigned to the Purchaser on the issuance of the defects liability certificate, save only for any warranties which relate to the design of the civil works which shall be assigned on the expiry of the .... year period specified in clause 36.12.

36.14 The contractor shall, prior to the issue of the taking over certificate, provide the Purchaser with the retention bond.

36.15 The contractor shall, upon the issue of the defects liability certificate provide the Purchaser with a bank guarantee (the "latent defects bond") duly executed by an internationally recognised first class bank acceptable to the Purchaser in the sum of 0.5% of the contract Price and in the form set out in Annexure 17 (latent defects bond).

Article 37: Vesting of Plant

37.1 All plant shall, subject to clause 37.3, become the property of the Purchaser at whichever is the earlier of the following:
   (a) on negotiation of ex-works despatch documents, which shall be copied to the Purchaser, in the case of plant comprising indigenous equipment;
   (b) on negotiation of .... shipping documents, which shall be copied to the Purchaser, in the case of Plant comprising Imported Equipment

37.2 The contractor shall procure that title to all plant vested in the purchaser under clause 37.1 shall, save only as created by the Purchaser, be free from any lien, charge or any other security interest and that no person shall have any claim to title thereto. If, notwithstanding this clause 37.2, any such Plant is subject to any lien, charge or other security interest, the Purchaser may discharge the lien, charge or security interest and recover all costs thereby incurred from the contractor on demand or by deduction from the contract price.

37.3 As soon as property passes to the Purchaser pursuant to clause 37.1 the contractor shall set such plant aside and mark it as the purchaser's property in such manner as may reasonably be required by the engineer.

37.4 Until any such plant has been so set aside and marked, the Purchaser shall not be obliged to pay any amount included in any interim payment certificate in respect of such plant.

37.5 The contractor shall permit the Engineer, the Purchaser and any person authorised by them at any time upon reasonable notice to inspect any Plant, which has become the property of the purchaser and shall grant or procure access to the contractor's premises or to any other relevant premises for such purpose.

37.6 All such plant shall be in the care and possession of the contractor solely for the purposes of the contract and shall be at the risk of the contractor in accordance with clause 43.

Article 38: Contractor's Equipment

38.1 The contractor shall within .... days prior to the commencement of work on the site provide to the Engineer a list of all major items of the contractor's equipment that the contractor intends to use on the Site and shall amend and resubmit such list as and when reasonably required by the Engineer.

38.2 All contractor's equipment shall when brought onto the Site be used exclusively for the Works. The contractor shall not thereafter remove the same or any part thereof from the Site without the consent of the Engineer, save that no such consent is required where the Contractor removes such contractor's equipment in compliance with clause 18.3.

38.3 The contractor shall be liable for loss of or damage to any contractor's equipment which may occur otherwise than through a default of the Purchaser or those for whom the Purchaser is responsible (including, for the avoidance of doubt, any other contractor working on the site).

38.4 The contractor shall at all times maintain the contractor's equipment on the site in safe working order.

Article 39: Certificates and Payment

39.1 The purchaser shall pay to the contractor the contract price and any additions thereto or deductions therefrom made pursuant to the contract in accordance with the payment Schedule and subject to the following:

39.2 Payment of the total contract price for the .... (Foreign Money) portion as well as for the Rupee portion shall be made out of two separate irrevocable, transferable and revolving Letters of Credit to be opened by .... Bank, at ...., prior to the Date of Effectiveness of the contract in favour of contractor (respectively contractor's designated subcontractor).

The Letter of Credit will allow partial shipments, will be valid for a period of 29 months from the effective date of the contract, and shall be extended at the Contractor's request.

The costs incurred for opening and possible extension of these letters of credit are for purchaser's account. The costs for confirmation of the letters of credit, if required by contractor, are for contractor's account.

39.3 The payment for the .... portion shall be effected as follows:

    39.3.1 30% will be paid as down payment against contractor's invoice.

    39.3.2 10% will be paid upon approval of drawings for the basic engineering (applicable drawings to be defined until.....................) against

      - invoice

      - approval –certificate of the Engineer

    39.3.3 45% will be paid on a pro-rata basis upon dispatch of materials against

      - Invoice

      - shipping documents or warehouse receipt

      - packing list.

    39.3.4 15% will be paid against taking over certificate and a bank guarantee of 0.5% of the price of the ....-portion valid until submission of As-Built documents. In case taking over is delayed due to reasons for which the contractor is not responsible, this instalment shall be paid against submission of a bank guarantee of 14.5% of the ....portion valid until Taking Over is deemed to have taken place plus a bank guarantee of 0.5% of the .... (Foreign Money) portion valid up to submission of As-Built-Document.

39.4 The payment for the rupees portion, except for piling works, shall be effected as follows:

39.4.1 Supplies

39.4.1.1 15% of the supply price will be paid as down payment against contractors Invoice.

39.4.1.2 5% of the supply price will be paid upon approval of:

drawings (applicable drawings to be defined until....) against

- Invoice

- approval-certificate of the Engineer.

39.4.1.3 65% of the supply price will be paid on a pro-rata basis upon dispatch of materials against

- invoice (6) copies

- railway receipt/lorry receipt or warehouse storage receipt

- packing list (6) copies

39.4.1.4 15% will be paid against taking over certificate and a bank guarantee of 0.5% of the supply portion valid until submission of As-Built-documents. In case taking over is delayed due to reasons for which the contractor is not responsible, this instalment shall be paid against submission of a bank guarantee of 14.5% of the supply portion valid until taking over is deemed to have taken place plus a bank guarantee of 0.5% of the supply portion valid until submission of As-Built-documents.

39.4.2 Civil works

39.4.2.1 15% of the price for civil works will be paid as down payment against contractor's Invoice.

39.4.2.2 5% of the price for the civil works will be paid upon approval of drawings (applicable drawings to be defined until....................) against

- invoice

- approval-certificate of the Engineer.

39.4.2.3 65% of the price for civil works will be paid on a pro-rata basis against

- monthly invoice

(the minimum value for any Invoice will be Rs. .... (amount)

- Contractor's statement of monthly progress of work certified by the Engineer.

39.4.2.4 15% will be paid against taking over certificate and a bank guarantee of 0.5% of the price for the civil works valid until submission of As-Built-documents. In case Taking over is delayed due to reasons for which the contractor is not responsible, this instalment shall be paid against submission of bank guarantee of 14.5% of the price for civil works valid until taking over is deemed to have taken place plus a bank guarantee of 0.5% of the price for civil works valid until submission of As-Built-Documents.

39.4.3 Erection, testing and commissioning

39.4.3.1 15% of the price for erection, testing and commissioning will be paid as down payment against contractor's invoice.

39.4.3.2 5% of the price for erection, testing and commissioning will be paid upon approval of drawings (applicable drawings to be defined until....................) against

- Invoice

- approval - certificate of the engineer.

39.4.3.3 65% of the price for Erection, Testing and Commissioning will be paid on a pro-rata basis against

- monthly invoice

(The minimum value for any invoice will be Rs. ....)

- Contractor's statement of monthly progress of work certified by the Engineer.

39.4.3.4 15% will be paid against taking over certificate and a bank guarantee of 0.5% of the price for erection, testing and commissioning valid until submission of As-Built-documents. In case taking over is delayed due to reasons for which the contractor is not responsible, this instalment shall be paid against submission of a bank guarantee of 14.5% of the price for erection, testing and commissioning valid until taking over is deemed to have taken place plus a bank guarantee of 0.5% of the price for erection, testing and commissioning valid until submission of As-Built-documents.

39.4.4 Services, training (when provided within the rupees-portion).

15% of the price for services, training will be paid as down payment against contractors' invoice.

70% of the price for services, training will be paid against contractor's statement on progress of Services, training certified by the Engineer.

15% of the price for services, training will be paid against taking over certificate and a bank guarantee of 0.5% of the price for services, training valid until submission of As-Built-documents. In case taking over is delayed due to reasons for which the contractor is not responsible, this instalment shall be paid against submission of a bank guarantee of 14.5% of the price for services, training valid until taking over is deemed to have taken place plus a bank guarantee of 0.5% of the price for services, training valid until submission of As-Built-documents.

39.4.5 The payment for the piling works (Rupees Portion) shall be effected as follows:

39.5.1 15% of the piling will be paid as down payment against contractor's Invoice.

39.5.2 85% of the piling price will be paid on a pro-rata basis as per progress of work against contractors statement of monthly progress of work certified by the Engineer and submission of a bank guarantee for 15% of the price for piling valid until Taking Over or Taking Over is deemed to have taken place.

39.6 Payments out of this letters of credit will be effected against first presentation to the opening bank or to the confirming bank, if so chosen by contractor.

39.7 All banking charges for the execution of this contract incurred in the .... shall be borne by the purchaser and those incurred outside the .... shall be borne by contractor.

39.8 The Letters of Credit are subject to the uniform customs and practice for documentary credits (................... Revision) International Chamber of Commerce (Publication No. ....).

39.9 No interim payment certificate shall be relied upon as conclusive evidence of any matter stated therein.

39.10 Not later than 56 days after the issue of the taking over certificate, the contractor shall submit to the Engineer four copies of a draft final statement with supporting Documents showing in a form approved by the Engineer;

    (a) the total amount payable in respect of all work done in accordance with the contract; and

    (b) any further sums to which the contractor considers he is entitled to payment under the contract.

If the Engineer disagrees with or cannot verify any part of the draft Final Statement, the contractor shall submit such further information as the Engineer may reasonably require.

39.11 Within .... days following receipt of the draft final statement or following receipt from the contractor of the further information required by the Engineer in relation thereto, the Engineer shall issue to the purchaser, with a copy to the contractor, the final payment certificate stating:

    (a) the contract price with all additions thereto and deductions therefrom made pursuant to the contract; and

    (b) after giving credit to the purchaser for all amounts previously paid by the Purchaser and for all sums for which the purchaser is entitled, the balance, if any, due from the Purchaser to the contractor or from the contractor to the Purchaser as the case may be.

If, the contractor has not issued a draft final statement in accordance with clause 39.10, the Engineer shall request the contractor to do so. If the contractor fails to make such an application within a period of .... days, the Engineer may issue the final payment certificate showing such amounts as he considers due.

39.12 (a) The contractor shall pay to the Purchaser any liquidated damages or other sums as due to the Purchaser as per the provisions of the contract:

(b) Subject to clause 39.12 (a) the Purchaser shall pay to the contractor the sums certified as due to the Contractor in interim payment certificates issued pursuant to clause 39 within .... days after the respective dates of issue.

39.13 If payment of any sums payable under the contract, whether payable by the purchaser to the contractor or by the contractor to the Purchaser is made later than the date for Payment, the contractor or the Purchaser as the case may be shall be entitled to interest on the amount unpaid during the period of delay at the rate stated in the Appendix. Such entitlement to interest shall arise automatically, without formal notice and without prejudice to any other right or remedy.

39.14 Each payment certificate shall not be withheld solely on account of defects of a minor character which are such as to affect the use of the .... plant or the Works.

> 39.15.1 For clauses 39.4.2 (Civil works), 39.4.3 (erection, testing and commissioning), 39.4.4 (Services, Training) and 39.4.5 (Piling) the following shall be applicable.
>
> 39.15.2 At least 14 days prior to making any application for an interim payment certificate the Contractor shall submit to the Engineer such particulars as agreed between the purchaser and the contractor.

Article 40: Void

Article 41: Claims

41.1 Where under the contract or otherwise the contractor is or considers himself entitled to be paid or to have included in or added to the contract Price any extra or additional payment the contractor shall if he intends to make any claim in respect thereof:

> (a) within .... days of any circumstance arising which the contractor considers entitles him to such extra or additional payment give to the Engineer and the Purchaser notice of its intention to make a claim stating its reasons for making the claim; and
>
> (b) as soon as reasonably practicable thereafter and not later than the expiry of .... days after the issue of the provisional taking over certificate, submit to the Engineer and the Purchaser full particulars of its claim. The contractor shall thereafter as soon as reasonably practicable submit such further particulars as the Engineer or the Purchaser may reasonably require.

41.2 When the Engineer has received full and detailed particulars in accordance with clause 41.1 and such further particulars as he may reasonably have required, he shall as soon as reasonably practicable and, in any event, within .... days of receipt of such particulars, determine whether the contractor is entitled to additional payment and notify the Parties accordingly.

41.3 The contractor shall not be entitled to any extra or additional payment in respect of which he has not complied with the requirements of this clause 41.1, strict compliance with which shall be a condition precedent to payment.

Article 42: Patent Rights, etc.

42.1 The contractor shall indemnify the purchaser against all actions, claims, demands, costs, charges, expenses and other liabilities arising from or incurred by reason of any infringement or alleged infringement of any patent, registered design, copyright, trade mark, trade name or other intellectual property right protected in India or elsewhere by the use or possession of any plant, materials or equipment supplied by the contractor under the contract.

42.2 If any claim is made or legal proceedings commenced against the purchaser arising out of the matters referred to in clause 42.1, the Purchaser shall notify the contractor thereof and the contractor may at its own expense on behalf of the Purchaser conduct any such legal proceedings and/or negotiations for the settlement of the same, subject to the Purchaser being kept reasonably informed. The conduct by the Contractor of such proceedings or negotiations shall be conditional upon the Contractor having first undertaken to the Purchaser to indemnify the Purchaser on such reasonable terms as may be required by the Purchaser against the amount ascertained, agreed or estimated, as the case may be, of any compensation, damages, expenses and costs for which the Purchaser may become liable. The Purchaser shall, at the request and cost of the Contractor, afford all available assistance to the contractor for any such purpose and shall be repaid all reasonable expenses incurred in so doing.

42.3 If the purchaser is prevented from using the works in consequence of any infringement of any patent, registered design, copyright, trade mark, trade name or other intellectual property right the contractor shall, after notice thereof from the Purchaser, procure the removal, at its own expense, of the cause of prevention. This may be achieved by the contractor replacing infringing plant, materials or equipment with non-infringing plant, materials or equipment or by the Contractor modifying the infringing plant materials or equipment, so that they no longer cause an infringement, provided that the modified plant, materials or equipment comply with the requirements of the contract.

If the contractor is unable to do so within .... days after notice thereof from the purchaser then the purchaser may treat such prevention as a default by the contractor and exercise the powers and remedies available under clause 46.

Article 43: Accidents and Damage

43.1 Subject to clause 43.2, the contractor shall bear and be responsible for all risk of loss or damage to the works and any Plant notwithstanding that the same may have become the property of the Purchaser and for all risks relating to and the care of the works until taking over. The contractor shall also be responsible for the care of any outstanding work, which he has undertaken to carry out during the Defects Liability Period until all such work is complete.

43.2.1 If the works shall suffer loss or damage whilst the contractor has responsibility for the care thereof, the same shall be made good by the contractor at its own expense:

(a) except to the extent that such loss or damage shall be caused by:
  (i) a purchaser's risk which is not covered by insurance, where clause 45.2 shall apply; or
  (ii) *Force Majeure* which is not covered by insurance, where clause 43.2.2 shall apply; and
(b) subject, in all other cases, to the receipt by the contractor of the proceeds of the "all risks" insurance for the works required to be maintained pursuant to clause 47.

The contractor shall, subject as aforesaid, also at its own expense make good any loss or damage to the works occasioned by it in the course of completing any outstanding work or of complying with its obligations under clause 36.

43.2.2 In the event, that the works shall suffer loss or damage whilst the contractor has responsibility for the care thereof which is caused by *Force Majeure* and which is not covered by the insurances required pursuant to clause 47, the same shall, if required by the Purchaser within 6 months after the happening of the event giving rise to loss or damage, and subject to the prior receipt by the Contractor of an extended or a new letter of credit in the amount of the reasonable price referred to in this clause, be made good by the contractor. Such making good shall be at the expense of the Purchaser at such reasonable price, and subject to such reasonable extension of time (subject to clause 33) and in such reasonably expeditious manner as may be agreed between the contractor and the Purchaser or failing agreement, determined by reference to the Dispute Resolution Procedure. The price or sum so agreed or determined shall be added to the Contract Price (subject to clause 41).

43.3 The contractor shall be liable for and shall indemnify the Purchaser against all claims in respect of personal injury or death and in respect of loss of or damage to any property (other than the Works) which arises out of or in consequence of the execution of the works whilst the Contractor has responsibility for the care thereof and against all demands, costs, charges and expenses arising in connection therewith, except to the extent that such claims arise due to any breach of contract, neglect or default of the Purchaser or any person for whom the Purchaser is responsible.

43.4 If, there shall occur any death or injury to any person or loss of or damage to any property (other than the Works) after the responsibility for the care of the works shall have passed to the Purchaser the contractor shall be liable for and shall indemnify the Purchaser against all such claims and all proceedings, claims, demands, costs, charges and expenses arising in connection therewith to the extent that such death or personal injury or loss of or damage to property was caused by the negligence or other breach of legal duty of the contractor, any of its sub-contractors, suppliers or agents or by any defective design, materials or workmanship for which the contractor is responsible, but not otherwise.

43.5 The contractor shall indemnify the Purchaser against all proceedings, claims, damages, costs, charges and expenses arising in connection with the death of or injury to any person employed by the Contractor or any of its sub-contractors or suppliers for the purposes of the Works. This indemnity shall not apply to the extent that any such death or injury results from any breach of contract or negligence of the Purchaser or any neglect or default of its agents or others for whom it is responsible. The Purchaser shall indemnify the Contractor against all proceedings, claims, damages, costs, charges and expenses to such extent.

43.6 In the event of any claim being made against the Purchaser arising out of the matters referred to above the Contractor shall be promptly notified thereof and may at its own expense conduct on behalf of the Purchaser all negotiations for the settlement of the same and any legal proceedings that may arise in relation thereto. The conduct by the contractor of such negotiations or proceedings shall be conditional upon the contractor having first undertaken to the purchaser to indemnify the Purchaser on such reasonable terms as may be required by the Purchaser against the amount ascertained, agreed or estimated, as the case may be, of any compensation, damages, expenses and costs for which the Purchaser may become liable. The Purchaser shall at the request of the Contractor afford all available assistance to the contractor for any such purpose and shall be repaid all reasonable expenses incurred in so doing.

43.7 For the avoidance of doubt, the persons for whom the Purchaser is responsible include the Engineer, and any other contractor employed by the Purchaser (including the Power Plant EPC contractor), and their respective employees, agents and contractors of any tier.

43.8 The provisions of this clause 43 shall survive termination of this contract.

Article 44. Limit of Liability and Indirect or Consequential Damage

44.1 In all cases the party seeking to establish or alleging a breach of contract or other breach of a legal duty or right to be indemnified under the contract shall take reasonable measures to mitigate the loss which has occurred provided that it can do so without unreasonable inconvenience or cost.

44.2(a) Notwithstanding any other provision to the contrary, except as provided in clause 44.3, the contractor shall not be liable to the Purchaser and the Purchaser shall not be liable to the contractor by way of an indemnity, or by reason of breach of contract or breach of any other legal duty or for any loss of profit, loss of use, loss of production, loss of contracts or for any indirect or consequential loss or damage whatsoever, including financial and economic loss that may be suffered by the other of them as a consequence of such breach; and

(b) Clauses (28, 34.2, 34.3, 36.11, 36.12, 44.4, 44.5, 44.6 and 46.3) shall apply so as to limit and/or exclude (as the case may be) the contractor's liability, as provided therein.

44.3 Clause 44.2(e) shall not effect:
(a) any obligation of the contractor to pay liquidated damages;
(b) any liability of either party arising as a result of the gross negligence or wilful misconduct of such party;
(c) any liability of either Party in respect of a specific payment obligation under clause 46; or
(d) any liability of the Purchaser to pay to the contractor costs wherever the contractor is entitled to recover the same under the contract and any liability of either Party to pay interest in accordance with the contract;
(e) any liability of the contractor to the Purchaser in respect of a specific payment obligation under clauses 13.1, 23.6, 28 and 29.4.
(f) any specific payment obligation of either Party under clause 48;
(g) any liability of either party to the other in respect of third party claims for personal injury, death or damage to property.

44.4 The aggregate liability of the contractor to the Purchaser for liquidated damages under clauses 34 and 28 in respect of any and all acts, defaults or delays or failures giving rise to such liquidated damages shall not exceed the limit of total liquidated damages.

44.5 No action arising out of or in relation to the contract or the works shall be commenced later than 3 months from the date of expiry of the Defects Liability Period (or, if more than one, the last of such periods to expire), or, in the case of latent design defects resulting in major damages to the Civil works .... months from the date of expiry of the three year period specified in clause 36.12, or from the date of termination of the contract, if earlier.

44.6 The total liability of the contract to the purchaser under the contract, including any liquidated damages and any liability whatsoever arising out or related to the implementation or performance of this contract shall not exceed the contract price.

Article 45. Purchaser's Risks

45.1 The Purchaser's Risks are:
(a) war, hostilities (whether war be declared or not), invasion, act of foreign enemies;
(b) rebellion, revolution, insurrection or military or usurped power, or civil war, within India;
(c) ionising radiations, or contamination by radioactivity from any nuclear fuel, or from any nuclear waste from the combustion of nuclear fuel, radioactive toxic explosive, or other hazardous properties of any explosive nuclear assembly or nuclear component of such assembly except as may be attributable to the Contractor's use thereof;

(d) pressure waves caused by aircraft or other aerial devices travelling at sonic or supersonic speed;

(e) loss or damage due to the use of or occupation by the Purchaser of any part of the works;

(f) any operation of the forces of nature against which an experienced contractor could not reasonably have been expected to take precautions; and

(g) man-made underground obstructions, which were not disclosed in the soil survey, carried out by the contractor pursuant to the Articles of Agreement.

45.2 The contractor shall give notice to the Engineer of a purchaser's risk upon it being foreseen by or known to the contractor. If a Purchaser's risk results in loss or damage to the works, which is not covered by the insurances required pursuant to clause 47, the Contractor shall, if required by the Purchaser, rectify such loss or damage to the extent required in writing by the Engineer. Such rectification shall be at the expense of the purchaser at such reasonable price, and subject to such reasonable extension of time (subject to clause 33) and in such reasonably expeditious manner as may be agreed between the contractor and the Purchaser provided however, the Purchaser establishes a letter of credit for the agreed amount referred to hereinabove within .... working days of the Agreement if, any.

In the absence of any agreement, the Engineer may nevertheless direct the contractor to rectify such loss or damage subject to determination of the outstanding matters by reference to the dispute resolution procedure, and the contractor shall carry on such works pending determination of such outstanding matters. The price or sum so agreed or determined shall be added to the contract price (subject to clause 41).

Article 46. Termination

46.1 Termination upon contractor and purchaser events.

This clause 46 sets out the exclusive rights of the Parties to terminate the contract.

46.1.1 Contractor remediable Events.

Each of the following events shall be a contractor remediable event:

(a) failure of the Contractor within .... days after the effective date to commence the works as evidenced by the undertaking of the activities usually and customarily undertaken under internationally accepted construction standards and practices in connection with the commencement of construction of projects similar to the .... plant;

(b) after commencement of construction of the .... plant, a general suspension or abandonment by the Contractor of the construction of the .... plant for more than 5 consecutive days other than due to *Force Majeure;*

(c) failure by the Contractor to make any payment under the contract when due and payable;

(d) breach by the contractor of any of its obligations under the contract other than as provided in clause 46.1.1. or 46.1.2 which is not remedied within .... days after notice from the Purchaser to the contractor stating that such breach has occurred, identifying the breach in question in reasonable detail and demanding remedy thereof; and

(e) breach by the Guarantor of any of its obligations under the Guarantee which is not remedied within .... days after notice from the Purchaser to the Guarantor stating that such breach has occurred, identifying the breach in question in reasonable detail and demanding remedy thereof.

46.1.2 Contractor non-remediable events.

Each of the following events shall be a contractor Non-Remediable Event:

(a) the occurrence of any of the following:

   (i) the passing of a resolution for the bankruptcy, insolvency, winding up, liquidation or other similar proceedings in relation to either the contractor or the guarantor;

   (ii) the appointment of a trustee, liquidator, custodian, provisional manager or similar person in a proceeding referred to in clause (I) above, which appointment has not been set aside or stayed within .... days of such appointment;

   (iii) the making by a court having jurisdiction of an order winding up or otherwise confirming the bankruptcy or insolvency of the contractor or the guarantor, which order has not been set aside or stayed within .... days;

   (iv) the occurrence of any equivalent proceedings in any jurisdiction;

   (v) the unenforceability, cancellation or other failure of any advance payment guarantee or the performance Bond, or the bankruptcy or other proceedings of the type described in the immediately preceding sub-clauses (i), (ii), (iii) and (iv) affecting the APG guarantor or Surety provided that, in either case the contractor has not provided a replacement guarántee or bond either in the same terms (*mutatis mutandis*) or otherwise on terms acceptable to the Purchaser within .... days after the occurrence of any such event;

   (vi) the guarantee ceases to constitute the valid, binding and enforceable obligation of the guarantor in accordance with its terms, and the contractor does not replace the guarantee with another guarantee in all respects acceptable to the Purchaser (both as to the form of such guarantee and the identity of the new guarantor) within .... days after the Contractor becomes aware of the occurrence of any such event;

(vii) the assignment of the benefit of the contract by the contractor in breach of its terms;

(viii) any unlawful or negligent act or omission of the Contractor, which will result in:

   (1) the contractor being prevented from meeting its obligations under the contract; and

   (2) such prevention having a materially adverse effect on the Purchaser:

   Provided, that the purchaser has given notice to the contractor containing reasonable detail of the grounds upon which the purchaser believes that the contractor will be so prevented, and the contractor has not demonstrated to the reasonable satisfaction of the purchaser that the contractor will be able to meet its obligation under the contract within a period 14 days from its receipt of the Purchaser' notice.

(b) the occurrence of any of the following events after a contractor remediable event shall have occurred and a Remedial Notice shall have been given by the Purchaser to the Contractor pursuant to clause 46.1.5.

   (i) in the case of a contractor remediable event described in clause 46.1.1(a), the failure of the Contractor to commence the works (evidence as provided in clause 46.1.1(a) within .... days after receipt of the Remedial Notice;

   (ii) in the case of a contractor remediable event described in clause 46.1.1(b), the failure of the contractor to resume construction of the .... plant within .... days after receipt of the Remedial Notice;

   (iii) in the case of a contractor remediable event described in clause 46.1.1(c), failure by the contractor to make such payment in full within .... days after receipt of the Remediable Notice;

   (iv) in the case of a contractor remediable event described in clause 46.1.1(d), the certification of the Engineer that any of the following have occurred;

   (1) the failure of the contractor to furnish the purchaser with a remedial programme in accordance with clause 46.1.5(b), or

   (2) the failure of the contractor to implement such remedial programme with due diligence, or

   (3) the manifest or demonstrated inability of such remedial programme to be capable of reasonable implementation, or

   (4) the manifest or demonstrated inability to remedy the contractor remediable event notwithstanding the exercise of due diligence by the contractor in implementing such remedial programme.

   (v) in the case of a contractor remediable event described in clause 46.1.1(e), the failure of the contractor to procure the remedy of such

contractor remediable event within .... days after receipt of the remedial notice.
  (c) failure by the contractor to complete the works in accordance with the terms of clause 34.4.
  (d) the contractor being unable to demonstrate that the works have achieved the minimum performance criteria, which entitles the purchaser to reject the same under clause 46.3.1(a)(ii).

46.1.3 Purchaser Remediable Event

Each of the events described below shall be a Purchaser Remediable Event:
  (a) failure of Purchaser to make any payment under the Contract when due and payable or to extend or issue a new letter of credit when required to do so under the terms of the Contract;
  (b) breach by the Purchaser of any of its other obligations under the contract which will affect the performance of the contractor and which is not remedied within .... days after notice from the contractor to the Purchaser stating that such a breach has occurred, identifying the breach in question in reasonable detail and demanding remedy thereof;

46.1.4 Purchaser non-remediable event

Each of the events set forth below shall be a purchaser non-remediable event:
  (a) the occurrence of any of the following:
    (i) the passing of a resolution for the bankruptcy, insolvency, winding up, liquidation or other similar proceedings in relation to the Purchaser;
    (ii) the appointment of a trustee, liquidator, custodian, provisional manager or similar person in a proceeding referred to in clause (i) above, which appointment has not been set aside or stayed within .... days of such appointment;
    (iii) the making by a court having jurisdiction of an order winding up or otherwise confirming the bankruptcy or insolvency of the Purchaser, which order has not been set aside or stayed within .... days;
    (iv) the occurrence of any equivalent proceedings in any jurisdiction;
    (v) the unenforceability, cancellation, non-renewal (pursuant to its terms) or other failure of any letter of credit, or the bankruptcy or other proceedings of the type described in the immediately preceding clauses (i), (ii), (iii) and (iv) affecting the .... Bank, provided that the Purchaser has not provided a replacement Letter of Credit or bond either in the same terms (*mutatis mutandis*) or otherwise on terms acceptable to the Contractor within 14 days after the occurrence of any such event;
    (vi) the assignment of the benefit of the contract by the Purchaser in breach of its terms;

(b) the occurrence of any of the following events after a Purchaser Remediable Event shall have occurred and a Remedial Notice shall have been given by the Contractor to the Purchaser pursuant to clause 46.1.5:

   (i) in the case of a Purchaser Remediable Event described in clause 46.1.3(a), the failure of the Purchaser to make such payment or to provide the extended or new Letter of Credit (as the case may be) within 15 days after receipt of the Remedial Notice;

   (ii) in the case of a Purchaser Remediable Event described in clause 46.1.3(b), the certification of the Engineer that any of the following have occurred;

   (1) the failure of the Purchaser to furnish the contractor with a remedial programme within the time provided in clause 46.1.5(b) or

   (2) the failure of the Purchaser to implement such remedial programme with due diligence; or

   (3) the manifest or demonstrated inability of the Remedial programme so furnished to be capable of reasonable implementation; or

   (4) the manifest or demonstrated inability to remedy the Purchaser Remediable Event notwithstanding the exercise of due diligence in implementing the Remedial programme.

46.1.5 Remedial procedures

Upon the occurrence of a Contractor Remediable Event or a Purchaser Remediable Event, the following procedures shall be strictly followed by the Parties;

(a) the purchaser may give notice to the Contractor of a Contractor Remediable Event and the contractor may give notice to the purchaser of a Purchaser Remediable Event (a "Remediable Notice") such notice to contain full particulars of the facts and matters relied upon and of the provisions of the Contract pursuant to which it is issued:

(b) upon the contractor's receipt of a Remedial Notice notifying the contractor of a Contractor Remediable Event described in clause 46.1.1(d) and upon the purchaser's receipt of a Remedial Notice notifying the purchaser of a Purchaser Remediable Event described in clause 46.1.3(b), the Party receiving the Remedial Notice shall promptly prepare and furnish to the other party (in any event within .... days) a detailed programme (the "Remedial Programme") showing the steps to be taken to remedy such Remediable Event.

46.1.6 Termination upon Contractor or Purchaser Non-Remediable Event.

Upon the occurrence of a contractor non-remediable event or a Purchaser Non-Remediable Event, the following procedure shall apply:

(a) The Party wishing to rely on such event may give a notice (the termination notice") to the other party, specifying the Contractor Non-

Remediable Event or the Purchaser Non-Remediable Event, as the case may be, giving rise to such Termination Notice, and the date on which the party giving such Termination Notice proposes to terminate this contract, which date shall not be less than .... days after the date of such notice.

(b) During the period of .... days (or such longer period set forth in the Termination Notice or as the Parties may agree) following the giving of such Termination Notice, the Parties shall consult as to what steps shall be taken with a view to mitigating or remedying the consequences of such event having regard to all the circumstances.

(c) If the party receiving the Termination Notice intends to dispute the right of the other Party to give effect to the Termination Notice and to refer such dispute to the dispute resolution procedure, such Party shall within .... days of receipt of the Termination Notice so inform the party giving the Termination Notice and shall immediately refer such dispute for resolution in accordance with the Dispute Resolution Procedure the question of whether the Party receiving the Termination Notice has a reasonable basis to dispute the other Party's right to give effect to the Termination Notice which reference shall instruct the arbitrator to render such determination not later than .... days after service by each of the parties of their respective pleadings.

(d) At any time after the expiry of the period referred to in clause 46.1.6(a) and unless:

  (i) the parties shall have agreed in writing that the Party which has given the Termination Notice shall not terminate the contract, either at all in connection with the event that gave rise to such Termination Notice or for such further period as may have been agreed by that party;

  (ii) the event giving rise to the Termination Notice shall have been remedied by the expiry of the period referred to in clause 46.1.6(a); or

  (iii) a reference to the dispute resolution procedure pursuant to clause 46.1.6(c) has been made and has not yet been concluded; or

  (iv) the dispute resolution procedure referred to in (iii) above has concluded with a final determination that the party having given the Termination Notice does not have a right to give effect thereto;

The Party that has given the Termination Notice may terminate the contract by giving written notice thereof to the other party, whereupon the contract shall terminate on the date specified for termination in such notice or such later date as the Parties shall have agreed and clause 46.3 shall apply.

46.2 Termination other than upon contractor non-remediable events or purchaser non-remediable events.

46.2.1 Termination in the event of certain events of *Force Majeure*

If:

(a) any event of *Force Majeure* prevents, or the contractor and the purchaser agree that such an event of *Force Majeure* will prevent, the contractor or the Purchaser from fulfilling all or substantially all of its obligations under the contract for a continuous period of more than six months; or

(b) an event of *Force Majeure* shall have occurred as referred to in clause 49.5(c) and the parties shall have followed the procedures described in clause 49.5(c) and the Parties do not agree on an adjustment of the contract price;

either party may terminate this contract upon .... days prior written notice to the other Party.

46.2.2 Termination for convenience.

The Purchaser may terminate the contract at any time by giving not less than 15 days' notice thereof to the contractor.

46.3 Consequences of termination

46.3.1 Financial consequences.

46.3.1(a) (i) In the event of termination of the contract pursuant to clause 46.1.6 due to a contractor non-remediable event, except where the Purchaser is entitled under the contract, and elects to, reject the works for failure to achieve the minimum performance criteria, the financial consequences are as follows:

(A) as soon as practicable after the Purchaser has given written notice referred to in the last paragraph of clause 46.1.6 to terminate the contract to the contractor, the Engineer shall value the works and all the sums then due to the contractor as at the date of termination in accordance with clause 39 and shall certify the amount thereof. The amount so certified is herein called "the termination value". For the avoidance of doubt, the termination value shall include the contract value of any works for which an interim payment certificate has not been issued; and

(B) the Purchaser shall not be liable to make any further payments to the contractor until the direct cost of completing the works actually incurred and documented by the Purchaser has been ascertained and the amount thereof certified by the Engineer (who shall take into account the Purchaser's obligation to minimise such costs by obtaining international and local market competitive prices for the completion of the works ("the cost of completion").

The Purchaser shall make all documentation supporting the amount of the cost of completion freely available to the contractor. The contractor shall be entitled, upon request, to review and receive from the Purchaser a copy of all such documentation.

If the cost of completion less the amount paid by the contractor by way of liquidated damages for failure to achieve the Performance Guarantees, plus the total amount already paid to the contractor (such amount being hereinafter called "the total cost of completion" as at the date of termination exceeds the total amount which the Engineer certifies would have been payable under the contract to the contractor if the Contract had not been terminated ('the notional contract price") the Engineer shall certify the amount of such excess. The contractor shall upon demand pay to the Purchaser the amount of such excess, provided that the liability of the contractor under this clause 46.3.(a)(i) shall not exceed the contract price.

Any excess payable by the contractor under this clause 46.3.1(a)(I) shall be deemed a debt due by the contractor to the purchaser and shall be recoverable accordingly.

If there is no such excess, the contractor shall be entitled to be paid the lower of:

(1) the Termination Value less the total of all payments received by the Contractor as at the date of termination, for the execution of the Works; or

(2) the notional contract price less the total cost of completion.

46.3.1.(a)(ii) In the event of termination of the contract pursuant to clause 46.1(b) due to a contractor non-remediable event, for failure to achieve the minimum performance criteria, the Purchaser alternatively may reject the works at its sole option. Such rejection shall however, be subject to determination by the Expert acting in accordance with the Annexure 21 (Dispute Resolution Procedure) that the rejection of the Work is justified in the overall facts and circumstances of the case. For the purpose of this clause, the Expert shall be .... He/She shall make his/her determination within .... days after rejection of the works by the Purchaser.

Upon final rejection of Works:

(i) The contractor shall forthwith return to the purchaser the entire contract price, which it has received less any amounts paid as liquidated damages, if any.

(ii) Subject to the aforesaid payment being made, the title to the works shall vest in the contractor and the contractor shall be entitled to dismantle, demolish or otherwise remove the works from the site within a maximum period of .... months from the date of decision of the Expert, or of the Arbitrators, (in the event the dispute is referred to arbitration under Annexure. 21). All such dismantling and demolitions shall be carried out so as not to affect any other property of the Purchaser or its sub-contractors or otherwise affect the right of ingress and agress to the Site.

(iii) Any part of the works not removed from the site within the aforesaid period of .... months shall deemed to have been vested in the Purchaser and the purchaser may deal with it in such manner as, it deems fit.

46.3.1(b) In the event of termination of the contract pursuant to clause 46.1.6 due to a purchaser non-remediable event or pursuant to clauses 46.2.1 or 46.2.2, the Engineer shall certify, and the Purchaser shall pay to the contractor the amount stated in the cancellation Schedule for the month in which the Termination Notice is issued in addition to the actual payments due under the terms of the contract for the relevant month and the contract value of any works which are not yet included in an interim certificate of payment and any amount if due to the contractor under the contract but remaining unpaid.

46.3.2. Discontinuance of the works.

In the event of termination of the contract pursuant to clauses 46.1.6, 46.2.1 or 46.2.2, the contractor shall;

(a) discontinue the works in an orderly manner, save only that it shall carry out such work as may be necessary and instructed by the Engineer for the purpose of making safe and/or protecting those parts of the works already executed; and

(b) not place any further orders or sub-contracts in respect of the .... plant or the Works.

46.3.3 Plant

In the event of termination of the contract pursuant to clauses 46.1.6, 46.2.1 or 46.2.2, the contractor shall, upon the written request of the Purchaser, take such steps as are necessary and specified in the Purchaser's request, to transfer to the Purchaser, free from and clear of all liens and encumbrances, all of the contractor's rights, title and interest in the following:

(a) all raw materials, consumables and spare parts;

(b) all buildings and fixtures;

(c) warranties of equipment, materials and workmanship referred to in clause 36.13.

(d) contracts between the contractor and its vendors, suppliers and contractors;

(e) all work in progress under contracts with vendors, suppliers and contractors; and

(f) all rights with respect to any insurance proceeds payable to or for the account of the contractor, but unpaid at the date of termination of the contract, in respect of the contractor's right, title and interest in the .... plant and the works but excluding the amount of any of the contractor's own costs which are covered by such insurance.

And the contractor shall provide the Purchaser with a copy of computerised and non-computerised records, reports, data, filed and information in respect of the works excluding proprietary pricing and cost information of the Contractor and all drawings, test results, and other design documentation relating to the works.

Provided that the contractor's obligations set out in this clause 46.3.2 are subject to receipt by the contractor of all amounts due to it under clause 46.3.1. The Purchaser may withhold such amount as is, in the circumstances, fair and equitable, if the Contractor has failed to provide satisfactory evidence to the Purchaser, of the steps it has taken to comply with the above obligations.

46.3.4 Survival

The provisions of this clause 46.3 shall survive the termination of the contract.

46.3.5 Other rights and remedies.

Upon the breach by either Party of any covenant or warranty hereunder, the Party damaged by any such default or breach may, in its sole discretion, in addition to exercising any other remedies provided for hereunder, proceed in accordance with clause 50 to protect and enforce its rights, to recover any damages to which it may be entitled (including all costs and expenses reasonably incurred in the exercise of its remedy) or to seek specific performance by the other Party of such other Party's obligations under the contract.

Article 47: Insurance

47.1 The purchaser's Insurances

47.1.1 Without limiting the obligations, responsibilities and liabilities of the parties under the contract, the purchaser shall, at its expense, take out and maintain in effect (or cause to be taken out and maintained in effect) during the performance of the Contract those insurances specified in the draft insurance policy which is set out in Part I of Annexure 7 (Insurance) for the Policies period(s) specified therein (or, if earlier, on the date of termination of the Contract) in the sums and with the deductible and other terms therein specified.

47.1.2 The lenders (and governmental instrumentality where appropriate), the contractor (its affiliates) the Power Plant EPC contractor, all sub-contractors (of any tier... shall be named as co-insured under all such policies (save only as otherwise provided in Part I of Annexure 7 (Insurance) in respect of the insurance for Advance Consequential Loss).

47.1.3 The purchaser shall ensure that the "material damage" insurance is renewed on the same terms and conditions as set out in Part I of Annexure 7 (Insurance) so that such insurance remains in place until the expiry of the defects liability period.

47.2 Contractor's Insurances

47.2.1 Without limiting the obligations, responsibilities and liabilities of the parties under the Contract, the Contractor shall, at its expense, take out and maintain in effect, or cause to be taken out and maintained in effect, during the performance of the Contract, those insurances specified in Part II of Annexure 7 (Insurance) in the sums, for the period(s) specified therein (or, if earlier, on the date of termination of the Contract) and with the deductibles and other conditions therein specified.

47.3 Sub-Contractor's Insurances

The Contractor shall ensure that, where applicable, its sub-contractors shall take out and maintain in effect adequate insurance policies against liability for the death or injury of their own employees (and vehicles).

47.4 Evidence of Insurance

47.4.1 Each party shall, in relation to insurance policies which it is obliged to effect and maintain, shall ensure that—

(a) satisfactory evidence that the required insurances are in full force and effect is delivered to the other party prior to that party running the relevant risk covered by such insurance; and

(b) the relevant policy is endorsed so as to require the insurers to give not less than .... days notice to the other party prior to any cancellation (where applicable) or material modification of the policy (including any reduction in limits or coverage, any increase in deductibles).

47.4.2 Each party shall also, whenever reasonably requested by the other party, produce (or procure the production of) the policies or certificates of all insurances which it is obliged to effect and maintain evidencing the policies and endorsements obtained, together with receipts for the premiums.

47.5 Compliance with Terms of the Insurance Policies

The Purchaser and the Contractor shall comply, (and the Contractor shall procure that its sub-contractor will comply)... with all terms (other than those relating to the payment of premiums) of the policies of insurance to be effected under this clause 47, including the procedures for the notification and administration of claims thereunder and shall not do anything or commit to do anything which might render such polices voidable or entitle insurers to avoid liability thereunder.

47.6 Notification of changes

47.6.1 Each party shall notify the insurers of any fact, change of circumstances or occurrence which is material to the risks being insured against.

47.6.2 Neither party shall make any material alteration to the terms of any insurance without the other party's prior written approval. Each Party shall immediately notify the other of all changes made to the insurances.

47.7 *Losses not Insured.*—Any loss not insured or not recovered from insurers or any deductibles shall be borne by the Purchaser or the Contractor in accordance with their responsibilities under the contract.

47.8 *Indemnity.*—Each party shall indemnify the other party for any loss which it suffers as a result of not being able to recover under the insurances as a result of any mis-representation, non-disclosure or breach of any declaration, condition or warranty contained in the relevant insurance policy by the other party.

47.9 *Failure to Insure.*—If either party fails to provide or maintain in effect, or ensure the provision or maintenance in effect of, any of the insurance cover required under this clause 47. The other party shall be entitled (but not obliged) to provide or maintain such cover and the failing party shall reimburse the other party for the costs incurred by such party in so doing.

47.10 *Provision of Assistance in Connection with claims.*—Each party shall give to the other party all such reasonable assistance as the other party may require in connection with any claims that may be made under the policies of insurance effected pursuant to this clause 47. Neither party shall give any release or make any compromise with any insurers without the prior written consent of the other Party.

47.11 *Application of insurance proceeds.*—In the event of any loss or destruction of the Works, all insurance proceeds received as a result of such loss or damage under the material damage and additional cost of completion insurances, shall be paid to the Contractor and applied in or towards the replacement and repair of the works lost, damaged or destroyed.

Article 48: Environmental Claims

48.1 The Contractor shall not, in the course of carrying out the works:
(i) cause or knowingly permit the entry, discharge, escape, release or migration of pollutants or contaminants (together, a "Contamination") in, on, above or under the Site; or
(ii) cause a Contamination elsewhere,

which, in either case, results in or where it is reasonably foreseeable that it would result in any action, proceedings, claim or demand commenced by any person or regulatory authority under any relevant environmental law against the Purchaser or the Contractor (together, an "Environmental Claim").

48.2 The Contractor shall not be liable in respect of an environmental claim:
(i) arising due to any incorrect or misleading information (referred to in clause 5.3) provided to the Contractor by or on behalf of the Purchaser; or
(ii) arising from the entry, discharge, escape, release or migration of pollutants or contaminants in, on, above or under the Site from areas outside the Site; or
(iii) arising from any Contamination existing in, on, above or under the site or elsewhere as at the effective date (including any Contamination arising from any works carried out in, on, above or under the Site prior to the Effective Date).

48.3 The Purchaser shall not cause or knowingly permit, and shall procure that all of other contractors working on the Site and any of their respective visitors and invitees shall not cause or knowingly permit, any Contamination in, on, above or under the Site or elsewhere which results in or where it is reasonably foreseeable that it would result in any Environmental Claim.

48.4 If either Party becomes aware or receives notice (whether oral or written) of any environmental claim or the existence of any contamination which will result or it is reasonably foreseeable that it may result in any Environmental

Claim, it shall immediately notify the other Party and provide it with all necessary information relating thereto.

48.5 Each Party shall indemnify the other Party against all actions, claims, demands, costs, charges, expenses and other liabilities whatsoever arising out of any failure on its part to comply with its obligations under this clause 48. The Purchaser shall further indemnify the Contractor against any Environmental Claim referred to in clause 48.2.

Article 49: *Force Majeure*

49.1 *Instances of Force Majeure.* An "event of *Force Majeure*" shall mean an event or circumstance not within the reasonable control, directly or indirectly, of the Party affected, but only if and to the extent that:

   (i) such event or circumstance, despite the exercise of reasonable diligence, cannot be (or be caused to be) prevented, avoided or removed by such Party;

   (ii) such event or circumstance materially adversely affects (in cost and/or time) the ability of the Party to perform its obligations under the contract, and such Party has taken all reasonable precautions, due care and reasonable alternative measures in order to avoid the effect of such event on its ability to perform its obligations under the Contract and to mitigate the consequences thereof; and

   (iii) such event or circumstance is not the direct or indirect result of the failure of such Party to perform any of its obligations under the Contract.

Subject to the foregoing, the events of *Force Majeure* shall include:

   (a) war, hostilities (whether declared or undeclared), invasion, act of foreign enemies;

   (b) rebellion, revolution, insurrection or military or usurped power or civil war;

   (c) epidemic, explosion, major fire, flood, earthquake or other exceptional natural calamity and exceptional act of God;

   (d) ionising radiation or contamination by radioactivity from any nuclear fuel, or from any nuclear waste from the combustion of nuclear fuel, radioactive toxic explosive, or other hazardous properties of any explosive nuclear assembly or nuclear component of such assembly, except as may be attributable to the Contractor's use thereof;

   (e) riot, commotion or disorder, unless solely restricted to employees of the Contractor or any of its sub-contractors or suppliers;

   (f) expropriation or compulsory acquisition of the .... plant and/or the Power Plant;

   (g) any act or omission of any Government instrumentality;

   (h) a Change in Legal Requirements;

   (i) strikes (whether or not nation-wide) and any lock out or other industrial disturbance; and

(j) extraordinary weather or sea conditions including tempest, lightning, hurricane, typhoon, exceptional monsoon rain and exceptional temperatures.

49.2 *Certain Events not Excused.*—Notwithstanding, that an event of *Force Majeure* otherwise exists, the provisions of this clause 49 shall not excuse:

(a) late delivery of equipment or materials caused by negligent acts or omissions on the part of the Contractor, or any sub-contractor or supplier of the Contractor;

(b) delays in progress of the works caused by the Contractor's failure to engage competent sub-contractors or suppliers or to hire personnel or labour; or

(c) in relation to the performance by the Purchaser of its obligations under Annexure 2 (Purchaser's Obligations), any of the matters referred to in (a) and (b) above caused by any other contractor engaged by the Purchaser (or any of their sub-contractors or suppliers of any tier);

(d) delays resulting from unsuitable ground conditions (whether foreseeable or not); or

(e) the payment by either Party of any amounts due to the other Party save only where the event of *Force Majeure* affects the transmission of funds through the banking system.

An event of *Force Majeure* affecting certain of the affected Party's obligations shall not excuse such Party's failure in timely out the remainder of its unaffected obligations.

49.3 *Notice of* Force Majeure: *Procedure.* Relief under this clause 49 shall not be given unless the Party intending to claim relief has, by notice to the other Party within .... days of becoming aware of an event of *Force Majeure* or if later, within .... days of an event of *Force Majeure* having an effect upon the performance of such Party's obligations under this Contract, informed the other Party that it desires to claim relief under this clause 49. Such notice shall include such relevant information as is available, including a description of the event and the date of its occurrence, the effect of such event upon the performance of such Party's obligations, the expected duration of such event of *Force Majeure* and its effects and the actions it is taking in order to comply with this clause 49.

49.4 *Obligations of Parties upon Force Majeure.* As soon as practicable after the occurrence of an event of *Force Majeure*, the Party affected shall:

(a) use all reasonable endeavours to prevent and reduce to a minimum and mitigate the effects of the event of *Force Majeure*, including where appropriate by having recourse to alternate acceptable sources of services, equipment and materials; and

(b) use all reasonable endeavours to perform its obligations to the maximum extent practicable.

Relief under this clause 49 shall cease to be available to a Party to the extent it fails to use such best endeavours.

49.5 Effect of *Force Majeure*

(a) Except as provided in clauses 49.2 and subject to clauses 49.3 and 49.4 either Party shall be relieved from liability and shall not be construed to be in default in respect of any obligation hereunder to the extent that and for so long as the failure to perform such obligation shall be due to an event of *Force Majeure*.

(b) If the Contractor suffers delay and/or incurs additional Cost as a result of the occurrence of an event of *Force Majeure*, the Contractor shall give further notice to the Engineer and the Engineer shall determine (subject to clause 33) any extension of time to which the Contractor is entitled.

(c) In case of an event of *Force Majeure* according to clause 49.1 which is not covered by Purchaser's insurance to be effected under clause 47, and such event of *Force Majeure* continues for a period ending .... months after beginning of such event of *Force Majeure*, Parties shall enter into good faith negotiations regarding an adjustment of the Contract Price, notwithstanding that the Contractor has been granted extension of time as per clause 33.1. The Contractor shall not be required to complete the works or to repair the damage of the works being due to the respective events of *Force Majeure*, and such failure to complete or repair the works shall not constitute a Contractor Remediable or Non-Remediable Event, until the Parties have agreed to the respective adjustment of Contract Price. If the Parties do not reach such agreement within .... months after end of such event of *Force Majeure*, either Party may terminate the Contract as per clause 46.2.1. During such period if required by the Purchaser the Contractor shall only be obligated to perform such parts of the works as are reasonably required by the situation being the consequence of the respective event of *Force Majeure*, subject to the Parties Agreement on appropriate compensation therefor.

(d) In case an event of *Force Majeure* described in clause 49.5(c) continues for a period of .... months, either party may terminate the Contract in accordance with clause 46.2.1. Such termination shall not effect the validity or effectiveness of the Contractor's claims being referred to in clause 49.5(c), in respect of which the Parties have arrived at an agreement.

Article 50: Dispute Resolution Procedure

All disputes shall be resolved in accordance with the provisions set out in Annexure 21 (Dispute Resolution Procedure) to the Articles of Agreement.

Article 51: Applicable Law

The Contract shall in all respects be governed by and interpreted in accordance with the Law of ....

Article 52: Miscellaneous

52.1 *Language and Measures.*—This Contract is being executed and delivered in the English language and all modifications, amendments, waivers of any provision of this Contract, all documents, notices and communications between the Parties under this contract shall be in the English language. The metric system of measurement shall be exclusively used in the Contract.

52.2 *Severability of Provisions.*—The invalidity, illegality or unenforceability in whole or in part of any of the provisions of this contract shall not affect or impair the validity, legality or enforceability of the remaining provisions of this contract.

52.3 *Waiver.*—Save where this Contract otherwise expressly provides, neither Party shall be deemed to have waived any right under this Contract, unless such Party shall have delivered to the other Party a written waiver signed by an authorised representative of such waiving Party. No delay or omission in the exercise of any power or remedy shall be construed to be a waiver of any default or an acquiescence therein.

52.4 *Amendment.*—This Contract may only be amended or modified by a written instrument signed by a duly authorised representative of each of the Parties.

52.5 *Entire Agreement.*—This Contract constitutes the entire agreement between the Purchaser and the Contractor concerning the subject matter hereof. All previous documents, undertakings and agreements (to the extent not forming part of this Contract), whether verbal, written or otherwise, between the Parties concerning the subject matter hereof are hereby cancelled and shall not affect or modify any of the terms or obligations set forth in this Contract.

52.6 *Further Acts and Assurances.*—Each of the Parties agree to execute and deliver all such further instruments, and to do and perform all such further acts and things, as shall be necessary or convenient to carry out the provisions of this Contract.

52.7 *Expenses.*—Each Party shall pay its own costs and expenses (including, without limitation, the fees and expenses of its agents, representatives, advisors, counsel and accountants) necessary for the negotiation, preparation, execution, delivery, performance of and compliance with this contract.

52.8 *No Partnership.*—Nothing contained in this contract shall or shall be deemed to create an association, trust, partnership, or joint venture or impose a trust or partnership duty, obligation, or liability on or with regard to either Party.

52.9 *Compliance with Laws.*—In the performance of their obligations under the Contract, the Parties shall, and shall cause their respective affiliates, officers, directors, agents and employees to, comply strictly with all applicable Legal Requirements.

52.10 *Exclusive Remedies.*—The Parties intend that this Contract alone shall govern their respective rights, obligations and liabilities in relation to the matters referred to herein. Accordingly, the remedies arising under this Agreement (or otherwise at common law for breach of contract) in respect of or in consequence of:

(a) any breach of contract;

(b) any negligent act or omission;

(c) death or personal injury; or

(d) loss or damage to any property,

to be to the exclusion of any other remedy (whether in tort or otherwise) that either may have against the other.

52.11 *No other representations.*—For the avoidance of doubt, the Contractor gives no representations, guarantees or warranties and assumes no obligations to the Purchaser except as expressly stated in the contract.

52.12 *Change over to Euro.*—Purchaser and Contractor agree that the contractual obligations regarding payment, in particular monetary values, shall be deemed as agreed upon in .... when the .... becomes the only admissible currency in .... (name of the country). The conversion shall be made on the basis of the official exchange rate.

The other parts of the Contract shall not be affected by the changeover to the .... The Parties agree in particular that no party shall have the right to terminate, withdraw from, contest, or change the contract in any other way because of the changeover to the ....

APPENDIX TO THE CONDITIONS

[Note: the Appendix will need to be agreed following the "split contracts"]

Matter	Clause No.	
Articles of Agreement		
Amount of performance bond price	2(b)	(....................) % of the contract
Amount of advance Payment guarantee	2(b)	Equal to the amount of advance Payment
Amount of advance payment	5	....................% of the Contract Price
Conditions		
Time for completion	1.1	.... months after effective date
Person and address for service of notices etc.	10.1	Purchaser: Contractor: Engineer:
Date of legal requirements, standards etc.	13.3(d), (e) and (j)	[The signing date of the Contract]
Rate of liquidated damages for performance	35.4	Liquidated damages for failure to demonstrate satisfaction of the performance guarantees shall be:

Rate of liquidated damages for delay	34.1	(foreign currency) .... per day
Limit of liquidated damages for delay	34.2	.... % of the contract price
Limit of liquidated damages for performance guarantees	35.5	.... % of the contract price
Limit of total liquidated damages	44.4	.... % of the contract price
Rate of interest on overdue payment	40.2	[Base lending rate plus .... %]

ANNEXURE 9
FORM OF PERFORMANCE BOND

[Note: all forms of the bonds (*i.e.* Performance Bond, Advance Payment Bond and Retention Bond) are subject to confirmation by the commercial department of TSOA. The Retention Bond is not included as part of this document. Amendments reflecting those made for the Performance Bond will be required.]

BY THIS BOND we ....

of ....

(hereinafter called "the Surety") are held and firmly bound unto .... of .... ("the Purchaser") in the sum of .... being ....% of the Contract Price for the payment of which sum the Surety binds itself its successors and assigns by these presents.

WHEREAS, ... (name of Contractor) of .... (registered address) ("the Contractor") has by an Agreement made between the Purchaser of the one part and the Contractor of the other part entered into a Contract ("the Contract") for the design, construction and completion of a non-recovery .... oven plant with a gross output of .... tonnes per annum of Coke .... on a dry basis at .... (place) as more fully described in the said Contract ("the Works") and for the consideration of payment for the amount stated therein ("the Contract Price"), subject to the provisions of the Contract. Any capitalised terms used and not defined herein shall have the meanings attributed thereto in the Contract.

Now the Condition of this Bond is such that if the Contractor shall duly perform and observe all the terms, provisions, conditions and stipulations of the Contract on the Contractor's part to be performed and observed or if the Contractor is in default under the Contract and the surety shall satisfy and discharge the damages sustained by the Purchaser up to the amount of this Bond or if the Contract is terminated and it is either agreed by the Parties or determined in accordance with the Dispute Resolution Procedure that the Contractor was entitled to terminate the Contract, then this obligation shall be null and void but otherwise shall be and remain in full force and effect.

The obligations of the Surety hereunder shall, except as provided in the previous paragraph, and until this performance bond expires, remain in full force and effect and shall not be affected or discharged by any act, omission, matter or thing which but for this provision might operate to release or otherwise exonerate the Surety from its obligations hereunder in whole or in part, including without limitation and whether or not known to the Surety or the Purchaser:

(a) any time, waiver or indulgence granted to the Contractor or any other person;

(b) the taking, variation, compromise, renewal or release of or refusal or neglect to perfect or enforce any rights, remedies or securities against the Contractor or any other person;

(c) any legal limitation, disability or incapacity relating to the Contractor or any other person;

(d) any variation of or amendment to the contract or in the nature or extent of or method of carrying out of the works or the obligations to be performed thereunder or any other document or security so that references to the contract in this Bond shall include each such variation or amendment; and

(e) any unenforceability, invalidity or frustration of any obligations of the Contractor under the contract [or any other document or security].

The benefit of this Bond may be assigned by the Purchaser to the [Finance Parties] as collateral security and any other assignment shall be subject to the prior written consent of the Surety (such consent not to be unreasonably withheld).

This Performance Bond shall automatically expire upon the provision by the Contractor of the Retention Bond (whether or not returned to the Contractor).

[Note: The above was agreed by the parties, as recorded in the Position paper dated 11-09-98.]

The above-written Bond and all matters relating thereto shall be governed by .... (name of the country) law and the Surety hereby irrevocably submits to the non-exclusive jurisdiction of the (name of the country) Courts.

Executed as a Deed by the Surety on the   Day of
Executed as a Deed by   )
the Surety   )
)
in the presence of:)

ANNEXURE 10
FORM OF ADVANCE PAYMENT GUARANTEE
(Note: Proposed amendments to follow shortly)

To: [PURCHASER]

From:.................... Bank

Dear Sirs,

Advance Payment Performance Guarantee Number

We are informed [name of Contractor] (hereinafter called "the Contractor") has entered into a Contract ("the Contract") with you for the design and construction of a Coke.................. plant at .... and that under the terms of the contract the payments you are to make to the Contractor will include the sum of .... as an advance payment ("the Advance Payment") on the delivery of this guarantee. Any capitalised terms used and not defined herein shall have the meanings attributed thereto in the contract.

In consideration of your agreement to make the advance payment above to the Contractor we Bank hereby irrevocably guarantee to pay to you any amount or amounts demanded by you not exceeding in aggregate ....(immediately on)/(within .... days of) receipt of your first demand in writing without objection or contestation whatever from our part or from the Contractor without the necessity on your part to pursue or exhaust any remedy against the Contractor and notwithstanding that the contract may be unenforceable in whole or in part.

Our obligations hereunder shall remain in full force and effect unless and until the Contract is terminated and it is either agreed by the Parties or determined in accordance with the Dispute Resolution Procedure that the Contractor was entitled to terminate the contract and subject only as aforesaid, our obligations shall not be affected or discharged by any act, omission, matter or thing which but for this provision might operate to release or otherwise exonerate us from our obligations hereunder in whole or in part, including without limitation and whether or not known to us or you:

    (a) any time, waiver or indulgence granted to the Contractor or any other person

    (b) the taking, variation, compromise, renewal or release of or refusal or neglect perfect or enforce any rights, remedies or securities against the Contract or any other person;

    (c) any legal limitation, disability or incapacity relating to the Contractor;

    (d) any variation of or amendment to the Contract or in the nature or extent of or method of carrying out of the works or the obligations to be performed thereunder or any other document or security so that references to the Contract in this guarantee shall include each such variation or amendment; and

    (e) any unenforceability, invalidity or frustration of any obligations of the Contractor under the Contract [or any other document or security].

This guarantee shall come into force upon receipt by the Contractor of the Advance Payment in accordance with the terms of the contract.

The amount of this guarantee will automatically be decreased [upon receipt by us of a copy of each [interim certificate] issued by the Engineer certifying the amount certified therein as representing the amount of the pre-payment by the Contractor of the amount of the Advance Payment.]

Upon receipt by us of a copy of provisional taking over certificate issued by the Engineer under the Contract the outstanding amount of this guarantee shall reduce to nil (whether or not it is returned to the Contractor).

This guarantee shall be null and void when its value has reduced to nil (which shall not be later than the date of a copy of provisional taking over certificate), and as soon as it has been reduced to nil, this Guarantee shall be returned to the Contractor.

The benefit of this guarantee may be assigned by you to the [Finance Parties] as collateral security and any other assignment shall be subject to our prior written consent (such consent not to be unreasonably withheld).

This Guarantee and all matters relating thereto shall be governed by German law and we hereby irrevocably submit to the non exclusive jurisdiction of the .... courts.

IN WITNESS whereof, we have duly executed this guarantee as a Deed on this Day of

    Executed as a Deed by   )

    [ ]   )

    in the presence of:)

ANNEXURE 14
DEFECTS LIABILITY CERTIFICATE

TO: CONTRACTOR DATE:
FROM: PURCHASER
(SHORT DESCRIPTION OF WORKS)

1. It is hereby certified that the defects liability period for the works expired on [ ] and that the Contractor has fulfilled all its obligations under the contract for defects therein.
2. The Purchaser shall within .... days after the date hereof return to the Contractor the Retention Bond provided by the Contractor.
3. [The Contractor shall forthwith provide the Purchaser with the Latent Defects Bond duly executed by an internationally recognised first class bank acceptable to the Purchaser in the sum of ....% of the contract price and in the form set out in Annexure 17 to the Articles of Agreement.]

   [Note: This is not agreed.] Engineer

ANNEXURE 17
FINAL PAYMENT CERTIFICATE

[Note: This is subject to the "split contracts" and Letters of Credit]

TO: CONTRACTOR DATE:....................
FROM: PURCHASER
(SHORT DESCRIPTION OF WORKS)

1. In accordance with clause 39 of the conditions either:
   (a) Having considered the Contractor's Final Account it is hereby certified that the value of the works is as follows:
   or
   (b) No final statement having been submitted by the Contractor in accordance with clause 39.6 of the Conditions it is hereby certified that the value of the works has been determined as follows:

   Contract price
   Adjustment for variations
   Reductions
   Claims for additional payment
   Amounts due to purchaser
   TOTAL VALUE OF WORKS
   Less Payments Previously Certified
   BALANCE DUE TO CONTRACTOR

2. The Purchaser shall pay the amount due to the Contractor within .... days after the date hereof.

3. Payment by the Purchaser of the amount due to the Contractor hereunder shall constitute conclusive evidence that the Purchaser has performed all its obligations under the Contract, provided that it is not so conclusive:

    (a) to the extent that fraud or dishonesty relates to or affects any matter dealt with in this Certificate, or

    (b) if any arbitration or court proceedings under the contract have been commenced by either Party before the expiry of .... days after the date hereof.

Engineer

CHAPTER 7
DEEDS

SYNOPSIS
PRECEDENTS
- Assignment of Business with Goodwill and Tenancy Rights
- Assignment of Simple Contract Debts
- General Power of Attorney
- Special Power of Attorney in respect of entering into and concluding one Transaction
- Special Power of Attorney for Admitting Execution before Sub Registrar of Document already executed
- Release and Indemnities
- Guarantees
- Guarantee, Deposit and Charge as Security for Advances to a Third Person
- Agreement Of Reference – To Arbitration

In India English forms are still useful guide for the preparation of deeds. They are adopted as such by conveyancers in India.

Generally speaking, English forms of conveyances divided into several parts, each of which bears a technical or descriptive name. The deeds begin with what is called *Introductory* or the *Commencement clause*. This clause begins with a description of the nature of the document and contains the date of its execution. It also contains the names and description of the parties is not ordinarily stated in the documents, but in India this must as a rule, be done in order to identify the executants properly. It is well-known that ordinarily there is no identifiable family name in India, as is the case in England, and this is an essential difference between the two countries.

The *commencement clause* is followed by the clause called the *recitals*. This clause generally contains a description of the Title of the Transferor and a narrative of the circumstance which have led to the necessity or desirability of executing the deed. It is not, however a necessary part of a deed and no substantial injury is done to the document, or the transaction evidenced by it, if this clause is omitted altogether. But, it is desirable to include it as, *inter alia*, it is sometimes useful in ascertaining the intent one of the parties, if operative part of the documents defective obscure. Previously, it was the practice to state the whole history of the previous tenures and transfers of the property intended to be transferred, so that from a study to the recitals alone, it was possible to form an opinion about the nature of the title which had from time to time been transferred and of the existing title of the transferor.

PRECEDENTS

ASSIGNMENT OF BUSINESS WITH GOODWILL AND TENANCY RIGHTS

THIS INDENTURE made at .... (place) this.................... day of .... 20..... BETWEEN (1) .... and (2) .... both of .... Indian inhabitants carrying on business in partnership in the firm name and style of .... (hereinafter called "The assignors") (which expression shall unless it be repugnant to the context or meaning thereof be deemed to mean and include the partners of the said firm for the time being and the heirs, executors and administrators of the last surviving partner and persons for the time being carrying on the said business) of the ONE PART; AND

(1)

(2)

(3)

(4)

all Indian inhabitants, carrying on business in partnership in the firm name and style of M/s .... (which expression shall unless it be repugnant to the context or meaning thereof be deemed to mean and include the partners of the said firm for the time being and the heirs, executors and administrators of the last surviving partners and persons for the time being carrying on the said business) of the OTHER PART:

WHEREAS the Assignors have been carrying on business of ...... in the firm name and style of .... hereinafter called "the said business" in Shop No. .... on the ground floor of the building known as .... situated at .... whose landlords are .... and which property bears Cadestral Survey No..... of Fort Division within the registration and sub-registration District of .... City and .... District hereinafter called "the said shop premises";

And, whereas the Assignors in respect of the said business should licences and certificates and are the owners of furniture, articles, and things including Air-conditioning machine, other machines etc. a list whereof is hereto annexed and marked 'A';

And, whereas the Assignors have represented to the Assignees that the said licences and certificates are valid and subsisting and there is no action pending in respect of the same against the Assignors for breach of any of the covenants and conditions of the said licences;

And, whereas the Assignors are the tenants of the said shop premises and paying monthly rent of Rs. .... per month and the tenancy in respect of the said premises is valid and subsisting;

And, whereas the Assignors have also represented to the Assignees that they have neither charged, mortgaged or otherwise encumbered the said business either together, with the goodwill, tenancy rights, benefit of telephone number..... and or the said furniture, articles, things, and machines etc., a list whereof is annexed hereto and marked "A: and the same are free from encumbrances and there is no debt due and payable in respect of the said business including income tax and sales tax;

And, whereas the Assignors have agreed to sell and assign and the Assignees have agreed to purchase the said business from the Assignors together with the good will as a running concern together with the benefit of tenancy rights as incidental to the said assignment of the business but for no monetary consideration and also the benefit of telephone No. .... and of licences etc., at or for the price Rs. ....(Rupees ....);

And, whereas the Assignors have also agreed to sell and the Assignees have agreed to purchase the said furniture and articles and things including air-conditioning machine, other machines etc. a list whereof is hereto annexed and marked "A" at or for the price of Rs. .... (Rupees....) which has been delivered to the Assignees on or before the execution of these presents which are capable of passing by manual delivery (the payment and receipt in respect whereof has been acknowledged separately).

Now, this indenture witnesseth that in pursuance of the said agreement and in consideration of the sum of Rs. .... (Rupees....................) paid on or before the execution of these presents (the receipt whereof the Assignors do hereby admit and acknowledge and of and from the same and every part thereof do and each of them doth hereby acquit, release and discharge the Assignees forever) AND ALSO in consideration of the covenants hereinafter contained the Assignors do hereby assign unto the Assignees all the beneficial interest and goodwill of the said business carried on by them in the name of M/s. .... as aforesaid as a running concern together with the benefit of all licences and certificates in relation to the said business and the right title and interest of the Assignors in the tenancy of the said shop premises being shop No. .... Survey No. .... of .... Division within the registration and Sub Registration District of .... city and .... District but for no monetary consideration and the benefit of telephone no.... and the deposit made for the same TO HAVE HOLD, RECEIVE AND TAKE the premises unto and to the use of the Assignees absolutely as regards the said business and goodwill thereof forever and as regards the said tenancy of the said shop premises subject to the terms and conditions of the tenancy in respect thereof and subject to the payment by them the Assignees of the monthly rent to the land lords;

And further that the Assignors do hereby covenant with the Assignees that notwithstanding any act, deed, matter or thing whatsoever by the Assignors or by any person or persons lawfully or equitably claiming from under or in trust for them made, done, omitted or executed or knowingly or willingly suffered to the contrary the hereinbefore recited tenancy is now valid and subsisting of the said premises hereinbefore expressed so to be hereby assigned and is not void or voidable AND that notwithstanding any such thing as aforesaid all the rents reserved and the covenants by the Assignors and the conditions of the tenancy have been paid, observed and performed up to the date of these presents AND the Assignors do hereby covenant with the Assignees that They the Assignors have now good right to assign the said premises and business and good will hereby assigned or expressed so to be unto the Assignees in the manner aforesaid and that They the Assignees shall and may at all times hereafter peaceably and quietly possess and enjoy the same and receive the issues and profits thereof without any lawful eviction interruption claim and demand whatsoever from or by the Assignors or any person or persons lawfully or equitably claiming as aforesaid and further that They the Assignors and all persons having right title or interest in the said premises hereinbefore expressed to be hereby assigned or any of them or any part thereof from under or in trust and at all times hereafter at the request and cost of the Assignees do and execute or cause to be done and executed all such acts, deeds and things whatsoever for further or more perfectly assuring the said premises and every party thereof unto and to the use of the assignees in manner aforesaid as shall or may be reasonably required AND it is hereby expressly agreed by and between the parties hereto that all outstanding of the Assignors and of the said business upto the date of giving possession to the Assignees shall belong to and be the absolute property of the Assignors and shall be recoverable by them for their own use and benefit or otherwise and that the Assignors shall satisfy and discharge all the debts and liabilities of the business including the liability for payment of income-tax, Sales-tax, or the liability or claim made by any employees for salary, leave pay, retrenchment compensation, gratuity or any other claim upto the date of carrying on the said business and shall indemnify the Assignees against all claims and demands in respect of the said business;

And this indenture also witnesseth that in pursuance of the said Agreement in this behalf and in consideration of the aforesaid terms, the Assignors shall indemnify and keep indemnified the Assignees from and against all rents, claims and demands, contracts and engagements in respect of or in connection with the said business or any claim made by any other person uptodate;

And the assignees do hereby covenant with the Assignors that They the Assignees will henceforth during the said term pay the rent reserved and perform all the covenants and conditions of the said tenancy and keep indemnified the Assignors from and against the payment of the said rent and the observance and performance of the said covenants and all actions, proceedings, costs, damages, claims, demands and liability whatsoever for or on account of the same or in anyways relating thereto.

IN WITNESS WHEREOF, the Parties hereto have hereunto set and subscribed their respective hands the day and year first hereinabove written.

SIGNED AND DELIVERED by the

With named....................

And....................

Partners of M/s. ....

In the presence of:

SIGNED AND DELIVERED by the
With named (1)....................
(2)....................
(3)....................
Partners of M/s. ....
In the presence of:

RECEIVED the day and year first hereinabove written of and from the within named Assignees a sum of Rs. .... (rupees....................) by cheque No. .... dated .... drawn on .... Being the full consideration amount within mentioned to be by them paid to us.

Rs. ....

WITNESSES: WE SAY RECEIVED:

Annexure "A"

List of licences and certificates and furniture, articles and things including air-conditioning machine, other machines, etc.

[LIST TO BE PREPARED ACCORDINGLY]

ASSIGNMENT OF SIMPLE CONTRACT DEBTS

THIS ASSIGNMENT made on the .... day of...................., 20....

BETWEEN

AB of etc. (hereinafter called "the Vendor") of the ONE PART

AND

CD of etc. (hereinafter called the "the Purchaser") of the OTHER PART.

WHEREAS:

(1) The several persons, firms and companies described in the first column of the Schedule hereto are indebted to the Vendor in respect of the matters mentioned in the second column thereof in the several sums set opposite their respective names in the third column thereof.

(2) The Vendor has agreed with the Purchaser for the absolute sale to him of the said debts for the sum of Rs. ....

NOW THIS DEED WITNESSETH as follows:

1. In pursuance of the said Agreement and in consideration of the sum of Rs...... paid by the Purchaser to the Vendor (receipt of which sum the Vendor hereby acknowledges) the Vendor as beneficial owner hereby assigns unto the Purchaser all the several debts and sums of money specified in the Third column of the Schedule hereto due and owing to the Vendor from the several persons, firms and companies mentioned in the First Column thereof in respect of the matters mentioned in the second column thereof TO HOLD the same Unto the Purchaser absolutely.

2. The Vendor hereby covenants with the Purchaser that the several debt and sums of money hereby assigned are still due and owing in full to the Vendor from the several persons, firms and companies aforesaid.

IN WITNESS, etc.

THE SCHEDULE ABOVE REFERRED TO:

GENERAL POWER OF ATTORNEY

(Make use of such clauses as are necessary and appropriate)

TO ALL TO WHOM these presents shall come I .... of .... Indian Inhabitant SEND GREETINGS: WHEREAS I am desirous of appointing some fit and proper person to look after all my affairs and requested.... Also of ..... Indian Inhabitant (hereinafter called the "Attorney") to act for me and manage and look after my affairs which the Attorney has consented to do NOW KNOW ALL AND THESE PRESENTS WITNESS that I the said .... do hereby nominate, constitute and appoint the Attorney the said .... my true and lawful attorney to act in, conduct, manage and look after all my affairs in the Republic of India and for the purposes aforesaid, I hereby confer upon the Attorney the following powers and authorities:

1. To ask, demand, sue for, recover and receive from every person and every body politic or corporate in India whom it shall or may concern all sums of money, rents, issues, profits, debts, dues, goods, wares, merchandise, chattels, effects and things of any nature or description whatsoever which now are or which at any time or times during the subsistence of these presents shall or may be or become due owing payable or belonging to me in or by any right title ways or means howsoever and upon receipt thereof or of any part thereof to make sign execute and deliver such receipts releases or other discharges for the same respectively as the Attorney shall think fit or be advised.

2. To settle any account or reckoning whatsoever wherein I now am or at any time hereafter shall be in any wise interested or concerned with any person whosoever and to pay or receive the balance thereof as the case may require.

3. To receive every sum of money whatsoever which now is or at any time hereafter may be due arising or belonging to me upon or by virtue of any mortgage, charge, pledge, hypothecation or other security whatsoever and on receipt thereof to make, sign, execute and give good and sufficient releases, acquittances or other discharges for the same and also to sign, seal, execute, make and deliver all proper and sufficient reconveyances releases and other assurances of the lands tenements hereditaments and property which shall have been mortgaged or charged as security thereof and also to consent to any such alternation or modification of the nature or conditions of the said securities as the Attorney shall think fit.

4. To compound with or make allowances to any person for or in respect of the aforesaid debts or any other debt or demand whatsoever which now

is or shall or may at any time hereafter become due or payable to me and to make or receive any composition dividend thereof or thereupon and to give receipts, releases or other discharges for the whole of the same debts, sums or demands or to settle compromise or submit to arbitration every such debt or demand and every other claim, right matter or thing due to or concerning me as the Attorney shall think most advisable for my benefit and for that purpose to enter into make, sign, execute and deliver such bonds of arbitration or other deeds or instruments as are usual in like cases.

5. To accept service of any writ, summons or other legal process or notice and to appear and my persons to represent in any court and before all Magistrates, judicial revenue or other officers and Tribunals whatsoever as by the Attorney shall be thought advisable and to commence any suit action or other proceeding in any court of justice and before any public officer or tribunal for the recovery or enforcement of any debt sum of money, right, title, interest, property matter or thing whatsoever now due or payable or to become due or payable or in anywise belonging to me by any means or on any account whatsoever and the same action suit or proceeding to prosecute or discontinue or become non-suit therein if the Attorney shall see cause and also to take such other lawful ways and means including proceedings in execution, distress, distraint and the like for recovering or getting in any such sum of money or other thing whatsoever which shall by the Attorney be conceived to be due owing, belonging or payable to me by any person whosoever and also to appoint pleaders, advocates, solicitors and legal advisers to prosecute or defend in the premises aforesaid, or any of them as occasion may require and from time to time them or any of them to remove and other or others to appoint in their place and to pay them such fees and remuneration as the Attorney shall think fit or be advised and for all or any of the purposes aforesaid to sign, execute, deliver, file all necessary Vakalatnamas, Warrants of Attorney, plaints, petitions, applications, defences, statements, accounts, declarations, affidavits, and other documents, papers and writings.

6. Also to make any declaration or affidavit in proof of any debt or debts due or claimed to be due to me in any proceedings taken or hereafter to be taken by or against any person, firm or company under any Act or Ordinance for the time being in force for the relief or otherwise of insolvent debtors or the winding up of companies and to attend all meetings of creditors under any such proceedings and to propose, second or vote for or against any resolution at any such meeting and generally to act for me in all proceedings whether by way of bankruptcy or liquidation by arrangement or by composition which may be taken against or for the relief of any debtor as the Attorney shall think fit.

7. To enter into and upon any messuages, lands, hereditaments and immovable properties whatsoever and to view the state and defects of the repairation thereof and forthwith to give proper notices and directions for repairing the same and to let manage and improve the same to the best advantage and to make or repair drains and roads thereon.

8. To pay or allow all taxes, rates, assessments, charges, deductions, expenses and all other payments and outgoings whatsoever due and payable or to become due and payable for or on account of my said lands, hereditaments, estates and premises.

9. To contract with any person for leasing for such period at such rent subject to such conditions as the attorney shall see fit all or any of the said premises and any such person to let into possession thereof and to accept surrenders or leases and for that purpose to make, seal, deliver and execute any lease or grant other lawful deed or instrument whatsoever which shall be necessary or proper in that behalf.

10. To ask, receive and recover from all receivers, farmers, tenants and all other occupiers whatsoever whether holding under a written lease or Agreement or otherwise of my said lands, hereditaments, all rents, arrears of rent, services, issues, profits, emoluments and sums of money now due, owing and payable or at any time hereafter to become due, owing and payable in respect of the same premises in any manner whatsoever and also on non-payment thereof or of any part thereof to take summary proceedings to distrain or distress according to law and to give notices to quit, and vacate and file suits and proceedings in ejectment and to recover rents and compensation for use and occupation and to make, like and appropriate demands and take, like and appropriate actions proceedings against trespassers.

11. To appoint any fit persons to be steward, bailiff, receiver or servant for the management of my lands, hereditaments and premises and to recover rents thereof and the same or any of such stewards, bailiffs, receivers or servants at pleasure to remove and displace as the attorney shall think fit.

12. To sell (either by public auction or privately) or exchange and convey transfer and assign any of my lands, tenements or hereditaments and property for such consideration and subject to such covenants as the Attorney may think fit and to give receipts for all or any part of the purchase or other consideration money and the same or any of them with like power to mortgage, charge of encumber and also to deal with my immovable personal property or any part thereof as the Attorney may think fit for the purpose of paying off, reducing, consolidating or making substitution for any existing or future mortgage, charge, encumbrance, hypothecation or pledge thereon or thereof or any part thereof and to make or concur in any transfer of or alteration in the terms of any existing or future mortgage, charge, hypothecation or pledge of the same or any part thereof as the Attorney shall think fit and in general to sanction any scheme for dealing with mortgages, charges, hypothecation or pledges of any property or any part thereof as fully and effectually, as I myself could have done.

13. To purchase, take on lease or otherwise acquire such lands, houses, tenements and immovable property generally as the Attorney may think fit or desirable.

14. To sell or to concur in selling either by private sale or in any other manner any of my stock, merchandise, goods, chattels and other effects, articles and things for such consideration and subject to such conditions as the Attorney may think fit and to receive the proceeds thereof and to give receipt for all or any part of the sale proceeds or other consideration money.

15. To pledge, hypothecate or charge or concur in pleading, hypothecating or charging with, to or in favour of a respectable bank or banks (and not individual banker or shroff or firm of bankers or shroffs) any personal or moveable properties, goods, chattels, merchandise, commodities, effects and things for such consideration and subject to such conditions as the Attorney may think fit and for that purpose to sign, seal, execute and deliver all necessary instruments and deeds of mortgage, charge, hypothecation, pawn, pledge, lien and trust receipts and to receive the consideration money or otherwise for such pledge, pawn, hypothecation, charge, mortgage, lien and the like.

16. Also to draw, make, sign, accept or endorse, pledge, hypothecate or otherwise negotiate all or any foreign or inland bills of exchange, hundi, cheques, orders for payment of money and promissory notes and to sign, seal, execute, deliver, endorse, accept, assign or transfer all mortgage deeds, bills of lading, delivery orders or other symbols or indicia or of documents of title relating to goods or merchandise policies of assurances charter parties ships' certificates, bills of sale, securities of any Government, empire, kingdom, republic, State, territory, colony, country, municipality or local authority wheresoever situate or other stocks, shares, debentures, mortgages, obligations or other securities of any company or corporation whether commercial, municipal or otherwise and all and every other public or other securities, stocks or shares, foreign or otherwise and to deal with the same and to receive the proceeds thereof respectively.

17. To purchase, take on hire, borrow or otherwise acquire machinery, tools, spare parts, raw materials, merchandise commodities, goods, wares, articles, effects and things and to deal in and deal with the same and to dispose of the same in such manner and for such consideration as the Attorney may think fit.

18. To borrow any sum of money on such terms and with or without security as the Attorney may think fit for any of the purposes of these presents.

19. To deposit any money which may come to his hands as such attorney with any banker, broker, or other person and any of such money or any other money to which I am entitled which now or hereafter is or shall be deposited with any banker, broker or other person, to withdraw and either employ as the Attorney shall think fit in the paying of any debts or the keeping down of interest payable by me or the creation of sinking fund for the liquidation of any charges or encumbrances affecting my moveable and immovable property or any part thereof or in or about any of the

purposes mentioned in these presents or otherwise for any use and benefit or to invest in any such stocks, funds, shares or securities as the Attorney may think proper and to receive and give receipts for any income or dividends arising from such investments and the same investments to vary or dispose of as the Attorney may think fit.

20. To continue and or to open new, current and or overdraft accounts in my name with any banks or bankers and also to draw cheques and otherwise to operate upon any such account.

21. To engage, employ and dismiss any agents, clerks, servants or other persons in and about the performance of the purposes of these presents as the Attorney shall think fit.

22. To sell any of my present or future investments and for that purpose to employ and pay brokers and other agents in that behalf and to receive and give receipts for the purchase money payable in respect of such sales and to transfer any of my investments so sold to the purchaser or purchasers thereof or as he or they may direct and for these purposes to sign and execute all such contracts, transfer deeds and other writings and do all such other acts as may be necessary for effectually transferring the same.

23. To accept the transfer of any shares, stocks, debentures, annuities, bonds, obligations or other securities of whatever nature that may at any time be transferred to me.

24. To attend vote at and otherwise take part in all meetings held in connection with any company or corporation with which I am concerned or in relation to any of my investments and to sign proxies for the purpose of voting threat or for any other purpose connected therewith as freely as I myself could do.

25. Out of any of my moneys in his hands or under his control to pay all calls that may be lawfully made upon me or other expenses that may be incurred in relation to any of my investments and to give security for payment of the same.

26. To exercise all other rights and privileges and perform all other duties which now or hereafter may appertain to me as a holder of debentures or shares or stock of or otherwise interested in any company or corporation.

27. To exercise any power and any duty vested in me whether solely or jointly with another or others as executors, administrator, trustee, or in any other fiduciary capacity (including powers and trusts to sell or lease land or to receive and give good receipts for money) so far as such power or duty is capable of being validily delegated.

28. And also to appear before the Registrar of any district or sub district registrar of deeds appointed or to be appointed under any act or law for the time being in force or otherwise for the registration of deeds, assurances, contracts or other instruments and then and there or at any time thereafter to present and register or cause to be registered any deeds, assurances, contracts or other instruments in which I am or may be by the

Attorney be deemed to be interested and also these presents and to pay such fees as shall be necessary for the registration.

29. To enter into, make, sign, seal, execute, deliver, acknowledge and perform all engagements, contracts, agreements, indentures, declarations, bonds, deeds, assurances, documents, papers, writings and things that may be necessary or proper to be entered into, made, signed, sealed, executed, delivered, acknowledged and performed for any of the purposes of the presents or to or in which I am or may be party or in any way interested.

30. In general to do all other acts, deeds, matters and things whatsoever in or about any estate, property and affairs or concur with persons jointly interested with myself therein in doing all acts, deeds, matters and things herein either particularly or generally described as amply and effectually to all intents and purposes as I could do in my own proper person if these presents had not been made.

31. For all or any of the purposes of and powers, authorities and discretions conferred by these presents, to use and sign my name or in which I am or may be in anywise interested or to use and sign his name as the Attorney shall think fit.

32. To appear on my behalf and to represent my interest before the income tax, wealth tax and gift tax and/or other taxing authorities in respect of my income tax, wealth tax, gift tax, as also before any tribunal or court.

33. To sign on my behalf Income tax, wealth tax and gift tax returns and to submit the same on my behalf to the respective taxing authorities.

34. To execute, declare and affirm on my behalf all the applications, documents, declarations and affidavits as may be necessary for the purposes of the income tax, wealth tax and gift tax affairs and to submit and file the same with the respective taxing authorities.

35. To file appeals and references as the attorney may be advised and as he may deem fit and proper against the orders and decisions of the income tax, wealth tax and gift tax authorities in respect of my assessment proceeding.

36. To appoint on my behalf such auditors, accountants and advocates as the said Attorney shall deem fit and proper for representing me before the income tax, wealth tax and gift tax and/or Taxing Authorities or any other tribunal or court in respect of the income tax, wealth tax and gift tax assessments and to discharge them and appoint new auditors, accountants and advocates as the case may be in their place.

37. To compound, compromise and settle with the income tax, wealth tax and gift tax authorities the orders and assessments made by them.

38. To apply for time for payment and to apply for instalments for the payments of the amounts assessed and to be paid by me to the income tax, wealth tax and gift tax or other taxing authorities.

39. And also for the better and more effectually doing, effecting and performing the several matters and things aforesaid to appoint from time

to time or generally such person or persons as the Attorney may think fit as his substitute or substitutes to do execute and perform all or any such matters and things as aforesaid and any such substitute or substitutes at pleasure to remove and to appoint another or others in his or their place and I hereby agree at all times to ratify and confirm whatsoever the Attorney or any such substitute or substitutes shall lawfully do or cause to be done in or about the premises.

40. And for more effectually removing any doubt which may arise as to the true meaning of these presents or as to the construction or application of the powers, authorities and discretion hereby conferred I do hereby declare that the powers, authorities and discretions hereby conferred shall not in any case be deemed to revoke any powers or authorities or discretions before given by me to the attorney or to any other person or persons or be deemed to be limited by any such previously given powers, authorities and discretions or be deemed to be limited to such transactions and matters as are herein expressly mentioned but the same are intended to be extended and shall in all cases extend to any other matters or transactions not herein precisely mentioned or defined which in the course of any of my businesses, concerns or affairs may by the Attorney be deemed to be requisite or expedient to be done or performed.

41. And I do hereby declare that all the powers and authorities and discretions hereby conferred upon the Attorney shall be available for exercise by him both during my absence as also at the same time and place along with the Attorney.

AND, I the above named................... do hereby undertake to ratify whatever the Attorney or any substitute or agent appointed by him under the power in that behalf hereinbefore contained may lawfully do or cause to be done in and by virtue of these presents.

IN WITNESS WHEREOF, I the abovenamed.... Have here unto set my hand and seal this................... day of .... in the .... Christian year ....

SIGNED, SEALED AND DELIVERED

By the within named................... in the presence of:

SPECIAL POWER OF ATTORNEY IN RESPECT OF ENTERING INTO AND CONCLUDING ONE TRANSACTION

TO ALL TO WHOM THESE PRESENTS shall come, I..................., Indian Inhabitant,

Whereas I am the owner of the land, hereditaments and premises situate at .... and more particularly described in the Schedule hereunder written.

And, whereas I am desirous of disposing of the said property I am desirous of appointing some fit and proper person to act for me and do all necessary acts and things in connection with the sale of my said property more particularly described in the Schedule hereunder written;

NOW, KNOW ALL AND THESE PRESENTS WITNESSETH that I do hereby nominate, constitute and appoint.... To be my true and lawful attorney for the purpose hereinafter expressed that is to say:

1. To negotiate for sale of the said property more particularly described in the Schedule hereunder written with the intending purchasers and to conclude such agreement for sale, sign the agreement for sale of the said property and receive deposit or earnest from the purchaser of the said property and give receipts and discharges for the same.
2. To appoint advocates/solicitors in connection with the sale of the said property and pay, their remuneration.
3. To apply for and obtain permission/sanction if required from the Competent Authority appointed under the Urban Land (Ceiling and Regulation) Act, 1976 or from any other officer or authority and to make application for that purpose and appear before the officer concerned if necessary in connection with obtaining sanction to the sale of the said property more particularly described in the Schedule hereunder written.
4. On receiving the balance of the sale price to sign and execute conveyance and other documents and assurances in favour of the purchasers or their nominee or nominees as the case may be and to do all other acts, deeds, matters and things in relation thereto.
5. To apply for and obtain income tax clearance certificate under section 230A of the Income Tax Act, 1961 in connection with the sale of the said property and to do all acts and things in connection therewith.
6. To appear before the sub registrar of Assurances or any other competent authority and lodge the document of conveyance or assurances for registration and to admit execution of the said deed as my said Attorney shall find necessary.
7. To appear before talati, mamlatdar, collector, municipal corporation, or any other authority in connection with the said property more particularly described in the Schedule hereunder written for effectuating the transfer of the said property in favour of the intending purchaser.

AND, I DO HEREBY for myself, my heirs, executors and administrators agree to ratify and confirm all and whatsoever my said attorney shall or purport to do or cause to be done by virtue of these presents.

IN WITNESS WHEREOF, I have hereunto set my hand at..................... this.................... day of....................

THE SCHEDULE ABOVE REFERRED TO:

All that piece of parcel of land or ground with messuage tenement or bungalow and other erections standing thereon and being at ... in the registration sub district and district of ... city by admeasurement... sq. metres or thereabouts and registered in the books of the Collector of Land Revenue Under Olds Nos... and New Survey No. .... Cadastral Survey No. .... of ....l. Division which said premises are assessed by the .... Municipal/Rates and Tax under.................... Ward No. ....and Street No.... and bounded as follows:

On or towards the East

On or towards the West

On or towards the North

On or towards the South

SIGNED AND DELIVERED by the
Within named....................

In the presence of

Before me,

SPECIAL POWER OF ATTORNEY FOR ADMITTING EXECUTION BEFORE SUB REGISTRAR OF DOCUMENT ALREADY EXECUTED

(This Power of Attorney must be authenticated before the Sub Registrar)

TO ALL WHOM THESE PRESENTS shall come, I.................... of...................., Indian inhabitant SEND GREETINGS;

WHEREAS I was the owner of land, hereditament and premises situate at .... and more particularly described in the Schedule hereunder written:

And, whereas I executed a Deed of Conveyance of the said property in favour of.... The Purchasers;

And, whereas I am unable to go to the office of the Sub Registrar for admitting execution of the said Conveyance as I am leaving....................

And, whereas therefore I am desirous of appointing.................... as my Constituted Attorney to attend the office of the Sub Registrar to admit execution of the said Conveyance.

NOW, KNOW YOU ALL THESE PRESENTS WITNESSETH that I do hereby nominate, constitute and appoint.................... to be my true and lawfully Attorney for the purposes expressed that is to say:

1. To present and lodge in the office of the Sub Registrar of Assurances at Bombay and to admit execution of the conveyance dated... executed by me in favour of ... the Purchasers and to do all acts and things necessary for effectively registering the said conveyance.

2. AND, I DO HEREBY for myself, my heirs, executors and adminsitrators agree to ratify and confirm all and whatsoever my said Attorney shall or purport to do or cause to be done by virtue of these presents.

IN WITNESS WHEREOF, I have hereunto set my hand at.................... this.................... day of....................

THE SCHEDULE ABOVE REFERRED TO:
Signed and delivered by the
Within named....................

In the presence of

Before me,

RELEASE AND INDEMNITIES

(Indemnity to a Company and its Directors on issue of a Duplicate to replace lost Share Certificate.)

To, ... Limited and M/s *ABCD* and *EF* its Directors.

Gentlemen,

I have lost or mislaid the certificate of title dated..... and numbered.... Relating to ... (fully paid up) (ordinary) Shares in the above named Company of Rs. .... each numbered .... to .... both inclusive of which I am the registered holder.

The said certificate has not been pledged or deposited by me by way of security, nor have I sold or transferred any of the shares to which it relates, and I am entitled to the custody of the certificate of title relating to such shares.

I request you to issue to me a fresh certificate of title to the said shares and I hereby undertake to indemnify you and each of you against all proceedings, claims, expenses and liabilities whatsoever which may be taken or made against or incurred by you or any of you by reason of the issue of such fresh certificate or the registration of a transfer of the said shares or any of them without the production of the said original certificate.

Dated the .... day of..................

Signed..................

WITNESS Signature of the

Said..................

GUARANTEES

Guarantee for payment of goods to be supplied to Tradesman.

To Messrs. *AB* and *CD* of .... Trading as .... & Co.

IN CONSIDERATION of your supplying goods and giving credit to *EF* of etc. I hereby guarantee to you the payment of all moneys (nor or) at any time of times (hereinafter) to become due to you in respect of any goods but so that my liability to you is in no event to exceed the sum of Rs.....

I agree that you are to be at liberty to grant to the said *AB* such extension of credit or time for payment or other indulgence as you may think proper without discharging or impairing my liability hereunder.

This guarantee is to be a continuing guarantee and is to continue to binding notwithstanding any change in the constitution of your firm abo named.

I reserve the right to myself or my personal representatives by (one month's) notice in writing to your above-named firm at any time to revoke this guarantee as to all future dealings by you or your said firm with the said *EF*.

Dated the .... day of....................

Signed....................

Witness to the signature of the said....................

Guarantee for payment of arrears of rent about to be distrained for

To

CD

IN CONSIDERATION of your having at my request agreed not to enforce by distress or otherwise the payment of Rs. .... Being arrears of rent now due and owing to you from AB of etc. under a lease dated....................whereby you demised to him for the term and at the rent therein mentioned the premises therein described and situate at.................... I hereby guarantee to you the payment of the said arrears of rent on or before the.................... day of....................

Dated the.................... day of....................

Guarantee for payment of debt by Instalments in consideration of creditor foregoing or discontinuing legal proceedings.

To

AB of etc.

IN CONSIDERATION of your refraining from instituting any legal proceedings which you may be entitled to institute against CD (or you discontinuing the action which you have begun against CD in the Queen's Bench Division of the High Court of Justice 20..... B. No. ....) for the recovery of the sum of Rs. .... Now due to you by him I hereby guarantee the payment to you of that sum together with the further sum of Rs. .... For your costs making in all the sum of Rs. .... by equal (weekly) instalments each of Rs. .... Beginning on the day of .... and further that if default shall be made for (one week) in the payment of any instalment the whole of the said sum of Rs. .... Or the balance thereof for the time being remaining unpaid shall forthwith be paid to you.

Dated the.................... day of....................

Signed....................

Witness to the signature of the

Said....................

GUARANTEE, DEPOSIT AND CHARGE AS SECURITY FOR ADVANCES TO A THIRD PERSON

IN CONSIDERATION of your advancing to A of etc. at my request the sum of Rs. .... As a loan to carry interest at the rate of .... per cent per annum (or the sum of Rs. .... As a loan at the date hereof and such further sums as the said A may request from time to time but before the expiration of two years from the date hereof the whole of such sums including the loan of Rs... granted at the date hereof not to exceed the sum of Rs..... and the whole of such loans as from the date upon which the advance is made to carry interest at the rate of .... Per cent per annum).

I, the undersigned hereby agree with you as follows:

1. (Subject to the provision of clause 5 hereof) to make good any default by said A or his estate in the payment of the loan(s) and of all interest due thereon.
2. To deposit forthwith with you the securities mentioned in the schedule hereto as collateral security for the said loan(s) until payment thereof with interest as aforesaid.
3. The said securities are hereby charged by me with the payment of the said loan(s) and interest and shall not be encumbered by me in any way without your consent in writing first obtained so long as the said loan(s) or any part thereof shall remain due to you from me hereunder.
4. I will whenever required by you so to do execute at my own expense a proper transfer or transfers to you of such of the said securities as are capable of being transferred together with power of sale and all other necessary powers for securing and enforcing the payment of the said loan(s) and interest.
5. The period of said loan(s) shall expire on.... (and all my liability hereunder shall cease on ... and any of the said deposited securities not then realised shall be forthwith returned to me).
6. No change whatsoever, in the constitution of your firm shall impair or discharge my liability hereunder notwithstanding the provisions of the Partnership Act or any other enactment.

THE SCHEDULE ABOVE REFERRED TO

(List of Securities)

Guarantee for the Performance of a Contract

THIS AGREEMENT is made the .... day of ..... BETWEEN (guarantor) of etc. (hereinafter called "the Guarantor") of the one part AND (part guaranteed) of etc. (hereinafter called "the Principal" of the other part

WHEREAS:

(1) This agreement is supplemental to a contract (hereinafter called "the Contract') dated... and made between (contractors) (Hereinafter called "the Contractors") of the one part and the Principal of the other part whereby the Contractors agreed and undertook to (state nature of works or other obligation undertaken) for the sum of Rs. .....

(2) The Guarantor has agreed to guarantee the due performance of the contract in manner hereinafter appearing.

NOW THE GUARANTOR HEREBY AGREES with the principal as follows:

1. If the Contractors (unless relieved from the performance by any clause of the contract or by statute or by the decision of a tribunal of competent jurisdiction) shall in any respect fail to execute the contract or commit any breach of their obligations thereunder then the Guarantor will indemnify the Principal and his personal representatives against all loses, damages, costs, expenses or otherwise which may be incurred by him by reason of any default on the part of the Contractors in performing and observing the agreements and provisions on their part contained in the contract.

2. If any question or dispute shall arise as to the amount of any such losses, damages, costs, expenses or otherwise the amount thereof shall be determined by (architect, engineer or trade expert according to the nature of the contract) whose decision shall be final.

3. The Guarantor shall not be discharged or released from this Guarantee by any arrangement made between the Contractors and the principal with or without the assent of the Guarantor or by any alteration in the obligation undertaken by the contract or by any forbearance whether as to payment time performance or otherwise.

As WITNESS, etc.

AGREEMENT OF REFERENCE – TO ARBITRATION

ARTICLES OF AGREEMENT made at Bombay this................... day of ....20..... BETWEEN.................... of Bombay Indian Inhabitant residing at ... hereinafter person called "the said.................... (which expression shall unless repugnant to the context or meaning thereof mean and include his heirs, executors and administrators) of the one part AND.................... Also of Bombay Indian Inhabitant residing at... hereinafter called the said.................... (which expression shall unless repugnant to the context or meaning thereof mean and include his heirs, executors and administrators) of the OTHER PART;

WHEREAS certain disputes and differences have arisen between the said.................... and the said.................... as regards contract dated.................... Made by and between the Parties hereto;

AND WHEREAS the parties hereto have agreed to refer the said disputes between them to the sole Arbitration of.................... upon the terms and conditions hereinafter contained;

NOW THIS AGREEMENT WITNESSETH as follows:

1. All disputes and differences between the Parties hereto regarding the contract dated... made by and between the Parties hereto and mentioned in the schedule hereto are hereby referred to the arbitration, determination and award of the said sole arbitrator...

2. The arbitrator shall have summary powers and may take such evidence, documentary or oral as he may in his sole and absolute discretion think proper and the said arbitrator shall have power to record only such evidence as he may in his sole and absolute discretion think fit and proper

and shall also have such powers and authorities as are granted to an arbitrator under the Indian Arbitration Act, 1940 (Act X of 1940).

3. The arbitrator will be at liberty to take the assistance of any technical expert or engineer of his choice on such matters on which he may decide to take such assistance.

4. The arbitrator shall be entitled to use personal knowledge relating to the matters referred to his sole arbitration.

5. The venue of the arbitration proceedings and the fee of the arbitrator will be as may be fixed by the arbitrator himself.

6. The arbitrator shall make and publish his award within four months from the date of entering upon the reference. In the event of the said period becoming insufficient the arbitrator shall have power with the consent of the parties hereto from time to time extend time for making and publishing his award.

IN WITNESS WHEREOF, the parties hereto have hereunto set and subscribed their respective hands and seals the day and year first hereinabove written.

THE SCHEDULE ABOVE REFERRED.

SIGNED, SEALED AND DELIVERED
By the within named.....................
In the presence of....................
SIGNED, SEALED AND DELIVERED
By the within named
In the presence of....................

CHAPTER 8
BONDS

SYNOPSIS

FORM
USE OF BONDS
HEIRS AND REPRESENTATIVES
TWO RATES OF INTEREST
STAMP DUTY
REGISTRATION

PRECEDENTS
- Simple Money Bond for money borrowed
- Simple Money Bond, for Money due with Recitals
- Instalment Bond
- Equated Instalments Bond
- Bond by a Debtor and his Surety for a Loan
- Bond by a Debtor and his Surety for an Existing Liability
- Instalment Bond, with Surety, for an Existing Liability (in the form of a deed)
- Bond with Sureties for a Loan Repayable in Equated Instalment with Hypothecation of Property (in the form of a deed)
- Bond with Sureties for Loan (in the form of a deed) with Provision for lower Rate of Interest in case of Punctual Payments
- Administration Bond by a Person Obtaining Letters of Administration (section 291, Succession Act)
- Security Bond given for the Grant of a Succession Certificate (section 375, Succession Act)
- Administration Bond by Guardian Appointed under the Guardians and Wards Act
- Security Bond by a Debtor (under section 21, Provincial Insolvency Act)
- Security Bond by a Receiver Appointed in a Suit: Order 40, Rule 3(a), C.P.C.
- Cash Security Bond by an Employee of Government (in the Form of Agreement)
- Personal Security Bond by an Employee, with Sureties, Pending the Execution of a Hypothecation Bond
- Security Bond by Sureties on behalf of a Claimant to Money due from Government to his Deceased Ancestor
- Security Bond by Surety of the Manager of an Estate (Hypothecating Property)
- Security given by a Legatee under a Lost Will to a Purchaser of Bequeathed Property (with Hypothecation)
- Security Bond with two Sureties, the Principal Agreeing to Deposit Cash Security by Monthly Deduction from Pay
- Bond by Sureties of a Student Admitted to a College to Secure the Performance of an Agreement
- Bond by Surety for Due Observance by Another of Terms of Partnership Deed
- Bond by a Trainee (if minor, by his Guardian) with Sureties
- Performance Guarantee Bond
- Deed of Indemnity
- Indemnity Bond

A bond is an instrument by which a person obliges himself to pay money, deliver or supply grain or other agricultural produce to another. In sec. 2(v) of The Stamp Act, 1899 bond is defined as including,

"(a) any instrument whereby a person obliges himself to pay money to another, on condition that the obligation shall be void if specified act is performed, or is not performed, as the case may be[1]

(b) any instrument attested by a witness and not payable on order or bearer, whereby a person obliges himself to pay money to another; and

(c) any instrument so attested, whereby a person obliges himself to deliver grain or other agricultural produce to another."

Thus, there are two kinds of bonds, simple and conditional.

Form

A bond is usually drawn up in the form of deed poll. A conditional bond consists of two essential parts, *viz.* (1) the obligation, and (2) the condition. Sometimes recitals are introduced between the two parts for the purpose of explanation of the conditions, which follow them. Usually the executant is a debtor who executes the bond in favour of the creditor. However, the sum named in the bond is sometimes intended to be a penalty, and sometimes liquidated damages. The question whether a sum stipulated for in a contract is a penalty or liquidated damages is a question of law. The intention of the parties is material.[2] When it amounts to a penalty, the obligee is not entitled to recover for the breach of conditions the whole amount but only a reasonable compensation not exceeding such sum (*vide* sec. 74, the Contract Act). In any case it is advisable to fix the sum for which a bond is taken at the maximum figure to which damages apprehended from the breach can possibly go, as the sum entered in the bond is the maximum which the obligee can claim, even if damages actually incurred are larger.

The bond is usually commenced by saying "By this bond I bind myself, etc." or "THIS bond executed by, etc." If a departure from the usual practice prevailing is intended, then any of the different forms given in the precedents can be adopted for drafting a bond[3].

Use of Bonds

The object in view in the execution of a bond can as well be served by an agreement. The difference between the two is purely formal. Bond is executed in the form of a deed poll and its conditions are mentioned in an indirect form, that is, not that the obligor will do this or that and will pay so much as damages or compensation if he does not do so, but that he will pay so much unless he does this or that. An agreement is executed as a deed between two parties and directly

---

1. This is also the definition of "bond" in sec. 2(d), the Limitation Act, 1963.
2. K.P. *Subbarama Sastri* v. *K.S. Raghvan*, (1987) 2 SCC 424: AIR 1987 SC 1257.
3. A simple bond is to be distinguished from a promissory note (*see* NEGOTIABLE INSTRUMENTS, post) inasmuch as money payable under the bond is not payable to the order of the obligee or to the bearer of the instrument.

expresses the real obligation intended to be created, *e.g.*, A covenants with B that he will do so and so or will not do so and so and that if he commits a breach he will pay the sum stipulated. Both forms are equally good, but in some cases, the later is preferable. For security bonds when the liability is necessarily limited to the amount of security offered, the bond form is more suitable.

Heirs and Representatives

Under section 37, Contract Act, promises bind the representatives of the promisors and the right to enforce a promise descends, under the general law. To the heirs and representatives, unless a contrary intention appears from the contract, either expressly or impliedly. The common instance of a contrary intention being implied from the nature of the contract is that of contracts of a purely personal nature, such as a contract to marry, a contract to paint, etc. It is, therefore, unnecessary to mention the personal representatives or successors in title of the obligor or obligee in the "obligatory" part of the bond. In the "condition" part, however, the "heirs and representatives" of the obligor and the heirs, executors, representatives and assigns of the obligee have to be mentioned, because the condition refers not to the persons upon whom the obligation is binding or for whose benefit it endures but the persons by whom and to whom the act or acts is or are to be done, by the doing of which the obligation is avoided, and they are not necessarily the same as the persons bound by, or entitled to enforce, the obligation. For instance, if an obligor promises that he will pay a sum of money on a certain date, the promise can be enforced after his death against his representatives (section 37, Contract Act). But if the bond is in English form and contains the condition that it shall be void if the obligor pays the money on a certain date[1], there is no law under which it can be said that the bond would be equally void if the obligor's heir pays the money and after obligor's death the bond can be enforced against his heirs under section 37, even though he has paid the money, as it was not the payment by the obligor's heir which could avoid the bond.

Two Rates of Interest

Sometimes the parties agree that in case of default of payment on a certain date, a higher rate of interest would be payable. Such an agreement is penal under section 74 of the Contract Act. In *Nagewaraswami* v. *Viswasundara*,[2] a stipulation to pay compound interest on default was held penal. In order to avoid this possibility of the covenant being regarded as penal it is desirable to mention the higher rate of interest originally and provide that if the debtor shall pay on or before a certain date the principal and interest at a specified lower rate, the creditor would accept such lower rate and would not insist on the higher rate originally fixed. Such a contract is, however, possible only when the deed is between parties and is signed by the creditor also and is not in the form of a deed poll, as the covenant about acceptance of reduced interest is one by the creditor and not by the debtor.

---

1. cf precedents 10 to 14, post.
2. AIR 1953 SC 370.

Stamp Duty

Article 15 of the Schedule I to The Stamp Act, 1899 governs the Stamp duty on bonds of different valuation. There are separate Articles 34 and 57 for Indemnity Bond and Security Bond respectively. Security Bond, even if it creates a charge on immovable property, has been held not to amount to mortgage. This would be so only if such bond is signed by the surety alone as provided by Article 57.

For distinction between bond and simple agreement for purposes of the payment of stamp duty under The Stamp Act, 1899 reference may be usefully made to the decision of a special bench of seven Judges in *Mahabir Prasad* v. *Peer Bux*[1].

Registration

Registration is not necessary unless, as in security and hypothecation bonds, any immovable property is charged or hypothecated.

PRECEDENTS

SIMPLE MONEY BOND FOR MONEY BORROWED

I, *AB* son of *CD* (or, We, *AB*, etc. and *XY*, etc.) .... and resident of .... having borrowed Rs. .... from *EF*, etc., son of *GH* .... and resident of .... (or, being indebted to *EF*, etc., to the extent of Rs. .... due to him on account of the price of .... purchased by me, or under a previous bond dated....................) hereby promise (or, ourselves jointly and severally promise) to pay to the said *EF* the said sum of money on demand (or, on the...................., or, within.................... years of this date) with interest thereon from the date of this bond at the rate of.................... per cent per annum with half yearly rests).

Dated the.................... day of....................

                       (Signed)....................

Witness....................

Witness....................

SIMPLE MONEY BOND, FOR MONEY DUE WITH RECITALS

THIS BOND is made on the .... by me, *AB*, etc.

Whereas I owe Rs. .... to *EF*, etc., on the following accounts:

(i) On account of the principal and interest due under a bond executed by me in his favour on the.................... Rs. ....;

(ii) On account of the price of a bullock purchased by me from him on the...................., Rs. ....;

---

1. AIR 1972 All 466.

(iii) On account of various loans taken by me from him on *bahi khata* from... to................., Rs...................;

(iv) On account of rent for the years................... Rs...................;

(v) On account of a decree of the Court of................... dated................... in his favour and against my deceased father CD, Rs. ....

Now in consideration of the aforesaid liabilities I hereby promise to pay to the said *EF* the said sum of Rs. ... within ... years and interest thereon or on so much thereof as shall for the time being remain unpaid at the rate of................... percent per annum payable half yearly on the................... day of................... and the................... day of................... in each year;

And, I hereby agree that in case any interest is not paid on due date the same shall be added to the principal and shall bear interest at the rate and payable on the dates hereinbefore mentioned.

In witness whereof, I, the said *AB*, have put my signature hereunder.

INSTALMENT BOND

I, *AB*, etc., having borrowed Rs. .... from *CD*, etc., hereby promise to pay to the said *CD* the said sum of Rs. .... in twelve equal half yearly instalments payable on the .... and on the .... in each year (or, in twelve instalments of the amounts and payable on the dates hereinafter mentioned) and also on the same dates interest at the rate of .... percent per annum from the date of this bond on the said sum or on so much thereof as shall remain due on the said dates;

And I hereby agree that in case I fail to pay up any two consecutive instalments of principal with interest due hereunder on the due dates, the whole amount then due under this bond shall become payable at once.

Details of instalments:

Amount   Due Date.
***   ***

EQUATED INSTALMENTS BOND

I, *AB*, etc., having borrowed Rs. .... from *EF*, etc., hereby promise to pay to the said *EF* the said sum of Rs. .... and interest at the rate of .... percent per annum in twelve equated instalments of the principal and interest combined of Rs. .... each payable on the .... day of .... and the .... day of................... in each year, the first instalment being payable on the................... day of ....;

And I hereby agree that in case any such instalment shall remain in arrears for one month the whole money then due on account of the principal and interests shall thereupon become payable at once.

BOND BY A DEBTOR AND HIS SURETY FOR A LOAN

THIS BOND is executed on the .... day of .... by us *AB*, etc. (debtor) and *CD*, etc (his surety);

Whereas *EF*, etc., has this day advanced a loan of Rs. .... to me, the said *AB*, at the request of my surety the said *CD*, on the terms and conditions hereinafter appearing;

Now, we the said *AB* and *CD* hereby jointly and severally bind ourselves to pay to the said *EF* the said sum of money on demand with interest thereon from the date of this bond at the rate of .... per cent per annum with half yearly interests.

BOND BY A DEBTOR AND HIS SURETY FOR AN EXISTING LIABILITY

THIS BOND, etc. (as in Form 5).

Whereas, I the said *AB* owe Rs. .... to *EF*, etc., on the following accounts (as in Form 2).

And, Whereas in consideration of the said *EF* refraining from instituting a suit for the said sum, I, the said *AB*, have agreed to give this bond with the said *CD* as his surety.

Now we, the said *AB* and *CD*, hereby, etc. (as in Form 5).

INSTALMENT BOND, WITH SURETY, FOR AN EXISTING LIABILITY (IN THE FORM OF A DEED)

THIS BOND is made on the .... day of .... between *AB*, etc (hereinafter called "the debtor") of the first part and *CD*, etc., (hereinafter called "the surety") of the second part and *EF*, etc., (hereinafter called "the creditor") of the third part.

Whereas, Rs. .... is still due to the creditor from the debtor under the decree dated ...., passed in suit No. .... (name of parties) by the court of ... on account of the arrears of rent for house ....

And, whereas the lease of the said house has again been settled with the debtor on the debtor agreeing to undertake payment of the said sum due under the said decree;

And, whereas on the application of the debtor, the creditor has agreed to accept an instalment bond with surety for the said sum due under the said decree without interest;

And, whereas in consideration of the creditor having agreed to accept payment of the said sum by instalments, the surety has agreed to guarantee payment of the said sum in accordance with the terms of this bond.

NOW THIS BOND WITNESSES and it is hereby agreed and declared as follows:

1. For consideration aforesaid the debtor and the surety hereby jointly and severally covenant with the creditor to repay to him the said sum of Rs. .... in six equal half yearly instalments on the .... day of .... and the .... day of .... in each year commencing from the .... day of .... next.

2. If any of the said instalments or any part thereof shall be in arrear for thirty days after the said instalments shall have become payable as aforesaid, then the whole of the said sum of Rs. .... or such part thereof as shall for the time being remain unpaid shall immediately become due and payable with interest thereon at .... per cent per annum upto the date of actual payment thereof and the debtor and the surety hereby jointly and severally covenant to pay the same to the creditor.

IN WITNESS WHEREOF, etc.

BOND WITH SURETIES FOR A LOAN REPAYABLE IN EQUATED INSTALMENT WITH HYPOTHECATION OF PROPERTY (IN THE FORM OF A DEED)

THIS DEED is made on the .... day of .... BETWEEN *AB*, etc. (hereinafter called "the borrower") of the FIRST PART AND *CD*, etc., (first surety) and *EF, etc* (second surety) (hereinafter collectively referred to as the "sureties") of the second part AND *GH*, etc., (hereinafter called "the creditor") of the THIRD PART;

Whereas the borrower has requested the creditor for the advance of a loan of Rs. .... repayable with interest at .... per cent per annum by instalments hereinafter specified;

And, whereas the sureties have agreed to give security for the repayment of such loan in the manner hereinafter appearing, and the creditor has agreed to advance such loan on such security.

NOW THIS DEED WITNESSES as follows:

1. Covenants

In pursuance of the said agreement and in consideration of the sum of Rs. ... advanced by the creditor to the borrower (the receipt of which is hereby acknowledged) the borrower and the sureties hereby jointly and severally covenant with the creditors as follows:

(i) To pay in instalments.

The borrower and the sureties will pay to the creditor the said sum of Rs. .... with interest thereon at the rate of .... per cent annum computed from the date hereof by four, half yearly instalments of principal and interest combined of Rs. .... each payable on the following dates:

Instalment	Due Date
First instalment	
Second instalment	
Third instalment	
Fourth instalment	

(ii) Penalty for default

If any of the instalments aforesaid shall be in arrears in whole or part, the whole sum then remaining due to the creditor under this deed on account of principal and interest shall thereupon become payable at once and the borrower and the sureties will be liable jointly and severally to pay the same.

2. Hypothecation

For the consideration aforesaid and in further pursuance of the aforesaid agreement the borrower/first surety/second surety[1] hereby grant(s) and transfer(s) by way of simple mortgage to the creditor all that property described in the schedule hereto, to the intent that the said property hereby mortgaged shall remain and be charged by way of simple mortgage as security for the payment to the creditor of the said principal money and interest in accordance with the covenants herein contained.

3. Covenant of no Charge

The said borrower/ first surety/second surety hereby covenant(s) with the creditor that the said property is free from encumbrances.

4. Enforcement of Mortgagee's Remedies

It is hereby agreed and declared that in case of default in the payment of such sums on account of principal and interest as may become due under the covenant hereinbefore contained and creditor may forthwith enforce against the said property hereby mortgaged or any part thereof, all or any of the remedies of the holder of a simple mortgage.

IN WITNESS, etc.

BOND WITH SURETIES FOR LOAN (IN THE FORM OF A DEED) WITH PROVISION FOR LOWER RATE OF INTEREST IN CASE OF PUNCTUAL PAYMENTS

THIS DEED etc. (as in Form 8).

Whereas, the creditor has agreed to advance to the borrower a loan of Rs. .... repayable in .... years with interest at the rate hereinafter specified on the security of the sureties.

---

1. If the mortgage is made by one strike off the other two. If it is made by two strike off the third and add "and" between the two. If it is made by all the three, substitute "and the sureties" for "first surety/second surety".

NOW THIS DEED WITNESSES, as follows:

1. In pursuance of the said agreement and in consideration of the said sum of Rs. ... advanced by the creditor to the borrower (the receipt of which is hereby acknowledged) the borrower hereby covenants with the creditor that he will repay the said sum of Rs. ... to the creditor within ... years from this date and will in the meantime and for so long as any part of the said principal sum or any money to be treated as principal hereunder remains unpaid pay interest on the said sum or on so much thereof as shall for the time being remain unpaid at the rate of fifteen per cent per annum half yearly on the ... and ... in each year:

Provided always that the creditor shall accept interest at the reduced rate of twelve per cent per annum *in lieu* of the rate of fifteen per cent per annum for any half year in respect of which the borrower shall pay interest at such reduced rate not later than ... days after the due date.

2. In consideration of the creditor advancing the said loan to the borrower the sureties hereby jointly and severally guarantee the repayment of the said loan with interest to the creditor in accordance with the covenant hereinbefore contained.

IN WITNESS WHEREOF, etc.

ADMINISTRATION BOND BY A PERSON OBTAINING LETTERS OF ADMINISTRATION (SECTION 291, THE SUCCESSION ACT)

KNOW ALL MEN that we, *AB*, etc., and *CD*, etc., (surety for the said *AB*) hereby bind ourselves jointly and severally to Shri[1] .... District Judge of .... for the payment to him or his successor in office of the sum of Rs. ....

Whereas by an order of the court of the said District Judge of .... made on the .... day of .... the above named *AB* has been appointed administrator of the estate of *XY* deceased subject to the said *AB* entering into a bond of Rs. .... with one surety in the same sum for the due collection, entering upon and administering the estate of the deceased;

And, whereas the said *AB* had agreed to enter into the above-mentioned bond and the said *CD* has agreed to enter into the said bond as surety for the said *AB*.

Now the condition of the above written bond is this that if the said *AB* do and shall within six months from the grant of letters of administration of the estate of *XY* deceased, or such further time as the said court may appoint, exhibit in the said court an inventory containing a full and true estimate of all the property, in possession, and all the credits, and also all debts owing by any person to which the said *AB* is entitled as administrator, and do and shall, within one year from the said grant, or such further time as the said court may appoint, exhibit an account of the estate of the said deceased, showing the assets which

---

1. As stated in INTRODUCTION, ante, a court is not a juridical person, hence the bond has to be executed in favour of its presiding judge and his successors in office.

have come to his hands and the manner in which they have been applied or disposed of and do and shall, justly and truly administer, the said property, credits and estate according to law, and shall deliver and pay to such person or persons, as shall be lawfully entitled thereto, all the rest and residue of the said property, credits and estate which shall be found remaining upon the said administration account, then the above written bond shall be void but otherwise it shall remain in full force.

Signed, etc.

SECURITY BOND GIVEN FOR THE GRANT OF A SUCCESSION CERTIFICATE (SECTION 375, THE SUCCESSION ACT)

KNOW ALL MEN, etc., (as in Form 10)

Whereas the court of the said District Judge has on the .... passed an order for the grant to the said *AB* of a succession certificate to the estate of *XY* deceased on condition of the said *AB* executing a bond with one surety for the amount of Rs. .... for the purpose hereinafter appearing.

And, whereas the said *AB* has agreed to enter into the above bond and the said *CD* has agreed to enter into the above bond as surety for the said *AB*.

Now the condition of the above bond is this that if the said *AB* shall justly and truly account for the debts and other securities of the said *XY* deceased received by him and shall indemnify the persons who may be entitled to the whole or any part of such debts and securities then, the above written bond shall be void but otherwise it shall remain in full force.

ADMINISTRATION BOND BY GUARDIAN APPOINTED UNDER THE GUARDIANS AND WARDS ACT

KNOW ALL MEN, etc. (as in Form 10).

Whereas by an order of the court of the said District Judge made on the .... day of .... under section 15 of the Guardians and Wards Act, 1890, the abovenamed *AB* has, subject to his entering into a bond for Rs. ...., with a surety in the same sum, been appointed guardian of the property, movable and immovable of *EF*, minor son of *GH*;

And, whereas the said *AB* has agreed to enter into the above written bond, and the said *CD* has agreed to enter into the same bond as surety for the said *AB*;

Now, the condition of the above bond is that if the said *AB* do and shall justly and truly account whenever called upon to do so for what he may receive in respect of the property of the said *EF* and do and shall carefully observe, perform and keep all orders and directions of the said court touching or concerning the estate and effects of the said minor and his property, and touching and concerning all such moneys as he, the said *AB*, shall receive as such guardian as aforesaid, and in all things conduct himself properly, then the above written bond shall be void but otherwise it shall remain in full force.

SECURITY BOND BY A DEBTOR (UNDER SECTION 21, THE PROVINCIAL INSOLVENCY ACT)

KNOW ALL MEN, etc. (as in Form 10)

Whereas *AB* has been ordered under section 21(1) of The Provincial Insolvency Act to give reasonable security for his appearance until final orders are made upon the insolvency petition filed by him (or, his creditor);

And, whereas *CD* has consented to be the surety for the said *AB*.

NOW, the condition of the above obligation is this that if the said *AB* shall appear before the court whenever called upon by it to do so, then the above written bond shall be void but otherwise it shall remain in full force.

SECURITY BOND BY A RECEIVER APPOINTED IN A SUIT: ORDER 40, RULE 3(A), C.P.C.[1]

KNOW ALL MEN, etc. (as in Form 10)

Whereas, a suit has been filed in the court of the District Judge - by *EF*, etc., against *GH*, etc., for the possession of the immovable and movable property entered in the schedule to the plaint in the said suit;

And, whereas by an order of the said court, *AB* has been appointed receiver of all the property in suit on the terms and conditions mentioned in the said order and subject to his entering into a bond for Rs. .... with one surety for the purpose hereinafter appearing;

And, whereas the said *AB* has agreed to enter into the above bond and the said *CD* has agreed to enter into the above bond as surety for the said *AB*.

Now, the condition of the above bond is this that if the said *AB* shall duly account for all and every sum and sums of money which he shall as such receiver receive on account of the rents and profits of the immovable property and in respect of the movable property mentioned in the plaint in the said suit and shall submit his accounts at such period and in such form as the said court shall direct and shall duly pay the balances which shall from time to time remain in his hands and such damages for any loss occasioned to the said property by his wilful default or gross negligence as the said court shall direct and shall during the period of his appointment as such receiver fully obey and follow all the orders and directions passed and issued or which may hereafter be passed or issued by the said court to or for the guidance of the said *AB* as such receiver, then the above written bond shall be void but otherwise it shall remain in full force.

Forms of the bonds of security for stay of execution by original court, and by appellate court and for courts of appeal (Order 41, Rules 5, 6 and 10) are given in Forms Nos. 2, 3 and 4 in Appendix G to the Code of Civil Procedure and as

---

1. It is not necessary for the court to file a suit for recovery of the amount of the bond as under sec. 145, C.P.C. the court's order is directly executable in the manner provided in the Code for the execution of decrees.

they are statutory forms they may be used for these purposes. The court may execute its order holding the obligor to be in breach of the bond as if such order were a decree (sec. 145, CPC). Similarly, security bonds under the Code of Criminal Procedure are in prescribed Forms Nos. 3, 12, 13, 28 and 29 in Sch. II to that Code. They all provide for forfeiture of the specified amount to Government. The amount forfeited is recoverable as fine under that Code: [See sec. 546, Cr. P.C.]

CASH SECURITY BOND BY AN EMPLOYEE OF GOVERNMENT (IN THE FORM OF AGREEMENT)

THIS AGREEMENT made on this .... day of .... BETWEEN AB (hereinafter called "the depositor") of the one part AND the Governor of the .... (hereinafter called "the Government") of the OTHER PART;

Whereas the depositor has been appointed to the post of .... in the .... Department;

And, whereas it was a condition of his said appointment that the depositor should deposit security to the amount of Rs. ... for the discharge of his duties in the said appointment;

And, whereas the depositor has made the said deposit in cash (or, has paid Rs. .... in cash and has agreed to pay the balance by monthly instalments of Rs. ....).

NOW, THESE PRESENT WITNESS and parties hereto hereby agree as follows:

(1) Deposit to be applied to indemnify

The said deposit or any part thereof may be taken by the Government for the purpose of indemnifying it, the Government, from any loss caused by an act, negligence, or default of the depositor in losing, misappropriating, injuring, or failing to prevent injury to, and money or property while in his custody or under his supervision as a servant or officer of the said Department, or in permitting or failing to prevent the loss or misappropriation of, or any injury to, any such money or property as aforesaid by any person whosoever.

(2) To realise penalty

The said deposit or any part thereof may be applied for the purpose of realising any penalty for which the depositor may become liable under the conditions of his service in force for the time being.

(3) To be retained for six months

The said deposit may be retained by the Government for six months after the depositor has either died in the said service or has ceased to be in that service.

(4) To be repaid

On the expiration of the said period of six months the said deposit will be repaid to the depositor or to the person then entitled to his property after his accounts have been passed by the officer authorised under the rules of the said Department to examine and pass the same and after all sums to which the Government may be entitled under the first two clauses hereof has been deducted therefrom.

(5) Additional deposit

Any additional sum deposited by the depositor, stated in the schedule hereto, verified by the signature of the depositor, of the officer accepting the same may be applied in the same manner, and shall be refunded subject to the same conditions as the said deposit.

(6) Depositor to make up deficiency

If the said deposit is insufficient for the purpose set forth in the first and second clauses hereof, the depositor will pay to the Government such sum as may be necessary to make up such deficiency.

(7) Repayment not to exonerate

The repayment either in whole or in part of the said deposit or any additional deposit made under the fifth clause hereof shall not exonerate the depositor or his estate or effects from liability to make good to the Government any loss or damage for which the depositor was liable under the terms of these presents or the rules of the said Department or the conditions of his service and which was not made good before such repayment, as aforesaid was made.

IN WITNESS whereof, etc.

PERSONAL SECURITY BOND BY AN EMPLOYEE, WITH SURETIES, PENDING THE EXECUTION OF A HYPOTHECATION BOND

KNOW ALL MEN that we *AB*, etc. (Principal), *CD*, etc. (First Surety) and *EF*, etc. (Second Party), bind ourselves jointly and severally to *XY*, etc., for the payment to the said *XY* of the sum of Rs. ....

Whereas the above bounden *AB* was on the .... day of .... appointed to and now holds and exercise the office of treasurer of the estate of the said *XY*.

And, whereas the said *AB* has been called upon to furnish security to the extent of Rs. .... indemnifying the said *XY* against all loss and damage which he might suffer by reason of any property entrusted to the care of the said *AB* in the course of his duties as such treasure being wasted, embezzled, stolen, misspent or lost dishonestly, negligently or otherwise by the said *AB*;

And, whereas the said *AB* has offered such security in landed property and as the verification of the value and adequacy of the security offered by the said *AB* is likely to take sometime and the execution of the security bond will consequently be delayed;

And, whereas the said *XY* has called upon the said *AB* to execute a personal bond with two sureties temporarily for such time as the security bond aforesaid is not executed and registered;

And, whereas the said *AB* and the said *CD* and *EF* as the said *AB*'s sureties have entered into the above written bond in the penal sum of Rs. ... conditioned for the due performance of his duties by the said *AB* and for the indemnity of the said *XY* against loss from the acts or defaults of the said *AB* until such times as the said *AB* offers adequate security and executes a registered security bond;

Now, the condition of the above written bond is that if the said *AB* has whilst in the service of the said *XY* duly performed and fulfilled the duties assigned to him or if the said *AB* and the said *CD* and *EF* shall indemnify the said *XY* from all and every loss and damage caused to the said *XY* from any act, omission, neglect or default of the said *AB* in the course of discharge of his duties while in the service of the said *XY*, or if the said *AB* shall offer adequate security and execute a regular security bond as promised, then the above written bond or obligation shall be void and of no effect, otherwise the same shall be and remain in full force;

Provided, always that immediately on the said *AB* executing, registering and delivering in the security bond hereinbefore referred to, this bond shall cease to have an effect:

Provided, also that neither of them, the said *CD* and *EF*, shall be at liberty to terminate their suretyship except upon giving to the said *XY* six calendar months' notice in writing of his or their intention to do so and their joint and several liability under this bond shall continue in respect of all omissions and defaults on the part of the said *AB* until the expiration of the said period of six months

Forbearance of Obligee not to Effect Liability

Provided further, that any forgiveness or forbearance on the part of the said *XY* or his administrators or executors or any of them towards the said *AB* in respect of his failure or neglected to perform such services and duties shall not in any way release or exonerate the said *CD* and *EF* or either of them or either of their executors or administrators in respect of their or his liability under the above written bond.

IN WITNESS to the above written bond and to all the terms and conditions hereinbefore contained, we have signed hereunder this .... day of ....

SECURITY BOND BY SURETIES ON BEHALF OF A CLAIMANT TO MONEY DUE FROM GOVERNMENT TO HIS DECEASED ANCESTOR

KNOW ALL MEN that we, *AB*, etc., *CD*, etc. and *EF*, etc., hereby bind ourselves jointly and severally to the Governor of Assam (hereafter called the "Government") for the payment of the said Government of the sum of Rs. ....

Whereas *XY* was at the time of his death in the employment of the Government (or, was receiving a pension of Rs. .... from the Government);

And, whereas the said *XY* died on the ... and there was then due to him the sum of Rs. .... for pay and allowances in respect of his said office (or, in respect of his said pension);

And, whereas the above bounden *AB* (hereinafter called "the Claimant") claims to be entitled to the said sum as heir of the said *XY* but has not obtained letters of administration of or a succession certificate to the property and effects of the said *XY* or a succession certificate in respect of his said dues;

And, whereas the Government after making due inquiry is satisfied that the claimant is entitled to the said sum and that it would cause undue delay and hardship if the said Government insisted upon the production by the claimant of letters of administration of or a succession certificate to the property and effects of the *XY* or a succession certificate in respect of his said dues.

And, whereas the said Government desires to pay the said sum to the claimant but under government rules and orders it is necessary that the claimant should first execute a bond with two sureties to indemnify the said government against all claims to the amounts so due as aforesaid to the said *XY* before the said sum can be paid to the claimant;

NOW, THE CONDITION of this bond is that if, after payment has been made to him, the claimant shall refund to the said Government the sum of Rs. ...., if the said Government so requires, and shall in any event indemnify and save the said Government harmless from all liability in respect of the said sum and all costs incurred in consequence of any claim thereto then the above written bond or obligation shall be void, otherwise the same shall remain in full force.

IN WITNESS to the above - written bond and the condition, thereof we, *AB*, *CD*, and *EF* have signed hereunder this .... day of ....

SECURITY BOND BY SURETY OF THE MANAGER OF AN ESTATE (HYPOTHECATING PROPERTY)

KNOW ALL MEN that I, *AB*, etc., hereby bind myself to *CD*, etc., for the payment to the said *CD* of the sum of Rs. .... to be paid to the said *CD*;

Whereas, *EF*, etc., has been appointed by the said *CD* to the post of manager of his estate on the condition that he shall furnish security to the amount of Rs. ...... for the faithful and honest performance of all such duties as may be required of him as such manager as aforesaid;

And, whereas the said *AB* has in consideration of such appointment being made by the said *CD* agreed to give security for the said *EF*, in the manner hereinafter appearing.

Now, the condition of the above written bond is that if the said *EF* shall faithfully and honestly perform all his duties as such manager as aforesaid and shall at all times account for, render and deliver in such manner and to such persons as the said *CD* may appoint in that behalf all moneys, securities for money and property of any kind whatsoever which he, the said *EF*, may recover or be entrusted with by virtue of his office as such manager as aforesaid and shall not lose, injure, destroy or in any way take or apply either for his own use or for any purpose other than those for which the same have been received by or entrusted to him any such moneys, securities for money or property as aforesaid then the abovewritten bond or obligation shall be void but otherwise it shall remain in full force and effect.

And, these presents also witness that for the consideration aforesaid and as a security for the payment to the said *CD* of the said sum of Rs. ...... or any part thereof according to the terms and conditions hereof the said *AB* (hereinafter called the "mortgagor") hereby transfers to the said *CD* hereto, to the intent that the same shall remain and be charged by way of simple mortgage in the manner following, namely that for the purpose of recovering the said sum of Rs. ... or any such lesser sum as may become due by the mortgagor to the mortgagee by virtue of these presents, the mortgagee may enforce against the said property or any part thereof all or any of the remedies of the holder of a simple mortgage AND the mortgagor hereby covenants with the mortgagee, that the said premises are free from encumbrances:

Provided always that the mortgagor may terminate this aforesaid surety ship on the expiration of six calendar months' notice in writing given by him to the said *CD*:

Provided also that notwithstanding the termination of this said surety ship the mortgagor shall remain liable under these presents for any such act or default as aforesaid committed by the said *EF* before the termination of the mortgagor's suretyship and that for the enforcement of such liability the mortgage hereby created shall continue until released by the mortgagee.

IN WITNESS whereof the said *AB* has signed hereunder on the .... day of ....

SECURITY GIVEN BY A LEGATEE UNDER A LOST WILL TO A PURCHASER OF BEQUEATHED PROPERTY (WITH HYPOTHECATION)

KNOW ALL MEN, etc. (as in Form 10).

Whereas by the last will dated the .... *EF* devised the lands known as ... described in the First Schedule hereto, to the above bounden *AB* absolutely;

And, whereas the said *EF* died on the .... but probate of the said will was never obtained;

And, whereas the said will has been diligently sought for by the said *AB* but cannot be found;

And, whereas by a deed dated the .... all the children of the said EF have released the said lands from any claim which they or any of them might have thereto whether under the said or any other will or by inheritance if the said *EF* had died intestate;

And, whereas the parties to the said deed of .... are the only descendants of the said *EF*;

And, whereas the said *AB* has in this manner come to be the sole owner of the said land;

And, whereas by a deed of even date hereto the said *AB* has sold and transferred the said lands to the said *CD* absolutely;

And, whereas it has been agreed between *AB* and *CD* that for the better protection of the said *CD* and in addition to the ordinary covenants for title contained in the said sale deed, the said *AB* should execute the above written bond subject to the condition hereinafter contained.

Now, the condition of the above written bond is that if the said *AB*, his heirs, executors, administrators or assigns do and shall from time to time and at all times hereafter save harmless and keep indemnified the said *CD* from all suits, losses, costs, charges whatsoever in respect of the said land in case it shall appear that the said will does not devise the said land to the said *AB* absolutely or that the said will is for any reason invalid or that the said *EF* died intestate, then and in such case the above written bond shall be void but otherwise the same shall remain in full force:

Provided always that in the event of any suit being brought or claim being made against the said *CD*, in respect of the said lands for any of the reasons aforesaid the said *CD* will forthwith give notice of such suit or claim to the said *AB* or his heirs, executors, administrators or assigns and will at his or their expense diligently contest such suit or claim if required by him or them to do so.

And, whereas *CD* has required security for the payment of the sum named in the above written bond, the said *AB* in consideration of the purchase from him of the said lands by the said *CD* hereby grants and transfers by way of simple mortgage to the said *CD* the property mentioned in the schedule hereto to the intent that if the said *AB*, his heirs, executors, administrators or assigns made default in paying any such which may become due to the said *CD* under the conditions of the above written bond the said *CD* shall have a right to cause the said property to be sold and the proceeds of the sale applied as far as may be necessary in payment of the said sum AND the said *AB* and *CD* hereby agree that all the conditions, covenants and stipulations set forth in the aforesaid bond shall form part of this mortgage.

SECURITY BOND WITH TWO SURETIES, THE PRINCIPAL AGREEING TO DEPOSIT CASH SECURITY BY MONTHLY DEDUCTION FROM PAY

KNOW ALL MEN that I *AB*, etc., (Principal) and *CD*, etc. (First Surety) and *EF*, etc., (Second Surety) hereby bind ourselves jointly and severally to the Governor of West Bengal (hereinafter referred to as the Government) for the payment to him of the sum of Rs. ....

Whereas, the above bounden *AB* was on the .... appointed to, and now holds and exercises the office of....................;

And, whereas by virtue of his appointment as such the said *AB* has, amongst other duties, the care of, and responsibility for the safe and proper handling and keeping in the places appointed for custody of Government proper and money;

And, whereas the said *AB* is bound, whenever called upon to do so, to show to his superior officer that the said property and money is at all times intact in the places aforesaid and is bound to keep true and faithfully account of the said property and money;

And, whereas the said *AB* in consideration of the said appointment has promised to pay the amount of security of Rs.... in monthly instalments of not less than 10 per cent of his pay for the purpose of securing and indemnifying (the Government) against all loss and damage which it might suffer by reason of the said property and money or any part being wasted, embezzled, stolen, misspent, loss dishonestly, negligently, or otherwise by himself, the said *AB*.

And, whereas the said *AB*, and the said *CD* and *EF* as his sureties, have entered into the above bond in the penal sum of Rs. ... conditioned for the due performance by him of the duties of the said office and of the other duties appertaining thereto or lawfully required of him and for the indemnity of the Government against loss from the acts or defaults of the said *AB*.

Now, this condition of the above written bond is that if the said *AB* has, whilst he has held the post of ...... always duly performed and fulfilled the said duties of the said office and the other duties aforesaid or if the said *AB* or the said *CD* and *EF* shall indemnify the Government from all and every loss or damage which during the time the said *AB* has held, executed and enjoyed the said office has happened, then the above written bond or obligation shall be void otherwise the same shall be and remain in full force:

Provided always and it is hereby agreed and declared that neither of them the same *CD* and *EF* shall be at liberty to terminate their suretyship except upon giving to the government six calendar months' notice in writing of his or their intention to do so, and their joint and several liability under this bond shall continue in respect of all omissions and defaults on the part of the said *AB* until the expiration of the said period of six months;

And it is hereby lastly agreed and declared by and between the said *AB* and the said *CD* and EF as his sureties and the Government that on the realisation of the required security of Rs. .... in cash by monthly deductions from the pay of the said *AB* as aforesaid the above bond will cease to be in operation.

IN WITNESS, etc.

BOND BY SURETIES OF A STUDENT ADMITTED TO A COLLEGE TO SECURE THE PERFORMANCE OF AN AGREEMENT

BY THIS BOND we, *JK*, etc., and *LM*, etc. (hereinafter called "the sureties") are bound jointly and severally to the trustees of the .... college (hereinafter called "the trustees") for the payment to the trustees of the sum of Rs. ....

Whereas by a deed of agreement dated the .... executed by the trustees and *AB*, etc., (or *XY*, etc., acting as guardian of *AB*, etc) the trustees have agreed to educate the said *AB* at the .... college and to make him certain payments therein stipulated on the terms and conditions therein specified.

And, whereas for the purpose of securing and indemnifying the trustees, their assigns and successors against all loss and damage which they might suffer by reason of the said *AB* (or, the said *XY*) making default in the observance and performance of any covenant on his part to be performed and contained in the aforesaid agreement and in consideration of the said education and payment to be given and made by the trustees to the said *AB* it has also been agreed that the sureties should execute the above written bond subject to the condition hereinafter contained.

Now, this condition of the above written bond is that if the said *AB* (and the said *XY*) shall duly and faithfully observe and perform all the stipulations and conditions on his (their) part to be observed and performed and contained in the aforesaid agreement dated the .... then the above written bond or stipulation shall be void otherwise the same shall remain in full force.

BOND BY SURETY FOR DUE OBSERVANCE BY ANOTHER OF TERMS OF PARTNERSHIP DEED

KNOW ALL MEN that I, *AB*, etc., hereby bind myself to *CD*, etc., and *EF*, etc., for the payment to them of Rs. ....

Whereas the said *CD* and *EF* have by a deed of partnership dated ... taken *GH*, etc., into partnership within the firm styled....................

And, whereas it was part of the arrangement for taking the said *GH* into the said partnership that, the said *AB* shall enter into and execute a bond for the due observance by the said *GH* of the terms of the said partnership deed.

Now, the condition of the above written bond is that if the said *GH* shall faithfully perform and observe each and every term and all provisions and agreements contained in the said partnership deed and on his part to be performed and observed and if the said *AB*, his heirs and executors or administrators shall at all times hereafter keep indemnified the said *CD* and *EF* and their respective heirs, executors and administrators for all losses, costs, charges and expenses which they or any of them shall or may incur or sustain by reason of the breach or non-performance on the part of the said *GH* of any of the terms, provisions and agreements aforesaid or by reason of the said *GH* not doing, performing, observing and complying with any award made by any arbitrator or arbitrators appointed under the terms of the said partnership deed, so and in such manner that he, the said *AB*, his heirs, executors and administrators shall be answerable to the said *CD* and *EF* and their respective heirs, executors and administrators for such losses, etc., in the same manner as if the said *AB* had been a party to the said partnership deed in the place of the said *GH* and not further or otherwise AND so that any alteration which may be made in the terms of the said partnership deed or the neglect or forbearance of the said *CD* and *EF* in enforcing payment of any sums which may become due to them from the said *GH* on account of breach or non performance aforesaid or the giving of time to him for the payment thereof should not release the said *AB*, his heirs, executors and administrators in respect of his or their liability under the above written bond THEN the above written bond shall be void but otherwise shall remain in full force.

Signed, etc.

BOND BY A TRAINEE (IF MINOR, BY HIS GUARDIAN) WITH SURETIES

KNOW ALL MEN that we *AB*, etc. (or XY guardian of *AB*), *CD* etc., (surety No. 1) and *EF*, etc., (surety No. 2) bind ourselves jointly and severally to the Governor of .... (hereinafter called "the Government") for payment to the Government of the sum of Rs. ....

Whereas the above named bounden *AB* has under the order .... notification dated .... been selected to get training for .... at .... in...................

Whereas by a deed of Agreement dated .... executed between the Government and the said bounden *AB* (or, his guardian XY) the Government has agreed to bear all the expenses in relation to the said training including the passage of the said *AB* at .... for .... and to make certain payment to the said *AB* on the terms and conditions therein specified.

And, whereas for the purpose of securing and indemnifying the Government against all losses and damages which the Government may suffer by reason of the said *AB* making default in the observance and performance of any covenant on his part to be performed and contained in the said Agreement and in consideration of the expenses to be incurred on the said training and payments thereof to be made to the said *AB*, it has been agreed that the said sureties (*CD* and *EF*) should execute the above given bond subject to the condition hereinafter contained.

Now, the condition of the above written bond is that if the said *AB* (or, the said XY his guardian) shall duly and faithfully observe all these stipulations and conditions on his part to be observed and performed and contained in the aforesaid Agreement dated ... then the above written bond or stipulation shall be void otherwise the same shall remain in full force.

Signed, etc.

PERFORMANCE GUARANTEE BOND

To: *Alpha*

....

...................(address)

From: ....Bank

Dear Sirs

(i) We....................Bank acknowledge that in relation to the above subject you have entered into a consulting services agreements dated .... with *Beta Technologies Limited* ('*Beta*') (hereinafter called 'the Agreement').

Any capitalised terms used and not defined herein shall have the meanings attributed thereto in the Agreement.

We hereby unconditionally and irrevocably guarantee to pay to you any amount or amounts demanded by you from time to time upto the maximum aggregate value of this Performance Guarantee Bond immediately on receipt of your first demand in writing without objection or contestation whatever from our part or from *Beta* and without the necessity on your part to pursue or exhaust any remedy against *Beta* and notwithstanding that the Agreement may be unenforceable in whole or in Part.

The value of this Performance Guarantee Bond shall be [insert sum].

Our obligations hereunder shall remain in full force and effect and shall not be affected or discharged by any act, omission, matter or thing which but for this provision might operate to release or otherwise exonerate us from our obligations hereunder in whole or in part, including without limitation and whether or not known to us or to you:

(a) any time, waiver or indulgence granted to *Beta* or to any other person;

(b) the taking, variation, compromise, renewal or release of or refusal or neglect to perfect or enforce any rights, remedies or securities against *Beta* or any other person;

(c) any legal limitation, disability or incapacity relating to *Beta* or any other person;

(d) any variation of or amendment to the Agreement or in the nature or extent of or method of carrying out of the services or the obligations to be performed thereunder or any other document or security so that references to the Agreement in this Performance Guarantee Bond shall include each such variation or amendment; and

(e) any unenforceability, invalidity or frustration of any obligations of *Beta* or any other person under the Agreement or any other document or security.

This performance guarantee shall come into force on ....

Our obligations under this Performance Guarantee Bond shall cease upon expiration or termination of the Agreement, except in relation to demands made by you prior to that date, which *Beta* has not satisfied.

This performance Guarantee Bond and all matters relating thereto shall be governed by Indian law and the courts of .... shall have jurisdiction.

IN WITNESS whereof we have duly executed this Performance Guarantee Bond

on this .... day of

Executed by

(.....................)

in the presence of:

DEED OF INDEMNITY

This Deed of Indemnity (the "Deed") is executed this .... day of .... 20..... by Mr. .... (name) son of Late .... resident of .... and Mrs. .... (name) wife of Mr. .... (name) resident of .... (hereinafter jointly and severally referred to as the "Legal Heirs") in favour of *Alpha* FINANCES INTERNATIONAL (herein after the "*Alpha*")

Whereas:

1. The elder brother of the Legal Heirs, Mr. .... (name) son of Late .... ("Mr. .... (name)") has deposited with the *Alpha* certain amount of money accounts known as .... deposit A/c # .... (Account No.) (Along with any other deposit of Mr. .... (name) with the *Alpha*, herein after referred to as the "Deposits")

2. The Legal Heirs are the only brother and sister respectively of Mr. .... (name) and are the only persons entitled to inherit Mr. .... (name)'s assets as per the provisions of the Indian law.

3. Mr. .... (name) under in his registered Will dated.................. 20..... (Annexure-2) has named Mr. .... Advocate, Mrs. .... (name) (one of the Legal Heirs) and Mrs. .... daughter of Mr. .... (name) as the executors of the Will. (Hereinafter jointly the "Executors")

4. Mr. .... (name) is in a critical condition and he is not in a position to take any decision in connection with his affairs as he has lost his mental faculties and is terminally ill since [ ]. A doctor's certificate to this effect is enclosed as Annexure-1 to this Deed.

5. Large sum of money is required to be drawn from the Deposits to meet the necessities of Mr. .... (name) business and medical expenses.

6. As Mr. .... (name) is not in a position to take any decision with respect to the Deposits, the Legal Heirs have requested the Alpha to act on the instruction of the Executors and allow the withdrawal of money from the Deposits on the instructions and advice of the Executors. For this the Legal Heirs have agreed to indemnify the Alpha for any loss or expenses that it may incur on this account.

NOW, THIS DEED WITNESSETH AS UNDER

In consideration of Alpha's acting on the instruction and advice of the Executors in connection with the Deposit including any withdrawals therefrom, the Legal Heirs jointly and severally covenant and undertake at all times to indemnify Alpha and keep Alpha indemnified from and against all action, proceedings, claim, demands, costs and expenses that Alpha may have to incur or bear, occasions on its acting on the instructions and advice given by the Executors from time to time.

IN WITNESS WHEREOF, THE LEGAL HEIRS EXECUTES THIS DEED ON THE DATE MENTIONED ABOVE HERE IN........................ (Name of the place)

....
..................(name)   ....(name) (Mrs.)

INDEMNITY BOND

THIS DEED OF INDEMNITY is made on this .... day of ...., 20.....

BETWEEN

Mr. ...., son of ...., resident of ...., (hereinafter called the "SELLER") of THE ONE PART;

AND

Mr. ...., son of Mr. ...., resident of ...., (hereinafter called the "BUYER") of the OTHER PART;

AND

Mr. .... son of Mr. ...., resident of ...., (hereinafter called the "SURETY")

WHEREAS the Parties have entered into an Agreement to Sell dated .... whereunder the Buyer has agreed to buy and the Seller has agreed to sell his property No. (Description of the property), (hereinafter called "the said Property").

AND WHEREAS the Seller has agreed to indemnify and keep indemnified the Buyer and the Surety has agreed to stand Surety, as stated hereinafter.

NOW THEREFORE, THIS DEED OF INDEMNITY WITNESSETH THAT:

1. In consideration of the Buyer agreeing to buy the said Property for a consideration of Rs. ...., the Seller hereby assures the Buyer that the said Property is free from all encumbrances and the Seller has the right to enter into an Agreement in the nature of the Agreement to Sell to transfer rights in the said Property.

2. The Seller covenants with the Buyer that the Seller will hold the Buyer and/or his nominee(s) indemnified against all losses, expenses, damages etc. accruing to the Buyer and/or his nominee(s) as a result of any of the assurances of the Seller, as set out above or in the Agreement to Sell, being shown otherwise, and against any claims made with respect to the said property by any person or authority including all costs and charges and the legal expenses incurred in defending any proceedings which may arise therefrom, or in the event of the sale being voided by any order, law or Act of the Government [and that the Seller shall be liable to incur all expenses of whatever nature and to pay the consideration for the purchase of, and to put the Buyer and/or his nominee(s) in possession and ownership of premises which is equal in size to the said Property and in a locality of the same standard as the one in which the said Property is situate, and which is acceptable to the Buyer and/or his nominee.]

3. The Surety agrees that in the event that the Seller breaches any of the covenants as stated above, the Surety shall be liable, in the stead of the

Seller and to the same extent as the Seller, as set out above and any extension or time given or any other indulgence shown by the Buyer will not discharge the Surety, nor will any other act of omission or commission on the part of the Buyer have the effect of discharging the Surety.

4. The parties hereto agree that the Buyer has the option to enforce his rights as provided for herein against the Surety in the first instance without taking any recourse to any remedy against the Seller.

IN WITNESS WHEREOF, the Parties hereto have signed this Deed on the date first above-written in the presence of witnesses.

....

SELLER

....

BUYER

....

SURETY

WITNESSES:
1.
2.

THIS INDEMNITY is made by deed on the day of ...., 20.....

BY .... (name) of .... (address) and Mrs. .... (name) of .... (address), (hereinafter jointly referred to as the "Potential Legal Heirs") AND .... (name) of, ... (name) of, ... (name) of, ... (name) of................... and .... (name) of................... (all hereinafter collectively referred to as "the Potential Will Beneficiaries").

IN FAVOUR OF:—

(1) *ALPHA* BANK AND TRUST COMPANY LTD., a Company incorporated under the laws of the................... (Name of the country) and having its registered office at .... (address), and

(2) *THETA* FIDUCIARY SERVICES LTD., also a Company incorporated under the laws of the .... (name of country) and having its registered office at .... (address).

WHEREAS:

(A) .... (name) a domiciliary of the Republic of India but a non-resident of that jurisdiction (hereinafter "...................(name)") executed a Corporate Services Agreement dated the................... day of................... 20..... Between .... (name), *Alpha* and *Beta*, under which *Alpha* agreed to provide certain corporate services to *Beta*, including the provision of a registered office and the services of one or more nominee shareholders of the Company and the services of an affiliate company of *Alpha* as a Director of *Beta*.

(B) *Theta*, is now and has at all material times been the sole Director of *Beta*,

(C) .... (name) has fallen terminally ill and is now in a coma and is not in a position to manage his own affairs [check]

(D) .... (name) made a Will dated.................... 20..... which he therein declared to be his Last Will and Testament and that Will has been registered in the registry of Wills of the High Court of .... (Registration no....................) on the .... day of.................... 20.....

(E) To the best of the knowledge, information and belief of the Potential Legal Heirs and the Potential Will Beneficiaries, the aforesaid Will is the Last Will and Testament of .... (name).

(F) Under the terms of the aforesaid Will, the Potential Will Beneficiaries and the Potential Legal heirs are the principal beneficiaries of that Will.

(G) In the event that the aforesaid Will should not for any reason be probated and .... (name) is declared to have died intestate the Potential Legal Heirs will be his legal Heirs under the terms of the Succession Act of India.

(H) *Beta* is the holder of a brokerage account with Alpha and Gamma Inc.

(I) In view of the critical condition of .... (name) the Potential Will Beneficiaries and Potential Legal Heirs have requested *Alpha* and *Theta*, to release sufficient money to defray current and future medical expenses of .... (name) and to reimburse those persons who have paid for .... (name) medical expenses since he became ill;

(J) *Alpha* and *Theta* have agreed to consider such requests for payment and reimbursement of medical expenses and the Potential Legal Heirs and the Potential Will Beneficiaries have agreed to exonerate and indemnify *Alpha* and *Theta* for any loss or expenses that they may incur in so doing;

NOW THIS DEED WITNESSETH AS FOLLOWS:

(1) The parties hereto hereby agree that *Alpha* and THETA shall not be held liable for any loss to *Beta* unless such loss shall result from their actual fraud or wilful misconduct.

(2) The Potential Legal Heirs and the Potential Will Beneficiaries hereby unconditionally agree to indemnify *Alpha* and *Theta* and each of them in full on demand against all claims, demands, actions, proceedings, losses, costs, charges, expenses and any other liabilities whatsoever suffered or incurred by *Alpha* and *Theta* and each of them arising from or in connection with any or all of (a) the payment or reimbursement of medical expenses as aforesaid and (b) the management of the investments of *Beta*.

Protections

The liability of the Potential Legal Heirs and the Potential Will Beneficiaries under this indemnity shall not be reduced, discharged or otherwise adversely affected by:

(A) Any variation, extension, compromise discharge dealing with exchange or renewal of any right or remedy which *Alpha* and/or *Theta* may now or hereafter have against *Beta* or any other person;

(B) Any Act or admission by *Alpha* and/or *Theta* or any other person taking up perfecting or enforcing or the non-enforcement of any security or guarantee from or against;

(C) Any grant of time, indulgence, waiver or concession to the Potential legal Heirs or Potential Will Beneficiaries.

All sums payable by the Potential Legal Heirs or the Potential Will Beneficiaries under this indemnity shall be paid to *Alpha* or *Theta* in full:—

(a) Without any set of or counter claim whatsoever;

(b) Free and clear of all deductions or withholdings whatsoever, save only as may be required by law.

The parties hereto each acknowledge that they have separate and independent legal advice prior to the execution of this document.

This indemnity is governed by and shall be construed in accordance with the laws of the ....

IN WITNESS THEREOF, the Potential Legal Heirs and the Potential Will Beneficiaries have entered into this indemnity as a deed with the intention that it be delivered on the day and year first before written.

.... (name)   ....

IN THE PRESENCE OF: ....

Witnesses Name: ....

Witnesses Address: ....

                              ....

Occupation: ....

Etc.

CHAPTER 9
PLEDGES

SYNOPSIS

"PLEDGE", "PAWNOR AND "PAWNEE" DEFINED
DOCUMENTS AND SECURITIES

PRECEDENTS
- Pledge Deed
- Pledge of Term Deposit as Additional Security for NCDs subscribed by *Beta* Bank

Pledge is handing over of goods as security for payment of a debt or performance of a promise. The person who hands over the goods is called bailor or pawnor and the person who takes it as security is called bailee or Pawnee.

Section 172 of the Indian Contract Act gives definition of pledge pawnor and pawnee. It runs as follows:

"Pledge", "Pawnor and "Pawnee" defined

The bailment of goods as security for payment of a debt or performance of a promise is called *"pledge"*. The bailor is in this called the *"Pawnor"*. The bailee is called *"Pawnee"*.

A pledge is not exactly a mortgage. It is something between a simple lien and a mortgage. As the pawnor has no right of foreclosure since he has no absolute ownership at law and his equitable title cannot exceed what is specifically granted by law.[1]

Documents and Securities

The law relating to Pawns contained in the Contract Act is not applicable to pledge of all clauses of documents. Title deeds of property are not "goods" that may be pledged within section 172. Government securities which are not specifically mentioned in section 173 cannot be pledged except by endorsement by the owner even if they are already in possession of the pledgee.[2]

A saving bank book can also be validly pledged. A saving bank book falls within the definition of goods. The pledge of a saving bank book must be held at least to stand on the same footing as pledge of scrip unaccompanied by blank transfer.[3]

---

1. *Bal Krishna Gupta* v. *Swadeshi Polytex Ltd.*, AIR 1985 SC 520.
2. *Jyoti Prakash* v. *Mukti Prakash*, 22 CWN 297: 33 IC 89.
3. AIR 1959 J&K 67.

PRECEDENTS

PLEDGE DEED

THIS DEED made at .... this .... day of ...., 20.....
BETWEEN *Alpha* AIRWAYS INDIA LIMITED, a Company existing within the meaning of the Indian Companies Act, 1956 having its Registered Office at .... (address) hereinafter called the "Company" (which expression shall include its successors and assigns), of the ONE PART; AND .... hereinafter referred to as either as the "Debenture Trustee" (which expression shall include its successors and assigns) of the SECOND PART;

WHEREAS

(A) The Company is engaged in the business of ....;

(B) On the invitation of the Company, Theta Bank Limited (the 'Bank') has agreed to subscribe, by private placement, non-convertible, non-marketable, secured, redeemable debentures (hereinafter referred to as the "Debentures"), issued by the Company to the Bank in the aggregate amount of Rs. .... (Rupees .... only), on the terms and conditions contained in the Subscription Agreement signed by the Company and the Bank this day (hereinafter called the "Subscription Agreement");

(C) Under the Subscription Agreement, the Company has agreed to secure the Debentures together with interest, costs and charges, by a hypothecation and mortgage on certain aircraft and equipment owned by the Company, and by a pledge of certain term deposits of the Company, in favour of a trustee for the benefit of the Debenture holders (as defined in the Subscription Agreement);

(D) The Debenture Trustee has agreed to act as the trustee to hold the aforesaid security interest created for the benefit of the Debenture holders in accordance with a Debenture Trust Agreement between the Company and the Debenture Trustee (the 'Debenture Trust Agreement').

(E) Contemporaneously with the allotment of the Debentures to the Bank and the execution of this Deed, the Company has created a security interest in certain aircraft and equipment owned by the Company in favour of the Debenture Trustee by entering into a mortgage deed with the Debenture Trustee (the 'Mortgage Deed').

NOW, THEREFORE, in pursuance of the documents exchanged between the company and the Bank and in consideration of the Bank having subscribed to the Debentures in the aggregate amount of Rs. .... (Rupees .... only) on the terms and conditions as contained in the said documents and in the Subscription Agreement, the Parties hereby covenant that:

Article 1: Definitions

The capitalised terms used but not defined herein shall have the meaning as defined in the mortgage deed, unless otherwise indicated.

Artilce 2: Grant of security

2.1 To secure the due and complete redemption by the Company to the Debenture holders of the Debentures together with payment of all interests, additional interests, costs, charges, expenses and all other monies payable by the Company to the Debenture holders in respect of and/or on account of and/or by virtue of the Debentures, as well as any renewals, extension or changes in the form of said obligation or indebtedness, and the performance of its obligations, in accordance with all the terms, conditions, provisions, covenants and stipulations contained in the Debenture documents, the Company hereby mortgages, pledges, assigns, transfers and grants to the debenture trustee a security interest by way of an exclusive first charge in the term deposits of the Company aggregating Rs. .... (amount in figure) .... (amount in word) maintained with the *Theta* Bank, ... Branch (the "Term Deposits") by handing over the instrument evidencing the term Deposits to the Debenture trustee or to any person nominated by the Debenture trustee.

2.2 *Irrevocable instructions.*—The Company shall instruct the Term Deposit Bank with respect to the Term Deposits to act on the instructions of the Debenture trustee, *inter alia*, to .... The instructions to the Term Deposit Bank shall be irrevocable until receipt by the Company of a certificate of the Debenture Trustee confirming the receipt by the Debenture holders and the Debenture trustee of all monies secured pursuant to this Agreement and the performance by the company of its obligations under the Debenture documents.

Artilce 3: Company's representations and warranties

Except for the security interest granted herein, the company warrants that it is (or, to the extent security interest is created hereinafter, will be) the owner of the Term Deposits free from any Lien. The company further warrants that it will defend the term deposits against all claims and demands of any person claiming any interest therein by virtue of any Lien. The company represents and warrants to the Debenture Trustee that this Agreement, upon execution and delivery, will constitute the legal, valid and binding obligation of the Company and shall be enforceable in accordance with its terms. The company agrees to furnish the Debenture trustee with written legal opinions, satisfactory in form and substance to the Debenture trustee, verifying the aforesaid; representations and warranties.

Artilce 4: Maintenance of security interest

4.1 *General principle.*—The company shall neither do nor allow anything that may prejudice the security interest hereby created or whereby the recovery or realisation thereof may be delayed, impeded, prejudiced, prevented or become time-barred nor create any security ranking *pari-passu* with the security hereby created.

4.2 *Company to take steps.*—The company shall promptly, at its own expense, take all steps, as may be necessary to safeguard the security interest of the Debenture trustee in the Term Deposits, and without limiting the generality of the foregoing:

4.2.1 not do or knowingly permit to be done or omit or knowingly permit to be omitted to be done any act or thing, which might reasonably be expected to jeopardise the security interest of the Debenture Trustee under this Agreement or the validity, enforceability or priority thereof;

4.2.2 on all occasions when the ownership of the Term Deposits is relevant, make clear to third parties that the Debenture trustee has a security interest under this Agreement in the Term Deposits;

4.2.3 not at any time pledge the credit of the Debenture holders or the Debenture trustee;

4.2.4 not create or knowingly permit to exist any Lien upon the Term Deposits other than permitted liens;

4.2.5 not do or knowingly permit to be done anything which may reasonably be expected to expose the Term Deposits to penalty, forfeiture or appropriation, and without prejudice to the foregoing, if any such penalty, forfeiture, or appropriation, occurs, give the Debenture trustee notice and use its best endeavours to procure the immediate release of the Term Deposits , as the case may be;

4.2.6 pay and discharge or cause to be paid and discharged when due and payable or make adequate provision by way of security or otherwise for all debts, damages, claims and liabilities which have given or might give rise to a Lien over or affecting the Term Deposits; and

4.2.7 not attempt, or hold itself out as having any power, to sell, assign, pledge, mortgage, or otherwise dispose of the Term Deposits.

4.3 *Continuing security.*—The security interest hereby created shall be a continuing security for payment of the monies due to the Debenture holders and the performance of its obligations by the Company under the Debenture documents and shall not affect, impair or discharge the liability of the company by winding up (voluntary or otherwise) or by any merger or amalgamation, reconstruction or otherwise of the company with any other company, or the take-over of the management or nationalisation of the undertaking of the company, or otherwise.

Artilce 5: Books and Records

The company shall keep proper books of accounts of its business and carefully keep and preserve all the documents, papers and vouchers in connection with or relating to the Term Deposits and will at any time when required produce such books, documents, papers and vouchers for inspection thereof by the Debenture trustee and its officers and agents and allow them access thereto and allow them to make copies or extracts from the same.

Artilce 6: Taxes

The company shall duly pay and discharge all contractual and statutory outgoings including all rents, rates, taxes, assessments, dues and duties including income-tax, sales tax, excise duties, customs duties, including those in respect of, the Term Deposits, this Agreement, any payments made hereunder or under any of the Debenture documents and duly perform and discharge all its obligations under the Debenture documents according to law and shall immediately upon any proceedings being adopted against the company for violation or alleged violation of any law or regulation give notice of such action or proceedings to the Debenture Trustee. The debenture trustee shall have the right to intervene in any such actions or proceedings entirely at the cost of Company and also a right to redeem the from confiscation and/or forfeiture by payment of such rates, rents, taxes, assessments, dues or duties and fine or penalty, etc., as may be payable by or levied on the company and the company shall on demand pay to the debenture trustee all such claims, rents, rates, taxes, assessments, dues or duties, fine or penalty, etc., as may have been paid by the Debenture trustee and also the cost of any such actions or proceedings including costs on full indemnity basis for legal counsel, with default interest (as defined in the Subscription Agreement) thereon until payment by the company of the same, the same shall be a charge on the Term Deposits.

Artilce 7: Indemnities

7.1 *Company's indemnity:* The company undertakes to indemnify the Debenture trustee and the Debenture holders against any cost, claim, loss, expense (including legal fees) or liability together with any value added or singular tax thereon, which it may sustain or incur, as a consequence of the entering into, delivery or performance of this Deed or the occurrence of any Event of Default (as hereinafter defined) or any default by the company in the performance of any of the obligations expressed to be assumed by it under the Debenture documents or otherwise.

7.2 *Survival of indemnities*: The indemnities by the company in favour of the Debenture trustee and the Debenture holders contained herein shall continue in full force and effect notwithstanding the termination or expiry of this Agreement.

7.3 *Payment after-tax:* Any payment, which the company shall be required to make to or for the account of the Debenture trustee or the Debenture holders with respect to any losses, which are subject to indemnification by the company under this Clause, shall be made on a net after-tax basis, if any taxes are imposed with respect to such payment.

Artilce 8: Information

The company will promptly furnish to the Debenture trustee all information the Debenture trustee from time to time reasonably requests regarding the Term Deposits.

Artilce 9: Company's Default

9.1 The company agrees that the occurrence of any of the following events shall constitute an "Event of Default" for the purposes of this Agreement:

    (a) An event of default under the Mortgage Deed;

    (b) Any misrepresentation made by the company to the Debenture Trustee in connection with or under this Deed;

(c) The prospect of payment, performance or realization of the Term Deposits, in the opinion of the Debenture trustee, is or becomes significantly impaired;

(d) The Company's failure to perform any promise, Agreement, obligation, warranty or covenant made by it under this Deed, if such failure continues for a period of .... business days after the Debenture Trustee has given the company notice of such failure.

9.2 *Default notification.*—NOTWITHSTANDING, anything else stated above and elsewhere in this Deed, the company will notify the Debenture Trustee immediately of the occurrence of any Event of Default and in all cases, such notice would be given within .... hours of the occurrence of such Event of Default.

9.3 *Remedies.*—Should an Event of Default occur, the Debenture Trustee may employ all remedies allowed by law, including declaring all indebtedness of the Company owed under the Debenture documents, as well as any other indebtedness or liability of the company owed to the Debenture Trustee or the Debenture holders, immediately due and payable.

9.4 *Rights upon default.*—The Debenture Trustee and/or its nominee/s shall, without assigning any reason and at the risk and expenses of the company and if necessary as attorney for and in the name of the company, be entitled to take charge and/or possession of, seize, encash, recover, receive, appoint receiver of, or otherwise deal with the Term Deposits and enforce, realise, settle, compromise, refer to arbitration and deal in any manner with any rights or claims relating thereto, and to complete any engagements and carry on the business of the company through any agents, managers or otherwise without being bound to exercise any of these powers, or be liable for any losses in the exercise or non-exercise thereof and without prejudice to the Debenture trustee's rights and remedies of suit or to the rights and remedies which the Debenture trustee may have under the Debenture Documents.

9.5 *Application of moneys.*—It is agreed that all moneys realised by enforcement sale or realisation of the Term Deposits or otherwise shall with all convenient dispatch be applied in the manner provided in the subscription Agreement (clause 1.12).

9.6 *Costs.*—The Company shall accept without question the Debenture trustee's account of the costs, charges and expenses incurred in connection with the realisation of the Term Deposits by any agent or other authorised officer as the conclusive proof of the amount due from the company to the Debenture holders or the Debenture Trustee, the amount realised and expenses incurred and the Company shall forthwith pay to the Debenture trustee on demand any shortfall or deficiency, together with Default Interest and until such payment by the company the same shall be a charge on the Term Deposits.

9.7 *Debenture Trustee's directions.*—As and when the Debenture Trustee seeks to enforce the security hereby created, the company shall comply with all such directions, as may be given by the Debenture Trustee.

9.8 *Receivers.*—The Debenture trustee, at any time after the security hereby created has become enforceable and whether or not the Debenture Trustee shall then have taken possession of the Term Deposits, and in addition to the powers hereinbefore conferred upon the Debenture Trustee, may have a receiver or receivers appointed of the said Term Deposits or any part thereof. The following provisions shall apply to such receiver/s:

(i) unless otherwise directed by the Debenture Trustee, such receiver/s shall have and exercise all powers and authorities vested in the Debenture Trustee;

(ii) such receiver/s shall, in the exercise of his powers, authorities and discretion, conform to the regulation and directions from time to time made and given by the Debenture Trustee;

(iii) the Debenture Trustee may, from time to time, fix the remuneration of such receiver/s and may direct payment thereof out of the proceeds of the said Term Deposits but the company alone shall be liable for the payment of such remuneration;

(iv) the Debenture Trustee, may from time to time and at any time, require such receiver/s to give security for the due performance of his duties as such receiver and may fix the nature and amount of the security to be given to the Debenture Trustee but the Debenture Trustee shall not be bound to require such security in any case;

(v) the Debenture Trustee may hand over to such receiver/s any monies constituting part of the Term Deposits with the intent that the same may be applied for the purpose hereof by such receiver/s and the Debenture Trustee may, from time to time, determine what funds the receiver/s shall be at liberty to keep in hand with a view to the performance of his duties as such receiver/s;

(vi) every such receiver/s shall be the agent of the company for all purposes and the company alone shall be responsible for his acts and defaults, loss or misconduct and liable on any contract or engagement made or entered into by him and for his remuneration and the Debenture Trustee shall not incur any liability or responsibility therefor by reason of its making or consenting to his appointment as such receiver/s.

9.9 *Liens.*—All proceeds from the realisation of the Term Deposits shall always be kept distinguishable and held as the exclusive property of the Debenture Trustee specifically appropriated to this security and to be dealt with only under the directions of the Debenture Trustee and the Company shall not create or suffer or attempt to make or suffer any Lien upon or over the same or any part thereof except the security interest of the Debenture Trustee hereunder.

9.10 *No Prejudice.*—Nothing herein shall prejudice the rights or remedies of the Debenture Trustee in respect of any present, future, further or other security, guarantee obligations or decree for any indebtedness or liability of the company to the Debenture Trustee. Nothing herein contained shall prejudice or affect any general or special lien to which the Debenture Trustee is or may by law or otherwise be entitled or any rights or remedies of the Debenture Trustee in respect of any present or future security, guarantee obligations or decree for any other indebtedness or liabilities of the company to the Debenture holders or the Debenture Trustee, nor shall anything herein contained prejudice the right of the Debenture Trustee to enforce or have recourse to the securities under this Deed without enforcing or having recourse in the first instance to any other security held by the Debenture holders or the Debenture Trustee from the Company including without limitation under the Mortgage Deed and the Debenture Trustee shall be entitled to sue on any one of such securities without being bound to sue on all such securities.

Artilce 10: Execution and delivery of documents by company

10.1 *General principle.*—The company shall, at its own costs, execute/sign and deliver such other deeds or documents and do all such acts and things as may be required by the Debenture Trustee to establish, maintain or further perfect to the Debenture Trustee's satisfaction, and/or enforce the security created hereunder Further, the Company shall promptly furnish such information and documents as the Debenture Trustee may reasonably request. The company will pay the cost of filing all appropriate documents in all public offices where the Debenture Trustee deems such filings necessary or desirable.

10.2 *Indemnity.*—The company shall pay on demand to the Debenture Trustee the costs on full indemnity basis incurred by the Debenture Trustee or the Debenture holders in connection with the preparation, engrossment and stamping in duplicate and execution of these presents or other security executed contemporaneously herewith in connection with the moneys hereby secured and of the registration of this security with the Registrar of companies and all other costs, on full indemnity basis, incurred or to be incurred by the Debenture Trustee in connection herewith, or with the enforcement or attempted enforcement of the security created or the protection or defence or perfection thereof or for the recovery of any moneys secured and of all suits and proceedings of whatsoever nature for the enforcement or realisation of the security created or the recovery of such moneys, or otherwise in connection herewith or in which the Debenture Trustee may be joined as a party or be otherwise involved in by reason of the existence of the security hereby created in favour of the Debenture Trustee.

Artilce 11: Miscellaneous

11.1 *Debenture Trustee's records.*—The Company acknowledges and agrees that the Debenture Trustee's records (including, without limitation, account balances and transaction and statement details) shall be conclusive proof of the matters to which they relate. The company shall honour all its obligations to the Debenture Trustee, to the satisfaction of and as required by the Debenture Trustee and as per the records of the Debenture Trustee.

11.2 *Waivers.*—No waiver of any covenant, warranty or condition of this Deed, nor of any breach or default hereunder, shall be effective for any purpose whatsoever unless such waiver is in writing and signed by an officer of the

Debenture Trustee. It is expressly agreed that the Debenture Trustee's waiver of any breach or default by the company shall constitute a waiver only as to such particular breach or default and not a waiver of any further breach or default.

11.3 *Governing Law.*—The law governing this transaction shall be that of India as it may from time to time exist. The law of India shall apply to any and all matters arising from or related to this Deed and transaction, including any action to obtain possession of and foreclose upon the Term Deposits, and all other remedies which may be available including seeking a deficiency judgement against the company.

11.4 *Arbitration.*—Any dispute or difference which may arise out of this Deed or in relation thereto, including any dispute relating to its interpretation, validity or effect, shall be settled finally in accordance with the Rules of Conciliation and Arbitration of the International Chamber of Commerce (ICC). The arbitration proceedings shall be initiated by the party asking for arbitration submitting its request for arbitration to the Secretariat of the ICC. In such request for arbitration, the party shall nominate its arbitrator for confirmation by the ICC. The other Party shall nominate its arbitrator in its answer to the request for arbitration, which shall be supplied to the party asking for arbitration and the ICC within a period of .... days of the receipt of the request for arbitration. The two arbitrators thus appointed shall within a further period of 30 (thirty) days elect the Chairman of the Arbitration Tribunal. In the event that the other party should fail to appoint its arbitrator within the .... days or in the event the two arbitrators appointed for the parties do not agree on the appointment of the Chairman within .... days of their appointment the ICC shall make the appointment of the Chairman or the appointment of one the arbitrator not timely made or as the case may be, and any such appointment shall be final and binding upon the Parties. The venue of the arbitration shall be .... Notwithstanding the above, in the event an Event of Default should occur, the Debenture Trustee (at its sole option) may institute a legal proceeding in any jurisdiction as may be appropriate in order for the Debenture Trustee to realise the Term Deposits.

11.5 *Severability.*—The provisions of this Deed shall be severable and, if any provisions are for any reason determined to be invalid, void or unenforceable, in whole or in part, the remaining provisions shall remain in full force and effect; provided that the purpose of the remaining valid, effective and enforceable provisions is not frustrated; and provided further that no party is substantially and materially prejudiced thereby.

11.6 *Assignability.*—The Debenture Trustee shall have the absolute right to assign, transfer or sell any of its rights under this Deed to any party of its choosing upon giving written notice thereof to the company. The company shall not assign or delegate any of its rights or obligations hereunder without the prior written consent of the Debenture Trustee.

11.7 *Binding Agreement.*—All obligations of the company hereunder shall bind the successors, and assigns of the company. If there be more than one, the Company hereunder, their liabilities shall be joint and several. All rights of the

Debenture Trustee hereunder shall inure to the benefit of its successors and assigns.

11.8 *Entire Agreement.*—This Deed and the Debenture Documents constitute the entire agreement between and among the parties hereto with respect to the subject, matter hereof. There are no verbal understandings, agreements, representations or warranties between the parties, which are not expressly set forth herein. This Deed shall not be changed orally, but only in writing signed by the parties hereto.

11.9 *Notice.*—Any notice pertaining to this Deed shall be deemed sufficiently given if personally delivered or sent by registered or certified mail, return receipt requested, to the party to whom said notice is to be given. Notices sent by registered or certified mail shall be deemed given on the third day after the date or postmark. Until changed by written notice given by either party, the addresses of the Parties shall be as follows:

Company

Debenture Trustee

The designated address of both parties must be located within India. The company shall immediately notify the Debenture Trustee in writing of any change of address from that shown in this Deed.

IN WITNESS WHEREOF, the company has caused these presents to be executed on the day, month and year first hereinabove written, as hereinafter appearing.

The Common Seal of....................has been hereunto affixed pursuant to the Resolution passed at the meeting of its Board of Directors held on the .... day of .... in the presence of (AS PER MEMORANDUM AND ARTICLES OF ASSOCIATION)

SIGNED AND DELIVERED by .... Constituted Attorney for ....

PLEDGE OF TERM DEPOSIT AS ADDITIONAL SECURITY FOR NCDS SUBSCRIBED BY *BETA* BANK

Alpha Airways India Limited, (the "Company") have issued non-convertible, secured, redeemable debentures of the face value of Rs. .... (amount) each aggregating to Rs. ....(amount) (the "Debentures") to *Beta* Bank Limited (the "Debenture holders"), under the Subscription Agreement dated .... 20..... (hereinafter called "the Subscription Agreement"). The company has mortgaged two Boeing 737-400 aircraft, bearing registration nos. .... and Registration .... and .... and Registration .... (together the "Aircraft"), in favour of State Bank of India (the "Debenture Trustee") under a Debenture Trust and Mortgage Agreement executed on .... 20..... between the Company and the Debenture Trustee (the "Debenture Trust and Mortgage Agreement") to secure the performance of its obligations and payment of all monies payable under the Subscription Agreement and the Debenture Trust and Mortgage Agreement.

As additional security for the performance of its obligations and payment of all monies (under the Subscription Agreement and the Debenture Trust and Mortgage Agreement) as aforesaid, the Company hereby pledges to the Debenture holders its rights, title and interest in three term deposits of .... (amount) (initially bearing nos. .... along with interest accrued thereon and not paid to the company ("Term Deposits"), with *Beta* Bank, ... (address) ("Term Deposit Bank") by handing over the three receipts in respect of the Term Deposits. The company undertakes to maintain the Term Deposits until the release of the Security as described under the Debenture Trust and Mortgage Agreement and Subscription Agreement.

The company irrevocably undertakes to the Term Deposit Bank that the Term Deposit Bank can act and do such acts and deeds, at the cost of the company, to preserve the interest of the Debenture holders in the Term Deposits.

The company hereby authorises the Term Deposit Bank to utilise the Term Deposits to pay the Debenture holders in full or partial settlement of claims arising under the Subscription Agreement and the Debenture Trust and Mortgage Agreement upon the happening of an Event of Default (subject to any cure periods as provided therein) under the Debenture Trust and Mortgage Agreement.

IN WITNESS WHEREOF, *Alpha Airways (India) Ltd.* has caused its Common Seal to be affixed to this Pledge and to the duplicate hereof and the Debenture Trustee have caused this Pledge to be executed in duplicate on the day, month and year first above written.

The Common Seal of *Alpha Airways* (India) Ltd. has been hereunto affixed pursuant to the Resolution passed at the meeting of its Board of Directors held on the .... day of ...., 20..... in the presence of .... (name) and .... (name) who have in taken thereof affixed, their respective signatures, hereto.

SIGNED AND ACCEPTED by the within named *Beta* Bank by the hand of its Constituted Attorney for the Debenture holder.

CONFIRMED, by the Term Deposit Bank

CHAPTER 10
ARBITRATION

SYNOPSIS

DISPUTE SETTLEMENT: ALTERNATE DISPUTE RESOLUTION
DRAFTING AN ARBITRATION AGREEMENT/Clause
   Arbitration Agreement
   Judicial Analysis
   Halsbury's Laws
INTERNATIONAL COMMERCIAL ARBITRATION
   Advantages of alternative dispute resolution
   Disadvantages of alternative dispute resolution:
ENFORCEMENT OF ARBITRAL AWARDS
   Detrimental Reliance
ARBITRATION CLAUSE
DAMAGES IN ARBITRATION

Dispute Settlement: Alternate Dispute Resolution

The Arbitration and Conciliation Act, 1996, consolidated and amended the law relating to domestic arbitration, international commercial arbitration and enforcement of foreign arbitral awards. It also defines the law relating to conciliation of disputes. The Act was enacted in pursuance of the recommendations of the general assembly of the United Nations stressing the desirability of uniforming the law relating to arbitral and conciliation procedures and is largely based on the model law on International Commercial Arbitration and Model Conciliation Rules adopted by the United Nations Commission on International Trade Law (UNCITRAL).

It is an essential pre-requisite of the arbitration law in India that parties to a contract can demand resort to arbitration, if and only if, there is an arbitration agreement between them and it is further necessary that the arbitration agreement must satisfy the legal requisites. In the Arbitration Act, 1940, the legal requisites are set out in section 2(a). In the Arbitration and Conciliation Act, 1996, these requisites have been elaborated in greater detail, but the substratum has been retained with further additions and refinements.

Drafting an Arbitration Agreement/Clause

The Arbitration and Conciliation Act, 1996, came into force on and from 16 August 1996. Section 2(1)(b) of the Act defines arbitration agreement to mean an agreement referred to in section 7 of the Act. Chapter II of the Act deals with arbitration agreements.

Arbitration Agreement

Section 7 of the Act defines arbitration agreement to mean an agreement by the parties to submit to arbitration all or certain disputes which have arisen or which may arise between them in respect of a defined legal relationship, whether contractual or not. Section 7(2) provides that an arbitration agreement may be in the form of an arbitration clause in a contract or in the form of a separate agreement. In particular, section 7(3) mandatorily provides that an arbitration agreement shall be in writing.

According to section 7(4), an arbitration agreement is in writing, if it is contained in—

(a) a document signed by the parties;

(b) an exchange of letters, telex, telegrams or other means of telecommunication which provide a record of the agreement; or

(c) an exchange of statements of claim and defence in which the existence of the agreement is alleged by one party and not denied by the other.

It is further stipulated in section 7(5) that the reference in a contract to document containing an arbitration clause, constitutes an arbitration agreement, if the contract is in writing and the reference is such as to make that arbitration clause as part of the contract. Therefore, the emphasis under the Arbitration and Conciliation Act, 1996, is clearly and unambiguously on an arbitration agreement in writing as the basis for invoking the proceedings for arbitration and/or conciliation.

The expression 'arbitration agreement' as defined in section 2(a) of the Arbitration Act, 1940 (which has since been repealed by the Arbitration and Conciliation Act, 1996) had been defined earlier to mean a written agreement to submit present or future differences to arbitration, whether an arbitrator is named therein or not. Therefore, in the absence of a written agreement between the parties, the nature of the dispute as well as the terms of reference to the arbitrator(s) cannot be determined and, hence the agreement in writing is insisted upon as a pre-requisite for ascertaining the dispute(s) and for making reference thereof to the arbitrator(s). The statute does not recognise any oral or implied agreement for arbitration.

The very purpose of requiring in section 7(3) of the Act that the arbitration agreement shall be in writing – is to secure that an oral agreement is not recognised in Law and, hence, does not constitute an arbitration agreement. The cases and circumstances in which an arbitration agreement is to be regarded as being in writing, have been narrated in section 7(4) and the instances given therein are illustrative and cannot be regarded as exhaustive.

The English Arbitration Act, 1996, also contains special provisions in section 5(2) to secure that there is an agreement in writing, if the agreement is made in writing whether or not it is signed by the parties, or if the agreement is made by exchange of communications in writing or if the agreement is evidenced in writing.

Judicial Analysis

The requirement of arbitration agreement in writing is also taken note of by the Supreme Court in *M.M.T.C. Ltd* v. *Sterlite Industries (India) Ltd*, AIR 1997 SC 605 in which it has been made clear that—

> "Sub-section (3) of section 7 requires an arbitration agreement to be in writing and sub-section (4) describes the kind of that writing. There is nothing in section 7 to indicate the requirement of the number of arbitrators as a part of the arbitration agreement. Thus the validity of an arbitration agreement does not depend on the number of arbitrators specified therein. The number of arbitrators is dealt with separately in section 10, which is a part of machinery provision for the working of the arbitration agreement. It is, therefore, clear that an arbitration agreement specifying an even number of arbitrators cannot be a ground to render the arbitration agreement invalid under the new Act as contended by the learned Attorney General."

It may be noted that prior to the enactment of the Arbitration Act, 1940, oral agreements for arbitration were considered as valid in law and any award made in pursuance of such oral agreements could validly form the basis for the suit as also for reference to arbitration and/or as a defence in the suit. After the requirement of arbitration agreement in writing became statutorily mandatory, the determination of how to find an arbitration agreement in writing, became necessary in various cases, as may be seen from the various cases decided by the courts. The signatures of the parties to the agreement was not considered essential earlier, but in view of section 7(4) of the 1996 Act, the signature of the parties is essential. The insistence on identity of parties to the agreement for arbitration and the signature of the parties is essential. The insistence on identity of parties to the agreement for arbitration and their signature is only to secure that the parties are *ad idem* so that the arbitration agreement could be read to ascertain and establish that the Parties agreed to the same thing in the same sense. The absence of *ad idem* would invalidate the arbitration agreement and make the proceedings for arbitration unsustainable in law.

The judgement of the Supreme Court in *U.P. Rajkiya Nirman Nigam Ltd.* v. *Indure (P) Ltd*, AIR 1996 SC 1373 illustrates a case in which there was no arbitration agreement between the parties and, hence, the plea for reference to arbitration was rejected because an agreement for arbitration cannot be inferred, nor could be implied. After referring to the earlier decision in *Ramji Dayawala & Sons (P) Ltd* v. *Invest Import*, AIR 1981 SC 2085, the court held that, in the facts of a given case, acceptance of a suggestion may be *sub silentio* reinforced by subsequent conduct. It was further held that—

> "Where there is mistake as to terms of a document, amendment to the draft was suggested and a counter offer was made, signatory to the original contract is not estopped by his signature from denying that he intended to make an offer in the terms set out in the document. Where the contract is in a number of parties, it is essential to the validity of the contract that the contracting party should either have assented to or taken

to have assented to the same thing in the same sense or as it is sometimes put, there should be consensus *ad idem*. In that case, a sub-contract was signed and executed by the managing director of the appellant company, but part of the contract was altered subsequently since counter proposal was given by the respondent. This court had held that one such case is whether a part of the offer was disputed at the negotiation stage and the original offeree communicated that fact to the offeror saying that he understood the offer in a particular sense; this communication probably amounts to a counter offer in which case it may be that mere silence of the original offeror will constitute his acceptance. Where there is a mistake as to the terms of the documents as in that case, amendment to the draft was suggested and a counter offer was made, the signatory to the original contract is not estopped by his signature from denying that he intended to make an offer in the terms set out in the document; to wit, the letter and the cable. It can, therefore, be stated that where the contract is in a number of parties, it is essential to the validity of the contract that the contracting party should either have assented to or taken to have assented to the same thing in the same sense; or as it is sometimes put, there should be consensus *ad idem*. It was held that there was no consensus *ad idem* to the original contract. It was open to the party contending novation to prove that he had not accepted a part of the original agreement though it had signed the agreement containing that part."

It was accordingly held that—

"There is no signed agreement by a duly competent officer on behalf of the appellant. The doctrine of indoor management cannot be extended to formation of the contract or essential terms of the contract unless the contract with other parties is duly approved and signed on behalf of the public undertaking or the Government with its seal by an authorised or competent officer. Otherwise, it would be hazardous for public undertakings or Government or its instrumentalities to deal on contractual relations with third parties. In view of the fact that section 2(a) of the Act envisages a written agreement for arbitration and that written agreement of submit the existing or future differences to arbitration is a pre-condition and further, in view of the fact that the original contract itself was not a concluded contract, there existed no arbitration agreement for reference to the arbitrators. The High Court, therefore, committed a gross error of law in concluding that an agreement had emerged between the parties, from the correspondence and from submission of the tenders of the Board. Accordingly, it is declared that there existed no arbitration agreement and that the reference to the arbitration, therefore, is clearly illegal. Consequently, arbitrators cannot proceed further to arbiter the dispute, if any."

Where the Parties to the arbitration agreement are not *ad idem*, the arbitration by reference to the arbitrators of any dispute cannot be justified and the reference would be bad and unsustainable in law as held in *Sheodutt* v. *Pandit Vishnudutta,* AIR 1955 Nag 116.

Halsbury's Laws

It is stated by Lord Halsbury in Laws of England, 4th Edn., vol. 2, page 267, para 522:

> "If the agreement is written, it may be included in a particular contract by reference or implication. The agreement between the parties may incorporate arbitration provisions, which are set out in some other documents, but in order to be binding, the arbitration provisions must be brought to the notice of both parties...
>
> "It is inherent in cases of incorporation by reference that the parties are concerned not with one document alone, but with at least two one of which contains an arbitration clause and the other of which does not. In some case, the one document may constitute a contract between other parties. A common case is where the two documents concerned are a charter party and a bill of lading. If the relevant contract between the relevant parties is contained in the document, which does contain the arbitration clause, no question of incorporation arises. Where this is not the case, the question whether the document containing the arbitration clause is incorporated in the relevant contract between the relevant Parties is, always, a question of construction.

A brief epilogue

The need for an arbitration agreement in writing between the parties is to secure that the terms and conditions of the agreement are clear and certain and they are capable of being enforced to give effect to binding legal relationships between the Parties in regard to their rights and obligations. In the absence of an agreement in writing between the same parties, there can be no arbitration of a dispute which needs to be resolved and in every such case where no arbitration is permissible, the only remedy is to pursue civil suit in accordance with the law of contract and the Indian Civil Procedure Code. The significance of a written arbitration agreement cannot, therefore, be under-estimated, nor could it be disregarded for settlement of any dispute between the parties to decide whether the arbitration is permissible or not and whether civil suit is the only remedy left to be pursued by and between the parties to the dispute.

International Commercial Arbitration

Commercial arbitration has been going through incredible growth over the last decades and has become a "hot-topic". An entire industry has developed around alternative dispute resolution. (ADR) Certain countries have even adopted arbitration laws that limit judicial reviews of arbitration awards (Belgium, Switzerland, and England) in order to facilitate this growth market and get their share of this multimillion-dollar industry.

If the parties to a contract decide to use commercial arbitration to resolve any dispute they might have, they will have to do so either by inserting a clause to that effect into the written agreement, or agree to submit a conflict to arbitration when it arises. Since it can be safely stated that parties in dispute will be having a hard time agreeing on, anything, it is better to include an arbitration clause in the original agreement.

Advantages of alternative dispute resolution

Familiarity with the procedure: when international contract disputes are brought before a national judge there is normally one party unfamiliar with the procedure. In case of arbitration with one of the international institutes this is not the case. Furthermore the procedures in arbitration are simple compared to the civil procedure of many countries.

No home-court advantage: Even when it is not justified, there will always be distrust towards a foreign court, especially when the court is from the homeland of the opposing party. This is not the case with arbitration before an impartial tribunal, and sometimes even on neutral ground.

Choice of Law: National judges will often "lean" towards the laws of their own country and resist the use of transnational laws and trade usage. (*lex mercatoria*).

Clear Jurisdiction: There is no doubt in case of an arbitration clause regarding the tribunal, which would have jurisdiction over the dispute. The question of jurisdiction however is an issue, which can be the grounds for expensive and tedious jurisdictional law-suits.

International Enforcement: This is probably the most important reason to elect arbitration for dispute settlement. About 100 countries are signatories to the 1958 New York Convention, which makes the enforcement of an arbitration award a "shoe-in" compared to enforcing monetary judgments from a national court in another country.

Confidentiality: The proceedings before the tribunal and the final award are normally kept confidential. This protects business secrets and can facilitate settlement by reducing the opportunities and incentives for "media-play" by the parties.

Disadvantages of alternative dispute resolution:

High Costs: The costs of conducting an international arbitration are considerable. Actually, with the legal fees, administration costs and arbitration fees, the average arbitration can be more expensive than a lawsuit.

Delay Tactics: Speed used to be one of the advantages of arbitration. This is no longer so. In case of a technical or legal complex matter the arbitration can last just as long, or even longer, than a lawsuit. Furthermore, there are ways in which an arbitration procedure can be delayed, not unlike the delays experienced in a lawsuit.

Limited Judicial Review: With legal systems all over the world more positive towards arbitration, the judicial reviews of the arbitration procedure and subsequent rewards are being limited to procedural or "public policy" checks only (not a review of the merits of the case). This means that there now exists the risk that one has to take defense against an obvious erroneous arbitration award in each country where one has assets and that is a signatory to the New York Convention, since the arbitration award can no longer be annulled in the country of the arbitration situs.

Different Arbitration Laws: Contrary to its name, international arbitration is not regulated by international treaties but governed by the arbitration laws of the location of the arbitration situs.

With arbitration becoming less of a "quick fix", mediation is gaining in popularity as it still holds many of the informalities and speed that were once the reasons for arbitration's original popularity.

Enforcement of Arbitral Awards

Under the Indian Arbitration Act, an award is enforceable on its own force without the need for any ratification or approval by the court.

However, an opportunity to challenge the award is afforded to the aggrieved party. Under section 34 (a) of the Arbitration Act, an award can be challenged only on certain limited grounds, as follows:

(i) incapacity of the party;

(ii) invalidity of the arbitration agreement;

(iii) lack of proper notice to the aggrieved party of the appointment of the arbitrator or of the arbitration proceedings;

(iv) inability of a party to present his case;

(v) the arbitral award dealing with disputes not contemplated by or falling within the terms of submission to arbitration;

(vi) the procedure not being in accordance with the agreement of the parties.

An award can also be set aside under sub-section (b) of section 34, if the court finds that the subject-matter of the dispute is not capable of settlement by arbitration or that the arbitration award is in conflict with the "public policy" of India. Public policy is not defined. The *Explanation* to section 34 states that the Award is bad on the grounds of public policy, if it is induced or affected by fraud or corruption or is contrary to section 75 (duty of conciliator to maintain confidentiality) or section 81 (non-admissibility of evidence relating to conciliation proceedings). Mere error of law would not render an award bad on the ground of public policy.

The time limit for filing objection to an award is three months, extendable by 30 days at the discretion of the court. An appeal would lie from the order of the court, setting aside or refusing to set aside the award. Thereafter a second appeal may lie to the Supreme Court, purely at the discretion of the court. This would only be if an important question of law or of public interest is involved. Subject to the aforesaid, an award is executable, as soon as the period for filing objections is over.

Detrimental Reliance

In India, the cause of action would not be based on "detrimental reliance" but on "estoppel". Estoppel is defined in section 115 of the Indian Evidence Act as follows:

"115. When one person has, by his declaration, act or omission, intentionally caused or permitted another person to believe a thing to be true and to act upon such belief, neither he nor his representative shall be allowed, in any suit or proceeding between himself and such person or his representative, to deny the truth of that thing."

Estoppel is based on the principle that it would be inequitable and unjust if one person by a representation made, or by conduct amounting to a representation, had induced another to act as he would not otherwise have done. The person who made the representation should not be allowed to deny or repudiate the effect of his former statement, to the loss and injury of the person who acted on it.

One species of estoppel is Promissory Estoppel which creates an estoppel as to future promises. The law of promissory estoppel is well settled by the Supreme Court of India in *M.P. Sugar Mills* v. *State of U.P.*, AIR 1969 SC 621 and in *Union of India* v. *Godfrey Philips*, (1985) 4 SCC 369 (both decided by Justice Bhagwati). For this equitable doctrine to operate there must be:

 (i) a legal relationship giving rise to certain rights and duties between the Parties;

 (ii) next there must be, a promise which is intended to affect the legal relationship between the parties and which indicates that the promisor will not insist on his strict legal rights, arising out of that relationship, against the promisee;

 (iii) an intention on the part of the former Party that the latter will rely on the representation and such reliance by the other Party.

Even if these requirements are satisfied, the operation of the doctrine may be excluded if it is, nevertheless, not inequitable for the first party to go back on his promise, *i.e.*, the promisee must have acted in reliance on the promise, in a way, so that he cannot be restored to the position in which he was before he took such action.

In the present factual situation, *prima facie* the above requirements are not fulfilled. Further, estoppel cannot be invoked also for the following reasons:

 1. *Written contract.*—It has been held by the Supreme Court that the doctrine of promissory estoppel cannot be on a higher pedestal than a written contract between the parties. [*The State of Himachal Pradesh* v. *Ganesh Wood Products*, 1995 (6) SCC 363.]

 2. *No damages.*—The only relief in an action for promissory estoppel is by way of Injunction. No award of damages can be made.

Arbitration Clause

(a) Any dispute, controversy, or claim by or among the parties hereto arising out of or relating to or in connection with the transactions contemplated hereby or the Project, including, without limitation, under this Agreement or the Organizational Documents, or the breach, termination or validity hereof or thereof (a "Dispute") shall be finally settled by arbitration in accordance with the

Arbitration Rules of the United Nations Commission on Trade Law (UNCITRAL) then in effect (the "Rules"), except as modified therein.

(b) There shall be three arbitrators. In the case of a Dispute between any two (2) persons Party hereto, each shall select one arbitrator. The two arbitrators thus appointed shall select the presiding arbitrator of the arbitral tribunal who shall act as chairman of the arbitral tribunal within twenty days of the appointment of the second arbitrator. If any arbitrator has not been appointed within the time limits specified herein and in the Rules, the appointment of such arbitrator shall be made by the International Court of Arbitration of the International Chamber of Commerce upon the written request of any party to any such dispute within twenty (20) days of such request.

(c) Any arbitration proceedings or award rendered hereunder and the validity, effect and interpretation of this Agreement to arbitrate shall be governed by the laws of .... The arbitration proceedings shall be conducted in ...., ..., and the award shall be rendered, in the english language.

(d) The award shall be final and binding upon the parties thereto, and shall be the sole and exclusive remedy between them regarding any claims, counter claims, issues, or accountings presented to the arbitral tribunal. The arbitrators award shall, as between the disputing Parties and those in privity with them, be final and entitled to all of the protections and benefits of a final judgment, *e.g.*, *res judicata* (claim preclusion) and collateral estoppel (issue preclusion), as to all claims, including compulsory counterclaims, that were or could have been presented to the arbitrators. The arbitrators' award shall not be appealable to any court.

(e) The parties hereto expressly agree that leave to appeal under section 45 or section 69 of the English Arbitration Act of 1996 shall not be sought with respect to any question of law existing in the course of the arbitration or with respect to any award made. Furthermore, each party hereto hereby waives irrevocably any rights of application or appeal to the courts of India and the courts of the United States to the fullest extent permitted by law in connection with any questions of law arising in the course of the arbitration or with respect to any award made except for actions to obtain a judgement recognising, enforcing or setting aside an arbitral award and except for actions seeking interim or other provisional relief in any court of competent jurisdiction in aid of arbitration.

(f) It is the intent of the parties hereto that the arbitration proceeding shall be conducted expeditiously, without initial recourse to the courts and without interlocutory appeals of the arbitrators' decisions to the courts. However, if a disputing party refuses to honour its obligations under this agreement to arbitrate, any other disputing party may obtain appropriate relief staying litigation and/or compelling arbitration in any court having jurisdiction over the disputing parties; the order compelling arbitration shall require that the arbitration proceedings take place in ...., ..., as specified above. The disputing Parties may apply to any court having jurisdiction for orders requiring witnesses to obey *subpoenas* issued by the arbitrators. Moreover, any and all of the arbitrators' orders and decisions may be enforced if necessary by any court having jurisdiction. The arbitrators' award may be confirmed in, and judgement upon the award entered by, any court having jurisdiction.

(g) The validity, construction, and interpretation of this agreement to arbitrate, and all procedural aspects of the arbitration conducted pursuant to this agreement to arbitrate, including, but not limited to, the determination of the issues that are subject to arbitration (*i.e.*, arbitrability), the scope of the arbitrable issues, allegations of "fraud in the inducement" to enter into this Agreement to arbitrate, allegations of waiver, laches, delay or other defences to arbitrability, and the rules governing the conduct of the arbitration (including the time for filing an answer, the time for the filing of counter-claims, the times for amending the pleadings, the specificity of the pleadings, the extent and scope of discovery, the issuance of subpoenas, the times for the designation of experts, whether the arbitration is to be stayed pending resolution of related litigation involving third parties not bound by this agreement to arbitrate, the receipt of evidence, and the like) shall be decided by the arbitrators.

(h) Any monetary award shall be made and promptly payable in dollars and the arbitral tribunal shall be authorised in its discretion to grant pre-award and post-award interest at commercial rates. However, the arbitrators shall have absolutely no authority to award treble, exemplary or punitive damages of any type under any circumstances, regardless of whether such damages may be available under applicable law. The arbitrators shall have the authority to assess the costs and expenses of the arbitration proceeding (including the arbitrators' fee and expenses) against one or more of the disputing parties in whatever manner or allocation the arbitrators deem appropriate, provided that each disputing party shall bear its own attorneys' fees, and the arbitrators shall have no authority to award attorneys' fees.

(i) Each party hereto acknowledges and agrees that in the event of any breach of this Agreement by it, the other parties hereto would be irreparably harmed and accordingly agrees (i) to waive the defence in any arbitration proceeding conducted hereunder that a remedy at law would be adequate, and (ii) that the other parties hereto, in addition to any other remedy to which they may be entitled at law or in equity, shall be entitled to compel specific performance of this Agreement.

(j) To the extent that any party hereto (including assignees of any party's rights or obligations under this Agreement) may be entitled in any jurisdiction, to claim for itself or its revenues, assets or properties, sovereign immunity from service of process, from suit, from the jurisdiction of any court, from an interlocutory order or injunction, from any order of specific performance or order for the recovery of any property, or from the enforcement of the same or any arbitral award against its revenues, assets or property in such court or otherwise, from attachment prior to judgment, from attachment in aid of execution of an arbitral award or judgment (interlocutory or final), or from any other legal process, and to the extent that, in any such jurisdiction there may be attributed such a sovereign immunity (whether claimed or not), each party hereto hereby irrevocably agrees not to claim, and hereby irrevocably waives, such sovereign immunity and consents to such matter, to the extent that, without prejudice to the generality of such Agreement and waiver, in any proceeding taken in .... the foregoing agreement and waiver of sovereign immunity shall have effect under, and be construed in accordance with, the State Immunity Act of 1978.

(k) A disputing Party's breach or alleged breach of this Agreement shall not affect this agreement to arbitrate. Moreover, the obligations of the parties hereto under this arbitration provision are enforceable even after this Agreement has terminated. The invalidity or unenforceability of any provision of this agreement to arbitrate shall not affect the validity or enforceability of the obligation of the parties hereto to submit their claims to binding arbitration or the other provisions of this Agreement to arbitrate. This Agreement to arbitrate shall be binding upon the successors, assigns and any trustee or receiver of each party hereto.

Damages in Arbitration

Arbitration a Judicial Process: It is a settled principle of law that "Arbitration is a process by which a dispute or difference.................... is referred to and determined judicially." Halsbury Law of England 4th Edition, Reissue, Volume 2 page 332 – 333; *See* also *Dobson* v. *Groves*, 1844 (6) QB 637, 647. Hence, an arbitration tribunal is bound to determine the dispute in a judicial manner.

Indian law regarding award of damages.—Indian law stipulates that in case of breach of contract, damages may be awarded by way of compensation for any loss or damage which naturally arose in the usual course of things, or which the parties knew when they made the contract likely to result from the breach thereof. Further, compensation is not to be given for any remote and indirect loss or damage sustained by the breach (the Contract Act, section 73). As regards, liquidated damage, the Act provides that where such damages are stipulated, the party complaining of breach is entitled to receive "reasonable compensation" not exceeding the amount stipulated (section 74). A bare perusal of sections 73 and 74 makes it clear that in law damages can only be compensatory in nature and not penal and must be such which naturally arose in the usual course of things. Further remote or indirect damages cannot be awarded. Even where the parties have stipulated liquidated damages, the court can only award "reasonable compensation". Any award of damages, which is contrary to sections 73 and 74, would be an award contrary to Indian law.

Scheme of Arbitration Act.—Section 28(1)(b) mandates that the arbitral tribunal shall decide the dispute "in accordance with the rules of law designated by the parties". In the present case, the parties have agreed (*vide* Article 12.1 of the JDA) that the governing law shall be the law of India. Hence, the arbitrators have to decide the dispute in accordance with (*inter alia*) sections 73 and 74 of the Contract Act. Further, under UNCITRAL Rules if a party so requests, the arbitral tribunal shall hold hearings for the presentation of evidence including experts witnesses.

Consequence of literal interpretation of Article 13.4.—It cannot be that after taking evidence, hearing arguments, establishing correct facts and legal position, the arbitrators cast aside all this, and merely select the position of one of the parties.

The arbitrators cannot abdicate their role of deciding in accordance with law. Such an award would be a mockery of the law and the arbitration proceedings, and hence invalid and unenforceable under Indian law.

The above proposition can be supported by the following illustrative Indian and International arbitration cases:

- The Delhi High Court has held that if the arbitrators have not decided the dispute in accordance with the law, the award can be set aside [1998 (2) Arb. LR 345].
- ICC Case No. 4462 Year Book Commercial Arbitration Volume XVI page 54. In this case, the arbitration tribunal disregarded the liquidated damages contractually agreed between the parties holding the same to be "grossly exaggerated" and awarded a lesser sum based on the applicable law and evidence presented to it.
- ICC Case No. 5759; Year Book of Commercial Arbitration, Volume XVIII page 39. It was held that failure to provide sufficient evidence to prove damages and failure to mitigate the loss was a ground for the arbitrators to reduce damages from the contractually stipulated amount.

Interpretation of the Article 13.4.—A perusal of Article 13.4 shows that the Clause is perhaps intended to apply only to a certain class of disputes. These are disputes where the project has to be proceeded with, but the parties have differences between two commercial viewpoints. Here, the arbitrators are directed to adopt one of the parties' position, giving due considerations to the commercial reasonableness of each party's position. It is for this reason, that it is stipulated, that the parties should not only state their position to the tribunal, but also state the "proposed resolution" (line 2 of Article 13.4). The types of disputes, which would fall under Article 13.4, would be perhaps choice of EPC/O&M Contractor, selection of Suppliers, Manufacturers or other commercial decisions. These are disputes which are not suitable for a judicial determination, and hence the arbitrators, have to give due consideration to the "commercial reasonableness" of each Parties case, and then select one Party's position. Article 13.4 cannot apply to a claim for damage which has to be judicially determined in accordance with law, nor can it compel the arbitrators to decide contrary to established facts and settled law. Such a decision would be invalid in law, contrary to public policy and liable to be set aside.

CHAPTER 11
LEASE

SYNOPSIS

PARTIES
CONSIDERATION
COVENANTS ENTERED INTO BY THE LESSEE
COVENANTS BY THE LESSOR
PROVISO FOR RE-ENTRY

PRECEDENTS
- Agreement of Lease

Parties

A lease must be executed by both lessor and lessee. An instrument signed by the lessor alone or lessee alone, in the eyes of law, would be a mere agreement to lease. It was general practice in Punjab that a lease was executed solely by a lessee. This practice was rendered illegal by the Transfer of Property Amendment Act, 1929, which had added third paragraph to section 107. This paragraph runs as follows:—

> *"Where a lease of immovable property is made by a registered instrument such instrument, or where there are more instruments than one, each such instrument shall be executed by both the lessor and lessee".*

Consideration

Consideration for lease would be the rent reserved or payable thereunder as well as under the covenants entered into by the lessee.

Covenants entered into by the lessee

These covenants vary according to the nature of the property leased and the purpose for which the lease is made. More important of these may be summarized:

(i) Covenant to pay a rent on a fixed period;

(ii) Covenant to repair;

The lessor is under no liability to repair the lease-hold premises in the absence of a covenant to the contrary. Section 108(m) of the Transfer of Property Act, shows that the liability to repair is that of the lessee. If a lessor who is liable to make, within a reasonable time after notice, any repairs which he is bound to make, to the property, the lessee may make the same himself and deduct the expenses of such repairs with interest from the rent or otherwise recover it from lessor, (section 108(f), Transfer of Property Act);

(iii) Covenant not to sublet or assign the lease without the written consent of the lessor;

If there is a condition of forfeiture in the lease on branch of this covenant and the lessee commits default, the lessor is entitled to enforce this condition and the court cannot believe him. (See section 114A, Transfer of Property Act);

(iv) Covenant to pay rates and taxes but not the property tax which generally falls on the landlord;

(v) to permit the lessor or his servants to enter at reasonable time to inspect the condition of the property;

(vi) Not to commit any nuisance or noisome trade or business;

(vii) To insure;

(viii) After the expiry of the term of the lease to hand over the lease hold premises in as good condition as it was at the beginning of the lease barring ordinary wear and tear.

Covenants by the lessor

This generally provides that if the lessee performs the covenants entered into by him, he will have quiet and undisturbed possession without any interruption by the lessor of any person claiming through him.

Proviso for re-entry

This is the forfeiture clause. This provides that if the lessee does not pay the rent reserved or commits default in observing or performing other terms, the lessor may avoid the lease and enter into possession.

The forfeiture clause about non-payment of rent must be read in the light of provision of section 114 of the Transfer of Property Act, according to which the court has discretion to grant relief to the lessee under certain circumstances. Section 114A of the said Act, requires the lessor before enforcing such a clause in other cases to serve the lessee with a notice specifying the particular breach complained of and requiring him remedy if it is capable of remedy and it is only when he failed, that a suit for enforcing such a condition can lie.

Agreement of Lease

This Agreement made at .... (Name of the place) on this ....20....., BETWEEN *Alpha*, residing at .... (address), hereinafter referred to as the 'LESSOR' of the one Part AND *Beta*, ... S/o *Gama*, residing at .... (address), hereinafter referred to as the 'LESSEE' of the other Part;

WHEREAS the Lessor is the lawful owner of, and otherwise well sufficiently entitled to .... (address), falling in the category, ... (name of the category of flat) and comprising of two bedrooms, one hall, one dining room, one kitchen, two bathrooms and one scooter garage on the ground floor hereinafter referred to as the 'said premises';

AND WHEREAS the Lessee being in need of an accommodation, approached the Lessor with a request to permit the Lessee to occupy the said premises on lease for a temporary period and for purposes of residential use for a period of Twelve (12) months commencing from.................... 20.....

AND WHEREAS the Lessor has agreed to allow the Lessee to use and occupy the said premises for the above period of .... months;

AND WHEREAS the Lessor has necessary permission of the concerned authorities for this lease and will pay any charges, if any;

NOW THIS AGREEMENT WITNESSETH AND IT IS HEREBY AGREED BY AND BETWEEN THE PARTIES AS UNDER:

1. That the Lessor hereby grant to the Lessee, the right to enter into and use and remain in the said premises alongwith the existing fixtures and fittings listed in the Annexure 1 to this Agreement and that the Lessee shall be entitled to peacefully possess, and enjoy possession of the said premises, and the other rights herein.

2. That the lease hereby granted shall, unless cancelled earlier under any provision of this Agreement, remain in force for a period of .... months. The Parties however shall have the right to extend the lease for a period of .... months with mutual consent.

3. That the Lessee will have the option to terminate this lease by giving one month's notice in writing to the Lessor.

4. That the Lessee shall have no right to create any sub-lease or assign or transfer in any manner the lease or give to any one the possession of the said premises or any part thereof, except for his family.

5. That the Lessee shall use the said premises only for residential purposes.

6. That the Lessor shall, before handing over the said premises, ensure the working of sanitary, electrical and water supply connections and other fittings pertaining to the said premises. It is agreed that it shall be the responsibility of the Lessor for their return in the working condition at the time of re-possession of the said premises (reasonable wear and tear and loss or damage by fire, flood, rains, accident, irresistible force or act of God excepted).

7. That the Lessee is not authorised to make any alterations in the construction of the said premises. The Lessee may however install and remove his own fittings and fixtures, provided this is done without causing any excessive damage or loss to the said premises.

8. That the day to day repair jobs such as fuse blow out, replacement of light bulbs/tubes, leakage of water taps, maintenance of the water pump and other minor repairs, etc., shall be effected by the Lessee at its own cost, and any major repairs, either structural or to the electrical or water

connection, plumbing leaks, water seepage shall be attended to by the Lessor. In the event of the Lessor failing to carry out the repairs on receiving notice from the Lessee, the Lessee shall undertake the necessary repairs and the Lessor will be liable to immediately reimburse costs incurred by the Lessee.

9. That the Lessee shall be entitled to install air conditioners, water pumps, telephone, room coolers, TV Antenna/cable connection, etc., at its own cost in the demised Premises and make any alteration to the Demised Premises for the purpose of such installation. The Lessor hereby agrees to provide sufficient electrical power to install and run such appliances.

10. That the Lessor or its duly authorised agent shall have the right to enter into or upon the said premises or any part thereof at a mutually arranged convenient time for the purpose of inspection with a minimum 24 hours notice.

11. That the Lessee shall use the said premises along with its fixtures and fittings in careful and responsible manner and shall hand over the premises to the Lessor in working condition (reasonable wear and tear and loss or damage by fire, flood, rains, accidents, irresistible force or act of God excepted).

12. That in consideration of use of the said premises the Lessee agrees that he shall pay to the Lessor during the period of this agreement, a monthly rent at the rate of Rs. .... (amount in figure) Rupees .... (amount in word). The amount will be paid in advance on or before the .... day of english calendar month.

13. That in addition to the compensation mentioned above, the Lessee shall pay the actual electricity and water bills for the period of the agreement directly to the authorities concerned. The relevant 'start date' meter readings are those set out in Annexure 1 of this Agreement.

14. That the Lessee has paid to the Lessor a sum of Rs.................... (Amount in figure Rupees .... (amount in words) as deposit, free of interest, which the Lessor does accept and acknowledge. This deposit is for the due performance and observance of the terms and conditions of this Agreement. The deposit shall be returned to the Lessee simultaneously with the Lessee vacating the said premises. In the event of failure on the part of the Lessor to refund the said deposit amount to the Lessee as aforesaid, the Lessee shall be entitled to continue to use and occupy the said premises without payment of any rent until the Lessor refunds the said amount with interest @ 24% p.a. from the date the Lessee offered to vacate the said premises till the date of refund of the deposit to the Lessee (without prejudice to the Lessee's rights and remedies in law to recover the deposit).

15. That the Lessor shall be responsible for the payment of all taxes and levies pertaining to the said premises including but not limited to House Tax, Property Tax, other cesses, if any, and any other statutory taxes, levied by the .... (name of corporation) and other Government

debenture or similar instrument, (3) any other transaction having the commercial effect of a borrowing or raising of money or (4) any uncontested liability or a final judgment for a monetary amount with respect to borrowings from a bank or other financial institution.

"*Extended Lease Term*" means such period extending the Lease Term up to three periods of 12 months each commencing on the expiry date in accordance with clause 3.2.

"*Flight Hour*" shall mean each hour or fraction thereof elapsing from the moment at which the wheels of the Aircraft or, in the case of any Part or engine temporarily installed on another aircraft, that other aircraft, leave the ground on the take-off of such aircraft until the wheels of such aircraft touch the ground on the landing of such aircraft following such take-off.

"*Lease Period*" means the period during which the Lessee shall be entitled to the possession and use of the Aircraft in accordance with this Agreement, including the period during the Extended Lease Term and, for the avoidance of doubt, shall include any period during which the leasing of the Aircraft is extended pursuant to clause 18.1.

"*Lease Term*" means the period commencing on the delivery date until expiry date, which for the purposes of this Agreement shall be deemed to include the Extended Lease Term following its becoming effective.

"*Lessee*" includes the successors of the Lessee.

(**Note.**—In this section a coneyancer is supposed to mention important terms and expressions with their respective meanings. For the sake of brevity only few of technical terms with their meanings have been given in this draft.)

Article 2: Representations and Warranties

(**Note.**—In this part of agreement a conveyancer is supported to give terms & conditions relating to representations and warranties. For the sake of brevity only few of the following points are given in this draft.)

Article 3: Term of Lease

3.1 Lease Term

The Lessor shall lease and the Lessee shall take on lease the Aircraft, subject to the terms and conditions of this Agreement, for the Lease Term.

3.2 Extended Lease Term

Provided that no Relevant Event has occurred and is continuing, and subject to the terms and conditions agreed in writing executed by both Lessor and Lessee no later than 12 months prior to the end of the Lease Term, as such Lease Term may be extended in accordance with this Agreement, Lessee shall be entitled to continue the leasing of the Aircraft for an additional 12 months following the end of the Lease Term. Lessee shall be entitled to exercise such extension right for up to three periods, each such period being of twelve months, the first such period commencing at the end of the initial Lease Term on ....20....., and each subsequent such period commencing at the end of the immediately preceding such period.

Article 4: Conditions

4.1 Lessor conditions on and following execution

Lessee shall provide to Lessor on or prior to execution of this Agreement the documents and evidence specified in Part 1 of Schedule 2 in form and substance satisfactory to the Lessor.

4.2 Lessor conditions precedent on or prior to delivery

The obligation of the Lessor to lease the Aircraft to the Lessee under this Agreement is subject to the condition that on or prior to the delivery date the Lessor shall have received the documents and evidence specified in Part 2 of Schedule 2 in form and substance satisfactory to the Lessor.

4.3 General conditions precedent

The obligation of the Lessor to lease the Aircraft to the Lessee under this Agreement is subject to the further conditions that:—

(1) the representations and warranties set out in clause 2.1 are true and correct as if each were made with respect to the facts and circumstances existing immediately prior to the time when delivery is to take place;

(2) no Relevant Event shall have occurred and be continuing or would arise by reason of delivery taking place;

(3) the Aircraft shall have been delivered to the Lessor pursuant to the Sub-Purchase Agreement.

(4) no Total Loss in respect of the Aircraft or Airframe and no damage shall have occurred which in the reasonable opinion of the Lessor could have an adverse effect on the expected residual value of the Aircraft upon the expiry date.

4.4 Lessor conditions subsequent

Lessee shall ensure compliance with the conditions listed in Schedule 2, Part 3 in accordance with their terms (conditions subsequent), the non-occurrence of any of which shall constitute a termination event and entitle Lessor to exercise any and all remedies available to Lessor.

4.5 Lessee Conditions Precedent

Lessee's obligations to accept delivery of, and take on lease, the Aircraft under this Agreement are subject to the receipt by the Lessee from the Lessor not later than delivery of:—

(1) certificate of a duly authorised officer of the Lessor attaching a copy of an up to date extract from the corporate registration setting out those persons entitled to bind the Lessor together with a power of attorney duly executed authorising a specified person or persons to execute this Agreement and the Assignment of Insurances on its behalf;

(2) a letter from an entity located in .... agreeing to receive service of process referred to in clause 25.2;

(3) an undertaking letter from .... in a form agreed between Lessor and Lessee.

category of flat) and comprising of two bedrooms, one hall, one dining room, one kitchen, two bathrooms and one scooter garage on the ground floor hereinafter referred to as the 'said premises';

AND WHEREAS the Lessee being in need of an accommodation, approached the Lessor with a request to permit the Lessee to occupy the said premises on lease for a temporary period and for purposes of residential use for a period of Twelve (12) months commencing from..................... 20......

AND WHEREAS the Lessor has agreed to allow the Lessee to use and occupy the said premises for the above period of .... months;

AND WHEREAS the Lessor has necessary permission of the concerned authorities for this lease and will pay any charges, if any;

NOW THIS AGREEMENT WITNESSETH AND IT IS HEREBY AGREED BY AND BETWEEN THE PARTIES AS UNDER:

1. That the Lessor hereby grant to the Lessee, the right to enter into and use and remain in the said premises alongwith the existing fixtures and fittings listed in the Annexure 1 to this Agreement and that the Lessee shall be entitled to peacefully possess, and enjoy possession of the said premises, and the other rights herein.

2. That the lease hereby granted shall, unless cancelled earlier under any provision of this Agreement, remain in force for a period of .... months. The Parties however shall have the right to extend the lease for a period of .... months with mutual consent.

3. That the Lessee will have the option to terminate this lease by giving one month's notice in writing to the Lessor.

4. That the Lessee shall have no right to create any sub-lease or assign or transfer in any manner the lease or give to any one the possession of the said premises or any part thereof, except for his family.

5. That the Lessee shall use the said premises only for residential purposes.

6. That the Lessor shall, before handing over the said premises, ensure the working of sanitary, electrical and water supply connections and other fittings pertaining to the said premises. It is agreed that it shall be the responsibility of the Lessor for their return in the working condition at the time of re-possession of the said premises (reasonable wear and tear and loss or damage by fire, flood, rains, accident, irresistible force or act of God excepted).

7. That the Lessee is not authorised to make any alterations in the construction of the said premises. The Lessee may however install and remove his own fittings and fixtures, provided this is done without causing any excessive damage or loss to the said premises.

8. That the day to day repair jobs such as fuse blow out, replacement of light bulbs/tubes, leakage of water taps, maintenance of the water pump and other minor repairs, etc., shall be effected by the Lessee at its own cost, and any major repairs, either structural or to the electrical or water

connection, plumbing leaks, water seepage shall be attended to by the Lessor. In the event of the Lessor failing to carry out the repairs on receiving notice from the Lessee, the Lessee shall undertake the necessary repairs and the Lessor will be liable to immediately reimburse costs incurred by the Lessee.

9. That the Lessee shall be entitled to install air conditioners, water pumps, telephone, room coolers, TV Antenna/cable connection, etc., at its own cost in the demised Premises and make any alteration to the Demised Premises for the purpose of such installation. The Lessor hereby agrees to provide sufficient electrical power to install and run such appliances.

10. That the Lessor or its duly authorised agent shall have the right to enter into or upon the said premises or any part thereof at a mutually arranged convenient time for the purpose of inspection with a minimum 24 hours notice.

11. That the Lessee shall use the said premises along with its fixtures and fittings in careful and responsible manner and shall hand over the premises to the Lessor in working condition (reasonable wear and tear and loss or damage by fire, flood, rains, accidents, irresistible force or act of God excepted).

12. That in consideration of use of the said premises the Lessee agrees that he shall pay to the Lessor during the period of this agreement, a monthly rent at the rate of Rs. .... (amount in figure) Rupees .... (amount in word). The amount will be paid in advance on or before the .... day of english calendar month.

13. That in addition to the compensation mentioned above, the Lessee shall pay the actual electricity and water bills for the period of the agreement directly to the authorities concerned. The relevant 'start date' meter readings are those set out in Annexure 1 of this Agreement.

14. That the Lessee has paid to the Lessor a sum of Rs..................... (Amount in figure Rupees .... (amount in words) as deposit, free of interest, which the Lessor does accept and acknowledge. This deposit is for the due performance and observance of the terms and conditions of this Agreement. The deposit shall be returned to the Lessee simultaneously with the Lessee vacating the said premises. In the event of failure on the part of the Lessor to refund the said deposit amount to the Lessee as aforesaid, the Lessee shall be entitled to continue to use and occupy the said premises without payment of any rent until the Lessor refunds the said amount with interest @ 24% p.a. from the date the Lessee offered to vacate the said premises till the date of refund of the deposit to the Lessee (without prejudice to the Lessee's rights and remedies in law to recover the deposit).

15. That the Lessor shall be responsible for the payment of all taxes and levies pertaining to the said premises including but not limited to House Tax, Property Tax, other cesses, if any, and any other statutory taxes, levied by the .... (name of corporation) and other Government

Departments. During the term of this Agreement, the Lessor shall comply with all rules, regulations and requirements of any statutory authority, the .... (name of corporation) and other Government Departments, and any local, State or Central Governmental authority in relation to the said premises.

IN WITNESS WHEREOF, the parties hereto have set their hands on the day and year first hereinabove mentioned.

SIGNED AND DELIVERED BY *Alpha*
IN THE PRESENCE OF:
SIGNED AND DELIVERED BY *Beta*
IN THE PRESENCE OF:

Annexure 1

Lease Agreement dated .... between
Alpha (Lessor) and *Beta* (Lessee)
List of fixtures and fittings provided in..................... (Address)

Item	Quantity
1. As per inventory Schedule A.	
2. Ceiling Fan	- 4 nos.
3. PVC Tank	- 1 in scooter garage
4. Motor Pump	- 1 in scooter garage
5. Meter reading as on	: Electricity.....................
	Water ....

....
Alpha   *Beta*

PRECEDENTS

AGREEMENT OF LEASE

AIRCRAFT LEASE AGREEMENT ("Agreement") dated and effective as of ....20.... made

BETWEEN

Alpha, whose registered office is at (.....................address) ("Lessor")

AND

Beta whose registered office is at (..................... address) (the "Lessee").

BY WHICH IT IS AGREED as follows.

Article 1: Definitions

1.1 In this Agreement, unless the context otherwise requires, the terms and expressions specified below shall have the following respective meanings:

"Acceptance Certificate" means a certificate in the form set out in Part 2 of Schedule 3 to be signed by the Lessee as required under Schedule 3, Part 2.

"Acceptance Flight" means the flight referred to in clause 19.4(1).

"Agreed Value" means Rs. ....

"Aircraft" means the Airframe together with the engines (whether or not any of the Engines may from time to time be installed on the Airframe) and, where the context permits, references to the "Aircraft" shall (1) include the Aircraft Documents, and (2) mean the Aircraft as a whole and any part thereof.

"Aircraft Documents" means all records, logs, manuals, technical data and other materials and documents (whether kept or to be kept in compliance with any regulation of the Aviation Authority or otherwise) relating to the Aircraft, including the documents, data and records identified in Part 2 of Schedule 1 and all additions, renewals, revisions and replacements from time to time made thereto in accordance with this Agreement or provided by the Lessor to the Lessee.

"Approved Maintenance Performer" means, subject to receipt of all necessary approvals of the Aviation Authority, the Sub-Lessee or, with the consent of Lessor, such consent not to be unreasonably withheld, any independent maintenance performer to perform all major maintenance work on the Aircraft.

"Approved Maintenance Programme" means the Sub-Lessee's maintenance programme based upon the Manufacturer's Maintenance Planning Data for aircraft of the same make and model as the Aircraft approved by the Aviation Authority.

"APU" means the Auxiliary Power Unit installed on the Aircraft at Delivery or any replacement auxiliary power unit title to which has or should have passed to the Lessor in accordance with this Agreement, but excluding any replaced Auxiliary Power Unit title to which has or should have been passed from Lessor in accordance with this Agreement.

"Assignment of Insurances" means the assignment executed or to be executed by the Sub-Lessee in favour of the Lessor in respect of certain of its rights under the Insurances, in form and substance satisfactory to the Lessor.

"Aviation Authority" means each person who shall from time to time be vested with the control and supervision of, or have jurisdiction over, the registration, airworthiness and operation of Aircraft or other matters relating to Civil Aviation in the State of Registration contemplated at the date of this Agreement to be the Director General of Civil Aviation in India.

"Banking Day" means a day (other than a saturday, sunday or holiday scheduled by law) on which banks are open for business in .... (name of place) and (if payment is required to be made on such day) in....................

"Basic Lease Term" means the period commencing on the delivery date until ....20.....

"Borrowed Money" means indebtedness incurred in respect of (1) money borrowed or raised and debit balances at banks, (2) any bond, note, loan stock,

Article 4: Conditions

4.1 Lessor conditions on and following execution

Lessee shall provide to Lessor on or prior to execution of this Agreement the documents and evidence specified in Part 1 of Schedule 2 in form and substance satisfactory to the Lessor.

4.2 Lessor conditions precedent on or prior to delivery

The obligation of the Lessor to lease the Aircraft to the Lessee under this Agreement is subject to the condition that on or prior to the delivery date the Lessor shall have received the documents and evidence specified in Part 2 of Schedule 2 in form and substance satisfactory to the Lessor.

4.3 General conditions precedent

The obligation of the Lessor to lease the Aircraft to the Lessee under this Agreement is subject to the further conditions that:—

(1) the representations and warranties set out in clause 2.1 are true and correct as if each were made with respect to the facts and circumstances existing immediately prior to the time when delivery is to take place;

(2) no Relevant Event shall have occurred and be continuing or would arise by reason of delivery taking place;

(3) the Aircraft shall have been delivered to the Lessor pursuant to the Sub-Purchase Agreement.

(4) no Total Loss in respect of the Aircraft or Airframe and no damage shall have occurred which in the reasonable opinion of the Lessor could have an adverse effect on the expected residual value of the Aircraft upon the expiry date.

4.4 Lessor conditions subsequent

Lessee shall ensure compliance with the conditions listed in Schedule 2, Part 3 in accordance with their terms (conditions subsequent), the non-occurrence of any of which shall constitute a termination event and entitle Lessor to exercise any and all remedies available to Lessor.

4.5 Lessee Conditions Precedent

Lessee's obligations to accept delivery of, and take on lease, the Aircraft under this Agreement are subject to the receipt by the Lessee from the Lessor not later than delivery of:—

(1) certificate of a duly authorised officer of the Lessor attaching a copy of an up to date extract from the corporate registration setting out those persons entitled to bind the Lessor together with a power of attorney duly executed authorising a specified person or persons to execute this Agreement and the Assignment of Insurances on its behalf;

(2) a letter from an entity located in .... agreeing to receive service of process referred to in clause 25.2;

(3) an undertaking letter from .... in a form agreed between Lessor and Lessee.

debenture or similar instrument, (3) any other transaction having the commercial effect of a borrowing or raising of money or (4) any uncontested liability or a final judgment for a monetary amount with respect to borrowings from a bank or other financial institution.

"*Extended Lease Term*" means such period extending the Lease Term up to three periods of 12 months each commencing on the expiry date in accordance with clause 3.2.

"*Flight Hour*" shall mean each hour or fraction thereof elapsing from the moment at which the wheels of the Aircraft or, in the case of any Part or engine temporarily installed on another aircraft, that other aircraft, leave the ground on the take-off of such aircraft until the wheels of such aircraft touch the ground on the landing of such aircraft following such take-off.

"*Lease Period*" means the period during which the Lessee shall be entitled to the possession and use of the Aircraft in accordance with this Agreement, including the period during the Extended Lease Term and, for the avoidance of doubt, shall include any period during which the leasing of the Aircraft is extended pursuant to clause 18.1.

"*Lease Term*" means the period commencing on the delivery date until expiry date, which for the purposes of this Agreement shall be deemed to include the Extended Lease Term following its becoming effective.

"*Lessee*" includes the successors of the Lessee.

(**Note.**—In this section a coneyancer is supposed to mention important terms and expressions with their respective meanings. For the sake of brevity only few of technical terms with their meanings have been given in this draft.)

Article 2: Representations and Warranties

(**Note.**—In this part of agreement a conveyancer is supported to give terms & conditions relating to representations and warranties. For the sake of brevity only few of the following points are given in this draft.)

Article 3: Term of Lease

3.1 Lease Term

The Lessor shall lease and the Lessee shall take on lease the Aircraft, subject to the terms and conditions of this Agreement, for the Lease Term.

3.2 Extended Lease Term

Provided that no Relevant Event has occurred and is continuing, and subject to the terms and conditions agreed in writing executed by both Lessor and Lessee no later than 12 months prior to the end of the Lease Term, as such Lease Term may be extended in accordance with this Agreement, Lessee shall be entitled to continue the leasing of the Aircraft for an additional 12 months following the end of the Lease Term. Lessee shall be entitled to exercise such extension right for up to three periods, each such period being of twelve months, the first such period commencing at the end of the initial Lease Term on ....20....., and each subsequent such period commencing at the end of the immediately preceding such period.

4.6 Lessor Waiver

The conditions specified in clauses 4.1, 4.2, and 4.3 are for the sole benefit of the Lessor and may be waived in whole or in part and with or without conditions by the Lessor.

4.7 Lessee Waiver

The conditions specified in clause 4.5 are for the sole benefit of the Lessee and may be waived or deferred in whole or in part and with or without conditions by the Lessee.

Article 5: Delivery and Acceptance

5.1 Scheduled delivery month and scheduled delivery date

Lessor and Lessee have agreed that the Delivery of the Aircraft is scheduled to occur in the expected delivery month. The expected delivery date, unless otherwise agreed, shall be....................20.....

5.2 Commencement

Subject to the terms of this Agreement, the Lessor will offer the Aircraft for delivery and the Lessee will accept Delivery of the Aircraft on or about the expected delivery date at the delivery location in an as-is, where-is condition. The Lessee shall not, subject to clause 4.5, be entitled to refuse to accept Delivery of the Aircraft hereunder once the Aircraft has been delivered to and accepted by the Lessor under the Sub-Purchase Agreement. The Lessor will lease the Aircraft to the Lessee and the Lessee will take the Aircraft on lease in accordance with this Agreement for the duration of the Lease Term. The Lessor shall not be liable to the Lessee for any loss or damage of any kind or any loss of profit, resulting directly or indirectly through any physical defects, alleged physical defect in, or the lack of required condition, quality, suitability and fitness for the purpose of the Aircraft.

5.3 Delay

The Lessor shall not be responsible for any loss or expense, or any loss of profit, arising from any delay in the delivery of, or failure to deliver, the Aircraft to the Lessee under this Agreement including, but not limited to, any excusable delay.

5.4 Cancellation

If for any reason, other than a default by the Lessor or the Lessee, the Aircraft shall not have been tendered for delivery to the Lessee in accordance with this clause 5 on or before......................20....., then the Lessor (if there is no default of the Lessor) or the Lessee (if there is not default of the Lessee) may cancel the obligation contained in this Agreement to lease the Aircraft by giving notice to the other party to that effect.

5.5 Indemnity

Without prejudice to the Lessor's obligations under the Loan Agreement, neither the Lessee nor the Lessor shall be liable to the other or any Relevant Party in respect of any liabilities, damages, losses, costs or expenses incurred by the

5.6 Risk

other or such Relevant Party as a consequence of any delay in the delivery of or non-delivery of the Aircraft to the Lessee save and to the extent that such delay in delivery or non-delivery arises as a direct consequence of a breach of the Lessee (in the case of the Lessee) or the Lessor (in the case of the Lessor).

5.6 Risk

After delivery and until the date on which the Aircraft is returned by the Lessee to the Lessor in the condition required and in accordance with the terms of this Agreement, the Aircraft and every part thereof will, as between the Lessor and the Lessee, be at the sole risk of the Lessee, who will bear all risk of loss, theft, damage or destruction or any total loss in respect of the Aircraft.

Article 6: Lessor's Warranties

6.1 Quiet enjoyment

The Lessor warrants that, provided that no termination event has occurred and is continuing, the Lessor shall not, through its own acts, interfere during the Lease Period with the use, possession and quiet enjoyment of the Aircraft by the Lessee.

Article 7: Payments

7.1 Rent instalments

7.1.1 Fixed rent

During the Basic Lease Term, the Lessee shall pay the Lessor on each payment date instalments of rent for the Aircraft in advance as provided in Schedule 4.

7.1.2 Floating Rent

(a) During the Extended Lease Term, on each payment date, the Lessee shall pay to the Lessor in advance an instalment of Rent for the Aircraft, being the aggregate of the Base Instalment and the Variable Instalment applicable to such payment date.

(b) For the purposes of this clause 7.1.2:

"Base Instalment" means, in relation to any payment date, the amount specified opposite such payment date in column (2) of Part 2 of Schedule 4;

"Interest Determination Period" means each of the semi-annual periods, which commences, in respect of the first such period, on the payment date falling on....................20......, and thereafter on the date falling at intervals of six months.

"Instalment Payment Period" means each of the periods commencing on a Payment Date and ending on the next succeeding payment date, provided that the first instalment payment period shall commence on ....20..... and end on the next succeeding Payment Date;

"Outstanding Balance" means, in relation to any Instalment Payment period, the outstanding balance set out in column (3) of Part 2 of Schedule 4 opposite the payment date upon which such Instalment Payment Period commences; and

"Variable Instalment" means, in relation to any payment date and for any instalment payment period falling in any Interest Determination Period, the amount equal to the amount of accrued interest for such Instalment payment period calculated at LIBOR applicable to such interest determination period on the outstanding balance outstanding at the commencement of such Instalment Payment Period plus one point eight five per cent. (1.85 %) per annum.

(c) For the purposes of this clause 7.1.2, interest will accrue from day to day and shall be calculated on the basis of actual number of days elapsed and a year of .... days.

7.2 VAT and taxes

Subject to clause 10.2, rent and all other sums payable by the Lessee to the Lessor under this Agreement are exclusive of any value added tax or similar tax payable in respect thereof which shall in each case be paid in addition.

7.3 Unconditional obligation

The Lessee's obligation to pay rent and make other payments in accordance with this Agreement shall be absolute and unconditional irrespective of any contingency whatsoever including, but not limited to, (1) any right of set-off, counterclaim, recoupment, defence or other right which the Lessor or the Lessee may have against the other or against any Relevant Party, (2) any unavailability of the Aircraft for any reason, including, but not limited to, any lack or invalidity of title or any other defect in the title, airworthiness, merchantability, fitness for any purpose, condition, design, or operation of any kind or nature of the Aircraft, or the ineligibility of the Aircraft for any particular use or trade, or for registration or documentation under the laws of any relevant jurisdiction, or the Total Loss of, or any damage to, the Aircraft, (3) any failure or delay on the part of the Lessor or the Lessee, whether with or without fault on its part, in performing or complying with any of the terms or conditions of this Agreement, or any misrepresentation, negligence, misconduct, action or inaction, by any Relevant Party, but in each case without prejudice to any rights at law or in equity which the Lessee may have arising by reason of any such failure, delay, misrepresentation, negligence, misconduct, action or inaction; or (4) any insolvency, bankruptcy, administration, reorganisation, arrangement, readjustment of debt, dissolution, liquidation or similar proceedings by or against the Lessor or the Lessee or any other person, or (5) any lack of due authorisation of, or other defect in, this Agreement or any other document, or (6) any event beyond the control of Lessee which would prevent Lessee from making any payment required hereunder, including, but not limited to *force majeure*.

Article 8: Payments and Calculations

8.1 Payment account

All payments to be made by the Lessee to the Lessor under any Lessee Document shall be made without (unless specifically otherwise provided in such Lessee Document) prior demand and in full, without any set-off or counterclaim whatsoever and, subject as provided in clause 10.2, free and clear of any deductions or withholdings in dollars (or, in the case of indemnity payments, in the currency claimed by the Lessor) for value on the day on which payment is due to the account of the Lessor opened with .... (name of the branch) or at such other bank in such other place as the Lessor may have notified to the Lessee.

8.2 Banking days

When any payment under any Lessee Document would otherwise be due to the Lessor on a day which is not a Banking Day, the payment shall be made on the immediately preceding Banking Day.

8.3 Default interest

If any payment by the Lessee hereunder is not received on or before the due date thereof in the manner herein provided, the Lessee shall pay interest on the same for the period commencing on such due date until such date on which the same is received or recovered in full at the overdue rate (such interest to accrue from day to day and be due and payable on the demand of the Lessor).

8.4 Calculations

All interest relating to payments of an annual nature under this Agreement shall accrue from day to day and be calculated on the basis of actual days elapsed and a 360 day year.

8.5 Certificates

Any certificate or determination of the Lessor as to any rate of interest (including default interest) relating to any amount pursuant to and for the purposes of this Agreement shall, in the absence of manifest error, be conclusive and binding on the Lessee.

8.6 Currency Indemnity

If any sum due from the Lessee under any Lessee Document or under any order or judgement given or made in relation thereto:—

(1) has to be converted from the currency ("the first currency") in which the same is payable under such Lessee Document or under such order or judgement into another currency ("the second currency") for the purpose of (a) making or filing a claim or proof against the Lessee, (b) obtaining an order or judgement in any court or other tribunal, or (c) enforcing any order or judgement given or made in relation to such Lessee Document; or

(2) is paid to Lessor in the second currency instead of the first currency; the Lessee shall indemnify and hold harmless the Lessor from and against any loss suffered as a result of, in the case of (1) above, any difference between (a) the rate of exchange used for such purpose to convert the sum in question from the first currency into the second currency and (b) the rate or rates of exchange at which the Lessor may in the ordinary course of business purchase the first currency with the second currency upon receipt of a sum paid to it in satisfaction, in whole or in part, of any such order, judgment, claim or proof, and in the case of (2) above, any shortfall in the

amount of the first currency due after conversion by Lessor of the amount received in the second currency. Any conversion made under this clause 8.5 shall be made at the market rate of exchange available in .... at or around .... noon on the date of such conversion. Any amount due from the Lessee under this Clause 8.6 shall be due as a separate debt and shall not be affected by judgement being obtained for any other sums due under or in respect of any Lessee Document and the term "rate of exchange" includes any premium and costs of exchange payable in connection with the purchase of the first currency with the second currency.

Article 9: Costs and Indemnities

9.1 General indemnity

The Lessee shall pay promptly all costs or expenses of, or arising from, the certification, manufacture, testing, delivery, import, export, registration, ownership, title, possession, control, use, operation, leasing, sub-leasing, insurance, maintenance, repair, refurbishment, service, overhaul, modification, change, alteration, replacement, loss, damage, storage, removal or re-delivery of, in or to the Aircraft, and all costs or expenses otherwise arising in connection with the Aircraft or the performance of the Lessee's obligations under any of the Lessee Documents, the Purchase Agreement or the Sub-Lease.

9.2 Costs and expenses

Each of Lessor and Lessee shall bear its respective costs and expenses incurred in connection with the negotiation, preparation, and execution of this Agreement and any additional documentation thereto in pursuance of the execution of this Agreement.

9.3 Default Indemnity

The Lessee shall indemnify and hold harmless the Lessor, without prejudice to any of the Lessor's other rights under any of the Lessee Documents, from and against any Taxes, costs or expenses which the Lessee has agreed to pay and which shall be claimed from or assessed against or paid by the Lessor, and against any liability incurred by the Lessor by reason of any delay or failure of the Lessee to pay any such Taxes, costs or expenses.

9.4 Aircraft indemnity

Without prejudice to the Lessee's obligations under this clauses 9, the Lessee agrees at all times, whether before, during or after the Lease Period, to indemnify and hold harmless the Lessor and each indemnitee from and against all costs, expenses, payments, charges, losses, demands, liabilities, claims, actions, proceedings, penalties, fines, damages, judgements, orders or other sanctions (in this clause 9, together referred to as "Losses"), where such Losses arise from events which occur at any time:

(1) *Aircraft*: relating to, or arising directly or indirectly in any manner or for any cause or reason whatsoever out of the Aircraft, the Airframe, any Engine or engine installed on the Aircraft or Part or any Aircraft

Documents or other thing delivered under this Agreement or any other Lessee Document;

(2) *Operational*: relating to, or arising directly or indirectly in any manner or for any cause or reason whatsoever out of, the certification, design, manufacture, testing, delivery, import, export, registration, ownership, possession, control, use, operation, leasing, insurance, maintenance, repair, refurbishment, condition, service, overhaul, modification, change, alteration, loss, damage, removal, storage, re-delivery, sale, purchase or disposition of, in or to the Aircraft, or otherwise in connection with the Aircraft, or relating to loss or destruction of or damage to any property, or death or injury of, or other loss of whatsoever nature suffered by, any person caused by, relating to, or arising from or out of (in each case whether directly or indirectly) any of the foregoing matters;

(3) *Design*: which may at any time be made or brought on the ground that any design, article or material in the Aircraft or the operation or use thereof constitutes an infringement of any patent, intellectual property right or any other right whatsoever;

(4) *Arrest*: which may at any time be incurred by the Lessor or any Indemnitee in preventing or attempting to prevent the arrest, confiscation seizure, taking in execution, impounding, forfeiture or detention of the Aircraft or any enforcement of any encumbrance in respect of the Aircraft, or in securing the release of the Aircraft; and

(5) *Default*: which the Lessor or any indemnitee shall certify as sustained or incurred by it as a consequence of any default by the Lessee in the due and punctual performance of any of its obligations under any of the Lessee Documents or as a consequence of any Relevant Event.

(6) *Preservation*: which the Lessor or any Indemnitee shall certify as sustained or incurred by it as a consequence of preservation and enforcement of the indemnitee's rights under the Lease Documents:

Provided always that, subject to the prior written approval of the Lessor, unless and until a Relevant Event shall have occurred, the Lessee shall be entitled to take, in the name of the Lessor, such action as the Lessee shall see fit to defend or avoid any such Losses as are referred to in this clause 9.4 or to recover the same from any third party, subject to the Lessee first ensuring that the Lessor is indemnified and secured to its reasonable satisfaction against all losses thereby incurred or to be incurred.

9.5 Exceptions to aircraft indemnity

The indemnity provided for in section 9.4 will not extend to any of the following Losses of any Indemnitee:

(1) Losses which would not have occurred but for the gross negligence or willful misconduct of any Indemnitee (other than negligence imputed to such Indemnitee solely by reason of its interest in the Aircraft);

(2) Taxes and Losses which Lessee has expressly not agreed to indemnify against pursuant to the other provisions of this Agreement or any other Lessee Document;

(3) Losses resulting solely from acts or events which occur after the date of return of the Aircraft to Lessor in the condition required and in accordance with the terms of this Agreement after the expiration or termination of the Lease Term, and not attributable to or arising as a consequence of (i) any act, omission, event or circumstance occurring prior to such return or (ii) any default by the Lessee in the due and punctual performance of any of its obligations under any of the Lessee Documents or any Relevant Event;

(4) Losses arising solely as a result of any Lessor's encumbrance; and

(5) Losses arising solely as a result of any sale, transfer or disposition of the Aircraft by or on behalf of the Lessor (including any sale, transfer or disposition of the Aircraft by any trustee or administrator in insolvency proceedings for the Lessor) other than, in any case, any sale, transfer or disposition of the Aircraft following any Relevant Event.

9.6 Duration

Notwithstanding anything to the contrary contained in this Agreement, the indemnities by the Lessee in favour of the Lessor and the other Indemnitees contained in this Agreement shall survive and continue in full force and effect notwithstanding any breach by the Lessor or the Lessee of the terms of this Agreement, the termination of the lease of the Aircraft to the Lessee under this Agreement, the repudiation by the Lessor or the Lessee of this Agreement, or the expiration of the Lease Period by effluxion of time or otherwise.

9.7 Indemnity payments

Moneys becoming due by the Lessee to the Lessor under the indemnities contained in this clause 9 or elsewhere in this Agreement shall be paid on demand made by the Lessor.

Article 10: Taxation

10.1 General indemnities

10.1.1 The Lessee shall pay when due and shall indemnify and hold harmless each Indemnitee for, from and against all Taxes levied, assessed or imposed on or in respect of the Lessee and any Indemnitee, the Aircraft, the Airframe or any engine or part, any payments made under any of the Lessee Documents or any of the transactions contemplated by any of the Lessee Documents or the certification, design, manufacture, testing, delivery, import, export, registration, ownership, possession, control, use, operation, leasing, insurance, maintenance, repair, refurbishment, condition, service, overhaul, modification, change, alteration, loss, damage, removal, storage, re-delivery, sale, purchase or disposition of, in or to the Aircraft, or otherwise in connection with the Aircraft, but, subject to the remaining provisions of this clause 10, excluding in respect of any Indemnitee;

(1) Taxes imposed based on or measured by or with respect to gross or net income (including, without limitation, capital gains taxes, minimum taxes, income taxes collected by withholding and taxes on tax preference items) or receipts (excluding, however, sales, use, rental, license, *ad valorem*, VAT or property taxes or taxes in the nature of the foregoing), or taxes which are capital, doing business, franchise, excess profits, net worth taxes, or Taxes imposed in lieu of an income tax, or interest, additions to tax, penalties, fines or other charges in respect of the foregoing Taxes, in each case imposed on any Indemnitee by any Government Entity in the place of incorporation or principal place of business of any Indemnitee;

(2) Sales or similar transfer taxes imposed on any Indemnitee upon any sale, transfer or disposition (excluding a sale, transfer or disposition following a Relevant Event) by any Indemnitee (including any trustee or administrator in insolvency proceedings for such Indemnitee) of any equitable or legal interest in the Aircraft, Airframe, any engine or Part on this Agreement to any person;

(3) Taxes caused solely by a breach by any Indemnitee of any covenant or by the inaccuracy of any representation or warranty made by such Indemnitee in this Agreement;

(4) Taxes caused solely by the gross negligence or wilful misconduct of any Indemnitee; and

(5) Taxes imposed on any Indemnitee resulting solely from, or which would not have occurred but for, a Lessor's encumbrance created by any Indemnitee.

(6) Taxes imposed as a direct result of the activities of any Indemnitee in any jurisdiction which are unrelated to dealings with the Lessee, transactions contemplated by this Agreement or the other Lessee Documents, the Purchase Agreement or the Sub-Lease, or operation of the Aircraft during the Lease period.

10.1.2 Third party liabilities

If and to the extent that any sum payable to the Lessor or an Indemnitee by the Lessee under any Lessee Document by way of indemnity or reimbursement proves to be insufficient, by reason of any Taxation suffered on that sum, for the Lessor or such Indemnitee to discharge the corresponding liability to a third party, or to reimburse the Lessor or such Indemnitee for the cost incurred by it in discharging the corresponding liability to a third party, the Lessee shall pay the Lessor or such Indemnitee such additional sum as (after taking into account any Taxation suffered by the Lessor on that additional sum) shall be required to make up the relevant deficit.

(**Note.**—In this part of agreement conveyancer should give all the technical details on Taxation liabilities. The same are not given in this model draft for the sake of brevity.)

Article 11: General Undertakings

11.1 The Lessee undertakes with the Lessor:

(1) *Status report*: to provide the Lessor by the 12th Banking Day of every calendar month during the Lease Period, and whenever reasonably requested by the Lessor, with a status report in the form of Schedule 8 in respect of the Aircraft and the engines containing or indicating the matters required in that form;

(2) *Information concerning the aircraft*: promptly to provide the Lessor with such other information regarding the location, operation, use, insurance, maintenance and condition of the Aircraft as the Lessor may from time to time reasonably require, and without prejudice to the generality of the foregoing, shall, if requested, supply the Lessor with copies of any Agreement relating to the Aircraft in the Lessee's possession;

(3) *Inspection*: throughout the Lease Period to permit the Lessor and/or its agents or representatives, and procure that they are afforded all necessary facilities, to inspect or survey the Aircraft at any reasonable time upon giving the Lessee reasonable notice. All time taken in respect of such inspections or surveys shall form part of the Lease Period. The Lessor shall have no duty to make any such inspection or survey and shall not incur any liability or obligation by reason of not making any such inspection. Any inspection conducted hereunder shall not disrupt the normal operation of the Aircraft;

(4) *No operational interest*: to procure that neither the Lessor nor any Relevant Party is at any time represented as carrying goods or passengers on the Aircraft, or as being in any way connected or associated with any operation of carriage which may be undertaken by the Lessee or any other operator of the Aircraft, or as having any operational interest in, or responsibility for, the Aircraft;

(5) *Compliance with insurances*: to comply, and procure compliance by any other operator of the Aircraft, with the terms and conditions of the Insurances, and not do, consent to, or permit any act or omission which might invalidate or render unenforceable the whole or any part of the Insurances;

(6) *Financial statements*: to cause to be prepared in each financial year and cause to be certified by its auditors financial statements and consolidated financial statements required by law which are prepared in accordance with generally accepted accounting principles and practices in .... which have been consistently applied (save as disclosed in the relevant financial statements), and deliver to the Lessor a copy of such audited financial statements as soon as practicable but not later than 180 days after the end of the financial period to which they relate and a copy of every report, notice or like document issued by it to its creditors generally (in each case at the time of issue thereof);

(7) *Information concerning the lessee and the guarantor*: to promptly provide the Lessor with such financial and other information concerning the Lessee and the Guarantor and its affairs material to the performance of its obligations under this Agreement, the Guarantee and the other Lessee Documents as the Lessor may from time to time reasonably require.

(8) *Governmental and other Approvals*: to obtain or cause to be obtained, maintain in full force and effect and comply in all material respects with the conditions and restrictions (if any) imposed in, or in connection with, every consent, authorisation, licence or approval of governmental or public bodies or authorities or courts and do, or cause to be done, all other acts and things, which may from time to time be required or recommended under applicable law for the continued due performance of all its obligations under this Agreement or the other Lessee Documents;

(9) *Disposal of Aircraft*: not to attempt or hold itself out, and procure that any Sub-Lessee will not attempt or hold itself out, as having the power to sell or dispose of the Aircraft;

(10) *Encumbrances*: not to create or suffer to exist Encumbrances (other than Permitted Liens) in respect of the Aircraft;

(11) *Notification of termination event*: promptly inform the Lessor of any occurrence of any Termination Event forthwith upon becoming aware thereof;

(**Note.**—Other technicalities haven't been given in this model draft for the sake of brevity.)

Article 12: Operations and Maintenance

12.1 The Lessee further undertakes with the Lessor that throughout the Lease Period it will, or will procure that any other operator of the Aircraft will, at the Lessee's own cost and expense:

(1) *Certificates and licences*: obtain and maintain in full force and effect all necessary certificates, licences, permits and authorisations required for the use and operation of the Aircraft, including, without limitation, an air operator's certificate, an unrestricted certificate of airworthiness with respect to the Aircraft in the public transport category (passenger) issued by the Aviation Authority, and such certificates of maintenance, review and release to service as are required for the Aircraft to be used for the public transport of passengers and will from time to time provide to the Lessor copies of the same on request;

(2) *Operation and use*:

(a) procure that the Aircraft is used, operated and controlled in accordance with all Applicable laws (including I.A.T.A. regulations) affecting the Aircraft in any jurisdiction and in accordance with all certificates, licences, permits, authorisations and registrations relating to the Aircraft, and regardless of upon whom any of the same are by their terms imposed, and so as not to invalidate any manufacturer's warranties;

(b) procure that the Aircraft will not be used for any purpose for which it is not designed or reasonably suited, or outside the tolerances and limitations for which the Aircraft was designed and will be operated in accordance with the Aircraft Documents and that the Aircraft shall not be utilized for the purposes of (x) the carriage of goods, materials or items which could be reasonably expected to cause damage to the Aircraft or of (y) training, qualifying or reconfirming the status of cockpit personnel, except for the benefit of the Sub-Lessee's cockpit personnel, and then only if the use of the Aircraft for such purpose is not disproportionate to the use for such purpose of other aircraft of the same type operated by the Sub-Lessee;

(c) procure that the Aircraft will not be used for any purpose or in any manner not fully covered by the insurances, or outside any geographical limit imposed by the insurances, or for any illegal purpose or in any illegal manner; and

(d) procure that the Aircraft will be operated only by personnel approved by the Aviation Authority.

Article 13: Aircraft Documents

13.1 Documents and data

All documents and data (including technical and engineering data, calculations and drawings) evidencing or produced in connection with compliance with any of the requirements or procedures set out in this clause 14 shall form a permanent part of the Aircraft Documents.

13.2 Records

The Lessee will procure that accurate, complete and current records of all flights made by, and all maintenance (scheduled or unscheduled) carried out on, the Aircraft (including in relation to each engine, Landing Gear, APU and Part subsequently installed) are kept in such manner as the Aviation Authority may from time to time require, and ensure that they comply with the recommendations of the manufacturers of the Aircraft and any Engine, Landing Gear, APU or Part and shall cause the Sub-Lessee to allow the Lessor and its agents and representatives to inspect the Aircraft Documents at any reasonable time.

13.3 Language

The Aircraft Documents shall be maintained in accordance with the regulations of the Aviation Authority in the english language. All Aircraft Documents shall be in plain language and all coded forms must have cross references, including but not limited to parts numbers, engineering order numbers and service bulletin numbers.

13.4 Regulatory Requirements

The Aircraft Documents shall at a minimum meet all FAA (or their equivalent) or Aviation Authority requirements and shall be prepared and maintained in hard copy format.

13.5 Possession

The Lessee shall keep all Aircraft Documents in its possession and shall not, except as required by any Government Entity or in connection with any judicial tribunal or similar proceedings as notified in advance to the Lessor, permit any other person, agency or vendor to have possession of or control over any of the Aircraft Documents, except with the prior written consent of the Lessor, which consent shall not be unreasonably withheld or delayed.

Article 14: Title and Registration

14.1 Lessor's title

Title to the Aircraft shall remain vested in the Lessor subject to any assignments, charges or other disposals the Lessor may make under clause 23.

14.2 Parts and engines

(1) *Parts*: the Lessee agrees that all Parts at any time installed on the Airframe or any Engine, except borrowed Parts, shall be the property of the Lessor;

(2) *Engines*: the Lessee agrees that all engines at any time installed on or removed from the Airframe shall be and remain the property of the Lessor (save as provided in clause 13.6); and

(3) *Further assurance*: the Lessee shall execute and do all such acts, deeds, assurances or things as may be reasonably required by the Lessor to ensure that all replacement or substitute engines or Parts installed in or attached to the Airframe or any engine shall become and remain part of the Airframe or the relevant Engine and the property of the Lessor and subject to the rights of any Relevant Party.

14.3 Registration

Throughout the Lease Period the Lessee shall ensure that the Aircraft is duly registered in the name of the Lessee and/or Sub-Lessee on the Aircraft Register of the Aviation Authority with the interest of the Lessor as owner thereof and of any Relevant Party noted thereon, as the Lessor may so request and the Lessee shall not do, and shall use its best endeavours to procure that no third party does, any act or thing which might change, prejudice or cancel such registrations, without the prior written consent of Lessor.

Article 15: Insurance

The Lessee covenants and undertakes to comply with the provisions of Parts 1 and 2 of Schedule 5 in respect of the insurances.

Article 16: Loss and Damage

16.1 Pre-delivery

If a Total Loss occurs prior to the delivery of the Aircraft to the Lessee under this Agreement, this Agreement will immediately terminate and, except as expressly stated in this Agreement, neither party will have any further obligation or liability under this Agreement other than pursuant to clause 9.2.

16.2 Post-delivery

Notwithstanding clause 6.1, throughout the Lease Period, the Lessee shall bear the full risk of any loss, destruction, hijacking, theft, condemnation, confiscation, seizure or requisition of or damage to the Aircraft and of any other occurrence of whatever kind which shall deprive the Lessee or the operator of the Aircraft for the time being of the use, possession or enjoyment thereof.

16.3 Information

(1) *Notice*: the Lessee shall give the Lessor immediate notice in writing of the occurrence of any circumstance referred to in clause 17.2 (other than repairable damage the likely cost of rectification of which will not exceed the Damage Notification Threshold) or any other occurrence of whatever kind which shall deprive the Lessee or the operator of the Aircraft for the time being of the use, possession or enjoyment thereof; and

(2) *Information*: the Lessee shall supply to the Lessor all necessary information, documentation and assistance which may be required by the Lessor in connection with making any claim under the Insurances and to the extent the Lessee may make a claim under the Insurances the Lessor shall supply to the Lessee all necessary information, documentation and assistance which may be required by the Lessee in connection with such claim.

16.4 Agreed value, timing of total loss

(1) *Agreed Value*: if the Aircraft shall become a total loss during the Lease Period, the Lessee shall pay, or procure that the insurers or reinsurers pay, to the Lessor or other agreed loss payee under the Insurances on or prior to the earlier to occur of (a) the date falling 30 days (or such longer period as may be agreed in writing by the Lessor) after the date on which the Total Loss is deemed to have occurred as provided, in clause 17.4(2), and (b) the date on which payment is made under the Insurances in respect of such total loss, the agreed value as at the date of payment thereof together with all amounts of Rent and any other amounts then due and payable under the Lessee Documents.

(2) *Timing*: for the purposes of this Agreement a total loss shall be deemed to have occurred:

  (a) in the case of an actual total loss, at or about noon (.................... time) on the actual date the Aircraft was lost or, if such date is not known, noon (.................... time) on the day on which the Aircraft was last heard of;

  (b) in the case of any of the events described in sub-paragraph (1) of the definition of total loss (other than an actual total loss), upon the date that notice claiming the loss of the Aircraft is given to the relevant insurers, unless the insurers do not forthwith admit such claim, when such total loss shall be deemed to have occurred at the date and time at which either a total loss is subsequently admitted by the insurers or a competent court or arbitration tribunal issues a judgment to the effect that a total loss has occurred;

(c) in the case of any of the events described in sub-paragraph (2) of the definition of total loss, upon the date of occurrence of such destruction, damage or cessation;

(d) in the case of compulsory acquisition, upon the date upon which the relevant requisition of title or other compulsory acquisition, requisition, appropriation, expropriation, deprivation or confiscation occurs; and

(e) in the case of any of the events described in sub-paragraph (4) of the definition of total loss, upon the expiry of the period of 180 days referred to in such sub-paragraph (4) after the date upon which the relevant hijacking, theft, condemnation, confiscation, capture, detention, seizure or requisition for use or hire occurred.

16.5 Rent

The Lessee shall continue to pay rent on the days and in the amounts required under this Agreement notwithstanding any total loss; provided always that no further instalments of rent shall become due after the date on which all sums due under clause 17.4(1) shall have been paid in full, and the Lease Period shall terminate on the date of such payment.

Article 17: Requisition

17.1 Continuing obligations

If the Aircraft suffers any hijacking, theft, confiscation, capture, detention, seizure or requisition (excluding any Compulsory Acquisition) (each a "Contingency Event") during the Lease Term then, unless and until the Aircraft becomes a Total loss following such Contingency Event and the Lessee shall have made payment of all sums due pursuant to clause 17.4(1), the lease of the Aircraft to the Lessee under this Agreement shall continue in full force and effect (and if any Contingency Event extends beyond the end of the Lease Term, the leasing of the Aircraft hereunder shall be extended until the Lessee or the Sub-Lessee recovers possession of the Aircraft, but subject always to the provisions of clause 21) and the Lessee shall remain fully responsible for the due compliance with all its obligations under this Agreement (including the payment of Rent in respect of any period of such Contingency Event extending beyond the end of the Lease Term at the higher of the rate at which rent was payable at the end of the Lease Term and the rate which the Lessor certifies to the Lessee is the market rate of rent applicable to the Aircraft (provided that if the Aircraft subsequently becomes a total loss and the Agreed Value is paid to the Lessor pursuant to clause 17, subject to the Lessor not being liable to repay or refund the Agreed Value in accordance with any applicable law, the Lessor shall reimburse to the Lessee without any interest an amount equal to the total Rent so paid by the Lessee during the period during which the leasing of the Aircraft hereunder is extended, or the leasing of the Aircraft is otherwise continued under this Agreement beyond the Lease Term, due to such Contingency Event)) other than such obligations which the Lessee is unable to comply with solely by virtue of such Contingency Event.

17.2 Requisition Compensation

If the Lessee shall duly comply with all its obligations under this Agreement and provided no Relevant Event shall have occurred and be continuing, save as mentioned in clause 18.1, the Lessee shall, during the Lease Period, be entitled to all Requisition Compensation or, subject to clause 18.4, other compensation for any Contingency Event (as defined in clause 18.1) paid to the Lessor or to the Lessee on account of such Contingency Event.

17.3 Condition

The Lessee shall, as soon as practicable after the end of any Contingency Event (as defined in clause 18.1), cause the Aircraft to be put into the condition required by this Agreement and if that Contingency Event has ended prior to the end of the Lease Term by the end of the Lease Term, and where that Contingency Event shall end after the expiry or termination of the Lease Period, the Lessee shall, as soon as practicable, cause the Aircraft to be put into the redelivery condition required by clause 19 and the Lessee shall compensate the Lessor on demand for any Losses (as defined in clause 9.5) incurred or suffered by the Lessor as a consequence of the Aircraft not being redelivered to the Lessor on the date of expiry or termination of the Lease Period as a consequence of such Contingency Event.

17.4 Structural change

The Lessor shall be entitled to all compensation payable in respect of any change in the structure, state or condition of the Aircraft arising during the period of any Contingency Event (as defined in clause 18.1). The Lessor shall apply such compensation in reimbursing the Lessee for the cost of complying with its obligation under clause 18.3: provided always that if a Relevant Event has occurred and is continuing, the Lessor shall be entitled to apply such compensation in or towards settlement of any amounts owing by the Lessee under any Lessee Document.

Article 18: Redelivery

18.1 Delivery and De-registration

At the end of the Lease Period (including, for the avoidance of doubt, where the leasing of the Aircraft is extended pursuant to Clause 18.1, but in any event other than following a total loss) the Lessee at its own expense shall redeliver the Aircraft to the Lessor at the redelivery location, and the Lessee shall pay all expenses, Taxes and duties and provide such assistance as the Lessor may reasonably require in connection with the de-registration and export of the Aircraft from the State of registration.

18.2 Requirements

On redelivery:—

(1) Schedule 7 shall apply and the Lessee shall comply and ensure the Aircraft complies with its provisions;

(2) the condition of the Aircraft shall be such as to demonstrate that the Lessee has in all respects complied with the obligations on its part contained in this Agreement;

(3) the Engines shall be installed on the Aircraft;

(4) the Aircraft shall be free and clear of all Encumbrances other than any Lessor's encumbrance;

18.3 Final inspection

(1) *Notice*: the Lessee shall notify the Lessor of the expected commencement date of the return inspection ("Final Inspection") of the Aircraft not later than 25 Banking Days prior to the expected commencement of the return C or D-Check referred to in clause 1.1(6) of Schedule 7, such scheduled commencement to be finalized 3 Banking Days prior to the actual scheduled commencement. In addition, the Lessor and its duly appointed representatives shall be permitted to be in attendance during the performance of such return C or D-Check.

The Lessee shall notify the Lessor of the schedule for the borescope inspection referred to in clause 19.5 to permit the Lessor and its representatives to be present during the accomplishment of such inspection.

(2) *Availability*: the Aircraft shall be made available to the Lessor and its duly appointed representatives for such period as is reasonably necessary at or around the time of the return C or D-Check referred to in clause 1.1(6) of Schedule 7 in order to perform the Final Inspection and verify that the Aircraft is in compliance with the requirements specified in this Agreement. The Lessor shall cooperate with the Lessee to minimise the time required for the final inspection.

(3) *Inspections*: during the Final Inspection, the Lessor and its representatives shall be permitted to:—

(a) inspect the Aircraft Documents;

(b) inspect the Aircraft and uninstalled Parts;

(c) be present during a complete video borescope inspection.

(4) *Discrepancies*: the Final Inspection shall be conducted in accordance with the specifications and requirements of the Manufacturer's maintenance manuals as a standard. Any item or discrepancy resulting from the inspection which is found to be non-compliant with the limitations and requirements specified in this Agreement or manufacturer's manuals and documents shall mean that the Aircraft is not in the condition required by this Agreement.

(5) *Manufacturer's manuals*: non-compliance with the Manufacturer's maintenance manual requirements will be viewed as a condition of non-airworthiness.

Article 19: Termination Events

19.1 The Lessor and the Lessee agree that it is a fundamental term and condition of this Agreement that none of the following events or circumstances shall occur during the Lease Period and that the occurrence of any of the following events and/or circumstances shall constitute a repudiatory breach of this Agreement.

(1) *Non-payment*: the Lessee fails to pay any sum due from it under this Agreement or any other Lessee Document in the currency and in the manner stipulated in this Agreement or, as the case may be, such Lessee Document on the due date therefor (and so that, for this purpose, sums payable on demand shall be treated as having been paid on the due date if paid within 5 Banking Days of demand); or

(2) *Insurances*: the Insurances are not obtained and maintained in full force and effect in accordance with the provisions of Schedule 5; or

(3) *Breach*: the Lessee or the Guarantor commits any breach of or omits to observe any of the obligations or undertakings expressed to be assumed by it under any Lessee Document [other than those referred to in clauses 20.1(1) and 20.1(2) above] and, in respect of any such breach or omission which in the opinion of the Lessor is capable of remedy, such action as the Lessor may require shall not have been taken within 14 days of the Lessor notifying the Lessee or the Guarantor of such default in writing and of such required action;

(4) *Representations*: any representation or warranty made or deemed to be made or repeated by the Lessee or the Guarantor in or pursuant to any of the Lessee Documents is or proves to have been incorrect in any material respect; or

(5) *Consents*: any consent, authorisation, licence or approval of, or registration with or declaration to, governmental or public bodies or authorities or courts required by the Lessee or the Guarantor to authorise, or required by the Lessee or the Guarantor in connection with, the execution, delivery, validity, enforceability or admissibility in evidence of any of the Lessee Documents or the performance by the Lessee or the Guarantor of its obligations under any of the Lessee Documents is modified in a manner unacceptable to the Lessor or is not granted or is revoked or terminated or expires and is not renewed or otherwise ceases to be in full force and effect; or

(6) *Voluntary proceedings*: the Lessee or the Guarantor shall (a) commence any proceeding or file any petition seeking relief under any applicable bankruptcy, corporate reorganization, insolvency, liquidation or other similar Applicable Law, (b) consent to or acquiesce in the institution of, or fail to contravene in a timely and appropriate manner, any such proceeding or the filing of any such petition, (c) apply for or consent to the appointment of a receiver, trustee, examiner, administrator, custodian, sequestrator or similar official for itself or for a substantial part of its respective property or assets, (d) file an answer admitting the

material allegations of a petition filed against it in any such proceeding, (e) propose or enter into any composition or other arrangement, or make a general assignment, for the benefit of creditors, (f) suspend payments on or become unable, admit in writing its inability or fail generally to pay, any material portion of its debts as they become due, (g) seek its own liquidation, re-organization, dissolution or winding up, (h) take steps to agree with its creditors a composition, extension or adjustment of any borrowed money or (i) take any corporate action for the purpose of effecting any of the foregoing; or

(7) *Involuntary proceedings*: a proceeding shall be commenced or a petition shall be filed, in either case, without the consent or application of the Lessee or the Guarantor, as the case may be, seeking (a) relief in respect of the Lessee or the Guarantor, as the case may be, or of a substantial part of its respective property or assets under any applicable bankruptcy, insolvency, receivership or similar applicable law, (b) the appointment of a receiver, trustee, examiner, administrator, custodian, sequestrator or similar official for the Lessee or the Guarantor, as the case may be, or for a substantial part of its respective property or assets or (c) the liquidation, reorganisation, dissolution or winding up of the Lessee or the Guarantor, as the case may be,; and such proceeding or petition shall continue undismissed for 45 days or an order or decree approving or ordering any of the foregoing is made, provided however that to the extent the Lessee or the Guarantor, as the case may be, can demonstrate to the Lessor's satisfaction (the Lessor acting reasonably and after consultation with independent English counsel) that any such action is frivolous, vexatious or an abuse of process of the court, then such action shall not be regarded as falling within this clause 20.1(7); or there occurs, in relation to the Lessee or the Guarantor, as the case may be, in any country or territory in which any of them carries on business, or to the jurisdiction of whose courts any part of their respective assets is subject, any event which, in the reasonable opinion of the Lessor, appears in that country or territory to correspond with, or have an effect equivalent or similar to, any of the events mentioned in clause 20.1(6), 20.1(7), 20.1(8) or 20.1(9), or the Lessee or the Guarantor, as the case may be, otherwise becomes subject in any such country or territory to the operation of any law relating to insolvency, bankruptcy or liquidation;

(8) *Cessation of business*: the Lessee or the Guarantor suspends or ceases to carry on a substantial part of its business; or

(9) *Nationalisation*: all or a material part of the undertakings, assets, rights or revenues of, or shares or other ownership interests in, the Lessee or the Guarantor are seized, nationalised, expropriated or compulsorily acquired by or under the authority of any Government Entity; or

Article 20: Lessor's Rights following a termination event
20.1 Rights

At any time after the occurrence of any Termination Event (and provided that the same is continuing) the Lessor may, by notice to the Lessee, immediately terminate the Lease Period (whereupon, as the Lessee hereby agrees and acknowledges, the Lessee's right, to possess and operate the Aircraft, along with any other interest provided under this Agreement, shall terminate) and retake possession of the Aircraft (and the Lessee shall immediately return the Aircraft to the Lessor in the condition required by this Agreement (including clause 19 and Schedule 7)), and the Lessee agrees that the Lessor may for this purpose enter upon any premises where the Aircraft or any part thereof may be located, and, subject to the Lessor's duty to mitigate, the Lessee shall pay to the Lessor forthwith upon such termination (or where any sums cannot be then determined by the Lessor or where the Lease Period has already terminated, upon determination) such sum as shall equal the aggregate of:

(1) all amounts due under the Lessee Documents as shall then be due and payable and remain outstanding;

(2) all losses incurred by the Lessor in connection with such Termination Event including, without prejudice to the generality of the foregoing, (x) all costs and expenses incurred in recovering possession of the Aircraft, and in carrying out any works or modifications required to bring the Aircraft up to the condition required by this Agreement upon redelivery and (y) any loss suffered by the Lessor because of the Lessor's inability to place the Aircraft on lease with another lessee on terms as favourable to the Lessor as this Agreement or because whatever use, if any, to which the Lessor is able to put the Aircraft upon its return to the Lessor, or the funds arising upon a sale or other disposal of the Aircraft, does not yield to the Lessor revenue or income equivalent to the sums which would otherwise have been recoverable by it under or pursuant to this Agreement had the Lessee returned the Aircraft to the Lessor strictly in accordance with the provisions of this Agreement;

(3) any loss suffered by the Lessor because of the Lessor's inability to place the Aircraft on lease with another lessee on terms as favourable to the Lessor as this Agreement or because whatever use, if any, to which the Lessor is able to put the Aircraft upon its return to the Lessor, or the funds arising upon a sale or other disposal of the Aircraft, does not yield to the Lessor revenue or income equivalent to the sums which would otherwise have been recoverable by it under or pursuant to this Agreement had the Lease Period not been terminated;

(4) any losses, premium, penalty or expense which may be incurred in repaying funds raised to finance the Aircraft or in unwinding any swap, forward interest rate agreement or other financial instrument relating in whole or in part to the Lessor's financing of the Aircraft ; and

(5) all liabilities, losses, costs and expenses incurred by the Lessor under agreements with any Relevant Party providing finance to the Lessor in connection with, or as a consequence of, such termination.

20.2 Cure rights

If the Lessee fails to comply with any of its obligations under this Agreement or any other Lessee Document the Lessor may, without being in any way obliged so to do, or responsible for so doing, and without prejudice to the ability of the Lessor to treat that non-compliance as a Termination Event, effect compliance on the Lessee's behalf, and if the Lessor incurs any expenditure in effecting such compliance the Lessor shall be entitled (without prejudice to clause 21.1) to recover such expenditure from the Lessee).

20.3 Termination on change of ownership

If any single person, or group of persons, acquire (a) more than half in nominal value of the equity share capital of the Lessee or (b) control of the Lessee, in each case without the previous consent in writing of the Lessor, such consent not to be unreasonably withheld (and for the purposes of this clause 21.3, "control" means the power to direct the management and policy of the Lessee whether by control of the composition of the board of directors (or similar governing body) of the Lessee or of the voting capital of the Lessee, by contract or otherwise), then the Lessor shall be entitled to terminate the leasing of the Aircraft under this Agreement by not less than .... Banking Days notice to the Lessee, such notice to be given not later than .... days after the earlier of (i) the time when the Lessor became aware of such change of control, and (ii) receipt by the Lessor from the Lessee of notice of change of control. The Lessee shall notify such change of control to the Lessor immediately upon the occurrence thereof.

20.4 Continuation

All the indemnities and the Lessor's rights contained in this Agreement will continue in full force after the expiry date, notwithstanding the termination of this Agreement or of the leasing of the Aircraft for any reason whatsoever and notwithstanding the cessation of business of the Lessee, dissolution of the Lessee or any other event, fact or circumstance of any kind whatsoever whether similar to the foregoing or not.

20.5 Illegality

Following the occurrence of a Relevant Event described in clause 20.1(11) but without prejudice to the Lessor's rights under this clause 21, the Lessor shall consult in good faith with the Lessee regarding the steps (if any) that may be taken to restructure the transaction to avoid that unlawfulness. Notwithstanding the foregoing, the Lessor shall not be obliged to take such steps and avoid that unlawfulness.

Article 21: Notices

Save as otherwise expressly, provided in this Agreement, every notice, request, demand or other communication under this Agreement shall:—

(1) be in writing by mail, courier or delivered personally or by or by facsimile, and shall be effective on receipt;

(2) be deemed to have been received, subject as otherwise provided in this Agreement or any other Lessee Document, in the case of a facsimile upon receipt at the number specified below (provided that, if the time of despatch is not within normal business hours on a Banking Day in the country of the addressee it shall be deemed to have been received at the opening of business on the next such Banking Day), and in the case of a letter, when delivered personally or by mail or courier to the following address:

(3) be sent:

    (a) to the Lessee at:

        Address: ....

        ....

        ....

        Attention: ....

        Facsimile: ....

        Telephone: ....

    (b) to the Lessor at:

        Address: ....

        ....

        ....

        Attention: ....

        Facsimile: ....

        Telephone: ....

or to such other address, telex or facsimile number as is notified by one party to the other under this Agreement.

        with a copy to Crédit....................

        Address: ....

        ....

        ....

        Attention: ....

        Facsimile: ....

        Telephone: ....

Article 22: Assignment, Transfer

22.1 The Lessee may not assign or otherwise transfer any of its rights or obligations under this Agreement or any other Lessee Document without the prior written consent of the Lessor.

22.2 Lease assignment/novation

(1) The Lessor may assign or novate all or any of its rights and/or obligations under the Lessee Documents and in the Aircraft pursuant to a sale, financing arrangements or otherwise (and the Lessee hereby consents to such assignment or novation and to any steps for any sale or financing arrangements or otherwise, subject to the following) and the Lessor will, in the case of an assignment or novation other than by way of security, have no further obligation under a Lessee Document following the assignment or novation of all its rights and/or obligations under such Lessee Document but notwithstanding that assignment will remain entitled to the benefit of each indemnity under such Lessee Document, as will each Indemnitee.

(2) No such assignment or novation will result in a material change in the terms of a Lessee Document, any prejudice to the Lessee's operation of the Aircraft, any overall diminution in the Lessee's rights hereunder or any increase in the Lessee's overall obligations hereunder or impose on the Lessee any additional expense or cost not reimbursed by the Lessor (and where any such assignment or novation would do so, the Lessor shall not assign or novate without the prior written consent of the Lessee, such consent not to be unreasonably withheld), and the Lessee shall receive from any successor or assignee of the Lessor a letter of quiet enjoyment addressed to the Lessee acknowledging the Lessee's rights and interest in and to the use and operation of the Aircraft under this Agreement.

(3) The Lessee will comply with all reasonable requests of the Lessor, its successors and assigns in respect of any such assignment or novation, including without limitation the provision and execution of any documents and the making of any filings or registrations which the Lessor or any of its successors or assigns may reasonably require, the Lessor will promptly notify the Lessee of any assignment or novation, and the Lessee shall continue to name the Lessor as an additional assured in the liability insurances for a period of .... years after the date of such assignment or novation.

22.3 Financing

(1) Without prejudice to any other rights of the Lessor under this clause 23, the Lessee hereby acknowledges that the Lessor may enter into certain financing arrangements with respect to the Aircraft and consents to any such steps as the Lessor may require in order to facilitate or effect such financing, including, without limitation, the execution of any documents.

(2) No such financing arrangements will result in a material change in the terms of any Lessee Document, any prejudice to the Lessee's operation of the Aircraft, any overall diminution in the Lessee's rights hereunder, any overall increase in the Lessee's obligations hereunder or impose on the Lessee (other than in respect of the Lessor Assignment or the Mortgage and save as expressly provided herein) any additional expense or cost not reimbursed by the Lessor (and where any such assignment or novation would do so, the Lessor shall not assign or novate without the prior written consent of the Lessee, such consent not to be unreasonably withheld).

(3) The Lessee will at the cost and expense of the Lessor comply with all reasonable requests of the Lessor, its successors and assigns in respect of any such financing arrangements, including without limitation the provision and execution of any documents and the making of any filings or registrations which the Lessor may reasonably require and any amendment to the Insurances to protect Relevant Parties and their interests.

22.4 Costs and expenses

Provided no Relevant Event has occurred and is continuing and save as expressly provided herein, the Lessor agrees to pay the actual reasonable costs and expenses incurred by the Lessee in complying with any request of the Lessor under this clauses 23.2 and 23.3.

22.5 Benefit of Agreement

The agreements, covenants, obligations and liabilities contained in this Agreement or any other Lessee Document, including, but not limited to, all obligations to pay Rent and indemnify the Lessor, are made for the benefit of the Lessor, any assignee or transferee of the Lessor and their respective successors and assigns.

22.6 Third Parties

Any person which is a Relevant Party from time to time shall be entitled to enforce such terms of this Agreement as provide for the obligations of the Lessee to such Relevant Party, subject to the provisions of clause 25 of this Agreement and the Contracts (Rights of Third Parties) Act, 1999 (the "Third Parties Act"). The Third Parties Act applies to this Agreement as set out in this clause 23.6. Save as provided, above a person who is not a party to this Agreement has the right to use the Third Parties Act to enforce any term of this Agreement.

Article 23: Miscellaneous

23.1 Entire agreement

The Lessee Documents (together with all documents which are required by their terms to be entered into by the parties or any of them) contains the entire agreement and understanding between the Lessor and the Lessee relating to the leasing of the Aircraft, and the terms and conditions of the Lessee Documents shall not be varied otherwise than by an instrument in writing of even date herewith or subsequent hereto executed by or on behalf of the Lessor and the Lessee.

23.2 Rights, waivers and consents

(1) The powers, rights and remedies conferred on the Lessor under this Agreement and the other Lessee Documents are cumulative and are additional to, and not exclusive of, any powers, rights or remedies provided by law or otherwise available to it.

(2) No waiver shall be effective unless specifically made in writing and signed by a duly authorised officer of the Lessor.

(3) Subject to clause 24.2(4), neither the single or partial exercise or temporary or partial waiver by the Lessor of any right, nor the failure by the Lessor to exercise in whole or in part any right or to insist on the strict performance of any provision of this Agreement or any other Lessee Document, nor the discontinuance, abandonment or adverse determination of any proceedings taken by the Lessor to enforce any right or any such provision shall (except for the period or to the extent covered by any such temporary or partial waiver) operate as a waiver of, or preclude any exercise or enforcement or (as the case may be) further or other exercise or enforcement by the Lessor of, that or any other right or provision.

(4) clause 24.2(3) is without prejudice to clause 21 and to the time limits in clause 20 (for which purposes time shall be of the essence). All references in clause 24.2(3):—

(a) to any right shall include any power, right or remedy conferred by this Agreement or any other Lessee Document on, or provided by law or otherwise available to, the Lessor;

(b) to any failure to do something shall include any delay in doing it; and

(c) to the giving by the Lessor of any consent to any act which by the terms of this Agreement or any other Lessee Document requires such consent shall not prejudice the Lessor's right to withhold or give consent to the doing of any similar act.

23.3 Time of essence

Subject to the periods of grace referred to in clause 20, time shall be of the essence of this Agreement as regards any time, date or period, whether as originally fixed or altered by Agreement between all the Parties or in any other manner provided in this Agreement, for the performance by the Lessee of its obligations under this Agreement.

23.4 English language

All certificates, instruments and other documents to be delivered under or supplied in connection with this Agreement or any other Lessee Document shall be in the English language or shall be accompanied by a certified English translation upon which the Lessor shall be entitled to rely.

23.5 Counterparts

This Agreement may be entered into in the form of any number of counterparts, each executed by at least one of the parties and, provided that all the parties shall so enter into this Agreement, each of the executed counterparts, when duly exchanged or delivered, shall be deemed to be an original, but, taken together, they shall constitute one instrument.

23.6 Severability

Each provision of this Agreement and each of the other Lessee Documents is severable and distinct from the others and, if any provision is or at any time becomes to any extent or in any circumstances invalid, illegal or unenforceable for any reason, it shall to that extent or in those circumstances, be deemed not to form part of this Agreement or, as the case may be, such other Lessee Document but (except to that extent or in those circumstances in the case of that provision) the validity, legality and enforceability of that and all other provisions of this Agreement or, as the case may be, such other Lessee Document, shall not be affected or impaired, it being the parties' intention that every provision of this Agreement or such other Lessee Document shall be and remain valid and enforceable to the fullest extent permitted by law.

23.7 Delegation

The Lessor may delegate to any person or persons all or any of the trusts, powers or discretions vested in it by any Lessee Document and any such delegation may be made upon such terms and conditions and subject to such regulations (including power to sub-delegate) as the Lessor in its absolute discretion thinks fit.

23.8 Appropriation

If any sum paid or recovered in respect of the liabilities of the Lessee under the Lessee Documents is less than the amounts then due, the Lessor may apply that sum to amounts due under the Lessee Documents in such proportions and order and generally in such manner as the Lessor may determine.

23.9 Set-off

The Lessor may set-off any matured obligation owed by the Lessee under any Lessee Document or any other agreement between the Lessor and the Lessee (each an "Other Agreement") against any obligation (whether or not matured) owed by the Lessor to the Lessee, regardless of the place of payment or currency. If the obligations are in different currencies, the Lessor may convert either obligation at the market rate of exchange available in .... (Name of the place) or, at its option, ... (Name of the place) for the purpose of the set-off. If an obligation is unascertained or unliquidated, the Lessor may in good faith estimate that obligation and set-off in respect of the estimate (of which estimate Lessor will notify Lessee along with documentation in support of the calculated estimate), subject to the relevant party accounting to the other when the obligation is ascertained or liquidated. The Lessor will not be obliged to pay amounts to the Lessee under any Lessee Document or any other Agreement so long as any sums which are then due to the Lessor by the Lessee under any Lessee Document or any other Agreement remain unpaid and any such amounts which would otherwise be due will fall due only if and when the Lessee has paid all such sums except to the extent the Lessor otherwise agrees or sets off such amounts against such payment pursuant to the foregoing.

23.10 No implied waivers; rights cumulative

(1) No failure on the part of the Lessor to exercise and no delay in exercising any right, power, remedy or privilege under any Lessee Document or provided by statute or at law or in equity or otherwise shall impair, prejudice or constitute a waiver of any such right, power, remedy or privilege or be construed as a waiver of any Termination Event or as an acquiescence thereto, nor shall any

single or partial exercise of any such right, power, remedy or privilege impair, prejudice or preclude any other or further exercise thereof or the exercise of any other right, power, remedy or privilege. No acceptance of partial payment or performance shall, whether or not expressly stated, be or be deemed to be a waiver of any Termination Event then existing or a waiver or release of full payment and performance. No notice to or demand on the Lessee shall in any case entitle the Lessee to any other or further notice or demand in other or similar circumstances or constitute a waiver of the right of the Lessor to any other or further action in any circumstances without notice or demand.

(2) Nothing contained in any Lessee Document shall be construed to limit in any way any right, power, remedy or privilege of the Lessor hereunder or under any Lessee Document to which the Lessee is a party or now or hereafter existing at law or in equity. Each and every right, power, remedy and privilege of the Lessor in respect of the Lessee under the Lessee Documents to which the Lessee is a party (a) shall be in addition to and not in limitation of, or in substitution for, any other right, power, remedy or privilege under any Lessee Document to which the Lessee is a party or at law or in equity, (b) may be exercised from time to time or simultaneously and as often and in such order as may be deemed expedient by the Lessor and (c) shall be cumulative and not mutually exclusive, and the exercise of one shall not be deemed a waiver of the right to exercise any other to the extent permitted by Applicable Law.

(3) The rights and remedies of the Lessor provided in this Agreement and the other Lessee Documents are cumulative and are not exclusive of any rights and remedies provided by law.

23.11 Non disclosure

Lessor and Lessee agree that neither party will disclose the terms of this Agreement or any information derived as a result of the discussions, negotiations, or any writing relating to this Agreement, including, but not limited to documentation or information delivered to either party in accordance with the terms of this Agreement, to any third Party, without the prior written consent of the non-disclosing party, except (i) as may be required by applicable laws or governmental regulations, (ii) as may be necessary in connection with any enforcement of the terms and conditions of this Agreement, (iii) any disclosure to Relevant Parties, or (iv) any disclosure to any adviser to the parties hereto or the Relevant Parties. In the event such disclosure is required by applicable law or governmental regulation, the party disclosing the information shall exercise its best efforts to obtain from the entity to whom such disclosure is made its agreement to be subject to the obligations with respect to non-disclosure as contained herein.

Lessee agrees to indemnify, defend and hold harmless Lessor against any and all liability, loss or damage, together with all reasonable costs related thereto (including legal fees and expenses) arising from any breach resulting from an unauthorized disclosure of information under this clause by Lessee or any of its directors, officers, agents, or employees.

Lessor agrees to indemnify, defend and hold harmless Lessee against any and all liability, loss or damage, together with all reasonable costs related thereto (including legal fees and expenses) arising from any breach resulting from an unauthorized disclosure of information under this clause by Lessor or any of its directors, officers, agents, or employees.

Article 24: Law and Jurisdiction

24.1 Law

This Agreement is governed by and shall be construed in accordance with the Governing Law.

24.2 Dispute resolution and arbitration

(1) For the benefit of each of the parties hereto, each of the Lessor and the Lessee agrees that the courts of .... are to have non-exclusive jurisdiction to settle any disputes arising out of or relating to this Agreement and each submits itself and its property to the non-exclusive jurisdiction of the foregoing courts with respect to such disputes.

(2) Without prejudice to any other method of service, (a) the Lessee hereby irrevocably designates, appoints and empowers ....(address) at present of .... (Address) to receive for it and on its behalf service of process issued in connection with any proceedings in .... courts arising out of or in connection with this Agreement and/or any other Lessee Document and (b) the Lessor hereby irrevocably designates, appoints, and empowers .... at present of .... (address) to receive for it and on its behalf service of process issued in connection with any proceedings in .... courts arising out of or in connection with this Agreement and/or any other Lessee Document.

(3) Lessor and Lessee undertake to procure that letters of acceptance from each entity designated to receive service of process for the respective party, will be received by the recipient party, within .... days of execution of this Agreement.

24.3 Immunity

(1) The Lessee agrees that in any legal action or proceedings against it or its assets in connection with this Agreement and/or any other Lessee Document no immunity from such legal action or proceedings (which shall include, without limitation, suit, attachment prior to judgment, other attachment, the obtaining of judgment, execution or other enforcement) shall be claimed by or on behalf of the Lessee or with respect to its assets, irrevocably waives any such right of immunity which it or its assets now have or may hereafter acquire or which may be attributed to it or its assets and consents generally in respect of any such legal action or proceedings to the giving of any relief or the issue of any process in connection with such action or proceedings including, without limitation, the making, enforcement or execution against any property whatsoever, (irrespective of its use or intended use) of any order or judgment which may be made or given in such action or proceedings.

(2) The Lessor agrees that in any legal action or proceedings against it or its assets in connection with this Agreement, no immunity from such legal action or proceedings shall be claimed by or on behalf of the Lessor.

Article 25: Waiver and Disclaimer

25.1 The lessee expressly agrees and acknowledges that, save only as expressly provided in clause 6.1, no condition, warranty or representation of any kind is or has been given by or on behalf of the lessor in respect of the aircraft or any part thereof, and accordingly the lessee confirms that it has not, in entering into this agreement, relied on any condition, warranty or representation by the lessor or any person on the lessor's or any relevant party's behalf, express or implied, whether arising by law or otherwise in relation to the aircraft or any part thereof, including, without limitation, warranties or representations as to the description, airworthiness, suitability, quality, merchantability, fitness for any purpose, value, state, condition, appearance, safety, durability, design or operation of any kind or nature of the aircraft or any part thereof, and the benefit of any such condition, warranty or representation by the lessor or any relevant party is hereby irrevocably and unconditionally waived by the lessee. To the extent permissible under applicable law, the lessee hereby also waives any rights which it may have in tort in respect of any of the matters referred to above and irrevocably agrees that neither the lessor nor any relevant party shall have any greater liability in tort in respect of any such matter than it would have in contract after taking account of all of the foregoing exclusions. No third party making any representation or warranty relating to the aircraft or any part thereof is the agent of the lessor nor has any such third party authority to bind the lessor thereby. Notwithstanding anything contained above, nothing contained herein is intended to obviate, remove or waive any rights of warranty or other claims relating thereto which the lessee or the lessor may have against the manufacturer or supplier of the aircraft or any third party.

25.2 Confirmation

Lessee confirms that it is fully aware of the provisions of this clause and acknowledges that rent and other amounts have been calculated notwithstanding its provisions.

IN WITNESS whereof the parties hereto have caused this Agreement to be duly executed the day and year first above written.

EXECUTED and DELIVERED
for and on behalf of
Beta
By:....................
Title:....................
Location:....................
Witnessed By:....................
EXECUTED and DELIVERED
for and on behalf of

Alpha
By:....................
Title:....................
Location:....................
Witnessed By:....................

SCHEDULE 1
PART 1
DESCRIPTION OF AIRCRAFT

PART 2
AIRCRAFT DOCUMENTS

SCHEDULE 2
LIST OF DOCUMENTS AND EVIDENCE

SCHEDULE 3
PART 1
AIRCRAFT DELIVERY CONDITIONS

PART 2
ACCEPTANCE CERTIFICATE

SCHEDULE 4
RENT INSTALMENTS DURING LEASE TERM

SCHEDULE 5
PART 1
INSURANCE REQUIREMENTS

PART 2
INSURANCE REQUIREMENTS

SCHEDULE 6
FORM OF BROKERS' LETTER OF UNDERTAKING
[Insurance Brokers Letterhead]

SCHEDULE 7
OPERATING CONDITION AT REDELIVERY

SCHEDULE 8
MONTHLY AIRCRAFT UTILISATION & STATUS REPORT

CHAPTER 12
TRUST

SYNOPSIS

THE GOVERNING LEGISLATION
    The Nature of an Indian Trust
    Requirements of a Trust
        Trust deed
        Complete constitution of a trust
    Legislation relating to trusts
    Trustees
    Trustees' Duties

REGULATORY ENVIRONMENT AND LIMITATION ON TRUSTS
    Courts
    Breach of Trust
    Limitation on trusts
        Perpetuities and accumulations
        Remuneration
        Exoneration clauses
        Public policy
    Who can act as a trustee?

REASONS FOR THE CREATION OF TRUSTS AND THEIR USES
    Personal or Private Trusts
    Pension and employee benefits
    Collective investment schemes
    Charities
    Non-Charitable Purpose Trusts

CONCLUSION

PRECEDENTS
- Agenda of meeting of Board of Trustees
- Appointment of additional members to Board of Trustees
- Deed of Family Trust Settlement
- Rules and Regulations Governing the Management of "Nature For Children"
- Trust Deed
- Alteration of A Trust Deed

The Governing Legislation

The Nature of an Indian Trust

The *Indian Trusts Act, 1882* (hereinafter referred to as "the Act") defines a trust as "an obligation annexed to the ownership of property, and arising out of a confidence reposed in and accepted by the owner, or declared and accepted by him, for the benefit of another, or of another and the owner."

The basic classification of trusts in India is between private and public trusts, the Act only being applicable to the former. The latter (public trusts and public charitable trusts) are governed by other legislation such as the *Charitable & Religious Trusts Act, 1920*; the *Religious Endowments Act, 1863* and the *Bombay Public Trusts Act, 1950*. Since a study of charitable trusts is beyond the scope of this chapter, attention has been focused here on private trusts.

The distinction between a private and public trust is that whereas in the former the beneficiaries are specific individuals, in the latter they are the general public or a class thereof. Thus, in the former the beneficiaries are persons who are ascertained or capable of being ascertained, in the latter they constitute a body, which is incapable of being ascertained. It is to be noted that the above definition does not set forth any distinction between an equitable and legal ownership.

The person who reposes or declares the confidence is called the "author of the trust"; the person who accepts the confidence is called the "trustee"; the person for whose benefit the confidence is accepted is called the "beneficiary"; the subject matter of the trust is called "trust property" or "trust money"; the "beneficial interest" or "interest" of the beneficiary is his right against the trustee as owner of the trust property; and the instrument, if any, by which the trust is declared is called the "instrument of trust".

Requirements of a Trust

Certainty

In general, the creation of a trust necessitates:
- certainty of words;
- certainty of subject-matter; and
- certainty of objects.

Courts look at the intention conveyed through the words used in a trust rather than the form in which it is created. Indeed, no particular form is required for creation of the trust. If an intention to create a trust can be deduced without ambiguity, the court will give effect to that intention. The persons stated in the trust deed should be certain or capable of being rendered certain. The subject matter may not be considered uncertain by the courts only because it does not contain a quantified description.

Under the Act, in order to create a valid trust, an author of the trust should indicate with reasonable certainty by any words or acts:

(a) an intention on his part to create a trust;
(b) the purpose of the trust;
(c) the beneficiary; and
(d) the trust property.

Unless the trust is created by a will or the author of the trust himself is to be the trustee, he should transfer the trust property to the trustee.

Trust deed

Although the conventional way of creating a trust is by written document, there is no general requirement that it must only be created by deed or in writing. The interpretation of trust under the Act says that ".... and the instrument, *if any*, by which the trust is declared is called the instrument of trust." However, where it concerns an immovable property, no trust in relation to such immovable property is valid unless declared by a non-testamentary instrument in writing, signed by the author of the trust or the trustees, and registered; or by the will of the author of the trust. A trust can be created orally, it can be imposed by statute and it can be imposed by a court as a result of the conduct of the parties (a constructive trust). However, wherever possible the use of a professionally drafted trust deed is recommended.

A significant proportion of personal trusts still arise by Will. In this connection, it should also be said that under some circumstances the laws of intestacy impose a trust on the estates of those who die without a valid Will. These trusts can be for minor beneficiaries, usually children and the surviving spouse of the deceased. The requirements for, and conduct and administration of Will and intestacy trusts is the same as for *inter vivos* or lifetime settlements.

Complete constitution of a trust

Under the Act the creation of a trust is complete when the author indicates the intention, purpose, etc., as mentioned above, and transfers the trust property to the trustee, unless the trust is declared by a Will or the author himself is to be the trustee. A trust is created only if the settlor manifests clear intention to that effect. The manifestation of intention may be by written or spoken words or by conduct. No particular form of words or conduct is necessary.

Although the creation of a trust includes the transferring of the trust property to the trustee, there is no requirement that in order to be valid; a trust must have a trustee. A trust will not fail for lack of a trustee and if no trustee is appointed or if the deed does not provide for further trustees, the statute or, ultimately, the court will provide for the appointment or appoint one. Where a composition deed is executed by the debtor who has earmarked some immovable properties for payment of debts, the names of debtors also being mentioned, such deed is a constructive trust and does not fail because no trustee is named.[1]

Legislation relating to trusts

The principal statute relating to private trusts, which is the focus of this Chapter, is the *Indian Trusts Act, 1882*. This statute provides administrative powers for the trustees that are additional to the powers in the deed, but are subject to any restrictions if any in the deed.

It should be stressed that most modern trust deeds do not rely on the statutory administrative powers available to trustees. The current approach, in professionally drafted deeds, is to confer on trustees such powers of administration wide or narrow as may be appropriate to the size and purpose of

---

1. *Ebrahim Peer Mohamed* v. *K. Gopal Bagree*, AIR 1937 Cal 180.

the trust. This is especially true for investment powers, given the very limited list of permitted investments set out in the Act.[1]

Trustees

In general, any individual, limited company or other corporation may act as a trustee. The Act provides that every person capable of holding property may be a trustee. It further provides that "where the trust involves the exercise of discretion, he cannot execute it unless he is competent to contract". Therefore, the person should be mentally competent and of age. Curiously, a minor can become a trustee by circumstances - a constructive trustee - but cannot be expressly appointed as a trustee as under Indian law, a minor is not capable to be a trustee as he is not competent to contract. The Act does not forbid the beneficiary of a trust from being appointed as trustee. But, as a general rule, it is advisable to avoid appointing a beneficiary as a trustee as there may arise a conflict between his interest and his duty. It has been held by courts that the same person may be both a trustee and a beneficiary.[2]

There is no bar to a non-resident acting as a trustee although it is questionable if someone outside the country should act in this capacity, given the difficulty of enforcing the terms of the trust against a trustee who is out of the jurisdiction.[3] This is only a permissive ground, not a mandatory disqualification, and requires an application to court. This is clarified by a statutory illustration, which provides that where a trustee goes to reside permanently out of India, the beneficiary may institute a suit to have such trustee removed and to appoint a new trustee in his place. Section 73 of the Act provides that where a person appointed as a trustee is absent from India for a continuous period of six months or leaves India for the purpose of residing abroad a new trustee may be appointed in his place.

Unless the trust deed restricts the number, there is no restriction under law on the number of persons who may be appointed trustees. When the administration of the trust involves the receipt and custody of money, the minimum number of trustees should be two.[4]

A trustee will contract for all services to be provided for the trust in his personal capacity. Lenders to a trust, have no original right to claim payment of their debts out of the trust estate even though they may have made such payments against the requisition of the trustee. The remedy of creditors is against the trustee as an individual. The personal funds of the trustee are at risk and despite the trustee's right to be reimbursed for all properly incurred debts on behalf of the trust, if the trust funds are insufficient the trustee will not be reimbursed. A decree will be passed against the trustee personally who has made the contract or borrowed the money. It may also be enforced against his

---

1. Section 20.
2. *M.C. Mohapatra* v. *R. Mohapatra*, AIR 1951 Ori 132.
3. This point is recognised by *Explanation* 1 to section 60 of the Act, which provides that a person domiciled abroad is not a proper trustee.
4. *Explanation* II to section 60 of the Act.

beneficial interest in the estate.[1] Trustees must therefore be very cautious in incurring financial obligations in the course of trust business and ensure that sufficient trust funds are available to meet its obligations.

Trustees' Duties

Upon acceptance of the trust, the trustee remains under duty to the beneficiary to administer the trust. Simply stated, a trustee's duty is to fulfil the purpose of the trust, and to obey the directions of the author of the trust given at the time of its creation, except as may be modified by the consent of all the beneficiaries being competent to contract. However in the performance of his duties, a trustee must have regard to certain additional duties, in particular:

(a) to inform himself of the state of trust property;

(b) to protect title to trust property;

(c) not to set up title adverse to beneficiary;

(d) to act with care;

(b) to act impartially with respect to beneficiaries;

(d) to prevent waste;

(e) to keep and supply clear and accurate accounts of the trust property and other information and to inform the beneficiaries of the same;

(f) to invest the trust funds and manage them prudently; and

(g) to act jointly and unanimously with co-trustees, unless the governing deed permits otherwise.

The duty of care has been examined particularly in connection with the standards to be applied to trust investment. A trustee has duty to take such care as an ordinary prudent person making investments for his own benefit. In the matter of investments the *Indian Trusts Act* is not as elaborate as the English Law contained in the *Trustee Investment Act, 1961*. Even though investment of trust property is the most critical factor among the duties of the trustees, Indian law contains no express provision to prevent ineffectual or motivated investments by self-seeking trustees. Courts in India are quick to provide redress to beneficiaries of a trust in the event of mismanagement. Lord Watson in *Learoyd* v. *Whitely*, (1887) 12 App Cas 727, spelled out the trustee's duties as regards investment of trust properties:

" . . . Businessmen of prudence may, and frequently do, select investments which are more or less of a speculative character but it is the duty of a trustee to confine himself to the class of investments which are permitted by the trust and likewise to avoid all investments of that class which are attended with hazard . . ."

The law now clearly recognises that a higher standard of care and diligence applies to paid trustees. The trustee is bound in a fiduciary character to protect the interests of another person and not to put himself in a position where his interest and duty conflict.[2] In cases where the trustee enters into a transaction in

---

1. Mackintosh Burn Ltd. v. *Shivakali Kumar*, AIR 1933 Cal 668.
2. Section 88, Indian Trusts Act, 1882.

regard to property whose interest he is to protect, onus lies on him to prove that he did not gain any pecuniary advantage by such transaction.[1]

Sections 49, 51 and 52 of the *Indian Trusts Act, 1882* enjoins the trustees to be faithful to the trust and execute it with reasonable diligence in the manner an ordinary prudent man of business would in the conduct of his own affairs. A person in a fiduciary position like a trustee is not entitled to make a profit for himself or a member of his family. It can also be said that he is not allowed to put himself in any such position in which a conflict may arise between his duty and his personal interest. The above sections cast a heavy responsibility in the matter of discharge of his duties as a trustee.[2]

When there are more than two or more beneficiaries in a trust, the trustee is under duty to deal impartially. The rule is applicable whether the beneficiaries are entitled to interest in the trust property simultaneously or successively. The trust instrument may sometime give discretion to favour one beneficiary over the other. The court will not control the exercise of such discretion, except to prevent the trustee from abusing it.[2]

When following the duty to invest it is important for the trustee to exercise an impartial judgement, free from prejudices or outside non-financial considerations. A trustee is bound to make the trust fund productive for the beneficiary by investing it in proper securities.

It is not a duty of a trustee to give a beneficiary the information as to the way in which the beneficiary has to deal with his interest, for it is not the duty of a trustee to assist the beneficiary in squandering or anticipating his fortune.

The trustee is under duty to the beneficiary to keep clear and accurate accounts with respect to the administration of the trust and to supply them on demand. The expenses incurred for supplying any information, which the beneficiary demands shall be paid by the beneficiary. The trustee also bears a duty to the beneficiary to allow the beneficiary or his agent to inspect or make copies of all title deeds and other documents relating to the trust estate which are in his own possession.[3] The liability to render accounts is irrespective of any question of negligence or wilful default. The period for which the trustee is made liable to render accounts depends upon the facts and circumstances of each case.[4]

A beneficiary is entitled to inspect deeds and documents representing trust investment. He is also entitled to inspect most other documents relating to the trust as the beneficiaries are the equitable owners of the trust property, and therefore they are also the equitable owners of the documents which have arisen in the course of the trust administration. The beneficiary is entitled to see all trust documents, because they are the trust documents and because he is a beneficiary. They are, in this sense, his own.[5] While a beneficiary is entitled to inspect trust

---

1. *Pierce Leslie & Co. Ltd.* v. *Miss Violet Ouchterlony Wapshare,* AIR 1969 SC 843.
2. *M.V. Rama Subbiar* v. *Manicka Narasimhachari,* AIR 1979 SC 671.
3. *Cowin (in re:),* 1886 33 Ch D 179.
4. *Sri Yadagiri Lakshmi Narasimha Swami Temple* v. *Induru Pattabhirami Reddi,* AIR 1967 SC 781.
5. *O'Rourke* v. *Darbishire,* 1920 AC 581.

documents, this rule would conflict with the rule that the trustees are not obliged to give reasons for their decisions. The English Court of Appeal (which has persuasive value in India) has held, in effect, that the rule enabling a beneficiary to inspect trust documents did not extend to documents which gave reasons for the trustee's decisions. If the document was one that the beneficiary was entitled to inspect, and if it also contains trustee's reasons for decision, passages containing those reasons should be covered up when the document is produced to the beneficiary.[1]

A trustee is in a fiduciary relation to the beneficiary and therefore remains under a duty to perform his duties personally as a fiduciary with only limited statutory provision for delegation and the employment of agents. Delegation by a trustee is not illegal when such delegation becomes a matter of necessity for an efficient management of the trust. However, unless the original trust deed contains provisions permitting a trustee to delegate his duties to some of the trustees, those trustees cannot be asked to act according to the instructions of the delegating trustee.[2] In the case of a private trust where there are more trustees than one, the concurrence of all is in general necessary in a transaction affecting the trust property and a majority cannot bind the trust estate. In order to bind the trust estate, the act must be the act of all. They constitute one body in the eyes of the law, and all must act together. This is subject to any express direction by the settlor.[3] The existing statutory provisions permit the delegation of many administrative functions and the employment of agents to do them, but it is the delegation of discretion and decision-making that falls outside of these powers.

An exception to this as provided in the *Explanation* to section 47 is the ability of a trustee to delegate his functions with respect to appointing an attorney or proxy to do an act merely ministerial and involving no independent discretion by power of attorney. The appointment of a proxy to do a job which is purely clerical or secretarial and which does not involve the task of taking an independent decision will not amount to delegation.[4] A trust deed may provide that the trustee may not delegate for more than a specified period.

Arrangements made by trustees among themselves for effective management of the trust are not treated as alienation of office or delegation of duties since such arrangements will remain with the persons who are jointly entitled to act as trustees.[5]

Regulatory environment and limitation on trusts

Courts

Although the courts are the ultimate control of the conduct and administration of trusts, they provide, in many respects, a light hand of control.

---

1. *In re Marquess of Londonderry's Settlement*, 1964 Ch 594.
2. *Sree S M Jew v. B K Vyas*, AIR 1952 Cal 763.
3. *Shanti Vijay and Co. v. Princess Fatima Fouzia*, (1979) 4 SCC 602.
4. *Shanmuga Mudali v. Arungiri Mudali*, AIR 1932 Mad 658.
5. *Nilamani Poricha v. Appanna Poricha*, AIR 1936 Mad 14.

There are no requirements for regular court approval of accounts or lodgement of documents with the court nor any requirement for registration or validation of trust deeds with the court nor a public inspection of trust documents, with the notable exception: Under the *Bombay Public Trusts Act, 1950* an act to regulate and to make provision for the administration of public, religious and charitable trusts in the State of Bombay (now Maharashtra). It includes provisions regarding the registration of public trusts, budget, accounts and audit of public trusts etc. Another exception is of trusts created by Wills. All Wills once admitted to probate after death are available for public inspection. Even this can be avoided by the use of secret trusts. The notification of the trust and its acceptance by the trustee precedes death and on death the Will merely leaves an unqualified legacy to the trustee, thus completing the constitution of the trust. The basis of the doctrine of secret trust is that the trust operates outside the Will, and the *Indian Succession Act, 1925* is not concerned with a secret trust at all. The Indian courts have lesser power than the English courts to modify the trust or alter the directions of the author of the trust or authorise specific dealing with the trust property. Under the Act, the courts have been conferred the power to resolve disputes and to compel due administration. These powers of the court are wide and include, *inter alia*, the power to:

(a) prescribe where the trust money should be invested;[1]
(b) extend the time within which a trustee is directed to sell property under the deed;[2]
(c) render opinion, advice or direction on any present questions regarding the management or administration of the trust property, on application by a trustee;[3]
(d) permit a trustee to lease trust property for a term exceeding 21 years from the date of executing the lease;[4]
(e) permit the trustee of a minor to apply the whole or any part of the trust property for or towards the minor's maintenance, education, advancement or expenses when the income from the trust property is insufficient for the same;[5]
(f) control a discretionary power conferred on a trustee if the same is not exercised reasonably and in good faith by the trustee;[6]
(g) permit a trustee to buy or become mortgagee or lessee of the trust property or any part thereof for the advantage of the beneficiary;[7]
(h) execute a trust when there is no trustee, on the beneficiary's application, until the appointment of a trustee or new trustee;[8]

---
1. Section 20(f) of the Act.
2. Section 22 of the Act.
3. Section 34 of the Act.
4. Section 36 of the Act.
5. Section 41 of the Act.
6. Section 49 of the Act.
7. Section 53 of the Act.
8. Section 59 of the Act.

(i) discharge a trustee from his office on the application of a trustee;[1]
(j) appoint trustees, when no other way of appointment can be use;[2]
(k) consider and award damages for breach of trust;
(l) determine the true construction of the terms of the trust; and
(m) remove a trustee on the application of beneficiaries of a trust or any other interested party.

Breach of Trust

The court will be the arbiter of allegations that a trustee has breached trust, provided that there is no prior negotiated settlement. A breach of trust results from some improper act or omission relating to the administration of the trust or the interests of the beneficiaries arising under it. It involves some failures to carry out the general duties of the trustees as laid down by the Act. A trustee can breach trust in a myriad of ways (an exhaustive list is probably not possible) and in general the trust is entitled to be reconstituted financially as though the breach had not occurred. Examples of situations involving breach of trust by the trustee include paying trust property to the wrong person, purchasing trust property without authorisation, taking a profit from the trust property without authorisation, investing trust funds in unauthorised investments, failure to have trust funds transferred into his name, etc. In principle, a trustee is not liable for a breach of trust committed by his co-trustee but there may be a few circumstances in which he may be held liable where a breach of trust has been committed by his co-trustee for which he himself may be seen to be in some way at fault. The Act provides that in the absence of an express declaration to the contrary in the instrument of trust, a trustee will be liable for a breach of trust committed by his co-trustee in the following circumstances:

(a) where he has delivered trust property to his co-trustee without seeing to its proper application;

(b) where he allows his co-trustee to receive trust property and fails to make due enquiry as to the co-trustee's dealings therewith, or allows him to retain it longer than the circumstances of the case reasonably requires; and

(c) where he becomes aware of a breach of trust committed or intended by his co-trustee, and either actively conceals it or does not within a reasonable time take proper steps to protect the beneficiary's interest.

Where co-trustees jointly commit a breach of trust, or where a trustee by his neglect enables his co-trustee to commit a breach of trust, each is liable to the beneficiary for the whole of the loss occasioned by such breach. A trustee pursued successfully in this manner has a right of contribution against the other trustees. However the right of contribution is no authority for compelling contribution in the event of a fraud.

---

1. Section 72 of the Act.
2. Section 74 of the Act.

Limitation on trusts

In the context of regulation of the operation of trusts, it is pertinent to look at the limitations on their operation imposed by law.

Perpetuities and accumulations

The rule against perpetuity is a rule of common law. Broadly, a trust cannot exist for longer than a life in being (at the time of its creation) plus a further period of 21 years. A similar issue is the equally complex subject of the bar against excessive accumulation of income. In broad terms this can be considered to prevent income from being retained within the trust for a period greater than 21 years or for the life of the settlor. Thereafter it must be distributed.

Under Indian law, a trust may be created for a lawful purpose. Every trust of which the purpose is unlawful is void. And where a trust is created for two purposes, of which one is lawful and the other unlawful, and the two purposes cannot be separated, the whole trust is void.

Every future limitation, whether by way of executory devise, or trust of real or personal property, the vesting of which absolutely as to personality, or in fee as to realty, is postponed beyond the lives in being and 21 years afterwards (with a further period of gestation where it exists), is void. This rule does not apply to charitable trusts.

Where the settlor gave benefit also to unborn children under a charitable trust deed which already had 12 beneficiaries and where he stipulated that the duration of the trust was 18 years from the date of the trust deed or his own death, whichever was later, the trust was held not to be invalid as it did not attract the rule of perpetuity.[1]

Where a Will provided for a trust for two minor children and any after-born children or their surviving issue, interests which were invalid under the rule against perpetuities were separable from valid interests and did not invalidate trust in its entirety.[2]

A trust which will not vest until a time beyond 21 years after the death of the last survivor of the testator living at the time of the testator's death is illegal but that portion of the trust which can be performed within the proper period does not fail when it can be separated from the illegal provision.

Remuneration

The Act does not entitle a trustee to charge for his services. Reimbursement for expenses incurred is however allowed by section 32. A trustee must not profit from neither his office nor use or deal with the trust property for his own profit in any way and this includes remuneration. In the absence of express directions to the contrary contained in the instrument of trust or of a contract to the contrary entered into with the beneficiary or the court at the time of accepting the trust, a trustee has no right to remuneration for his trouble, skill and loss of time in executing the trust.

---

1. *N. Chordiya Family Beneficial Trust* v. *Income Tax Office*, 1989 30 ITD 373 (Pune).
2. *In re Micheletti's Estate*, 24 Cal 1944 2d 904.

However, an Official Trustee, Administrator General, Public Curator or a person holding a certificate of administration is excepted from the application of the above principle.

The general rule that a trustee must not profit from his office extends further than the mere charging of fees. Two main points should be noted. *Firstly*, this rule prevents self-dealing so that a trustee cannot purchase trust property on sale. Similarly a trustee for purchase of particular property for the beneficiary cannot buy it for himself. The permission of a principal civil court of original jurisdiction is necessary for a trustee to buy or become mortgagee or lessee of the trust property and such permission shall not be given unless the proposed purchase, mortgage or lease is manifestly for the advantage of the beneficiary.

Secondly, it makes a trustee liable to account to the trust for any incidental profits. For example, trustees who were empowered to appoint two directors appointed themselves. They were held liable to account for remuneration received as directors, since their appointment had resulted from their use of trust powers.[1] It is because of the difficulty with incidental profits that most trust companies" general terms and conditions of business (which are specifically authorised in their appointment in the trust deed) make provision for incidental remuneration for providing other services, such as acting as banker to the trust. It should be made clear that this does not affect the trustee's right to be reimbursed for expenditure properly incurred on behalf of the trust, as this is not remuneration.

Exoneration clauses

The *Indian Trusts Act, 1882* enumerates certain duties and liabilities of the trustee. Thus, it is submitted that a trust, contrary to the provisions of the Act governing such duties and liabilities of the trustee would be severable from the trust deed. Therefore, the trustee is required by law to fulfil the duties enumerated. The Act lays down that a trustee is bound to:

(a) fulfill the purpose of the trust;

(b) be acquainted with the nature and circumstances of the trust property; and

(c) protect the title to the trust property.

The test of standard of care laid down is one of ordinary prudence, failing which, liability would lie on the trustee.

Public policy

As stated earlier, under Indian law a trust may be for any lawful purpose. The purpose of a trust is lawful unless forbidden by law, or is of such a nature that if permitted, would defeat the provisions of any law or is fraudulent or involves or implies injury to the person or property of another or the court regards it as opposed to public policy. The courts will hold a trust or a provision in the terms of a trust as invalid if the enforcement of the trust or its provisions would be against public policy, even though its performance does not involve the

---

1. *Re Gee* 1948 Ch D 284, *Re Orwell's W.T.*, [1982] 3 All ER 177.

commission of a criminal or tortious act by the trustee. Examples of trusts found to have been against public policy include those that attempt or intend to:...

— be in restraint of marriage;
— induce separation of husband and wife or parent and child;
— publicise pornographic works, etc.

It should also be noted that the if the settlor becomes bankrupt or liquidates his affairs within two years, or after two but within 10 years in some cases, the trust will be void or voidable as against the settlor's creditors. Also, other settlements of property capable of being taken in execution will be void if executed with intent to defeat or delay the claims of creditors. Intent to defraud the creditors must however be proved against the settlor.

Who can act as a trustee?

For personal trusts usually there are three main types of trustees: corporate trustees, professional individuals (such as solicitors and accountants) and private individuals (usually friends or relatives of the settlor). There is a wide choice within the professionals as most major banks increasingly act as trustees. Similarly most solicitors and accountants are often called upon to so act. Naturally, professional trustees are only prepared to act where they will be remunerated and where the risk of a particular trusteeship is perceived to constitute an acceptable business risk.

Reasons for the Creation of Trusts and their Uses

The English doctrine of privity of contract limits third-party rights under contracts, thus making a trust an ideal vehicle for enforceable third-party rights. This section does not provide an exhaustive list of all possible uses of trusts, but instead it is intended to give an indication of the very considerable breadth of use and diversity of purpose.

Personal or Private Trusts

The purpose of trusteeship is not to protect the rights and interests of persons who for any reason are unable to effectively protect them for themselves. The law vests those rights and interests for safe custody, as it were, in some other person who is capable of guarding them and dealing with them, and who is placed under a legal obligation to use them for the benefit of him to whom they in truth belong. Therefore, the object behind the development of trusts was the preservation of wealth and to allow for the ability to direct the devolution of that wealth through future generations. Although this use of trusts has declined to some extent (principally because of taxation and the costs of trust administration) it still remains a key use. Taxation has curtailed some advantages and it has positively penalised the use of certain types of trusts that have been the instrument of tax evasion, but the social need for trusts remains. Although taxation is a disincentive in some areas, the ability of trusts to adapt to changes in tax legislation means that there are taxation advantages that can be exploited in other areas. The effect of this is an increasing trend for trusts to be drawn on the most flexible terms possible, in order to give scope to change and adapt benefits with future changes in taxation provisions.

Trusts created with the intent to defraud creditors are void. Any gift can be set aside if it was made within two years of bankruptcy.

Trusts can be used to meet a variety of family circumstances, such as to provide for those who are incapacitated to the degree that they lack the capacity to handle their own affairs or trust for the benefit of minor children or grandchildren for their education, marriages or general advancement in life. Usually such trusts are of a discretionary nature in order to permit the trustee flexibility in the application of income. Giving the beneficiary an absolute right can lead to complications if the income is greater than is needed.

Trusts for the maintenance and education of children and more generally for the protection of minors" interests are created so that their prospective fortune is managed on their behalf by a trustee with clear fiduciary duties.

Discretionary trusts enable the exact nature and amounts of the distributions among a family class to be postponed and assessed by the trustee in the light of circumstances when the distribution is due.

Pension and employee benefits

The application of trust law also provides the basis for the operation of many employee benefit schemes. A gratuity fund trust may be created for employees of a company. A trust may be constituted to establish a provident, superannuation, welfare or any other fund for the benefit of the employees.

Collective investment schemes

These are mutual funds, otherwise known as "unit trusts", which enable investors (unit holders) to pool their capital for investment. The governing instrument for such vehicles is the trust deed, which defines the relationship between the investment managers of the fund, the trustee of the funds and the unit holders themselves. In broad terms, the major functions of the trustee are to hold the assets, maintain the register of unit holders, distribute income and ensure that the investment dealings of the manager remain within the terms of the trust. The trustee may also under some circumstances remove the manager. Such trusts are currently exempted from paying income tax to encourage capital market investment.

Charities

The *Indian Trust Act, 1882* does not apply to public or private religious or charitable endowments. The distinction between private and public trusts is that in private trusts, the beneficiaries are defined and ascertained individuals but in a public trust interest may be vested in an uncertain and fluctuating body of persons.[1] The conduct of public religious and charitable trusts in the State of .... is subject to regulation by the Charity Commission appointed under the *Bombay Public Trusts Act*, 1950. The *Charitable and Religious Trust Act*, 1920

---

1. *Shanti Devi* v. *State*, AIR 1982 Del 453.

provides for more effectual control over the administration of charitable and religious trusts and enables the trustees of such trusts to obtain the directions of a court on certain matters, *vide* Section 7.

Charitable trusts are exempt from the rule against perpetuities and have considerable taxation exemptions. However, in view of these considerable advantages there are controls as to what constitutes a charity. *The Indian Trusts Act* does not define the term charity. One has to import the legal meaning of the word charity from other related legislation. The definition can be found under the *Income Tax Act 1961*, wherein "charitable purpose" includes the relief of the poor, education, medical relief and the advancement of any other object of general public utility.[1]

In India, it has been held that relief of the poor by itself would not be a charitable object unless it involved an object of public utility. It is impossible to contend that relief of poverty, when that relief is restricted to members of one's family, can be a charitable object, which is of general public utility.[2]

Non-Charitable Purpose Trusts

The basic rule is that trusts created for abstract or impersonal purposes are void as there is no beneficiary to enforce the terms against the trustee, provided that the purpose is not charitable. Under provision 11 of the *Bombay Public Trusts Act, 1920*, a public trust created for certain purposes, some of which are charitable or religious and some are not, shall not be deemed to be void in respect to the charitable or religious purpose, only on the ground that it is void with respect to the non-charitable or non-religious purpose.

Conclusion

Trusts in India are being used increasingly as a form of business organisation as they offer a number of advantages, particularly to hold and control shareholding in companies. In one particular structuring exercise, this instrument was used very effectively to give the benefit of earnings in a vast industrial empire with cross-border interest to the family members without giving them the liberty to interfere with the professionally managed group companies and also to continue the benefit for the next generation. In certain circumstances trusts can still be effective tax planning tools. It is said about trusts that those who use them are unable to understand how they were ever able to live without them.

PRECEDENTS

AGENDA OF MEETING OF BOARD OF TRUSTEES

Agenda for the Meeting of the Board of Trustees of .... (name) Charitable Trust held on ...., 20...... at .... hours at .... (address).

---

1. *Municipal Corporation of Delhi* v. *Children Book Trust*, (1992) 3 SCC 390.
2. *Trustees of Govardhandas Family Charitable Trust* v. *Income Tax Commissioner*, AIR 1952 Bom 145.

Item No.	Contents
1.	To appoint additional members to the Board of Trustees of the.................... TRUST, thereby raising the strength to....................

MINUTES

Minutes of the Meeting of the Board of Trustees of .... (name) Charitable Trust held on ...., 20..... at .... hours at .... (address).

Present:

1.	....	President
2.	....	Chairman
3.	....	Trustee
4.	....	Trustee
5.	....	Trustee
6.	....	Trustee

In Attendance

Shri ....

Shri ....

Shri ....

Shri ....

(for discussion only)

Item No. ....

APPOINTMENT OF ADDITIONAL MEMBERS TO BOARD OF TRUSTEES

.... (name), President informed that it was necessary to appoint .... persons as members of the Board of Trustees of .... with provision for an alternate member for each. In this connection the following resolution was passed:

"RESOLVED that the consent of the Board of Trustees be and is hereby given to the appointment of Mr./Mrs. ...., representative of .... as a member of the Board of trustees and Mr./Mrs. .... as a member of the Board of Trustees."

.... (name) CHARITABLE TRUST

(address),

....

Dated:....................

To

(to all four Founder Trustees, to be sent)
Shri....................

Dear Sir,

Notice is hereby given that a meeting of the Board of Trustees which will be held at .... (address), on ...., 20..... at .... hours to consider there at the matters as per the enclosed agenda.

Yours faithfully,

For .... (name) CHARITABLE TRUST

Hony. Secretary

DEED OF FAMILY TRUST SETTLEMENT

Date of Execution:

Date of Commencement:

SETTLOR

Ms. .... (name)

TRUSTEES

1. Ms. .... (name)
2. Mr. .... (name)
3. Ms. .... (name)

BENEFICIARY

Master .... (name)

This INDENTURE made this .... day of .... 20..... BETWEEN Ms. .... d/o.................... resident of .... hereinafter referred to as the Settlor of the ONE PART AND Mr/Ms. .... son/daughter of.................... resident of ...., AND Mr/Ms. .... son/daughter of .... resident of ...., hereinafter collectively referred to as trustees (which expression shall wherever the context so admits or requires be deemed to include the said trustees and the survivor/survivors of them and the heirs, executors and administrators of the survivor, their or his or her assigns and the trustees or trustee for the time being of these presents) of the OTHER PART.

WHEREAS the Settlor is absolutely seized and possessed of and otherwise well and sufficiently entitled to an amount of Rupees .... only; and

WHEREAS the Settlor desires to provide a fund to be applied for the benefit of Beneficiary mentioned hereinafter and accordingly to create such trustees in the manner and subject to the powers, provisions, agreements and declarations declared and expressed hereinafter, and

WHEREAS for the purpose of effectuating such desire, the Settlor has handed over a cheque No. .... dated....................in favour of the trust drawn on .... bank of an amount of Rupees.................... only, to the trustees intending that the said amount and future net income thereof shall be held by the Trustees upon the following Trust and subject to the powers, provisions, agreements and declarations hereinafter declared and expressed of and concerning the same which the trustees have agreed to do.

NOW THIS INDENTURE WITNESSETH:

1. For effectuating the settlement, the Settlor hereby irrevocably transfers and assigns unto the trustees all the said amount of rupees .... only and her beneficial interest in the said amount to have and to hold and stand possessed of the same, the trust fund and net income of the trust fund upon the trust and for the purpose hereinafter declared and expressed of and concerning the same.

2. The trust shall be known as .... and shall carry on activities from .... (address) and/or such other place or places as the trustees may agree upon from time to time.

3. In these presents, the following terms where the context admits, shall have the following meanings:

(A) *'the trust fund'* means and includes;

   (i) the sum of Rs. .... settled by the settlor; and

   (ii) any other amounts, stocks, securities and other investments, business, properties and funds which may be substituted or added, the conversion thereof and/or accumulation, addition and accretion thereof by gift and/or otherwise, and/or the investments, or conversion of such accumulations, additions and accretion thereto.

(B) *'the Beneficiary'* means:

   .... (name)

(C) *'the Trustees'* means the original trustees and the survivor of them and the heirs, executors and administrators of such survivor and their or his or her assigns and the trustees or trustee as may be appointed from time to time under these presents.

(D) *'the date of distribution'* means:

   (i) the day on which the beneficiary shall attain the age of thirty five years; or

   (ii) the day of death of the beneficiary; or

   (iii) such earlier day than either of the dates mentioned in (a) or (b) as the Trustees for the time being may, at any time, after the execution of these presents, fix as 'the date of distribution'.

(E) *'the net income'* means the balance of interest, dividends, business profits, capital gains and other income of the trust fund after paying there out or providing for all the costs, charges and expenses incurred in or about the administration of the trust of these presents including any income-tax, wealth tax or other rates, assessments and duties and costs of ordinary rebates to immovable property, if any, forming part of the trust fund.

4. On the consideration aforesaid the trustees hereby covenant with the settlor, his heirs, executors and administrators that the trustees and other trustees for the time being shall stand possessed of the trust fund to receive the annual or other net income arising therefrom upon the trusts and subject to the powers, provisions, agreements and declarations hereinafter declared and expressed of and concerning the same.

5. The trustees shall, till the date of distribution, hold and stand possessed of the trust fund upon the following trusts:

(A) On the date of distribution, the trust shall cease and the trustees shall pay, transfer and handover the trust fund to the beneficiary:

Provided that if the beneficiary shall die before the date of distribution, the trust fund which would have been taken by him had he not died shall be taken by his legal heir excluding the Settlor:

[Provided, further, if there shall be no legal heir of such person, the trust fund shall be handed over to a public charitable trust as may be decided upon by the trustees.]

(B) Pending the date of distribution, the trustees shall pay, transfer, distribute and/or hand over the net income of the trust fund to the Beneficiary at the end of each accounting year of the trust.

Explanations:

(i) For the purpose of sub-clause (B) above, the expression 'accounting year' shall mean:

(a) in respect of the first such accounting year, the period beginning on the day hereof and ending on ....; and

(b) in respect of the subsequent accounting year the period beginning on the .... every year and ending on the .... every year.

(ii) For the purpose of sub-clause (B) above, the net income of the trust fund shall be deemed to have accrued on the last day of each accounting year of the trust.

6. The trust established hereby shall be irrevocable. The trust fund and the net income thereof shall be possessed and enjoyed by the person beneficially entitled thereto by virtue of these presents to the entire exclusion of the Settlor and or any benefit to him by contract or otherwise and no part of the trust fund or the net income thereof shall be paid to or be paid for the benefit of the settlor in any circumstances whatsoever.

7. The trustees shall be free to sell or exchange or otherwise dispose of any assets, movable or immovable forming part of the trust fund and to invest all moneys which shall require investment in any manner they may think fit without being obliged to invest the same in the investments authorised by law or the investment of the trust fund and to sell or exchange such investments and other

properties both movable and immovable as are forming part of the trust fund whenever they may think fit desirable to do so and.

8. Without prejudice to the generality of the foregoing powers, the trustees may invest any moneys requiring investment:

(i) in the purchase of any immovable property situated in India or elsewhere and for the development thereof the trustees may borrow money at such interest as they may think fit for the purchase without security of the trust fund or any property forming part of the trust fund;

(ii) in the purchase of or subscription to debentures, stocks, funds, shares and securities of any company or corporation whether incorporated in India or elsewhere;

(iii) in making loans to or deposits with any person, firm or company or corporation;

(iv) in making loans upon the security of any immovable property or movable property.

(v) In any business, if permissible under the provisions of law, fiscal or otherwise which may be carried on by the trustees as such trustee for and on behalf of the trust hereby established or in partnership with any other person or persons;

(vi) In the purchase of any immovable property or acquisition of flats by becoming member of co-operative societies;

(vii) In such other investments of whatsoever nature and wheresoever whether involving liability or not or upon such personal credit with or without security as the trustees may think fit to the intent that the trustees shall have the same full and unrestricted power of investing and transposing the investments in all respects as if they were absolutely entitled hereto beneficially.

9. The Trustees may engage in carrying any activity for providing services or any business for and on account of the trust established by this deed and may invest any part of the trust fund in such activity, business or businesses and in course of such business, trustees may enter into contract for purchase or hire of equipment, sales or purchases, may borrow funds without security or on security of the trust fund at interest or free of interest as they may think fit, and engage and discharge executives, manager clerks and other staff and hire premises and open and operate banking account and take all legal and other proceedings and obtain and hold such licenses as may be necessary and apply for such registration under such laws relating to any activity, trade commerce or industry or sales or purchases or otherwise as they may think fit. The trustees may pay out of the trust fund and the income of the trust, such losses, damages, costs, charges, and expenses and as they may incur sustain or be liable for in such activity or business or otherwise as trustees may think fit. The trustees shall have all such power for the management and conduct of such activity or business as any individual proprietor has. The trustees may carry on any activity or business in partnership with any person, firm or company and may for that purpose execute

such deed or deeds containing such terms or provisions as the trustees may think fit and they may retire from or dissolve any such partnership and may invest any trust fund as capital or as loans or advance to any such partnership with interest or at such rate of interests as they may think fit and may execute any guarantee or indemnities or bonds in course of or for the purpose of the business of this trust and/or in connection or for the purpose of the business or other activity of any such partnership. The trustees may exercise all such power and they have as if they alone carried on such activity or business. The trustees may nominate any one of them to be a partner in such partnership for and on behalf of this trust though ostensibly such nominee may appear in such partnership as a partner in his/her individual name and the trustees shall out of the trust fund be found to indemnify such nominee against all losses, damages, expenses and all liabilities which such nominee may incur or sustain as partner in such partnership and such nominee shall have recourse to the trust fund for full indemnification.

10. The Trustees are hereby expressly authorised to accept gifts of moneys and/or property (movable or immovable) for the benefit of this trust from the Settlor and/or other person or persons and any such gifts shall be held by the trustees as accretion to or augmentation of the trust fund the money or other property received by way of such gift and future income thereof shall be held in like trusts in all respects as are herein contained and are applicable to the trust fund and the net income of the trust fund and shall be subject to the same trusts, powers and provisions as are contained in these presents and applicable thereto as if such money or property had formed part of the original trust funds.

11. (i) The powers of appointing new trustees shall vest with the trustees for the time being:

(ii) All acts in carrying out these presents if done and carried out by a majority of the trustees for the time being shall be valid and effectual as if such acts had been done by all the trustees;

(iii) Should any difference of opinion at any time exist between the trustees for the time being in relation to the commission or omission of any act or otherwise however, in the execution of this deed the opinion of the majority of such trustee shall prevail.

(iv) Trustees may resign office as trustee by giving notice in writing to his/her co-trustees:

(v) Without prejudice to the generality of their powers the trustee shall have powers:

- (a) to employee clerks and other employees, agents, brokers, bankers, lawyers, accountants and others and at such remuneration as they may think fit;
- (b) to delegate any powers to one or more of their body;
- (c) to appoint any one from amongst them as a managing trustee with such powers as may be delegated to him/her;
- (d) to delegate any powers as they can lawfully delegate to any person and to execute such power of attorney as they may think fit for the purpose

(e) to withdraw any power or revoke any appointment of any employee or attorneys;

(f) to let any portion of any immovable property forming part of the trust fund at such rent and for such period on such terms and conditions as they may think fit and to accept surrender of any lease;

(g) to open and maintain banking accounts in the name of the trust or in the name of any business which the trustees may start or in the name of such one or more of the trustees as they may think fit and to make the account operable by such one or more of them as they may think fit;

(h) to determine who shall be the first named as regards investments in shares, stocks, debentures and other securities and other investments;

(i) to appoint proxy or proxies for voting at any meeting of creditors, contributors, shareholders or others; and

(j) to allow any investments to stand in the name of any bank.

12. A resolution in writing circulated among all the trustees and signed by a majority of them present in India shall be as valid and effectual as if it has been duly passed at a meeting of the trustees duly called and convened.

13.(i) No trustee purporting to act in the execution of the trusts and powers of these present shall be liable for any loss unless it is attributable to his/her own dishonesty or to the wilful commission or omission by him/her of any act which commission or omission is known to his/her to constitute a breach of trust.

(ii) A trustee or trustees of these present sign good faith paying over any moneys under the trust of these presents to his/her or their co-trustees or doing any act facilitating the receipt thereof for the purpose of the trusts of ..... shall not be answerable for the .... or non-application thereof.

IN WITNESS WHEREOF, this Deed is executed on the day and year first above written.

By

.... (name)

IN THE PRESENCE OF:

RULES AND REGULATIONS GOVERNING THE MANAGEMENT OF "NATURE FOR CHILDREN"

1. Board of Trustees

1.1 The NATURE FOR CHILDREN (hereinafter referred to as "NATURE FOR CHILDREN") will be managed by a Board of Trustees having no more than six and not less than four members at any point of time. The DONOR shall be the President of the Board of Trustees. The Board will appoint a Chairman and an Hony. Secretary from amongst its members. The Hony. Secretary will summon the meetings of the Board on the instruction of the President as and when necessary. The quorum for the meeting of the Board of Trustees shall be four Trustees present and voting. All affairs relating to the Trust will be decided by a simple majority. In the event of a tie, the President will have a casting vote. The DONOR Trustee will have a right of veto in all decisions.

1.2 The following will be deemed to be the Founder Trustees:

1. Shri "X" resident of....................
2. Shrimati "X" w/o Shri "X",
3. Shri "A" s/o Shri "X",
4. Shri "B" s/o Shri "X" and their successors.

1.3 The Founder Trustees will have the power to name and appoint the remaining Trustees to the Board of Trustees.

1.4 The Founder Trustees will hold office until their death, resignation or incapacity. Any vacancy so caused will be filled by appointment made by a majority decision in a meeting of remaining Founder Trustees. The Founder Trustees shall have the right to nominate the direct lineal descendants and immediate family members in their place with the same powers. Upon nomination, such Trustees will also be called 'Founder Trustees'.

The Trustees other than the Founder Trustees shall hold office until their death, resignation or incapacity. The Founder Trustees will also have the power to remove any of the Trustees other than the Founder Trustees without assigning any reasons. Any vacancy so caused will be filled by appointment made by a majority decision in a meeting of the Founder Trustees.

2. Membership

Membership of NATURE FOR CHILDREN shall be open to a person who is 18 years of age or above and who is interested in carrying out the aims and objectives of NATURE FOR CHILDREN and who has been accepted by the Board of Trustees. Each member shall pay the prescribed subscription and also accept to abide by the Rules and Regulations of NATURE FOR CHILDREN.

3. Subscription

The Board of Trustees of the NATURE FOR CHILDREN will have the power to nominate members as Patrons, Life Members, Ordinary Members and Honorary Members and may fix such fees as deemed fit by them.

4. Disqualifications

A member shall be liable to be disqualified in the following circumstances:....

(a) (i) If his/her activities are contrary to the aims and objects of the NATURE FOR CHILDREN or

against its interests;

(ii) if he/she is convicted for any offence involving moral turpitude by a court of law;

(iii) if he/she has become insolvent;

(iv) if he/she does not pay arrears of subscription and the money due to the NATURE FOR CHILDREN within one month of issuance of notice for the said purpose, on him/her;

(b) Any person sought to be disqualified as a member of the NATURE FOR CHILDREN, shall be given a show cause notice of two weeks as to why he/she should not be disqualified.

(c) The show cause notice and reply, if any, received from the member shall be placed before the Board of Trustees of the NATURE FOR CHILDREN and the member shall stand disqualified, if his/her disqualification is approved by a majority decision.

5. The Managing Committee

The Board of Trustees, may by majority from time to time, form a Managing Committee for the management of the Hospital, set up by the NATURE FOR CHILDREN, or for other activities that may be set up, which will hold office at the pleasure of the Board of Trustees and will report its activities to the Board of Trustees. The said Managing Committee or any of its members will hold office without any remuneration unless there is a contract to the contrary with any one of them and will retire on the 31st of March, every year but if otherwise eligible can offer themselves for re-appointment. The Managing Committee can be dissolved by the Board of Trustees by a simple resolution. The terms of any of the members of the Managing Committee can also be terminated in the same manner. The constitution and the meetings of the Managing Committee will be governed by such rules as may be framed by the Board of Trustees from time to time.

6. Powers of the Managing Committee

The Managing Committee shall exercise all powers for carrying out the aims and objects of NATURE FOR CHILDREN, including NATURE FOR CHILDREN Child Care Centre, which have been delegated to the managing Committee for carrying out and more specifically the following:

(a) for the purpose of running the hospital, the Managing Committee will have the authority, subject to the approval of the Board of Trustees to incur such expenses, enter into such contracts, buy and sell such assets, appoint or discharge such personnel and do all other deeds, acts and things as the Board of Trustees may in their absolute discretion may think it fit;

(b) the Management and Administration of various activities of NATURE FOR CHILDREN, including that of NATURE FOR CHILDREN Child Care Centre;

(c) the appointment of persons as employees with or without remuneration and to take such disciplinary action as may be necessary;

(d) specifying the duties and powers of the employees;

(e) the realisation of all subscription, dues or other moneys in any manner deemed expedient;

(f) all acts and things, which are conducive to the efficient administration and fulfillment of the aims and objects of NATURE FOR CHILDREN and its activities.

7. The Trust Fund

7.1 The Trust fund shall be deposited by the Trustees at any reputed Bank, as the Founder Trustees may think proper and convenient, in the name of the Trust. The DONOR and any other Founder Trustees as may be named by the DONOR will have the power to operate the same, withdraw money from such account for the benefit of the Trust and to endorse, negotiate all instruments such as cheques, drafts, promissory notes for and on behalf of the Trust. All receipts of money for and on behalf of the Trust shall be deposited in such account and all withdrawals for and on behalf of the Trust shall be so debited to such accounts. This clause will not restrict the right to keep the Trust funds and assets in such security and other assets as the DONOR and such other Founder Trustees as named by the DONOR may from time to time determine.

7.2 Fees received from patrons and life members shall form part of the capital and reserve fund. The interest accruing therefrom may, however, be used towards the current expenses of NATURE FOR CHILDREN and its activities.

7.3 Funds received from ordinary members, donations from general public and interest that accrues from the investment of the capital and reserve fund shall form the general fund for the expenses of the NATURE FOR CHILDREN and its activities. Any balance from the general fund or any portion thereof might be transferred to the capital and reserve fund at the end of the year by a decision at the meeting of the Board of Trustees.

7.4 The Board of Trustees shall invest the money not required immediately for the Trust in accordance with the decision taken in that regard at a meeting of the Board of Trustees and keep accounts thereof.

7.5 The Board of Trustees shall maintain regular books of accounts of Trust moneys, receipts, out goings and other dealings. The Board of Trustees shall have the powers to take steps for the growth of the hospital or any other institute that may be set up and if necessary to erect or construct a hospital or any other such building on the land.

7.6 The Board of Trustees shall forward the Annual audited statement of accounts to .... India and .... (UK) [patron body, if any] within six months of the close of the financial year.

The above mentioned, clause will be effective till such time as there is a valid memorandum of understanding between the .... India, ... (UK) and ....

8. Miscellaneous

8.1 There will be no bar for appointment of any of the Trustees to serve the hospital on payment of salary or other compensation as long as the said Trustee is a qualified doctor or other professional.

8.2 The Founder Trustees shall have the power to make and alter the above rules and regulations with regard to the conduct of the Trust and all other matters in respect of which any power or duty is hereby vested in them as they may think proper for the enhancement of the object of the Trust and its better management.

Such alteration or modification will not effect any acts, things or deeds already performed, including any act of the Trustees nor will it have the effect of revoking the Trust or of the donation.

8.3 In the event of any conflict between the above Rules and Regulations and the provisions of the Trust Deed, the Rules and Regulations as altered from time to time will take precedence over the provisions of the Trust Deed.

TRUST DEED

THIS DEED OF TRUST is made on this .... day of...................., 20....

BETWEEN

Mr. *Alpha*, s/o Mr. *Alpha*, aged .... years, resident of.................... (address), of the FIRST PART,

AND

Mrs. *Beta*, w/o Mr. *Beta*, aged .... years, resident of .... (address), of the SECOND PART,

AND

Mr. *Gama*, s/o Mr. *Gama*, aged ...., resident of .... (address), of the THIRD PART.

The Parties of the FIRST PART and of the SECOND PART shall hereinafter collectively be referred to as the "Settlors".

The Settlors and the part of the THIRD PART shall hereinafter collectively be referred to as the "Trustees" which expression shall, unless repugnant to the context or the meaning thereof, mean and include their survivor or survivors, and such other Trustees as may be appointed in the manner laid down hereinafter.

The Trustees, both present and future, shall constitute the Board of Trustees of the Trust (hereinafter referred to as the "Board of Trustees").

WHEREAS the Trustees are desirous of carrying on certain public charitable activities.

AND WHEREAS the Settlors for this purpose are desirous of settling upon a public charitable trust certain monies.

AND WHEREAS the Trustees have agreed to become the Trustees of the charitable trust and carry out the obligations of the Trust.

NOW THIS DEED WITNESSETH AS FOLLOWS:

1. The Trust shall be known as "Nature for Children Public Charitable Trust" (hereinafter referred to as the "Trust"). The registered office of the Trust shall be situated in .... and shall for the present be at .... (address).

2. For affecting the objects of the Trust, the Settlors hereby assign and transfer absolutely unto the Trust a sum of Rs. .... (amount) (hereinafter referred to as the original corpus of the Trust).

For effectuating the desires of the Settlors and in consideration of the premises, the Trustees agree and declare that they shall stand possessed of the original corpus of the Trust and such further sums of donations and subscriptions in cash or kind as may from time to time be received by the Trust and the income with all the accumulations thereof and the additions and accretions thereto and the investment for the time being representing the same (all of which shall hereafter be referred to as the "Trust Fund") upon trust and under the considerations, provisions and declarations concerning the same set out herein.

3. The objects and purposes of the Trust are as follows:

(a) To ameliorate the living conditions of the poor and the needy and the physically handicapped in whatsoever manner and through whatsoever programmes or schemes as may be deemed fit by the Trustees.

(b) Without prejudice to the generality of the aforesaid, the Trust may run orphanages, homes for the old and disabled, organise food camps for the poor, adopt poor families in villages and uplift their economic living standard; ameliorate the health conditions of the poor and needy or disabled and do all whatsoever is necessary, incidental or ancillary to the object of ameliorating the living conditions of the poor and needy and physically handicapped whether such activities are economical, education, social or cultural.

(c) To establish and operate centres of education through schools, colleges, public libraries or vocational training centres or other centres for imparting formal or non-formal education.

(d) To establish and operate centres for sports and physical activity.

(e) To establish and operate centres for development of children by providing for activities, which stimulate the mental and physical growth of children.

(f) To establish and operate centres for the care of animals and birds, such as hospitals, sanctuaries etc.

(g) To establish and operate centres for the protection and growth of the natural fauna and flora of India from the viewpoint of protecting the ecology.

(h) To establish and operate centres for promotion of art and culture of India.

(i) To make such monetary and other donations and contributions as the Trustees deem fit to any organisation and/or programme engaged in any of the activities mentioned hereinabove:

Provided, however, that the activities of the Trust do not involve the carrying on of any activity purely for profit.

4. The party of the FIRST PART shall be the first Chairman of the Board of Trustees (hereinafter referred to as the "Chairman"). In the event he is unwilling or unable to continue as the Chairman, he shall nominate one of the existing Trustees to be his successor in office. Thereafter, the Chairman of the Board of Trustees shall be appointed by a majority vote of the Board of Trustees.

5. The number of Trustees shall not exceed .... persons and shall not be less than 3 (three) persons. The Trustees may, from time to time by majority vote, appoint such further and additional persons as Trustees as they may deem fit, provided, however, that the Chairman of the Trust may in his sole discretion veto the appointment of any further Trustees, in which event such persons will not be appointed as Trustees of the Trust. All such appointments shall be within the maximum number prescribed hereinabove.

6. The Trustees shall hold office as Trustees for life unless and until they are unwilling or unable to discharge their duties. Not withstanding the following, any Trustee may be removed from office by a majority vote of the remaining members of the Board of Trustees on the grounds of moral turpitude, or in the event the majority of the remaining Trustees feel that such Trustee is unable to carry on his duties as a Trustee.

A Trustee shall continue to hold office until such time as his resignation is accepted by the Board of Trustees, and in the event he is discharged from his duties by the Board of Trustees, with effect from the date on which such decision to discharge is taken.

7. The Board of Trustees shall have the following rights and powers:
   (i) To manage the properties of the Trust and to solicit and receive and administer funds, received from any lawful source and to dispose of the same for any purpose of the Trust in any, lawful manner.
   (ii) To acquire by gift, purchase, exchange, lease or otherwise lands, buildings or other properties – movable or immovable, together with all rights appurtenant thereto.
   (iii) To contract, incur obligation and otherwise make legally binding agreements of whatever kind and purpose upon such terms and conditions as the Board of Trustees deem advisable.
   (iv) To receive monies, securities, instruments or other movable property for and on behalf of the Trust.
   (v) To raise funds for the Trust by gift, donations or otherwise.
   (vi) To invest the monies of the Trust upon such terms and conditions as the Board of Trustees deem fit and advisable.
   (vii) To sue and defend the legal proceedings on behalf of the Trust including compromise, settle or refer to arbitration all such proceedings.
   (viii) To make, sign and execute all such documents and instruments as may be necessary or proper for carrying on the management of the property or affairs of the Trust.
   (ix) To grant receipts, to sign and execute instruments and to endorse or discount cheques or other negotiable instruments through its accredited agents.
   (x) To do any other act or thing and exercise any other function or power permitted by law to the Trust which is incidental and conducive to the

attainment of any of the aforesaid rights and duties and incidental or conducive to attainment of any other objectives of the Trust.

8. The Trustees shall, at all times, be empowered to accumulate the whole or any part of the income of the Trust for the purpose of achieving and/or furthering the object of the Trust set out hereinabove provided that such accumulation shall be in accordance with the requirement of the Income-Tax Act and the Rules made thereunder from time to time.

9. The accounts of the Trust shall be maintained with such bank as the Board of Trustees may determine, and cheques on such account shall be drawn by any or all of the parties of the FIRST PART, the SECOND PART and the THIRD PART, and any such Trustee or Trustees as the Board of Trustees may decide upon.

10. The Board of Trustees shall cause to be kept true accounts relating to the said Trust and such accounts shall contain proper particulars of the money received and expended by the Board of Trustees and the matters in respect of which such receipts and expenditure take place as also such other particulars as may be usual in the account of a like nature. The books of accounts and other papers and documents relating to the said Trust shall be kept at the office of the Trust and shall be open to inspection by the Board of Trustees at all reasonable time.

11. The accounts of the Trust shall be audited every year by an auditor appointed by the Trustees for the purpose and shall be placed before the annual meeting of the Board of Trustees to be held within two months of any expiry of the official year of the said Trust.

12. Except in so far as may be otherwise provided, all decisions of the Board of Trustees shall be taken by a majority vote of the Trustees; in the event of a tie, the Chairman shall have the casting vote.

13. The quorum for any meeting of the Board of Trustees shall be two Trustees. All meetings shall be presided over by the Chairman. In the event the Chairman is unable to attend any meeting of the Board of Trustees, he shall nominate a presiding officer from amongst the Trustees to preside over the meeting. Such presiding officer shall have the casting vote in the event of a tie, but shall not be entitled to any other powers of the Chairman.

14. The Board of Trustees shall meet at least once every calendar year. A special meeting of the Board of Trustees may be summoned by requisition by any of the Trustee(s). The Board of Trustees may pass resolutions by circulation.

15. The Trustees shall be individually accountable only for such moneys, securities and other properties, as they shall actually receive, notwithstanding their signing any receipt. Each Trustee shall be answerable and accountable for his own acts, receipts, neglects or faults and not for those of the other Trustee(s), not for the insufficiency or deficiency of any funds, securities or other properties, nor for any other loss, unless the same is a consequence of any act and/or omission or any wilful default or negligence by the said Trustee.

16. Upon any sale by the Board of Trustees under the aforesaid power of sale,

it shall be no concern of the Purchasor(s) dealing *bonafide* with the Board of Trustees to inquire as to whether the occasion for executing or exercising such power has arisen or whether the provisions as to the appointment or retirement of the Trustees contained herein have been properly and regularly observed and performed, nor shall it be any concern of the Purchasor(s) to see the application of the purchase money.

17. In the event of dissolution of the Trust, the assets of the Trust, after clearance of all debts and liabilities, shall be transferred to such organisation and/or programme having object similar to that of the Trust, as the Board of Trustees may deem fit. No part of the properties and assets of the Trust shall be distributed amongst the Trustees.

18. The Trustees shall not be entitled to any monies or monetary compensation for services rendered by them in the discharge of their duties for the business of the Trust.

19. The funds of the Trust shall be invested and deposited in the forms and modes specified in sub-section (5) of section (13) of the Income-tax Act, 1961.

20. The Trust shall not spend its funds in any activities outside India without the prior approval of the Central Board of Direct Taxes.

21. The Board of Trustees shall have power from time to time to make such rules and regulations as may be necessary and as the Board of Trustees may think fit for the management and administration of the Trust, and also from time to time to set aside and vary any such rules and regulations provided, however, that no such rules and regulations shall in any manner be inconsistent with any of the provisions of this Trust Deed.

22. All questions of interpretation of the scope and ambit of any provisions of this Trust Deed shall be decided by the Board of Trustees, in the first instance by consensus, and failing that by a majority vote. No Trustee holding a minority opinion shall be entitled to raise any dispute regarding the interpretation of the Trust Deed in any form whatsoever. The interpretation of the majority shall also be binding upon the beneficiaries of the Trust.

IN WITNESS HEREOF the parties hereto have set their hands hereunto respectively the day and year first here-in-above written.

....
A

....
B

....
C

WITNESSES:
1. ....
2. ....

attainment of any of the aforesaid rights and duties and incidental or conducive to attainment of any other objectives of the Trust.

8. The Trustees shall, at all times, be empowered to accumulate the whole or any part of the income of the Trust for the purpose of achieving and/or furthering the object of the Trust set out hereinabove provided that such accumulation shall be in accordance with the requirement of the Income-Tax Act and the Rules made thereunder from time to time.

9. The accounts of the Trust shall be maintained with such bank as the Board of Trustees may determine, and cheques on such account shall be drawn by any or all of the parties of the FIRST PART, the SECOND PART and the THIRD PART, and any such Trustee or Trustees as the Board of Trustees may decide upon.

10. The Board of Trustees shall cause to be kept true accounts relating to the said Trust and such accounts shall contain proper particulars of the money received and expended by the Board of Trustees and the matters in respect of which such receipts and expenditure take place as also such other particulars as may be usual in the account of a like nature. The books of accounts and other papers and documents relating to the said Trust shall be kept at the office of the Trust and shall be open to inspection by the Board of Trustees at all reasonable time.

11. The accounts of the Trust shall be audited every year by an auditor appointed by the Trustees for the purpose and shall be placed before the annual meeting of the Board of Trustees to be held within two months of any expiry of the official year of the said Trust.

12. Except in so far as may be otherwise provided, all decisions of the Board of Trustees shall be taken by a majority vote of the Trustees; in the event of a tie, the Chairman shall have the casting vote.

13. The quorum for any meeting of the Board of Trustees shall be two Trustees. All meetings shall be presided over by the Chairman. In the event the Chairman is unable to attend any meeting of the Board of Trustees, he shall nominate a presiding officer from amongst the Trustees to preside over the meeting. Such presiding officer shall have the casting vote in the event of a tie, but shall not be entitled to any other powers of the Chairman.

14. The Board of Trustees shall meet at least once every calendar year. A special meeting of the Board of Trustees may be summoned by requisition by any of the Trustee(s). The Board of Trustees may pass resolutions by circulation.

15. The Trustees shall be individually accountable only for such moneys, securities and other properties, as they shall actually receive, notwithstanding their signing any receipt. Each Trustee shall be answerable and accountable for his own acts, receipts, neglects or faults and not for those of the other Trustee(s), not for the insufficiency or deficiency of any funds, securities or other properties, nor for any other loss, unless the same is a consequence of any act and/or omission or any wilful default or negligence by the said Trustee.

16. Upon any sale by the Board of Trustees under the aforesaid power of sale,

it shall be no concern of the Purchasor(s) dealing *bonafide* with the Board of Trustees to inquire as to whether the occasion for executing or exercising such power has arisen or whether the provisions as to the appointment or retirement of the Trustees contained herein have been properly and regularly observed and performed, nor shall it be any concern of the Purchasor(s) to see the application of the purchase money.

17. In the event of dissolution of the Trust, the assets of the Trust, after clearance of all debts and liabilities, shall be transferred to such organisation and/or programme having object similar to that of the Trust, as the Board of Trustees may deem fit. No part of the properties and assets of the Trust shall be distributed amongst the Trustees.

18. The Trustees shall not be entitled to any monies or monetary compensation for services rendered by them in the discharge of their duties for the business of the Trust.

19. The funds of the Trust shall be invested and deposited in the forms and modes specified in sub-section (5) of section (13) of the Income-tax Act, 1961.

20. The Trust shall not spend its funds in any activities outside India without the prior approval of the Central Board of Direct Taxes.

21. The Board of Trustees shall have power from time to time to make such rules and regulations as may be necessary and as the Board of Trustees may think fit for the management and administration of the Trust, and also from time to time to set aside and vary any such rules and regulations provided, however, that no such rules and regulations shall in any manner be inconsistent with any of the provisions of this Trust Deed.

22. All questions of interpretation of the scope and ambit of any provisions of this Trust Deed shall be decided by the Board of Trustees, in the first instance by consensus, and failing that by a majority vote. No Trustee holding a minority opinion shall be entitled to raise any dispute regarding the interpretation of the Trust Deed in any form whatsoever. The interpretation of the majority shall also be binding upon the beneficiaries of the Trust.

IN WITNESS HEREOF the parties hereto have set their hands hereunto respectively the day and year first here-in-above written.

....
A

....
B

....
C

WITNESSES:
1. ....
2. ....

ALTERATION OF A TRUST DEED
MINUTES OF THE BOARD MEETING

Minutes of the meeting of the *Board of Trustees of Helping Hands Public Charitable Trust (the "Trust")*, held on .... day of .... 20.....

Present

1.
2.

This was the first meeting of the Board of Trustees, which took place on ...., when it was placed on record that the Trust was formed and functional on the .... day of ...., 20.....

It was further placed on record that it was the intention of the Settlors to induct .... (name) s/o Mr./Mrs./Ms. .... (name), aged ...., resident of.................... (address), as a Trustee, which was not possible on the date of creation of the Trust and registration of the Trust Deed with the Sub-Registrar at ...., as he was out of the country at the time. It was unanimously agreed that .... (name) be invited to be a Trustee of the Trust. It was further placed on record that the informed consent of .... (name) to become a Trustee has already been obtained.

Accordingly, ... (name) has been appointed a Trustee of the Trust, as per the rules and regulation of the Trust for a period of .... years (in perpetuity), subject to the terms and conditions, rules and regulation of the Trust.

RESOLVED ACCORDINGLY

Signed

1.
2.

CHAPTER 13
SOCIETY

According to section 1 of The Societies Registration Act, 1860, any seven or more persons associated for any literary scientific or charitable purpose, may, by subscribing their names to a memorandum of association and filing the same with the Registrar of joint-stock companies form themselves into a society.

Section 2 of The Societies Registration Act, 1860, gives that the memorandum of association shall contain the following things.

(1) The name of the society

(2) The objects of the society

(3) The name, address, and occupations of the governors, council, directors, committee, or other governing body to whom by the rules of the society, the management of its affairs is entrusted.

It also directs that a copy of the rules and regulations of the society, certified to be a correct copy by more than two of the governing body, shall be filed with the memorandum of association.

PRECEDENTS

(The Societies Registration Act, 1860)

BYE LAWS

OF

Alpha RESIDENTS WELFARE ASSOCIATION,

NEW DELHI

CHAPTER I

PRELIMINARY

1. The name of the Association is *Beta* and its registered address is .... (address), ... (place).

Any change in the address shall be notified to the Registrar within .... days.

2. A. In these Bye Laws (the "Bye Laws") unless there is any thing repugnant to the subject or context, the expression "the Act" means the Societies

Registration Act, 1860 and its words and expression defined in the Act and used in these Bye Laws shall have the same meaning as assigned to them in the said Act.

B. *"Association"* means the *Beta*.

C. *"President"* means the president of the Association.

CHAPTER II
OBJECTS

3. The objects of the Association shall be as under:

(a) For the welfare of the owners and residents of .... at .... (place).

(b) For provision and supplementation of civic amenities, to create a body of representation of rights of the owners and residents with the respective concerned authorities (governmental and non-governmental) in connection with electricity, water and tax.

(c) to foster a spirit of neighbourliness, enhanced social interaction and exchange of information.

(d) to immediately, take in hand the provision of roads, drainage, security, lighting, sign posting and beautification.

(e) to carry out such other objectives, as the members may decide from time to time.

CHAPTER III
MEMBERSHIP

4. The members of the association shall consists of:

(a) The persons joining in the application for registration.

(b) Persons admitted in accordance with these Bye Laws.

(c) The Association may admit joint members, provided they make a declaration in writing that the person whose name stands first in the share certificate shall have the right to vote and all the liabilities will be born jointly and severally by them, as provided in the Act, Rules and Bye Laws.

(d) In accordance, with the procedure laid down in the Bye Laws and the Rules for admission of any member, the Association may admit minors and persons of unsound mind inheriting share or interest of deceased members as its members through their legal representatives or guardians respectively. The member so admitted will enjoy such rights and liabilities as are laid down in these Bye Laws and which are consistent with the Act and Rules.

5. (i) Any person shall be eligible to be admitted as a member of the association provided:

(a) he/she owns a Flat in ...., at ....(place).
(b) his/her written application for membership has been approved by a majority of the Managing Committee;
(c) his/her age is more than 18 years, except in the case of minor heir of a deceased member;.

(ii) Every member on admission shall pay Rs. .... (Amount in fugure) (Rupees.................... (amount in word) admission fee, which shall not be refunded in any case.

(iii) The association shall not admit member one month prior to the date of the annual general meeting.

6. A member of the association may be expelled by a two-third majority of votes of the members present at a general meeting, which shall be called by the Managing Committee for this purpose, within one month of the date of suspension of the member concerned after giving him reasonable opportunity to submit his explanation:

(a) if, he applies for bankruptcy; or
(b) if, he is convicted of a criminal offence involving dishonesty and moral turpitude; or
(c) if, he intentionally does any act likely to injure the credit of the association or fails to observe proper discipline in regard to work of the association; or
(d) for any action which may be held by the Managing Committee or a general meeting to be dishonest or contrary to the stated objects of the Association; its activities or to he spirit and interest of co-operation

An opportunity shall be given to a member, before expulsion from membership to represent his case to the Managing Committee.

7. A person ceases to be a member:
(i) on death; or
(ii) when his resignation is accepted by the Managing Committee; or
(iii) on expulsion under bye-law ....; or
(iv) on withdrawal after .... months notice in writing to the Secretary, provided that the member with drawing does not owe anything to the Association and is not a surety for an unpaid debt.

CHAPTER IV
CAPITAL

8. The capital shall be composed of:
(a) membership fee.
(b) donations and grants;
(c) contributions towards the maintenance of roads, drains and parks;
(d) other funds;
(e) realised profits.

The capital of the association shall be used in carrying out its object. Surplus funds of the association, not likely to be immediately required, shall be invested in such securities as the Managing Committee may deem fit. The borrowing and/or liabilities of the association shall not exceed at any time its total capital as mentioned above.

CHAPTER V
GENERAL MEETING

9. The first general meeting of the members shall have the same powers, as are herein given to the annual general meeting.

10. (a) The first general meeting shall be called within a period of not more than three months from the date of its registration. In first general meeting, the following business shall be discussed and decided.

   (i) Approval of amount collected and amount spent in connection with the registration of the Association before registration;

   (ii) election, if any, of the members of the Managing Committee other than seven members as mentioned in clause 4 of the Memorandum of the Association.

   (iii) programme of activities and budget estimate for ensuing year;

(b) The annual general meeting shall be called within a period of three months of the close of the accounting year. A special general meeting may be called at any time by the Managing Committee and shall be called on the requisition from $1/5^{th}$ of the total number of members of the association.

(c) In case of the annual general meeting, time and place of the meeting shall be announced at least .... days clearly in advance and in case of special general meeting at least .... days in advance, by a written notice along with agenda of the meeting.

(d) The presence of the $1/3^{rd}$ of the total number of the members subsisting as such on the date of notice of the meeting subject to a minimum of five members shall be necessary for the disposal of any matter at general meeting. Each member shall have one vote irrespective of his contribution to the Association. In case of equality of the votes on any matter, the President shall have a casting vote.

(e) If, within thirty minutes from the time appointed for the meeting a quorum is not present, the meeting shall stand adjourned ordinarily to the same day in the next week, at the same time and place but if the meeting is called upon the requisition of the members it shall stand dissolved:

Provided, that at the adjourned meeting, no quorum shall be necessary.

(f) If, at any time during the meeting, sufficient number of members is not present to form a quorum, the President of the meeting on his own motion or on his attention being drawn to this act shall adjourn the meeting at such convenient time date and place as he thinks fit and the business to be transacted at the adjourned meeting shall be transacted in the usual manner even if no quorum is present.

11. The duties and powers of the general meeting are:
   (a) to elect, suspend or remove members of the Managing Committee including its President;
   (b) to receive from the Managing Committee a report on the preceding year's working of the association together with a statement showing the receipts and expenditure, asset and liabilities and profit and loss for the year;
   (c) to consider the audit note or any financial statement or report of any person authorised to inspect the records of the Association;
   (d) to dispose off profits in accordance with the Act and the Bye Laws.
   (e) to amend the Bye Laws;
   (f) to expel members;
   (g) to consider any other business brought forward;
   (h) to appoint the auditors of the Association for the ensuing accounting year.

12. All business discussed or decided at a general meeting shall be recorded in proceedings book, which shall be signed by the President of the meeting.

13. Amendments to the Bye Laws shall only be carried out by a majority of not less than $2/3^{rd}$ of the members present in a general meeting in which due notice of the intention to discuss such amendments has been previously given. Such amendments shall be forwarded to the Registrar for Registration.

All other questions, before the general meeting shall be decided by a majority of votes.

CHAPTER VI
MANAGING COMMITTEE

14. (a) The Managing Committee shall consist of at least seven members of the Association and not more than 15 over the age of 21 years including its President. Each member of the Committee shall have one vote, but the President shall have a casting vote, in addition.

(b) Except for the first members, each of the member of the Managing Committee shall be elected and shall hold office for a period of two years and shall be eligible for re-election, but no member inclusive of the President shall hold office for a period exceeding six years consecutively.

15. A member of the committee shall cease to hold office, if, he:
   (a) ceases to be a member of the Association; or
   (b) applies for insolvency or is declared insolvent; or
   (c) becomes of unsound mind; or
   (d) is convicted of any offence involving dishonesty or moral turpitude; or
   (e) resigns and his resignation is accepted by the committee; or
   (f) fails to attend three consecutive meetings without leave of the Managing Committee.

16. The Managing Committee shall exercise all the powers of the Association except those reserved for the general meeting, subject to any regulation or restrictions laid down by the Association in a general meeting or in the Bye Laws and in particular shall have the following powers and duties:

   (a) to observe in all their transactions the Act, the notified rules and the Bye Laws;

   (b) to maintain true and accurate accounts of all money, received, expanded and all stock bought or sold;

   (c) to keep a updated register of members of the association;

   (d) to keep true account of assets and liabilities of the association;

   (e) to prepare and lay before the general meeting the annual profit and loss account and audited balance-sheet;

   (f) to examine the accounts, sanction contingent and other expenditure and supervise the maintenance of the prescribed registers;

   (g) to admit new members;

   (h) to summon general meeting in accordance with the Bye Law;

   (i) to contract loans subject to any restrictions imposed under the Bye Laws;

   (j) to appoint, suspend, punish and dismiss employees subject to the provisions of these Bye Laws, and fix their remuneration;

   (k) through any member or the officer or employee of the Association or any other persons specially authorised to institute, conduct, defend, compromise, refer to arbitration or abandon legal proceedings by or against the association or committee or the officers or employees concerning the affairs of the association;

   (l) to arrange for the custody of books and to appoint one of its member or one of officers of the Association, resident in the area of operation, to take charge all the registers and papers prescribed in these Bye Laws and rules;

   (m) to invest the surplus funds of the Association, in accordance terms of the Bye Laws;

   (n) to acquire and hold property and to enter into contracts on behalf of the association;

   (o) to decide the manner of execution of work and its allotment to members and employees;

   (p) to appoint a treasurer, to keep the money of the Association and to require him to give such security as it may deem sufficient;

   (q) to select and appoint a secretary and to fix his remuneration, if necessary;

   (r) to distribute the duties between the secretary and manager, if necessary;

   (s) generally to carry out the activities of the association.

In exercise of its rights, the Managing Committee shall exercise the prudence and diligence of ordinary men of business and shall be responsible for any loss sustained through acts contrary to the law, the notified rules and these Bye Laws.

17. No member of the Managing Committee shall receive any remuneration for his work as its member.

18. All matters discussed or decided at a meeting of the Managing Committee be recorded in a proceeding book which shall be signed by the President of the meeting and all the members of Managing Committee present.

19. The Committee may appoint from amongst its own members a sub-committee and may delegate to it or any officer of the association such of its own powers as it may consider desirable for the better conduct of the Association's affairs. The Sub-Committee or officer, shall in the discharge of the function entrusted to them confirm in all respects to these Bye Laws and to the instructions given by the Managing Committee.

20. The Managing Committee of the Association shall specify which of the officers of a Association shall:

   (a) keep the books of accounts;

   (b) keep other books and registers; and

   (c) prepare returns and statements:

   Provided, that a person charged with the keeping of accounts shall not be the in-charge of cash.

If, the Managing Committee of the Association has not specified the officers as aforesaid, notwithstanding anything contained in the Bye Laws, the following officers shall be responsible for keeping accounts, record etc.

   (a) TREASURER

   He shall keep or cause to be kept all the books of accounts and vouchers and shall prepare or caused to be prepared annual profit and loss account, receipt and disbursement account and the balance-sheet, whosoever may be writing these books of accounts, they shall always be deemed to be in his custody, possession, power and control. He shall be responsible for their safe delivery to his successor after making a list of documents handed and taken over.

   (b) SECRETARY

   He shall keep or cause to be kept all other records of the association and shall be responsible for preparation and submission of various returns to the Registrar, whosoever may be keeping these records, these shall always be deemed to be in his custody, possession, power and control. He shall be responsible for making over the charge of this record to his successor under proper charge report to be signed by the relieving and the relieved officers.

   (c) PRESIDENT

   Cash balance in hand shall always remain in the hands of the President.

CHAPTER VIII
REGISTERS

21. The following registers and papers shall be maintained and shall be open to the inspection of any member during an hour on each working day, as may be specified by the Managing Committee:

   (a) a register of members; showing the name, address and occupation of every member, the date of admission to membership date of termination of membership;

   (b) a cashbook showing the income, expenditure and cash balance on each day.

   (c) a minute book;

   (d) the register of application for membership containing the name and address of the applicant, the date of receipt of application;

   (e) any other register as may be prescribed under the Act.

22. Copies of the Bye Laws and balance sheet shall be supplied free on demand to any member.

23. The Managing Committee shall appoint one of its members to take hold and keep in safe custody all the registers prescribed under the Bye Laws or under the Act.

CHAPTER IX
GENERAL

24. AUDIT

The Accounts of the association shall be audited at least once a year by an auditor appointed at the annual general meeting. The first auditor shall be appointed by the Managing Committee, who shall hold office until the conclusion of the first annual general meeting. The association shall pay such audit fee, as may be fixed by the Managing Committee.

25. DISPUTE

If in any dispute touching the constitution of the association arises between members or past members of the association or person claiming through a members or past member or past members or persons so claiming and an officer, agent or employees of the association (past or present) or between the Association or its Managing Committee, sub-committee shall be referred to the Principal court of original jurisdiction of the district, in which the registered office of the Association is situated at the time of such reference.

26. MISCELLANEOUS

All matters not specifically provided for, are to be decided in accordance with the Societies Registration Act, 1860 and the rules, if any notified thereunder.

The Managing Committee with the approval of the general meeting may frame rule to carry out its activities not inconsistent with the Act and the Bye Laws and can may make addition or alterations in them from time to time.

We the undersigned are desirous of forming a Association namely .... under the Societies Registration Act, 1860 in pursuance the Memorandum attached and adopt the above as the Bye Laws of the Association.

S. No.	Names and Addresses	Occupation	Signature
1.			
2.			
3.			
4.			
5.			
6.			
7.			

(The Association Registration Act, 1860)

MEMORANDUM OF ASSOCIATION
OF ....

1. Name of the Association

The name of the Association shall be .... (Name of Welfare Association).

2. Registered office

The registered office of the Association shall remain in the State of .... and at present it is at the following address:

....

....

....

....

3. Aims and Objects

The aims and objects for which the Association is established are as under:

(a) for the welfare of the owners and residents of .... (Name of Area).

(b) For provision and supplementation of civic amenities, to create a body of representation of rights of the owners and residents with the respective concerned authorities (governmental and non-governmental) in connection with electricity, water and tax.

(c) to foster a spirit of neighbourliness, enhanced social interaction and exchange of information.

(d) to immediately take in hand the provision of roads, drainage, security, lighting, sign posting and beautification.

(e to carry out such other objectives as the members may decide from time to time.

4. Governing Body

The names, addresses, occupation and designation of the present members of the governing body to whom the management of the Association is entrusted as required under section 2 of the Association Registration Act, 1860 are as follows:

5. Desirous persons

We the undersigned are desirous of forming a Association namely under the Association Registration Act, 1860, in pursuance of this Memorandum of Association.

Sl. No.	Names and Addresses	Occupation	Signature
1.			
2.			
3.			
4.			
5.			
6.			
7.			
8.			
9.			
10.			

MEMORANDUM OF ASSOCIATION

1. Name of the Society

The name of the society shall be ....

2. Registered Office

Registered Office of the society shall remain in the State of .... and at present it is at the following address:

....

....

3. Aims and objects

The aims and objects for which the society is established are as under:

(a)

(b)

(c)

....

....

(add the following as the last paragraph)

All the incomes, earnings, movable and immovable properties of the society shall be solely utilized and applied towards the promotion of its aims and objects only as set forth in the Memorandum of Association and no portion thereof shall be paid or transferred directly or indirectly by way of dividends, bonus, profit or in any manner whatsoever, to the present or past members of the society or to any person claiming through any one or more of the present or the past members. No member of the society shall have any personal claim on any movable or immovable properties of the society or make any profit, whatsoever, by virtue of his membership.

4. Governing Body

The names, addresses, occupation and designation of the present members of the governing body to whom the management of the society is entrusted as required under Section 2 of the Societies Registration Act, 1860, are as follows:

Sl. No.	Name(in capital)	Addresses	Occupation	Designation in the society
(1)				
(2)				
(3)				
(4)				
(5) & so on				

5. Desirous person

We the undersigned are desirous of forming a society namely "....................." under the Societies Registration Act, 1860 in pursuance of this Memorandum of Association of the Society.

Sl. No.	Name & Addresses	Occupations	Signatures
(1)			
(2)			
(3)			
(4)			
(5)			
(6)			
(7) & so on			

RULES AND REGULATIONS

1. Rules and Regulations

   (i) Name of the society:
   (ii) Membership definition:
   (iii) Admission and Qualification of membership:
   (iv) Subscription:
   (v) Cessation of membership:
   (vi) Rights and privileges of Membership:

2. General Body
   (i) Definition of the General body
   (ii) Powers and duties/functions of the general body
   (iii) Quorum and notice of meeting and periodicity of meetings.

3. Managing/Governing Body/Executive
   (i) Definition of Managing/Governing/Executive Committee
   (ii) Composition
   (iii) Minimum and maximum strength including office bearers
   (iv) Election and its mode
   (v) Term of the office of the governing body
   (vi) Powers/duties/functions of the managing/governing body/committee
   (vii) Powers and duties of the office-bearers
   (viii) Quorum and notice of the meetings
   (ix) Filling up of casual vacancies.

4. Sub-Committee (if any)
   (i) Formation
   (ii) Composition
   (iii) Duties and functions

5. Sources of income and utilization of funds

6. Financial year

7. Audit of Account

8. Operation of Bank Account

9. Annual list of Managing/Governing Body (Section 4 of the Act)

- Once in every year a list of the office-bearers and members of the Managing /Governing body shall be filed with the Registrar of Societies, as required under Section 4 of the Societies Registration Act, 1860.

10. Legal Proceedings (Section 6 of the Act)

The Society may sue or be sued in the name of the President / Secretary as per provision laid down under section 6 of the Societies Registration Act, 1860.

11. Amendment/alteration, extension or abridgement of 'purposes' aims and objects or change of name, sections 12 and 12A of the Societies Registration Act. The amendment shall be made under this section.

12. Dissolution and adjustment of affairs

If the society need to be dissolved it shall be dissolved as per provisions laid down under sections 13 and 14 of the Societies Registration Act, 1860.

13. Application of the Act

All the provisions under all the sections of the Societies Registration Act, 1860 shall apply to this society.

14. Certificate

Certified that this is the correct copy of the rules and regulations of the society.

(Sd)	(Sd)	(Sd)
President	Secretary	Treasurer

From:

....

....

....

To,

The Registrar of Societies,

.... (address).

Sir,

Re: *Registration of a society under the name* ....

A society by name .... has been formed on .... day of ...., 20...... I have been elected its first Secretary and have been authorised to complete the formalities of registration.

Please find enclosed

(1) Two copies of Memorandum duly signed and completed.

(2) Two copies of Rules and byelaws of the society.

(3) Affidavit duly attested.

(4) House tax receipt/No objection certificate.

(5) Registration fee of Rs. .... (Amount) in cash.

Please register the society under the Societies Registration Act, 1860 and issue a Certificate of Registration.

I have been authorized by the society to sign this application on behalf of all the subscribers of Memorandum.

Thanking you,

Your faithfully

AFFIDAVIT

I, ... S/o .... R/o.................... aged about........................ years do hereby solemnly affirm and state as under:

1. That a society under the name and title .... has been formed and has its main office at....................

2. That I am one of the subscribers of the memorandum of the abovenamed society.

3. That I am also a member of the first Governing Body of the abovenamed society and have been elected its Secretary.

4. That I have been authorized by all the members of the abovenamed society to sign and execute all documents required for registration of the abovenamed society as also to swear and execute this affidavit.

5. That none of the members of the society or the Governing Body are related to each other.

Place....................

Date....................

DEPONENT

VERIFICATION

I, the abovenamed, do hereby verify that the contents of paras 1 to 5 are true and correct to the best of my knowledge and belief and nothing material has been concealed therefrom.

Verified at .... on .... day of ...., 20.....

DEPONENT

In .... a society can be registered for the following purposes:

1. Promotion of social welfare
2. Activities conducive to the protection and improvement of the natural environment (including forests, lakes, rivers and wild life)
3. Compassion for living creatures
4. Sports, games
5. Fine Arts.

CHAPTER 14
POWER OF ATTORNEY

SYNOPSIS

DEFINITION
ELEMENTS OF POWER OF ATTORNEY

PRECEDENTS
- IRREVOCABLE POWER OF ATTORNEY
- POWER OF ATTORNEY – 1
- POWER OF ATTORNEY – 2

Definition

Power of Attorney is the authority to act for another person in legal or financial matters.

Section 2(21) of Indian Stamp Act gives definition of power of attorney.

Elements of Power of Attorney

Following are to important elements of a Power of Attorney.

1. No particular form is prescribed and all that is necessary is that the power of attorney should indicate with sufficient clearness certain power given to a specific person to act for and in the name of the person executing it.

2. If a power of attorney appoints more than one attorneys they should be appointed as follows:—"Jointly and every two or more and each of them severally my attorney or attorneys". If the appointment is not joint and several all the attorneys appointed must act jointly. One attorney acting alone cannot bind the principal and his act is not valid.

3. Power of attorney after giving specific powers to the attorney usually winds up with these general words: "Generally to do all such other lawful acts and things as my attorney shall think advisable for the purposes aforesaid as fully and effectually in all respects as could do myself". It is necessary to point out that these general words do not extend or widen the authority of the power of attorney to do other acts besides those which he is specifically authorized to perform.

4. A power of attorney appointing attorneys without in terms limiting the duration of their power but with a recital that the principal was going abroad and was desirous of appointing attorneys during his absence.

5. After a power of attorney is written out, it is desirable that it should be attested by witness. In order to dispense with proof the execution of a power of attorney the provisions of section 85 of the Indian Evidence Act, should be followed.

6. Stamp—(a) As already stated the Indian Stamp Act section 2(21) gives definition of a power of attorney. Following this definition it has been ruled that when *A* writes a letter to *B* to send him money through *C* the bearer of the letter, and takes his acknowledgement, then the above instrument is not a power of attorney.

(b) For purposes of stamp, powers of attorney may be classed as general and special. The stamp is provided for in Article 48 of the Indian Stamp Act.

(c) If a power of attorney is executed outside India but relates to any property situated or to any matter of thing done or to be done in India and is received in India it must be stamped within three months of its arrival in this country.

PRECEDENTS

IRREVOCABLE POWER OF ATTORNEY

Be, it known to all that We, *Alpha* (the '*Alpha*'), having our registered office at .... (address) hereby appoint and constitute *Beta* (the '*Beta*'), with offices at................... (address), as our lawful attorney to act in our name and on our behalf in the manner hereinafter mentioned.

WHEREAS, pursuant to the terms of an Agreement (the '*Beta* Loan Agreement') dated as of date between the *Beta* and us, the *Beta* has made a program related investment loan of Indian Rupee equivalent of................... (amount in word) (................... amount in figure) (the '*Beta* Loan'), which *Beta* Loan is to be utilised by us to capitalise our subsidiary, *Omega* (the 'Company');

WHEREAS, as security for the payment and performance, of the *Beta* Loan, an agreement of lien ('...................') dated as of date has been entered into between us and the *Beta* and it is a condition of the Lien Agreement that we shall grant as security, *inter alia*, an irrevocable power of attorney authorising the *Beta*, to deal in its sole discretion, with the shares, both equity and preference, (the 'Shares') held by us at present and to be acquired by us in the Company in the future by utilising the proceeds of the *Beta* Loan, if an Event of Default (as defined in Article VII of the *Beta* Loan Agreement) occurs.

NOW, THEREFORE BY THESE PRESENTS, we hereby authorise and empower our attorney that in the Event of Default, it shall be entitled, to the exclusion of all others, to do any or all of the following acts, deeds or things as it may, in its sole discretion, deem fit:

(i) Sell or cause to be sold, mortgage, pledge, create a lien, security interest or encumbrance of any nature, or deal with the Shares in any manner whatsoever;

(ii) Cause the name of the transferee to be registered in the books of the Company and if necessary to apply to any court or take any other proceedings so as to complete the said sale;

(iii) Receive the proceeds of any sale of the Shares in cash or otherwise and apply the proceeds in fulfilment of our obligations under the *Beta* Loan Agreement;

(iv) To do all such other acts, whatsoever, as are expedient, incidental or necessary to effectuate any or all of the aforesaid;

(v) To delegate all or any of the above powers to such persons as it may deem necessary or expedient.

And, we hereby agree to ratify and confirm and hereby ratify and confirm all such acts, things, deeds and assurance that may be done or caused to be done by the said attorney. IN WITNESS WHEREOF, we hereby execute this power of attorney on this .... day of .... 20.....

In consideration of the Foundation Loan received by the company and the interest of Foundation in the Shares, this power of attorney shall be irrevocable.

We further agree, that we shall not question or contest and shall accept without demur or protest any written communication by our attorney to us that an event of default has occurred.

For *Alpha*

By Authority of the Board of Directors.

POWER OF ATTORNEY – 1

I, ... (name), S/o.................... (name), resident of .... (address), one of the subscribers to the Memorandum and Articles of Association of the Proposed Company, '.................... (name)' ('proposed company') appoint and authorize.................... (name) and.................... (name) Associates of.................... (name), Advocates and Solicitors, ... (address), as my Attorneys and authorise them jointly and severally to do all or any of the following:

1. To file the Memorandum and Articles of Association of the proposed company, Forms 1, 32, 18 and any other documents as may be necessary for the incorporation of the proposed company, with the requisite fee, and to make corrections, changes alteration in the above documents or any other documents as may be filed in the above matter.

2. To represent me before the Registrar of companies, ... (place) and .... (place) in all the matters connected with the incorporation of the Proposed Company and to collect the Certificate of Incorporation of the Proposed Company or any other document, letter, record, notice etc. and to give acknowledgement for the same.

3. All actions of my Attorneys under this power of attorney shall be binding on me and shall be deemed to have been taken by me.

Date....................

....
(EXECUTOR)

ACCEPTED

....

(ATTORNEY)

....

(ATTORNEY)

POWER OF ATTORNEY – 2

I, ... (name), D/o .... (name), resident of .... (address), one of the subscribers to the Memorandum and Articles of Association of the proposed company, ... (name) ('proposed company') appoint and authorize .... (name), Associate of .... (name), Advocates and Solicitors, ... (address), as my Attorney and authorise her to do all or any of the following:

2. To file the Memorandum and Articles of Association of the proposed Company, Forms 1, 32, 18 and any other documents as may be necessary for the incorporation of the proposed company, with the requisite fee, and to make corrections, changes alteration in the above documents or any other documents as may be filed in the above matter.

3. To represent me before the Registrar of companies, ... (place) and .... (place) in all the matters connected with the incorporation of the proposed company and to collect the certificate of incorporation of the proposed company or any other document, letter, record, notice etc., and to give acknowledgement for the same.

4. All actions of my Attorneys under this power of attorney shall be binding on me, and shall be deemed to have been taken by me.

DATE

....
(EXECUTOR)

ACCEPTED

....

(ATTORNEY)

....

(ATTORNEY)

SUBJECT INDEX

A

Actor Employment Agreement, 425
Additional Contribution, 63
   by company, 63
Administration Bond, 686, 687
   by a person obtaining letter of administration, 686
   by guardian, 687
Advance Payment Guarantee, 655
   form of, 655
Agency Agreement, 163
Agreement, 34, 251, 252, 253, 539, 728, 731
   commencement of, 34
   extending time for completion of purchase, 252
   for sale and purchase and delivery of coat, 539
   for sale made by a vendor in favour of purchaser, 251
   for sale of property, 253
   of lease, 728, 731
Agreement
   for actor employment, 425
   for arbitration, 715, 716, 717, 719
   for confidentiality, 496
   for confidentiality and non-disclosure, 503
   for consultancy, 111, 499
   for consultancy service, 115
   for consultants non-disclosure and non-compete, 159
   for co-production, 405
   for dialogue and vocal replacement, 411
   for employees non-disclosure and non-compete, 506
   for employes innovation, 109
   for ERL facilities, 181
   for exclusive reseller, 254
   for facilities sharing, 191
   for financial collaboration, 196
   for franchise, 514, 515, 521
   for fuel supply, 550
   for joint venture, 275
   for know-how assignment, 467
   for marketing assistance, 206
   for office refreshment, 218
   for power purchase, 545
   for research and development, 239
   for share holder, 295, 316
   for share transfer, 319
   for shores acquisition, 337
   for software services supply, 171
   for sound recording and distribution, 393
   for subscription, 354
   for technology and marketing collaboration, 460
   for technology assignment, 484
   for technology transfer and licences, 446
   for trade mark licence, 380
   for trade name licence, 386
   of written employment, 394
Agreement of reference, 676
   to arbitration, 676
Agricultural Land, 17
Alternate Dispute Resolution, 715, 720
   advantages of, 720
   disadvantages of, 720
Application form, 44
   for availability of names, 44
Arbitration, 158, 725
   damages in, 725
Arbitration Act, *1940*, 716

Subject Index

Arbitration Agreement, 715, 716, 717, 719
   drafting of, 715
   judicial analysis, 717
   Halsbury's laws, 719
Arbitration and Conciliation Act, *1996*, 715
Arbitral Awards, 721
   enforcement of, 721
Arbitration Clause, 715, 722
   drafting of, 715
Area, 18
Articles, 316, 317
   effect of, 316
   enforceability of, 316
   interpretation of, 317
Articles of Association, 59, 61, 316
   definition of, 61
   drafting of, 59
Assignment 371, 660
   disputes between parties, 371
   of business with goodwill and tenancy rights, 660
   of rights in invention, 483
   of simple contract depts, 663
Attorney, 11
   in deed, 11
Authorised Capital, 62
   of company,

B

Bailments, 30
Board of Directors, 68
   meetings of, 68
Board of Trustees, 778
   appointment of additional members, 778
Bond, 679, 680, 683, 684, 685, 695, 696, 697
   by debtor and his surety for loan, 683
   by sureties of student, 695
   by surety for due observance of partnership deed, 696
   by trainee with sureties, 697
   form of deed poll, 679
   heirs and representatives, 680
   use of, 679
   with sureties for loan payable in equated instalment, 684
   with sureties for loan with provision for lower rate of interest, 685
Breach, 29
   of contract, 29
   remedies for, 29

C

Cash Security Bond, 689
   by government employee, 689
Chairman, 68
   of board, 68
Charge, 674
   as security for advances to third person, 674
Check list, 36
   of contract, 36
Common Seal, 69
   of company, 69
Companies, 41
   types of, 41
Companies Act, *1956*, 40, 41
Companies, 63, 65, 66, 67, 316, 333
   additional contribution, 63
   analysis of relationship with member, 316
   borrowing power, 67
   director of, 65, 66
   managing director, 66
   take over of, 333
   transfer of shares, 63
Confidentiality Agreement, 492, 496
Confidentiality and Non-disclosure Agreement, 503
Consideration, 15
   as contract, 15
Consultancy Agreement, 111, 499
Consultants Non-disclosure and Non-Compete Agreement, 159
Construction Deeds, 26
   rules of, 26
Consulting Services Agreement, 115
Contract, 29, 30, 31, 32, 34, 35, 36, 37
   administration phase, 36
   analytical phase, 35
   breach of, 29
   capacity to, 32
   checklist of, 37

drafting of, 34
drafting phase, 35
engagement phase, 35
excuse for non-performance of, 30
execution phase, 36
for sale of goods, 32
formal requirement, 32
interpretation of, 31
management of, 34
remedies for breach of, 29
types of, 36
written agreement, 32
Contract of Employment, 101, 104
for junior level employee, 101
for senior level employee, 104
Conveyance, 3
forms of, 3
Conveyancing, 2
in India, 2
Co-production Agreement, 405
Copyright, 369, 371, 394
assignment of, 369
infringement of, 371
Consideration, 727
for lease, 727
Court, 770
control of conduct and administration, 770
Covenants and undertakings, 19

D

Damage, 376, 544
contract, 544
liquidated, 544
proof of, 376
Data Collection, 36
during engagement phase, 36
Deed, 4, 5, 6, 7, 8, 9, 10, 11, 21, 22, 23, 25, 26, 392, 409, 699, 779, 788, 793
alteration of, 793
attorney, 11
capital, 4
date, 5
delivery of, 22
description of, 5, 7, 26
division of, 5

endorsement, 23
errors, 23
firm, 11
government, 11
Hindu coparcenary, 10
insolvent, 10
juridical person, 7
mentally ill person, 10
minors, 9
of assignment of copyright, 409
of assignment, 392
of family trust settlement, 779
of indemnity, 699
of transfer, 21
of trust, 788
omissions, 23
paragraph, 4
parties to, 6
person under disability, 8
post script, 23
precautions, 25
punctuation, 4
registration, 25
sign, 21
supplemental, 23
third person, 7
trustee, 10
Deed Drafting, 2
in India, 2
Deed of Transfer, 4
general requirement, 4
Deeds Poll, 3
Defects Liability Certificate, 657
Delivery, 22
of deed, 22
Deposit, 674
as security for advances to third person, 674
Dialogue and Vocal Replacement Agreement, 411
Director, 65
of company, 65
Dispute Settlement, 715
Distributor, 154, 155, 156
non-remediable events, 155
procedure for remediable events, 155
remediable events, 154

termination on remediable events, 156
termination other than non-remediable, 156
Documents, 704
Drafting, 271, 715
   of joint venture documentation, 271
   of Arbitration Agreement, 715
   of Arbitration clause, 715
Draftsman, 27
   of deed, 27
Due Diligence Report, 74

E

ERC Facilities Agreement, 181
Employee Innovation and Proprietary Information Agreement, 109
Employees Non-Disclosure and Non-Compete Agreement, 506
Employment Contract, 101
Endorsement, 23, 24
   form of, 23
   stamp duty on, 24
English Arbitration Act, *1996*, 716
English Common Law, 374
   passing off action, 374
Equated Instalments Bond, 682
Exceptions and Reservations, 19
Exclusive Reseller Agreement, 254
Executed Deeds, 26

F

Facilities Sharing Agreement, 191
Figures and Words, 4
Final Payment Certificate, 658
Financial Collaboration Agreement, 196
Firm, 11
   in deed, 11
Forms, 3, 22
   of conveyance, 3
   of attestation, 22
Franchise Agreement, 514, 515, 521
   law relating to, 575
   drafting of, 521
Franchising, 515, 516, 526
   agreement, 526
   Area Development agreement, 516, 526
   direct, 515

   joint venture, 516
   master agreement, 516,
   subsidiary or branch office, 516
Fuel Supply Agreement, 550, 551, 552
   default, 552
   dispute resolution, 551
   force majeure, 551
   infrastructure, 550
   payment, 551
   pricing, 551
   project financing, 550
   quality and rejection, 552
   remedies for breach, 552
   scheduling, 552
   transportation, 552

G

General Meeting, 69
   quorum for, 69
General Power of Attorney, 664
General Words, 17
Government, 11
   in deed, 11
Grove, 18
Guarantee, 30, 673, 674
   as security for advances to third person, 674
   for payment of goods, 673

H

Habendum, 19
Heirs and Representatives, 680
Hindu Coparcenary, 10
   in deed, 10
Hindu Minority and Guardianship Act, *1956*, 9
House, 18

I

Indemnity, 30, 69, 699
   deed of, 699
   out of assets, 69
Indemnity Bond, 681, 700
   stamp duty for, 681
Indenture Bilateral, 3
India, 2, 238, 379, 443
   conveyancing in, 2

deed drafting in, 2
Mareva injunction in, 379
patent in, 443
patent licensing, 443
patent protection, 443
product liability, 235
product standard, 238
Indian Contract Act, *1872*, 27, 250
Indian Law, 374
  passing off action, 874
Indian Law of Contract, 28
  general concepts, 28
  notes on, 28
Indian Trust
  nature of, 764
Indian Trust Act, *1882*, 764, 774, 776
Insolvent, 10
  in deed, 10
Instalment Bond, 682, 683
  with surety for existing liability, 683
Interest, 680
  two rates of, 680
International Commercial Arbitration, 719
International Trade, 235
  impact on, 235
Issue of Capital, 62
  by company, 62

J

Joint Venture Agreement, 275
Joint Venture Documentation, 271
  drafting of, 271

K

Know-how Assignment Agreement, 467

L

Legal Due Diligence Report, 70
Lease, 727, 728, 731
  agreement of, 728, 731
  consideration for, 727
  execution of, 727
Lessee, 727, 728
  covenant by, 728
  covenant entered into by, 727
  proviso for re-entry, 728

Lender, 542
  diligence, 542
  project finance structure, 542

M

Managing Director, 66
  of company, 66
Map or Plan, 16
Mareva Injunction, 379
  in India, 379
Marketing Assistance Agreement, 206
Members, 316
  analysis of relationship with company, 316
Memorandum of Association, 45
  drafting of, 45
Memorandum of undertaking, 430
  between two media companies, 430
Minors, 9
  in deed, 9

N

Non-agricultural Land, 18
Non-disclosure and non-compete agreement, 509
Non-OECD Countries, 234

O

OECD Countries, 234
Office Refurbishment Agreement, 218
Operative Words, 16

P

Parties, 13
  reference labels of, 13
Parcels, 16
Partnership Act, *1932*, 11
Passing Off, 375, 376, 377, 378
  in Indian courts, 378
  in professional practice, 377
  methods for, 377
  modern formulation of Law of, 375
  remedies for, 378
  remedies, 376
Passing-off Action, 374
  under English common law, 374
  under Indian, 374

Subject Index

Subject Index

Patent, 443
  in India, 443
Patent Agreement for Employees, 442
Patent Licensing, 443
  in India, 443
Patent Protection, 443
  in India, 443
Pawnee, 704
  meaning of, 704
Pawnor, 704
  meaning of, 704
Performance Bond, 654
  form of, 654
Performance Guarantee Bond, 697
Personal Security Bond, 690
  by an employee, 690
Pledge, 30, 704, 705, 713
  deed of, 705
  meaning of, 704
  of term deposit, 713
Power Purchase Agreements, 545, 546, 547, 548, 549
  counter guarantee, 547
  financing, 547
  force majeure, 549
  judicial inquiry, 549
  payment risk, 548
  pitfalls, 545
  price mechanism, 548
  pricing risk, 548
  remedies, 545
  tariff, 546
  tax holiday, 549
  third party sale, 549
Power of Attorney, 808, 809, 810, 811
  definition of, 808
  elements of, 808
  irrevocable, 809
Power of Attorney Act, *1882*, 11
Private Company, 41, 62
  meaning of, 62
Private Limited Company, 41
  formation procedure, 41
Product Liability, 233, 234
  analysis of, 233
  and consumer protection, 233

Product Liability Land Suits, 236
Product Standard, 236
  in India, 236
Project Developer, 539
  risk matrix, 539
Project Financing Structure, 554
  diligence deliberations in, 554
Provisional taking over Certificate, 657
Public Companies, 41
Purchases, 31
  bona fide, 31

R

Recitals, 13, 14, 15
  caution, 14
  form of, 15
  introductory, 14
  kinds of, 13
  narrative, 13
  order of, 14
Receipt, 15
  acknowledgement of, 15
Registration, 25, 681
  of deed, 25
  for immovable property, 681
Registration Act, *1968*, 3
Release and Indemnities, 673
Religious or Charitable Endowments, 770
Research and Development Agreement, 239
Residential Welfare Association, 794
  bye-laws of, 794

S

Sale of Goods, 250
Sale & Purchase & Delivery of Coal Agreement, 550
Sale of Goods Act, *1930*, 250
Securities, 704
Security, 693
  by a legatee under a lost will, 693
Security Bond, 681, 687, 688, 691, 692, 694
  by a debtor, 688
  by a receiver, 688
  by sureties on behalf of claimant, 691
  by surety of manager of estate, 692
  for grant of succession certificate, 687

stamp duty for, 681
with two sureties for monthly deduction from pay, 694
Share Transfer Agreement, 319
Shareholder Agreement, 295, 316
Shares, 331
transfer of, 331
Shares Acquisition and Reconstruction Agreement, 337
Sign, 21
meaning of, 21
Signature and attestation, 20
Simple Money Bond, 681
for money borrowed, 681
money due with recitals, 681
Societies Registration Act, *1860*, 794
Society, 794
nature of, 794
object of, 794
Software Services Supply Agreement, 171
Sound Recording and Distribution Agreement, 398
Special Power of Attorney, 670, 672
for admitting execution before sub-registrar, 672
in respect of entering into and concluding one transaction, 670
Stamp Act, *1899*, 3
Stamp Duty, 24, 681
for indemnity bond, 681
for security bond, 681
on endorsement, 24
on supplemental deeds, 24
payment of, 24
Standard Clauses Check-list, 37
Subscription Agreement, 354
Supplemental Deed, 24
form of, 24
stamp duty on, 24
Supply contract, 165

T

Technical Barrier to trade, 235
Technology and Marketing Collaboration Agreement, 460
Technology Assignment Agreement, 484

Technology Transfer and Licence Agreement, 446
Testimonium, 20
Trade Mark Licence Agreement, 380
Trade Name Licence Agreement, 386
Transfer of Property Act, *1882*, 7
Transfer of Shares, 63, 331, 332
refusal to register, 332
Transfer of Undertaking Agreement, 347
Transfer Price, 64, 332
calculation of, 64, 332
Trees, 18
Trust, 764, 765, 766, 770, 773, 775, 776, 777, 788, 793
agenda for meeting, 777
alteration of deed of, 793
charitable, 776
complete constitution of, 766
deed of, 766, 788
for pension and employee benefits, 776
governing legislation, 764, 766
limitation on, 770, 773
non-charitable, 777
personal, 775
private, 775
reason for creation of, 775
regulatory environment on, 770
requirements of, 765
Trustees, 10, 767, 768, 772, 773, 774, 775
breach of trust, 772
condition to become, 775
duties of, 768
exoneration clauses, 774
in deed, 10
public policy, 774
remuneration of, 773

U

Unit Trust, 776
collective investment scheme, **776**
United Nations Commission on International Trade, 715

W

Witness, 22
World Trade Organisation, 235
Written Employment Agreement, 394
Written Agreement, 32
for contracts, 32